CHARLES EVANS HUGHES

© *Harris & Ewing*

Charles E. Hughes

BY MERLO J. PUSEY

Charles Evans Hughes

IN TWO VOLUMES

Volume One

COLUMBIA UNIVERSITY PRESS

New York and London

1963

First published by The Macmillan Company, 1951
Third printing, Columbia University Press, 1963
Library of Congress Catalog Card Number: 51-7851

PRINTED IN THE UNITED STATES OF AMERICA

To

my wife and co-worker,

DOROTHY RICHARDS PUSEY

PREFACE

Charles Evans Hughes himself contributed more to this volume than any other individual. In declining many requests that he write his own story, he used to say that personal memoirs had a way of turning into apologia and therefore did not interest him. Knowing, however, that others would write about him, he wished them to have the facts. Through thirty-five years of public life he carefully preserved important documents and letters, and after his retirement as Chief Justice of the United States he wrote several hundred pages of biographical notes. These have been my primary sources of information.

Even more fruitful in some respects were my interviews with Mr. Hughes in the latter years of his retirement. During the spring and fall months that he spent in Washington, I visited him once or twice a week over a period of two and a half years. Seated at his desk in a reminiscent mood, he would often answer my questions for three hours without a break, speaking with candor and clarity—drawing upon his amazing memory of events over fourscore years. In this manner we reviewed his experiences as a youth and as a young lawyer and discussed all the momentous events of his public career.

Through the six years required to complete this biography, I had exclusive access to Mr. Hughes' voluminous papers in the Library of Congress and the Supreme Court and to part of his private correspondence. Among the former are extensive memoranda prepared in 1933 and 1934 by Henry C. Beerits with the aid and supervision of Mr. Hughes. These too proved to be an excellent source of background material. Mr. Beerits had also arranged and classified the Hughes Papers—those now in the Library of Congress—so as to make them more readily accessible.

Several interviews with Charles Evans Hughes, Jr., gave me new insight into his father's personality and an array of facts about their joint practice of law. In one of the busiest years of his career, the younger Mr. Hughes read my earlier chapters and offered many constructive suggestions. His untimely death in 1950 robbed his profession of one of its ablest and most eminent practitioners and deprived me of counsel that had proved of the utmost value.

Other members of the Hughes family have been most cooperative. I am especially indebted to Catherine Hughes Waddell and Elizabeth Hughes Gossett for permission to use many of the personal letters written by their father, mother, and grandparents—letters discovered on a closet shelf during the last illness of Chief Justice Hughes. Mrs. Waddell and her husband, Chauncey L. Waddell, and Mrs. Gossett and her husband, William T. Gossett, also read the entire manuscript and suggested corrections and additions. In no instance, however, did they request me to alter any conclusion. Responsibility for the tone of the work, for its imperfections, and for its appraisal of Charles Evans Hughes as a man and a public figure is entirely mine. It is an authorized but not an official biography.

Many of Mr. Hughes' friends and former associates gave invaluable help by way of interviews, letters, and criticism of different parts of the manuscript. Especially outstanding in this group are former Justice Owen J. Roberts, Chief Justice D. Lawrence Groner of the United States Court of Appeals (retired), and Edwin McElwain, Mr. Hughes' last law clerk, all of whom read the chapters on the Chief Justiceship; also Justices Felix Frankfurter, Robert H. Jackson, and Hugo Black of the United States Supreme Court; Chief Judge John J. Parker of the United States Court of Appeals, Fourth Circuit; Henry P. Chandler, Director of the Administrative Office of the United States Courts; Charles Elmore Cropley, clerk of the Supreme Court; Thomas E. Waggaman, marshal of the court; also former President Herbert Hoover; William D. Mitchell, former Attorney General; Sumner Welles, Joseph C. Grew, and Henry P. Fletcher, all former Undersecretaries of State; J. V. A. MacMurray, William R. Castle, Charles Cheney Hyde, A. W. Dulles, and William H. Beck.

I am heavily indebted to John Lord O'Brian for his advice and criticism of the governorship chapters; to Herbert Elliston and Francis White for similar aid in regard to some of the State Department chapters; to Joseph M. Lalley for his comments on the early chapters; to Dr. Anna Youngman for reading several chapters on economic policy; to Dr. Frederick M. Davenport for his help with the chapters on 1916; to Judge Meier Steinbrink for his stories and counsel, chiefly in connection with the aircraft investigation; to Henry M. Wriston for criticism of the chapter on Brown University; and to Allan Nevins and Charles E. Cuningham for many suggestions regarding the entire manuscript.

I wish also to thank Milo R. Maltbie, Grenville Clark, Roscoe Pound, Francis V. Keesling, Laurence H. Green, former Ambassador Edwin C. Wilson, Harvey D. Hinman, Senator Joseph C. O'Mahoney, former Senator Burton K. Wheeler, J. Reuben Clark, Jr., Edward M. Bassett, Mrs. J. Butler Wright, Mrs. Ruth B. Shipley, Michael J. McDermott, former Congressman James W. Wadsworth, William F. Unger, Ambassador David Bruce, Randolph Paul, John W. Davis, Fred K. Nielsen, G. Howland Shaw, Roy Vallance, Oscar R. Ewing, Harold L. Ickes, Mark DeWolfe Howe, E. Kimball MacColl,

Judge William H. Wadhams, and Charles Warren, historian of the Supreme Court; also Mrs. Franzetta DeGooyer, who typed the manuscript.

Finally I wish to thank Eugene Meyer, chairman of the board of the *Washington Post,* and Mrs. Meyer for their generous aid and encouragement, and Philip L. Graham, president and publisher of the *Washington Post,* for many helpful suggestions.

MERLO J. PUSEY

CONTENTS

Volume One

Volume Two

ILLUSTRATIONS

Volume One

Volume Two

CHARLES EVANS HUGHES

Chapter 1

HOUR OF TRAVAIL

THE HOT wave of rebellion sweeping up from the South aroused Glens Falls to fighting fury. The townsfolk marched with torches—a "veritable river of fire" —for Abraham Lincoln. They recruited the stoutest of their sons for the Union Army. Patriotism mounted to a high pitch, but it did not save the picturesque paper-mill town on the Hudson River from the repercussions of the catastrophe that was shaking the nation.

Greenbacks drove hard money out of circulation, and the local authorities were forced to issue "shinplasters" to keep the economy functioning. Copperheads held clandestine meetings and openly raided the first drafting booths set up in the town. From New York City came news of a secession movement led by Mayor Fernando Wood himself, and the election of Horatio Seymour as governor of New York in 1862 was soon to add fears of revolution in the North to the perils of the war. Worst of all was the news of disaster following disaster that came from the battle fronts. As the stagecoach completed its run from Fort Edward, a flag would go up and the people would gather on the porch of the Glens Falls Hotel to hear the war news. Not infrequently some pair of these stern Hudson Valley folk went away sobbing over the loss of a soldier son.

In the cold spring of 1862, however, a temporary wave of cheering news reached the upper Hudson. The *Monitor* had met the *Merrimac* and forced that menacing raider to withdraw to Norfolk. Pensacola had been captured, and Grant was pounding his way through Tennessee. McClellan had begun his Peninsular Campaign. The North had found renewed hope, even though the war was making a heavy drain upon its resources and the peril overhanging the great American experiment was still keenly felt. It was in this hour of the nation's exertion to redeem itself from calamity that Charles Evans Hughes was born on April 11, 1862.

Outside of the Hughes household the event caused no stir. It had no announcement in the local press. The child's parents, the Reverend Mr. David Charles Hughes and Mary Catherine Connelly Hughes, had lived in Glens Falls only a year and a half—since the young pastor had accepted a call from the First Baptist Church in the autumn of 1860. Only five years before he had landed on the shores of America from the Old World, alone and friendless. Fervent, energetic, and adventurous, he was one of the millions of poor immigrants who looked upon the United States as a land of promise.

In a brief period the young pastor had been absorbed into the New World ferment, becoming an evangelist for unity and freedom as well as Christian doctrine. Two months after his ordination at Glens Falls, he had been employed to fill a second pulpit—that of the First Baptist Church of near-by Sandy Hill (now Hudson Falls). This added $300 a year to his meager income and gave an additional outlet for his untiring efforts. In both churches he labored "with great acceptance," [1] preached the doctrine of abolition and pounded the pulpit in indignation over the activities of the Copperheads.

Through this exciting period the Hughes family lived humbly in a small one-story frame house, with the living-room door and two windows opening on quiet Maple Street a short distance from the church. Incidentally, this house was to be moved in the seventies from 135 Maple Street to its present location at 16 Center Street, and this would later give rise to a controversy as to whether it was actually the birthplace of Charles E. Hughes. At one time the State of New York would accept the claim that Governor Hughes came into this world within the house at 47 Maple Street.[2] But that claim would be undermined by eyewitnesses of the moving previously referred to [3] and by the recollections of old-timers in Glens Falls, including Mrs. Celia Gould Ames who took care of Mary Hughes during her confinement and gave the infant Charlie his first bath.[4]

David Charles Hughes was a product of the Wesleyan movement that had claimed the devotion of his forebears in the middle of the eighteenth century.[5] Of Welsh descent, he had been born in Monmouthshire, England, migrating in 1855 because he had been favorably impressed by Franklin's *Autobiography* and because he thought he had a "providential call" to preach in America. We first hear of him in the United States when he presented his credentials to the New York Conference of the Methodist Church.

"Well, young man," said the presiding elder, "I see that you are from Hingland."

"No, sir," David Charles replied, "I am from England."

"You'll do," was the presiding elder's abrupt decision.[6]

In three days the young Welshman who wished to become an American was sent to a little parish at Vails Gate on the slope of Storm King on the Hudson. His good English had given him a favorable introduction to America, and his

[1] A. W. Holden, *A History of the Town of Queensbury*, p. 203.
[2] *State Service* (New York State publication), November, 1919.
[3] Author's interview with Dr. Frederick G. Streeter, July 30, 1946.
[4] Author's interview with Mrs. William H. Barber, July 30, 1946.
[5] For details of David Charles Hughes' ancestry, see Appendix I.
[6] CEH, Biographical Notes, p. 9.

fluency and clear enunciation would further contribute to his early success in the ministry.

As a member of the New York Conference "on trial," he was appointed to the New Windsor Circuit, Newburgh District, and there he served until December, 1856. A letter of commendation from the presiding elder indicates that he gave up this work "to enter school & prepare for College." A private school in Maryland afforded him the opportunity of supporting himself by teaching some subjects while he studied others. About a year and a half later, however, he was in charge of a Methodist parish at Eddyville on Rondout Creek, New York, and it was there that he met and fell in love with Mary Catherine Connelly, whose parents' home was then at New Salem on the opposite side of the creek. By dint of preaching and teaching, he earned enough to carry him through a year at Wesleyan University in 1858–1859. At the end of that precious year he went cheerfully back to preaching and continued his scholastic efforts in his spare time. Having become proficient in Latin and Greek, he studied Hebrew during his thirties, aided at first by the instruction of a rabbi.

Mary Connelly became a great influence in his life from the moment he met her. Her father, William Connelly, Jr., invited the young preacher to go with him to the station at Rhinebeck to meet his daughter who was apparently returning from a year of schooling at Fort Edward Institute. David Charles saw her smile; he admired her golden hair and light blue eyes; he noted that she was delicate and reserved. When she spoke, he felt an intellectual kinship between them. Before he left her at this first meeting, he realized that he was in love.

His affection struck a responsive chord in Mary Connelly. They were drawn together by a common zeal for study, by the depth of religious feeling which they shared, and by their evangelical conceptions of Christian truth. There were sharp contrasts between them—between her fair complexion and his typically Welsh black hair, snapping black eyes, and swarthy skin. While she was cautious and reflective and of strong will, he was emotional, impulsive, generous, and sociable, with a flair for adventure. But these differences were complementary rather than antagonistic. The only real threat to their happiness was her mother's deep suspicion of this "foreigner" who had the audacity to fall in love with her daughter.

Margaret Ann Terpenning Connelly was a positive character who dominated her entire household, including her mild-mannered, blue-eyed husband. She viewed the courtship of her daughter by a young immigrant as many another clannish American mother has done. "Who was this upstart, this dark-hued Welshman? Who knew but that he had left a wife in Wales? Who really knew anything about him?" [7] Considering the fact that David Charles Hughes was a

[7] *Ibid.*, p. 20.

stranger in a strange land and that Mary Connelly was a reserved and cautious young lady, his courtship could not be an easy one.

But Mary Connelly, despite her quiet nature, had a mind of her own.[8] She had escaped the limitations of her environment in the little Dutch community where she lived by attending two of the leading institutions of learning then open to young women. First, at Ford Edward Institute, she had delved into history, logic, the United States Constitution, Evidences of Christianity, Kames' *Elements of Criticism*, Cicero, French, and German. The following year she had spent at the Hudson River Institute at Claverack, where she specialized in French. Then she had taught in the little district school in Esopus and later established her own school for girls at Kingston.

It was soon evident that she loved the dark Welshman who persisted in courting her in spite of her mother's hostility. As to their religious differences, it was her influence that proved decisive. She had been brought up a Baptist. Her faith was "like that of the Christian martyrs," and those who knew her best felt that, notwithstanding her natural timidity, "she would have gone to the stake rather than be untrue to her religious convictions." [9] Through her persuasion the young Methodist preacher who had fallen in love with her became a Baptist. A certificate from Pastor William S. Mikels shows that David Charles Hughes joined the Sixteenth Baptist Church in New York on October 5, 1860. He married Mary Connelly in Kingston on November 20 of the same year.

The only child of this marriage has written of his parents: "They were brought together in a spiritual union which held them in the closest companionship as they pursued the same aims and cherished the same hopes. . . . Their love for each other, which at the outset had surmounted the obstacles raised by the differences in their early environment and in temperament, grew in strength throughout the forty-nine years of their union, as they labored together in unity of spirit for a common cause and with a profound faith. I have never known any persons more sincere in what they professed or more constantly dominated by a sense of religious duty." [10]

When their son was born, they looked upon him as a precious soul entrusted to their care, and, in spite of poverty, war, and political ferment, they bent every effort toward dedication of his life to the church.

[8] For details of Mary Connelly's ancestry, see Appendix II.
[9] CEH. Notes, p. 20. [10] *Ibid.*, pp. 2, 20.

Chapter 2

HOTHOUSE ENVIRONMENT

CONSCIOUSNESS of the world about him had scarcely dawned for young Charlie Hughes when his parents moved to Sandy Hill. Like Glens Falls, Sandy Hill was a thriving paper-mill town. Its Baptist congregation raised the salary of the Reverend Mr. Hughes to $500 with a donation, or $600 without a donation, and he decided to devote himself exclusively to that parish. His family was received into the Sandy Hill church on May 15, 1863.[1]

Young Charlie learned to go to Church while he was still a toddler. For a time his mother's cousin, Kate van Nostrand, had been his nurse, but after a year or two his mother managed the household without assistance. Going to church thus became a necessity, for his father conducted the services and his mother sang in the choir. The strain of sitting through religious services was relieved in some measure when a close friend of his parents, Mrs. Charles Stone, gave him a little rocking chair that could be placed beside his mother in the choir gallery. He became very fond of that chair, and it has been handed down through the Hughes family as a relic.

At Sandy Hill, too, he made an impressionable acquaintance with Nellie, the family's cream-colored mare. Nellie was accustomed to both saddle and harness. On her back, or behind her in buggy or sleigh, Pastor Hughes made the rounds of his parish. Sometimes Nellie hauled the whole family on excursions to Fort Edward or Glens Falls. The exciting trip behind Nellie to the Stones' residence where he was given the little chair was Charlie Hughes' earliest recollection.[2] From these days he also retained dim memories of the martial music that was frequently heard in Sandy Hill—of his father giving words of encouragement to the men who were ready to march away in defense of the Union. Still more memorable was "the awful strain, the cry of anguish, when the news came of the death of our martyred President." [3] Young Charlie had good reason to remember the assassination of Lincoln. When his father came bursting into the house with the tragic news from Washington, he was in a state of grief that the child had never before witnessed. "Mary," cried the distracted pastor to his wife, "I could not feel worse if you had been killed." [4]

The reputation of the Reverend Mr. Hughes for enthusiastic preaching and

[1] *The First Baptist Church of Hudson Falls, N.Y.: A Brief History.*
[2] CEH, Notes, p. 43. [3] Governor Hughes' speech at Sandy Hill, August 27, 1907.
[4] CEH, Notes, p. 21.

devotion to his parish spread to other New York towns in spite of the meager communications of the day. On February 14, 1866, Deacon Harmon, speaking for the pulpit committee of the West Baptist Church at Oswego, suggested that the congregation extend a call to "Rev. Mr. Hews of Sandy Hill to become our pastor." [5] Brother Thomas Kingsford, who had made starch big business in Oswego even in the sixties, moved to offer "Rev. Mr. Hews" $1,200 annually. To this the congregation added a "donation." The Sandy Hill Baptists were reluctant to let their pastor go and did not accept his resignation when he first tendered it. Nor did he accept the new call immediately, but went to Oswego for four weeks "that he might become acquainted with the church and they with him." [6] The tryout brought mutual satisfaction, and the new pastor plunged into the work of building up the parish and getting its $70,000 meeting-house completed.

The Hugheses' new home at 40 West Oneida Street was a two-story white frame house with green shutters and front porch set back a respectable distance behind an ornamental picket fence. Here Charlie found new playmates, including Ginny (Virginia) Kingsford, who was about his own age, and Florence Sprague, who was somewhat older than he. Charlie was a delicate little fellow. Although a vigorous infant at birth, he had suffered, at the age of two, an attack of what was called "inflammation of the lungs," which left him an easy prey to several maladies. The winter winds off Lake Ontario seemed to cut through him, producing chronic catarrh. He suffered much from tonsilitis; no one in those days suggested the removal of tonsils. Nearly all the usual diseases of childhood came his way, including a serious case of scarlet fever, but that was not until he was ten. Contributing further to his lack of robustness was a very whimsical appetite. "For years," he tells us in his Biographical Notes, "I did my best to resist the efforts to persuade me to eat meat and vegetables. My diet was chiefly milk, graham bread, griddle cakes and maple syrup, 'johnny-cake' and honey."

But for the devotion and intelligent care of his mother, a born nurse, Charlie probably would not have lived to maturity. As he was an only child, his mother could give most of her attention to his physical well-being and his spiritual and mental training. He was taught to read at the age of three and a half. Memorizing was easy for him, and he soon had a fairly large repertoire of biblical lore. Weakness of the eyes—a handicap which persisted in some degree throughout his youth but which he fully overcame in later life—threatened to impede his progress. When he was five, his mother gave him a *New Testament and Psalms* with large type so that he could take his turn in reading the verses at family prayers, and when even that help proved insufficient he would recite verses from memory.

[5] West Baptist Church Record Book No. 1. [6] *Ibid.*

Religious zeal and moral fervor infused all his early education. His precocity encouraged his mother to believe that he would have a great career in the ministry, and she redoubled her efforts to prepare him for it even before he reached school age. The youngster had scarcely a waking moment in his mother's presence without being instructed in one way or another. As an experienced teacher, she was elated by practicing her pedagogical art on so receptive a pupil. And for him the absorption of information was a fascinating experience.

Strict discipline accompanied her teaching. While Charlie was encouraged to pursue the studies he especially liked, he was not permitted to neglect any subject that his mother regarded as essential. As he advanced in the "three R's," he was started in Fasquelle's *Lessons*, which gave him at least a foundation in French. His mother also took him through a German primer. She was strong in mathematics, and her exercises in "mental arithmetic" gave Charlie the most useful training he ever had.[7] She would have him toe a mark on the floor and, without changing his position, "do in his head" the various sums she gave him. He was urged to think quickly and accurately without recourse to paper or pencil—a faculty that would add greatly to his prowess as investigator, advocate, and public speaker.

At six Charlie was sent to school in Oswego and acquired an acute dislike for it. School meant for him unnecessary confinement and an incredible waste of time. He listened with increasing boredom to the teacher's repetition of morsels of learning that were already familiar to him. In later years he denied that he had been in any sense a prodigy, and insisted that some descriptions of his early performances were overdrawn.[8] But he had certainly experienced a hothouse intellectual growth that left him quite out of place in the Oswego school.

After three or four weeks he begged for the privilege of resuming his studies at home. Having planned his campaign carefully, he walked into his father's study and handed him a neat little document entitled "Charles E. Hughes' Plan of Study." With initiative, order, and foresight that are certainly rare in a youngster of six years, he had listed in separate columns each subject that he wished to study at home and the hour that he would give to it. Of course, this does not mean that he had no interests beyond books, study, and religion. Years later, when his father, with understandable parental pride, had informed the press of the "Plan," Hughes dismissed it as solely a means of giving him more time to play "when the studying was done."[9]

The "Plan" was accepted, and Charlie made a practice of beginning his lessons early in the morning, before his parents were up. He sat by the great stove in the living room—the "Morning Glory," very high and imposing, sending out its heat to the room above as well as to the main living quarters. The

[7] CEH, Notes, p. 26. [8] *Ibid.* [9] *Outlook*, Oct. 20, 1906, p. 405.

memory of its red coals shining through the isinglass became inseparably associated in his mind with the studies he pursued under his "Plan." [10]

Charlie's father sought to guide the boy's reading, which soon became extensive. The elder Hughes had an unquenchable desire for books, and this had led him to extravagances in accumulating a large library. Mrs. Hughes' thrift and caution saved the household from debt in spite of these outlays. But the family experienced many privations, and its treasures (such as were not laid up in Heaven) were very largely contained between the covers of books.

When Charlie was five, his father gave him a copy of Miss Corner's *England and Wales*—a history "adapted for youth, schools and families." Fact and not fiction was what the elder Hughes prescribed. One day he found his son engrossed in a story book from the Sunday School library, his cheeks flushed with pleasure and excitement. The lad was invited to walk with his father along the shore of Lake Ontario.

"Charlie, do you know why these stones are of different colors?" the father asked as he gathered up a handful of pebbles.

"No, sir, I don't."

"Do you know why they are smooth and round?"

"No, sir."

"Would you like to know?"

"Yes, sir." [11]

The elder Hughes then said that it is much more important to know why pebbles are round and smooth than to have the most intimate acquaintance with Jack the Giant Killer or the Forty Thieves. On his sixth birthday, Charlie received *The Wonders of Science, or Young Humphry Davy*—the boy "who taught himself Natural Philosophy." A complete set of *Chambers's Miscellany* was also put into his hands, and he spent many hours browsing over its carefully digested information and selected literature.

Charlie's father tutored him in Greek, and on his eighth birthday presented him with a Greek *New Testament with Lexicon.* The lad could not do much with this, but he learned the alphabet and he liked to look up words in the lexicon. "I remember," he wrote in his old age, "that I was able, to the amusement of the family and others, to rattle off the genealogy of the first chapter of Matthew. My efforts were aided by another Greek *Testament* with the English version in a parallel column and in a childish way I liked to compare the Greek and English words." [12]

Meanwhile the Reverend Mr. Hughes had greatly enriched the spiritual life of Oswego. In appreciation the congregation raised his salary to $1,800 a year in 1867 and agreed to give him an additional $200 at the end of the year

[10] CEH, Notes, p. 27.
[11] Burton J. Hendrick, in *McClure's Magazine*, March, 1908, p. 521.
[12] CEH, Notes, p. 28.

"provided there be money in the church treasury not otherwise appropriated." In January, 1869, the pastor conducted a week of prayer meetings, "and such a week," the clerk recorded, "has not before in years been enjoyed by our church."[13] So rich was the manifestation of the spirit that the congregation voted to continue the meetings for two more weeks. In three years the pastor's untiring zeal had brought 106 souls into the church.[14]

Nevertheless, dissension arose. The warmhearted and impetuous pastor had endeared himself to the rank and file, but he had also antagonized a few powerful members. In a meeting on March 25, 1869, Brother Kingsford reported a prospective indebtedness of $700. It was a sign of discontent. The pastor summoned Brother Harmon to the chair, reviewed "in a few feeling words" his three years spent with the congregation, and tendered his resignation.

Young Charlie, aged seven, sat alone in the minister's pew, listening to these strange proceedings with increasing apprehension. Should he stay, he asked himself, when the other nonmembers filed out at the conclusion of the religious services? His father had asked all *members* to remain, and he was not yet a member. In spite of this, he decided to sit tight because his father was still there. When his father offered his resignation and withdrew to the study, however, the lad was frightened and followed his father into retreat.[15]

A flood of protests then broke loose against acceptance of the pastor's resignation. "Remarks expressive of the highest esteem for Bro. Hughes were indulged in by Brethren William H. Harmon, Burt, Rope, Colby, Selden Clark, Thompson, and Sister Smith."[16] The congregation unanimously resolved not to accept the resignation, and the Reverend Mr. Hughes withdrew it. A few weeks later, however, after he had attended the "anniversarys" at Boston, he again resigned, with the explanation that two or three influential brethren were trying to prejudice the people against him. Since the Lord had opened another field of labor to him, he said, his resignation would have to be considered irrevocable. "This was very unexpected," the faithful clerk wrote into his minutes, "and many were there that wept like children in fact the whole assembly did save a few, it was to [*sic*] much for them to bear, to think that they have got to part with a Bro. and Pastor whom they so much loved."[17]

Emotion was also at a high pitch on the last Sunday that the Hugheses spent at the Oswego church, on June 6, 1869. The members expressed their "affectionate esteem" and resolved that "in the labors of Bro. Hughes and his devoted wife, we have discovered the power of an earnest Christian life. We

[13] West Baptist Church Record Book No. 1, Jan. 9, 1869.
[14] *History of West Baptist Church, Oswego, N.Y., 1853–1897*, p. 41.
[15] Author's interview with CEH, Oct. 15, 1946.
[16] Church Record Book No. 1, March 25, 1869.
[17] *Ibid.*, May 30, 1869.

beg to assure them that their unselfish labors among us will never be forgotten and that our prayers . . . will follow them."[18]

With the memory of this friendly farewell warming their hearts, the Hugheses moved to Newark and were soon settled in the parsonage of the Fifth Baptist Church. Being an evangelist at heart, David Charles Hughes rejoiced in the enlarged opportunity which Newark offered. Here he was close to the throbbing pulse of the new America that was in the making. Here was greater need for his unflagging industry, for his ministrations to the afflicted and the unfortunate, and for his spirited sermons. In financial reward, too, he had probably made some gain, for free use of the parsonage at Newark supplemented his $1,500 a year. The Hugheses thanked God for all these blessings and entered upon a new chapter in their ministry with intensified devotion to the Christian ideal.

[18] *Ibid.*, June 6, 1869.

Chapter 3

SCHOOL AT LAST

MRS. HUGHES, as well as her son, was "delicate" in health. When she was a child, the family doctor had once brusquely remarked, "Mary, you will never make old bones." In her mature years that prognosis gave her husband many anxious hours, and one day he communicated his uneasiness to his son. Charlie, with the budding self-assertion of a nine-year-old, had spoken rudely to his mother. "My boy," his father rebuked him in private, "you must never speak to your mother in that way. She will not be with us very long." From that time on, Hughes tells us, "I always regarded my mother with a certain anxiety, but she well understood the care of the body and had her little remedies for temporary ailments. She bore all the burdens of a pastor's wife with unfailing regularity and with a constant joy in the performance of duty." [1]

Charlie continued to be afflicted with various ailments. The parsonage at 164 Elm Street was near what were then unreclaimed marshes, and fever and ague (*malaria*) were prevalent. But he was wiry and took great pains to develop his physical strength with the aid of a horizontal bar and two flying rings that his father had erected in the yard back of the parsonage.

Adjoining the parsonage was a vacant lot where he played baseball with the boys of the neighborhood. "One old cat" and "two old cat" were their favorite forms of the national game, and over the fence was "out." When Charles E. Hughes, candidate for the Presidency of the United States, revisited this spot in 1916, he recalled that one day while he was playing there as a youngster a friend aimed a chestnut burr with unfortunate accuracy at the head of a passer-by. The friend disappeared with lightning speed, while Charlie stood in his tracks, laughing. The man with the stinging cheek came over and knocked him down, and he rolled all the way to the foot of a high bank on which he had been standing.[2]

Charlie Hughes and his friends had no television, no motion pictures, no comic strips, no radio. But they did not know what they missed. Interspersed among their glorious days of baseball were happy hours given to "cops and robbers," "red lion," and other games. In winter the Chief Justice-to-be had great fun with his sled "hooking rides" behind passing carts.

For the days when Charlie could not play outdoors, he had other diversions.

[1] CEH, Notes, p. 21. [2] Author's interview with CEH; *New York Times*, Oct. 7, 1916.

As he had no brother or sister, he learned to play alone. At one time his parents thought of adopting a child to give him companionship, but Charlie, overhearing the discussion and knowing the family's meager resources, marched into the room and said he thought it would be a mistake. It was more important, he said, to give him an education than companionship at home.

"One of my favorite sports was 'travel,'" he tells us. "In the attic in the Newark parsonage, I had a large playroom. One of my father's parishioners gave me an enormous hobby-horse, about as big as a small pony, and I rigged up a shoe-box, with a driver's seat and whipsocket, and with trunk straps for reins I set forth on my journeys which were very extensive. I loved to get hold of a travel book and pretend, with the book before me, to go with my stout steed from place to place. Especially helpful in these excursions was Thomson's *Land and the Book*, descriptive of Palestine with inset pictures, and I traveled up and down that land, reading the descriptions to aid my imagination, as they seemed very familiar in view of my Bible lessons." [3]

In this period, too, Charlie became more familiar with his father's library. It consisted mainly of theological works, commentaries, histories, biographies, and works of reference—a formidable mental diet for a youngster. But he learned to know each book at least from its cover, and he catalogued a "good part of them." While he completed his "required reading" willingly, his real delight came from browsing through the library for interesting stories. These he seized upon with the zest of an explorer entering a choice but unknown land.

When he discovered *The Pilgrim's Progress*, he read it several times. This led him to Bunyan's *The Holy War*. At the age of eight a large volume of Shakespeare's plays piqued his curiosity, and he struck up a fascinated acquaintance with the Bard. "Of course I could not appreciate Shakespeare at so early an age," he wrote from the viewpoint of mature reflection, "but I loved the stories. *The Tempest, Twelfth Night* and *The Merry Wives of Windsor* were my favorites." [4] In the same manner he discovered Byron, Tom Moore, and a book of anecdotes for ministers. On his ninth birthday his father gave him a copy of Coffin's *The Seat of Empire* which he had obtained in Minneapolis while attending a religious meeting there. Charlie was so thrilled by this description of the Northwest that he resolved that he would make his home in Minneapolis when he grew up. His choicest possession, however, was a profusely illustrated copy of *Robinson Crusoe* which had been brought from England and given to him by James Clare.

This young Englishman, James Clare, who lived with the Hughes family in Newark for some time and taught Charlie in Sunday school, described his pupil as being "wrapped up in his books" and as a proficient Bible student. But he never regarded Charlie Hughes as a bookworm. "Withal he was a regu-

[3] CEH, Notes, pp. 28, 29. [4] *Ibid.*, pp. 29, 30.

lar boy," Clare once told the press, "delighting in boyish pranks, even if his father or his Sunday school were the victims." [5] Fun of every sort had a strong attraction for Charlie, although his bent toward mischief was restrained by the keen sense of discipline implanted in him by his parents.

Charlie made a "second experiment in attending school" at the age of eight and again gave it up. The following year, however, he attended the Tenth Ward Public School in Oliver Street, entering one grade below the graduating class. "My chief interest in the school work," he wrote of this experience, "was in the course in American History, taught by Mrs. [J. A.] Hallock, the wife of the Principal. She was one of the best teachers I ever had. She seemed to give me special attention and I loved her dearly." [6] His scholastic record hovered close to the perfection mark. In 1873, the year of his graduation, his report card bore seven marks of one hundred, two of ninety-nine, one of ninety-eight, and two of ninety-seven.

The happiest times of Charlie Hughes' early youth came in the long summer days that he spent on Grandfather Connelly's fruit farm at Port Ewen. The place had a restful and enticing atmosphere, with stately fir trees on each side of the walk leading to the house and other fine trees shading the front lawn. More important to a youngster of Charlie's fertile imagination was its enchanting view of the Hudson River.

"My outing began," he recalled, "with a trip on the 'Mary Powell,' the fastest and most graceful steamer on the Hudson River, leaving New York in the afternoon and reaching her berth at Rondout between eight and nine in the evening. I generally went on Saturday with my Uncle 'Simmie' [7] (whose family made their home with my grandfather). I sat on the deck with him and a number of his cronies from the Custom House (who also had their families up the river) and I heard endless discussion on New York politics which seemed to me a world of extraordinary cunning. Then, there were the good playtimes with my cousins. I took my part in berry-picking, but when I was nine or ten, being overcome by the heat, I was made paymaster, receiving the berries and paying the berry-pickers. Then there was the gathering of apples, a chore I never liked. But it was fun to drive with my grandfather in the late afternoon to Rondout Creek where the fruit was put on the steamer for New York. I recall that my father, who had been much on horseback in his first parishes, and prided himself on his horsemanship, wished me to learn to ride and sent the saddle he had used to my grandfather's place. So I saddled 'Billy'—the trusted family horse—and galloped about on the dusty country roads. Best of all, there was a rustic seat under an apple tree at the far end of the orchard which lay on the crest of a knoll commanding an extensive view up the river. I never tired of that

[5] Newark *Sunday Call*, Feb. 9, 1930.
[6] CEH, Notes, p. 30. [7] Carey Simpson Connelly.

charming scene. Immediately below was the mouth of Rondout Creek with its busy boats, the most of which I learned to know as well as the larger steamers which called across the river at Rhinebeck. The river teemed with life, always interesting, but I loved the river itself, with its broad sweep and majestic serenity, and the view of the rolling upland toward the Berkshires on the East and of the Catskills to the North,—the wonderful heights, as they then seemed to me, full of mystery and legend. On the warm summer days, whenever I had a chance, I would sit and watch the river in a sort of enchantment." [8]

On June 14, 1875, Charlie wrote to his parents from Port Ewen the first letter of his that has survived:

> I again have the pleasure of writing from this little Paradise. The country air surrounds me while the sun shines forth in its brilliancy and Grandpa's well welcoming the thirsty to draw and drink. Such is my situation, and now I guess I am beginning to see the loveliness, beauty and glory of nature. . . .
>
> This morning I rode "Billy" very long, first with the sheepskin, and I got him so he can run as fast as you please and don't hurt me. He does not canter a bit. I put the saddle on him afterward and it went just as well. I can harness, unharness, put saddle on and off and tend to him, clean him, etc.
>
> I hope you have a pleasant time on the excursion. Please excuse my absence and give my love to all who inquire after me. Write as soon as you receive this. Grandma and Grandpa are well and send their love to you—so are Aunt Hattie, Charlie, Henry, Mamie, Maggie. Charlie is as cunning as he can be. He is our pet and it has been very curious to me to see the different phases of character—first, in Charlie, 16 months old—then, in Henry, a boy of 4—then, in Maggie, of 8 and then, Mamie, 10. And, then, myself, 13 . . .
>
> But I must draw to a close. I hope that you will pray earnestly for me. That, if it be possible, I may regain some of the spiritual power I once possessed and more completely obey the sentiments expressed in Ephesians 6:1. [The citation reads: "Children, obey your parents in the Lord: for this is right."]

Here is the first intimation that the intense religious zeal that Charlie's parents had instilled into him was beginning to wane. The lad was starting to think for himself, and while his budding sense of differing with his parents disturbed him at first, it did not seem to interfere with his enjoyment of life.

In the summer of 1873 came an entirely new thrill. The Hugheses decided to treat themselves to the almost incredible luxury of a trip to Europe. The journey they had often dreamed of became feasible when Leonard W. Cronkhite of Sandy Hill, a friend at whose home the Hughes family frequently visited during their August vacations, advanced the necessary funds on easy terms. The trip was planned primarily in the interests of Mary Hughes' health, but her husband was eager to visit his relatives in England and Wales, and their son was panting for adventure. They sailed in June on the *City of Antwerp*,

[8] CEH, Notes, pp. 31–32.

landed at Liverpool, and went directly to Abertillery, Monmouthshire, where Mr. Hughes' sister lived.

Charlie was keenly disappointed in his Aunt Jane. She was postmistress of Abertillery and obviously a woman of ability. Since the death of her husband, Edward Jones, she had also continued his business—a general store. But she had opposed her brother's migration to the United States, and now, after eighteen years, it was apparent that she had never forgiven him for becoming an American and marrying an American woman. One night in a London lodginghouse Charlie was awakened by his father's sobbing because of the icy reception his sister had accorded him. The lad pretended to remain asleep and overheard his mother's efforts to soothe his father's grief. The incident widened the gulf that already existed in his mind between himself and his Aunt Jane.

David Charles Hughes had become thoroughly Americanized by early naturalization as well as by habit and turn of mind. Young Charles' upbringing had been completely dominated by American thought and custom; he never acquired any feeling of identification with his father's kin abroad. On the steamer he had fought over the American Revolution with an English boy, and when he got to Wales his relatives there seemed entirely foreign to him. In later years, when his name had become well known in Europe, the Welsh effusively claimed him as their own, and the University of Wales twice offered him an honorary degree. He accepted neither the adoption nor the degree. While he greatly admired the character of the Welsh, he refused to forget the Dutch, Scotch-Irish, English, and German strains in his ancestry; and his feeling of oneness with a people was reserved for his own American countrymen.

Charlie was much more favorably impressed by his uncles. His father's brother Jabez, whom they visited in South Wales, proved to be "a kindly man, full of humor." His uncle John Richard Hughes was an eminent preacher of the Calvinistic Methodist denomination at Anglesey, North Wales. Charlie went to hear his Uncle John preach in Welsh and was deeply affected even though he could not understand a word of it. Uncle John had what the Welsh call *hwyl*—that mysterious power which seems to give a Celtic orator unexplained eloquence and excites his listeners without their knowing why they are excited.

Taking leave of relatives, the Hugheses were lured by the scenes that have drawn many thousands of Americans to the Old World. Charlie found Warwick Castle so fascinating that he wrote a theme on the subject when he returned to school. The armor, jewels, and ancient furniture held his interest, but most curious of all was the "famous iron porridge pot, which holds 102 gallons, and which he [Sir Guy, the giant, Earl of Warwick in the tenth century] had filled every morning for his breakfast." In London they took a room in a King Street lodginghouse with only one bed for three, but spent two exciting weeks sightseeing. Religion was not forgotten. Twice they went to hear Charles Spurgeon, and father and son made notes on his sermons. After London, came the thrill of exploring Paris. Charlie's enjoyment of the journey was "beyond words." He devoured the guidebooks with unflagging enthusiasm and became so well informed on London and Paris that his parents permitted him to plan many of their excursions. His mind registered so faithfully what he saw that when he again visited Europe as a young man these two cities seemed very familiar.

Returning to Wales from Paris, they took passage for New York on the *City of Richmond*. It was the first trip for this steamer, and she was trying to undercut the record of a sister ship which was said to have crossed the Atlantic in seven days. Engine trouble developed, however, and, as the vessel approached Nantucket Shoals in a dense fog, a shrill feminine scream of terror turned the anxiety of the passengers into panic. Frightened men and women in their night attire filled the passageways. Rumors of a terrible accident ran through the disheveled crowds. Charlie Hughes thought the ship might be going down, and he never forgot the excitement of that scene. Not until the next morning did they learn the reason for the commotion. A young actress who had imbibed too much at a gay champagne supper had gotten into the wrong stateroom. After disrobing in the dark, so as not to disturb her companion, she had aimed at the top berth and happened to grasp its occupant by the beard. Her screams as she ran from the room had been given an absurd misinterpretation because of the prevailing anxiety.[9]

At the age of eleven Charlie entered the Newark High School. It was an excellent school, and he looked forward to preparing for college by the fall of 1877. Especially to his liking was the Latin course taught by John L. Heffron, a tall, handsome young graduate of Madison (now Colgate) University. But high-school days for Charlie Hughes were to be very brief. During the recess one day in January, 1874, he joined in a game of "red lion," as he had often done before. A group of boys with their hands linked together chased and caught him. In accord with the rules of the game, he joined the line and the chase continued, the line growing ever longer. With all the heedlessness of adolescents acting in unison, the line whipped its center link into a stone pillar. That center link was Charlie. He lost his two upper front teeth and was badly hurt. Before he recuperated from this experience, his father resigned his pastorate in Newark and the family moved to New York.

[9] CEH, Notes, p. 33.

Chapter 4

SIDEWALKS OF NEW YORK

CHARLES E. HUGHES was to become the most conspicuous figure in New York, and, later on, its foremost lawyer. His name and his doings were to fill many thousands of columns in the city's leading newspapers. In 1874, however, his introduction to the great metropolis was very humble. His father accepted a secretaryship in the American Bible Union, and the family found lodgings in the four-story brownstone house at 32 Great Jones Street in which the Union had its headquarters. The remainder of the house was rented to other lodgers, with Mrs. Hughes acting as landlady.

The boy's schooling became a baffling problem. New York had no public high school that he could attend. Graduates of the public schools entered the College of the City of New York, which offered a five-year course. But the college would take no student under the age of fourteen, and Charlie was not yet twelve. His only chance of getting back into school was to join the graduating class of a New York public school, and even for this he would have to wait until the following September. Circumstances thus conspired to give him more than six months of freedom in a city that held unlimited fascination for him.

Up to this time Charlie had visited New York only occasionally in the company of his father when he attended the Ministers' Conference on Mondays. He had been much excited by the crush of traffic on lower Broadway, with irate policemen and swearing drivers trying to extricate the stalled buses and trucks. Now he was free to explore all the city's wonders, and in spite of the inferiority complex he had acquired because of his missing front teeth, he lost no time in getting his excursions under way.

Being near the center of the city, Great Jones Street was an ideal base for the young explorer's operations. That oddly named thoroughfare was really the part of Third Street which lay between Broadway and the Bowery. "The neighborhood to a considerable extent was still residential," Hughes recalled in his later years. "Lafayette Street had not been cut through, and from Astor Place to Great Jones Street was known as Lafayette Place and had a number of commodious homes as well as the Astor Library. On the corner of Lafayette Place and Great Jones Street, next to our house, was the church building which had recently been St. Thomas's, then removed to Fifth Avenue. This building bore an enormous sign with the words 'Moral Amusements.' Across Lafayette Place and on the western corner of Great Jones Street was a large mansion occupied by the Columbia Law School. Many a time I climbed up the iron fence which surrounded it to see Professor Dwight, with the white pitcher of water on his table, lecturing to the law school students."[1] Several years were to elapse, however, before any thought of growing up to be a lawyer himself ever entered Charlie Hughes' mind.

His expeditions took him as far as the Battery on the south and Central Park on the north. No one interfered with his wanderings, and that undoubtedly added to the sheer joy he found in them. Equipped with a little street directory and a willing pair of legs, he commanded the entire town. For New York in the 1870's consisted of Manhattan; a break at Central Park separated the metropolis from Harlem, Bloomingdale, and the other communities beyond. Down in the Wall Street area the Trinity Church steeple dominated the skyline, and the old Equitable Building was the chief mecca for sight-seers.

Sometimes Charlie indulged in the luxury of a ride in one of the quaint old buses that came to typify "little old New York." And there were other means of getting about. When he was tired of walking, he would jump on the tail-end of an empty horse-drawn truck and "ride joyously with dangling legs."

Bustling, skyscraperless New York was in the throes of its last fight with Boss Tweed. Corruption and crime were a part of its nature, and this too held an interest for young Hughes. On one of his later excursions he saw political workers near the polling places with greenbacks in their hands, marshaling the voters, and never forgot that experience. In his Notes he tells us:

> Any part of New York that had a bad reputation was particularly interesting. I wandered about Chatham Street, the Five Points, Cherry Hill and various places that were notorious. The Bowery was a fascinating place and little escaped my curious eye. On Broadway, around the corner from Great Jones Street, stood the Grand Central Hotel, one of the leading hotels of the City, where but a short time before Stokes had shot Jim Fisk. I regarded it with awe. The stretches of the lower East Side, then predominantly Irish, became very familiar. I went to Sunday School at an old Baptist Church on Stanton Street, east of the Bowery, an institution which already seemed sadly out of touch with the neighborhood. I loved to sit in the small parks. Union Square was a beautiful park with fountain and trees. Madison Square was also a delightful spot, but best of all to my mind was Stuyvesant Square and broad Second Avenue with its spacious residences and shade trees. Central Park, then a sylvan retreat of the "horse and buggy" age, was a dream of beauty, and when I had a visiting cousin we would make a day of it, investigating its by-paths. I have known New York through all the transformations of the past sixty-eight years but the memory of the old town as I first became intimately acquainted with it stands out most vividly.[2]

[1] CEH, Notes, pp. 36–37. [2] *Ibid.*, pp. 37–38.

In September, 1874, Charlie took the entrance examination of Public School No. 35 on Thirteenth Street and was admitted to the graduating class, A First. No. 35 was at that time the most famous of the New York public schools for boys, having won great distinction under the principalship of Thomas Hunter. That eminent teacher had left the school to head the Normal College for Girls (now Hunter College) before young Hughes arrived, but the fame of No. 35 for scholarship and discipline was maintained under his successors. The school attracted students from all parts of the city and boasted that its graduates became leaders in many walks of life.

Despite the fact that he was in the highest of four units of the graduating class, Charlie found himself covering a great deal of familiar ground. No Latin was offered. The teacher of "A First" was middle-aged Charles Gates, who was later to become principal of No. 35. He was an able instructor, but the students were most impressed when he asked them to put aside their books and talked about his philosophy of life or the great world outside. Specialists came in once or twice a week—a French teacher with purple hair, who amused the students but taught them virtually nothing, and a lecturer in chemistry, who was almost toothless and not easily understood. The one terrifying hour of the week was that given to drawing, for which young Hughes had not the slightest talent. He toiled longer over the required sketches than over anything else, but to no purpose. So futile were his efforts that his father had him excused from that course.[3]

Charlie had been at No. 35 only a few weeks when his parents moved to Greenpoint, Brooklyn. Although it was a long journey from Greenpoint to No. 35, he would not hear of shifting to another school. Usually he took the Twenty-third Street ferry and walked (except in bad weather) from Avenue A to the school at Thirteenth Street and Sixth Avenue, carrying his books and lunch box. Ice in the ferry slips frequently caused delay in winter, but Charlie did not object so long as he could continue on at No. 35.

Whenever possible, he also sought his recreation among his school friends in New York. Skating became his favorite sport, and Central Park offered many opportunities to indulge in it. No palatial apartment houses then obstructed the sweep of wintry winds across the park. Eighth Avenue west of the park was a haven for squatters living in little shanties and tending their chickens, goats, and pigs. On the Fifth Avenue side of the park, according to the recollections of the enthusiastic skater from Greenpoint, there were only two houses —on the corners of Sixty-second and Sixty-fourth streets.

The most notable burgeoning of young Hughes' talents at No. 35 came in writing. Early in the term Mr. Gates called for an essay on "Bones." That was

[3] *Ibid.*, p. 40.

a stumper, but Charlie laboriously produced a paper which met the test. Then came an invitation to put in voluntary essays. At the suggestion of his father, Charlie wrote expansively on "The Elements of Success." Three such elements held his attention: "Knowledge, Determination and Industry." Knowledge, he thought, "also involves thoughtfulness and clear headedness." Determination could be exemplified by Grant's decision to "fight it out on this line if it took all summer." Industry? "The well known Latin proverb, 'Perseverance conquers all things' should be stamped on the memory of every person who wishes to succeed. Without industry no man can succeed."

This effort pleased the authorities so much that the young essayist was asked to read his paper in chapel. With such encouragement, he produced a series of essays,[4] making an ambitious choice of subjects. "Happiness and Its Constituents" was a ringing youthful appeal for virtue: "Happiness is that state of mind produced by the enjoyment of good . . . and an untroubled conscience. . . . For as soon as evil is committed, its loud and thunderous notes peal and echo through the regions of the soul. . . . Whenever we turn aside from following Duty's beckoning finger, that moment happiness ceases." This paper was marked "Excellent," and another straight dose of moralizing entitled "True Manhood" brought a similar reward.

The most controversial essay of the series was "Light Reading and Its Consequences." Written language was a great blessing, Charlie pontificated, "but like all other human inventions this has been put to base uses and to one of these corruptions has been assigned the name of light reading." The gist of his complaint was that "light reading will not educate our moral sense, but will blind, pervert and weaken it. . . . Light reading is fanciful," he continued, "and its chief power consists in working up the imagination to such a degree, that we will either go off in ecstasy of delight or sink into tears on account of the good or bad luck of our fictitious hero . . . if one were never to see a book nor learn a letter he would be in a more hopeful condition for true progress than one who confines himself wholly to light reading."

This boyish rehashing of countless admonitions he had received from his parents and Mr. Gates is the source of various absurd stories to the effect that Hughes grew up in ignorance of fictional literature. Actually, he was devoted to Shakespeare, Byron, and Moore long before this essay was written; he never thought of their works as "light reading." A year later he was to discover a volume of Smollett in his father's library and become absorbed in the adventures of Peregrine Pickle and Roderick Random, and he was soon to be reveling in many works of the great novelists. The target of this essay was the drivel to be found in the *New York Weekly* and similar sensa-

[4] All these essays have been preserved among CEH's personal papers.

tional publications of the time, which some of the boys devoured during their lunch period.[5]

In any event, these preachments reflected but a temporary phase of his intellectual development. An impressionable boy of twelve, Charlie got a regular diet of moralizing at the family table. Visiting grownups, usually preachers, added quantity but seldom variety to the wisdom offered him. Accompanying his parents to church gatherings, he heard innumerable discourses on moral and religious subjects. Occasionally, too, his father took him to hear an eminent lecturer. Henry Ward Beecher and Wendell Phillips held the boy spellbound. His extensive notes on these lectures and sermons were a natural source of material for his essays. When No. 35 offered "merits" for such papers plus the distinction of reading each of them in chapel, he reproduced, almost as faithfully as a dictaphone, the platitudes that had been dinned into him.

Charlie's chief competitor, R. Floyd Clarke, won his "merits" by declamations. At chapel, Clarke recited "The Battle of Ivry" and other pieces with fine effect. Another classmate, Harry G. S. Noble, was to become president of the New York Stock Exchange. It was a less conspicuous lad, Harry G. Tobey (later of Charleston, South Carolina), who became Charlie's seatmate and best friend at No. 35.

Their commencement in June, 1875, was an affair of distinction. The well drilled graduating class, with its four divisions, marched from the school to the old Academy of Music at Fourteenth Street and Irving Place and was seated in tiers on the stage. The boys' parents and friends filled the boxes and orchestra seats and the general public the balconies. Charlie Hughes delivered the "salutatory" on the subject of "Self-Help," inspired by his reading of Samuel Smiles. In addition to that signal honor, the school gave him a silver medal inscribed "For Composition."

Young Hughes thus found himself graduated from a public school for the second time, but he was still a year short of the minimum age for admittance to college. Rebelling against the arbitrary rules that held him back, he resolved that he would graduate from some college in 1880 when his classmates at No. 35 would be getting their A.B. degrees. With that determination goading him —determination which was one of "The Elements of Success"—he once more took up a course of study at home.

Greenpoint in the 1870's was an attractive village. It was the seventeenth ward of Brooklyn, but a stretch of undeveloped land separated it from other built-up sections; it was connected with Williamsburg by only a one-horse car line using queer little vehicles with a single door at the rear. "Filled with

[5] CEH, Notes, p. 41.

people who were always friendly and neighborly in the true sense of the word," [6] it was a community of self-respecting families of moderate income. For a few months the Hugheses occupied part of a three-story shingled rowhouse at 109 Oak Street. Then for nine years they lived in a modest red brick rowhouse at 127 Milton Street. Directly opposite their house lived Ralph Albert Blakelock, celebrated painter of Brooklyn. A few houses down the street lived Herbert Baker, future oil magnate, and, up the street, Thomas C. Smith, who built the Little Church Around the Corner in Manhattan.

Charlie Hughes played baseball with the boys of the neighborhood on Paddy Flood's lots. He had a velocipede on which he used to scoot along the otherwise quiet and uncongested residential streets. Swimming in the East River was a favorite sport for the Greenpoint lads. They left their clothes on the docks and swam sans trunks without being molested. Charlie looked on enviously without joining in this fun; he did not know how to swim.

To the rural charm of Greenpoint was added the glamour of the shipbuilding industry extending along the shores of Newtown and Bushwick creeks. Of still greater interest were the Greenpoint churches, which were thronged every Sunday. During the Reverend Mr. Hughes' pastorate at the Union Baptist Church, more than four hundred new members were added to his congregation. His parish boasted that its Sunday school, with approximately a thousand members, was one of the largest, if not the largest, in the state. Brooklyn was a paradise for Protestant ministers.

The Sunday-school May Walk, which brought together the children and young people of most of the Protestant denominations, was a leading event of the year. Each class marched as a unit under its own banner, the little girls dressed in their best finery, the boys in their Sunday clothes. Reverend Hughes, grave and erect, led his own special division. The procession moved slowly through lines of spectators on Manhattan Avenue to the ringing of firehouse bells. At the end of the Walk came "union services"—inspirational but in a lighter vein. Then the serving of ice cream and strawberries in the cool groves of what had been the Meserole farm gave the day a happy climax.

Even more enjoyable were the annual midsummer excursions. Two barges were lashed together to accommodate Pastor Hughes' Sunday school on such occasions, with a gangway providing easy access from one to the other. A tugboat would pull the barges up the Hudson to Iona Island (or down to Long Branch or some pleasant resort on Long Island Sound) while bands played and a holiday atmosphere prevailed. The young people were inclined to dance in spite of lifted eyebrows. At the picnic grounds the boys went swimming, played games, and devoured incredible quantities of food.

The Reverend Mr. Hughes once more made his influence strongly felt, as

[6] Granville F. Sturgis in the *Brooklyn Eagle*, June 9, 1940.

he had done at Glens Falls, Sandy Hill, Oswego, and Newark. Liquor and tobacco took the place of the Copperheads as the chief objects of his reforming zeal.[7] His parishioners thought of him as a lovable character who stimulated them to the attainment of new self-respect, a balanced budget, and a new house of worship. His salary of $2,000 a year without a parsonage, a maximum that he was never to exceed, was often in arrears,[8] but not his fidelity to what he believed to be the work of God.

[7] Brooklyn *Daily Eagle*, Feb. 9, 1930. [8] CEH, Notes, p. 22

Chapter 5

EMANCIPATION

IN HIS rambles about the city, young Hughes had often visited Washington Square and observed the dignified buildings of New York University with profound respect. The idea of entering there made his heart tingle with excitement. In the summer of 1875, however, chance suddenly shifted his interest to an even bolder venture.

The Hugheses visited their friends, the Cronkhites, at Sandy Hill, and Charlie was thrown into the company of Mr. Cronkhite's nephew and namesake, who had just finished his sophomore year at Madison (now Colgate) University. Young Hughes was flattered by the companionship of this college man several years his senior and thrilled by the stories he heard of college life on the hill at Hamilton. Up to this time schooling outside of New York had seemed utterly beyond his reach. Now the idea of going away to college was suddenly made to appear feasible. He began a whirlwind campaign to win his parents' consent.

In concept as well as in results this campaign may be regarded as Charles E. Hughes' second big case. The first, of course, was when, at the age of six, he won the privilege of studying at home instead of going to school. In neither instance was he attempting to imitate a lawyer's methods. Courts and law were utterly foreign to his experience. Nevertheless, his logical young mind formulated a set of convincing arguments, and his fervor gave them a real impact. Obtaining a Madison catalogue from his friend, he studied it with the object of proving that he could prepare at home during the following year for the entrance examinations. The expenses would be light, he argued, especially in view of the reductions in room rent and tuition granted to ministers' sons. His friend Cronkhite, without that advantage, got along on an allowance from his uncle of $300 a year. Then came the clincher: "Was not Madison University a Baptist institution, with many studying for the ministry? Was not Hamilton a safe and wholesome place, and did I not need the invigoration of life in the country, among the hills? I would be so careful, so obedient!" [1]

Remembering his college life at Wesleyan, Charlie's father soon capitulated. His mother was more hesitant. She could not bear to think of her "little boy" (for he was not only young but also slight and small for his age) being away

[1] CEH, Notes, p. 47.

from her constant care. But Charlie was determined and did not relax his efforts until he had "carried the day."

Behind his adolescent enthusiasm for a rural college was another powerful motive that he diplomatically concealed from his parents. He was eager to get away from home.[2] The strict regimen to which he had been subjected since his infancy had created in him a distaste for religious formalities and a longing for freedom to follow his own inclinations. As a minister's son, he had been expected to be a little angel—to attend all the church gatherings, to be an example to the other boys, to neglect nothing. Anything resembling sports or even pleasure on Sunday was tabooed. While his mind was receptive to religious teachings, his parents overgorged him, with the effect of defeating the very purpose to which they were so conscientiously devoting themselves.

In later life Hughes discussed this experience with candor that could not have been attained at the time:

It was the fondest hope of my parents that I should enter the ministry and I was early "dedicated." Their chief concern was that as soon as possible I should apprehend religious truth as they understood it, and whatever precocity I had was utilized for that purpose. My childish peccadilloes were evidence of the sinful nature of which I partook with the rest of humanity, and I was constantly warned of the necessity of subduing my evil inclinations, lest they "grow with my growth and strengthen with my strength," as my mother was wont to say. It was natural that when I was caught in a grievous fault I should have a conviction of sin. I readily absorbed the doctrines I was taught, and when at the age of nine I was admitted to membership in the Church, the Deacons who examined me were amazed—as I was later informed—at the "mastery" I displayed of the tenets of the denomination. As I look back upon that training at home, in the light of subsequent views and experiences, I realize that what interested me most was the dialectic rather than the premises. In that period, as soon as it was practicable, I also assumed certain duties of leadership. At Newark, I organized a boys' club which for about a year met regularly at the parsonage and I addressed the club from time to time. I took an interest in my father's classes for the Sunday school teachers and prepared references for his syllabi.

But with all this unusual sort of activity for a small boy, I retained a healthy love of play and frolic . . . and I was always eager for new experiences. A year or more before I left home for college, my spirit had begun to flutter in its cage. I recognized my parents' sincerity—I responded to their warm affection—I would not wound them for the world—but I became restive at required attendance at so many meetings and wished greater freedom. Then I began to question my father about the problem of evil and I wanted to know how what I observed in the ways of nature and of men could be reconciled with the goodness, the omniscience and the omnipotence of the Creator. Despite these disturbing thoughts I still had a deep religious feeling and I was more inquiring than rebellious. I also became increasingly conscious of internal difficulties in the church administration, due as I imagined to the shortcomings of church trustees which were fully discussed at the family table.

[2] Author's interview with CEH, Dec. 4, 1945.

Tiring of the routine of services and observing my father's pastoral troubles, I concluded that I would not enter the ministry. My parents hoped that I would have a different, and in their eyes a truer, vision of opportunity and duty as I matured. But in this they were destined to be disappointed.[3]

The Hughes family returned home about the end of August, and Charlie took up his preparatory studies with unbounded enthusiasm. His father now took him in charge, directing his study and occasionally holding recitations. This supervision was an inadequate substitute for the drill of a preparatory school, but it enabled young Hughes to set his own pace, and he lost no time in school exercises. At first he found it "very hard going," but he was soon advancing rapidly. In a period of nine months he did his lessons regularly in Latin and Greek grammar and prose composition, brushed up on Caesar's *Commentaries,* read six books of the *Aeneid,* four orations of Cicero, and three books of the *Anabasis*. In English and mathematics he had comparatively little to do to complete his preparation. His "emancipation" was now definitely in sight.

Charlie's father took him to Hamilton for the entrance examination in June, 1876. "With one exception," he wrote of this experience, "I took the regular written examinations which I passed without difficulty. The exception was in Greek, in which I had, for some reason unknown to me, a separate and private examination. By appointment, I went to the home of Dr. N. Lloyd Andrews, professor of Greek, and to my surprise he took me into his library, handed me an *Anabasis* and pointed out various passages. He left me for a few minutes and then put me through an oral examination, which satisfied him. Perhaps, because of my extreme youth, he sought to try me out in order to see whether it was worth while to let me enter. Anyway, I was duly matriculated, selected my room in old West College (I believe it was No. 39), observed with wonder and admiration the Commencement exercises and returned home the happiest of boys.

"In the following September, I went back to Hamilton to enter the freshman class and a new life began. As my mother often said—her 'little boy left home and never came back.' It was a different youth, with a broadened outlook, who visited his parents in the later vacation periods." [4]

Young Hughes' morale was at a low ebb, however, in his first hours alone at Madison. After his father had left him, he watched the students arrive in the stages from the railroad station. They clustered about the dormitory steps cheering and singing lustily "The Bull-Dog on the Bank" and "The Son of a Gambolier." The uninitiated little freshman felt lonely and unprotected. What would these gay and boisterous youths do to a newcomer so completely at their mercy when they discovered him? But these fears soon melted away; he

[3] CEH, Notes, pp. 44–46. [4] *Ibid.*, p. 48.

found that he was well received and quickly entered into all the joys of their common campus life.

What was then Madison University was beautifully located on a hill overlooking the lovely, picture-book village of Hamilton. In the 1870's the university had three main buildings—East and West College (the dormitories) and Alumni Hall, which contained the classrooms, library, chapel, and a large hall at the top for commencements. Some distance beyond was the building which housed the Theological Seminary. Below the hill, across what was then a treeless meadow, was the preparatory school known as Colgate Academy. Dr. James Morford Taylor had not yet begun his transformation of the campus, which was to make the bog into a lake mirroring lacy willow trees and the rough meadow into lawns with charming roads and paths. Indeed, the editor of the *Madisonensis,* biweekly publication of the senior class, was so unimpressed by the rustic charm of the campus in 1876 that he likened it to "a vast wilderness unfrequented by man, inhabited only by wild beasts and such things." [5]

The college's accommodations and physical equipment were primitive. The dormitories lacked central heating, lighting, running water, and, of course, bathtubs. The unfurnished rooms were in suites of two, a small study, with one large window and window seat, and an adjoining cubicle. Most of the students had small cylindrical stoves in one corner of their study. On these they heated whatever water they used for bathing or washing—water carried from an outside pump which, in cold weather, was surrounded by ice several inches thick. Coal purchased by the students for their stoves was kept in bins lining the halls. Their toilet was a little stone outhouse at the far end of the campus, with the rudest accommodations. As there were no servants, the boys took care of their own rooms—after a fashion.

Charlie Hughes took furniture from home for his "suite." In his study he had a round deal table with a black oilcloth cover, which served as a desk; a lounge, two straight-backed chairs, one camp chair, and a small bookcase. Certainly it was a modest abode. But he was filled with pride and happiness as master of his little domain, "unconscious of lacking anything which a collegeman could rightly expect." [6]

All the students took their meals in the town, walking down the hill, across the swamp, and back again, three times a day. This was exercise enough for even a lively, undersized freshman determined to build up his physique, and the barnlike structure called a gymnasium was little used. At first Charlie boarded with the mother of one of his Greenpoint friends, Ralph W. Thomas, who had entered the academy; but he was soon to be drawn more closely into the bosom of the college.

[5] Nov. 18, 1876. [6] CEH, Notes, p. 50.

Madison had a faculty of about ten professors, including the president, Ebenezer Dodge, a Baptist preacher and professor of metaphysics. Charlie's favorites were N. Lloyd Andrews, professor of Greek, the students' beloved "Καὶ γὰρ"; and James M. Taylor, professor of mathematics. Professor "Jim," as he was affectionately called, was an ideal teacher, helpful, precise, and thorough—a man who made mathematics a "window to the universe."

The young freshman from Greenpoint concluded that the number of good students was relatively large, and some were of outstanding ability. In his own class of 1880 were George A. Williams, who became a professor of Greek at Kalamazoo College, and Edward F. Waite, for thirty years an eminent judge in Minneapolis. Heading the sophomore class was Albert Perry Brigham, who was to leave the ministry and become professor of geology at Colgate, winning high distinction as an author of standard works on physical geography. The leader of the junior class was Benjamin S. Terry, later professor of English history at the University of Chicago. Foremost among all the young men at Madison that year was David Call, valedictorian of the class of 1877, who was soon to be president of Des Moines University, although his career was to be cut short by death.

Lonesome and uneasy over their son's absence, the Reverend and Mrs. Hughes continued by letter the intensive training and character-molding efforts in which they had been engaged since his birth. On September 4, 1876, his mother wrote to him:

My dear Charlie,

Your letter of Monday morning gave us much pleasure and I can assure you we praise God for his loving care over you. . . . We are in usual health, though somewhat pressed with care in consequence of the backwardness of ——— in meeting your Pa's salary. We had hoped to send you the money for your board today (we fear that Mrs. Thomas may be burdened also). But, as yet, the money is not received. Pray that God will give our people a liberal spirit. . . .

Charlie, I fear you don't sleep enough. I think you get up too early. Remember, you will be able to do more and better work in the same time if your brain is *thoroughly rested.* Don't commit the blunder in the beginning of your college course of *overdoing.* You will never amount to anything in the world of letters, etc., if you *overwork now.* Do be guided by us in this respect as well as in other respects.

Now a word in regard to your washing. Don't wear your clothes too long—especially, your flannels.

I do wish to know whether you have been troubled at all with sore throats since you have been in Hamilton. Be frank, my dear boy, about the state of your health, mind and experiences. . . .

We miss you, O, so much. Still, the Lord helps us to bear your absence, knowing it is for your good. . . .

Well, goodbye. May the Lord bless you, my boy, in all your efforts is the constant prayer of your loving,

Mother

On September 18 Charlie's father gave expression to his feelings:

It was an unspeakable relief to receive from the hand of the letter carrier this Monday morning your anxiously expected and thrice-welcome letter. And when I read its contents . . . and found how good the Lord had been to our dear, dear child, I need not assure you that our hearts were uplifted to God in praise and thanksgiving—warmed with an unusual inspiration of gratitude.

When I arose this morning, I remarked to your dear Ma that I had had not the remotest conception of the place that you filled in my heart. From the moment I bid you adieu on Thursday morning until your letter came, your form was constantly before my mind's eye. It is most emphatically proved that—"where our treasure is, there our heart is also." Don't misunderstand me in what I have said. I was not *anxious* about you. I felt perfectly free from any solicitude about you. I had perfect confidence that that covenant keeping God, to whom we have ever commended you, and who has so wonderfully cared for and guided you up to the present time, will not forsake you now. We were very thankful that you could commend yourself to God in believing prayer; and that you were so signally heard and that the God of peace had filled you with all peace and joy in believing. And our prayer is that your life will always be characterized by prayerfulness, trustfulness, purity of heart, sincerity of motive, unreserved consecration to God in your relations to God; and industry, thoroughness in your studies, undeviating courtesy to all around you, and an honest, manly, frank, generous and gentlemanly treatment of everybody without exception—however others may treat you. . . .

Ma joins me in tenderest love and interest. She will answer your next letter. Write soon and believe me,

As ever your loving
FATHER

A week later Charlie received these questions and instructions from his father:

MY DEAR CHARLIE,

Your thrice welcome letter reached us on Saturday afternoon. To say that we were glad to receive it, is speaking very moderately. . . . And, that you could say that, "in spiritual matters," the Lord is blessing you, filled our hearts with joy and thankfulness. Our prayers constantly ascend, our dear boy, for your *spiritual* as well as your *temporal* good. Indeed, we know if you are faithful to your obligations; if, in all things, you have an eye to the glory of God; living in fellowship with the Father and His Son, Jesus Christ; habitually walking in the light as He is in the light; and daily equipped in the armor of God; we will have no solicitude in respect to your college, social or other personal duties.

There are a few things which you have not yet mentioned, which we should like to know.

1. Your management of your stove.
2. Does your stove kettle work as you expected?
3. Do you air your bedding and bedroom every morning?
4. Are you careful to keep your neck and ears and wrists and nails perfectly clean every morning?

5. How about table manners? (I noticed when I took tea at Mrs. Thomas's that you sat with your elbows on the table: see to it that you refrain from any such breach of good manners.) Be gentlemanly at table. "Familiarity," remember, "breeds contempt."
6. At what temperature do you keep your room?
7. Do you practice on the piano?
8. What is your hour for retiring?
9. *Be sure you do not for once overdo in the gymnasium.*
10. What is the result of the Dodge Prize Exam?
11. Do you find it difficult to keep up with your class without over-much studying?
12. How many hours do you give to your respective studies?
13. Have you yet recited: if so, how did you get along?

In regard to college and other bills, I will be able, I think, in a week or so to meet them all. . . .

Mama joins in tenderest love. Don't forget our instructions. Continue to pray for us, as we pray for you.

From your affectionate Pa

Other letters written to him that fall provide additional insight into the Hughes home:

Sept. 30, 1876

MY DEAR BOY

. . . The Lord has heard prayer & relieved my mind from anxiety concerning you, but you are continually in my thought. Often I start up to call you to do this or that, only to awake more thoroughly to the fact that we are indeed alone. Well, we trust it is all for the best, & if you are a good, obedient, Godfearing boy, I *know* all things will work together for your good. We were happy in the fact that you passed your Examinations so finely. However we feared that your brain might have been overtaxed. How is it? Are you well? Don't be reticent on this point. Remember advice given & taken in time saves great trouble. I send you enclosed, directions for the use of your medicines. I thought perhaps in the excitement of getting away you might forget. Put them in your box for reference. I also enclose instructions for the regulation of your bed &c. all of which I wish you to heed. One thing more. *Don't forget to hang your flannels & sheets & stockings around the stove when they are returned from the wash.* Some wash women always send home the clothing before it is *dry*. If you were to put on damp flannel or stockings or sleep in damp sheets, the result might be, rheumatism, or, consumption, if not death in a short time.

How I wish I could see your room. Pa says it looks so pretty. . . . Pa sent much love. He misses you so much. He said you must try to send a postal or a little letter in the middle of the week. We can't wait a whole week. With much love & many prayers,

From your loving
MAMA

127 Milton Street,
October 16, 1876

My dear Charlie,

We have come to expect a greeting from you before breakfast every Monday morning. We were not disappointed this morning. For which we were thankful to our Father in Heaven. Thankful for the health and strength you report; thankful for the success in your studies; and, above all, that you are able to say: "God has filled my heart with peace and joy." This, indeed, filled our hearts with joy unspeakable. . . .

In respect to your debates, let me say: I do not want you to take any side, pro or con, which you cannot *conscientiously* maintain. *It is a vicious habit.* There are plenty of questions on which there are honest differences of opinion. Let such be selected. . . . But, NEVER *for the sake of argument*, take a wrong side. . . .

Be sure you remember all the advice we give you. Have a little memorandum with a classification of rules. And write down our counsel under the respective heads. eg—Rules for Health—Rules for Conduct, at table, in families, in college, in classrooms, among fellow students, in Society rooms.—Rules for Religion—Scripture Reading, Prayer, Meditation, etc., etc. . . .

Your loving
Pa

October 23, 1876

My dear, dear Charlie,

. . . Let me beg of you, dear Charlie, don't overtax your energies. Your physical constitution is something like my own. You can do good service up to a certain limit. Then you just give out. . . . The barrenness of your mind—when you tried to prepare your composition—is explained on the principle of an overtaxed brain. And you must not accept any Society work when you have a composition to write. And let me caution you again, my dear boy, in respect to accepting so much Society work. I understand that you have 30 members in your Society. If four took part in rotation every week, the same person would not have to take part again under six or seven weeks. But *you* have already taken part two or three times.

Do your regular work in regular time. Do not deviate from your systematic plan. . . . Let nothing but absolute physical inability interfere with your methods of study—I mean your regular daily and hourly routine. Don't ramble over hills on Saturday unless your work for Saturday is done. I regret that you yielded even for once to writing up to 12 o'clock at night. You must not do so again. Believe me, my darling boy, the points I am now making will be found the best in the end. . . .

We were truly thankful, our darling boy, that you could say: "Whatever I do, wherever I go, when the question of right or wrong comes up, it is decided by what will Pa or Ma say if I did it." My dear boy, this has been our prayerful aim all your lifetime—to so instruct you and train you that, if we were called away from you, our teaching would not have gone for naught. Continue thus, dear Charlie, and remember to walk in the fear of God all your days. Ma joins me in love,

Pa

Nov. 22, 1876

MY DARLING BOY,

. . . We praise God for these blessings to you every day, but we desire to see manifestations of *quiet* in the midst of your great and numerous duties. . . . I don't wish to lessen your enthusiasm, but I desire to see you pull steadily—with dignity—with quiet composure of soul, so that you may at all times *realize* what you do, why you do it and that it is well and carefully done.

Pa, too, is under the whip all the time,—scarcely gets time to take his meals properly. He looks almost like a walking skeleton—grows thinner and weaker, week by week, and works harder and harder. . . .

Now, I am doing very little better than either of you. I feel like panting for breath all the time—in sympathy with my hurried loved ones. May God in His infinite mercy bless you and keep you is the earnest prayer of your loving mother.

M. C. C. H.

In his first months at Madison, Charlie was responsive to his parents' admonitions, at least in his letters. "You know how it is," he wrote on December 2, "when you have your soul fired with love to God, how you feel. . . . Pray for me that I may be a useful servant in God's vineyard."

Finances were a difficult problem. On October 7 Charlie's father sent him $12, and his mother added this advice:

Pa says, as soon as you get the money, ask Mrs. Thomas for your bill for the month. That will give her an opportunity to decide as to the price per week. You know, we have not asked the question—we have only taken it for *granted* that she will board you for $3 per week. We hope it is all right. Still, *this* method will be a delicate way to relieve us from setting the price. Then, Pa says pay her and take her receipt and send it back to him so that he may know you have done the business, *business-like.*

The precocious freshman from Greenpoint was "rushed" by Delta Upsilon, one of the two national fraternities on the campus, and by a local society, the Adelphian. "My friend Cronkhite," he tells us, "was a member of the Adelphian and some of his society brethren went to extremes in their insistence. They contended that I should be entering on slippery paths if I joined either of the fraternities and went so far as to try to hold a prayer-meeting in my room in the interest of my soul. But I was attracted by the scholastic standing of Call, Terry and Brigham, all of whom were members of Delta Upsilon, and by the obvious good fellowship of others of that chapter, and I joined it with much gratification at the opportunity." [7]

His affiliation with a fraternity gave his parents some concern, and two other youthful requests—for permission to have a roommate and to join a boarding club so that he could "be with the boys"—were at first denied. His father wrote to him on November 6:

[7] CEH's Notes, pp. 52–53.

My Darling Boy,

There are two or three things which have caused us both some solicitude of late, and your last letter has increased it rather than diminished it. I refer to your Society matters. There are 3 things which I have always feared in respect to college Societies:

1. The cultivation of a party spirit, which leads to envy and jealousy. . . .
2. . . . the consumption of time which ought to be devoted to private meditation or to thorough and systematic reading—you ought rigidly to pursue a systematic course of reading to which every hour, which can be conscientiously spared for that purpose, may be given. . . .

I notice a parenthetical sentence in your letter which revealed much to me. It is this: "I am quite lonesome some evenings." It indicated to me that there is danger of your losing sight of some of the things to which I have just referred, in respect to the field of exploration beyond the mere narrow routine of college life. You can never feel lonesome if you have enough to do.

3. The third danger arising from college Societies is the difficulty of maintaining a strictly *spiritual* life. I will not dwell on this point. A suggestion must be sufficient to you.

Now, in regard to two requests mentioned in your letter, namely—

1. To board in the DU Club and
2. To take a DU chum.

In regard to the first, it would be a most welcome request financially considered. But there are other considerations. . . . Wait until the close of the present term at all events and then we will *see* you and talk the matter over.

In regard to the second request our judgment is the following . . .

1. It would seriously interfere with your religious privileges. Freedom to throw yourself on your knees frequently and whenever you were inclined to do so, would be out of the question.
2. A chum would increase the number of callers upon your room.
3. A chum would lead to time spent in conversation, which would be better spent in meditation and research.
4. A profitable chum is so rare a thing, that the risk is too great for us to give our permission without being personally acquainted with him. . . .

Write soon and ever believe me, with love from your dear

Pa

Three days later the Reverend Mr. Hughes wrote Charlie another long letter beginning:

To say that we were highly gratified and truly thankful to God for the tone of your letter and the excellent spirit with which you took the advice I gave you, coming as it did from the depths of my heart, is expressing our feelings very mildly. O, Charlie, I can sincerely assure you that these evidences of your love for your parents, your pious submission to their counsel, your implicit confidence in their judgment, are to us more gratifying than the most brilliant evidences of unusual genius could be; however much the latter might dazzle and excite and crown you with worldly honor.

Within a few weeks, however, young Hughes had joined a boarding club, along with fifteen or twenty of his new friends. In the following letter he tries to convince his parents of the wisdom of his step:

HAMILTON, December 13, 1876

DEAR MA AND PA,

At present I am perfectly well and hearty and I like it at the DU Club first-rate. Our board is splendid. Mrs. ——— knows how to make good pies. They are not those unbaked crusts as sometimes Mrs. Thomas has, but real good and thoroughly baked. We have pancakes in the morning and they tasted a good deal better than those Mrs. Thomas has. Their bread and butter too is excellent.

Then, in regard to general deportment, I never in my life saw better. There is not even loud laughter but conversation in groups—there being 19 at the table. . . .

In regard to my spiritual welfare. The Lord is abundantly blessing me with tokens of His love and mercy. I am so thankful to Him to think that here I am far away from you and, yet, He has not suffered me to be afflicted in the least, nor a hair of my head to be touched. But I must close. You have my heart's best love more than tongue can tell. So goodbye,

Your affectionate son,
CHARLIE

Eager though he was to get home for the Christmas holidays, Charlie was soon irked by his parents' continuous preaching and overweening concern for his soul. On their part, his parents were obviously shocked by the "worldliness" their "darling boy" had acquired. Shortly after his return to Madison his mother wrote him:

Now, my dear boy, will you remember the counsel of your father and mother. I am so apprehensive that you may be turned from the path of rectitude, by the influence of your worldly associates, that I feel that I was under the shadow of great sorrow. I have committed you to God's care, praying daily that you may be kept from the evil—not only kept from the evil, but be *active* in doing good. . . . In order that you may realize the blessings prayed for, treasure up in your mind the precious promises of God's word, think on them as you used to, write on them also. And, in respect to song, treasure up hymns of praise to God, instead of foolish, pointless college songs—worse than nothing, for it is like feeding on husks, causing one to be full of emptiness.

This week, rather tomorrow, begins the week of prayer, and I trust you will seek opportunity to pray with us sometime between the hours of 7½ and 9 o'clock every evening. Pray for a manifestation of God's power to save in our church and Sunday School and the community, generally.

Well, my *dear, dear* boy, once again I close another letter to you. May you have great success in your studies, the approval of God your Father and Christ your Saviour, and may this year be *characterized* in your life as a year of great progress in Truth and Holiness. May God's word be truly your counsel and your guide is the continued prayer of

Your loving
MOTHER

When he thought of his parents, Charlie felt both penitent and obedient. "In regard to my inner life," he wrote on January 2, 1877, "the Lord is caring for me and watching over me. I am weak & helpless but with his strength may overcome. Pray for me. . . . It is my desire to have my treasure in Heaven where it may be kept free from corruption." But his chief interests were study, fiction reading, and Delta Upsilon. On January 13, he wrote to his mother:

Studies are going on swimmingly and, really, Williams says, if he don't look out, the little tortoise may beat him . . . yet. I found out my standing in Geometry—and it was 4.87, the maximum being 5.00. Williams and I are pretty good friends, and he told me his standing. It was 4.88—only one-one hundredth ahead. We both obtained 5.00 in our examination.

We are still going on with our "Geometrical inventions." Last week we had two demonstrations to work out. . . . The professor asked one day for an original demonstration, ie.—we were to conjure up a figure ourselves and then work out a demonstration. Williams got a very nice one up and was highly complimented. I thought I couldn't let him go ahead there, so I got up a figure even better than his in which I did not even have to draw auxiliary lines, but he had to draw three. The professor said they were better than any in the book. We were the only successful men in that field.

Well, here I am, again, as usual talking about studies. Well, the fact is, I talk and think about very little else than studies. It's my food, my life and my spirit.

On January 24 he wrote again to his mother:

Your letter saddened me somewhat, as it reminded me by the pictures you drew that, indeed, as I richly deserved, your confidence in me had been shaken—if not wholly removed. But, I hope that in the future I may merit better things. I *am* trying to do your will.

But, I must hasten for I have very little time indeed. I had a chance to get a $6 DU pin for $4.50. As this chance will probably never happen again, and as many were after it, I secured it by paying 75 cents down, and saying that I would write and see if I could keep it. If so, I will pay balance when Fortune should give me a chance—if not, he will give me my 75 cents and I, his pin.

Please answer immediately, as there is no time to lose. It is a very pretty pin and awfully cheap. I hope you will consent to my keeping it.

The Reverend Mr. Hughes gave vent to his apprehensions in his letter of February 6:

My own Darling Boy,

Your long looked-for letter was most heartily greeted yesterday morning. Its tone was more like your own real self than any in some time. The obtaining of that precious prize—a DU pin—opened your *heart*. . . . Is it not so? For me, my dear boy, it gave me great pleasure to have the opportunity of proving to you once more how real, deep, and abiding is our love of you. The marked improvement in your spirit—and I trust in your piety since your visit home—has given us, as your parents, unfeigned gratification. It is, indeed, our constant prayer that the Lord will never allow you again to fall into the snares into which you were inveigled last term. Let Joseph's question be ever uppermost: "How can I do this great evil and sin against God?" There is nothing of permanent value in man except character. . . .

We were glad to see that you make a distinction between what we should have as *aims* and what we should desire as results. Never forget these three essential elements of every true life, and every action of every true life: (1)—*the supreme aim:* THE GLORY OF GOD. (2) *the supreme motive:* THE LOVE OF GOD. (3) *the supreme law:* THE WILL OF GOD. . . .

Again on February 21 Charlie's father wrote:

O, yes, my dear, dear boy, believe it, it is what we *are* that makes our life a success or failure. *Character* is the mighty power, not only of the preacher but of the student, of the boy, of the man. . . . And pray tell me, my dear Charlie, what is the very essence, spirit, vital breath of character, if it be not *true piety*? . . . It is, indeed, what we *are* and not what we *seem* to be, that constitutes real power. O, remember, my dear boy, that there are but two masters—God or Satan. . . . O, see to it ever, child of my heart, that to you God in Christianity shall be your all in all.

Charlie replied on February 24: "I try to follow your injunctions, in regard to everything." But his hunger for scholastic honors seemed to play havoc with his pursuit of piety and moderation. His mixed emotions are clearly evident in his February 11 letter:

I hope, dear Pa, that you will forgive me, for this once, for sitting down on a Sabbath afternoon, but the past week has seen me so busily engaged that it was impossible to write. . . .

I am sure that when you learn what has this week been accomplished, both your heart and Ma's will be in unison with mine, in rendering to God praise. . . . Successes have attended me on every side, and I have done more to raise myself in the esteem of those around me than ever before. . . .

In the afternoon, I spoke before the college and God helped me, and I did better than ever before. But I was very nervous about the evening, for—on account of much drilling—everything in my oration seemed trite to me and unworthy of speaking. I drilled most of the afternoon and after committing all to the Lord, my head and heart grew clearer and more easy—finally I was left without the slightest dread.

When my name was called and as I walked on the platform, every eye was upon me, for never before has anyone in Hamilton so young appeared on the platform of a Society. Every movement I made was watched and, when I had stopped, I found my audience delighted. Success was complete. To God be all the glory! They said I had the best of the evening. . . .

This letter—as usual—is full of *self*, unworthy, abominable, selfish self. How I wish I could—as it were—get out of *self* and know that God's glory is my only aim. Pray for me.

Elocution and literary contests in the 1870's held much of the interest and glamour that today go into college football. Hughes got a good deal of training in Delta Upsilon, which gave part of its weekly meetings to debates, declamations, and essays. His rousing declamation about a cavalry charge in the Civil War won him a place in the Royce contest in his freshman year. In later life he often laughed at the spectacle he must have made—a small boy shouting, "Come on, old Kentucky, I am with you!" But this cry of the cavalry commander seemed to stir the audience, and he took second prize.

When Charlie plunged into Livy and the Orations of Lysias, he realized how inadequate his preparations at home had been. Once this initial handicap had been overcome, however, he carried his courses easily. While he was no "grind" and was sometimes inattentive in class, he seemed always to be prepared. Professor "Jim" confessed in later years that on several occasions he had tried to "catch Hughes napping" but had never succeeded.

By midyear Charlie was able to write to his mother:

Work tells, and all say that indisputably I stand second only to Williams. I can hardly hope to stand any higher. For no one does his work easier than Williams and he has an immense amount of reserve force. Well, for that matter, I have a little too.

A letter written on January 20, 1877, gives us a glimpse of the work he was doing:

In Greek, also, we are having a very interesting time. Next Friday, I have to prepare and deliver an article on Dr. Schliemann and his discoveries. Then, we will have written debates on the question "Has Dr. Schliemann actually discovered the site of Troy?" "Were the Iliad and Odyssey the work of one author?" "Is the Iliad based on historic fact?" "When did Homer live?" So, you see, we are having a very interesting time now. Then, in the "History of Greece" we learn about all the old legends which are very pleasing to study.

This week I have made a splendid bargain. Hearing that, by writing and stating that you were a ministerial student, you could get a copy of "Channing's works" free, and, knowing that it was so, I wrote and got it. It is neatly bound, worth about $3.00, and I did not even have to pay the postage. Besides a full canvassing of Unitarian doctrines, it has fine lectures on "Self Culture,"—"Elevation of Laboring Classes"—"Slavery" and 10 or 12 other subjects.

Pleased though she was by his high standing, his mother sent a note of caution: "Well I always felt your little head was worth a good deal, but don't forget the source of power—all power. It is God who gives wisdom." On April 17 she offered Charlie a pretty stiff bracer for his sense of responsibility:

How truly should gratitude of heart constantly characterize your life. You *are*, highly favored with mental gifts and special privileges for their development—with blessings too numerous to mention in this hurried letter,—for which you will be held accountable in the great future. Make good use of them now remembering the promise, "To him that hath shall be given,"—"He that is faithful in little shall also be faithful in much."

Social life at Madison was meager. Occasionally the Delta Upsilon held a "private-public" (*private* because admittance was by invitation and *public* because others than members were invited) at which members demonstrated their skills in song and speech. These occasions afforded the boys a chance to escort the "sem" girls—students of the Hamilton Female Seminary described by the *Madisonensis* as "handsome, witty and clever as country school marms."

Charlie Hughes became a devotee of whist. Card playing had been tabooed at home, and that made it seem all the more alluring. Occasionally he also played chess with an upperclassman who roomed near him. His venture into baseball, the only athletic sport then in vogue at Madison, is memorable solely because his heroic attitude toward a swift grounder in the sophomore-freshman game cost him a tooth. This misfortune brought a pointed reminder from his father: "Do not forget what I have said about violent exercise and those club competitions in physical skill. *I do not wish you to take part in those things.*"

As spring came to Hamilton, young Hughes reported to his father:

There has been a phrenologist around telling for 50 cents what the boys have in their heads. I would have had mine examined, but I have no money to lose. Well, my birthday passed without my thinking of it. Such is life. My high standing has done one good thing for me, at least. The boys no longer think of me as a little fellow but as one whom they can esteem and regard with respect. My smallness saves me from all rough handling and so I have a happy and unmolested life.

. . . My money record for the last week is as follows:

Balance on hand—as of last letter. .	$.73
Postage	.03
Crystal for watch	.25
On hand now	.45

On March 3 he had written to his mother:

You ask how my clothing is holding out. I think my shirts will last till June easily. My Sunday clothes are all right. My blue coat and vest is growing shabby. My pants (those you made from Pa's) are threading out. I cannot explain it. The outer thread split. My shoes are miserable. The soles are all right but the leather splits. Two big splits nearly across my foot. . . . My collars and cuffs are all in order but that cravat is about worn out. I wish you would send me one of that kind or some stylish silk neckties for my standup collars.

His father wrote him on May 10:

Well, of this you may be assured,—that there will be two pairs of eyes to speak "Welcome Home" and two pairs of arms to clasp you at home.—O, my dear boy, how little you dream of the height and depth, the length and breadth, of a father's and a mother's love! May the Divine Grace enable you to live worthily of a love that transcends even a parent's love—"The love of God in Jesus, our Lord."

On May 31 his father wrote again:

I was not surprised that you shall be "on for Royce." It was what I expected. Now do your best. But trust implicitly in God for every need and assistance and for success. Do not be too elated, too sanguine or too ambitious. May the Lord help you to do your duty from right motives is my prayer. . . .

It is now quite doubtful whether both your Ma and myself will be permitted to visit Hamilton at Commencement. The truth is, my dear boy, "impecuniosity" has visited us and we do not seem to rally from it. I trust that either the one or the other of us will be there.

Charlie Hughes returned to Madison for his sophomore year in the fall of 1877, and his mother's admonitions soon followed him:

How thankful we are for God's loving care over you & how pleased that you are attentive to your studies & doing well. *Be thorough.* BE THOROUGH. BE THOROUGH in all you undertake. In your reading also, let your motive be improvement. Dwell upon the page long enough to get it into the mind. Inattention in reading injures the mind—weakens the memory. . . .

In respect to your washing neck &c., don't ignore your feet. If you persist in washing them every day, you will cure them of sweating.

Don't play croquet in the evening. I was astonished that you have taken again to the "worn out game." *Well don't play it at night. Take good care of your health in all respects.* HEED THIS WARNING!

Charlie's interest was centered in the Delta Upsilon convention, which brought an engaging group of college men to Madison. Their leader, E. Benjamin Andrews, young president of Denison University, an eminent educator who was later to become the most popular president of Brown University, made a profound impression on Hughes. Here is a man, he thought, who embodies my ideals. The enthusiastic sophomore wrote a detailed account of the convention to his mother on October 27:

DEAR MA:

. . . Well, as you say, our Convention is now a thing of the past. You can't tell how inexpressibly lonely I feel, when all the boys (our delegates) have gone. It seems as if I had known all of them through my whole college life. All our delegates were true men. You may imagine a crowd of about 60—the most of them holding highest positions in our largest and most influential colleges—all of them just completing a long college course and you may form an idea of the strength and talent represented in our Convention . . . some of them I am confident will be heard of throughout our land in coming days . . . all the discussions proved that there were long heads at work behind those shining faces.

On Thursday evening, everything gave way to our grand Promenade Concert. It was the most promising feature of the Convention and it was a grand success. . . . First, our Hall—the largest auditorium in Hamilton was fitted up splendidly. . . . The platform was all festooned and the words—Delta Upsilon—hung over it in letters of evergreen. . . . The most beautiful flowers that could be obtained were placed in urns in the middle of a hall and on the front of the platform. Most of the ladies present were in full dress, and the gentlemen were all dressed as well as possible with white kid gloves. The ladies were escorted to and from the Hall by young gentlemen with carriages. The band was on the platform and discoursed sweet music, while delegates and our own boys became acquainted with [the] ladies . . .

If ever I thought anything of Delta U my thoughts went up 10,000 per cent after our Convention. And, although it will probably cost us a great deal, yet it is in a noble cause. . . .

Now, I come to money matters. This term I am afraid expenses will be large on account of this Convention. That Concert obliged me to buy a pair of white kid gloves. I am sorry I had to get them but I got a six and three-quarter size, so that I can wear them on similar occasions in my college course. My college tuition tax of $13 really ought to be paid now. . . .

I will try to tutor at 20 cents per hour which will help some. I will do anything, but please don't think hard of our heavy tax in D.U.

Charlie's father tried to moderate his excitement and got this reply on November 3:

You speak of the excitement I was laboring under in my last letter. I have now had time to cool off, but I would still reiterate my statements of the DU Convention, and would say in addition, that it did me a great deal of good. We are apt to become narrow and straightened in our ideas, but such occurrences make us liberal and free.

Toward the end of the school year the sophomore class formed a good-fellowship society that indulged in raw oysters, cider, and cigarettes at the old Eagle Hotel. Hughes began to smoke on these convivial occasions. In his Notes he confesses also to taking part in some of the minor pranks at Madison. As a freshman he had joined a group of students campaigning for Hayes and Wheeler, and when (on returning to the campus in the early morning hours after a rally at Morrisville) they had rung the chapel bell in happy disregard of the rules he had felt duly initiated into the ways of college men. But his pranks were as harmless as the snowball fight and mild revolt against overwork that he described to his mother on January 19, 1878:

We met on the hill, and as we were marching downtown, the Academes snowballed us from behind an embankment. The College immediately charged on them, and a vigorous fight ensued, (with snowballs at about two feet apart) which resulted in the entire discomforture [*sic*] of the Academes. I came out all right, except one bad blow in the ear. A good many of the boys had black eyes the next day and sore heads. Well, so much for college fun.

In studies, we go along as usual. Prof. Andrews kept increasing our lessons until patience ceased to be a virtue, and a committee was appointed to tell him how much we would learn and no more! He acceded to our demands, and though we have hard work enough now, yet it is easy in comparison to what it might have been.

Charlie's parents knew nothing of his smoking, but they kept up a constant effort to keep him in the straight and narrow way. After a brief visit at home in April, he felt very penitent over the heartaches he had caused his parents. On April 13 he wrote to his father:

I am well and happy, but I don't know when I have felt so disconsolate on a return as I have this time. I feel alternately sad and joyous. I am trying to live as a Christian should before the world. But it is so hard. It is uphill work. But it is my aim, by the grace of God, to make my life a truly spiritual one. Pray for me, dear Pa, that I may live to the honor and glory of my Savior and please, please forgive the cruel heartaches I occasioned you on my last visit. I do want to become a truly Christian gentleman.

In April, 1878, the Reverend Mr. Hughes was expelled from the Greenpoint Pastors' Conference, apparently on a charge of unfair proselyting. While the incident caused something of a furor, which was magnified by garbled reports, he was easily vindicated. ". . . blessed be God," he wrote to his son, "I can use the language of Joseph to his Brethren: 'Ye meant this for evil; but God meant it for good.' "

Charlie replied on May 11, almost rivaling the numerous classical references in his father's letter:

DEAR PA,

I am glad . . . to know that you are coming into a safe harbor after a perilous storm. Neptune, with his trident has appeared amid the troubled waters of an Etruscan sea, and ordered Eurus and Notus and Zephyrus to their homes. . . .

However perilous the storm may seem, however violent may be the winds of adversity, the Christian is sure to come off triumphant. In what strange way does Providence lead. Here an attempt to do you the grossest injustice ends in giving encomiums of praise to the pastor of the little church in Greenpoint.

No one knew about it up here until the issue of the last Examiner when I was troubled on every hand by questions of every description. "Is D. C. Hughes your father?" "Quite a gun." "It don't do for them to tackle him." "Tell us all about it."

And so it goes. Well, as you well know, I did all that I could to set you up in the estimation of Hamilton students. You are "quite a gun," and it takes such circumstances as these to show it. I think it will do you and the church good. Nothing like a little stimulating excitement to make the brain quiver and burn with a sense of injustice done and wrong received. How it swells and strains every fibre of one's nature, and what a grand victory it is to establish one's self as inviolable before those who have attempted to stain one's reputation. Self is a mighty power. Bad, when too highly favored. But, when once roused in the cause of right, sets on fire the whole man, and makes him glow with zeal in the cause of truth. . . .

In two weeks from today the ordeal of a thorough prize examination will be passed, the Rubicon crossed—my hard work will be over. O, how I dread it! I will do my best but I cannot beat Williams. I feel it in my bones. If only I can get the second prize. Hoopla! Well, if work will do it it is mine. . . .

Just before the end of his sophomore year, Charlie had one of his few sick spells in college and feared that he was coming down with diphtheria. "Last Tuesday afternoon," he wrote to his mother, "I felt the sore throat coming on me, and before night my throat was nearly shut. I bound it up with a stocking and went to bed. When I got up the next morning, my legs sank from under me, and my eyes blurred, and I was compelled to fall right down on the lounge. It was a long while before I could get down to breakfast. I felt miserably. I couldn't swallow anything and was as weak as a rat." But a doctor supplied him with pills, and he was soon well again.

The extent to which his illness interfered with his competition for the Dun prize is not clear, but he blotted a page of his essay and in recopying it left out ten or twelve lines. Williams got the first prize, as Charlie had anticipated, and he got only honorable mention. "Well," he wrote to his mother, "a disappointing failure. But while sorry, I feel that [it] is a punishment for a pride that must inevitably precede a fall. Well, such is life." There was no cause for disappointment, however, in his scholastic standing. The Madison (now Colgate) records show that his rating was 4.91 in rhetoric (four meaning "superior" and five being the maximum grade), 4.84 in French, 4.71 in Greek, 3.92 in Latin, 4.90 in calculus, and 4.97 in analytical geometry.

Chapter 6

BROWN UNIVERSITY

"EACH man begins with his own world to conquer," Charles E. Hughes once said, "and his education is the measure of his conquest." [1] During his second year at Madison the urge in him to expand the "measure of his conquest" became very strong. He was approaching sixteen. Growing fast in body and intellect, he began to yearn for the more liberal atmosphere and wider opportunities that a larger college could be expected to offer. A survey of the possibilities indicated that the most favorable shift he could hope to make would be to Brown University. Brown, with its Baptist tradition, would appeal to his parents. At the same time it would give him the privileges of city life in Providence besides the freedom of living away from home.

Charlie wrote to Professor Poland at Brown and found that the requirements for admittance were stiffer than he had expected. Brown students finishing their sophomore year had had two years of college French and had begun German and mechanics. It was doubtful whether he could catch up with them by devoting the entire summer to hard study. Professor Poland argued persuasively that, in any event, three years at Brown would give a more solid foundation for his career, and he could still graduate at nineteen. That was early enough. Hughes recognized the good sense of this advice and decided to follow it.

Still there was the question of expense. His entire outlay at Madison (exclusive of clothes) had been $250 for the first year and not more than $275 for the second. At Brown the cost would be higher. Charlie's plan became feasible only when his father got a promise from President Ezekiel G. Robinson of Brown that he could have a scholarship with an income of $60 a year and, as the son of a minister, would not have to pay room rent. On learning the good news from his mother, Charlie wrote:

> You cannot imagine how it thrilled me with joy and delight to hear the good tidings of your last letter. It, indeed, was so sudden and so unexpected that I hardly knew how to contain myself. The pent up longing of a whole year to burst forth in such a pleasing fruition was almost too much for me. My joy knew no bounds. How I wish I could see you and have a long talk. How many things I thank you for and how many joyous prospects come up before me.

[1] Address to Brown alumni, Feb. 1, 1929.

Entering Brown in September, 1878, Hughes was delighted with the college on the "high and pleasant hill." Manning, University, Slater, and Rhode Island halls and especially Hope College and the new library at Waterman and Prospect streets were soon familiar to him—a familiarity that was to extend throughout his lifetime. The president's house stood opposite the front campus on the site later occupied by the John Hay Library. Slater Hall had just been opened, and its suites were thought to be luxurious. But Dr. Robinson made no effort to conceal his disgust over the "battered doors . . . defaced walls, the gaping flooring" in the halls and "the unmistakable odor of decay pervading" University Hall; and Hope College, built in 1822, was "only a little less uninviting."

Nevertheless, the rooms were in such demand that Charlie Hughes and his roommate, Cornelius W. Pendleton, who had also come from Madison, could not at first obtain accommodations. For a time they lived together in a boardinghouse at 171 Congdon Street, paying $6 a week apiece. Eager to reduce this expense and live on the campus, they moved at the first opportunity to the ground floor of Hope College. Kerosene lamps provided their light, and a Franklin stove with open grate kept them warm in winter. Coal for this stove was stored in one of their two closets. In the other they kept their washstand and clothes. There was no running water or baths, although toilets were provided in University Hall. Servants ("slaves" to the students) kept the rooms in good order. The Hughes-Pendleton pair moved to Hope No. 22 on the second floor in their junior year, and often found it necessary to grope their way up and down unlighted halls.

Brown had about 250 students—a jovial lot with an abundance of college spirit. Hughes got a prompt introduction to Brunonian tradition in the sophomore-freshman class fight called a football game in deference to the fact that a football was somewhere in the center of the melee. A few days later came the forbidden cane rush, which also led to fist-swinging of the free-for-all variety. The specialty of Brown students in forbidden amusements was bonfires. A great blaze was likely to flare up on the College Green in spring or fall whenever there was a varsity triumph or other cause for an eruption of college spirit. Human moths seemed to fly toward the flames, and for a few precious moments there would be boisterous singing and dancing. They would scatter with even greater speed, however, when their sounds of mirth brought Brown's tall, gray-haired, sexagenarian president running to the fire at a deer's pace. Occasionally he would catch one of the students "and act at once as both policeman and committing magistrate." [2]

But not all their fun was of the *verboten* variety. They often gathered on the chapel steps after supper and sang their glees, and accepted rituals were some-

[2] CEH, Notes, p. 63.

times given an amusing twist. Instead of slavishly following the tradition of burying its Chaucer text when the course had been completed, Hughes' class dressed up to represent the characters in *The Canterbury Tales* and paraded through the streets of Providence. Charlie's chief regret about this was that it cost him $4 to help pay for the "grounds, band, advertisements, horses and costumes."

The freedom Charlie found in Providence brought many satisfactions. Up to this time he had never been in a theater. Now he eagerly seized upon every opportunity to see drama, taking the poor along with the good. This experience was high-lighted, however, by such memorable performances as Edwin Booth's in *Hamlet,* Lawrence Barrett's in *Richelieu,* Joseph Jefferson's in *Rip Van Winkle*, and Mary Anderson's in *Ingomar*. His first opera was *Aïda* with Clara Louise Kellogg and Annie Louise Cary. Providence also offered good light opera, such as *The Chimes of Normandy* and in the early part of 1879 the campus resounded with the catching airs of *Pinafore*. To pay for these diversions, Hughes took to tutoring boys who were behind in their work.

Frequently he played poker with his college friends, using matches instead of money. But whist continued to be his favorite. He joined the Brown whist club and played with experts whenever possible. As a mark of his good-fellowship, his friends nicknamed him "Hughsie," "Hughie," or, more frequently, "Huggis." He smoked more than previously. Occasionally, too, he could be seen at a beer garden patronized by the students. When he was studying German, he thought it good sport to drop in at Karl's beer hall and converse with the German proprietor in his native tongue. One day Hughes recited a portion of Schiller's *William Tell* in German for old Karl, who was so delighted that he "set 'em up" for all the boys.

Social opportunities at Brown were few so far as Hughes was concerned. It is more amusing than significant that the satirists of the *Liber Brunensis*, that "amiable catalogue of college follies," as he once called it, listed him as one of the eight foremost members of the Brown University Mashing Association and gave him the special title of "Bewitching Enchanter of Female Hearts." [3]

While Hughes' slight physique and his father's admonitions discouraged any direct participation in athletics at Brown, he became an ardent baseball fan. The Brown team was riding a wave of victories, thanks largely to J. Lee Richmond's mastery of the new curve-ball technique. In the spring of 1880 Brown defeated both Harvard and Yale and won the intercollegiate baseball championship. The fascination that this aspect of college life held for young Hughes stands out from a letter to his father on May 24, 1879:

[3] *Liber Brunensis*, April, 1880, p. 37.

Well, Saturday this afternoon, was taken up with the most exciting game of baseball I have ever witnessed between Yale and Brown, resulting in a victory for the latter by a score of 7–5. The greatest enthusiasm prevails. I can hardly write I am so excited. About a hundred of the Yale boys were down here. In all the games with her rival colleges, Brown has not been beaten once. She has the college championship within her grasp. Even the steadygoing Professors are excited. Professor Lincoln said "it was as good for the college as a new dormitory." You see, the boys always want to go to a college that holds up its head and beats all the others.

Probably, the best game so far this year will be played with Harvard at Cambridge next Saturday. About 150 of our boys are going down. The round trip will not cost more than $1.50, as the Harvard boys will treat all who go to supper and dinner, as they have always done and as we do when they come here. Won't you please let me go with them? Just think, I will be shown all through Harvard University as well as the renowned city of Boston with its historic Green and historic memories. Please grant me this great favor and I will assure you that all I do will be done as becometh a Christian and your son.

Brown University in those days was a classical and literary institution, giving only meager recognition to science and none to the professions. It had a strong faculty. "Such men as J. Lewis Diman, John L. Lincoln, Albert Harkness and Alpheus S. Packard would have been distinguished in any university faculty. Alonzo Williams was an excellent teacher in the modern languages. Nathaniel Davis, in mathematics, had already shown conspicuous ability. The students were brought into direct contact with these and other professors, and there was no reason to complain of lack of competent guidance in the various courses. The president was a powerful directing force." [4]

Hughes started at Brown with light work. Having completed geometry and calculus at Madison, he was excused from mathematics for the first semester. Latin and Greek were easy for him. Consequently, he had an unusual amount of time to give to his French and indulge his passion for literature. On October 21, 1878, he wrote to his father:

Though I am not studying very hard, I am doing an immense amount of reading. I have already read and am reading several of Thackeray's works and miscellaneous Addison's writings in the "Spectator" and Macaulay's essays. . . . I have read a couple of volumes of Addison's work but I don't like him very much. . . . There is in it something which leads me to think more of the great mind of Addison who writes, than of the great thought written. But, when we come to Macaulay's works, all this is gone. Take Macaulay's essay on "Milton." We lose all thought of Macaulay in the thought of the grandeur of the author of "Paradise Lost."

O! How much we lose sight of this all important essential to oratorical success—to make everything bend to the exaltation of the theme. This we see in Demosthenes. The Athenians did not say, "O! what a wonderful speech," but "we must fight Philip." And in this very fact did Demosthenes make the overwhelming power

[4] CEH, Notes, p. 63.

Charlie Hughes with his father and mother, about 1868

Young Hughes at fourteen, at Madison University

Graduation picture—Brown University, 1881

The Delta Upsilon Camp at Lake George, 1880

Hughes at the extreme left

of his oratory appear. Well, I must close this sort of thing. But, I have been thinking of this a good while and, at last, it has found expression.

Dickens and Thackeray were his favorites, but dozens of other authors also held his attention, including Irving, Ben Jonson, Gray, Hugo, Scott, De Quincey, Lamb, Emerson, Carlyle, Sterne, Goldsmith, Hawthorne, Balzac, Kingsley, and Schiller. When he learned French, he also read extensively in French fiction. In his later college years the fiction he read was generally interspersed by history and philosophy. He had already acquired the habits of rapid reading and absorption of what he read that were to amaze his associates in official life.

At the end of his first year at Brown, Hughes was a little disappointed in his Greek course, for while Professor Harkness was a great scholar and a most gracious and careful teacher, he kept hammering away at construction, and Hughes felt that they did not fully enter into the spirit of the classics they were studying. Latin was a delightful contrast. Professor Lincoln embodied the Latin spirit, and his familiar talks gave the students a sense of the most charming fellowship. Everyone loved "Johnny Link" with his smooth upper lip, bearded chin, and winning smile. Excepting only Professor Lincoln's course, which opened a treasure house of classical literature, Hughes concluded that he had learned more from his extra curricular reading than from the classroom. But this did not disturb him; he was now disposed to follow his own bent, with less concern for marks and credit than he had had at Madison.

As Hughes settled down to study in his junior year, the ever present problem of paying his expenses seemed to be especially bothersome. He wrote to his father on October 20, 1879:

I received your welcome letter last Wednesday with the enclosed check for $15. I paid my three weeks board, got our pail and oilcloth, paid my Society tax ($2) to meet our expenses at the Convention, paid $.75 for voting and football taxes, went to a college ballgame (25¢), got a lamp chimney (10¢), got a lead pencil and a rubber and find myself, at present, with 32¢ in my pocket. How money does go! I am so sorry to have to keep asking for money when I know how short you are and how you have to pinch. But, I am trying to spend just as little as possible—to meet my honest dues and spend none needlessly. I am sorry I went to that ballgame. But it was the closing game of the season between Harvard and Brown and I very much wanted to go.

Our landlady is very good to us and I can say I never have been so hearty and had such a first rate appetite right along as now. We have splendid meals. I will give you an idea of our bill-of-fare. In the morning, first oatmeal, then coffee, baked potatoes and our choice—generally, between nice beefsteak, tripe, pork steak and sausage, as well as hot rolls. At dinner—first some nice vegetable soup—then, vegetables, splendid boiled potatoes and either roast beef, lamb chop, beef pie and occasionally chicken—as well as nice desserts, consisting of good pies and puddings. At tea, we have tea, toast, cake and sauce. So you see, I live pretty well and feel quite strong and hearty.

I am going to the Gymnasium as soon as I have the money to pay in advance—$3 (for the year). I went once, but was respectfully informed that they must have pay in advance.

My shoes are in very poor condition. . . . My hair also needs cutting and my term's reading room tax ($1) should be promptly paid. Such is the constant demand. But, of course, it lessens as we get along further in the term.

His chronic shortage of funds led him into a shabby ghost-writing venture to pay for a pair of skates. The details come to light in the following letter:

PROVIDENCE,
Feb. 11, 1880

DEAR PA,

I just received your postal, giving me my marks for last term. I believe I am bewitched. By what possible means of legerdemain could my poor work be transmuted into perfection or nearly so? Truly, for ways that are dark & tricks that are vain, the Profs are peculiar. But, however it may be, I am extremely grateful & I know you & Ma will join me in fervent thankfulness to our Heavenly Father, who works everything for our good. . . . In a couple of weeks as soon as my hair grows long enough I will have my pictures taken. I am going to have ½ dozen taken standing up, with my ulster on, open, & hat & cane in hand. Such pictures are very stylish here now. Also ½ dozen in a rational posture. I will send you one as soon as I can get them. . . .

I have bought a pair of skates. You wonder, & think of my promise. Well, I will tell you all about it. Know therefore that when I told you I would never ask you for a pair, on account of my overcoat, I nevertheless intended to have a pair & earn them myself. A fellow hard up, offered me his skates (American Club, like my other pair, in fine condition, polished, sharpened, & new last year & cost $5.00, as you know) for $3.00. I took them. You ask, where did you get the money? A Sophomore came to me one day, told me he had to have an essay in three days, & couldn't spare the time to write it. He only wanted a fair one. I wrote it & received $1.00, which I laid away. He told another one, who is a fine scholar & for him I wrote a fine essay, got him an "ex." & received $2.00, which added to my $1.00 gave me a pair of skates, all for about ten hours work as they had to do the copying.

I shouldn't wonder if I had more such jobs. You see I read over some of the man's essay & imitate his style just as nice as you please. Don't mention this as it is strictly confidential between these fellows & myself. It don't make any difference to me, but the fellows would be in a nice pickle if it got out. We have had skating for a week & I never enjoyed it so much in my life. . . . To-night I am going to a social at Central Baptist Church; to-morrow night I have an engagement out, & Friday, Society, all of which with skating, studying & eating keep me pretty busy. I am progressing nicely in study. 14 ex's out of 15 marks since I have been in Brown. Hurrah! Much love to Ma & you from

C. E. H.

Four months before, Charlie had sharply condemned "one of the boys" who had cribbed an oration from an old magazine. "It doesn't pay in a selfish sense," he had written his mother, "and we all know its real name—*theft.*" When his mother chided him for being a party to a similar bit of trickery, however, he vigorously defended his action:

BROWN UNIVERSITY
Feb. 17th, 1880

DEAR MA,

I received your kind letter the other day, & took great pleasure in reading it. For, besides the interest you naturally feel in me, I was much pleased that the way I earned my skates had been a subject of discussion among you. For, I supposed it would be a foregone conclusion. Now, I will give you a few reasons why I think my conduct proper. (1) The aim I had in view. Now you know, skating is a very healthy exercise & also pleasing. It is the very best means of quieting the brain & stimulating physical health. Now to buy a pair of skates without asking my father for money was a very laudable aim. (2) Earning money is also a fine thing for the young. (3) The advantages accruing to myself from much writing. (4) I don't regard myself as placed in any predicament whatever. It is no worse to write an essay for a fellow than to help him out with his lesson. And no blame could attach itself to me in any case. Hack writing, or writing for money is a perfectly legitimate business. I am not supposed to know for what it is to be used. I wrote a certain paper, received so much for it & it is the responsibility of the man himself whether he uses it for himself. (5) Writing like everything else can be bought & sold. If I buy a pencil I have a right to use it as my own, & if a fellow buys an essay of me as merchandise, the only copy in the world, it passes out of my hand & he has a right to do as he wills with it.

Now I wouldn't care if the whole faculty knew of it for with me it was only a business transaction & the other fellows must settle the moral point with themselves. . . . Now about going into society, I think it does a world of good to me, as I am having an easy time with my studies. It polishes one's rough edges & counteracts the influence of being wholly with the boys. Now I don't want you to think I am shirking my work, for I do my duty just as faithfully as I know how.

Although none of the letters written to Charlie by his parents while he was at Brown has survived, it is obvious from his own letter of February 22 that his father also criticized the ghost-writing venture. Charlie then acknowledged his error and asked forgiveness:

As I see it, all your arguments are pointed at the other man. Although you may not see it, I know perfectly well, that my course is not reprehensible before the faculty or before justice. I could cite similar cases in past college history. But, if I have laid myself open to the slightest moral crimination, I am willing to repent and beg your forgiveness. You know the proverbial rashness of youth. You also know my fondness for skating. You know my desire of independence & my aptitude for easy writing. I hope that in view of these facts, you will consider my conduct, if not morally right, as excusable & pardonable. Well, I might as well say out & out that I will pull in my horns & you stand victor of the arena.

Now I have been sick. . . .

Charlie's retreat from his fallacious reasoning was somewhat grudging, but it is evident that his father's strictures found their mark. The net effect of this experience was not to give him a precedent for closing his eyes to moral consequences but to sharpen his conscience. It is significant that at no time in his later career did he use a ghost-writer, and his high sensitivity to moral considerations will be apparent as this story unfolds.

Hughes had plunged into the work of his junior year with the liveliest expectations, and these were not disappointed. Astronomy, chemistry, physics, and German now came within his intellectual ken. On October 27 he wrote to his mother:

> But our work in Chemistry is to me the best of all. It is taught so splendidly. If I ever thought I could be a great chemist, I would make it a specialty. It is more interesting to me than any other study I have yet taken up, notwithstanding my love for Mathematics. Professor Appleton is the best chemist in the state and he never says a single word in class but what means something and which gives some exact information.
>
> . . . A day never passes over my head in which I do not feel profoundly grateful for the advantages I enjoy, and none the less anxious, lest I in my after life—should fail to show the fruit of so much thorough teaching and untiring study.

At the end of the semester he gave his father a rather enthusiastic appraisal of his progress:

> I suppose you will get my marks soon. I expect an ex in German, English Literature and Astronomy and a vg in Physics and Chemistry. I know I won't get an ex in Physics, but I would expect one in Chemistry if the professor wasn't such a hard marker. However, I don't believe a fellow in our class will get five exs, as it is not so easy to recite perfectly in science as in language.
>
> Well, I am glad I am through. I never got so much stuff in my head in a given time in my life. But Chemistry was the worst. I got up at four o'clock Monday morning and worked 'til eight. We had the very hardest possible examination he could have given. I knew it all and wrote just as fast as I could make my pen fly for two hours. But, as I got along very nicely, I felt happy when I got all through —even if I was tired out. . . .
>
> My studies for the coming term are very nice. Logic will, of course, demand much study. Chaucer will be pleasant and easy. Physiology is quite interesting. . . . Political Economy is immense. Our professor, Diman, is about the biggest gun on the Faculty and a clear-headed, shrewd man. You have to pay attention to everything he says and just jot down what you can get of it.

J. Lewis Diman was the pride of Brown. This dignified but unpretending thinker had had numerous attractive offers from Harvard, Princeton, and other universities, but he loved Brown and chose to remain there. When he delivered a special lecture on "Immanent Finality," students flocked in as if it had been a baseball game. His earnest face, creased forehead, and long flowing sideburns were accepted as a sort of symbol of intellectual mastery. He talked with freedom, brilliance, and a fidelity to truth, as he saw it, that lifted the sensitive and receptive Charlie Hughes into a "new and exalted sphere of intellectual activity."[5]

Special notice from Professor Diman was a high distinction. Once Hughes wrote to his father: "On Friday, I was up in History on Guizot's lectures on the Medieval Church. Professor Diman complimented me very highly, saying that it was the best analysis he had during the term." Some weeks later the devoted student again reported, "By the way, Professor Diman bowed to me yesterday and, as he never bows to college boys, it augurs well."

Near the end of the scholastic year Professor Lincoln threw out a challenge: "Hughes, why don't you take examinations for freshman year rank. You ought to do it. You will be sorry in later life if you graduate without class standing."[6] This was a new and appealing idea. By taking a few examinations, Hughes established his class standing and was one of the five members of his class admitted to Phi Beta Kappa at the end of his junior year.

Happy summer days came as a further reward. Marcus C. Allen, scion of the Allen family that had been close to the Hugheses in Sandy Hill, set up a Delta Upsilon camp on an island in Lake George, off Bolton, in 1877, and young Hughes became one of the first to enjoy a vacation there. During the summers of 1879 and 1880 he spent two or three weeks at this rustic camp consisting of tents and a messroom built of rough boards. Hughes and Pendleton (his roommate), Charles C. Mumford, and William Jillson joined a number of fraternity brothers from other colleges, taking along a guide and a cook. They jaunted by buckboards from Glens Falls to the beautiful lake region, and rowed to the island in small boats.

Days at the camp were a merry round of boating, hiking, eating, reading, and tomfoolery. Jillson tells us that Hughes' tent was well stocked with books and that he had a seemingly endless fund of humor and stories. In the evenings the campers sang their college songs so lustily that an audience from the near-by inns often clustered about their tiny island in boats. It was still more fun for the young men to serenade the hotels in their own boats. On these occasions, according to Jillson's account, girls would flock out to the porches. The boys found ways of introducing themselves and sometimes went into the inns to dance—square dances and the Virginia reel.

Hughes returned to Brown in September, 1880, determined to devote to the studies of his senior year all the energy he possessed, but first he became entangled in college politics. He wrote to his father on September 25:

> Today was the time for class elections for officers next spring. Each society constituted a clique to run in their men. A combination would be formed & then a

[5] CEH, Notes, p. 67. [6] CEH, Notes, p. 69.

counter-combination against it. I never saw such a terrible state of affairs. We met this morning & after a two hour's stormy session adjourned in the wildest confusion. For the last three days, class politics have taken the class by storm. The professors are wild & say they have never seen anything like it in the annals of the college. . . .

As I was in it heart & soul, I was naturally terribly excited. I am yet. The class is becoming thoroughly aroused at the mean chicanery of some members, which was brought out today. From morning to night, new schemes are formed, old ones thrown up. Every little while someone comes to my room to know if I will vote for this or that, & then I must go & get the Neutrals to vote in such a way & so & so, it is a complete picture of politics, on a small scale, except it is bitter war to death bet. the secret societies united & the Delta U's & Neutrals. Unfortunately we have just the same number of votes on each side & are fearfully worked up. Pray for me, that I may let my moderation be known. I never was more worked up. I got up this morning in class-meeting & talked about 20 minutes, I haven't the slightest idea what I said only that I sat on cliques generally. But when I got through I was bathed wet through with perspiration & almost wilted out. But the boys all acknowledge that I did more to break up the secret clique than has been done yet. At last accounts, 3 votes have come over to our side.

His studies were now more exacting. There was medieval and modern history under Professor Diman, an elected course in Italian, and psychology and philosophy under Dr. Robinson. At first he thought both history and psychology were "terrible." These two subjects required more work than all his studies combined in junior year. "They give us references every day of 100 pages or so," he complained, "on which we are thoroughly questioned, and the main point of their teaching is to get away from the habit of memorizing a certain number of words, to hard & independent research." But after a few months he was enjoying research—a fact of the utmost importance in his later career. On November 21 he wrote to his father:

You can hardly understand my interest in the term's work. With practical history and philosophy to study and not the ideal and fanciful traditions of Latin and Grecian lore—however beautiful and instructive—I have found a new fondness for research awaken in me. To sit down and develop a closely fact-compacted history is now the same—as a few months ago—to devour the last novel. Sometimes, I look upon this new feature of my character as startling. May it not betoken inconstancy to readily grasp and become enthusiastic in every new branch brought under my consideration?

Dr. Robinson was short on inspiration but had a way of goading his students into self-expression. In his letter of October 6 Hughes gives a vivid picture of how the president badgered him and of his own reaction to it:

We are very busy now looking at the germs of European Civilization among the Goths and Vandals, and deciding that momentous question, as to whether we have a mind or not, or rather whether there is "a conscious cognizing soul or spirit distinct and separable from the material organism, or whether the soul or spirit is a function of the entity called body, i.e. the product of the organs of sense?" This momentous question will probably be decided by the end of the week, and meanwhile I would humbly suggest that all philosophers and sages hold their breath till the decree of fate, personified in E. G. Robinson D.D., LL.D. has gone forth and the question whether there is an entity called soul, distinct and separable from the bodily organism is settled for all generations. Although in this position of undeniable doubt and loss of breath, still I cannot but state that I am perfectly well, and that whatever is learning within me is getting along first rate. . . .

I think I have had the good or bad fortune (as result will prove) of falling into the graces of the aforesaid "fate personified" for whenever with stern eye and solemn phiz he cracks a joke at the other half of the class, he invariably turns suddenly with relentless gaze to my corner only to subdue my hilarious ha ha into a mournfully dying gasp. Then (this is the part of the fortune I deem bad) he always has me up on the hardest parts of the lectures (which I understand is a token of favor), and then suddenly in the midst of my flowing recitation, cuts it off sharply, by asking me what Des Cartes would have thought if I talked such stuff to him. I tremblingly reply, meanwhile flatteringly giving his lectures a better cognomen than stuff, by plunging into Des Cartes philosophy (crammed up the night before) when I am again hauled up with, "What are *you* sir?" That being a much pondered and never satisfactorily answered query, I indulge in a blank stare, which is hewed down . . . by, "Well, if you don't know yourself, what do you expect to know outside of yourself"! I gently advise that a much older and much grayer head than mine attack that problem, when a shout of, "Go on sir," drums my wearied faculties into action & I trot on again in good style when my gait is broken by the following: "What have you been talking about all this time"? This floors me completely, and dissatisfied with all mankind, I repeat my former eloquent appeals to consciousness with broken and failing utterances, when suddenly I find myself sitting down and "fate-personified" telling the class that that is the kind of recitation he likes to hear.

I recover my shattered senses and my spirit once more breathes the pure air, when I am once more sunk in "ungeheures Unheil" by 6–100 pages of references, "which, gentlemen, must be perused by tomorrow morning." No wonder the poet sings "I would not live alway," taking alway in the sense of all manner, method, &c. . . . For my part, if my hair leaves the top of my head, I will never originate a new theory to perplex the students under "fate personified."

On one occasion "fate personified" caught the young man completely off guard but not vacant-minded. As he related it:

I came nearly fizzling yesterday. We are on the question of Moral Taste as contrasted with Conscience. Just as I was called on, the precise point escaped me and, to save myself from a complete flunk, I asked Prex. to answer a hard question I had been thinking of and he entered into a discussion with me about it,—never asked for his point at all and concluded the recitation by saying that nothing pleased him so much as to see original thought on the part of his students. How is that for luck?

A sharp summons to the president's office in October caused Hughes' heart to sink, but he came out walking on air and wrote to his mother:

PROVIDENCE,
Oct. 17th, 1880

DEAR MA,

After recitation in psychology, the President loudly and rather roughly said, "I wish to see Mr. Hughes in my office immediately." Well, I was so scared, I turned white as a sheet, for this is his invariable manner of "hauling up" the boys as it is called. I went quaking to his office with him. He looked me all over carefully and took a piece of paper from his pocket—handed it to me—meanwhile, talking something about "gratifying my father"—"highest marks"—"rhetoric," etc., which in my confusion I did not understand. I hoped most vainly to get from under his stern eye. Slowly, I opened the paper and read an order on the Treasurer for $50 for the Dana Premium. Shortly to say Ma I had received a prize of $50 for having the highest standing in the class in our rhetorical studies, commencing with elocution and rhetoric in sophomore year and ending with our oration and work in English literature. You could have knocked me over with a feather. I thanked the President and made my way to my room and devoutly thanked my Heavenly Father.

I had forgotten all about this prize and if I had thought of it, so many stood high in the rhetorical studies that I could never have supposed myself the highest. The $50 is safe in the best bank in Providence. I want to keep it as a nest egg for my future career. It will be a good thing to have after graduation.

Another honor is put upon me. I am unanimously elected senior delegate to represent the Brown Chapter at the Delta Upsilon Convention at Amherst which means all expenses paid and free leave from college from October 26–29. Think of that! Poor little I am selected to represent Brown in Convention. Well, I will have to buy a new hat and please send me Pa's black coat and vest which I wore last winter as I must have it to go to Amherst with. I will bring it back Thanksgiving or Christmas whenever I go home. *Please, send them as soon as possible.*

Dear Ma, I wish I could see you when you read this letter and kiss you and Pa many times. Think of it, $50 and a delegate to Amherst. Now, please, let me keep that $50 secure until after I graduate so that I can have something to start with. Please excuse this scrawl. You and Pa have my best love, I remain your loving son.

CHARLIE

Write soon

A few days later he was pleading again for his father's coat and vest, for money to buy a new hat and pay his DU tax. "I hope the prize was not too much for you," he wrote. "I have been dazed for almost two or three days."

The Delta Upsilon convention at Amherst in October, 1880, proved to be one of his most memorable college experiences. In the D.U. chapter at Brown he had found stimulating companionship, and many of the friendships formed there were to be lifelong. One of his D.U. friends, William H. P. Faunce, a young man who "represented all that was best in student life," was to be president of Brown University for thirty years. At Amherst, Hughes encountered other keen young fellows who impressed him most favorably. Among them were Starr J. Murphy (later counsel to John D. Rockefeller for investigation of proposed philanthropic enterprises), Frank C. Partridge (later solicitor of the State Department, diplomat, and for a brief period United States Senator from Vermont), and William Travers Jerome, who was to win fame as district attorney for New York County.

It was on this occasion, when he was only eighteen, that Hughes first discovered his power to sway a crowd—a power that was to remain with him throughout his life. Losing himself in his speeches, he demonstrated in marked degree the Welsh *hwyl* that he had so admired in his Uncle John. His excitement over this discovery about himself was poured out in a letter to his father:

PROVIDENCE, Oct. 31, 1880.

DEAR PA,

. . . Last Monday night was a great night in Providence. The grand state demonstration on behalf of Garfield & Arthur took place & as it was to pass the campus, we were busy all afternoon in illuminating our rooms and the outside grounds. I did not get to bed till quite late & on Tuesday morning, I was very much hurried in preparing for my departure. You must know, that in a certain sense, that was the proudest day of my life. To go out from the finest society in college, which contains the best scholars, speakers &c. to go forth as her representative to meet in convention with representative men from all the principal colleges of the United States, you may well suppose was the highest honor to which I could look in college. . . .

Starting off then as Senior Delegate, at 2-o'clock on Tuesday afternoon, I arrived in Amherst at 9.00 P.M. & was at once met by the Amherst boys, who conducted me to their rooms. . . . I certainly never made the acquaintance of a finer set of fellows. . . . I went to chapel the next morning with the Amherst boys & inspected their buildings &c. . . . The convention assembled at 10 A.M. received the credentials of the delegates, laid out an order of business & adjourned. At 2 P.M. they again assembled & listened to fine reports from all the chapters. I wish you could have been there, to see how high D.U. stands at all the colleges, not from words only but from the immense number of prizes & honors secured. My head was almost turned. You know how ardent a Delta U. I have been, but do not be surprised, when I say that I never had half an idea of the greatness of Delta U. It is wonderful.

When the report of the Brown Chapter was called for, I arose with fear and trembling to tell what the boys were doing at Brown. I gradually warmed with my theme, till it actually seemed as if something gave way in my head & I ran on in the most profuse style, words succeeding words, & climax, climax, without effort and wholly extemporaneous, till I sat down amid sounds of applause & feeling as if I had dropped from a cloud. Please do not imagine me egotistical, for I have been longing to pour out my heart to someone, & I dare do it to no fellow, as I am afraid, he will regard me conceited, but you know how afraid to speak I have been, & you will appreciate my spirit, when I say, that from that morning to this, I have made numerous speeches & in none of them have I had the least trouble in saying just what I wanted to, with well-rounded periods & good climaxes. Well, to return, after that session, I was the centre of an eager crowd of boys, gathering around me & congratulating me on my report. Ever after when I rose to speak, I was greeted with loud applause, and never did my newly-obtained faculty fail me.

In the evening, the question of camping was brought up, & I rose to say only a few words & I spoke to an interested audience for half an hour. Anecdotes, humorous expressions & pithy sentences came unbidden to my lips & when I was through, the Junior delegate said to me—"Hughes, a wonderful change has come over you; you have no idea how finely you have spoken. Why," said he, "the way you kept us laughing & at the same time brought out your point in a steady stream of good English was marvellous." Nor had I an idea of what I was saying. I knew I was speaking very fast & that once in a while I was interrupted with applause & loud laughter & when I sat down I found myself bathed in perspiration & amid a crowd of fellows cheering for the Brown delegate. Now please, dear Pa, don't smile at what you may consider a conceited young fellow, whose head is turned. I have been home two days, am perfectly cool, with my pulse at 70, & I assure you that I never felt more humble than at the present. It seems to me as if a higher power had taken me from myself & given the faculty of unhesitating speech.

Certainly I made many friends & at each session I spoke on some topic or other to an interested audience. I proposed the adoption of resolutions, I had drawn up, with reference to our support of Garfield, the President of the D.U. Fraternity [then the Republican candidate for the Presidency of the United States] & took a prominent part in the business of the convention. I am on a dozen or more committees & never worked harder than when enjoying those two days of respite. . . . Garfield sent us a splendid letter, congratulating the Fraternity, & expressing his sorrow at his inability to meet with us. Then succeeded the banquet & I arrived at Providence at 12 o'clock on Friday & have since been busy in making up lessons &c.

At society meeting, I gave my report & again was blessed with wonderful success. To be able to get away from myself, to live only in my speech, to think only of my point & not of how many buttons there are on my waistcoat, is a gift for which I have longed & sighed in vain till last Wednesday. And, then when thoroughly aroused, not to forget the requirements of rhetoric & accurate oratory, is a matter of constant wonderment to me. The Junior delegate brought back to Brown wonderful accounts of me & the boys have been around me, congratulating & talking to me, ever since my return. Now may my Heavenly Father, the giver of every good gift, bless & sanctify me to his service. This is my constant. Never have I felt more solemn & subdued, than at the very instant of success, when I could hear the echoes of the dying applause.

Your loving son,
CHARLIE

In spite of his feeling of dedication, religion was claiming less of Hughes' attention. Occasionally he prepared a synopsis for one of his father's expository articles in the *Homiletic Review*, and he often went to church. But the sermons he liked best were those of Dr. A. J. F. Behrends of the Union Congregational

Church and Dr. David H. Greer of the Grace Episcopal Church (later Bishop of New York) instead of those to be heard at the First Baptist Meetinghouse. In a letter to his father he riddled a casuistic lecture by Henry Ward Beecher, and a year later he was challenging and seeking to modify some of his father's views:

> Well, you may be sure, I will be glad to greet you next Christmas and we will have many a good chat . . . as of yore. Only I hope my major premise will be more acceptable and my conclusions more worthy of your approbation. I am intent on reforming many of your opinions and I hope, aided by the lectures of our redoubtable Professors and a little subtly turned English, for once to conquer some of the notions coming out of long established and stereotyped methods of thought. In short, I bring this letter to a close—sending you and Ma my dearest love and throwing down my glove before the most terrible of all debaters.
>
> Yours affectionately,
>
> CHARLIE

Another letter, written on his nineteenth birthday and signed "Your little Charlie," shows pretty clearly where he stood:

> I verily believe you would have wondered at the scion of your stock, if you had seen me argue for three hours yesterday afternoon with one of the boys, impassionately & laboriously endeavoring to show the necessity of accepting the whole word of God, of an overruling Providence & a future punishment. I declare it is impossible to get outside of one's early training. Whatever I may do or become, there is no danger that I ever will be able to rid myself of the truths implanted in early child-hood.

In November, 1880, Hughes was elected one of the editors of the *Brunonian,* the student newspaper. This he accepted enthusiastically, but when he was elected president of the Brown chapter of Delta Upsilon a few months later he declined to serve because of the extra work it would involve. While his editorials ranged over a wide field, the most notable one concerned a tragedy at Brown. The inimitable Professor Diman, twirling his glasses as he explored the great epochs of history, had become the center of an intellectual ferment on the campus. His lectures seemed more fascinating than ever before. Then, with shocking suddenness, in February, 1881, Professor Diman died. Hughes wrote a vivid account of the incident to his mother on February 6:

> On Thursday, as you have probably heard, occurred the death of our much loved Professor Diman. I have never in my life been so stunned. Not only was he my best loved Professor, not only did I reverence him and listen with the greatest respect to all his teaching, but I looked up to him as the greatest embodiment of true scholarship I had ever met. He was taken sick the day after my return from home (Jan. 28). He gave us our first lecture on International Law in the forenoon and returned home to illness and death. . . . On Thursday, noon, I heard he was

seriously ill and told the boys so at dinner—but they all laughed at me and said it was all a hoax and so I thought myself. . . . After dinner, Bean [George F. Bean, managing editor of the *Brunonian*] and I got together some of our class and proposed sending a bouquet. So we went down, got a most lovely bouquet and sent it to him at four o'clock. He took it, smelled of it, expressed his gratification very pleasantly and at five-thirty the same afternoon he passed away. . . .

I heard of it first at supper where I arrived late, but would not credit it for a long time, till the blank faces of the boys told me the astounding truth. . . . I felt in a dream. I could not eat. Had I heard of anything incredible I could not have been more stunned. I thought more of him than any man living, outside of my own relatives. . . . You, who know how often and how fondly and reverently I spoke of him, can imagine my utter bewilderment . . . I went to my room and remained in a stupor for some time. About eight o'clock, Bean came to me and said, as the Brunonian was already in press for Saturday, we must get out a great supplement with a memorial.

We immediately went to Prex and Professor Lincoln for facts of his career and at nine and a half o'clock sat down to write. Bean wrote the little editorial at the head and I wrote the account of his life up to the last week and Bean wrote the account of his illness and death, and then I finished with the eulogy (the last column and a half beginning with "The Sudden Removal"). We distributed the parts before we sat down and wonderful to tell it was finished at ten and a half and carried down and was printed by next morning. I wrote faster than Bean and, as you will see, wrote the larger part of it. We were both under a spell and it would be utterly impossible for us to do the like again except as then under the greatest nervous excitement. The next morning, in chapel, Pres. Robinson arose and in a broken voice read and prayed, and then postponed college exercises till after the funeral. Among the Seniors there was not a dry eye and we all left chapel sobbing as if suddenly deprived of parents and friends. . . .

A pall seemed to fall on everything. The boys (Seniors) talked to each other in whispers and burst into tears when vivid recollections would occur. It did seem as if the stars had fallen. . . . In this time of gloom and sadness, it seems as though the joy had faded from the world and, as I try to shake off this mournful feeling, every now and then there rises before me that manly form, whose like I shall never again behold. Oh! if I could but give you an adequate description of him and our relations to him. All I can say is that, in his death, the University has suffered the greatest possible loss and the class of '81 has lost its kindest instructor, its most cheerful advisor, its most cherished friend.

Sickness at Brown caused much concern that winter. Hughes complained in an editorial that students in chilly classrooms were "whirled from serene meditation on . . . modern philosophy to a sudden consciousness of freezing feet and hands." [7] Before Professor Diman's death one of Hughes' intimate friends, Frederick L. Gamage, had gone to bed with typhoid fever. For a time Hughes took care of him, as there was no college infirmary. The consequent loss of sleep, added to his hard work, drained him of his vitality, and he went home sick for the first time in five years at college. After a week of his mother's

[7] *Brunonian,* Feb. 5, 1881.

nursing, however, he was back at Brown for the final sprint toward graduation.

As his senior year approached an end, he wrote to his parents, "I am thoroughly tired of college life, and when once, I grasp my diploma it will be with no mawkish or sentimental sorrow at leaving the Lyceum of my youth." In part this feeling may have resulted from the continued struggle to pay his bills. It seemed a last straw when he had to ask his father for $18 for the alumni dinner. "Think of paying $18," he wrote, "to see a lot of gray-haired alumni gorge themselves. Then I am having the hat made over $3.00 & the pictures (extra dozen standing ones) $3.00 more & I suppose the Finance Committee ought not to be obliged to delay their wonderful proceedings to accommodate the downtrodden and poverty-stricken Senior. At least they will not."

One other worry was what he would turn to when he left college. Dr. Robinson had told the father of one of his students that there were two or three men in the class who would "amount to something"—Hughes, Chase, and Bean. He had also given Hughes a suggestive bit of advice: "Now above everything else don't let yourself sink out of sight after you graduate." But Hughes had only vague ideas as to how his talents might be employed. On November 7, 1880, he had written to his father:

> I am quite intimate, now, with a DU graduate of '80 who is studying medicine in the city. I have become quite interested—picking up information here and there and have attended one dissection and one operation. Who knows? I may become a doctor. Hoping the Lord will direct me in the way He has chosen for me, I am looking in all directions to ascertain my fitness for some pursuit.

A week later he was very much at sea:

> I was somewhat amused at your observation on my courage and my approaching manhood. I assure you, that I really am afraid that I am too much the dear little boy of yours and not enough the dignified and reverent Senior whom Prex thinks is so responsible for the well-being of our Seminaries of learning. However, I never could be and never hope to be anything else to *you* than a dear little boy, although in Providence it is Sir, Mister, etc. That is one reason why I also feel as if I have tumbled off an elevation to which I had no right and been respectfully reminded of my real position when I come home. Well, my dear Ma, a long intercourse with the world has taught me much that will be of benefit to me (please supply after "long" in the above, "for my age" and be sure you don't laugh).
>
> Well, if I only knew what I should do when I left college, I would feel more cheerful and manly than I do now. I never was more respected in college than at present, never was more honored, yet, I always feel as if—when I left college—I would drop unminded into oblivion as far as the professors and the boys are concerned.
>
> Dave Call has now been made President of Des Moines University, Iowa. Think

of it and the rapid rise of that most fortunate young man. It is truly wonderful. Now, don't think I am ambitious, but I would like to be something in this world.

Within a fortnight he was talking of medicine again, although in a rather facetious vein:

I am thinking more and more of medicine as a profession. During vacation, I have talked several times with my friends—and, in fact, am almost enthusiastic over dry bones and sticking plasters. There is something enchanting about the study and, were it not for the long course necessary, I am almost afraid, dear Ma, I should usurp your functions and take your place as the family doctor. What a team we would make! I would have you to entertain and nurse the nervous—Pa can give them lectures on morals and myself to supply the pills. . . .

The one certainty was that he did not wish to go into the ministry. Replying to his mother's urgings, he made this clear on December 7:

I have carefully weighed what you said in your letter & have reached this conclusion. I want to do just that which will enable me to do most for the world around me according to the divine will. As yet, I feel no *call* to the ministry, & I know that such a sphere of life is not exactly suitable to my abilities. In the other professions, I see no special choice, except I have felt of late a drawing toward medicine, although all the boys declare that my business should be that of law. Now I know that I [could do] well in law, but the profession is repugnant to me.

This letter is the first indication that he had given any thought to the legal profession as his life's work. His fellow students continued to point to his special talents in this field, and the law gradually became less repugnant to him. By January 9, 1881, he was at least neutral toward it:

I had a good sober talk with the boys last night on our future, and everyone said that, in every respect, I was cut out for a lawyer—that I would be foolish to think of anything else. Well, time will tell. At present, I am grateful to do my regular work, trusting in Providence for future favors.

A month later he was "thrown into a whirl of excitement" by the prospect of becoming a university professor. In response to a letter from Hughes' father, David Call, Charlie's esteemed friend from Madison who was now president of Des Moines University, wrote that, while he could offer no opening in 1881, he would be happy to give young Hughes the chair of modern languages and belles-lettres the following year. Overjoyed by this promise, the young man began to dream of spending the intervening year on a scholarship at Johns Hopkins University.

By March 6, however, he was definitely warming up toward the law. He wrote to his mother:

The more I think of the future, the more I incline toward the legal profession, as the one for which I am most fitted & the one most favorable to a high ambition. However, I am now settled down into a quiet, inoffending drudge, whose pleasant anticipations of the future are mere dry leaves blown about by the present duties, which operate on my mind like a chill October gale.

There are other indications of his growing interest in the legal field. Digging into the antiquated rules of the university, he wrote two editorials for the *Brunonian* ridiculing the prohibitions against playing cards, using profane language, going to the theater, or entering a tavern where liquor was sold. It was already evident that his investigative instinct, his logical mind, his quick grasp of intricate problems, and his powers of lucid expression were made to order for the law. But the question of his future was still wide open as he finished his work at Brown. Having been chosen class prophet, he was pondering over the future careers of his fellow students one day when John Murray Marshall, the songfest leader, came in and asked, "And what are you prophesying about yourself?"

"I don't know," Hughes admitted, ". . . I rather think I'll take up teaching."

"Of course, you'll be a lawyer," his friend retorted. "I've picked out law for myself, and if you are not a lawyer too I'm no prophet." [8]

Young Marshall's confident prognostication gave Hughes another strong push toward the legal profession. For the present, however, all dreams of the future had to be subordinated to the pressing realities of commencement week. As usual, Hughes had made an enviable record. In his sophomore year he had earned nine ratings of "excellent" and one of "very good"—in Latin; in his junior year all his marks were at the maximum, excepting a "very good" in physics. Only his French dropped one notch below the maximum in the first term of his senior year, and in the last term he had the coveted "ex." in everything.[9] After the final examination he was assigned the "Classical Oration" at commencement, which meant that he stood third in the class. He and Charles C. Mumford (later associate justice of the Superior Court of Rhode Island) were singled out for the Carpenter awards; in the judgment of the faculty they united "in the highest degree the three most important elements of success in life, ability, character, and attainment." Although he was the youngest member of a class of forty-three, Hughes' intellect and capacity for work had made a deep impression upon professors and students alike.

The commencement festivities began with class day on Friday in mid-June. Custom dictated that the seniors wear full-dress suits and silk hats throughout the day and every day following until the commencement exercises came to a close the next Wednesday night. In this garb they went to the formal

[8] CEH, Notes, p. 76. [9] Brown College Register, 1880–1881.

class-day ceremonies, to a tree-planting in the afternoon, a promenade concert in the evening (balls had not yet come in), and then to their class supper. This convivial affair began about midnight after the seniors, escorted by their band, had marched down college hill to the Narragansett Hotel. It was on this occasion that Hughes delivered his "Class Prophecy." At the end of their festivities, about four or five o'clock in the morning, the hilarious seniors marched back to the campus and attempted, in accordance with the tradition, to play a baseball game.[10] With his "swallowtails" and pumps and his pompadour haircut, young Hughes must have been an amusing spectacle on the baseball field at sunup that morning.

On Wednesday the academic procession formed on the campus and the "Officers of the Corporation, the faculty, the seniors and alumni marched to the old First Baptist Meeting House, 'built for the worship of God and to hold commencements in.' " Walter J. Towne, who was to become a teacher in the schools of Providence, delivered the valedictory. Hughes' classical oration was on "The First Appearance of Sophocles." George F. Bean (a future lawyer and mayor of Woburn, Mass.) was salutatorian; William C. Ladd (later professor of French at Haverford College) gave the philosophical oration; Frederick R. Hazard (future president of the Solvay Process Company of Syracuse, New York) was class president. Among other prominent members of the class were William Sheafe Chase, who was to become a canon of the Episcopal Church and a noted crusading reformer; John Murray Marshall, who was to practice law in Los Angeles; and Morgan Brooks, future professor of electrical engineering at the University of Illinois.

Looking back at his college experience across half a century, Hughes once remarked that he was impressed by two facts—"first, that there was so much that we did not learn, and, second, that we learned so many things that were not so." [11] But this whimsical hindsight does not obscure the extraordinary intellectual growth that his letters from Brown reveal. In those three years he had felt the inspiration of Diman and the imperious challenge of Robinson, and he had discovered the power of his own mind. While he had turned definitely away from the ministry, the moral essence of his home background had been transfused into his thinking and his new activities. The young man had found himself. Throughout his days Hughes never ceased to be grateful to Brown for the good fellowship it afforded, the standards it upheld, the scientific method or "way of knowing" that it taught, and the windows it opened upon "a world so full of riches of culture that no one with eye and ear need ever be poor." [12]

[10] CEH, Notes, p. 74.
[11] CEH's address to Brown alumni, June 15, 1931. [12] *Ibid.*

Chapter 7

LAW TAKES COMMAND

WITH college days behind him, Hughes' uppermost thought was that he must begin to make a living. The idea that he might become a lawyer now fascinated him. He nursed it fondly every time he went over the question of his future career. But he did not feel that his parents should be burdened with the expense of a law-school course. Law was something to reach for in the future. Just now he had to make some money by means already available to him.

In the days when he thought of teaching as his métier, Hughes had a vague notion that he might make enough money to enable him to study for a year or two in Germany in preparation for a college position. That dream was now fading before the onslaught of a new ambition, but teaching still seemed to afford him the best opportunity of earning some money in the year ahead; so he registered with a teachers' agency, hoping for a place as an instructor in Latin or Greek in a secondary school.

Several schools showed an interest in his application. When they learned that he was only nineteen, however, negotiations were quickly terminated. One of his best prospects seemed to be the Pennsylvania Military Academy (now College) at Chester. Colonel Hyatt, the principal, had been pleased with Hughes' letters, but when they met for an interview in New York he exclaimed, "Why, you could never maintain discipline with my cadets!" [1] The only satisfaction Hughes was to get out of this experience was postponed until 1928, when, on receiving the degree of doctor of laws from the Pennsylvania Military College, he told the alumni how much easier it was to get that degree than to enter the faculty.

Young Hughes was keenly disappointed over these rejections. Yet he could scarcely complain; for, while he had attained his maximum height of five feet eleven inches, he was still slight and looked younger than he was. The beard that was to become famous in many lands had not even begun to grow. He had a fine, intelligent face, but it was the face of youth and inexperience.

Turning to other fields, Hughes secured his first job in the midsummer of 1881—a truly novel undertaking. Property in certain parts of Brooklyn had been heavily assessed for local improvements in advance of immediate needs, and the unpaid taxes and assessments exceeded the then assessed valuation of

[1] CEH, Notes, p. 77.

the property. The legislature offered the owners relief, and it became necessary to calculate the amounts of the arrears in each case. The owners offered this job to the young master of mathematics from Brown University. Hughes worked ten hours a day for six weeks at a wage of $6 a week.

Just as he was finishing this job, he was pleasantly surprised by an offer from the Delaware Academy at Delhi, New York. The salary was only $200 for the school year, with board and room. But he would be free each afternoon, and if he desired to study law he could do so in a good office. Hughes accepted with alacrity and went to Delhi at once.

Dr. James O. Griffin, principal of the academy, went to the station on a September afternoon to meet his new teacher. When the lanky young man from Greenpoint alighted from the train and introduced himself, he could see a shadow of disappointment cross the principal's face. Dr. Griffin held his tongue until he had reinforced the eager young man by taking him home to supper. Then his misgivings could no longer be restrained. "I had not supposed," he began, "that you looked so young—quite as young as many of my students." [2]

One account of this interview has the principal exclaiming, "Why, you've no more beard than an egg." Such a statement would have been accurate, but Hughes carried away no recollection of such bluntness on the part of Dr. Griffin. Certainly the inference that this chiding caused Hughes to grow a beard in later years is without foundation. The significant point is that Dr. Griffin voiced his fears that Hughes would be unable to handle the job, and Hughes, seeing his last chance to teach that year slipping away, summoned all his powers of persuasion. What he pleaded for was a test of his teaching ability. At least he had self-confidence and enthusiasm, and, in the circumstances, a tryout could scarcely be denied him. Dr. Griffin assented.

One reason for Dr. Griffin's initial reluctance became apparent when Hughes was shown to his room. It was near the center of a long hall on the second floor of the dormitory, with the girls' rooms on one side and the boys' on the other. He was expected to maintain order in the hall. The academy had all grades from the primary to full preparation for college. Some of the young farmers who would come in later for a winter of schooling—steady, industrious, and ambitious fellows—were older and huskier than the new teacher. But from the beginning Hughes' students responded to his enthusiasm and vitality, and, except on rare occasions, noise in the hall ceased to be a problem. Even without a whisker to shave, he had enough magnetism about him to command a rare combination of loyalty, attention, and respect.

"Do I stay longer?" Hughes asked the principal as soon as he dared to raise the issue.

[2] *Ibid.*, p. 78.

"You may stay the rest of your life if you wish," Dr. Griffin replied.[3]

Delhi was a charming village among the hills. The academy had a delightful setting in spacious grounds with beautiful trees. Its main building, with cupola and broad veranda, and the separate hall which served as a commodious dormitory had the atmosphere of an old and honored institution. Professor Griffin, a man of exceptional talent who had studied abroad and was later to become professor of German at Leland Stanford University, came to be listed among Hughes' best friends. Teaching in this congenial atmosphere proved to be one of the happiest experiences of a long lifetime.[4]

Hughes fell in with a number of forward-looking young men at Delhi. As an informal club, they would meet at the American Hotel on Saturday evenings for whist and other games and "raids" upon the hotel larder at the invitation of the proprietor's genial son, who was one of the intimates. Hughes' reputation as a wit also won him an invitation from the townspeople of Scottish descent to eat the haggis in honor of Robert Burns and respond to a toast. At Dr. Griffin's urging the young instructor also "broke through the fetters" of his work-study system and "sought both health and pleasure in a genuine fishing excursion." Describing this experience to his father, he wrote on April 30, 1882:

> We reached Delhi about six P.M.—bringing home as nice a mess of trout as could well be caught—they numbered 42 in all, and a large number were these large, beautiful ones, which make the heart of the angler palpitate. Although I did not do as well as Mr. Griffin, I secured some rare beauties, and with the exception of a slight lameness, feel much the better for the trip, which we hope soon to repeat. I wish you could make such a trip. It would do you more good than a pound of medicine—put new blood in your veins and harden your muscles. . . .
>
> I am making the most of my time and trying to do my work in a conscientious manner. I have countless desires and yearnings, which I repress in paying strict attention to the demands of the present. That is the best cure for all mental ailments—*work.*

The following week Hughes wrote to his mother:

> I was thinking over my relations with Delhi people the other day. I never found more cordial and whole-souled friends. I never received so many kind attentions, and I don't think that I have a single enemy. May these blessings continue. My health is good. I weighed 130 the other day. I hope to return to you without any ill health caused by my year of hard work.

At the academy Hughes taught Latin, Greek, algebra, and plane geometry and drilled the boys in their declamations. One of his outstanding students was

[3] Clipping in Mr. Hughes' personal papers, quoting Cornelia Raymond, Delhi teacher.
[4] CEH, Notes, p. 78.

James E. Russell, who became dean of Teachers College, Columbia University. "Many of our students are so eager & enthusiastic," Hughes wrote to his mother, "that I find myself passionately fond of instructing them." "They were 'my boys,' " he said in later years, ". . . and . . . I have never had a warmer glow of satisfaction than I felt when the boys of the academy came through their tests and went forth to justify their training." As a sideline, he tutored two young women of Delhi in advanced French. At first he declined to attempt French conversation, but when the girls insisted (one of them was soon to be married and go to Belgium) he guided them in a series of talks based on a French translation of *The Vicar of Wakefield.* Apparently this was the basis of his quip when he was Secretary of State that he did not speak French but had once taught it.

Hughes began his study of law in the office of William M. Gleason, former Delaware County judge and a lawyer of high repute in up-State New York. Especially stimulating was his association with the judge's son and partner, John B. Gleason, a graduate of Yale and of Columbia Law School, who had one of the keenest minds Hughes had encountered. First he read Maine's *Ancient Law* and followed with Kent's *Commentaries* and the first volume of Washburn on *Real Property,* making elaborate notes. Most of his afternoons and many evenings were spent in the Gleasons' law offices. Occasionally John Gleason would prod him with questions. During this period he also got his first glimpse of the judiciary in action by attending sessions of the New York Supreme Court held regularly in Delhi, the county seat.

The sense of duty that his parents had implanted in him was driving him to great efforts. Two days before his twentieth birthday he wrote to his mother:

> When I cast myself into a reflective mood, and think how I have been cared for, how every wish has been met, how every want provided for, I am constrained to cry out at the terrible responsibility that rests upon me, and as I look at the future, that distant shadow gradually creeping on and becoming lost in the light of the present, I feel a weight resting on me, and a consciousness of utter lack & need, such as almost to overwhelm,—but the power, which has led & cared for & protected me for the past 20 years . . . is able to hold me to the end . . .

Before commencement time rolled around, Hughes had made a decision. The law had hold of him. He was determined to have a career at the bar, and he was not satisfied with his progress from reading in a law office. Only a few months ago he had pleaded for a chance to teach at $200 a year. While he had found that experience most congenial, and Dr. Griffin now offered him $800, with board and room, for the ensuing year, he turned it down. Nor would he consider the offer from David Call, his friend at Madison, to join the faculty of Des Moines University. Some of his Delhi friends suggested that, if he were admitted to the bar and practiced in an up-State community, he would have political opportunities. But this prospect had no more interest for him than further teaching. He was intent on thorough preparation in law and had sufficient confidence in himself to move directly toward that goal. "If you could possibly see me through two years at Columbia," he wrote to his father, "I am sure it would pay in the end." [5] Apparently the Reverend and Mrs. Hughes were by this time reconciled to their son's rejection of the ministry; but they still believed he would have a great future and agreed to put him through law school.

Hughes returned to New York in June, 1882, found a job for the summer, and soon embarked upon an eye-opening experience. His employer was handsome and agreeable Edgar Gray, then in his forties, promoter of the Gill Rapid Transit Company. When Hughes answered Gray's advertisement for a secretary, the latter spoke of his cab service enterprise in the most alluring terms and offered the young man $200 a month, which he thought a princely sum. So attractive was the opportunity, the promoter said, that Hughes might give up the idea of studying law and become a permanent officer in the company.

Hughes was asked, incidentally, of course, to make a small investment in the company "so that he would feel identified with it." He did not like that idea, but he was eager to have the job and thought he could recoup from his salary the small amount required. After making inquiry of W. Fearing Gill, the originator of the company, and of its bankers, a reputable Wall Street firm, Hughes' father borrowed money from a parishioner and made a small payment to Gray for stock to be delivered later.

One of the new secretary's first assignments was to index Gray's press-copy letter books. Uneasiness began to creep into his mind when he saw letters apparently in Gray's handwriting signed by other names. One day Gray blandly informed him that, not wishing to be known personally in a certain matter, he was signing his (Hughes') name to a telegram. Further use of his name was apparent when he found a note addressed to him by a woman, expressing regret that he had not kept an appointment of which he knew nothing. The young secretary was alarmed. The affairs of the company seemed to be in good order, and he did not wish to lose his job, but he felt that this duplicity could not be tolerated. His anxiety sent him to the Astor Library to see what information about Mr. Gray and his enterprises could be gleaned from the newspaper files.

Hughes soon discovered that Gray was a notorious character. Armed with extensive data from the newspapers, he went straight to Mr. Gill, who again assured him that Gray had been introduced to him by General Daniel E.

[5] *Ibid.*, p. 81.

Sickles and was "all right." Hughes disclosed his ammunition, and Mr. Gill was greatly shocked. He said they must confront Gray in his office the following morning and promised that the money "invested" by Hughes' father would be returned. Mr. Gill, too, was eager to get back the power of attorney he had given Gray.

There was a dramatic scene when Hughes and his father called on Gray the next morning and Mr. Gill promptly joined them. Hughes told Gray that he had learned his real name—William E. Gray. He recounted the charges that Gray, while employed by a Wall Street banking firm, had raised the amounts of checks and fled the country with about $300,000; that Gray had been arrested in London, where he had been for several years a dashing member of the Prince of Wales' set; that he had escaped and had again been arrested after a long period in Paris; that he had been extradited to New York, tried and convicted, and that on appeal he had won the right to a new trial. Hughes also said that he knew of the failure of Gray's electric-light venture during the period (apparently several years) while he had been awaiting a new trial. With his employer thus completely unmasked, the aspiring young lawyer-to-be demanded the return of his father's money.

The suave Mr. Gray could not blot out his record, but he insisted on his right to take stock subscriptions. Mr. Gill denied it, and Gray then flashed his power of attorney. Hughes asked to see it and then handed it over to Mr. Gill. "As a result," he once wrote, "my father got his money back and I left Gray's employment with my salary for two weeks' services and with a new insight into the ways of men." [6]

Even before entering law school, Hughes thus conducted his first successful investigation into financial corruption. Apparently Gray was never brought to retrial. Hughes saw him some fourteen years later as Gray—in evening dress, escorting a beautiful woman—entered the dining room of the Hotel Victoria in London. Despite the repeated exposure of his operations, he was reported to be engaged in an investment business.

Left without a job, the young investigator decided to resume his preparations for Columbia. A friend of his father gave him a letter of introduction to General Stewart L. Woodford, United States Attorney for the Southern District of New York. The general assigned the young man to a desk in a room adjoining his own in the Federal Building and thus made it possible for him to use the library of the Law Institute on the floor above. Hughes was delighted and made the most of his privilege. When Elihu Root became United States Attorney in March, 1883, Hughes, coming last in the line as the office staff paid its respects, explained his status and said that his desk was, of course, at Mr. Root's disposal. Root had already acquired an enviable stature in the

[6] *Ibid.*, p. 84.

law, and Hughes looked upon him with the admiration of a young hero worshiper. "The impression," he said forty-two years later, "was too deep ever to be effaced."

The Columbia Law School had a two-year course, with each of its classes divided into morning and afternoon sections. Entering in the fall of 1882, Hughes chose the afternoon section and continued to spend his mornings in the Law Institute Library. His class began with Chase's *Blackstone*. Then came a course in Contracts, guided by Parsons' treatise, and in the second term they concentrated on Washburn's *Real Property*. Hughes had the good fortune to take both the latter courses from Professor Theodore W. Dwight, a teacher of remarkable powers, who had fascinated him as a youth peering through the windows of the Columbia Law School. Dwight's head was "crowned with the distinction of age while his countenance gleamed with the fire of youth." [7]

The "Dwight Method" was frequently contrasted with the Harvard system. This eminent Columbia professor used no case books. His method was to assign portions of the textbook and hold recitations accompanied by his running comments, with an occasional dictated note. By this means he gave his students a ready grasp of fundamental legal principles. Of course he did not ignore the leading cases, and he supplied a profusion of citations. But in the absence of daily drill in the analysis of cases, many students left his classes with "a delusion of acquisition, which was the undoing of those inclined to avoid toil." Hughes knew little of the different methods of teaching law at the time, but he ran down the cases that Professor Dwight cited and carefully digested them in his notebook. This library work brought to his attention numerous other cases which he also digested. By systematically adhering to this practice, he doubtless taught himself more law than he learned from even the brilliant Professor Dwight. "The great lawyer," he once said, speaking of his illustrious predecessors, "has always been a great teacher and his best pupil is himself." [8]

Hughes was soon filling his nights as well as his days with law. He joined a small private "quiz" conducted two nights a week by capable young lawyers—Walter Leggat and Lewis Burchard. Other nights were given to the moot court and "quizzes" sponsored by his legal fraternity, Phi Delta Phi. Some of the latter were conducted by his rival from Public School No. 35, R. Floyd Clarke, who had been graduated by Columbia Law School the previous June. Hughes was also one of the seven members of "The Law Club," which held a moot court fortnightly at the home of John S. Melcher, its organizer. In this exclusive group were Frank C. Partridge, his old friend of Amherst, and Sherman Evarts, son of William M. Evarts. Hughes was making new friends and going ahead at full steam.

[7] CEH's address to Dwight Alumni Association, April 12, 1917.
[8] Address to Alumni of Harvard Law School, June 21, 1920.

Not content with living and breathing the law in a scholastic atmosphere, Hughes thought he ought to have his foot in a law-office door. With this in mind, he went to see Eugene H. Lewis, the junior member of the well known firm of Chamberlain, Carter & Hornblower. He had a letter of introduction from a young lawyer in his father's congregation at Greenpoint, but Mr. Lewis was not interested. He did not even seem to remember the lawyer who had taken the liberty of introducing the young man. Crestfallen and preoccupied by this rebuff, Hughes was making an inconspicuous retreat when, turning at the doorway, he bumped headlong into Walter S. Carter. That was a most fortunate collision which was to change the whole course of his future career. Chance, fate, or Providence had given him a jarring introduction to the best friend of young lawyers in New York—a man who was to be his future partner and father-in-law.

While Hughes was apologizing, Mr. Carter gave him a sharp glance and asked him what his business was. Hughes said that he had been seeking a place in the Carter firm. To his surprise, this brought an invitation to step into the lawyer's private office. There the young man was put through a stiff examination concerning his antecedents and aspirations. Mr. Carter, the antithesis of his junior partner, was a man of hobbies. He "collected" young men with the same enthusiasm with which he collected etchings. Having by accident encountered an interesting specimen, he proceeded to advise the young man as to his future education. German universities, he said, offered some remarkable opportunities. As he was planning ambitiously for his son George, then a student at Yale, he drew German university catalogues from his desk and described their courses in jurisprudence.

"If I were your son, sir," Hughes replied, "I might hope for such advantages. But I am not your son—I must earn a living right away. What I would like to know is whether I may enter your office." [9]

This brought from Mr. Carter a sharp attack upon the idea that anyone should attempt to work in a law office while going to law school. Before he dismissed the young man, however, Mr. Carter told him that if he wished to come into his office during the summer "to see the wheels go 'round"—on "the usual terms"—he could do so. Hughes eagerly accepted the invitation, and as soon as the law-school term ended he became a nonsalaried clerk.

At fifty, Walter S. Carter, with his iron-gray hair and closely trimmed beard, was a successful lawyer of most pleasing personality. Since coming to New York from Chicago, he had had partnerships with such able men as Leslie W. Russell, later attorney general of New York, and Sherburne B. Eaton, who became counsel for Thomas A. Edison. When Daniel H. Chamberlain, former governor of South Carolina, joined the firm, it became Chamberlain, Carter &

[9] Brooklyn *Daily Eagle*, Feb. 9, 1930; author's interview with CEH, Nov. 19, 1947.

Eaton. Then William B. Hornblower, a graduate of Princeton and of Columbia Law School who was rapidly rising to eminence in the profession, took the place of Eaton.

Mr. Carter had also gathered around him a notable group of young men. He was perhaps the first of the New York lawyers to make a practice of keeping in close touch with the law schools so as to single out their most promising students and take some of them into his office after their graduation. As a result, students trooped from Harvard, Columbia, and other schools to interview him, and, aside from those who entered his own office, he was able to place many of these young men in law offices throughout the country. In this he was aided by a wide acquaintance with lawyers and the remarkable ability of remembering the names—even the middle names—of everyone he had met. The achievements of his "kids," as Mr. Carter called them, were a source of great satisfaction to him.

When Hughes entered Mr. Carter's office in the summer of 1883, the managing clerk was Lloyd W. Bowers, valedictorian of the class of 1879 at Yale. Bowers was to become, in the opinion of the Justices of the United States Supreme Court, one of the best solicitors general ever to appear before them, and he probably would have been appointed to the supreme bench had it not been for his untimely death in 1910.[10] Next to Bowers sat James Byrne, a graduate of Harvard Law School in 1882, who was to become one of the leaders of the New York bar and chancellor of the University of the State of New York. On the other side of the clerks' room sat Starr J. Murphy, Hughes' friend from the Delta Upsilon convention at Amherst.

Association with this group of brilliant young men became a great stimulus to Hughes. His chief assignment was to assist Bowers. This was a pleasure, for Bowers possessed personal qualities conducive to the highest professional success. Both Bowers and Hughes worked largely on cases in charge of Mr. Hornblower. This was less of a pleasure, for the third member of the firm was irritable and difficult to work for. Nevertheless, he had a keen intellect, a clear voice, and an incisive manner which commanded respect. A decade later Mr. Hornblower was to be nominated as Associate Justice of the United States Supreme Court, but Senator David B. Hill was to block his confirmation out of resentment over the part Hornblower had played in investigating a contested election.

One of the most memorable events of the summer was a blunder. Mr. Hornblower was engaged in a savage fight with E. Payson Wilder, a terror of the New York bar, over the assets of an insolvent firm. Throughout their battle of motions, appeals, and so forth, Wilder never failed to begin his argument by saying, "My friend, Mr. Blowhorner, I beg pardon, Mr. Hornblower"—

[10] CEH, Notes, pp. 89–89*a*.

a jest that left the victim livid with rage. An important brief in the case was given to Bowers one Friday afternoon to be printed, proofed, and put in readiness by Monday morning. Being addicted to italics, capitals, and bold-face type, Mr. Hornblower had reached the climax of his argument in this outstanding line: "And the firm paid *seven thousand dollars* in CASH." On Monday morning the printed brief was on his desk, but he soon appeared at the door of the clerks' room so full of wrath he could hardly speak. As he pointed to the climax of his brief, the two young men who had labored over it read with amazement and horror: "And the firm paid *seven thousand dollars* in COAL."

"Bowers and I did not know which one of us was responsible for this egregious error," Hughes wrote many years later, "whether it was due to a misreading of Mr. Hornblower's script or to a failure to catch the mistake in the print, and we both took Hornblower's unsparing denunciation with abject humility and contrition. Thenceforth, I was the most careful of proof-readers, quite sure that the mistake most likely to be overlooked would be on the title page or in some conspicuous place where it would stand out like a monument." [11]

Adhering to his agreement, Hughes left the office as soon as the law school opened. At their parting, Mr. Carter sent a tingle up the young man's spine. "Hughes," he said, "when you get through the law school, you can come back and I will put you on a salary." The lawyer-to-be walked home on air, thinking his future was now secure.

At Columbia, Hughes plunged into Equity under Professor Benjamin F. Lee and into Torts, Evidence, and the New York Code of Civil Procedure under Professor George Chase. He also took the course in Common Law Pleading, not because he had any intention of practicing outside New York but because he wished to be familiar with the subject. Chase was utterly uninspiring; he had none of Dwight's magnetism; but he was precise and accurate, and the students came to have a high regard for him. Hughes and a number of his classmates made a practice of attending the junior as well as the senior lectures in order to review the previous year's work.

During the summer this young disciple of the law had spent his evenings in a commercial school studying stenography. He left with a diploma saying that he could write 150 words a minute. This new skill enabled him to make copious notes of everything Professors Dwight and Chase had to say, and those notes proved invaluable when he later began teaching law. After leaving law school, however, he never used shorthand.

In the spring of 1884 Hughes' father resigned his pastorate in Greenpoint and moved to Jersey City Heights, where he had become pastor of the Summit

[11] *Ibid.*, p. 92.

Avenue Baptist Church. Not wishing to lose his residence in New York, young Hughes went to live with a classmate, Emerson Hadley. They shared a small room—fourth floor back—in West Thirty-fourth Street, then a desirable street of brownstone fronts. Here they crammed for the final examinations. Hughes did not enter the voluntary competition for the law-school prize given for the best essay and the highest marks in a special examination, but he was given the prize fellowship for his class. Columbia thus rewarded the outstanding graduate of each senior class with a salary of $500 a year for three years, in return for tutoring in the law school. Hughes accepted gladly with the understanding that his duties would involve only the holding of a "quiz" two nights a week, and would thus not interfere with his plan to become a law clerk in Mr. Carter's office.

Then came the New York County bar examination. Hughes passed with a high mark, took the oath, and was admitted to the bar in June, 1884. Sixty years were to elapse before the star performer at that bar examination was to learn of his real standing. One day in the late fall of 1944, Michael H. Cardozo IV called at the home of Chief Justice Hughes, then retired, carrying the original record of the bar examinations which his grandfather, Michael H. Cardozo, had helped to conduct in 1884. Hughes' mark in this record is 99½.

Chapter 8

FIRST YEARS AT THE BAR

CHARLES E. HUGHES had invested his lifeblood as well as his father's money and all of his own time in a legal education. After his admittance to the bar, even he had to acknowledge that his relentless toiling day and night had impaired his health. Fully clothed, he weighed only 124 pounds. A severe cold had left him with an obstinate cough. It was evident that he would have to take a long rest if he were to enter upon his duties as a law clerk with his customary zest.

Good fortune came his way. De Witt J. Seligman, who had been a classmate of Hughes in law school, asked him to tutor Larry Bernheimer, Seligman's brother-in-law, in preparation for the bar examination in the fall. Since the young man's family was to spend the summer at Long Branch, Hughes could thus have several months at the seashore. The tutoring would require only two hours a day. Hughes was very pleased with the arrangement and systematically applied himself to the task of improving his health.

During his sojourn at Long Branch, Hughes escorted two girls from the boardinghouse where he was staying to a "hop" at the West End Hotel. While they were sitting on the veranda, up came Albert Cardozo, a friend of one of the girls, with his young brother, Ben, a shy lad of fourteen, in knickerbockers.[1] They spent a large part of the evening together, not dreaming that in a distant future the gay law-school graduate and the shy lad would sit together as judges of the highest court in the land.

Later on, Hughes moved to Asbury Park but returned by train every day to do his tutoring. His summer of leisure was terminated by a note from Mr. Carter in these words: "What do you say to coming 1st Sept. instead of 1st of Oct.? We need you now." [2] Hughes was ready. A summer of sunshine, sea air, and exercise had added eight pounds to his weight, fully restored his health, and left him in the best of spirits.

Several changes had taken place in the firm of Chamberlain, Carter & Hornblower since Hughes had watched "the wheels go 'round" during the previous summer. When Eugene H. Lewis left the firm, Lloyd W. Bowers had succeeded him as junior partner. Bowers, too, had left to form a partnership

[1] CEH, Notes, p. 95; G. S. Hellman's *Benjamin N. Cardozo*, p. 221.
[2] Hughes Papers, Library of Congress, Item 24.

with Judge Thomas Wilson of Winona, Minnesota, and James Byrne had stepped up to the position of junior partner. About the same time Robert Grier Monroe, a grandson of Mr. Justice Robert C. Grier of the Supreme Court, entered the office as a clerk.

Hughes was full of regret over the departure of his brilliant friend Bowers and the circumstances contributing to it. Bowers had suffered an unmerciful tongue-lashing from Justice Abraham R. Lawrence, a choleric gentleman with wavy white hair and florid complexion, who seemed to have a special contempt for young lawyers. In closing his argument on a motion, Bowers had ventured to suggest that it was highly important that the question be speedily decided. Procrastination being a well known failing of Justice Lawrence, his vanity was wounded. Pounding with his gavel, he shouted that "it did not lie in the mouth of a young lawyer whom he had never seen before to tell him when to decide his cases"; he wanted "the young lawyer" to know that he would not "tolerate such an innuendo by any member of the bar"; that "a more experienced lawyer" would have known better than to make such an "unjust imputation." [3] Bowers went back to his office fuming and vowed that he would never set foot in a New York court again. Apparently he never did. The incident deeply impressed Hughes with the importance of good manners on the bench.

In those days the best law firms were engaged in general practice, with many cases in the courts, and the most highly prized professional opportunities in New York City still lay in advocacy. The business of Chamberlain, Carter & Hornblower was largely commercial. Most of it was brought in by Mr. Carter, but he did little law work himself. His attention was given chiefly to managing the office, correspondence, and interviewing clients, whom he would usually turn over to Hornblower or Byrne.

Hughes' job was to assist members of the firm in whatever was assigned to him. He helped on briefs, acted as junior in cases in court, and did general office work. For this he received $30 a month, with an increase of $5 every two months. His chief reward was experience. He especially prized the privilege of being about the court house, "for any morning one might see Joseph H. Choate, Benjamin F. Tracy, Frederic R. Coudert, Edward C. James, or some other distinguished advocate, ascending the stairs to one of the court rooms and one might find a few minutes to hear part of some important trial and observe a great lawyer in action." [4]

Hughes' first case proved to be a dramatic affair. Mr. Carter brought in a German street broker named Wellenkamp, who had suffered painful injuries and some disfigurement in rescuing his two young children from a fire in his home. While Wellenkamp had been recovering in a hospital, his wife had

[3] CEH, Notes, p. 97. [4] *Ibid.*, p. 98.

deserted him and thereafter refused to allow him to see his children. Mr. Carter correctly concluded that there was no prospect of a fee in the case, but he liked to give young lawyers a chance to prove themselves; so he dumped the Wellenkamp mess into young Hughes' lap and told him to see what he could do with it.

His first step was to bring a habeas corpus proceeding to assert Wellenkamp's rights as a father. There followed a long and bitter controversy which attracted a good deal of attention in the press. Mrs. Wellenkamp was defended by her brother into whose home she had gone when she deserted her husband. "This precious pair," as Hughes called them, "she a virago and he a pugnacious lawyer and glib witness, piled up accusations regardless of truth or decency against the unfortunate Wellenkamp." [5] The hearings before a referee continued for many months, and almost every detail of the Wellenkamps' married life was laid bare. Hughes almost lived with Wellenkamp for a year. By rigorous cross-examination of the brother and sister he succeeded in breaking down the stories they had fabricated. The referee, Samuel A. Blatchford, decided in Wellenkamp's favor, awarding him custody of the children. The court confirmed the referee's report. The children were well cared for by their father, and years later Hughes had the pleasure of hearing from the daughter, who was then living under much happier circumstances.

Under his scholarship at Columbia, Hughes was quiz master for about two hundred students two nights a week, and two other nights were given to a private quiz which he undertook at the request of about a dozen seniors. At the end of these grilling two-hour periods, he had a long journey every night—by the elevated railroad to Cortlandt Street, by ferry to Jersey City, and by horsecar for twenty-five minutes to Jersey City Heights, where he was living with his parents. This extra work thus proved to be a heavy burden, but it gave him a wide acquaintance with, and a most favorable reputation among, the coming young men of the bar. One of his former classmates, Scott Hopkins, was so firmly convinced that Hughes was destined for the Supreme Court that he always greeted him as "Mr. Justice." But Hughes thought this ridiculous.[6]

Meanwhile his reputation in the Carter firm was rising with the swiftness of the morning sun. Mr. Carter declared that of all the young men with whom he had been associated "not one of them, in pure intellect and legal scholarship, compared with Hughes." [7] That amiable connoisseur of men was delighted by his young clerk's industry, his searching mind, his thorough knowledge of the law, his systematic habits, personal honesty, and high pro-

[5] *Ibid.*, p. 99. [6] Author's interview with CEH, Dec. 4, 1945.
[7] Burton J. Hendrick, in *McClure's Magazine*, March, 1908.

fessional ideals. But Hughes was by no means swept off his feet by this happy appreciation of his qualities.

"Mr. Hughes," said his employer in one of their early conferences, "I am told that you are the brightest man ever graduated from Brown University."

"Mr. Carter," Hughes replied, "hearsay evidence is not trustworthy." [8]

In terms of financial reward Hughes was also doing remarkably well. The firm paid him $500 for his year's work. His fellowship brought him $500, his private quiz a similar amount, and fees from cases coming to him from outside the firm amounted to nearly $1,000, of which he was allowed to keep 50 per cent. His total income for his first year at the bar amounted to nearly $2,000.

Worn out but happy over his initial success, Hughes concluded in the midsummer of 1885 that he should take a good vacation. The firm agreed. With Colin S. Carter, son of his employer, as a traveling companion, he sailed on the *State of Nevada* for Glasgow, taking advantage of the old State Line's return-trip fare of $75 for first-class passage. The two young men parted at Glasgow, and Hughes went to Oban and Inverness, then to Edinburgh and through the Trossachs. Journeying then to Wales, he visited his Aunt Jane Jones and Uncle John Richard Hughes, crossed the St. George Channel to Dublin and went north to Belfast.

On the return voyage Hughes made an acquaintance that brought him into a highly sensational affair. His stateroom companion was Gerard Murray, son of the "keeper of the petty bag" of the British Court of Chancery, who was traveling with his brother, an Episcopal clergyman living in Virginia. Young Murray soon confided to Hughes that he had failed in an attempted elopement with the daughter of a tavern keeper and was being shipped to America to finish his medical education at the University of Virginia. He swore that he would marry the girl in spite of his family. This he did a few months later after returning to England on funds supplied by his prospective mother-in-law. Bringing the girl to New York, he left her in a boardinghouse while he went to Charlottesville for his books and clothes. She disappeared, and detectives found her in a brothel whence she had been taken by a merchant with whom she had struck up an acquaintance on the voyage while Murray had been seasick. When Murray was arrested for allegedly threatening to kill his bride, Hughes defended him in police court and later got the charges dismissed. The girl was sent back to England, and shortly afterward Murray died of a sudden illness.

During part of the second year of his fellowship at Columbia (1885–1886) Hughes taught, at the insistence of Professor Chase, the regular course in

[8] Recorded in letter, Frederick L. Gamage to Hughes, July 27, 1945.

common-law pleading, also continuing his private quiz. At the office, Hughes stepped into the position of junior member of the firm. Governor Chamberlain withdrew to practice alone, and the firm became Carter, Hornblower & Byrne, with Hughes as fourth man. He was kept on salary, as was customary with the junior, but his bimonthly increases brought his salary for the second year to nearly $900. His own business also expanded, and occasionally he was asked to write briefs for other lawyers. Eugene H. Lewis, who had turned Hughes away so abruptly when he first knocked at the door of the Carter firm, now asked him to write briefs in two or three important cases and to join the staff of Eaton & Lewis. A large firm, Turner, Lee & McClure, offered Hughes a place at more than twice the salary he was receiving, and several young lawyers sought a partnership with him. But Hughes appreciated the special opportunity he already had for important work and continued advancement in a firm of excellent standing, and this meant more to him than larger compensation.

Hughes and Colin Carter went abroad again in 1886. After jaunting about Holland, the young men roved through Paris and London. In London, Hughes read in a newspaper that Parliament was assembling. "Listen to this, Colin," he said, ". . . I'm going to try to get in." Young Carter laughed and insisted that any such attempt would be futile on the opening day, without a card from the American Legation; he refused to go. As the more venturesome traveler encountered a "bobby" near the entrance, he had an inspiration. "Where are Mr. Parnell's headquarters?" he asked. He followed the "bobby's" directions and presented his card showing that he was an "Attorney and Counsellor at Law, 346 Broadway, New York City." "I was soon introduced," Hughes recalled, "to an agreeable young man who said he was on his way to the House and would take me over. He was none other than John Redmond, then at the outset of his parliamentary career and destined to become the leader of his party. Full of inquiries about the States and our public opinion on the Irish question, he proved a most amiable escort. He took me to the lobby of the House, pointed out some of the most distinguished members who were about, and left me with one or two of his friends,—an exciting and unforgettable adventure." [9]

The young travelers returned on the *W. A. Scholten,* an ancient vessel that went down a short time later. Their adventure abroad together had been so pleasant that they now decided to live together in New York. Hughes had concluded that he could no longer endure the inconvenience of living in Jersey City Heights. He and young Carter took rooms at the Murray Hill Hotel, then new, with a first-class clientele, rivaling the Windsor. The arrangement did not last long; for when the Reverend Mr. Hughes accepted a call to the Trinity

[9] CEH, Notes, p. 105.

Antoinette Carter and Charles E. Hughes
at the time of their wedding, 1888

Mrs. Hughes with Charlie and Helen, Cornell University, 1892

© Pach Brothers, N.Y., 1905

© Pach Brothers, N

The uncompromising investigator

Baptist Church on East Fifty-fifth Street, New York, his lawyer son returned to the parental roof at 110 East Eighty-first Street.

In the third year of his Columbia fellowship, Hughes was relieved of the course in pleading and acquired a partner in his private teaching. Mr. Carter had asked him who was the most promising man in his quizzes. Hughes had replied, "A great big fellow by the name of Cravath." Paul D. Cravath, the six-foot-four prize fellow of the class of 1886, thereupon became a clerk in the office. Cravath agreed to share Hughes' private quiz so that each would give only one night a week to it. Hughes' happy relations with his students was warmly attested when, at the end of his fellowship, they presented him with a handsome gold watch that he was to carry for more than sixty years.

His most disagreeable experience in this period was an emergency appearance before Justice Van Brunt, known as "Sitting Bull." Mr. Byrne was seeking an attachment on the ground of fraudulent disposition of property. Moving with all possible speed, this ordinarily meticulous practitioner based his case on a sheaf of affidavits, without waiting to assemble his facts in more orderly form. When a motion to vacate the attachment came up before Justice Van Brunt, Byrne had a severe cold and sent word that Hughes should appear for him. Hughes had not previously worked on the case, and before he had a chance to master all the facts he found himself in court listening to a vehement attack upon the papers Byrne had offered. Abram Kling, counsel for the defendants and a companion of Justice Van Brunt on summer trips, used the strategy of selecting insignificant affidavits and holding them up to ridicule. His close friend on the bench was favorably impressed.

"Who appears on the other side?" the judge shouted. "It's an imposition on the court to present such papers. I'll vacate the attachment!" [10]

Hughes arose, inwardly trembling with excitement but giving the impression of cool discipline and determination. The judge's tongue-lashing was then directed straight at the young lawyer. He remembered the searing experience of his friend Bowers, and his fighting disposition was aroused. He insisted on being heard. In the circumstances he could have disavowed all personal responsibility for the state of the papers, but his loyalty to his firm prevented him from doing so. In spite of repeated interruptions by the judge, he succeeded in pointing out certain affidavits containing admissions by the defendants which, under a decision of the General Term, justified the issue of the attachment. Doggedly he held his ground, and Van Brunt (who was an able judge in spite of his overbearing attitude) eventually sustained the attachment rather than risk reversal on appeal. Throughout the ordeal Hughes "suffered keenly" and was once more deeply impressed by the importance of judicial manners.[11]

[10] *Ibid.*, p. 107. [11] *Ibid.*

Hughes' work load was too heavy to permit another vacation abroad in 1887, but his two weeks at Block Island brought unexpected pleasures. As he sat in the smoking room of the Ocean View Hotel on the evening of his arrival, an imposing man of stocky build appeared at the door, glanced about, and asked, "Young man, do you know how to play whist?" Hughes admitted that he did.

"Come into my apartment," the imposing gentleman commanded, "we need a fourth hand."

Chance thus threw the energetic young lawyer into the company of Mr. Justice Samuel F. Miller of the United States Supreme Court, and he had the "inestimable privilege" of playing whist with this eminent jurist every evening of his stay at Block Island.

"To be his partner," Hughes wrote, "was a tough experience. He played without signals and expected one to divine his hand without the aids which modern whist had provided. When things went wrong, he used his objurgatory vocabulary without restraint. We cut for partners every rubber and it was a joy occasionally to get the best of him. Despite his brusquerie, he had a very kindly disposition and took a genuine interest in young lawyers." [12]

Justice Miller plied Hughes with questions about the practice of law in New York. "It is hard to make a good lawyer in New York," he once observed. "You try to get an injunction or an attachment or something right at the start, and if you don't get it you drop the case. What we want at the bar is thoroughness." On the last evening of their play together the Justice made up for the severe discipline to which he had subjected the young lawyer by saying, "Well, Hughes, if you will practice law as well as you play whist, I think you will get along." [13]

During his stay at Block Island, Hughes also encountered Justice George C. Barrett of the New York Supreme Court, whom he regarded as the best of the New York judges. Justice Barrett asked the young lawyer to join him in an afternoon walk and talked at length on the legal points at issue and the basis for his rulings in the trial of Jacob Sharp for bribery in obtaining the Broadway street-car franchise. When Hughes returned to work, he had been intellectually stimulated as well as physically refreshed.

There is other evidence that young Hughes was very pleasant company. Within his circle of friends his wit and his skill in self-expression made him a favorite toastmaster at dinners. In June, 1885, Charlie Hughes, Mark Allen, "Ned" Bassett, Fred Crossett, and "Ot" and "Robe" Eidlitz went to Easton to install a Delta Upsilon chapter at Lafayette College. Hughes was the youngest member of the group, but he entertained his fraternity brothers in the sleeper until late into the night with an "inexhaustible fund of stories." [14] At

[12] *Ibid.*, p. 108. [13] *Ibid.*, p. 109. [14] New York *Herald*, Jan. 5, 1908.

Easton he took the initiative in carrying out the business of the trip. In the fall of 1886 he was toastmaster at the Delta Upsilon convention at Madison University. As his reputation grew, he was frequently invited to add sparkle to a festive occasion.

Hughes had no time for politics. His first vote had been cast for Seth Low in the Brooklyn mayoralty election of 1883. In the following year he lost his opportunity of voting for Blaine or Cleveland by moving from New York to his parents' home in Jersey City. After settling once more in New York, he joined the Republican Club and the Association of the Bar. With other young lawyers, he campaigned unsuccessfully in 1887 for De Lancey Nicoll, prosecutor of Jacob Sharp and rising hope of the independent bar, who was running for district attorney. But these were minor events in a life given almost wholly to law. "Many nights Hughes and I sat reading law together," Cravath once said, "but at two o'clock in the morning I was usually on the sofa, dozing, despite black coffee and wet towels, but Hughes was still reading." [15] One of Hughes' resolutions was to get in a good deal of reading outside the law, but that sort of self-education was confined largely to weekends and to his devouring of the daily papers on horsecars and elevated trains.

William Hornblower's practice in connection with the Grant & Ward receivership and the New York Life Insurance Company had become so extensive and so lucrative that he decided to pull out of the Carter firm in the fall of 1887. James Byrne agreed to go with him. Their decision was a matter of deep regret to Hughes. Hornblower's clarity, precision, and exacting demands upon his associates and Byrne's extreme care and caution had afforded an excellent discipline. Intimate contacts with these men had given their junior partner "a constant awareness of the best traditions of the bar."

Walter Carter looked around for an outstanding lawyer to fill the gap in his firm. When he discussed several possibilities with Hornblower, the latter suggested, "Why not take young Hughes?" Mr. Carter repeated this to Hughes, and he was "greatly surprised and overjoyed at the opportunity." [16] "But," he said, "we should hold Cravath." Mr. Carter agreed.

That evening the jubilant new second partner took Paul Cravath to dinner at the famous Martinelli restaurant, where they reviewed the whole situation over a bottle of Chianti.

"Cravath," he said, "this is an extraordinary chance. We would be a young firm with a good business at the start and every opportunity for making an independent reputation instead of virtually being clerks." A young firm, indeed! Hughes was twenty-five and Cravath twenty-six. Mr. Carter was the business-getter and gave little attention to legal work as such. To clinch the argument with his associate, who had had a tempting offer from Hornblower

[15] *Outlook*, Oct. 20, 1906. [16] CEH. Notes, p. 110.

and Byrne, Hughes declared, "We will make the firm Carter, Hughes and Cravath."

"Make it Carter, Hughes *and Cravath*," the big fellow thundered, bringing his fist down on the table, "and I'll join."

Carter, Hughes & Cravath it became. They agreed to a division of the fees from the general business of the firm, giving Carter, who owned the library and office furniture, 60 per cent, Hughes 24 per cent, and Cravath 16 per cent. In addition, Hughes and Cravath continued to have 50 per cent of the fees from business that each brought in. Their junior partner was John W. Houston, a graduate of Harvard Law School who had shown exceptional talent as a clerk. Among the new crop of clerks were such promising men as Thaddeus D. Kenneson, Howard A. Taylor, and Harry W. Mack.

Hughes could scarcely believe that fortune had smiled upon him so favorably. At the age of twenty-five he had become the number one lawyer of a highly respected firm with an extensive practice. By dint of industry, intelligence, and frequent reorganizations he had moved from the bottom to the top rung in the firm, so far as handling the legal work was concerned, in only three years. That remarkable success was shortly to lead to the happiest venture of his life.

Chapter 9

OVERFLOWING CUP

LOVE had little chance to blossom in Charlie Hughes' heart in his first quarter-century. At Madison he had shown some interest in the "Sem" girls, but at Brown and Columbia Law School his experience was almost devoid of social contacts. In his first years at the bar his work and his quiz classes four nights a week left little time for dates. When girls whom he had known elsewhere came to visit New York he used to "beau them around." [1] But the law had first call upon him. Feminine charm was a negligible factor in the range of interests that he permitted himself to pursue.

He had been with the firm a year before he knew that Mr. Carter had a daughter. One day Mr. Carter took from his drawer a watch—a birthday gift to his daughter—and showed it to Hughes. A few months later the young clerk met the daughter herself. The firm had hired two new graduates of Columbia Law School—Ethelbert Dudley Warfield (later president of Lafayette College) and Charles B. Storrs. In December, 1885, Storrs accepted an offer to teach law at the University of Tokyo, and the firm gave him a dinner at old Delmonico's. Standing with Mr. Carter as he received the guests was his tall and attractive twenty-one-year-old daughter Antoinette. She was dressed in black and seemed to Hughes a vision of loveliness. He had "but a word with her," and the opportunity of taking her in to dinner was not to be his. Instead, he escorted Mrs. Thomas Wilson. But at the table, he once related, "I happened to catch Miss Carter's eye when we both saw the same joke which others seemed to miss, and a certain understanding was then and there established, although it was some time before this ripened into the love that never failed." [2]

Hughes made no immediate effort to follow up this favorable introduction. Months of hard grinding in the law enveloped him—months in which Antoinette Carter was only a vivid and pleasing memory. Then he was invited to the Carter home for Sunday dinner, and on various occasions he played whist in the same alluring environment. On one of these visits he stayed overnight with Antoinette's brother Colin. About 2:00 A.M. Antoinette awakened the young men and asked them to go for a doctor; her stepmother had become dangerously ill. She spent the night taking care of her stepmother, but

[1] Author's interview with CEH, Dec. 5, 1945. [2] CEH, Notes, p. 103.

the next morning Hughes found her as radiant and good-humored as if nothing had happened. Such poise and even temperament were typical of her. His admiration was lifted several notches higher. Still Hughes made no concerted effort to court the young lady.

Antoinette Carter had attained her sunny disposition in spite of a harried childhood. Born in Milwaukee on September 14, 1864, she was christened at the funeral service for her mother, Antoinette Smith Carter. Her father, a direct descendant from Elder William Brewster of the *Mayflower,* had gone to Milwaukee as a young man and returned there to practice law after serving as a member of the United States Christian Commission in the Civil War. As the youngest of four children orphaned by her mother's death, Antoinette was placed under the care of a nurse, Mrs. Sarah Williams. In her old age Mrs. Williams remembered Antoinette as "an unusually beautiful little child with dark hair and eyes and sweet little vivacious ways" [5] and a captivating lisp that gave special charm to her recitation of "A Little Thip Thailed on the Thea."

Mr. Carter married again, but his second wife died within a year. A sister of the second Mrs. Carter (Mrs. W. J. Bridges of Baltimore) then induced him to "lend" Antoinette to her for a few months. The child's sojourn with the Bridges lengthened to six years—until she reached the age of ten. At Washington, Pennsylvania, Antoinette went to a private school kept by Miss Nannie Stewart in West Maiden Street. Later she moved with the Bridges to Princeton, having become so much a part of the family that she was often called "Nettie" Bridges.

Meanwhile Mr. Carter had moved to Chicago and then to New York and had acquired a third wife who became the mother of Walter F. ("Dutch") Carter, the great Yale pitcher of his day, and Leslie Carter. When Antoinette rejoined her father's family, therefore, she came under the influence of her fifth mother. Yet she remained a serene and sweet-tempered girl. At Wells College in Aurora, New York, and at Wellesley College, she was a good student and acquired the habit of extensive reading. Like her father, she found much interest in art and music as well as literature. But she was also athletic, and her face was a beaming reflection of good health. Hughes regarded her as a perfect specimen of womanhood.

For two and a half years after their meeting at Delmonico's, Antoinette Carter and Charlie Hughes were merely friends. During the second year of their acquaintance, he took her to the theater twice and saw her on a few other occasions. But he would not permit himself to fall in love with her. She was the daughter of his employer. Contrary to the oft-repeated statement that Hughes "married the boss's daughter," he deliberately avoided courting her so long as he was a clerk in her father's firm. The idea of marriage to further

[5] Undated letter in the Milwaukee *Daily News.*

his ambition was highly repugnant to him; [4] it stood as a barrier between them. And that barrier was not removed until after he had become a full-fledged partner in the firm of Carter, Hughes & Cravath.

Meanwhile Antoinette had gone to Rochester, where she and her friend Marie B. Pond opened a gymnasium for women and children on November 3, 1887. When she returned to New York the following summer, Hughes (now a full-fledged partner with excellent prospects) saw her more frequently. In the course of their excursions to Manhattan Beach, Bridgehampton, and elsewhere, their mutual attraction ripened into a close friendship—so close that Hughes began to unburden his heart to her concerning a personal matter that was troubling him. Antoinette proved to be not only a delightful companion but also an eager confidante and clear-headed adviser. It must have been apparent to everyone but him that she loved him.

After she returned to Rochester in September, Hughes became a persistent correspondent. One of Antoinette's letters in reply seemed to strip a blindfold from his eyes, and love for her suddenly filled his whole being. No longer could he suppress his feelings. Proposing by letter, he got a prompt and favorable reply and almost flew to Rochester with an engagement ring. From that moment to the end of their days his devotion to her was intense and unwavering.

Antoinette's happiness was bubbling over when she wrote the good news to her father. He replied on October 11, 1888:

MY DEAR DAUGHTER:

The subject called for a good letter and *you wrote it.*

Yes, that is all right. There are *very* few abler, and certainly there are no better, fellows than Hughes. If I'd been going to choose for you, I should have selected him over all I know.

For the remainder of the autumn, Hughes was a faithful week-end visitor in Rochester. Stopping at the Powers Hotel, he would take a sitting room so that they could be indoors together, but as tongues began to wag, they soon shifted their meeting place to the home of Miss Pond's sister. Each visit deepened Hughes' conviction that his fiancée was the one woman in the world with whom he could be happy.

We get some indication of Antoinette's emotions (as well as an index to her disposition) from the following letter which she wrote on October 16 to her future mother-in-law:

MY DEAR MRS. HUGHES:—

My heart was full of gratitude when I read your letter welcoming me as a *daughter* to your "heart and home."

[4] Author's interview with CEH, Dec. 5, 1945.

Office of

Carter, Hughes & Cravath,

Attorneys & Counsellors at Law,

346 Broadway,

Walter S. Carter,
Charles E. Hughes,
Paul D. Cravath,
John W. Houston.

New York, Oct. 11th, 1888.

My dear daughter:

The subject called for a good letter & you wrote it.

Yes, that's all right. There are very few abler, & certainly there are no better fellows than Hughes. If I'd been going to choose for you, I should have selected him, over all I know.

Lovingly,

Father.

For Charlie's sake, because you are *his Mother,* though we have but met, I love you and think of you as *my Mother* already. When I come to you, I shall love you, I know, for your own sake as well as his and find you indeed a Mother. All that I feel for you, I feel for your husband also. Will you tell him for me, and I hope it will not be long before we shall see each other face to face.

If I could not rely upon your charity it would be with grave fears of sadly disappointing you that I look forward to that day, for do you not know that Charlie paints me in colors altogether too bright, that he looks at me with a lover's eyes, blind to faults and seeing virtues which I do not possess? If however *love* for *him* and his can "cover a multitude of sins" and over balance many failings, all will be well.

You will spare Charlie to me next Sunday? Even gladly, if you knew how I long to see him and how anxiously I am awaiting that day.

Many bright visions of the future float through my mind. I see a *very* happy, a very united family, myself one of its members and as such to be to each all that I should be is my fondest hope, the most earnest prayer of

Your daughter to be

ANTOINETTE CARTER

They were married on the following December 5. It was a simple ceremony at the Carter home, 176 Brooklyn Avenue, Brooklyn. Officiating were Hughes' father and the Reverend Mr. E. H. Dickinson, husband of Antoinette's sister Emma, and only members of the families were present.

"Hughes," said Mr. Carter as the newlyweds were leaving the house, "you'll find that Nettie is a good person to live with." [5]

The groom concluded that this was the most masterly understatement of which his father-in-law was capable.

Plans for their honeymoon were a deep secret. When Mr. Carter asked where they intended to go, Hughes replied, "You might guess Canada." But he did not deceive his shrewd father-in-law. Mr. Carter telegraphed to Judge Thomas Wilson (then in Congress) to expect the newlyweds at the Arlington Hotel in Washington. The judge was on hand to greet them. On the train they had encountered Mayor Hugh J. Grant of New York, and it was to him that Hughes had the privilege of first introducing his "wife."

Washington favored them with delightfully mild and sunny weather. They drove about in one-horse victorias and went by steamer to Mount Vernon. Visiting the Supreme Court, they watched its solemn proceedings with reverence. Hughes was proud to point out to his bride his erstwhile partner in whist, Mr. Justice Miller. The memory of this first glimpse of the Supreme Court in action would often flash upon his mind when he himself came to look out upon wide-eyed visitors from that mighty seat of judgment. But in December, 1888, his imagination would not stretch so far as to place himself on the supreme bench. To friends who assumed that at least he must

[5] CEH, Notes, p. 121.

have cherished such an ambition, his reply was always: "Not for an instant! . . . I dreamed of nothing more than a reasonable measure of professional success." [6]

The blissful days in Washington, and a few more in Baltimore, passed all too quickly. Back in New York, Hughes took his bride to live with his parents in the three-story brownstone house at 129 East Sixty-second Street. Being relatively prosperous, he had become responsible for the rent ($1,200 a year) when the family first moved to this house the previous May. With his mother still inclined to call him to account for any shortcoming, real or imagined, the arrangement was probably not a happy one; but within a few months his parents moved to Scranton, where his father had accepted a call from the Jackson Street Baptist Church.

The newlyweds spent most of their first summer together at Lake Mahopac, with Hughes commuting to and from New York every weekday. His exacting legal work was interrupted for a vacation of two weeks in the Adirondacks. On November 30, 1889, a son was born to them and promptly named for his father. His coming convinced them that they should establish a permanent home, and, thinking Brooklyn might be the most desirable location, they rented a house on the Park slope, No. 117 St. John's Place.

Hughes had found new bearings. His love for his wife knew no bounds, and that love was now extended to include his son. The marriage on which he had embarked was to be one of the happiest imaginable. It made all his other causes for satisfaction seem "trivial by comparison." To draw further upon his own words, written after more than half a century of married life: "Our cup of happiness was full at the beginning and has been full and overflowing ever since. In all my privileges and responsibilities, in good times and bad, in success and defeat, in joy and sorrow, we have had a perfect union of minds and hearts. Whatever I have accomplished has been made possible by that strong, unselfish, ever radiant spirit, constantly by my side." [7]

In the summer following the birth of his son, Hughes also acquired a new badge of identification—his beard. His decision to join the ranks of his be-whiskered elders—his father, father-in-law, grandfather, and several uncles—had nothing to do with his prolonged beardlessness as a youth. The family took a little cottage at Siasconset, Nantucket, for the summer, and Hughes let his beard grow during his holiday of three weeks as a matter of convenience. He had never learned to shave himself. When he returned to the office, he simply rebelled at the idea of resuming his daily visits to the Hotel Astor barbershop, where he had kept a shaving cup for several years. He had previously worn a mustache by choice, but the auburn stubble on his chin was allowed to take its own course solely as a matter of saving time. Had the

[6] *Ibid.*, p. 122. [7] *Ibid.*

safety razor come within the range of his experience, the famous beard would never have been grown.[8]

After living in Brooklyn for a year, Charles and Antoinette Hughes concluded that the upper west side of Manhattan was a more desirable place for a permanent residence. Early in 1891 they bought the house at No. 318 (apparently later numbered 320) West Eighty-eighth Street, near Riverside Drive. That is, they bought the equity subject to the building loan. This four-story red brick house, with its bay windows and spacious rooms, was a very attractive residence, and they decorated and furnished it to their complete satisfaction. Their cup of happiness was truly overflowing. Only one circumstance arose to cloud their bliss, and that can better be seen from the vantage point of Hughes' law office.

[8] Author's interview with CEH, Dec. 26, 1945.

Chapter 10

BREAKNECK STAIRS

IT WAS a proud moment for Charles E. Hughes when, on the first day of 1888, he took possession of Mr. Hornblower's room and assumed the leading role in the legal work of Carter, Hughes & Cravath. At an age when most young lawyers are pleased to be clerks, he was the head of a little legal domain.

Compared with present standards, the firm was small and its equipment meager. Indeed, when Hughes had first joined the firm, it had but one telephone placed in the outer hall of the office and but one stenographer who copied all the important court papers (when not printed) in "copperplate" longhand. By 1888, however, typewriting had become the rule. Carter, Hughes & Cravath began with two stenographers and two law clerks, and their staff was soon reinforced by two graduates of Columbia Law School—Philo P. Safford and Frederic R. Kellogg.

While office arrangements were simple and staffs small in even the best law firms, the 1880's were, in several respects, the golden age of the bar. The legal profession was riding a high wave of prestige. Roused by the scandals of the Tweed régime, William M. Evarts and Samuel J. Tilden had led public-spirited lawyers in founding the Association of the Bar in 1871. Its meetings still brought forensic clashes among great men of the law. Hughes was especially intrigued by the verbal battle over the advisability of codifying the common law in which James C. Carter led the opposition and David Dudley Field defended the proposed code of which he was the author.

The art of advocacy had reached a high state of development. Evarts was approaching the close of his distinguished career. Joseph H. Choate, James C. Carter, William Allen Butler, Frederic R. Coudert, Wheeler H. Peckham, and other leaders were in their prime. These giants of the profession seemed to hold an enduring grasp upon the best professional opportunities and to leave little room for young aspirants outside the favored groups. But this gave Hughes little concern. He was "intent on the day's work with the single ambition to do it well." As the years passed, he was impressed by the gradual disappearance of the old masters and the emergence of new leaders in a constant fructification of the bar. "If the young lawyer sees to it that his work is of the best and if by intelligence and industry he stands well in his own generation," Hughes reflected, "he can afford to await his share of the privileges and responsibilities which to that generation are bound to come."[1] This is precisely the course that he followed.

The practice that Hughes began to direct was largely in the field of commercial law. Among the firm's clientele were importers, jobbers, commission merchants, and leading houses in the drygoods business with many claims against insolvent debtors. Since there was no bankruptcy law and the state insolvency law was seldom invoked, failing debtors usually made general assignments for the benefit of creditors. Often, however, they concealed property or made separate transfers to relatives and friends on pretended claims. Shrewd and unscrupulous lawyers aided these fraudulent schemes. It required both mental agility and resourcefulness to unmask such operations and induce the courts to set aside transfers and assignments tainted with fraud.

In one difficult case involving a general assignment without preferences, Hughes succeeded in getting attachments sustained by the Special Term, but they were upset by the General Term. While the proceedings were under way, an employee of a brokerage house told Hughes that the debtor in question had purchased shares of stock shortly before his assignment. The stock had not been delivered to the assignee or even mentioned to him. When the debtor was examined in supplementary proceedings, he again concealed this information. Hughes brought a creditors' bill and successfully resisted a motion for a bill of particulars. A long time elapsed before the case was tried, but Hughes kept his secret, and the devious debtor walked straight into the trap. After he had given his testimony without a word about the concealed transaction, Hughes produced his evidence to the debtor's dismay. That dramatic exposure clinched the case for the creditors, and the assignment was held invalid as part of a fraudulent scheme.[2] Hughes' success in so difficult a case did not go unnoticed at the bar.

Early in 1888 Hughes tried a case involving the ownership of a deposit with the Consolidated Stock and Petroleum Exchange before Justice Alton B. Parker. He won both the case and a friend. Parker was a man of pleasing personality and courtly demeanor as well as an excellent judge. He did not get Hughes' vote when he ran for the Presidency against Theodore Roosevelt in 1904, but their friendship was broken only by Parker's death.

That tantrum of nature known as the Blizzard of 1888 dealt roughly with Hughes. Not accustomed to being intimidated by either man or weather, he went to the office as usual on Monday, March 12, in disregard of a heavy fall of snow, which had left the streets impassable to vehicles and stalled the elevated on Third Avenue. Wading over to Second Avenue, he took the elevated to Chatham Square and again waded to his office on Broadway. No one else

[1] CEH, Notes, p. 115.

[2] *Passevant* v. *Cantor, Cases and Points,* Vol. I. (This set of eight volumes consists of Mr. Hughes' printed records and briefs assembled in 1891.)

had arrived. Indeed, most New Yorkers had recognized that they were snowed in and had stayed home. Seeing that no business could be done on such a day, Hughes decided to get home as soon as possible.

By this time the trains as well as the cabs and buses had stopped running. Hughes and a number of other defiant souls plowed up Broadway single file, stopping to rest at the hotels. The chance of getting home was nil, but he thought he could make it to the Murray Hill Hotel. "A furious blinding gale that made exposure to it an exquisite torture" [3] disputed his decision. The upper layers of a snowfall that would reach a depth of 20.9 inches were being distorted into fantastic drifts. All the perils of polar exploration seemed suddenly to have invaded the great metropolis.

"Fifth Avenue between 23d and 40th Streets," according to Mr. Hughes' account of the storm, "was a wild scene. There were no vehicles and almost no pedestrians. The wind was blowing a gale and the drifts not only covered the street but the lower parts of the dwellings. There was no place to stop on that leg of the journey and it was all I could do to finish it. I arrived at the Murray Hill almost exhausted and remained there for a couple of days while the City sought with difficulty to renew its life." [4]

Hughes had scarcely any acquaintances in business circles other than those he had made through the office and consequently brought in little business of his own as distinct from that of the firm. Cravath was in a very different position. His uncle, Caleb H. Jackson, who was the right-hand man of George Westinghouse, began to direct Westinghouse cases to Carter, Hughes & Cravath. Within a year the firm was almost swamped by this new type of business.

The most important litigation resulting from this contact was the overhead wires case. The New York electric-light companies were furnishing current by means of poorly insulated wires strung on poles above the streets. One lineman had been roasted alive from contact with a defective wire in front of the courthouse; deaths from this cause became so common that the city was aroused. Relying upon an act of the New York Legislature requiring the companies to put their wires underground, Mayor Grant ordered the overhead wires to be torn down. The companies, including the United States Illuminating Company represented by the Hughes firm, brought suit for an injunction against the city.

Hughes drew the papers and prepared the brief, and on the motion for injunction he opened the case, stating the facts and the questions involved. The firm retained Joseph H. Choate as counsel, and one of the other light companies brought James C. Carter into the case. This array of legal talent induced the Special Term to give the companies an injunction, but the General Term, not unexpectedly, found "a shameful condition of affairs" and sustained the right

[3] New York *Tribune*, March 13, 1888. [4] CEH, Notes, p. 121.

of the city to remove wires that were not adequately repaired and constituted a public nuisance.[5]

A good deal of criticism has been directed against Hughes for his participation in this case. The companies' negligence had properly aroused intense public feeling. But there is not the slightest indication of any unethical conduct on his part. He argued against destruction of an essential utility in the process of abating a nuisance. The companies had erected their poles and strung their wires with proper authority, and bad though the situation was, they could not shift to underground cables immediately because only a small part of the city had been supplied with the necessary subways.

With the overhead wires outlawed, the fight for underground conduits became intense. The Westinghouse interests arranged to make use of subways to be provided by a new company under authority granted by the Board of Electrical Control. But the board's action was challenged in two suits, one brought by a group of taxpayers and the other by Elihu Root in behalf of an electric-light company.[6] Wheeler H. Peckham, one of the most eminent lawyers of his day in spite of his rejection when nominated for the Supreme Court, appeared in support of the board, and Hughes helped to prepare his briefs. Once more they were successful in the Special Term, but the General Term held that the contract between the board and the new subway company was invalid.

The part Hughes played in these complicated legal tussles was relatively minor, but they gave him experience in a new field and brought him into close personal contact with the top men of the bar. He made the most of this by observing the great lawyers' methods. James C. Carter, he shrewdly noted, bore heavily on the legal rights of property and was not as persuasive as Choate, who skillfully presented the practical problem of supplying current to consumers and the earnest efforts of the companies to repair the defects in their lines.

Choate was a delightful personality as well as a brilliant advocate. When Hughes would arrive at the Choate home in the early morning, eager and tense after a long night of labor, he would find the great lawyer in his library reading some literary work and serenely looking forward to the heavy tasks of the day without a suggestion of strain. His invincible calm in difficult situations, his easy mastery of his cases, his unvarying geniality and air of complete confidence won the younger man's unbounded admiration.

The great lawyer's advice thus fell upon fertile ground. It was a mistake, he told Hughes, for a busy professional man to accustom his system to more physical exercise than it was feasible for him to take. Find some method of

[5] *U.S. Illuminating Co.* v. *Grant,* 55 Hun 222.

[6] *Manhattan Electric Light Co.* v. *Grant,* 56 Hun 642; *Armstrong* v. *Grant,* 56 Hun 226.

moderate daily exercise, he advised, that would not take much time and would yet keep one fit despite hard day and night work. Walking could best serve the purpose. Hughes followed this counsel for the remainder of his life. Choate also talked about the great importance of being able quickly to relax and find some agreeable diversion. "Hughes," he said, "if you don't get your fun as you go along, you will never have it." [7]

In studying the technique of eminent practitioners, Hughes had no thought of emulating Choate's scintillation, Coudert's charming pleasantries, or James C. Carter's profundities. He realized that "there are gifts which belong to one's native endowments and are not to be had by laborious effort." While the young lawyer can "aim at equanimity, clarity and force," he said, "he must succeed, if at all, by being himself." [8] But Hughes proved to his own satisfaction that the young lawyer can improve his technique by observing the most able of his elders.

When the firm established a branch office for Cravath at 120 Broadway, because of his rapid development of a distinct line of legal business, Hughes tried to keep abreast of the firm's commercial cases while at the same time helping Cravath to carry the Westinghouse load. This finally proved to be an impossible task, and they agreed to dissolve the firm. Cravath took Houston with him. Carter and Hughes advanced Frederic R. Kellogg into third place in their firm, and the fourth place went to Edward F. Dwight, nephew of Professor Dwight and a prize fellow at the Columbia Law School.

The new firm had plenty of work. Hughes and Hornblower won a ten-year-old case when the Court of Appeals ruled that the promoters of a corporation must account to subscribers to its shares for secret profits.[9] During the following year Hughes took several cases to the Court of Appeals, writing the briefs and presenting the arguments. In one of these he succeeded in convincing the court that a section of the Code of Civil Procedure was unconstitutional as depriving his client of real property without due process of law.[10]

Despite his gratifying professional success and his happy marriage, Hughes was worried and nervously depressed. In seven years of practice he had driven himself at a terrific pace. His steady grind of day and night work had reduced his weight to 127 pounds in his shirt sleeves. Every application he had made for life insurance had been rejected. The examining doctors could find no ailment or physical defect; they classified him as a poor risk solely because of his emaciated condition. "I found it easier to get married," he once remarked to a group of incredulous insurance men, "than to get insured. She thought I was a good risk. The life insurance companies thought I was a lightweight." [11] His

[7] CEH, Notes, p. 125*a*.
[8] *Ibid.*
[9] *Brewster* v. *Hatch*, 122 N.Y. 349.
[10] *Gilman* v. *Tucker*, 128 N.Y. 190.
[11] Address to Life Underwriters Association, May 22, 1906.

anxiety over the lack of protection for his family and the seemingly endless drain upon his strength was intensified by the fact that he was soon to be the father of a second child.

Hughes had been stimulated to extraordinary efforts by an ambition that was deeply imbedded within his nature. It was not political ambition, nor was it a passion for wealth. He labored as indefatigably on cases involving small fees, or no fee at all, as he did on cases that might bring large returns and professional distinction. It was the work itself that drove him on, and when he had a vacation he applied himself to the task of recouping his strength so that he could return to the legal treadmill with renewed vigor.

"I inherited a continuing ambition to excel in good work," he said, "and to do my job as well as it could be done. I couldn't bear the thought of leaving undone anything which could be done or of not doing my particular work as well as it could be done within my limitations." [12]

What troubled him was that his driving passion for self-fulfillment seemed to lead only to more of the routine drudgery that was impairing his health and thus threatening to blight his fondest hopes. His faculty for cool self-analysis and his profound respect for facts, however disagreeable they might be, led to drastic action. He decided to give up his great opportunity in New York and go back to teaching.

The door of escape was opened by Hughes' old friend James O. Griffin under whom he had taught at the Delaware Academy. Griffin was now assistant professor of German at Cornell University. Visiting the Hugheses in New York, he asked if his friend would consider a professorship of law. "I would jump at the chance," [13] Hughes replied. Professor Griffin repeated this conversation to President Adams, and he asked Hughes to come to Ithaca. At the conclusion of their interview, he offered a full professorship in the Law School, and Hughes accepted it.

Mr. Carter was dumfounded. The idea of giving up a promising career at the bar for a professorship, he told his son-in-law, was absurd. Hughes had done remarkably well at the bar. He had a great opportunity, Mr. Carter insisted, to build up a practice that would bring him "opulence." [14] But "opulence" was not an irresistible attraction for the younger man. It was the intellectual stimulus of the law, the interests of his clients, and especially the opportunity for advocacy that had appealed to him. Now he was tired, and the offer of an academic retreat, affording what he thought would be abundant time for study and reading, seemed so attractive that he could not reject it. Mrs. Hughes, with characteristic loyalty and unselfish interest in her husband's well-being, strongly supported him despite her father's opposition. In September, 1891, they gave

[12] Author's interview with CEH, Dec. 4, 1945. [13] CEH, Notes, p. 129. [14] *Ibid.*

up their new home in New York, after living in it only a few months, and moved to Ithaca.

Dejected, Mr. Carter gave Hughes' place in the firm to George M. Pinney, Jr. His sharp disappointment over the loss of his young partner may nevertheless have been tinged by prophetic insight, for at the luncheon given Hughes at the Lawyers' Club before his departure the firm presented him with two volumes—*Lives of the Lord Chancellors* and *Lives of the Chief Justices.*

Chapter 11

HAPPY INTERLUDE

HUGHES went to Ithaca with a sense of emancipation from the grinding toil, the hustle, and tension of the great metropolis. For one in this mood, Cornell was a charming refuge with its broad lawns, stately elms, and quiet walks, with its superb setting on the hill—"far above Cayuga's waters." The Hugheses took a house on State Street about halfway up the hill, and the new professor walked to and from the campus. The air, the exercise, and the associations were exhilarating, and he soon found himself gaining in vigor and thoroughly enjoying life.

Being only twenty-nine, Hughes believed himself to be Cornell's youngest full professor, but he and Mrs. Hughes were received with the utmost cordiality. This was not surprising, for the outstanding members of the university faculty were still young. Jacob Gould Schurman, who was to become president of Cornell a year later, was only thirty-seven. Benjamin Ide Wheeler, future president of the University of California, was about the same age. Liberty Hyde Bailey, at thirty-three, had begun his climb toward recognition as one of the country's most distinguished agricultural experts. James Laurence Laughlin, future head of the political economy department of the University of Chicago, was forty-one. Harry Burns Hutchins, soon to be dean of the Cornell Law School and later president of the University of Michigan, was forty-four. Among these men on the threshold of outstanding careers Hughes formed lasting friendships.

The social life into which Professor and Mrs. Hughes were initiated was most agreeable. Andrew D. White, cofounder of Cornell, still had his residence on the campus, and in the town Henry W. Sage and his sons had large mansions in which they gave generous entertainment. "On the campus," Hughes recorded, "the professors had frequent dinner parties which were simple, but conducted with *savoir-faire*, and afforded the most delightful contacts. Some of us became close companions, playing whist from time to time in each other's homes, trudging about the campus in daily walks, or bowling in the excellent alley of the Town and Gown Club." [1]

Hughes' thoughts were much upon his family as the year 1892 dawned, with

[1] CEH, Notes, p. 131.

the result of enhancing his appreciation of his own parents. On January 3 he wrote to them from Ithaca:

DEAR PA AND MA,

Antoinette continues extremely well. Baby, ditto. They told me in New York that I had not looked so well in many years. Certainly, I am highly favored—and would much prefer my pleasant, quiet and healthful life in the retirement of this small city than the active, abnormal existence (however materially successful) of those who are devoting all their energies to the pursuit of gains in the great centers.

Baby grows more and more lovely. His mind is expanding rapidly. He has a wonderful memory and a love of humor which daily gives us new cause for wonder. What a happy home ours is! And it is not rarely that I think of my great debt to you, for the quiet, wholesome training in childhood—the learning to live contentedly without luxury or extravagance—the fondness for books—for the really good things of life—above all for the constant incitements to probity and integrity, which your examples will ever furnish. I begin now to realize and appreciate the love you have lavished upon me as I begin to know the daily strengthening hold our little one has upon my heart, which he, in turn, will take as a matter too much of course, until, if he has his father's and his grandfather's rare happiness, he will find a corresponding love welling up within him, for a child born out of the pure love which only a true and noble woman may inspire. So that these days, I revisit the scenes of boyhood the more frequently—and I think the more tenderly of the kind hands that led me and the care that kept my feet from slipping, as "with heedless pace I ran." With me the New Year is full of thoughts of fatherhood—thoughts which embrace not only my own duty but my own privilege. Antoinette joins me in much love to you both,

CHARLIE [2]

His domestic bliss rose to new heights on January 11 when his daughter Helen was born. Antoinette Carter Hughes was indeed proving to be an ideal wife and mother. She managed the household without the slightest friction. She was never ill, except in her periods of confinement, and, while she had plenty of spunk and determination, she never lost her serenity. She knew precisely how to handle the children—how to keep them well and happy and how to train them in the essentials of civilized living. Little Helen was not a strong child, but she responded well to her mother's expert care. So adept was Mrs. Hughes in the delicate art of rearing a family that her husband could devote himself to his work without a moment's anxiety about the children.

Her presence was also sweet balm to Hughes' nervous tension. He had come to think of her as "a perfect companion whose spirit was a constant benediction." [3] His reliance upon her was evident whenever they were separated.

[2] CEH's private papers.
[3] Author's interview with CEH, Oct. 24, 1946.

"There is no doubt of my need of you," he wrote her in this period. "You are my 'strong tower.' Without you, I feel helpless (sort of a one-legged feeling, if you know what that is)—Such a sense of incompleteness." [4]

At the first opportunity the Hugheses moved to the campus. With a few thousand dollars of savings, they bought at a bargain the commodious frame and shingle house that Professor William Gardner Hale had built at No. 7 on shady East Avenue before he left Cornell for the University of Chicago. Cornell encouraged its professors to acquire homes on the campus by renting plots at nominal sums and making substantial building loans. This house had an especially fine library and an attractive outlook over the campus. Moving there in the summer of 1892, the Hugheses seemed to be settling down to a long period of campus life.

Cornell was completing an extensive building program that would add Barnes, Morse, and Boardman halls and the library to its plant. During Hughes' first year the Law School occupied the top floor of Morrill Hall. In the fall of 1892, however, attractive Boardman Hall, built of gray Ohio sandstone, provided ample quarters for the two hundred law students.

The faculty was small but painstaking and full of zeal. Judge Francis M. Finch of the New York Court of Appeals, was the titular dean. As acting dean, Professor Hutchins handled the administrative work with tact and dispatch. Professor Charles A. Collin, the oldest member of the law faculty, was an expert in corporation law and legal adviser to Governor Hill. William A. Finch was an able associate professor.

Hughes had many subjects: elementary law, contracts, agency, partnership, mercantile law, suretyship, sales, and evidence. To cover all this ground, he taught no less than fifteen hours a week, in addition to holding moot courts, and, in his second year, giving considerable time to graduate students taking advanced work. While he used textbooks, he insisted on the study of cases, with analysis and discussion of the leading cases in the classroom. Already well versed in the law of New York, Hughes determined to make up for any deficiencies in his own legal training by giving himself a course in the Harvard casebooks. Langdell's, Ames', and Thayer's casebooks became his guides in this one-man venture. "Whether or not the students were benefitted by my teaching," he commented, "I got the advantage of a self-conducted but thorough post-graduate course which in my later practice proved to be invaluable." [5]

In the minds of his students there was no doubt about the value of his teaching. "He created in all of us," wrote Harry L. Taylor, justice of the

[4] CEH to his wife, Sept. 15, 1892.
[5] CEH, Notes, p. 134.

New York Supreme Court, "respect for his extensive and (so far as we could judge) accurate learning, his uncanny memory and his ability to 'put over his messages.'"[6] President Schurman's appraisal was:

> Hughes would lecture for three hours, always without a note, citing perhaps a hundred cases, and quoting the opinion verbatim. It is a matter of record, too, that his pupils did not "cut" his lectures. Nor should one miss the human note amid all this labor. Apart from his regular hours, Professor Hughes gave up his own time, his own recreation periods, to help the less brilliant . . . among his pupils. Students who marveled at his scholarship were still able to profit by his friendship.[7]

The New York Law School made a bid for Hughes' services in December, 1891, offering a salary of $5,000 and a share in receipts that would bring it close to $6,000. Gratified by this recognition, Hughes nevertheless declined for reasons stated in a letter to his father and mother:

> I shall stick to Cornell, however—as I prefer the quiet of this University town to the attempt to teach law in the midst of the busy metropolis with all of the *dis*advantages of a metropolitan residence and none of the *ad*vantages in the way of money-getting. I assure you that I appreciate the offer—coming, as it does, from my former instructor [Professor Chase]. I found the "office" thriving—and all friends revelling in a prosperity and living in a luxury which seemed dazzling to my already-grown-provincial eyes.

In his second year at Cornell, Hughes was asked to take over the course in international law while Professor Herbert Tuttle was away on sabbatical leave. His protests on the ground that he was not familiar with the subject were overridden. While he embarked upon this new assignment with misgivings, because it meant devoting all the time he could spare from his other courses to a study of international law, it proved to be a "most satisfying diversion." "Little did I dream," he tells us, "that many years later I should find that year of special and exacting study a highly important, if not an indispensable, preparation for my service in connection with our foreign relations."[8]

The Hugheses had been settled in their new home on the campus for only a few months when they came face to face with a difficult decision. Messrs. Carter and Pinney had come to a parting of the ways, and Carter and Kellogg insisted that Hughes should resume his old position. Their offer was tempting, but the genial atmosphere of Cornell still had a strong appeal. To be sure, the Law School had proved to be a "hive of industry," and Hughes had found little of the leisure that he craved for general reading and contemplation. Nevertheless, his purpose in coming to Ithaca had been attained. He had re-

[6] *Cornell Law Quarterly*, December, 1940.
[7] *Outlook*, Oct. 20, 1906, p. 405. [8] CEH, Notes, p. 134.

gained his poise and a sound physical condition, and had been accepted for life insurance. The strongest argument for returning to practice was the fact that he was drawing upon his savings to make both ends meet. In his last year of practice Hughes had earned $13,500. At Cornell he had dropped to a salary of $3,000. With his increased family responsibilities and two mortgage loans to repay (he had been unable to sell his house in New York and had carried it for some time without a tenant), he concluded that he would have to increase his income or retrench to the point of serious inconvenience.

Eager to have Hughes back, his father-in-law bore down heavily on the financial sacrifice that a professorship entailed. On December 21, 1892, he wrote to Hughes:

I felt, when you first spoke to me of going to Cornell, that you were making a very great mistake, and time has only served to strengthen that conviction. Moreover, I have never yet talked with a friend of yours, who did not agree with me,—with the exception of Houston and I have always thought that he was so much of a friend of yours that he felt he must offer some sort of a defense of your course. . . .

I want to say this, not only for your eye, but Antoinette's also. Nothing has ever made me more furious than to hear it urged that you left because you were afraid of your health. Who under the sun ever asked or ever wanted you to work yourself into the grave? You know—and no one knows better—that I am never happier than when I have an office full of bright young fellows whom I have a patent on being able to find. I don't know but you thought, at the time, that if you didn't do these things, they wouldn't be done well. But, Kellogg and Dwight and Rounds have shown since—by uniformly good work in this office—that they are able to take up and carry forward successfully any work which you may not have time or strength to do. You can come back and play just as ornamental a part as anybody at the Bar. You can come down late and go home early and get something more than $3,000 a year! In a word, there is open to you today here, an opportunity the like of which has never been offered to any man of your age in this country.

The business will be the most varied that ever came to a law office. It is going to come from all nations and tribes and kingdoms under the sun, and there is going to be a great deal of it. . . .

I don't know whether you have found it out or not, but I want to say to you that the man who has a wife and two children has got to everlastingly twist and turn—economize in all directions—to get along and make both ends meet. Of course, he can do better on $4,000, but even that is pretty scanty. Here you can have income enough from the very start to live as you please—with the probability that it will grow every year. . . .

Tell that girl, A. Carter Hughes, that I should think life in a one-horse town like Ithaca would remind her that "a little thip was on the thea" and that both "thip" and "thea" were very small. The very idea of bringing up two such lightning calculators as you have got in Ithaca! You ought to be "batted in the beak" —both of you—for even thinking of such a thing.

Walter Carter followed up this tour de force with further argument on December 27:

> So, you see, the way is clear for you to come so far as things here are concerned. Now, let me say, that I want you to come first and foremost on my own account. I shall be 60 years old in a few days, and I ought not to be compelled to undergo the agony of change of firm anymore. There is going to be business enough—the opportunity is a magnificent one—and, in asking you to do this, I am sure I am demanding no sacrifice.
>
> Of course, I realize that you will not have the pleasure of life in a university town, but you will have in its place plenty of money for all reasonable wants, and the leading Court position in one of the best equipped and successful law firms in the country. . . .
>
> And, now, I want to record a prediction which I would like to have you remember. It is this—that the firm of Carter, Hughes and Kellogg, in 1893, with you away nine months of the year, will do a cash business of at least $60,000:—that, in 1894, with you present *all* the time, its cash receipts will be at least $80,000 . . . and that before the 1900 point shall have been passed, we will have a business where the net amount to be divided is $100,000 per year.
>
> Now, if you don't preserve this letter as a whole, just clip this part out, put it away in an envelope, seal it up and write across the face of the envelope—"Mr. Carter as a Prophet."

The letter found its mark. Receiving it at Palmer House, Chicago, Hughes read it and reread it. His father-in-law's logic seemed irresistible. The lawyer-professor went out and bought a hat—one of the slouch variety that made him "look like a cross between a minister and a cowboy." Then he read the letter again and sat down in a whimsical mood to write to his wife:

> He [Mr. Carter] asked no sacrifice—if it were a sacrifice he would not ask it, but would suffer in silence (heroic). He only asks that I should not sacrifice *myself* and thus he hopes to prevent what our theatrical friends would call a "grand double bill" consisting of two high class immolations on the altar of consummate folly.
>
> I do not see (at present) my way clear to destroy your Father's hopes and to frustrate his cherished plans when I'm by no means sure that the course he wishes me to take is not the best for us both . . . the strongest argument he could have used was to appeal to me to show *him* some consideration as well as to protect myself.
>
> I do not mean that I think this argument so well founded that I would be led by it to do what I otherwise could not approve—but the case on its merits is so nicely balanced that this is enough to turn the scale. And I think before you have this letter, I will have telegraphed him that I will come—if interests are adjusted harmoniously—as I've no doubt they will be. . . . But, after sleeping over it, I may change my mind.

The next morning his resolution was strengthened. It was the natural and proper thing, he told himself, to help retain the large business his father-in-law had built up. His desire to stay at Cornell was a fancy—a whim. It was doubtful whether, after a few years of routine, he would continue to enjoy teaching more than practice. In any event, he had the dearest wife in the world, the most promising son, the sweetest daughter. It was his duty to make their future secure. He wired Mr. Carter that he would come and dictated letters to Dr. Schurman, Judge Finch, and Professor Hutchins. When the letters were finished, however, he withheld them from the mail, visited some lawyer friends, and went to see *The Professor's Love Story*, a "most charming comedy."

Late that night he wrote a full account of his doings and thinking to his wife with this conclusion:

> And now last and best of all. I got this evening your dear letter. Oh my darling, I would give up all for you—and when I am asked to stretch forth my hand and take the good things of life for your sake—how can I refuse? Yes, I will take them and if there is anything in this big moneymaking world I can win, I will win it for wife and babies. I have no business to be out of the great rush. There is my place—and, if I fail and troubles come, you will know, dearest, that I did what I thought best for the little family. I could not do otherwise and think of you. Now goodnight, sweet one, it will be all right. We have each other and that makes everything right.

Back in Ithaca, however, Hughes ran into a powerful barrage of arguments from his associates as to why he should not go. When he went to New York to consult Messrs. Carter and Kellogg, Professor Hutchins telegraphed that the trustees had agreed to raise his salary to $4,000. Hughes felt that his family could live comfortably on that. Touched by this evidence of his high standing at the Law School, he again wavered. He was not yet finally committed to the law firm. Going to see President Schurman, who was also in New York, Hughes was strongly inclined to accept the anticipated offer. But Dr. Schurman said nothing about the action of the trustees and merely urged Hughes to remain because of his interest in teaching. This lack of candor provoked the professor into a firm decision to return to practice, and when Schurman got around to offering the salary increase it was too late.[9]

Dr. Schurman expressed his regrets on January 3, 1893:

> I greatly regret, but I must accept as final, your decision to leave Cornell. To the University it is a loss whose magnitude I do not care to contemplate. In view of the splendid opening before you, your decision is not surprising,—and though your colleagues would all fain have prevented it, now that the die is cast, they will, I am sure, all join me [in] wishing you all success and happiness.
>
> In expressing my own sincere regret at your withdrawal from Cornell, I desire to add that nothing could have been more courteous, honorable, and straightforward than your conduct of this business.

[9] *Ibid.*, pp. 136–137.

Mr. Carter celebrated his victory with this note to his daughter:

December, 30, 1892

Well, Madame Hughes OF NEW YORK, how are you?

There never was anything so "perfectly lovely" as the way we have fixed things for the prodigal's return. . . .

We shall welcome you all gladly. Love to the young folk,

WSC

Hughes left Cornell in June, 1893, thus ending one of his happiest experiences. "As I look back over a life of varied activities," he said nearly a half-century later, "I think that I enjoyed teaching most of all." [10] In September the family moved back to New York, settling at 229 (later renumbered 329) West End Avenue. The burden of their frequent moves fell upon Mrs. Hughes, but she bore it with patience and good humor. No lack of cooperation on her part would ever interfere with her husband's career.

Back in the role of advocate, Hughes in some small measure satisfied his urge to teach by returning to Ithaca for a week in each year to lecture on "Assignments for the Benefit of Creditors." He also lectured for several years at the New York Law School. Despite his enjoyment of these contacts with the oncoming generation of lawyers, the increasing pressure of his practice finally drove him out of the teaching field.

[10] Letter from CEH in *Cornell Law Quarterly*, December, 1940.

Chapter 12

ATTAINING STATURE

BEFORE Hughes had a chance to plunge into practice again in New York, he went to the Far West to safeguard Rowland Hazard's investment in bonds of the Oregon Pacific Railroad. While he had regained his poise at Ithaca, he was still far from being sure of himself. One of his letters to Mrs. Hughes, written from Portland on June 20, 1893, contains this revealing paragraph:

MY DARLING WIFIE,

Today I have written for about six straight hours. Then my long letters to Mr. Martin. I suppose I'm foolish to write them. Better to be Napoleonic and give a word and a hint—saving myself trouble and increasing his respect. As it is, I turn my mind inside out, tell him just what I'm doing—everything as to my proceedings. So that if I'm not coming up to his standard, he has full chance to know it. I'm not posing a bit, wifie, treating him as a real friend & giving him my complete confidence. I lack *nerve*—wifie—*confidence, cheek*—I could [do] so much better if I had it. And the older I get the less I have. I'm so anxious that he shall be satisfied, I go far to make it likely that he will not. So I write—when I'm tired out—hurriedly to catch the mail, etc. But I really think I am doing well. Between you and me I don't see how any one could do more or better. Only others might appear to be doing more than any one could, or at least leave something to a friendly imagination.

Lonely but full of faith in her husband, Mrs. Hughes replied:

SWEET DARLING —

Do not wish yourself other than you are. Your perfect candor and frankness with Mr. Martin, I am sure he will appreciate, and as for the work you are doing, that will tell, as your thorough and self-sacrificing work has ever told. . . .

Dear darling, I want to tell you of my love each time I write you. I long to but how can I? Words are inadequate. . . . I can but assure you, not of the continued existence of that love but of its growth. Oh, dearest, it is so sweet to love and be loved.

Goodbye,
WIFIE

The Oregon Pacific case was a difficult one involving a grandiose venture promoted by a notorious character—T. Egenton Hogg. The railroad was projected to run from the Oregon coast to Boise, Idaho, but one disillusioned bondholder described it as connecting "a snowbank on the Cascades to a mudhole on the Pacific." [1] Hogg had induced Rowland Hazard and other Eastern investors to put $15,000,000 into Oregon Pacific bonds. His success in collecting money had not been matched by the laying of rails. When the depression of 1893 hit his mismanaged enterprise, Hogg had nevertheless become the receiver and induced the bondholders to take receiver's certificates to the amount of several hundred thousand dollars.

In one of their conferences Hogg told Hughes that in his younger days in Illinois, on an occasion when he had hired a rig to take him to Springfield, an innkeeper induced him to take along a lawyer who could find no conveyance. It was Abraham Lincoln. On arriving at Springfield, Lincoln thanked Hogg and said, "If I can ever do anything for you, let me know." Hogg remembered this, and when he was thrown into jail for hauling down a Union flag in the early days of the Civil War, he succeeded in having his card taken to the White House. Lincoln sent for him, asked "what scrape he was in" and what he wanted.

"I want to go South," said the Confederate sympathizer.

"What for?" asked Lincoln.

"I want to save my country," Hogg replied.

Lincoln turned to his desk and wrote on a card addressed to the commander of the defenses of Washington: "Pass the bearer T. Egenton Hogg through the lines. He is going to save his country. A. Lincoln." [2]

Hughes later learned that Hogg's effort "to save his country" consisted of a scheme to seize a merchant vessel in the Port of Panama and convert her into a Confederate cruiser. He was caught, convicted, and sentenced to be hanged,[3] but succeeded in having his sentence commuted and then in obtaining his release. With similar adroitness, he had later exploited Eastern investors and Western dreamers of empire.

Hughes made a careful firsthand examination of the whole enterprise, spending several weeks at Corvallis, Oregon, where the railroad crossed the Willamette Valley. Returning to New York, he reported that the Oregon Pacific could not pay expenses unless it was extended at a cost of several million dollars. Without further improvement, it was not worth anything like the amount of the receiver's certificates. On the basis of this report the burnt-fingered bondholders organized a committee to seek a solution. Hughes worked with the committee, and his self-confidence grew as he began to submit plans of his own "instead of being merely a reservoir of facts and a critic of the plans of others." [4]

In December, 1893, the bondholders sent Hughes and Fabius M. Clarke to

[1] CEH, Notes, p. 138. [2] *Ibid.*, p. 140.
[3] Footnote in *Ex Parte Quirin* (saboteurs' case), 317 U.S. 32.
[4] CEH to wife, Aug. 31, 1893.

Oregon to bid in the property at the foreclosure sale. They succeeded in doing so at a price of $200,000—the minimum fixed by the court and the maximum fixed by the bondholders. But confirmation of the sale was violently opposed.

In his letters to his wife Hughes gives a vivid account of his discouragement over the case and his loneliness. It was the first time they had experienced a lengthy separation. On December 23 he wrote from Portland:

MY OWN DARLING,

. . . Of course, our position is one easily understood by reasonable men—but these men are not reasonable. We have put up all the money our principals are willing to invest in an almost hopeless enterprise & if it is not enough to pay these claims [for wages, materials and so forth], we are sorry—but we cannot give more for the luxury of owning a railroad in the condition this one is in. . . . Then certain attorneys here—who think we have supplanted them have worked hard to prejudice us. Pressure of every sort has been brought to prevent the Judge from confirming the sale—& we think it will succeed—nor in view of the conditions will we be very sorry if it is not confirmed.

The next day, Christmas eve, he wrote again:

MY OWN SWEET WIFIE,

. . . the Angel Gabriel couldn't do much with this situation and would be extremely fortunate to escape with his wings in good order and a good note in his trumpet. . . .

God bless you my darling—I cannot keep back the tears as I think of your loving heart—your true devotion. And how I love you—and the dear babies—well, well, this is not a merry Xmas for poor ———. I rebel when I think of how I have toiled for these past few years and the little I have to show for it.

In court Hughes argued earnestly that the only hope of saving the Oregon Pacific and protecting the community lay in confirmation of the sale. Never again, he said, would the court see an offer of as much as $200,000 for the railroad as it stood. But Hogg's fantastic visions still dominated the thinking of the local people. At a junction hotel where Hughes was waiting for his train, the proprietor told him that the barroom below was filled with cursing railroad men who were threatening to avenge their wrath upon his person in good old Western fashion. "Come this way," the proprietor said, "I have a rig waiting at the back to take you to the neighboring town."

"Where is this barroom?" Hughes demanded, suddenly finding more nerve than his task required, in spite of his meager 135 pounds. Walking into the midst of the hostile crowd, he said: "Good evening, gentlemen. Will you join me? What will you have?" Hughes stayed in the barroom until a few minutes before train time, discussing his clients' offer man to man.[5]

[5] John Palmer Gavit in New York *Evening Post*, June 10, 1916.

Because of the unfriendly atmosphere, the bondholders obtained the consent of the court to withdraw their offer, take their losses, and give up the enterprise. The road is reported to have been sold later for half the sum Hughes offered. Incidentally, his pessimism as to his own reward proved to be well founded. Two years later at a Swiss resort he met one of his Oregon Pacific clients, the wealthy J. J. Belden of Syracuse, and reflected bitterly that Belden had not paid his bill. "The old boy, . . ." Hughes remarked contemptuously, "hasn't sensibility enough to maintain the ideals of a wild boar." [6]

His trips in connection with the Oregon Pacific case gave Hughes his first opportunity to see the West, and he made the most of it. What impressed him deeply were the great pine forests along the projected line of the railroad, the trip to San Francisco by way ot Siskiyou Pass, and the acute depression he found in that city as well as in Portland, Tacoma, and Seattle. Despair pervaded everything. Lawyers who had gone to new settlements in Washington and Oregon with the brightest prospects found themselves in wretched plight.

In New York, too, the bar felt the effects of the depression. There was no diminution of work in the office of Carter, Hughes & Kellogg, but fees had shrunk and were not easily collected. The firm was established at a new location—96 Broadway in the old Schermerhorn Building (later replaced by the American Surety Building). Arthur C. Rounds, graduate of Amherst and the Harvard Law School, had become a strong pillar of the firm. Randall J. Le Boeuf (later to practice in Albany and to be appointed to the New York Supreme Court by Governor Hughes) had become managing clerk on his graduation from Cornell Law School, and Hughes now brought into the office one of his graduate students, George W. Schurman, brother of President Schurman. Rounds' keen mind and thorough training and Schurman's special aptitude for legal work won Hughes' admiration, and they were to remain associated with him for many years.

Kellogg left the firm about 1896, and it became Carter, Hughes & Dwight, with Edward F. Dwight as third man. Within five years, however, Dwight was stricken with a fatal illness. George W. Schurman, who had left the office to become assistant district attorney under William Travers Jerome, then returned, and the firm became Carter, Hughes, Rounds & Schurman. In June, 1904, death again invaded the firm, this time claiming Walter S. Carter. After his father-in-law's funeral, Hughes sorrowfully reorganized the firm once more as Hughes, Rounds & Schurman.

Activities of the organized bar claimed Hughes' interest and support whenever his work permitted. At a meeting of the Montreal bar he addressed the banquet as a representative of the American Bar Association and met many leading Canadian judges and lawyers. For the last two years of the old century,

[6] CEH to wife, Aug. 20, 1895.

he was a member of the committee on admissions of the Association of the Bar of the City of New York, and from 1906 to 1908 he was a member of its executive committee.

That "legal monstrosity," the Code of Civil Procedure, engaged his special attention in 1898. Numerous changes and additions had robbed the code of its simplicity and made it an instrument of confusion. As a member of a New York State Bar Association committee, Hughes helped to bring to light the code's shortcomings and pleaded for its revision.

Hughes, the reformer, came to the fore again with a denunciation of the imprisonment of men for debt. The New York law was "unsound in principle" and stupid in practice. "While it is ordinarily ineffective as a remedy for *bona fide* enforcement of just demands," he declared, "the existing law is easily made a means of extortion and oppression in the case of the ignorant and friendless poor. It is a ready instrument of blackmail." He called for complete abolition of imprisonment for debt, save in cases of contempt of court.[7]

Nor was his interest in civic and human affairs narrowed to legal outlets. His face became familiar at the Social Reform Club, where he met John Spargo, the prolific Socialist writer. That club was, as Spargo said, "both a symbol of racial and religious equality and a conscious protest against every kind of intolerance and bigotry." Some forty-six years later Spargo would look back over the years and congratulate his friend for never having compromised on these aspects of "genuine liberalism." [8]

Hughes' political activities were casual and local. He always attended the primaries in his district and voted the Republican ticket in state and national elections. The Democratic Party was associated in his mind with the rebellion, the fight against Lincoln, and, more currently, with the heterodox economic schemes of William Jennings Bryan. That was enough to keep Hughes steadfastly Republican. On election days he served as legal watchdog for the Republican Committee on the lower East Side. Local fusion campaigns and independent candidates for judicial office had his support. Frequently he was named vice chairman of a political meeting, but no one asked him to make a political speech, and he made none.

Abe Gruber, Republican leader, argued that the wholehearted manner in which Hughes threw himself into every case gave him a natural aptitude for public office. In the late 1890's the New York County chairman suggested that Hughes come around to the Republican Club more often. "We might want to run you for the Supreme Court some day," he said.[9]

"I'm too busy," Hughes replied, "and I don't want a judgeship or any other office."

[7] Speech before New York State Bar Association, January, 1905.
[8] John Spargo to CEH, April 8, 1947.
[9] Author's interview with CEH, Dec. 3, 1947.

A few years later he replied in the negative when a White House intimate asked if he would be interested in a federal district judgeship. Considering his family obligations and the salary then paid federal judges, he thought he could not afford to go on the bench.

The church claimed more of Hughes' time than did politics. He joined the Fifth Avenue Baptist Church about 1889, when his college friend William H. P. Faunce became pastor, and resumed active relations with that congregation on his return from Ithaca. Actually the church was not on Fifth Avenue. A wave of depression had induced the parish to sell its Fifth Avenue lots and build its edifice on the adjoining property facing Forty-sixth Street. But the authorities held doggedly to the name. At a meeting of the Baptist Association, Dr. Robert S. MacArthur, pastor of the Calvary Baptist Church, took occasion to twit the Fifth Avenue Baptists for perpetuation of this misnomer. The dry rejoinder of Dr. Thomas Armitage was, "The Fifth Avenue Baptist Church is a great deal nearer to Fifth Avenue than the Calvary Church is to Calvary." [10]

Dr. Faunce asked his college chum to teach the young men's class in the Sunday school. Hughes consented with the understanding that, instead of following the scheduled lessons, he would be at liberty to concentrate on the teachings of Jesus. "While I maintained my Baptist connection," he tells us, "I had long since ceased to attach any importance to what many regard as the distinctive tenets of the denomination. Rather, I cherished the noble tradition of the Baptists as protagonists in the struggle for religious liberty. I wished to throw what influence I had to the support of Christian institutions, and so far as the dogmas of the creeds were concerned I saw nothing to be gained by leaving the Church in which I had been brought up and joining another denomination." [11]

At Cornell he had conducted a Sunday afternoon course in the Old Testament prophets, with special reference to their place in the evolution of religious thought. At the Fifth Avenue church his lessons on the ethical and literary aspects of the New Testament brought together a large group of interested young men, and Hughes continued to teach the class for several years. When the pressure of his legal work finally compelled him to give it up, the class continued under one of his pupils, John D. Rockefeller, Jr., and became widely known as the Rockefeller Class.

Hughes was elected a trustee of the Fifth Avenue church and held that position until shortly before he entered public life. For two or three years he was president of the Baptist Social Union in New York and presided at its dinners. At one of these he invited Booker T. Washington to be the principal guest and was surprised at the protests from some of the good Baptist brethren.

[10] CEH, Notes, p. 156. [11] *Ibid.*, pp. 158–159.

They were especially resentful over the fact that Mr. and Mrs. Hughes escorted the eminent Negro educator and Mrs. Washington to seats at the guest table. Hughes thought this display of prejudice on the part of those who were supposed to be the least susceptible to it was ridiculous and tried to ignore it.[12]

Membership on the board of the Fifth Avenue Baptist Church brought Hughes into frequent contact with its president, the elder John D. Rockefeller. In his church work the tycoon of Standard Oil was unassuming and affable. Occasionally he asked Hughes to join his golf parties at Pocantico Hills. But Hughes had no business dealings with him or the companies in which he was interested. At Rockefeller's request, Hughes did take up the case of a young church member in need of legal advice, and he reported on the case several times to the multimillionaire, also at his request. But his service was rendered gratis, and he received only Rockefeller's thanks.

Many good stories passed between members of the board. Rockefeller was fond of telling about the Swedish immigrant in his employ who wandered into a Salvation Army meeting on the Bowery. One of the army lassies sat down beside him and said, "Wouldn't you like to work for Jesus?" The Swede stiffened and shook his head. She would not be put off. "Why wouldn't you like to work for Jesus?" Again the Swede shook his head: "I have a very good yob with Rockefeller."

While he was Governor of New York, Hughes was chosen president of the Northern Baptist Convention, and continued to respond to the church's demands upon him whenever it was feasible. The essence of what he distilled from Christian teachings may be found in the following excerpt from his remarks to the Vaughan Class of the Calvary Baptist Church in Washington:

> We need to cultivate the spiritual life, not by centering our attention upon dogma, or by sacrificing intellectual honesty, but by reflection upon the spiritual verities of the Sermon on the Mount.
>
> A truly Christian character is revealed in a balanced life. . . . What does the Christian character or balanced life mean? It is this:
>
> Faith without credulity; conviction without bigotry; charity without condescension; courage without pugnacity; self-respect without vanity; humility without obsequiousness; love of humanity without sentimentality; and meekness with power.
>
> That is our ideal.[13]

Hughes' disinterest in ritual and his lack of orthodoxy was a continued source of grievance to his mother, and she never ceased to let him know it. On August 31, 1893, he wrote to his wife:

> I got a sermonic letter from mother this morning. (Poor mother, she didn't expect to see me so soon, when she wrote it.) I know just how she feels. Sermons

[12] *Ibid.*, p. 158. [13] Address, Feb. 20, 1925.

prompted by a sense of duty may be ignored, but this was an appeal of love—the result of Ocean Grove experiences. Well, dearie, it's hard to be misunderstood by those we love. But it would be cruel to meet such a loving appeal in any other way than lovingly.

On November 30 he replied to his mother with a touching defense of his own convictions and a sad realization that she would never understand his feelings:

DEAR MOTHER:—

You must not think that my silence indicates indifference to your reproaches. I have felt them keenly. I have been anxious to write you fully in regard to the questions which trouble you, but I have not had the opportunity. Then, too, I may say frankly that I have had little hope that you would understand me. You know, of course, to what I refer.

I know how far short I fall of that ideal you have always set before me and which I have set before myself. If you knew my heart you would not think me complacent and certainly you would not find me indifferent to those interests which we would both call highest.

But, when we come to formal religious observances, your thinking and the circumstances of your life make it difficult for you to judge me either justly or leniently. Many things you would have me do, I cannot do with sincerity and I know that you would not wish me to act otherwise. But you grieve that I cannot enter—as you do—into certain religious exercises and this you attribute to a "religious declension." It cuts me to the heart that you should grieve and the more painfully that it should be on my account. But, while in important matters we are in entire accord, you give special prominence to certain forms which in many cases are indeed "means of grace," but which cannot be or, at least are not, in mine.

Now, I hold what religious convictions I have, as sacredly as you do yours. I am perplexed by many questions, but I believe my heart is open to the truth. I want to be honest with myself. I do not want to use the form of prayer when I am not praying, and whatever may be the mysterious connection between ourselves and the unseen world, and whatever the secret of that communion with the Father of Spirits for which we all yearn, it is too wonderful and mysterious and sacred to be cheapened by formalism and vain repetitions. When I really want to *pray* I want to be *alone*—and it is at those times when the reality of the unseen comes upon one irresistibly and the sense of one's own littleness and helplessness draws one, half-doubtfully—half-trustfully but altogether reverently to the Father of all.

Would that I were always, or often, on the "mountain top"! But one thing's certain, I will not imitate this most sacred communion by unworthy pretense of devotion. I believe in the "life of prayer," in the ever-abiding spirit of prayer—in the sense that we may live always conscious in a meaure of a connection, however ill-defined, with the unseen. But they are few—who take their places in the world's conflicts—who are not compelled to draw themselves away to the secret place to fit themselves for prayer. You and Father are peculiarly circumstanced. Your daily work is intimately connected with your religious emotions. As for me, I try to be true and do right, but the attempt to adopt your methods would end sadly enough.

And whatever else my children may find to condemn, I do not wish to be found guilty of trifling with that which is Holiest or of setting a daily example of insincerity. For most people, prayers before meals and the so-called family prayers are a wretched business. There is a *life*, of the possibilities of which I am keenly sensible, so far above these petty observances,—a *faith*, of which I sometimes feel the power, so transcending the narrow limits of our church creeds that I have little patience with the tests commonly proposed to determine one's religious condition. And it sometimes seems to me that these tests should be wholly done away with. But this is not so. They have their uses. But they are not for many, of whom I am one.

So believe me, dear Mother, though you may not understand, though you may grieve, we have the same desire to serve God though the methods of our service may differ.

I cannot write you more fully. I had hoped to see you before this. Can you not make it convenient to visit us soon? Any time! We would all be so glad to see you and Father, too, if he could come with you. . . .

I manage to keep well despite the work. I hope you and Father are in good form. Antoinette sends her love and, whatever else you may think, you know you have the devoted love of your boy,

CHARLIE

In his practice Hughes was unassuming, independent, and increasingly effective. Almost everything he did was carefully planned and reduced to order and system. His planning was especially fruitful because of his faculty for seeing the possibilities for trouble in every situation. Instead of merely fussing over such difficulties, he went to extraordinary pains to overcome them. "Hughes never wins a case," his father-in-law used to say, "until it's won."

Nor was planning enough. He taught himself to work rapidly with a minimum of error. As he improved his technique, he could dictate a brief with such precision that the first draft would be ready for the printer and would stand with only minor changes in proof. His method was to assemble all the data he would need and make a brief outline high-lighting his chief points. Then he would begin dictating. Augustus L. Richards, who went to the firm's office hoping, as he said, to "hitch his wagon to a star," found Hughes "pacing the floor like a lion in captivity, roaring dictation to a stenographer." [14] His method accounted in large measure for his fabulous capacity to get work done.

At no time did he accept a general retainer that might have required him to render all kinds of legal service. In this respect he was not a corporation lawyer. To be sure, he took many corporation cases, but always on his own terms. Clients came to him because they knew they would get a candid and independent opinion of what the law required.

Judges began to take special note of his work and to send him hotly contested or highly entangled legal controversies. Judge Alton B. Parker told

[14] Richards to CEH, March 25, 1940.

friends that of all the lawyers appearing before the Court of Appeals none was abler than Hughes, who was still in his thirties.[15] "I guess we better take that to Hughes" became a common reaction to a complicated legal problem.[16] He could carry a thousand details in his mind. He was always ready for any emergency. The man who wished to remain a professor had become one of the most resourceful lawyers in New York.

Hughes acted as junior to James C. Carter in *Stokes* v. *Stokes,* writing the brief in the Court of Appeals and drafting the papers in subsequent proceedings. In Albany the two lawyers discussed the case in a hotel lobby the night before Mr. Carter was to make his argument. Hughes excused himself and said that he would like to make a memorandum on certain points they had talked over. Suspecting that Hughes would work most of the night, Carter related that on one occasion, after he had worked until 4 A.M. boiling down an argument, he lost his train of thought before the court and found it impossible to continue. "Hughes," he advised, "never work the night before an argument." To the younger man this seemed a "counsel of perfection." For many years he put in his hardest licks at night in preparation for trials and arguments.

Hughes won an interesting case against the New York *Sun*. Chester S. Lord, managing editor of the *Sun*, had chartered a yacht to obtain news in Cuban waters during the Spanish-American War. When the yacht was lost by stranding, the owner brought suit in admiralty against the *Sun*. The owner's attorney, George Zabriskie, took sick and Hughes was retained to try the case. The publishers insisted that their managing editor had no authority to bind the *Sun*. Hughes brought in an abundance of evidence to show the broad authority of the managing editor to get the news. Addison Brown, the eminent admiralty judge, decided against the *Sun*, awarding judgment for the agreed value of the yacht ($75,000) less the amount of the charter hire ($10,000),[17] and this decision was upheld by the United States Supreme Court.

A happier contact was soon established with the New York *World*. Several leading lawyers had given Joseph Pulitzer cautious and conflicting opinions as to whether his newsprint contract was enforceable. At the suggestion of Justice Edward Patterson of the New York Supreme Court, Bradford Merrill, managing editor of the *World*, walked into Hughes' office and asked for his opinion. He got a candid and forthright reply.

Pulitzer then asked Hughes to visit him at Lakewood for a consultation. Almost blind, the famous publisher passed his hands over Hughes' face to get an idea of his features. For an hour or so he then put the lawyer through a rigorous examination on all the points involved in the paper contract. As he left, he called a stenographer and asked Hughes to dictate what he had said.

[15] Cuthbert W. Pound to CEH, April 27, 1910.
[16] Burton J. Hendrick in *McClure's Magazine*, March, 1908, p. 521.
[17] *Moore* v. *Sun Printing & Publishing Ass'n*, 95 Fed. Rep. 485 (1899).

Staying for lunch, Hughes was fascinated to see a journalistic genius in action. Surrounded by his editors and secretaries, Pulitzer seemed to be in touch with everything of importance. "One would have supposed that Mr. Pulitzer was sitting as the judge of all the earth," Hughes said, "and I was vastly entertained by the way in which this man, so physically dependent, dominated all by his intellectual power." [18]

During an afternoon drive Pulitzer consulted Hughes about his will. Their conference left each with the most favorable impression of the other. They were not to meet again, but representatives of the publisher frequently came to Hughes for legal advice, and he drafted contracts for the *World*. When Hughes entered public life, Pulitzer became one of his most enthusiastic supporters. In 1910 the publisher named Hughes in a codicil to his will as a trustee of the Press Publishing Company, with the understanding that, at Pulitzer's death, Hughes would become the directing influence behind the *World*. When he ascended the bench a few months later, however, Hughes informed Pulitzer that he would not be able to continue as trustee. A cablegram from the publisher on May 1 begged Hughes to let the arrangement stand, insisting that it would "not interfere with your high integrity and sensitive independence." Pulitzer died in October, 1911, leaving a will that still named Hughes as trustee and provided that he should receive a fee of $100,000 for his services—twice the amount fixed for the other two trustees.[19] But Hughes could not imagine himself directing the policies of a newspaper from the inner sanctum of the Supreme Court. He renounced both the appointment and the fee.

The most important retainer in this period, in its relation to Hughes' future career, was that in the beet-sugar case. A group of enterprising young men of Detroit had employed a German firm to build a beet-sugar factory at Caro in the Michigan Thumb. The work was miserably botched. When the antiquated machinery installed by the contractor went to pieces under use, the owners sued Speyer & Company of New York on their bond of $300,000 guaranteeing performance of the contract. Hughes was brought into the case because his firm was correspondent in New York for Charles Beecher Warren, who represented the factory owners in Michigan. Other lawyers were shaking their heads over the case because of the extensive technical knowledge required to prove the inadequacy of the machinery. But Hughes went to Caro, made a thorough study of beet-sugar manufacturing, and came back with enough technical details and expert testimony to overwhelm the opposition.

After many months of testimony-taking, the referee died. As Henry W. Taft, the opposing attorney, would not stipulate before the new referee the evidence already taken, Hughes began the weary task of presenting it a second time. Baffled at last by the thoroughness of the case he had built up, the opposi-

[18] CEH, Notes, p. 150. [19] *Ibid.*, p. 151.

tion caved in, agreeing to a settlement which gave Hughes' clients a very substantial sum. Hughes did not know it at the time, but he was acquiring a reputation in legal circles that was certain to carry him to a wider field of activity.

Retained by David Belasco, Hughes successfully resisted an attempt to stop the production of *The Music Master* starring David Warfield. In 1903–1904 he gave an opinion as to the validity of the charter of the New York, Westchester and Boston Railway Company, which was seeking, and finally attained, a franchise to lay tracks in New York City. Critics attempted to discredit him in this case as a tool of J. Pierpont Morgan and the New York, New Haven and Hartford Railroad in attaining the franchise to promote a monopolistic scheme. But Hughes represented neither Morgan nor the New Haven. He appeared only for the local company, which was later acquired by the New Haven; his work was confined solely to the legal issues and had nothing to do with any negotiations for absorption of the New York, Westchester and Boston project by the New Haven. The senior attorneys in the case were John G. Johnson, leader of the Pennsylvania bar, and William Hornblower.

In the year that Theodore Roosevelt was elected President, Hughes had his first brush with the life-insurance scandal. James W. Alexander, president of the Equitable Life Assurance Society, who had locked horns with James Hazen Hyde in one of the most famous struggles in the history of American finance, hired a number of lawyers to back up his efforts to mutualize the company. Among them were Bainbridge Colby, William D. Guthrie, William N. Cohen, Adrian H. Joline, Hornblower, and Hughes. They consulted and prepared opinions while New York seethed with excitement over the threatened crumbling of a great financial empire. Within four months, however, Hughes dropped this engrossing task for a much larger undertaking.

Increasingly he had become a lawyer's lawyer, with wide recognition of his talent within the legal profession. Yet he was not conspicuously successful financially. Associates estimate his income during this period at $20,000 to $25,000 a year. Often he reduced by half the fees suggested by his partners. Hughes had acquired none of the beautiful houses, private art galleries, or spacious country estates that were common to successful New York lawyers of the day. While some of his friends were making fortunes out of corporate mergers and reorganizations, he was plodding along with difficult cases and modest rewards. Up to this time (1905) he had had no opportunity to argue a case in the United States Supreme Court, although three of his cases were then on their way to the highest bench. His independent course and herculean efforts often seemed to be leading nowhere.

To the public he was quite unknown. Seldom did his name appear in the newspapers. One evening, as he and Mrs. Hughes sat in their library looking at the papers, the absence of his name from stories about an important case on which he was working seemed especially strange because his associates were mentioned.

"My dear," Hughes said, "you must know that I have a positive genius for privacy." [20]

Little did they realize that he was soon to be caught in a wave of publicity that would broadcast his name throughout the land, or that the public eye would be focused upon his activities for the next thirty-seven years.

[20] CEH, Notes, p. 160.

Chapter 13

STRENGTH FROM THE ALPS

TWO POWERFUL forces were at war within Charles E. Hughes. His irresistible will to succeed repeatedly drove him close to the breaking point of his nervous and physical strength. At the same time his yearning for a fullness of life stirred up rebellion against this seemingly endless drudgery. The clash of these inner stimuli left him alternately happy and miserable.

Nature had given him an unusual mind. His home training and his own philosophy of life made intensive use of that mind one of the imperatives of his being. In spite of his moments of self-deflation, he recognized within himself the makings of a great lawyer. For realization of that dream no effort was too strenuous. But it was a well rounded self-fulfillment that he sought, and this often seemed to be thwarted by the heavy drain upon his energy and reserve.

No greater mistake could be made about Hughes than to assume that he was merely a thinking machine. On the contrary, he was a bundle of nerves. Having inherited a mercurial temperament from his Welsh-Irish-Scotch forebears, he shifted easily from elation to depression and back again. At the office he was called "the ship," and his associates would say that "the ship" was "plowing along steadily" or sometimes that it was "in stormy seas" and "pitching heavily."

Such a volatile personality could not thrive on the dry dust of the law alone. Greater than the law was life, and the life for which he was struggling was made up of love, freedom, aesthetic interests, humor, and bracing mountain air no less than of professional achievement. His eager pursuit of the good things of life and the resulting conflicts within must be given a good deal of attention if we are to understand the complex forces that shaped his career.

Along with most other New Yorkers, he and Mrs. Hughes found pleasure in bicycling in the gay nineties. On holidays, whenever possible, they took long cycling excursions into the country as far as Babylon, Long Island. The theater, too, was a constant lure. The Hugheses found keen delight in the productions of the stock companies, notably the Daly company with Ada Rehan, John Drew, and George Lewis, and the Frohman company with Herbert Kelcey and Georgia Cayvan, in addition to the more famous stars of the period. "Musical comedy still had standards of decency, and such inimitable comedians as

Francis Wilson, De Wolf Hopper, and Jefferson De Angelis, afforded the best light entertainment." [1] Occasionally they went to the opera, but more frequently Mrs. Hughes attended the afternoon performances, sometimes, after the turn of the century, taking her son.

Sunday was Hughes' day with the children, who were devoted to him. It was rarely that he allowed his work to interfere with a Sunday-afternoon excursion with young Charlie and Helen. They rowed or took swan boats on the Central Park lake, visited the zoo, the Museum of Natural History, and the Metropolitan Museum of Art, went coasting or took sleigh rides in the winter and victoria rides in the warmer weather, took the ferries to Fort Lee or Staten Island or the "Iron Steamboats" to Coney Island, and generally availed themselves of whatever made for a companionable afternoon. One memorable day, when the fleet came up the river after the Spanish-American War, they visited the battleship *Indiana*. On another there was the first ride in one of the "horseless carriages." Sometimes the whole family spent Sunday afternoon visiting the children's grandparents. Often, too, Hughes took long walks with his son, discoursing zestfully on many subjects and punctuating his talk with such enthusiastic gesticulations that the lad, who was at the self-conscious age, thought his father ought to be ashamed to make such a spectacle of himself in public.[2]

At home Hughes found time to read to the children, usually dialect stories such as "Uncle Remus" or "Mr. Dooley," and to write whimsical rhymes for their birthdays. He was especially adept at reproducing Mr. Dooley with a fine Irish brogue. Being a born mimic, he was in danger, even in later years, of unconsciously slipping into the accent of anyone he happened to be conversing with. Being also an incorrigible tease, his humor sometimes cropped out at the least suspected moments. He had a habit of reading aloud interesting bits from the newspapers while the family was at breakfast or in the study after dinner. Then, with his face still in the paper and without changing his expression, he would tell a fictitious story involving a member of the family in some humorous situation. His pretense to be reading this imaginary tale would continue until the credulity of his listeners would give way to laughter.

Sometimes he would "blow off steam" at the piano. The only piece he ever played certainly did not come from his music-lesson days. It was a rollicking number of unknown origin, in octaves for both hands, and devoid of harmony. He played it presto and fortissimo, with great verve, and ended by running up and down most of the keyboard with his thumb and adding a couple of resounding thumps. His "piece" was reserved for moments of extreme exhilaration, and when he played it without urging from the children, the family knew that something good had happened at the office. To amuse the children, there

[1] CEH, Notes, p. 160. [2] Author's interview with CEH Jr., Aug. 13, 1948.

were also "stunts" carried over from his boyhood, such as the "Evangeline Walk" and a series of rapid manual convolutions ending with crossed hands pinching his nose and ear, which he performed with a comical expression of self-consciousness.[3]

The Hughes household was a place of relaxation and happiness as well as an intellectual workshop. The rugs, books, and pictures contributed to its quiet, harmonious atmosphere. There was evidence of refinement and comfortable living, without ostentation. The study was the favorite room. In this second-floor retreat looking out over West End Avenue, the walls banked with bookcases and a large picture of Gladstone giving a legal touch, Charles and Antoinette Hughes spent many an evening together; she in an easy chair with a book, he at a great central desk covered with manuscripts, letters, and telegrams.[4]

Any placid attorney at law might well have found in these happy circumstances an ample offset to the tensions generated at his office. Hughes did not. With the approach of summer, he would be physically worn out and subject to "fits of depression."[5] By 1894 his "unrequited drudgery" had pulled him down so near to the breaking point that both he and Mrs. Hughes concluded he would have to have the relaxation of an ocean voyage and a few weeks of complete freedom. It was a difficult decision to make, for Mrs. Hughes, with a baby only two years old, could not go, and her husband was as loath to be parted from her as she from him. As he boarded a Dutch steamer for Boulogne, regret thus mingled with his determination to regain his strength and peace of mind.

Mrs. Hughes and the children spent the lonely weeks in a cottage in the Connecticut hills. On the boat her husband wrote to her:

Darling Wifie,

I have slept every afternoon from one to three hours and managed about eight more at night. . . . I have about as much thought as a jelly fish. Reading is out of the question—talking is laborious—and this is my first attempt at writing. . . .

I am afraid I am reputed to be rather misanthropic—at least I have not tried to be "sociable." Aside from two or three pleasant men—who know how to enjoy their hard-won leisure, I have talked with few. . . .

But to sit by the hour and watch the sea is my chief enjoyment—though my stare is a vacant one. I have tried desperately to get up a little mental friction by worrying—but it's out of the question. There is an abiding peace of mind which resists all shocks. I feel like one benumbed or bewitched—and the senses, or rather the faculties—you see how my psychology has suffered—won't work.

Darling, it is hard for me to realize that I am "here" and you are "there." I have not allowed myself to get moody or "maudlin" but "from morn to afternoon, from afternoon to night, from seven o'clock till two, from two till broad daylight," you have been in my thought—the thought of my heart. "Far and away to me is

[3] *Id.* [4] New York *Evening Post*, Oct. 20, 1906. [5] CEH, Notes, p. 160a.

near." And I shall have you with me every hour of my trip. Too bad you can't know at the time how much fun we are having—you and I. . . .

I am daily renewing my youth. By the time I get back, I shall skip like the "little veals" a German doctor on board talks of.

Now, darling one, you said you loved me well enough to let me leave you. I love you too much to leave you again. And when I take a similar outing, we will have a "vacation built for two" and wifie will be the other.

Darling, this voyage would have been of three times the benefit if you had been with me. As you once said, every pleasure is halved when it might have been doubled. But all in good time. This trip will accomplish the purpose for which it was taken, I don't doubt, and I shall be happier for it. . . .

Bye bye, darling. Kisses for the babies and a wealth of love for them and for the dearest one on earth.

CHARLIE [6]

After a day in Paris he left for Lausanne. His first glimpse of the Alps from the pass over the Jura almost took his breath away. An intense lover of mountains, he found here the greatest exhilaration that nature had ever afforded him. The transformation that came over him is evident from the letter he wrote on August 8:

MY DARLING WIFE,

. . . The day has been perfect—the scenery all beautiful but the last few hours gave me a delight I shall never forget. We went through the Jura Country—the mountains richly wooded—the valleys richly cultivated. And then about seven the Alps rose before us en masse—peak above peak—dark, rugged, snow-capped. And at 8:30 after twelve hours travelling, I reached Lausanne—near the shore of Lake Geneva—with the grand mountains on the other side. A "petit diner" enjoyed all the more for the reason that a "station lunch" was all that I had had, a pipe—and then my letter to my darling. I want to say *mon ange—mon trésor—ma femme, la femme, la plus belle et la plus chère dans le monde.* But I will forbear, and you can dream in English all that I cannot say in French.

Oh! my love—if you could share this with me. You would have been in ecstasy today. . . .

This letter, darling, if it represents my feeling has love all over it—"not jes' bedobbled but jes' civired" as Uncle Remus would say.

But I must add it in words, my love; you are my idol—and the wealth of this beautiful world is nothing in comparison with my darling's true heart. Kiss the little doddies and tell Charlie his papa is riding on the funniest "choo-choos"—little Brownie "choo-choos." Tell both Charlie and Helen how much their Papa loves them.

Bye bye, darling,

CHARLIE

He took the boat to Geneva. Then came Chamonix, where he again wrote on August 10:

[6] All the letters quoted in this chapter are in CEH's private papers.

MY DARLING WIFE,

. . . Your letters have thrilled me many times—but I have never had such a thrill as your little letter of this morning gave me. Darling one, I do love you so devotedly.

Well, at last, I am in the Alps and my vacation seems to be just beginning—that is, I feel that sense of freedom, that exhilaration which is borne to one on the cool mountain breezes. Here I am at Chamonix with the great peaks of the Mont Blanc range towering above me—Mont Blanc itself—monarch of the European mountains—rising to a height of 15,780 feet. Even this valley is 3445 feet above sea level. The great glaciers are close at hand, stretching their icy arms toward the valley—but all about them are fine trees and grassy slopes. It is such a contrast—grim death and verdant life side by side—for you know the vegetation extends even to the ice line.

Before dinner I took a three-mile walk and observed the "lay" of the valley. I am feeling very well, and have improved twenty-five per cent since I reached here. . . .

I am delighted to get away from the cities and out into the open—into God's country. . . . I shall not be content until you can make this trip with me. I could almost hear your outcries of delight as we drove into the valley. In fact, most of the time I am thinking—"What would wifie say? What would wifie do?"

On the "diligence" from Cluses, where the train journey then ended, Hughes fell in with a young Londoner who proved to be a good companion. Together they walked up to Montanvert, crossed the Mer de Glace, and found shelter in a little inn at La Flégère on the other side of the valley. A thick fog obscured the mountains, but at five o'clock the next morning the excited traveler from New York had a thrilling view of the Mont Blanc range in the gleaming sunshine. Nature had lifted her curtain on one of her most inspiring sights at the most dramatic moment.

Hughes and his new-found friend returned to the valley and set out for Martigny, walking over the Col de Balme. Taking the train, they traveled through a gorge and emerged into a "valley of rare beauty" where "under the Matterhorn—lies quaint little Zermatt." [7] They walked to the Riffel Alp, and, the following day, to Gornergrat and back to Zermatt. Here they parted, and Hughes went on to Leuk, where he took to his boots again to cross the Gemmi Pass to Kandersteg. Then came Spiez, Interlaken, and Meiringen. In passing over the Grimsel Pass to the Rhone Glacier he was caught in a snowstorm.

At the inn Hughes sent his only suit to the drying room and went to bed to await its return. The gong for table d'hôte awakened him out of a sound sleep at seven. His clothes had not been returned, and the electric bell would not ring. He was ravenous and could scarcely face the thought of missing dinner. Opening his door a crack, he summoned a chambermaid and tried to explain his predicament. She brought him "nearly everything in the hotel" except his

[7] CEH to his wife, Aug. 15, 1894.

clothes. Finally he made her understand that he was *"sans habits"* by shaking his foot at her through the doorway, and his clothes were returned in time for him to "connect with dinner in good shape."

Crossing Furka Pass by "diligence," he took a boat to Lucerne and returned to Boulogne by way of Basel. "Thirteen glorious days!" [8] Hughes came home a new man. No outing had ever given him so much reinvigoration of body, mind, and spirit. In consequence, walking in the mountains became his hobby. While he was never to become a real mountaineer, he "did all that a sedentary man, with a young family dependent upon him, should attempt." [9]

In the following winter, Amelia Edwards' *Untrodden Peaks and Unfrequented Valleys* filled the ambitious climber with a desire to visit the Dolomites. Again it was impossible for Mrs. Hughes to go, but she raised no objection to his plan. After he had sailed she wrote to him on August 9, 1895, from Chesham, New Hampshire:

MY DARLING,

. . . you are nearly two days and a half out now and I am constantly wondering how you are faring on the "Teutonic." . . . I know that you can't but enjoy it my darling—and wifie is glad for you. I can't say that I don't miss you, dearest. On the "Priscilla" Wednesday evening after the babies were tucked away in their little berths . . . I went out on deck alone and saw the moon rise. I was very sure that on another ship deck you were looking at the same . . . sight—and though very near to you in spirit I longed to be *really* near you and was so oppressed by the thought that each moment took you further from me that I couldn't stay out under that starry sky very long, though it was so beautiful and in a way so fascinating. I went in to my little ones and busied myself with practical affairs. . . .

ANTOINETTE

When Hughes wrote a few days later, he was again looking forward to the trip they would someday take together:

My dearest,

. . . Sweet wifie, you have spoiled me for friendship. The sweet quiet restful companionship of love unfits me for the conventions of social intercourse. [There follows a complaint about the passengers encroaching upon his rest.]

I have a room picked out for "wifie" when we can go together—with the little ones "hard by." What wouldn't I give to take you and them into my arms at this moment. My darling, I must try to get into a normal condition so that we may make more of our home life. A separation like this makes us feel its worth. I feel guilty in running away from you—but I know it will be best for us all.

Hughes had been near to nervous exhaustion when he left, and he had some difficulty in regaining his composure. After a walk of seventy miles in three days (over the passes to Caprile, Canazei, St. Ulrich, and Bolcano) he felt

[8] CEH, Notes, p. 161. [9] *Ibid.*

reinvigorated, but the edge of exhilaration was dulled by loneliness. From Pontresina he wrote on August 30:

My precious one—were it not for my constant—rather "continual" journeyings what would I do? As soon as I halt there comes over me such a sense of loneliness and homesickness. One by one my illusions are passing—and now the illusion of travel is fast going. I realize that after all my soul anchor is wifie. Oh my precious one—how dreary, dreary would be life anywhere and everywhere were it not for your love—not that your *love* alone is everything, but it is *your* love—the love of the dearest, truest, noblest woman on earth. And how blessed we are in having such sweet little ones to care for and treasure. It is at a time like this, when I am away from the cares of business, that I fully understand how small a part of life they are.

Their separation was brief in 1896. Mrs. Hughes spent July at Chesham with the children, while Hughes' mother and father came to stay with him in New York. On July 4 he wrote a self-revealing letter from his library:

DARLING WIFIE,
This is Independence Day—but I find myself more dependent than ever—on wifie. . . .
Mother is watching the books and making valiant struggles toward economy. Poor mother—she is so tyrannized by trifles. It's in the blood. I have a big dose of it. But everything is going smoothly and both father and mother are doing all possible to make me comfortable—and I am comfortable. Happy? Well, that requires wifie. Love and kisses to the doddies.

Lovingly,
C.

At the end of the month his father and mother went to Chesham to stay with the children while Hughes introduced his wife to the beauties of Switzerland. In happy anticipation he wrote on July 19:

DARLING "WIFIE,"
. . . at the prospect of our outing I'm as happy as a tinker. Only ten days—and what's more only six days till I see "wifie." Then opens a "vista!" Well, dear one, you have had the burden and heat of the day—and very little freedom from care since we have been married. And if I can make this little excursion pleasant for you—I will. How often I thought yesterday of our walks on Manhattan [Beach] about eight years ago. We haven't much to regret have we? Our sorrows are yet to come. And with the love that soothes and sustains we can bear whatever there is in store. Our separation, darling, is a good appetizer for the coming feast—isn't it? I have a very busy week ahead, but I can't very well break down in five days. . . .

By by, Sweetheart
C.

They reached Switzerland by way of Liverpool, London, and Paris. Starting at Lausanne, they covered much of the charming mountain and lake country that had so fascinated Hughes on his first trip. Arriving at Zermatt in a fog, the Alpine enthusiast from New York could scarcely wait to show his wife the Matterhorn. "Can't you just see it through the mist!" he exclaimed, as he outlined the position of the famous peak from their hotel window. When the sun lighted up the mountains the next morning, the Matterhorn was indeed visible from one of their windows but in the opposite direction from where Hughes had described it.

From the Riffel Alp above Zermatt they walked to Gornergrat, and on the way to the Rhone Glacier they ascended the Eggishorn, Mrs. Hughes riding a mule halfway up. The day was bright, and they could "see plainly most of the great peaks of the Alps." [10] At Interlaken they visited Mürren and Grindelwald and then went on to the blue waters of Lake Lucerne.

Having planned another jaunt to Switzerland alone in 1897, Hughes began to protest the separation from his wife before he embarked. Mrs. Hughes was at Littleton, New Hampshire. On July 11, he wrote to her from Asbury Park:

MY DEAREST,

. . . I thought I might get rid of my loneliness, or some of it, as well as the heat, but the sight of these papas and mammas and the host of little ones makes me feel worse than ever. And so while gazing at the blue ocean what I have really seen is the peaceful cottage under the elms and the widespread view of wooded hills stretching far away to the southwest and wifie dear in her chic little summer dress (with the pink ribbons) and little Charlie and Helen playing gleefully on the lawn. And every now and then I must wipe my glasses to get a better view. Oh! my darling, how I rebel against this cruel separation. Why should it be so, I ask again and again, only to review all the "logic of the situation" and once more come to the conclusion that it is for the best. I have been over my continental time tables which I got yesterday and planning my trip in detail—not a difficult task—for I know pretty well what I want to do. Only I don't want to do it at all. The present is but an earnest of the wretchedness to come. Even when I think of Pontresina and try to picture that lovely valley—the most vivid recollection is that of my lonely tramps on each one of which I vowed I would never do it again. Really if I hadn't that return passage and my tickets paid for, I should give it up. What I should do, I don't know. But anywhere *with* wifie—nowhere *without*, I would like to make my motto. Sweet one, our lives are so intertwined, neither is complete without the other. And to make one happy, both must be made happy. We can have no separate pleasures. . . .

I haven't met a soul I know—and if I don't uncork soon, I shall "bust."

Bye-bye, wifie dear. To think that you—so even, so normal—so reasonable—so sane—should have such a neurotic, abnormal, cranky, crotchety, absurd husband. I think you are my steering gear and when I lose you, I flounder about like an old hulk in a swell.

[10] Mrs. CEH to Mrs. D. C Hughes, Aug. 24, 1896.

Dearest, I owe so much to you. As the years go by, I feel that I am accomplishing very little—but I know that I am far more of a man than I ever should have been, had we not met and loved.

Now a thousand kisses and a heart full of love.

C.

After saying goodbye and just before sailing, he wrote her:

How is my brave little wifie this morning? How fondly we shall cherish the memory of yesterday, darling. I must confess that I was badly broken up last evening. The little girl's sorrow touched me deeply and brought such a vivid realization of all I had to be thankful for and the beautiful love of our home life that I couldn't control myself. That last incident I shall never forget and the darling one's remembrance—"The Shield of Faith" never meant so much to me before—I shall always have with me. Now that our separation has actually begun and the ordeal of parting is over, I feel stronger. As you say, "I have shut my teeth." I'm going through with the program and get all the benefit I can out of my vacation, which costs us so much in many ways, and come back as vigorous as possible to do my best for the dear ones I love so devotedly and of whose love I feel so unworthy.

You are the most unselfish—the bravest, truest wife a man ever had. You let me go without a murmur—indeed, urge me to go because you believe it best. Darling, I know what it means to you—I know what must be the monotony of the life at Elin Cottage and how eagerly you will follow my travels and how much you long to be with me. I know it all—and it makes me feel like a worm in the dust. . . .

The next day Mrs. Hughes wrote:

I am trying to fix my mind to the weeks of separation to come. As you say there is a great deal in what you set your mind to—and I believe it. The hope of our sweet reunion buoys me up. . . .

But, my sweet one, I must stop. I know you won't have time to read a long letter, and you know how truly and undividedly *I love you.*

On the boat he took to imagining that he was walking the deck with her:

I have seen your nose wrinkle with delight as you entered with me into the pleasures of this delightful journey.

My own—I feel newly wed—I want to say it all over again. And yet if you were here, I should probably be silent. For we have been too long together to need *words.* To be with each other—to see love in every glance of the eye—to have the joy of constant companionship—that is what we want. And we shall have another happy year—my loved one—and if I can, by being happier and more thoughtful of you, repay you for the unselfishness which permits a vacation like this—darling one—you shall be repaid.

Pontresina now fascinated him more than any other retreat. From that delightful spot he wrote on August 8:

The past two years seem almost like a dream, and the old spell is over me. For one thing, the air is so exhilarating that Chamonix with its lower level is not to be compared with it for healthfulness, and one has that *joie de vie* which gives so much zest to every undertaking. Then there is so much more that the ordinary mortal can do than at Zermatt, while the town itself is clean and picturesque. . . .

I am not as worried as I was two years ago—I distinctly remember my endless calculations. Now I am at peace. . . .

Do the little ones think of Papa sometimes—or is he simply one who works and plays all by himself?

Climbing Piz Languard (10,715 feet), he found the view "too wonderful to describe," conversed in a high state of good humor with a German couple, and came away so excited that he left his Baedeker on top. In the course of a letter to Mrs. Hughes he wrote on August 11:

If I could only feel as well as this in New York! My heart is where wifie is, my business is in New York—but my "Gesundheit" is in the Alps. I went up the Piz Languard two years ago. I would like to go up every year. Precious one—I have just been up a mountain and I am very happy. But this after dinner—when I wander about in solitude, I am so lonely. But luckily I am tired and can sleep. And so I drown in slumber the thought of our separation.

At first Hughes spoke to hardly anyone at the inn. "Almost everybody is in some party and somehow opportunities for making acquaintances have been rare," he reported. "I have a pleasant neighbor on my right, a recent Cambridge graduate, but after a half hour of 'No, really!' 'Well, rather,' and 'Very jolly, isn't it,' I give it up." [11] As the days passed, however, he became better acquainted. Every night he dressed for dinner—"for the honor of my country," he said. "No Englishman could be more fastidious. Every man at our table is in full dress—'thriving' is a mild description."

Before leaving on a jaunt to the Italian Lakes, he wrote on August 16:

This is certainly the air I need. I have never anywhere felt so well—continuously. No "downs"—all "ups" in this climate. . . .

One thing [is] sure. This is my last trip to Switzerland without wifie— For I have done Pontresina so thoroughly, I know I shall not want to come again *alone*—and I love Pontresina so much, I shall not be contented to go anywhere else. So some day, when we can come together, we shall—and until then we shall stick together and to our own country. For Switzerland, for me eclipses all else—and Pontresina is the best of Switzerland. . . . Well I have had four great years. And possibly hard work may drive me over here again—but the charm of novelty will be gone and the other charms can only be enjoyed with "my charmer." . . .

Well, dearest, two weeks from today I sail for home. Sometimes I feel uncertain as I think of that dreadful office with its constant demand—but I am inclined to be stout-hearted—and ready to do my best. The most disheartening thing is the growing

[11] CEH to his wife, Aug. 14, 1897.

conviction that my best is not much. But I have what counts most—a happy home and what counts next—good health—and to tell the truth what I have not weighed in true balance is not worth much—that is money and fame.

The birth of their third child kept the Hugheses away from Switzerland in 1898. They took a cottage at Twilight Park in the Catskills so that Hughes could spend week ends with his family and be close by at the time of Mrs. Hughes' confinement. Daughter Catherine arrived earlier than was expected, however, and caught her father off guard. He had gone to Canada for a few days and learned at Quebec of her advent on August 11. Hurrying to Twilight Park, the happy father had scarcely made the acquaintance of his daughter when he was summoned to New York to handle litigation over a city bond issue. Returning again to his family, he was soon snatched away by Frederick R. Hazard for a business trip to Belgium.

The Hugheses returned to Twilight Park the following summer, but the call to Switzerland would not be denied. When Hughes had to go to London in June to take depositions in a will case, he finished his work and went straight to Geneva. Soon he was off to Fayet and St. Gervais to make a tour of the southern side of Mont Blanc. Here is his own account of it:

I walked over the Col du Four and the Col du Bonhomme, passed through L'Allée Blanche—directly below the great massive of Mont Blanc, and by the Lac de Combal to Courmayeur, which lies across the Mont Blanc range from Chamonix. I then proceeded to Aosta and Valtournache. From there I walked over the Theodule Pass to Zermatt. On the way I stopped at the Alpine hut on the side of the Theodule Glacier and from there made the ascent of the Breithorn, for me a memorable climb.[12]

Back at Zermatt, he described the climb in a letter to Mrs. Hughes on July 17:

. . . at half past three in the morning, I am waked and make ready for the Breithorn. The stars are shining peacefully in the dark blue sky and we are sure of a clear sunrise. We take our coffee black (we have no milk) and set out. I am securely fastened to my guide by a stout rope—and away we go over the snow, now hard and firm. The morning is beautiful—every mountain unclouded. Soon the Matterhorn is tipped with rosy light and one by one the mountain peaks are lit like torches. We cross the Theodule Glacier, then on over a fairly steep ascent of snow until we reach the Breithorn plateau and so to the base of the summit, if I may so express it. . . . We climb the steep sides, digging our shoe nails vigorously into the snow and zig-zag up. There is no suggestion of danger, and there was none beyond the risk of losing one's head and consequently his footing, and sliding "quite indefinitely." Once we came to a little level space and stopped to rest. "No," says the guide, "you are over a crevasse." So I must rest on the steep slope leaning

[12] CEH, Notes, p. 163.

on my stick. The morning air is cool and we go rapidly and reach the top in 2½ hours—all over snow and ice. The summit is a ridge of ice . . . with precipitous descents on both sides. I spread out my mackintosh and sit down to enjoy "the finest view in Europe." So many call it and I have never seen anything approaching it. Well, I won't say that, but anything as superb. . . . I have had the best the Alps can give, and that is saying a good deal.

In another letter written at Vevey he described himself as "frisking like a youngster, sleeping like a deacon." After a "wheel voyage" of thirty-six miles, he reported, "I was all right, though, of course, after so many revolutions, the seat of government was much disturbed." There were some discouraging moments. "The weather changed," he wrote, "and I left [Bel-Alp] yesterday in the midst of thick clouds, picking my way along the path I could hardly see and followed by my pack mule who no doubt thought me more of an ass than he himself for coming out on such a beastly day." [13] By the time he finished his excursions on the Aletsch Glacier, however, and visited Sass Fee, he concluded that this was his best trip.

Meanwhile the family had taken up a new diversion. Hughes returned to find his wife, his son, and his father playing golf on a little course near their cottage in the Catskills. He joined in the fun and soon became a golf enthusiast. Almost every free Saturday or holiday thereafter he could be found chipping the turf at the Scarsdale or the Englewood golf club. Hughes "played with his nerves" and never became a good golfer, but his zeal was boundless, as illustrated by the fact that on one Washington's birthday he played with red balls in the snow. Years later, when he golfed with his debutante daughter Elizabeth, he used to call her "Deb, the daughter of Dub."

In 1901 Hughes also began to bolster his strength with regular exercises. At first he followed, morning and night, a system prescribed by Swoboda. After a few years he trimmed this down to a workout of about ten minutes each morning. His slender frame began to fill out. Within two years his previous maximum of 140 pounds had been increased to 153 pounds. By 1907 another twelve pounds had been added. When he attained "a proper weight" of 173 pounds (stripped before breakfast), he was to hold it with little variation for more than twenty years by the simple expedient of adding a slice of toast for breakfast when he began to lose and reducing the pile of toast when he began to gain. His regimen of exercise was to be faithfully adhered to until he reached the age of seventy-seven.

The enthusiastic Alphine climber had to be content in 1900 with a summer place at Mount Menagha near Ellenville, New York, and a two weeks' holiday with Mrs. Hughes on the Maine coast. But the following year they sailed together again, visiting Bremen, Hamburg, Berlin, Dresden, Prague, Vienna,

[13] CEH to his wife, July 26, 1899.

Salzburg, Munich, and Innsbruck as a preliminary to Thusis and The Engadine. Then came the Italian Lakes and the thrill of their first trip to Venice.

Left behind with Grandpa and Grandma Hughes at Mount Menagha, young Charlie and Helen, then aged eleven and nine, experienced difficulties which they had not sensed during their parents' first European trip five years earlier, and to which Catherine, being only three, was even then immune. The grandparents were not convinced that their son and daughter-in-law had put sufficient zeal into training the children along religious lines, and they devoted themselves assiduously to supplying the lack. When Charlie was caught with a Sweet Caporal breath, which he had not had time to disguise, he was knelt down by the bed, between the grandparents, who prayed alternately for nearly an hour for his salvation from evil companions. The crowning indignity for both children was when their grandparents assembled them on the porch of the cottage to sing old revivalist hymns, grandpa singing a resonant and breathy bass and grandma a piercing, flutelike treble. Thoroughly miserable because of the snickers of their playmates from the near-by cottages and hotel, the children would steal away hand in hand to some secluded spot and hold an indignation meeting.

At the age of twelve Charles Junior was initiated into the pleasures of European travel. His father took him on a jaunt to London, Paris, Switzerland, Germany, and Belgium. The trip was especially notable, however, for an event which temporarily robbed the elder Hughes of the peace of mind he customarily found in Europe. At Strasbourg they visited the cathedral, and being fresh from the Alps, decided to climb the spire. Charlie and the guide went rapidly ahead. Hughes followed at a slower pace with increasing concern over the narrowness of the spiral stair and the great Gothic apertures in the spire, which gave a full view of the street 464 feet below the pinnacle.

The steps became almost too narrow for a secure footing. Hughes wanted to turn back, but his son was nowhere in sight. He had to go on. As he came to the final pinched stairway, he spied the guide standing on the outside of the spire above, with only one foot on a narrow perch quite devoid of protection. In his best German, Hughes shouted, "Where is my son?" The guide pointed upward and said something like "Hinauf." Keeping far ahead, Charlie had passed the precarious spot where the guide was now standing, and, without the slightest concern, climbed a straight metal ladder outside the spire to the highest point that could be reached.

"Get him down!" commanded the frantic father.

There followed a period of mental torture while the agile youth came down the ladder, squeezed himself into the spire, and joined his elders in descending the open stair, which seemed to Hughes as unprotected as a great corkscrew reared into the sky. He reached the ground in a nervous chill. It is scarcely necessary to add that the incident became a family saga.

In the summer of 1903, the Hugheses returned to the delights of Maine, camping on the western side of Moosehead Lake about ten miles north of Kineo. One of their excursions took father and son to Lobster Lake and to the summit of Spencer Mountain. Another took them by canoes and carries by way of Chesuncook, Chamberlain, Eagle, Churchill, and Umsaskis lakes and the Allagash River to Fort Kent. On the return trip they climbed Mount Katahdin, reaching the summit in a driving rain. Moose and other big game often crossed their trail, but Hughes never carried a gun. Nor would it likely have been different if his tramping had been done in the hunting season. He went to the wilds for relaxation and a sense of inward enrichment, without the slightest desire to kill anything.

Every trip into the mountains was an uplifting experience. Hughes thrived on the high altitude, the bracing air, the sense of achievement in climbing, the awareness of natural beauty, and the delight of satisfying an appetite whetted by exercise. As he found renewal of vigor year after year, even at a heavy cost of loneliness, he came to believe that Switzerland had saved his life and made it possible for him to carry a work load that otherwise would have pulled him down in middle age. Not only that; the mountains calmed his feverish ambition, gave him perspective, and in this sense prepared him for the larger responsibilities ahead.

Chapter 14

THE GAS INQUIRY

AMERICAN industrialism was undergoing what is probably its sharpest transformation in the early years of the twentieth century. Big corporations were in their heyday of mergers. Sprawling financial empires were in the making. Men of vision and daring were creating vast new industries and amassing fortunes, and unscrupulous promoters were taking their toll through the watering of stock, the capitalization of franchises, the exaction of exorbitant rates, and, not infrequently, the corruption of lawmaking bodies.

Against this background the great investigations that made Charles E. Hughes a national figure were undertaken. New York was most concerned in 1904 and early 1905 about the exorbitant rates charged for gas and electricity. The city was fighting the trust over the cost of municipal lighting. "For Half Light," screamed a New York *World* headline, "New York Pays Double Price." [1] Mayor George B. McClellan was advocating construction of a municipal lighting plant. The City Club and the Merchants' Association were clamoring for an investigation. Rousing editorials protested that the people were being "shamelessly robbed." Even "thief-ridden Philadelphia" was getting light at rates much lower than those prevailing in New York.[2] The Board of Aldermen concluded that something would have to be done, but when Charles F. Murphy, leader of Tammany Hall, poured cold water on the idea of an investigation the Tammany aldermen once more turned their backs upon the scandal. At last, in the spring of 1905, the legislature at Albany was goaded into ordering an investigation, to the dismay of the gas lobby, which was said to be offering high prices for opposing votes.

Governor Francis W. Higgins hastened to name the investigating committee, representing both the Senate and the Assembly, with Senator Frederick C. Stevens as chairman. The committee went to New York in March and began its search for an eminent lawyer to direct the inquiry. At the suggestion of former Judge William N. Cohen, Governor Higgins had recommended Charles E. Hughes for this assignment.[3] Cohen and Hughes had crossed swords years before in several hotly contested creditors' suits involving the analysis of complicated accounts, and the judge was keenly aware of Hughes' resourcefulness. But the Stevens committee was not immediately impressed. It was looking for

[1] Dec. 7, 1904. [2] New York *World*, Dec. 8, 1904. [3] CEH, Notes, p. 169.

a lawyer with a name that would instantly command public confidence. The assignment was offered to Henry Taft, brother of the Secretary of War, and to several other eminent lawyers. Obviously inspired by his defeat at the hands of his auburn-whiskered friend in the beet-sugar case, Taft advised: "Take Hughes; if any one can take you through the maze of technical testimony about the practical business as well as the stock manipulations, it is Hughes." [4] Suggestions to the same effect came from other lawyers and from Bradford Merrill and Frank McCabe of the *World*, without any knowledge on Hughes' part that his name was being mentioned to the committee.

Senator Stevens then went to Hughes' office and encountered another rejection. "I knew nothing of the gas business," Hughes later explained. "I had little or no confidence in the integrity of legislative investigations, and I feared that, with the great financial interests involved, the investigation would be thwarted in some way and I should be in a position of apparent responsibility and debited with a conspicuous failure in a matter in which there was intense public interest." [5] His skepticism was shared by the public. So many investigations had fizzled that the new venture was looked upon as just another excursion in political plunder.

Stevens would not take No for an answer. "The more I think about it," he said on his second visit to Hughes' office, "the more I am convinced that you're the man to take charge of the investigation." [6] The committee was determined, he further insisted, to make a thorough inquiry without political hindrance. As counsel, Hughes would have a free hand to bring out the facts and would have assurance in advance that he would not be "called off." Stevens also sent Senator Page around to reassure the lawyer of the committee's intentions.

Hughes then began to think more seriously of the offer. His first step was to investigate the committee chairman. Senator Stevens had been president of an electric-lighting company in Washington, D.C., but he was a man of independent mind and complete integrity. Although he was a millionaire and "desperately solvent," as Job Hedges put it, his devotion to the public interest seemed to be well established. Satisfied on this score, Hughes then scrutinized his own qualifications. He had had no experience whatever in legislative investigations. He distrusted his capacity and "hated the idea of work where the public eye would be upon every step, with the newspapers keen on the scent for any political intriguing and the Hearst press ever ready to make sensational charges." [7] All these objections he laid before Senator Stevens with complete candor.

"Mr. Stevens," Hughes then said, "I belong to the same church as Mr. Rockefeller."

[4] *Outlook*, Oct. 20, 1906, p. 406.
[5] CEH, Notes, p. 170.
[6] Beerits' Memorandum, II, p. 4.
[7] CEH, Notes, p. 171.

"What bearing does that have on the matter?" the senator asked.

"Well," the cautious lawyer replied, "some might mention it later." [8]

Stevens assured him that the committee was convinced of his integrity, and Hughes finally concluded that it would be "cowardly" to reject the committee's urgent appeal to him on grounds of his own inadequacy. "There is a public service of importance to be rendered," he told himself, "and if I go at it with the single purpose of doing a thorough professional job, that attitude will be recognized and in some way I shall get through." [9]

In announcing the committee's choice of counsel, Stevens said: "It was purely a Diogenes search, and we found an honest man. Furthermore, I think it will be conceded that we obtained one of the most eminent as well as one of the most able attorneys in the city." [10] Hughes promptly nailed down the pledge he had received by telling the reporters who swarmed around him: "I told Senator Stevens that I would not become counsel to the committee unless I could be absolutely free from political dictation of any and every sort. When we get this investigation started we will follow the trail that leads us to the information we desire, no matter where that trail takes us. . . ." [11]

But skepticism was rampant. The press introduced Hughes "with a groan." He was a friend of Rockefeller (who was supposed to control the gas monopoly) and a former partner of Cravath, now attorney for big utilities. William Randolph Hearst's *New York American* carried a three-column headline on the front page: "Friend of Rockefeller, Long a Fellow Trustee of his Church, Leader in his Son's Sunday School Class, Counsel for Gas Investigators." Beside this smear in words was a cartoon depicting Rockefeller and Hughes, Bible in hand, passing the plate. Hughes' straightforward attitude was described by cynical newsmen as being "hard, cold, and flinty." His recreation was said to be "climbing icy crags." When he gave his days and nights to preparing for the inquiry, he was suspected of being closeted with the gas tycoons. Before the hearings got under way, he had been associated in the public mind with "coldness, solitude, aloofness, silence, frigidity, ice." [12]

The first few days of the inquiry did nothing to alter the gloomy forecast that it would be a "whitewash expedition." Hughes offered only dull figures for the record. The press yawned. Even the company officials under investigation acquired a feeling of reassurance. "If Hughes gets out of a witness anything he does not wish to reveal," one journalist wrote, "it will be a surprise to those who watched his initial operations." [13] Senator Owen Cassidy described the committee members as "running around like a lot of children with toy bal-

[8] Stevens, quoted in *New York American*, March 26, 1905.
[9] CEH, Notes, p. 171 [10] *New York Journal*, March 24, 1905.
[11] New York *Daily Tribune*, March 25, 1905.
[12] William Brown Meloney in *Everybody's Magazine*, October, 1916, p. 389.
[13] James Montague in the *New York Journal*, March 31, 1905.

loons, gas balloons, you know." [14] Here was, in strident and voluminous detail, precisely the sort of public reaction that Hughes had feared.

The investigation went forward, nevertheless, without heeding the skeptics. Hughes had had only a week to prepare for the hearings. He was still feeling his way. Then a deluge of malodorous facts began to pour out of the aldermanic chamber of City Hall where the inquiry was being held. Through the press and by word of mouth it flowed out through the city in astonishing volume. The public attitude was changed almost overnight. At last it appeared that an investigating committee was actually investigating.

NEXT!

From the *New York American*, 1905.

Hearst's yellow journals, which had ridiculed Hughes and called him a "trust lawyer," now begged their readers to follow the reports of the investigation. Even some of the chief counsel's friends were surprised at his ability to elicit vital information from reluctant witnesses, without bluster, rudeness, or even impatience. With the suddenness of an eruption, a striking new figure burst in upon the public consciousness.

Newsmen took great delight in publicizing their "discovery." Here is a sample of many descriptions: "Mr. Hughes is a large man, not burly, but with the appearance of one who is built on big, broad lines. He looks strong. His shoulders are square, his limbs solid, his teeth big and white and his whiskers thick and somewhat aggressive. His voice is loud, but not rasping, his manner that of one sure of himself and his position." [15] Photographers and cartoonists exploited his whiskers with brashness characteristic of the great

[14] *New York Times*, March 26, 1905. [15] New York *Evening Mail*, April 1, 1905.

untamed metropolis, and the *World* assured its readers that "in real life they are broader, braver, bigger, bushier" than they appeared in pictures, and that "when in action they flare and wave about triumphantly like the battle-flag of a pirate chief." [16]

In three toilsome weeks Hughes examined the chief executives of all the gas and electric companies operating in the five boroughs of New York, in addition to various city officials and Boss Murphy and his brother. He showed that the Consolidated Gas Company (popularly known as the gas trust) was charging the city $80,000 for the same amount of electric current it supplied to large private consumers for only $25,000. One unit of the monopoly was supplying electric current to the city at a cost of 4.86 cents per kilowatt hour and reaping a profit of 2.44 cents per kilowatt hour.[17]

Small private consumers were similarly "gouged." Hughes proved that the New York Gas and Electric Light, Heat and Power Company, which was entirely owned by the gas trust, produced and distributed electric current at a cost of 3.664 cents per kilowatt hour and sold it at an average rate of 8.042 cents, the net earnings being substantially larger than the costs.[18] Many consumers were paying 15 cents a kilowatt hour for this current.

The chief target of the inquiry was the gas trust itself. This gigantic combine had absorbed six gas companies back in 1884. Only one company manufacturing and selling gas in New York, the Mutual, had been able to remain outside the trust, and that was only because its charter provided for the imprisonment of its officers if they should consent to its merger with any other company. In 1902 even Mutual had surrendered by entering into an agreement to supply all its gas to the trust.

Hughes compelled officers of the monopoly to admit that when the consolidation was effected the plants and other property belonging to the six companies, which had cost them $20,942,632, were capitalized at $37,971,419 without any additional contribution. Good will, franchises, and rights had been capitalized at $7,781,000. Hughes vigorously challenged the right of the company to base its earnings on any such inflated valuation. "The fact that the company, by rendering competition impossible, has been able to earn large dividends," he wrote into the report he prepared for the committee, "does not justify it in adding to the value of its plant an additional amount for good-will or earning capacity, and thereby justify a continuance of excessive charges. If this were permitted, . . . extortion for a series of years would be sufficient excuse for further extortion. . . . The company is entitled to a fair return upon its capital actually invested, but it is not entitled to capitalize its grip upon the public." [19]

[16] March 25, 1905. [17] *Committee Hearings*, I, 802.
[18] *Committee Report*, p. 94. [19] *Ibid*, pp. 17–18.

In attempting to justify its exorbitant rates, the trust claimed a book value of $47,183,455 for its assets employed in the making and distribution of gas. But when it reported to the State Board of Tax Commissioners, the trust cut this down to $35,079,576. The actual value of the company's plant, the investigation showed, was little more than $27,000,000. When various trust officials were unable to explain these appalling discrepancies, Hughes called Robert A. Carter, secretary of the company. The suave witness drew elaborate distinctions in terms of high finance, but before his grilling was completed he had entangled himself in the ridiculous contention that the value of the company's plant was greater than its worth and that its worth was greater than its value. There was no escape from the fact that the trust was juggling its figures to the extent of more than $12,000,000 in order to keep taxes down and rates up.

The company's inflated valuation had been built up by adding the cost of every new unit and every improvement of its plant, with only meager allowances for depreciation. "For eighty or a hundred years we have been building up this plant to an investment of $48,000,000," cried Charles F. Matthewson, counsel for the trust. "It is utterly preposterous to say that you can take what it might cost to reproduce a plant today."

"I once had an umbrella . . . for fifteen years," Hughes replied dryly. "I had it recovered every year . . . and I suppose that covering of the umbrella dating back would amount to $50 or $60 at the end of that time. Would you say therefore that the value of that umbrella might be $50 or $60?" [20]

Even with its inflated capitalization, the trust's profits were so enormous as to be embarrassing. In 1904 its dividends were 10 per cent, not on the real value or even the inflated book value of the plant, but on the $80,000,000 par value of the stock. Hughes also brought out that the stockholders were receiving an additional 6 per cent on $19,857,600 of debentures convertible into stock of the company at par. When new stock was issued, favored stockholders reaped additional millions through the privilege of buying it at from forty to fifty points below the market price.

Nor was Hughes content to expose financial trickery and ruthless profiteering. One of his witnesses testified that adulteration of the gas created a deadly poison, even when it was burning. New York had suffered 130 accidental deaths from gas in a single year. The investigation also brought forth charges that the company increased the pressure in its mains in order to make a poor quality of gas supply the required illumination, thus forcing unwitting consumers to pay for wind as well as gas. There was no inspection of gas pressures, except occasional inadequate tests in Manhattan.

[20] *Committee Hearings*, I, 383.

Taken as a whole, the picture was one of brazen corporate pillage and governmental ineptitude. At last an unassailable case for reform had been made. New York's exploited masses were delighted. The press applauded heartily. "Admirably conducted," exclaimed the *World*. "The people wanted to know the facts; and the facts have been brought out beyond cavil." [21] "A model inquiry," said the *Globe*, "under able and adroit direction." [22] The Stevens committee, which had remained true to its pledge giving Hughes a free hand, was no less pleased. "Mr. Hughes has shown ability of a high order," Senator Stevens commented. "The committee is more than satisfied with the way he has handled the case." [23]

Hughes had no time to contemplate the plaudits that came his way. The inquiry had ended abruptly, leaving some leads unexplored, because of the committee's rush to get corrective bills before the legislature while it was still in session. Taking his voluminous data to the Fifth Avenue Hotel, Hughes plunged into the writing of the report and did not leave the hotel until it was finished a week later at two o'clock in the morning. Six and a half hours later he was on the Empire State Express en route to Albany, where he delivered the report to the committee.

The report was factual and restrained. Hughes concluded that the gas company could earn a reasonable return upon its capital actually invested in the gas-making business by charging 75 cents per thousand cubic feet for its product instead of a dollar; that electric current could be furnished for light, heat, and power purposes at a maximum of 10 cents per kilowatt hour in place of the 15 cents then being charged; and that charges to the city for street lighting should be substantially reduced. On the basis of these conclusions he submitted specific recommendations.

The proposal for 75-cent gas and 10-cent electricity won the warmest response from the public. Far more important, however, was Hughes' last recommendation calling for a public service commission to supervise all the activities of the gas and lighting companies in New York State in order to compel their operation in the public interest. "The gross abuse of legal privilege in overcapitalization and in the manipulation of securities, for the purpose of unifying control and eliminating all possible competition," he wrote, "shows clearly that there can be no effective remedy by general legislation or through ordinary legal proceedings, and that for the protection of the public there should be created a commission with inquisitorial authority, competent to make summary investigations of complaints, to supervise issues of securities and investment in the stocks or bonds of other companies, to regulate rates

[21] Editorial, April 24, 1905. [22] April 24, 1905.
[23] *New York Press*, April 22, 1905.

and to secure adequate inspection, or otherwise to enforce the provisions of the law." [24]

Hughes turned his back upon the vain hope that competition could be restored. Only through effective governmental regulation could the public hope to obtain fair treatment from the giant utilities that had made their services indispensable. In that forward-looking stand he was joined by all but two of the investigating committeemen.

At Albany, Hughes spent several days briefing legislators in gas economics. Six weeks before, he had known nothing of the gas business or of legislation controlling it. Now he was generally regarded as the leading expert in this field. His close-up view of the New York Legislature in action was not impressive. Before settling down to a morning conference, Chairman Malby of the Finance Committee, Speaker Merritt, Senator Raines, and others fortified themselves with whisky. After observing their hard drinking and irregular living for a few days, Hughes told one of his companions: "I'll give those fellows five more years. They can't live any longer than that." Within a few years the only survivor of the group was in a sanatorium.

All the bills which Hughes helped to draft to carry out the recommendations of his report were promptly passed, except the eighty-cent gas bill, which was rejected by the Senate and did not become law until 1906. Timorous legislators had lifted Hughes' maximum price by five cents. Nevertheless, the trusts challenged the constitutionality of the act, and Hughes led the fight to have it upheld in the courts, serving entirely without compensation. The legislature also created a State Commission of Gas and Electricity with the powers Hughes had requested for it. Saving in New York City's light bills alone were later estimated at $780,000 a year.[25]

The lift in spirits that came to Hughes through this experience was temporarily reversed, however, as he was taking his son to Old Point Comfort for a breathing spell over Memorial Day. He chanced to pick up a paper carrying an editorial to the effect that, since he had been restrained in his treatment of Boss Murphy on the witness stand, Tammany Hall might use its influence to have him nominated for justice of the New York Supreme Court.[26] Hughes had tried so hard to avoid any appearance of currying favor with any person or group that he was unprepared for such a cynical jibe. Wounded and perturbed, he yearned for the bracing air and the majestic detachment of Switzerland. As soon as he could tie up the loose ends of his neglected practice, he followed Mrs. Hughes and the children to Europe.

[24] *Committee Report*, p. 94.

[25] New York *Evening Post*, Oct. 20, 1906.

[26] Beerits' Memorandum, II, 8.

Chapter 15

THE INSURANCE INVESTIGATION

WHILE Hughes reveled in his freedom, New York was seething with excitement from a new source. The almost sacred temple of life insurance was being shaken by dissension within and sensational rumors without. As early as February 12, 1905, the *World* had dragged into public view the dramatic struggle between James Hazen Hyde and James W. Alexander. This put many hounds of the press on the trail, and they brought in, as Mark Sullivan has recorded, "morsels of rumor about scandal in the very highest financial circles of New York, of charges and counter-charges, of rival committees wrangling, of the pot calling the kettle black, of violent quarrels, of bitter invectives hurled across mahogany tables in closed directors' rooms. . . ." [1]

There had been no sudden revolution in the life-insurance business. Rather, the public had acquired a new awareness of long-standing exploitation, and the chief eye opener seemed to be young Hyde's unbecoming display of his inherited wealth and power. He affected French clothes and spiced his conversation with Gallic witticisms. His fabulous parties at his "château" on Long Island, the elegance of his town house and of the private hansom that carried him to his office caused widespread wagging of tongues as well as the clatter of typewriters. "Dumas' riotous, turbulent imagination," cried the *World,* "never conceived of such a situation."

Five years after his graduation from college, Hyde was drawing a salary of $100,000 as vice president of the Equitable Life Assurance Society. Under the terms of his father's will, moreover, he was about to inherit absolute ownership of 502 shares of Equitable stock, which carried with it control of a company with assets of more than $400,000,000. So fastidious and so favored a youth, strolling jauntily through the Wall Street jungle, was "little Red Riding Hood to the wolves." [2] Financiers and directors of life-insurance companies as well as policyholders were alarmed. James W. Alexander, president, and thirty-five other officers and agents of Equitable brought serious charges against Hyde and asked the board of directors to mutualize the company. It was in connection with this effort that Hughes had been retained by Alexander before he took up the gas investigation. Hyde countered with charges against Alex-

[1] *Our Times* (New York, Scribner's, 1933), III, 49–50. Copyright, 1933, by Charles Scribner's Sons.

[2] *Ibid.*, p. 35.

ander. Henry Clay Frick, hard-boiled steel magnate of Pittsburgh, was named chairman of a committee to sift the charges, and his report called for dismissal of both Hyde and Alexander, drastic reorganization of the company, and restitution of certain ill gotten profits. When the report was rejected by the board, Frick, E. H. Harriman, and Cornelius N. Bliss resigned. The following week Hyde sold his 502 shares to Thomas Fortune Ryan for $2,500,000.

This turn of events convinced thousands of people that their policies were mere pawns in the hands of unscrupulous czars of finance fighting among themselves. Under the law, dividends on Hyde's stock could not exceed $3,514 a year. Yet before he parted with it under pressure for $2,500,000, Frick had offered him $5,000,000 for it and George W. Young had offered $7,000,000.[3] Obviously it was not an investment they were seeking but the privileges of high finance manipulation that control of the Equitable would afford.

The demand for an investigation grew so loud that it could no longer be ignored. The *World* carried a series of more than one hundred editorials under the heading "Equitable Corruption," numbering them one, two, three, and so forth, for greater effect. Still the major facts behind the life-insurance scandals remained unknown. Only a full-fledged legislative investigation could bring them to light. At last Governor Higgins yielded, although insisting that "nothing is to be gained by it," and the legislature approved his request for an investigation just before its adjournment.

Senator William M. Armstrong was named chairman of the investigation committee, the other members being Senators William J. Tully and D. J. Riordan and Assemblymen James T. Rogers, Robert Lynn Cox, W. W. Wemple, Ezra P. Prentice, and John McKeown. Armstrong, Tully, and Rogers went to New York to employ the ablest lawyer they could find having no connection with insurance litigation. They called on Ervin Wardman, editor of the *New York Press*. Wardman telephoned Don C. Seitz of the *World* to ask for his suggestion.

"What's the matter with Charley Hughes?" asked Seitz, remembering the gas inquiry.

"He's in Europe," the committeemen replied through Wardman.

"Well, there are cables aren't there?" was the journalist's response.

"They will cable," came the reply.[4]

"The committee could do no better," the *World* declared editorially, than to select as its counsel "the patient and persistent prober of the gas trust abuses. . . . Mr. Hughes would get the facts."[5]

[3] *Hughes Report*, p. 94.

[4] Don C. Seitz, *Joseph Pulitzer, Life and Letters*, (New York, Simon and Schuster, 1924), pp. 278–279. Copyright, 1924, by Simon and Schuster, Inc.

[5] New York *World*, Aug. 4, 1905.

Apparently the committee had similar advice from various sources, including Governor Higgins. At first Hughes' connection with the Alexander case had caused some hesitation, but inquiry showed that he was one of the few outstanding lawyers in New York who were free from entangling alliances with corporate wealth. "No one," as Ida Tarbell said, "held a mortgage on his ability." His independence and unquestioned integrity, in addition to his ability as a fact-finder, had singled him out as the logical director of the great investigation.

Hughes himself was oblivious to all this. Catching up with his family for a happy reunion at Nuremberg, he concentrated all his energies upon the thrilling business of showing his two daughters, his son, and Mrs. Hughes through the Dolomites. They took delightful excursions out from Cortina. Father and son wheeled to Belluno, on a trip to Venice. After leaving the Dolomites, the Hugheses journeyed to the Carinthian Alps and set up new headquarters at idyllic Heiligenblut. In this remote and picturesque retreat the stern-faced investigator was a youth again, drinking in the beauty around him. New York with its toil and corruption seemed a million miles away. The climax of his enjoyment came in a long day's trip to the Gross-Glockner Glacier. Tired and happy, he was eating a hearty dinner with his family when a messenger put a cablegram from Senator Armstrong into his hand.

Hughes was almost stunned.[6] There was little sleep for him that night. At 4:00 A.M. he aroused his family and began a thirty-mile drive down the valley to the nearest railway station. All the glory of morning in the Alps burst upon them as they jaunted from Heiligenblut to the Pusterthal, but now it was Antoinette Hughes who repeatedly exclaimed over the panoramic views unfolding before them.

"Look, sweetheart!" she finally chided him for his silence, "we may never see such a scene again."

"My dear," he expostulated, "you don't know what this investigation would mean. It would be the most tremendous job in the United States." [7]

Hughes' first thought was that he was not free to act because of the work he had done for James Alexander. At the railway station, he so cabled Senator Armstrong before taking the train for Munich so that cable communication could be more readily maintained. Armstrong brushed this objection aside. Hughes then insisted in his second cable that the committee chairman see Hornblower, Cravath, Alexander, and others to make certain that the Alexander case left him under no disqualification. Again he was reassured. Still he was tempted to decline. The responsibility that would go with this assignment would be staggering. When the showdown came, however, his sense of duty and his ambition to advance in his profession pushed him forward. His next

[6] CEH, Notes, p. 172. [7] *Ibid.*

From the New York *World*, September 14, 1905.

THE GRIDIRON

cablegram laid down the condition that he be given a free hand to conduct the investigation. When the committee gave such a promise, he at once cabled his acceptance, arranged for passage home, and arrived about the middle of August, "bubbling over with enthusiasm for the work ahead of him." Doubt and hesitation had given way to determination supported by boundless energy.

There was no time for adequate preparation. The press was hammering away at the Equitable scandal, and the committee felt that it had to open its hearings at the earliest possible moment. The Hyde-Alexander imbroglio was only one phase of a much broader degeneration of standards that threatened the whole life-insurance business. The investigation would have to deal comprehensively with all the New York companies and with many kinds of slick practice. Facts and responsible recommendations would now have to take the place of rumors and sensational reporting. A hurried survey of what the newspapers had disclosed gave few leads of importance. After subpoenaing records and books of the insurance companies and obtaining transcripts of many accounts, Hughes outlined a tentative plan of procedure and plunged into the taking of testimony.

Several hundred persons were in the aldermanic chamber of City Hall an hour before Chairman Armstrong, "watchdog of the Senate," brought down his gavel at the first public hearing on September 6. The committee occupied an improvised platform in front. Reporters, photographers, and sketch artists swarmed into the hall as if the proceeding had been a notorious murder trial.

Forty-four company officials, some under subpoena and some voluntarily present to get the lay of the land, occupied conspicuous seats, flanked by a cordon of lawyers. Among these distinguished fellow practitioners, now lined up in bitter opposition to what Hughes was undertaking, were former Governor Frank S. Black (Equitable), Paul D. Cravath, personal counsel to Ryan; James M. Beck (Mutual), and Richard V. Lindabury (Metropolitan). With so many adroit legal minds seeking to thwart him and so many nimble writers itching for sensation, Hughes would have to watch every move. Keenly he realized that he was walking the edge of a precipice, with his future career at the bar the price of a serious misstep.

James McKeen, associate counsel, made the opening statement for the committee. Then Hughes quietly began the examination of witnesses. From that point on, the investigation was unmistakably a Hughesian performance. His reddish-brown beard, piercing steel-blue eyes, and large teeth (which the *New York Times* spoke of as rivaling "the famous Roosevelt collection in size, prominence and regularity") made him a striking figure at any gathering. More impressive than physical features, however, were the wit and mental agility that kept him in the center of the controversy.

James McKeen had been named counsel to the committee on ostensible terms of equality with Hughes. Actually, however, McKeen's appointment was a sop to the interests opposed to the investigation. Some soft-pedaling committeemen had sought to have him appointed chief counsel and consented to naming Hughes only on condition that McKeen should be associated with him. In spite of this, Senator Armstrong informed Hughes that he was expected to take full charge of the examination of the witnesses. The latter chose as his general assistant Matthew C. Fleming, who had been with him in the gas investigation, and Miles M. Dawson, an independent actuary. Fleming worked with Hughes at his home in the evenings preparing for the public hearings. There was no time to consult McKeen on every step; so Hughes was soon playing virtually a lone hand.[8]

When Emory McClintock of the Mutual Life Insurance Company took the stand, McKeen asked if he might conduct the examination. Hughes readily assented, but after the questioning had proceeded for some time Chairman Armstrong intervened.

"You must take charge of this," he whispered to Hughes. "McKeen is not getting anywhere. McClintock hasn't even opened his brief case." [9]

Hughes replied that he did not wish to offend his fellow counsel; if the chairman wished McKeen to step aside, he himself should make the request. The Senator then asked McKeen to give way, and within a few minutes Hughes had McClintock diving into his brief case. McKeen did not again attempt to examine any witness. Indeed, he appeared quite willing to let Hughes take the full responsibility, as the investigation began to rock the insurance business to its foundations.

Hughes moved slowly at first, as he had done in the gas inquiry. A publicity seeker would have plunged into the seething Equitable scandal. Hughes began with almost colorless details about Mutual and New York Life. The hungry press had to be content with the disclosure of a few exorbitant salaries and the farce that some companies were making of "mutualization." Mutual had boasted that its governing authority rested with more than 400,000 policyholders. Under Hughes' prodding, however, vice president Robert A. Granniss confessed that in practice voting was confined to about 200 policyholders, nearly all of them officers or employees of the company. And in case the policyholders should manifest any tendency toward independence, the officers were ready to squelch it with 20,000 long-standing proxies.

The disclosures began to take on a sensational cast as soon as Hughes was able to follow up the leads he gleaned from detailed examination of company books and records. Often he was as surprised by the outcome as anyone else. Great scandals grew out of the most trivial clues. He would plan each day's work, "but almost invariably something would soon be developed in the

[8] *Ibid.*, p. 174. [9] Author's interview with CEH, Dec. 3, 1947.

course of the examination of witnesses which would give a lead that had to be followed up at once,—and in so doing new and important facts would be elicited." [10] Headlined in the press, these disclosures became very disquieting to the companies, the politicians, and even to some committee members.

At first the insurance executives were reluctant to unburden their souls. "Those relations are confidential, sir," one of them replied to Hughes' searching questions, "and I must decline to answer."

"There is nothing confidential about the insurance business now," he replied, and went right ahead with his probing. He asked several New York Life representatives what had happened to the money received for some Erie stock that had been carried as a nonledger asset. No one seemed to know. The mystery whetted his interest. Finally a bookkeeper produced a card on which sale of the stock was recorded, with no indication as to what had happened to the money. In one corner were three tiny letters, "H.B.O.," so inconspicuous that they might easily have escaped notice. "What do these letters mean?" Hughes asked. They signified the Hanover Bank Office, he was told.

So New York Life had an office at the Hanover Bank! Hughes demanded the books from that office. Officials promised to produce them at once. Hours passed, and the books did not arrive. Visibly annoyed, Hughes went to the bench and whispered to Chairman Armstrong, "I think I shall have to have those books by four o'clock or issue a public statement drawing attention to the fact that the company has failed to submit for examination the books we have requested." [11] Armstrong urged patience, and Hughes agreed to wait until the next morning.

Political temblors of alarming proportions shook New York that night. Every influential person in the state seemed to be telephoning members of the insurance investigating committee. Former Governor Odell, the Republican boss, summoned Senator Armstrong and said it would be inadvisable for the committee to demand the missing books. Armstrong replied that the committee had accepted its assignment with the understanding that it would go to the bottom of the insurance irregularities. Odell frowned and mumbled that he was afraid the missing evidence "might actually lead to the door of the White House." [12]

The next morning the committee asked Hughes what he wanted from the missing books. With complete candor, he replied that he did not know but that it was essential to examine the books to make his investigation complete. At last the books were brought in. Hughes scanned them eagerly, finding many items that he wished to explore. Near the end of one book was a mysterious item of $48,702.50 which the witness then under examination could not

[10] CEH, Notes, p. 174. [11] Ida Tarbell in *American Magazine*, March, 1908.
[12] James Creelman in *Pearson's Magazine*, September, 1907, p. 246.

explain. "Who can explain it?" the patient counsel asked. "George W. Perkins," was the reply. Perkins was called to the stand.

This suave partner of J. P. Morgan & Company and vice president of New York Life began by telling the story of his life and expatiating upon his principles and motives. Hughes let him ramble on, then gradually brought him around to the business at hand. When the committee adjourned for lunch, with the mystery still unexplained, Perkins sought the investigator's private ear.

"Mr. Hughes," he said, "you're handling dynamite. That $48,000 was a contribution to President Roosevelt's campaign fund. You want to think very carefully before you put that into the evidence. You can't tell what may come of it."

"After lunch," Hughes replied, "I'm going to ask you what was done with that $48,000; and I expect a candid answer." [13]

When Hughes put the momentous question, he had already offered the telltale check as evidence.

"What was the payment for?" he persisted.

"That was money paid to Mr. Cornelius N. Bliss," Perkins admitted, with a characteristic flourish, "on account of the Republican National Committee Campaign account of last year. . . . I am very glad you brought that out." [14]

"Yes," Hughes replied with a broad grin parting his whiskers, "I intended it should be brought out."

Reporters raced to the telephones. Telegraph wires throughout the land clicked out news stories of "widows' and orphans' money" swelling the coffers of big politics. Meanwhile Hughes coolly drew from the hapless Morgan partner the fact that similar sums had been contributed to the Republican Party by the New York Life in 1896 and 1900. A later parade of witnesses showed that Mutual had contributed $40,000 to the Grand Old Party in 1904; Equitable had given $50,000; and smaller companies, lesser sums.

"If no other or further information about the life insurance business were elicited by the Armstrong Committee," said the *New York Times*, "the ordering of the inquiry would be fully justified. . . ." [15] The *World* expressed doubt, "if any legislative investigation in the history of the state was ever conducted more ably or more acutely or more rationally." A wave of resentment against giant corporations marshaling stockholders' and policyholders' funds for political purposes swept over the nation and hastened the outlawing of that vicious practice.

"Hughes calls himself a Republican," the bosses wailed, "but he's ripping the party wide open." Under the bosses' badgering, several members of the committee became restive and asked for an executive session to seek a show-

[13] Beerits' Memorandum, II, 19.

[14] *Armstrong Committee Hearings*, I, 751–752.

[15] Sept. 16, 1905.

down with Hughes. Instead of openly opposing him, however, a spokesman complained that the committeemen never knew in advance what course the investigation would take. They were caught utterly unprepared for Hughes' shocking revelations. Could not their counsel keep them informed as to what line he was going to take?

Hughes protested that this would be impossible. Usually he did not know what he would find until he came to the end of the trail. How could he give them information he did not have? Some members were nevertheless persistent. After all, they intimated, it was the committee's investigation.

"I understand that perfectly," Hughes replied. "I am only your counsel. Of course, you are free to give me explicit instructions, and if you do so I shall follow them, or I shall resign and tell the public why." [16]

Senator Tully walked over to the lawyer's side. "I am with Mr. Hughes," he said. Others followed suit. Public sentiment was such that the committee could not have provoked Hughes' resignation on the issue of continuing the investigation free from boss domination without committing political suicide. Every member knew it. Hughes had become, as one commentator said, "the personification of outraged America." From this point on there was no further effort to interfere with his direction of the inquiry.

Outside the committee, however, tremendous forces buffeted the determined investigator. A clamor arose for further light on the "buying of public office" with corporate funds. Hughes had courageously exposed the tie-in of his own party with the "big three" in life insurance. Now, the argument ran, he must summon Cornelius Bliss and Postmaster General George B. Cortelyou, chairman of the Republican National Committee, and probe further into the relations between big business and the political machines. The pressure behind this demand was especially intense because it came chiefly from those individuals and newspapers (including the *World*) that had given the investigator the most enthusiastic support. But Hughes refused to budge. He was investigating life insurance, not political corruption. He fought with dogged persistence to get a complete picture of the hidden campaign expenditures of insurance companies spread upon the record; these were part of the mismanagement that he had been retained to expose and correct. At the same time he refused to jeopardize the insurance inquiry by going off on a tangent. If he deviated from his central aim, the inquiry would be smothered by politics and nothing of value would be accomplished. His friends were no more successful in diverting him from his purpose than were his opponents.

Meanwhile the Republican bosses advanced his name as the logical candidate for mayor of New York City. Hughes correctly saw that it was a plot to break up the insurance investigation and tried to withdraw his name from con-

[16] CEH, Notes, p. 175; author's interview with CEH, Dec. 3, 1947.

sideration. Odell persisted, however, in refusing to believe that a hitherto obscure lawyer would turn down a chance to be mayor of New York when the final showdown came.

The evening of Friday, October 6, 1905, was one of the few occasions during the insurance investigation when Hughes found it possible to snatch two or three hours for relaxation. He took his wife to the theater. Meanwhile a drama of a very different sort was taking place at Carnegie Hall, where cheering and waving of flags greeted Senator Nathaniel Elsberg's declaration that Hughes was "the man to meet a great emergency." Returning from the theater, the investigator found his house brilliantly lighted and the street full of cabs and excited people. He had been nominated for the mayorship in spite of his prior refusal to run. A large delegation of party leaders was awaiting his return, determined to high-pressure him into acceptance of the honor.

Hughes took the "notification committee" up to his library. There were Herbert Parsons, the county chairman; Julius Mayer, attorney general of the state; Senator Page and Ezra Prentice of the insurance investigation committee, and several others. Flattery was the foremost arrow in their quiver. Hughes was the only man, they said, who could beat Mayor McClellan. If he should refuse to run, McClellan would be reelected mayor, then governor, then President of the United States. Hughes must step in, he was told, to save his party and his country from this dire chain of contingencies. His nomination had been pressed against his wishes because of these peculiar circumstances, and now he could not let his party down.

The dilemma confronting the party leaders, Hughes replied, was entirely of their own making. He had told them in unmistakable terms before they had acted that he could not accept the nomination. Their heedlessness had not in any way changed his situation. Nor would he attempt to look into the future. It was enough that he had an immense job to do in the present.

"If I were free to take the nomination for mayor," the harassed investigator continued, "I cannot say what I would do, for I have never desired to enter public life. My wish is to practice my profession and to support my family with my earnings from that work. If I were free, however, to take a nomination, it might seem to be my duty to do so against my wishes and the interests of my family. But I am not free." [17]

Every suggestion that he could continue the investigation and run for mayor at the same time he brushed aside. To permit entanglement of the investigation in politics would be to defeat its purpose and subject himself to justifiable attack. Such G.O.P. wheelhorses as Platt, Depew, and Odell were yet to be called. How impossible it would be to question them if he were their candidate for mayor! The argument went on until two o'clock in the morning, the pressure

[17] An eyewitness, Ervin Wardman in *Review of Reviews*, November, 1906, p. 552.

gathering such intensity that Mrs. Hughes, listening in an adjoining room, did not see how her husband could hold out. No one present would accept his point of view. Finally the politicians implored him to delay announcement of his decision until Monday. When he agreed to this, they went home.

The telephones at Hughes' home and office buzzed almost incessantly through Saturday and Sunday, and his desk was banked with telegrams. Every cog in the Republican machine seemed to be grinding out an appeal to him to bow to the good of the party. Nor was the pressure confined to Republican sources. So intense was Hearst's bitterness against McClellan that he sent a message to Hughes through Ervin Wardman, editor of the *New York Press*. If Hughes would run, the message informed him, Hearst would support him, or, alternatively, Hearst himself would run in order to split the opposition and ensure the election of Hughes.[18]

The investigator remained unshaken. On Monday he issued a crisp statement explaining why it was impossible for him to accept the nomination:

> In this dilemma I have simply to do my duty as I see it.
>
> In my judgment, I have no right to accept the nomination. A paramount public duty forbids it. . . .
>
> You know how desirous I have been that the investigation should not be colored by any suggestion of political motive. Whatever confidence it has inspired has been due to absolute independence of political consideration. It is not sufficient to say that an acceptance of this nomination, coming to me unsought and despite an unequivocal statement of my position, would not deflect my course by a hair's breadth, that I should remain, and that you intend that I should remain, entirely untrammelled. The non-political character of the investigation and its freedom from bias, either of fear or favor, not only must exist, they must be recognized. I cannot permit them, by any action of mine, to become matters of debate. . . .
>
> Were I with the best of intention to accept the nomination, it is my conviction that the work of the investigation would be largely discredited; its motives would be impugned and its integrity assailed. To many it would appear that its course would be shaped and its lines of inquiry would be chosen, developed, or abandoned as political ambition might prompt or political exigency demand.
>
> Such a situation would be intolerable. There is but one course open. The legislative inquiry must proceed with convincing disinterestedness. Its great opportunities must not be imperilled by alienating the support to which it is entitled or by giving the slightest occasion for questioning the sincerity and single-mindedness with which it is conducted.[19]

Ten days after Hearst had failed to induce Hughes to accept the mayoralty nomination, his *New York American* (October 16, 1905) was denouncing the Republican bosses for trying "to take away the brilliant and uncompromising investigator who is following the trail of financial perfidy and crime" in the in-

[18] Author's interview with CEH, Dec. 3, 1947.
[19] New York *Evening Post*, Oct. 9, 1905.

surance investigation. "It is to the everlasting honor of Charles Evans Hughes," Hearst's organ continued, "that he saw through this intrigue and refused to be the dupe of Ryan and Odell." Hearst ran against McClellan and William M. Ivans, the Republican nominee, and came close to equaling McClellan's vote.

Hughes assumed that he had burned his political bridges. His chance of receiving another Republican nomination seemed about equal to that of the bosses putting their fingers twice into the same fire. But this consequence of his independence did not disturb him, and it immeasurably enhanced his standing with the public. ". . . his refusal to be a Mayoralty nominee is as praiseworthy as his nomination by the party managers in convention was reprehensible," commented the *New York Herald*. "This action," chimed in *World's Work*, "is a good measure of the quality of the man." "His declination was so fine," declared the *Evening Post*, "that everyone wishes his duty had allowed him to make it an acceptance." In contrast to the "mire of moral rottenness" that the insurance investigation was exposing, Hughes' conduct stood out as a beacon of new hope for democratic government.

The investigation went forward without interruption. Hughes keenly felt its responsibility. The future of a great business and billions of dollars belonging to policyholders were at stake in addition to the reputations of numerous business and political leaders. Because the committee did not allow counsel to appear for witnesses or to cross-examine them, Hughes took special precautions to avoid any unfairness. He encouraged witnesses to explain or defend any conduct that had been brought into question. When the phalanx of lawyers in the front seats suggested questions, he himself would pass them along to the witnesses.

Not content to get the whole truth into the record, Hughes often called in the newsmen to make certain that they understood complicated or elusive testimony. The public as well as the committee, he felt, was entitled to the facts. Almost to a man, the reporters were friendly to him, although some were doing their utmost to sensationalize the investigation. By his frequent seminar sessions Hughes took the rough edges off many stories and convinced the reporters that he was "trying to cut out a cancerous growth and restore the victim to health—not to slay dragons for the sake of public applause." [20]

Sometimes the burden seemed too heavy to be borne. Night work, often continuing as late as 2:00 A.M., repeatedly cut into his rest. When he did get to bed, his nerves would be too taut to be relaxed in sleep. Indeed, his capacity for quick relaxation was permanently impaired. He began to take an alcoholic drink each night before going to bed to help release his mind from its charge.

"I can't see an end to this," he exclaimed to his wife on several occasions when his feeling of depression seemed especially acute. "It is too much.

[20] Author's interview with CEH, Oct. 17, 1946.

I simply can't go on." [21] But after a night's rest he would start again with unrelenting vigor.

Great reputations began to crumble. Men who dealt in millions and were mentally conditioned only to the giving of commands suddenly found themselves accounting to a lean and persistent lawyer for transactions they had supposed to be safely hidden by the trickery of bookkeeping. It became a common experience for them to come into the hearing room with lordly self-assurance and leave in a gray fog of disgrace.

Portly Richard A. McCurdy, president of Mutual Life, came breezing into the limelight with an air of aloofness to petty inquisitions. Elegantly dressed and wearing a large seal ring, McCurdy seated himself with enviable composure, removed his gold-rimmed pince-nez, and asked that the shades be drawn to shut out the glare of the sunlight. Having seen a dozen insurance investigations that had come to nothing, he intended to take this one in stride.

When Hughes pressed him on the exorbitant salaries and commissions paid by his organization, McCurdy expatiated grandly upon the virtues of life insurance. It is no ordinary business, he boasted. The men who organized Mutual did so "from a pure spirit of philanthropy" on the theory "that it was a great beneficent missionary institution."

"Well," Hughes replied, "you have made a very full explanation. . . . The question comes back to the salaries of the missionaries." [22]

"Well, all right," the witness snorted.

Hughes showed that "Missionary" McCurdy and his vice president held enough proxies from policyholders to control the election of the trustees who had increased his salary over a period of years from $30,000 to $150,000 annually. Another of the "missionaries," Robert H. McCurdy, the president's son, had received $530,788 from the company in sixteen years, in addition to commissions on the company's foreign business (at first calculated at 5 per cent and later reduced at his own request) amounting to $1,268,390, part of which was paid to an associate. The president's son-in-law, Louis A. Thebaud, had drawn $147,687 in commissions in 1904. The *World* estimated the "take" of the McCurdy clan, including syndicate and trust-company profits, at $15,000,000 [23] during their reign over this "autocracy, maintained almost without challenge."

In an effort to determine how much the $150,000 president knew about the business of the company, Hughes asked him a simple question about calculation of premiums.

"You are trying to prove me a fool," McCurdy retorted. "I refer you to the actuary."

"Without commenting upon that, Mr. McCurdy," dryly replied the investi-

[21] CEH, Notes, p. 177. [22] *Hearings*, II, 1842. [23] Oct. 15, 1905.

gator, "I want to ask *you*. . . ." [24] He repeated his question about premiums. McCurdy stubbornly refused to venture upon any such demonstration of his knowledge of the business. But in the course of his examination he said enough to show that his ignorance of his own company was astounding.

From the *Denver Post*, October 19, 1905.

SOME OF THEM ARE COMING OUT OF
THE LITTLE END OF THE HORN!

What Mutual called "legal expenses" amounted in 1904 to the exorbitant figure of $364,254. Many payments from this "legal expense" fund were made at the behest of Andrew C. Fields, head of the "supply department." Fields maintained a house at Albany—promptly dubbed the "House of Mirth" by the press—at which lawmakers were entertained in gratitude for their work in controlling legislation. Senators William J. Graney and Charles P. McClelland, of the Senate's Insurance Committee, had lived at the "House of Mirth" as the guests of Fields. Before his election McClelland had had $3,000 a year from Mutual as an "adviser on legislation." For other favored legislators there were poker games in which lawmakers always won.

Fields left for parts unknown soon after the committee began its hearings.

[24] *Hearings*, II, 1870–1872.

But Hughes showed that all the expenses of the "House of Mirth," including the wages of the cook, the rent, and all the supplies used, were charged to "legal expenses." Fields also acted for Equitable. The investigation brought to light numerous memoranda from Equitable's Thomas D. Jordan (who also had disappeared) instructing Fields to oppose, or in some cases to promote, legislation in which the big insurance companies were interested. The evidence also showed that an examiner in the State Insurance Department had been appointed on requests from Fields and a Senator living at the "House of Mirth."

Hughes laid bare an organized scheme on the part of the big insurance companies to control legislation throughout the United States. To avoid duplication of effort, they had divided the country into four districts. Lobbyists for Mutual undertook to "kill" all "unfavorable" legislation in one of these districts; New York Life lobbyists took over the second, and Equitable lobbyists the third, the fourth being regarded as open territory.

"They have been organized into an offensive and defensive alliance," Hughes concluded, "to procure or to prevent the passage of laws affecting not only insurance, but a great variety of important interests to which, through subsidiary companies or through connections of their officers, they have become related." [25]

In addition to large gifts to the Republican war chests in 1896, 1900, and 1904, Mutual had helped to elect Republican congressmen and New York legislators. McCurdy claimed not to have heard of any Mutual contributions to state or local campaigns; but Senator Platt later admitted that he had had $10,000 from Mutual "from time to time," and his recollection was that it had come in response to his requests to McCurdy. The president of Mutual admitted that the company had paid $1,000 to William Barnes, Sr., father of the Albany boss, for fighting a change in the insurance law.[26]

Insurance money also flowed freely for the purpose of corrupting the press and influencing public opinion. The companies paid some newspapers for advertisements disguised as news and greased the palms of venal reporters. Even during the investigation, Hughes showed, Mutual sent out "colored statements of its proceedings," which were published in numerous papers throughout the country "at a cost of one dollar a line." [27]

While the income of executives and concealed expenditures for illegitimate purposes had skyrocketed, Mutual's dividends had taken a nosedive. Between 1885 and 1904 the company's total income had increased from $20,214,954 to $81,002,984, but dividends to policyholders had fallen from $3,183,023 to $2,674,207. Total payments to policyholders had also fallen drastically in

[25] *Hughes Report*, p. 394. [26] New York *World*, Oct. 18, 1905.
[27] *Hughes Report*, p. 22.

relation to total income. McCurdy's explanation was that "large rewards" are justified in return for "large achievements."

Not all the foregoing details about Mutual were elicited from President McCurdy himself. But his "terrible hours" of writhing, twisting, and blustering on the witness stand brought the story of scandalous mismanagement of a great enterprise to a fitting climax. As McCurdy's confessions entangled him deeper and deeper in a web of ignominy, his counsel, James M. Beck, arose and charged Hughes with giving cues "to the most sensational newspaper attacks." "I don't impute to Mr. Hughes any intention to be unfair," he said, "but I do say that the net result is quite as unfair to the witness as if it were Mr. Hughes' intention that it should be unfair."

"The record is far more eloquent than anything I can possibly say," Hughes replied, "of the extreme courtesy and fairness with which this investigation has been conducted. . . . The witness who gets himself into a false position has only himself to blame. Candor and straight-forwardness will ever be treated as they deserve to be treated, and evasion will always be held up to the contempt which it also deserves." [28]

Round after round of applause came from the big audience in the chamber. Chairman Armstrong pounded with his gavel and threatened for the seventh time to clear the room. As soon as he had a chance to speak, McCurdy cut the ground from beneath his counsel by saying: "May I avail myself of the opportunity to express myself in entire concurrence with the remarks of Mr. Hughes . . . the self-restraint that he has imposed upon himself . . . I have noticed with admiration, not to say gratitude." [29]

Probably McCurdy realized at the time that he was ruined. Within a month he voluntarily slashed his salary from $150,000 to $75,000. Several weeks before the investigation was finished, he resigned from the company, as did his highly paid son and son-in-law and vice presidents Granniss and Gillette. Broken in health, McCurdy went abroad and died. The McCurdy family restored $815,000 to Mutual.[30]

John A. McCall, president of New York Life, was 225 pounds of self-assurance when he took the witness stand. A former superintendent of insurance in New York and a man who commanded wide respect in business circles, he drew a salary of $100,000 and completely dominated the company through proxy votes.

"As president of the New York Life Insurance Company," Hughes asked, "have you had occasion, from time to time, to direct the drawing of checks on executive order?"

[28] *Hearings*, III, 2021f. [29] *Ibid.*, p. 2024.

[30] Marquis James, *The Metropolitan Life*, (New York, Viking, 1945), p. 161. Copyright, 1945, by Viking Press, Inc.

"Yes, I have," McCall replied.

"Without approval or reference to any committee of the company?"

"Absolutely."

"Has that been a frequent occurrence?"

"Daily."

"For large amounts?"

"For large amounts."

"Amounts in excess of $25,000?"

"Yes."

"In what way is the propriety of the payment determined by other officers of the company?"

"I am the sole judge of that." [31]

Of the $48,000 gift to Theodore Roosevelt's campaign McCall said: "I took the responsibility. The blame is mine." He defended his action as a legitimate effort to maintain a proper monetary standard, although sound money was not an issue in 1904. In addition to by-passing the trustees in this matter, he had made every effort to conceal the nature of the item in the company's books. In the "Hanover Bank Office account," which had concealed the political contributions, Hughes also found a disbursement of $235,000 which tripped McCall into a pathetic series of evasions and contradictions. McCall had authorized the spending of this money, but he would give no clear indication as to what it had been used for. Public confidence suffered a reverberating shock.

Hughes knew precisely how to deal with quibbling. "If a witness evades him," said the *New York Times*, "he is willing to go around the irresponsive answer with infinite patience and elicit a whole body of collateral facts." [32] Sometimes he was criticized for not being brutal enough, but his method brought results. When McCall came back to the stand, Hughes had already assembled proof that the $235,000 could not have been used for any legitimate aspect of the insurance business. No avenue of escape from candor was left. Shaken and worried, McCall began to unfold the full story of his relations with "Judge" Andrew Hamilton.

Hamilton was the key lobbyist of the whole corrupt alliance between the political bosses and the insurance magnates. Supplied with enormous resources, he made a big business of influencing legislators and press agents in many states. McCall admitted that Hamilton was expected to deal with the men who could "produce the results" and "to do whatever was necessary to prevent the attacks the companies feared." In defense of the system he insisted that the insurance executives in every state were "badgered and harassed to death . . . by the introduction of bad bills." "I believe that three-quarters of the

[31] *Hearings*, I, 788. [32] Oct. 1, 1905.

insurance bills introduced in the United States," he said, "are blackmail bills." [33]

New York Life had paid Hamilton $1,312,197 in eleven years. In addition, he had been getting substantial sums from other life-insurance companies. Big insurance was "feeding a monster whose appetite could not be sated."

Hamilton himself had fled to Paris, claimed to be ill, and refused to return until after the investigation was finished. When the committee demanded an accounting for the funds that had been turned over to him, McCall sent his son, John C. McCall, the company's treasurer, to Paris. Young McCall brought back a statement from Hamilton purporting to account for $720,550 which he had retained as compensation or expended during the years 1899 to 1905. But Hamilton had not kept any books or accounts; he had obtained no vouchers from the people to whom he had paid money; he offered no checkbooks, since most of his disbursements had been made in cash—for obvious reasons. In these circumstances his statement was obviously worthless.

Most embarrassing of all was the mysterious $235,000 which McCall had secretly advanced to Hamilton in 1903 and 1904 without authorization from any source. The lobbyist already had ample funds to carry on the work of his "department of legislation and taxation." No purpose whatever could be found for advancing him an additional $235,000. McCall said it had been anticipated that this money might be used in connection with the purchase of a mortgage, but Hughes showed that that purchase had not been made. The fact that Hamilton had charge of purchasing land for the company's "Home Office Annex" was used as a pretext for charging the $235,000 to the real-estate account. But Hughes dug into the records and disclosed the cost of every piece of property bought for the annex and the source of the money used to pay for it. Hamilton could not have spent the $235,000 for that purpose. Moreover, he had cashed the mysterious checks in Albany. At last McCall admitted that the $235,000 belonged to the company and gave a pledge to repay it by December 31, 1905, if Hamilton had not previously done so.[34]

In order to comply with the prerequisites for doing business in Prussia, New York Life had pretended to sell 15,300 shares of stock and thereafter reported to the Insurance Department that "the Company does not invest in stocks of any kind." Actually, Hughes proved, it had not sold its stock. The shares were in the keeping of the New York Security & Trust Company, but they were held as collateral for "dummy" loans in the names of a New York Life bond clerk and a messenger in an aggregate amount of $3,357,000.

Before the inquiry ended, McCall's health was shattered, as well as his reputation. Making arrangements to repay the New York Life the mysterious $235,000 he had turned over to Hamilton, McCall resigned his presidency

[33] *Hearings*, II, 1415. [34] *Hughes Report*, pp. 51–53.

and in a few weeks was dead. His tragedy left him without resentment against the man who brought about his undoing. "Mr. Hughes has been eminently fair," the broken executive told Haley Fiske, later president of the Metropolitan Life.[35] Hughes had only disclosed the truth. It was McCall's misfortune that this lighting of dark corners tended to obscure the constructive work he had done for life insurance in his long career.

George W. Perkins was in a less vulnerable position, but Hughes bore down heavily upon his dual role as a vice president of New York Life and a representative of J. P. Morgan & Company. In a $4,000,000 bond deal Perkins had represented both Morgan, the seller, and New York Life, the buyer.

"When you bargained for the bonds," Hughes asked, "did you bargain for them with any person other than yourself?"

"I can't recollect," Perkins stammered, "but I think I did it myself, probably."

"You were dealing with yourself," Hughes persisted.[36]

Perkins also provided details of a trick to deceive the public and the Insurance Department. New York Life had participated in the Navigation Syndicate and received an allotment of $4,000,000 from the Morgan company. Upon this $3,200,000 was called in 1902, and this amount appeared in the company's annual statement. But the Navigation Syndicate proved to be one of Morgan's most disastrous ventures. When the remaining $800,000 was called in 1903, the insurance company was loath to admit any additional involvement. So it effected one of those familiar year-end "sales" of the stock to Morgan. Three days later, however, it repurchased the stock at the same price—far above its market value. Obviously there had been no bona fide sale. Having arranged this deceptive loan for both companies, Perkins insisted that he had acted "to protect our situation."

"But the only situation you had to protect . . ." Hughes retorted, "was the situation exigent by reason of your making your report to the superintendent of insurance." [37]

New York Life ultimately lost $80,000 on this venture. Perkins was forced to admit the anomalous nature of his dual role and resigned from the insurance company.

James Hazen Hyde's appearance on the witness stand was almost an anticlimax. Hyde had already sold his Equitable stock. The company that he had planned to dominate had undergone an extensive housecleaning. Claiming to act out of philanthropic motives, Thomas F. Ryan, purchaser of the Hyde stock, had placed the shares in a voting trust composed of former President Grover Cleveland, Justice Morgan J. O'Brien, and George Westinghouse. The

[35] Address by Haley Fiske to Association of Life Insurance Presidents, Dec. 4, 1925.
[36] *Hearings*, II, 1219. [37] *Hearings*, I, pp. 758f.

From the *Brooklyn Eagle*, December 8, 1905.

THE PIED PIPER OF LIFE INSURANCE

new chairman of the board of directors, Paul Morton, had effected economies estimated at more than $600,000 a year before the investigation was completed.

After trying to explain to the committee his lavish use of policyholders' funds to give a party for the French ambassador, Hyde's conscience prompted him to repay the $12,000 in question. Hughes also focused attention upon numerous slick practices in which the men of Equitable had indulged. Equitable controlled the Mercantile Trust Company and had very large interests in two other trust companies. "The relations to the Trust Companies have been used," the investigator showed, "to aid in carrying of irregular accounts and to further the interests of individual officers." [38] Equitable maintained cash balances, largely in these trust companies, in the enormous sum of more than $36,000,000 in 1903 and 1904. The obvious purpose, Hughes said, was to enhance the prosperity of the trust companies in which various Equitable bigwigs were interested. To conceal the extent of these unprofitable cash balances, year-end loans were made to Kuhn, Loeb & Company (later in the name of clerks of that company), the cash balances being correspondingly decreased for a few days while the Equitable made its sworn report to the Insurance Department. With the annual report thus safely falsified, the "dummy" loans were promptly canceled.

The inquiry brought out that Jacob Schiff of Kuhn, Loeb & Company had sold to Equitable, of which he was a director, securities valued at $49,704,408 in five and a half years—in the teeth of a state law requiring the dismissal and permanent disqualification of any life-insurance director who profited by "selling or aiding in the sale of any stocks or securities to or by such corporation. . . ." But the basic complaint ran deeper than manipulative abuses and laxity in enforcement of the law. In his report Hughes deplored the whole tie-up between insurance and speculative finance.

The insurance companies were not chartered, he asserted, to make money by speculation, barter, or the development of industry. "They were chartered to furnish life insurance, and the true measure of their power and their duty in the handling of their funds is to invest them with due conservatism, to the end that they may be able to discharge their obligations." [39] The mingling of life insurance with banking and industrial finance was tending toward vast combinations of capital. That dangerous trend should be broken up, he concluded, by forbidding insurance companies to invest in stocks.

Edward H. Harriman brought the committee a tale of sordid intrigue that had failed. With his 16,000 miles of railroad and forty steamships, the hard-boiled financier said that he had little time to think about life insurance. Yet he had moved in to shape the destiny of the great Equitable Society when dissension arose among its officers. Under Hughes' probing, he admitted that he

[38] *Hughes Report*, p. 122. [39] *Ibid.*, p. 384.

had prevented bills from being introduced in the legislature to aid James Alexander's efforts to mutualize the Equitable. Incidentally, Alexander was in a sanatorium and did not appear at the investigation.

"I had the matter watched at Albany," Harriman said, "to see what attempts were being made to use legislation improperly." [40] The men on whom he relied for this service, he claimed, were Governor Higgins and Speaker Nixon.

Harriman had boasted to Hyde that he controlled the New York Legislature.[41] Now he openly proclaimed his political prowess.

"Were you in politics?" Hughes asked.

"No, sir."

"Did you have any political influence?"

"I think I have," Harriman responded.

"Well, it has been openly charged that through your relations with Mr. Odell you have political influence: what would you say to that?"

"Well," the railroad magnate boasted, "I should think Mr. Odell [the former governor and at the time of the inquiry Republican leader in New York] had political influence because of his relations to me." [42]

Harriman's confidence in his political power had led him to believe that he could recoup his lost opportunity even after Ryan had tricked him by buying Hyde's Equitable stock. Apparently he had helped Ryan get his nominee, Morton, elected chairman of the Equitable board and Ryan had then agreed to consult Harriman before taking any further move in the matter. Harriman waited in vain for a call from Ryan. When a message finally came, through Ryan's attorney, it was to the effect that the controlling Equitable stock had been purchased. Harriman was furious. He offered to buy half the stock from Ryan, on condition that he be permitted to name two additional trustees, and, according to Ryan, threatened his rival with adverse legislative action if he should refuse to comply. "Ryan," the *World* aptly commented, "assumed he had become the Equitable. Harriman assumed he was the government of New York." [43] Harriman left the witness stand very little ruffled, but he had contributed greatly to public knowledge of the corrupt working arrangement between the lions of finance and the jackals of politics.

Thomas Fortune Ryan, cool and reserved, came to the witness stand assuming that he could withhold from the Armstrong Committee whatever he did not care to see in print. When Hughes asked him about Harriman's alleged threats, Ryan flatly refused to answer. Here seemed to be an opportunity to entangle the inquiry in a legal contest. Ryan's attorney, Paul Cravath, who had been one of Hughes' first partners, called the investigator by telephone and said that if Hughes would get out an order to show cause, he would be glad to

[40] *Hearings*, VI, 5155. [41] Philip C. Jessup, *Elihu Root*, p. 440.
[42] *Hearings*, VI, pp. 5152–5154.
[43] Editorial, "Equitable Corruption," No. 150, Dec. 13, 1905.

cooperate in having Mr. Ryan's right to decline to answer the questions tested in court.

"Oh, no!" Hughes instantly replied, "I'm going to have him indicted." [44]

Cravath was indignant, but Ryan came back a few days later and answered everything Hughes asked him.

That incident alone is enough to dispose of Hearst's trumped-up charge, in the 1906 campaign, that Ryan had selected Hughes as counsel to the committee. And it does not stand alone. A few weeks later, when Hughes probed into the affairs of the Washington Life, he showed that, under Ryan's management, it had become a heavy buyer in what were known as "Ryan securities," and most of its stock and bond purchases had been made through a brokerage firm of which Ryan's sons were members. Hughes' treatment of Ryan was the same fair, fearless, and impartial treatment that was accorded every other witness.

Senator Thomas C. Platt was probably the most candid of the New York bosses who paraded before the committee. Before leaving his office to testify, he put into his pocket letters from several members of the committee asking contributions in their campaigns of former years.[45] But no committeeman attempted to prevent Hughes from calling the "easy boss" or to interfere with his examination.

Platt confessed that each of the big insurance companies customarily gave him $10,000 which he turned over to the Republican State Committee for the election of pliable legislators. After some preliminary fencing, the ugly truth came out in this colloquy:

> HUGHES. Now, isn't that the way it really comes about, Senator, that the use of these contributions in the election of candidates to office puts the candidate more or less under a moral obligation not to attack the interest supporting him?
>
> PLATT. That is naturally what would be involved.
>
> HUGHES. But isn't that really what is involved?
>
> PLATT. I should think so.
>
> HUGHES. That is what you meant when you said that they would expect you, through your relations to the State Committee, to defend them?
>
> PLATT. Yes, sir.[46]

Platt had previously admitted that, in return for these contributions, he held himself in readiness to fight bills in the legislature hostile to the insurance interests. It was a triangular arrangement. The "interests" controlled the bosses by paying them "boodle"; the bosses controlled the legislature by use of this money in campaigns; and the legislature protected the "interests" in their exploitation of the public. "The frank admission that moneys have been obtained

[44] Author's interview with CEH, April 16, 1946.
[45] *Outlook*, Vol. 84, pp. 404–407. [46] *New York Times*, Nov. 23, 1905.

for use in state campaigns upon the expectation that candidates thus aided in their election would support the interests of the companies," Hughes wrote, "has exposed both those who solicited the contributions and those who made them to severe and just condemnation."

Senator Chauncey M. Depew shamefacedly told of drawing a $20,000 annual retainer from Equitable, of which he was a director. The arrangement had been made by the elder Hyde, whom Depew advised as to investments and various "troublesome questions," and was continued by his successors for many years. "The testimony as to the services [rendered] is very general," Hughes commented with characteristic understatement, "and it does not appear that outside of those which the society was fairly entitled to receive from him as a director, the services were such as to warrant the payments made."[47] The reformed management cut off this retainer, and Depew resigned as a director. An attempt was made to force his resignation from the Senate, but he held on until the end of his term.

Benjamin B. Odell, Jr., came before the investigators haggard and angry. The man who had refused to accept nomination for the mayorship of New York at Odell's hands now put the former Governor through a searching examination as to an alleged shakedown of the Mercantile Trust Company. Odell had invested $184,171 in bonds of the United States Shipbuilding Company, for which Mercantile was trustee. Having sold the bonds at a loss of $125,482, he brought suit against Mercantile to make it good. Before the suit was filed, however, bills were introduced in both houses of the legislature for repeal of the law incorporating the Mercantile Company.

In these circumstances the Mercantile Company settled Odell's claim through negotiations for $75,000. Odell vehemently denied that any threat was made and insisted that the bills had not been introduced at his request. Yet the fact remained that he knew about and approved the bills to repeal the company's charter before they were introduced, and his guardian in the financial world, Mr. Harriman, had suggested to Mr. Hyde, vice president of the trust company, that the claim be settled "in view of the powerful interests in Albany which were antagonistic to the Mercantile Trust Company."

The nature of Hughes' findings was not changed much when he turned to the State Insurance Department. Superintendent Francis Hendricks' stock reply to questions put to him on the witness stand seemed to be, "I don't know." For six years he had been complacently examining insurance companies' reports without exposing any of the irregularities that Hughes uncovered within a few months. Ample authority was at his command, but he had not used it. Companies were deceiving the department by "glaringly false returns," and the department did not even recognize the fact. No attempt had

[47] *Hughes Report*, p. 106.

been made to ascertain the nature of the companies' expenditures. Not one of the sinkholes into which vast sums were being poured for lobbying and vote-buying had been uncovered. In short, the reports of the superintendent of insurance were nothing more than misleading propaganda. "Most of the evils which have been disclosed by the investigation," Hughes concluded, "would have been impossible had there been a vigorous performance of the duties already laid upon the department." [48] Hendricks recognized that his position was untenable and retired.

In spite of the drama of crumbling reputations and falling official heads, Hughes was not primarily concerned with personalities. Wasteful, hazardous, and dishonest practices were his chief target. When District Attorney Jerome started a movement to have Hughes prosecute all the culprits exposed as law violators by the insurance investigation, the latter promptly scotched it.[49] His job was to diagnose the sickness of the business and to prescribe a remedy, and he refused to be diverted to the building up of criminal cases. Several insurance-company officials were later indicted, but the cases against them came to nothing. It was the housecleanings that the investigation inspired and the legislation that it brought about which gave it a significant place in American history.

Every detail of the policies that the companies sold to their patrons came under scrutiny. Were the terms fair to policyholders? What was the record of performance on the contracts? Was the cost of getting new business excessive? Frequently it was an idea that cracked up under Hughes' cyclotronic bombardment. That is what happened to the idea of deferred-dividend policies which had been popular with various companies. The scheme of these policies called "tontine" was to hold back for ten, fifteen, or twenty years all accumulations that would otherwise have been available for dividends. In the case of death before the expiration of the fixed period, only the face value of the policy would be paid. If a policy lapsed, everything would be lost. At the end of the period, the survivors would share the accumulated profits.

The advantages of such policies went largely to the companies. "They permitted the accumulation of profits for long periods without accounting," [50] and the tendency was for those profits to be frittered away through exorbitant salaries, commissions, and other expenses for obtaining new business. Hughes concluded, with the concurrence of the full committee, that no more deferred-dividend policies should be written in New York.

Through fifty-seven public hearings over a period of four months the exposé continued. The press carried the story to every town and city. University presidents and preachers joined editors and humble citizens in condemning the

[48] *Ibid.*, p. 356. [49] Author's interview with CEH, April 16, 1946.
[50] *Hughes Report*, pp. 421–422.

men in places of trust who had proved to be "reckless speculators" and "pilferers with the savings of the poor." The life-insurance business throughout the country was shaken to its foundations, but the result was to dislodge the exploiters and their practices and leave the business infinitely sounder than before.

The investigation had not been a complete success. The committee decided to close its hearings before Hamilton, Fields, Jordan, and other key figures could be found within its jurisdiction. "At the close of the investigation," Hughes said, in a statement praising the committee for its fairness, courage, and intelligence, "I am impressed more with what we have failed to do than what we have done. So many phases of life insurance developed that it is a matter of regret to me that we have not been able to go on and do thorough work in all the directions that have been suggested." [51] But that modest appraisal found slight echo in the public response.

The investigation, said the *World*, "has restored faith in legislative committees as a means of bringing the truth to light. It has given us Charles E. Hughes as another magnificent example of the man who is willing to serve the public, who has a service of the highest order to give to the public, and who can be neither intimidated nor betrayed." [52] "Nobody in New York," agreed Hearst's *American*, "will question the excellence of the work done by the counsel for the people, Mr. Charles E. Hughes. . . ." [53] Hughes, the chorus continued, is "the chief figure on the right side of the most important inquiry of its kind in recent American history." "This man ought to be kept in public life if possible, why not make him governor?" [54]

Probably the most significant comment was that of the *Outlook*: "It has been a dash of cold water upon the face after a time of moral drowsiness. It has set the public conscience stirring." [55] Hughes, too, believed that the public awakening was the most striking aspect of the inquiry. A "vindication of the sound moral sense of the American people," he called it. He had brought into public life in New York a new standard of morality, a new concept of the public interest and of the power of the people to make their will prevail.

In Montreal, where he had gone with Mrs. Hughes for a few days of rest, the acclaimed investigator was amused to encounter, at the top of Mount Royal, an exiled lobbyist by the name of Buckley whom he had been trying to subpoena. One glance at the whiskered nemesis put Buckley in flight, while Hughes laughed heartily.

Back in New York, Hughes plunged into the writing of the report. Several insurance men had importuned the committee to forgo a formal report, and

[51] New York *World*, Dec. 31, 1905. [52] Jan. 1, 1906. [53] Dec. 30, 1905.
[54] Public reaction reported by Ida Tarbell in *American Magazine*, March, 1908.
[55] Nov. 4, 1905.

Counsel McKeen emerged to support the argument. But Hughes insisted that a comprehensive report be made. Chairman Armstrong and a majority of the committee agreed and gave Hughes a broad mandate to finish his work. In six weeks of day and night toil he brought together in fewer than five hundred pages the salient facts about every New York life-insurance company, summarized the abuses he had found, and concluded with sweeping recommendations for legislative action. Every word of the report was his, although it carries only the names of the committee members.

From the *New York Herald*, January 2, 1906.

PREPARED FOR THE WORST

After conferring with the committee, Hughes also drew up bills to carry out his recommendations. Then he went to Albany to explain the bills to legislators and the press. By April, 1906, the legislature had completed enactment of these bills, giving New York what Haley Fiske later declared to be "the best insurance legislation the world has ever known." [56]

One of these measures prohibited insurance companies (and other corporations) from making contributions to political campaigns. Another forced

[56] Fiske's address to the Association of Life Insurance Presidents, Dec. 4, 1925.

the registration of lobbyists, with public disclosure of the nature of their services, expenses, and compensation. Congress soon followed the first of these leads with its Corrupt Practices Act of 1907, but forty years passed before it similarly required the registration of lobbyists at Washington.

The acts dealing more directly with insurance provided machinery for mutualizing stock companies; outlawed existing proxies and required new elections with wider policyholder participation; prohibited the writing of the unsound deferred-dividend policies and required dividends to be paid annually; prescribed standard policies "simple in form and clear and concise in language"; required the companies to give to policyholders who discontinued the payment of premiums policies representing an appropriate ratio to the premiums already paid; limited the amount of new insurance that any company could write in one year so as to minimize the wasteful scramble for new business; required action by the full board of directors to approve all salaries over $5,000 a year; limited commissions and other expenses; required vouchers for all expenditures of a hundred dollars or more and annual reports in much greater detail, including data on lobbying expenditures; tightened up the law against making false reports; made triennial examinations of all companies mandatory; required the companies to dispose of speculative securities within five years and forbade them to hold stocks in banks, trust companies, or other corporations; forbade participation in syndicates; prohibited officers and agents from holding pecuniary interests in transactions with their companies; and opened the courts to suits by policyholders against the companies.

These laws were widely copied in other states and became the foundation on which modern insurance in America rests. Temporarily the investigation and the new laws hurt some of the New York companies. A survey in 1909 by William H. Hotchkiss, New York superintendent of insurance, indicated that insurance in force with New York companies decreased $126,213,453 in 1906, the first year following the investigation. But in the same period the business of companies organized outside of New York increased by more than twice that sum, and the purged New York companies soon regained their losses.

More significant is the estimate by Hotchkiss that in 1908 the savings in general management expenses of thirty-four New York insurance companies amounted to $4,817,500. Savings in the cost of writing new policies he placed at $4,864,500, making a total saving of $9,682,000 to policyholders in a single year as a result of the insurance investigation.[57]

Some resentment against Hughes lingered among insurance men. One critic went so far as to denounce the investigation as a "Socialistic assault on the pillars of civilization." But the more intelligent insurance men realized that Hughes had given their business an invaluable charter of reform. When he addressed

[57] Hotchkiss' report, CEH's private papers.

the Life Underwriters Association of New York shortly after the new insurance laws had been enacted, he was greeted by applause, cheering, and waving of napkins for "what seemed an interminable length of time." [58] Thirty-four years later Frederick H. Ecker, chairman of the board of the Metropolitan Life, concluded that Hughes was "in considerable part" responsible for the prosperity of the life-insurance business.[59] Especially during the great upheaval of the thirties, insurance men and informed policyholders alike felt in their bones a deep thankfulness to Charles E. Hughes. He had transformed the insurance business from "a public swindle to a public trust."

[58] *Life Insurance Notes*, June, 1906.

[59] *St. Louis Post-Dispatch*, March 26, 1939.

Chapter 16

THE CAMPAIGN AGAINST HEARST

PRESIDENT THEODORE ROOSEVELT had followed the insurance investigation with keen interest and approval. Apparently he took no offense at Hughes' exposure of the lavish corporate gifts that had gone into his campaign fund in 1904. In any event, he concluded that he could make good use of an investigator of Hughes' ability and asked him to take charge of an inquiry into combinations in restraint of trade and other illegal practices in the coal industry. Hughes acquiesced.

Roosevelt tested the temperament of his new investigator by asking for advice on an appointment. He wished to know whether the insurance investigation had reflected upon the individual in question so as to make his appointment inadvisable. Hughes answered the President's letter with great care, setting forth the facts in the case and concluding that the proposed nominee had not really been discredited. Roosevelt was "DElighted" and said that Hughes' fair and impartial answer reflected a commendable freedom from vindictiveness.[1]

These two striking personalities met for the first time on Easter Monday, 1906. A conference on the coal investigation had taken Hughes to Washington. He found Attorney General William H. Moody eager to get the investigation completed before the transfer of Secretary of War William H. Taft to the Supreme Court, then scheduled for the coming fall. Actually it was Moody and not Taft who went to the Supreme Court, and the coal investigation, too, was to be left to other hands. Indeed, the President was already thinking of Hughes in a quite different role. When the investigator went to the White House with the Attorney General—his second visit there that day—Roosevelt and his secretary, William Loeb, were standing by a window in a holiday mood. Hughes joined them in watching the Easter egg-rolling festival on the lawn. As his guest was leaving, the President said, "In the next Republican convention you will have two votes for governor—mine and Loeb's." [2]

Pleased by this compliment, Hughes nevertheless dismissed it as "only a pleasantry." [3] The idea of exploiting his prestige as an investigator to win public office struck no responsive chord in him. His primary interest still lay in the

[1] Beerits' Memorandum, III, 8. [2] *Ibid.*, p. 9. [3] CEH, Notes, p. 178.

law, and, aside from some preliminary work on the coal inquiry, his whole energy was devoted to picking up the threads of his neglected practice. But talk of his nomination for governor spread like ripples on the disturbed surface of a pond.

Hughes got a firsthand report on these political reverberations when he chanced to drop in at the University Club while working with Samuel Untermyer on a big shipbuilding case. There he met Frank H. Simonds, Albany correspondent for the New York *Daily Tribune*, whom he had come to know well through the insurance investigation. Simonds predicted with remarkable foresight that his whiskered friend would be the Republican nominee for governor and that William Randolph Hearst would run against him.

Hughes protested that during the insurance investigation he had been gall and wormwood to many Republican leaders. By exposing the failings of the Insurance Department he had subjected the Republican régime at Albany to an avalanche of criticism. When he refused to run for mayor after his nomination in 1905, the party leaders had been highly irritated. They would never consent to his nomination for governor, Hughes said.

"But the governor elected this year may occupy the White House in two years," Simonds persisted.

"That, too, has no attraction for me," Hughes replied. "My one desire is to be left alone in my profession." [4]

In June, 1906, Brown University conferred an honorary degree of Doctor of Laws upon her distinguished alumnus and trustee. President Faunce's salutation is still remembered: ". . . investigator without malice and without fear, skillful to use the probe but not the rake, through whose labor the public conscience has been quickened and purified." Charles Junior proudly witnessed the ceremony as a freshman completing his first year at Brown.

More concerned with recuperation from the strain of past toil than with any political future, Hughes took his son to Europe in July. His disinterest in politics stands out from the following paragraph of a letter written to his father and mother from Edinburgh on July 26:

> I was informed yesterday by the Cable Company that a code name had been registered for Communications with Timothy L. Woodruff—and I suppose there will be cables ere long. (Keep this to yourselves of course.) As soon as I have an opportunity I shall put a quietus on the whole business. It's the only thing that worries me. It gives me a cold sweat to think of going through a Campaign with the alternative of defeat or two years at Albany. I don't [know] which would be worse. I can be of more service and far happier in my chosen profession. So "fling away" any political ambition you may have for your son—and take counsel of your philosophy—for of all vanities there is no vanity like that of politics.

[4] *Everybody's Magazine*, October, 1906.

In his letters to his wife it was their separation and not politics that concerned him most. His letter of August 3 reechoes a familiar refrain:

YOU DEAR OLD SWEETHEART,

To think of one at my age receiving such a love letter as I received this morning! Dearest, we must arrange in the future not to be separated in our holidays—life is too short and our love is too strong. Your letter was like a long draught from the old home well. And the sweet poem, darling, I shall always cherish. You must *not* worry about me, sweetheart—I am doing pretty well. . . .

C.

While Hughes and his son were "doing London," he wrote:

Charlie left his watch under the pillow at Oban and I was duly superior, paternal and severe. But alas! I left my drawers at Edinburgh (Ramie's at that) and I have walked humbly (and somewhat coolly) ever since. If I do not recover my reason, I may have to come home in kilts—à la "Hielan Willie." Charlie wrote for his watch and it came today—wonderful to tell! I didn't have the nerve to write for my panties and of course they haven't come. Charlie is a good boy and doesn't say much.[5]

Walking quietly together one evening, each began to wish they were in Switzerland. As soon as they realized they were of the same mind, they changed their plans and revisited the old haunts they loved so well. While there, Hughes received word that Odell had suggested his nomination for governor, but he refused even to nibble at the bait. Continuing his relaxation into September, he returned to New York only two and a half weeks before the Republican state convention at Saratoga.

Governor Higgins, who was too ill to consider another term, had thrown his support to Lieutenant Governor M. Linn Bruce. But astute politicians saw no hope of victory in Bruce or in any candidate from their own circle. The people of New York were in open revolt against bossism and the exploitation that had characterized Republican rule for many years. Even Theodore Roosevelt, who had been elected governor by a narrow margin in 1898 on the strength of San Juan Hill, had sought his reforms by working with the bosses. Once when he had a judge to appoint he had said over and over again to Odell that he wanted to name a certain individual. "Well," Odell had replied, "why don't you?" "Can I? Can I?" T. R. had queried.[6]

After Roosevelt, Odell had given the state four years of direct boss control. Then came the Higgins administration, carried into office by the strength of the Roosevelt presidential campaign in 1904. Quiet and honest, Higgins had ousted some of the exploiters but he could not control the organization. By 1906 even the bosses had to admit that only a miracle could save them from

[5] CEH to his wife, Aug. 10, 1906.
[6] Odell to Hughes to author, interview April 16, 1946.

resounding defeat. In their desperation it became increasingly difficult to suppress the name of the now famous insurance investigator.

Hughes himself remained silent, apparently forgetting the quietus that he had talked about in July. To his friends he said: "I do not desire office; I am not a candidate; any man who knows me knows that. But, in the present emergency, to declare myself out of the field would be to put myself forever beyond the possibility of rendering a public service, if the peculiar conditions now prevailing should later lead that way." [7]

Herbert Parsons, the Republican committeeman for New York County, took the lead in pressing for a candidate who could arouse the enthusiasm of the people. That meant Hughes. Parsons aired his views at the White House and obtained a hearty endorsement from the President. Going to Saratoga for the convention of September 25, he began to sound out the delegates. He found Odell, who controlled about one-third of the delegates, trying to swing the nomination to former Governor Black. Other bosses were promoting their favorites. In a long conference before the final session of the convention, Parsons and Senator Page talked earnestly in favor of Hughes as "the strongest man." But the bosses were not convinced. What assurance did they have that Hughes would be loyal to the party?

"I never spoke to this man," blurted William Barnes, Jr., boss of Albany, whose letter chiding an insurance company because of its delay in forwarding the "usual honorarium" to his father had been read at the insurance investigation.

"I never saw him," protested George W. Aldridge, chief political dictator of up-State New York.

"Gentlemen, I have met him—once," [8] lamented Francis Hendricks, boss of Syracuse and former superintendent of insurance, with understandable acerbity.

Parsons and Page sent word to Oyster Bay that they needed help. Roosevelt replied through Postmaster General Cortelyou and Congressman William W. Cocks: "I think that Mr. Hughes is the strongest candidate before the convention. We need just his qualities in the coming campaign." [9] With this emphatic endorsement on record, the convention could not reject Hughes without also repudiating Roosevelt. The bosses bowed to "mournful necessity." The next morning Job E. Hedges presented Hughes' name, and he was unanimously nominated by a convention in which he had no instructed delegates, no partisan politicians and only hostility on the part of the bosses. His only asset was the confidence of the people.

Hughes responded with a telegram that rubbed salt into the bosses' wounds:

[7] *Outlook*, Oct. 20, 1906. [8] *Ibid.*
[9] B. J. Hendrick in *McClure's Magazine*, March, 1908.

I thank you for your confidence. . . . I shall accept the nomination without pledge other than to do my duty according to my conscience. If elected, it will be my ambition to give the State a sane, efficient and honorable administration, free from taint of bossism or of servitude to any private interest.[10]

President Roosevelt wired Hughes, "I rejoice for the sake of the cause of good citizenship in your nomination." T. R. was enjoying "the astonishment of many of the Republican leaders of my native State and city at finding how very respectable their party has suddenly become." In some measure Roosevelt shared the bosses' concern about the rise of a popular and independent figure in his home state. At the moment, however, it was a welcome alternative to "disaster at the polls." "Hughes' nomination," the President wrote, "is an excellent thing for the morale of the Republican party . . . he is identified in the public mind as a reformer, but a sane and sincere reformer, who really has fought against the very evils which Hearst denounces, while yet free from any taint of demagogy." [11]

The President's attitude failed to dispel the gloom at Saratoga. Some of the organization men hoped that their candidate, in divorcing himself from bossism, was indulging in campaign buncombe. But those who knew Hughes best saw in his declaration of independence a gage of battle within the party. Dark forebodings were held in check only by the ominous news that had come from Buffalo, where the Democratic Party had nominated William Randolph Hearst for governor.

Hearst was at the apex of his political career. In 1904 he had spent $600,000 trying to get the Democratic presidential nomination and had won a substantial following in the West. His drive for a political stronghold in the East had carried him within a few thousand votes of capturing the mayoralty of New York in a three-cornered race in 1905. Now he was making a determined drive to obtain the New York governorship so as to strengthen his bid for the Presidency in 1908.

When Hearst lost the mayoralty, he had accused the Tammany boss, Charles F. Murphy, of stealing the election. Murphy had been cartooned in the Hearst press in prison stripes and called an "evil specimen of a criminal boss." [12] A year later, however, Hearst accepted Murphy's support in grabbing the Democratic gubernatorial nomination. His ambition had to be gratified at any price. Edmund Wetmore caught the essentials of the situation in a verse in which he had Hearst saying,

So I lashed him and I thrashed him in my hot reforming zeal,
Then I clasped him to my bosom in a most artistic deal.

[10] New York *Daily Tribune*, Sept. 27, 1906.

[11] *Selections from the Correspondence of Theodore Roosevelt and Henry Cabot Lodge*, (New York. Scribner's, 1925), II, 239. Copyright, 1925, by Charles Scribner's Sons.

[12] Oliver Carlson and Ernest Sutherland Bates, *Hearst: Lord of San Simeon*, p. 150.

Murphy was willing to team up with his former enemy because he had broken with Mayor McClellan and was frightened by Hearst's vote-getting power. Together they took control of the Democratic convention by throwing out anti-Hearst delegates from twenty-one districts and seating rival groups that were prepared to do their bidding. The powerful Tammany machine was thus harnessed with the country's greatest journalistic rabble-rouser. Hearst also had in his favor a wave of popular sympathy resulting from the widespread belief that he had been swindled of the 1905 election.

It was against this background that Hughes weighed his "call to duty." "If there appeared to be a contest between two forces equally worthy," he told an interviewer, ". . . there would be nothing in the office for which I have been nominated that could appeal to me." [13] His innate modesty did not prevent him from seeing that he was the only man in the state who had a chance of defeating Hearst. Roosevelt also saw it; the Republican bosses saw it; and so did a great majority of the informed voters.

Hughes mapped out the strategy of his campaign the night after his nomination. His acceptance speech at the Republican Club in New York City on October 3—the first political address he ever made—set the tone of his appeal. It began with a bow to "the achievements of our great leader, Theodore Roosevelt," and then swung sharply to state issues. In contrast to the "noisy pretensions of the hour," he pointed to the substantial achievements of the gas and insurance investigations and the legislation they had produced. But the real issue was not the Republican record or any difference of principle between the old-line parties. It was not a partisan issue at all. "It is," he said, "the vital issue of decent government. The question is whether the unholy alliance that succeeded at Buffalo shall capture the State of New York." The choice between orderly reform and the play upon ignorance to further selfish ambition, he felt, should array on one side all lovers of truth and sobriety, whether they be Republicans, Democrats, or Independents.[14]

Some feared that Hughes would not be an effective campaigner. The insurance investigation had given rise to rumors that he was a "mental machine, a human icicle" devoid of emotions and lacking any warmth of personality. A cartoonist had pictured the ship which brought him back from Europe on a hot day in 1906 as draped with icicles and smothered with frost because of his presence on it. Many who had witnessed the intensity of his efforts in the two legislative inquiries were ready to accept this view. In those tense and dramatic situations he had had no time or inclination to be a good fellow. Nor did he play to the galleries with the expectation of emerging a popular hero. In this sense Hughes *was* unusual; there was a good deal of justification for writing

[13] Ervin Wardman in *Review of Reviews*, November, 1906, p. 550.

[14] CEH, *Addresses 1906–1916* (New York, Putnam, 1916), p. 60. Copyright, 1916, by G. P. Putnam's Sons.

him down as a *rara avis*. But the assumption that he was a cold fish or a sort of legal calculating machine without human feelings was a mile wide of the mark.

When he began to campaign, people were relieved to note that he told amusing stories, that he laughed spontaneously with his whole body, that he was a good handshaker, and that he met men and women in all walks of life with friendliness and keen interest in their problems. The public began to learn what Hughes' close friends had always known—that beneath his reserve he was "a buoyant and joyful person, fond of books of all sorts, music, golf, mountain climbing, friends, family, college and church." [15] John Palmer Gavit of the *Evening Post* described him as "the most straightforward, intellectually honest, transparently sincere person I ever have known; at the same time one of the most companionable, most *human* men it has been my fortune to meet." [16]

Hughes often turned the reports of his icy disposition to good account. Once when some one urged him to "warm up" and suggested that every candidate had the duty of kissing babies, he replied, with a twinkle in his eye, "No, I will not make any appeal to the passions of the populace." [17] On another occasion when he encountered a ridiculous yarn illustrating his supposed frigidity, he exclaimed, "I hope that, if an autopsy is ever performed upon me, you will find something besides sawdust and useful information." [18]

As the campaign warmed up, Hughes bore down heavily on Hearst's demagogy while sparing his private life. "The man who would corrupt public opinion," he declared, "is the most dangerous enemy of the state. . . . As against reckless denunciation, I set fair criticism. As against indiscriminate attacks upon business organizations, I set a serious and determined attempt to ascertain the evil and to remedy it." Here is an issue, he continued, which transcends all the questions on which we may differ. "When, in a flame of passion, you once get a feeling existing which ignores reason and dispassionate discussion, how are you going to make progress? Flame feeds flame . . . let us settle once for all that this is a government of sound public opinion and not a government of insanity and appeal to the passions of the ignorant and the thoughtless." [19]

His faith in public opinion ran deep. "We have in this country," he declared, "but one security. You may think that the Constitution is your security—it is nothing but a bit of paper. You may think the statutes are your security—they are nothing but words in a book. You may think that elaborate mechanism of

[15] Ida M. Tarbell in *American Magazine*, March, 1908, pp. 451–464.
[16] New York *Evening Post*, June 10, 1916.
[17] Frank H. Simonds in *Putnam's Monthly*, October, 1907.
[18] B. J. Hendrick in *McClure's Magazine*, March, 1908.
[19] *New York Times*, Oct. 6, 1906.

government is your security—it is nothing at all, unless you have sound and uncorrupted public opinion to give life to your Constitution, to give vitality to your statutes, to make efficient your governmental machinery." [20]

When Hearst assailed him as a corporation lawyer, Hughes showed that Hearst himself was the head of fourteen corporations, some of them organized to evade taxes and responsibility for libel. Hearst's response took the form of ridicule and defamation. His newspapers pretended to believe that Ryan had chosen Hughes as counsel in the insurance investigation. One of his papers said that the attorney general of New York had retained Hughes to assist in arguing a case growing out of the gas investigation and that Hughes had taken the fee and gone to Europe. Actually, Hughes had argued the case and had neither asked nor received one cent of compensation for it.

Hearst reached the nadir of his campaign when he called his bewhiskered opponent an "animated feather duster." Hughes made no effort to reply in kind. Ridicule was the weapon of petty or malicious minds. Keeping his speeches and his thinking free from animosity, he drove home the importance of the choice voters had to make without the slightest effort to insurrect the public mind or to match the extravagant promises of his opponent.

Traveling widely over the state, Hughes sometimes attended five or six rallies in an evening and made as many as twenty speeches in a single day. Mrs. Hughes did not attempt to take the strenuous up-State trips, and experienced newspapermen grew weary of trying to follow him, but Hughes kept up his pace until the end. "Whatever the result," he would say, "I want to know that the fight has been fought for all it is worth."

At home Antoinette Hughes watched the campaign with great interest. On October 25, 1906, she wrote:

DEAREST,

I have just been reading of the demonstrative welcome accorded you in Cortland—and I can't help rejoicing through and through that the good work goes on. I know how you feel about it all in your inmost heart, and I wish you might be spared the immense personal sacrifice. But, as the wife of a Columbia professor said to me this morning, "When I think of Hearst, it must be, it *must* be!"

We are following your strenuous career through the papers and in thought and spirit, darling. I am with you *always*. I am not without my anxieties, of course, for you were weary when you left us. I hope you are standing the heavy strain in your usual, wonderful and surprising manner and that your voice is holding out well.

Devotedly,

ANTOINETTE

The non-Hearstian press was strongly for Hughes. Every man who is not "ready to see the Empire State sold to a reckless adventurer," said the *Daily*

[20] Speech at Kingston, Oct. 23, 1906.

Tribune, was lined up behind the investigator.[21] The *Sun*, the *New York Times*, and the *Evening Post* were working for him, but it was the *World* that continued to give him the most spirited and effective support. "I am simply crazy about Hughes, so vitally important do I regard his work," wrote Joseph Pulitzer to Frank I. Cobb, chief editorial writer of the *World*. "Support Hughes with all the fire and force you possess." [22]

President Roosevelt repeatedly put in his oar. Returning to Washington from Oyster Bay after the Saratoga convention, he asked Hughes to join him at Jersey City and ride to Trenton. They went over the strategy of the campaign and agreed upon the desirability of concentrating all effort on state issues. Roosevelt was fearful of trickery and fraud on the part of the Hearst-Murphy combine. On October 2 he wrote to Hughes:

> The situation is certainly very serious in New York, and we must get out the reserves of decent citizenship in order to upset the apostles of unrest and their huge and misguided following. Hearst will of course use money like water and with shameless corruption wherever he gets a chance. . . . I earnestly hope you will thru Woodruff see to it that our up State leaders are thoroly on the alert and watchful about any . . . move by Hearst's people to cut down our vote in the Republican counties, either by downright corruption or by an unrebuked and uncontradicted appeal to envy and hate. I regard your triumph as of more consequence than anything else at stake in this election.[23]

"I cannot tell you," Hughes replied, "how much I appreciate your cordial support. This fight must be won." [24] To this he added on October 7: "Your letter was a most inspiring one. Needless to say that in the campaign for decency and sanity you and the achievements of your administration are our tower of strength."

Roosevelt offered his advice on the importance of appealing to the Catholic vote. Hughes replied that he had addressed the YMCA at Carnegie Hall by invitation accepted before his nomination, but that he would not speak before any other Protestant group. Parsons was making the candidate acquainted with the labor leaders. Roosevelt drew attention to his own speech at Harrisburg to emphasize the difference between sensibly curbing the great corporations and the "hideous orgy of misdoing" that would follow a victory by "a mixt crowd of wild zealots and crafty corruptionists." [25] T. R.'s enthusiasm for Hughes reached its zenith in these words:

> My dear Sir, I feel that you are fighting the battle of civilization. If you were an ordinary time-serving politician, if you had the slightest taint of subserviency to the great moneyed interests, I would not give a rap for your success. But you are

[21] Sept. 27, 1906. [22] Don C. Seitz, *Joseph Pulitzer, Life and Letters*, p. 309.
[23] Hughes Papers, Library of Congress. [24] CEH to T. R., Oct. 4, 1906.
[25] T. R. to CEH, Oct. 5, 1906.

an honest, fearless, square man, a good citizen and a good American first, and a good Republican also—a Republican who believes in Abraham Lincoln's principles. You believe in reforming the relations between the Government and the great corporations as drastically as is necessary to meet the needs of the situation; but you believe in having it done in a spirit of sanity and justice. If I were not President I should be stumping New York from one end to the other for you. As it is I can not do much of anything save to hope that my own record and the way I stand towards these questions will help and not harm you.

The first differences between Roosevelt and Hughes arose over the "Judiciary Nominators'" ticket. It had been named by a committee of lawyers of which Hughes, Henry Taft, and Judge Cohen had been members. They chose outstanding men who would make good judges. The ticket was weak from the viewpoint of the party leaders because no Republican lawyer of real stature in New York thought he had a chance of being elected. The organization was dissatisfied and appealed to the President. Roosevelt complained to Hughes. The candidate replied that the situation had been straightened out in Brooklyn, but he stood firm against loading the judicial ticket with politicians and especially against any deal with Hearst and Murphy. To select men who had been more active in politics than at the bar, he wrote the President, would "turn a current of criticism against us at a critical time. It would seriously reflect upon the sincerity of the position we have taken." [26] Secretary of State Root took a similar view. But the President was not wholly satisfied. "As you know," he lectured Hughes two weeks later, "I did not think they [the judiciary nominators] displayed great wisdom in their ticket in any event, and nothing but the fact that the Republican organization was in mighty good hands enabled us to avoid a break. We are going to have with us anyway the people whom the great lawyers could influence. We don't want to drive away the others." [27]

In itself this disagreement was of little significance. But it was symptomatic. Hughes would not bid for votes by any sacrifice of principle that he considered vital to good government, while Roosevelt was willing to play the game of politics in the politicians' way. Such a difference between two men of strong will and tough fiber could scarcely portend a smooth relationship. Their cordiality would, however, outlast the campaign.

The New York managers were "continually having fits" over the strategy of the campaign. National issues were rigorously excluded. Only one Cabinet member—Root, a New Yorker—was to speak. Then the strategists became panicky over what Hearst might say of Root's former connections with Ryan and the big corporations. Contrary to Hughes' wishes, they decided that Root's speech might be a liability. Before the campaign ended, however, the man-

[26] CEH to T. R., Oct. 7, 1906. [27] T. R. to CEH, Oct. 21, 1906.

agers' fears were running in the opposite direction. Hearst's followers were interpreting the seeming aloofness of the White House as indifference. So the strategists frantically urged the President to come to New York. Instead, he persuaded Root to carry out his original plan to speak at Utica and issued the following statement: "Anyone who believes or tries to convey the impression that I am not heart and soul for Mr. Hughes is either wilfully or inadvertently laboring under a delusion. I am first, last and all the time for Mr. Hughes, because I know he stands for concisely [*sic*] the same principles that I stand for. I authorize you to make that statement to your friends, and to my friends on the East Side with all the emphasis that is in you." [28]

Root prepared his speech before leaving Washington and took it to the White House. Roosevelt penciled in stiffer language in one portion to express his view of Hearst. In Utica, Root and Hughes rode together from the station to the hall. Newsboys threw into their carriage Hearst's reply to Root, as the latter's speech had been given out in advance to the press. Across the front page was a cartoon of "Root, the Rat" nibbling at the defenses of the common people. Republican supporters were buying up these copies of the *Evening Journal*, tearing them into shreds, and littering the streets.

Tammany Hall had sent a gang to Utica to break up the meeting. But every act of rowdyism was suppressed by the spirited audience. One of the hecklers yelled at Root, "It's a lie!" The crowd roared, "Throw him out!" Root quelled the uproar with his raised hand and said, "No, let him stay and learn."

Root rebuttressed Hughes' accusation that the publisher-politician was using his great wealth to sow the seeds of dissension, strife, and hatred throughout the land. "Once only," he said, "has this method of incendiary abuse wrought out its natural consequence—in the murder of President McKinley. For years, by vile epithet and viler cartoons, readers of the *Journal* were taught to believe that McKinley was a monster in human form, whose taking-off would be a service to mankind."

From Hearst's *New York Journal*, Secretary Root quoted the fatal quatrain:

> The bullet that pierced Goebel's breast
> Cannot be found in all the West:
> Good reason; it is speeding here
> To stretch McKinley on his bier.

"In President Roosevelt's first message to Congress, in speaking of the assassin of McKinley," Root continued, "he spoke of him as inflamed by the reckless utterances of those who, on the stump and in the public press, appeal to the dark and evil spirits of malice and greed, envy and sullen hatred. . . . I say, by the President's authority, that in penning these words, with the horror

[28] *New York Times*, Oct. 28, 1906.

of President McKinley's murder fresh before him, he had Mr. Hearst specifically in mind.

"And I say, by his authority, that what he thought of Mr. Hearst then he thinks of Mr. Hearst now." [29]

Election day came with forecasts ranging erratically from a 200,000 majority for Hughes to a similar majority for Hearst. Party lines had been extensively broken. The first returns suggested that the voters had administered a severe drubbing to the entire Republican ticket. But the gloom in Hughes' headquarters was short-lived. Soon it was evident that he was pulling ahead of the other Republican candidates and ahead of Hearst. The final count stood: Hughes, 749,002; Hearst, 691,105, giving Hughes a comfortable plurality of 57,897 votes. Hearst had spent $500,000 out of his own resources and brought upon himself probably the bitterest disappointment of his career. Hughes' campaign had cost him only $619, largely spent for travel and secretarial service,[30] and he had won a striking manifestation of public confidence even while the party which sponsored him was being repudiated. All the other Republican candidates for state executive offices were defeated.

"I am much gratified," the new Governor-elect said as soon as the returns seemed to leave no doubt of the outcome, "but, regardless of the size of the plurality, my feeling is not one of elation, but of deep responsibility." [31]

The staggering obligation he had taken upon himself was all too apparent. He would go to Albany to preside over an administration composed of his political opponents and cope with a legislature still in the grip of the bosses who had fought his nomination. For the moment, however, there was great rejoicing over his victory. The President was elated. "I doubt whether in this crisis," he wrote to Hughes, "we could have elected any other man but you. . . . I feel that you and I, my dear Mr. Hughes, approach our work in the same spirit: and I wish you Godspeed in performing the heavy task which the people of the State of New York have laid on your shoulders." [32]

The 1906 campaign left Hearst so discredited that he would never again become "a national peril." Some writers expressed the belief that this elimination of Hearst as a contender for the Presidency was perhaps Hughes' greatest public service. Today that negative view is amply contradicted by history, but in November, 1906, when Hughes' ability in public office was yet to be tested, his awakening of the people to the distinction between fair reforms and hate-producing slander could well be regarded as his crowning achievement.

[29] Reprinted by permission of Dodd, Mead & Company from *Elihu Root* by Philip C. Jessup, p. 120. Copyright, 1938, by Dodd Mead & Company, Inc.

[30] Sworn statement to New York Secretary of State, Nov. 16, 1906.

[31] New York *Daily Tribune*, Nov. 6, 1906.

[32] T. R. to CEH, Nov. 7, 1906. Theodore Roosevelt Papers.

Chapter 17

FIGHTING GOVERNOR

THE GREAT battle of 1906 was followed by brisk maneuvering for position among the victorious forces. Woodruff, Barnes, and Parsons took the initiative. The chairman of the Republican State Committee invited Hughes to relax at Camp "Kill Kare" in the Adirondacks, along with Dr. Schurman, Senator Page, and other friends. Hughes accepted the invitation and found himself surrounded by the Old Guard instead of the friends he had expected. This did not interfere with his enjoyment of the sleigh riding and other sports that the camp offered, but it excited the newspapers. When he returned to New York, they were expressing fear that he had been "taken into camp" in more ways than one. Woodruff clearly won this first skirmish.

William Barnes, Jr., Republican boss of Albany, followed up his none too subtle suggestions at Camp Kill Kare with a letter bluntly denouncing several reforms that the Governor-elect had favored and arguing for restoration of "the power of the organization." [1] The implication was that the bosses understood the purpose of Hughes' campaign oratory, but with the votes safely counted, they expected him to be a regular Republican. Hughes countered in a friendly vein, although he rejected Barnes' major premise. Harmony was not enough, he said. The party would also have to give "aggressive and convincing" leadership in the public interest.[2] While he was trying to avoid an immediate showdown, he held stoutly to his own principles.

Parsons, who was a man of character and in general a "good-government" Republican, kept his maneuver strictly under cover. As committeeman for New York County and one of Roosevelt's close friends, he suggested that the Governor-elect go to Washington to write his message. Hughes interpreted this as a White House hint that the President would like to keep his hand on the Governor's shoulder.

"No," he replied, "I'll gladly talk with the President about the points to be dealt with in my message; but the people of this state elected me to be Governor of New York and not an agent by which they might be governed from Washington. To write the message in Washington wouldn't be a good thing for the

[1] William Barnes, Jr., to CEH, Nov. 26, 1906.
[2] CEH to Barnes, Dec. 3, 1906.

party, or for the President, or for me. But I hope that the President and I will have the most cordial relations." [3]

This skirmish was a Hughes victory, but the public knew nothing about it.

The President's direct maneuver was to give a stag dinner for Hughes at the White House in December. It was a sort of initiation for a neophyte into big-league politics. Secretary Taft, Senator Henry Cabot Lodge, Speaker Joseph G. Cannon, James S. Sherman (later to become Vice President) and most of the other Republican leaders were there to take the measure of the rookie Governor. Roosevelt was the acme of cordiality. After dinner he accompanied Hughes to his room, sat on the edge of the bed, and chatted about New York politics in the most entertaining Rooseveltian manner for an hour and a half.

Hughes entered fully into the spirit of the occasion. With complete candor, he discussed the high points of what he intended to do as governor; Roosevelt gave his endorsement, and the two seemed to have reached a cordial understanding.[4] T. R. was especially pleased with Hughes' idea of recommending a recount of the Hearst mayoralty vote of 1905. The President and Governor-to-be parted in an aura of friendship and apparent mutual admiration.

If this meeting can be regarded as a skirmish, it ended in a draw. Hughes took the oath of office on January 1, 1907, with the question as to who would actually exercise the powers of governor in the Empire State still wide open.

The Hughes family moved to the Executive Mansion on Eagle Street shortly after Christmas. On inauguration day the Governor-elect was escorted from the mansion to the Capitol by a parade. Promptly at twelve o'clock a colorful ceremony was held in the assembly chamber. Hughes and his staff marched to their appointed places following the official entrance of the outgoing Governor and his staff all decked out in uniform. Ailing Governor Higgins spoke briefly; then Hughes took the oath from Secretary of State John S. Whalen and delivered his inaugural address while Mrs. Hughes and the children looked on beaming with pride. At the public reception which followed in the executive chamber, the bewhiskered chief of state and his graceful spouse had an opportunity to greet almost every outstanding figure in the state.

The façade of gaiety at the official ceremonies could not dispel the awareness of impending upheaval that pervaded Albany and radiated through the state. New York seemed to be on the verge of a revolutionary shakeup of the established political and economic order; yet the nature and extent of the changes to be effected remained a mystery.

Hughes' inaugural address heightened the tension without offering any specific clues as to what his course would be. "We have reason to congratulate ourselves," he said, "that coincident with our prosperity, there is an emphatic assertion of popular rights and a keen resentment of public wrongs. . . .

[3] Beerits' Memorandum, III, 17. [4] Author's interview with CEH, Jan. 7, 1946.

Slowly but surely the people have narrowed the opportunities for selfish aggression, and the demand of this hour . . . is not allegiance to phrases, but sympathy with every aspiration for the betterment of conditions. . . ."

The speech was Lincolnesque in its sense of dedication:

> I assume the office of Governor without other ambition than to serve the people of the State. I have not coveted its powers nor do I permit myself to shrink from its responsibilities. . . .
>
> I believe in the sincerity and good sense of the people. I believe that they are intent in having government which recognizes no favored interests and which is not conducted in any part for selfish ends. They will not be, and they should not be, content with less.[5]

The next day came a detailed Hughesian program outlined in his message to the legislature. He requested a recount of votes in the Hearst-McClellan contest in 1905 and amendment of the law to provide a summary recanvass in any future contest. "Our entire system of government," he said, "depends upon honest elections and a fair count."[6] The victor was demanding justice for his bitterest enemy not only because it was the right thing to do but also because a recount would probably deprive Hearst of an issue that had won him much sympathy.

Disregarding the advice of Boss Barnes, the Governor asked for reforms in the method of voting and limitation of the amount that a candidate could spend "to procure his election." Defying all the bosses, he asked for an experimental direct-primaries law to be applied on a voluntary basis. More important still, he urged abolition of the Board of Railroad Commissioners (a haven for boss-controlled timeservers), the Commission of Gas and Electricity, and the Rapid Transit Board of New York City. In their place he suggested two broad-gauged public service commissions, one to operate in New York City and the other in the remainder of the state, with ample power to control utility corporations in the public interest.

Here was the direct and powerful blow to special privilege that the bosses and the utilities had feared. In the teeth of their opposition, the new Governor had translated his campaign promises into specific legislative proposals. That seemed intolerable conduct for a tyro who had no standing in political circles.

While the bosses fumed, the press and public loudly applauded. "Mr. Hughes presents the first comprehensive plan advanced by any governor within a generation," declared the exultant *World*, "for dealing adequately with the complicated questions of election reforms and the regulation of public utilities." "It is pregnant with enormous possibilities," said the *New York Press*. ". . . filled with words of wisdom," echoed the *Binghamton Herald*.[7] "Specific, candid and

[5] *Public Papers of Charles E. Hughes 1907*, pp. 7–9. [6] *Ibid.*, p. 24.
[7] Fuller Collection, New York Public Library, Vol. 49.

progressive . . ." added the *Outlook.* "Seldom has a . . . message been so freighted with promise to American democracy." [8]

"It is none of my business," wrote President Roosevelt, with unmistakable irony, "but I cannot deny myself the pleasure of writing to congratulate you as well as our party and our State upon your admirable message and upon the admirable way in which you have begun your term." [9]

The response of the Republican organization was to assign the key posts in the legislature to anti-Hughes men. The time-honored custom at Albany had been for the machine to boss the governor and the governor to boss the legislature. In accord with this tradition leaders of the Assembly and Senate called on Hughes and asked for his views as to the selection of committee chairmen. He replied simply that that was the task of the Senate and the Assembly. While he was eager to cooperate in every way in suggesting legislation and putting it into proper form, he had no intention of trying to control the committees or of resorting to any kind of dictation. As a practical matter, he could not have organized the legislature to his own liking without inviting its leaders to make patronage demands upon him; and Hughes was determined that the employees of his administration should be chosen for their competence in the jobs at hand—not for their service to any party machine.

The party leaders guffawed over this strict regard for constitutional functions and entrenched the Old Guard in the committee chairmanships. The liberal Senators, including Page, Saxe, Agnew, and Tully, were given insignificant assignments. The only concession to the Hughes men was the chairmanship of the Committee on Miscellaneous Corporations assigned to Senator Harvey D. Hinman. The vital Railroads Committee went to Senator Benjamin N. Wilcox, who for years had produced a stream of procorporation laws, and the Judiciary chairmanship to Senator George Davis, who had fought Hughes' 80-cent gas bill after the 1905 investigation. "So offensive to decency" was the committee list, one observer said, "that there was a state-wide howl of rage when it was published." [10]

Governor Hughes was shocked. His education in the ways of politicians had been greatly enhanced by the gas and insurance investigations and his gubernatorial campaign. By the time he took the oath of office he knew all the political leaders of the state and was no "babe in the woods," as some of the party leaders supposed. But he had misjudged the temper of the Republican leaders. He had supposed that, after his election, they would accord him some degree of loyalty in spite of disagreements over policy. Instead, they had unmistakably thrown down the gage of battle.

Hughes took up the gage, but without any show of hostility toward the or-

[8] Jan. 12, 1907. [9] T. R. to CEH, Jan. 6, 1907, Hughes Papers.
[10] Christian MacDonald in *Harper's Weekly,* Feb. 2, 1907.

ganization leaders themselves. In reply to questions from the press, he completely dissociated himself from the committee assignments. About an hour later came the first inkling of what his course would be. "The only strength that I or my Administration may have," he said in a speech to the Albany Chamber of Commerce, "is the confidence of the people of this State, and, in any difficulty that may arise, to the people of this State I propose to appeal." [11]

The bosses laughed at this sally. Nor was the Governor's talk of going to the people the only executive antic that set legislative tongues to wagging. Hughes was actually trying to conduct the public business in public. The press was talking about "daylight government." The politicos who gathered in the bar of the Ten Eyck Hotel close to the Capitol alternately snickered and cursed as they reviewed the indignities to which their fraternity was being subjected.

The New York executive chamber is a large, high-ceiling room in the southeast corner of the Capitol beautifully paneled in Santo Domingo mahogany. On two sides are five huge arched windows; on the walls are the portraits of past governors, a sprinkling of presidents, and other historic figures. Here the governors had presided at occasional hearings and conducted ceremonies of state, but until 1907 none of them had ventured to use this room as an office. Rather, they had secluded themselves in the inner sanctum reached by way of a swinging panel in the wall of the great chamber. Tradition said that a secret stair gave the political bigwigs access to this private suite without danger of being observed in their comings and goings.

Hughes surveyed the situation and decided to see visitors in the big room. It was a symbol of his break with the back-door methods of the past. Of course, his private office remained open to department heads and others who came in by appointment with important state business to transact. But during his "morning hour," which was given over to the hearing of complaints, suggestions, and comments from citizens, he operated almost exclusively in the big room. The rule was first come, first served, whether the visitor was a humble farmer or a powerful boss. It amounted to a revolution in the conduct of state affairs.

The Governor sat at an elaborate desk in the far corner of the room beneath the "fighting and squinting" portrait of Theodore Roosevelt. On the right was his secretary, Robert H. Fuller, a former newspaper man. On his left was his military secretary, Colonel George Curtis Treadwell, who had a fondness for swank uniforms and decorations. Waiting visitors occupied the chairs and sofas around the room and moved over to the big desk as their turns came. Hughes listened attentively, kept the discussions on the points at issue, and usually promised to give prompt attention to the problems laid before him.

As one delegation moved away, a clever little man darted back to the big

[11] New York *Evening Post*, Jan. 10, 1907.

desk. "Now, Governor," he said, "I know a lot about this thing that you ought to hear. I'd like to talk to you about it."

"There is no time better than the present," Hughes replied. "I want to get all the facts."

He instructed his messenger to call back the other members of the group who were leaving the room. The puzzled citizens returned, but the little man who had stayed behind, hoping to whisper privately into the Governor's ear, had little to say.

The politicians were furious over having to wait in line and then talk with the Governor under the watchful eyes of other citizens. The size of the executive chamber made it possible to carry on a conversation at the Governor's desk without being overhead by visitors awaiting their turn, but the atmosphere conducive to undercover bargaining was gone. And to put the party hierarchy on a par with ordinary citizens added insult to injury. Hughes was not only taking over powers that the bosses had traditionally exercised; he even made a show of his independence. Woodruff publicly complained that "things are in a bad way at Albany."

The press was delighted with the arrangement. It meant that the state government would be operating out in the open where editors and reporters could see the wheels go around. "Sly party Nicodemuses no longer go to the executive chamber by night . . . or the back door," rejoiced the *Evening Post*. "We have a governor again." [12]

The showdown with the party leaders was not long in coming. Woodruff and Parsons were in agreement that two political plums—the offices of superintendent of public works and superintendent of elections for the New York Metropolitan district—should fall promptly into their hands. At their behest Governor Higgins had given Lewis M. Swasey a recess appointment as superintendent of elections, but his tenure would soon expire unless Hughes renominated him. Before acting, Higgins had asked the Governor-elect for his advice, and Hughes, knowing nothing about Swasey and being preoccupied with his message and other affairs, had declined to commit himself. After his inauguration he inquired into the nominee's fitness and found no evidence of the ability and character which he thought a superintendent of elections should have. Swasey was a Republican district leader in Brooklyn, "a mere tool of the machine." To entrust the supervision of elections to him would make a mockery of Hughes' promise to give the state a clean and efficient administration "free from taint of bossism."

Woodruff rounded up the legislators from Brooklyn and sent them to the Governor to plead the cause of Swasey. "While I thank you very much for what

[12] Feb. 6, 1907.

you have said," the Governor responded, "I shall have to use my own judgment, even though it may be erroneous." [13]

Woodruff then insisted on making the reappointment of Swasey a test of power. He and Parsons called on the Governor and bluntly told him that Swasey would have to be retained. Hughes replied with equal candor that he did not intend to renominate the unqualified Swasey, but he would be glad to appoint anyone else whom they might recommend, "provided he was a fit man for the place." [14] His offer was spurned. The party leaders were thinking only of maintaining their power.

The issue was much broader, Hughes told them, than the question of this particular appointment. The people had elected him governor because they trusted him to stand on his own feet and use his best judgment in directing the affairs of the state. If he should appoint Swasey, the people would know that he was sacrificing their interest to party organization. Woodruff and Parsons ought to sympathize with his efforts to bring the Republican Party back to popular esteem, he told them, and not take a stand that would hinder essential changes.

At one o'clock in the morning Woodruff and Parsons were still insisting that Swasey be appointed. Hughes ended the argument at that point with a flat No. As the conference broke up, Parsons turned to the Governor and said, "I think we'll find a way." [15] Hughes did not know what the New York County leader meant, but it was soon to be evident.

The press detected the scent of battle and knew that Hughes would have to win this fight if he were to make good his promise of an unbossed administration. When the Speaker of the Assembly, James W. Wadsworth, Jr., went to Washington, therefore, amid reports that he would bid for the President's support of Swasey, the outcome of his mission was followed with intense interest. Roosevelt apparently concluded that in this instance "opportunism could be one of the major virtues." Washington dispatches of patent White House origin reported that the President had no intention of giving Governor Hughes any advice on appointments or other state affairs unless the Governor should ask for it, and Wadsworth told reporters that he had not received any "orders or instructions." [16]

When he called on the Governor, however, Wadsworth did have a message—a message which, he said, he was sorry to have to deliver. "The President said," the Speaker reported, "that while of course he thought the Governor should do what he thought right, he felt that he should appoint Swasey, and that if he (Roosevelt) were governor, he would appoint him." [17]

[13] New York *Evening Post*, Jan. 10, 1907. [14] CEH, Notes, p. 182.
[15] Beerits' Memorandum, IV, 5. [16] New York *Evening Post*, Jan. 14, 1907.
[17] Beerits' Memorandum, IV, 5.

"I'm sorry to get this message," Hughes replied. "I would be very glad if it were possible to accept the President's advice. However, I wish you would tell the President that I have thought over this matter very carefully and that I'm sending in the nomination of William Leary this evening." He had already ordered the nomination to be written out and saw no reason to reconsider it.

Leary's name had been suggested by Job E. Hedges, one of Hughes' most enthusiastic supporters in the 1906 campaign. The nominee was a Republican of good standing, a friend of Roosevelt, and Parsons' former campaign manager. He also had the endorsement of many independents. Hughes felt that Leary was so well qualified both as a public servant and as a party man that the Senate could not turn him down.

The implied rebuff to Roosevelt was a matter of "deep regret" to the Governor.[18] He was eager to maintain friendly relations with the President and to have his advice. But when the issue was whether he should be governor in his own right, Hughes felt that he had to adhere to his own principle. Woodruff and Parsons had acted foolishly in trying to dictate to him and then in bringing the President into the affair. It was they who had insisted on a showdown, and only they could be blamed for the outcome.

Scarcely less jolting to the organization was the appointment of former Senator Stevens of Attica to be superintendent of public works. Stevens was a man of integrity and executive talent whose business and political experience especially fitted him for this major administrative task. Hughes had learned to trust him when Stevens was chairman of the gas investigating committee. But Stevens was anathema to the Wadsworth clan of western New York. He had helped to unseat James W. Wadsworth, Sr., from Congress, and the Wadsworths had gerrymandered him off the political map. The junior Wadsworth, Speaker of the New York Assembly, now visualized Stevens using the vast Public Works Department, which was constructing the new Erie Canal at a cost of more than $100,000,000 as a source of patronage for anti-Wadsworth men.

Hughes had discussed this appointment with several advisers without reference to politics. He was determined to rescue the department from the aura of scandal surrounding it and did not know that Stevens was involved in a political feud.[19] To quiet the furor he issued a statement explaining why Stevens had been chosen and disavowing any antagonism toward Speaker Wadsworth. It was nevertheless a bitter pill for a high-minded legislator whose aid the Governor needed.

There was no foundation, however, for the Speaker's fears that the Public Works Department might become an anti-Wadsworth machine. "I want you to conduct this office with an eye solely to efficiency and the public interest," Hughes instructed his number one administrator. "The one thing you must

[18] CEH, Notes, p. 183. [19] *Ibid.*

not do is to try by the use of patronage to build any 'Hughes machine.' "[20] This was typical of his attitude. He preferred to appoint Republicans and gladly accepted the candidates of professional politicians whenever they measured up to the standard he set. But the primary consideration was to get trained and competent men.

Friendship with the Governor was likely to be a liability to job seekers. After the new public service commissions had been authorized, Job Hedges dropped into the Governor's office, reminded him of the part he (Hedges) had played in the campaign, and said frankly that he would like a place on one of the commissions. Hughes expressed his high regard for Hedges. "But you see, Job," he added, "I can't very well appoint you because you're a personal friend." "By God," Hedges replied, "you need no longer consider that an obstacle."

In spite of its shock, the Senate promptly confirmed the Leary and Stevens appointments. The anti-Hughes men had not surrendered. They were merely waiting for firmer ground on which to make their stand.

Meanwhile the public found new hope and amusement in the turn of events at Albany. Frank H. Simonds declared that Woodruff had been eliminated as a political figure and that the reactionaries would now have to fight or run. "To listen to the stupefied comments of the old-line politicians," he wrote, "to watch the inextinguishable mirth of the independents and unaffected onlookers, and to mark the confusion of the people who said two weeks ago, 'Oh, Hughes will be a Republican,' is to understand fully what has happened, and why the appointments for two comparatively small jobs are regarded as indicative of a revolution. It is worth recalling, also, that the Hughes Administration is not yet two weeks old."[21]

John Kendrick Bangs expressed the prevailing sentiment in verse:

> O woe is me! O woe is us
> That it should come to pass!
> That gum-shoe King Politicus
> Should go at last to grass.
> It is the dee-dash-dernedest thing
> That ever we did see!
> A Governor a-governing
> At ancient Albanee.[22]

Hughes himself managed to squeeze more than a little ironic humor out of the situation when he spoke at the dinner welcoming James Bryce, the new British ambassador to the United States. Dipping into Bryce's *The American Commonwealth*, which other speakers had been lauding extravagantly, Hughes

[20] John Palmer Gavit in New York *Evening Post*, June 10, 1916.
[21] New York *Evening Post*, Jan. 15, 1907. [22] *Current Literature*, June, 1907, p. 622.

came up with a passage saying that the men who managed state governments "turn out to be insignificant" persons who fail to hold the public interest.[23]

"I find no flattering word for the governor in *The American Commonwealth*," Hughes bantered—to the great amusement of an audience keenly aware of what was happening at Albany.

"Oh, yes, Governor," Lord Bryce spoke out, "there is another passage there."

"Perhaps our good friend refers to this," the Governor replied, quoting again: " 'The State Executive, it is said, has little to do and comparatively small sums to handle. . . . A State Governor, however, is not yet a nonentity.' Now, while there is life there is hope," Hughes commented, "that we may be able to supply material for a new edition."

Whatever his discomfiture may have been at the time, Lord Bryce wrote to the Governor two months later, congratulating him on his "great success" and penciling on the bottom of the note: "I shall indeed have to rewrite that chapter in my 'American Commonwealth' in order to show what may be accomplished by the firmness, tact and courage of a State Governor." [24]

[23] Speech of March 23, 1907, Hughes Papers, Library of Congress.
[24] Bryce to CEH, June 18, 1907.

Chapter 18

THE BOSSES RUN RIOT

BEFORE he had been in office a week, Governor Hughes embarked upon a systematic housecleaning. His pledge to the people made it necessary to break the hold of the political machines and the big corporations upon the state's service and regulatory departments. In the face of the opposition now lined up against him this was a herculean task; yet he could not fail without risking loss of all the public confidence that he had attained.

His first effort was successful. Banking Superintendent Kilburn stepped out and was replaced by Charles Hallam Keep, a trained executive of high standing recommended by President Roosevelt. The Insurance Department presented a more delicate problem, but the Governor hoped that by tact and candid reasoning he could quietly effect a change there also. In this he was to suffer a sharp disappointment of historic consequences.

Otto Kelsey was strongly entrenched as superintendent of insurance. A former legislator and comptroller, an ally of Odell and a friend of the Speaker, he commanded powerful support and had a reputation for simple honesty that seemed to make him invulnerable to attack in the 1907 political climate in and about Albany. In deference to these facts Hughes looked for a less strategic position into which Kelsey could be eased without loss of face.

When Kelsey refused to budge, the Governor laid his case before a group of the superintendent's organization friends. Eight months had elapsed since the insurance reforms had been enacted, and Kelsey, ostensibly named to make the new laws effective, had done nothing. Senator Armstrong and Hughes had met with Kelsey shortly after he took office and explored the relationship between the department's laxity and the insurance scandals.[1] Kelsey had seemed sympathetic to reform at the time, but he went right on operating his department as if the insurance investigation had never been held.

"If I can appoint Kelsey to any other position for which I think he is qualified," Hughes promised the organization men, "I'll do it. He is honest, and I don't want his removal to reflect on him. But he is not the man to head this department. I want you to get him to resign." [2]

Kelsey stood pat. Being an amiable and spineless fellow, he might well have yielded to avoid a fight if the organization had left him free to make a choice.

[1] CEH, Notes, p. 184. [2] Beerits' Memorandum, IV, p. 9.

But the political satraps could not afford to let the Insurance Department—one of the foremost political levers in dealing with big business—slip out of their control. Nor could they let an "honest man" be ousted for any such reasons as the Governor advanced. The case against Kelsey was that "he owed a duty to the people of the state" and had failed to perform it. Albany understood the eclipse of political figures for opposition to a boss or a governor or for conduct bringing the individual into open disgrace. But here was a new and frightening test. Kelsey was to be sacrificed because he had been loyal to the machine instead of the people. Judged by this criterion, who would be safe? The Governor's revolutionary idea could obviously be turned against every bosslet holding a political job.

The leaders felt especially sure of themselves because, under the statute, Kelsey could not be removed without the consent of the Senate. How could Hughes go before the Senate and demand the removal of a public servant admitted to be honest when no well defined charges had been brought against him? Certainly this time they had an issue on which they could show up the Governor for the babe in the woods they believed him to be.

As Kelsey consulted a wide circle of friends, the story leaked out to the press. Further scrutiny of his record then indicated that the assets of a savings and loan association of which he had been receiver had dwindled disastrously. Five million dollars' worth of stock-transfer stamps, almost as good as money, were reported to have disappeared while he was comptroller. Ostensibly they were burned because of defects, but no record had been kept. These disclosures further stiffened Kelsey's fighting spirit.

Defeated in his persuasive efforts, Hughes openly demanded Kelsey's resignation. Kelsey flatly refused to make any such "admission of wrongful conduct in office," but invited the Governor to tell him what he wished to have done in the Insurance Department. To Hughes' mind this was a confession of Kelsey's unfitness. The Governor's demand was not for a lackey but for a superintendent who could clean out the department's dead wood and corruption and administer it as an alert and virile instrument of public policy.

The fight was temporarily interrupted by the death and funeral of former Governor Higgins. Then Hughes took the offensive with a brilliant maneuver the like of which Albany had never seen. In response to Kelsey's request for further consideration of his fitness, the Governor unearthed an old statute authorizing him to "take proofs" before recommending a removal and summoned Kelsey to the executive chamber on February 18 for an informal examination.

Kelsey came to the hearing wrapped in his honesty, which the Governor had not challenged, but utterly unprotected against the sort of probing to which he was subjected. The superintendent admitted that the negligence of the examiners he had inherited from his predecessor amounted to a "public scandal," but he had not dismissed any of them. The chief examiner of the old regime had resigned of his own accord. Other examiners who could see no evil and hear no evil were still at their desks because Kelsey did not wish to hurt their feelings and felt a need for "experienced men." Oblivious to the revolt against the old order which he represented, Kelsey had plodded along with his eyes fastened on routine trivialities.

Ida M. Tarbell called the examination of Kelsey the most cruel stripping of a man in public ever seen.[3] In answer to the Governor's searching questions, Kelsey had prepared his own indictment before the Senate. Some critics who knew nothing of the Governor's efforts to save Kelsey's face felt that this public exposure of his incompetence was unnecessarily harsh. But it was Kelsey himself who had brought the case into the open. Hughes could only choose between making an example of Kelsey and making a shambles of his own program. The Governor "has handled the case of the people vs. Kelsey with such skill and fairness," rejoiced the *New York Press*, "that we almost hesitate to praise him for fear of intoxicating ourselves with the adjectives that flow in streams to the lips." [4]

By this time it was evident, however, that Kelsey was only a pawn in a major struggle for political power. The men who had said at Saratoga that "even Hearst wouldn't hurt *us* as much as Hughes" were now shaking their heads and telling each other how right they had been. The Governor could not be controlled. He would not play the political game. The only course open to the bosses was to attack him and all that he stood for. Kelsey had merely supplied a name, as Frank H. Simonds said, "for Hughes' political rubicon." "Henceforth," he added, "the issue is not Kelsey, but progress or reaction at Albany." [5]

For weeks the Senate did nothing in response to the Governor's appeal for Kelsey's removal. The Republican leader, John Raines, whose long drooping mustache seemed to symbolize the old order, formed a coalition with Democratic legislators captained by the sharp-faced and sinister Patrick H. McCarren and Thomas F. Grady in order to block the Governor's reforms. They braced themselves for what they believed to be the inevitable swinging of the Governor's patronage and veto clubs. But Hughes made no effort either to coerce or to punish them for their opposition. Instead, he announced that his powers would be used solely in the interests of good legislation and efficient administration. The Senate would have to act on its own responsibility without fear of retaliation against Kelsey's supporters or promise of reward for those who stood by the Governor. This strict adherence to the principles of

[3] *American Magazine*, March. 1908, p. 460.
[4] Feb. 20, 1907.
[5] New York *Evening Post*, Feb. 18, 1907.

representative government amused the rough-hewn legislators and spurred them to bolder measures of revolt. Hughes' prestige in Albany visibly sagged.

Throughout this period the Governor was fighting doggedly—in his own way. He held two press conferences every working day that he was in the capital, talking freely with the news-gatherers about what he had done and what he planned to do. In confidence he unfolded background information and news not yet ready for release to the public, thus discouraging uninformed speculation and preparing the way for intelligent handling of each story when it broke. Hardheaded newsmen paid him the great compliment of saying, "Hughes is on the level." [6] Such keen observers of public affairs as Louis Howe, who represented a Saratoga paper, John Palmer Gavit of the Associated Press, and Frank H. Simonds of the New York *Evening Post* became enthusiastic exponents of the Hughes policies. The newsmen's confidence in the new Governor filtered through to editorial offices that were already friendly, and Hughes had an exceptionally favorable press.

The extraordinary flow of good will between the Governor and the press was demonstrated when newspaper men pretended to "impeach" him at a dinner of the "Amen Corner" in the Fifth Avenue Hotel. Hughes was acquitted of the accusation that he was a Republican. But the most "heinous crime" charged against him was a different matter. "He does wear upon his face," the "impeachment" read, "certain long and dark curtains, portieres, lambrequins or draperies of an impenetrable texture, which make it impossible to tell whether he is stringing a statesman or not." Hughes laughed heartily at this ribbing. When he arose to speak, several diners shouted, "The next President of the United States," and the audience roared its approval.[7]

As a novel and striking figure in the political firmament, Hughes was much in demand as a speaker. He accepted as many invitations as possible for the sake of acquainting the public with his program. In his campaign he had promised that he would be close to the people. Now he realized that he would have to rely upon their support if he was to accomplish anything at Albany. His heavy duties as Governor left him little time to prepare speeches, but he talked out of the fullness of his daily experience, hiring stenographers in relays to take down his extemporaneous remarks so that accurate copies would be available to the press a few minutes after he had finished speaking.

Often he spoke at three dinners in a single evening by hurrying from one to another. If the audiences expected to hear oratorical gush or sparkling pleasantries, they were disappointed. Hughes packed his speeches with facts about the public business and reasoning on the basis of those facts, laying each issue candidly and persuasively before the people for their own decision.

[6] Samuel G. Blythe in the *Saturday Evening Post*, March 16, 1907.
[7] *New York Press*, Feb. 10, 1907.

The Governor threw his challenge directly into the teeth of the politicians when he spoke to the Republican organization of Albany on February 27. He knew that Barnes had asked him to dine with the machine in the hope of softening him to its pressures. The big red-faced, loud-talking Albany boss was clearly the most formidable leader of the Old Guard. Keen and eloquent in a bullish sort of way, a graduate of Harvard University and a grandson of Thurlow Weed (one of the founders of the Republican Party), his dominant purpose was to restore the party machine in New York to "fighting trim." To Barnes' mind this meant tight control of the three P's—patronage, privilege, and police. In his letter written shortly after the election, he had warned Hughes: "There are breakers ahead unless the faddist [meaning reformer] as well as the political crook is exposed in his folly." Apparently Hughes decided that one of the best places for a breaker to strike was the organization dinner.

Party harmony was desirable and party loyalty was a fine quality, he told the machine. But they did not require support of anything wrong either in policy or administration. Organization too was essential, of course. But "no matter how skilfully constructed or astutely led," Hughes solemnly warned, "the people will smash any organization that is devoted to selfish interests." They had rebuked the Republican Party for overreaching itself. Hughes supplied the facts and figures. "It is clearly evident," he insisted, "that on state issues the Republican Party will be doomed to defeat unless it gives new assurances to the people of its capacity to govern in their interest. No man is a friend of the Republican Party," he continued, "who asks me or anyone in authority to appoint a man or to retain a man who is not equal to his job. . . . Let there be a demonstration that we are a party of the people and that the interests of all citizens are safe in our keeping." [8]

The politicians who had come to believe that Hughes was already beaten and in retreat were stupefied. "It was like a skeleton in armor," one of them exclaimed. Barnes' anger flared openly. As soon as the Governor had left—apparently to make another speech—the bullish boss unloosed a passionate tirade in defense of the old order and in denunciation of the Hughes reforms.

As the months passed, Hughes' appeal to the people became increasingly direct. "When any proposal is made that is right . . . which the people recognize as demanded for mischiefs that exist," he urged, "then let public opinion assert itself and make it impossible to defeat such a proposition upon any ground of expediency or because of the opposition of any interest." [9] But while the Governor talked, the situation at Albany went from bad to worse. Near the end of March, John Raines, leader of the Senate, let it be known that he had "decided to fight Mr. Hughes tooth and nail for the rest of the ses-

[8] Text of address in Hughes Papers, Library of Congress.
[9] Brooklyn *Daily Eagle*, Feb. 12, 1907.

sion."[10] The legislature had done nothing. Two irreconcilable forces were locked in what seemed to be hopeless combat that thwarted the plans of both.

A wave of dissatisfaction swept in upon Albany, and some of it hit the Governor. Several newspapers commented sharply on the apparent failure of his tactics. The people will look elsewhere for a Governor, next time, said the *Hornell Times*, unless Mr. Hughes can produce results.[11] Some of the legislators themselves, accustomed to being told what to do, were obviously embarrassed by the freedom and responsibility that Hughes forced upon them. Many resented his inclination to play a lone hand and his genius for holding the spotlight of publicity on his own program.

Then came an incident that seemed to align the White House with the bosses. President Roosevelt was eager to see the Hughes Administration succeed. At the same time he was irritated by Hughes' uncompromising attitude toward the organization. The party leaders ran down to Washington with numerous complaints, and the Governor did nothing to counteract their wailing. When the Kelsey incident produced an open split, Roosevelt saw in it dangerous potentialities. He called Woodruff to Washington and urged him to swing the organization behind the Hughes program in order to keep New York in the Republican column in 1908.

About the same time the President ousted Collector of Customs Archie Sanders of Rochester, one of the minor figures in the anti-Hughes fight. Undoubtedly he thought he was doing Hughes a favor. Superintendent of Public Works Stevens had visited the White House and asked for Sanders' political scalp, apparently not mentioning that he spoke without Hughes' knowledge or consent. Roosevelt may well have assumed that Stevens was reflecting the Governor's wishes. As Sanders was a partisan of the Wadsworth clan, however, both Stevens and Roosevelt had personal motives for moving against him, apart from any interest in the Hughes program.

Congressman James W. Wadsworth, the Speaker's father, had denounced Roosevelt's meat-inspection bill, and, losing his fight, had called the President "a humbug and a faker."[12] Wadsworth's "federal appointees" were thereafter removed "one by one."[13] When the ax fell upon Archie Sanders, Wadsworth accused the President of persecuting his (Wadsworth's) friends because of his opposition to the meat-inspection bill. Reporters carried the accusation to the White House, where a statement was given out saying Sanders was being removed to "uphold the hands of Governor Hughes." "It is the President's intention," said the *Tribune*, "to strengthen Governor Hughes' stand at every opportunity."[14]

[10] *New York Press*, March 29, 1907.
[11] Fuller Collection, New York Public Library, Vol. 101.
[12] CEH to Mark Sullivan, Oct. 22, 1929. [13] Brooklyn *Daily Eagle*, Dec. 13, 1907.
[14] April 20, 1907.

Hughes read this news with dismay. The President's interest in what he was trying to do was indeed gratifying, but Roosevelt was using patronage as a club in Hughes' behalf—a method the Governor had repeatedly pledged himself not to use. If he had had any inkling as to what Stevens was up to, Hughes would have scotched the proposal before it had been made. Newsmen flocked into the executive chamber to learn whether he had changed his policy. In response to their questions, he admitted that he had not requested the President to remove Sanders. Even at the risk of offending the President, Hughes would not be a hypocrite. He told the correspondents the simple truth, without authorizing quotation of what he had said.

"It was stated from excellent authority today," the *New York Times* reported the next morning, "that Governor Hughes was not consulted . . . and knew nothing about it [Sanders' resignation] until it was announced to the public." [15] Hughes' matter-of-fact explanation was to be grossly distorted by another newspaper to feed the fires of personal resentment. But that story can best be told in another connection. For the moment it is sufficient to note that the Governor's failure to fall in with Roosevelt's "big stick" tactics brought a sudden cooling off at the White House.

At first the order for Sanders' removal had been a jolt to the bosses. Opposition to the Hughes program was temporarily relaxed. But when the Governor dissociated himself from the Sanders incident and the resentment of the White House became evident, the anti-Hughes forces cut loose. Albany witnessed the amazing spectacle of Republican leaders in the Senate violently denouncing the Republican Governor. "Even the Governor's friends confess," wailed the *Tribune*, "that he is about defeated on all the things he suggested in his message." On May 3 the Senate demonstrated its control of the situation by voting 27 to 24 to reject the Governor's request for the removal of Otto Kelsey.

The immediate effect of this defeat was a tragedy in the Governor's official family. Through all his darkest hours at the executive chamber Hughes had had the unfailing aid and support of Ernest W. Huffcut, his legal adviser. Huffcut had succeeded Hughes as professor of law at Cornell University in 1893 and moved on to become dean of the law school. Handsome, vigorous and amiable as well as intellectual, the young bachelor was a man of inestimable promise. Governor Higgins had made Huffcut his legal adviser, and Hughes induced the dean to remain with him in the same capacity on extended leave. They had been good friends, and now the bond between them was greatly strengthened as they fought together in a cause that had the undivided loyalty of both.

Huffcut went to the Governor's office on the morning of Friday, May 3, with an armful of bills. He found Hughes dictating a speech to be delivered at Elmira that night. The governor had planned to go directly from Elmira to New York

[15] April 21, 1907.

City, where he was to speak the following night, but when Huffcut said the bills would have to be signed or rejected by Monday night he agreed to return to Albany on the night train.

The dean was dejected because of the Senate's refusal to remove Kelsey. Along with other members of the Governor's staff, he had nervously awaited until 2:00 A.M. that very morning for the Senate to vote. The Governor himself had gone to bed. Being extremely sensitive, Huffcut probably feared that Hughes might be overwhelmed by this defeat.

"Now, Governor," he said, putting his arm around his friend's shoulders as they walked together to the waiting carriage, "don't feel badly about this Kelsey business. It will hurt them more than you. You don't need to worry. Everything will come out all right." [16]

"I'm not disheartened at all," Hughes replied, without a trace of regret in his voice. "I simply showed the people that I was trying to do all I could to reform the Insurance Department. The conduct of that department is now the responsibility of the Senate."

After the speech at Elmira, Hughes took the train for Albany by way of Binghamton. But when the locomotive broke down in the early morning, he gave up trying to get to Albany and wired Huffcut to bring the bills down to the Astor Hotel in New York, where they could work on them together. Instead of Huffcut, an undertaker called on Governor Hughes and his military aide at breakfast that morning. Someone from the Governor's office, he said, had committed suicide on the night boat from Albany. They hastened to the morgue, and there lay Huffcut with a bullet wound in his temple.

Hughes' suffering over the incident was the more acute because Huffcut's action seemed so inexplicable. To be sure, Huffcut had been under severe pressure from a long and exasperating legislative session. But his work had been less exacting than that of Fuller and the Governor himself, and Huffcut had given no indication of undue fatigue. Apparently the Kelsey vote convinced him that he had failed, and the strain was too much for his sensitive and somewhat morbid nature.

Months later the *Ithaca Journal* intimated that Huffcut's death might have been traceable to an interview with the Governor about a legislative blunder.[17] A bill passed by the legislature and signed by the Governor was discovered to have no enacting clause. Someone jumped to the conclusion that Hughes might have reproved his legal aid for failure to note the oversight. Owen L. Potter, who had been assistant to Huffcut, hastened to point out, however, that the bill in question had not been signed until after Huffcut's death and the mistake was not discovered until a week later.[18] The unfortunate dean went to his

[16] Author's interview with CEH, April 16, 1946. [17] Dec. 3, 1907.

[18] *Ithaca Journal* carries Potter's letter dated Dec. 4, 1907, Fuller Collection, Vol. 149.

death without the slightest shadow on his relationship with Hughes. The Governor so highly appraised Huffcut's ability that he had planned to offer him a judgeship.

Nevertheless, the suicide of the Governor's brilliant adviser deepened the gloom that overcast Albany. Hughes had lost the support of the bosses, the legislature, and the White House, and even Fate seemed to have turned her back upon him. The bleak outlook might well have discouraged any lone-handed fighter without a high degree of iron in his will.

Chapter 19

RETAINER FROM THE PEOPLE

NO DOMESTIC issue was more troublesome to the untamed United States of America in 1907 than control of the big public service corporations. Hughes had wrestled with one segment of the problem in the gas and electric-light investigation. On his advice, the state had created in New York City a Commission of Gas and Electricity and, incidentally, Hughes had declined Governor Higgins' offer of its chairmanship. When he was elected governor, he saw that the regulation of utilities would have to be approached on a much broader base. The state had been creating special regulatory bodies for some time, but their jurisdiction was narrow and their powers were meager. The usual outcome was not commission control of the utility but utility control of the commission.

The necessity of prompt as well as comprehensive action was impressed on Hughes when, as governor-elect, he made a firsthand investigation of the "bridge crush." Taking his chance along with thousands of other New Yorkers trying to get across the Brooklyn Bridge in the "rush hour," he was jolted, trodden, and squeezed by a seething mass of men and women fighting for a ride home. He narrowly escaped being pushed into the pathway of the cars. The bridge crush was only a small part of the railway safety problem. The railroads in Greater New York were killing more than 500 persons a year and injuring 2,000. And safety was only one of many neglected phases of utility regulation.

Hughes' broader investigation showed that railroads were practicing "pernicious favoritism"—granting secret rebates and discriminating as to rates and transportation service. "Those who have sought to monopolize trade have thus been enabled to crush competition and grow in wealth and power," he said in his message to the legislature, "by crowding out their rivals who have been deprived of access to markets upon equal terms. These abuses are not to be tolerated." [1] The Board of Railroad Commissioners was an important, machine-controlled body with only the power to make recommendations for enforcement of the law. Its expenses were paid by the railroads as if in cynical recognition of the fact that it was used by them to deceive the people into thinking that regulation existed when it did not.

[1] *Public Papers of Charles E. Hughes, 1907*, p. 29.

In Boston, Hughes' friend Louis Brandeis had successfully concluded a few months earlier a fight for the adjustment of gas rates by a sliding-scale formula.[2] Progressive Mr. Brandeis was still trying to cope with the big public service corporations through specialized commissions and direct action of the legislature. Hughes thought the time for such halfway measures had passed, so far as New York was concerned. He asked that the whole welter of special regulatory bodies be swept away and that two powerful public service commissions be set up in their place—one to regulate transportation and utilities in New York City and adjacent counties and the other to have jurisdiction throughout the remainder of the state. Only strong and expert administrative agencies armed with a mandate from the people could end the era of governmental shadow boxing with gigantic utilities.

Each of the new public service commissions, the Governor said, should have "power to act upon its own initiative as well as upon complaint; to pass upon the issue of stocks and bonds; to examine properties, books and accounts; to require detailed reports in prescribed form; to prescribe reasonable rates; to require adequate and impartial service; to provide for the safety of employees and for the protection of the public; and generally to direct whatever may be necessary or proper to safeguard the public interest and to secure the fulfillment of the public obligations of the corporations under its supervision." [3] The regulatory bodies were to have ample powers of inspection in order to detect abuses before they assumed serious proportions. Their orders were to be enforced through legal action to be brought by themselves and given preference in the courts.

The Governor provided a blueprint for the modern type of public service commission that was to become an increasingly important factor in American life during the next half-century. Wisconsin was pioneering in the same field, and Congress had extended the regulatory power of the Interstate Commerce Commission, but nowhere in America was there a regulatory body of the scope and power that Hughes sought to give his commissions.

The Governor worked with Senator Page and Assemblyman Merritt in preparing the bill, which was introduced on March 6, 1907. He had loyal support, too, from Senators Hinman and Agnew, Assemblyman John Lord O'Brian, and many others. Secretary of State Elihu Root also contributed valuable advice, being especially concerned over the corporations' prevalent practice of issuing watered stock on the basis of mergers.[4]

To facilitate the selection of experts, the bill authorized $10,000 salaries (later raised to $15,000) for the five members of each commission. It gave each commission jurisdiction over railways, pipe lines, tubes, express, gas, and

[2] Alpheus Thomas Mason, *Brandeis*, pp. 137–138.

[3] *Public Papers, 1907*, pp. 31–32.

[4] Root to CEH, Dec. 20, 1906.

electric-light companies. It forbade special rates, rebates, free tickets, and unjust discrimination by any device. Fares and rates would have to be posted for the information of the public. The commissions could not authorize the capitalization of franchises, except to the extent that they represented actual payments made to the state or a municipality. Mergers could not be capitalized beyond the amount of the capital stock of the two merged companies. The commissions could quickly abolish discriminatory rates and fix fair ones. Penalties as high as $5,000 could be assessed for each separate day's violation of a commission order, or officers and employees of the offending corporation could be sent to jail. Finally, the commissions would have to keep their offices open from 8:00 A.M. to 11:00 P.M. to hear complaints from the public.

But the commissions could not act arbitrarily. Before filing an order, they would have to give the interested corporation a hearing and make a thorough investigation. The rates they fixed would have to be "fair and reasonable." Hughes looked upon his proposed commissions as ideal agencies that could utilize "special knowledge, flexibility, disinterestedness and sound judgment in applying broad legislative principles that are essential to the protection of the community, and of expanding enterprise."

The Page-Merritt bill, as it became known, commanded enthusiastic support from the press. From the bosses and the corporations seeking to avoid control came a barrage of epithets: "Confiscation . . . violation of vested rights . . . usurpation of power . . . ruination of our prosperity." Never had a bill so stirred up the legislature. The betting odds against it would be one hundred to one, a senator commented, except for one thing—the man behind the bill.[5]

The man behind the bill had concluded that his one chance of getting it enacted lay in mobilizing the people behind it. In two months, early in 1907, he preached his public service commission doctrine at forty dinners and meetings. At first his appeal to the people became a "riotous joke" at Albany. The bosses rubbed their hands in delight and talked of tying ribbons in the Governor's whiskers. As the debate continued, however, they found it increasingly difficult to devise any convincing argument against the bill. The opposition concentrated, therefore, on two objections: first, the power the bill gave the Governor to remove the commissioners, and, second, the limitations it placed upon review of the commissions' orders in the courts.

Hughes had insisted upon giving the Governor power to remove members of the commissions for neglect of duty, inefficiency or malfeasance, without requiring the consent of the Senate.[6] His critics said that this would put the commissions under the Governor's control. It is the duty of the Governor, Hughes replied, to see that the laws are faithfully executed, and the removal of

[5] *New York Press*, March 8, 1907. [6] CEH, Notes, p. 191.

commissioners who are failing in their assignment is a suitable incident to the discharge of that duty. The inability of the Governor to remove bungling Mr. Kelsey and other timeservers in important administrative posts was a perfect illustration of his point. "It is a great mistake," he said, "to be so intent on preventing bad administration as to make difficult a good one. . . ."[7]

As to judicial review, Hughes drew a fine line of distinction that was profoundly to influence the relationship between administrative bodies and the courts through the following decades. Thirty-three years later Majority Leader Alben W. Barkley of the United States Senate was to insert into the *Congressional Record* Hughes' then famous speech favoring limited judicial review as a guide to Congress in legislating on judicial supervision of administrative agencies.[8] In 1907, however, the corporations had strong backing in insisting that the courts be given "a general review" over all the orders of the commissions. That view was widely accepted at the time. It was championed in the hearings on the bill by a battery of lawyers selected no doubt with the object of impressing the Governor as well as the legislature. There were Joseph H. Choate, Hughes' former mentor and senior associate in various legal battles; Paul D. Cravath, Hughes' former partner; De Lancey Nicoll, a friend of the Governor; and Edward M. Shepard.

Hughes insisted that the commissions should operate without interference from the courts unless they should exceed their statutory authority or issue an unconstitutional order. "In either of these cases," he said, "there should be full judicial review." But the courts should not be asked to make decisions properly within the sphere of the legislature or an administrative body. It was not their province to upset administrative findings supported by evidence and not shown to be arbitrary. "To provide a right of appeal to the courts from every order of the commission," he argued, "not only invites delay and an unnecessary multiplicity of proceedings, but has for its object the substitution of the judgment of the court for the action of the commission. To give the court power to hear such appeals, to take evidence, and to reverse or to modify the orders of the commission comes simply to this: that the court becomes in effect the ruling commission, and the commission created by the Legislature is simply a board to take evidence and make what are, in effect, recommendations."[9] The Governor based his case on the bedrock principle of keeping fact-finding and policy decisions in the commissions and legal and constitutional issues in the courts.

Administrative agencies were then in their infancy, so far as the United States was concerned. But their essential place in modern government was as clear as sunlight to Hughes. It was not difficult to frame legislation establishing general standards, but to translate accepted principles into regulations wisely

[7] CEH, Speech at Glens Falls, April 5, 1907.
[8] *Congressional Record* (appendix) Vol. 85, Pt. 15, p. 2686.
[9] Address at Elmira, May 3, 1907

adapted to particular cases required an experienced body sitting continuously and removed so far as possible from the blandishments and intrigues of politics. Complaints had to be heard, expert investigations conducted, complex situations deliberately and impartially analyzed, and legislative rules intelligently adapted to a myriad of instances. Only a commission acting under authority appropriately delegated by the legislature could do this job, and only special knowledge, flexibility, disinterestedness, and sound judgment could save the commission from lapsing into a stultifying bureacracy that would not benefit the community but would hurt it.

It was at Elmira in the midst of this fight over the public service commissions that Hughes uttered his most frequently quoted phrase: ". . . the Constitution is what the judges say it is." Through the remainder of his life he was to hear and see this casual phrase, torn from the context of an extemporaneous speech, repeated again and again as if he had, in a moment of candor, exposed the solemn function of judging as a sort of humbuggery. Of course he had done nothing of the sort. "The inference that I was picturing constitutional interpretation by the courts as a matter of judicial caprice," he wrote in his Biographical Notes, ". . . was farthest from my thought. I was not talking flippantly or in disrespect of the courts, but on the contrary with the most profound respect. I was speaking of the essential function of the courts under our system in interpreting and applying constitutional safeguards, and I was emphasizing the importance of maintaining the courts in the highest public esteem as our final judicial arbiters and the inadvisability of needlessly exposing them to criticism and disrespect by throwing upon them the burden of dealing with purely administrative questions." [10]

The inexcusable nature of the distortion to which this segment of his speech has been subjected may be readily seen from the following paragraphs of the text:

> I have the highest regard for the courts. My whole life has been spent in work conditioned upon respect for the courts. I reckon him one of the worst enemies of the community who will talk lightly of the dignity of the bench. We are under a Constitution, but the Constitution is what the judges say it is, and the judiciary is the safeguard of our liberty and of our property under the Constitution. I do not want to see any direct assault upon the courts, nor do I want to see any indirect assault upon the courts. And I tell you, ladies and gentlemen, no more insidious assault could be made upon the independence and esteem of the judiciary than to burden it with these questions of administration,—questions which lie close to the public impatience, and in regard to which the people are going to insist on having administration by officers directly accountable to them.
>
> Let us keep the courts for the questions they were intended to consider . . . there will be abundant opportunity for review of everything that should be reviewed.

[10] CEH, Notes, p. 193.

But to say that all these matters of detail which will be brought before the commission,—matters requiring men to give their entire attention to the subject, to get their information in a variety of ways, to have hearings of those interested, and to deal with questions from a practical standpoint,—should, at the option of the corporations, be taken into court, is to make a mockery of your regulation. And, on the other hand, if that policy should succeed, it would swamp your courts with administrative burdens and expose them to the fire of public criticism in connection with matters of this description, from which I hope they will be safeguarded.

The much quoted phrase lacks the deliberate quality usually associated with the Chief-Justice-to-be. But, left in its context, its meaning is unmistakable. So widespread has been the distortion of this phrase, however, that any attempt to restore it to its original meaning suggests Pandora's difficulty in trying to return the ills of life to her box.

The fight for the public service commissions bill took the Governor to many different parts of the state. The joy of combat was aroused in him, and he threw himself into the campaign as if the whole American experiment of government by the people were at stake.

On the fiftieth anniversary of the Buffalo Chamber of Commerce, April 18, 1907, he went to a banquet prepared to eulogize the progress of Buffalo. When the assembled businessmen made it an opposition meeting to the public service commissions bill, however, he put aside his prepared speech and ripped into the contention that the reforms he was championing would wreck legitimate business. The prevailing sentiment of the country, he said, rejoiced in the extension of commerce and the development of industry. It extolled prudence; revered achievement; but it also demanded honesty. "The people . . . have no inclination to hamper industry," he added, "but they are tired of financial jugglery, and they demand proper service."

At Elmira on May 3, Hughes learned from his host, Judge Walter Lloyd Smith, that he was scheduled to speak first at the Chamber of Commerce that night. The privilege of having the last word had been reserved for John B. Stanchfield, prominent up-State lawyer, legislator and former mayor of Elmira. Hughes suspected rigging and asked Judge Smith to have the program altered so that he would speak last. His suspicions were fully confirmed when Stanchfield launched into a slashing attack upon the public service commissions bill, speaking as a citizen "under no retainer from the railroads."

Once more Hughes discarded his prepared speech. "In distinction from my learned friend," he asserted, "I am here under a retainer. I am here retained by the people of the State of New York, to see that justice is done, and with no disposition to injure any investment, but with every desire to give the fullest opportunity to enterprise, and with every purpose to shield and protect every just property interest. I stand for the people of the State of New York against extortion, against favoritism, against financial scandal, and against everything that goes to corrupt our politics by interference with the freedom of our Legislature and administration."

In spite of the country's prosperity, he said, there was a general feeling of discontent. Why? "Will anyone suggest to an intelligent audience that American citizens are in revolt against their own prosperity? What they revolt against," the Governor declared, "is dishonest finance. What they are in rebellion against is favoritism which gives a chance to one man to move his goods and not to another; which gives to one man one set of terms and another set to his rival; which makes one man rich and drives another man into bankruptcy or into combinations with his more successful competitor. It is a revolt against all the influences which have grown out of an unlicensed freedom, and of a failure to recognize that these great privileges, so necessary for public welfare, have been created by the public for the public benefit and not primarily for private advantage."

As he scored point after point, with his profoundly serious and forceful delivery, the applause rose by jumps. The speech attained a power that reverberated throughout the state. Hughes' happy phrase "retained by the people" echoed and reechoed as the battle approached a climax. "People do listen to the fellow," one old-time boss exclaimed with an oath, "and when he sticks his thumbs into his vest pockets and puts his head down, that's the time to watch out!" [11]

The people recognized not only that the Governor was right but also that he was fighting gallantly for their interests without regard for his own political future. A Citizens League was organized to blanket the state with information concerning the Governor's program and the legislative rebellion at Albany. Wave after wave of public sentiment favorable to the Hughes reforms began to roll toward the capital. The Governor's candid communion with the people was bringing results.

After their victory in the Kelsey affair, the legislators rewarded themselves with a week end at home. Instead of congratulations, they encountered a "torrent of reproach." [12] Almost to a man the people said the Governor was right. "When I got home," one senator reported, "the people fairly mobbed me. They took me to task on the street corners and called me up on the telephone in the middle of the night. They said: 'Look here, young man, why aren't you standing with the Governor? Are you tired of political life? You go back to Albany and line up with Hughes, or never dare to ask again for votes in this district.' " [13]

The Capitol was deluged with mail—entreaties, threats, and scathing denun-

[11] Author's interview with John Lord O'Brian, July 25, 1950.
[12] Ida M. Tarbell in *American Magazine*, March, 1908.
[13] *World's Work*, March, 1908, p. 41.

ciations from constituents. The same flood of indignation was reflected in the press. Never within the memory of men had the machine been subjected to such a bombardment from so many sources. Republican bosses who had been laughing at what they called Hughes' "babe-in-the-woods" tactics now turned and ran to cover in almost a panic of submission. Woodruff assembled the Republican State Committee "to demonstrate to the people that the Republican organization is with the Governor." Securing a resolution of unanimous support for the Hughes policies, he rushed to Albany to save the Republican Party from suicide. Senator Raines flip-flopped with astounding dexterity and called a caucus to get his followers on the bandwagon. Speaker Wadsworth also surrendered, and the Assembly passed "the Governor's bill," substantially as it had been introduced, without a dissenting vote. The Senate soon fell into line. Three weeks after Hughes' "appeals to the intellect" began, one journalist observed, "an insolent and hostile legislature was on its knees." [14]

One Assemblyman said that not more than twenty of his colleagues were in favor of allowing the Governor to remove commission members. They voted to give him that power in order to save their necks. Hughes made no bargain with the machine. Armed only with his principles, with public confidence, and the gift of couching his message in terms that galvanized the people, he swept all opposition before him.

Having joined lustily in the fight, the press was delighted by the outcome. "Not since Tilden's day," boasted the *World,* "has New York had a governor who was mentally, morally, professionally and politically capable of carrying out such a policy." [15] James Creelman, writing in *Pearson's Magazine,* pronounced the new Act "the most remarkable and, in its significance, far-reaching law passed by any state in the last quarter of a century, a law that may profoundly affect the whole future of the nation." [16] There was some scattered criticism. But the protests were lost in the avalanche of praise. The Act soon became a model for legislation in other states.

The Governor chose William R. Willcox, former park commissioner and postmaster of New York, to be chairman of the Public Service Commission's metropolitan branch. Other members were Edward M. Bassett, former Democratic member of Congress and traffic expert; Milo R. Maltbie, economist and expert in the utilities field; William McCarroll, merchant; and John E. Eustis, lawyer and experienced public official. When Dr. Schurman turned down the chairmanship of the up-State commission, Hughes named Frank W. Stevens, a practicing lawyer of East Randolph and Jamestown. The other members were James E. Sague, engineer and experienced railroad man; Martin S. Decker, who got his training with the Interstate Commerce Commission;

[14] Frank H. Simonds in the *Independent,* June 27, 1907, p. 1495.
[15] June 3, 1907. [16] September, 1907.

Thomas Mott Osborne, businessman and former mayor of Auburn; and Charles Hallam Keep, who had been Hughes' superintendent of banks. Not one of them was a political hack. Only one, Bassett, was a personal friend of Hughes, and he stood out as the best transportation expert available.

Both commissions began their work in the Hughesian tradition, operating without demagogy or outside control. The corporations as well as the consumers were treated fairly, and the previous haughtiness of the interests melted to a spirit of cooperation. It was the beginning of a revolution in the regulation of utilities. Some of the commissions' rulings met with disapproval, but on the whole they functioned efficiently and held the confidence of the people.

While Hughes was working to get the new regulatory system into operation, the legislature passed a bill limiting passenger fares on the railroads of New York State to two cents a mile. He was well aware of the popularity of this measure and of the railroads' past exploitation. Yet he coolly analyzed the bill and vetoed it. The following year a bill forbidding the collection of fares of more than five cents on street railways operating within the limits of a city was to meet the same fate.

No other governor had rejected a two-cent fare bill when confronted by a *fait accompli*. Support of such measures was regarded as the acid test of a governor's loyalty to the people. But Hughes was convinced that public opinion was wrong in this instance and refused to follow it. His reasoning was impeccable. Passage of the bill had not been preceded by a legislative investigation. He did not contend that the two-cent fare would be unreasonably low; it might be high enough in many cases. But the legislature had not attempted to find a proper balance between consumer and corporate interests. It had substituted "unreason for sound judgment . . . a policy seriously mistaken and pregnant with disaster." The Governor insisted that "injustice on the part of railroad corporations toward the public does not justify injustice on the part of the State toward the railroad corporations." [17]

There was, moreover, a better way. The Public Service Commissions now had ample powers to conduct investigations and fix rates in a scientific manner. The Governor insisted that they be allowed an opportunity to do their job free from capricious restrictions.

The two-cent-fare veto brought widespread criticism from those who put immediate relief above principle. But it was hailed by thoughtful commentators for its "statesmanlike quality" and its "soberness and wisdom." Out in Wisconsin Senator Hudnall lauded the courage of the New York Governor and, using Hughes' arguments, defeated a similar two-cent-fare bill that was up before the legislature.[18]

The success of this refreshing renaissance of principle in government brought

[17] *Public Papers, 1907*, p. 89. [18] *New York Times*, June 16, 1907.

Hughes to nationwide attention. He had suddenly become a giant in public affairs. "In six months," wrote Frank H. Simonds, "the quiet corporation attorney, lacking in political training, destitute of even rudimentary partisan experience, has subjugated a state machine, overthrown a legislative cabal and secured for the people of New York the passage of more progressive legislation than the legislative mills of Albany have ground out in a decade." [19]

More than thirty years later an able and progressive member of the 1907 Assembly, John Lord O'Brian, would still be deeply impressed by the Governor's performance. He wrote:

> It is impossible to reproduce for the present generation the aggressive personality, the seemingly inexhaustible energy, the unrelenting insistence of Governor Hughes. It is equally impossible for those who were not eye witnesses to appreciate the dramatic qualities which characterized his efforts, or the overpowering quality of his arguments during those stormy years. . . . Without creating a political faction of his own, he brought to New York State an entirely new kind of political leadership, the effects of which still remain potent. His genius for evoking by personal persuasion the support of popular opinion was as unique as it was successful. The numerous statutes enacted on his insistence present, in themselves, a remarkable record of achievement. But over and above these reforms, it was the force of the man's personality, his genius for masterly exposition and the great confidence of the public in his personal integrity which brought to him the support of the electorate and challenged the attention of the Nation at large.[20]

[19] The *Independent*, June 27, 1907, Vol. 62, p. 1495.
[20] *American Bar Association Journal*, July, 1941, p. 413.

Chapter 20

CRUSADER FOR DEMOCRACY

NOWHERE was Hughes' independence more evident than in the wielding of his veto power. In his first year at Albany he vetoed 297 bills and various items in six appropriation measures. His secretary also estimated that 200 bills were withdrawn because of the Governor's opposition. His firm belief that "our government is one of principle and not of favor" appears to have resulted in the greatest slaughter of special legislation since the days of Cleveland.

One popular measure that went down was a bill to equalize the pay of men and women holding the same positions in the New York City school system. Hughes rejected it because it applied to New York City alone and was an invasion of the powers of the local Board of Education. Another bill designed to force a three-platoon system upon the New York police was vetoed as an encroachment upon home-rule powers. In many instances the Governor wielded his veto to impress upon the legislature the desirability of establishing broad general policies instead of making the law a "patchwork of favoritism."

With the aid of Assemblyman "Al" Smith, Hughes induced the legislature to enact a "clean elections" bill limiting the amounts that candidates for various positions could spend in their campaigns and requiring strict accounting for such expenditures. The Governor's proposed recount of the votes in the McClellan-Hearst mayoralty contest was approved, but the Court of Appeals held the act to be unconstitutional, and a court proceeding under the old law was necessary to lift the cloud of doubt that had hung over McClellan's title and given Hearst a disguise of martyrdom.

Hughes had to call the legislature back into extraordinary session in 1907 to bring about the enactment of a fair bill reapportioning seats in the Senate and Assembly. Subdued by his appeals to the people, the lawmakers also granted the Governor sweeping new power to investigate the organization and conduct of the executive departments and the militia. In one respect this victory seemed to be an extra dividend from his work as a professor of law. At Cornell a student by the name of Sherman Moreland had faithfully stoked Professor Hughes' furnace. Now leader of the Assembly, Moreland was once more disposed to stoke the Hughes furnace. It was he who, at the Governor's request, put through the executive investigations bill, which resulted in numerous probes and enabled Hughes to tie his administration together more securely.

Alert and dynamic though he was, Hughes was caught off guard by the financial panic of 1907. Having transferred Superintendent of Banks Charles H. Keep to the new up-State Public Service Commission, he found it difficult to get the type of man he wanted at the head of the Banking Department for the $7,000 salary the position paid. The post remained vacant for three months. Meanwhile panic was brewing in Wall Street and along with it dissatisfaction over this neglect of the Banking Department. At last Hughes gave the post to Luther Mott of Oswego, son of a Republican state committeeman. Bankers raised their eyebrows in surprise if not dismay. While he was an amiable fellow and had been well recommended, young Mott was inexperienced and proved utterly unequal to the task of nursing the New York banking system through the convulsions that were beginning to shake it.

Within a fortnight Mott went to pieces under the strain. Hughes quickly recognized his mistake and told Mott that he would have to resign.[1] Meanwhile the Governor asked A. Barton Hepburn of the New York Clearing House Committee to name the ablest banker in the state who could be drafted to take over the Banking Department. Hepburn suggested Clark Williams, and under the pressure of the panic Hughes induced Williams to leave the vice presidency of the Columbia Trust Company for this trouble-shooting role at Albany at a small fraction of the salary he had been drawing. Williams took office on October 23, the day after the Knickerbocker Trust Company, with assets of more than $68,000,000, closed its doors following a frantic run by depositors.

A strong and alert banking department might have averted the crisis or at least mitigated its effects. Undoubtedly the Governor had not lived up to his reputation for forehand action. But he quickly recovered his fumble, and induced the banks to cooperate in averting further disaster. Then he named an unpaid commission consisting of Hepburn and five other leading bankers to investigate the causes of the panic and suggest how the state banking laws should be changed to avoid similar emergencies in the future. On the basis of the experts' findings he sponsored bills enlarging the powers of the superintendent of banks, curbing speculation, protecting depositors, and subjecting trust companies that were doing a banking business to the regulations applicable to banks.

The Governor named another group of experts headed by Horace White to delve into the whole broad question of speculation in a free economy and the proper relation of the state to it. While the committee's report was largely devoted to explanation of the economic function performed by the stock and

[1] Author's interview with CEH, Oct. 29, 1947.

commodity markets, it urged that promoters be punished for false statements about securities offered for sale to the public. This idea was to find expression in the federal Securities and Exchange Act a quarter of a century later.

Labor legislation became a specialty of the Hughes régime. John Williams, a practical carpenter, was made state labor commissioner and given the assignment of rescuing the Labor Department from the grip of machine politics. With his aid, Hughes put through a safety measure for railway engineers and firemen, a prohibition against working train-service men more than sixteen consecutive hours, and an eight-hour-day law for railway telegraph and telephone operators and signalmen. Child-labor laws were strengthened and extended, and the working hours of women were limited. Inspection of factories, mines, and tunnels was tightened up; new safeguards to health were established; employees' rights in the courts were more clearly defined, and all New York children were guaranteed an education, with special emphasis on industrial training.

Alarmed by the terrible waste of life and limb in industrial accidents, Hughes named a committee under the chairmanship of Senator Wainwright to devise a new approach to the problem. Industrial America was killing and injuring more workmen in proportion to the number employed than any other country in the world. And the cost of these tragedies was falling largely on the families of the unfortunate workmen themselves. Employers thus had no economic incentive to make their mines, factories, and railroads safe. When the committee brought in its report, the Governor secured the enactment of the first workmen's compensation laws in the United States. One of these provided for an elective compensation plan; the other made compensation for injuries compulsory in certain hazardous industries.

Part of this good work was undone when the New York Court of Appeals upset the compulsory statute as a violation of due process of law.[2] In 1913, however, New York corrected its Court of Appeals by constitutional amendment. That broke the backbone of resistance to industrial insurance. By 1916 thirty-two states had workmen's compensation laws—a belated but nonetheless significant tribute to Hughes' pioneering in this field.

By the end of his second term Hughes' name was on fifty-six statutes for the benefit of labor, "including many of the best labor laws ever enacted in this or any other state." "Now, that Gov. Hughes has retired from politics . . ." commented the *Legislative News*, union labor organ in New York, "the fact can be acknowledged, without hurting anybody's political corns, that he was the greatest friend of labor laws that ever occupied the Governor's chair at Albany."[3]

[2] *Ives* v. *South Buffalo Ry. Co.*, 201 N.Y. 271, 317.
[3] *Legislative News*, October, 1910.

New social legislation and improved state service were largely responsible for the increase in New York State expenditures from $26,978,928 in 1906 to $39,601,224 in 1910. Using his item veto, the Governor stripped appropriation bills of graft and waste but encouraged spending for what he regarded as essential institutions and public functions.

The conservation of forests, water, and natural scenery was a vital concern of the Hughes régime. The guiding principle that the Governor laid down was that "these resources should be preserved and held for the benefit of all the people and should not be surrendered to private interests." [4]

Disregarding the Governor's advice, the legislature granted a charter to the Long Sault Development Company authorizing the construction of dams in a section of the St. Lawrence River, with perpetual rights to the water power thus created. The lawmakers asked nothing in return for this favor. Donation of public rights for private benefit was still the order of the day. But Hughes rebelled. When the innocent-looking bill reached his desk, he sent for Superintendent of Public Works Stevens and asked him to determine how much power the project would generate, what return it would give the company, and what would be a fair amount for the company to pay the state for the rights granted in the charter. Stevens secured the aid of one of the best engineers in the country. When their report reached the Governor, he called in the sponsors of the charter bill and told them it would have to be rewritten so as to require an immediate payment to the state of $100,000 and annual rental charges thereafter. At last an effective blow had been struck at the profligate policy of giving away the state's natural resources. Although the Long Sault charter was later repealed because the company claimed the rights it had obtained were perpetual, the importance of the precedent it had set remained.

President Roosevelt gave the conservation movement great impetus in May, 1908, by assembling a conference of governors at the White House. One of the highlights of the gathering was a speech by Governor Hughes in which he declared that New York was allowing 550,000 horse power of energy worth $6,600,000 to run to waste each year because the state had failed to develop a comprehensive plan for its utilization. Experts were then at work on the problem, but it was not until 1910 that sufficient data had been assembled to permit the formulation of an intelligent water power policy looking toward systematic development of New York's larger rivers.

On the basis of the Water Supply Commission's reports Hughes asked the legislature to accept the following principles as a guide to future action: (1) River flow should be regulated and water power developed "to the fullest extent that may be practicable." (2) Only the state should build and own regulatory or power-generating reservoirs on streams originating in or flow-

[4] *Public Papers, 1907*, p. 37.

ing through public parks or state reservations. (3) Hydroelectric power projects should be undertaken by the state "whenever such action appears to be feasible and for the general interest." (4) Power so developed should be made available on "equitable terms and conditions." (5) Rigid scrutiny should be provided to see that the public interest in the state forest preserves would not be jeopardized by water-power projects.[5]

Hughes had no opportunity to carry this forward-looking policy into effect. But it may well have influenced a young legislator who was just then entering the New York Senate and who would later have much to do with the public development of water-power resources both at Albany and Washington—Franklin D. Roosevelt. In his last years at Albany, Hughes also pleaded for larger purchases of land in the areas of the Adirondack and Catskill Parks. And a gift to the state of ten thousand acres of land in the Hudson highlands of Orange and Rockland Counties by Mrs. E. H. Harriman (in addition to large monetary gifts from Mrs. Harriman, John D. Rockefeller, J. Pierpont Morgan and others) made it possible for Hughes to send to the legislature a $5,000,000 project for extension of Palisades Park. This was one aspect of his work as governor that brought much satisfaction.

Hughes took advantage of the summer, when the legislature was not in session, to visit the state institutions and county fairs and to talk with the people. Everywhere he was greeted enthusiastically; the fairs especially gave him rousing receptions. His finger was close to the public pulse. The result was to solidify his strength at the grass roots in preparation for the new tests that awaited him at Albany.

Wherever he went he preached the doctrine of good government or his philosophy of the good life. A powerful current of optimism ran through all his speeches. At no time did he yield to the "destroying cancer of cynicism." To him the United States was a land of unparalleled prosperity and future promise. No country had ever enjoyed a "larger degree of equal rights and equal opportunities." To be sure, rapacity and corruption had attained unconscionable proportions, but this could be attributed in part to the newness of the country—to the rawness resulting from sudden exploitation of a rich continent. More important was the fact that the people were rising to curb rapacity.

Young America was also confidently moving toward a larger degree of stability. "By stability," he said, "is not meant fixity of things or relations, but steadiness. It may be steadiness in motion. Paradoxical as it may seem, human society cannot be stable unless it is progressive. That is because growth and progress are the law of our nature."[6] In his lectures at Yale University he

[5] *Public Papers, 1910*, pp. 22–25.
[6] *Addresses 1906–1916*, p. 247. Copyright, 1916, by G. P. Putnam's Sons.

added: "The peril of this nation is not in any foreign foe! We, the people, are its power, its peril, and its hope." [7]

"Under certain forms of government," he said, "stability has been maintained by force exercised for the benefit of a privileged few. . . . In a democracy stability depends upon the reign of reason, and it is the fact that we are a common-sense people that gives us assurance for the future. Reason demands the facts . . . not scrappy sensationalism or distorted emphasis" and open conduct of public affairs that will give the people "the truth, the whole truth and nothing but the truth in regard to matters that concern them."

Good administration, he contended, required a concentration of executive powers in the hands of the governor. Hughes was not, however, reaching out promiscuously for more power. When county delegations came to him and urged that the state take over local functions because of the difficulty of getting local boards to act, he would reply: "My friends, that means that you have no confidence in free institutions . . . the first principle of administration is to keep things in connection with local government locally administered so far as possible. . . . It is the greatest mistake in the world to run to Albany to hold the men whom you elect accountable for the discharge of their duties when you can tend to the matter at home." [8]

Nor was he jealous of the Federal Government's expanding powers. The people had many interests beyond the reach of state authority. The future distribution of governmental powers would be determined, he said, "not by sentiment nor by repetition of arguments regarding the original sovereignty of the states, but will result from considerations of paramount public advantage. If it should appear that the powers of the States are inadequate to deal with a subject hitherto retained in their keeping, and that the interests of the people as a whole imperatively demand the assumption of a power by the Federal Government, the people will provide the assumption of that power." [9]

"The people . . . have reached the conclusion," he added on Washington's birthday at the University of Michigan, "that there should be no limit to the exercise of federal power in connection with interstate commerce short of absolutely securing the people in the freedom of that commerce, and of putting an end to the discrimination and unlawful preferences which have afflicted interstate commerce in the past." It is interesting to note that this concept as to the breadth of the power of Congress to control business reaching across state lines—a concept that was later to be written into many of Hughes' opinions as a judge—was well rooted in his mind even while he was wrestling with state problems and might have been assumed to be partial to states' rights. His sojourn at Albany had not upset his objectivity.

[7] *Conditions of Progress in Democratic Government*, p. 8.
[8] *Addresses 1906–1916*, pp. 219–221. [9] New York *Sun*, Feb. 13, 1907.

Apostle of hard work though he was, Hughes took delight in spreading "the gospel of play." "The successful worker," he said, "must have the spirit of play in his heart, and the successful man is only a boy with a man's experience. He must have the zest, the devotion, the spirit of comradeship, the capacity for self-forgetfulness, the boy's wholesome outlook upon life, if he is to do a man's work in the world." [10] His address on "Why We Want Playgrounds" was reprinted many times and thirty-nine years after the speech was made the National Recreation Association was still expressing its sense of indebtedness to Hughes.

In lifting up the people, he discarded racial distinctions. The Negro, he said,

> is entitled to the advantages of training and education. He is entitled, under the stimulus of free institutions, to an opportunity to prove by his works what is in him and to make his contribution, according to his talent and aptitude, to the sum of our productive labors and of our national life; and he is entitled to the rewards which his character and industry may deserve. There is no color line in good work, whether of hand or brain. . . . It has well been said that whatever problem the progress of the Negro may present, it is not comparable with that which will be presented by stagnation or retrogression. In this land the door of opportunity must be wide open to our citizens. We want neither slaves nor serfs, nor any body of citizens permanently below the standards which must be maintained for the preservation of the Republic. We cannot maintain our democratic ideals as to one set of our people and ignore them as to others.[11]

Democracy, he thought, should secure to every man an opportunity "to make the most of himself." But it also demanded that "no man should construe his opportunity to mean license to exploit his fellow men and unjustly profit himself at the expense of their equal chance. The cry 'Every man for himself' is out of date," the Governor exclaimed. "The demand of the future will be 'Every man for the people!' " [12]

"If the term Bolshevik had been invented then," said Oswald Garrison Villard some years later, "the business community would have applied it to Charles E. Hughes." [13] Yet there was nothing revolutionary in his program. "It is not our part to plan an ambitious scheme for the reconstruction of society," he said. "Our immediate duty is more practical than that. It is to obtain from our existing institutions that full measure of freedom of political action and of equality of opportunity which they were intended and are able to confer." [14]

What Hughes preached night after night and week after week was the more

[10] Address to the Recreation Congress, 1908.
[11] Speech in behalf of Tuskegee Institute, Jan. 17, 1908.
[12] *Addresses 1906–1916*, p. 270.
[13] *Prophets True and False*, p. 38. Copyright, 1928, by Alfred A. Knopf, Inc.
[14] *Utica Press*, Dec. 14, 1906.

effective because he practiced it by day. He became not merely the evangelist of democracy but also the practitioner who employed its principles to produce far-reaching social improvements. Aware of the unrest that permeated the nation, he held unwaveringly to the conviction that that unrest could be cured by courageous leadership and faithful application of the representative principle. Ida M. Tarbell caught the gist of what he was trying to do when she wrote: "Charles E. Hughes is engaged in a passionate effort to vindicate the American system of government." [15]

[15] *American Magazine*, March, 1908, p. 464.

Chapter 21

MAN BEHIND THE WHISKERS

INSIDE the Executive Mansion the Hughes household was managed primarily for the Governor's convenience. Antoinette Carter Hughes presided there with the same natural poise that had always endeared her to husband, children, friends, and servants. But there was a new light in her eye. Her unwavering faith in her husband had been vindicated. He was well launched upon what she knew in her bones would be a great career. Within her own realm of activity she bent every effort to smoothing his way.

No craving for the spotlight actuated her avid interest in his career. She was the antithesis of a social climber. In 1906 she had refused to let her picture be published until after the election, and she assumed her new station as the first lady of New York without a trace of hauteur. Her freedom from pretense even went to the extreme of admitting that she was forty-two. But her ambition to see her husband succeed in whatever he undertook was boundless. She never permitted the children to break in on him or create a disturbance when he was at work. Knowing his excitable nature and his keen sensitivity to his surroundings, she shielded him in a hundred ways without any suggestion from him and in many instances without his knowledge.

The family routine was a reflection of the Hugheses' orderly habits and their love of privacy. Breakfast was always served at precisely the same hour with all members of the family present. Mrs. Hughes invariably came downstairs dressed as if she were going out for the day. The Governor, too, was always fully dressed for the office before he left his room. At bedtime a cordial "Good night" went the rounds, and when their door was closed it remained closed for the night. None of the children thought of intruding or even knocking until father and mother appeared the next morning.

Yet there was neither stiffness nor stuffiness in their family relationships. Both parents set great store upon their offspring. Mrs. Hughes had come to Albany, as she had gone to Ithaca, expecting a baby. On August 19, 1907, she had the distinction of bringing into the world the first child (Elizabeth) ever born in the Executive Mansion. The event seemed to demonstrate the primacy of her conjugal and maternal interests. She was immensely pleased to be the mother of four children. Young Charlie would be a junior when he returned to Brown University in the fall. Helen and Catherine ("Caca" within the family after her baby sister began to talk) were going to the Albany Girls Academy. The Hugheses were so sufficient unto themselves and so wrapped up in their own activities that they felt little need for intimate friendships outside the family circle.

The comfortable old Executive Mansion on Eagle Street often resounded with merriment. Sometimes, to be sure, Hughes would come home with a Sisyphean burden on his mind and sit through a meal scarcely uttering a word. Sometimes he would unloose a flow of serious talk as if to relieve accumulated pressures. But more often his humor would bubble up through whatever responsibility he carried. One story that brought gales of laughter was a garbled newspaper account of a speech the Governor had made during one of his fights with the bosses. He had characterized them as "petty satraps" but was solemnly quoted as calling them "petty rat traps."

In the bosom of the family he remained a persistent funmaker. He had a habit of winking at his daughters with a meaningful twinkle in his eye and of waving at them with a congenial wagging of the fingers. His reputation for austerity in official life did not restrain him from causing a riot at home by mimicking a cat, lion, or monkey. A stern and uncompromising governor he might be, but to his children he was still a warm, human, and companionable father and the funniest man they had ever known.[1] A visitor privileged to look in upon his antics would have accepted quite literally a comment he once made to a group of school children to the effect that "while men grow to look old . . . every man is a boy in his heart, and he finds it difficult as he grows older to understand why other people do not take him that way." [2]

Contributing also to the homely atmosphere of the Mansion was Mrs. Hughes' canary and the children's mongrel bull terrier named Petie. Hughes had a fondness for animals and was even tolerant of the duck that had been given to the children when they visited the Home for Incurables. Cats won his special favor, and it was not unusual for him to sit down to read with a kitten on his shoulder.

Except during brief vacations, the Governor had no time to take the children on fun-seeking expeditions, as he had done in New York. Their principal playmates were the orphans of St. Joseph's Catholic Home, which adjoined the back yard of the Executive Mansion. Mrs. Hughes had groups of these children over several times a year for games, cake, and ice cream.

In spite of their self-sufficiency, the Hugheses did not neglect the social amenities. Mrs. Hughes readily adjusted her thinking from the small and simple dinner parties that she had given in New York and Ithaca to the large

[1] Author's interview with Catherine Hughes Waddell, June 16, 1948.
[2] Washington's birthday speech in Chicago, 1908.

official receptions that were expected of her in Albany. Her first step was to replenish her wardrobe. She loved beautiful clothes and had always dressed well but in keeping with the needs of the occasion. Now she felt that some elegant gowns would be appropriate and did not hesitate to buy them. Hughes watched approvingly the transformation that was effected by her bright red dress, her canary yellow dress, and the others. But he could not refrain from teasing. "Now, my dear," he would say, "what you need is jewels."

Even during her pregnancy Mrs. Hughes gave two large receptions, in honor of the legislators and the judges, sending out more than 2,500 invitations for each. After her child was born, she made a practice of receiving the ladies of Albany almost every week during the social season. These were memorable occasions. The tall, slender hostess, looking beautiful in her new canary yellow or bright red dress, won the hearts of her guests by cordial greetings, by her intriguing combination of vivacity and dignity, and by her democratic practice of widely distributing the honor of acting as co-hostess. Music by the National Guard band ensconced on the stairway added an official touch. But a homelike atmosphere prevailed when the infant Elizabeth was brought down and invariably screamed instead of cooing for the guests. Helen and Catherine played a part no less domestic but much less conspicuous. It was their task to keep Petie, the bull terrier, in a back room and prevent him from barking, which seemed to necessitate continuous throwing of horse chestnuts for him to chase around the room.

The Hugheses frequently accepted dinner invitations and returned the compliments with dinners at the Executive Mansion. Mrs. Hughes was "queenly and gracious" on such occasions but left most of the talking to others. Seldom did she enter a discussion of public affairs even with her husband. Usually the Governor dominated the conversation regardless of who the guests might be. His dynamism, his impressive manner of speaking, and his good memory combined to give him the center of the stage.

In their four years at Albany the Governor and Mrs. Hughes met and worked with all kinds of people. In many instances there came to be a mutual exchange of high regard and affection. Yet these relations stopped short of intimate friendship. Mrs. Hughes' natural reserve kept friendships on an impersonal basis. She would freeze up in a moment if she thought a visitor was trying to pry into her personal affairs. As for the Governor, personal friendships were less important to him than his work, which absorbed most of the time that other men gave to casual friendly intercourse. And he felt no need to seek personal understanding, sympathy, or solace outside his home. If the events of the day caused him to boil inside, the woman he loved was at hand to soothe his troubled spirit. Sometimes, to be sure, she chided him for trying to do too much, saying that he carried the burdens of office along with him.

But she never nagged him and never sought to restrain him from doing anything she knew he wished to do or believed it his duty to do.

To the bosses, Hughes was still a formidable figure, and many were afraid of him. His extraordinary self-containment and the absence of political intermediaries in the executive chamber encouraged the belief that he was cold and aloof. To the Albany crowd he was "Charles the Baptist" or "Whiskers" —but only behind his back. His secretary confirmed the fact that no one ever slapped the Governor on the shoulder and called him "Charlie." Among those who worked with him, however, he inspired an astonishing degree of loyalty that cannot be explained as devotion to the principles he espoused. One editor concluded that, so far from being an icicle, Hughes had become "a remarkable example of the live, glowing wire." [3]

Traveling from western New York one night with Colonel Treadwell and John Palmer Gavit, the Governor discovered that only one berth had been reserved on the sleeper for his party. Gavit and Treadwell insisted that he should take it. His rest, they said, was of public importance. Hughes laughed and insisted on sharing the inconvenience. Through most of the night they exchanged stories and, according to Gavit, had "a jolly time." It was after this experience that Gavit described Hughes as "phenomenally clear-headed, single-minded . . . inconceivably industrious, absolutely fearless . . . but humanly approachable and friendly, good natured, reasonable, jovial—and on the level with his job." [4]

The Governor took a party of Civil War Veterans and state officials to Gettysburg in September, 1907, to dedicate the Greene Monument on Culp's Hill. General Alexander S. Webb, who had commanded the New York troops at the Bloody Angle, and General Sickles, who had lost a leg at Gettysburg, gave them a memorable account of the battle that saved the Union. In the evening, as Hughes' brilliantly lighted car lay in the railroad yards, he entertained a group of his guests with stories. When he repeated the tale of his son's eerie ascent of the Strasbourg cathedral spire, he danced about, gesticulating excitedly, throwing all his energy into the drama of the story. Then suddenly he caught a glimpse of the large crowd of spectators who had gathered outside to see the show, although they could hear nothing of what he was saying. For a moment Hughes had the look of a dignitary who had been caught clowning, but he joined in the general laughter at his expense.

"That comes of drinking three cups of tea at dinner," he said. "I shall never again be able to tell that story without chills of the spine." [5]

At the Jamestown Exposition of 1907, Governor Hughes first met the man whom he was later to challenge for leadership of the nation. Woodrow Wilson

[3] *Kansas City Times,* Oct. 28, 1908.
[4] New York *Evening Post,* June 10, 1916. [5] *Ibid.*

was then the suave, learned, and conservative president of Princeton University. He had been invited, along with the Governor of New York, to address the descendants of the signers of the Declaration of Independence on July 4. Both were breakfast guests of Henry St. George Tucker in Norfolk before going to the exposition grounds. Later they accompanied General Frederick Grant to Old Point Comfort, reviewed the fleet, and watched the fireworks. It was a full day they spent together as members of an eminent group of officials and dignitaries. Hughes found Mr. Wilson "a most charming conversationalist" and reported that he had "a thoroughly enjoyable time." [6]

Wilson's enjoyment of the occasion seems to have been less pronounced, at least when the formal speaking began. On several visits to New York, Wilson had spoken disparagingly of Hughes' reforms. The courts, he insisted, could do more purifying than the "new instrumentalities [Hughes' regulatory commissions] now being unthinkingly elaborated." His scorn for regulatory commissions was as well defined as his contempt for Bryanism and for Theodore Roosevelt's assault on big business. At Jamestown, after listening to Hughes' speech, Wilson altered the entire plan of his own address.[7]

Intellectual fencing gave way to less weighty matters, however, at the Tucker house. One of Mr. Wilson's sallies brought an expression of surprise from a guest who said she thought the president of Princeton had to be a clergyman. Wilson replied that others had had that erroneous notion and that the university, he feared, had lost a large gift because he had given some offense in repeating a favorite limerick in the presence of an old Presbyterian lady. The amused guests demanded the limerick, and Wilson responded as follows:

> There was a young monk of Siberia
> Whose life grew drearier and drearier,
> So he burst from his cell
> With a hell of a yell
> And eloped with the Mother Superior.

In later years, when the once conservative university president surprised the country with the liberal measures he promoted as Governor of New Jersey, Hughes thought Mr. Wilson's limerick might be taken, in a figurative sense, to be autobiographical.[8]

Hughes' yearning for the wilds had to be restrained in the years of his governorship. The family remained in the Executive Mansion all summer in 1907, when daughter Elizabeth was born, and the Governor had only a few days of fishing and tramping with his son in the Adirondack woods, using a forester's camp for their headquarters. In the following two summers the family took

[6] CEH, Notes, p. 201. [7] New York *World*, Jan. 6, 1908.
[8] CEH, Notes, pp. 201–202.

a cottage at Saranac Inn, which became in effect a summer executive office. Hughes spent most of his time there dictating letters, making appointments, granting extraditions, ordering investigations, and replying to appeals for aid.

In the summer of 1908 he broke away for a brief walking trip with his son and the latter's college chum. From Lake Placid they tramped through the Indian Pass to the Tawahus Club, fished in Lake Colden, and climbed to the top of Mount Marcy. At forty-six he still had an urge to climb every mountain in sight. At the summit they encountered a party of young people, and one of the girls pampered the Governor with a generous offering of huckleberries. In return he gave the party a beefsteak and some tea. At the great campaign meeting in Madison Square Garden that fall, as Hughes was being ushered through the crowd to the speaker's stand, a young woman thrust out her hand and gave him a card. While waiting for the audience to quiet down, he read the card: "Good luck! We ate your steak and drank your health in the tea." [9]

The Governor found some opportunities for reading. While waiting for the balky legislature to act on his measures in 1907, he read six of Dumas' swashbuckling novels. "If the session keeps up much longer," he told one interviewer, "I'll have to begin on Gaboriau." Sometimes he read Ibsen and Henry James. But Ibsen tried to make life too dismal, and Hughes was never persuaded that life was as complex as "Henry James has almost persuaded us that it is." [10] Hardy distorted his characters. Shaw was not to be taken seriously. As an escape from tension, Hughes came to like "blood-and-thunder romance" better than any other type of literature. There is nothing like a good thriller or detective story for a weary brain and a tired back, he said, nothing like it in the world.

His work habits were even more extreme than they had been in his practice of law. He arrived at the executive chamber as soon as the mail was ready. His office received from forty to four hundred letters a day. Usually he ate lunch at his desk in the Capitol—merely a sandwich, an apple, and tea. While eating he listened to complaints or advice from visitors and then resumed his work until six or seven in the evening. When he carried work home —a frequent occurrence—it was not unusual for him to keep at it until midnight or even 2:00 A.M.

There was neither showmanship nor masochism in this performance. Hughes felt that he must handle every problem that called for exercise of the gubernatorial judgment, and he had to have the facts to go on. "No duty was ever too small to receive the closest attention," his secretary tells us, and no obligation was ever so great as to cause him to shrink from its performance.[11] "His

[9] CEH, Notes, p. 205. [10] *Current Literature*, February, 1906, pp. 207–210.
[11] MS by Robert H. Fuller, Hughes Papers, Library of Congress.

work literally takes possession of him," said Dr. Schurman. "It is consequently impossible for him to do anything he undertakes in a half-hearted or slipshod manner." [12]

New challenges repeatedly reenergized his powers. So far as it was humanly possible, Hughes insisted on finding not merely an answer to each problem but the right answer. Every issue had to be weighed with the deliberation of a judge; then the Governor sat in judgment on his decisions. He had a rare ability to survey even his own work and conclusions with objectivity.

Given his generous measure of common sense, his methods narrowed the margin in which errors were likely to be made. And he had learned as a young man to correct his discoverable errors promptly instead of capitalizing them as precedents for future action. In New York and over an expanding area beyond, therefore, few were disposed to challenge Frederick Boyd Stevenson when he declared, "Hughes is unlike any other man who ever held public office." [13]

[12] Introduction to Hughes' *Addresses 1906–1916*, p. lv.
[13] *Harper's Weekly*, May 9, 1908.

Chapter 22

FIGHT WITH THE GAMBLERS

THE NEW YORK legislature reassembled in January, 1908, with blood in its eye. Now fully conscious of the Governor's power, the lawmakers were nevertheless emboldened by the prospect that his stay in Albany might be short. It seemed improbable that he would seek renomination or that the organization would ever renominate him if he did. Stiff opposition to his policies thus appeared to be a fair gamble.

As for the Governor, he drove straight ahead toward the reforms he believed to be necessary and desirable. He asked for new banking laws; for extension of the public service commissions law to cover telephone and telegraph companies; for a simplified ballot; for a direct-primaries act; for classification of salaries in the state institutions; for several labor and conservation measures and a pure food law. It was a sweeping program that was about as palatable to the Old Guard as earthworm soup.

Nor was the Governor willing to let sleeping dogs lie. After the Senate had refused to remove Otto Kelsey in 1907, charges were filed against him and Hughes appointed Matthew C. Fleming, his assistant in the insurance investigation, to look into the affairs of the Insurance Department. Fleming brought in a report that showed some improvement but also continuation of gross irregularities and inefficiency in Kelsey's organization. Hughes sent the report to the Senate in February along with a stiff message again demanding the removal of Kelsey. "The work of the department," he insisted, "had been a travesty on State supervision." [1] Two weeks later the Senate lashed out with a negative reply—thirty votes to nineteen.

In areas where the Senate's voice was not controlling, the Governor's housecleaning was going forward. Charges of gross negligence had been brought in 1907 against John F. Ahearn, president of the Borough of Manhattan. There was no showing that Ahearn was personally corrupt. The question was whether the Governor could remove a local official for shocking neglect of the streets and flagrant mismanagement of the borough's affairs. Seeing that the case would become a precedent, Hughes presided in person at a hearing, took voluminous evidence, and listened to legal arguments. Ahearn said he wished to thank the Governor for his fair examination regardless of what his decision

[1] *Public Papers, 1908*, p. 179.

might be. But neither his courtesy nor his honesty saved him. Hughes sustained the right of the Governor to act in such cases, and, finding the charges of inexcusable dereliction proved, he removed the borough president.

Similarly he removed Louis F. Haffen, president of the Borough of the Bronx, and Joseph Bermel, president of the Borough of Queens, resigned when summoned by the Governor to face his accusers. Charges were brought against numerous other local officials, including William Travers Jerome, district attorney for New York County. In each case Hughes ordered a thorough investigation and let the evidence dictate his action. Jerome and many others survived this scrutiny, but enough official heads toppled to indicate that New York was an unsafe place for faithlessness and inefficiency in office—enough also to keep the bosses in a state of continuous irritation.

The most dramatic fight of the year came over enforcement of the constitutional mandate against gambling. Hughes gave this issue only casual attention in his message. Following his suggestion, Senator Agnew and Assemblyman Hart introduced a bill for repeal of the Percy-Gray law, under which race-track gambling flourished, but the Governor did not then see it as a cause of major combat. He was not opposed to horse racing and did not take a puritanical attitude toward betting. It was only when bookmaking at the races loomed up as a crass and deliberate violation of the state constitution and when torrential opposition to any change in that special license swept in upon Albany that Hughes' fighting blood was aroused. Then the gray shading disappeared; it became a struggle between right and wrong with Hughes passionately determined to win.

Heavy pressure came from both sides. As letters from the people poured into the executive office, the Governor was made poignantly aware of the relation of gambling to poverty and crime. The politically powerful agricultural societies got little comfort, therefore, when they sent a delegation to the Governor to complain that the Agnew-Hart bill would deprive them of certain benefits obtained from the race tracks. Hughes told them that they knew in their hearts he was right. "The test of respect for law," he said, "is where . . . it is upheld in its majesty even though it hurts."

As the contest began to warm up, the Governor's life was threatened. This was followed by threats to kidnap his baby daughter. Another letter reported that the gambling lobby was preparing to hand out $200,000 in bribes to legislators in order to defeat the bill. The furious Assembly passed a resolution requesting that this letter and any similar communications received by the Governor be turned over to it. Hughes refused to comply. Transmission of the letter could serve no purpose, he said, except, perhaps, to expose the author to revenge.

Opponents of the bill had hoped to place him in the position of antagonizing the Assembly by seeming to endorse the bribery charge. Instead of falling into their trap, Hughes declared, probably with tongue in cheek, that he had "implicit confidence" that the legislature would do its duty—that it would "purge our State of this source of misery and vice which exists only because the will of the people, flatly declared in the fundamental law, has not been carried into effect." [2]

Because of indifferent application of the old laws against gambling the people had written into the constitution of 1894, as amended in 1895, an absolute prohibition against "any lottery, the sale of lottery tickets, pool-selling, bookmaking or any other kind of gambling." They had directed the legislature, using the word "shall," to pass appropriate legislation to effectuate this policy. The legislature had pretended to do so in the Percy-Gray Act, but actually it provided that if no token of racetrack wagers were delivered the only penalty for such gambling would be a civil suit for recovery of losses. This made a mockery of the constitution.

"We either have constitutional government or we do not have it," the Governor told an audience of businessmen. ". . . If it is an easy thing to override the Constitution in order to protect gamblers, some day it will be an easy thing to override the Constitution in its protection of property." [3]

The Agnew-Hart bill passed the Assembly by an overwhelming vote but provoked a hurricane of opposition in the Senate. What at first had appeared to be a majority for the bill began to fade before the onslaught of the racing interests. Bitterness permeated the debate. Mrs. Hughes, who had been listening in the Senate gallery, left before the acrimony reached a climax. Senator Grady, hatchetman in the Hearst-Murphy deal of 1906, assailed the Governor as "a whited sepulchre," and others accused him of deceiving the people. "The name of Governor Hughes will be remembered as a synonym for honesty," Senator Armstrong retorted prophetically, "long after the name of every man occupying a seat in this chamber has been forgotten." [4]

Lobbyists swarmed through the corridors. The press accused them of using money lavishly. Fake letters purporting to be from constituents cluttered the mail of senators. One legislator's investigation showed only four out of one hundred letters written to him in opposition to the bill were genuine.

Boss Barnes tried openly to subvert the legislative will. Both Barnes and Senator Grattan of Albany had assured Senator Agnew that Grattan would vote for the bill. Then Barnes changed his mind, summoned Grattan out of a committee meeting, and brutally ordered him to vote the other way. When Senator Agnew protested and told Barnes that an open switch would disgrace him before the community, Barnes replied that his antagonism toward Hughes

[2] *Ibid.*, p. 39.

[3] Speech to Northside Board of Trade, Bronx, New York, March 5, 1908.

[4] *New York Times*, April 9, 1908.

overcame every other consideration.[5] Grattan's humiliating conformity to his master's demands was openly flaunted in brazen defiance of Hughes' own scrupulous methods.

Senator Knapp also switched his vote overnight, and only the alertness of the sergeant at arms of the Senate saved the antigambling forces from losing Senator Fancher at the crucial moment. The night before the vote was to be taken, Fancher was lured to a residence in Albany by a telephone message to the effect that some friends had a little surprise in store for him. What the surprise turned out to be was not disclosed, but the senator was found asleep at the rendezvous at noon the next day with his watch turned back to indicate that it was only nine o'clock. Located by tracing the telephone number that had been left for him the previous day, he reached the Senate in time to vote but could not stem the tide. The Agnew-Hart bill went down by a tie vote of twenty-five to twenty-five.

On April 23 the legislature adjourned in open defiance of the Governor. Once more a wave of anger swept over the state, leaving a heavy deposit of letters in Hughes' office. The press, even the Hearst papers, gave him strong encouragement to continue the fight. Indignation meetings were held all over the state. Churches turned out dozens of resolutions. The City Club of New York, the International Reform Bureau, the Brooklyn League, and a special Anti-Race-Track-Gambling Committee joined in the crusade. Aid came also from such men as Haley Fiske, Henry L. Stimson, Horace White, Andrew Carnegie, Jacob Gould Schurman, Seth Low, Judge Thompkins, Oswald Garrison Villard, Spencer Trask, Charles S. Whitman, Louis Wiley of the *New York Times*, former Ambassador Stewart L. Woodford, and Edward B. Whitney. Some felt that Hughes' fight was "toughening the moral fiber of the whole country." A. B. Humphrey wired: "Looks like you are deserted by everybody except God Almighty and The People." [6]

One of the Governor's strong supporters, Thomas P. Peters, editor of the Brooklyn *Daily Times*, tried to induce him not to risk calling a special session. Another defeat, he feared, would seriously jeopardize Hughes' chance for renomination.[7] Some of his ablest political associates gave similar advice. But the Governor had the bit between his teeth. Two days after the Senate had defeated the Agnew-Hart bill, he ordered a special election in the Niagara-Orleans district where the death of Senator Stanislaus P. Franchot had left a vacancy. On the very day of the legislature's adjournment he signed a proclamation calling it back into extraordinary session on May 11, the day before the special election was to be held.

Throughout the long fight Hughes kept up a drumfire of speeches. The

[5] Agnew to James Fenimore Cooper, April 22, 1908, Agnew Papers, New York Public Library.
[6] April 24, 1908. [7] Peters to CEH, April 22, 1908.

racing interests attempted to seize the initiative by denouncing him for trying to coerce the legislature. "Since when," he retorted, "did those who profit by gambling privileges become the guardians of the honor and independence of the Legislature? . . . I have used no weapon but that of reason. I have exercised no prerogative but that of recommendation and argument."[8] If there were any coercion in what he had done, it was the coercion of presenting to New York citizens a cogent array of facts which influenced their judgment and stirred their conscience.

Hughes bore down with special relish on Boss Barnes' perversion of representative government. "What a humiliation it is for a community," he exclaimed, "and what an abuse of leadership, when any man is able to say that he assumes responsibility for the vote of a Senator . . . no party leader has a right to assume the role of dictator, or so to violate the manhood of elected officials as to parade them before the people as subject to his domination."[9] Nothing less than representative government was on trial, and Hughes insisted that it be vindicated.

Then, taking his political life in his hands, the Governor went on a stumping tour of the Niagara-Orleans district in behalf of William C. Wallace, whose sole distinction was his pro-Hughes stand in the antigambling fight. The racing interests flushed the district with campaign money in behalf of the Democratic candidate, and some votes were bought on election day in spite of the private detectives hired to check corruption.[10] Hughes had no campaign fund, and the Republican machine men either went fishing or remained on the sidelines to sneer at "Charles the Evangelist."

Hughes told the voters that when his recommendations were challenged he felt it his duty to lay his case before the people, thus placing the responsibility for the outcome where it belonged. That deference to the people's judgment brought thundering applause and a sense of close identification with the cause. Humble men became warriors against corruption and lawlessness. "Leave your farms and your work shops on Tuesday," the Governor specifically charged them, "and remember that the people throughout the state are watching you, to see whether my confidence in the people and their sobriety, and their strength of character in such an emergency, has been misplaced."[11] To another group his plea was even more direct—"Rise in your might."[12]

So it went at Medina, Lockport, Holley, Albion, Middleport, Niagara Falls, and North Tonawanda. The indignant evangelist of the new democracy fought against seemingly hopeless odds with a sense of complete dedication. The struggle against race-track gambling was almost lost to sight in the larger cru-

[8] Speech to Ulster County Republican Club, March 20, 1908.
[9] Speech at Albany Mass Meeting, April 26, 1908.
[10] Report of detectives in Agnew Papers.
[11] Speech at Medina, May 8, 1908. [12] Speech at Tonawanda, May 9, 1908.

sade for uncorrupted government. "The history of politics," the Governor admonished the voters, "has been the history of men struggling for freedom and for individual rights against all sorts of special privileges. Tyranny and despotism have had their day, and in one place after another have finally been overthrown because they have represented the interests . . . and the will of the few against the interests and the inalienable rights of the many." [13] His faith in another uprising through the ballot box seemed implicit. And it was justified, even though Wallace won by a very slender margin.

Back in Albany, Hughes came down upon the legislature with a series of demands in addition to enactment of the Agnew-Hart bill. Three days later the Senate met for its crucial vote. Tension had been heightened by the fact that even Hughes' dramatic victory in Niagara-Orleans carried no assurance of a majority for the bill. Senator Otto G. Foelker of Brooklyn had undergone an appendectomy on May 10, and for several weeks his condition had been critical. On June 9 the Albany flier had stopped at Staatsburg at the Governor's order and brought Foelker to the capital looking very pale under his black derby. Groaning at every step, he declared that he would vote tomorrow on the antigambling bill "if there is breath in my body." But no one knew how he would vote. In the previous test he had stood with the Governor, but racetrack money had been flowing freely and Foelker was reported to have given promises to both sides.

As the final debate crackled in the tense atmosphere of the Senate Chamber, legislators shifted in their seats and asked one another if Foelker could make it to the floor. Just before the roll call on a motion to recommit the bill to the committee where it originated they had their answer. Leaning heavily upon his physician and Canon Chase, Foelker entered the chamber. Advocates of the bill cheered gleefully. The voting went forward. Foelker sat nervously waiting. His lips twitched convulsively and his hands dropped into his lap; he was bewildered by the nature of the motion. "What is it?" he asked, and being uncertain, refrained from voting when his name was called.[14] Other Senators continued to vote. A tremor of excitement ran through the chamber. It was one of the most dramatic moments that the legislature had ever experienced. Catching the import of the recommittal motion, Foelker at last voted No, sank back into his seat, and looked as if he would collapse.

The sick Senator had to remain in the chamber for the final vote on the bill. Senator Cohalan tried to extend the debate, apparently in the hope of driving his ailing colleague back to his bed. But Majority Leader Raines, who in this fight was with the Governor, intervened as a matter of "humane duty," and Foelker was able to cast the winning vote.

Senator "Long Pat" McCarren gulped and then resumed chewing his tooth-

[13] Speech at Albion, May 8, 1908. [14] Albany *Journal*, June 11, 1908.

From the New York *World,* May 14, 1908.

STILL "ANIMATED"

(Here Hughes is pictured sweeping into the Senate the vote needed to win his fight against race-track gambling.)

pick, his eyes blazing with fury. The lobbyists were dumfounded. Hilarious supporters of the bill went cheering through the city. Hughes was elated. His smile created a great unconformity between his upper and lower whiskers. "I am deeply gratified," he said simply. "It is a victory for law and order, the importance of which cannot be overestimated." Foelker's courage, he added, merits the same praise that we give "to distinguished service on the battle field." [15]

A fresh current of admiration for the Governor swept over the state. The New York *Evening Mail* commented:

> While the legislative record completed today embodies the policies and evidences of the triumph of Charles E. Hughes, it is not in the measures themselves that the greatest achievement is to be found. That lies in the demonstration that public opinion, when rightly interpreted and courageously expressed, will assert itself and dominate every situation. . . . Government for the people and not for politics was the text of every utterance made by Governor Hughes before he went to Albany, and has been ever since. . . . The house of politics is cleaner than it was thanks to the "animated feather duster." [16]

William Barnes' *Evening Journal* (Albany) characterized the defeat of its publisher as an "absurd blunder" attributable to agitation stirred up by sensational newspapers and "public officers who aim at cheap notoriety." But it was a voice in the wilderness. The *Daily Tribune* summed up the predominant feeling: ". . . the victory in the anti-gambling fight will only serve to intensify the public unwillingness to see him [Hughes] retire."

Once more Hughes' victory had been achieved without intrigue, alliances, threats, or use of patronage. The bosses accused him of destroying his party, and some of them were saying that, for their own preservation, they would have to destroy him. So far as their political future was concerned, they had good reason for complaint. Five of the eight Republican Senators who voted against the Agnew-Hart bill were defeated when they sought renomination. But the party was notably strengthened. What the Governor had spoiled was only the old game of using the machine for personal advantages.

The Governor's crusade put out of business many of the New York race tracks that had flourished solely as gambling enterprises, although horse racing continued on a smaller scale. The bookmakers experienced a long period of idleness. The law that the Governor had wrung from an unwilling Senate was to remain on the books until displaced some years later by the pari-mutuel betting system. Within twenty-four months California, Texas, Louisiana, and Georgia paid Hughes the compliment of imitating his anti-race-track-gambling law.

[15] *Ibid.* [16] June 26, 1908.

Chapter 23

WHITE HOUSE ON THE HORIZON

As soon as Hughes proved his vote-getting power in New York, in a contest with the most formidable demagogue of the time, men began to talk seriously of electing him President. The key to the whole situation was held by President Roosevelt. Following his election in 1904, T. R. had announced that he would not again be a candidate, but it was clear that, if he held to this decision, he would name his own successor. William Howard Taft, the Secretary of War, appeared to have the inside track, but he was willing to abide by Roosevelt's wishes, and the President's mind remained open. Watching Hughes campaign in New York, they both concluded that he would make an admirable presidential contender, and T. R. told Mrs. Taft that he might feel it his duty to be for Hughes in 1908.[1]

The events of 1907 greatly strengthened Governor Hughes' hold on the public imagination. By comparison, the men who were actively seeking the Presidency seemed to lack spirit and conviction. In his candid discussion of the outlook with Taft in September, 1907, the President admitted that the strongest candidate of all was Governor Hughes.[2]

Many others were saying the same thing publicly. Hughes is "the only man in the party, aside from Roosevelt," said the *St. Louis Mirror*, "who means anything in and of himself. . . . Hughes is the coming man." Returning from the Far West, Oscar King Davis, Washington correspondent for the *New York Times*, reported: "I heard enough Hughes talk in those three months to satisfy me that, if the New York Governor should be the Republican nominee, he would start with a first-class chance of carrying all that part of the country." [3] Most of T. R.'s insurgent friends, including the La Follette group, and the second-string leaders around the President also favored Hughes over Taft.[4] In an open contest there can be little doubt as to who the nominee would have been. In spite of the brevity of his experience in public life, Hughes had the advantage of being personally identified with the fight against exploitation and privilege in which the people were primarily interested.

[1] Henry F. Pringle, *The Life and Times of William Howard Taft*, I, 318.

[2] *Ibid.*, p. 331.

[3] *Released for Publication* (Boston, Houghton Mifflin, 1925), pp. 57–59. Copyright, 1925, by Oscar King Davis.

[4] William Allen White, *Autobiography*, p. 528.

But the decisive factor, it must be remembered, was not Hughes' standing with the people but his standing with President Roosevelt. The Governor had done nothing to encourage the belief that, as President, he would unswervingly walk in T. R.'s footprints. While he had given strong support to the Roosevelt Administration, he had followed his own independent course. As one commentator expressed it, "He would rather be Hughes than President."

Roosevelt's coolness toward the Hughes régime approached frigidity only after the Sanders incident.[5] In removing Sanders from his federal job in Rochester, T. R. was punishing a critic, but he also doubtless sincerely intended to help Hughes in his fight for good government. On his part, Hughes was glad to have the President's aid, even though he deplored the President's use of the patronage club in his behalf. He scrupulously avoided any flaunting of their differences as to methods. But Frank H. Simonds made it his special business to fashion the incident into a red flag and wave it in the President's face from the front page of the anti-Roosevelt *Evening Post.*

Simonds was a brilliant journalist whose facile stories about the new régime created the impression that, of all the Albany correspondents, he was "the closest to Hughes." Actually he was no more intimate with the Governor than were Louis Howe, John Palmer Gavit, Louis Seibold, and several others. Hughes did not play favorites. But Simonds' alertness in picking up information and his shrewdness in forecasting what was going to happen led many to believe that he had an inside track, which irked the other reporters.

On March 29, 1907, a correspondent brought a copy of the *Evening Post* into the Governor's press conference determined to have a showdown. "Governor Hughes will veto the public utilities bill if the corporations succeed in inserting the broad court-review feature," said a front-page Albany dispatch. "He will then call an extra session of the Legislature. . . . This is the programme that the Governor's friends are confidently predicting." Had the Governor, the correspondent asked, given this advance information to Simonds?

Much as he admired Simonds' ability and appreciated his friendly dispatches, Hughes concluded that this story went too far in presuming to speak for him. A careful reader would see that Simonds was relying upon "the Governor's friends," but the casual reader would assume that he was echoing the Governor's own words. The forecast was erroneous, and Hughes felt that the net effect was to put him in a false light before the other reporters and the public. "No statement has been made with my authority," he said. "No one is in a position to predict what course I shall take. . . . when there is occasion to state my attitude with regard to public questions I shall state it myself." [6]

Simonds left the executive chamber deeply offended and did not return for a long time. But he continued to write as if he were the Governor's alter ego.

[5] See pages 196-197. [6] New York *Tribune*, March 30, 1907.

The Sanders affair gave him a unique opportunity for revenge, and he made the most of it. In two special articles, he wrote that the descent of T. R.'s "big stick" in New York "had made Hughes, in the minds of the politicians, a Roosevelt governor." For that reason the support of the President had "not been welcomed entirely." Simonds intimated that the Governor would have preferred "to win alone"—that he resented "playing 'second fiddle' to Roosevelt." Working both sides of the street, Simonds then pictured Roosevelt as trying to edge himself under the umbrella of Hughes' popularity. "The truth, of course, was that the President desired to punish James W. Wadsworth, Sr., and in order to make a neat cover for this, he announced that it was an action to aid Hughes. It is entirely possible," Simonds continued, "that the governor will repudiate this assistance given through federal patronage." [7]

Roosevelt read this posturization of the Governor as a self-seeking egotist and this assault upon his own motives as if the words had come straight from Hughes' mouth. The dispatch had all the earmarks of a spite story planted by an official speaking off the record. The President did not know that Simonds was no longer seeing Hughes. His anger was kindled, as indicated by a subsequent letter to Taft in which he referred to Hughes as "a thoroly selfish and cold blooded creature." ". . . when I strove to help him," T. R. complained, "he started the entire mugwump press cackling with glee about the way in which he had repudiated my help . . . and relied purely on the people." [8]

After this incident there was no probability of Hughes being chosen as Roosevelt's successor. Hughes didn't "play the game." He was not a Roosevelt man in the sense of subordinating his judgment or his individuality to that of the famous Rough Rider. Roosevelt's dislike for Hughes was apparently communicated to Taft. Since Hughes was the only rival who offered any real challenge to Taft's nomination, the White House circle assigned itself the task of eclipsing his popularity.

Only a determined and spectacular campaign by a new leader of commanding popular strength could have overcome this handicap, and Hughes would not lift a finger in his own behalf. There had been high expectation that he might declare himself a receptive candidate when he addressed the Republican Club dinner in New York on October 18, 1907. Instead, he declared: "I do not seek any public office. . . . To me public office means a burden of responsibility . . . it is far from being an object of ambition."

There was no posing about this seeming indifference to the glittering prize of American politics. Hughes had not been touched by the power complex that afflicts so many politicians. While he would meet the responsibilities of the White House unflinchingly if they should fall to his lot, he did not wish

[7] *Evening Post,* April 22 and 23, 1907.
[8] T. R. to Taft, Aug. 14, 1908, Roosevelt Papers.

them and would not reach out for them. Nomination for the Presidency, he said—laying down a rule that would guide him in 1916 as well as 1908—is an honor that no citizen should either seek or decline.

There was another restraining factor. "I thought," he admitted many years later, "that the position of a successor to Theodore Roosevelt would not be an attractive one. I was sure that, although out of office, he would still desire to have a dominating influence and that he would have a large following which would make the way of his successor hard. Nor did I think that, with his temperament and enjoyment of the strenuous life and especially of political activity, he would long be content to remain out of office. In all probability he would be at least a receptive candidate four years later." [9]

Hughes' high regard for Taft relieved him of any sense of duty in connection with the nomination. Throughout the period when he was being hailed as "the next President," he stood ready to support the Secretary of War—"a most worthy selection." In part this deference to Taft seemed to reflect Hughes' native humility. He was slow in learning to appreciate his own ability. For the first forty-three years of his life he had worked prodigiously without any public recognition. Then suddenly he had risen to the pinnacle of public acclaim in New York. That was difficult enough to swallow. Now the clamor for his advancement to the Presidency of the United States seemed strangely unreal. When his own family began discussing the prospect for his nomination, he dismissed it with a wave of the hand and a flat declaration that "it wouldn't ever happen."

"Oh, yes, it will," Mrs. Hughes contradicted, "you're a man of destiny, my dear." [10]

Hughes was finally persuaded to make a public statement of his views on national issues. People who were promoting his nomination had a right to know what he stood for. When the Republican Club of New York formally made him its candidate, he agreed to address the club on January 31. Meanwhile the New York County Republican Committee passed a Hughes-for-President resolution in spite of much maneuvering and delay tactics on the part of the President's supporters.

Hughes' "announcement" speech was widely heralded. The newspapers gave him an impressive build-up as the only rival to Taft. Might he not sweep the country with an unanswerable speech, as he had often swept New York, and upset the scheme to give Taft the nomination on a silver platter? Roosevelt, who had thrown all his energy into the fight for Taft, decided to take no chances.

What the people saw when they scanned their newspapers the morning after Hughes' speech were blazing headlines of a very different sort: "ROOSE-

[9] CEH, Notes, p. 195. [10] Author's interview with CEH, Jr., July 8, 1948.

"SO LONG, CHARLIE! WE'D LIKE TO SEE YOU GO!"

(This cartoon was mailed to Governor Hughes during the preconvention fight for the Republican presidential nomination in 1908, with the above comment penciled in.)

VELT'S ONSLAUGHT . . ." "BIG MEN ROASTED . . ." "HOTTEST MESSAGE EVER SENT TO CONGRESS . . ." "MESSAGE DAZES." The President had sent to Congress "the most provocatively sensational utterance" of his career, with careful timing so as to smother the Hughes speech.

Most newspapers that had reserved front-page space for the so-called "Hughes platform" had to use it for the verbal explosion in Washington. "Hughes' temperate, sane, well-thought-out discourse could no more compete for public attention with Roosevelt's effulgence," as Mark Sullivan wrote, "than a crystal spring with a volcanic eruption." [11] Hughes had argued persuasively for effective regulation instead of government ownership of the railroads, for an expert commission to prepare the ground for an equitable revision of tariff rates, for a modified employers' liability law, for improvement of the Sherman Antitrust Law, and for progressive and orderly government. "The battle for free institutions," he had said, "has been a struggle against special privilege." He had had only praise for the Roosevelt Administration and had made no direct bid for the nomination. "I ask no favor and I make no claim," he had said. "I desire that the party shall act for its best interests." T. R. did not know the nature of Hughes' speech when he threw out his trip line, but there can be no doubt as to what his intention was. Newspaper men asked him if his outburst had been maliciously timed, and he replied, "If Hughes is going to play the game, he must learn the tricks."

Hughes' good will toward Taft remained unimpaired. Both candidates were speakers at the annual dinner of the Friendly Sons of Saint Patrick on March 17. In the course of a glowing eulogy of everything Irish, Taft claimed to have visited historic Blarney Castle near Cork and to have "kissed the stone with all its mellifluous consequences." When it came Hughes' turn to bid for Irish favor, he said that he did not doubt Mr. Taft had given a "veracious chronicle" of his experience, but it would have been a joy to have taken a picture of the Secretary "pressing his ruby lips to the famous stone." [12] Gazing on Taft's enormous hulk and knowing full well the inaccessibility of the Blarney stone, the Friendly Sons howled with delight. (The next day a cartoonist pictured Taft being hoisted by a derrick to reach the stone.) To prove his own standing in that genial company, Hughes then trotted out his Irish great-great-grandfather, Michael Connelly. But he also warmly complimented Taft.

When Woodruff wrote to ask his pleasure as to the selection of delegates to the national convention, Hughes said no pressure should be exerted in his behalf and asked for a "free expression" of Republican voters' wishes through their own representatives in the state convention.[13] Part of the delegation

[11] *Our Times* (New York, Scribner's, 1932), IV, 297–304. Copyright, 1932, by Charles Scribner's Sons.

[12] New York *Herald*, March 18, 1908.

[13] CEH to Woodruff, April 4, 1908.

finally chosen was sincerely devoted to Hughes; others merely hoped to get him out of Albany. The Barnes outfit left for Chicago singing, "Goodbye, Charlie, we'll be glad to see you go." The Governor himself was still unconcerned. He went so far as publicly to repudiate the announcement that Hughes headquarters had been opened in Chicago to secure his nomination.

Before the convention opened on June 16, the nomination of Taft was a certainty. Being eager to capture the vice-presidential nomination and feeling inhibited so long as the New York delegation was holding out against Taft for first place, Herbert Parsons asked Hughes to release the delegation from its instructions to vote for him. Hughes replied that he had had nothing to do with instructing the delegates in the first place and therefore had no right to release them. Barnes was furious. Overriding his instructions, he voted for Taft, taking nine New York delegates with him. "This is the end of Hughes," he railed. That defection left Hughes third on the list of candidates, with one vote less than Senator Philander C. Knox's 68 and wholly out of range of the 702 votes that nominated Taft on the first ballot.

At two o'clock on the morning of June 19, Governor Hughes was awakened to receive the following telegram from Elbert F. Baldwin, one of Roosevelt's friends on the staff of the *Outlook:*

> The Republican Presidential nominee asks me to telegraph you that he considers you far and away the strongest man for the Vice Presidency if you can be induced to take the nomination. He, the party, and thousands irrespective of politics call for you. As he and the President said to me tonight, no other candidate could add such moral strength to the ticket. Mr. Taft earnestly urges you to stand with him on that ticket, assured of hearty Washington and general support. As your admirer, as Roosevelt's and Taft's friend, I implore you to recognize that Republican success or failure may hang upon your decision, for the Democratic ticket is to be unexpectedly strong.

Hughes could see no challenge whatever in the Vice Presidency and felt that, without a compelling reason, he could not afford to make the financial sacrifice it would entail. His reply was a courteous but unequivocal No, and the nomination went to another New Yorker, James S. Sherman.

The hard-fighting Governor of New York ended his first cool and hesitant flirtation with the presidential bee without rancor or regret. It was to have a more dramatic sequel in 1916. Yet he never lost the conviction that shaped his action in 1908—the conviction that to be fit for high office a man must be willing to forgo it or to leave it at any time.

Chapter 24

SECOND GUBERNATORIAL CAMPAIGN

GOVERNOR Hughes was not inclined to seek a second term because his two years at Albany had left him nervously worn and $20,000 poorer than he had been in 1906. Now a family of eight (the Governor's parents were living with him), the Hugheses had found it impossible to maintain the Executive Mansion and finance the large receptions and dinners it was customary to give on the Governor's $10,000 salary and the meager additional allowances. The $100,000 fortune that he had accumulated from his law practice was thus undergoing what seemed to be a most imprudent shrinkage.

The drain upon his savings was especially heavy because, on his numerous forays to arouse public opinion, he paid his own way and that of his military secretary as well as the fees of the stenographers who took down his speeches for the press. Only if he traveled strictly on state business did he send in an expense voucher. One day Comptroller Martin H. Glynn, a Democrat, brought into the Governor's office a handful of vouchers indicating that Theodore Roosevelt had charged to the state the entire cost of his travels as governor. "It is absurd," he said, "for you to finance so many of your activities when your whole time is devoted to state business." But Hughes continued to draw upon his own resources for every outlay that was not directly essential to his official duties.

The only public intimation of the Governor's intention was his offhand remark to the National Guard Association early in 1908 that he was making his "second and farewell appearance as commander-in-chief." At that time he hoped that his reform program would be fully enacted at the 1908 legislative session. As the revolt against his policies spread, however, it became apparent that he could not retire without appearing to forsake much of what he stood for.

While the Governor was debating with himself what course to take, Dean Hutchins of the Law School of the University of Michigan (his old associate at Cornell) paid him a visit to ask if he would entertain an offer of the presidency of the university. Hughes had stirred the hearts of the students, faculty, and trustees when he delivered a Washington's birthday address at Ann Arbor in 1907 and was entertained at luncheon by President James B. Angell, who was now about to retire. While still sensitive to the lure of campus life, the

JUST A WHISPER

(Cartoonist Bradley's comment on the reluctance of the New York Republican organization to renominate Governor Hughes in 1908.)

Governor declined because of his feeling that he should take advantage of the great opportunity awaiting him at the bar.

As the weeks passed, his supporters clamored for a fresh subordination of his personal preference to his public duty. "The plain people understand you, love you and are for you," Stewart L. Woodford had written him. "If the people want you for governor again in order to force this reform [the direct primary], I do not see how you can consistently refuse." [1] Similar urgings came through the mails, in speeches, and direct conversation. The Governor saw that he could not relinquish his post without leaving his faithful followers in the lurch. On July 24 he announced that, "upon further reflection," he had decided to accept a renomination, if tendered, in spite of the "entirely personal reasons" that had previously inclined him against it. "But it is my desire," he added, "that the will of the party to which I belong should be freely expressed and that it shall take such action as shall be most closely in accord with public sentiment." [2]

To the Republican leaders, who had been smirking over the prospect of recapturing the governorship, Hughes' announcement was vinegar and hemlock. To President Roosevelt it brought a new dilemma. His dislike for Hughes had not evaporated with the nomination of Taft. The White House was now deluged, moreover, with predictions of Republican defeat in New York if T. R. should permit the renomination of Hughes. The bosses were moving heaven and earth to save themselves from two more years of frustration. Barnes wrote to Secretary Root on August 14 that under no circumstances would the Albany delegates vote for Hughes. Roosevelt, as he wrote to Taft on August 3, was at his "wit's end as to whether it is absolutely necessary to nominate Hughes or whether it would be suicidal to do so." [3]

Taft probably did more than anyone else to soften Roosevelt's attitude. Hughes must be renominated in spite of the Old Guard, he replied, because of the strength he would add to the national campaign, especially in the West. T. R. was inclined to agree, but he was still worried. "There are any number of thoroughly good people," he wrote to Taft on August 12, "who violently object to his [Hughes'] nomination, and we may get beaten out of our boots with him." Relying on his distorted view of the Sanders incident, he conjured up fears that Hughes might accept a nomination dictated from the White House and then repudiate his (T. R.'s) interference.

In his letters to Woodruff, T. R. also accused Hughes of "wantonly and needlessly" insulting the party workers and of allying himself with "some peculiarly malevolent and underhanded enemies of the party." But having aired his ill-founded resentment, Roosevelt bowed to expediency. Frank H. Hitch-

[1] Woodford to CEH, March 28, 1908. [2] *New York Times*, July 25, 1908.
[3] Taft Papers, Library of Congress.

cock, chairman of the national committee, had returned from the West with the conviction that Republican chances would be seriously jeopardized in that area by any sacrifice of Hughes at the behest of the bosses. After a series of conferences at Oyster Bay, T. R. concluded that it would be safer to dragoon the politicians than to antagonize the rank and file. He explained his position in a letter to Taft:

> Hughes is not a man I care for; he is not a man whose actions have really tended to the uplifting of political life; but he is financially an entirely honest man and one of much ability, and I am concerned that while to nominate him will do harm, not to nominate him will do more harm because I am convinced that the bulk of the Republicans, including the best men in the party outside the active organization, are for him.[4]

The only real complaint against the Governor was that he had refused to play the politicians' game. The fact is he did not know how to play politics, and he would probably have been beaten if he had tried. Roosevelt's irritation over Hughes' inability to get along with the bosses seems especially strange in the light of his own tirades against the bosses when they opposed him in 1912.

Hughes' reaction to the claim that he was not a good Republican was given pointed emphasis one day when he visited a mental hospital accompanied by a committee of the legislature. An inmate accosted him and inquired, "Are you Governor Hughes?" When Hughes assented, the inmate said, "I don't know whether you're a Republican or not."

"Did you hear that, Governor?" exclaimed Senator Raines, chuckling with delight.

"Yes," Hughes replied. "He's insane."

Taft was so confident that Hughes was an asset to the Republican Party that, even before Hughes announced his decision to run again, he asked the Governor to open the national campaign with a speech at Youngstown, Ohio. It will be "perhaps the greatest meeting of the campaign," Taft said. "I don't know anybody whose words will have more weight than yours."[5] Hughes sensed the compliment and readily acquiesced. It was the first bid for his aid in a national campaign.

Youngstown did its utmost to make this opening rally for Taft impressive. On the morning of September 5 Hughes joined Senator Beveridge, Governor Andrew L. Harris of Ohio, and other notables in reviewing a parade of 15,000 workingmen. It seemed endless. Noon passed and the reviewers got nothing but coffee for lunch. As soon as the last marcher had gone by, they hastened to Wick Park where a large crowd was waiting to hear the oratory. The chairman

[4] Roosevelt Papers. [5] Taft to CEH, July 16, 1908.

spoke for forty minutes and Governor Harris for an hour. Hughes had been scheduled to speak next but he agreed to exchange places with Senator Beveridge when the Senator explained that Mrs. Beveridge was about to give birth to a baby. The Senator's concern over the forthcoming event was not sufficient, however, to end his peroration on the tariff before 5:30 P.M. Hughes felt that the situation was hopeless.

"I have a dry speech consisting only of reasoning," he told James R. Garfield. "The people are so tired they will probably walk out. I suggest that you call it off."

"You don't know Western reserve," Garfield replied. He insisted that the meeting go forward, and the audience vindicated his judgment by listening courteously. Hughes turned his devastating power of analysis upon Taft's opponent, William Jennings Bryan. Recognizing Bryan as an eloquent critic, he nevertheless insisted that if all the schemes the Commoner had advocated in the previous twelve years had been enacted "we should have been overwhelmed with disaster." Bryan's plan to curb the trusts by forbidding any corporation to control more than 50 per cent of the total amount of "any product consumed in the United States" came under an especially withering examination. What was the meaning of that elusive phrase "any product consumed in the United States"? Would it exclude patented articles which the Government had given the owners exclusive rights to manufacture and sell? "When . . . we consider these . . . remedies that are proposed for the trusts," Hughes declared, "we find ourselves journeying in a land of dreams. Again the magician of 1896 waves his wand. . . ."

At the dinner given that evening by James G. Butler in honor of Governor Hughes, there were no repercussions from the speech. No one congratulated him; no one thanked him; no one even mentioned it. The thin-skinned Governor felt depressed. Like Lincoln after Gettysburg, he went home fearful that he had fumbled a great opportunity.

The following day, however, it appeared that the weary Youngstowners who heard the speech were the only ones who had missed its significance. Encomiums for the Governor's "sanctified common sense" all but dripped from the press. "What a masterly speech Hughes made when he opened the campaign in Ohio," exclaimed Roosevelt. "How he cut into Bryan! It is far the best thing yet done in this campaign."[6] Two days later T. R. advised Taft to paraphrase the Hughes speech in his own campaign addresses. Republican headquarters sent out more copies of the Youngstown speech than of any other except Taft's acceptance speech.

Throughout the remainder of his campaign Bryan refrained from pressing the portion of his platform that Hughes had riddled. Taft's speeches and Roose-

[6] T. R. to John A. Sleicher, Sept. 19, 1908, Hughes Papers.

velt's statements drew the Commoner's fire, but he attempted no reply to Hughes. Mark Sullivan credited Hughes with "crumpling" Bryan's campaign in a single speech.[7] Henry L. Stoddard reported that, after the Hughes speech, "the election, though six weeks distant, was only a matter of totalling the vote against Bryan." [8]

So far as Hughes' political fortunes were concerned, the chief importance of the Youngstown speech was its impact on the Old Guard in New York. It blasted the hope of Barnes and his associates that they might be able to unite upon a candidate whom the administration in Washington would have to accept. Root and former Governor Black declined to be used against Hughes, and the bosses were no more successful in their overtures to Joseph H. Choate, Ambassador Horace Porter, and Seth Low. Choate had been asked to be permanent chairman of the convention, but when he let it be known that he was an ardent Hughes man, the organization decided that it needed a chairman more familiar with parliamentary law than the president of the last constitutional convention.

As the convention met at Saratoga on September 14, the only anti-Hughes candidates who had shown any strength whatever were Speaker Wadsworth, with 122 delegates, and William Berri, who had most of the Kings delegation. Wadsworth refused to release his delegates to any compromise candidate. The frustrated bosses went into a huddle and made another appeal to Root. Root repeated that the defeat of Hughes would be a critical blow to the national ticket and produced a statement from the President saying that "while he had no intention of dictating, yet to all his friends who have spoken to him on the matter he has said in the strongest possible terms that he favored the renomination of Governor Hughes." [9]

Hughes himself remained completely aloof from the convention. There were no Hughes headquarters at Saratoga, no organization representing him, no one authorized to speak for him or to promise any favor in return for support. No delegate had been importuned by him. There was no picture of him in the convention hall. When Secretary Root mentioned the Governor's name in his keynote speech, the galleries cheered and shouted but the delegates sat stonily silent. The phrase "Nobody wants Hughes but the people" was eloquently descriptive of the situation.

The final postmidnight conference of the Old Guard hatched a scheme to nominate David Jayne Hill, the American Ambassador to Germany, without his knowledge, so that if he should refuse to run after the convention adjourned the leaders would be free to fill the vacancy as they pleased. Root appears to

[7] Mark Sullivan, *Our Times*, IV, 306.

[8] *As I Knew Them* (New York, Harper, 1927), p. 280. Copyright, 1927, by Harper & Brothers.

[9] New York *World*, Sept. 15, 1908.

have broken up this midsummer night's dream by bringing the wrath of T. R. and Taft upon the hapless Woodruff.

Barnes shook his clenched fists and worked himself into a "frenzy of rage" as he denounced Hughes in the process of seconding Wadsworth's nomination. The main speech for Hughes was "chanted" by Senator Page in a monotonous fashion, but Assemblyman John Lord O'Brian and William A. Prendergast cut loose with seconding speeches that raised the rafters. The first ballot gave Hughes 827 votes to 151 for Wadsworth and 31 for former Congressman John K. Stewart. Barnes swallowed his anger and moved to make the nomination unanimous.

Roosevelt wrote to Taft that he had used every ounce of power he possessed to bring about Hughes' renomination. Root, too, concluded that, without the President's help, Hughes would have had no more than 200 votes in the convention. Certainly the President's influence was effectively used in the Governor's behalf, but the underlying fact was that the bosses could choose only between the renomination of Hughes and a still more costly defeat. Actually the bewhiskered executive at Albany had won his own fight simply by being Hughes. "The renomination of Governor Hughes," boasted the *Nation,* "must be reckoned as one of the most significant political events in the last quarter century. It is a sheer triumph of naked principle, and as such it must mightily strengthen the forces of good government." [10]

Hughes' campaign was a whirlwind affair beginning with his acceptance speech in Brooklyn on September 26. The Old Guard had given him a platform of generalities and weasel words which approved no more of his achievements than was necessary and, without directly saying so, attempted to close the door against the simplified ballot and primary nominations. But Hughes was his own platform. The question before the voters was simply whether or not his administration should be returned to power.

The Democrats had favored him with a weak opponent in the person of Lewis Stuyvesant Chanler. As lieutenant governor from 1906 to 1908, Chanler had proved to be an amiable fellow who worked in harmony with Hughes and often expressed admiration for him. Selected by his party to oppose the Governor, Chanler found himself in an embarrassing position. His struggle to differentiate himself from Hughes and take advantage of the Republican schism led to the inference that he accepted boss rule. Indeed, he was indebted to Bosses Murphy and Conners for his nomination. Chanler's assault on "government by commission" won applause in some quarters, but it brought him into direct collision with Hughes' most successful reform. Trying to back away from that unpopular stand, Chanler urged retention of the Public Service Commissions with election of their members—an artful way of destroying

[10] Sept. 17. 1908.

them. Trying to lure the race-track interests, Chanler also accused the Hughes administration of invading "personal liberty," and a Personal Liberty League spent a good deal of money conjuring up bogies. But this sham issue fell flat when Chanler was finally badgered into saying that he did not favor repeal of Hughes' anti-race-track-gambling law.

The campaign in New York had scarcely begun when Republican national headquarters once more importuned Hughes to make a Western tour. His New York followers were indignant. Because of the combination of interests opposing him and the disaffection among the Old Guard, the need of his campaign talents was greater at home than in the West. After continued urging, however, Hughes promised to make eight speeches on condition that they be indoors, that they be limited to two a day, with no speaking at night. The G.O.P. managers agreed, but as soon as he got on the road he found himself speaking outdoors and indoors, twenty times a day through Nebraska, Kansas, and Illinois.

One incident during this trip always stood out in Hughes' memory "as an illustration of the friendliness and generosity of the American people which even the bitter contests of political campaigns cannot wholly obscure." He tells the story in his Notes:

> One evening, shortly before my train arrived at Hastings, Nebraska, there was a severe storm which tore down the tent in which I was to speak. The only hall in the town at that time was taken and already filled by the Democrats who were awaiting the arrival of their speaker. We concluded that we could not have a meeting, but a committee of the Democrats came to the train and invited me to speak at their hall. Their orator's train was an hour or so late. They made the condition that I should appear on the platform alone, without any Republican associates, as their invitation was a courtesy extended to me as Governor of New York,—but I was at liberty to speak as I pleased.
>
> A straggling lot of Republicans followed me to the hall and crowded in as best they could. To the amazement of the Democratic audience I appeared on the platform, introduced myself, thanked the Democratic committee for its courtesy and said that they would not have any respect for me if I did not make the speech I had intended to make at Hastings. I then launched out as usual. The audience gave me a rousing welcome and the hall rang with their applause as I extolled the American spirit of fair play and concluded with a number of questions for the Democratic orator to answer on his arrival, which was shortly after I left.

The tour heightened disappointment among the Hughes men outside New York that he was not the presidential candidate. "If the Chicago convention were to do its work over, in the light of recent events," said the *Cleveland Plain Dealer* on October 25, "there would be but one name considered, that of Hughes."

Roosevelt was delighted with the response to this trip and swallowed enough of his pique to tell the Governor so.

> Permit me to congratulate you [he wrote on October 14] upon the admirable campaign work that you have been doing. I think it has been of the greatest service in the West; and what is more, I think it has been of great service in New York, not only to Taft but in the State campaign, to have had you do just what you did in the West. I have kept in the closest touch possible with the different organization men, and I believe now that you will have their hearty and undivided support. I was amused the other day to find that one of the leaders, who had originally been very much opposed to your renomination, was now your enthusiastic backer, having been completely converted by your speeches in the West. . . .[11]

On his return to New York, however, Hughes was confronted by a forecast in the *World* that he would be beaten by 200,000 votes. Wall Street feared a stock market investigation and sought emancipation of the public utilities from the Public Service Commissions. Traveling men were irate over his veto of the two-cent-fare bill. Firemen similarly resented his veto of an unsound insurance bill that would have given them certain benefits. The Prohibition State Committee also fought him on the ground that he was a drinking man, opposed prohibition of the liquor traffic, and had been a director in a liquor-selling company. This brought great amusement in Albany, where the take-it-straight men joked about the Governor's occasional highballs made with one tablespoonful of whisky. As for his directorship in a liquor company, it referred to a title he had once assumed for a few months in connection with the reorganization of an ale-bottling business for which he was counsel. Malicious anti-Hughes propaganda was likewise disseminated among insurance men and other factions supposedly hurt by legislation the Governor had sponsored.

Hughes had only two and a half weeks, after he returned from the West, to answer his opponents. Almost every moment of it he turned to good advantage. Racing from one meeting to another, he sometimes continued to speak until after midnight. His audiences, ranging from up-State businessmen or farmers to Italians, Jews, or Negroes in New York City, were asked to restrain their applause to save his tired voice and conserve the precious moments. Sometimes he talked humorously and sometimes with the deepest seriousness, but always there was keen sensitivity to the wants and aspirations of the people coupled with an appeal to their powers of reason as stalwart citizens. After the meeting at Long Island City, the crowd went "almost wild" in efforts to reach him and shake his hand or even touch him as he passed.[12]

Chanler helped his opponent by asking him ten questions that were supposed to be embarrassing. Newspapers carrying the questions were distributed on the Governor's train at six o'clock the next morning at Rouses Point. Hughes

[11] Hughes Papers. [12] Henry P. Huling to Robert H. Fuller, Oct. 28, 1908.

called a stenographer and dictated frank, crisp, and satisfying answers to every question. By the time the train reached Malone, he had a typewritten copy of his replies, all numbered and tagged, ready for each of the reporters. In his speech at Malone he threw Chanler's questions back at him with such fervor that one observer thought the townsfolk would "tear the opera house down." Then he asked Chanler some questions that the latter could not answer without spilling some of the water he was trying to carry on both shoulders. The press repeatedly challenged him to be as candid as Hughes had been until he was finally forced to attempt some answers which proved to be pallid and equivocal.

By the end of the campaign Hughes and Roosevelt were almost chummy again. After Hughes had reported on his "hot fight" and warmly thanked T. R. for his help, the President wrote on October 20:

> That is such an extremely nice letter of yours that I can not forbear taking up your time by a line of acknowledgment. I have, naturally, the keenest sympathy for you in this campaign, because of the very fact you point out; that is, the two-fold type of attack made upon you: the attack upon you because you stood for the corporations where they were right or where improper measures were aimed at them, and the attack upon you because you have declined to sanction abuses in their management or to refrain from trying to better their management. . . .
>
> Now one word. You say that your feeling is that "if the Republican support is energetic I shall unquestionably be elected." Is there any way that I can help in this matter of the Republican support? Pray let me know if you think that there is.
>
> Taft, by the way, mentioned to me his great sense of obligation to you for your part in the campaign and his purpose to lay all possible emphasis upon the need for electing you, when he makes his speeches in New York.[13]

Hughes replied on October 25:

> The week has been very successful, and unless I am very much mistaken it has been the decisive week in the campaign. Chanler's questions were a stupid blunder, of which we lost no time in taking advantage. It seems to me that his candidacy is hopelessly weak; it is evasive, shifting, and stands for nothing whatever. It promises nothing to the radicals and it offers no assurance, in any promise of steadiness or of convictions, to the conservatives. His effort has been simply to capitalize in his favor the various elements of opposition. . . .
>
> I have been very much gratified by the assurances of Republican support that I have received and the many evidences of loyal party activity. . . . The situation is apparently much better than it was two years ago. . . . I have no complaints to make with regard to anybody, anywhere,—for I do not make them unless I have the facts—and I haven't the facts.

The entire Republican ticket was elected, including Horace White as lieutenant governor and Samuel Koenig as secretary of state. Both houses of the

[13] Hughes Papers.

legislature remained strongly Republican. Hughes was cut heavily in New York and Buffalo, where the sporting element was strong, but he finished with a vote of 804,651, which gave him a plurality of 69,462 or 11,565 more than his margin over Hearst. His campaign had cost him $369 as against Chanler's $7,305. "With this expression of the confidence of the people," he said, "I shall devote myself with renewed zeal to their service." [14] Once more he faced the people with no political debts to pay and without having compromised any principle for which he stood.

To Roosevelt's bubbling congratulations, the Governor replied:

> I warmly appreciate your kind letter. It was a good fight; and I enjoyed it thoroughly. More than anything else, I enjoyed stumping through the Middle West and the opportunity of speaking for Mr. Taft, whose splendid victory over Mr. Bryan is a tonic to the entire country.
>
> We had a desperate time in New York, and when I consider the variety of influences, powerful and unscrupulous, that were working against me, I confess that I marvel at the result; though all along I felt, for some reason, a strong confidence that we should be successful. These are good Republican days, and I rejoice with you and must congratulate you upon the course of events.[15]

The Governor's enviable position appealed so strongly to the retiring President that he appended the following wistful and prophetic paragraph to a letter thanking Hughes for a trivial favor:

"Good luck to you! I believe and hope that you have a long career in public life ahead of you. As I shall soon leave public life, and in all human probability permanently, I feel a real interest in a man who is in the middle of his career." [16]

[14] New York *World*, Nov. 4, 1908.

[15] CEH to T. R., Nov. 7, 1908.

[16] T. R. to CEH, Dec. 7, 1908.

Chapter 25

THE GOVERNOR'S CONSCIENCE

CEREMONY, drama, and nerve-fraying toil were copiously mingled in Hughes' last years at Albany. The new cordiality between him and Theodore Roosevelt brought him prominently into the Washington scene as the old administration gave way to the new early in 1909. With Mrs. Hughes, he was a guest at the last state dinner given by T. R. on January 28 in honor of Chief Justice Fuller and other members of the Supreme Court. When the men went into the breakfast room to smoke, the President turned his back upon the long-haired Chief Justice and talked exclusively to the Governor about New York until Hughes felt embarrassed by such discourtesy to the guest of honor.

On February 22 the Governor was again in Washington to address the convocation of the George Washington University and receive an LL.D. degree, and on March 2 he and Mrs. Hughes attended the dinner party given by Oscar Straus, the Secretary of Commerce and Labor, in honor of President Roosevelt. Once more there was animated conversation between the President, sitting on Mrs. Straus' right, and the Governor, sitting on her left.

"Well, Mr. President," Hughes consoled the great man who was giving up the big game in America for comparatively dull hunting abroad, "when you come back from Africa we'll all be down on the shore to greet you."

"Will you? Will you?" he exclaimed as if a little incredulous.

That evening in the smoking room the retiring President told the story of his political life—a long and interesting tale that was not inappropriate to the occasion. Hughes saw the President again the next day at the White House levee and was greeted effusively amid a huge crowd. Then—on March 4—came Taft's inauguration.

The Capital awoke almost smothered by snow, with a furious blizzard howling through the streets. Frigid temperatures seemed to augment the coolness between Taft and Roosevelt as they took their last ride together down Pennsylvania Avenue. The inaugural ceremony was held in the Senate Chamber and T. R. hastened to his train to avoid playing second fiddle to Taft in the traditional return to the White House. A new chapter in American history thus began. Its first colorful event was the struggle of the inaugural parade down the Avenue from the Capitol to the White House in heroic defiance of the elements. Governor Hughes, who rode at the head of the New York troops, gives the following account of the incident:

> Immediately after the ceremony . . . I went to a designated place southeast of the Capitol where Squadron A of the New York Cavalry was stationed. We waited for over an hour before we could take our position in the inaugural parade. The horses were very restive as the icicles dropped from the trees upon their backs. As customary, I wore a silk hat and a frock coat,—with my Marshal's scarf, and thinking an overcoat too clumsy I had protected myself with a chamois vest. But my hands inside my gloves were very cold and I had to dig them into the horse's flesh to keep them from freezing. As we came down the hill from the Capitol our horses almost slid on the icy street. My horse had always been in the ranks, and it was with difficulty that he could be persuaded to take his place at the head of the procession. But with the cheers of the crowd as we came to the large stands, he seemed to realize that this was his day and he went along at the head, proudly arching his neck and acting his part as a well trained horse of the Commander in Chief should. I made my bows with all the grace I could command and managed to get through without mishap. I dismounted at 19th Street and Pennsylvania Avenue, Northwest, (where the parade broke up) with a keen sense of relief. The storm was so severe that the Seventh Regiment of New York failed to get to Washington in time and President Taft gave it a special review on the next morning, asking me to join him.[1]

Other accounts of the impression the Governor made, riding with uncovered head, are less modest. The *Washington Post* reported that he aroused "the wildest enthusiasm." [2] According to Senator Davenport, a continuous roar of applause . . . greeted him from one end of the avenue to the other." [3] Hughes returned to Albany with a devoted friend in the White House and a gratifying sense of public appreciation for his work.

June, 1909, brought the Alaska-Yukon-Pacific Exposition in Seattle. The New York legislature had voted funds for a special train to ensure the attendance of a large delegation from that state. Hughes vetoed the bill and went to the exposition himself, taking only his military aide and paying the expenses from his own pocket. Once more he was lionized.

After delivering his speech on "New York Day" to an audience of ten thousand people, Hughes felt the joyous release of a schoolboy on a holiday. He had already traveled through Yellowstone National Park in a special relay of buckboards. From Seattle he took a boat to Vancouver, then spent a day at Banff and a day or two at Lake Louise. Still eager to climb every peak he saw, he induced Colonel Treadwell to accompany him to the top of Sulphur Mountain. It was not a severe climb, compared to what he had done in the Alps, but stiff enough to be exhilarating.

[1] CEH, Notes, pp. 202–203. [2] March 5, 1909.
[3] New York *Tribune*, April 2, 1909.

Other events interrupted the grinding routine of the governorship. A telephone call from Brown University brought the alarming news that son Charles, who was nearing the end of his senior year, had suddenly been stricken by cerebrospinal meningitis after a night of toil on an essay. Mrs. Hughes caught the first train to Providence while the Governor continued to labor over his thirty-day bills in a state of high nervous tension. Young Charlie had the good fortune to fall into the hands of the only doctor in New England who was skilled in administering Dr. Simon Flexner's serum for meningitis and was soon on the road to complete recovery. Incidentally, his paper won first prize. He was following in the Hughesian tradition.

Only a few weeks later, in June, 1909, the Governor's father suffered a stroke while preaching in New York. The Reverend Mr. Hughes had retired from active service as a pastor in 1901, but the spirit still burned within him and he had continued to preach in a number of pulpits in the vicinity of New York. In 1908, while his son was bearing down on the corruptionists at Albany, he was demanding from the pulpit that the New York police stop Gertrude Hoffman's "indecent and demoralizing" Salome dance at Hammerstein's. When his stroke put an end to his preaching, he and Mrs. Hughes went to Albany to spend the remainder of their days with their son. On December 15, 1909, David Charles Hughes died at the Executive Mansion at the age of seventy-seven.

Governor Hughes was still fighting doggedly for some of his reforms. His bill for the regulation of telephone and telegraph companies had been voted down again in April, 1909, and it was not until the following year, after an investigation of the subject by a legislative committee, that a satisfactory measure was finally passed.

Early in 1910 Hughes created a stir by opposing ratification of the proposed Sixteenth Amendment. The Supreme Court had struck down the federal income tax law of 1894, and Congress in turn was trying to strike down the court's decision by changing the Constitution. Governor Hughes felt that the aim was good, but the instrument fashioned to effect it was inept. It would give Congress power to tax incomes *"from whatever source derived."* These comprehensive words, if given their natural meaning, he argued in a strong message to the New York legislature, "would include not only incomes from ordinary real or personal property, but also incomes derived from State and municipal securities." They would enable Congress to limit the borrowing power of the states and "make the performance of the functions of local government a matter of Federal grace." [4]

Hughes did not quibble about the income tax; he favored it and was certain that an amendment making it legal could be drafted without danger of crip-

[4] *Public Papers, 1910,* p. 74.

pling the states. To be sure, Senator Root and others argued that the amendment then awaiting ratification would merely remove the necessity of apportioning income taxes among the states according to population and would not permit federal taxation of state or local bonds. The other interpretation, however, was clearly permissible. Hughes insisted that the amendment should be stripped of its ambiguity. His influence caused rejection of the amendment in New York, but other states supplied the requisite number of ratifications. When the scope of the amendment was tested in the Supreme Court, Chief Justice White chose the Root interpretation and Hughes, then an Associate Justice, assented. In his Chief Justiceship he treated the issue as closed by White's opinion, but many of the states are still fearful that federal taxation of income from state and municipal bonds may impair the federal system.

Nerve-racking pardon cases weighed heavily upon the Governor's conscience. The law gave him power to commute sentences as well as to pardon convicts, which meant that pleas came up to him in behalf of every person convicted of murder. The first time that a human life hung upon his word he listened to pleas on behalf of the two condemned boys, read the record of their trial with the utmost care, and scrutinized the jury's findings. At the end of his ordeal he came out of his office, white and haggard, and said that he could find no reason to interfere with the judgment of the court. "It was the hardest work I ever did," he confessed to a reporter.[5]

This was typical. Hughes would move heaven and earth to make sure that justice was being done. But he resolutely refused to take over the function of the court or to substitute his own personal caprice for the orderly operation of the law. "I have no right to pardon a man," he would say, "in order to make certain people happy or because I might feel particularly good-natured at the time."

The case of Chester Gillette, out of which Theodore Dreiser was later to fashion *An American Tragedy,* was an acid test of the Governor's sense of justice. Gillette was convicted of drowning the girl to whom he had been engaged by tipping over their canoe out on a lake. His sensational trial rocked the state. The Court of Appeals upheld the judgment of the lower court even though the evidence against the young factory worker was wholly circumstantial. Hughes reviewed the case and declined to interfere. The frantic supporters of Gillette then besieged the Governor for a reprieve in order to permit the presentation of new evidence, but the new evidence proved to be worthless.

Gillette came from a good family, and his mother proved to be one of his strongest defenders. "I'm not going to appeal to sympathy," she said when

[5] Ida M. Tarbell in *American Magazine,* March, 1908, pp. 451–464.

she called on Governor Hughes. "I understand your position. But Chester is not guilty, and I want to prove it." [6] For two hours she reviewed the facts and the trial as if she had been the lawyer in the case.

The Governor promised to read the three volumes of testimony once more. The effect was to buttress his conviction of the young man's guilt. Gillette had insisted that the girl's death was the result of an accident. But the boat had been found bottom side up with her coat lying on top. The totality of the evidence pointed to foul play. Hughes felt certain of his ground. Yet a life was at stake and his conclusion could be wrong. With the execution set for Monday morning, the Governor heard a final plea for Gillette on Saturday. On Sunday, after a terrible day of soul searching, he walked to his office and said the execution would be carried out. About ten o'clock that evening his secretary called to say that Gillette had confessed to his religious adviser.

The Farmer case added physical peril to mental anguish. Farmer and his wife killed an old lady who lived next door, hid the body in a trunk, moved into the old lady's house, forged a deed in favor of themselves, and told inquirers that she had gone to visit friends in the West. The trunk was found, with its gruesome and incriminating evidence, in their possession. Both were convicted. At her separate trial Mrs. Farmer appeared oblivious to what was taking place. Later she gave birth to a child in prison, and these facts were used to whip up a tornado of sentiment against her execution.

Because Hughes did not respond to the clamor, Hearst's *Evening Journal* launched an execrable attack upon him. In an editorial reminiscent of the slander that led to McKinley's assassination, the *Journal* said that if Hughes should permit this woman to be murdered, he would be a legal murderer himself and would get what was coming to him. As this calumny reverberated through the state, Police Commissioner William Bingham warned the Governor of his danger and sent him a special guard. District Attorney Jerome of New York telephoned to say that he was going after Hearst for criminal libel. "Hearst is simply trying to stir up a sensation," Hughes replied. "If you prosecute him, you will keep the sensation alive for a year. The best thing to do is to let it die."

The Governor himself was worried about Mrs. Farmer's apparent stolidity at the trial. He asked for the prison physician's reports, and was sent a large box containing hundreds of little slips of paper. His tedious task of examining these slips one night at the Executive Mansion seemed to be futile until he discovered a sealed envelope containing pieces of rough brown wrapping paper covered with scribbling. Investigation proved the writing to be Mrs. Farmer's. She had recorded the whole story of the trial. She knew the witnesses and had carefully analyzed the testimony. Hughes felt that the assumption of her de-

[6] Beerits' Memorandum, VI, 28.

fenders that she might have been insane at the time of the trial was completely undermined.[7] He permitted the execution to be carried out.

Still more disturbing to the Governor's peace of mind was the stench of corruption that continued to hang over Albany. For many years the legislature had been the venal tool of unscrupulous bosses and corporate interests. Hughes had cleaned out the executive departments and broken the control of legislation by the corruptionists. But the "Black Horse Cavalry," as the newspapers called the combination of exploiters representing both parties in the legislature, was far from being subdued.

The struggle between these forces and the Governor dramatically erupted again with the death of John Raines, the Senate majority leader, on December 16, 1909. To succeed Raines the Old Guard chose Jotham P. Allds, who had been a youngster in Hamilton when Hughes was attending Madison (now Colgate) University. Their personal relations had always been pleasant, but Allds had faithfully served Platt and Odell when he was a member of the Assembly. The elevation of this slow, ponderous, and unprincipled politician to the Senate leadership could be regarded only as betokening last-ditch resistance to the Hughes reforms.

While the caucus was nominating Allds, seven disgusted Senators met separately in protest, and Senator Benn Conger informed his colleagues that he had personal knowledge that Allds had accepted a bribe.[8] Josiah T. Newcomb repeated the story to Oswald Garrison Villard of the New York *Evening Post*. Allds tried to suppress the story, then begged for mercy and threatened a libel suit. When the *Evening Post* printed the story [9] nevertheless, and Conger himself unfolded the sordid details, the state was shaken as if by a delayed-action bomb. Allds demanded an investigation which only confirmed the charges. Several years before the advent of the Hughes régime the American Bridge Company, fighting to defeat a bill that would have upset its monopoly, had sent Hiram T. Moe to Albany with $6,500 in a satchel. In addition to the $1,000 paid to Allds,[10] the testimony showed that $4,000 had gone to Assemblyman Jean L. Burnett, presumably for division among several legislators, and $1,000 to the late Speaker Nixon. Although still asserting his innocence, Allds resigned before the Senate found him guilty by a vote of 40 to 9.

President Taft and Governor Hughes met at the Republican Club dinner in New York on February 13 and surveyed this grim political mess. Both threw their influence on the side of complete exposure of the corruptionists. "This is not the time to retire in dismay from any disclosure," the Governor declared two days later. "The party . . . needs to purge itself of evil." [11] Hughes

[7] *Ibid.*, p. 31. [8] Burton J. Hendrick in *McClure's Magazine*, September, 1910.
[9] *Evening Post*, Jan. 18, 1910. [10] New York *Evening Post*, Feb. 11, 1910.
[11] Buffalo *Commercial*, Feb. 12, 1910.

sought an investigation broad enough, as Senator Hinman put it, to uncover "all the crawling things which have been leaving their trails of slime in the legislative halls at Albany." But the Old Guard, with its back to the wall, doggedly fought off every effort to turn the light upon a broader area of its machinations.

The obvious answer to Allds' disgrace was to select the Governor's most conspicuous friend in the Senate, Harvey D. Hinman, as majority leader. Senator Root came out strongly for the nomination of Hinman "as the only course which will . . . correctly exhibit the real relation of the party as a whole to the principles and policies for which Governor Hughes stands and will rightly represent the wishes of the voters of the party." [12] Hughes publicly announced his agreement with this view. So much was at stake that he could no longer remain entirely aloof from the organization of the legislature, as he had done in 1907. But Hinman, sponsor of the direct-primaries bill, was anathema to the bosses. Woodruff and Barnes rallied their forces and elected Senator George H. Cobb as both floor leader and president pro tempore.

As the fight went on, other scandals came to light. In a special message to the legislature on April 11, Hughes asked for an investigation that would be "immediate, impartial, thorough and unsparing." [13] "You know that for years," he said in a public address a few days later, "we have not had decent government in this state but government that has been disreputable and indecent. I am convinced that the time has come when this must stop. The people are aroused. They will stand for nothing less than honest and fair dealing in the public service. Rip the cover off. Let in the light. Get the hooks out of the state departments. For years votes have been shamelessly bought and sold at the Capitol. Send one of the bribe-takers properly branded through the state so that he may be scorned by all honest men and it will have an inestimable effect for good and wholesome things in the service of the state and of the people." [14]

The legislature authorized a limited and restricted inquiry as if it were afraid of what might be turned up. Hope of securing a more thorough exposé was one of the Governor's chief reasons for calling a special session in June, 1910, when he also pressed his primary reform bill for the last time. But his efforts were futile.

This blind repudiation of his leadership quickened his yearning to shake the dust of politics from his feet. For some months his disgust had been mounting. In a postscript to a letter that he wrote to his father and mother on April 11, 1909, his feelings were laid bare:

[12] *New York Journal*, March 11, 1910. [13] *Public Papers, 1910*, p. 97.
[14] *New York Times*, April 14, 1910.

Your words are encouraging—and certainly I feel the need of inspiration. It seems at times so hard that I have to bear this burden. You have no idea how I dislike public life—and what one can do seems so little. Well, it will be only for a few months longer. My only desire is to do all that I can to make things wholesome—it isn't much—but life is merely doing what you do with all your might. And so, I try to take things philosophically and while my life is far from what I should like to have it, I am not downcast—but rather the more determined, on this my 47th birthday, to make the most of the rest of it.

Chapter 26

FAREWELL TO POLITICS

TWO YEARS of breaking lances with the Republican bosses taught Governor Hughes one paramount lesson: New York would have to improve its governmental machinery if the will of the people were to be translated into workable public programs. In his first term he had struck chiefly at evils produced by the boss system. In his second term he was to strike more directly at organizational defects that made it possible for the czars of politics to use government as a means of powering the chariot of special privilege.

The Empire State boasted of its democracy. Yet it permitted self-appointed satraps to name the candidates for whom the people might vote. It used ballots so lengthy and so baffling as to defeat the central purpose of taking a popular canvass. It maintained an executive branch in which powers were so carelessly diffused that the ship of state seemed to be guided by a dozen different tillers, which caused it to creak and wobble instead of steering a straight course to the desired port.

After his reelection, Hughes seized the first opportunity—his inaugural address—to lay the case for more responsive and more efficient government before the people. The President of the United States, he pointed out, had a Cabinet of his own choice whose members directed the great Executive departments. The Governor of New York had no such opportunity to prove himself. The state comptroller, treasurer, attorney general, and engineer were elected. Sometimes, as in Hughes' first term, these officials were of a different party from that of the governor. Many of the administrators appointed by the governor held their offices for terms longer than his. In most instances they could be removed only with the consent of the Senate.

What Hughes asked of the lawmakers was not a Utopia but feasible, concrete improvements for which the need could be readily demonstrated. One was abolition of the Senate's power to block removal of incompetent administrative officials. The second was a simplified form of ballot. The third was a system of direct nominations that would enable the people to choose their party nominees.

He had already made extensive progress in getting control of his own official family. Investigations under the Moreland Act had helped to ferret out sloth and corruption. After the election of 1908, even Otto Kelsey gave way to the buffetings of public opinion and resigned as superintendent of insurance. The Governor was so swept off his feet that he made a hasty and ill-advised nomination and then withdrew the appointee's name before charges that were bruited about in the corridors of the Senate could be aired on the floor.[1] Having recovered his own fumble, he sent in the name of William H. Hotchkiss of Buffalo, and a new era of thorough and strict regulation of the insurance companies began.

With the aid of Clark Williams, who had become state comptroller in 1909, Hughes initiated a systematic study that led to the establishment of an executive budget in New York. Departmental requests for funds had previously been sent to the legislature in haphazard isolation. Hughes and Williams whipped together an experimental budget in 1910, and at Hughes' request the legislature enacted the rudiments of a budget-making system, although a good many years were to elapse before the executive budget would be fully established at either Albany or Washington.

The fight for ballot reform and direct primary elections had really begun with Hughes' first message in 1907, but the climax came in his second term. He pounced with special vehemence on the monstrosity that passed as a ballot in New York City elections. It was about four feet wide and had nineteen columns for city candidates. The names of some candidates appeared four, five, and even eight times in separate columns. "The use . . . of such an unwieldy ballot with its absurd duplications, in the most important municipal election held in this country," the Governor said indignantly, "is such a serious reflection upon our capacity to devise suitable election methods that we should hasten, out of very shame, to make needed correction." [2]

His attitude toward the direct primary underwent a progressive stiffening as the legislature persistently resisted his appeals. Hughes had no faith in the wide-open primaries that were being used in the West. To avoid similarly disappointing results, New York would have to feel its way cautiously. The Republican organization of Kings County had committed itself to direct primary nominations, and Hughes thought it would be a good idea to let that local group experiment with a permissive form of the primary. When the fight waxed hot, however, this permissive feature became the focal point of attack. Woodruff succeeded in beating the bill on the ground that its application would not be general, but as soon as the Governor suggested a general primary system Woodruff turned his full fury against that also.

In deference to public opinion, the lawmakers finally passed bills with some primary trappings but actually designed further to entrench the party machines. Hughes vetoed these and renewed his pleas for genuine primaries. After his

[1] Author's interview with Harvey D. Hinman, Aug. 15, 1948.
[2] *Public Papers, 1910*, p. 30.

reelection in 1908, he made a compulsory direct-nominations bill the leading item in his reform program, frankly describing his fight as "a late phase of the long struggle against the control of the powers of government by selfish interests." [3] The convention method of choosing candidates perpetuated the power of the bosses and the interests that financed them. Delegates to such conventions were "mere pieces on the political chess board." Only by drastic action could the rank and file make their influence felt under such a system. "All that is worst in our public life," the Governor declared, "finds its readiest means of access to power through the control of the nominating machinery of the parties."

What he recommended was a system of direct nominations for all elective offices, excepting presidential electors. As the debate proceeded, however, some of his ideas underwent further evolution. There was no point in taking power from unscrupulous bosses and handing it to unprincipled demagogues. The party would have to be preserved as a center of cohesiveness in government, while being brought under popular control. "Those who would use the direct primary to destroy party organization," he once said, "not only fail in their purpose, but they simply embarrass the efforts of those who are endeavoring to secure clean, wholesome and effective group action for political purposes."

In his fully matured plan, therefore, Hughes struck at the root of the evil by trying to democratize the parties themselves. The people should be able to throw out faithless party leaders as well as faithless public officials. The Hughes plan called for division of the state into small primary districts. The voters of each party in these districts would elect a committeeman. Within each Assembly district the committeemen would meet to select their candidates for assemblyman. Larger groups of the same committeemen would meet in the Senate districts to choose their senatorial candidates. The party committee of each Assembly district would name one of its members to represent it in a statewide committee for selection of candidates for governor and other statewide offices and formulation of a party platform.

Here was a bold scheme to retain the advantages of party leadership and at the same time require party chieftains to seek election on the same ticket with the men whose nomination they advocated. The voting for such leaders would be strictly a party affair. Hughes thought it was absurd to let Democrats vote in Republican primaries and Republicans in Democratic primaries. That confused party responsibility instead of sharpening it.

With party leaders answerable to the rank and file, Hughes believed that most of the defects in the direct primaries then in use could be corrected. High-caliber men who would not go out and campaign for a nomination on

[3] *Public Papers, 1909,* p. 36.

their own initiative could be drafted as the candidates of the party committee. Tickets could be made up with some balance as to geography and representation of various groups within the party. No doubt these tickets would be accepted nine times out of ten. But the Hughes plan left the door open for rebellious party members to enter their own candidates in the primaries by petition if the leaders should botch their opportunity.

Under this system a legislator who had refused to bow to the special interests could not be thrown out for his independence (as he often was under the old system) if his constituents were willing to fight for him. The grip of the bosses could be broken. The plan had its origin in Hughes' own experience. Twice the people had given him a vote of confidence but in each case they had an opportunity to vote for the man of their choice chiefly because Theodore Roosevelt and Elihu Root had overridden the bosses who held the nominating power. Hughes had set his mind firmly against a third term, but he was loath to leave Albany with the boss system still entrenched.

Barnes, Woodruff, and Wadsworth ridiculed the Hughes plan as legalized bossism. Raines and Barnes pleaded with Elihu Root, whom the legislature had just elected to the United States Senate, to come out with a statement that would kill the primaries bill. Divide and rule was their strategy. Root candidly replied at the annual dinner of Barnes' Albany machine. "I count him [Hughes]," he told the hostile Barnes men, "as I count all lovers of their country and their party to be for party organization." As questioning "ohs" resounded through the hall, Root let loose another challenge: "The wide popularity of Governor Hughes, not only with the State of New York, but in the West, is based on the presumption that he has jumped on the politicians." The grand old statesman brought his speech to a climax with a full endorsement of what Hughes was trying to do.

Reason and argument had no more chance in that sea of skepticism, however, than a fisherman on the back of a whale. The legislative correspondents at Albany correctly diagnosed the situation when they gave their annual dinner in the spring of 1909. Across the room was hung a huge banner bearing the words, "CHARLIE, QUIT DREAMING." When Hughes arose to respond to the newsmen's bantering, he said, "I may be a dreamer, but I'm not a quitter." Then he launched into his dream of what New York might be and what its public-spirited citizens and the legislators sitting before him might accomplish by working together in the public interest. His idealism won hearty applause but few legislative votes.

Once more Hughes carried his fight to the people. "I know of no better way of insuring the people against exploitation from corrupt political methods," he told a Rochester audience on the night of April 8, "than by making political managers account directly to the voters of their party and giving to the voters the right of final decision by direct vote upon the candidates that are presented. It is not loyalty to party spirit which occasions the trouble, but loyalty to special interests, which seem to control the party and utilize the party machinery." [4]

That very night the Assembly riddled his primaries bill by a vote of 112 to 28. Against these odds it was futile to call a special session. Governor Hughes awaited the convening of the legislature in January, 1910, to renew the fight. The Hinman-Greene bill was reintroduced with improvements but without change in principle. This time the bosses came forward with a bill of their own resulting from a legislative inquiry into the primary laws of other states. While it incorporated some of the Hinman-Greene provisions, it denied the voters any chance of passing upon party nominees. The *New York Press* accurately characterized it as "a fake bill designed to preserve the power of the bosses." [5]

Barnes also pressed his fight against the Governor personally. Both were guests at the legislative correspondents' dinner on April 7. When the good-natured journalistic ribbing of the distinguished guests was concluded, the Albany boss, fortified by intoxicants, launched into a tirade of abuse against reformers in general and Hughes in particular. It was the most caustic assault upon himself to which Hughes had ever listened or ever would listen. Anger may have burned within him as he arose to reply, but what came to the surface was only an unruffled flow of words that laid bare the sordid triangle of bossism, corruption, and exploitation of which Barnes was the central figure. "Look into each other's eyes," the Governor cried, "and know the truth." Seldom has the despicable business of perverting a government and plundering a people been more skillfully stripped to the core. To those who listened, Hughes seemed to become the embodiment of eloquence, sincerity, and power.[6]

The crowd gave way to delirium. Men stood on their chairs and shouted themselves hoarse. Bosslets and toadying politicians joined in the impulsive demonstration, as if in unavoidable admiration for a man who could shrink the big boss to peanut size without resorting to rancor or distortion of fact. As soon as the excitement subsided, however, they hastened down to the bar and cursed themselves for having lost control of their emotions.

Senator George H. Cobb attempted to save the day for the reformers by drafting a compromise bill applying the Hinman-Greene provisions only to congressmen, members of the legislature, and county officers. Hughes stood ready to approve it as half a loaf, and the Senate passed it by thirty-four to thirteen. Once more, however, the Assembly turned it down and passed its

[4] New York *Tribune*, April 9, 1909. [5] March 17, 1910.
[6] Author's interviews with John Lord O'Brian and Harvey D. Hinman, eyewitnesses.

own "fake" primaries bill. Without waiting for the official copy to reach his desk, the Governor announced he would veto it.

Hughes decided to try once more. His influence as Governor had gone into partial eclipse because of his impending resignation, but the outlook was not hopeless. The country was bestirring itself to welcome back its hero fresh from new conquests in Africa and Europe—Theodore Roosevelt. Six days before the special session convened T. R. wrote Hughes from aboard ship on the Atlantic:

> Are you going to be in New York any time during the next month or two? If so, would you care to come out and spend the night with me, or come out and take lunch with me—whichever you choose? Now, my dear Governor, I know how busy you are, and this may be utterly inconvenient, and if so you must not think of coming; but it would be a very great pleasure to see you and talk over many things with you. If you would prefer, I would gladly meet you in New York, and we could lunch together, but of course it would be a pleasure to me to have you in my house.[7]

Two days later the former President landed in New York amid great popular acclaim and ceremony. The Governor had no part in these events; nor was he able immediately to accept T. R.'s invitation. The delay in their meeting unloosed fresh rumors of coolness between the two men, and Hughes sought in his letter of June 25, 1910, to dispel any misunderstanding:

> I beg you not to believe the stories which the mischief makers are endeavoring to circulate, and which here and there find some reflection in the press. I have said nothing directly or indirectly save that I was very glad to receive your invitation and accepted it with pleasure,—the date of the visit yet to be fixed.
>
> In truth, the work has been so insistent—not only days, but night after night until the morning hours—during the past month that I have about reached my limit and am nearly exhausted. I shall not finish the 30-day bills until Sunday night, and I must be in Cambridge Wednesday morning. Not a line of my Phi Beta Kappa address has yet been written.
>
> I am sure you will understand all this, but I do not wish you to have the faintest doubt as to my attitude. I am looking forward with much pleasure to seeing you in Cambridge, and I shall be glad to visit you at Oyster Bay when we are able to fix a mutually convenient date.

Roosevelt replied on June 27:

> Indeed, I shall pay no heed whatever to those stories. I believe that you are backed up by the best people of this State, and one of my main reasons for desiring to see you is to tell you so.

Meanwhile William M. Chadbourne had dropped in at the Governor's office to say that he thought Roosevelt would lend his aid to a compromise primaries

[7] T. R. to CEH, June 14, 1910.

bill. Chadbourne undertook to sound out T. R. with respect to the Cobb bill. But the answer came straight from Roosevelt himself when he encountered Hughes in the Yard of Harvard University on commencement morning, June 29. It was their first meeting since the inauguration of Taft sixteen months before. The atmosphere was heavy with speculation as to what the return of T. R. would mean as to both the Hughes policies in Albany and the Taft policies in Washington. Instinctively the other men in the parties fell back and left the two giants of New York politics together under the Harvard elms. The conversation soon turned to the situation at Albany and the fight for direct nominations.

"I don't wish to say anything about this matter," the former President said.

"Colonel," Hughes admonished, "silence means opposition." The Hearst press had been saying that the bill would be beaten because of Roosevelt's disapproval.

"Opposition!" T. R. exclaimed. "Silence means opposition! I'll speak." [8]

The marshal of the parade broke up the conversation by asking the two distinguished visitors to move into the hall. They sat together on the platform and during intervals in the ceremony Hughes whispered to T. R. a more detailed explanation of what he was trying to do at Albany. On the other side of Roosevelt sat Senator Henry Cabot Lodge. His opposition to any participation by the former President in the New York fight resulted in a whispered debate between the Senator and Governor across T. R.'s chest.

At noon Roosevelt presided over the alumni luncheon. "Our Governor has a very persuasive way with him," he said. "I had intended to keep absolutely clear from any kind of public or political question after coming home, and I could carry out my resolution all right until I met the Governor this morning, and he then explained to me that I had come back to live in New York now: that I had to help him out, and after a very brief conversation I put up my hands and agreed to help him." [9]

Roosevelt agreed to accept the Cobb bill, with an amendment excluding candidates for city office so as not to interfere with municipal fusion campaigns, and telegraphed his endorsement to Senator Davenport. President Taft also lent his aid. Big names were not enough, however, to turn the tide of revolt at Albany. The antiprimary forces condemned Roosevelt's intervention in the same terms the Governor had used to condemn the interference of the bosses. There was a difference, of course: neither Roosevelt nor Hughes used the patronage club or any of the forces of invisible government. Their appeal was to public opinion. Nevertheless, the Senate rejected the amended Cobb bill by one vote, and the irate Assembly brought up the old bill and scuttled it again in a petty display of resentment.

[8] Beerits' Memorandum, VI, 18. [9] *Outlook,* July 9, 1910.

Governor Hughes thus lost one of the hardest battles of his career. Yet he had given the state and nation, as Burton J. Hendrick pointed out, a "clearly outlined picture of what the old party system means."[10] He had shown the people in unmistakable terms what they must do to bring government under their control. It is true that his plan had the defects of its virtues: it presupposed an alert and intelligent citizenry, which does not always exist. It called for unselfish leaders of the type of Hughes himself, who are difficult to find. In a more friendly climate, however, his direct-nominations plan might well have become the pattern for a great rejuvenation of popular government through the two-party system. New York was ultimately to acquire a primary system less bold in scope and design. A shorter ballot, too, was to be achieved along with reorganization of the executive branch and strengthening of the governor's powers. As several of Hughes' successors fought for these reforms, they realized that their tasks had been made easier by his vigorous spadework.

In those gloomy days of 1910, however, recriminations multiplied. T. R.'s friends were piqued because he had been led into a losing fight. His foes were disgruntled because, having dipped his toe into the hot water of the primaries contest, Roosevelt plunged headlong into the New York political caldron. If Hughes had left the colonel alone, some conservatives were wont to lament, the whole catastrophic split between Roosevelt and Taft might have been avoided. What naïveté! Once back in his native habitat, T. R. could no more avoid politicking than the sun can avoid radiating heat. While still in Europe, he had written Lodge that he was aware of Taft's mistakes and implied that he would have "to plunge into this caldron of politics."[11] Hughes merely offered the colonel a convenient springboard.

Professor George Edwin Mowry goes so far as to accuse Hughes of drawing Roosevelt into the fight and then, belatedly accepting a seat on the Supreme Court, withdrawing himself from the political arena. "The air around Oyster Bay must have been electric," he writes, "after that incident."[12] The facts are that Hughes had accepted the Supreme Court nomination two months before he ever talked with Roosevelt on the primaries bill. So far from being deceived about it, T. R. wrote to Lodge before sailing for home, "Hughes' nomination is excellent."[13]

The air at Oyster Bay may have been electric, but if so it was from the intensity of discussion when the retired President and the retiring Governor met there in July, 1910, for their long postponed visit. Hughes was accom-

[10] *McClure's Magazine*, September, 1910.

[11] *Selections from the Correspondence of Theodore Roosevelt and Henry Cabot Lodge* (New York, Scribner's, 1925), II, 380. Copyright, 1925, by Charles Scribner's Sons.

[12] *Theodore Roosevelt and the Progressive Movement* (Madison, University of Wisconsin Press, 1946), p. 136. Copyright, 1946, by University of Wisconsin Press.

[13] *Selections from the Correspondence of Theodore Roosevelt and Henry Cabot Lodge*, p. 380.

panied by Chairman Willcox of the Public Service Commission and Frederick M. Crossett, his new military secretary. Colonel Roosevelt greeted him effusively. After dinner the two hitched their chairs close together at one end of the capacious veranda, far from the other guests, and plunged into a prolonged discussion of the state of affairs at Albany. From time to time the colonel strode with quick steps up and down the veranda. Then he would resume his seat beside the Governor, talking even more earnestly than before. T. R. seemed to be wholly in sympathy with the Hughes program. Once more they were drawn together in a common cause.

Later that evening the colonel took his guests to his library and humorously described his hobnobbing with foreign potentates on his trip abroad. Speaking of his interview with the Kaiser, he pointed to an enormous but unlovely vase that had been given him and snapped in his inimitable manner, "A bit of German crockery; I will send it to the Germanic Museum at Harvard." Then he brought out a folio on art, with a full-page inscription written in English by the Kaiser, who seemed to regard himself as the highest authority on that subject. T. R. read the inscription with great gusto and observed with a chuckle, as he got to the "Wilhelm I.R." signature, "Slightly ungrammatical." The one gift from the Kaiser that he really prized was a copy of the *Nibelungenlied.* "The Kaiser showed it to me," the irrepressible colonel boasted, "and said something which I at once interpreted as an offer and immediately accepted." [14]

For some months Taft, too, had interested himself in the Republican schism at Albany. His first effort had been to keep Hughes in the saddle as a means of averting disaster. Taft had come to have an unbounded admiration for the Governor in spite of his fear that Hughes might be his rival for the presidential nomination in 1912. "If I am defeated for the next nomination," he had told Captain Butt, "I think it will be by Hughes. And I don't think he will allow his name to be used unless he really feels that I have no chance to win. . . . But I always think of Hughes as President." [15]

In March, Taft went to Albany. The Governor met the presidential party at the station and took Taft to the Executive Mansion with a cavalry escort. Both were speakers at the Tuberculosis Congress before going to the University Club banquet at the Ten Eyck Hotel. Back at the Mansion, they talked politics until two o'clock in the morning, Hughes presenting a full-scale sketch of the debauchery and reaction in the legislature. Taft responded that it was the Governor's duty to run again. Root shared that feeling, he said. The entire hope of the party rested on Hughes.

"I do not dare to run the chance of breaking down mentally," Hughes re-

[14] CEH, Notes, p. 204.

[15] *Taft and Roosevelt: the Intimate Letters of Archie Butt* (New York, Doubleday, 1924), I, 223. Copyright, 1924, by Doubleday, Page & Co.

plied, citing warnings from his doctor. "I must get out and make my family safe while I am able." [16]

Taft spent all day Sunday with the Hugheses, and they had a delightful time together. Baby Elizabeth, having been coached on how to behave in the company of the President, created a riot of laughter when she sat on his ample lap as long as she could stand it, then ran to her mother and exclaimed, "Oh, what a big man!" The Hugheses gave a luncheon for the President at which the guests included the governor general of Canada (Lord Grey), President Nichols of Dartmouth College, former Governor David R. Francis of Missouri, and Mayor McEwan. They took Taft to church, went driving in the afternoon, and arranged a press conference for him at the Executive Mansion.

"I don't know the man I admire more than Hughes," said Taft to Captain Butt two days after they had left Albany. "If ever I have the chance I shall offer him the Chief Justiceship." [17]

A week later the death of Justice David J. Brewer gave the President a seat on the Supreme Court to fill and he decided not to wait for a vacancy in the Chief Justiceship to get Hughes on the bench. Albany was dumfounded by Hughes' acceptance. The bosses rejoiced, and the Governor's political supporters put on sackcloth and ashes. They realized that his administration, like Samson, had been suddenly shorn of its power. Their hopes of rescuing the Republican Party in New York from its corrupt machine control were utterly shattered. Wails of despair crept into dozens of the congratulatory letters that were showered upon the Governor. Even more general was a profound sense of regret that he had turned his back upon his bright prospect of being elected to the Presidency.

"If your confirmation were submitted to the country," wrote former Governor Black, "I think it would fail, for I believe the sentiment is strong, widespread and active in favor of a career for you more public and conspicuous than that you have chosen." "I cannot but feel," declared E. J. Ridgway, "that the Nation is paying a frightful price for your peace." The most pointed comment of all was the friendly and prophetic warning from Nathaniel Myers, New York lawyer. "If an exigency shall arise and you shall be needed,' he wrote, "the People will pull you off the Bench for the higher position." [18]

Hughes had little sympathy with these lamentations. Undoubtedly he could have had a third term as governor. Then he would have been, in 1912 the logical man to have saved the Republican Party from its tragic split between Taft and Roosevelt. But he had had enough of politics. The law was calling him back. He regarded the work of the Supreme Court as of the highest importance and of course he realized his own peculiar fitness for public service

[16] *Ibid.*, p. 309. [17] *Ibid.*, p. 310.
[18] These letters and comments are in the Hughes Papers.

of that type. "I had no right to refuse," he wrote to Ridgway. "A refusal on the ground that some time or other I might be a candidate for the Presidency, particularly in view of the record of the disappointed ambition of so many historic worthies, would have been absurd." [19]

The chorus of regrets was significant chiefly as a measure of the impression Hughes had made upon public opinion in his four years at Albany. He had infused new vigor and new meaning into democratic government. He had taught the people how to use new instruments for their protection and advancement of their interests. The example he set for integrity, efficiency, and judicious use of power had never been surpassed. The *World* unhesitatingly singled him out as the one New York governor who had "done the most toward purifying the State government and re-establishing rule of the people." [20] "This new breath of life which he breathed into our political methods," wrote the *Evening Post*, "came largely from his steadfast reliance upon reason and justice. No public man ever treated a democracy more consistently as a fair-minded court that could be prevailed upon to see where the weight of argument lies and what is the right thing to do. . . . We gratefully acknowledge that he has ennobled our public life and quickened our hope in democracy." [21]

In the years that followed, governors in New York and elsewhere paid him the great compliment of emulating his methods. Henry L. Stimson ran as the Republican candidate for Governor of New York in 1910, supporting all the Hughes issues, but could not overcome public disgust with the machine. A few years later, Governor Martin H. Glynn, a Democrat, who had been comptroller during the first Hughes administration, announced publicly that he intended "to follow Hughes' footsteps" in dealing with the legislature.[22] Woodrow Wilson won the governorship of New Jersey in 1910 after a campaign in which he promised to do in that state what Hughes had done in New York.

Time further magnified Governor Hughes' achievements. After a quarter of a century had passed, Russell McInnes of the legislative committee of the New York Citizens' Union analyzed the records of all the New York governors from Hughes to Franklin D. Roosevelt to determine how successful they had been in getting their recommendations adopted by the legislature. Of all the recommendations made by governors from 1907 through 1931, 43.6 per cent had been adopted. Popular and strong though he was, Governor Alfred E. Smith had a batting average of only 33.5 per cent. "And Governor Hughes, who was the most successful of the governors during these twenty-five years," wrote McInnes, "had 56.5 per cent of his recommendations adopted by the legislature." [23]

[19] CEH to E. J. Ridgway, April 27, 1910.
[20] April 26, 1910.
[21] New York *Evening Post*, Oct. 6, 1910.
[22] Utica *Daily Press*, Nov. 13, 1913.
[23] *National Municipal Review*, May, 1934.

On his last day at Albany, Oct. 6, 1910, the Governor cheered his melancholy staff with a gay stag dinner. Mrs. Hughes had already gone to Washington to get their new household in order. In the course of the evening the staff presented him with a large loving cup filled with champagne. When the wine was gone and the regret-tinged hilarity was at an end, Hughes took his hat and bag and walked out of the Executive Mansion never to return. His carriage whisked him to the station and the train carried him, in a contemplative mood, to a new life that was to be totally different from anything he had known before.

The fighting Governor

By L. E. Shattuck, 1908

On top of Mount Marcy

By L. E. Shattuck, 1908

Helping daughter Catherine sail her boat

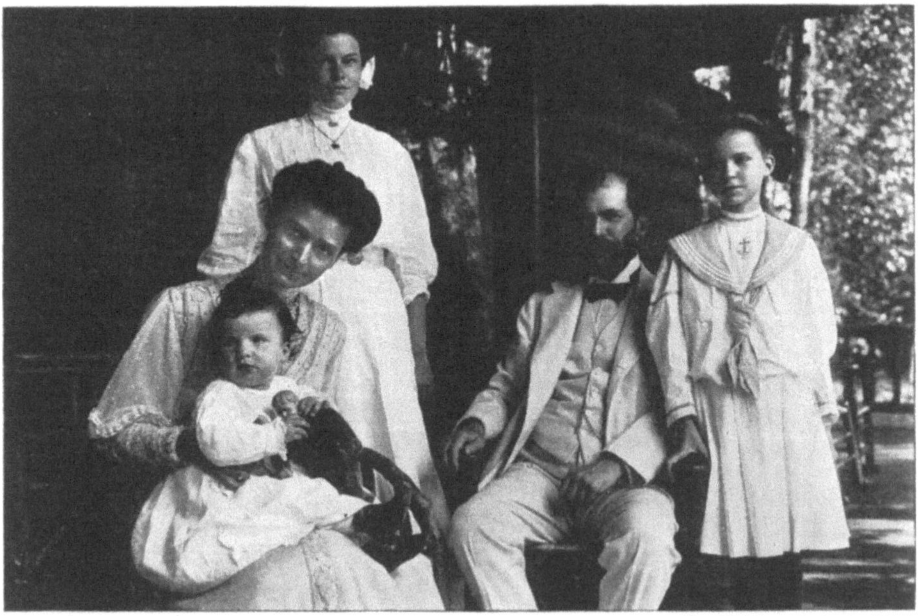

By Waldon Fawcett, 1908

Governor and Mrs. Hughes and their daughters at their summer cottage on Upper Saranac Lake

Chapter 27

ASCENDING THE SUPREME BENCH

THE SUPREME COURT in the first year of the Taft Administration was in a sorry plight. Four of its members, including Chief Justice Melville W. Fuller, were aged and slow, and Justice Moody was ill from overwork. Its calendar was overloaded with stale cases. The President was irate over the unwillingness of "those old fools," as he called them, to retire. "It is an outrage," he wrote to Senator Lodge, "that the four men on the bench who are over seventy should continue there and thus throw the work and responsibility on the other five." [1]

Taft's eagerness to get vigorous new blood on the court impelled him toward Hughes as soon as he learned that the Governor was determined to get out of politics. "I know the reasons that suggest themselves against your acceptance and I do not minimize them," he wrote in offering Hughes the place vacated by Justice Brewer. "I believe as strongly as possible that you are likely to be nominated and elected President some time in the future unless you go upon the Bench or make such associations at the Bar as to prevent." [2] But the court needed Hughes, the President argued, to add strength to its membership and to buttress public confidence in its work. Taft strained himself to overcome the objection that he feared would arise in the Governor's mind. It would not be necessary, he wrote, for Hughes to resign the governorship until October, leaving only two and a half months of his term. The court position was for life. While the salary was then $12,500, Taft said that in all probability it would be increased to $17,500 at the next session of Congress—an overly optimistic prediction, for the increase would be to $14,500.

Then Taft openly dangled the most powerful judicial position in the world before the Governor. "The Chief Justiceship," he wrote, "is soon likely to be vacant and I should never regard the practice of never promoting Associate Justices as one to be followed. Though, of course, this suggestion is only that by accepting the present position you do not bar yourself from the other, should it fall vacant in my term. . . ."

In a postscript he added:

Don't misunderstand me as to the Chief Justiceship. I mean that if that office were now open, I should offer it to you and it is probable that if it were to become

[1] From *The Life and Times of William Howard Taft*, by Henry F. Pringle, I, 530. Copyright, 1939, by Henry F. Pringle and reprinted by permission of Rinehart & Co., Publishers.
[2] Taft to CEH, April 22, 1910.

vacant during my term, I should promote you to it; but, of course, conditions change, so that it would not be right for me to say by way of promise what I would do in the future. Nor, on the other hand, would I have you think that your declination now would prevent my offering you the higher place, should conditions remain as they are.

Hughes was not swayed by this talk about a position that was not yet open. By nature he always avoided counting his chickens before they were hatched. The reasoning that led him to accept the Associate Justiceship is clearly evident in his reply to Taft on April 24:

My dear Mr. President,

A careful consideration of the questions raised by your offer to nominate me for the Supreme Court to succeed Mr. Justice Brewer has convinced me that I should accept it. The honor of this appointment, great as it would be in any case, is especially enhanced in my estimation because it comes from you,—in view of your distinguished judicial career and your intimate knowledge of the requirements of the office. So far as my personal inclinations are concerned, they lie in the direction of judicial work. My training and professional interest have been such that I should undertake this work with a personal satisfaction which no other line of effort could command in the same degree. No one could have a more profound sense of the vast responsibilities of the Supreme Court than I have, and while this makes me realize the more keenly my shortcomings, it also disposes me to welcome the opportunity to devote my life to such important service. Against such a life-work, to meet the conditions of which an adjustment could be made, I should not for a moment set any prospect of money-making at the bar.

I trust that I should be able, however, to withstand any personal inclination and not permit it to control my decision, if it were opposed to the obligations of public duty. This is the only question which has occasioned any difficulty. But reflection has re-assured me upon this point. There is no definite sphere of public usefulness, other than the place you offer, which would be open to me at the close of this year and my circumstances would permit me to accept. The opportunities of the future are conjectural. The alternative of your proposal is private practice. Undoubtedly this would permit public service in many ways, but there would also be the exacting demands of active work at the bar. Against this division of effort, and its doubtful fruition, I should have on the bench a definite field of usefulness in the discharge of a function of national government of the gravest consequence to our people and to the future of our institutions.

The question seems to me to be really,—What right have I to refuse this opportunity of public service which is now presented by you and upon what ground could I justify myself in turning aside from such a plain path of usefulness?

I confess that I know of none unless it be found in my present obligations as Governor of this State. But you point out that I need not qualify as Justice of the Supreme Court or resign as Governor until the second week of October. . . . I should regard a refusal to take up at your request this life-work solely because I should have to leave my office here in October instead of remaining until the close of December as based on ground too trivial to be just to you or worthy of myself. . . .

Your expressions regarding the Chief Justiceship are understood and most warmly appreciated. You properly reserve entire freedom with respect to this and I accept the offer you now make without wishing you to feel committed in the slightest degree. Should the vacancy occur during your term I, in common with all our citizens, should desire you to act freely and without embarrassment in accordance with your best judgment at that time.

Assuring you of my esteem and warm personal regard, and expressing again my deep sense of the confidence you repose and the responsibility it involves, I am

Very sincerely yours,

CHARLES E. HUGHES

Had he chosen to return to private practice, Hughes could have earned from $100,000 to $400,000 a year, as indicated by the fact that his fees did reach the latter maximum after he had left the bench. He was well aware of the financial sacrifice he was making. But what was wealth compared to the satisfaction of a judicial career? Were not the courts in the truest sense "the expert agencies of democracy"—the democracy that he cherished? "I am very glad," he wrote to his son, "that you are so entirely satisfied with the decision I have made. . . . We shall have to live within rather narrow bounds; but we can stand that. My only desire is to be able worthily to perform the duties of the office. And I confess that the congratulations and friendly comments that have been coming in have made me feel very humble and have deepened my sense of responsibility." [3]

The President fairly beamed with delight over Hughes' acceptance.

"Yes, Archie," he told Captain Butt, "that is a great appointment. How do you think it will be taken?"

"It will be a monument to your administration," Butt said. "There was every political reason why you should not have made it, and apparently every reason why he should not have accepted it."

"Yes," Taft answered reflectively, "such an appointment makes politics look petty." [4]

The Senate was equally pleased. On May 2, 1910, it confirmed the Hughes nomination in a five-minute executive session without a negative vote being cast. Senator Chauncey Depew, who had been besmirched by the insurance investigation, nevertheless took the lead in pressing the nomination through.

Considering the President's feeling of virtue in making this appointment, it is difficult to account for his next move. En route to Albany by train, he asked Hughes to join him at Pittsfield. His purpose was to induce the Governor, who had not yet taken his seat on the bench, to make a campaign speech in Ohio. When Taft came to the point of voicing his request, however, he couched it as if he were only feebly echoing a suggestion from other sources.

[3] May 2, 1910.
[4] *Taft and Roosevelt: the Intimate Letters of Archie Butt*, I, 336–337.

Hughes immediately said that he thought it would be highly improper for him to make any campaign speeches even in his own state, and the embarrassed Chief Executive dropped the matter.

Mr. Justice Hughes met with his brethren of the bench for the first time on October 10, 1910, only four days after he had resigned as governor. All the Justices greeted him warmly as they assembled in the robing room. Every one of them was pleased to have him added to the court.[5] Hughes donned his flowing black robe, which seemed a little out of place on so active a man, and took the oath of allegiance. Then followed the awe-inspiring procession across the corridor and through the courtroom—the old Senate Chamber in the Capitol where the court had sat since the days of Taney. First in the line was Harlan of Kentucky, huge of frame, shaggy, with heavy brows half covering his eyes. Then came White of Louisiana, with his plump, kindly face looking grave; McKenna of California, with a neat fringe of whiskers on his squarish chin; Holmes, looking at once wise and frisky behind his long white mustache; William R. Day of Ohio, keen but frail; and Horace H. Lurton of Tennessee. Hughes, with his graying beard, thinning hair, firm step, and serious demeanor, looked every inch a judge before he ever ascended the bench. At the end of the line came the retired Justice Brown.

Every seat in the historic, half-circular courtroom was taken. The Cabinet was represented by Attorney General Wickersham and Secretary Nagel. Antoinette Carter Hughes had been waiting for half an hour for the ceremony to begin. Beside her sat her daughter Catherine and the new Justice's mother. Their eyes fastened upon Harlan as he announced the appointment and confirmation of Charles E. Hughes to take the place of Justice Brewer and directed Clerk McKenney to read the new member's commission. "The court extends a cordial welcome," Harlan said.

At the clerk's desk Hughes took the oath of office in a voice that was vibrant with conviction: "I, Charles E. Hughes, do solemnly swear that I will administer justice without respect to persons, and do equal right to the poor and to the rich. . . ." "So help me God," said the clerk at the end. Hughes repeated, "So help me God."

The marshal escorted Hughes to his seat, but not at the extreme left of the Chief Justice where a newcomer customarily sits. Because of the vacancy on the court, he went at once to the seat at the extreme right of the bench. Here Oliver Wendell Holmes shook his hand, and the brief induction ceremony was at an end. While Harlan paid a brief tribute to Chief Justice Fuller prior to adjournment of the court in his honor, Holmes beckoned to Hughes to move up and take the vacant seat of the ill Justice Moody which separated them. The new member knew enough of the traditions of the court not to make such

[5] Judge Peter B. McLennan to CEH, June 14, 1910, quoting Justice Harlan.

a *faux pas*. "I tremble to think," he once said, "what might have happened if I had been innocent enough to follow Justice Holmes' kindly but rather thoughtless suggestion. The other Justices would have regarded me as a fresh and bumptious newcomer, and even the Chief Justices in their marble busts might have raised their eyebrows." [6]

Everything about the court seemed compact and conservative. Its atmosphere was satisfyingly rich in dignity and tradition. Hughes was conscious of the lingering influence of Marshall, Story, Field, Curtis, Bradley, and Miller. Great minds had been at work in the court for more than a century. One could not study their lives and decisions without gaining confidence in their sincerity and independence. Truly they had created a noble institution. De Tocqueville had rightly called it "the head of all known tribunals."

Yet in its physical facilities the court was astonishingly barren. In the absence of a dining hall the Justices lunched together, when the court was in session, in their robing room. Below was the judges' conference room and library, small and cluttered, where they assembled about a table to make their momentous decisions. During the long conferences the room became overheated and stuffy because some of the nine objected to having windows open.

The snug courtroom itself was so poorly ventilated as to be a source of friction. Within their own restricted circle the judges passed down a story of how Justice Gray, a large and full-blooded man, insisted on keeping a window open behind the screen. One day frail Justice Brown, feeling the draft, asked a page to close the window. Justice Gray, overheated, arose from the bench and went behind the screen to confirm his suspicions. "What damn' fool told you to close that window?" he asked the frightened page. "Mr. Justice Brown," the page admitted. "I thought so," sputtered Gray as he stormed back to the bench.

Even less commodious was the clerk's office. Lawyers who wished to smoke or chat while waiting for their cases to be called had to crowd into the entrance room of this office or stand in the corridor outside the courtroom. Probably no high court in the country had fewer conveniences. Yet most of the Justices were loath to leave the Capitol. President Taft was eager to initiate the construction of a Supreme Court building, but the Chief Justice threw cold water on the idea. He feared that the public might lose interest in the court if it sat outside the Capitol—a fantastic notion in view of the thousands of visitors to the white marble temple of justice that has housed the court since the thirties.

At that time none of the Justices had an office at the Capitol. Writing their opinions and doing their research at home, they had to provide working space for themselves and secretaries. The Government supplied furniture for their

[6] CEH, Notes, p. 209.

home offices and lent each member of the court a working library. Hughes found it difficult to rent a house in Washington with space enough to accommodate a family of seven (his mother was still living with him) and afford the necessary office space. At first he leased the house at 2401 Massachusetts Avenue, Northwest, and fitted up an office in the basement. That proved to be unsatisfactory, and he decided to put what was left of his savings into a permanent home. "At a very low price" he purchased a lot on the northwest corner of Sixteenth and V streets, Northwest, from former Senator John B. Henderson. It was then a very quiet and pleasant neighborhood, with no buildings at all on the east side of Sixteenth Street between Meridian Hill and U Street. Here in 1911 the Hugheses built a commodious four-story brick house in which they expected to live for the remainder of their days.

The clerical help provided was meager. Each Justice had only $2,000 a year to pay a secretary. Hughes hired a young lawyer to do this work—three of them served him in succession while he was Associate Justice—but, hating to write in longhand, he kept the young man busy with dictation and did most of his own research. The question of securing more help was occasionally discussed, but some of the Justices feared that if they had law clerks the public might suppose that the clerks were writing their opinions.

Hughes was shocked by the work load that loomed up ahead of him in his very first week on the bench. As he listened to the arguments, he thought he could be ready to make his decisions within a month or so. To his consternation he learned that he would be expected to vote in the Saturday conference on all the cases heard during the week. And they were important Government cases that had been advanced to the beginning of the session because the court was so far in arrears in its calendar. This demand upon his legal judgment sent him delving into the law books far into the night hours in spite of his weariness from a summer of toil at Albany.

Soon he was able to keep up with the work of the court, but he was not content merely to analyze each case as it came along and wait for experience on the bench to fill the gaps in his knowledge. Nothing less than a comprehensive view of the jurisprudence of the court would satisfy him. That could come only from intensive outside reading; so his night work continued far beyond the period of his initial "boning up" on litigation immediately at hand.

Justice Hughes was keenly aware of the difference between the outlook and training of the advocate and of the judge. "The advocate," he said, "is looking for something to support a particular argument and too often seizes upon any sentence in an opinion which he thinks will help him win his case." The jurist must study the whole range and scope of the law. "He learns the points of view of the Justices and to read their reasoning and various *dicta* in that light. Not infrequently a sentence or phrase, or even a paragraph, will get into a majority opinion which really does not have majority support and the effect of which one or more of the majority may be desirous of destroying as soon as they get a chance. A new Justice is not at ease in his seat until he has made a thorough study of lines of cases, so that when a case is argued he at once recognizes, or by looking at a key case brings back to his memory, the jurisprudence of the Court upon the general subject and can address his mind to the particular variant now presented. That is the explanation of the ability of experienced Justices to dispose rapidly of their work, and also of the difficulties the new Justice encounters in going over ground which is more familiar to his seniors on the bench." [7] By his intense application Hughes shortened his novitiate and was soon taking some of the court's most difficult assignments.

At first the atmosphere of the court was less agreeable than he had expected it to be. His only acquaintance among the Justices when he came to Washington was John Marshall Harlan, who had occasionally written to him at Albany. On one of the Governor's visits to Washington in 1909, the giant Justice had also driven him about the city and introduced him to Justice Brown at the latter's reception. Now on the bench together, Harlan was like a father to the new member.

Among some of the older judges, however, Harlan generated unmistakable friction. Harlan and White, both powerful men in the court, had apparently disliked each other since their first dramatic meeting in the spring of 1877. The story came out one day as the Justices lunched together in the robing room. President Hayes had sent a commission to Louisiana to bring about a settlement of local controversies. White, as spokesman for a Louisiana delegation, met the commission and freely described conditions within the state. When he finished speaking, a huge man wearing a buff-colored vest came over to him and said, "Well, you are damned frank." It was Harlan.

The stalwart Harlan, who seemed to embody the strength and dignity of the old court and who was somewhat overbearing in spite of his warm heart, also found much about Holmes that set him on edge. Holmes' opinions abounded in "obscure phrases" and his constitutional views were "unsound." The philosophic judge from Boston reciprocated in kind. He liked to refer to Harlan as the last of the tobacco-spitting judges and insisted that the old man's opinions were verbose and demagogical. While each respected the soldierly qualities of the other, the clash of their personalities often enlivened the judicial conference. Harlan would tartly challenge Holmes' conclusions, and the latter, always urbane, would refer to Harlan as "my lion-hearted friend." [8]

Those trying first months were further complicated by the fact that, with Justice Moody still sick, the court was sitting with only seven members and no

[7] *Ibid.*, pp. 211–212. [8] *Ibid.*, p. 216.

Chief Justice. Fuller had died in July, 1910, and Taft was still giving "prayerful consideration" to the naming of a successor. Various lawyers and newspapers had suggested Hughes for the post immediately after Fuller's death, and it seemed to be generally assumed that Hughes would be the President's choice, even though nothing was known of his letter to Hughes on April 22. Taft had seemed to confirm this impression when he told Justice Moody that he wished to appoint "someone young and vigorous enough to go into the question of methods in equity cases, and if possible revise the entire procedure of this country and put it more in line with that of Great Britain." [9] Hughes admirably met these qualifications. At forty-eight he was nine years younger than any man then on the supreme bench. Vigor was his dominant characteristic. While the President procrastinated, however, Hughes had taken his seat as Associate Justice.

The age factor turned the President definitely against Elihu Root, who was sixty-five, and he exploded when word reached the White House that Justice Harlan, then seventy-seven, thought he should receive the appointment "as a final ornament to his judicial career." Attorney General Wickersham was delegated to ask the preference of the Justices, other than Hughes, and came back with the reply that Associate Justice White was the court's first choice.[10] But White was the same age as Root. The President continued to survey every possibility to make certain that Hughes was the best choice.

Beneath the smooth dignity of the court it was evident that the vacant Chief Justiceship was causing no little irritation. Harlan was obviously hungry for the honor. He thought the President could reasonably reward him for long service rendered and then, after a comparatively brief period, make Hughes his successor. White felt just as strongly that he was entitled to the place. With Harlan presiding as senior Associate Justice, White had little to say in conference and his usually amiable disposition seemed to have passed under a cloud. Throughout the fall he was offish and disgruntled.[11]

Hughes, too, was irritated by the President's indecision. The way in which the press was bruiting his name in connection with the Chief Justiceship made his position in the court very difficult. He quickly sensed that the brethren were allergic to inexperienced men in the presiding chair. The appointment of Chief Justice Waite directly from the bar, without any experience in court work and without any great prestige in the profession, had created resentment on the bench. Fuller, too, had become Chief Justice with little knowledge of how the court operated. The standing of Hughes in the legal profession in 1910 was much higher than that of either Waite or Fuller had been at the time of their appointments. His investigative work had given him a national reputation; his governorship had lifted him into the realm of high officialdom; and many

[9] Butt, *op. cit.*, I, 438–439. [10] Pringle, *op. cit.*, p. 534. [11] CEH, Notes, p. 216.

regarded him as presidential timber. Still, judicial work was new to him, and he feared that he would have a difficult time of it if he should be placed over the wise old men then on the bench. Cool reason told him that the President, now that he actually faced the awesome business of naming a Chief Justice, might regard him as too young and inexperienced.

Nor did Hughes think that the President was in any way committed to him. His irritation was solely a product of the embarrassment the President was causing him by his failure to make up his mind. "I thought," he said years later, "that if the President was not going to appoint me he should say so frankly and proceed promptly to appoint someone else . . . it is a mistake for the President to delay making judicial appointments." [12]

As the weeks passed, the public assumption that Hughes would be promoted seemed to be confirmed. "Hughes to Head Court," declared a headline in the *Washington Post* of November 11. On the same day a dispatch to the New York *Sun* asserted that Hughes was still the President's choice for Chief Justice in spite of objections from two members of his Cabinet who thought the former Governor was too uncompromising and from businessmen who feared that he was "a little too progressive." Those objections had been offset by impressive endorsements, including a letter of glowing praise from Francis Lynde Stetson, a Democrat who was president of the New York Bar Association and one of the country's foremost lawyers.

"I should bet," wrote Justice Holmes to his friend Pollock, "that he will appoint Hughes, who has given up a chance of being Republican nominee for the Presidency. . . ." [13] Justice Lurton, a close friend of Taft's since they had sat together on the circuit bench in Cincinnati, intimated to Hughes as he drove him home from the court one crisp December afternoon that he had recently seen the President. "I really think," he said, "you are going to be our Chief Justice." [14] A few days later Justice Day, another of Taft's close judicial friends, told Hughes that he understood that all question as to his elevation had been removed.

On Saturday, December 10, Taft called in the White House reporters and told them that he had made his decision as to the Chief Justiceship and that the nomination would go to the Senate on Monday or Tuesday. Still the finger of destiny seemed to point at Hughes. Toward evening of the next day, Sunday, came a telephone call from the White House.[15] "Would Mr. Justice Hughes please come over to see the President!" The cautious judge suppressed a surge of excitement. He would take nothing for granted. Yet here was a

[12] *Ibid.*, p. 217.

[13] Reprinted by permission of the publishers from *Holmes Pollock Letters: The Correspondence of Mr. Justice Holmes and Sir Frederick Pollock, 1874–1932*, edited by Mark DeWolfe Howe, I, 170, Harvard University Press, 1941.

[14] Beerits' Memorandum, VI, 42. [15] CEH, Notes, p. 217.

summons. It linked itself with Taft's letter, with the reports in the press and the tidings from Lurton and Day. He hastened to dress for the interview.

The telephone tinkled again. Once more it was the White House. "Please cancel the appointment with the President!" Less than half an hour had passed since the appointment had been made. The next morning Hughes read in the newspapers that the nomination of Edward Douglas White to be Chief Justice would be sent to the Senate at noon.

Why and when did Taft change his mind? One account of the incident has Taft handing the nomination of Hughes to Vice President Sherman when the latter called at the White House. As Sherman was leaving, Senator Joseph Bailey of Texas was announced, and Taft is said to have asked Sherman to hold the Hughes nomination in abeyance until he received further word from the White House. Sherman is reported to have returned to the Capitol in a state of gloom and to have told a friend: "I am afraid that Joe Bailey is going to talk President Taft into cancelling this appointment and appointing Justice White to the Chief Justiceship." Sherman's friend, a Mr. McMurray, asserted years later that he had asked if he might see the "very historic document" naming Hughes Chief Justice and that he had been allowed to read it.[16]

In their many associations thereafter Taft offered Hughes no explanation for passing him over or for cancellation of his White House appointment that Sunday evening. What we do know, however, suggests that the President did not change his mind in the brief interval between the telephone calls to Hughes. On the previous Saturday night, while dressing for the Gridiron dinner, Taft had told Archie Butt that he had got the Supreme Court off his mind. His chief concern then was how he was going to break the news to the friend who had been his first choice and was being shunted aside.

Another version has Taft's switchover coming after a delegation of six members of the Senate Judiciary Committee had called on the President. Not one of the Senators attacked Hughes; his position as Associate Justice was unassailable. But as a lawyer he had never argued a case before the Supreme Court, and he had sat on its bench only two months. The older and more experienced Justices, the Senators said, would not care to be presided over by the junior member who had just been admitted to their fraternity.[17] Taft, a former judge himself, saw the point (as Hughes had done) and decided to enshrine experience instead of vigor in the highest judicial post. There are also indications that White's sponsors convinced the President that selection of Hughes would arouse the ire of Roosevelt.

[16] McMurry to Sam Hobbs to author, letter of Nov. 2, 1951.

[17] Stephen Bonsal in *New York Times*, Jan. 16, 1921, on authority of a Senator who was present.

"Hughes is young enough to wait," the President said, "and if he makes good on the bench I may yet be able to appoint him." [18]

Official and journalistic Washington almost gasped with surprise, although some rumors that a change was in the making had leaked out. Hughes himself was the soul of equanimity. "An admirable appointment," he said. "I hold Mr. Justice White in the highest esteem and his appointment is in every way fitting." [19]

When the uncertainty was over, Hughes was genuinely glad that he had not been chosen.[20] Devoid of any hunger for power, he was fully content to serve under Chief Justice White. Within the bosom of the court White expressed his humility in accepting his new assignment, and Hughes responded with a warm tribute to the new chief without the slightest trace of resentment. In the tradition that is handed down from judge to judge, this feat of unselfishness has few equals.

From the hindsight of four decades, it would have been no mistake for Taft to have carried out his original intention. Hughes would have found it rough going for a time, but he would soon have been master of the situation, and the tenure of his Chief Justiceship would have rivaled Marshall's and Taney's. His executive ability and his keen legal mind were ultimately to give him power within the court that Chief Justice White never succeeded in attaining.

It is interesting to contemplate the changes in history resulting from Taft's vacillation. Had Hughes become Chief Justice in 1910, he would not likely have resigned to run for the Presidency in 1916, and he would not have arrested the naval armament race in 1922 as Secretary of State. From 1910 to 1930 he would probably have led the court in more sweeping and successful adaptations of the law to our changing industrial civilization than either the White court or the Taft court achieved. And of course Taft would never have realized his great ambition to be Chief Justice. Taft privately lamented in 1910 the irony of fate that forced him to give to another the one position in all the world that he coveted for himself. We may reasonably assume that the possibility of cutting off his last chance to be Chief Justice by naming a man as young and hardy as Hughes flickered through the President's mind. But it must have been a remote factor. In any event, the President was right in saying that Hughes was young enough to wait. Yes, he would still be young enough in a distant day to take the Chief Justiceship from Taft's own dying grasp.

[18] Butt, *op. cit.*, I, 567.
[19] *New York Times*, Dec. 13, 1910.
[20] Author's interview with CEH, April 30, 1946.

Chapter 28

WHITE, HOLMES, AND HUGHES

THREE strong men emerged in the "new court" of 1911. As Chief Justice, Edward D. White held the spotlight at the time, although his renown would ultimately appear dim beside either Hughes' or Holmes'. White was a Louisiana sugar planter who had been successively rebel soldier, Democratic politician, state judge, and United States Senator before ascending the supreme bench. A powerful man, full of integrity and jealous of the good reputation of the court, he presided over it with extraordinary relish.

White underwent a happy transformation as soon as he moved his chair beneath the bronzed eagle. The gloom and offishness that had afflicted him while the leadership of the court was in doubt now gave way to graciousness and solicitude.[1] He radiated friendliness among all the brethren, and the court entered upon one of its most remarkable eras of good feeling. White was so eager to meet every requirement of his new office that he even dropped the undignified habit of breaking up five-cent cigars and chewing the pieces.

Despite his buoyancy and good humor, the new Chief Justice found his duties a heavy burden. His eyes were beginning to fail; he had to rely increasingly upon his memory of the oral arguments. The judges said he played by ear. To buttress his health he took up walking and was often to be seen trudging homeward in earnest conversation with Holmes or Van Devanter, stopping every few blocks to rest his feet. As the years passed, his ailments degenerated into disabilities, but he continued his work with determination, fidelity, and a keen sense of justice.

White came to rely upon Hughes for counsel in numerous matters before the court. Walking from his home in Rhode Island Avenue, he frequently dropped in at the Hughes home without prior announcement. "Green," he would say to Hughes' secretary, "is the great man in? I'm in trouble. I want to talk with him."[2]

Hughes, for his part, became very devoted to the Chief Justice and many confidences passed between them. His affection for the older man never wavered even though he deplored White's lack of mastery as a judicial helmsman. Sometimes the Chief Justice would bring to conference cases on which he could

[1] CEH, Notes, p. 218.
[2] Author's interview with Laurence H. Green, Nov. 14, 1948.

reach no decision. "Here is a difficult case," he would say with a gesture of despair. "God help us!" [3] In presenting cases to the conference he was seldom clear and concise. He would permit the other judges to ramble far from the points at issue. This inefficient manner of directing a court that seldom came within 150 cases of finishing its work at the end of the term became irksome to the industrious junior member. Hughes made a practice of going to the Saturday conference armed with compact notes and prepared to render a clear-cut decision in every case. When it came his turn to speak, he went straight to the point, analyzed the issues down to the bare bones, and then briefly stated his conclusions. It was the same method he had always used. His efficiency, industry, and keen perception enabled him to cut through many a fog-bound argument. But the operations of the court as an institution reflected the less systematic habits of the Chief Justice.

In spite of the rambling and windy arguments, Justice Harlan thought the court was much too serene. The massive, organ-voiced Kentuckian had swallowed whatever disappointment he may have felt at not being appointed Chief Justice and continued his work with little apparent abatement of his vigor. But, having written 316 dissenting opinions in his thirty-four years on the bench, he complained to Hughes that there was too little division in the court. As if to demonstrate his point, he brought his service to a conclusion with a tirade against the Standard Oil decision that almost rattled the benches in the staid old courtroom. His tongue loosened by whisky, he bellowed bitter invectives that caused his brethren to blush with shame. "It was not a swan song, but the roar of an angry lion." [4] Hughes was strongly tempted to reply, but he held his tongue. A few days after the next term opened in October, 1911, Harlan was dead.

Joseph McKenna moved up to the seat of the senior Justice. Friendly and deferential, he had little to say in conference. For a Californian he seemed unusually hesitant about expressing a definite view and often withheld his vote until he could "see the opinion."

Both Lurton and Day had sat with Taft in the Sixth Circuit Court of Appeals, which their brethren accordingly called "the learned Sixth." Because of their close friendship, they were often thought of as a team, but they were a study in contrasts. Lurton, with his walrus mustache, was a typical judge of the old school—solid, experienced, deliberate, and conservative. Day's delicate physique was most aptly described by Justice Holmes when he referred to one of Day's husky sons as "a block off the old chip." But Day was mentally vigorous, clear-thinking, precise, and witty. Proud of his service as Secretary of State under President McKinley, he never failed to give each Justice a carnation to wear on the anniversary of McKinley's birth.

[3] Author's interview with CEH, May 15, 1946. [4] CEH, Notes, p. 219.

When Congress passed a special law to let Justice Moody retire, Taft nominated Willis Van Devanter of Wyoming, a former assistant attorney general and federal circuit judge. The vacancy left by the promotion of Justice White went to Joseph R. Lamar, formerly of the Supreme Court of Georgia. Lamar won the esteem of his brethren by his gentleness as well as his ability. Van Devanter brought from the West not only judicial experience and an intimate familiarity with the public land laws but also remarkable perspicacity and common sense. "His careful and elaborate statements in conference, with his accurate review of authorities," Hughes commented, "were of the greatest value." His advice was widely sought; Chief Justice White leaned upon him, as Taft was later to do. In those days Van Devanter was by no means an ultraconservative, as indicated by his opinion upholding the right of Congress to regulate virtually every phase of the relationship between the railroads and their employees.[5] His chief difficulty was what Justice Sutherland was later to call "pen paralysis." In conference his statements were so lucid and complete that, had they been recorded, they might have served, with a little editing, as good opinions. But when he sat down to write, the words would not flow. Procrastination in getting out his opinions thus became a habit—a habit that time was to magnify into a real handicap.

To succeed Justice Harlan, Taft appointed Mahlon Pitney, who had been a member of Congress and of the Supreme Court of New Jersey. Pitney's clean-shaven face was a mirror of the sincerity and strength of mind that were to win him the high regard of his brethren. The judges appointed by Taft were now in the majority. On the whole, they were much younger than the men they had replaced. It was indeed a "new court"—and much of its attention was centered on new legal problems.

In point of time and age Holmes belonged to the "old court," but in judicial philosophy and buoyancy of spirit he was often ahead of the new Justices. Of all the judges Hughes came to know intimately, Holmes was the most fascinating personality. It was not that Holmes was a more admirable character than any other. Rather, it was his rare combination of qualities—his intellectual power and literary skill, his freshness of view and inimitable way of expressing it, his enthusiasm and cheerful skepticism, his abundant vitality and gaiety of spirit. The man radiated a constant charm.[6] From beginning to end Hughes' relationship with him was of the happiest sort.

Holmes appears to have enjoyed their association no less than did Hughes. "I shall miss him consumedly," Holmes would write to Pollock on Hughes' resignation from the court in 1916, "for he is not only a good fellow, experi-

[5] *Second Employers' Liability Cases,* 223 U.S. 1.
[6] CEH, Notes, p. 221.

enced and wise, but funny, and with doubts that open vistas through the wall of a nonconformist conscience." [7]

Indicative of the occasional notes that passed between them is the following undated letter in the Holmes Papers:

DEAR JUDGE—

Many thanks for your kind note. I was nearly knocked out and it is very refreshing to be fanned and sponged off. I am more pleased than I can tell you that you approve.

Sincerely

HUGHES

The Magnificent Yankee was interesting even in his method of work. He was the only member of the court who attempted to make comprehensive notes during the oral arguments—a formidable task. Though he greatly admired Holmes, Hughes did not try to imitate this note-taking feat. Apparently he did not think it was necessary. Hughes' amazing memory enabled him to keep in mind the intricate details of many cases. Walking home together after arguments, the two Justices often talked law, and Hughes noted on several occasions when he referred to a troublesome point in a case argued a few days before that Holmes would ask, "Have we that point before us?" Hughes would then recite enough details to bring the issue back to his colleague's mind. In conference, with his sheaf of notes, however, Holmes was armed cap-a-pie.

As soon as Holmes had a case worked out to his satisfaction, he would relax completely. Even on the bench he would snatch a little sleep after lunch while resting his head in his hands over his desk as if in deep study. On one occasion he awoke from such a nap and found a prosy lawyer still droning on with a repetitious argument. "Jesus Christ!" he muttered loud enough to be heard out in the courtroom, and went to sleep again.

Once an opinion was assigned to him, Holmes was miserable until he had finished it. Such assignments were usually made on Sunday, following the Saturday conference. As each Justice completed his opinion, he had it printed and circulated the proof sheets among his brethren for approval or dissent. Holmes worked with such intensity that he would often have his proof sheets ready to distribute three days after getting an assignment. While most of the Justices were laboring on their opinions during the recesses, Holmes was thus free after a few days to indulge his passion for philosophy, social theory, and fiction.

Holmes was not then as popular with the bar as he later became. His

[7] Reprinted by permission of the publishers from *Holmes Pollock Letters: The Correspondence of Mr. Justice Holmes and Sir Frederick Pollock, 1874–1932*, edited by Mark DeWolfe Howe, I, 237, Harvard University Press, 1941.

opinions, always written in his own hand, were short and pungent but sometimes lacking in body and clarity. Chief Justice White occasionally showed Hughes letters from lawyers complaining that Holmes did not adequately spell out the position the court had taken and that his language was frequently vague. Hughes thought it was amusing to have the Chief Justice, who was none too clear in his own style, refer to Holmes' "obscurities." [8]

White was not alone, however, in squirming over Holmes' expansive generalities. Fearful of hidden implications, the brethren frequently insisted on stripping Holmes' opinions of their more fanciful images and seemingly reckless phrases. The good-natured Yankee would agree, reporting at conference that he had the concurrence of his brethren but the "fizz" had been taken out of his opinion. When he wrote to Pollock about drafting opinions some years later, it was not merely the loss of "fizz" about which he complained. "The boys," he said, "generally cut one of the genitals out of mine." [9]

If Holmes liked an opinion written by some other Justice, he would inscribe a gay comment or a bit of verse on the proof sheets. On a Hughes opinion holding that corporate books and papers in possession of an officer may be subpoenaed despite the provisions of the Fifth Amendment as to self-incrimination,[10] Holmes penned, "Yes—twice if I can get in two votes." Another Hughes opinion upholding a West Virginia law imposing heavier criminal penalties on second offenders [11] won the Holmesian accolade, "Clear as a bell and sound as a nut—Yes."

Hughes appears to have fended off a dissent by Holmes in *Peabody* v. *United States*.[12] His opinion held, for an ultimately unanimous court, that the mere location of a battery of guns which had not been fired for more than eight years, and which the Government had no intention of firing, except in case of war, was not an appropriation for military purposes of the land within their firing range. Holmes wrote on the proof sheets:

> How sweet a countenance tyranny endues
> What reverend accents and what tender Hu(gh)es
> Such seeming modesty and justice blent
> Smile at the futile claims of long dissent.
> So I expect to shut up.
>
> O. W. H.

Hughes was inclined to return the compliment when Holmes wrote an opinion for the court construing the Opium Registration Act of 1914 solely as a revenue measure.[13] "I am not convinced that this could not be worked out the other way—as I voted," he penciled on Holmes' proof sheet. "But I am not

[8] CEH, Notes, p. 224. [9] *Holmes Pollock Letters*, I, 258.
[10] *Wilson* v. *United States*, 221 U.S. 361. [11] *Graham* v. *West Virginia*, 224 U.S. 616.
[12] 231 U.S. 530. [13] *U.S.* v. *Jin Fuey Moy*, 241 U.S. 394.

disposed to dissent alone. For the present, I sit mute and sorrowful." When Pitney dissented, however, Hughes joined him.

The fascinating candor that Holmes brought to his daily task stood out in his comment on a Hughes opinion involving the effect of a writ of error in a criminal case.[14] "Yes, with humility," he wrote. "I now see what you have been about when I was giving parties their constitutional right to jaw while I slept." Another Hughes opinion [15] brought from his jovial Boston friend this idyllic assent: "Wee—Mussoo—I float in a fairy bark to the bight and serenely anchor there with you." [16]

The New York jurist could not match Holmes' sparkle and incisiveness, but his proof-sheet comments had a charm and spontaneity of their own. On one Holmes opinion he inscribed: "This is as beautiful as an impressionist picture which it requires a wide knowledge of art fully to appreciate. I compliment myself by expressing admiration." Sometimes his *entre nous* comments took on a decidedly unjudicial tone, as when he jotted on Holmes' opinion in *International Harvester Company* v. *Kentucky:* "Yes. Fine! I think this will hold 'em for a while." [17]

When the two went separate ways in a decision, the one in the majority would say to the other, with a twinkle, "You were in the wrong, as usual." Sometimes they even indulged in pig Latin together. Holmes also spiced the conversation at the court with downright vulgar talk. He would "run the full gamut of pungent utterance," enlivening many a legal argument with unprintable phrases. His descriptions were as fresh and down to earth as Dickens'. The huge men on the court he called "mastiffs." Lawyers he divided into three categories: the ordinary run of legal minds were "kitchen-knives"; the sharper ones, "razors"; and the top men of the bar, "stings."

The Oliver Wendell Holmes whom the judges knew had little in common with the humanitarian crusader of the same name who has so often been extolled in print. Holmes' brethren knew that he didn't care a straw for the "social" or "progressive" legislation that he was said to be heroically defending. What he did believe in profoundly was the constitutional right of legislatures to experiment. "In my epitaph," he humorously remarked to Hughes, "they ought to say: 'Here lies the supple tool of power.' " [18] Soon after Hughes' arrival from Albany, he fell into a discussion with Holmes of certain labor laws and spoke of the need for impartial and efficient administration to fulfill their promise. "I don't care anything about these fool statutes," the Yankee jurist replied, "unless they go to the nape of the neck."

Strength was what Holmes really prized and respected—the survival of the fittest. Even ruthless men of power won his admiration. Empire builders

[14] *U.S.* v. *Mayer*, 235 U.S. 55. [15] *New York* v. *Becker*, 241 U.S. 556.
[16] These comments are in the Hughes Papers. [17] Oliver Wendell Holmes Papers.
[18] CEH, Notes, p. 226.

such as Hill, Rockefeller, and Harriman might be "malefactors of great wealth" to Roosevelt, but Holmes thought "they should have statues erected to them." His brethren who listened to his candid glorification of power were not surprised when, in his will, he ignored all the "causes" and left the residue of his estate to the United States Government.

The first major opinion Hughes wrote for the court in January, 1911, brought him into friendly collision with the Great Dissenter.[19] The case was brought by Lonzo Bailey, an Alabama Negro, who had been sentenced to 136 days of hard prison labor under the Alabama peonage law. Once before, in 1908, Bailey had appealed to the Supreme Court, and Holmes had written the opinion saying that the constitutional issue had been raised prematurely. Over the dissents of Harlan and Day, the court had sent the case back to Alabama for trial. When it reached the supreme bench a second time, Hughes emerged in conference as the ablest champion of the view that the Alabama law was unconstitutional. Chief Justice White asked Hughes to write the opinion, and Holmes and Lurton dissented.

Bailey had contracted to work on a farm for a year at $12 a month. After about thirty days he quit and did not return the $15 that had been advanced to him. Under Alabama law this sort of conduct was a crime if done with fraudulent intent, and failure of the employee to perform the work or to refund the money advanced was considered prima-facie evidence of his intent to defraud. Alabama's rules of evidence did not permit a man caught in this net of circumstances to testify belatedly that his intentions had been good.

"We cannot escape the conclusion," Justice Hughes wrote, "that, although the statute in terms is to punish fraud, still its natural and inevitable effect is to expose to conviction for crime those who simply fail or refuse to perform contracts for personal service in liquidation of a debt. . . ." Thus judged by its effect rather than its pretense, the statute was a violation of the Thirteenth Amendment. In an almost passionate rejection of the idea that that amendment prohibited only slavery, Hughes asserted:

> It was a charter of universal civil freedom for all persons, of whatever race, colour or estate, under the flag. . . . The plain intention was to abolish slavery of whatever name and form and all its badges and incidents; to render impossible any state of bondage; to make labour free, by prohibiting that control by which the personal service of one man is disposed of or coerced for another's benefit which is the essence of involuntary servitude. . . .
>
> Without imputing any actual motive to oppress, we must consider the natural operation of the statute here in question, and it is apparent that it furnishes a convenient instrument for the coercion which the Constitution and the act of Congress forbid; an instrument of compulsion peculiarly effective as against the poor and the ignorant, its most likely victims. There is no more important concern than to

[19] *Bailey* v. *Alabama*, 219 U.S. 219.

safeguard the freedom of labour upon which alone can enduring prosperity be based. The provisions designed to secure it would soon become a barren form if it were possible to establish a statutory presumption of this sort and hold over the heads of the labourers the threat of punishment for crime, under the name of fraud but merely upon evidence of failure to work out their debts.

On finishing his opinion, Hughes went over to Chief Justice White's home and read it to him. White was delighted. "Cannot be improved on," he later penciled on the proof sheets. "Clear, convincing and in my opinion unanswerable." "I am with you 'through & through,' " said a note from Harlan. "Count me that way."

Holmes' dissent took strange refuge in mere legalism as if, to borrow Max Lerner's conclusion, he were leaning backward to get away from a "humanitarian" opinion.[20] "If it is a perfectly fair and proper contract," he wrote, "I can see no reason why the State should not throw its weight on the side of performance." Holmes' brethren were well aware of his scorn for any deviation from the result he thought the law required because that result might be "unjust" to the individuals concerned. It was "the stinking sense of justice," he used to say, that bedeviled a proper administration of the law.[21] In *Bailey* v. *Alabama,* however, he slipped into a superficial regard for procedural law that he himself would lay great store upon in later cases. Hughes' complete triumph over the Magnificent Yankee in this instance was further confirmed many years later when a unanimous court[22] followed the tightly reasoned and forceful opinion that had kept farm-hand Bailey out of jail.

In several other civil rights cases these two leading liberals of the 1911 court stood side by side against a majority of their brethren. Hughes' first dissenting vote after he ascended the bench had been cast in company with Harlan and Holmes in behalf of the emancipation of women in the District of Columbia.[23] In *Frank* v. *Mangum,*[24] Hughes worked with Holmes on his dissenting opinion, and in circulating it Holmes wrote a note saying, "I think it would be fairer to say (if you agree) that you and I think the judgment should be reversed and to put *we* for I all through." The opinion came down that way after Hughes had replied, "I shall be proud to be associated with you in this opinion."[25]

Both the dissenters believed that Frank was being sent to his death without a fair trial. Georgia had convicted this young New Yorker of murdering a girl who had worked in the pencil factory of which he had been manager. His trial had been conducted in an atmosphere of intense anti-Semitism plus Southern antagonism against "foreigners" from New York. An angry mob had packed

[20] *The Mind and Faith of Justice Holmes* (Boston, Little, Brown, 1943), p. 338.
[21] CEH, Notes, p. 227. [22] *Taylor* v. *Georgia,* 315 U.S. 25, 29.
[23] *Thompson* v. *Thompson,* 218 U.S. 611. [24] 237 U.S. 309.
[25] Holmes Papers.

the courtroom and jammed the street outside. The clapping of hands and the stamping of feet in the courtroom had not been controlled. The judge had suggested to Frank's lawyer that there would be "probable danger of violence" if the jury should bring in an acquittal or be in disagreement, and Frank had been kept out of the room when the verdict was announced. It had brought such a roar of applause and such prolonged disturbance that the judge had great difficulty in polling the jury.

In the face of this psychological coercion, which had brought the case to national attention, Georgia's highest court had taken evidence and given no weight to Frank's charge of "mob influence" on the jury. On that basis the United States District Court had denied Frank's petition for a writ of habeas corpus. A majority in the Supreme Court was willing to let it go at that. Holmes and Hughes insisted that the federal courts had a duty to inquire into the facts to determine for themselves whether "the trial was dominated by a hostile mob and was nothing but an empty form."

"This is not a matter for polite presumptions," they asserted; "we must look facts in the face . . . we think the presumption overwhelming that the jury responded to the passions of the mob . . . it is our duty . . . to declare lynch law as little valid when practised by a regularly drawn jury as when administered by one elected by a mob intent on death."

Frank never got a fair trial. Hoodlums took him from a prison farm and lynched him. But the dissenting judges' appeal to "the brooding spirit of the law" was successful. Eight years later, after Hughes had left the bench, Holmes reiterated the doctrine they had worked out together, and this time he spoke for a majority of the court.[26]

The liberals of the court prevailed when Arizona's antialien statute was challenged.[27] That law, requiring employers to hire not less than 80 per cent native or naturalized citizens, caused a restaurant owner in Bisbee, Arizona, to discharge an immigrant named Raich, who carried his demand for "equal protection of the laws" all the way to the Supreme Court. It was not unnatural that Justice Hughes should have been asked to write the opinion. As Governor of New York, he had worked conscientiously to improve the conditions under which immigrants were living, and a commission which he had appointed in 1908 had given New York a leading position in the "Americanization" movement. It was with much satisfaction, therefore, that he expounded the rights of aliens under the Constitution.

Writing for the entire court, except Woodrow Wilson's new appointee, James C. McReynolds, Hughes declared that in spite of the breadth of the states' power to make reasonable classifications in legislating to promote the public health, safety, and morals they could not "deny to lawful inhabitants,

[26] *Moore* v. *Dempsey*, 261 U.S. 86. [27] *Truax* v. *Raich*, 239 U.S. 33.

because of their race or nationality, the ordinary means of earning a livelihood." He continued:

> It requires no argument to show that the right to work for a living in the common occupations of the community is of the very essence of the personal freedom and opportunity that it was the purpose of the [Fourteenth] Amendment to secure. If this could be refused solely upon the ground of race or nationality, the prohibition of the denial to any person of the equal protection of the laws would be a barren form of words.

Congress, having full authority over immigration, had invited Raich to these shores. Arizona could not nullify the invitation by threatening him with pauperization.

More liberal opinions came from the court in this period than the country had witnessed in many years. It outlawed the "Grandfather Clause" by which various Southern states had disfranchised the Negro.[28] In another case Hughes took occasion to sound a warning against the denial of equal travel facilities to colored passengers. Five Negroes of Oklahoma had petitioned a federal court to restrain the railroads from complying with that state's "Separate-Coach Law." A unanimous court concluded that there was no ground on which the judiciary could hold up the operations of this statute providing for separate coaches and waiting rooms for the white and Negro races with accommodations "equal in all points of comfort and convenience." [29] It had been well settled that "equal" but "separate" accommodations met the requirements of the Fourteenth Amendment. In writing the opinion, however, Hughes singled out for condemnation a weasel-worded proviso in the Oklahoma law intended to authorize the hauling of dining cars, sleeping cars, and chair cars exclusively for the white race.

The lower court had approved the legislature's deft phrasing, and it appears to have found some support on the high bench. Holmes sent Hughes a memorandum on the point, but Hughes flatly rejected the idea that equality could be found in providing sleepers for white men and forcing colored men to sit up all night until the railroad could make a "black sleeping car" pay. "I don't see that it is a case calling for 'logical exactness' in enforcing equal rights," he replied to Holmes, "but rather as it seems to me it is a bald, wholly unjustified discrimination against a passenger solely on account of race." [30] In his opinion Hughes virtually invited Negroes to bring their complaints to the federal courts if they were in fact denied equality. Holmes, White, Lamar, and McReynolds concurred only "in the result."

Holmes won a short-lived victory over his whiskered friend in *United States*

[28] *Quinn* v. *U.S.*, 238 U.S. 347.
[29] *McCabe* v. *Atchison T. & S.F. Ry. Co.*, 235 U.S. 151
[30] CEH to Holmes, Nov. 29, 1914, Holmes Papers.

v. *Johnson.*[31] The question was what Congress had meant when it prohibited the "mis-branding" of drugs in the Food and Drug Act of 1906. Johnson was charged with delivering for shipment in interstate commerce a worthless fluid called "Cancerine" and tablets of inert matter which together were sold as "Dr. Johnson's Mild Combination Treatment for Cancer." Holmes contended that, as Congress had meant to penalize only misstatements of fact, quacks could be prosecuted for misrepresenting the quality, strength, or ingredients of their nostrums, but not for saying what they would cure, for that was a matter of opinion. This time Holmes carried a majority of the court with him, and Hughes wrote his first dissenting opinion with the concurrence of Harlan and Day.

Hughes conceded that the medical profession was in disagreement as to the curative properties of numerous medicines. But this case concerned worthless stuff about which there was no controversy whatever. To create the impression in a label that it was a cure for cancer was not merely an expression of judgment but also a "downright falsehood." Hughes argued persuasively that Congress must have aimed at false statements of *fact* as to the curative properties of a drug as well as false statements as to what the drug contained. Nor was there any question as to the power of Congress to give its statute this broader meaning. "Why should not worthless stuff, purveyed under false labels as cures, be made contraband of interstate commerce as well as lottery tickets?"

While Holmes carried the court, Hughes carried the country. The following year Congress passed the so-called "Sherley Amendment" in order to give the Food and Drug Act precisely the meaning that the dissenting Justices had attributed to it. In 1916, when a case involving the misbranding of another worthless concoction reached the high bench, a unanimous court, with Justice Hughes as spokesman, upheld the seizure of the drugs and confirmed the constitutionality of the Sherley Amendment.[32] The shrewd, lanky jurist from Massachusetts did not again challenge his keen-witted colleague from New York in a Food and Drug Act case, although Hughes wrote many opinions in this field.

In *Slocum* v. *New York Life Insurance Company,*[33] Hughes and Holmes were together again (joined also by Pitney and Lurton), with Hughes writing a fiery dissent in spite of Holmes' eminence in the common law with which the opinion dealt. Slocum's heirs had sued in a federal court in Pennsylvania on a life-insurance policy that had expired four days before he died. After a jury had heard the evidence, the company's request for a directed verdict had been denied, and the jury had awarded the plaintiff $18,224. The Circuit Court

[31] 221 U.S. 488. [32] *Eckman's Alternative* v. *U.S.*, 239 U.S. 510.
[33] 228 U.S. 364.

of Appeals found that, under the evidence, no such verdict could be legally sustained. Acting under a practical reform adopted by the Pennsylvania state courts, the Circuit Court granted a motion for denial of judgment. In the Supreme Court a bare majority said that the Court of Appeals had properly reversed the judgment but that the case would have to go back for a new trial. The decision meant in effect that the suit should be tried over again even though there was no possibility of winning it.

Hughes thought the majority was grafting onto the Constitution wholly unwarranted impediments to simplified legal procedure. There had been no invasion of the province of the jury. "Whether there was any evidence for the jury," he insisted, "was a question of law." It had not been converted into a question of fact by the trial court's error. The avoidance of futile retrials commended itself to both bench and bar. Hughes' long and vigorous opinion bristled with impatience over the court's superficial legalism. "Excellent," Holmes penciled on the proof sheets, "I am with you *totis viribus*." As in *Frank* v. *Mangum* and *Coppage* v. *Kansas*, this dissent too was to become the accepted statement of the law.

In spite of the far-reaching influence of their joint dissents, Hughes never shared Holmes' reputation as the Great Dissenter. To him the minority opinion was a device to be used with the utmost restraint. It was "an appeal to the brooding spirit of the law, to the intelligence of a future day, when a later decision may possibly correct the error into which the dissenting judge believes the court to have been betrayed." [34] Where unanimity could not be obtained without a sacrifice of conviction, he thought dissents should be openly expressed; for in the long run it was the character and independence of the judges that sustained the court in public confidence. But the right of dissenting ought never to be used, he felt, merely for self-expression. On many occasions he dissented "without memorandum" or joined in another Justice's minority opinion to save the court from becoming a Babel.

When he wrote for the court, Hughes had a genius for warding off possible dissents by other judges. In his hands an opinion never became a stump speech, a personal essay, or a vehicle for display of his learning. Hughes stated the law, as the court had agreed upon it, in the simplest, most direct and forceful language at his command. Writing as a member of a judicial team and never as a lone ego craving self-expression, he left dissenters little ground on which to stand. In the 150 cases in which he spoke for the court while he was Associate Justice, dissents are recorded in only nine instances and only three of these had the adherence of more than one Justice.[35]

Probably because of their differences, Hughes and Holmes learned much

[34] Charles Evans Hughes, *The Supreme Court of the United States* (New York, Columbia University Press, 1928), p. 68. Copyright, 1928, by the Columbia University Press.

[35] William L. Ransom, *Charles E. Hughes, the Statesman*, p. 9.

from each other. Holmes was the embodiment of law in the grand manner. To live in his presence was a rich experience—an experience that undoubtedly intensified Hughes' intellectual curiosity and broadened his judicial perspective. And it would be difficult to believe that as wise and genial a man as Holmes did not profit from his numerous brushes with the dynamic intellect of the younger man, as in *Bailey* v. *Alabama* and *United States* v. *Johnson*. For in the memorable cases in which they differed it has been Hughes' viewpoint which has thus far weathered the test of time.

Chapter 29

A FLAT "NO" IN 1912

THE QUIET life of study and contemplation that Hughes had sought without success at Ithaca again eluded him in Washington. Days were crowded with sessions of court, conferences, and toil over opinions, nights with social activities and reading of law.

The "new court" was in the midst of Washington's social whirl. Hostesses swamped Justice and Mrs. Hughes with invitations, as they did the Holmeses and other couples in the judicial hierarchy. Because of the pressure of his work, Hughes tried to limit his social engagements to two nights a week, but when invitations had been accepted on this basis far in advance along came others that could scarcely be declined. Seeking balm for his troubles, President Taft began to favor private hostesses with his ample presence. As he was known to be very fond of Hughes, the latter was repeatedly asked "to meet the President," and in the etiquette of the Capital such invitations were obligatory. Justices of the Supreme Court were also expected to attend all the receptions at the White House. Hughes could enjoy a good dinner and the conversation that went with it as much as any man in Washington, but this multiplicity of parties became a real burden. His best defense, he discovered, was to break away about ten o'clock and return to his library for three or four hours of reading before going to bed.

Hughes had come to Washington weary from overwork, for he had spent all the summer of 1910 reviewing hundreds of applications for pardons and clearing his gubernatorial desk to avoid leaving an accumulation of work for his successor. As a result, he had entered upon his engrossing judicial work nervously worn and lacking his usual zest and vigor.

Worried over her husband's health, Mrs. Hughes bought an electric automobile, with the object of giving him needed relaxation. Several of the Justices had electric cars, which were more common than gasoline-driven vehicles. Only McKenna drove a "gas" car, and Harlan and Holmes still preferred their horses. At the end of the day Antoinette Hughes would call for the weary judge in her new contraption, and they would go for a brief drive together before dinner.

As he fought off fatigue and toiled to extend his grasp of the court's jurisprudence, Hughes looked forward eagerly to the long summer vacation of

1911. In March of that year, however, Taft induced Congress to create a commission to determine the cost of handling second-class mail. One of the three commission members, under the resolution, had to be a Justice of the Supreme Court. Taft informed Hughes that this provision had been inserted for the special purpose of drawing upon his investigative skill. Hughes strongly resisted. Aside from his hangover of weariness, he did not believe that the vital work of judges should be interrupted by administrative assignments. But Taft was insistent; the Justice finally bowed to what seemed to be the inevitable.

His associates in the undertaking were President Lowell of Harvard University and Harry A. Wheeler, Chicago businessman. Taft had assured them that the task would not be difficult—that all the necessary calculations had been made by the Post Office Department. But those calculations were sharply challenged, and the commission had to spend most of the summer of 1911 in public hearings, taking technical evidence on which to make its own calculations. Hughes caught a severe cold and suffered much from lumbago. Still the work went on. Through the fall he had to meet his judicial obligations in addition to poring over postal figures late into the night hours. Holmes thoughtfully offered to relieve his hard-pressed friend by taking some of his cases, but Hughes rebuffed him as if the offer reflected upon his capacity.

The commission's report, finally completed in February, 1912, recognized the desirability of keeping second-class postal rates low so as to encourage the dissemination of news and current literature. It recommended, however, "a moderate increase"—from one to two cents a pound—as a means of relieving the burden on the Post Office without seriously impeding newspaper and magazine circulation. Taft sent the report to Congress with his blessing, but nothing came of it. Because of Hughes' extraordinary efforts, the President ordered that he be paid $2,000 more than the other members of the commission. He refused to accept it, and the President modified the order accordingly.[1]

Looking back upon this disagreeable experience and other demands upon Justices of the Supreme Court for service on administrative commissions, Hughes' opposition to the practice hardened into a firm conviction. While he recognized that, because of their aloofness from politics, judges may often render unique service in an administrative inquiry, this fact was outweighed in his mind by the effects upon the courts. The work of the Supreme Court is so important and so heavy that no outside demand can be made upon its members without seriously impairing the judicial system. If nonjudicial work takes a judge from the bench, moreover, the court may be left evenly divided on some cases. "Again," Hughes wrote in his Notes, "these administrative commissions bring the Justice into a realm of controversy with which he should not be associated. It is best for the Court and the country that the Justices should

[1] Taft to CEH. March 11, 1912.

strictly limit themselves to their judicial work, and that the dignity, esteem, and indeed the aloofness, which attach to them by virtue of their high office as the final interpreters of legislation and constitutional provisions, should be jealously safeguarded."

Except for his one deviation under pressure and his presidency of the board of Garfield Memorial Hospital, Hughes gave himself up wholly to his judicial task. In his office he worked with speed that amazed his secretary, Laurence H. Green. His eye was trained to take in a whole paragraph at a glance, and his photographic mind stored information with almost the accuracy of a microfilm. Green would spend hours running down cases with some bearing on a point at issue. With only the sweep of his eye across a few pages, Hughes would select some of these for citation and discard others.

When he dictated an opinion, he would stride up and down the bare floor as if to get the vigor of physical motion into his words. Often his mind worked on two different aspects of the case at the same time, and Green found it difficult to relegate each sentence to its proper place. In spite of his intensity, the judge's courteous manner never wavered. Sometimes he was positively deferential to his secretary, although he occasionally snorted over an incompetent brief submitted to the court. Shiftlessness and bungling always irritated him. "Green," he would say with a deep awareness of the spotlight of history on the court, "we are building either monuments or tombstones to ourselves." [2]

When he had a baffling decision to make, he would fret and stew over it as if it were a child with an undiagnosable ailment. "I can't see my way out of this one," he would say to Mrs. Hughes at the end of a troubled day.

"You always say that," she would reply with an implication of unlimited confidence in his ability to work it out.

"This time it is different," he would lament.[3]

His worry would intensify his concentration until the light would somehow break through. Then his gloom would pass as quickly as the darkness of an eclipse. His triumph over the intricacies of the law would be written all over his whiskered face. "It's all right now," he would say to Mrs. Hughes, giving her a hearty slap on the back. Or his exuberance might send him to the piano to pound out his one rollicking piece.

Out on the street, when he sought to recharge his dynamo by vigorous walking, a troublesome case was likely to pursue him. If his mind happened to be free on these excursions, he would chatter volubly and gaily to his companion—usually one of his daughters. But if a legal dilemma closed in on him, he would walk in unbroken contemplation. Elizabeth became so accustomed

[2] Author's interview with Laurence H. Green, Nov. 14, 1948.
[3] Author's interview with Catherine Hughes Waddell, July 1, 1948.

to walking silently by her father's side that one day years later when she happened to meet Chief Justice Taft on Connecticut Avenue and walked a short distance with him in animated conversation, she blurted out, "You don't have to talk to me if you don't want to." Taft chuckled with delight when he related the incident to Mrs. Hughes.

The family life was still geared to Hughes' convenience, the more so because he had to work at home. Catherine, who was budding into young womanhood, chafed a little under her mother's restrictions against bringing home crowds of young people who might interrupt the writing of an important opinion. But there were compensations during vacation time. Once the second-class mail investigation was out of the way, delightful summers were in store for the whole family, including grandma, the servants, and the canary bird. A Justice's salary could not be stretched to cover a trip to the Alps, but the Hugheses found delightful retreats in the Adirondacks and Maine. It was nearly always a lake in the mountains rather than the seashore that attracted them. Hughes loved to row as well as to climb. Taking a large boat with two sets of oars, he would assail the water with short impetuous strokes, Helen and Catherine taking turns at trying to keep pace with him. Invariably he played with the same vigor and spurts of energy that marked his work. Even choppy waters did not deter him. Considering the fact that neither he nor Mrs. Hughes could swim, their habit of rowing in all kinds of weather seems strangely out of harmony with his cautious nature. The only explanation one can find is that he was so fond of gliding over a blue mountain lake that he disregarded the risk of an upset during a storm.

Grandma Hughes was no longer with them after December, 1914. That rigid disciplinarian had lived long enough to see her only son and best pupil become famous, though not in the ministry as she had hoped. At eighty-four she died in quiet defiance of the doctor who had said she would never make old bones.

It was during the period of his Associate Justiceship that Hughes began strictly to adhere to a time schedule. His working habits had always been systematic. Now even greater regularity was feasible, and, finding that this increased his capacity, he adhered closely to his routine. His children said they could set the clock by the time he came down to breakfast. As this habit grew upon him, he took his walk, ate his meals, and began his work at precisely the same moment every day. It was not a matter of being a slave to the clock, he insisted, but of taking full advantage of precious moments.

Still feeling as if he were carrying a ball and chain, he also resurveyed his personal habits. Since the insurance investigation he had often sought relaxation in a highball before going to bed. Concluding that a man ought to run on his own steam, he gave up this habit and restricted his indulgence to an occasional light drink at social functions. In the spring of 1914 he began also to look with increasing suspicion upon his cigars.

Hughes had smoked continuously since his admission to the bar, save for a few months in 1895. Being high-strung and inclined to tenseness, he thought smoking helped to maintain his poise. Under pressure at Albany he smoked excessively, in Washington more moderately. His physician advised him that complete abandonment of smoking might be a severe shock to his system, but he felt in his bones that it would be good for him. As he sat smoking with the men at a dinner party one night, he said to himself, "I think I won't smoke any more for a little while." He never smoked again.

The decision brought a transformation in his working habits and apparently in his health. "After breakfast," he said, "instead of sitting with my cigar and morning paper, I started out for a walk of half an hour. I soon found that I came back full of ideas and eager to get to my desk. In the evening, instead of indulging in a last cigar in the late hours, I went to bed. Instead of working late at night, I found that I was at my best in the morning. This gave me confidence, and when I was dealing with difficult problems I would say—'It will all clear up in the morning.' And so generally it did. While I suppose that the final result was no better than in my smoking days, I worked more rapidly, with less friction, and with a much greater sense of *bien être*. . . . Giving up smoking improved my health and increased my efficiency at least twenty-five percent." [4] To his last days Hughes clung steadfastly to the belief that abandonment of his cigars had not only given him new energy and freed him from excessive nervousness but also prolonged his life.

Justice Hughes' conduct completely dispelled any idea that he might keep one foot in the political arena, as Chief Justice Chase and several other members of the court had done. He went out of his way to break off all political ties. In Albany newspaper men had trooped to his door and had seldom left without a story. In Washington he avoided any contact with the press. His rigid adherence to the judicial tradition of aloofness gave rise once more to newspaper stories about his "austerity," a characterization that had been generally abandoned during his governorship.

His invitations to speak in public were multiplied by reason of the fact that he succeeded Justice Brewer, the court's most inveterate speechmaker. Several organizations that had been accustomed to paying Mr. Justice Brewer up to $500 for his speeches sought a similar arrangement with Hughes, without success. He no longer felt free to discuss public affairs, and he never accepted money for making a speech.

[4] CEH, Notes, p. 228.

A few invitations he found it impossible to decline. At a heart-warming dinner given him by the Lotos Club in New York on November 19, 1910, he spoke "under limitations wholly unfamiliar" and centered his brief comments on the theme, "Justice must ever be the chief concern of democracy." Occasionally he addressed legal groups, and he delivered the historical address at the sesquicentennial of Brown University in October, 1914. In this new life, however, his task was, as he told the Lotos Club, "to hear appeals and not to make them." Not for a moment did he forget it.

The rumble of impending battle between Taft and Roosevelt could be heard throughout the land by the end of 1911. Hughes watched the widening of the breach between his two friends with a feeling of deep regret but absolute detachment. From time to time it was suggested that only the nomination of Hughes could save the Republican Party from disaster. The unhappy Taft would have gladly withdrawn in Hughes' favor if he had seen any opportunity of doing so. As early as 1910 he had said that he would favor Hughes if party success seemed to demand someone stronger than himself. "If I could nominate . . . Hughes by a withdrawal it would give me great pleasure to bring it about," he wrote to Hilles just before the 1912 convention. "My chief purpose in staying in is to defeat Mr. Roosevelt, whose nomination . . . would be a great danger and menace to the country." [5]

Holmes thought in April that a certain reserve in Hughes' speech left "possibilities open." His surmise was high and wide. Hughes remained silent because he feared that any statement on his part would be regarded as presumptuous. As the Republican delegates assembled in Chicago, however, ominous rumors reached Camp Abenaki on Lake Placid, where the Hugheses were spending the summer. A prolonged fight between Taft and Roosevelt, it was said, would probably swing a majority of the delegates to Justice Hughes in order to avert calamity. New York leaders sent Judge William H. Wadhams to urge Hughes to permit use of his name. The Justice emphatically refused.[6] Later he issued a public statement through Rabbi Stephen S. Wise outlining his reasons for turning down any conceivable nomination before it could be made. If men were to step from the bench to elective office, he said, Supreme Court decisions might be rendered for their political effect and certainly they would be subjected to partisan criticism. The independence of the judiciary would be weakened along with the nation's confidence in its courts. When the rabbi asked him point-blank whether an extraordinary crisis might "make it your duty to accept the nomination for President," Hughes unhesitatingly replied, ". . . no man is as essential to his country's well being as is the unstained integrity of the courts." [7]

[5] Henry F. Pringle, *The Life and Times of William Howard Taft*, II, 794.

[6] Judge Wadhams to author, May 20, 1949.

[7] *New York Times*, June 21, 1912.

He also wrote to Root, chairman of the Republican National Convention:

I am informed that, notwithstanding my published statement, efforts are being made to bring about my nomination. It should be understood, not only that this use of my name is unauthorized, but that, whatever the result, my decision will not be changed. The highest service that I can render in this difficult situation is to do all in my power to have it firmly established that a Justice of the Supreme Court is not available for political candidacy. The Supreme Court must be kept out of politics. I must add, to avoid all possible misunderstanding, that, even if nominated, I should decline.[8]

"I am clearly of the opinion you took a wise and patriotic course," Root replied after the convention was over. "It seems to me that keeping the Supreme Court out of politics is more important than the Presidency." [9] If T. R. had stayed in the convention and a deadlock had developed, Root nevertheless concluded, only a strong expression of Hughes' reasons for declining would have prevented his nomination. William Barnes, the New York boss, three times urged Senator Borah to let his name be used as a running mate for Hughes on a compromise ticket.[10] "If Mr. Hughes had been nominated for President instead of Mr. Taft," commented the New York *World* during the course of the campaign, "there would be no Roosevelt third term candidacy, no Progressive party, no wreck of the Republican organization, no certainty of Republican defeat." [11]

The Republican schism brought Woodrow Wilson to power in March, 1913, without disturbing the equilibrium of the Supreme Court. Hughes occasionally met the new President at official receptions, thus renewing the friendly relationship begun at Jamestown in 1907. Cordial letters passed between them at the time of the first Mrs. Wilson's death and later when the President married again. In November, 1913, the President's daughter Jessie married Francis B. Sayre, who had been a close friend of Charles E. Hughes, Jr., at Harvard Law School, from which both had been graduated in 1912. Young Sayre stayed at the Hughes home for a few days before the wedding. After the honeymoon a White House luncheon was given for the young couple at which the Hugheses were guests. As the President and the Justice sat together after lunch, only one ripple disturbed the placid flow of their chat. Hughes made some joking remark about William Jennings Bryan, who, as a bungling Secretary of State, was giving the President some of his most difficult problems. Wilson stiffened and said in all seriousness, "I have the highest respect for Mr. Bryan." [12]

Nothing in their friendly differences suggested a feud or even any deep-seated antagonism between Wilson and Hughes. On the contrary, Wilson's

[8] CEH to Root, June 21, 1912. [9] Root to CEH, June 30, 1912.
[10] Claudius O. Johnson, *Borah of Idaho*, p. 139.
[11] New York *World*, Sept. 24, 1912. [12] Author's interview with CEH, Jan. 7, 1946.

growing liberalism since he had entered public life had given them much in common. He often spoke to his secretary, Joseph P. Tumulty, "in warm and generous terms of the work of Mr. Hughes as Governor of New York, which he admired because of its progressive, liberal character." [13] Wilson also recognized that the idea of a presidential nomination "was not even remotely in the thoughts of the then Justice of the Supreme Court." [14] Little did either realize, as they sat together on that pleasant afternoon, that they would fight each other for the Presidency two and a half years later.

[13] Joseph P. Tumulty, *Woodrow Wilson As I Know Him* (New York, Doubleday, 1921), p. 192. Copyright, 1921, by Doubleday, Page & Co.

[14] *Ibid.*

By Frederick J. Weber

Taft begs to be commanded in the 1916 campaign

Underwood & Underwood

Candidate for President

Martin Photo Service, Spokane, Wash.

On the Campaign Special en route to California

Underwood & Underwood

All campaigns are alike. In a copper mine at Butte

Chapter 30

WELLSPRING OF FEDERAL POWER

HUGHES' greatest contribution to judicial thinking in this period came in the adaptation of law to the control of national economic policy. The whole country was wrestling with the question of whether the big utility corporations could be effectively regulated in the public interest. At Albany, Hughes had met the problem as a policy maker. Now he encountered it again in the judicial sphere. The question before the court was whether it could fit broader use of the national and state police powers into the constitutional concept of limited government operating according to law.

Congress was relying primarily upon its power over interstate commerce to check the abuses of the new industrial age. It was "cementing the union" with new controls over transportation, trusts, adulteration of foods, meat inspection, and various types of criminal activity. Hughes joined with his brethren in a broad interpretation of the commerce clause which gave vitality to the Pure Food and Drug Act [1] and later to the Mann Act forbidding the transportation of women and girls across state lines for purposes of prostitution.[2] "Congress is not to be denied the exercise of its constitutional authority over interstate commerce, and its power to adopt not only means necessary but convenient to its exercise," he pointedly declared in another case, "because these means may have the quality of police regulations." [3] His most notable commerce-clause opinions, however, were primarily concerned with the regulation of railroad rates.

Armed with new powers under the Hepburn Act of 1906 and the Mann-Elkins Act of 1910, the Interstate Commerce Commission was clamping national regulations upon exploiting carriers. The states, too, were laying down new rules and rates for railroads operating within their borders. Regulation from both these sources was meeting stubborn resistance on the part of the carriers in the courts. State control over rates was denounced as being not only confiscatory but also beyond the power of the states because it impinged upon instrumentalities used in interstate commerce. Conversely, the efforts to make fair and effective national regulations were condemned as an invasion of rights reserved to the states. It was the problem of many governments in

[1] *Hipolite Egg Co.* v. *U.S.*, 220 U.S. 45. [2] *Hoke* v. *U.S.*, 227 U.S. 308.
[3] *Eckman's Alternative* v. *U.S.*, 239 U.S. 510.

one nation dealing with different portions of unified economic organisms. How could these conflicting regulatory systems be reconciled? How could the overworked Supreme Court possibly hear and decide all the complicated rate cases, with their voluminous records, that were piling up on its calendar? To many it seemed that the decisive challenge to the whole idea of regulating the railroads had come. If the railroads could entangle the Supreme Court in the intricacies of rate making under the constitutional guarantee of property rights or in the rivalries of national and state regulatory agencies, the experiment in rate control for the public benefit could be expected to collapse.

The problem came to a head in the *Minnesota Rate Cases* [4] argued April 9 to 12, 1912. Pierce Butler, later to become a member of the court, put in a 900-page brief for the railroads. Twenty-one states intervened because the lower court's decision threatened to destroy their rate controls. The immediate question was the validity of an order by Minnesota's Warehouse Commission fixing rail rates within that state. Behind it loomed the greatest constitutional issue of the first half of the twentieth century—the relative power of Congress and the states to control the national economy.

In the judicial conference the case proved so complicated and baffling that the judges decided to postpone voting on it. There was a multitude of decisions bearing on different facets of the question, and it seemed impossible to reduce them to an orderly system.[5] Some of the brethren were in doubt as to whether an opinion could be written that would properly guide regulatory commissions and courts through the morass of conflicting claims and rights. At the end of the conference Chief Justice White, conscious of the importance of the outcome both to the country and to the court, decided to dump the whole problem into the lap of the court's most vigorous and perhaps most experienced member in this field—Justice Hughes. In effect he asked Hughes to see if he could work out to the court's satisfaction a comprehensive judicial doctrine on railroad rate control.

Hughes toiled over this case through the summer recess of 1912 and on through the fall and spring, although he also wrote twenty-one other opinions for the court and an important dissent in this period. As soon as he had finished the first section of his opinion dealing with the interstate commerce issue, he took it to the Chief Justice. After reading the proof sheets, White ambled over to the Hughes home in a state of high animation. For Hughes had thoughtfully weighed every national and state claim to power over transportation and come out with a statesmanlike apportionment that would have done credit to John Marshall himself. He had written:

> The power of Congress to regulate commerce among the several States is supreme and plenary. . . . The conviction of its necessity sprang from the disastrous experi-

[4] 230 U.S. 352. [5] Justice Lamar to CEH, June 3, 1913.

ences under the Confederation when the States vied in discriminatory measures against each other. In order to end these evils, the grant in the Constitution conferred upon Congress an authority at all times adequate to secure the freedom of interstate commercial intercourse from State control and to provide effective regulation of that intercourse as the National interest may demand. . . . There is no room in our scheme of government for the assertion of State power in hostility to the authorized exercise of Federal power. The authority of Congress extends to every part of interstate commerce, and to every instrumentality or agency by which it is carried on; and the full control by Congress of the subjects committed to its regulation is not to be denied or thwarted by the commingling of interstate and intrastate operations.

Here was a doctrine pregnant with future possibilities. The fact that local transactions became interwoven with commerce extending across state lines did not give supremacy to state regulations. Nor did it create a no-man's land in which governmental power was paralyzed. Rather it swept those local transactions within the reach of congressional power to any extent necessary for effective regulation of interstate commerce. "This conclusion necessarily results," Hughes asserted, "from the supremacy of the National power within its appointed sphere." Congress, he added, "must be the judge of the necessity of Federal action."

The court decided, however, that the wide range of local activities affecting interstate commerce in some degree but not requiring uniform treatment could be regulated by the states until Congress saw fit to exercise its overriding authority. The states could not prohibit legitimate articles of commerce from moving across their boundaries. They could not discriminate against the products or the corporations of their sister states or fix interstate rates. But a state could govern its internal commerce and "adopt protective measures of a reasonable character in the interest of the health, safety, morals and welfare of its people, although interstate commerce may incidentally or indirectly be involved."

These state powers were not to be stricken down in the absence of conflict with valid federal legislation simply because Congress might at some later date occupy the field. ". . . our system of government," the opinion asserted, "is a practical adjustment by which the National authority as conferred by the Constitution is maintained in its full scope without unnecessary loss of local efficiency."

Turning to the troublesome question of fixing the value of property for rate-making purposes, Hughes struck a blow at inflated valuations.[6] The ascertainment of "fair value," he said, "is not controlled by artificial rules." "It is not a matter of formulas, but there must be a reasonable judgment having its basis in a proper consideration of all relevant facts." The cost-of-reproduction

[6] 230 U.S. 450-454.

method could be used when reasonably applied and when such costs could be accurately determined. Current value, because of price changes and growth of the country, might be more or less than the amount of the original investment. It was the property actually used in service to the public, Hughes pointed out, not the original cost of it, of which the owner could not be deprived without due process of law.

But in this case the railroads had tried to apply the cost-of-reproduction formula to their lands. The result was to give them a speculative "railway value" that "would make the public use destructive of the public right." The court refused to countenance such "conjectural values" and said that railway yards, terminals, and rights-of-way should not be valued at more than "the fair average of the normal market value of land in the vicinity having a similar character." As for plants and equipment, Hughes insisted that proper allowance be made for depreciation through use.

The great decision was handed down on June 9, 1913. In spite of White's unusual procedure in asking Hughes to write the opinion before a vote was taken, there was no dissent, although McKenna concurred only in the result because he found the hundred-page decision too long to read. Mrs. Hughes went to court for the occasion and dutifully listened as the reading went on and on. Justice Day scribbled a note and sent it to her:

"Your husband has done a great work this day—the effects of which will be beneficially felt for generations to come."

Lurton, too, sent down his penciled congratulations: "The subject is not interesting to you and is very complex. But I want to say to you what I have already said to Judge Hughes that his opinion now being delivered is as able and important as any opinion from this Bench since the foundation of this court."

Hughes was apologetic for the length of the opinion, but he had no need to be. With its sweeping survey of what the court had previously said on this subject and its cogent adjustment of constitutional doctrine to twentieth century economics, the opinion was to become a sort of Bible for the court. Holmes heartily endorsed it. Lamar was certain that the opinion "will be a landmark in the history of the court." Pitney scrawled on the proof sheets: "To my mind, they [these 'admirable' opinions] far outclass any of the previous opinions of the Court upon subjects of this character." Even more glowing was the comment of Chief Justice White: "Yes. Admirably well done. The country and Court owe you a debt they would have to go into bankruptcy if called upon to pay." [7]

Former President Taft, now Kent Professor of Law at Yale, sent his comment by letter: "I write to thank you as a struggling teacher of constitutional law

[7] CEH's private papers.

for the benefit you have conferred on my newest profession by your opinion in the Minnesota Rate Cases. . . ."

About a year later the profluent doctrine of the *Minnesota Rate Cases* was directly invoked to upset discriminatory state railway rates. Again Hughes wrote the opinion of the court.[8] The Interstate Commerce Commission had found that the Houston and Texas Railway was charging much lower rates from Dallas to other cities in Texas than from Shreveport, Louisiana, to Texas cities over like distances. It was a clear case of favoritism for traffic within Texas as against interstate commerce, but the railroads argued that the ICC could not touch rates effective only within one state.

Hughes thoroughly shattered that argument with the plenitude of the commerce power. He did not believe in stretching the commerce clause, but he did believe in applying it in the light of current economic facts. "By virtue of the comprehensive terms of the grant," he said, "the authority of Congress is at all times adequate to meet the varying exigencies that arise and to protect the national interest by securing the freedom of interstate commercial intercourse from local control. . . ." Congress was free to regulate local operations "having such a close and substantial relation to interstate traffic that the control is essential or appropriate to the security of that traffic, to the efficiency of the interstate service, and to the maintenance of conditions under which interstate commerce may be conducted upon fair terms and without molestation or hindrance." The effect of intermingling transactions in which both the nation and the states had legitimate interests, he said, reechoing his opinion in the *Minnesota Rate Cases*, was to give Congress the dominant voice:

> It is immaterial, so far as the protecting power of Congress is concerned, that the discrimination arises from intrastate rates as compared with interstate rates. The use of the instrument of interstate commerce in a discriminatory manner so as to inflict injury upon that commerce, or some part thereof, furnishes abundant ground for Federal intervention.

In the former cases the court had upheld the state in the use of its rate-making power because the effect on interstate traffic had been incidental, and there was no conflict with national authority. In the *Shreveport Case* it upset the state rates and gave effect to the ICC order because a direct injury had been inflicted on interstate commerce in violation of an Act of Congress. Never before had the commerce power been given such broad scope. This "charter of a vitalised nationalism," as Judge Ransom called the two opinions,[9] would echo down through the decades and come to the fore again in an hour of great peril for the Supreme Court.

[8] *Shreveport Case*, 234 U.S. 342.

[9] William L. Ransom, *Charles E. Hughes* (New York, Dutton, 1916), p. 19. Copyright, 1916, by E. P. Dutton & Co.

"I heartily agree with this admirable opinion," was Holmes' comment on the "Shreveport" proof sheets.

"Yes," White assented. "Clear, powerful, and sound to the core."

"This had to be," wrote Day. "You have written a clear and convincing opinion which all may comprehend."

"I voted to reverse," Lamar admitted, "but my views are much shaken by your opinion. The conclusion is so desirable and the reasons for unanimity so great that, unless others do, I shall not dissent." [10]

Lamar's conversion held even though Lurton and Pitney did dissent.

Hughes also spoke for the court [11] in upholding an ICC limitation of working hours for railway employees. "The length of hours of service," he said, "has direct relation to the efficiency of human agencies upon which protection of life and property necessarily depends." Here again the national power was not to be defeated by any commingling of interstate and intrastate activities.

In *Philadelphia Company* v. *Stimson* [12] a unanimous court, with Hughes as spokesman, upheld the right of the Secretary of War to fix harbor lines on navigable streams. The company claimed that construction of the Davis Island Dam in the Ohio River near Pittsburgh had flooded part of its land on Brunot's Island and deprived it of rights granted by the State of Pennsylvania. But the court held that federal control over this "highway of commerce" could not be fettered by any state action or minimized by changes in the course of the river. The public right of navigation follows the stream, Hughes said, and the authority of Congress goes with it.

Hughes joined with his brethren in upholding President Taft's order withdrawing from public entry extensive public lands on which oil had been discovered.[13] He refused to interfere with the findings of immigration authorities as to the citizenship of a person seeking entry to the United States.[14] And he gave free rein to the new administrative agencies so long as they did not overstep their authority or encroach upon the constitutional rights of the individual.

Hughes was not, however, an extreme nationalist. "An over-centralized government," he said, "would break down of its own weight." What he contended for and what he found in the Constitution was ample power both for the national and for state governments to carry out their functions in a changing world, with no stultifying vacuum between them. His routine practice was to explore every possibility of upholding a public policy. He had a passion for making government successful so long as it did not encroach upon the basic rights of the individual. The intensity of that passion may be noted in his numerous opinions upholding the police powers of the states.

[10] CEH's private papers. [11] *Balt. & Ohio R.R. Co.* v. *ICC*, 221 U.S. 612.
[12] 223 U.S. 605. [13] *U.S.* v. *Midwest Oil Co.*, 236 U.S. 459.
[14] *Tang Tun* v. *Edsell*, 223 U.S. 673.

The Fourteenth Amendment, he said, was not designed to fasten the states in an archaic strait jacket. Its sponsors had not attempted "to make improvement or rational experimentation impossible." Rather, the amendment sought "to preserve and enforce the primary and fundamental conceptions of justice which demand proper notice and opportunity to be heard before a competent tribunal in advance of condemnation, immunity from the confiscation of property, and, with respect to every department of government, freedom from the exercise of purely arbitrary power." [15]

What chiefly distinguished Hughes as well as Holmes from a majority of their brethren was their freedom from cliché thinking in regard to the rights thus protected. Whenever a person or a corporation claimed to have been deprived "of life, liberty or property, without due process of law," the Holmes-Hughes team brushed away slogans and looked at the substance of the rights granted against the background of modern society. This did not imply any carte blanche for the states. Their power was limited, and those limits could not be overstepped by the simple expedient of declaring legislatively that whatever the state wished to do was in accord with due process. Conformity to "due process" was a test for the courts to make, and the courts could not escape that obligation because "due process" was a vague and elastic concept. Hughes was keenly sensitive to the purpose of the Constitution-makers when they used these words of "indefinite content." "They wanted protection against tyranny," he said, "wherever and however it might hit." [16]

Holmes invoked the due-process clause against state legislation deemed to be utterly unreasonable and arbitrary in *Chicago, Milwaukee & St. Paul Railway Company* v. *Polt.*[17] The following year the court upset a North Dakota statute which had fixed intrastate rates on coal so low as to require its transportation at cost or below.[18] Holmes wholeheartedly approved Hughes' opinion in this case, inscribing a big "A1 (first class)" beside his initials on the proof sheets. White thought the opinion was "masterful and could not be better." "Admirable," commented Lamar in giving his assent. "The argument is irresistible. I take it all, especially the clear statement of the underlying principles."

Hughes had written, ". . . broad as is the power of the regulation, the State does not enjoy the freedom of an owner." The state could prevent extortion, require equal treatment of shippers, and promote safety, good order, and convenience on railroads operating in its territory. But even the public interest could not be invoked to force a carrier to haul commodities with no profit to itself. Nor could the state disguise the actual cost of carrying coal by shifting

[15] Address to New York Bar Association, January 14, 1916.

[16] *The Supreme Court of the United States* (New York, Columbia University Press, 1928), p. 186. Copyright, 1928, by the Columbia University Press.

[17] 232 U.S. 165.

[18] *Northern Pacific Railway Co.* v. *North Dakota,* 236 U.S. 595.

all the expense for maintenance of roadbeds upon the carriage of wheat or other commodities.

With the demands of "due process" satisfied, however, Hughes saw the states possessed of a wide range of police power. He had joined with Holmes in asserting that the police power extends to all the great public needs. The court, with his assent, upheld a Kansas statute regulating fire-insurance rates.[19] He wrote for the court in sustaining, in the absence of a conflicting congressional Act, a California pilotage law affecting interstate and foreign commerce.[20] Likewise, he found nothing in the Constitution to prevent Indiana from regulating "concentrated commercial food" for livestock.[21]

Franchise rights were a subject of much controversy in the court, with Hughes repeatedly contending for the right of states and municipalities to alter or revoke such privileges. When a majority, including Holmes, agreed with a telephone company that the franchise granted it by the City of Owensboro was perpetual and could not be revoked, Hughes strongly dissented along with Day, McKenna, and Pitney.[22] Only Pitney stood with Hughes in protest when the court held that South Bend could regulate the use of a railway franchise but could not withdraw it.[23]

The hot controversy of the day was over the extent to which "freedom of contract" restrained the states from passing social legislation. Hughes made his position unmistakably clear in the McGuire case.[24] Various railroads had set up "relief funds" to which both the companies and employees contributed and from which workers injured in the course of their employment were paid benefits. Employees participating in these relief plans had to sign contracts limiting their common-law right to recover damages for injuries. Iowa outlawed such contracts and the Supreme Court upheld the statute. Hughes' opinion was emphatic in declaring that private companies and individuals could not upset a public policy within the power of the legislature by making contracts in conflict with that policy. He said:

> Freedom of contract is a qualified and not an absolute right. There is no absolute freedom to do as one wills or to contract as one chooses. The guaranty of liberty does not withdraw from legislative supervision that wide department of activity which consists of the making of contracts, or deny to government the power to provide restrictive safeguards. Liberty implies the absence of arbitrary restraint, not immunity from reasonable regulations and prohibitions imposed in the interests of the community. . . .
>
> The right to make contracts is subject to the exercise of the powers granted to

[19] *German Alliance Insurance Co.* v. *Lewis*, 233 U.S. 387.
[20] *Anderson* v. *Pac. Coast S.S. Co.*, 225 U.S. 187.
[21] *Savage* v. *Jones*, 225 U.S. 501. [22] 230 U.S. 58.
[23] *Grand Trunk Western R.R. Co.* v. *South Bend*, 227 U.S. 544.
[24] *Chicago, B. & Q. Ry. Co.* v. *McGuire*, 219 U.S. 549.

Congress for the suitable conduct of matters of national concern, as for example the regulation of commerce with foreign nations and among the several States. . . . It is subject also, in the field of State action, to the essential authority of government to maintain peace and security and to enact laws for the promotion of the health, safety, morals and welfare of those subject to its jurisdiction.

Hughes reiterated a well established doctrine that the court would not interfere with legislative acts having a "reasonable relation to an object within governmental authority." It was concerned with the power invoked, not with the policy effected. Whether an act was wise or unwise, whether it was economically sound or the best means of achieving the desired result was not a question for the courts. "In dealing with the relation of employer and employed," he said, "the legislature has necessarily a wide field of discretion in order that there may be suitable protection of health and safety, and that peace and good order may be promoted through regulations designed to insure wholesome conditions of work and freedom from oppression."

In a later case [25] Hughes applied the same principle in declaring that the federal Employers Liability Act superseded "relief funds" set up through contracts between railroads and their employees. Here was the bedrock on which his famous opinion in the *Gold Clause Cases* would be based many years later.

When the question of the so-called "yellow dog" contract came before the court in *Coppage* v. *Kansas*,[26] a majority of the brethren veered away from the sound principle of the McGuire case. Only Holmes, Hughes, and Day held the fort of liberal thinking. The court had previously upset a federal statute making it a crime for an interstate carrier to discharge an employee because of his membership in a labor union.[27] Now it was a question of whether a Kansas law forbidding an employer to require of his employees a pledge that they would not join a labor organization could be reconciled with the Constitution. To the majority it was simply a matter of constitutional "freedom of contract." Labor was essentially a commodity about which every man had the right to contract. A law interfering with complete freedom in this field was a "substantial impairment of liberty." Consequently, the statute was at war with the Fourteenth Amendment.

The dissenters looked much deeper into the actualities about which Kansas had legislated. Holmes wrote what was to become a famous opinion pleading for the right of the state "to establish the equality of position between the parties in which liberty of contract begins." Hughes concurred in the longer dissent of Justice Day. "The preservation of the police power of the States . . . ," Day asserted, "is of the utmost importance. . . . The law should be as zealous

[25] *Phil., Balt. & Wash. R.R. Co.* v. *Schubert*, 224 U.S. 603.
[26] 236 U.S. 1. [27] *Adair* v. *U.S.*, 208 U.S. 161.

to protect the constitutional liberty of the employee as it is to guard that of the employer."

Thirteen state laws restraining use of the "yellow dog" contract went down because the court closed its eyes to a teeming industrial civilization and held fast to an outmoded slogan. Holmes tilted at this strait-jacket thinking because he believed in the right of the legislature to experiment. Hughes shared that view, but, having intimately felt the pulse of the people, he was also warmly devoted to the democratic ideas of fair play, justice, and reasonable use of public power for advancement of the general welfare. When these aims could be attained within a broad concept of the constitutional framework, he was loath to accept any tradition-crusted dogma that might stand in the way. The Constitution was made for the people and not the people for the Constitution.

In upholding the Illinois child-labor law, Hughes said frankly that "freedom of contract" could be a trap for helpless persons in need of the protection of the police power.[28] Two other Hughes opinions gave new underpinning for the right of the states to limit the working hours of women. In *Miller* v. *Wilson*[29] the court sustained the conviction of a hotel proprietor for working a chambermaid nine hours a day, finding no infirmity in California's eight-hour day for women in various industries. California was also free, Hughes wrote in the other case,[30] to apply its eight-hour regulations to some groups of women and not to others, such as graduate nurses. Both cases had been argued by Louis D. Brandeis. They loosened the judicial joints a trifle more than they had been loosened in *Muller* v. *Oregon*[31] a few years before.

The case of the paper-box factory girl was more difficult. It came up to the supreme bench for argument on December 16 and 17, 1914, with Brandeis again pleading for a broad interpretation of the police power. This time it was an Oregon law prescribing minimum wages for women in industry that was challenged; similar laws in Colorado, Minnesota, Utah, Washington, Wisconsin, and California were hanging in the balance. The question was whether the Oregon Industrial Welfare Commission could compel Frank C. Stettler to add sixty-four cents a week to the meager wage that he had been paying Elmira Simpson for working in his box factory. The Oregon Supreme Court had unanimously upheld this minimum-wage law. But the company's attorneys brought to Washington, D.C., vehement arguments to the effect that the regulation of wages, regardless of the employee's efficiency and other sources of income and of the employers' ability to pay the fixed rate, was a deprivation of property without due process of law and an encroachment upon the "freedom of contract" guaranteed by the Fourteenth Amendment. Exercise of the police power, counsel said, had never been invoked and could not be invoked

[28] *Sturges* v. *Beauchamp*, 231 U.S. 320.
[29] 236 U.S. 373.
[30] *Bosley* v. *McLaughlin*, 236 U.S. 385.
[31] 208 U.S. 412.

to supply an individual's needs which were merely *incidental* to employment. Minimum-wage laws might be ethically right and even economically sound, but they were impossible under our form of government. Brandeis argued masterfully on the consequences of paying women so little that they could dress decently and get enough to eat only at the expense of morality.

All the judges were intensely interested in the case. Chief Justice White asked counsel whether such a regulation would not drive some employers out of business. Holmes probed into the degeneracy of the working classes in England before the factory acts curbed absolute "freedom of contract." Hughes listened quietly until he saw an opportunity to cut to the heart of the issue. Then he leaned forward and questioned former Senator Fulton, who was summing up the case for the company.

"Do you base your argument on the theory of freedom of contract?"

"Yes."

"Then is there not a precedent in the Ohio case in which this court held constitutional the 54-hour [week] for women in industry?"

"No, there is a difference between hours and wages."

"What is it?" Hughes persisted.

"Long hours," the lawyer replied, "break down women so that they become public charges; it is a condition growing *out* of employment. The amount of wages has no relation to health and morals."

"But," Hughes retorted, "suppose it has; suppose this court finds that these evils *are* in consequence of wages paid in employment?" [32]

Here was the crux of the issue. Would the court recognize the grim facts of industrial life or decide the case on the fantastic theory that wages of $6 to $8 a week had no relation to health and morals that need concern the community? In conference Hughes and Holmes stood fast for upholding the Oregon statute. The court was sharply divided. Chief Justice White, who always approached a controversy of this sort after the manner of a skittish horse going up to a brass band, failed to bring the case to a vote. When the court met for the October term in 1915, Justice Lamar was too sick to take his seat. He died in January, 1916, and that appears to have left the court evenly divided. Even after Lamar's successor won confirmation by the Senate following a long fight, he could be of no help in this decision, for he was Mr. Brandeis, who had argued so persuasively for the state. The case was finally reargued in January, 1917, and the judgment of the state court was upheld by a four-to-four decision.[33] Hughes had then left the bench, but he was destined finally to settle the question in *West Coast Hotel* v. *Parrish* [34] on a historic occasion two decades in the future.

[32] Mary Chamberlin in *Survey* magazine, Dec. 26, 1914.
[33] *Stettler* v. *O'Hara*, 243 U.S. 629. [34] 300 U.S. 379.

In six years on the supreme bench Hughes had attained a judicial stature not often equaled in a similar period. His grasp of the law was comprehensive as well as profound. He had persistently avoided the mental grooves that judges sometimes fall into. Without the slightest hesitation, his decisions followed wherever the facts and a statesmanlike view of the law might point. In one case he carried his objectivity so far as to reverse himself in the midst of an opinion he was writing. Convinced by deeper probing that the vote of the court to which he had assented was wrong, he took the case back to conference, converted his brethren, and wrote the opinion to support a verdict precisely opposite to that previously agreed upon.[35]

In protecting civil liberties, Hughes had been more alert to realities than Holmes. By broadly interpreting the states' police powers, he had sought to make the law the servant and not the master of the people's will. Without jeopardizing federalism, he had taken the lead in forging the commerce clause into a potent tool for congressional control over the national aspects of our economy. One observer concluded that Hughes' opinions ranked "among the most important and able pronouncements upon the principles of constitutional law that have come from the Supreme Court during its entire history." [36] Still young for a Supreme Court Justice, he was well launched upon what promised to be one of the greatest judicial careers in America when fate or the voice of the people intervened.

[35] Author's interview with Laurence H. Green, Nov. 14, 1948.
[36] Arthur M. Allen in the *Columbia Law Review*, Nov. 1916, p. 566.

Chapter 31

THE 1916 NOMINATION

WAR FLAMED across Europe in the summer of 1914 and aroused the whole world from its complacency. Belgium and France were invaded. Slaughter in the trenches and on the high seas mounted to incredible totals. It was as if humanity had suddenly given free play to all its worst passions.

America was bewildered. Men hustled to supply the Allies with wheat, machinery, and guns. In their moral sympathies, too, they were drawn ever closer to the cataclysm, like neighbors to a fire. Yet there was much resistance to proposals to strengthen the country's defenses, and a general determination to keep out of the war. It was a period of intense activity and fantastic illusions.

Against this background, the forthcoming presidential contest of 1916 took on epic proportions. Wilson, it was assumed, would make a strong bid for reelection. But the Republican leaders saw in the world crisis an implied mandate for their party. Had they not elected every President since the Civil War. excepting only Cleveland and Wilson? And was not Wilson's victory in 1912 owing solely to the tempestuous quarrel between Taft and Roosevelt? With Europe tearing itself apart and Wilson talking nonsense about the United States being "too proud to fight," the Republicans felt a powerful urge to take the helm once more. But where was the candidate who could run successfully against the popular Mr. Wilson?

Taft had been buried, politically speaking, in 1912. Roosevelt had left his party and sown a whirlwind of bitterness. Root, too, was involved in the schism. Only Charles E. Hughes had a real chance of harnessing the Elephant and the Bull Moose to a victory chariot.

Talk of Hughes for President thus began more than two years before the nominating conventions assembled. Taft feared that "the Hughes talk is absurd, because Hughes would not permit himself to accept a nomination." [1] While Roosevelt was floundering, he said as early as July, 1915, that the Progressives would support Hughes if he were nominated.[2] More impressive was the increasing stream of letters which advised the hard-working judge that he was the only man who could reunite the Republican Party and shape an adequate foreign policy for the United States in a world at war. "If an exigency shall

[1] Taft to W. L. Fisher, Jan. 3, 1914. [2] *New York Times*, July 20, 1915.

arise," Nathaniel Myers had prophesied in 1910, ". . . the People will pull you off the Bench. . . ." Now the ferment was beginning to work.

Hughes' reaction was first indifference, then irritation. Since 1910 his mind had been closed to political vistas. The idea of a Supreme Court Justice engaging in politics was abhorrent to him. Like most of the other judges, he had even given up voting because a journey to New York for that purpose took too much time away from the work of the court. On May 20, 1915, he dictated an emphatic reply to a query by former Governor Edward C. Stokes of New Jersey as to whether his flat refusal to run in 1912 still stood:

> It seems to me very clear that, as a member of the Supreme Court, I have no right to be a candidate, either openly or passively. I cannot remain working here and hold an equivocal position before the country. I must, therefore, ask that no steps be taken to bring my name before the convention.[3]

Stokes announced on August 18 that Hughes would refuse to accept the nomination if it were proffered, although the letter did not go that far. It is incontrovertible that Hughes wished to continue the work he was doing. The companionship on the bench was most agreeable. He thrived on the intellectual stimulus of the courtroom and the judicial conference. Aware of his growing contribution to the law of the country he loved, Hughes asked only to be left alone. The picture we get of him, as he walked down Capitol Hill at the close of a day's work, is that of a happy marcher "with chest well out, head held erect, full beard breasting the wind, arms loosely swinging, the face of one who is at peace with the world." [4]

But his friends and admirers would not leave him alone. Politicians repeatedly put his name forward, and the press teemed with speculation as to whether the Republicans would go to the Supreme Court for their candidate. Roosevelt sent William Noble to tell Hughes that Roosevelt considered him "the brainiest man now in public life in the United States" and "the best equipped man" for the Presidency.[5] Hughes was "sane, safe and progressive" and the only man upon whom both the Republican and Progressive parties could unite.

The hard-pressed judge reiterated his desire to stay on the bench, and thereafter refused to make appointments with persons he suspected of wishing to talk politics. After this negative response, T. R. found "a considerable feeling that it is not wise to establish a very bad precedent and take a candidate from the Supreme Court." [6] Hughes' disinterest probably reminded the colonel afresh of how disappointed he had been by Hughes' independent course as Governor of New York.

[3] *Ibid.*, June 2, 1916. [4] *Nation*, Sept. 30, 1915.

[5] Noble to CEH, Jan. 5, 1921, Hughes Papers.

[6] Roosevelt-Lodge *Correspondence* (New York, Scribner's, 1925), II, 468. Copyright, 1925, by Charles Scribner's Sons.

In November, 1915, the men who were trying to "smoke out Hughes" circulated a petition to have his name put on the ballot in Nebraska's presidential preference primary. The Justice sharply declined the nomination,[7] and when this proved ineffective, he threatened court proceedings to get his name off the ballot. The sincerity of his effort to squelch any political movement in his behalf was widely recognized and commended. Yet the press was quick to point out that it did not place Justice Hughes beyond the reach of his party. ". . . no man would be given the Presidency merely because he desired it," commented the *Washington Post*, "and no man can keep himself out of it if the people want him in."

"There is not a flicker of suspicion in anybody's mind," asserted the *Nation* a few months later, "that he has used his judicial office as a steppingstone to political office. . . . It is not Hughes the judge who is discussed as a candidate, but Hughes the fearless investigator, Hughes the Governor who put moral courage into his reforms and gave a fighting edge to his constructive plans, Hughes the campaign speaker of 1908 who deeply impressed himself on the country as a man who carried heavy guns." [8]

The politicians, however, found it difficult to believe that Hughes was sincere in rebuffing their efforts to hand him voluntarily the great prize for which most men were so eager to fight. There seemed to be no end to their "smoke out" efforts. To a letter from Representative C. Bascom Slemp of Virginia, Hughes replied on February 9, 1916:

> I am entirely out of politics, and I know nothing whatever of the matters to which you refer. I am totally opposed to the use of my name in connection with the nomination and selection or instruction of any delegates in my interest, either directly or indirectly.[9]

Taft's hopes were dashed. "I am quite sure that Justice Hughes will not be a candidate," he wrote to G. V. Howard. "He is not a man who says a thing without meaning it." [10] Nevertheless, Taft continued to pull every string within his reach to bring about the nomination of the judge he himself had appointed to the supreme bench, despite Hughes' wish to remain there. On April 11 he carried his campaign directly to Hughes' chambers with a long and persuasive confidential letter.[11]

> MY DEAR JUSTICE HUGHES,
>
> I presume your correspondence in these days is increasing. Perhaps it would be more accurate to say that your correspondents are increasing. I have been moved . . . to write you for several months past but refrained. I do not write now for a

[7] *New York Times,* Nov. 17 and 19, 1915.
[8] April 6, 1916, p. 376. [9] *New York Times,* Feb. 10, 1916.
[10] Henry F. Pringle, *The Life and Times of William Howard Taft,* II, 890.
[11] Taft to CEH, April 11, 1916; Hughes Papers.

reply because I hope you will not send me one. I write to express a view to you contrary to that of Mr. Choate in his letter to the New York Times of yesterday. I believe myself to be as anxious to keep the Supreme Court and Supreme Judges out of politics as any one; but there are few general rules of policy, not involving moral considerations, to which circumstances of the country's need may not justify an exception.

What is the country's great need? It is the restoration of the Republican party to power to do the constructive work needed in carrying out a policy of reasonable preparedness which involves financial and economic preparedness. The Democratic party is what it has always shown itself to be—the organized incapacity of the country. I am no partisan but I cannot escape this conclusion. The Republican party was split in two in 1912. The great body of Progressives have enrolled themselves again in the party. To retain them, however, and to win over the others, we must have a candidate who will not revive the enmities of that internecine struggle and who will because of his record stimulate the enthusiasm of both elements and give them confidence in victory. In looking over the candidates, most Republicans and Progressives in their hearts find you to be the only available man. Bridging the chasm of 1912, they all go back to you as the leader of real progress in New York, and the one acknowledged to be your own master under every environment. Your position in this regard is unique. It appeals to all the voters.

Mr. Root is admirably qualified to be President but he will not be a strong candidate. He will not lead a united party. I admire him as a jurist and a statesman and I love him as a friend; but I state the truth.

Mr. Burton is a statesman of long legislative experience, lacking somewhat in the executive quality of decision, but a man of high ideals, studious habit and real ability. He is not a leader of magnetic qualities, either personal or on the stump. Both he and Root are burdened with association with my fortunes in 1912. I think Burton more available than Root but I fear he would not lead a completely united party.

Assuming that Roosevelt is to be preferred to Wilson and the Democracy—a violent assumption which I do not discuss—he cannot be elected. Many who supported me would support him, but a considerable number—enough to turn the scales in doubtful states—would desert him because they feel, whether justly or not, that he is responsible for the present conditions. Then he is the conspicuous candidate who would drive the Germans to Wilson. . . .

Of the other men named, Fairbanks is the best qualified for the Presidency but he labors under the cloud of staleness and he would not attract the Progressives. I have thought McCall a strong man and a possible successful candidate in the last resort but I fear that the Presidential bee has tested his head with its buzzing and the result has not been reassuring.

Now, my dear Justice, you may not agree with my summary of the candidates. I have reviewed all who call for consideration. But what I have said the great body of the American [people] are thinking, and they are going to manifest their thoughts through the Republican Convention and the delegates. They are going to nominate you unless you announce before the convention acts that you will not accept the nomination under any circumstances. I know that if you followed your preference, you would do that now. I know that you prefer your life on the Bench and that should a Republican come to the Presidency, you would in all probability be put at the head of the Court with the acclaim of the country. I know that you are properly most sensitive in respect to the nonpartisan attitude of the judges of the Court and deeply deprecate making a precedent which might inspire other judges to an ambition which would demoralize them and destroy their usefulness and affect the high position of the Court. But I beg of you to consider that your position in the peculiar situation of affairs is so exceptional that it cannot afford a dangerous precedent. You have been most scrupulous to discourage all effort to nominate you. You have declined to express your opinions on any issue of current importance lest it may be inferred that you are a candidate in any sense. The whole country knows your attitude of antagonism to the canvass of your name but in spite of that, the movement grows and the result will be, I verily believe, your unanimous nomination.

Mr. Roosevelt is thundering. He is a genius. In certain ways he commands my admiration more than he ever did for his genius. His powers over correspondents, due to his marvellous personality. His courage to ignore obstacles and inconsistencies of his own creating and what is more his power to induce others to ignore them are sublime. But I cannot think it on the cards for him to win.

I do not conceal from myself his influence in the Election in uniting the party; but he has put himself in a position which makes it absolutely necessary for him to support you if you are nominated. Moreover, he will, after his disappointment, do so with fervor. He saves his face in supporting you as he does in supporting no one else. He is sincerely opposed to Wilson. He is really anxious to defeat him. He will be sincerely for you.

You will certainly be elected if you accept the nomination and you will reunite the only party from which constructive progress can be expected at a most critical time in the country's history. Your opportunity as President to guide the country through the trials bound to come after the war will be as great as Washington's or Lincoln's. And you are equal to it. Strong men will respond to your call because you are yourself so satisfying in strength and in your political courage and patriotism.

In view of all this, my dear Justice Hughes, I appeal to you not to decide the question until the Convention acts. Then approach its decision, as you will, with a solemn sense of the responsibility on you and with the willingness to make the sacrifice if your duty to accept appears clear.

I have written long and perhaps without the force I would like to give to what I say, but I believe sincerely and deeply all I have written. I think I was discharging a duty to myself in writing you. It cannot hurt, even if it does not help what I urge. It may put something in a light to help.

Sincerely yours,
WM. H. TAFT

I have written without any one's knowledge. I have not copied this letter. I do not expect an answer. Indeed I would rather not have one.

The next day Taft added a few more arguments. If Hughes were nominated, Wilson would of course name his successor to the Supreme Court. But that was no reason for not leaving the court, Taft insisted: ". . . think of the vacancies he is likely to fill if he is to be re-elected. He can almost destroy the court." Roosevelt, should he be reelected, would likely "get us into war," and his appointments to the bench might be "in many ways quite as bad as Brandeis." But even Roosevelt would be less distasteful, Taft wrote, "than . . . Wilson whom I regard as the greatest opportunist and hypocrite ever in the White House. . . . As I conceive it, therefore, the exigency presented to you is whether you will save the party from Roosevelt and the country from Wilson." [12]

Taft visited Washington on May 14, and newspaper gossip said that he called on Hughes. The *Chicago Tribune* and some other papers even claimed that Taft went away with Hughes' assurance that he would accept the nomination.[13] But there was no word of truth in either report. Hughes did not reply to the Taft letters; no emissary passed between them, and they did not meet in 1916 until after the convention.

Meanwhile the snowball of Hughes sentiment was rolling at ever increasing tempo. He was the unmistakable favorite in several polls. Republican leaders of New York came out for him on January 13. Governor Whitman added his endorsement two days later. Colonel George Harvey, the political godfather of Woodrow Wilson, concluded in the *North American Review* that the people wanted Hughes. On May 3 he was singled out as the favorite candidate by the Michigan Republican Convention and on the 16th by the Vermont primaries. The Oregon primaries gave him a landslide on the 20th, and Senator Borah said that Hughes would have carried every state primary if his name had been on the ballots.

More important than any of these events was the work being quietly done by Eugene Meyer and Frank H. Hitchcock, who had managed Taft's successful campaign in 1908. With Meyer's encouragement and financing, Hitchcock had surveyed public opinion in many of the big cities and reported that Republican voters favored Hughes over Roosevelt by a large margin. Hitchcock then began to round up delegates for Hughes. It proved to be an easy task, for politicians are always eager to clamber aboard a band wagon that gives real promise of ending its journey at the White House.

Hughes repudiated this work in his behalf and denied through his secretary that he had had any communication whatever with Hitchcock. The latter was well aware of Hughes' irritation over what he was doing, but that did not stop him. As soon as the convention was over, he wrote to Hughes: "I realize that I must have been acting counter to your wishes in advocating your nomination but I have felt that my activities were justified by the exigencies of the situation. I believed you were the man above all others to reunit [*sic*] our party and lead it to victory." [14]

Through the last trying months before the convention, Hughes was the pic-

[12] Taft to CEH, April 12, 1916.
[13] Harold L. Ickes, in *American Historical Review*, January, 1941, p. 316.
[14] Hitchcock to CEH, June 12, 1916.

From the New York *World*, June 4, 1916.

HIS NIGHTMARE

ture of a man wrestling with his own conscience. No longer could he blind himself to the power of the movement in his behalf. Yet he continued to hope that it would prove to be only a passing nightmare. Looking out over the war-torn world, he foresaw the next President carrying an unconscionable share of humanity's burdens and going to an early grave. While his fifty-four years had scarcely impaired his vigor, he would not choose such a role for himself. "I seek no new titles," he told Henry L. Stoddard, editor of the New York *Evening Mail*, "and I do not want the work that is before the next president. He may wear a crown, but it will be a crown of thorns." [15]

Hughes remembered also that he had left Albany in a mood of disgust with politics and politicians. The Presidency would take him back to many of the old controversies, to squabbles with the bosses who did not like his ways, and to political jockeying that was distasteful to him. "I do not pretend to be more than reasonably well adapted for the work I am doing," he told Stoddard in a confidential interview at his home, "but I feel that I can say that I am better adapted for it than for the work of the White House. . . . My reluctance to think of the Presidency is not because I regard it as an office below my abilities; but because I think it so great and beyond my abilities. Nor am I afraid to risk the possibility of defeat and thus lose my place on the bench and the Presidency, too. It is no time to consider such things when and if as a citizen you are called to a post of duty."

Stoddard said the nomination lay between Hughes and Roosevelt. "Then I hope T. R. will be named," the Justice replied. "I would not put a straw in his way. He is a wonderful man, and I have long believed that he has struck the dominant note of the country. . . . The newspaper stories that Roosevelt is stronger and I am weaker since he spoke out so boldly from Trinidad please me immensely. They are a ray of hope—a rift in the clouds." [16]

In spite of his strong desire to remain on the bench, Hughes could not bring himself to a flat refusal to run in any circumstances. He had done so in 1912, but no national crisis had then complicated his decision, and the rift in the Republican Party had not yet become an open schism. The question of reuniting his party was an issue of no minor importance in his mind, for a permanent rupture would have meant an end of the two-party system and might have destroyed the Republican Party as a useful instrument of government.

Hughes felt, moreover, that it was highly desirable for the Republican

[15] *It Costs to Be President* (New York, Harper, 1938), p. 114. Copyright, 1938, by Harper & Brothers.

[16] Stoddard made detailed notes of what had been said as soon as he got back to his hotel room. When he published a summary of those notes in 1938, Hughes saw no reason to question their accuracy, but Stoddard had slipped in one particular when he previously wrote about the Justice's mental ferment in this preconvention period. He had said that the dominant thought in Hughes' mind was to return to the practice of law to rebuild his depleted fortune (*As I Knew Them*, p. 447). Not for a moment did Hughes entertain such an idea. His firm intention was to remain on the bench the remainder of his active life (CEH, Notes, p. 230).

Party to return to power. Wilson's foreign policy had been weak and vacillating. Military preparedness had been "shockingly neglected," and the resulting weakness of the United States in a war-mad world was an invitation to disregard American rights. If these policies based on dangerous illusions and backed only by words were to be changed, the Republicans would have to change them. And if Hughes were the only man who could reunite the party and win the election. as his supporters insisted, then he was the only man who could swing the country away from the perilous course it was pursuing. Duty to country thus merged into concern for the future of the party.

In the face of these considerations personal wishes shrank to minor proportions. As Hughes pondered his dilemma against the onrush of the world crisis, he visualized people coming into the Supreme Court in future years and pointing him out. "There is the man," they would say, "who placed his own comfort and preference for the life of a judge above his duty to the nation." That thought was as abhorrent to him as politicking from the bench.[17] He was torn between a profound desire "to keep the judicial ermine unsullied" and another profound desire "not to fail in meeting what might be a duty to the country." [18]

Nomination for the Presidency, he had said in 1908, should neither be sought nor refused. Now he was told on every hand that, if nominated, it would be his duty to run. The advice of Roosevelt, Taft, and other party leaders was not essentially different from that he got within the court and at home. Justice Van Devanter was one of those who expressed sympathy with Hughes' efforts to prevent political use of his name. "But if they should nominate you nevertheless," Van Devanter added, "I think you could not rightly decline." Chief Justice White, in referring to a newspaper comment, expressed the same opinion.[19]

When the children were present, the Hugheses avoided all mention of the momentous events that were threatening to upset the family routine. But the heart of Antoinette Hughes beat faster with the conviction that she had expressed in 1908. Now it was more than ever apparent that he was "a man of destiny." If the convention should summon him from the bench, she said, he would have no right to refuse. Once when she pressed her point he exclaimed, "When you see me in my coffin, remember that I did not want to take this burden on myself."

At various times while Hughes was undergoing his ordeal he felt the pull of partisan forces trying to keep him on the bench as well as those that were trying to get him off. Vice President Marshall praised him in an address before the Chicago Bar Association for not seeking the presidential nomination. Sev-

[17] Author's interview with CEH, Oct. 24, 1945.
[18] CEH, Notes, p. 231. [19] *Ibid.*

eral Senators urged him in public speeches to announce a positive refusal to run in any circumstances. The Wilson forces favored Roosevelt as the opposition candidate, believing that he could be easily beaten on the war issue. The President himself indicated that a Roosevelt candidacy would give him no concern, but Hughes, if nominated, would "have to be met." [20]

The safest way of dealing with Hughes, of course, would be to keep him on the bench. Apparently in pursuit of that aim Franklin K. Lane, Secretary of the Interior, took Hughes aside at a dinner party and dropped a hint to the effect that if he stayed on the court he would be appointed Chief Justice.[21] Was Lane merely indulging his fancy? That seemed probable at the time. Hughes dismissed the suggestion as of little significance, but after the election Lane again approached him at a Brown alumni dinner and said, "You know what I told you, and what might have been."

Shortly before the date set for the Republican National Convention, Chief Justice White, looking old and worried, came toddling over to the Hughes home. It was evident that he had not just dropped in to discuss a court problem, as he had often done before. The Chief Justice had something special on his mind. Within a few minutes he came out with it.

"Before you decide on what course you will take," he said with unnatural tensity, "I feel that you should know that I am going to retire and that if you do not resign you will succeed me."

"Why," Hughes exclaimed incredulously, "President Wilson would never appoint me Chief Justice!"

"Well," White answered solemnly, "he wouldn't appoint anyone else, as I happen to know." [22]

Hughes was more deeply perturbed than before. White was a man of integrity and a dear friend. In saying that he was going to retire, the Chief Justice must have spoken with complete candor and sincerity. Could his assurance as to the President's intention in naming his successor be any less forthright and well founded? Hughes concluded that White must have spoken with authority from Wilson.[23] In any event, the suggestion that the President would make him Chief Justice if he did not run against the President had the smell of a deal. The people would so regard it. The Chief Justiceship would become the price of his honor. Hughes recoiled from the suggestion and told the Chief Justice that he intended to follow the lead of his conscience without being influenced by what he had just heard. As he pondered over the incident, he came to realize that if he should remain on the bench and if Wilson should offer him the Chief Justiceship, he would be condemned in the public mind, even in the absence of any deal.

[20] Ray Stannard Baker, *Woodrow Wilson—Life and Letters* (New York, Doubleday, 1937), VI, 267. Copyright, 1937, by Doubleday, Doran & Co.
[21] CEH, Notes, p. 231. [22] *Ibid.*
[23] Author's interview with CEH, Jan. 7, 1946.

The anxiety that pervaded the office of Mr. Justice Hughes was relieved temporarily by a letter from his old friend John Palmer Gavit, then managing editor of the New York *Evening Post*. Noting that William Jennings Bryan, former Secretary of State, was to report the national conventions for a syndicate of newspapers, Gavit offered a similar commission to Justice Hughes. "Notwithstanding your lack of actual newspaper experience," Gavit wrote, "I am sure your reports of and comments upon these gatherings would be readable. I believe I can guarantee you a position on the first page, next pure reading matter; we might even be able to syndicate your dispatches to our mutual advantage."

Hughes expressed his gratitude for the offer on May 19:

DEAR GAVIT:

I cannot tell you how deeply touched I am by your kind offer. At last my secret ambition is laid bare. For many weary years I have longed to be a newspaper correspondent and say a few things. But my talent for up-to-date, virile, philosophical, prophetical, cinematographical correspondence has been unrecognized, and one exigency after another has compelled me to make other arrangements. I am now under contract for work, relatively unimportant, which, however, will detain me here during the time the Convention is held. I put aside my longing to see a Convention; that is very great, but it is as nothing compared to my wish to write one up and to show the best of newspapers how it may be improved.

Faithfully, CHARLES E. HUGHES[24]

Two days before the convention opened, Hughes was under the embarrassing necessity of having to make a speech. Throughout the period while public opinion in his favor was gathering force, he had avoided any utterance that might spark a political movement. Not a word he had written for the court could be regarded as politically slanted. His address to the New York State Bar Association in January, 1916, which had been arranged a year in advance, was cool, philosophical, and entirely nonpartisan. Thereafter he refrained from making speeches, except to carry out his promise of the previous October to present an American flag to two honor students of the graduating class of National Cathedral School of which his daughter Catherine was a member.

"It is a beautiful prize that I am privileged to give. . . ." he said. "It is the symbol of our national unity, our national endeavor, our national aspiration. . . . It means America first: it means an undivided allegiance. It means America united, strong, and efficient, equal to her tasks. . . . There is not a thread in it but scorns self-indulgence, weakness and rapacity. . . ."[25]

The occasion was entirely unheralded, and what he had to say was precisely what he would have said if his name had never been mentioned for political office. The speech was noticed only because a news-hungry press, which had had no other scrap of information as to what Hughes was thinking, blazoned

[24] New York *Evening Post*, June 10, 1916. [25] Hughes Papers.

it on the front pages. Through his secretary, he denied that it had any political significance.

News of the great Battle of Jutland and a preparedness parade in Chicago heightened the tension as the conventions opened on June 7. The Republicans were seething with disgust over Wilson's attitude toward the war. The Progressive convention was meeting separately in Chicago at the same time. In the preceding weeks Roosevelt had been contemptuous of Hughes because the latter had neither denounced Wilson nor come out with a clear-cut declaration of where he stood.[26] While trying to find another candidate who would be acceptable both to the Progressives and to the Republicans T. R. was still hoping that the country might be in a "heroic mood" and that the lightning might therefore strike in his direction. Gloom hung over the Bull Moose gathering because most of the delegates knew that the colonel had no chance of reuniting the party.

At the request of the Progressives, "peace committees" were named by both conventions. The Republican conferees—Senators Reed Smoot and William E. Borah, former Senator Murray Crane, Dr. Nicholas Murray Butler, and Congressman A. R. Johnson—were not at first unanimous for Hughes. The Progressives, headed by George W. Perkins and Hiram Johnson, talked only of Roosevelt. The conference broke up in disagreement.

Aside from Hughes, the strongest man before the convention was Elihu Root. But Root was only a halfhearted candidate. Earlier in the year he had said that he was too old to run and that the effort to nominate him was ridiculous. Yet he was so disturbed over Wilson's foreign policy that he apparently began to think his tag of "corporation lawyer" might be overlooked in the kind of campaign that would have to be waged.

The only real groundswell at the convention centered in the name of the silent man still wearing his judicial robe in Washington. Hughes had no headquarters at Chicago, no representative, no badges, buttons, or literature. Yet his name seemed to dominate every discussion of potential nominees. Frank Hitchcock, whose work for Hughes had earned only repudiation, kept repeating that Hughes would be nominated on the third ballot. "Nobody seemed to be for Hughes," he said, "except the people." Joe Mitchell Chapple reported that the undercurrent of demand for Hughes was "unfathomable."

Nominations began on the third day, June 9, in the crowded Coliseum "resplendent with color." Alabama passed, and Arizona yielded to New York so as to give Governor Charles S. Whitman the opportunity of placing Hughes in nomination first. "We bring you today," the Governor said, with typical convention eloquence, "the name of a man trained for the battle for the truth. . . .

[26] T. R. to William Noble, May 2, 1916, Roosevelt Papers.

We have seen him the man of action, the champion of the people, the idol of the electorate, the faithful public servant, the profound thinker on national affairs. . . . I do not speak for any man or for any candidate. I do not claim to represent any man or any candidate. The great State of New York offers you . . . her son—her noblest and best." [27]

An audience that had clung to every word broke into sustained yelling and applause. The New York, Michigan, Maine, Vermont, and Mississippi delegates swarmed into the aisles for a demonstration of astonishing warmth considering the absolute silence of their hero in matters political for six years. Leo Weinburg of Maryland and Charles W. Fulton of Oregon made the seconding speeches.

Roosevelt's nomination by Senator Albert B. Fall brought an eruption in the galleries but also hisses and cries of, "Throw him out." On the first ballot Hughes led with 253½. Senator Weeks had 105; Root, 103; Senator Cummins, 85; Theodore E. Burton, 77½; Lawrence Y. Sherman, 66; Roosevelt, 65. The New York vote was split: Root 43, Hughes 42. The second ballot raised Hughes' vote to 328½. Weeks dropped to sixth place. Root was second with 98½ and Roosevelt fifth with 81. As the convention adjourned for the night, Hughes was still 170 votes short of a majority.

In Washington, Hughes heard the repercussions of these events in a solemn mood. He was still trying to work on cases before the court. Stoddard had called on him again on his way to Chicago, and Hughes had conceded privately that it looked as if the forecasts of his nomination were coming true. But he felt that his position had been made unmistakably clear and held to his resolution not to interfere.

As the convention began to vote, he asked Robert H. Fuller, his secretary and political adviser at Albany, to come to Washington. By that time he had probably made up his mind to accept the nomination, if it should be made without compromising circumstances. But he reserved final judgment. When the convention adjourned after the second ballot, he felt that his maximum strength had probably been reached.

"That settles it," he said to Mrs. Hughes. "I shall not be nominated. I am going to bed." [28] He slept soundly.

The reports that filled the newspapers the next morning made it evident that there had been no foundation for Hughes' impulsive conclusion. The judge was agitated. He took his after-breakfast walk as usual. He tried to work and found it impossible. He talked with Fuller. He strode up and down the room, mulling over and over again the predicament he was in.

[27] *Official Report of Proceedings.*
[28] Edward Marshall in the New York *Sun*, Aug. 20, 1916.

"Green," he exclaimed to his secretary, "if they will only choose some one else at Chicago today and let me go out West with my family this summer, I'll be the happiest man in the world." [29]

While Hughes had been sleeping peacefully, the "peace committees" in Chicago had again sought a compromise. Three of the Republican members were still opposed to Hughes, and the Progressives declined to receive a suggestion that was not unanimous. At 3:00 A.M. the conference adjourned. At 4:00 A.M. Dr. Butler talked with Roosevelt over a private wire to Oyster Bay, suggesting agreement on Root, Knox, or Fairbanks. T. R. himself had suggested Root to William Allen White the day before, although he had previously said the nomination of Root would "cut the throat of the Republican Party from ear to ear." [30] Now he refused to discuss Root and felt that neither Knox nor Fairbanks would do. T. R.'s own suggestions—Leonard Wood and Henry Cabot Lodge—aroused consternation among the Progressives and left the Republicans cold. The politically astute colonel must have known what the reaction would be. In the light of subsequent events it is reasonable to suppose that this was his way of throwing his support to Hughes, although he was still unwilling to say so openly in the face of Hughes' silence on the issues of the day.

Charles J. Bonaparte had carried to Chicago a Roosevelt letter intended to thwart the nomination of Hughes.[31] But its wording was evasive, and Bonaparte concluded that its publication would be futile in the face of the sentiment prevailing at Chicago. Hughes could be stopped only by Roosevelt's unqualified condemnation. T. R. refused to gratify the anti-Hughes men by any such maneuver, so the letter was never used.

When the "peace committees" met again at nine o'clock on Saturday morning, the Republicans were unanimously for Hughes. Hiram Johnson and John Parker had walked out in disgust over Roosevelt's suggestion of Lodge. It was then a foregone conclusion that the Republicans would name Hughes on the next ballot. Before the third roll call began, Weeks and Sherman withdrew, and Medill McCormick switched from Roosevelt to Hughes. Alabama, Arkansas, and California went solidly for Hughes. Burton's, Root's, and Fairbanks' names were withdrawn. When Illinois gave its fifty-eight votes to Hughes, it was clear to everyone that the stampede was in full swing.

As soon as New Jersey boosted the Hughes vote beyond the majority mark, bands broke in upon the roll call with patriotic airs, and a wave of hilarity swept through the Coliseum. Hughes' total ran up to 949½, with only scattering remnants left to other candidates. On motion of Alexander P. Moore the

[29] Author's interview with Laurence H. Green, Nov. 14, 1948.

[30] T. R. to E. C. Stokes, May 10, 1916, Roosevelt Papers.

[31] George Edwin Mowry, *Theodore Roosevelt and the Progressive Movement* (Madison, University of Wisconsin, 1946), p. 353. Copyright, 1946, by the University of Wisconsin.

nomination was made unanimous, while New York led a triumphal procession in which all the delegates joined. The nomination of Charles W. Fairbanks for Vice President completed the work of the convention.

The delegates still did not know whether Hughes would accept or whether if he did, Roosevelt would run against him. William Allen White says it was evident that Perkins and Hitchcock "knew definitely that Hughes would accept the nomination."[32] Others have made similar erroneous surmises. Neither Perkins nor Hitchcock nor anyone else could possibly have known what Hughes would do in the event of his nomination, for he had said nothing on that subject to anyone.[33]

Perkins faced a hostile crowd when he reported to the Progressives on the last meeting of the "peace committees." Protests rang through the hall at his suggestion of Lodge or Hughes as a fusion candidate. Being eager to swing the nomination to Hughes, Perkins tried to induce the convention to suspend deliberations until the Republicans had made their choice. John M. Parker insisted that Roosevelt be nominated. Pandemonium ensued. As soon as word came that the Republican roll call was under way, Raymond Robins, who was presiding, recognized Bainbridge Colby. Perkins leaped to the speaker's stand and began to shout. Apparently he had a letter from Roosevelt declaring that he could not accept the nomination.[34] But his loudest cry was lost in the din. Finally Colby placed T. R.'s name before the convention in less than a hundred words, and he was nominated by acclamation.

It was the Progressives' last act of self-intoxication and was swiftly followed by a hangover of disillusionment. Roosevelt wired his "conditional refusal to run"—conditional because he did not know "the attitude of the Candidate of the Republican Party toward the vital questions of the day."[35] Men who had yelled themselves groggy for T. R. a few hours before now roared with rage, tore Roosevelt pictures or badges from their lapels, and stormed out of the hall muttering "apostate," "running out," and similar expressions of disgust. Along with Roosevelt's subsequent support of Hughes, thus went a legacy of resentment against T. R. that was to cost the candidate dearly in terms of Progressive votes.

Mr. Justice Hughes was lunching with his family in the oak-paneled dining room on the second floor of his Sixteenth Street house (a mile due north of the White House) when the momentous news of his nomination came. A flash from Chicago was telephoned to one of the newsmen who were swarming over the premises or waiting on the street corner outside. Green bounded up the stairs three steps at a time.

Hughes came down immediately. Tears glistened in his eyes. Many of the

[32] White's *Autobiography* (New York, Macmillan, 1946), p. 523. Copyright, 1946, by The Macmillan Company.

[33] CEH, Notes, p. 229. [34] White, *op. cit.*, p. 526. [35] Mowry, *op. cit.*, p. 354.

newsmen who had seen him only on the bench realized for the first time that he had a heart-warming smile. All his agitation seemed to be gone now. He was the essence of cordiality as he shook the hands of the reporters, called them "you boys," and beamed for the photographers.

Soon the official telegram of notification arrived from Chicago. The nomination had come without prolonged opposition, without encumbrance or any embarrassing circumstance. No longer was there any doubt in Hughes' mind as to where his duty lay. He shut himself up with Fuller and Green to dictate his resignation and a message of acceptance to the convention. Not a word of his acceptance had been written in advance. His secretary did not know until after the telegram arrived from Chicago what Hughes' reply would be.

Catherine Hughes, seventeen, returned home while the hubbub was at its height, wondering what it was all about. She had been lying under a tree at the Cathedral School watching a tennis match when the principal told her she had better go home. She arrived, tennis racket in hand, wearing sneakers and a white sport dress—the picture of carefree youth—and could not get in. When she succeeded in breaking through the mob and learned what had happened, it was the first word she had heard within the family circle about the prospect of her father being made President.

The news reached Charles Evans Hughes, Jr., at the Citizens' Military Training Camp at Plattsburg where he was a rookie. "Has he accepted?" was the young man's first question.[36] "Son," as Hughes always called him, had captured the highest possible honor at the Harvard Law School, the editorship of the *Harvard Law Review,* at the end of his junior year. He had been secretary to Justice Cardozo of the New York Supreme Court for a brief period and had spent two years practicing in the firm of Cadwalader, Wickersham & Taft. In 1914 he had married Marjorie Bruce Stuart, and their offspring—Charles Evans Hughes 3rd and Henry Stuart Hughes—gave the Republican candidate the benevolent status of grandfather.

The Hugheses' eldest daughter Helen was visiting Vassar College, where she had been graduated in 1914. Perhaps most excited of all the children was eight-year-old Elizabeth. "If father is elected and we live in the White House," she exclaimed, "I can bathe in the fountains!"

The first message that came out of Hughes' besieged office went straight to the White House by messenger. It read:

June 10, 1916

To the President:

I hereby resign the office of Associate Justice of the Supreme Court of the United States.

I am, sir, respectfully yours,

CHARLES EVANS HUGHES

[36] *Washington Post,* June 11, 1916.

By Robert Carter in the New York *Evening Sun,* May 25, 1916.

PATRIOTISM WINS

Wilson was irked by the abruptness of the message. It *was* wanting in finesse, but it could scarcely be regarded as discourteous. Feeling that his resignation to run against the President was no occasion for expression of any regrets or for the conveyance of best wishes, Hughes couched his withdrawal from the Supreme Court in the simplest and most direct language at his command.

The second message to emerge was a lengthy wire to the convention:

> I have not desired the nomination. I have wished to remain on the bench. But in this critical period in our national history, I recognize that it is your right to summon and that it is my paramount duty to respond. You speak at a time of national exigency, transcending merely partisan considerations. You voice the demand for a dominant, thoroughgoing Americanism with firm protective upbuilding policies, essential to our peace and security; and to that call, in this crisis, I cannot fail to answer with the pledge of all that is in me to the service of our country. Therefore I accept the nomination.[37]

His statement of aims called for "firm and unflinching maintenance of all the rights of American citizens on land and sea," for industrial, economic, and military preparedness, undivided allegiance to the United States, "wise and practical measures" for the settlement of international disputes, and reunification of the Republican Party. The convention had adopted a strong and liberal platform almost identical in substance with the Progressive platform, and Hughes found it quite acceptable.

Having crossed the Rubicon, Hughes turned to the unjudicial business of greeting hundreds of visitors and reading a deluge of telegrams. A violent storm in the evening failed to dampen the spirits of his callers or to reduce their numbers. Prominent among them were Justice and Mrs. Brandeis, who were happy over the end of their long fight for the Justice's confirmation by the Senate.

The nomination of Hughes marked the first time that any major party had taken a presidential candidate off the supreme bench. Naturally, it set off an eruption. Many well informed people who had applauded Hughes' exemplary conduct in trying to avoid the nomination, and who recognized his obligation to take it when it came, nevertheless thought the Republican Party had made a grave mistake in going to the court for its standard bearer. Chief Justice White told James E. Watson that he looked upon the nomination "as a very great blunder and one from which we will be years in recovering."[38] This criticism was rightly directed at the party rather than at the man who had reluctantly responded to its call. The Chief Justice had previously counseled Hughes that he could not rightly decline if the call came. And after the nomi-

[37] Hughes Papers.

[38] From *As I Knew Them*, by James E. Watson, p. 164, copyright, 1936, used by special permission of the publishers, The Bobbs-Merrill Company, Inc.

nation had been made White (in spite of his Democratic affiliation) quietly favored the election of Hughes.

Holmes thoroughly understood his colleague's sacrifice and had no criticism to make. "It was not preference," he wrote to Pollock, "but simply and solely, as I believe, a sense of duty that led Hughes to accept the nomination."[39] To Hughes the genial jurist wrote:

June 11, 1916

DEAR HUGHES

Your first thought was of duty. I must confess that pretty near the first view here was the loss to the Court and especially to me. I shall miss you very much in every way—so much so that I wish the need of the country could have been postponed until I am out of this business. As it is I shall look back with affectionate regret at the ending of the time during which we sat (and stood) side by side.

O. W. HOLMES[40]

Justice Day wrote:

In your case the office has indeed sought the man, and your own conduct through all the trying months just past has been honorable and dignified, in every way worthy of yourself and the great office you now resign. . . . No man has filled the position more worthily than yourself.

Numerous comments in similar vein came from other judges, both Republicans and Democrats. Hughes was deeply grateful because he felt the judges especially would know his own feelings. "You can well understand the deep regret with which I severed my membership in the Court," he replied to Justice Day. "I don't think I have ever regretted anything more." To Judge Joseph Buffington's congratulations he responded:

I did not want to leave the Bench and I dreaded more than I can tell you the sort of activity in which I am now engaged. If there had been an honorable way out I should have taken that way. But under the conditions that existed I felt that I had no alternative and that I must do my best in the work to which I was summoned. Having decided upon this course I have followed it without allowing myself to indulge in vain regrets, and I have committed myself to the work with earnestness and enthusiasm.[41]

An attempt was made to write into the Democratic platform a condemnation of Justice Hughes for "dragging the Supreme Court into the mire of politics," but Wilson suppressed it. There were two compelling reasons for doing so: first, Wilson knew the charge was not true; second, in 1904 the Democrats had gone to the New York bench for their own candidate, Judge Alton B. Parker.

[39] Reprinted by permission of the publishers from *Holmes Pollock Letters. The Correspondence of Mr. Justice Holmes and Sir Frederick Pollock, 1874–1932*, edited by Mark DeWolfe Howe, I, 237. Harvard University Press, 1941.

[40] Hughes Papers. [41] *Ibid.*

Taft gurgled with glee over the success of the venture which he had helped to guide. The outcome, he wrote to Hughes, was a "testimonial to your standing as a statesman, citizen, and patriot—unique and unexampled in the history of American politics." [42] Lowell of Harvard was "delighted," and Root said it was the will of the rank and file. "No man in history ever has received such an expression of public confidence," exulted Wickersham, "and no man, I truly believe, ever deserved it more." [43]

Most heart-warming of all were the messages of confidence and affection that flowed in from the boys of Colgate, Brown, Columbia Law School, Cornell, and the New York bar of the nineties. "The biggest thing about it all," wrote Benjamin S. Terry, then head of the history department of the University of Chicago, "is its tribute to the character—the clean and honest spirit that we boys discovered and loved way back in Colgate." "Your whole career as a public man, culminating in the splendid triumph of yesterday," wrote Starr J. Murphy, brother in Delta Upsilon, "is the most inspiring event in American history since the Civil War." These alone were enough to illuminate the path of duty wherever it might lead.

[42] *New York Times*, June 11, 1916. [43] Hughes Papers.

Chapter 32

THE CALIFORNIA INCIDENT

HUGHES' first move, after the initial excitement of his nomination was over, was to flee from Washington. With swarms of visitors and reporters besieging him at home, there was no opportunity to work or to think. On Sunday night, June 11, he slipped away in company with William R. Willcox, who had come to visit him directly from the Chicago convention, and took a train to New York. Arriving at seven o'clock on Monday morning, he set up campaign headquarters at the Hotel Astor and gathered an ample staff around him.

Selection of a campaign manager was the most pressing business. Hughes returned to Washington on July 16 for a couple of days partly for political conferences on the choice of a manager. Advice flowed in from many sources. Taft proposed that Charles D. Hilles be retained, but he had managed Taft's sterile campaign of 1912. Hitchcock was automatically disqualified in Hughes' mind because his appointment might have suggested (contrary to fact) that his preconvention work had been done with Hughes' consent and approval. Hughes was determined, moreover, to find a manager who would reflect the standards of careful thinking and unbiased administration which he himself represented. In spite of his loss of contact with politics and politicians, he felt that he could not let the Old Guard name his manager. By a process of elimination the choice thus fell upon Willcox, whom Governor Hughes had named in 1907 as the first head of the Public Service Commission in New York City. Willcox had proved to be an able public servant, but in politics he was a novice who did not speak the language of the professionals. Taft regarded him as a "blunderhead." [1] The Willcox appointment was to prove Candidate Hughes' first major mistake.

It was fitting that Brown University, which he loved so well, should have been first to acclaim the new candidate with genuine campaign fervor. Attending the Brown commencement June 19–21, he was cheered at every step. In a great demonstration he marched with his classmates of 1881, hat in hand and "countenance wreathed in smiles," as the crowds yelled for "Charlie Hughes." At the corner of Waterman and Benefit streets a little boy stepped out from the crowd and worked desperately over his camera trying to snap a picture before the famous whiskers passed. Noticing the youngster's

[1] Henry F. Pringle, *The Life and Times of William Howard Taft*, II, 895.

difficulties, Hughes stopped, smiled, and waited until the camera had clicked. The crowd roared its approval. The candidate appeared to be thoroughly enjoying his rebaptism into politics.

Colonel Roosevelt swallowed his pique and on June 28 went to dinner with the man he had called a "bearded iceberg." Shortly after the conventions ended, he had announced that he would strongly support Hughes. In a letter to the Progressive National Committee he had candidly recognized that the hope for a new party was dead and urged his Bull Moose followers "not to sulk because our leadership is rejected." His unqualified endorsement of Hughes was followed by similar action on the part of the Progressive Committee.

Two days after the Hughes-Roosevelt dinner the candidate entertained former President Taft at luncheon at the summer home he had established at Bridgehampton, Long Island. Taft begged to be commanded in the campaign. Theoretically the schism in the Republican Party was thus closed. Three months later Roosevelt and Taft met, stiffly shook hands, and stood in the same line during a Hughes reception at the Union League Club in New York. But that reconciliation was even more superficial than the accord between Roosevelt and Hughes. And it was soon evident that there had been no real meeting of minds between the latter two men. Indeed, their mental processes differed so sharply that even when they started at the same point with the same premises, they were soon following divergent courses.

July was a month of reorientation. In those fleeting thirty-one days Hughes attempted to lift himself out of judicial seclusion into the role of a conquering hero. He talked with hundreds of visitors. He assembled stacks of magazines, newspapers, reports, and the *Congressional Record* and crammed for his campaigning ordeal. He analyzed issues and planned tours. Now that he was in the fight, he intended to win it. But he managed to retain his sense of humor. When a campaign committee, having produced a motion picture of the candidate, gave a private showing for Mr. and Mrs. Hughes at Montclair, he criticized his clothes, his walk, his haircut, and his whiskers. If the Republican candidate for President looks like that, he said, his place is not in the White House but in the morgue. At the conclusion he congratulated the committee and said that it had portrayed his character so perfectly that he had decided to vote for Wilson.[2]

His acceptance speech was delivered on the last day of the month. Every one of the 3,000 seats in Carnegie Hall in New York was taken, and large crowds milled around outside while Hughes responded to Senator Warren G. Harding's notification. It was the hottest day of the year. The sweltering crowd divided its enthusiasm between Hughes and Roosevelt, who was appear-

[2] Everett Colby in *Scribner's*, May, 1928, p. 559.

By Clifford Berryman in the Washington *Evening Star*, July 29, 1916.

THE LIVELY LEADER

ing at a Republican gathering for the first time since he had left the party. Hughes held his audience for an hour and a half, feeling it necessary to clarify his stand on all the issues because of his long absence from the political arena.

This speech fixed the tone of the campaign. Hughes gave it the title "America First and America Efficient," unwittingly taking, in the first part of the title, a slogan that Wilson had often used. In those days "America First" did not carry the blight that the isolationists were to give it prior to World War II. Rather it signified opposition to the divided loyalties of the "hyphenated Americans" who were trying to shape the United States' foreign policy to the interests of their ancestral homelands. The climax came in Hughes' cautious but none the less forthright declaration for an international court and for world organization at the end of the war to bring about disarmament and keep the peace. "Freedom from entanglements with interests and policies that do not concern us" was still desirable, he said.

> But there is no national isolation in the world of the Twentieth Century. If at the close of the present war the nations are ready to undertake practicable measures in the common interest in order to secure international justice, we cannot fail to recognize our international duty. The peace of the world is our interest, as well as the interest of others, and in developing the necessary agencies for the prevention of war we shall be glad to have an appropriate share. And our preparedness will have proper relation to this end as well as to our own immediate security.

On the whole it was a disappointing speech. It lacked the fire and the bold strokes that had been associated with the name of Hughes in his governorship days. He had not yet shaken off the excessive caution of his craft. If this is all he has to offer, some friendly critics asked, why did he leave the bench?

Before embarking on his series of tours—one of the most strenuous campaigning ordeals ever undertaken by any candidate—Hughes telegraphed George Sutherland of Utah his endorsement of the proposed woman-suffrage amendment to the Constitution, thus adding a plank that the platform makers at Chicago had ruled out. His first big rally was in Detroit, where he experienced a "wonderful demonstration," addressed 10,000 workmen, and leaped a rail at the baseball park to shake hands with the players and chat with Ty Cobb.

Hughes threw himself into the campaign with every ounce of energy he possessed. The Republican convention had ended on a note of perilous overconfidence, but the candidate took nothing for granted. He and Mrs. Hughes embarked upon a relentless round of interviews, luncheons, speeches, receptions, greetings, and travel with zest that seemed almost unlimited. Chicago, St. Paul, Minneapolis, Grand Forks, Fargo, Helena, Butte, Missoula, Coeur d'Alene, Spokane, Tacoma, Seattle: each stop was a milepost in an endurance contest. Crowds began rapping on the door of the candidate's car, appropriately designated the "Constitution," at five o'clock in the morning. "Charlie, come out," they would call. "Come out or we won't vote for you." It was a common experience to receive a telegram saying several thousand insistent persons were waiting at the next station where no stop had been scheduled. Usually he would squeeze another brief talk into his schedule.

At one stop of this sort in North Dakota an impromptu reception was held beside the tracks. While Hughes was talking to a group of farmers about their crops, the train began to move. Mrs. Hughes ran to catch it.

"Wait, Mother!" he called after her with a laugh. "These are pretty good people. Let the train go."

"Gosh!" a farmer remarked. "He ain't so unhuman after all."

It was a favorable omen. The austerity myth, which had been revived in some measure while he was on the bench, was wilting once more. But Hughes had not yet hit his stride. Sometimes he seemed to be groping for issues. With war inflaming the minds of the people, he talked about waste, extravagance, inefficiency, a scientific tariff, and the spoils system. Cautious legal phraseology sometimes dulled the impact of his speeches. His practice of having stenographers, working in relays, take down each unprepared speech as he gave it, so that carbon copies would be promptly available to the press, resulted in excellent local coverage. But the big Eastern papers, lacking a text prepared in advance, gave scant attention to his speeches in the West. Hughes spoke extemporaneously because he had no time to dictate speeches, and the idea of a ghost writer was abhorrent to him.

Mrs. Hughes was always with him. She tried to shield him from visitors when he was worn out, curtailed his talking when his voice was overstrained, and pulled his coattail when she thought he had spoken long enough. She won the heart of everybody. Tall, slight, and dressed with good taste, in spite of the fact that she "traveled in a hat box," she impressed thousands as the ideal companion for a presidential candidate. She met tobacco-stained rural politicians and overly perfumed hostesses without the slightest variation in her tact and good nature. Her manner reflected quiet simplicity. She seemed always to know the right thing to do. The first wife of a presidential candidate to make an extended campaign tour, she infused it with feminine charm and added immeasurably to the sense of high adventure that kept her husband in top fighting form. As she sat at a tiny table in the "Constitution," pouring grape juice for the men of the press, Hughes tenderly waved his hand toward her and exclaimed, "Gentlemen—the greatest asset of the Republican Party." [3]

Donning oilskins, she followed her husband to the bottom of a copper mine in Butte and climbed with him to Bear Lake at an elevation of 10,000 feet in the Rockies. Excepting the rallies for men only, she never missed a meeting

[3] *New York Herald*, Nov. 8, 1916.

on their trips. In Missouri a group of women made arrangements for her special entertainment while the men were attending to the dull business of politics. She insisted, instead, on being driven to the hall where she could watch his performance, and as the audience broke into tumultuous acclaim her eyes were luminous with tears. She kept a diary of their tours which gave almost as much space to their quiet meals together as to their big public receptions.

Long before the campaign special reached California, repercussions from the hot fight between Governor Johnson and the Old Guard were reaching its passengers. Johnson was campaigning for the Republican as well as the Progressive nomination for the United States Senate. With the collapse of the Bull Moose in Chicago, the Old Guard was making a ferocious effort to destroy Johnson and all the forward-looking reforms for which he stood. As a national force the Progressive Party might be dead, but progressivism was still an upsurging movement in California. The din of battle between the Progressives and the Old Guard beat with painful effect upon the harmony program that Hughes was so assiduously promoting.

The proud and vindictive California Governor, who had been Roosevelt's running mate in 1912, had left Chicago in a rage. "I'm too mad to be tired," he had told a friend on the day that T. R. deserted the Progressive cause.[4] Before returning to California, however, he had paid a friendly visit to Hughes at the Hotel Astor and pledged his support.[5] Back in Sacramento, he reiterated his commitment to the Republican-Progressive candidate because, he said, "I believe his record warrants it." [6] About the same time Chester H. Rowell, Progressive national committeeman and a member of the national campaign committee, wired Hughes, "I find Progressive sentiment here overwhelmingly and very cordially for you."

In opening his senatorial campaign on July 8, however, Johnson said that his choice of Hughes was a personal one and that each Progressive was free to "measure the candidates" for himself and make his own decision.[7] On the same day Hughes wired to the Governor at the California Progressive conference, appealing for harmony:

> The national aims to which we are devoted are so vitally important that I earnestly hope there may be that strong and effective cooperation which will assure their achievement. I desire a reunited Party as the essential agency of national progress, a Party drawing to itself the liberal sentiment of a quickened nation. . . . We are not divided in our ideals, let us work together to attain them.

In a series of telegrams the leaders of the warring factions were importuned to act jointly in making arrangements for Hughes' tour of California. Rowell

[4] *Washington Post*, June 11, 1916.
[5] Author's interview with CEH, April 9, 1946.
[6] *New York Times*, June 28, 1916.
[7] *San Francisco Examiner*, July 9, 1916.

met with Republican National Committeeman William H. Crocker and State Chairman Francis B. Keesling in response to these requests and tried to reach an agreement as to how the Hughes meetings should be handled. Deeper antagonism seemed to be the only result. Rowell complained to Chairman Willcox on July 19 that the Old Guard was going ahead with the arrangements without consulting him. Then both Crocker and Rowell suggested postponement of the tour until after the primaries had been held.[8]

Compliance with this request might have changed history in many particulars. But at the time it seemed impossible. There were two imperatives of the campaign. One was for Hughes to travel as widely and speak as often as possible to overcome the handicap of his long silence on the bench. The other was to confine his efforts in the final weeks to the big cities of the East where, it was believed, the fight had to be won. Both Hughes and Willcox reasoned that the Western tour would have to be made in August or it could not be made at all. But this decision was reached without any real understanding of the intense hatred between the Johnson and Crocker factions. As a matter of fact, Hughes often missed the significance of political feuds inflamed with malice. Being free from personal bitterness, he found it difficult to comprehend the marriage of hate to politics.

Hughes was eager to meet Johnson in his home state and asked that both Republican and Progressive delegations accompany him on his tour of California. A similar arrangement had worked well in Illinois. Campaign headquarters repeatedly urged the California factions to adhere to the spirit of the Illinois arrangement. But Crocker apparently could not endure the thought of the Progressives getting any advantage out of the presidential candidate's visit. He would not agree to Rowell's suggestion (made without Johnson's knowledge) that Governor Johnson preside at Hughes' San Francisco rally and Willis Booth, Johnson's opponent for the Republican nomination, at the Los Angeles rally, although Hughes and Willcox gave their blessing to this proposal. Crocker countered with a proposal that he preside at San Francisco and Rowell at Los Angeles. Rowell disagreed and renewed his charges that the Progressives were being cold-shouldered. Willcox urged Crocker to take note of the Progressives' grievances and to end the feuding. But the fight continued, with Crocker then insisting that he and Rowell, being national campaign officials, could not interfere in a "state matter," and that all arrangements for Hughes' visit be handled by Keesling's state committee.[9]

All efforts to bridge the gulf were futile. Hughes reviewed the row on a sweltering day in St. Paul, and at the suggestion of Frederick M. Davenport asked that Crocker and Rowell meet the campaign special at Portland, reserv-

[8] Charles W. Farnham's report on the California incident, p. 2; Hughes Papers.
[9] Frederick M. Davenport in *North American Review*, Feb. 17, 1917, p. 203.

ing final arrangements until the whole controversy could be threshed out with the candidate himself. Rowell agreed. Crocker wired that all arrangements had been completed. Finally Crocker suggested that Johnson and Rowell join him in conducting the Hughes party through the state. Rowell said this would be impossible because Johnson's own campaign itinerary had been fixed.[10]

Rowell joined the Hughes party at the Hotel Benson in Portland. After reviewing his efforts to reach an agreement with the Old Guard, he told Hughes that Governor Johnson was very popular in California and was almost certain to win. "For the sake of your own candidacy," he said, "you ought to come out for Johnson. If you do, you'll be elected. If you do not, you may not carry California." [11]

Hughes replied that he could not look at the California situation from the local point of view. To come out for Johnson might help him in California, but it would severely hurt him elsewhere. When he was Governor of New York, he told Rowell, many of the machine leaders accused him of not being a loyal Republican. That feeling had generally subsided with the widespread acceptance of what Hughes stood for. But it would be quickly rekindled if he should throw his support to Johnson in his fight against the old-line Republican candidate in California. "Moreover," Hughes said, "I should be 'yellow'—even dishonest—if I should play favorites in California simply because of Johnson's popularity. I couldn't possibly comply with your request," he told Rowell, "even if it should mean my defeat." [12]

Crocker and Keesling boarded the campaign special at Ashland, Oregon, accompanied by a reception committee of Republicans and Progressives—"tame" Progressives, according to Davenport. A memorandum written by Charles W. Farnham, Hughes' train manager, about five months after the incident reports a series of conferences aboard the train. "There did not appear to be any lack of harmony," he wrote, "and it was agreed Mr. Crocker was to preside at the meeting in San Francisco." [13] Davenport, who was traveling with Hughes as a friend and adviser and a representative of Chairman Willcox, insists that Crocker's arrangements were permitted to stand without any question being raised.[14] This is corroborated by Keesling, who says, "We refrained from referring to the senatorial contest in our conversations with Mr. Hughes." [15] In any event, Hughes did not take command of the situation as he certainly would have done in his governorship days. His mistake was in not softening his necessary rebuff to Rowell by insisting that Johnson preside

[10] Keesling to C. E. Kunze, July 31, 1923; Hughes Papers.
[11] Author's interview with CEH, April 9, 1946.
[12] *Id.* [13] Farnham's report, p. 7.
[14] Author's interview with Dr. Davenport, Dec. 20, 1948.
[15] Keesling's monograph, *Hiram Johnson and the Hughes Campaign in California*, p. 36.

at the San Francisco rally. Whether or not Johnson could have complied at that late date, such a friendly gesture—stopping short of endorsement—might have averted the series of unfortunate events that was to follow.

The name of Crocker, an amiable philanthropist of high personal repute, was linked to the odious Southern Pacific machine. What that machine stood for was as repugnant to Hughes as it was to Johnson. But Hughes, fresh from the bench, knew little of California politics. On the night of Friday, August 18, he faced a crowd of 14,000 in the San Francisco Civic Auditorium still hoping that he could ride through California with one foot on the back of the Elephant and the other on the back of the Bull Moose. Rowell was on the rostrum in a silent role. Keesling introduced Crocker. As Crocker concluded his presentation of Hughes, there was a shout from the gallery, "Three cheers for San Francisco's favorite son!" What appeared at the time to be an outburst of public acclaim was later shown to be only a sycophantic gesture from an employee in Crocker's bank.[16]

"Fellow citizens," Hughes began in a voice that was hoarse from too much speaking, "I salute with you San Francisco's favorite son, and express my deep appreciation for his very generous introduction."[17]

"I come as the spokesman of a reunited Republican Party to talk to you of national issues—with local differences I have no concern."

It was a naturally generous response to Crocker's greeting and an accurate statement of Hughes' aloofness from the California imbroglio, but it chilled the powerful Progressives. Later his denunciation of political bosses caused the Old Guard to squirm. The rally ended with cheers but no demonstration. Rowell told the press that "the meeting was a frost," talked of Wilson's popularity in California, and openly accused Hughes of abandoning the Progressives to the wolves.[18] The next morning Rowell quit the Hughes party, saying that his wife was undergoing an operation. "We still hope to carry the state for Hughes," he said, "but we won't get the majority that we expected."[19] No other Progressive leader was assigned to take his place.

Crocker and Keesling were enraged by Rowell's disaffection and declared that they would not permit Johnson to preside at Los Angeles or any Progressives to participate in the other Hughes rallies in California. The city seethed with animosity. Impetuous Progressives were hinting openly that unless they got "substantial recognition" many of their votes would go to Wilson. The reactionaries insisted that any gesture toward Hiram Johnson on Hughes' part would drive them into Wilson's arms. Hughes was caught in the cross fire of hostile forces each of which was more interested in destroying the other than in his election.

[16] Francis V. Keesling to Paul Edwards, Aug. 9, 1945.
[17] *San Francisco Examiner*, Aug. 19, 1916. [18] *Ibid.*
[19] Davenport in *North American Review*, Feb. 17, 1917.

It was painfully evident that the Old Guard was trying not only to keep Johnson from attending a Hughes rally but also to prevent the two candidates from meeting. Farnham discovered that no meeting had been arranged at Sacramento, the capital, apparently in furtherance of this scheme. He insisted on a rally being held there and tried to communicate directly with Governor Johnson.

Meanwhile another political *faux pas* reached its climax. Keesling had arranged a Saturday luncheon for the visitors at the Commercial Club. One of Hughes' advisers had urged him in Portland to cancel the luncheon because the waiters were preparing to strike. Such a course, Hughes replied, might cause the country to think he lacked courage. His managers then asked the union to postpone its walkout until after the luncheon had been held. The union leaders agreed on condition that the "open shop" sign in the window be removed during the luncheon. The Hughes men appealed to Crocker, Keesling, and other party bigwigs to get the sign temporarily removed, but nothing was done. Served by strikebreakers, the luncheon became a potent source of ill will among union men. Once more Hughes had fallen victim to an extraneous row and to the desensitization of his political acumen.

The campaign party left strife-ridden San Francisco at 8:00 P.M. on Saturday with a feeling of relief. Weary and perturbed, Hughes was especially glad that tomorrow would be a day of rest. He had made it a rule not to speak on Sundays. His anticipation of a pleasant and easy day was heightened when three prominent citizens boarded his train. "We think you should have a rest," they said, "and we're going to give you a real rest in Los Angeles."

There was a lively throng at the Alexandria Hotel, however, and the day began with much handshaking. Two old friends, C. W. Pendleton, Hughes' roommate at Brown, and John Murray Marshall, who induced him to go into law, were among the hosts and well-wishers. Immediately after breakfast Hughes was told that he was expected to attend a meeting of the Temple Baptist Church. He was applauded so enthusiastically when Dr. Len G. Broughton, the pastor, called him "the man of the hour" that he got up and bowed. At the end of the services two thousand persons insisted on shaking his hand.

While Farnham again tried to locate Governor Johnson, the candidate and his wife granted interviews to the press. Then their hosts casually suggested a drive to Pasadena. En route they stopped to see former Senator George F. Edmonds and Mrs. Garfield, widow of the martyred President. In Pasadena they also stopped to greet the children of the Boys' and Girls' Aid Society Home. By strange coincidence the Republican City Committee of Pasadena had arranged a luncheon for two hundred persons at which Mr. and Mrs. Hughes became the honored guests. Calls for a speech were heard, but he insisted that it was not one of his speaking days. Of course he could not refuse to shake the hands of the good people who had come out to greet him. Before the gathering dispersed, Hughes thought the entire population of Pasadena must have pumped his arm.

"Wouldn't you like to visit Long Beach on the way back to your hotel?" his escorts then asked. "It's a lovely drive." The idea of rest seemed to have gone a-glimmering. Hughes consented. Over a rough and dusty road they reached Universal City, a motion-picture center, and stopped to shake hands with the actors and impresarios. It was 5:00 P.M. when the automobiles drew up to the Virginia Hotel in Long Beach.

Ostensibly the guests were taken to the hotel to rest and to get a favored view of the Pacific. But word of their imminent arrival had gone up and down the beach, and 5,000 persons filled the hotel and blocked the entrance to it. The visitors succeeded in getting through the crowd, but the candidate and his wife had spent only a few minutes in their room when the clamor and shouting that came up from the street brought another surrender to the local committee's request that they "shake hands with the crowd." It was dusk when they walked to the parapet for a fleeting glance at the free-rolling Pacific; then the eight-car caravan got under way again.

Back in Los Angeles, they passed a brilliantly lighted building. "We have a wonderful museum here," an escort said with California fervor. "It has a fine collection of saber-tooth tigers and the world's best exhibit of prehistoric animals. We have arranged to have it all lighted so that you can see it now." As they went through the museum, the Hugheses were photographed beside the skeleton of a mastodon estimated to be 30,000 years old and felt a strange affinity to it.

At last they were back at their hotel, dirty, rumpled, and tired. Only a late evening was now left for relaxation. Optimistic Mr. Hughes was beginning to feel gratified that at least he could have a quiet dinner alone with his wife when a delegation called on him and said that the First Methodist Church was having a meeting in his honor, that the elders and congregation were waiting, and that he simply must come. Taking time only to wash, he went to the meeting without any dinner, made a brief speech, and submitted to another handshaking ordeal.

It was after ten o'clock when the exhausted candidate returned to his hotel and found Farnham waiting with a bombshell. While the Hughes party was at Long Beach, Farnham said, Governor Johnson had been there too in the same hotel.

"Why didn't you tell me at the time?" Hughes demanded with undisguised anger.

Farnham replied that he had no knowledge of Johnson's presence in the hotel until a newspaper man had passed the word to him after they had returned to Los Angeles.

"Drive down to Long Beach at once," Hughes ordered. "Explain to Governor Johnson that I did not know he was at the hotel and that I am sorry I did not meet him and ask him to preside at my meeting in Sacramento." [20] Farnham induced Keesling to go with him; Crocker refused.

At midnight on his "day of rest," with the burden of the Virginia Hotel mishap on his mind, Hughes left for San Diego, where he was to address a large crowd at the exposition on Monday.

"If I had known that Johnson was in the hotel," he told Davenport shortly before catching his train, "I would have seen him if I had been obliged to kick the door down." [21]

Governor Johnson had motored into Long Beach from Bakersfield. When he registered, he asked why the lobby was full of people and was told that Hughes was expected to arrive in a few minutes. As Johnson wrote his name, he overheard Frank Roberts, one of his most bitter political enemies, remark, "Wouldn't it be just like the Progressives to horn in on our party." [22] Bristling and resentful, Johnson went to his room, accompanied by E. A. Dickson and Paul Herriott, and remained there while the Hughes party came and went. His irritation was understandable, but he must have known that Roberts had no connection whatever with the Hughes party.

Johnson made no effort to see or greet the candidate whose cause he was espousing. He sent no one to let the Hughes people know he was in the hotel.[23] Several writers who have investigated the incident have concluded that the men around Hughes knew Johnson was in the hotel and deliberately kept the information from him. Keesling insists, however, that no member of the Hughes party, including the Southern California reception committee, had any inkling of the Governor's presence.[24] The hotel manager was a Republican politician who was doubtless eager to keep the candidates apart.

There are various conflicting accounts of what took place at Farnham's and Keesling's interview with Johnson. Some facts, however, can be nailed down. Admitting that he knew Hughes was in the hotel, Johnson said "that the people of . . . California would not wish their governor to break through any cordon surrounding him in order that he might shine in Hughes' reflected light. . . ." [25] Farnham reports Johnson as saying also that he had expected Hughes or Farnham to send for him before leaving the hotel.

[20] Author's interview with CEH, Oct. 24, 1945; CEH, Notes, p. 234.

[21] Author's interview with Dr. Davenport, Dec. 20, 1948.

[22] Keesling's interview with E. A. Dickson, recorded in a monograph by Keesling in 1943–1944, p. 51.

[23] John Murray Marshall, letter in Boston *Evening Transcript*, Dec. 16, 1916.

[24] Keesling's monograph, p. 51.

[25] Frederick M. Davenport in *American Political Science Review*, April, 1949, p. 328, quoting Johnson's letter to Rowell.

Farnham repeated what he had said in the beginning—that if Hughes had known of Johnson's presence he would have insisted upon seeing him without standing upon formalities. By any code of etiquette, however, Farnham reminded the Governor, it was his obligation to greet the visiting presidential candidate—not vice versa.

Johnson expressed regret that no meeting had taken place but said it was too late for him to go to Los Angeles or for Mr. Hughes to return to Long Beach. Farnham suggested that the Governor cancel his next speaking engagement so that he and Hughes could review the whole situation on Monday night; also that Johnson preside at the Sacramento rally. Johnson replied that the petty Republican politicians surrounding Hughes were determined to prevent any such meeting. According to Johnson's account, Keesling stalled and would not reply when Farnham asked him if he would object to the Governor's presiding at Sacramento.[26] Keesling says that he told Johnson that "the Republican committeemen had always desired his meeting and accompanying Governor Hughes throughout the state" and that if the presence of any Republican created an impossible situation arrangements could be made for Johnson to "continue with Governor Hughes under congenial conditions."[27] Johnson thought he left the door open to further discussion of the Sacramento meeting, but Farnham interpreted the Governor's remarks about the impossibility of changing his itinerary as a definite rejection.

The train manager's final request was an exchange of friendly telegrams between Johnson and Hughes. Johnson scoffed at the idea of greeting the visiting candidate on the eve of his departure from California. He said the question of telegrams should be taken up with Hughes. Farnham understood Johnson to agree nevertheless to send a telegram that could be read at the Sacramento rally. The conference trailed off into a Johnsonian scorching of Crocker, Keesling, and the Southern Pacific crowd. From the instant Hughes' coming to California was announced, he said, the trip had been used by Crocker and Keesling and those acting with them, not for the benefit of Hughes, but for the promotion of their petty ambitions, "so that the foul regime which had governed California prior to 1911 might again be fastened upon the state."

When the results of this conference were reported to Hughes on Monday morning, he approved an exchange of friendly telegrams, the texts to be agreed upon in advance to avoid any possible embarrassment to Governor Johnson. Farnham telephoned this suggestion to Johnson while Hughes was speaking at San Diego under extra guard because of a threat against his life. Johnson seemed to acquiesce, but when his telegram arrived it was addressed to Farnham rather than to Hughes as follows:

[26] *Ibid.*, p. 329. [27] Keesling's monograph, 1943–1944, p. 49.

LONG BEACH CALIF. Aug. 21, 1916.

Mr. Charles W. Farnham
Care Governor Charles Evans Hughes
Hotel Alexandria, Los Angeles, Cal.

MY DEAR MR. FARNHAM your early telephone message from San Diego this morning suggesting that I wire Mr. Hughes and that he would respond as well as your suggestion last night that I go to Sacramento and there preside at Mr. Hughes meeting I have thought of most carefully. It goes without saying that I wish and have wished to extend to Mr. Hughes a most cordial and hearty welcome to California and that in view of my advocacy of him I would be very glad to present him to my fellow citizens and to state to them the reasons for my advocacy. Until now it has been rendered impossible for me to do either. The men surrounding Mr. Hughes in California and who have been in charge of his tour are much more interested in my defeat than in Mr. Hughes election and they have made it manifest both publicly and privately that they would vote for Mr. Wilson if the commonest courtesies were exchanged between Mr. Hughes and myself. At this late day when both our itineraries are full and fixed and upon the eve of Mr. Hughes departure from California for me even at your suggestion to wire Mr. Hughes and for him to reply or for me to preside at his Sacramento meeting would be misunderstood and misinterpreted and maliciously distorted. I have just been informed that tonights meeting has been elaborately staged for a Booth demonstration by the very people who protest they wish Mr. Hughes California trip wholly divorced from local candidacies. Such a thing in my behalf I would not of course tolerate or permit and I do not wish to be open even to the unjust accusation that I have attempted it. With kindest regards to yourself and Mr. Hughes and with best wishes for his success I am very sincerely yours,

HIRAM W. JOHNSON

It was not a greeting but a partisan lament from an official whose inflated sense of dignity had been wounded. In part it was based on misinformation that Johnson could have readily corrected. Instead of being a demonstration for Booth, Johnson's opponent, the Los Angeles meeting was a model of interparty cooperation. Equal numbers of Republicans and Progressives sat on the platform and united in supporting Hughes' candidacy. It was the kind of meeting that he had planned to have throughout California and would have had, except for the blind stubbornness of Crocker and the irritability of Johnson.

Farnham telephoned Johnson that the telegram was not what he had promised. Once more the Governor agreed to send his greetings and asked what the nature of Hughes' reply would be. Farnham could say only that it would be a proper acknowledgment. Johnson then asked Farnham to readdress the telegram he had sent so that it would go to Hughes and to strike out everything except the greeting.[28] When Farnham declined to tamper with the telegram, Johnson again promised to send a message to be held until he had a satisfactory

[28] Farnham's report, p. 11.

reply from Hughes. It never arrived, and Farnham thereafter got no response to his telephone calls and telegrams to Johnson.

Hughes went on to Sacramento with an appeal for progressive policies but with only Crocker and Keesling accompanying his party. Through a large part of California he was thus presented to the people by political leaders who were about to lose their shirts. Both the candidate and his managers were worried, but Hughes felt that he could neither dismiss the official representatives of the Republican Party nor compel any Progressive to accompany him. He had done everything humanly possible to wipe out any offense that might have resulted from the misadventure at Long Beach, which was no fault of his in the first place. Certainly there is no ground for saying, as careless writers have repeated for more than three decades, that Hughes snubbed Johnson. If there was any snubbing, it was done by Governor Johnson himself. Many Californians were "disgusted and humiliated" [29] by the conduct both of Crocker and of Johnson.

After a great barbecue in Reno and a rally in the Mormon Tabernacle in Salt Lake City, Hughes went on to Estes Park, Colorado, for three days of rest. On the day of his departure Johnson won the Republican as well as the Progressive nomination for senator in California and complete control of the Republican Party in the state. Hughes wired his hearty congratulations, wishing Johnson great success in his campaign for election. "I was very glad to receive your telegram of congratulations," was Johnson's frigid reply, "and I thank you for it." [30] That alone was sufficient notice to Johnson's followers that he was nursing a grievance.

The severest test of the remarriage between the Republicans and Progressives had been bungled. The self-serving tenacity of the Old Guard and the vindictive attitude of Hiram Johnson had cast a shadow over the entire campaign.

[29] J. A. Hayes to CEH, Aug. 21, 1916. [30] Hughes Papers.

Chapter 33

THE WAR ISSUE

ONLY a few times in our history have the people had an opportunity of choosing between presidential candidates of the caliber of Charles E. Hughes and Woodrow Wilson. Both were men of high integrity and powerful intellect. The parallelism in their careers has often held attention. Both were the sons of clergymen; both had been university professors and progressive governors of their states; both had fought the bosses and the trusts and united divided factions of their parties; both were men of vision and idealism who foresaw that isolation for the United States was nearing an end and that peace and democracy could be made secure only by world organization. Even Roosevelt sometimes spoke of Hughes as "the whiskered Wilson."

In the sphere of domestic policy both candidates talked the language of progressivism and pointed to records of substantial achievement. "I would not be here," Hughes declared again and again, "if I did not think of the Republican Party as a liberal party." His program included control of public utilities, old-age pensions, safeguards for labor, and protective legislation for women and children. But the Wilson Administration could point to a creditable record in domestic reforms, including the Federal Reserve System, the Federal Trade Commission, and the Farm Loan Act, and these accomplishments were much fresher in the public mind than Hughes' fights for the people as Governor of New York.

The general similarity of their aims naturally made the campaign more difficult for Hughes, for Wilson already occupied the Presidency. Hughes' case had to be built, of course, on their differences and contrasts. These were momentous and offered ample scope for a great national debate. But here again Hughes was at a disadvantage because his main reason for challenging the Administration lay in the uncertain and treacherous sphere of foreign policy, and he refused to make foreign-policy commitments that might embarrass him in office. The course of the next administration, he knew, would be determined largely by what happened in Europe and not by any policy devised in advance at the White House. He would not pretend that he could change the inevitable. The result was a campaign devoted for the most part to secondary issues, which keenly disappointed many of his friends.

Willcox's mismanagement of the campaign was another source of much concern. "If the election were held in the next fortnight," Medill McCormick, the Chicago publisher, warned Hughes on the last leg of his Western tour, "Wilson would win." [1] Taft too was alarmed. In Washington Senators Smoot, Weeks, Wadsworth, and Curtis were so concerned over the blunders of Chairman Willcox that they asked Harvey D. Hinman to come to the Capital for a conference. Since their fights together at Albany, Hinman had been known as Hughes' best friend among the politicians. The Senators asked him to go to Hughes and convince him that, in order to win, he would have to name a first-class politician as a back-stage manager for Willcox.

Hinman met Hughes' train at Buffalo and frankly outlined the weaknesses of the campaign up to that point. Hughes listened without comment. Then for ten minutes he gazed out of the window in silence. It was a perfect autumn day that seemed to magnify his troubles by contrast. When he turned to Hinman, he unburdened his heart. The campaign was not going well. The California mishap had complicated the difficulty of uniting the Republicans and Progressives. Willcox had demonstrated far less political gumption than Hughes had attributed to him. Hinman was undoubtedly right in saying that an experienced politician was needed at campaign headquarters.

"But I can't take it up with Willcox," Hughes said.[2]

The upshot of the conference was that Hinman, at Hughes' request, visited Willcox on his farm and tried to make him see the necessity of grass-roots organization and basic campaign strategy. Willcox laughed and said that Hughes was a great candidate, the campaign was going well, and he had no question about the outcome. A sweeping Republican victory in Maine in September tended to confirm this view.

A few weeks on the hustings, moreover, greatly improved Hughes' campaigning technique. His skill in managing an audience was put to an extraordinary test in Nashville on September 4. When Republican State Chairman James Taylor had talked in unflattering terms about the Wilson Administration, pandemonium had broken loose. Judge George N. Tillman had tried to introduce Hughes and had been driven back to his seat by an outburst of hisses and boos. The candidate walked forward smiling and waited patiently for the uproar to subside. When there was a lull, he began speaking in a conversational tone about his delight in visiting Nashville and his gratitude for the many courtesies he had received from the good people there regardless of party affiliations. Men who had been hissing sat back abruptly "as if they had received a slap in the face." [3] Someone laughed. Then came a ripple of applause. Here was the opening Hughes had hoped for. He plunged into the strike issue and won lusty cheers. After that even the hostile part of the

[1] McCormick to CEH, Aug. 25, 1916.
[2] Author's interview with Harvey D. Hinman, Aug. 15, 1948.
[3] *New York Times*, Sept. 5, 1916.

audience listened while he drove home his points with more force and vigor than he had attained in any previous rally. When he talked about Mexico, a man in the top gallery called out, "What would you have done?"

"What would I have done?" he flashed back, shaking his finger at the questioner. "I would have protected the lives of American citizens." [4]

The audience sprang to its feet cheering. Even the *New York Times* dropped its drumfire criticism of Hughes long enough to applaud his skill in turning insult to advantage.

After attending the Republican rally at Lincoln, Nebraska, David Lawrence drew a vivid picture of Hughes on the stump. The candidate stood erect with head uplifted, except when he dropped his chin, with its now short-cropped beard, to emphasize a point. "Nobody shoots out thought after thought, idea after idea, with more marvellous clarity or rapidity than the Republican nominee for the Presidency," Lawrence wrote. "He talks faster than most people think. . . . He is rattling it off at the rate of 200 words per minute . . . when he gets to a climax he is pounding so hard . . . that as he touches top speed and stays there for several sentences at a time, he holds the applause in check until he rounds it off with an epigrammatic phrase, when he finally releases the pent-up enthusiasm of his crowd, and the effect is like a cannon shot. . . . Mr. Hughes reaches over, drinks a glass of water in the interval, steps forward and is ready to go on. There is a rhythm to it all, a grammatical perfection and rhetorical mastery that catches the ear and transfixes the mind." [5]

His seriousness was usually leavened by bits of humor. When Wilson, forgetting his heavy reliance on his unofficial adviser, Edward M. House, said that a return of the Republicans would mean "invisible government," Hughes fired back that he preferred "government through two Houses and not three." While he was often severe in his criticism, he avoided personal enmity and never hit below the belt. "We are all friends," he insisted, "however divided politically."

While Hughes campaigned in the West, Wilson made votes in Washington out of the threatened railroad strike. First, he summoned the disputants to the White House and asked them to arbitrate their differences. The brotherhoods refused and called a strike for September 4. Incredulous when he heard of it, Wilson nevertheless hastened to Congress and asked for immediate enactment of a law giving the brotherhoods most of what they demanded—an eight-hour day with payment of the same wages that had previously been paid for ten hours. With 400,000 labor votes at stake, Congress too gave way and passed the Adamson Eight-Hour Act in time to avert the walkout.

Hughes thought this action was a "shocking abandonment of principle"

[4] Mrs. Hughes' diary. [5] New York *Evening Post*, Oct. 17, 1916.

and condemned it in many speeches. He favored the eight-hour day, and as Governor of New York he had signed a bill prescribing an eight-hour day for railway telegraphers and signalmen. But he could not tolerate dictation to government. "Labor least of all can afford to surrender the rule of reason," he declared. "We must never permit any of the processes of government to be surrendered to the dictates of any power. That is the path of disaster. . . . I would rather stand on that principle and be defeated than yield one jot or tittle of it to get into office." [6]

Many workingmen applauded this forthright stand. At Terre Haute 400 laborers escorted Hughes and gave him a boisterous reception. It was not the labor vote that would cost him the election.

Preparedness was a hot issue throughout the campaign. "The President has never realized the gravity of our unprepared position . . ." wrote Colonel House in his diary. "If war comes . . . it will be because we are totally unprepared and Germany feels that we are impotent." [7] "The people here [in Germany]," said James W. Gerard, the American ambassador, "are firmly convinced that we can be slapped, insulted, and murdered with absolute impunity, and refer to our notes as things worse than waste paper." [8] Yet Wilson had continued a policy of weakness in the face of world upheaval.

When the President gave no support to Secretary of War Lindley M. Garrison's proposal to increase the Regular Army to 142,000 and set up a new "continental army" of 400,000 men, Garrison had resigned in protest. During the second year of the World War and the worst year of the difficulties with Mexico, the Administration had added only 227 officers and 1,248 men to the Regular Army. Wilson's biographer, Ray Stannard Baker, concludes that "the programme he approved was at best only a strong gesture." [9]

Hughes bore down heavily on this Wilsonian blind spot. "We have outlived the time," he asserted at San Francisco, "when Americans can go up and down the earth boasting of a free government and of the unparalleled resources of America and win respect for that declaration." [10] We must measure up, he declared, "in efficiency and strength." "Adequate preparedness," he said at Fargo, "is not militarism: it is the essential assurance of security," for "weakness breeds insult, insult breeds war: honest, firm, consistent, determined defense of rights establishes peace and respect throughout the world." The one hope of keeping out of the European war, he contended, lay in building up our military strength and protecting our rights with courage and firmness.

Probably the severest criticism of the campaign was leveled at Wilson's

[6] *New York Times,* Sept. 7, 1916.

[7] H. C. F. Bell, *Woodrow Wilson and the People* (New York, Doubleday, 1945), pp. 190–191. Copyright, 1945, by H. C. F. Bell.

[8] *Ibid.*

[9] *Woodrow Wilson: Life and Letters,* VI, 304, New York, Doubleday, 1937.

[10] *San Francisco Examiner,* Aug. 19, 1916.

Mexican policy. He had used the influence of the United States to drive General Huerta from power while pretending to follow a policy of "watchful waiting." Huerta was an adventurer who had seized the government by force, but he had won recognition from Great Britain, Germany, France, Russia, Spain, and Japan. The Mexicans failed to depose Huerta after the United States had withdrawn its embargo on arms in the hope of aiding the revolutionaries. Wilson then urged an election in Mexico and sent John Lind as his "personal spokesman" to the unrecognized Huerta to demand that Huerta should not be a candidate in that election. Lind told the German minister that "Huerta will be put out if he does not get out." [11]

In April, 1914, moreover, Wilson had ordered Admiral Mayo to "take Vera Cruz." The ostensible purpose was to enforce the admiral's demand for an apology and salute after the Mexicans had seized members of the crew of a United States steamship. Actually, however, this invasion of Mexican territory was ordered in a naïve effort to prevent a German ship from landing a load of munitions for Huerta, and, according to a Cabinet officer, "to show Mexico that we were in earnest in our demand that Huerta should go." Nineteen Americans and over a hundred Mexicans were killed in the fighting that ensued. Huerta got his ammunition through another port. Admiral Mayo did not get the salute and ignominiously withdrew after a short occupation of Vera Cruz. ". . . we intervened," Hughes declared, "but we didn't stay intervened. We had intervention for an ignoble purpose, and a retreat without accomplishing anything, except the destruction of the only government Mexico had." [12]

Hughes' second count against the Mexican policy was its failure to protect American citizens. After Villa's bandits had killed sixteen American mining men on a train and invaded, looted, and burned Columbus, New Mexico, an American military force had penetrated several hundred miles into Mexico without punishing anyone. "We have not helped Mexico," Hughes declared. "She lies prostrate, impoverished, famine-stricken, overwhelmed with the woes and outrages of internecine strife, the helpless victim of a condition of anarchy which the course of the Administration only served to promote. We have made enemies, not friends. Instead of commanding respect and deserving good-will by sincerity, firmness, and consistency, we provoked misapprehension and deep resentment. . . . We have resorted to physical invasion, only to retire without gaining the professed object. It is a record which cannot be examined without a profound sense of humiliation." [13]

The strangest issue of the campaign was the accusation that Hughes was truckling to the German-American vote. Many citizens of German extraction

[11] Lind to Nelson O'Shaughnessy, April 5, 1914; Hughes Papers.
[12] *San Francisco Examiner*, Aug. 19, 1916. [13] Acceptance speech, p. 6.

in New York had supported him as governor, and their loyalty carried over to 1916. Others rallied to him at first because they thought Wilson was pro-British. Hughes refrained from insulting these people, but there was never the slightest reason to suspect him of sympathy for the hyphenates. "Whether native or naturalized, of whatever race or creed," he had said in his very first political utterance in 1916, "we have but one country, and we do not for an instant tolerate any division of allegiance." That view was often reiterated, and Hughes made it unmistakably plain that, if elected, he would deal more severely with any German invasion of American rights than Wilson had done.

On October 22 the Democratic National Committee released a sensational charge that Hughes had secretly met German-American and Irish-American groups and made "a campaign deal" with them.[14] Four men representing the American Independence Conference had called on Hughes about the middle of September through arrangements made by Charles Beecher Warren. They were Carl E. Schmidt, wealthy Michigan manufacturer; Frank Seiberlich; William R. MacDonald, an organizer of the Embargo Conference; and Jeremiah O'Leary, chairman of the American Truth Society. Directly or indirectly, these latter organizations were getting German financial support. Wilson later rebuked O'Leary and said that he did not want his vote or the vote of anyone like him. At the time of the meeting, however, Hughes knew neither the individuals nor their connections. He listened to their views, as he had done with all other groups that came to see him, and reiterated his own determination, if he should be elected, to give protection to American lives, property, and commerce. Nothing that was said gave the slightest ground for suspicion of intrigue or an improper bid for votes.

News of the "sensation" reached Hughes at the Montclair Hotel in New Jersey where he was dining with Willcox, Colonel Harvey, Travis H. Whitney, and several others. Immediately he dictated a reply setting forth the facts and declaring, "I have said nothing in private that I have not said in public." Two days later, in speaking at Schuetzen Park in Queens to an audience largely of German ancestry, he said emphatically that he did not want the vote of anyone "who would not instantly champion the rights and interests of our country against any country on earth." [15]

Undoubtedly Hughes would have won votes by making this emphatic statement earlier in the campaign. But the absurdity of the charge against him two weeks before election day is magnified by the historic fact that the German vote went largely to Wilson. Josephus Daniels, who was Secretary of the Navy, noted that after T. R. began his bellicose speeches for Hughes "the trend of the German vote from Ohio to the Pacific set in toward Wilson." [16]

[14] *New York Times*, Oct. 23, 1916. [15] *Ibid.*, Oct. 25, 1916.

[16] *The Wilson Era: Years of Peace—1910–1917* (Chapel Hill, University of North Carolina Press, 1944), p. 466. Copyright, 1944, by the University of North Carolina.

The war issue overshadowed everything else. Hughes played it down because he was confident that he would be elected and was determined to remain free to deal with any emergency in accord with his best judgment when all the facts and circumstances could be known. In sharp contrast, the Wilson forces pitched their entire campaign to the key, "He kept us out of war." Martin H. Glynn, the temporary chairman of the Democratic National Convention in St. Louis, had reached his climax by citing historic occasions on which American rights had been violated. Each story had ended with the intoxicating declaration, "But we didn't go to war." Then Senator Ollie James, the permanent chairman, had credited Wilson with wringing from Germany an agreement to American demands, "without orphaning a single American child, without widowing a single American mother, without firing a single gun, without the shedding of a single drop of blood." [17] Even Bryan, who had resigned as Secretary of State because Wilson's policy was too "militant" for him, joined in the orgy, and the platform reiterated the kept-us-out-of-war theme.

Knowing how precarious was the peace the United States still enjoyed, Wilson himself avoided this opportunistic and deceitful slogan. "It begins to look as if war with Germany is inevitable," he had told Tumulty as early as June.[18] To a newspaper man he had said, ". . . we ought to be in [the war] now, for the conditions are getting desperate for the Allies, and it is possible we may come in too late." [19] One gets the impression that he had little hope of keeping the United States out of the war even though he had failed to prepare for the inevitable.

In spite of this, the President's followers chanted the "Wilson and Peace" slogan from one end of the country to the other, and for a time they seemed to have some ground for the claim, for Germany had temporarily suspended her attacks upon neutral shipping in the Atlantic. "Gerard's utterances had made it clear," the Kaiser said, "that Wilson was seeking a ladder for reelection. It was better, then, that we should offer him the ladder of peace than the ladder of war, which will eventually fall on our own heads." [20] Undoubtedly the moderate faction in Berlin succeeded in holding the murderous U-boats in leash in part because of the recognized advantage to Germany of keeping Wilson in the White House.

In October, 1916, however, that expedient arrangement began to crack up. Ambassador Gerard returned to the United States with an urgent message from von Jagow, German Secretary of State. Unless Wilson could do something quick for peace, von Jagow had said, "German public sentiment would compel

[17] Baker, *op. cit.*, pp. 250–253.

[18] Joseph P. Tumulty, *Woodrow Wilson as I Know Him*, p. 159, New York, Doubleday, 1921.

[19] Harold Garnet Black, *The True Woodrow Wilson* (New York, Revell, 1946), p. 161. Copyright, 1946, Fleming H. Revell Co.

[20] Bell, *op. cit.*, p. 256, quoting Count Bernstorff.

the government to give in to the demands" for resumption of unrestricted submarine warfare.[21] Before Gerard got across the Atlantic, it was evident that Wilson could do nothing. Briand and Lloyd George, feeling that Germany was on the ropes, had flatly rejected the idea of a negotiated peace.

Gerard's message became in effect, therefore, a warning that the slaughter of Americans on the high seas was soon to be resumed. His ill tidings were broadcast through the newspapers. Wilson thought it best to delay seeing Gerard until after the election in order to dispel the idea that a new submarine crisis was at hand. Trying to close his eyes to the ugly picture, he declared on October 21, "I am not expecting this country to get into the war." [22] He had previously declared that the Republican alternative to his policy would mean war.

After two weeks of hesitation Wilson saw Gerard and learned the painful truth firsthand. There was also a report from Joseph C. Grew, secretary to the American Embassy in Berlin, that the German Navy had asked the emperor to permit an immediate U-boat campaign. House carried to the President a secret memorandum from the Kaiser predicting that Germany would have to regain her "freedom of action." [23] The sinking of six steamships off the Island of Nantucket a month before the election gave special emphasis to these warnings and greatly alarmed the East. The juggernaut of war was rolling relentlessly toward American shores.

Burdened by this ominous knowledge, Wilson let his campaign run its course with increasing frenzy for peace. "He kept us out of war." "You are Working; Not Fighting!" "Alive and Happy;—Not Cannon Fodder!" "Wilson with Peace and Honor?" Or "Hughes with Roosevelt and War?" [24] The wild oratory for a peace that had already vanished was accompanied by a lavish display of posters depicting the carnage of war, with a horrified mother and her children looking on. Underneath the legend proclaimed, "He has protected me and mine."

It is doubtful whether any other presidential campaign has reached comparable depths of slogan intoxication. Wilson had been hoodwinked by the Germans; and now that his illusions were exploding, his followers were continuing to hoodwink the people for the sake of his reelection. The fact that he was to become a great war President does not minimize the disingenuousness of the means thus used to return him to power.

In contrast, Hughes did not have access to the confidential State Department reports or to Ambassador Gerard. He did not know that war was imminent. Yet he honestly reminded his audiences that it might be necessary to go to war to protect American rights and interests. He took note of the

[21] Baker, *op. cit.*, VI, 356.
[22] *Ibid.*, p. 360.
[23] *Ibid.*, 361.
[24] *New York Times*, Nov. 4, 1916.

pledge in the Democratic platform of 1912 to protect American citizens in all parts of the world. "That is good doctrine," he said at Seattle, "and I believe in making it real. I do not think that in making it real we should encounter the danger of war. I would not shrink if we did in performing our obvious duty." [25] "We have honest rights," he reiterated at St. Louis, "and, so far as I am concerned, I am not too proud to fight to maintain those rights." [26]

The crowd roared approval in Ogdensburg when he declared, "I do not want to be President of a people that are not ready to give their all for their liberties, their land, their country that they love." [27] He felt that the United States should stand as the champion of international law and human rights. If the country "thought more of dollars than of human lives," he said, it should not turn to him.

At Louisville on October 12 Hughes finally answered the question which the press had been throwing at him ever since the campaign began and which no one had given him a chance to answer in an open rally. As he condemned Wilson's shilly-shallying, Augustus J. Bizot, a Democratic lawyer, stood up and asked, "What would you have done when the *Lusitania* was sunk?"

"Put him out!" yelled the audience.

"Please permit the question to be asked," Hughes shouted. "I do not want any one shut off from a courteous question. Go on, sir."

It took half an hour to quiet the crowd so that the question could be answered. At last Hughes made himself heard:

> I would have had the State department at the very beginning of the Administration so equipped as to command the respect of the world [applause]; and, next, when I said "strict accountability," every nation would have known that that was meant; and, further, when notice was published with respect to the action threatened, I would have made it known in terms unequivocal and unmistakable that we should not tolerate a continuance of friendly relations . . . if that action were taken; and the *Lusitania* would never have been sunk.[28]

Hughes strongly insisted that he was a man of peace and that his policy of preparedness and firm protection of American lives would keep the country out of war. Possibly he was right. Germany unleashed her U-boats after Wilson's reelection because, as Admiral von Holtzendorff wrote on December 10, "There is reason to hope that . . . the United States will confine itself to the use of big words." [29] But it is more probable that it would have been too late in the winter of 1916–1917 for a policy of firm dealing and preparedness to succeed. Germany had one chance left, and she gambled on success before the befuddled and unarmed giant across the Atlantic could bestir him-

[25] *Ibid.*, Aug. 15, 1916. [26] *Ibid.*, Sept. 3, 1916. [27] *Ibid.*, Oct. 28, 1916.
[28] *Ibid.*, Oct. 13, 1916. [29] *Official German Documents*, II, 1183.

self. The fact remains that Hughes' policy of facing up to the German menace and of preparing to meet the consequences, whatever they might be, was infinitely more realistic than the "Wilson and Peace" slogan, which turned sour two months after the election.

In November, 1916, however, many Americans were intoxicated with the idea that they could reap the fabulous profits of war and let the Europeans do the fighting and dying. With this head-in-the-sand attitude encouraged by a great political party, the people of the West, feeling remote from the war, swarmed into the polls and voted their illusions.

Chapter 34

DEFEAT WITHOUT BITTERNESS

HUGHES closed his campaign at Madison Square Garden in New York, with 62,000 supporters parading and yelling their devotion to himself, Mrs. Hughes, and Theodore Roosevelt. When the cheering finally subsided that Saturday night, the candidate and his wife went to the Hotel Astor to catch up on sleep and await the voice of the people. Both had come through their ordeal in good health and excellent humor.

On election day, November 7, Mrs. Hughes took her three daughters to see *The Music Master*. The candidate had a good sleep. Awaking after dark, he looked out over Times Square, where a huge lighted signboard advertised, "U.S. Tires." "Perhaps they will complete that tomorrow," he joked, "by adding 'of Wilson.'" Many New Yorkers were betting that the people were tired of Wilson, the odds being ten to seven on Hughes.

As the family ate dinner, friends repeatedly burst into their suite to overwhelm them with good news, and an avalanche of favorable bulletins descended upon their table. Robert Fuller said Hughes had carried New York by 100,000. Governor Whitman telephoned his congratulations from Albany. Chester Rowell wired his from California. The *World* and several other New York newspapers conceded Hughes' election. Reporters begged for a statement. "Wait till the Democrats concede my election," Hughes replied; "the newspapers might take it back." [1] It began to appear that the Republican ticket might carry every state outside the solid South. Times Square flashed the news of a great Hughes victory to a crowd estimated at a hundred thousand.

An American flag was flung out from the roof of the Astor with two searchlights playing upon it. Beside it a huge electric sign blazoned "HUGHES" through the night. Delegations from the Republican and Union League clubs importuned the "President-elect" to appear on the balcony and accept the plaudits of the milling multitude below. "If I have been elected President," Hughes replied, "it is because the people of this country think that I'll keep my shirt on in an emergency. I'll start right now by not yielding to this demand when I am not positive that I have been elected." [2]

Meanwhile Mrs. Hughes aroused nine-year-old Elizabeth so that she might share the family's great moment in history. "Elizabeth, you should see this,"

[1] *New York Times*, Nov. 8, 1916. [2] Berrits' Memorandum, VII, 35.

her mother said as they went to the window. The *Times* was flashing the election of Hughes. A sea of humanity below was yelling, "Hughes! Hughes! Hughes!" The child rubbed her eyes and took in the scene with an inner glow of delight.

Excitement was still running high at midnight when Hughes concluded that he preferred sleep to further returns. It has been repeated ten thousand times that he went to bed assuming he was elected, but he did not. Hughes never took for granted anything that was uncertain. Wishful conclusions were utterly contrary to his nature. When he retired that night, his thinking went no further than that his election seemed probable.[3]

Another delightful bit of fiction is the story that a reporter bearing bad news to Hughes' door the next morning was informed by his son that "the President" could not be disturbed and replied, "When he wakes up tell him he's no longer President." Much repetition of this remark does not alter the fact that Charles Evans Hughes, Jr., did not stay at the Astor over election night. After leaving his parents about midnight, young Hughes and his wife spent a couple of hours at Republican headquarters and then returned to their own home in New York. Nor did any other member of the Hughes family talk with a reporter that morning. The story is "such stuff as dreams are made on."

When Hughes awoke about 8:00 A.M., he was still being greeted as President-elect by numerous newspaper editorials filled with gratuitous advice. But the returns then coming in told a different story. While Hughes had swept the East, Wilson had swept the South and West. As the day wore on, the count stood: Wilson, 251 electoral votes; Hughes, 247, with California, Minnesota, North Dakota, and New Mexico still doubtful. Hughes' restrained optimism of the night before quickly vanished, and he prepared to face defeat with good grace.

In the difficult two days that followed, the Hughes family went to the theater twice, drove about the city, received hundreds of friends, and waited for the final returns from California. Hughes' poise and dignity were utterly unshaken. On Wednesday, Chairman Willcox prepared a statement and asked Hughes' permission to release it. Hughes said it would not do and while he was still on the telephone dictated a wholly objective and unemotional statement of the situation as it then stood. It was not until Friday morning that Wilson's victory was confirmed. On Tuesday night the President had been dissuaded by Tumulty from conceding the election of Hughes. Because of the emergency he was prepared, moreover, to turn the Presidency over to Hughes immediately. He had written to Secretary of State Lansing asking him, in the event of Hughes' election, to resign along with Vice President Marshall. Wilson would then appoint Hughes Secretary of State and resign himself so that, under the law

[3] Author's interview with CEH, Jan. 7, 1946.

then in effect, Hughes would succeed him without waiting for the four-month interval separating election day from inauguration day.[4] Hughes never indicated whether or not he would have cooperated in this plan if he had been elected.

With some states going Democratic by only a few hundred votes, Republican cries of "fraud" were heard, but Hughes quickly suppressed them. When all the returns were in two weeks later, he sent his congratulations to Wilson:

> Because of the closeness of the vote I have awaited the official count in California and now that it has been virtually completed, permit me to extend to you my congratulations upon your reelection. I desire also to express my best wishes for a most successful administration.[5]

The final electoral vote was 277 to 254, and the popular vote stood: Wilson, 9,129,606; Hughes, 8,538,221. Each candidate received more votes than had ever been cast for a presidential nominee before. Since Hughes got about a million more votes than both Roosevelt and Taft had in 1912, he had succeeded reasonably well in reuniting the rank and file of the Republican and Progressive parties. But California had denied him the 3,775 votes he needed to win, while Hiram Johnson, on the same ticket, was carrying California by nearly 300,000 votes.

The delayed count in California and the closeness of the vote dramatically emphasized the part that state had played in Hughes' defeat. He had lost the Presidency on that "day of rest" in Los Angeles because, through no fault of his own, he had not shaken hands with Johnson. The Senator-elect from California was promptly accused by many Republicans of betraying his party's presidential candidate. The resulting controversy will probably never be finally settled, but a few facts appear to be well established. Johnson and some of his lieutenants continued to speak for Hughes after the Virginia Hotel incident, but the word went around among his followers to vote for Johnson and Wilson.[6] Hughes was severely cut in San Francisco, Sacramento, and Fresno—the Progressive strongholds. Southern California gave him a plurality of more than 40,000 votes. It is clear enough that Johnson's followers were disgruntled.

The initial mistake was Hughes' insistence on making the California tour while the primary fight was in progress, although the situation would have been even more complicated later if Booth had won the Republican nomination, as he came within 15,000 votes of doing. To this must be added Hughes' delay in asking Johnson to preside at one of his rallies and his overly generous words to Crocker. But these errors resulting from lack of familiarity with the California situation would have been erased from the mind of a less vindictive man

[4] Copy of Wilson's letter to Lansing in Hughes Papers.
[5] Ray Stannard Baker, *Woodrow Wilson: Life and Letters*, VI, 300.
[6] John Murray Marshall's letter in Boston *Evening Transcript*, Dec. 16, 1916.

than Hiram Johnson by Hughes' friendly overtures at Los Angeles. After failing to extend a minimum of courtesy to the visiting candidate, Johnson made it impossible to overcome the repercussions from his own aloofness at Long Beach.

Hughes harbored no animosity toward Johnson. Years later when he was Secretary of State one of his subordinates drafted a bristling reply to a query from Senator Johnson. Laughing heartily, Hughes exclaimed, "I may not feel like sending love and kisses to Senator Johnson, but I'm certainly not going to sign a letter of this kind." He ordered the letter to be redrafted to make it a courteous and considerate reply.[7]

More damaging to the Republican cause than the California incident was Willcox's general mismanagement of the campaign. Hughes could have won if he had had a few thousand additional votes in New Mexico, North Dakota, and New Hampshire or in several other states. In congratulating him when it was believed that he had been elected, the *New York Herald* said editorially that he had been "handicapped by bungling campaign management from the start." [8] "Mr. Hughes did better than the Republicans had any excuse for expecting," said the *New York Times*.[9]

Willcox had been quite unaware of the prairie fire of pacifism that was sweeping the West. Only Charles Beecher Warren had sensed it. At his request Hughes had returned to Michigan and, as a result, carried that state. Obviously he should have stayed in the Midwest instead of going to the border states. Hughes always felt that if he had discovered Will Hays in time to have made him campaign manager in 1916, his victory would have been assured.

Another incredible blunder that any experienced manager would have avoided was the women's campaign train sponsored by Mrs. Payne Whitney, Mrs. Cornelius Vanderbilt, Mrs. Mary Harriman Rumsey, Mrs. Elizabeth Stotesbury, and others. Not every woman on the train was the "incarnation of fat dividends," but enough were in that category to make their campaigning a source of irritation instead of good will. The train was promptly dubbed the "Billion Dollar Special." Western women who had the vote especially resented advice on how to use it from voteless Eastern moneybags. This venture may well have cost Hughes more votes than he won by his forthright stand for woman suffrage.

Finally, there was the incubus of Roosevelt's war speeches. Because of the previous split in the party, Roosevelt's good will was indispensable to Hughes. But T. R. campaigned more for war than for the Republican-Progressive ticket. Since it was widely assumed that if Hughes were elected Roosevelt would have a hand in formulating the policies of his administration, this line

[7] Author's interview with Mrs. Ruth B. Shipley, Sept. 9, 1949.
[8] Nov. 8, 1916. [9] Nov. 11, 1916.

of campaigning gave the Democrats an opportunity to exploit the war issue with devastating effect. A group of New York Democrats who had supported Hughes wired their congratulations to Roosevelt on the election of Wilson to which, they said, "you contributed more than any other person in America. . . . Wilson ought to give you a Cabinet position," the telegram continued, "as you elected him beyond doubt . . . you made Wilson a million votes." [10] Many Progressives also went over to Wilson to punish Roosevelt for his last-minute "betrayal" at Chicago.

Taft was filled with bitter regrets. On November 10 he wrote to Hughes:

My dear Governor,

The election seems to be against us. I write to express my profound disappointment at the result and my very great admiration for your bearing in the campaign, for the great speeches you made, for the unstinted energy with which you sacrificed yourself and the marvellous endurance you showed.

There never was a man in public life whom good luck has aided so much as Woodrow Wilson. Good luck and the most unblushing opportunism brought him his success. It makes one indignant to think how effective was his appeal to the opportunism of Americans. The Kansas farmers' motto was, "I don't care a dern what happens so long as it doesn't happen to me." This prevailed throughout the jack rabbit states. . . .

I feel myself conscience stricken in that I urged you to the great sacrifice you have made with so disappointing a result. What Wilson will do with the Court now, the Lord only knows. I hope that the brethren on the Bench will stay in the harness as long as possible to prevent any more injury than is inevitable. . . .

As I look through the States, I find you suffered much from the ill jointed condition of the party. If a candidate for Senator or Governor was a Republican, he gave his first attention to his own election—so too if he was a Progressive. Your interests were not made paramount as they should have been and as they would have been with a solid party. . . .

Please present my affectionate regard to Mrs. Hughes. . . .

Tell her that I know there are many worse things than defeat. I have had some experience in this. You have nothing to apologize for. You have nothing to take back. I hope to have the pleasure of talking the whole matter over at no distant day.

With great respect
greater than ever
Sincerely yours

Wm. H. Taft

Hughes was not cast down by his defeat. "I had done my best," he later wrote in his Notes. "While of course I did not enjoy being beaten, the fact that I did not have to assume the tasks of the Presidency in that critical time was an adequate consolation." His buoyancy of spirit is clearly reflected in his reply to Taft:

[10] Hughes Papers.

During the past few days I have been sitting up with the mourners and there has been no opportunity to answer your very kind letter. You must not chide yourself for urging me to make the fight. I had no honorable alternative in view of the action of the convention and I do not think that anyone of common sense has entertained the idea that my acceptance hurt the dignity of the Court. I did not wish to leave the bench, but it was a high privilege to be chosen to lead in the endeavor to establish sounder national policies and to make the Republican party once more an effective instrument of national service. So far as I am personally concerned, I have no complaints and no regrets.

There are some grounds for gratification. The miserable appeal to "Labor" as a class vote succeeded only in part. Its failure, for example, in New York was conspicuous. Apparently, it did succeed in Ohio, but that was an exception. The entire weight of Gompers' influence and the direct appeal of the federation were not sufficient to convince workingmen, as a class. There is hope in that. Then, the division was not along the lines of sympathy with the warring Nations. I am grateful for that also. On the other hand, it is mortifying that the cry of "peace and prosperity" was so potent. I fear that we shall suffer in the coming years through the revelation of our "soft spots." It is hard to understand California and Washington. They have not had the prosperity there that other parts of the country have enjoyed. The bitterness of the factional strife in California passes belief, and I presume it accounts for the result. Of course, I did not snub Johnson. I had no idea that he was in the Long Beach Hotel when I was there. . . . All the facts doubtless will appear in due time. . . .

It was a very difficult campaign—there were so many cross currents. At times, it seemed impossible—even here in the East—to hold together the groups whose support was essential to success. For your own able and untiring efforts I am most grateful. Your article in the "Yale Review" was a most convincing statement. Nothing fairer, more lucid, or more completely unanswerable appeared during the campaign. It seems incredible that the Administration of which such a criticism was possible should have received a vote of confidence. Despite its victory, I trust that the closeness of the vote and the manifest feeling in the most populous states will be heeded, and that hereafter the Administration will represent the Nation more worthily. If the recent contest has this result, it will not have been wholly in vain.

I have been waiting for the official count in California—the vote was so close, I could not do otherwise—to close this chapter, and on January first I shall return to the practice of the law in New York City with a feeling of eagerness for the varied activities which it permits.[11]

For a time Hughes was depressed when people stared at him on the subways or on the streets. But he persistently joked about his defeat in public as well as in private. Speaking to the New England alumni of Brown, he brought roars of laughter with his sallies at his own defeat. "This is a very happy time for me," he said, "for I have the pleasure of resuming entirely human relations." [12]

When Root welcomed him back to the law at a dinner given by the New York Bar Association and said that he was glad to see Hughes but "wished

[11] CEH to Taft, Nov. 20, 1916; Taft Papers. [12] *Boston Post*, Jan. 24, 1917.

he were somewhere else," the latter blasted all lamentations. "I have no wounds to exhibit," he said. "I shall say nothing of either battle or murder or sudden death. I have no desire to evoke sympathy by any suggestion of misfortune." [13]

As time rolled on he came to view the outcome in 1916 with philosophical satisfaction. When the United States went into the war in spite of the "Wilson and Peace" campaign, political differences were forgotten in that common struggle. Hughes could not help wondering whether the Democrats who had campaigned so vehemently for peace would have joined as wholeheartedly in the war effort if he had been President. Could Wilson have endured defeat and then urged his followers to support the new administration in the war effort without becoming bitter and vindictive? Wondering, Hughes told his friends, "It is better this way."

Again when Wilson went to his grave broken and disillusioned, Hughes expressed a thankfulness that he had escaped the tragic fate that fell to his opponent. "The Presidency in those war years would have killed me as it killed Wilson," he said. In his later life he thus came to look upon his defeat in 1916 as the key to a happy and fruitful future.

[13] *New York Times,* Jan. 23, 1917.

Chapter 35

CIVILIAN WAR WORKER

AFTER RESTING for a few weeks at Lakewood, Hughes embarked upon a new career for the fourth time in a decade. The idea of being President had been completely banished from his mind. He dropped the role of standard-bearer as completely as he had dropped the practice of law when he became governor and politics when he went to the Supreme Court. Now again he was a practicing lawyer. Instead of moping because he had been denied leadership of the nation, he set out to win leadership of the bar.

In order to finance his new venture, Hughes sold his Washington home and some furniture to Senator John W. Weeks, realizing $44,438.13. Aside from this, his assets consisted of $7,500 invested in mortgages. But money was no problem. One organization offered him $50,000 a year, without office expenses, to take charge of its legal work. Frank Munsey offered him an editorial berth on the New York *Sun* with a free hand in making policy. From Cadwalader, Wickersham & Taft came a still more attractive offer of the place in that firm vacated by the death of John L. Cadwalader in 1914. Hughes declined these enticing bids for his services because he wished to regain his position of independent counsel and to have his son, now a thoroughly trained and able lawyer, associated with him. Those objects could best be attained, he thought, by rejoining his old friends and partners, Arthur C. Rounds and George W. Schurman. His firm thus became Hughes, Rounds, Schurman & Dwight.

At once he was swamped with legal business and found it necessary to reject about as many cases as he accepted. As counsel for New York City, he gave an opinion that a proposed agreement between the city and the New York Central Railroad for West Side improvements was legal. He became referee in a suit by the Brooklyn Borough Gas Company to restrain enforcement of the eighty-cent gas law. When Mayor John Purroy Mitchel was cited for contempt by the New York Senate on a charge of having uttered a "false and malicious statement concerning Senator Robert F. Wagner," Hughes went to Albany to defend the mayor. In one of his patriotic outbursts, Mitchel had accused Wagner of being pro-German. There was a lively hearing and a heated argument that ended in the early morning hours with dismissal of the charges.

Relieved of official duties, Hughes also gave an enormous amount of time to civic work. In 1917 he was elected president of the Legal Aid Society, the

Union League Club, the New York State Bar Association, and the St. David's Society. A year later he became president of the Italy-America Society for encouragement of Italy's war effort. He made several speeches for the Red Cross and became chairman of the committee of lawyers conducting a special wartime Red Cross drive. In the field of politics he endorsed the Fusion Committee's renomination of Mayor Mitchel and spoke several times for him; he headed a committee working for the renomination and election of Justices McLaughlin and Cardozo and supported William L. Ransom for district attorney.

The impending involvement of the United States in the war overshadowed everything else in the winter and spring of 1917. Less than three months after his defeat Hughes was urging all Americans to "stand loyally behind the President, without a partisan thought." [1] On March 20, six hundred Republicans met at the Union League Club behind closed doors and virtually declared war on Germany ahead of the government. "Let us not delude ourselves," Hughes pleaded. "Germany is making war upon the United States, making war with a ruthless barbarity. . . . Our citizens have been murdered, are being murdered. Our ships have been sunk. . . . I regard these attacks, the method of their conduct, as an onslaught on liberty and on civilization itself." [2] Roosevelt, Root, and Joseph H. Choate joined in declaring that Germany's illegal attacks should be repelled. The resolution that was passed "begged the President to give the people a chance to defend themselves."

War talk continued when Roosevelt, Root, Robert Bacon, and Hughes foregathered in a café after the meeting. T. R. was bubbling over with fighting zeal and the conviction that he should have a military command abroad. "You must see Wilson," he declared, turning to Root and Hughes, "and get his consent to let me go." His voice deepened with solemnity and emotion. "I must go," he said, "but I will not come back. My sons will go too, and they will not come back." For a moment there was silence out of respect for T. R.'s evident sincerity. Then Root spoke up, with his unfailing humor, "Theodore, if you can make Wilson believe that you will not come back, he will let you go." [3]

Wilson summoned Congress to meet on April 2, and the war resolution was signed four days later. Hughes was delighted to see Wilson's policy transformed from hesitation and weakness to strong prosecution of the war, and he took advantage of every opportunity to throw his support behind the Administration.[4] While he did not speak as the leader of the opposition party, thinking it absurd for a defeated candidate to retain any such prerogative, he threw all the influence of his personality as a private citizen into the war effort.

[1] *New York Times*, Feb. 2, 1917.
[2] *Ibid.*, March 21, 1917.
[3] CEH, Notes, p. 239.
[4] *New York Times*, April 13, 26, and May 2.

At the same time he insisted on maintaining the rights of free criticism. Focusing the spotlight upon governmental mistakes was as much a part of the war effort as the making of steel and ships. No democratic leader could ask immunity from it. Much as he deplored politics in wartime, Hughes declared that if he had to choose between partisanship with criticism and the absence of both he would unhesitatingly take the former alternative. His acid test of criticism was its effect on the war effort. If it merely caused embarrassment, the people would have none of it. If it helped, the more of it, the better. For this high-minded attitude, the New York *Sun* dubbed him "the Patriotic Critic."

The country was in an intellectual ferment. Participation in a world war for the first time not only unleashed new powers; it brought also a flood of new problems for the traditionally isolated American Republic. Hughes could no more be impassive in this situation than could a bobolink at the burst of dawn. As his law practice took every moment of his office hours, he and Mrs. Hughes were often up at 5:00 A.M., he to write speeches and she to make coffee and lend moral support to his efforts.

At the first of a series of meetings held by the National Conference on Foreign Relations, he urged a concert of all the great powers after the war, with the United States taking the lead:

> If the world is to be made safe for democracy, it must be a world in which the nations recognize and maintain the supremacy of law. . . . If we can see at all into the future we know that it offers no chance for isolation to the United States. We have vast resources and extraordinary privileges and we cannot shirk our duty to mankind. Self-interest as well as a proper sense of obligation demand that we should aid in rearing the structure of international justice, and certainly that we should not make its establishment impossible by holding aloof.[5]

When the American Bar Association met at Saratoga in September, 1917, Hughes blasted the timorous and narrow-visioned groups that were saying America could not fight a modern war without destroying the Constitution. "While we are at war," he declared, "we are not in revolution. . . . The Constitution is as effective today as it ever was and the oath to support it is just as binding. But the framers of the Constitution did not contrive an imposing spectacle of impotency. . . . A nation which could not fight would be powerless to secure 'the Blessings of Liberty to Ourselves and our Posterity.'"

To those who were saying that the draft law which Congress had passed in May was unconstitutional, Hughes replied, "The power vested in Congress is not to raise armies simply by calling for volunteers, but to raise armies by whatever method Congress deems best, and hence must be deemed to embrace

[5] *Proceedings of the Academy of Political Science in the City of New York,* Vol. 7, No. 2, July, 1917, pp. 195–207.

conscription. The power to wage war," he went on, "is the power to wage war successfully." Since nations were fighting with all their economic strength, Congress could also regulate the food supply as well as industrial plants and materials essential to military success. At the same time, he said, the basic rights of the individual remained secure against "unwarrantable attack."

"It has been said that the Constitution marches," Hughes concluded. "That is, there are constantly new applications of unchanged powers, and it is ascertained that in novel and complex situations, the old grants contain, in their general words and true significance, needed and adequate authority. So, also, we have a *fighting* Constitution. We cannot at this time fail to appreciate the wisdom of the fathers, as under this charter . . . the people of the United States fight with the power of unity,—as we fight for the freedom of our children and that hereafter the sword of autocrats may never threaten the world." [6]

Distributed throughout the country, the speech was widely applauded, and its reasoning was reaffirmed by the Supreme Court. Hughes' happy phrase "a *fighting* Constitution" was to be reechoed by the Supreme Court in World War II, and the speech continues to be read as one of the most authoritative and compelling statements on "War Powers Under the Constitution" in our political literature.

On July 26, 1917, Hughes interrupted his strenuous regimen of legal work and speechmaking for a vacation in the White Mountains. The morning after his arrival Governor Whitman notified him of his appointment as chairman of the District Draft Appeals Board for New York City. Without even taking a day to indulge his regrets, he returned to New York and plunged into a most exacting task.

This appeals board consisted of thirty members, including Chief Judge Edgar M. Cullen of the New York Court of Appeals, former Presiding Justice George L. Ingraham of the Appellate Division of the New York Supreme Court, Judge Edwin L. Garvin, who was secretary of the board, George W. Wickersham, Louis Marshall, William N. Dykman, and other distinguished men. Its jurisdiction covered the entire city, with many local draft boards and nearly 600,000 registrants. When Hughes took over, a vast number of appeals were awaiting decision, and there was no organization to handle them. He had the baffling problem of "building a wagon and riding in it at the same time."

Mail poured in upon the board at the rate of 4,000 pieces a day. Crowds of men seeking to have their appeals heard overwhelmed its makeshift quarters in the old New York Post Office Building. The volume of work was staggering. Hughes borrowed a number of trained men from two leading banks and the New York Telephone Company. The board was divided into six subcommittees, each with many clerks and assistants, to which the appeals were

[6] Address of Sept. 5, 1917; Hughes Papers.

initially directed. When a subcommittee had about fifty cases ready, it would take the list to Hughes' desk, the committee would gather around, and each appeal for exemption from service would be granted or denied. In this manner the board decided about a thousand cases a day.

Since it might be a question of life or death, Hughes insisted on signing in person the papers of every man who came before the board. There were hundreds of these papers to be signed in quadruplicate every day. While the organization was taking shape, the chairman toiled until midnight or later every night. He and Judge Garvin were "nearly floored by the task." [7] His digestive system refused to function, and for a time it appeared that his health might be seriously impaired. Mrs. Hughes came back from the White Mountains to see that he got proper food, and, as always, her presence brought relief.

Overburdened though he was, Hughes found time to greet his daughter in verse on her nineteenth birthday, August 11, 1917:

To Catherine—

My dearest Katrine
As you are nineteen
It's time that I write you a letter;
Enclosed you will find
Not a piece of my mind
But a check which no doubt you'll like better.

My advice, it is slight
For I cannot indite
Any words which meet the occasion;
To a wise Sophomore
It is always a bore
To be subject to too much dictation.

It will not be amiss
To send you a kiss*
And the love which ever grows greater;
Once more I'm away
On your happy birthday
Here's hoping for better luck later.

Many happy returns and every good wish from

FATHER

* Meaning many kisses, but the miserable necessities of rhyme interfere with the expression of my affection.

His son's participation in the war gave him many anxious hours. Young Hughes enlisted as a private in November, 1917. in spite of the fact that, being the father of two children, he was not likely to be drafted. Both he and his

[7] CEH, Notes, p. 241.

Thirty-two East Sixty-fourth Street

To Catherine — Aug. 11, 1917

My dearest Katrine
As you are nineteen
It's time that I write you a letter
Enclosed you will find
Not a piece of my mind
But a check which no doubt you'll like better.

My advice, it is slight—
For I cannot indite—
Any words which meet the occasion
To a wise Sophomore
It is always a bore
To be subject to too much dictation

[not through yet — over]

It will not be amiss
To send you a kiss*
And the love which ever grows greater
Once more I'm away
On your happy birthday
Here's hoping for better luck later.

Many happy returns
And every good wish from
Father

*Meaning many kisses, but the miserable necessities of rhyme interfere with the expression of my affection —

father scorned any suggestion of special privilege for him. He went overseas with the 305th Field Artillery as a regimental sergeant major. Hughes had spoken with the utmost seriousness when he said, "We should spare nothing in prompt and intelligent preparation for the vigorous conduct of the war."

At the Draft Appeals Board he bore his burden patiently. When he was inadvertently kept waiting for an unconscionable period in the outer office of Major Judge Advocate Hugh S. Johnson (later administrator of the NRA), Johnson apologized profusely for wasting the time of so distinguished a citizen.

"There are no distinguished citizens," Hughes replied, "except as they are doing distinguished duty." [8]

During the fall and winter he resumed his speechmaking, but his law practice had gone to pot. Occasionally he took an hour or two off from his unpaid war work for consultation on a case, and once he dashed to Chicago overnight, argued the American Press Association case at a special session of the Circuit Court of Appeals, left Chicago two hours after his arrival, and was back at the Draft Appeals Board the next morning. Many cases that would normally have come to him went to other lawyers, and others piled up to await his resumption of active practice after the war.

Although he had sat on the Supreme Bench for six years, Hughes argued his first case before that court on December 12, 1917.[9] While in Washington he asked for an appointment with the President and found Wilson both courteous and agreeable. That was not surprising, for in spite of their spirited fight in 1916, Hughes had since generously and consistently supported the President. Now he offered to take any wartime assignment in which the President might find his services useful. Five months were to pass, however, before the President would take advantage of the offer.

The spring of 1918 brought a new German offensive, new horrors of gas warfare, and the disastrous treaty of Brest-Litovsk in which Russia's new Bolshevik government made a humiliating peace with an apparently victorious Germany. Root and Hughes had led a mass meeting which rejoiced in "the triumph of democracy in Russia" when the Romanoff dynasty had been overthrown, but the subsequent destruction of the Kerensky régime by Lenin and Trotsky had turned their hopes to ashes. Hughes promptly aired his profound distrust of the new dictatorship of the proletariat, and that distrust was to remain with him to the end of his days.

As if to add to the gloom of the war news from Europe, typewriters began to click and tongues to wag about a scandalous breakdown of the American aircraft program. The most alarming charges were made by Gutzon Borglum, the sculptor. Wilson had authorized Borglum to run down the facts, but he came up with only more fuel to feed the sensation he had created. With the

[8] Johnson's radio address, April 13, 1937. [9] *Towne* v. *Eisner*, 245 U.S. 418.

nation's resources at its command, he said, the Aircraft Board had not produced a single service or battle plane that could be ordered across the lines. Hundreds of millions of dollars had been squandered, he claimed, and enormous contracts given to men having no connections with aircraft production solely because of their "pull" with Colonel E. A. Deeds.[10]

Wilson repudiated Borglum and appointed a committee to examine his charges. By this time the aircraft program was under attack from many quarters. The Senate Committee on Military Affairs launched an investigation. The press drew pointed contrasts between the War Department's "almost boastful aviation promises" and its meager performance. Wilson ordered a full-fledged inquiry by Attorney General T. W. Gregory and was further criticized for having one segment of his Administration investigate another on the eve of the 1918 congressional campaigns.

The President's deep concern led him at last to appeal to Hughes, apparently at the suggestion of Colonel House. On May 13, 1918, he wrote to his former opponent:

> Because of the capital importance of this branch of the military service, I feel that these charges should be thoroughly investigated and with as little delay as possible. . . . I requested the Department of Justice to use every instrumentality at its disposal to investigate these charges, and, with the approval of the Attorney General, I am writing to beg that you will act with him in making this investigation. I feel that this is a matter of the very greatest importance, and I sincerely hope that you will feel that it is possible to contribute your very valuable services in studying and passing upon the questions involved.[11]

"You may be assured," Hughes replied, "that nothing would give me greater pleasure than to render any assistance within my power." [12]

Resigning from the Draft Appeals Board, he wound up his affairs in New York within three days and took the train to Washington. Actually he regarded the aircraft inquiry as a cross that had to be borne. While his appointment was being rumored, several Republican leaders had begged him not to pull Wilson's chestnuts out of the fire. "The country is at war," Hughes had replied. "Our troops at the front are fighting without aircraft." His long experience in investigative work told him that he had been drafted for one of the most unpleasant civilian assignments of the war, but he plunged into it without the slightest hesitation.

At the outset Hughes made certain that he would have a free hand and that the findings of the investigation would be made public.[13] One other condition he laid down was that he should select his own assistant. The young attorney to whom he turned was Meier Steinbrink of Brooklyn, who had been with him in

[10] New York *World*, March 21, 1918.
[11] Wilson to CEH, Hughes Papers.
[12] CEH to Wilson, May 14, 1919.
[13] CEH to T. W. Gregory, May 18, 1918.

the Draft Appeals Board and who later became a justice of the New York Supreme Court.

Arriving in Washington, Hughes almost took the Attorney General's breath away by saying that he would launch the investigation the next morning. The very first witness, Colonel S. E. Wolff, brought in evidence of gross inefficiency. Wolff insisted that he would have to go to Paris to find out the extent of the United States' commitments to supply airplanes to Great Britain and France. Contracts to build planes for our allies had been authorized up to $47,000,000, but from the reports he had been getting Wolff feared that "over commitments" had been made possibly to the extent of $304,000,000.[14] Hughes suggested that the information be obtained by cable. Wolff replied that his cables brought no satisfactory results. Hughes scrutinized the officer's stack of cablegrams signed "Pershing" and agreed that they added up to confusion. When Hughes called Secretary Baker, he knew nothing about the inadequacy of the records or of Wolff's plan to go to Paris for want of an accurate cablegram. But Baker hastened to cable General Pershing, and the information was then forthcoming.[15]

Colonel Wolff also supplied figures showing how much the Army had spent on aircraft up to that time. Nearly five months later, when Wolff brought in more recent figures, Hughes called for a comparison of the two totals, and Wolff could not remember the sum he had named in May. "Wasn't it so and so?" Hughes asked, drawing upon his amazing memory. Steinbrink checked the record and found that his chief was right, down to the last digit.[16]

To avoid embarrassment to the war effort or disclosure of military secrets the hearings were conducted *in camera*. Attorney General Gregory or his assistant, William L. Frierson, later Solicitor General, was always present and kept a close watch on everything Hughes did. The investigator welcomed this precaution as insurance against any charge of improper conduct. Only once, however, did the Attorney General ask a question. There was no interference. Nor was there any consultation between the investigators and the silent watchers as to how the inquiry should be conducted. Week after week the story of an infant industry struggling for mass production under loose and ineffective supervision was unfolded, until 280 witnesses had been examined and 17,000 pages of testimony had been taken. When the investigators moved from Washington to Dayton, Detroit, New Brunswick, and Buffalo, Hughes visited aircraft and "Liberty engine" factories, examined company books and records, and questioned executives without taking them away from their vital work for any length of time.

Because of the quiet nature of the investigation, many defects in the make-

[14] *Aircraft Hearings*, I, 1ff., National Archives. [15] CEH, Notes, pp. 242–243.
[16] Author's interview with Judge Steinbrink, July 24, 1947.

shift aircraft procurement system were corrected without publicity as Hughes brought them to official attention. He was thus successful in greatly stimulating the production of military planes. The exposure of official misconduct was a decidedly secondary aim.

While in Washington, Hughes and Steinbrink lived together in a little house on New Hampshire Avenue. They became good friends and shared all the work, disappointments, and exhilaration of the aircraft inquiry together. Steinbrink was fascinated by Hughes' companionability and his skill in distilling the essence of humor from the miscellany of each day's activities. One summer morning Steinbrink noticed through the open door of Hughes' room a strange shadow moving rhythmically up and down in the light of the rising sun. His curiosity impelled him to investigate. What he found was the supposedly austere gentleman who had missed the Presidency by a hairsbreadth down on the floor doing push-ups.

"Oh, it's you," said Steinbrink. "I couldn't imagine what on earth you were doing."

"Well, what do you think now?" Hughes asked as he continued his daily dozen.

"It looks as if you were sweeping up the floor with your whiskers," Steinbrink ventured. Hughes rolled over on his back and laughed convulsively.

"Steinbrink," he asked in the course of one of their congenial chats, "why does the public continue to regard me as a human icicle?"

"I think there are two reasons," his friend replied with the utmost candor. "First, the public doesn't know you. Second, you wear a full beard. Can you think of any public man with a big, formidable beard who has the reputation of being affable and friendly?"

A few days later Hughes trimmed his beard notably shorter. Al Smith was quick to observe the change when next they met at a Gridiron dinner. "Why, Governor," he exclaimed, "you've bobbed it!"

The most dramatic episodes of the investigation concerned the activities of Colonel Deeds, who had been in charge of the aircraft program as head of the Signal Corps' Equipment Division. Before taking that assignment, Deeds had been associated with H. E. Talbott and Charles F. Kettering in numerous business enterprises at Dayton, Ohio. Just before going to Washington in 1917, he had helped Kettering and Talbott organize the Dayton Wright Airplane Company (although he did not become a stockholder) which was subsequently given highly profitable Government contracts. Borglum had charged Deeds with staggering offenses, and one of Hughes' most important tasks was to sift out the facts regarding the colonel's interests and activities.

At Dayton, Talbott was examined in detail on his relations with Deeds. His memory seemed to be conveniently vague, and there was a good deal of difficulty in nailing down the facts. While Hughes was plying the witness with questions, Steinbrink walked over to the plant's filing room and told a clerk that Mr. Talbott would like to have the confidential file. The clerk yielded it without question, and the attorney, opening it to "Deeds" and "Talbott," found telegrams which established a confidential relationship between the two men after Deeds had taken charge of the aircraft production program for the Army. Confronted by this evidence, Talbott was compelled to shift his testimony from intellectual fencing to pertinent comment on concrete facts.

That evening the investigators shared a good deal of satisfaction as they walked together to their hotel. Steinbrink told the story of how he had obtained the confidential file. "Steinbrink," was Hughes' pithy comment, "Deeds not words!" [17]

It was late in October when the inquiry was completed. Hughes then worked frantically on his report. During the last three days he wrote steadily in longhand, stopping for very little sleep. Steinbrink checked the facts against the exhibits and testimony. On Saturday morning they delivered the report to the Attorney General. Gregory was very pleased with its objectivity and hastened to Hughes' office to tell him so. Frierson had independently written an elaborate report of the inquiry, but Gregory discarded it. "I have $100,000 available to pay for this excellent piece of work," he told Hughes, but the latter would take nothing more than reimbursement for his actual cash outlays. Steinbrink, conferring separately with the Attorney General, also refused compensation.

In sending the Hughes report to the White House with only a brief supplement of his own, Gregory called it "a remarkably accurate statement of substantially all the transactions had since the beginning of the war in the course of the development of the aircraft program." After carefully examining this statement, he informed the President, "I find myself in substantial accord therewith and do not consider it necessary to present to you a somewhat full report which has heretofore been prepared in the Department of Justice. . . . I also find myself in accord with the conclusions presented by Judge Hughes on questions of dishonesty and malversation." [18]

A wave of relief swept over the country when the President released the report on October 31, 1918. Hughes had found incompetence, confusion, a lack of central responsibility in the aircraft program, and some minor violations of law but no thievery or major corruption. That good news coincided with the collapse of the Austro-Hungarian Empire and the seizure of a large slice of Belgian territory from the collapsing German armies. With only a few days remaining before the congressional elections, supporters of the Adminis-

[17] *Id.*

[18] *U.S. Department of Justice—Aircraft Inquiry* (Government Printing Office, 1918), p. 2 of supplement.

tration took immediate advantage of the Hughes report to confound the critics who had been making capital out of the Borglum charges.

"Probably there has never been a more searching and thorough investigation under direction of the Government," said the *New York Times*.[19] Wilson put his praise into a brief note:

> I write to express to you my sincere thanks for the painstaking and exhaustive examination you personally gave to the aircraft production situation, in cooperation with the Attorney General. I appreciate as much as the Attorney General does the thoroughness of the investigation and feel confident that the results of it put the country in possession of all the pertinent facts.[20]

The significance of the aircraft report was minimized, of course, by the Armistice of November 11. With the war over, the public quickly lost interest in the efficiency of the aviation industry, and the report became a target for those who found its unbiased presentation of facts distasteful. Chief among these were the friends of Colonel Deeds who tried to make it appear that Hughes maligned him by distorting the facts.

Actually Hughes cleared Deeds of the most serious charges that had been made against him. There was no evidence, he reported, that Deeds was pro-German, that he was guilty of major corruption or the violation of any statute. But the report did present evidence of "reprehensible conduct" and recommended disciplinary action through a court-martial. Although Deeds was under military discipline, he had continued to act as confidential adviser to his former business associates. To avoid criticism he had also falsified his report to the Secretary of War as to his stock holdings in companies with which the Aircraft Board might be doing business. And he was held responsible for statements grossly misleading the public as to the progress of the aircraft production program.

Secretary Baker sent the Hughes findings to the Judge Advocate General's office and got back a reply saying that "the report of Judge Hughes . . . clearly indicates conduct calling for his [Deeds'] trial by general court martial."[21] Not satisfied, Baker called in Acting Judge Advocate General S. T. Ansell and indicated that he wished to have additional facts considered. That unusual procedure led to the appointment of a "board of review" for the Deeds case, although boards of review usually hear only appeals from men convicted by courts-martial. The board took statements from Deeds' attorney and two business associates connected with the contracts that had been under scrutiny and exonerated him. A select committee of the House of Representatives found this conduct "astonishing and significant."[22]

[19] Nov. 1, 1918. [20] Wilson to CEH, Nov. 7, 1918.

[21] *Hearings of House Select Committee on Expenditures in the War Department—Aviation*, Serial 2, Vol. 3, p. 2667.

[22] *House of Representatives Report 637*, 66th Congress, 2nd session, p. 19.

Colonel Deeds' biographer, Isaac Marcosson, draws heavily upon this board's findings in attempting to dissipate the uncomplimentary facts disclosed by the Hughes report. He points especially to a telegram from Deeds to the Dayton Wright Airplane Company on August 3, 1917, urging that a sample De Haviland airplane which was being shipped to the Dayton plant be put under guard. The De Haviland 4 had been chosen as the foreign plane most suitable for adaptation to mass production in the United States, and sabotage was feared. The telegram is said to have been opened by a secretary who bruited its contents among employees of the plant. A desire to assure more restricted handling of such messages, says Marcosson, prompted Kettering to wire Deeds on August 4 and ask that all future "confidential telegrams" intended for the Dayton Wright Company be sent directly to Talbott or George B. Smith, who was both Deeds' and Talbott's confidential agent.[23] Deeds telegraphed his agreement.

The Hughes report made no mention of the telegram of August 3, and that fact has led several of his detractors to accuse him of suppressing it. Had he included this telegram in his report, along with the exchange of telegrams between Kettering and Deeds on August 4, it is said, his charge that Deeds was continuing to act as "confidential adviser" to his former business associates would have fallen flat. But that conclusion utterly ignores the testimony that Hughes had taken from Kettering, Talbott, and Deeds themselves. Talbott at first denied that he had had an arrangement for receipt of confidential telegrams, and when Hughes showed him the wire of August 4 he explained it as merely a means of expediting the delivery of telegrams to him.[24] Kettering also examined the August 4 message and said that his purpose in sending it was merely to establish a central delivery point for wires from Deeds. "I do not know," he said, "why we called them confidential telegrams."[25] Deeds said the chief purpose of the arrangement was to get telegrams through "without delay," although he touched upon the security angle. None of the three mentioned the telegram of August 3 that Hughes was later accused of suppressing. Apparently its relation to Kettering's wire of the following day, if it had any, was an afterthought. To accuse the investigator of suppressing a telegram that none of the witnesses concerned seemed to regard as worthy of mention is absurd on its face.

More important is the fact that Hughes' charge of reprehensible conduct rested only slightly on the telegrams of August 4 and very heavily upon Deeds' wire to Talbott on September 16, 1917, as follows:

> For your personal information as coming from your local attorney. Judge Advocate General has ruled it legal for Government to select one, contractor one

[23] Isaac F. Marcosson, *Colonel Deeds: Industrial Builder*, pp. 278–280.

[24] *Aircraft Hearings*, X, 596–597, National Archives.

[25] *Ibid.*, p. 714.

and the two a third, as appraisers of market value of plant at expiration of contract. If you care to raise the question the above will be found to be the final ruling.[26]

Hughes insisted at the hearing that the information Deeds was thus passing on to his former associate was "an inside tip."

"It depends," Deeds countered, "upon what sense is implied by the word 'tip.' "

"You said, 'For your personal information as coming from your local attorney!' " Hughes repeated.

"Yes, sir," Deeds admitted.

"That meant that the information you were giving in this telegram should be treated by him as though he had received it from his local attorney, did it not?"

"I imagine it did," Deeds again affirmed. He admitted that he had given inside information and did not wish to be known as the source of it.[27]

"When this last telegram, which puts in a strong light the relations of the parties, was sent, Deeds was an officer in the Army," Hughes wrote in his report. "This highly improper conduct, in holding communication in this manner with his former business associates in a transaction pending between the Dayton Wright Company and the Government Department in Colonel Deeds' charge, demands the attention of the military authorities." [28]

The exonerating board said that Talbott had been holding up a contract until the question of plant depreciation could be settled, that the Judge Advocate General had made an oral ruling to be followed by a written ruling, and that the information which Deeds passed along to Talbott was available to other contractors. The fact remains that Deeds had done precisely what Hughes accused him of. The case against Deeds was based on his own admissions. To say, as Mr. Marcosson does, that "Hughes was out to 'make a case' regardless of how it conflicted with the facts" [29] is to turn away from facts and make words do the ugly duty of smearing.

Hughes also examined in detail the charges that Deeds had violated the criminal statute forbidding any official to represent the Government in the transaction of business with a corporation in which he has a pecuniary interest. He could find no evidence to sustain this charge and frankly said so. But in setting forth the facts he did show the falsity of Deeds' letter of August 28, 1917, to the Aircraft Production Board and the Secretary of War, claiming that he had "made a bona fide transfer to other parties" of all his stocks in the four companies with which he had been associated. Deeds' 17,500 shares of United Motors Corporation stock were transferred on October 13, not in August (and then only to his wife), although Deeds claimed a previous "informal transfer."

[26] *Ibid.*, XXIII. 88ff. [27] *Ibid.* [28] *Aircraft Report*, pp. 32–33.

[29] Reprinted by permission of Dodd, Mead & Company from *Colonel Deeds: Industrial Builder*, by Isaac F. Marcosson, p. 280. Copyright, 1947, by Dodd, Mead & Company, Inc.

Deeds admitted that he still held his stock in the Domestic Building Company more than a year after he had told Secretary Baker that he had disposed of it.[30] He had merely arranged with Kettering to take this stock off his hands "if it should prove necessary."

Hughes' second count against Colonel Deeds was that he had given representatives of the Committee on Public Information "a false and misleading statement with respect to the progress of aircraft production." The official release of February 21, 1918, for which Deeds was responsible, had boasted:

> The first American built battle planes are today en route to the front in France. This first shipment, though in itself not large, marks the final overcoming of many difficulties met in building up this new and intricate industry.

Actually no planes had at that time been shipped overseas. Only one had been delivered from the factory for the AEF, and it did not leave the United States until a month later. No other shipments were made until April 3.

In his brief supplementary statement Attorney General Gregory found Deeds "guilty of censurable conduct" and underscored Hughes' recommendation of "disciplinary measures."[31] That alone is sufficient to buttress the objectivity of Hughes' findings. It is true that Hughes measured Colonel Deeds by a rigid and unbending concept of public duty. But it was the concept that he had consistently applied to himself and his own associates. Some of the other accusations in his report were petty. Hughes frankly recognized that fact but thought the law should be enforced against even minor infractions as a warning against future laxity. To deride a great investigator because he refused to whitewash deception, falsehood, and clandestine dealings in the public service is like assailing Moses because some people do not live up to the Decalogue.

[30] *Aircraft Hearings*, XXII, 565–571.

[31] *Aircraft Report*, supplement, p. 7.

Chapter 36

CHAMPION OF LIBERTY

HUGHES celebrated the end of the aircraft investigation by plunging into practice once more and making a series of speeches. His long silence during the inquiry had been broken only on such occasions as Bastille Day. Now he felt a release of spirit. As the country reeled with emotion and confusion in its shift from war to peace, his voice was heard and applauded before all sorts of audiences.

On October 29, 1918, he welcomed Governor Whitman and his fellow Republican candidates to the Union League Club. Four days later he breathed a fine idealism into the Madison Square rally of the United War Work Campaign. "I have read your living words and I cannot be silent," wrote one of his admirers. "One sentence especially rings in my ears: 'Democracy is not of the flesh but of the spirit—its forms in themselves are vain, and its meaning and justification must be found in service to mankind.' I thank you for that sentence: it is immortal." [1]

As president of the Legal Aid Society, he attempted to give every man assurance of legal protection of his rights. "There is no more serious menace," he said, "than the discontent which is fostered by a belief that one cannot enforce his legal rights because of poverty. . . . Without opportunity on the part of the poor to obtain expert legal advice, it is idle to talk of equality before the law." [2] His influence was a great stimulus to the movement within the legal profession to offer free service to those unable to pay for it.

Fate seemed to be marking the end of an era by removing some of its most eminent figures. On May 14, 1917, Joseph H. Choate, diplomat and great man of the bar, wrote a note to Hughes, whose early practice he had so much influenced. On the same day came news of his death. Theodore Roosevelt's restless spirit was finally stilled on January 5, 1919. Six months previously Hughes had signed a round robin urging T. R. to become a candidate for Governor of New York. It had then been widely assumed that Roosevelt would be the Republican presidential candidate in 1920. But he was not to enjoy any such revenge against the man in the White House. Hughes delivered the Roosevelt memorial address at the Republican Club in New York on February 9, with a

[1] Mrs. Spencer Trask to CEH, Nov. 5, 1918.
[2] *New York Times*, Aug. 28, 1920.

warm tribute to T. R.'s industry, courage, self-discipline, and democratic instinct.

The former Justice was called upon to honor new leaders no less than to eulogize those who had passed on. At a Lotos Club dinner he joined in lauding the character and achievements of Governor Alfred E. Smith. Some months later he presented the Civic Forum's medal of honor to Herbert Hoover, the wartime food-control wizard who had made a name for himself at home and abroad.

There seemed to be no end to the demand for Hughes' speeches. While he declined at least 95 per cent of the requests made of him, he found himself accepting the colors of a Negro infantry division, condemning the crime of lynching, denouncing the massacre of Jews in Europe, pleading for the rehabilitation of disabled soldiers, weighing the values in education, condemning arbitrary government, and delving into dozens of other subjects of general public interest. Busy as he was at the bar, he gave approximately one-third of his time to speeches and civic work. In 1919 he became president of the New York County Lawyers' Association, head of a commission to study war-risk insurance, president of the National Municipal League, and chairman of various other civic groups.

In the legal sphere it seemed that almost everyone with an intricate or baffling case was beating a path to Hughes' door. Many of his cases were brought to him by other lawyers eager to take advantage of his skill in stripping involved problems to their bare bones and laying the most complicated issues before a court with unfailing clarity. While he rejected numerous cases for want of merit, he never hesitated to take a case in which the odds were against him if he thought the issues were such that they should be presented to the court. In twenty-eight months he argued twenty-five cases in the United States Supreme Court in addition to the numerous cases that took him into the lower federal courts and the state courts. His reputation entitled him to the cream of the legal business, and his energy enabled him to take a thick skimming.

Once he accepted a case, Hughes threw himself into it with the vigor of a dynamo. Every litigant, he used to say, is entitled to have his case handled with all the ability and the resources at his counsel's command. John D. Rockefeller wanted an opinion as to whether he could put anything in his will that would prevent his executors (who would be getting millions anyway) from being allowed their statutory commissions. Hughes assigned the research to a new lawyer in the firm—Oscar R. Ewing. When Ewing reported on every New York case he could find, Hughes said, "Well, that's fine. Now what have you from outside of New York?" Ewing said that, as Rockefeller lived in New York, he had not supposed there would be any interest in decisions from other states. "Why," Hughes came back, "I want the law looked up for every state in the Union." [3]

In an argument he made it his business to know everything that his opponent could say. When he arose to argue, it was always a tour de force. He seemed to lose himself in the intensity of his own effort, but behind each performance was a studied technique designed to get his case so clearly, quickly, and cogently before the court as to forestall any objection to the conclusions he wished to draw before such objection could arise in a judge's mind.

Hughes would come into court with banners flying—with the air of one who had a great cause to defend. The judges were well aware of his forensic power. Judge Cardozo of the New York Court of Appeals once said that he always reserved judgment for twenty-four hours in any case argued by Hughes to avoid being carried away by the force of his personality and intellect.[4]

Yet there was neither arrogance nor overconfidence in Hughes' attitude. He scoffed at the idea that anything was important merely because he said it. Never did he assume that his reputation would make his argument irresistible. On the contrary, he tended to magnify in his own mind the strength of the opposition. And while his poise suggested that he was master of every situation, he always addressed the court with fear and trembling inside. It was not unusual for him to lie awake most of the night worrying about a case he was to present to the Supreme Court the next day. Sometimes he would go before the court feeling almost that he had his life in his hands.[5] But his self-control enabled him to pour his agitation into his argument, with the effect of adding power to reason.

His first big case after the Armistice was a suit against Postmaster General Albert Burleson challenging the Government's seizure of the Atlantic and Pacific cable systems. The President's seizure proclamation was dated November 2, 1918, but the action was not announced until November 21 and the actual seizure was alleged to have taken place five days after the Armistice became effective. Burleson had taken drastic action because of disagreement over cable charges and alleged discrepancies in figures provided by the companies to different governmental agencies. Hughes insisted that the action was "wholly unwarranted and arbitrary" and "beyond valid authorization."

Arguing for nearly three hours before Judge Learned Hand, Hughes rattled off numerous cases with scarcely a glance at the law books before him. Judge Hand ruled against him, and he carried the case to the Supreme Court. While rumors of a decision in his favor were being circulated in the spring of 1919, the cable systems were returned to their owners and the cases became moot.[6]

[3] Oscar Ewing to author, March 24, 1950.
[4] Justice Cardozo to Justice Owen J. Roberts to author.
[5] Author's interview with CEH, May 15, 1946.
[6] *Commercial Cable Co.* v. *Burleson*, 250 U.S. 360.

Hughes also challenged the validity of the Food Control Act of 1917 in a series of cases.[7] This statute made it a criminal offense to charge excessive prices for necessaries, without forbidding any specific or definite act and without setting up any ascertainable standard of guilt. Just before Hughes' argument in one of these cases, Judge Augustus N. Hand had fined some people $10,000 for charging too much for potatoes. That was in accord with a ruling of the Circuit Court of Appeals, but Hughes was so persuasive that Judge Hand deferred further decisions under the Act until a case then before the Supreme Court was decided.[8] In the Supreme Court, Hughes argued three cases involving the Act, and the court followed his logic in holding it unconstitutional, although choosing a case which he had not argued—*United States* v. *Cohen Grocery Company*—as the subject of its controlling opinion.

The National Prohibition Cases [9] were a severe test of Hughes' independence at the bar. The State of Rhode Island, with the aid of Root and Guthrie and the opulent backing of the brewing and liquor interests, was challenging the constitutionality of the Eighteenth Amendment. Guthrie urged his friend Hughes to join in a grand assault upon the right of Congress and the states to write "basic changes" or "alterations" such as the Eighteenth Amendment into the Constitution. It was reported that a fee of $500,000 was dangled before the former Justice. Actually no sum was mentioned. The liquor interests made it clear to him that the financial reward would be enormous, but they did not get to the point of discussing terms, for Hughes insisted that what they were trying to do was absurd and refused to have any part in it.[10]

Acceptance of this retainer would also have given him a chance to strike a blow at a policy he distrusted. While he had taken no part in the debate over drying up the flow of liquor by law, he felt from the beginning that national prohibition was both unwise and impracticable. But that was beside the point. Whether they acted wisely or unwisely, the people had an unlimited right to amend their Constitution as they saw fit.

After rejecting the money of the brewers, Hughes filed a brief as *amicus curiae* on behalf of twenty-one state attorneys general in support of the Eighteenth Amendment, for which he received a comparative pittance. Going back to the records of the Constitutional Convention, he showed that the Founding Fathers drew no distinction between "amendments" and "alterations." By Article V they had left the door wide open to any change that experience might prove to be desirable. Should the court limit the nature of changes that could be made, Hughes argued, our political system would be in danger of degenerating into despotism or revolution. The fate of the Eighteenth Amend-

[7] *Tedrow* v. *Lewis*, 255 U.S. 98, etc.
[8] Hughes memorial address by Judge Hand; Dec. 12, 1948.
[9] 253 U.S. 350.
[10] Author's interviews with CEH, Nov. 19, 1946, and June 4, 1947.

ment was insignificant compared to maintenance of this safety valve in the Constitution. The Supreme Court held to this view.

A Hughes opinion prepared for private clients in this period helped to give constitutional footing to the broad social legislation of the thirties and forties. The Supreme Court had not then definitely passed upon the meaning of the clause giving Congress power to "lay and collect Taxes . . . to pay the Debts and provide for the common defence and general Welfare of the United States. . . ." Several bond houses sought Hughes' advice as to whether the Federal Farm Loan Act of 1916 was consistent with this general welfare clause and whether the tax-exempt bonds to be issued under that Act were valid. He wrote an elaborate opinion that was widely used in promoting the sale of these bonds. When their validity was attacked, he was retained by a Federal Land Bank to present to the courts the compelling view he had previously outlined.

The case was tried in the District Court in Kansas City with an eminent array of counsel, including, besides Hughes, William G. McAdoo, who had been Secretary of the Treasury when the bonds were issued, and former Attorney General Wickersham. Hughes challenged Madison's view that the general welfare clause is limited by the Constitution's enumeration of the powers given to Congress. Rather, he found "the most weighty support" for the view taken by Hamilton and Story that Congress could appropriate funds for "the general welfare" beyond the scope of its enumerated powers.

From this premise he concluded that Congress "necessarily has a wide range of discretion" in selecting the objects for which federal funds may be spent and that in these matters the courts have no warrant "to substitute their judgment for that of Congress." The taxing and spending power was not unlimited; it could not, for example, be invoked for "a purpose essentially private." But the agricultural interests of the country, broadly considered, he said, "are of National and not merely of State concern." [11]

In the Supreme Court, Hughes argued the case twice, and the Federal Farm Loan Act was upheld,[12] although on other grounds which he had also advanced —that the land banks were duly created depositaries of public money and purchasers of government bonds. Not until after Hughes had become Chief Justice did the court write the Hamilton-Story view of the general welfare clause into the basic law.

In *New York* v. *New Jersey*,[13] Hughes sought an injunction for his native state to prevent New Jersey and the Passaic Valley Sewerage Commissioners from polluting the Upper Bay of New York Harbor. At one point the argument became an intellectual fencing bout between Hughes and his good friend Justice Pitney of New Jersey, whose interruptions became so frequent as to

[11] Brief in CEH's private papers, p. 28.
[12] *Smith* v. *Kansas City Title & Trust Co.*, 255 U.S. 180.
[13] 256 U.S. 296, 314.

suggest that he was deliberately trying to confuse the attorney and prevent an orderly development of New York's case. When Hughes referred to the law of New Jersey on a certain point, Pitney cut in with, "That is not the law of New Jersey."

"Your honor has the advantage of me," Hughes lashed back at him. "I know the law only as I read it in the statutes or in the decisions of the courts."

Hughes' defense of John L. Lewis and forty-two other officials of the United Mine Workers of America is memorable largely because of his matching of wits with a czar on the bench, Judge A. B. Anderson of the Federal District Court in Indianapolis. The setting for the encounter was perfect. The courtroom was jammed with union officials, attorneys, reporters, and curious bystanders. Knowing Judge Anderson's arrogance and severity, the Indianapolis lawyers were delighted to let Hughes take the lead in the case.

"Your honor," he began, "I have a disagreeable duty to perform, but both justice and a proper administration of the law require me to perform it." He went on to show that Judge Anderson had prejudiced the interests of his clients by laying a false statement before the grand jury which had indicted them. The charge against the union officials was conspiracy with the mine operators to raise the price of coal in violation of the Lever Act. The judge had cited to the grand jury a speech by a congressman quoting John L. Lewis, then acting president of the United Mine Workers, as saying that the operators' association and the union were working together to wipe out competition. Actually, the statement had been made by Thomas L. Lewis, who was not then connected with the union. While Judge Anderson squirmed and spectators struggled to hold their elation in bounds, Hughes bore down heavily on this error. He could conceive, he said, "of no more prejudicial statement which could have been made to the grand jury." [14]

Judge Anderson denied Hughes' plea in abatement, and the argument was then shifted to constitutional grounds. When court adjourned, the judge sent for Hughes, and they chatted pleasantly in his chambers. While the case was not mentioned, Hughes told his clients that it would never be tried, and he was right. Judge Anderson could not face the embarrassment of such a trial.

Later in 1920 Hughes argued the appeal of the United Mine Workers in the first Coronado case.[15] The miners were being sued for treble damages under the antitrust laws in connection with a strike in Arkansas. He admitted that individual miners had destroyed company property, but insisted that the strike had no relation to interstate commerce that would justify action under the Sherman Act. "If whatever may be deemed to have an indirect . . . relationship to, or effect upon, interstate commerce were regarded as being within the

[14] *Indianapolis Star*, May 7, 1920.
[15] *United Mine Workers* v. *Coronado Coal Co.*, 259 U.S. 344, 350.

commerce clause," he asserted, "it would be difficult to find any activity of importance in any community that fell without it. Such a construction of the Constitution would destroy the Constitution itself." Speaking for the Supreme Court (after the case had been reargued in 1922 without Hughes' aid but on the basis of his brief), Chief Justice Taft followed this reasoning and complimented counsel for the plaintiffs on the "rare assiduity and ability" with which the case had been prepared.

Possibly the most controversial case of Hughes' entire career at the bar was that of Senator Truman H. Newberry, who had been Roosevelt's Secretary of the Navy. While Newberry was on duty in New York as an officer in the Navy in 1918, a group of Michigan Republicans had secured his nomination for the United States Senate in a primary contest with Henry Ford. In "averting the Ford peril" they had spent about $195,000, although the legal limit on the amount a senatorial candidate might spend in a primary was $3,750. At first charged with bribery and various other acts of corruption, Newberry had succeeded in stripping the case to the question of excessive campaign expenditures. But the trial judge had instructed the jury to find Newberry guilty if he became a candidate or continued as such after learning that more than the amount specified in the statute had been contributed and was being expended in the campaign, even if the candidate himself had made no contribution and had not caused others to contribute and if the expenditures had been made without his participation. It was a direct appeal for a finding of guilt by association.

Hughes had nothing to do with the trial, but he argued Newberry's appeal in the Supreme Court and won a unanimous reversal of the conviction.[16] Meanwhile, however, Newberry's name had become a symbol of vote-buying regardless of the legal merits of his case. The Senate did not seat him until January, 1922, and then by a margin of only five votes. At the same time it condemned the lavish use of money in his behalf as "being contrary to sound public policy, harmful to the honor and dignity of the Senate, and dangerous to the perpetuity of a free government."

When the Reverend Hugh B. MacCauley wrote to Hughes in pursuit of facts about the Newberry case, he responded with too little regard for the circumstance that he had ceased being Newberry's attorney and was then Secretary of State. After reviewing the case, he asserted: "The plain fact is that Senator Newberry was wrongfully and most unjustly convicted and his conviction was set aside. . . . Accordingly, Senator Newberry stood as a Senator duly elected by the people of the State of Michigan and entitled to his seat in the Senate of the United States. . . . There seems to be a general misconception of the nature of the litigation and its results, and Senator Newberry has suffered in consequence a most serious injustice."[17]

The letter fell into the hands of the Republican National Committee and was widely circulated, without Hughes' permission, as an offset to the anti-Newberry campaign. The result was a political tempest in which Hughes was denounced along with his former client. The *World* said the letter was "Mr. Hughes' dirtiest day's work." A "life-long" Republican described himself as

By Rollin Kirby in the New York *World*, 1922.

"SANCTIFIED"

"blushing with shame." Editors wrote of "shock and humiliating disappointment." Congressman Cordell Hull drew a highly inaccurate word picture of the Secretary of State stooping to a whitewash job at the behest of the Republican National Committee. And in the Senate, Joseph T. Robinson shouted that the letter "discredits the reputation for sincerity and fairness which Secretary Hughes long enjoyed." [18]

These barbs literally missed their mark, for shortly after writing the controversial letter Hughes had left for his long-scheduled trip to Brazil. Even after his return, however, the controversy continued. Few people seemed to

[16] *Newberry* v. *U.S.*, 256 U.S. 232.
[17] Associated Press dispatch, Aug. 21, 1922.
[18] *Literary Digest*, Sept. 2, 1922.

understand what Hughes had actually written in his letter. His comment had been confined solely to the nature of the litigation and its results. And this involved, he replied to a stinging editorial in the *World*, "as gross a miscarriage of justice as had ever come under my observation." [19] He also contended that "there is not a line in my letter which has been or can be contravened." [20]

The fact remains that Newberry's election to the Senate was an offense against a basic principle of popular government. In trying to correct a personal injustice, Hughes had ignored a public wrong. Certainly this was a lapse from his customary objectivity. His letter to the Reverend MacCauley is one of the few instances in his long official career in which his defense of a maligned individual was blurred by failure to take account of the public interest.

For the full flower of Hughes' passion for justice we must turn to his voluntary defense of the Socialists ousted from the New York legislature. For months after the close of the war he had watched with deep anxiety the mounting fever of intolerance that swept over America. The Department of Justice was making wholesale arrests without warrant or any process of law, holding men and women incommunicado, searching homes without warrants, seizing property, and shamefully maltreating workmen suspected of radical views. By January, 1920, the raids had reached a shocking peak of hysteria. Then the New York Assembly suddenly decided to suspend its five Socialist members merely because of the unpopularity of their beliefs. That seemed to Hughes a last straw.

The Socialist Party was legally recognized in New York. The five men—Louis Waldman, August Claessens, Samuel A. DeWitt, Samuel Orr, and Charles Solomon—had been duly elected and held proper certificates of election. Two of them had previously served in the Assembly without question. At the beginning of the 1920 session all five had been admitted to full membership and participated in the organization of the Assembly. Then they had been summoned to the bar of the House, lectured by the Speaker, denied their seats pending an investigation, and herded out of the chamber by the sergeant-at-arms.

Hughes' first step was to write a letter to Speaker Sweet protesting this outrageous invasion of the people's right to choose their own representatives:

> If there is anything against these men as individuals, if they were deemed to be guilty of criminal offenses, they should have been charged accordingly. But I understand that the action is not directed against these five elected members as individuals but that the proceeding is virtually an attempt to indict a political party and to deny it representation in the Legislature. This is not, in my judgment, American government.

[19] CEH to Walter Lippmann, June 13, 1924.
[20] CEH to William Jillson, Nov. 20, 1922.

> Are Socialists unconvicted of crime to be denied the ballot? If Socialists are permitted to vote, are they not permitted to vote for their own candidates? If their candidates are elected and are men against whom, as individuals, charges of disqualifying offenses cannot be laid, are they not entitled to their seats?
>
> I understand that it is said that the Socialists constitute a combination to overthrow the Government. The answer is plain. If public officers or private citizens have any evidence that any individuals, or group of individuals, are plotting revolution and seeking by violent measures to change our Government, let the evidence be laid before the proper authorities and swift action be taken for the protection of the community. . . . But I count it a most serious mistake to proceed, not against individuals charged with violation of law, but against masses of our citizens combined for political action, by denying them the only resource of peaceful government; that is, action by the ballot box and through duly elected representatives in legislative bodies.[21]

His next step was to move, at a special meeting of the Association of the Bar, that that august body defend the maligned Socialists. There followed a classic battle over civil rights, with the eminent and formidable William D. Guthrie contending that no Socialist could conscientiously take the oath of office and Hughes proclaiming the right of the people to elect and seat their legislators regardless of nonconformist beliefs. In the end the Hughes motion carried, and a committee was appointed under his chairmanship to argue the case at Albany. All the members of the committee were opposed to socialism, but they had a profound belief in freedom for minorities.

The committee of lawyers went to Albany to appear before the Assembly's Judiciary Committee that had the Socialist members "on trial." The excited legislators refused to let the lawyers testify, but Hughes filed a brief in behalf of himself, Morgan J. O'Brien, Louis Marshall, Joseph M. Proskauer, and Ogden Mills. The act of the Assembly in depriving its Socialist members of their seats and then putting the burden of proof on them to show that they had a right to be reseated, the lawyers asserted, "is a reversal of the rule applicable to the meanest criminal. . . . This is the first time in American history that one against whom treason and disloyalty are sought to be imputed has been called upon to establish the negative. It reminds one of the English State Trials in the sixteenth and seventeenth centuries. . . . We have passed beyond the stage in political development when heresy-hunting is a permitted sport. . . . If a majority can exclude the whole or a part of the minority because it deems the political views entertained by them hurtful, then free government is at an end." [22]

The legislature not only expelled the five Socialists; it also passed a law out-

[21] Zechariah Chafee, Jr., *Freedom of Speech* (New York, Harcourt, Brace, 1920), p. 337. Copyright, 1920, by Harcourt, Brace & Co.

[22] Hughes' brief, pp. 23–32.

lawing the Socialist Party. "The Assembly was past saving," wrote Zechariah Chafee, Jr., professor of law at Harvard University, an eminent authority on civil liberties, "but the nation was saved. The American people, long bedrugged by propaganda, were shaken out of their nightmare of revolution. . . . A legislature trembling before five men—the long-lost American sense of humor revived and the people began to laugh. That broke the spell. The light of day beat in not only upon the Assembly, but upon the Congress and the Department of Justice. . . . The raids of January 2nd were flood-tide, and with Governor Hughes' letter on the 9th, the ebb set in." [23]

Hughes broadened the scope of his assault on bigotry, witch-hunting, and official lawlessness. At every opportunity he pleaded for a new birth of freedom. "The most vicious wrong in democracy," he had once said, "is the abuse of power—the betrayal of the people by their own agents." [24] The Administration had talked of democracy and liberty, he later declared, "but these have been betrayed in its own house. We have been amazed at the abuses scathingly denounced by the Federal Court in Boston. We have burned with shame and indignation as we have read the report of the Committee of Twelve . . . charging and specifying atrocities committed by the American Government on American soil in the course of pretended vindication of American institutions by the Department of Justice. No one can be trusted to save democracy by methods which displace liberty and due process in favor of administrative caprice."

Let it be known, he urged, that we shall secure ourselves against the violence of those who would overthrow the government. "But let it also be known, as our surest protection, that with calmness and sanity we propose to maintain the guarantees of free speech, free assembly and the right of representation, and that no one, however poor, friendless or accused, shall be deprived of liberty without due process of law." [25]

Repeatedly he linked freedom with the progressive revision of policies within the constitutional framework, to meet the changing requirements of the times. "The lover of the institutions of liberty," he said, "never stands pat, he is always looking for their more perfect working, for a better adjustment to the great purpose of making life brighter and happier and more secure in all its resources." [26]

Intelligent conduct was always the twin brother of liberty. "Free speech," he said at the semicentennial of Cornell, "is essential to a republic, but free speech without the insistent demand by the community for fair speech is the opportunity of rogues and demagogues." [27] Law, too, had to justify itself by its

[23] Chafee, *op. cit.*, pp. 338–339.
[24] Speech of January 17, 1919.
[25] *New York Times*, Sept. 19, 1920.
[26] Address of June 21, 1920; Hughes Papers.
[27] Address of June 20, 1919; Hughes Papers.

intrinsic merits. "It is true that democracy cannot live without respect for law, but it must be remembered that law in democracy will have only the respect it deserves."[28] Champion of freedom and law though he was, he had only contempt for the prostitution of freedom to mean and unworthy ends and the debasement of law to selfish or arbitrary purposes.

[28] Address of June 21, 1920; Hughes Papers.

Chapter 37

FIGHT OVER THE LEAGUE OF NATIONS

THE MAKING of peace proved more difficult for the United States than the making of war had been. Suddenly catapulted into a new world role, the American people had no clear idea of what their postwar foreign policy should be. There was, however, a strong desire to see the "peace-loving" nations organized into a concert of power that might be able to prevent future wars. Hughes stood out as one of the leading exponents of this view.

Along with Taft and Root, he was prominently mentioned for membership on the Peace Commission. There was a good deal of feeling that Wilson owed him this recognition because of his generous support of the President throughout the war and his herculean work in the aircraft inquiry. Undoubtedly he would have accepted such a call, but Wilson selected a delegation that would readily follow his own wishes. Completely ignoring the Republicans' victory in 1918, which had given them control of Congress and would give them the last word in ratification of the peace treaty, the President named all members of the Peace Commission from his own party, with the exception of Henry White, a professional diplomat.

In February, 1919, the League of Nations Committee of the Peace Conference met in Paris and began work on Mr. Wilson's four drafts of the proposed Covenant. Within a few weeks a preliminary version of the Covenant was released. Hughes read it in his newspaper at the breakfast table with avid interest. When he came to Article X, he knit his brow in disapproval. It carried a commitment "to respect and preserve as against external aggression the territorial integrity and existing political independence of all Members of the League." Reading it to his wife, who sat across the table, he snapped, "The American people will never stand for that." [1]

Before venturing to discuss the proposed Covenant in public, however, he scrutinized it with typical Hughesian thoroughness. "It is a great American question," he told the New York County Bar Association at its victory dinner on March 9, "and whether we are on one side or the other, it has nothing to do with partisanship." [2] The more he thought about Article X, the more convinced he became that it was a grave mistake. Wilson had gone to Paris with a version of Article X that specifically made allowance for territorial adjust-

[1] Author's interview with CEH, Nov. 26, 1946. [2] *New York Times*, March 9, 1919.

ments. The text he brought back had no such flexibility. Hughes told the Union League Club on March 26:

> I regard this guaranty as a trouble-breeder and not a peace-maker. . . . its inflexibility should condemn it.
>
> Unless the League is disrupted, the guaranty may be regarded as a permanent one. The guaranty makes no allowance for changes which may be advisable. It ascribes a prescience and soundness of judgment to the present Peace Conference in erecting States and defining boundaries which no body in the history of the world has ever possessed. Even as to the new States, it attempts to make permanent existing conditions, or conditions as arranged at this Conference, in a world of dynamic forces to which no one can set bounds. It gives no fair opportunity for adjustments. It is in the teeth of experience. The limitation of the words "as against external aggression" is a frail reliance; no one can foresee what the merits of particular cases may be. . . .
>
> The guaranty would be unwise even if it could accomplish its apparent purpose. But I also think that it will prove to be illusory. . . .
>
> Certainly, each power will be the judge of what in good faith it should do. In the case of the United States, the guaranty will not be made good except by the action of Congress, and it will be for Congress to decide whether we are bound and what we should undertake. The course of recent debates has sufficiently indicated what the attitude of Congress is likely to be, if the resort to war pursuant to Article X is opposed to the opinion of the country. . . .
>
> I think that it is a fallacy to suppose that helpful cooperation in the future will be assured by the attempted compulsion of an inflexible rule. Rather will such cooperation depend upon the fostering of firm friendships springing from an appreciation of community of ideals, interests and purposes, and such friendships are more likely to be promoted by freedom of conference than by the effort to create hard and fast engagements.

This speech was part of the opening round in the great national fight over the League. Hughes offered seven specific amendments to the Covenant, some of which were similar to changes suggested by Taft, Root, and members of the Senate. Five of these were adopted in part when Wilson returned to Paris, although Hughes regarded the changes made as inadequate. The revised Covenant made provision for a nation to withdraw on two years' notice, instructed the Council not to go into purely domestic questions, and made a gesture toward recognition of the Monroe Doctrine. Taft thought it was acceptable in that form, but Hughes' objection to Article X was too strong to permit him to embrace any league embodying that "trouble-breeder."

With many protests against Article X ringing in his ears, Wilson tried to outmaneuver his opponents by incorporating the League Covenant into the peace treaty.[3] The European statesmen did not want it that way, but Wilson was insistent. At the same time he allowed the principles outlined in his Fourteen

[3] Lothrop Stoddard, *Lonely America*, p. 33.

Points to be dangerously whittled away to secure agreement. In June he returned with his treaty and revised League Covenant, and the historic debate over their approval by the Senate began to rock the country. The hatred of the Irreconcilables for Wilson and his denunciation of them as "a battalion of death" inflamed the contest and made it more a struggle for power than the hammering out of a sensible foreign policy.

This turn of events was very disappointing to Hughes, who was eager to have the United States join the League with reservations. In July he received a letter from Senator Hale saying that the treaty was in danger of being rejected and asking his view as to the validity of interpretative reservations and also what specific reservations should be made. Hughes replied that the Senate could consent to ratification of the treaty with a few clarifying interpretations that would leave its main provisions unimpaired and would not necessitate a resumption of the Peace Conference.[4]

"There is plain need for a league of nations," he advised, "in order to provide for the adequate development of international law, for creating and maintaining organs of international justice and machinery of conciliation and conference, and for giving effect to measures of international cooperation which from time to time may be agreed upon. . . . I perceive no reason why these objects cannot be attained without sacrificing the essential interests of the United States. There is a middle ground between aloofness and injurious commitments."

Hughes suggested four "reservations and understandings" to be made a part of the instrument of ratification. The first would have clarified the right of any member to leave the League on two years' notice, while closing the door to escape from debts or liabilities previously incurred. The second would have made clear that immigration and duties on imports are domestic questions outside the jurisdiction of the League. The third was a much too sweeping declaration that the United States need not "submit its policies regarding questions which it deems to be purely American questions to the League of Nations or any of its agencies. . . ." The fourth would have undercut Article X by declaring that only Congress should determine in each case whether the United States had an obligation under that Article and, if so, how its obligation should be fulfilled.

Hughes thus gave the Republicans a formula with which they could have defeated Wilson's extremism and saved the League at the same time. The *Providence Journal* thought his proposals "must commend themselves to anyone except deaf, dumb and blind admirers of the Administration."[5] But the Irreconcilables were no more open to reason than the President to compromise.

Sponsors of the League insisted that, without any reservations, the United

[4] CEH to Senator Hale, July 24, 1919. [5] July 30, 1919.

States would have a right to review the advice of the Council as to what means should be used under Article X to protect the territorial integrity and independence of fellow members. Hughes agreed. The right of Congress to declare war, he said, is basic in our constitutional system. His objection was that, by underwriting a blanket guaranty to every member, the United States would expose itself to charges of bad faith. He assumed that Congress would not declare war because of minor boundary changes in Europe or Asia and insisted that we should not pretend to make a far-fetched commitment to defend such boundaries.

In some instances, moreover, Article X pledged League members to the defense of gross injustices. Hughes feared that if China went to war with Japan over the theft of Shantung, to which Wilson had reluctantly acquiesced in the Treaty of Versailles, League members would be bound to support Japan. Sponsors of the League replied that boundary changes could be made under Article XIX. But Article XIX merely provided that the Assembly might "from time to time advise the reconsideration" of treaties "which have become inapplicable, and the consideration of international conditions whose continuance might endanger the peace of the world." At best it offered but a remote possibility of obtaining desirable territorial adjustments in a dynamic world.

What Wilson offered the nation, as Walter Lippmann has pointed out, was "a very bad choice: either to involve itself in every disputed European question or to withdraw from the organization of the general peace of the world." [6] Public sentiment had been favorable toward cooperation to keep the world at peace, but as the great debate rolled on month after month, it became evident that if the showdown came on the more extreme issue, the League would be defeated.

The President decided to stump the country in the hope of arousing the public and forcing the Senate into line. The day before he left, he invited Senator Irvine L. Lenroot of Wisconsin, a mild reservationist, to the White House. The only real obstacle to ratification of the treaty, Lenroot told him, was Article X. If the President "would agree to a reservation relieving the United States from the obligation of that article," Lenroot said, "ratification would be certain" and Mr. Wilson's speaking trip would become unnecessary.[7] Wilson replied that the League would be of no value in maintaining peace without Article X and declined to budge.

After the President was stricken during his tour, the fight continued without his leadership. The treaty went down to defeat in the Senate on November 19, 1919, by the combined votes of the "little group of willful men" and Wilson's

[6] *Washington Post,* April 1, 1943.
[7] Judge Lenroot's article in the Washington *Evening Star,* March 4, 1945.

own supporters. Sick and isolated, the President had instructed his followers to vote against the Covenant because of the reservations that had been attached. Had these Senators ignored the advice or had the advice never been given, says Stephen Bonsal, the Covenant would have been brought "into the haven of ratification" by a vote of 81 to 13.[8] The treaty, with the Lodge amendments attached, was again defeated in March, 1920, and the debate was transferred to the larger forum of national politics.

Hughes again became an active participant. To the Wilsonian argument that Article X was the heart of the Covenant, he replied, "If it is, the covenant has a bad heart." His attitude toward the League has often been described as "legalistic," but that is only because he insisted on calling a spade a spade. Wilson had said that Article X created an "absolutely compelling moral obligation." "What higher obligation can there be than this?" [9] Hughes asked. He was legalistic enough to insist that the United States should not give either legal or "compelling moral" promises which it was not ready to live up to.

Nor was the nature of the issue changed, he insisted, by the facts that the United States would have a representative on the Council and that the Council could act only by unanimous agreement. "Are we to put a representative on the Council," he asked, "for the purpose of welching on our undertaking?"

At no time did he have the slightest sympathy with the Irreconcilables. Their conduct was beyond the pale of reason. Yet he always believed that the direct cause of the United States' failure to enter the League was President Wilson's uncompromising attitude.[10] History has given strong buttressing to that view. Lord Grey, the British ambassador, indicated in a letter published in the *Congressional Record* that even the Lodge reservations would have been acceptable to Great Britain.[11] It was not Europe but Wilson who insisted on Article X. In 1920 Léon Bourgeois, president of the Council, said that "Article X could be eliminated without in any way modifying the effectiveness of the League of Nations."

In the actual operation of the League, moreover, Article X had little significance. Colonel House told Bonsal in 1929 that "by common consent of all who signed it" Article X "has become a dead letter." [12] More important is the fact that when the nations had an opportunity to start afresh on the task of shaping a world organization to keep the peace after World War II, they completely discarded Article X. The Charter of the United Nations contains nothing comparable to it. The wisdom of Hughes and Root prevailed on this

[8] Stephen Bonsal, *Unfinished Business* (New York, Doubleday, 1944), p. 278. Copyright. 1944, by Doubleday, Doran & Co.

[9] Speech at Youngstown, Oct. 30, 1920. [10] CEH, Notes, p. 259.

[11] Judge Lenroot's article in the Washington *Evening Star*, March 4, 1945.

[12] Bonsal, *op. cit.*, p. 288.

point at San Francisco. "The conference abstained," as John Foster Dulles pointed out, "from seeking to legislate perpetual peace by a single Article sanctifying for all time things as they are." [13] It is interesting to note that two of the other three objections to the Covenant set forth in Hughes' letter to Senator Hale are also fully satisfied in the United Nations Charter.

[13] *Foreign Affairs*, October, 1945, p. 3.

Chapter 38

BACK TO WASHINGTON

THE ROAD to the White House was clear in 1920. Defeated, bitter, and physically broken, Wilson was at the end of his tether. No Democrat of power and imagination had arisen to succeed him, and the country was recoiling from the fetid backwash of the war and European intrigue. It was bound to be a Republican year, and, with Roosevelt in his grave, Hughes stood head and shoulders above any other Republican in presidential stature. The great prize of American politics could have been his for the asking.

To be sure, Hughes had the handicap of his defeat in 1916, but he had lost by a narrow margin under circumstances that now seemed to redound to his favor. Since then he had shaken off the judicial reserve that had blunted the edge of his campaign. His acceptance of defeat with good humor, his war work, his emergence as a leading champion of liberty, and his efforts to secure a League of Nations without Article X made him the logical Republican candidate and the logical successor to Woodrow Wilson. At fifty-eight, he was still young enough to be President. But Hughes had never shared his wife's feeling that he was a "man of destiny"; he was even less interested in being President in 1920 than he had been in 1908 and 1916.

Looking back at his 1916 campaign, he saw it as an ordeal that he was determined not to repeat.[1] His great success at the bar, moreover, had fortified his disinclination to seek any office. There was a strong possibility that his party might override his resistance, as it had done in 1916, but even this prospect was changed by the heavy hand that sorrow laid upon the Hughes family.

Through three decades of married life, Hughes' adventures, triumphs, and disappointments had merged into a happy domestic background. In addition to the felicity between himself and Mrs. Hughes (she still referred to him privately as the dearest husband in the world), his children had been a source of much satisfaction. "No association that you will ever make in life," he told a friend, "will pay you greater dividends than association with your own children." Back from the war, "Son" had become his father's "right bower" in handling their enormous practice. His father spoke of him with a glow of pride. Helen, the eldest daughter, also won an overflowing measure of fatherly

[1] Author's interview with CEH, Nov. 5, 1946.

affection. "A ray of sunshine," he called her, or "just pure gold!" "A rare and joyous spirit," he once said of her, "radiating happiness not only in our home but in all her associations, dedicating her life to good works, she realized my ideal of a beautiful character." [2]

Graduated from Vassar College in 1914, Helen had taken up volunteer work for the YWCA, organizing "Friendship clubs" among high-school girls. Later she became a member of the YWCA War Work Council in Boston. When the influenza epidemic swept the country in the fall of 1918, she taxed her strength in hospital service, contracted the disease, and was then an easy victim of pneumonia. After recuperating at home, she returned to work in April, 1919. In June she attended her fifth class reunion at Vassar and a YWCA conference at Silver Bay, Lake George, having become a member of the YWCA traveling staff. Joining her family at the Lake George cottage they had taken for the summer, she was stricken with a high fever thought at first to be typhoid. About ten days later her doctor discovered that she had an advanced case of tuberculosis.

Hughes suffered the greatest shock of his life. As Governor of New York, he had taken an influential part in the fight against tuberculosis, not dreaming that it might invade his own family. He sent for Dr. Horace J. Howk, an eminent specialist, but all the medical skill that money could buy could not change the outlook. In the autumn they took a house on Warren Street in Glens Falls to avoid moving Helen to New York. Catherine went back to Wellesley. Mrs. Hughes, with her youngest daughter, remained at the Glens Falls house nursing Helen while her strength ebbed away. Burdened with work and sick with grief, Hughes lived alone in the family's New York apartment at 32 East 64th Street. Every Saturday he went to Glens Falls, always returning on Sunday night with his crushing weight of sorrow heavier than before.

In late winter Dr. Howk informed the grief-stricken parents that there was no hope for Helen. The depth of Mrs. Hughes' suffering may well be imagined from the following paragraph of a letter she wrote to her husband on February 10, 1920:

> Oh the pathos of it! I have never struggled with myself more desperately than I have this week, with the result that I have kept up through the day, but the nights have been hideous. I thought after all that we went through last summer I was prepared for anything but I was not prepared for the definiteness of Dr. Howk's statements. My imagination ran riot and the many practical matters with their complications nearly drove me mad.

Hughes carried the letter into his son's room at their law offices and wept like a child. It was the first time that Charles Junior had ever seen grief break

[2] CEH, Notes, p. 251.

down his father's self-control. Some weeks later Helen died at the untimely age of twenty-eight.

A beautiful memorial chapel bearing her name was erected at Silver Bay, Lake George, whence she had gone to her last YWCA conference. Through the subsequent decades her father still spoke of her with a quaver in his voice. Her passing "in the fullness of her young womanhood—a victim of devoted services—" still seemed to him "the saddest of life's ironies." [3] It left a wound that never healed.

When friends pressed him to "run again" in 1920, the wound was fresh and painful. In February he asked a group of admirers in Nebraska to withhold his name from the primaries. Will Hays, chairman of the Republican National Committee, put out a feeler to see if Hughes would act as temporary chairman at the national convention and deliver the keynote address. Senator Johnson frowned upon this idea when the National Committee met, but Hughes had previously dismissed the suggestion as soon as it had been made. With no dominant candidate in the race, he was fearful that if he made the kind of speech the situation demanded a draft-Hughes movement might sweep the convention.

Some of the kingmakers were not satisfied. Shortly before the convention opened, a conclave including Senators Lodge, Wadsworth, and Calder met in Washington and decided that, after initial honorary votes had been cast for favorite sons, their influence would be thrown behind the nomination of Hughes. Senator Calder asked Meier Steinbrink to sound out the prospective candidate.

"I'm going to ask you to do me a favor," Steinbrink began when he and Hughes were ensconced in a private dining nook at the Lawyers' Club. "Don't interrupt me until I have finished what is on my mind."

"Steinbrink," Hughes replied solemnly, "there is no subject that you can't talk about with me."

The younger lawyer told his story, concluding, "These Senators want to be able to vote for you as their presidential candidate."

Hughes' eyes filled with tears. "I beg of you to believe me," he said. "Since our daughter died, Mrs. Hughes and I are heartbroken. I don't want to be President of the United States. I request that my name be not even mentioned in the convention." [4]

"Whoever is nominated will be elected," Hughes predicted before the lunch was over, "but in my opinion he will not fill out the term." Doubtless he was thinking about the shattered man in the White House and the accumulation of postwar dilemmas that Wilson would leave to his successor, but the remark was to prove prophetic.

[3] *Ibid.* [4] Author's interview with Judge Steinbrink, July 24, 1947.

In conformity with Hughes' request his name was kept entirely out of the convention, and the New York vote went to President Butler of Columbia University. The Republican hierarchy in the smoke-filled room at Chicago took a long shot on Warren G. Harding without any advice whatever from the candidate of 1916. When he wired Harding after the convention, it was a routine congratulation from a former candidate who had no thought of ever returning to public life.

"I am just coming to the realization of the responsibilities which I have assumed," Harding replied. ". . . if I were undertaking the task in a reliance upon myself alone, I should not make the venture. . . . I very much wish your cooperation, your counsel, your advice and your assistance."[5] Late in August, when Hughes went to St. Louis to address the American Bar Association, he stopped over at Marion and briefly shared the spotlight of the "front porch" campaign with Al Jolson and the Harding and Coolidge Theatrical League. This was the second time he had met Harding, the first time having been the notification ceremony of 1916.

On leaving Marion the next day, Hughes issued a statement praising Harding and expressing the belief that his election would "afford the surest way of securing our proper relation to international cooperation."[6] The election of Harding, he implied, would mean United States adherence to a world court and the League of Nations without Article X. Harding had approved the statement and was obviously delighted to have Hughes' support. The candidate's pro-League attitude in his talk with Hughes was watered down in some of the speeches that George Harvey was writing for him, but, hoping for the best, Hughes took an active part in the campaign. In any event, the alternative to Harding was James M. Cox, the Democratic nominee, who was committed to Wilson's uncompromising stand. In that course Hughes could see neither reason nor hope. For even if Cox could have swept the country, he would have had no chance of getting the treaty through the Senate without reservations.

In October, Root initiated the statement of thirty-one distinguished Republicans who were eager to see the United States "do her full part in association with other civilized nations to prevent war." Hughes signed it in good faith, along with Hoover, Wickersham, Henry W. Taft, Stimson, Lowell, Butler, and William Allen White. They concluded that the "true course to bring America into an effective league to preserve the peace" was frankly to call upon other nations to agree to changes in Article X. "For this course," they said, "we can look only to the Republican Party and its candidate."[7]

The smashing victory of Harding and Coolidge followed. Wilson had called

[5] Harding to CEH, June 15, 1920. [6] *New York Times*, Aug. 26, 1920.
[7] *Washington Post*, Oct. 15, 1920.

for a solemn referendum on his treaty. Here was the answer. In retrospect it is difficult to tell whether Wilson or Harding was the more bewildered by the avalanche of "noes."

Harding's bewilderment sprang out of his own unfitness to be President and his lack of a national program. Few men seem big enough for the Presidency before they take over the office; Harding seemed only knee-high to it. A small-city editor who had ridden a streak of good fortune to the Senate, the President-elect had hoisted himself chiefly by his knowledge of politics, his affability, his old-fashioned oratory, and his skill in effecting compromises. His dislike for controversy had saved him from making enemies, and his follow-the-leader tactics had aroused among his cronies in the Senate hopes that the Marionite might serve them as a marionette. Senator Brandegee had frankly described Harding as "the best of the second raters." Even that could be said only because his inability to say No had not been tested under the merciless pressures of the Presidency.

Conscious of his own meager knowledge of economics, government, and world affairs, Harding sought to minimize his oppressive burden by assembling a Cabinet of the best minds in the country. At least that was his announced intention, although many posts went to his cronies. One Republican bigwig was so concerned over the prospect of Harding's Cabinet being filled with no-account politicians that he sent Everett Colby to ask Hughes if he would agree with various other high standing men in the party not to accept appointment unless all were invited to serve. Hughes replied, with his customary reluctance to pass judgment on other men, that it was not his business to dictate to the President-elect.[8]

While Harding was in Texas trying to dispel his misgivings in unpresidential hilarity, he asked Hughes to confer with him, after his return to Marion, on "the problem we have to solve in dealing with our new world relationship."[9] Hughes kept an appointment on December 10, expecting only to discuss the legacy of chaos in foreign relations that the old administration was passing on to the new. The outcome of the conference was a request that he head the Harding Cabinet as Secretary of State.

Senator Albert B. Fall once claimed that Harding first offered him the position of Secretary of State. Certainly Fall was seeking that appointment, but Harry Daugherty, who was playing Mark Hanna to Harding's McKinley, scouts the idea that his chief had any serious thought of Fall for the State Department, and Harding told Hughes that he had not offered the position to anyone else. Apparently Harding was sincerely eager to carry out his "best

[8] Everett Colby in *Scribner's*, May, 1928, p. 565.
[9] Harding to CEH, Nov. 13, 1920.

minds" pledge so far as the State Department was concerned. "I have simply got to have Hughes in my Cabinet as Secretary of State," he had told a friend. "There is nobody else who is in the same class with him." [10]

For his part, Hughes found the idea of being Secretary of State very enticing. He promptly accepted the offer, subject only to consultation with his partners. When his final acceptance was given, the President-elect replied: "I am sure the country will be glad, and welcome your return to public service in that capacity. Of course, the proffer itself is the best evidence of my own confidence. . . . The big thing is that you will serve. It strengthens my faith, because I believe in you, and feel that the American people share my high opinion." [11]

Finding it difficult to complete his Cabinet, Harding let two months elapse before publicly announcing Hughes' acceptance. Meanwhile Washington buzzed with rumors coupled with senatorial hostility to the idea that the "whiskered Wilson" might become Secretary of State. Hughes' stand in favor of the League of Nations made him anathema to the Irreconcilables. Other Senators, inebriated with power, openly scorned the liberalism both of Hughes and of Hoover. Harding was urged to place at the head of his Cabinet some "amiable and colorless futility" who would not irritate the Senate. Boies Penrose haughtily asserted that it would make no difference who was Secretary of State; the Senate would control all matters of foreign policy anyway. Others urged the substitution of Root for Hughes. By January the anti-Hughes sentiment in the Foreign Relations Committee was said to have reached the proportions of a "revolt."

Always thin-skinned to criticism, Hughes flinched under this flailing of a decision that had already been made. Harding's procrastination in making the announcement was embarrassing also because the Secretary of State-to-be could give no reason for refusing to take numerous lawsuits that were pressed upon him. But Hughes made no complaint. On the contrary, he was full of deference and good feeling toward his new chief. At Harding's request, he urged Hoover to join the Cabinet. Hughes was no Salmon P. Chase. "I cannot conceive of any greater privilege, or higher duty," he wrote to Harding, "than to serve under your leadership in carrying out a sound Administration policy at this difficult time." [12]

Harding remained unmoved by the senatorial ranting. By letter he asked Hughes to visit him at St. Augustine, Florida, in February for a discussion of top officials in the State Department. Hughes spent most of the morning with the President-elect, and they were still together when Harding held his press conference. "I invited Mr. Hughes here," he said, "in order to offer him for-

[10] Rev. Mr. William F. McDowell to CEH, Sept. 3, 1923.
[11] Harding to CEH. Dec. 22, 1920. [12] CEH to Harding, Dec. 25, 1920.

By Rollin Kirby in the New York *World*, February 21, 1921.

A MAN'S JOB

mally the portfolio of Secretary of State. I am very happy to say that he has agreed to accept."

The reporters seized upon the opportunity to ask the President-elect what his foreign policy would be. "You must ask Mr. Hughes about that," Harding replied. "That is going to be another policy of the next administration," he added, with a smile tilted at Wilson's domination over foreign affairs. "From the beginning the Secretary of State will speak for the State Department." [13] Obviously pleased by this candid delegation of control over foreign policy into his hands, Hughes would say nothing more than that he had regarded acceptance of Harding's offer as an "imperative obligation."

The President-elect's good will was overflowing, and he seemed to be genuinely desirous of keeping his administration on a high plane. Yet the atmosphere at St. Augustine was far from being auspicious. A horde of politicians and camp followers was hounding him for favors. Knowing her husband's inability to say No, Mrs. Harding told Hughes, "You've got to help Warren resist these demands." [14] But the head of the new Cabinet could not visualize his assignment as that of a special aide to keep the President out of trouble. He was "taking a new case for the people in foreign affairs," and it was obvious from the beginning that this would absorb his entire energy.

The selection of Hughes brought widespread applause and some carping here and there. "If the nation believed that all the Cabinet appointments were to be of similar calibre," asserted the *New York Times*, "it would thank God and take courage." [15] "Mr. Hughes' name is luminous throughout the country," said the Baltimore *Sun*. "No public man has set higher standards of public service," observed the New York *Evening Mail*. "Intelligence, courage, and experience," concluded the *Evening Post*, "predestine Mr. Hughes for a place with the best who have held that office." "Une belle intelligence," wrote Stéphane Lauzanne in *Le Matin* of Paris. "Un homme de droit et de droiture." [16] A digest of fifty-nine editorials, most of them in Democratic papers, showed almost unanimous approval.

In the Senate there was much grumbling but no rebellion. "Hughes won't last thirty days," one Irreconcilable forecast. But Harding's cronies in the Senate were not yet ready to fight. On the day of his inauguration the President presented the names of his Cabinet to the Senate in person, and they were unanimously confirmed. The following day Hughes took the oath of office from Mr. Justice Day in a simple ceremony attended by the retiring Secretary of State, Bainbridge Colby, Undersecretary Norman H. Davis, Undersecretary-to-be Henry P. Fletcher, Mrs. Hughes, Mr. and Mrs. Charles E. Hughes, Jr., and their two children.

[13] *New York Times*, Feb. 20, 1921. [14] Author's interview with CEH, Nov. 19, 1946.
[15] Feb. 21, 1921. [16] Clippings in the Hughes Papers, Library of Congress.

The new Secretary established himself in the large rectangular room on the second floor of the bizarre structure just west of the White House then known as the State, War, and Navy Building. It was a pleasant room with south windows affording a view across the Mall to the Washington Monument, with the portraits of many great Americans looking down from the walls, and with a huge mirror crowned by the coat of arms of the United States over the stone-faced fireplace. Here John Hay and Elihu Root had done their most distinguished work. Here also was the spirit of the great Secretaries of State of earlier days—John Quincy Adams and Webster as well as Jefferson, Madison, and Monroe. Hughes found a deep satisfaction in joining the select company of men who have directed the United States' foreign policy. It was good to be back in the public service. He plunged into his work with enthusiasm—in spite of the wound that would never heal.

Bei Fragen zur Produktsicherheit wenden Sie sich bitte an:
If you have any questions regarding product safety,
please contact:

Walter de Gruyter GmbH
Genthiner Straße 13
10785 Berlin
productsafety@degruyterbrill.com

CHARLES EVANS HUGHES

BY MERLO J. PUSEY

Charles Evans Hughes

IN TWO VOLUMES

Volume Two

COLUMBIA UNIVERSITY PRESS

New York and London

1963

First published by The Macmillan Company, 1951
Third printing, Columbia University Press, 1963
Library of Congress Catalog Card Number: 51-7851

PRINTED IN THE UNITED STATES OF AMERICA

CONTENTS

Volume Two

ILLUSTRATIONS

Volume Two

CHARLES EVANS HUGHES

Chapter 39

SECRETARY OF STATE

PROBABLY no Secretary of State has ever faced a more chaotic and perplexing situation than Hughes inherited from the Wilson régime. "The murk of the Paris peace settlement," as the London *Times* remarked, "lay over international relations." [1] Nearly two and a half years after the fighting had ceased the United States was still technically at war. Relations with Mexico were immersed in confusion and bitterness. Yankee imperialism in Santo Domingo, Nicaragua, and Haiti cast a shadow over our relations with Latin America. In the Far East suspicion and distrust were rampant. "There is hardly a phase of our foreign policy," observed *Current Opinion,* "that is not hanging in mid-air." [2]

In the face of this spreading demoralization, the State Department, as Root said, was "in a condition of virtual coma." [3] For months it had been feebly putting aside international problems against the day when a new hand could take over the helm. The United States' prestige abroad was in a state of eclipse. The big, sprawling democracy that had mustered so much power in wartime had lapsed into disorder and impotence—a fact that contributed greatly to the malaise afflicting the postwar world.

When the transition came, it was like a sudden passing out of fog into light. Moving with speed almost unknown in diplomatic circles, Hughes inaugurated firm, clear, simple, and straightforward policies in each area needing attention. Without forsaking idealism, he was realistic enough to talk about interests, islands, ships, and national rights when more lofty projects were unattainable. "Our foreign relations," as one commentator remarked, "had been the subject of passion. Mr. Hughes made them the subject of reason."

On his very first day in office the affirmative character of his policy was in evidence. Costa Rica and Panama were exchanging hot lead on top of hot words across their controversial boundary. Their dispute had been arbitrated years before by President Loubet of France and later by Chief Justice White of the United States, but Panama had reneged after the second award was made, and Costa Rica had resorted to force to take the territory that had been awarded to her. Hughes had begun probing into the controversy on inaugura-

[1] March 3, 1921. [2] April, 1921, p. 442.
[3] Speech, Nov. 10, 1925; Hughes Papers.

tion day even before he had been sworn in. The next day he conferred with Undersecretary Davis and Sumner Welles, chief of the Latin American Division, and got approval of his plans from the White House. Before nightfall, pointed notes had gone out to the two little Central American countries, telling them to stop fighting, and two warships had been dispatched to protect United States interests.

Costa Rica obediently withdrew her troops. Panama too ceased firing but stubbornly rejected the White award. Hughes sternly called upon Panama to live up to her solemn agreement. When the Panamanian National Assembly again turned down the award in secret session, Hughes threatened to take such steps as might be necessary to establish the line where the arbitrators placed it.[4] He felt that our protégé Panama simply could not be permitted to flout an arbitration award that she had pledged herself to accept. The United States had guaranteed the independence of Panama. In order to fulfill its obligations, the Secretary said, it would have to know where the Panama boundary lay. Moreover, a naked question of international justice had been raised—a question arousing the interest of all Latin America. On August 18 he informed Panama that the "reasonable time" allowed her to withdraw from the Coto region had expired and that Costa Rica would be justified in taking jurisdiction over it. United States marines were sent to the Canal Zone. A few days later Panama evacuated the disputed district, and the White award became effective.

Hughes' handling of the case was typical. His policy was to be underscored by prompt and vigorous action, an alert sense of justice, and firm insistence upon the recognition of rights and obligations.

The Secretary lost no time in gathering the numerous reins controlling foreign policy into his own hands. Even before he was sworn in he observed that Colby was preparing to make about twenty-five shifts in the diplomatic service and sent word to the retiring Secretary that he would prefer to make those changes himself. Colby acquiesced cheerfully.

Within the department Hughes had a free hand in shaping his organization and made the most of it to assemble a staff of career men. His first Undersecretary, Henry P. Fletcher, was a personal friend of President Harding's, but Hughes selected him. Fletcher was an able and experienced diplomat who had served in the United States legations in Cuba and China and had been ambassador to Chile and Mexico. Organization of the department became his special assignment while the Secretary gave most of his time to major questions of policy. Although Fletcher was devoted to his chief, he gladly left the department in 1922 to become ambassador to Belgium. The Undersecretaryship had proved to be a little dull because most of the work was done by the Secretary himself.

[4] *Foreign Relations of the United States, 1921*, I, 212.

William Phillips, another career man, then minister to the Netherlands, was brought in to take Fletcher's place. Hughes' third Undersecretary was Joseph C. Grew, who had made a brilliant record in Egypt, Mexico, Russia, Germany, the State Department, and the secretariat at the Paris Peace Conference, in addition to having been minister to Denmark and to Switzerland. The Secretary made a routine practice of bringing men home from foreign posts so as to enrich the department by contact with diplomats experienced in the field. At the same time he sent men from the department to foreign posts to broaden their outlook and give our diplomats abroad a better understanding of the policies taking shape in Washington.

Not a single expert in the department was ousted to create a vacancy for any deserving politician. Hughes leaned backward, as he had done at Albany, to avoid any suspicion that he might be building up any personal organization. He even retained Colby's secretary, William H. Beck, in the same capacity. Appointments were made on merit, and promotions went to the men who demonstrated the greatest capacity for advancement in the service. Some of the President's senatorial friends put him under pressure to set up in the State Department a sort of watchdog to look out for their political interests, but Hughes would have none of it, and Harding did not press his request. "I am the only politician in the department," the Secretary used to say.

He assembled a distinguished roster of Assistant Secretaries who later served in American embassies and legations. Among them were Fred Morris Dearing, later ambassador to Peru; Leland Harrison, later minister to Sweden, Uruguay, Rumania, and Switzerland; Robert Woods Bliss, later minister to Sweden and ambassador to Argentina; Wilbur J. Carr, later minister to Czechoslovakia; John V. A. MacMurray, who became minister to China, Estonia, Latvia, and Lithuania as well as ambassador to Turkey; J. Butler Wright, who presided over our legations in Hungary, Uruguay, and Czechoslovakia and our embassy in Cuba.

Men of training and ability were either retained or brought in to head the various divisions in the department. Sumner Welles remained head of the Latin American Division until 1922, when he was succeeded by Francis White, later minister to Czechoslovakia. William R. Castle, Jr., in charge of Western European Affairs, was later to become Undersecretary in the Hoover régime. Allen W. Dulles was chief of Near Eastern Affairs; John V. A. MacMurray, of Far Eastern Affairs (before his appointment as Assistant Secretary); and De Witt C. Poole, of Russian Affairs. Charles Cheney Hyde, later Hamilton Fish professor of international law and diplomacy at Columbia University, came in as solicitor in 1923.

Hughes' door was always open to these men. He dealt with them in the utmost frankness and exercised a profound influence over them. His manner, his integrity, his industry, and a sort of intellectual aura that characterized the man seemed to inspire his associates with his own zeal.

While he won the unbounded esteem of the men around him, some of them discovered that he had a temper. A piece of incompetent work would strike fire in his eye. With a few knife-edged words he could strip a blunder to appalling nakedness. Yet his indignation seemed always to have an inner lining of good humor. One day a document prepared by Undersecretary Grew brought a flare-up. "You've missed the whole point," Hughes impatiently complained. Grew was making an inconspicuous exit when the Secretary looked up at him and beamed, "Nothing personal, you know." [5]

Castle smelled trouble one morning when his buzzer sounded and he heard a sharp, "Come down." "How do you suppose I can do my work," the Secretary challenged as soon as Castle entered the room, "if you send me an idiotic paper like this?" [6] Castle murmured something about having honestly expressed his views and went back to his office thinking that the end of his career in the State Department was at hand. Hughes soon buzzed again and, instead of firing Castle, he apologized. His explosion had come after he had read only two pages of Castle's memorandum. Having now finished the document, he said he agreed with the conclusion but thought some of the reasoning was faulty.

A spirited encounter between the Secretary and Solicitor Hyde followed the accidental transfer of a carelessly drafted note to the President's office. As soon as the mistake was discovered, Hyde completely redrafted the note and sent it to the Secretary for a final check. Weary from overwork, Hughes sent for Hyde and irritably cross-examined him.[7]

"Look at this first sentence," he commanded. "What does it mean?" The solicitor explained. "And this third paragraph!" Again Hyde defended his product with facts and logic. "And what about this last sentence?" the Secretary finally challenged. As the solicitor finished his last explanation, a sudden flash of sunshine completely obliterated the scowl on the Secretary's face. "Hyde," he exclaimed, "you're all right." These two men came to understand each other so well that they sometimes conversed in racy, half-finished sentences.

The swiftness with which Hughes' mood could change from stern determination to affability is legendary among his associates. Butler Wright asked the Secretary if he would greet the students of a girls' school who were to visit the department. "You know I have no time for that sort of thing," was the testy reply. "You see them." When the young ladies arrived several days later, however, Wright tried again.

[5] Author's interview with Mr. Grew, March 4, 1949.
[6] Author's interview with Mr. Castle, March 31, 1949.
[7] Author's interview with Professor Hyde, Oct. 1, 1947.

"The young ladies are here," he said, peering into the Secretary's office.

"What young ladies?" Hughes demanded.

Wright repeated his previous explanation and urged the Secretary not to disappoint a group of young women who were eager to get a glimpse of him. Hughes resisted stubbornly.

"Couldn't you just take the bull by the horns and get it over with?" Wright pleaded.

"Don't you think you have your metaphor a little mixed, Mr. Wright?" the Secretary retorted, his whiskers suddenly dancing with merriment. "Show the young ladies in."

No one in the department cared to challenge Hughes. His prodigious industry made him master of every subject that was likely to come under discussion, and his keen mind cut through sham, sophistry, and superficiality with equal ease. "He has an amazing mind," Castle wrote in his diary, "but demands terrifyingly quick reactions from his subordinates. I should hate to be his undersecretary unless I had a mind which worked like lightning." [8] Yet Hughes was no intellectual tyrant. He highly respected a subordinate who could hold his ground with the support of facts and reason. None of his associates had cause to complain of unfairness, and he stood by the men under him with the same fidelity that he expected of them.

Solicitor Hyde was troubled by a summons from the House Committee on Foreign Affairs to testify on the constitutionality of the liquor-traffic treaty that the department had negotiated with Great Britain. "Don't you go," Hughes told him. "The House has no right to inquire into a treaty that requires ratification by the Senate only. You refuse, and if they put you in jail, I'll get you out." [9]

Hugh R. Wilson took over the Division of Current Information with some trepidation because of reports he had heard of Hughes' severity. "I soon found, however," he tells us, "that the inspiration and joy of working with him far outweighed any apprehension that might have come from his occasional caustic manner. . . . At times his booming laugh would burst forth, at times he would enter into reminiscence, and on those occasions no character could have been more interesting and more fascinating. Even after months of experience with him one was startled at the breadth of his knowledge, at the penetration of his intellect, at his ability to thrust unerringly and swiftly to the heart of any matter." [10]

Sumner Welles was especially impressed by the Secretary's generous recognition of the work done for him. "No chief," he said, "could better inspire his subordinates to the best that was in them. Those of us who served under him

[8] Castle's diary, 1924, I, 57.
[9] Author's interview with Professor Hyde, Oct. 1, 1947.
[10] *Diplomat Between Wars* (New York, Longmans, 1941), pp. 162f.

will always regard that experience as beyond price." [11] The personal loyalty and devotion that Hughes inspired in amazing degree was to survive as long as his associates lived.

In spite of his belief in experts, Hughes virtually acted as his own secretary, entering his office appointments in a desk diary and his social engagements in a little pocket diary. His secretary, William H. Beck, became his personal stenographer. Beck's ability to write shorthand at more than two hundred words a minute made it possible for Hughes to dictate at top speed. Beck would then read back his notes, with Hughes rapidly inserting punctuations, corrections, and additions. By this means the letter or statement would be whipped into final form before being typed, and no rewriting would be necessary. Often Beck would fill half a shorthand book at a sitting and then have to redictate part of it to two other stenographers. So devoted was he to his boss that he "gladly gave up social and other engagements" in the evening and on Sundays to take dictation.

In keeping his fingers on every major activity of the department, Hughes made a practice of calling in the experts and specialists as well as the division chiefs and Assistant Secretaries. Any one of them might be asked to perform a miracle on short notice. Late one afternoon Hughes handed Solicitor Fred K. Nielsen a stack of documents a foot high and asked for a report the next morning. Nielsen had to work most of the night. Incidents of this sort ruffled the department's customary placidity, however routine they might be to the Secretary himself.

His office hours usually stretched from 9:00 A.M. to 7:00 P.M. He used to say that he distrusted his judgment after five o'clock but had to use it anyway. Reports from the various divisions and dispatches from the embassies invariably accumulated on his desk near the end of the day. Nearly every night he took a pile of these home with him, and on Saturday night he always cleared his desk by taking home a suitcase or two full of papers for Sunday reading. The next morning he would dispose of these items with the dispatch of a naval captain giving orders from the bridge. At fifty-nine he had the energy and exuberance of a man of forty.

The Secretary frequently went home at noon to lunch with Mrs. Hughes. Walking briskly both ways and eating lightly, with no cigar to linger over, he would return promptly, swallow a dyspepsia tablet, and wonder why the department was almost deserted. His buzzer would buzz in vain, with consequent embarrassment to "the boys" of the department when they did return. The example of his industry had far more effect upon the department than did its leisurely customs upon him. "It is amazing," Castle wrote in his diary, "how the Department machine limps when Mr. Hughes' hand is removed."

[11] *Washington Post*, Sept. 7, 1948.

A page from the yearbook in which his engagements are listed will give an idea of the pressure he was under:

9:30 Senator Lodge.
10:45 House Foreign Affairs Committee.
12:00 General George W. Wingate.
12:15 White House to see the President.
12:45 Mr. Emery.
3:00 Mr. H. G. Chilton.
3:15 Minister Hugh Gibson.
3:45 Senator McCormick.
4:00 M. Francisco Peynado.
5:00 Ambassador Houghton.
5:15 Secretary Mellon.
8:00 Representative and Mrs. Ernest R. Ackerman—dinner in honor of Ambassador Houghton.

Hughes' freedom in managing the department did not extend to the selection of ambassadors and ministers. The President had incurred political debts, and in some instances he had made specific promises as to the pay-off. To be sure, the Secretary was able to get a good many careerists and outside men of distinction into diplomatic posts. Myron T. Herrick, former Governor of Ohio, became ambassador to France for the second time. Alanson B. Houghton left a seat in Congress for the ambassadorship at Berlin. Hughes' old friend Jacob Gould Schurman went to China as minister after twenty-eight years as president of Cornell University. But campaign contributors and misfits were chosen often enough to irk so ardent an apostle of merit appointments as Hughes. As he grew impatient of trying to work with some of the men that were sent to foreign capitals, his only consolation was that "his was the common lot of all Secretaries since John Quincy Adams."

Sometimes Hughes was able to scotch these raids, for Harding was reluctant to override the Secretary's judgment. One day he called Hughes on the telephone and said that he wished to give a specified diplomatic post to an individual he must have known to be unqualified. Hughes vigorously protested.

"But I want to appoint him," the President said; "I want to appoint him."

"Of course you are at liberty to do so," the Secretary retorted, "if that is your decision."

The appointment was not made.

Nothing could dissuade the President, however, from carrying through his most notorious pay-off. George Harvey, editor of the *North American Review*, had lived with Harding during much of the campaign and poured his fluency into many a Harding speech. Now he coveted the position of ambassador to the Court of St. James's. Harvey had broken with Wilson to support Hughes in 1916; there was no bad blood between him and Hughes. The Secretary recognized Harvey's ability and his journalistic knack for picking up information. But he also saw that Harvey's cocky manner and his "one notorious failing" (addiction to alcohol) would make him a liability to the diplomatic service. One night at a private dinner Hughes noted that the arrogant editor was intoxicated, that he talked recklessly and scarcely knew what he was saying. In trying to convince the President that Harvey was not the man for the embassy in London, Hughes made use of this incident. At the time Harding seemed to agree that the appointment should not be made.

But Harvey knew the President's weakness. When Harding taxed him with irresponsible conduct, the "passionate patriot" burst into tears and promised to give up drinking. That settled it. The President concluded that, in view of Harvey's great service in the campaign and his promise to reform, he would have to make good his pledge. For Hughes this meant repeated embarrassment. According to many reports reaching the department, Harvey did not keep his pledge to the President and at times became quite unreliable.[12] By nature he was always presumptuous, and on two occasions he went so far as to dispute the veracity of Lord Curzon, the British Foreign Minister. His speeches were often at variance with State Department policy. As if to add insult to injury, he appears to have inspired rumors that he was to become Secretary of State in Hughes' place.

On January 21, 1923, the *World* and several other newspapers published stories of sharp differences between Harding and Hughes, with Harvey on the side of the President, and indicated on the authority of "an informed and dependable administration source" that the Secretary was about to return to the practice of law. Hughes publicly denied the report and in private called it a "stupid lie." [13] In a tart radiogram telling Harvey, "you are reported to have given expression to this antagonism during your recent visit here," he asked the ambassador to help "squelch" the rumor by a statement if he approved of that course. Harvey sent a message to the *North American Review* saying that the statements attributed to him were "absolutely false" and that he was in complete accord with Secretary Hughes. Nothing could wipe out the friction between them, however, so long as Harvey remained in London.

Early in his régime Hughes reorganized the department and began a systematic campaign to improve the Foreign Service. Under the impact of war the department had undergone a sudden growth without much order or pattern. Hughes recast the department with special emphasis upon regional divisions devoted to distinct geographical areas, which greatly enhanced its capacity to deal with foreign affairs on a global scale.

In seeking reorganization of the Foreign Service by law, the Secretary out-

[12] CEH, Notes, p. 357. [13] CEH to Theodore T. Joslin, Feb. 6, 1923.

lined three major objectives. The first was to obtain men of special aptitude and training. He was full of sympathy for the practice of going outside the service for men of wide experience, sagacity, and ability to fill important diplomatic posts. Such men could reinvigorate diplomacy. Yet they would be helpless without the backing of trained staffs. The bulk of the work would necessarily have to be carried on by career officials, and the ablest young men simply would not be available for this work unless the service could offer them fair opportunities to become heads of missions.

With isolationism rampant, some extremists in Congress were saying that communications had improved so much that it was no longer necessary for the United States to have ambassadors in other countries. "An hour of direct intercourse between responsible ministers," Hughes pointedly replied, "is often worth months of written communications . . . it is a poor patriot who would scrap both his ships and his diplomats at the same time. . . . Every American should feel ashamed that any country in the world should have a better diplomatic organization than the United States. This is not a matter simply of national pride; it is a matter of national security." [14]

The second focal point of his attack was the salary scale that made the diplomatic service "a rich man's club." Budding young diplomats were hired at $2,500 a year and advanced to a maximum of only $4,000. "The salaries are so low in the classified Diplomatic Service," Hughes complained, "that the choice of candidates is largely restricted to young men of wealthy families who are able and willing to a considerable extent to pay their own way. It is a most serious thing to be compelled to say that a young man without means, who desires to marry and bring up a family after the American tradition, cannot be encouraged to enter upon one of the most important careers that the country has to offer. I say bluntly that no American can face the facts without a sense of humiliation, and he is compelled to qualify his boasting of our intelligence and civilization so long as this condition continues."

Hughes' third objective was to merge the Diplomatic and Consular services. The Diplomatic Service could not confine its work wholly to political interests; nor could the Consular Service devote itself wholly to commercial interests. By bringing the two units together into a single Foreign Service, the Secretary insisted, better use could be made of special aptitudes and talents and a wider range of opportunity would be opened to men interested in representing their country abroad.

These far-reaching reforms were finally achieved in the Rogers Act of 1924. Wilbur Carr worked out the technique of the measure in collaboration with Representative John Jacob Rogers of Massachusetts, but the inspiration for its enactment came largely from Secretary Hughes. The Act lifted the

[14] Speech to U.S. Chamber of Commerce, May 18, 1922.

upper limit on Foreign Service salaries from $4,000 to $10,000 and granted allowances for rent, light, and exchange-rate adjustments. It made all appointments and promotions in the Foreign Service contingent upon personal merit rather than upon politics. A contributory pensions system enabled aged employees to retire. The consular and diplomatic branches were consolidated, and the new Foreign Service at last emerged as a genuine career service.

Probably the most notable result of these changes was the democratization of the Foreign Service in the following decades. Men already representing the United States abroad also saw in the Act new incentives for exerting their best efforts. A "vastly superior organization" began to take shape.[15] The Rogers Act came to be recognized as "the great basic charter of the modern diplomatic service."[16] Not until 1946 was the Foreign Service extensively reorganized again and the Act of that year was essentially a refinement and extension of the principles that Hughes helped to shape in 1924.

In the social aspects of his assignment Hughes was no less wholehearted than in his official duties. While neither he nor Mrs. Hughes had any hankering for social life, they entered upon a program of entertainment as ambitious as any ever undertaken by a Secretary of State. Nor were they long-faced about it. At one of the gatherings of the State Department Club, composed of officers and personnel of the department, he gaily announced that he and Undersecretary Phillips were prepared "to dine for our country."

The Secretary could always be relied upon to attend any celebration at an embassy or legation, whether it was the wedding of a diplomat's daughter, the observance of a king's birthday, or a reception for a visiting dignitary. In addition, the Hugheses dined once a year with the heads of every diplomatic mission in Washington and entertained every chief of mission in their own home.

Mrs. Hughes brought to this task the same natural charm and grace that had previously distinguished her as a hostess. Her table was always beautifully arranged. Some thought that she went to extraordinary efforts to make up for the lack of alcoholic beverages at their dinners and receptions. The Hugheses served no intoxicants during the prohibition era, although the Secretary never hesitated to take a cocktail at the embassies or elsewhere beyond the reach of the "noble experiment."

Even if a diplomatic dinner were "deadly," it might yield dividends of intelligence. "I seldom went to a dinner party," Hughes said, "without gaining some information which helped me in my work. And many highly prized

[15] Hugh R. Wilson, *Diplomat Between Wars* (New York, Longmans, 1941), p. 167.

[16] Bertram D. Hulen, *Inside the Department of State* (New York, Whittlesey House, 1939), p. 89. Copyright, 1939, by Bertram D. Hulen.

friendships resulted from these meetings."[17] His extraordinary grasp on the forces and trends that were shaping the world had a direct relationship to his personal contacts with the diplomatic corps.

The diplomats learned that they could rely upon anything Hughes told them and that he always respected their confidence. He spoke to them with disarming candor and for the most part got candor in return. Sometimes his directness shocked the professionals in the department. In the traditional sense of the word, his approach was lacking in diplomacy, but that was because he believed sincerity, frankness, and a free meeting of minds were more important than any conventional jargon invented to conceal thought. Hating pomposity and duplicity, he was likely to be severe in dealing with either. When the Iranian minister called a third time in connection with his country's attempt to avoid payment of indemnity for an American who had been stoned to death in Iran, Hughes cut him off and gave his own review of the unsavory facts and ended by saying, "Good day, Mr. Minister." The chargé d'affaires of another country who had been given an appointment with the Secretary became so fearful that he could not answer Hughes' questions that he called to have his appointment shifted to someone else in the department. But if Hughes unceremoniously cut through pretense, he never took unfair advantage of a diplomat.

His method was open diplomacy, but he well understood that diplomacy must be secret in process if it is to be open in result. He had little patience with those who seemed to think that differences between sovereign governments could be settled in a sort of town meeting. Negotiators for each country had to be free to make tentative suggestions and later withdraw them without embarrassment—to make concessions without losing face before their own people. "Even the most democratic governments must desire to succeed in their negotiations," Hughes said, "and there is no reason why democracy should turn upon itself and deprive its agents of its essential means of defense."[18] Yet secrecy in negotiations was only a means of attaining relations between peoples that would be open, candid, and direct.

Hughes brought into our foreign relations a concept that was the reverse of diplomatic intrigue. What he asked of other nations was simply good faith, respect for American rights, equal opportunities, and honesty and fairness in the settlement of any differences that might arise. Anything smacking of deception or hidden purposes was beneath the dignity of a democratic power. Those were the tools of despotism. The United States had a mission to stand out in all its dealings with other countries as an exemplar of the justice that it sought to attain between man and man within its own jurisdiction. "The first

[17] CEH, Notes, p. 360. [18] Address at University of Michigan, June 19, 1922.

requirement of those who demand justice and security," he said, "is to give justice and security." [19]

Under his guidance, therefore, the department did not take up the fight of any American interest abroad simply because it was American. In each case he asked, not what American power might command, but where the equities lay. At no time, his associates say,[20] did he sponsor any unfair cause. His aim was to place international relations on a basis of high principle without departing from any legitimate national interest. "All things are possible," he said, "if nations are willing to be just to each other."

This pursuit of justice on a global scale was an expression of Hughes' deep interest in the welfare of mankind. He refused to fall in with any of the petty jealousies of nations or their short-sighted scrambling for power. Repeatedly he identified American interests with the peace, prosperity, and well-being of peoples in other parts of the world.

The legalism that sometimes pursues lawyers when they operate in other fields is noticeably absent from his conduct as Secretary of State. Indeed, he often irritated other lawyers in the department by subordinating law to common sense. After Congress passed the Immigration Act of 1921, William Roy Vallance of the Legal Division sought to have the department recognize boundary changes resulting from the war and its aftermath so as to facilitate the application of the new quotas. Castle and Dulles resisted on the ground that boundaries were then too fluid to be given formal approval. Vallance argued that the department should not recognize Rumanian visas for immigrants coming from Bessarabia unless it also recognized the transfer of Bessarabia from Russia to Rumania. Political refugees were coming to America from Bessarabia in large numbers, however, and Hughes declined to exclude them on a legal technicality.

"Vallance," he said, with a good-natured smile that seemed to take any sting out of his words, "you have made your record perfectly clear as a lawyer. As you say, your plan is legally simple. You can remain legally simple by remaining tightly shut in a hermetically sealed compartment. But I cannot afford to make this Government ridiculous. I must face facts and surmount difficulties arising from those facts. I have respect for the law but I am not willing to be a damn fool." [21]

The Secretary expressed this same guiding principle in more compact form when he addressed the Brazilian Bar Association in Rio de Janeiro on September 12, 1922. "I have great respect for the appropriate technique which is essential to correct administration," he said, "but I have no sympathy with those who lose the spirit of the law in the worship of its garments."

[19] Speech to Pan American Conference of Women, April 28, 1922.
[20] Sumner Welles, Charles Cheney Hyde, J. V. A. MacMurray, and others.
[21] Castle's Diary, 1923, p. 80.

Having a completely open policy, Hughes went to extraordinary effort to let the people know about it. "I always felt," he said, "that I should be greatly relieved if I could shout from the housetops every morning everything I had done or proposed to do." [22] That was not always possible, but Hughes' consistent effort was to see how much he could disclose and not how much he could withhold. He felt a special responsibility to educate the people in foreign affairs; for Americans were only beginning to think internationally at a time when the fate of the world truly hung on the decisions they would make.

Another factor counted heavily in determining his attitude. "A public officer has always got to remind himself," he told the press, "and he ought to say every morning as he approaches his task: 'I am a servant and it is my business to see what I can do for the American people. I am not a boss, and my little authority or great authority that I happen to have for a day, is not a personal perquisite.' " [23]

In spite of this attitude, his first brush with the press as Secretary of State brought sparks of friction. His notes in the flare-up between Panama and Costa Rica had been published by the newspapers without authorization before they could reach the recipient governments. Hughes expressed his displeasure and asked that all news concerning the activities of the department be funneled through himself or other high officials. Fearful of being "gagged," the press reacted with typical vehemence. But its complaint was soon forgotten because of the unprecedented flow of news that came from the Secretary himself.

Sweeping away the timorousness and taboos that had prevailed under his predecessor, Hughes became a bubbling fountain of information. He held two press conferences daily, with Henry Fletcher sometimes taking over one of them. The stilted and ponderous verbiage of the old school gave way to direct, lucid, and succinct answers to reporters' questions. In ten minutes he would range from Mexico to Yap, from China to Mesopotamia, with candor that sometimes brought applause from the blasé men of the press. "The lucidity and frankness of his press conferences," Sumner Welles was to write a quarter of a century later, "are a Washington tradition." [24]

Much of what he had to say to the press was "not for quotation." He spoke for enlightenment of the public and not to get his name in the newspapers. He gave the press the background facts of every situation affecting our foreign relations, in so far as the facts could be disclosed without jeopardizing negotiations that might be under way. In addition to his press conferences, his door was always open to reporters. "I wish every man in the newspaper work to feel that if there is anything that he wants to know, he can come to me at any time and ask," Hughes said. "If I can't tell him, I will say so, but there

[22] CEH, Notes, p. 358.
[23] *The Pathway of Peace* (New York, Harper, 1925), p. 247.
[24] *Washington Post*, Sept. 7, 1948.

is no reason why anyone should set afloat a doubtful report because he hasn't the opportunity at least to ask the Secretary whether his information is accurate or not." [25]

The Secretary further clinched his favorable standing with the press by strict adherence to two cardinal rules. The first was: Never lie to a newspaperman. Deceptive propaganda might appear to be useful in some instances, but it was a perilous indulgence. Hughes' experience had taught him that newspaper confidence in his integrity was the first essential to a successful public career, and he instinctively avoided anything that might cast a shadow upon that confidence. His second rule was to treat all newspapermen alike. No one of them could be favored without antagonizing all the others. It was only the experienced journalists in Washington to whom he spoke freely, however. Repeated misquotation had left him ultracautious about giving interviews during his travels to reporters he did not know.

Lighter touches often enlivened his press conferences. It was not unusual for Hughes to roar with laughter or banter the journalists about their inaccurate use of words. When classical-minded Matthew Tighe wrote Hughes a note in Latin to ask the substance of his conference with Ambassador Harvey, the Secretary replied to his "learned friend"—also in Latin. To a reporter who asked if "certain deductions" could not be drawn from the Secretary's silence on a subject about which he had been questioned, he laughingly said that the usual "deductions" of the press reminded him of a definition of oratory: "Unhampered by facts, unrestrained by circumstance, unlimited by time."

The newspapers and magazines broke out with a rash of exuberance over the Hughes policy of talking to the country through their columns. Day-to-day news of foreign affairs began to rival local murders and the Stillman divorce case for front-page space. The leading correspondents in Washington, in addition to the regular reporters covering the State Department, thronged the Secretary's conferences as they have never done since. In his relations with the press, wrote Arthur Wallace Dunn, Secretary Hughes is "the equal, if not the superior, of all his predecessors."

At the end of Hughes' first year in the State Department the Washington correspondents, whom Matthew Tighe had dubbed the Independent Order of Ungodly Intellectuals, presented him with a pair of golden shears in token of their "gratitude" for his "kindly assistance to them in their work." To this formal inscription on the shears Tighe added an expression of the correspondents' "personal esteem, regard and affection." Responding with a twinkle in his eye, Hughes said that he would use the gift, not to cut the Gordian knots of international diplomacy, as Tighe had suggested, but to clip from the news-

[25] *The Pathway of Peace*, p. 249.

papers the voluminous accounts of his activities so as to keep himself "duly humble" and avoid any "lack of understanding on my part of my duty." [26]

A wholly unpremeditated demonstration of the Secretary's mental endowments set tongues wagging in the press room. As he left his desk to hold his press conference, an official handed him a three-page memorandum that was ready for public announcement. While walking to the conference room, he focused his photographic mind on the three pages, then thrust them into an inside pocket and made the announcement from memory. Reporters later compared the stenographic record of the conference with the memorandum and found that Hughes had recited its content with the change of only one unimportant word.[27]

More astonishing to the press than Hughes' intellectual feats was his cordiality. While he had been in private life, his reputation as a "human icicle" had been refurbished. Such a man, the press had assumed, would direct our foreign relations with cold and unrelenting formality. Instead the correspondents found the new Secretary to be "a veritable spring of geniality."

So striking was the contrast between the austerity of his reputation and the good humor of his day-to-day performance that many journalists rushed into print with their "discovery." "The new Hughes" became the theme of a monotonous plethora of feature stories and articles. He was portrayed as being in his "second youth," as always smiling and radiating abundant energy, and as fast becoming "one of the most popular men in public life." A wit struck close to the truth when he said, "Mr. Hughes never lets his dignity get thawed or his geniality get frozen."

Hughes' close friends and some of the older correspondents who had known him at Albany smiled knowingly at these "discoveries." No doubt he had mellowed as most men do at the approach of sixty. But the only significant changes were in the nature of his work and his accessibility to the press. In the sense of controlling his appetites, of avoiding loose gossip and questionable conduct, of adhering steadfastly to his purposes, and of mastering each task with the utmost seriousness, he was as austere as he had ever been. What the news writers had really discovered was that the pressure under which he worked and his "moral unapproachableness," as William Hard called it, did not cloud his sense of humor or dull his enjoyment of living. Hughes could relish laughter, join wholeheartedly in funmaking, and sound the depths of emotion without wavering one iota from the path that his towering intellect marked out for him. In this we have perhaps the most striking aspect of his character.

[26] *Ibid.*, p. 248. [27] Hulen, *op. cit.*, p. 50.

Chapter 40

THE HARDING CABINET

PRESIDENT HARDING called his Cabinet together for the first time on March 8, 1921. For two hours the new presidential advisers sat around the big mahogany table in the White House Cabinet room discussing the responsibilities they had taken over and sizing up one another and their new chief. The Cabinet was a symbol of the changed order that had been established in Washington, but a many-sided symbol as diverse and complex as the character of Warren Harding himself.

On the President's left was a wizened and taciturn but shrewd and fabulously wealthy little man who was holding public office for the first time—Andrew W. Mellon, Secretary of the Treasury. Mellon seldom spoke, but when questioned about any business, economic, or financial matter he seemed always to know the answer. Beside him sat the smooth and sinister Harry M. Daugherty, whom Harding had rewarded with the Attorney Generalship over many vehement protests. The large, good-natured fellow of limited capacity sitting next in line was Edwin Denby, Secretary of the Navy. Then came short, thick-set Henry C. Wallace, publisher of an Iowa farm journal and now Secretary of Agriculture, and James J. (Puddler Jim) Davis, the Secretary of Labor.

At the far end of the table sat the "calm little Yankee," Vice President Calvin Coolidge, looking very much the fifth wheel that he was. Harding always gave the canny New Englander a chance to speak after members of the Cabinet had had their say. "Well," was Coolidge's typical remark, "I don't see anything we can do about the railroad situation." [1] But Coolidge let nothing escape him.

At the President's right was Hughes, looking the acme of dignity in his gray striped trousers, white-trimmed vest, and morning coat. Next to him was John W. Weeks of Massachusetts, engineer, banker, former Representative and Senator, and now Secretary of War. Trim and alert Will Hays, who had so ably conducted the Harding campaign and was now Postmaster General, sat between Weeks and Albert B. Fall, Secretary of the Interior. At the end of the row was Herbert Hoover, Secretary of Commerce, who was hated by the Old Guard and who, next to Hughes, held the distinction of having the best mind in the Cabinet.

[1] Author's interview with CEH, Nov. 19, 1946.

Shaggy, mustachioed Fall held a special distinction of a different sort. He was the most garrulous member of the Cabinet. Ranging over a wide field, he would chatter about anything outside the scope of his own department. Secretary Hughes summarized his impression of the New Mexican windbag in words much sharper than he was wont to use: "He would discourse at length on foreign affairs, showing neither acumen, discretion, nor accurate knowledge. But he thought he was an authority. His flow of words without wisdom was very boring to me at least, and I think to others. I had little to do with him, but I did not suspect him of anything worse than vanity and mental indigestion." [2]

Hughes assumed that the Cabinet would function as a team of presidential advisers. When the President called on him at the first meeting, he described rather fully the important business on which the State Department was currently working. Some others followed this example. The warp of administration and the woof of policy-making were thus woven together at the highest level of government.

This cooperative spirit quickly wilted, however, in the aftermath of the first Cabinet meeting. On Hughes' suggestion Harding had bound his advisers to secrecy as to Cabinet discussions. But full accounts of what happened at the meeting were on the front pages of the newspapers the next morning. On several other occasions confidential data that Hughes disclosed only to the Cabinet "leaked" to the newspapers.[3] Some member was obviously currying favor with the press by violating his pledge to the President. Concluding that the Cabinet was not a safe place to talk of anything confidential, Hughes soon confined his remarks there to matters that were ready for public announcement. "I have nothing to say now," he would respond to the President's invitation to speak, "but I should like to see you after the meeting."

Similarly embarrassed by "leaks," other Cabinet members began going to the President individually. Each member became wrapped up in the affairs of his own department and probably felt, as Hughes did, that he was scarcely in a position to offer useful comment on policy outside his own bailiwick. The Cabinet meetings thus came to be brief and not very helpful, the talk running to generalities and politics.[4]

Hoover, Hays, and Weeks were the only members of the Cabinet Hughes had known before his appointment. Mutual admiration as well as mutual interest in foreign commerce brought Hughes and Hoover frequently together. The long-existing conflicts between the State and Commerce departments concerning foreign representation in commercial matters quickly subsided under their cooperative techniques. In less than ten minutes they agreed that information on business and economic conditions abroad could best be gathered

[2] CEH, Notes, p. 253*d*. [3] *Ibid.*, p. 253*a*. [4] *Ibid.*, p. 253*d*.

by Department of Commerce men reporting to the American ambassador in each foreign capital.[5]

A "delightful friendship" sprang up between Hughes and the Secretary of Agriculture. Wallace was a man of character, strength, and common sense, with an earthy quality about him that appealed to the city-bred lawyer in Hughes. Early summer mornings often found them playing golf together at the Chevy Chase Club. During the summers of 1921 and 1922, when the Hughes family occupied Greystone on the edge of Rock Creek Park, Mrs. Hughes sometimes accompanied the two men around the course, although she no longer dabbled in golf. "Look at him," Hughes said to her, as Wallace followed a ball he had driven down the fairway. "He is the picture of health; he'll live forever." Within two years, however, Wallace was dead.

The President's manner of addressing the men in his Cabinet roughly divided them into two categories. Those who had been chosen for their ability or special knowledge were always Mister Hughes, Mister Hoover, Mister Mellon, or, more simply, Mister Secretary. The presidential cronies were called by their first names. Harding in turn was "Warren" to his personal friends, even "Wernie" to some, but Hughes always adhered to the formal "Mr. President." Their relations were close on an official plane but never intimate in the personal sense. Hughes himself is the best witness on this point:

> President Harding was a most kindly man,—always eager to please his old friends and to make new ones. He found it difficult to say No. To me, he was a most agreeable Chief, always accessible, anxious fully to understand each problem as it arose. I soon came to understand the limitations which were imposed upon him by the situation which had developed in the Senate in consequence of the wrangle over the Treaty of Versailles, and I sought to avoid embarrassing him by stirring up futile conflicts. I realized that I must take a full measure of responsibility when I felt definite action should be taken. I did not go to him with a statement of difficulties and ask him what should be done, but supplemented my statements of the facts in particular cases by concrete proposals upon which he could act at once, and to which he almost invariably gave his approval. Our relations were of the happiest sort. Engrossed as I was, night and day, in the work of the Department of State, I knew nothing of his intimacies with those who later abused his trust and brought his administration into disrepute.[6]

While Hughes kept the reins of foreign policy securely in his own hands, he never took advantage of the President. Going to the White House almost every day, he kept Harding thoroughly informed on everything of importance that the department proposed or had ascertained. The effect was to confirm the President's trust and bolster his willingness to follow Hughes' lead in any and all dealings with other countries. According to James Grafton Rogers,

[5] Herbert Hoover to author, March 14, 1949.
[6] CEH, Notes, p. 253*a*.

Hughes was allowed perhaps the widest range of discretion ever permitted an American Cabinet officer in this field.[7]

As a frequent visitor at the Executive Office, Hughes got a close-up view of the President's troubles. The waiting room was usually filled with people seeking access to the President's ear, and Harding's ambition to become the best-loved President seemed to make him available to all of them. When a White House aide would slip Hughes into the presidential office ahead of the other visitors, Harding would often put his arm across the Secretary's shoulders and exclaim, "Hughes, this is the damnedest job!"[8]

The President sought relief through golf in the afternoon and poker and parties at night. Secretary Hughes was frequently pressed to join in the golf, and occasionally he did so. During the Washington Conference, Harding, Hughes, and Arthur Balfour played eighteen holes at the Chevy Chase Club in the rain. For the most part, however, the Secretary of State found it impossible to squeeze an afternoon of golf into his busy schedule even at the request of the President.

Some of the politicians who had opposed Hughes' nomination claimed to have assurance that he would be shifted to the Supreme Court as soon as Chief Justice White had been given a graceful opportunity to retire.[9] Secretary Fall, the rumor ran, would then be elevated to the State Department. In spite of his great affection for the Supreme Court, Hughes found these rumors very irritating.

The venerable Chief Justice had clung grimly to his office even though his sight was virtually gone and he had been told that an operation was urgent—even though his intention to retire had been communicated to Justice Hughes back in 1916. White had later told Taft that he was holding the office open for him and that he would give it back to a Republican administration.[10] Whether this reflected only gratitude to Taft for his appointment of White or involved also some resentment against Wilson because of the 1916 incident may never be known. The Chief Justice's last opportunity to carry out any pledge was cut off on May 19, 1921, by his death from the operation that he had long postponed.

"William H. Taft, Charles E. Hughes and George Sutherland," said the *Washington Post* the next morning, "were the names most prominently mentioned . . . as possible successors of Edward Douglas White. . . ." At the State Department Undersecretary Fletcher carried the paper into Hughes' office.

"I hope this isn't true, so far as you are concerned," Fletcher said. "No," Hughes replied with typical finality. "If the President should offer me the

[7] *American Bar Association Journal*, July, 1941, p. 411.
[8] CEH, Notes, p. 253*b*. [9] New York *Call*, Feb. 27, 1921.
[10] Henry Pringle, *The Life and Times of William Howard Taft*, p. 955.

Chief Justiceship, I would not accept it and I would resign as Secretary of State." [11]

Hughes had no idea that the President was thinking of him for the Chief Justiceship. But, with the Irreconcilables still gunning for him, he wanted it clearly understood that he would regard any proposed shift as an indication of no confidence in what he had been doing at the State Department.

"I'm going to play golf with the President this afternoon," Fletcher volunteered. "Do you want me to tell him what you have just said?"

"Yes," was the clipped reply.

Out on the golf course Fletcher repeated the conversation. The President put his arm around Fletcher's shoulders and reassured him in typical off-the-record verbiage:

"No, I'm not going to disturb the 'old chief.' [Harding himself was only two years younger than Hughes.] I'm going to appoint old man Taft to the court."

The incident may well have strengthened Hughes' high standing with the President. It was a new application of the Hughesian principle that to be fit for high office a man must be willing to leave it at any time. Harding respected this attitude, and, since he was loath to lose the greatest asset of his Administration, he permitted nothing to come between them. The President's own attitude was reflected in a half-gay, half-rueful remark to the Reverend Mr. William F. McDowell, in praising Hughes' achievements. "The truth is," he said, "he ought to be President and then I would not have to be." [12] It is almost needless to say that Hughes had no such idea. He was wholly absorbed in the fascinating business of being Secretary of State and was happy to serve such an agreeable President as Harding always proved to be.

[11] Author's interview with Henry Fletcher, Aug. 10, 1946.
[12] McDowell to CEH, Sept. 3, 1923.

Chapter 41

POLICY OF THE FREE HAND

To JOIN or not to join the League of Nations was the first great question that arose to bedevil the Harding Administration. Having straddled the League issue in the campaign, Harding came to Washington free from entangling commitments, let alone convictions. The one thing certain about his attitude was that he was willing to be led, and his selection of Charles Evans Hughes to be Secretary of State indicated that he was not averse to being led toward the League.

Hughes' convictions had never been in doubt since his speech of March 26, 1919. Indeed, he had actively campaigned for American participation in an international organization to keep the peace when he ran for the Presidency in 1916. While he had fought for "mild reservations" to the Covenant that Wilson brought back from Paris, it was a forward-looking fight designed to improve and not to scuttle the League.

Harding was well aware of these facts when he gave Hughes a free hand in directing the nation's foreign affairs. In their conference at Marion, moreover, he had seemed to acquiesce in Hughes' candidly expressed desire to see the United States join the peace-enforcing organization.[1] His idea was that they could analyze the Versailles Treaty and decide what should be accepted and what rejected, and that the Senate would then consent to ratification of the treaty with the suggested reservations. The Secretary-designate went into office prepared to follow that course.

In Washington, however, it quickly became evident that sentiment against the League had hardened. Cox had made the League the "paramount issue," and the people had buried him under the Harding landslide—16,152,000 votes to 9,147,353. To be sure, Harding had the support of many pro-League Republicans, but the sweeping nature of his victory had sapped their influence. The strength of the Irreconcilables had been enhanced. Of the twelve Republican bitter-enders who had voted against the League in March, 1920, ten were still in the Senate and two had been replaced by other Republicans. Most of the Democrats who had voted against the treaty were also still there. It was clear to anyone who surveyed the outlook that the "little group of willful men" held the balance of power more securely than before the election.

[1] CEH, Notes, p. 258.

Their mood had been reflected in their stiff opposition to Hughes' appointment as Secretary of State. On that point their case was weak; but the two-thirds rule gave them the whip hand in respect of treaty ratification, and they were determined to use it. Hughes got a foretaste of what was to come when Senator Frank B. Brandegee went to the State Department to offer his advice. The Senator was blunt and blustering. Hughes replied in his most incisive and devastating manner. Waggling with excitement, Brandegee dashed back to the Capitol and told his colleagues they could expect the Versailles Treaty by the next White House messenger; that "whiskered" Secretary of State would soon have the country in the League of Nations.

There were many other conferences in which discussion waxed warm and intense. When Hughes continued to press for early consideration of the Covenant with reservations, Brandegee, Johnson, Borah, and others openly threatened, by way of retaliation, to block everything the Administration might attempt to do.[2]

Hughes went over the situation with Harding many times. Every exploration led back to the same stone wall of Senate opposition. Senator Frank B. Kellogg and other pro-League men in the Senate reviewed the situation with Hughes but could offer no hope of getting a two-thirds majority for the Covenant at that late date. A renewal of the struggle could result only in disaster for the Harding Administration without taking the United States any closer to the League.

Hughes concluded that he had no right to drag the Administration into the maelstrom that had engulfed Wilson. That decision not only blighted fond hopes; it also left him in the awkward position of failing to carry out the policy to which he had committed himself. "The Republican Party is bound by every consideration of good faith," the statement of the Thirty-One had said, "to pursue such a course [ratification of the Covenant with reservations] until the declared object is attained." The pro-League forces were counting heavily on Hughes to make this pledge effective. He could not forsake the League without subjecting himself to charges of breaking faith.

The situation was less embarrassing for Harding because he had never been a warm supporter of the League anyway. He announced his surrender to the Irreconcilables on April 12, 1921, in his message to Congress: ". . . there will be no betrayal of the deliberate expression of the American people in the recent election . . . the League Covenant can have no sanction by us."[3] In less than six weeks the new Administration had completely abandoned the chief objective of the foreign policy it had intended to pursue.

Having bowed to the inevitable, Hughes then had to decide whether to pro-

[2] Author's interview with CEH, Nov. 26, 1946.
[3] *Congressional Record*, 67th Cong., 1st session, Vol. 61, p. 172.

Harris & Ewing

Antoinette Hughes at home, about 1915

". . . a perfect companion . . ."

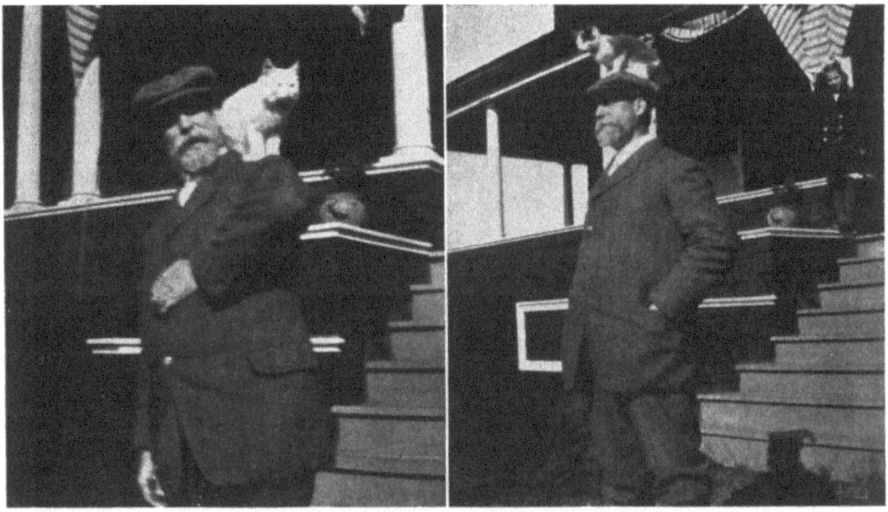

A strange sort of austerity—at Rangeley Lake, 1915

Underwood & Underwood

Three generations of Charles Evans Hugheses

ceed along other lines or to resign. His resignation so soon after taking office would have penalized Harding for not doing what Hughes knew he could not do.[4] It would also have deprived Hughes of the opportunity of carrying out other important policies that had begun to take shape and would probably have brought into power an anti-League Secretary of State. Pondering deeply on his predicament, Hughes decided that to resign would be a futile gesture unworthy of himself and unfair to the Administration. He had accepted office to do the best he could for the country in whatever circumstances might arise and he held on to his office for the same purpose.

That he made the best of a bad situation is scarcely open to question. His decision involved no sacrifice of integrity. While the Thirty-One had candidly voiced their hopes and convictions, they had not assumed the position of guarantors of American entry into the League. The inescapable fact was that the voters had made it impossible for the Administration to carry out the policy to which the Thirty-One had tried to commit it. The worst that can be said of Secretary Hughes in connection with this incident, therefore, is that he bowed to the will of the people and the Senate without an open fight.

Some of his friends concluded that he had lost his crusading zeal. In Albany when the bosses thwarted him he had gone straight to the people with his reforms. Could he not now similarly whip the Senate into line? Those who urged him to do so overlooked two compelling facts. In New York he had come into power as the head of a great popular movement that was demanding a housecleaning. As Secretary of State, he was an appointed official responsible to the President. No fight was possible without the President behind him, and in this matter the President was not behind him. In New York, legions of outraged voters had been eager to swoop down upon the hapless legislators who stood against his progressive measures. But in 1921 public opinion was running strongly against his plans for American adherence to the League.

Only a one-track mind would have carried over the Albany technique into these totally different circumstances. Hughes was not one to think in grooves, nor would he bankrupt statesmanship by clinging to the carcass of a dead policy. His willingness to be guided by facts and conditions beyond his control indicated a flexibility of mind and an attention to realities which are the beginning of wisdom in the conduct of foreign policy.

Repeatedly he was asked to explain the discrepancy between the pledge of the Thirty-One and his conduct as Secretary of State. Hamilton Holt, president of the Woodrow Wilson Democracy, wrote an open letter to the Thirty-One expressing the suspicion that they had been "betrayed and repudiated."[5] The *World* pointedly asked why a man who "is believed to represent the highest order of integrity in our public life" felt free to disregard his pledge and act

[4] CEH, to Edwin Gay, Aug. 1, 1922, p. 10. [5] *Independent*, Aug. 6, 1921.

contrary to it.[6] One of Thirty-One signers (Wickersham) indignantly accused the Secretary of being unfaithful to his trust. Discretion forbade Hughes to reveal the fight he had made for the League within the Administration, but he went as far as he could in defense of his position in a confidential letter to Wickersham:

> The plain fact is that President Harding, if he had undertaken to bring about our entry into the League, even upon the basis of reservations or a modified agreement, would have precipitated a controversy of the most serious character, but he could not have achieved the result. The opposition was too determined and resourceful. They had decided that there should be no participation in the League on any terms. No matter what Mr. Harding had said as a candidate, or the Thirty-One had said, the President was required as a statesman to take account of this condition. He would have been unworthy of his place had he not made the best appraisement possible . . . if he had proposed entry into the League with reservations, or modification of the Covenant, he would have wrecked the Administration by involving it in a most bitter fight and he would not have succeeded.[7]

Meanwhile the United States' strained relationship toward the League was a source of befuddlement abroad as well as controversy at home. Following the Senate's rejection of the Treaty of Versailles and Harding's election, the Wilson Administration had withdrawn from all contact with the League as if it had become contaminated. Communications from the League had been left unanswered. American officials had been instructed to go no more to the Council of Ambassadors. Even the "unofficial representative" on the Reparation Commission had been compelled to retire.[8] After March 4, Hughes tried to shake off this extremism so far as it was feasible. Ambassador Harvey was instructed to act as the President's representative in the Supreme Council, Ambassador Wallace in Paris to resume his status as "unofficial American observer" in the Conference of Ambassadors, and Roland W. Boyden to sit once more, unofficially, on the Reparation Commission. But a few months later the Senate attempted to slam the door upon any sort of American participation in League activities. Its consent to the peace treaty with Germany was given subject to the understanding "that the United States shall not be represented or participate in any body, agency or commission . . . unless and until an Act of the Congress of the United States shall provide for such representation." [9] The President accepted this probably unconstitutional invasion of the executive power as part of the instrument ratifying the treaty.

In these circumstances it was utterly impossible for Hughes to cooperate with the political agencies of the League, but he refused to close his eyes or stop his ears to what was going on in the world. By a liberal interpretation of the Senate's prohibition, he made increasing use of "unofficial observers"

[6] July 21, 1922.

[7] CEH to Wickersham, March 28, 1923.

[8] *Foreign Relations, 1921*, I, 2–6.

[9] *Ibid.*, II, 33.

in League agencies that were dealing with humanitarian problems or other issues in which the United States had a special interest. These "unofficial observers" became the butt of much ridicule in the United States and other countries. They sat in numerous League meetings without authority to join in the debate or to influence decisions. To be sure, they officially represented the United States in the only role it could play at Geneva. Still, they were merely outsiders listening in. The greatest power in the world was pretending to withdraw from world councils and then creeping back to learn what was happening.

While Hughes chafed under the limitations that had been laid upon him, he made no apology for doing the best he could in the circumstances. ". . . there is nothing obscure or reprehensible, nothing derogatory to our influence, dignity, or prestige, in the form of our cooperation," he said. "It is simply adjusted to an inescapable fact. Of course, as the United States has decided not to become a member of the League of Nations, this Government cannot act as though it were a member." [10]

While he was careful to avoid ventures that would be certain to start a cyclone of protest, the Secretary considered each separate proposal for joint efforts with the League on its merits. If it appeared that American interests were directly involved or that the general welfare of humanity would be promoted by an international undertaking, he went as far as he could in cooperating with the League. The United States named representatives to work with League committees in relation to opium, anthrax, public health, antitoxin serums, traffic in women and children, relief work, customs formalities, and the control of traffic in arms.

Some of the pro-League men expected Hughes to sponsor a new League as an alternative to securing ratification of the Versailles Treaty. The President had hinted that new "covenanted relationships" might be sought. Hughes explored the possibilities. He was convinced that Wilson had blundered in making this association for the promotion of peace an enforcing agency for the victors of the war. At one time he tentatively suggested that the League might be left to its task of "enforcing agency" and that "a new association on an acceptable basis not directly connected with the Peace Treaty might be formed for the broader purposes in view." Nothing came of it. Earlier he had put out a feeler that the League itself might become an acceptable peace agency if divorced from its enforcement function under the Versailles Treaty, but Ambassador Jusserand scotched the idea with a sharp declaration that it would never win approval in France.

Wickersham, Lowell, and others persistently clung to the fanciful hope of a new phoenix rising out of the supposed ruin of the League. But any Ameri-

[10] Speech to New York Republican State Convention, April 15, 1924.

can suggestion of a new peace organization just after this country had abandoned the existing League fathered by an American President would have been laughed to scorn in Europe. And it would have been little more acceptable to the Senate than was the experiment at Geneva. Hughes advised Lowell in July, 1922, that any further reference by the President to an association of nations would call for a more or less definite plan and that general conditions were such that it would be "impracticable to suggest a plan at this time." He added:

> We have been dealing with matters in a practical way and have accomplished a great deal. If there are those who think that they should renew a barren controversy, that is their right. Nothing good will come of it, and very likely it will stand in the way of much that might otherwise be accomplished.[11]

In the heat of the 1924 presidential campaign, Raymond B. Fosdick, former Undersecretary General of the League, fired a broadside of charges that were reechoed by disgruntled pro-League forces. The Secretary of State, he said, had slighted the League by failing to reply to many of its communications. He had snubbed the Barcelona Conference, put "wooden images" on League committees, and stooped to "indirection, deliberate obstruction and bad manners" in dealing with the League.[12]

The practice of ignoring League communications had begun, as previously noted, in the Wilson Administration. Of thirty-three notices, requests, and invitations from the Geneva organization, the department had replied to only fifteen when Hughes came in. For the next two and a half months a bungling career officer who remained in charge of the "desk" where League communications were received continued to file them in a sort of dead-letter drawer. As soon as the Secretary learned this, he angrily ordered the League communications to be answered and banished the hapless young man to the American Legation in Cairo. Whether or not we are in the League, he told his associates, we can at least be courteous.

As for the Conference on Communications and Transit held at Barcelona in the spring of 1921, Hughes was content to send no representative because of its preoccupation with European problems. But the invitation to attend it had been declined by his predecessor, Secretary Colby, in deference to the Senate's isolationism.

Another source of complaint was the State Department's brush-off of the League in connection with the arms-traffic convention. The Secretary General, Sir Eric Drummond, inquired on March 8, 1921, and again on November 21 whether the United States would ratify the Convention of Saint Germain. Hughes discussed the arms-traffic problem with the British at the Washington Conference, with Secretaries Denby and Weeks and President Harding. It was

[11] CEH to A. Lawrence Lowell, July 20, 1922. [12] *New York Times*, Oct. 19, 1924.

July 28, 1922, however, before he got around to informing Drummond that the United States did not approve the convention. Even then he communicated his reasons for disapproval only to the British Government, which had also been urging the United States to accept the convention. It was scarcely considerate treatment of the League.

Hughes declined to submit the convention to the Senate chiefly because it would have prevented the United States from supplying arms to many Latin American countries that were not signatories and because its provisions were so closely "intertwined" with the League. In 1924 he authorized Grew, then minister to Switzerland, to sit with the Temporary Mixed Commission, which was trying to work out a new agreement on control of the arms traffic. But, as the new draft treaty was drawn to buttress the League system of collective security, the State Department washed its hands of the whole business.

In seeking international control of narcotic drugs, the United States took the lead. The 1924 opium conference at Geneva was under the direction of a League committee, but the driving force behind the whole project was largely American. The comprehensive plan that Hughes cabled to Edwin L. Neville, the American representative on the preparatory committee, called for rigid control over production of the opium poppy and the coca-leaf plant in addition to control over transportation and manufacture of narcotic drugs. That plan was later embodied in a draft convention submitted by the American delegation to the conference. No real progress toward limiting the production of raw opium to the medicinal and scientific needs of the world could be made, however, and after two months of futile negotiations Hughes authorized the American delegation to withdraw.

The fiercely pro-League Americans often proved to be the League's worst enemies in its relations with the United States. If the State Department failed to do something that the League requested, they complained of "discourtesy." And when the department cooperated with the League, they shouted aloud that the United States was about to join, thus arousing a new wave of suspicion on Capitol Hill. Hughes had no sympathy with these short-sighted maneuvers. Yet he was often as irritated as the League enthusiasts by the handicaps under which he worked. Never was he free from petty obstruction. It is against this background that his work must be judged. If he "betrayed" the internationalists, it was only, as William Hard said, "in order to outwit and outflank the isolationists for the benefit of internationalism and international law and order." [13] Certainly his achievements would have to be sketched on a broader canvas if he had been Secretary of State when full cooperation with the world community was possible.

The chief difference between Hughes and the more passionate Leaguers

[13] New York *Herald Tribune*, Sept. 2, 1928.

was over the latter's faith in mere organization. Many Americans came to believe that our adherence would in itself make the League an effective organization and that peace would then be assured. Hughes never had any such illusions. "Had we entered the League," he said, "our cooperation would have been facilitated and our representatives would have taken an appropriate part in various discussions. This would have afforded a valuable training in participation in an international organization. Most likely it would have eliminated some of the fears, as well as dashed some of the hopes, created by the prospect of that participation. I question whether, with respect to important matters especially in relation to distinctly European questions, the actual results would have been different." [14]

As he watched the League struggle ineffectively with the postwar problems of Europe, Hughes asked himself philosophically what the United States might have done as a member to change the outlook. The League Council was impotent in all matters of larger importance because the great powers of Europe who were its chief members could not agree among themselves. They could not agree because their interests were diverse. The presence of an American representative on the Council would not have changed these basic facts. Nor would public sentiment have permitted the use of American arms abroad if League policies had called for such measures.

When the League buckled under the pressure of events that led to World War II, Hughes felt there was no justification for attributing its weakness to the continued absence of the United States. Secretary Stimson had seized the initiative in trying to curb Japan's aggression in Manchuria in 1931. He had worked openly with the League, in some instances spurring it into action and consistently demonstrating greater boldness than was evident at either London or Geneva.[15] "Certainly . . . there is no basis for saying that this result would have been altered by our membership in the League." [16]

Hughes was equally certain that our presence at Geneva would not have stopped Mussolini's imperialistic adventure in Ethiopia in 1935, or the "undeclared war" of Japan against China in 1937, or the rearming of Germany that led to Hitler's aggressive sprees. His reasoning is convincing:

> Hitler rearmed in violation of [the] treaty and in the presence of Europe. There was no real secret about it. His development of Germany's air power was his boast and was well known. The European Powers could easily have stopped him but they did not. Even when he sent troops into the Rhineland, they did not oppose him. Why? I suppose that the controlling thought in Great Britain was that Germany had been harshly treated and that if she were permitted to regain her prestige and take her place again as a Great Power, she could be dealt with satisfactorily by

[14] CEH, Notes, p. 261.
[15] A. Whitney Griswold, *The Far Eastern Policy of the United States*, pp. 417–418.
[16] CEH, Notes, p. 262.

diplomatic methods and war would be prevented. Neither Great Britain nor France wished war. And there was always the supposition that at the worst there was adequate protection in the redoubtable French Army.

Can any well-informed person, who looks at the matter realistically, believe that we should have taken a different view and as a member of the League would have thrown our weight against the policy of Great Britain and France, insisting on military action? They were immediately concerned and they, not we, had the military power to hold Hitler in check before it was too late. But they did not desire to use that power. It was in the absence of the exercise of that power that Hitler continued his aggressions and mocked at the efforts of appeasement; and when after overrunning Austria, Denmark, Norway, The Netherlands and Belgium, he invaded France, her great Army crumbled. It is vain to suppose that these tragic events would have been prevented if our Government had been a member of the League! [17]

To the end of his days Hughes' faith in international organization to keep the peace remained steadfast, and his thinking was to be reflected in the United Nations. But he never permitted idealism to blind him to the nature of national power. ". . . the experience of the League of Nations teaches," he wrote in his Notes, "that, despite international organization, when it comes to the use of force, the Great Powers who have the force and upon whose willingness to use it reliance must be placed will act or fail to act according to the policy which they believe to be dictated by their respective essential interests at the time. Formal international organization will provide a useful mechanism to facilitate united action in the interest of peace but will not insure that action."

This seasoned view was not entirely garnered, however, out of the League's failure. It is a reflection of the realism that Hughes consistently preached and practiced as Secretary of State. In a striking address to the Canadian Bar Association at Montreal on September 4, 1923, under the title "The Pathway of Peace," he exploded the idea that councils, rules, and formulas alone can insure peace.

"War should be made a crime," he said, "and those who instigate it should be punished as criminals." But, with the outlawing of war, he reasoned, other means of redress for injuries will have to be provided; and, since there is no lawgiver for independent states, the discipline essential to peace will have to come from self-imposed restraints. War can be abandoned, therefore, only by common willingness to let international law take the place of force. "As the restraint is self-imposed," Hughes emphasized, "it will prove to be of avail only while there is a will to peace.

"All contrivances for maintaining peace by economic pressure, as well as by military force, depend upon the sentiment which will apply the pressure and direct the force when the test comes. . . . There is no path to peace except as the will of peoples may open it. . . ." [18]

[17] *Ibid.*, pp. 263–264. [18] *The Pathway of Peace*, pp. 7–8.

Chapter 42

THE PEACE TREATIES

HOPE OF saving some portions of the Treaty of Versailles lingered for several months after the Harding Administration had turned its back upon the League of Nations. The two were not inseparable. And some means of ending the state of war between the United States and Germany had to be found. Secretary Hughes reasoned that the best way of safeguarding American rights as one of the victorious powers was to ratify the pertinent sections of the Treaty of Versailles, excluding the League Covenant.

It was vital, he thought, to protect American interests in Germany's overseas possessions. These had been ceded, not to the League, but to the five Principal Allied and Associated Powers, including the United States. We did not demand any of the former German territories for ourselves, but Hughes was determined that these colonies should not be disposed of without our consent. The much maligned treaty also provided that Germany should pay the costs of the armies of occupation. Without a treaty, these payments would be in jeopardy. Finally, the treaty set up an elaborate system of tribunals for the settlement of the claims of private citizens against Germany. Hughes thought it would be absurd to give up such obvious advantages merely because an emotional bias had come to be associated with the name "Versailles Treaty."

Sharply different views prevailed on Capitol Hill. On July 2, 1921, Congress passed a joint resolution declaring the war with Germany to be at an end and laying legislative claim to "all rights, privileges, indemnities, reparations, or advantages" to which the United States or its nationals had become entitled under the armistice and the Treaty of Versailles. But the rights to which the Government laid claim would still be insecure until directly confirmed in a treaty with Germany. Ratification of the pertinent sections of the Versailles Treaty, Hughes said, was still the best means of accomplishing this end.

The Secretary's earnest arguments won Harding to this point of view. When the President ran into senatorial hostility, he called a conference at the White House. About fifteen Senators attended. There was no roof-raising, but Hughes employed all his powers for logical, clear, and forceful exposition in an effort to make the Senators see the benefits that the United States would derive from ratification of the treaty. To give up this means of getting recognition for the very rights that the Senate had claimed in its resolution of July 2, he said, would be an act of incredible folly.[1]

The voice of reason beat in vain against the wall of passion which the Irreconcilables had put up. Some of them said bluntly that submission of the treaty to the Senate would provoke the same kind of futile struggle that the League Covenant had done, with a harvest of nothing but bitterness and trouble for the Harding Administration. Several mild Reservationists agreed that the outlook for approval of the treaty was hopeless.

Hughes saw that to proceed as he had planned would indefinitely delay the establishment of peace. That would be detrimental to American interests in addition to prolonging uncertainty and hampering economic recovery in Europe. Reluctantly he accepted another behind-the-scenes defeat, and began to rack his brain for ways and means of getting a new treaty with Germany that would satisfy the Senate.

The baffling nature of his task is apparent. He would have to draft a treaty that would look new to the Senate and old to Germany. The Treaty of Versailles was voluminous and complex. It seemed impossible to redraft its intricate provisions affecting American interests in a form that would be acceptable to Germany. New text covering the same ground as the text already in effect as between Germany and the Allies might plunge the peace settlements into an abyss of conflicting interpretations. Hughes shuddered as he thought of the Allies traveling one road with their treaty and the United States traveling another road with a separate treaty.

Of course, the new treaty would have to include all the rights and privileges reserved by the congressional resolution declaring the war at an end. If its language could be deemed to have a different significance from that contemplated in the joint resolution, the bitter-enders would tear it to pieces. Congress appeared to have given the Secretary a riddle impossible of solution.

One morning after Hughes had been mulling over his dilemma, he awoke with a brilliant idea that seemed to have taken shape while he slept. He could probably satisfy the Senate and avoid interminable negotiations with the Germans by incorporating into a treaty the specific language of the congressional resolution along with those parts of the Treaty of Versailles which stipulated rights and privileges for the benefit of the United States. In this way he could avoid redrafting either the treaty or the resolution.[2] Germany would have to accept such a treaty because the rights for which the United States would be asking had already been granted at Versailles. The Senate would have to accept it because it would be a verbatim compliance with congressional demands.

The Secretary went to his office that morning tingling with eagerness to get the job started. What had seemed hopelessly complex was now reduced to

[1] Author's interview with CEH, Nov. 26, 1946. [2] CEH, Notes, p. 273.

simplicity. He wondered why he had not thought of this solution before. Calling in Fred K. Nielsen, he told him precisely what the treaty should contain and asked the solicitor to draft it promptly. Before an hour had elapsed, he telephoned Nielsen to ask what progress had been made. His inquiry was repeated several times during the day, and, as Nielsen had still made no progress, Hughes threatened to take over the drafting himself.

The treaty finally took shape as he had visualized it. An extraordinary document it was, giving the United States all the benefits accruing to any power under the Treaty of Versailles and imposing none of the responsibilities assumed by the other victors. The United States could participate in the Reparation Commission or remain aloof at its discretion. Similarly, it could take advantage of the Mixed Arbitral Tribunal or work out a different arrangement for the settlement of claims. "This gives us a footing that is practically unassailable," Hughes wrote to his son on August 27, "and while it may be swallowed with a wry face, it is privately recognized by all those who have sense enough to appreciate the facts that it is the best that could be done."

In spite of the absence of American obligations, Germany accepted the treaty. It was signed in Berlin on August 25, 1921, and Hughes made his first appearance before the Senate Foreign Relations Committee to request its approval. "Never before had we met a Secretary of State," said one Democratic member of the committee, "who so thoroughly understood his subject and so clearly explained every phase of it." The Senate consented to ratification of the treaty the following October. Diplomatic relations with Germany were resumed a few weeks later, and similar treaties were negotiated with Austria and Hungary.

These separate peace settlements were criticized by the same groups that were hounding the Administration on the League issue. Hamilton Holt flatly charged Hughes with having abandoned the Allies. "The separate peace with Germany was concluded," Hughes replied, "for the sufficient reason that it became perfectly clear, after the most careful consideration, that the re-submission of the Treaty of Versailles with suggested reservations would have no other result than the renewal of the former controversy and its continuance for an indefinite period." [3]

Hughes had sought no special favors from Germany. He had merely refused to give up rights to which the United States was entitled, and he had recognized the practical necessity of restoring peaceful relations outside the Treaty of Versailles. The policy of "going it alone" was almost as disturbing to him as it was to his critics, but he was pragmatist enough to concentrate on what was possible instead of sighing over what might have been.

In the creation of claims machinery Secretary Hughes again ran head-on

[3] CEH to Holt, July 13, 1922.

into Senate opposition. His plan was to adhere to the Versailles pattern. In the Treaty of Berlin, as the separate peace settlement came to be known, he had made a special point of establishing the right of the United States to use the claims machinery that the Allies had already set up. But the prospect of battle with the Senate, when he had no legions at his command, caused him to change his mind and negotiate a separate claims agreement with Germany. It must be remembered that the Senate had attached to the Treaty of Berlin a reservation to the effect that the United States should not be represented on any body, agency, or commission without specific authorization from Congress.

Hughes began discussions with the German Foreign Office, through Ambassador Houghton, in the spring of 1922. His plan was to refer the claims of American nationals against Germany to a "mixed commission" on which Germany as well as the United States would be represented. While negotiations were going forward, Senator Oscar Underwood introduced a bill for settlement of these claims through a commission composed entirely of Americans. Claims thus approved would have been satisfied from German property in the United States which had been seized during the war under the Trading with the Enemy Act.

Chairman Knute Nelson of the Senate Judiciary Committee sent a copy of the bill to Hughes, and he tagged it a confiscation measure. Enactment of the bill, he wrote, would be "embarrassing to the Executive" and would make it necessary to abandon the plans under way to set up a mixed claims commission. The governments which would be asked to pay these claims, he argued, certainly ought to be represented on the commission that would fix the amounts. The fact that the United States held property from which claims might be satisfied made it the more important to avoid any unfairness. "I should hope," he declared, "that in any case no measure of confiscation would be adopted until there had been a failure, after reasonable opportunity, to provide for the satisfaction of the claims of American citizens, duly ascertained." [4]

Let us be just, his restrained language said in effect, even to our former enemies.

Hughes was fearful that the Senate would pass the Underwood bill in spite of his protests. Even if it did not, the bill would be a hazard to any treaty on German claims that he might submit to the Senate. Under this stimulus, he looked for other means of accomplishing his aim and hit upon the idea of setting up a claims commission by executive agreement without the advice or consent of the Senate.

Never a man to cut corners, Hughes carefully checked the authorities and found ample justification for what he wished to do. Settlement of the claims of nationals solely by executive action was an old practice going back to Jeffer-

[4] *Foreign Relations, 1922,* II, 252–255.

son's day. When he was ready to spring his surprise on the Senate, however, he asked the President to bring in Senator Borah for an interview. The Secretary poured out his abhorrence of confiscation and told the Lion of Idaho that the best way to avoid it was to set up an American-German claims commission by executive agreement. Borah asked for the authorities supporting this course of action, and when Hughes gave him the citations the Senator said he would raise no objection. The Secretary then wired Ambassador Houghton to close the agreement, and it was signed on August 10, 1922. In an exchange of notes the United States promised Germany not to press any claims of American nationals for pensions to disabled soldiers or "separate allowances" to their dependents, although claims of that sort were allowed under those sections of the Treaty of Versailles which had been incorporated in the Treaty of Berlin.

These American strokes for fair treatment of a defeated country were matched by a unique gesture on the part of Germany. The agreement called for an umpire on the mixed claims commission whose judgment would be decisive in case of disagreement between the American and German representatives in allowing claims and fixing their amount. The German Government suggested that a prominent American citizen be named by the President of the United States to act as umpire. It was a striking tribute to the sense of justice that characterized American foreign policy under Secretary Hughes.

Responding in the same spirit, the Secretary suggested that Justice Day of the Supreme Court be named as umpire. Day was acceptable to the German Government as well as to President Harding, but failing health compelled him to withdraw shortly after his appointment. Harding then named Edwin B. Parker of Texas. The commissioners were Chandler P. Anderson for the United States and Dr. Wilhelm Kiesselbach for Germany. Congress recognized the commission by appropriating its share of that body's operating funds, and a large part of the American claims against Germany was to be settled before Hughes left office.

Chapter 43

OPENING THE MANDATED ISLANDS

NO ASPECT of the peace settlement was more enmeshed in confusion in March, 1921, than Japan's mandate in the Pacific. Washington and Tokyo were exchanging heated notes over the Island of Yap. Great Britain was supporting the Japanese. The controversy was inflamed by conflicting reports as to what had happened in the Council of Four on May 7, 1919, when Japan had been awarded a class "C" mandate over the German islands in the Pacific north of the Equator. Suspicion and distrust were fast creeping in where understanding had vanished.

Yap is relatively a pin point in the Pacific 700 miles from the Philippines. But it happened to be the cable center for the German-Netherlands Telegraph Company from which cables ran to Shanghai, Manado (Dutch East Indies), and Guam, the latter cable making connections with lines to the United States, Japan, and the Philippines. Control of Yap meant mastery over the communications system of the Pacific. Wilson had insisted at Paris that Yap be internationalized so that all nations could be assured of equal access to its cable facilities. In the May 6 meeting of the Council of Four the President had agreed in principle that Japan should have a mandate over "certain islands" taken from Germany, believing that his prior objection to the inclusion of Yap would stand. The following day this decision had been formalized without further discussion. No reference to Yap had been recorded in the minutes of either day's proceedings.

This muddled situation made a perfect background for a battle of words. The British Foreign Office declared flatly that all the former German islands in the Pacific north of the Equator had been included in the mandate given to Japan. President Wilson had been present on that occasion and had offered no objection. "It does not appear to be open to His Majesty's Government," the note concluded, "to regard the decision of May 7, 1919, as other than definitive." [1]

Japan almost shrieked her arguments. If a decision to exclude Yap had been made at the May 7 meeting, at which no Japanese representative was present, said an arrogant note from Tokyo, "it could not but have been regarded as an

[1] *Foreign Relations, 1921*, II, 264.

act of entirely bad faith." [2] As to Wilson's prior reservations on Yap, Japan insisted that they amounted to only meaningless "preliminary conversations."

The United States informed the League of Nations that mandates could not be allotted without its consent, but the League Council replied that allocation of the mandates was the function of the Supreme Council, and that body had assigned the German islands to Japan in spite of Wilson's protests. Clearly the United States was losing its fight for a voice in the granting of mandates.

One of Wilson's last official acts was to send to the State Department on March 3, 1921, a communication as to his handling of the problem of Yap. Reviewing his efforts to have the island internationalized for cable purposes, he concluded:

> I never abandoned or modified this position in respect to the Island of Yap, and I did not agree on May 7, 1919, or at any other time, that the Island of Yap should be included in the assignment of mandates to Japan.
>
> As a matter of fact, all agreements arrived at regarding the assignment of mandates were conditional upon a subsequent agreement being reached as to the specific terms of the mandates, and further, upon their acceptance by each of the Principal Allied and Associated Powers. The consent of the United States is essential both as to assignments of mandates and the terms and provisions of the mandates, after agreement as to their assignment or allocation.
>
> The consent of the United States, as you know, has never been given on either point, as to the Island of Yap.[3]

When Hughes surveyed the situation, he encountered equally emphatic British and Japanese assertions that Wilson had given his consent. The great issue of the United States' relation to these strategic islands in the Pacific had boiled down to a contest in veracity between the former President and foreign chancelleries over the disposition of a single atoll. The larger American interests in the mandated territories seemed to be entirely forgotten. The nation which had turned the tide of victory had been reduced to squabbling for a crumb from the peace table.

Secretary Hughes' first conclusion was that the demands of the United States would have to be shifted to new ground. Important though it was, Yap was not the sum of our interests. Japan's acquisition of the Marshall, Mariana, and Caroline islands directly athwart the sea lanes from Pearl Harbor to the Philippines had a bearing of the utmost importance upon American security in the Pacific. Of course, there was no possibility at that late date of upsetting the mandate that had been given to Japan. Even at the peace conference Wilson had encountered a virtual *fait accompli*, as Hughes was soon to learn. But the United States could protect its rights in the islands, including the right to keep them demilitarized, and the Secretary decided that any lesser course would be a craven surrender of our basic national interests.

[2] *Ibid.*, p. 274. [3] *Ibid.*, p. 281.

It is not to be supposed that Hughes looked across two decades and foresaw the Japanese attack on Pearl Harbor that plunged the United States into World War II. But he did see that the mandated islands were potential strongholds for conquest in the Pacific. This was enough to convince him that the United States must have free access to the islands and equal rights with the League to see that no fortifications were built there. The absence of the United States from the League of Nations did not mean that we could safely draw into our shell or forsake rights that might prove to be vital.

In working out his new approach, Hughes pointed out that the right to dispose of Germany's overseas possessions had been acquired only through the victory of the Allied and Associated Powers. Consequently, that right was shared by the United States; there could be no valid disposition of German territories without the assent of the United States. The Supreme Council could not bind the American Government. Indeed, the rights accruing to this country by reason of the common victory could be ceded to Japan only by treaty, and no such treaty had been made.

Nor could the failure of the United States to ratify the Treaty of Versailles detract from the rights it had acquired. No country could be bound by a treaty to which it was not a party. It made no difference, then, what the Supreme Council had decided on May 7, 1919. It made no difference whether President Wilson had reiterated his reservations as to Yap. Under no circumstances would the allocation of the Pacific islands to Japan be final until confirmed by a treaty with the United States.[4]

Identic notes setting forth these views went out to Tokyo, London, Paris, and Rome on April 2, 1921. Since the Supreme Council had attempted to put into effect a mandate "purporting to be made in the name of the United States, but without the assent of the United States," Hughes expressed his trust that this action, presumably taken under "a misapprehension," would be reconsidered. What had appeared to be a humiliating rout for the United States was suddenly reversed with a stunning blow to Japanese hopes and British arguments.

At his press conference the Secretary insisted that his notes were not "sharp." The correspondents took him at his word and called them "blunt." The language he used was restrained enough, but his logic was devastating. It cut beneath all the petty squabbling and the contest in veracity; with typical Hughesian incisiveness it went straight to the fundamental issue. There was no valid argument left.

The Republican leaders in Washington, who had been watching Hughes with a fishy eye, hailed this stroke with unbounded enthusiasm. "Unambiguous," "masterly," and "unassailable" were the adjectives most frequently heard

[4] CEH, Notes, p. 269; *Foreign Relations, 1921,* II, 279–282.

in their comments. The Senate seemed especially delighted by this evidence that the Secretary's interest in international cooperation took no edge off his skill in upholding American rights.

France and Italy swung over to support of the American position. The British Ambassador, Sir Auckland Geddes, called on the Secretary to say, as an individual, that his government was bound by its agreement with Japan in 1916 to favor the awarding of the North Pacific islands to Japan. Hughes asked if President Wilson had been familiar with this agreement, and Geddes said that Mr. Balfour had given the President a copy of it when he was in Washington. Had Balfour called Wilson's attention to the document? the Secretary asked. Geddes did not know, but he was certain that Wilson knew of the secret deal when he reached Paris.[5]

Hughes talked earnestly to Geddes about the effect of the British position on American public opinion. Cooperation between Great Britain and the United States, he implied, could give the world stability. But little progress could be made in this direction if the American people should get the idea that Britain was making a secret engagement with Japan before this country entered the war the basis for resisting the very modest demands of the United States for equal rights in the mandated territories. Geddes replied that the British would have to stand by their agreement.

When the Japanese Foreign Office finally replied to Hughes' note, late in May, its tone was courteous and the door was left open to further discussion. Baron Shidehara, the Japanese ambassador, followed up with a call at the Secretary's office on June 3. He thought that an agreement might be reached on the division of the German cables and internationalization of Yap for cable purposes. Hughes replied that it was not merely a question of cables but of all means of communication. If Yap was useful for any other purpose, the United States should have a share in that use. Did Japan desire to fortify the island? he asked. Shidehara denied any such intention.[6]

Through a long period of negotiations the differences between the two governments were narrowed to the question of free access and equal opportunity. Japan complained on October 17 that acceptance of Hughes' open-door proposals would "virtually imply that foreign nationals and vessels shall have access, on the same terms as Japanese, to the territories and territorial waters committed to Japan's charge." This principle would be acceptable only if it were applied to territories held by other powers under class "C" mandates.

Once more Hughes interposed an unanswerable argument. The United States, he said, was not trying to force upon Japan the general principle of equality of opportunity. What he wished to emphasize was that the United States was one of the powers granting Japan the right to administer these islands as an integral

[5] *Foreign Relations, 1921*, II, 284. [6] *Ibid.*, p. 289.

part of its territory. If Japan had acquired the islands outright without our aid, they would have been open to American commerce under existing treaties. Obviously the United States could not yield its interest in the islands to Japan under a less favorable arrangement.[7]

The negotiations were still dragging on when the Washington Conference met in November, 1921. In the atmosphere of good will that pervaded the conference, Hughes finally induced the Japanese to accept his terms. The heads of the other Allied delegations acquiesced, and Hughes and Shidehara signed the treaty on February 11, 1922. The Senate voted its approval in less than three weeks.

The Secretary's persistence and skill had won for the United States every substantial advantage for which he had contended. As to Yap, free access was given for the operation of cables and radiotelegraphic service. The rights of residence and acquisition of property were guaranteed against restriction. Cable messages were to be free from censorship; persons and property were to have free entry and exit; they were to be free from taxes, landing charges or exactions, and discriminatory police regulations.

Agreement on the disposition of the Pacific cables came more easily. The cable from Yap to Guam was allocated to the United States; the cable from Yap to Shanghai and the Japanese mainland, to Japan; the cable from Yap to Manado, to the Netherlands. Mr. Balfour and M. Sarraut readily accepted the arrangement for Great Britain and France, and after Hughes repulsed a maneuver by Ambassador Ricci to hold up the Pacific agreement as a means of buttressing Italy's demands for cable facilities in the Atlantic the six-power treaty for allocation of the Pacific cables was eventually signed and ratified.

In later years Hughes negotiated treaties with France to protect American rights in several mandated territories: the Cameroons and Togoland in 1923, Syria and Lebanon in 1924. Belgium signed a similar treaty dealing with East Africa in 1923. The British put up much stiffer resistance, but finally signed treaties guaranteeing American rights in Transjordan and Palestine in 1924. The treaty as to Iraq was not concluded until 1930.

The mandate treaties would now be a comparatively minor item in Hughes' Secretaryship, except for Japan's notorious violation of her pledge not to fortify the islands entrusted to her. The failure of the ban on fortifications is a tragic chapter in the history of World War II and demands special attention.

As to all the islands mandated to Japan, Hughes' treaty provided for freedom of religion and protection of vested American property rights. It also extended to the mandated islands the Treaty of Commerce and Navigation of 1911 giving citizens of both countries the right "freely to come with their ships and cargoes to all places, ports and rivers in the territories of the other which

[7] *Ibid.*, p. 303.

are or may be opened to foreign commerce." Japan gave us a specific pledge not to establish any military or naval bases or fortifications in the mandated territories.[8] She even consented to send the United States a duplicate of her annual report to the League Council on the administration of the Pacific mandate.

Another of Hughes' suggestions ripened in an exchange of notes at the time the treaty was signed. The note of the Japanese ambassador, reaffirming the right of American nationals and vessels to visit the mandated islands, was as follows:

Japanese Embassy, Washington, February 11, 1922.

Sir:

In proceeding this day to the signature of the Convention between Japan and the United States with respect to the islands, under Japan's Mandate, situated in the Pacific Ocean and lying north of the Equator, I have the honor to assure you, under authorization of my Government, that the usual comity will be extended to nationals and vessels of the United States in visiting the harbors and waters of those islands.

Accept, Sir, the renewed assurances of my highest consideration.

K. SHIDEHARA

Honorable Charles E. Hughes,
Secretary of State.[9]

"Usual comity" means the courtesy which is normally accorded by one country to the nationals and vessels of another. Here was ample authority for the United States to keep watch over what Japan was doing in the mandated islands and to revoke our assent to the mandate if the treaty should be violated.

In spite of these thoughtful precautions, the islands became advance bases in Japan's war against the United States. Construction of the first naval base on the Island of Truk apparently began in 1930.[10] Reports that the islands were being fortified were numerous in 1932, and the State Department certainly knew of the violations as early as 1933. "As for Japan's action in fortifying Yap and the other mandated islands in contravention to express treaty stipulations," Ambassador Grew wrote into his diary in Tokyo on March 27 of that year, ". . . we have abundant firsthand evidence."[11]

Tokyo's reports to the League and the United States on administration of the Pacific mandate were masterpieces of evasion. Westerners were seldom allowed to visit the islands, and then under Japanese chaperonage.[12] In 1936 Secretary of State Cordell Hull was concerned about "a strong undercurrent of

[8] *Foreign Relations, 1922,* II, 601.

[9] *United States Statutes,* Vol. 42, Pt. 2, pp. 2149–2152.

[10] Navy's report to author, April 21, 1949.

[11] Joseph C. Grew, *Ten Years in Japan* (New York, Simon and Schuster, 1944), pp. 84f. Copyright, 1944, by Joseph C. Grew.

[12] Huntington Gilchrist in *Foreign Affairs,* July, 1944, p. 639.

suspicion and conjecture" as to fortification of the mandated islands and sought permission for the American destroyer *Alden* to visit the islands' unopen ports. As a means of allaying suspicions, the United States had consistently admitted Japanese vessels to harbors in Alaska and the Aleutian Islands not ordinarily open to foreign commerce. Hull cabled to Grew, ". . . it is unfortunate that the Government of Japan so far has not adopted an attitude similarly liberal in the face of allegations that in the Japanese mandated islands of the Pacific improvements are being carried out which are irreconcilable with Japan's treaty obligations not to fortify those islands." [13] Tokyo would not budge, and nothing was done.

In 1939 Secretary Hull admitted to the Senate Committee on Naval Affairs that the Japanese authorities had denied every request (four in number) that the department had made for the privilege of visiting harbors and waters of the mandated islands. At the same time he asked the committee to keep this information secret.[14] Under hush-hush precautions, the State Department replied to another query from the committee:

> With regard to the questions whether the terms of the treaty have been violated by Japan . . . the Government of the United States has at no time raised any question with the Japanese Government in regard to the obligations of Japan to the United States with respect to the Japanese mandated islands.[15]

The rights that Hughes had so carefully safeguarded were thus surrendered by subsequent régimes without raising a finger. The grave impairment of our security in the Pacific resulting from this course was then concealed from the public in an effort to avoid criticism and postpone a showdown with Japan. The effect was to encourage Tokyo in the belief that American rights could be flouted with impunity and to leave our own people asleep as to the perils mounting in the Pacific.

The Army's Pearl Harbor Board linked the disaster of December 7, 1941, directly to "our failure to have a showdown with Japan on her fortifications of the mandated islands." The board's report continued:

> Had the United States successfully insisted upon Japan living up to those treaty stipulations, the entire naval and military structure in the key Pacific islands erected by the Japanese might have been made impossible. Japan, without authority of international law and in violation of the treaties and mandates above referred to, for nearly twenty years successfully and completely excluded other nationals from the mandated territories, and during this time built up army, navy and air installations of tremendous strategical value.
>
> As a consequence of the foregoing, Japan gained the enormous advantage of a string of naval and air and army bases across our lifeline to the Philippines and

[13] *Foreign Relations—Japan, 1931–1941*, I, 307f.
[14] Sen. Doc. No. 202, 78th Congress, 2d session, pp. 8f. [15] *Id.*

rendered futile and impotent any fortification of our own islands, such as Guam, Midway, Christmas, Palmyra, etc. It also placed the dagger's point at the heart of the Hawaiian Islands because such a base at Jaluit in the mandated islands was a thousand miles closer to Hawaii than to the homeland of Japan.

Our policy through the successive years appears to have been based upon a combination of fear of the Japanese and of an obsession not to give offense to the Japanese; a policy which because of their temperamental characteristics, proved to be one of weakness rather than of strength.[16]

Nothing is to be gained by speculating as to what Hughes might have done if he had been Secretary of State in the thirties. But it is worthy of note that the price of his good will was honest fulfillment by every nation of its obligations to the United States. His technique was to offer each country friendship and just treatment while demanding, without fear of the consequences, that our rights be respected. Subsequent history has at least proved that relinquishment of rights and winking at treaty violations will buy neither friendship nor peace.

[16] *New York Times*, Aug. 30, 1945.

Chapter 44

THE WASHINGTON CONFERENCE

LESS than three years after the delirium of the Armistice, the ugliest word in the language—"war"—was creeping back into the headlines. Germany was crushed and Austria-Hungary dismembered, but new suspicions were clouding the relations of the victors. Especially in the Pacific, the march of events was in the direction of war.

Stimulating these postwar antagonisms was a naval armament race of proportions never before experienced. The United States had set out to build the largest battle fleet in the world. When the war ended, our Navy had under construction or authorized enough dreadnoughts and battle cruisers to add nearly 750,000 tons and 152 sixteen-inch guns to the American battle line.[1] Work on that program had begun in 1916. In December, 1918, the Wilson Administration had laid before Congress a request for 156 additional ships, including ten battleships, a duplication in all essential particulars of the 1916 program.

This gigantic paper fleet was the club with which Wilson had hoped to force the victorious powers to accept a league of nations, disarmament, and freedom of the seas. Fearing loss of her naval supremacy, Great Britain had come to an agreement with Wilson under which the proposed building program of 1919 was withdrawn. Then Wilson had offered the League to the American people as the only alternative to resumption of naval construction on a gigantic scale. When the League was rejected, the idea of building the largest navy in the world had naturally come to the fore again.

In this atmosphere the ultranationalistic press had whipped up a good deal of British-American discord. Some had gone so far as to visualize an Anglo-American war for commercial supremacy. Ill feeling had been accentuated by the Anglo-Japanese Alliance in spite of protestations that it would never be invoked against America. In March, 1921, London announced plans to resume the building of fighting ships on a scale that would keep His Majesty's fleet equal to, or superior to, any other navy. A futile and possibly ruinous struggle for supremacy on the sea was in the making. The two great English-speaking nations were unmistakably drifting apart.

[1] Harold and Margaret Sprout, *Toward a New Order of Sea Power* (Princeton, Princeton University Press, 1940), p. 53. Copyright, 1940, by the Princeton University Press.

In the Pacific, Japan was straining her resources to match the United States' expanding naval strength. Her substantial building program of 1917 had been stepped up in each of the following three years. In 1920 the Diet had approved plans designed to give Japan twenty-five capital ships by 1927, including eight new superdreadnoughts and eight giant battle cruisers. Japan had had her own way in Asia during the war. Now she seemed to be girding for further expansion. This menace to American insular possessions in the Pacific, to the open door in China, and to the peace and stability of the Orient was an ever-increasing source of apprehension.

Japan was equally alarmed by the sudden burgeoning of American sea power. Our Navy had established a separate fleet in the Pacific. Admirals were talking about a "strongly fortified naval base" on Guam and an improved secondary base in the Philippines. The Japanese interpreted this sudden rise of American navalism as a threat to the very existence of their empire. Relations were further strained, as we have seen, by the dispute over Yap. Washington and Tokyo were deadlocked at every point.

In each of the three leading sea powers, however, public sentiment was rising against the new navalism. Japan was spending nearly half its governmental revenue on its armed forces. Business groups, the press, and even politicians were beginning to cry out against the cost of meeting the American naval challenge. To the statesmen of Great Britain some means of curbing the naval race seemed imperative. While they had resumed naval construction, Britain's war-strained economy was in no condition to withstand an unrestrained shipbuilding race.

Men who have forgotten the spirit of the twenties sometimes assume that the Harding Administration thus had a golden opportunity to attain supremacy on the seas and enforce an era of peace. Actually, the revolt against navalism was running stronger here than in any of the other major powers. Many newspapers took up the cause, and the big-navy men encountered a veritable cyclone of opposition in Congress.

Late in 1920 Senator Borah introduced a resolution requesting the President to seek an understanding with Great Britain and Japan for curtailment of naval building by 50 per cent over the next five years. The movement won powerful support. General Pershing was among those who aroused the public with his plea for armament limitation to prevent us from plunging "headlong down through destructive war to darkness and barbarism." [2] The House slashed away almost half of the appropriation requested by the Navy Department, and Borah's filibuster when a more generous appropriation was sought in the Senate led to expiration of the Sixty-sixth Congress without any provision for support of the Navy having been made.

[2] *New York Times,* Dec. 30, 1920.

The Harding Administration was thus confronted, even before it took office, with a powerful demand for easing the burden of armaments. That was not disturbing, for both the President and Secretary Hughes were thinking favorably of an arms-limitation conference. Harding had expressed his willingness to cooperate with other powers for "approximate disarmament," but in their early discussions the first suggestion that it would be advisable to call an arms conference came from Hughes.[3] The President readily assented and said the conference could be called whenever Hughes thought the time was ripe for it.

In the first months of the new Administration the time was not ripe. The Secretary of State was immersed in the business of unscrambling the postwar chaos. He was also eager to avoid any positive commitment until the outlook for success of the conference was auspicious. At the same time he was aware of the danger of waiting too long. Determined that the conference should be held before the eyes of the American people, and that the initiative should remain in his own hands, he kept a hawklike watch over the situation to make certain that when the time came for issuing invitations they would go out from Washington rather than from any other capital.

Meanwhile the fight to reduce naval expenditures went forward in the extraordinary session of Congress which Harding had assembled. Senator Borah introduced a new resolution calling for negotiations among Great Britain, Japan, and the United States to halt the naval race. Similar proposals were made in the House. Harding attacked the Borah resolution and warned Congress to cease its efforts "to force the hand of the Executive" in this matter.[4] Ignoring the Borah resolution, big-navy Republicans in the Senate added $100,000,000 to the Navy supply bill for warship construction. But the foes of navalism redoubled their efforts. Pleas for disarmament rang from hundreds of pulpits as well as from the press and civic gatherings. The Administration promptly retreated, and Congress overwhelmingly adopted the Borah resolution as part of a sharply reduced naval appropriation bill.

Hughes had closely watched these events without being a direct participant. Now he would have to act with reasonable promptness. The people and the Congress had rebelled against further participation in the naval race. Only an international agreement could save the United States from being dangerously worsted in the armament competition that it had begun.

As the drama in Congress approached its climax, Hughes was besieged on July 7 by reporters who said that the British Government was about to call a conference on Far Eastern problems. Questioned on this subject in the House of Commons, Lloyd George had replied that he hoped to be able to make a statement on the following Monday if replies were received from the United States, Japan, and China. The Foreign Office hastened to explain that no

[3] Beerits' Memorandum X, 4. [4] *New York Times*, May 4, 1921.

"reply" was expected from the United States because there was nothing to reply to. But rumors of a forthcoming conference filled the air, and Washington reporters were indignant because they suspected Hughes of trying to keep it a secret.

While no inkling of these events in London had come through diplomatic channels, the press reports convinced Hughes that he would have to act immediately. Rushing to the White House, he told the President that "if the British got ahead of us in calling any kind of conference our show would amount to little." [5] Harding agreed. At four o'clock on Friday afternoon, July 8, the same day that the House and Senate conferees abandoned Harding's naval program, cables went out to four American ambassadors instructing them to inquire whether Great Britain, Japan, France, and Italy would agree to participate in a conference on limitation of armament to be held in Washington at a mutually convenient time.

A few hours after his instruction had gone out, Hughes received a long cablegram from Ambassador Harvey in London. Britain and the overseas Dominions were holding in London a conference on foreign policy and problems of the empire. Out of it had come a hot debate over Lloyd George's proposal to renew the Anglo-Japanese Alliance.[6] That bond between the British and Japanese empires was as obnoxious to Canada as it was to the United States. The cogent arguments of the Canadian Prime Minister, Arthur Meighen—added to Secretary Hughes' previous confidential and informal protests against the alliance—had finally convinced British statesmen that it should not be renewed in its then existing form. But something else would have to be put in its place. Britain would not suddenly abandon her ally of twenty years. As soon as plans for renewal of the alliance had run aground, therefore, the British Foreign Minister, Lord Curzon, had asked Harvey to propose to his government that the President invite the powers directly concerned to a conference on Far Eastern and Pacific questions, including the peaceful settlement of disputes and the elimination of naval warfare.

Curzon's request had been made on Tuesday evening, three days before Hughes sent out his proposal for an arms conference in Washington. Thinking there was no urgency about it, Harvey had delayed sending his message until Friday night, after Lloyd George had been questioned in Commons. Even then Curzon had had to prod Harvey into action. Laxity of this sort was always irritating to the Secretary, but in this instance it worked to his advantage. The two cablegrams proposing different kinds of conferences crossed in mid-ocean. Hughes insisted that his proposal would have to stand, as it had gone also to Tokyo, Paris, and Rome. "Limitation of armament question is vital here and

[5] Diary of William R. Castle, Jr., 1922, p. 182.
[6] A. Whitney Griswold, *The Far Eastern Policy of the United States*, p. 287.

is not confined to the Pacific," he cabled back to Harvey.[7] But as the Far Eastern questions in which London was primarily interested were related to the limitation of arms, he instructed Harvey to "ascertain and cable immediately" whether Britain would agree to enlargement of the American proposal so as to include all Far Eastern problems, with China as an additional participant.

While waiting for a reply on a hot July day, Hughes drafted informal invitations to be sent to the powers and a statement to be issued by the President. Harding's approval of both was obtained before he left on Saturday for a cruise down the Potomac. On Sunday afternoon Harvey showed Lloyd George a copy of the proposed statement, and the Prime Minister praised it as "admirable." [8] Harvey's report of this visit reached Hughes the same day at Greystone. He telephoned his assistants who were waiting at the State Department to cable the invitations and release the statement to the press. On Monday morning the whole world knew that the United States had invited Great Britain, Japan, France, Italy, and China to a momentous conference in Washington. "President Harding has taken a step," said the London *Evening Standard*, "which, whatever its results, must affect profoundly the history of the world." [9]

Although the British were delighted to have the United States take the initiative in calling the conference, they still expected to shape it to their own ends. Curzon immediately pressed for a preliminary meeting on Far Eastern and Pacific problems to be held in London for the convenience of the Dominion Premiers, who were still there. The disarmament section of the conference could then follow, he said, at Washington.

Hughes' ideas ran in a very different channel. A preliminary conference devoted to the Pacific would have the appearance of sidetracking the limitation of armament. It would give the British and probably the Japanese a chance to present their demands and to take positions that could scarcely be abandoned in Washington. France and Italy, left out in the cold, would certainly resent any preliminary understanding that might be reached. Concluding that Curzon's scheme would wreck the conference, Hughes firmly rejected it. Between the lines of his reply it is easy to read the prevalent American distrust of European diplomacy. The Secretary was determined that this conference should remain under American leadership.

Ambassador Geddes came in two weeks later, however, with a long telegram in which the British Foreign Office took the preliminary conference for granted. According to Geddes, Harvey had "warmly approved the idea" when he showed the President's statement to Lloyd George at Chequers on July 10 and had subsequently suggested to Curzon that a preliminary conference be

[7] *Foreign Relations, 1921*, I, 23. [8] *Ibid.*, p. 25.
[9] *Evening Standard*, July 11, 1921.

held at London or Havana.[10] Harvey hotly denied it by cable. Reading the cablegram aloud, Hughes slammed it down on his desk and exclaimed, "Who is the liar?" [11]

Curzon tried another tack. As the door had been closed to a preliminary parley in London, he sent word that Lloyd George and himself and the Dominion Premiers were ready to sail for Bar Harbor on August 12 if that would be acceptable to the United States. Hughes stood his ground. In a long cablegram for Curzon's attention he pointed out that he had taken pains to get British approval of the statement summoning the conference before it was released to the press. While he had later agreed to "consultations to facilitate preparation for conference," he had at the same time positively rejected anything that might be considered a preliminary conference. The meeting of top officials of several countries would be a conference regardless of what name might be given to it. The President could not possibly call such a gathering on American soil just after he had invited a larger group of nations to a conference on the same subjects.

Failing to get what they wanted, the British cooled toward the entire undertaking. Geddes said solemnly that his government would drop the idea of a preliminary meeting and "desired the United States to take full responsibility for arrangements in order to avoid possibility of further misunderstanding." [12] The implication of hand-washing was unmistakable, but this gave Hughes precisely what he wanted—the opportunity of planning the conference in his own way.

Apparently Lloyd George declined to attend the conference because he feared that Hughes would be "extremely *difficile*," somewhat dogmatic, and "not easily swerved" from a position he had taken.[13] The coolness between London and Washington was further emphasized when the British attempted to bring the question of Panama Canal tolls into the conference. Hughes' cutting reply to Geddes was that "the time had come when the constant sentiments and cordial expressions which were made at dinners and on various occasions with respect to the friendly cooperation between the two Governments should be translated into something definite." [14]

France and Italy had promptly accepted the conference invitation. Japan was skeptical. She wished to avoid scrutiny of her occupation of Chinese and Russian territory, but she could not afford to give up the Anglo-Japanese Alliance without getting something else in its place. While willing to discuss the limitation of arms, she wished to know the "nature and scope" of the Pacific and Far Eastern problems that would be taken up before making any commitment to attend.

[10] Memorandum of interview, July 30, 1921, Hughes Papers.
[11] Castle Diary, 1922, p. 183.
[12] *Foreign Relations, 1921*, I, 50.
[13] Harvey to CEH, Sept. 28, 1921.
[14] *Foreign Relations, 1921*, I, 73.

Hughes thought the agenda should be broad enough to embrace the open door, equality of commercial opportunity, the integrity of China and Russia, the status of the former German possessions in the Pacific, cable and radio communications, narcotic traffic, and other Far Eastern questions. Before replying to the Japanese, however, he asked the British view. Curzon sounded out the Japanese, and, finding them reticent, he urged that opium traffic, immigration, the mandated islands, and the integrity of Russia be excluded. Hughes had already excluded immigration as a domestic issue, and he agreed with Curzon as to opium traffic. Beyond that, however, he would not compromise.

Having been advised by the American chargé d'affaires in Tokyo that Japan would doubtless accept the invitation, the Secretary stood firm against the Japanese effort to restrict the scope of the conference. Any agreement of that sort as the price of Japan's participation, he said, might gravely minimize the usefulness of the gathering and "produce an unpleasant reaction." After two weeks of stalling, Japan yielded with a statement that Far Eastern questions should come into the conference only as a sideline to the limitation of armaments.

Long before the conference assembled, therefore, Hughes had clearly demonstrated that the reins were in his hands. Both the British and the Japanese were on notice that this was to be an American "show" and that its success or failure would depend largely upon the initiative of the Secretary of State.

Belgium, the Netherlands, and Portugal were belatedly invited to send delegates because of their interests in the Far East. The Secretary advised that all delegations be kept small so as to facilitate agreement. He also urged, much to the irritation of the armed services, that delegations be composed of civilians, with representatives of the Army, Navy, finance, and labor confined to advisory groups. All the principal powers except Japan followed this suggestion.

It was taken for granted from the beginning that Hughes would head the American delegation, and his high standing with the President enabled him to choose his own associates. Harding readily agreed that two of the four American delegates should be members of the Senate. There would be no repetition of Wilson's mistake at Paris. With his eye upon ratification of the treaties that would come out of the conference, Hughes selected Senator Lodge, chairman of the Foreign Relations Committee, and Oscar W. Underwood, the Democratic leader of the Senate.

The Secretary was well aware of the risk he would run in choosing a strong delegation. Three men of independent minds could take the conference out of his hands. That risk might have caused a less courageous man to take one of his own trusted followers for the fourth delegate. Instead, Hughes singled out the great elder statesman who had been Secretary of War as well as Secretary of State and Senator from New York and who was credited with more experience and wisdom in international affairs than any other living American—Elihu Root. Harding was lukewarm toward this selection because Root had antagonized the Irreconcilables, but Hughes was insistent, and the President yielded after conferring with Root.

With the conference now an approaching reality, the Hardings became apprehensive. Failure of this venture might be a fatal blow to the Administration. Mrs. Harding asked the Secretary one day how he was going to handle all the top-ranking statesmen who would descend upon Washington. "You've got to see this thing through," was the President's comment.[15] It was one thing, he seemed to imply, to call a conference and quite another to make it a success.

Preparations for the conference began on an elaborate scale. Hughes reviewed past efforts in disarmament and then turned to mountains of data related to the naval requirements of the three chief participants. His survey ranged also over the broad fields of Far Eastern policy, the Allies' venture in Siberia, the economic problems of China, the Shantung question, Japan's twenty-one demands on China, Japanese propaganda, American interests in the Far East, fortifications in the Pacific, gas warfare, submarines, and a host of other subjects. Days given to conferences, interviews, reports, and discussions were followed by nights of reading and deliberation.

From the beginning Hughes worked closely with the Navy, largely through its Assistant Secretary, Theodore Roosevelt, Jr.; the Chief of Operations, Admiral Robert E. Coontz; and Coontz' assistant, Captain (soon to be Rear Admiral) W. V. Pratt. Later on he used former Senator George Sutherland as liaison with the Navy. Hughes was scrupulous in exploring the Navy's point of view while insisting that civilian statesmanship rather than naval strategy should guide the conference.

Nothing in the voluminous data that came to him seemed to offer any plan, device, or theory by which naval strength could actually be limited. The Navy talked in terms of national needs. The admirals said they should have enough ships and men to protect all American territory, guard our commercial sea lanes, and defend the rights of citizens anywhere they might be menaced. In more specific terms this meant parity with Great Britain and twice the naval strength of Japan. "If the Anglo-Japanese Alliance is to be continued," the General Board added, "the minimum strength that the United States can safely accept for its navy is equality with . . . the two nations combined." [16] Similar elaboration of national needs was heard in other countries. On this basis every nation could make a convincing case for strengthening instead of limiting its fighting power on the high seas. There was scant hope of reconciling these claims. If the conference were to become entangled in controversy over relative

[15] Author's interview with CEH, Nov. 26, 1946.
[16] Report of General Board of Navy, Sept. 30, 1921.

naval needs, the result would probably be intensified competition and enormous expenditures, with no gain in security for any power. Hughes decided that some other formula would have to be found.

The Navy's first concrete proposal was that the United States insist on completing all the fifteen battleships and battle cruisers for which keels had been laid. Older ships would then be scrapped so as to fix the American and British capital-ship quotas at approximately one million tons. Against the world-wide outcry for reduction of armaments, such a proposal would have been farcical. Hughes discarded it at once. The General Board then suggested that four or five of the ships under construction might be scrapped. It was not enough. Roosevelt, Coontz, and Pratt worked up a third plan to scrap eight of the uncompleted ships,[17] but this too was to be discarded.

Pondering over the problem from every angle, Hughes was driven to the conclusion that the one hope of ending naval competition was to induce the powers to stop where they were.[18] No power could seriously object to a quota that would preserve its relative strength at the time the conference began. Only by this means, he reasoned, could the quandary of conflicting national needs be avoided. About October 1 he sent J. Reuben Clark, Jr., former State Department solicitor (later to become Ambassador to Mexico), to the Navy Department to find out what action on the part of Great Britain and Japan would be equivalent to the scrapping of all the American ships under construction.

This method of operation was to be followed consistently. While Hughes and his delegation fixed guiding principles, the Navy was always asked to fill in the technical details. On the basis of Clark's oral requests, the Navy prepared a chart showing what vessels Great Britain and Japan should scrap to maintain their relative standing if (*a*) the United States should give up all capital ships then being built and (*b*) if the United States should scrap its ships less than 60 per cent completed.

With these data, Hughes went to the White House and converted the President to the "stop now" formula. It was then presented to other members of the American delegation. Working independently, Root too had concluded that maintenance of relative existing strength was the only basis on which an agreement was likely to be reached.[19] The two Senators readily concurred. Underwood was especially enthusiastic in his approval.

The next question was how the relative strength of the existing navies should be measured. As this was a technical matter, Hughes relied wholly upon the Navy's contention that displacement tonnage of capital ships (battleships and battle cruisers) was the best yardstick. But what ships should be included? The American delegation took the position that paper programs should not be

[17] Colonel Roosevelt's diary, Oct. 24, 1921.
[18] CEH, Notes, p. 282. [19] Philip Jessup, *Elihu Root*, II, 448.

counted, but only ships laid down or upon which money had been spent. At the same time there was general agreement that ships under construction should be counted to the extent that construction had progressed at the opening of the conference.[20]

Using capital ships as an index to naval power and making allowance for ships under construction as well as the age, speed, gun power, and armor of ships then in service, the Navy calculated the existing relative strength of the British, American, and Japanese fleets at approximately the ratio of 5:5:3. With that ratio agreed upon as the basis of the American proposal, the logic of Hughes' drastic curtailment plan was obvious; for, if Congress intended to trim the American Navy anyway, our security would be promoted by a proportionate trimming of other navies by agreement.

Following this reasoning, the American delegation rejected the proposal fixing an upper limit of approximately 600,000 tons for the British and American navies and saving the ships that were more than 60 per cent completed. On October 25 Hughes formally asked the Secretary of the Navy what ships the British and Japanese ought to scrap to match a possible abandonment of "our entire building program for capital ships." [21] The next day the General Board of the Navy came back with a stern warning that such a proposition would be fraught with danger because Japan respected only force. "Our superiority today lies in these ships . . . ," the Navy's statement said. "If these fifteen ships be stricken from the Navy list, our task [in the western Pacific] may not be hopeless; but the temptation of Japan to take a chance becomes very great." [22] Denby sent the protest to Hughes. On October 30 the delegation decided, in spite of the admirals, to call for a naval holiday and the scrapping of all ships under construction.

The wisdom of this decision has often been challenged—more so in recent years since the facts before the conference have been forgotten. While conclusions must be left to a later chapter, it may be noted in passing that the problems which the Washington Conference faced were not those of 1937 or 1941. It had been assembled to meet an irresistible demand for curtailment of naval expenditures. Naval officers could close their ears to public opinion, but Hughes felt that he could not. His task was to safeguard American security and bid for peace and stability on the basis of irrefragable facts. The facts supplied to him by the Navy showed that, in spite of a strong drive for American superiority on the sea, Congress had trimmed appropriations for the Navy by $332,000,000 in the last year. Japan in the same period had increased her naval outlays by $61,000,000—in four years by $177,000,000. She was determined to go ahead, as events subsequently showed. The United States was not.

[20] CEH, Notes, p. 283. [21] CEH to Secretary Denby, Oct. 25, 1921.
[22] General Board to the Secretary of the Navy, Oct. 26, 1921.

Hughes had taken pains to inquire what would be the result of letting the naval programs then under way run their course. A Navy report to the American delegation indicated that, with the completion of the three shipbuilding programs (about 1928), the relative standing of the navies would be: United States, 100; Great Britain, 106; Japan, 87.[23] Under the Hughes proposal, of course, the ratio would remain: United States, 100; Great Britain, 100; Japan, 60—an enormous relative gain for the United States.

Great importance was attached to the unwillingness of Congress to vote funds for completion of the American ships. Root asked at one of the first preliminary meetings of the American delegation whether there was any likelihood that Congress would vote funds to continue the naval program and fortify the Philippines in accord with the policy the Navy then favored. Lodge, who had the reputation of being a big-Navy leader in the Senate, replied that there was no possibility of obtaining the necessary appropriations. Underwood supported that statement, and the President came to the same conclusion.[24] The unfinished ships were "frozen assets." Only one of the ten battleships authorized in 1916 had been completed. Three more were well along, but six were less than 20 per cent finished in January, 1921, and none of the battle cruisers was more than 11 per cent complete. Congress was abandoning the ships without any agreement.

It was perfectly clear, therefore, "that unless we could obtain an agreement for a limitation of naval armament, we were headed for a disastrous competition." [25] Distrust arising out of the naval race might have stimulated building in America, but in that event Great Britain and Japan were determined to launch still larger programs. The choice was between "wasteful and senseless" rivalry, in which the United States was virtually certain to be outclassed, and an agreement that would bite deeply into existing naval tonnage. Before the conference opened, the naval chiefs seemed to be reconciled to the "stop now" formula and prepared a memorandum showing why it was fair to each of the naval powers. Rear Admiral Pratt consistently stood by this far-sighted conclusion.

In twelve lengthy sessions the American delegates reached a complete understanding both as to strategy and as to the principles on which they would stand. There was no lack of teamwork among them, but the program that emerged had a very positive Hughesian cast; for the chairman followed his customary practice of presenting not merely problems but also solutions bearing evidence of long and careful deliberation.

As the opening date approached, a new danger loomed up. If the customary method of having each delegation present its demands behind closed doors

[23] *Book of Recommendations of the General Board of the Navy*, p. 196, Hughes Papers.
[24] CEH, Notes, p. 278. [25] *Ibid.*, p. 279.

should be followed, the conference might be embroiled in controversy before world opinion could be focused upon the American proposal. Clashing national interests would get the emphasis instead of the world-wide desire for relief from the armament burden. That danger might be minimized by a bold statement at the outset of what the United States was willing to do, but such an offer by itself would undermine our bargaining position. Weighing every element of strategy, Hughes finally decided to surprise the conference with a sweeping proposal that would slash into the British and Japanese navies as well as into our own. That technique involved some risk, but it seemed to offer the only hope of getting a fair hearing for genuine reduction of armaments.

Realizing the great importance of the surprise element in his strategy, Hughes guarded his secret with the utmost care. Only nine men, including the President, were permitted to share in the final consultations. So confidential was the American proposal that the final draft was mimeographed by an admiral, and all the copies were locked up in the Navy Department. No attempt was made to print copies until the morning the conference opened. The one copy of Hughes' speech was similarly under lock and key in his office.

It has sometimes been assumed that Hughes whispered his secret to Balfour when the chief of the British delegation called at the State Department on the afternoon of November 11. During the interview Balfour did make every gentlemanly effort to worm from his host the substance of the arms-limitation proposal he intended to make, but on this subject he found Hughes utterly uncommunicative.

"I am going to have the pleasure of nominating you as chairman of the conference," Balfour said as he was about to depart.

Thanking him, Hughes replied, "I have said nothing to you about what is in the speech I am going to make, and when you hear it I am sure that you will understand why." [26] There was no implication that Balfour could not keep a secret. Hughes was determined, however, to avoid any possible impression that the United States and Great Britain had entered into a deal which they wished to impose on the conference.

Most of Hughes' speech had been written on the train as he returned to Washington after spending election day in New York. As soon as he had finished it he called the American delegates together and got their approval. There had been no opportunity to show it to the President. Harding himself was to open the conference with a welcoming address on Saturday, November 12, following the dedication of the tomb of the Unknown Soldier on Armistice Day. Hughes' speech outlining the American proposal was to be reserved for the second plenary session on Monday or Tuesday.

On Thursday night before the opening, however, the Secretary became

[26] Author's interview with CEH, Nov. 26, 1946.

The Secretary of State found some moments for relaxation

Harris & Ewing

On the porch at "Greystone," 1922

National Photo Co., Washington, D. C.

Wide World Photo

worried over the possibility that news of his thunderbolt might leak out in the press over the week end. There was the additional danger that Borah might muddy the waters with a proposal of his own in the Senate. The tantalizing thought that months of careful preparation might be upset by some misstep drove Hughes to the telephone.

"I had not planned to make our proposal on the opening day," he explained to the President, "but I am so afraid that a leak or some other development might spoil its effect that I think I should get it off right away."

"Oh, that's all right," replied the agreeable Mr. Harding. "Go ahead." [27]

This timing was notably to enhance the explosive power of Hughes' message that was to be heard round the world.

[27] *Id.*

Chapter 45

INSPIRED HOUR

THE GREAT day dawned chill and blustery. Tension, excitement, and expectation were in the air. Traffic whisked through streets lined with thousands of spectators craning their necks to catch a glimpse of the eminent statesmen from many lands who were converging on Continental Hall. Swarms of newspapermen heightened the awareness of history in the making. For the first time Washington had become the center of the world stage.

In this Conference on the Limitation of Armament the hope of humanity was centered. Yet it was a tenuous and evanescent hope. No general disarmament conference had ever been successful. The conclave which the Czar of Russia had assembled at The Hague in 1899 had gone no further than the adoption of a resolution expressing the desirability of reducing the burden of armaments. Again in 1907 the powers had succeeded only in reiterating this futile gesture. Every country was eager to disarm its neighbors but not itself.

Fear that the great undertaking in Washington would simmer down to pious mouthings signifying nothing was dominant in the comment as the conference assembled. "The Washington Conference will be as useless as all those which have preceded it," forecast Maurice Maeterlinck. The Socialist *Daily Herald* of London said flatly that, so far as disarmament is concerned, "the conference will fail." [1] The British were especially dubious. They had had a surfeit of American idealism and were puzzled by Hughes' refusal to enter a preliminary conference. Pessimism from many sources underscored the forebodings of war that were rising out of the Pacific.

Nor was there anything in the public record since the President had summoned the conference in July to offset the prevailing skepticism. Even young America seemed to be infused with anxiety as the statesmen, diplomats, legislators, experts, distinguished guests, and journalists filed into the marble hall on Seventeeth Street. The major participants in the drama were observed to be "intensely nervous." Seldom if ever had American officials faced a greater challenge.

Official and social Washington thronged the conference chamber. Vice President Coolidge sat beside Mrs. Harding in a box. Near by were Mrs. Hughes, the wives of other delegates and Cabinet members, and Mrs. Longworth, the

[1] *Literary Digest*, Nov. 12, 1921.

daughter of Theodore Roosevelt. Among those in the section reserved for the Supreme Court were Chief Justice and Mrs. Taft and Justices Holmes and Brandeis. William Jennings Bryan, entering in his silk hat and old-fashioned cape, lent a touch of showmanship, but later, when the crowd called for "Briand"—the French premier, whose name they mispronounced—and Bryan arose to take a bow, his dignity was badly ruffled.

The delegates were seated at a specially constructed walnut table in the shape of a huge block U. Hughes, as chairman, occupied the key position at the bottom of the U, with Lodge, Root, and Underwood at his right. At his left was Arthur James Balfour, the tall, white-haired philosopher-statesman who headed the British delegation. At the left leg of the U sat the Italians headed by Carlo Schanzer, whom Root later described as "a German Jew, born in Vienna, speaking for Italy in French, to an audience that can understand only English." On the right leg were the French and the Japanese. Japan had sent, as window dressing, her Prince Tokugawa, descendant of the first ruling Shogun, and, as chief negotiator, her shrewd, impassive Minister of the Navy, Admiral Baron Tomosaburo Kato.

Under the alphabetical seating arrangement that had been copied from the Paris peace conference, the American and British delegates occupied all the places at the strategic end of the table. It happened that the French Premier, M. Aristide Briand, distinguished looking in spite of his short neck and drooping mustache, was just around the corner to the right. Briand was indignant and let it be known that he considered himself entitled to a seat at the "table d'honneur." Hughes said there was no "table d'honneur," but he diplomatically requested all the delegates to shift one chair to the left so that France's eloquent apostle of peace and European unity could face in the same direction as the Americans. That move averted what had threatened to be the first unpleasant incident of the conference.

Pent-up emotions broke loose in applause when the President, "groomed within an inch of his life," entered and took a seat next to Hughes. At 10:30 A.M. the chairman rapped for order, and a Baptist minister offered an uplifting prayer. Then came the President's speech, resonant in its fervor and spiritual overtones. "How can humanity justify or God forgive?" he asked in reference to the horrors that the world had recently witnessed. "Our hundred millions frankly want less of armament and none of war." [2]

While the European delegates were registering shocked surprise at the undiplomatic cheering started by the Senators at the close of Harding's remarks, Hughes grasped his chief's hand. Briand, Balfour, Viviani, and others followed suit. Soon the hubbub subsided and an easier atmosphere prevailed. English and French were announced as the official languages of the conference.

[2] *Conference on the Limitation of Armament*, p. 48.

Balfour arose to express what he believed to be the unanimous wish of the delegates—that Mr. Hughes should act as chairman throughout the conference. Responding gracefully, Hughes spoke with an easy mastery that belied the excitement boiling within him. It was his great hour.

> Born for success he seemed,
> With grace to win, with heart to hold,
> With shining gifts that took all eyes.

At first he dwelt upon the opportunities that the conference opened to the delegates sitting before him. The words rolled pleasantly off his tongue; he seemed to be inviting his listeners to relax. After a few minutes of this came a natural climax to his introductory remarks: "The world looks to this conference to relieve humanity of the crushing burden created by competition in armament, and it is the view of the American Government that we should meet that expectation without any unnecessary delay." [3] The audience applauded. Some thought he was finishing on a note of high-sounding generalities.

Instead of quitting, however, Hughes went on to review the "futile suggestions" that had come out of previous attempts to reduce the burden of arms by international agreement. Apparently he was enjoying this diversionary maneuver. Newspaper men dropped their alertness and began to whisper among themselves. In the galleries people were "looking about the room, recognizing acquaintances, and nodding to them." [4] The first session was proving to be a humdrum affair. Then all of a sudden the speaker assumed a commanding manner. His face, a mirror of health and good will, glowed with a kind of spiritual exaltation that gave tone and timbre to his voice.[5] As he turned from the past to the pulsating present, his words rang with sincerity and conviction stripped clean of sentimentality.

"We not only have the lessons of the past to guide us, not only do we have the reaction from the disillusioning experiences of war, but we must meet the challenge of imperative economic demands. What was convenient or highly desirable before is now a matter of vital necessity. If there is to be economic rehabilitation, if the longings for reasonable progress are not to be denied, if we are to be spared the uprisings of peoples made desperate in the desire to shake off burdens no longer endurable, competition in armament must stop."

The plaudits signified that the audience was now alert. Hughes followed up his advantage by increasing his tempo and driving home point after point. The

[3] *Ibid*, p. 52.

[4] Mark Sullivan, *The Great Adventure at Washington* (New York, Doubleday, 1922), pp. 19f. Copyright, 1922, by Doubleday, Page & Co.

[5] William Allen White, *Autobiography* (New York, Macmillan, 1946), p. 600. Copyright, 1946, by The Macmillan Company.

hour of great opportunity for the "liberty-loving and peace-preserving democracies" had come. "We can no longer content ourselves with investigations, with statistics, with reports, with the circumlocution of inquiry. . . . Power and responsibility are here and the world awaits a practicable program which shall at once be put into execution."

The immediate difficulty was the naval arms race. "Competition will not be remedied," he said, "by resolves with respect to the method of its continuance. One program inevitably leads to another, and if competition continues, its regulation is impracticable. There is only one adequate way out and that is to end it now.

"It is apparent that this cannot be accomplished without serious sacrifices. Enormous sums have been expended upon ships under construction and building programs which are now under way cannot be given up without heavy loss." Yet the nations would have to face these sacrifices, he declared with typical Hughesian candor, or yield their purpose.

"It is also clear," he continued, "that no one of the naval Powers should be expected to make these sacrifices alone. The only hope of limitation of naval armament is by agreement among the nations concerned, and this agreement should be entirely fair and reasonable in the extent of the sacrifices required of each of the Powers." In other words, navies should be trimmed so as to maintain their existing relative strength.

Now it was evident that Hughes was moving toward some momentous proposal. Each new sentence seemed to split the electric atmosphere with greater impact than the last.

"It would also seem to be a vital part of a plan for the limitation of naval armament that there should be a naval holiday. It is proposed that for a period of not less than ten years there should be no further construction of capital ships.

"I am happy to say that I am at liberty to go beyond these general propositions and, on behalf of the American delegation acting under the instructions of the President of the United States, to submit to you a concrete proposition for an agreement for the limitation of naval armament."

Men came forward in their seats. Looks of amazement were hastily exchanged, and ears were strained to catch every word of what this whiskered enigma was saying. While the import of a ten-year naval holiday was sinking in, Hughes explained that his immediate proposal concerned only the British Empire, Japan, and the United States, leaving the navies of France and Italy for later discussion. Then came his neat and precise "four general principles," hitting naval competition broadside with the impact of four sixteen-inch shells:

(1) That all capital shipbuilding programs, either actual or projected, should be abandoned;

(2) That further reduction should be made through the scrapping of certain of the older ships;

(3) That in general regard should be had to the existing naval strength of the Powers concerned;

(4) That the capital ship tonnage should be used as the measurement of strength for navies and a proportionate allowance of auxiliary combatant craft prescribed.

Delegates caught their breath and moistened hot lips as Hughes went on to detail the sacrifice that the United States was prepared to make. Only one of the ten battleships in our 1916 program had been completed. On the remaining nine battleships and six battle cruisers the nation had spent more than $330,000,000. "Still," the speaker's voice rang out, "the United States is willing in the interest of an immediate limitation of naval armament to scrap all these ships." Nor was this all. To the fifteen uncompleted ships to be scrapped the United States would add fifteen old battleships, making a total of thirty capital ships with an aggregate of 845,740 tons.

No nation had ever before made such an offer to reduce its own arms. For a moment the boldness of the American example seemed overpowering. The tumult that broke loose was more than applause. It was an outburst of joyous acclaim. Those foreign delegates who could believe their own ears were "resonant with enthusiasm." Even the British journalists, who had been exuding gloom ever since their arrival in America, were shocked out of their pessimism. Everyone seemed to take it for granted that the session would end with this glorious gesture in the hope that other delegations would prepare to match the American offer. The clamor in the hall seemed to be "an immense and burning ceremonial for the close of a day that had made unprecedented history." [6]

But as soon as the noise subsided, Hughes turned his devastating logic upon the other big navies. "The plan contemplates that Great Britain and Japan shall take action which is fairly commensurate with this action on the part of the United States." For Britain this would mean giving up "the 4 new *Hoods* . . . not laid down but upon which money has been spent" and the scrapping of nineteen first- and second-line battleships—an over-all total of 583,375 tons.

Balfour scribbled notes on an envelope without changing his expression while consternation spread over the faces of England's hard-bitten men of the sea. Admiral Chatfield "turned red and then white, and sat immovable." Lord Lee of Fareham, civilian head of the Admiralty, "half rose and whispered to Balfour." Admiral Beatty, First Sea Lord and the living embodiment of the idea that Britannia rules the waves, leaned forward with the belligerent expres-

[6] Sullivan, *op. cit.*, pp. 23f.

sion of a waking bulldog that had been "poked in the stomach by the impudent foot of an itinerant soap-canvasser." [7] But the general atmosphere was one of deep silence while Hughes sank more British battleships than "all the admirals of the world had destroyed in a cycle of centuries." [8]

Leaving his listeners no time to recover from this shock, Hughes turned to the Japanese, who were grinning over the idea of so many American and British ships going under. Smiles turned to stolidity or sagging gestures as the chairman named the ships Japan should scrap, including the giant *Mutsu,* pride of the empire. Four battleships and four battle cruisers not yet laid down should be abandoned. Three capital ships and four battle cruisers under construction should go, in addition to ten older ships, a total loss of 448,928 tons.

"Thus, under this plan," he summed up, "there would be immediately destroyed, of the navies of the three Powers, 66 capital fighting ships, built and building, with a total tonnage of 1,878,043."

After the ten-year holiday capital ships could be replaced at the age of twenty years; no single ship could exceed 35,000 tons; and the maximum tonnage of capital ships for the three powers during the life of the agreement would be:

United States	500,000 tons
Great Britain	500,000 tons
Japan	300,000 tons

"With the acceptance of this plan," Hughes concluded, "the burden of meeting the demands of competition in naval armament will be lifted. Enormous sums will be released to aid the progress of civilization. At the same time the proper demands of national defense will be adequately met and the nations will have ample opportunity during the naval holiday of ten years to consider their future course. Preparation for offensive naval war will stop now."

The conference went wild in its sudden release of emotion. From the galleries came a "tornado of cheering" initiated by Senators and Representatives. Exuberant democracy trampled down the rules of diplomacy. "Hats waved, handkerchiefs fluttered, men shook one another's hands, hugged one another, slapped one another, exhibited every kind of animal delight of which human beings are capable in their high moments." [9] Correspondent William Jennings Bryan looked on with tears streaming down his face. No such wave of exultation had ever swept an international conference within the memory of man.

[7] *Ibid.*, p. 26.
[8] H. W. Nevinson, *Manchester Guardian Weekly*, Nov. 18, 1921, p. 384.
[9] White, *loc. cit.*

Cries for Briand brought a warm but noncommittal statement from the alert little Frenchman, and various other delegation heads responded with brief tributes to American leadership. Then the conference adjourned until Tuesday, in accord with a prearranged plan, so that Hughes' words might echo around the globe and people everywhere might let the delegates know their wishes before those delegates would have a chance to make official responses.

Hughes had expected his speech to create a sensation, but he had no idea that it would loose such an avalanche of praise as now descended upon him. Members of Congress could scarcely contain their enthusiasm. A canvass revealed that a treaty embodying the Hughes plan would be approved by the Senate almost without dissent. Borah referred to the speech as "the first great triumph of open diplomacy."

The kind of stories that reporters wrote may be indicated by the fact that, almost to a man, they rushed into press headquarters "bubbling with happiness." Editors the nation over brought out their most scintillating adjectives. Hughes' proposal was a "master stroke"; "a most astounding and stupendous move"; an experiment in "practical idealism"; a "drastic but workable" plan. Like Napoleon, he was said to have stunned the enemy by a sudden, decisive, offensive blow.

"Yesterday Charles Evans Hughes was a big man in the United States," wrote one Democratic editor, "today he is one of the biggest men in the world." [10] "I'm going home," declared Ring Lardner. "This is going to be a bum show. They've let the hero kill the villain in the first act." [11] "It was probably the most wonderful and sensational thing that ever occurred in an international conference," observed Rollo Ogden, soon to be editor of the *New York Times*. "But it was entirely characteristic of the Hughes we have long known." [12] "Of all human conclaves I have ever witnessed," William Allen White was to write nearly a quarter-century after the event, "the gathering of the Disarmament Conference in Washington furnished the most intensely dramatic moment I have ever witnessed." [13]

The clergy was almost ecstatic. There was much repetition of Bishop William T. Manning's declaration from the pulpit of the Cathedral of St. John in New York that the Hughes speech was "one of the greatest events in history." Almost the sole discordant note came from the Communist American Labor Alliance, which ridiculed the idea of disarmament until the workers of the world had control of the armies and navies.

Touching compliments from old friends swelled the Secretary's mail. Among them was this note:

[10] Martin H. Glynn in the Albany *Times-Union*, Nov. 14, 1921.
[11] Mark Sullivan in New York *Evening Post*, Jan. 28, 1922.
[12] Ogden to H. H. Kohlsaat, Nov. 13, 1921.
[13] White, *op. cit.*, p. 598.

DEAR HUGHES

No answer—

This is simply to say that I was proud of your dignity and thrilled by what you said yesterday.

Your affectionate old colleague,

O. W. HOLMES

"It has given us more than we ever have dared to hope," wrote Judge Learned Hand; "it covers our country with glory more than ten victories. . . ." A note from Theodore Roosevelt, Jr., said, ". . . in my opinion, your speech is one of the great documents of American history." So it went. If Hughes had been a vain man, his head would certainly have been turned by the stream of unrestrained laudation that flowed into his office.

News pouring out of Washington choked the cables both to Europe and to Asia. Tokyo correspondents put the entire speech on the wire at $1.50 a word. The Japanese registered deep surprise, and many were critical. *Kokumin* saw it as a "plot" to place Japan at the mercy of Britain and America. *Nichi Nichi* said it was a hostile scheme by powers bent on humiliating Japan. But the keynote of the comment, according to Associated Press reports, was "keen satisfaction and admiration." France registered "almost unreserved approval." In London "nothing else was talked about." Winston Churchill told Harvey that "he could not find words to express his rejoicing as an Englishman and his pride in his American ancestry. His hat was not only off but as high as he could throw it." [14]

Balfour referred to the Hughes proposal as "one of the most remarkable utterances which has ever been made by any statesman under any circumstances. . . . I don't know," he added, "whether Mr. Hughes was conscious that he was at that moment not merely a great statesman but a great artist. But, to speak perfectly impartially, I say that he was both." [15]

At the end of the conference Balfour also acknowledged that "it was the inspired moment of November 12th on which all the greatness of this great transaction really depends." [16] Hughes had chosen the only technique that was likely to force a sweeping reduction of naval strength and create an atmosphere in which major causes of conflict could be removed. And he had carried out his plan with consummate skill. His tour de force gave him overnight the moral leadership of the world and brought the United States once more into an influential role in shaping the future. It commands a high place among the great gestures of men in behalf of world peace.

[14] Harvey to CEH, Nov. 14, 1921.

[15] *Current Opinion*, January, 1922, p. 36.

[16] *Conference*, p. 368.

Chapter 46

NEGOTIATING THE NAVAL TREATY

THE FEELING that it was a "time for greatness" carried over into the second plenary session on Tuesday, November 15. The delegates had worked feverishly since Saturday combing over the details of the "great American scheme" and getting instructions from their governments. Everyone seemed to come to the same conclusion. In the face of the almost universal acclaim, there could be no open rejection of the Hughes proposal.

"I count myself among the fortunate of the earth," Balfour told the conference, "in that I was present, and to that extent had a share in the proceedings of last Saturday . . . we felt that a new chapter in the history of world reconstruction had been worthily opened. . . . the United States have shown . . . that there is a way by which wars can really be diminished, by which the burdens of peace, almost as intolerable as the burdens of war, can really be lightened for the populations of the world. And in doing that . . . they have, believe me, made the first and opening day of this Congress one of the landmarks in human civilization." [1] Before he sat down, Balfour had accepted the Hughes plan "in spirit and in principle," with a few vague exceptions.

Baron Kato, in his solemn and matter-of-fact way, also accepted the Hughes principles subject to "a few modifications." "Mr. Hughes has quite rightly made it plain," said Briand, "that the duty before us is to find the straight path and to enter upon it at once; and he has set the example." At the end of the day one enthusiastic journalist wrote, "What was an impossibility is now a fact." [2] While this appraisal ignored the subtle reservations that had crept into the speeches, it was none the less clear that Hughes had the statesmen assembled in Washington coming his way.

The organization of the conference also made certain that it would operate with Hughesian efficiency. The heads of delegations constituted an unofficial steering committee. The detailed work of the conference was assigned to a Committee on Limitation of Armament representing five powers and a Committee on Pacific and Far Eastern Questions representing nine countries. In each of these fields there was also a committee on program and procedure and numerous working subcommittees. Hughes, Balfour, and Kato became a sort

[1] *Conference on the Limitation of Armament*, pp. 96, 98, 104.
[2] Edwin L. James in *New York Times*, Nov. 16, 1921.

of inner steering committee in working out the naval agreement. As soon as they could bring their respective governments into accord, they would meet with the heads of the French and Italian delegations. The conclusions of those five would be taken to the Subcommittee of Fifteen on Naval Limitation. At this stage the naval experts who were included among the fifteen had a chance to check and recheck the agreement. Then it would go to a drafting subcommittee to be put into treaty form and to a committee of legal advisers for further checking. At last the finished product would go to the Committee on Limitation of Armament and then to a plenary session of the conference itself for formal approval and signature.

As chairman of the conference, Hughes was also chairman of all its committees. Carefully budgeting his time, he attended more committee meetings than seemed possible for one individual. Nearly every morning he met the American delegates in his office, and he reported to the President every day. Before taking any step, he made certain that he had the approval both of the President and of the delegation.

Each afternoon Hughes held a press conference, with about 250 reporters from many different countries attending. The foreign reporters were admitted because the chairman of the conference was eager to have the whole world informed of what it was doing. Public opinion in Great Britain, Japan, and France was especially vital to achievement of his aim. Yet he felt that he could not talk to the reporters from all countries in the same confidential manner that marked his regular press conferences. In the words of one journalist, Hughes was "terribly outleaked." Lord Riddell, a brilliant newspaper man who was in the confidence of the British delegation, repeatedly divulged what had taken place behind closed doors. Even when Riddell did not know the facts, he was clever enough to put two and two together and accurately forecast what the conference would do. Reporters besieged Hughes for similar inside information without success.

Some of the world's most famous journalists were covering the conference. Among them were H. Wickham Steed, editor of the *Times* of London, H. W. Nevinson of the *Manchester Guardian*, "Pertinax" (André Géraud) of the *Echo de Paris*, H. G. Wells, William Allen White, Frank H. Simonds, Mark Sullivan, and many others. Keenly aware of the danger of antagonizing these molders of public opinion, the Secretary nevertheless held fast to his policy of not divulging confidential data. Being chairman of the conference, he knew everything that was going on. He could not speak freely without risking disruption of the negotiations. Neither the roasting that he got in the press nor his own distress over what Riddell was doing could induce him to incur the distrust of the delegates by forecasting unfinished agreements.

Hughes and Balfour ironed out the differences between their countries in a spirit of full cooperation. The obstacle to prompt agreement was Japan. In spite of their acceptance of the Hughes proposal "in principle," the Japanese brought in demands for a 10:10:7 ratio, parity with Britain and the United States in aircraft carriers, and retention of their new battleship, the *Mutsu*, on the ground that it was already completed. Anything less than 70 per cent of the tonnage allotted to the larger powers, the Japanese insisted, would undermine their national security. The argument was once more back on the basis of national needs. To buttress this demand, however, the Japanese asserted that the United States had miscalculated the relative strength of their navy. Giving no weight to American ships not yet completed, the Nipponese experts claimed that the ratio between the two fleets was somewhere between 69 and 86 to 100.

Tokyo's demands could not have been granted without upsetting the basic principle on which the American proposal rested and destroying the existing balance of power in the Pacific. Hughes held doggedly to his original stand. For several weeks this deadlock darkened the outlook for an agreement.

On December 1, Kato, who was affiliated with liberal elements in Japan and was genuinely eager to reach an agreement, came up with the suggestion of preventing new fortifications in the Pacific. He first presented the idea to Balfour, and Balfour passed it along to Hughes when they conferred at the Pan American Building later in the day. The Secretary's first reaction was that naval and military opinion would strongly oppose the proposal and that the American people probably would not wish to fetter themselves by giving up the right to fortify their own possessions.[3] His own idea was that the United States and Japan could agree that if either one or the other should wish to build fortifications in the Pacific it should give notice of its desire, and the opposite party would then have the right to terminate the whole naval agreement. Under these circumstances bases would probably never be built, he said. But he dropped the suggestion in deference to Balfour's fears that it would detract from the stability of the arms treaty.

Other members of the American delegation saw no objection to granting Japan's request when Hughes laid it before them. He especially questioned Lodge and Underwood on what the attitude of Congress would be. "There should be no hesitation in making the agreement," the Senators replied, "since Congress would never consent to spend the vast sums required in adequately fortifying these islands."[4] Root took the same view. Since Lodge had for a quarter of a century advocated a strong American policy in the Far East, his assurance on this point was especially impressive. "You're not giving up anything," he told the Secretary. When the fortifications agreement later was attacked in the Senate, Lodge became its foremost defender.

[3] *Foreign Relations, 1922,* I, 74.
[4] CEH, Notes, p. 286.

Admiral Coontz complained some years later that, to the best of his knowledge, neither the Navy nor the General Board was consulted about giving up the right to fortify our Pacific islands.[5] The implication seems to be that the delegation acted without technical advice. But the General Board's report to Hughes on October 14, 1921, amply covered the subject. That report vigorously opposed any agreement to dismantle fortifications and insisted that the security of American possessions in the Pacific was "dependent upon proper development and defense of Oahu, Guam, and Manila Bay." [6]

The Secretary also had the whole subject of Pacific bases investigated by Dr. George H. Blakeslee before the conference began. The Blakeslee report took note of the desire of the armed services for strongly fortified bases in Hawaii and Guam. So Hughes was well advised as to the views of the strategists. Confronted by the Japanese request, moreover, he discussed it with the Assistant Secretary of the Navy, assuming that Roosevelt would in turn consult the admirals.

In the end the Navy was overruled. The conference was, as Root said, "the complete negation of naval policy." Hughes was pursuing, not the chimera of an impregnable navy, but a policy of live and let live. His expert, Dr. Blakeslee, had pointed out that fortification of Guam, while it would assure earlier success of American naval operations in the western Pacific, was not essential to our national security or to the maintenance of American policy in the Far East. On the other hand, it would be an obvious menace to the security of Japan, which would doubtless prevent her from reducing her naval forces. The gain from fortifying Guam, he concluded, would not equal the loss resulting from failure of the conference and increased friction with Japan.[7] This reasoning harmonized with Hughes' keen desire to make offensive war more difficult while safeguarding defenses. And if bases would never be built in Guam and the Philippines anyway, maintenance of that sterile right at the cost of continuing the naval race would be a colossal blunder.

When the Big Three met again on December 2, after the failure of the technical experts to break the deadlock, Kato again defended his claim for a 10:10:7 ratio and retention of the *Mutsu*. Instead of being 98 per cent complete, as the American proposal indicated, the *Mutsu* was finished and had 500 miles of sea travel behind her. If he were to give up the pride of the Japanese Navy and accept the 60 per cent ratio, how could he justify it to the Japanese people? Certainly it would be of great assistance in getting agreement on the lower ratio, Kato said, if the United States would consent not to increase its fortifications at Guam, the Philippines, and Hawaii. Japan in turn

[5] *Hearings on the London Naval Treaty* (of 1930), p. 436.

[6] Copy of report is in the Hughes Papers; see p. 10.

[7] "The Existing Strategic Situation in the Pacific in Relation to Limitation of Armament," Hughes Papers.

would agree not to fortify Formosa, the Pescadores, and Oshima. Incidentally, Kato had admitted to Balfour that Japan was planning to fortify these islands.

Hughes began by saying that Japan was in the fortunate position of having no great naval power as a neighbor. The 10:10:6 ratio was entirely fair to Japan because it represented her own estimate of her national needs. To be sure, Japan could reject an agreement and build more ships, but that would be futile because the United States would build, too. In spite of his qualms about getting money from Congress, Hughes insisted that the ratio would be maintained as it was in any event.

To another of Kato's arguments, Hughes replied that American ships under construction must be counted as part of our naval strength. A warship 90 per cent complete would be an enormous asset in case of emergency. "Similarly," he added, "in the case of a ship 70 per cent or 50 per cent or other per cent completed, the work done was so much naval strength in hand . . . the American people would never consent to scrap the ships in course of construction, on which they had spent $330,000,000, and at the same time not count what they actually had in course of construction as a part of their naval strength."[8] Japan's naval experts were permitted to examine the pertinent Navy records to remove all doubt as to the work done on the unfinished ships. Under the pounding of Hughes' logic, Kato retreated from his contention that a ship was not a ship unless it was ready to fight.

Turning to the *Mutsu,* Hughes said that if Kato wished to know how he could justify this sacrifice to the Japanese people, "surely his best line of argument was to explain the sacrifices which America was making. She was not giving up merely one ship but three ships that were very little behind the *Mutsu,* and no less than fifteen capital ships which were under construction."

As to Kato's proposal to "freeze the Pacific" in regard to fortifications, Hughes said that the American delegation might be willing to consider it but only as part of a general agreement that would embrace the proposed four-power pact and the American plan for reduction of naval armament. And in no event could Hawaii, which was solely a defensive base, be included in any such agreement. The conference broke up with the understanding that Kato would seek further instructions from Tokyo. Because of the congestion of the cables, ten days elapsed before he was ready to talk again.

When the Big Three met in Hughes' office on December 12, Kato definitely offered to accept the 10:10:6 ratio in return for maintenance of the status quo as to fortifications and naval bases in the Pacific. The two proposals were inseparable in the Japanese mind. Kato said frankly that if naval bases were to be developed in the Philippines or Guam, "the better tendency in relations between the two countries which had lately been observable would be changed

[8] *Foreign Relations, 1922,* I, 75-82.

to hostility."[9] Hughes gave his blessing to the arrangement, again exempting Hawaii, and stating his assumption that Japan would refrain from fortifying her outlying islands and that existing fortifications would be left intact. Balfour likewise acquiesced.

The *Mutsu,* however, appeared more than ever to be a sacred cow. School children had contributed pennies to help finance her. She was now fully manned, Kato said, and could not be destroyed without striking a disastrous blow to Japanese morale. Kato offered to sink the old *Settsu* instead.

Both Hughes and Balfour argued powerfully against this course. Retention of the *Mutsu* would upset the carefully devised ratio of the American proposal. Japan could not camouflage that fact by offering to scrap an older vessel in place of her giant, modern man-of-war. Kato tried to squeeze out of the tight place he was in by saying that the 10:10:6 ratio was to apply at the end and not the beginning of the ten-year naval holiday. Hughes replied pointedly that he had always understood the ratio to be immediately applicable as a means of measuring what each country had to sacrifice. If Japan insisted on retaining the *Mutsu,* Great Britain would have to build and the United States would have to finish the construction of equivalent ships. Kato was sorry, but in any event the *Mutsu* had to be saved.

The Secretary was keenly disappointed over this defeat. All he could do, however, was to insist that the list of doomed ships be altered so as to maintain the 10:10:6 ratio with the *Mutsu* spared. Having consulted his naval advisers, he informed the Japanese the next day that the United States would have to complete the *Washington*[10] and the *Colorado,* the two ships farthest advanced, while scrapping the *Delaware* and the *North Dakota,* to match Japan's departure from the original plan. The result would be to give the United States roughly 525,000 tons of capital ships and Japan 315,000 tons instead of the 500,000-ton and 300,000-ton limits originally proposed.

Japan's intransigence convinced the British that they would have to build two of the enormous super-*Hoods* that were under contract. Unless building went forward, Britain would have no ships designed after the Battle of Jutland, except the *Hood,* which had been somewhat altered after Jutland. Britain was loath to spend money on new ships, but all agreed that it would be the only fair and feasible thing to do if the *Mutsu* were to be kept.

This raised a new difficulty, for the super-*Hoods* would far exceed the 35,000-ton limit that Hughes had proposed for all battleships. He strenuously objected to any further breach in the original plan. Neither Japan nor the United States would have a ship larger than 35,000 tons, he said. Could not Britain reduce the size of her ships and thus avoid excessive scrapping of

[9] *Ibid.,* p. 91.
[10] The Navy later decided to complete the *West Virginia* instead of the *Washington.*

existing vessels to keep within the maximum tonnage allowance? Balfour said that large sums had been spent in designing the super-*Hoods*. It would take a year to change the designs. Meanwhile Britain would be in a position of serious inferiority. The argument waxed warm for several days.

Two sessions were held on December 14, the final one at Secretary Hughes' home that evening. There was much talk about a plan under which Britain would build two 35,000-ton battleships and scrap four in the *King George V* class. The British experts and delegates strongly favored, however, the alternative plan of building two super-*Hoods* which would necessitate the scrapping of five older ships. Balfour begged Hughes not to ask the British to sacrifice the size and weight that would be necessary to give their ships adequate protection against submarines and airplanes. But Hughes was not convinced. By way of emphasis he questioned Balfour on what size the super-*Hoods* would attain.

"Would those ships displace more than 35,000 tons?"

Balfour said they would.

"As much as 40,000 tons?"

Again Balfour answered affirmatively.

"As much as 45,000 tons?" Hughes then asked with pointed emphasis on the figure.

"Yes," Balfour admitted, "the plans call for ships that would displace nearly 50,000 tons."

Kato agreeably consented to the British plan, but Hughes became increasingly alarmed over the prospect. The more he thought about it, the more indefensible it seemed for an arms limitation conference to put its stamp of approval on 49,000-ton battleships. When the Big Three met in his office on the morning of December 15, he launched a final assault on Britain's sea monsters. If we agree to this, he said, the British can go home from the conference and start building battleships of a magnitude never before seen on the oceans. Her example would quicken the desires of other countries for larger ships. Instead of encouraging peace and ending naval rivalry, the conference would thus be undercutting its own handiwork.

"How could we possibly defend such a decision before our peoples?" Hughes asked. "They are looking to us to curtail naval strength. We cannot be content with agreement upon mathematical formulas. No matter how we might try to justify the building of warships of such colossal size, most of the moral and psychological impact of the conference would be lost." [11]

Balfour was visibly shaken in his position. Excusing himself, he went across the hall to consult Admiral Chatfield. On his return he said frankly that the Admiralty would not agree to any reduction in the size of the super-*Hoods*. "But I think," he said dramatically, turning to Secretary Hughes, "that you

[11] Author's interview with CEH, Nov. 19, 1946; *Foreign Relations, 1922*, I, 125.

are right. I do not like to act without consulting my government, but what you have proposed is so manifestly just, and I am so impressed with the importance of avoiding further delay, that I will take the responsibility of accepting the scheme under which Great Britain would have the right to build two new ships of not more than 35,000 British tons." [12]

It was the most intense moment in all the negotiations of the conference. No other delegate could have taken so much upon himself. The courage and statesmanlike attitude of Balfour won Hughes' unbounded admiration, and it goes a long way toward explaining their close teamwork through the remainder of the conference. The French got little sympathy from Hughes when they later clashed with the British. "I can't go back on Mr. Balfour," he told Castle, "nor would you if you could have seen him day after day sitting beside me in this office and backing up all I had to say on the subject of destruction of capital ships, to the great amazement of Baron Kato, who had expected the British to support some, at least, of the Japanese claims." [13] Balfour's comment was that the three months he and Hughes spent together represented "the perfect ideal of that which international negotiations ought always to possess, but which too often are absent." [14]

Prior to Balfour's dramatic concession, Hughes had agreed to a second minor breach in his plan—that the limit of 35,000 tons placed on the two British battleships should be deemed to mean British tons, thus raising the limit to about 37,000 American tons. Except for this and the upward revision of the tonnage cuttings because of the *Mutsu,* the Hughes plan had come through the negotiations intact. On December 15 the Big Three announced their agreement to the world. They had accepted (1) the 10:10:6 ratio; (2) a ten-year naval holiday, except for two American and two British ships to offset Japan's retention of the *Mutsu;* and (3) maintenance of the status quo as to fortifications and naval bases "in the region of the Pacific." It was a notable victory for the patient and unrelenting statesman who had summoned the conference, fixed the scope of its undertakings, and nursed it through several crises.

A sea of trouble lay ahead, however, for this accord was contingent upon a satisfactory agreement with France and Italy. Those two countries had not been invited to the discussions of the Big Three because Hughes wished to avoid the intrusion of relatively minor issues into the major problem of arresting the Anglo-American-Japanese naval race. That was certainly the best strategy for hastening the major accord, but it aroused suspicions among the French and doubtless stiffened their demands. M. Briand had come to Washington without any program, hoping to play the role of mediator between the United States and Great Britain. No such opportunity arose. The weak bargaining

[12] *Id.* [13] Castle's diary, 1922, p. 29.
[14] Address to Pilgrims, London, July 21, 1924.

position of the French was further accentuated because the war had forced them to neglect naval building. As the conference seemed to move along without them, they felt frustrated and unhappy.

Sensing this restiveness among the French delegates, Hughes asked Theodore Roosevelt, Jr., to see Admiral de Bon and find out what total tonnage the French expected. The admiral declined to commit himself. Roosevelt and his naval experts concluded that France and Italy should agree to a replacement limit of 175,000 tons while retaining all the warships they then possessed. Hughes agreed that the proposal was reasonable. It asked nothing of France to match the 40 per cent reduction proposed for the British and American fleets.

Ambassador Jusserand attempted to sound out Hughes as to what he had in mind for France as the two climbed the stair at the Pan American building one day. Finding that Jusserand had no suggestion to offer, Hughes asked, "Would 175,000 tons be satisfactory?" Jusserand made no definite reply.[15]

It is not clear whether Jusserand passed along this suggestion to Premier Briand. The Premier returned home late in November before there was any opportunity for the French to enter the negotiations on naval limitation. He had, however, come to a friendly understanding with Hughes as to general policies. Just before Briand left Washington, he visited the Secretary at his home and they chatted amiably together without the aid of an interpreter, Briand speaking French, which Hughes understood, and Hughes speaking English, which Briand largely understood. The Premier said in no uncertain terms that he was in sympathy with what Hughes was doing, that although he was leaving he would still be head of the French delegation, and that if at any time during the conference he could be helpful the Secretary should call on him.

This offer assumed major significance when the French delegates in Washington demanded a quota of no less than 350,000 tons of capital ships. The Secretary had called in Albert Sarraut and Jusserand to tell them of the accord he had reached with Great Britain and Japan. In spite of previous indications of French pique, he was shocked by the unreasonableness of their stand. Sarraut was claiming the right to build a navy more than twice the size of France's existing fleet.

Seeing the great achievement for which he had labored so indefatigably slipping from his grasp, Hughes addressed the French delegates with bluntness approaching severity. France's economic position, he said, would not permit her to build so many ships. "Why," he undiplomatically exclaimed, with obvious reference to France's unpaid war debt to the United States, "you can't even pay your debts."

[15] *Foreign Relations, 1922*, I, 134.

"We are as proud of our debts," Jusserand came back, with a stiffening gesture, "as we are of our wounds."[16]

Hughes begged the French delegates not to announce their demand publicly. It would cause a revulsion of feeling throughout America. The numerous efforts of the American people to extend financial aid to the French would be left virtually without support. France, he said, would scarcely have a friend left in the United States. The irritable and quarrelsome Sarraut indicated that he would fight publicly for the 350,000-ton quota. He did so and brought a storm of indignation upon his head.

Rent by feuds among themselves and plagued by the incompetence of René Viviani and Sarraut, the French delegates were in a state of acute agitation. Hughes' proposal to limit their fleet to 175,000 tons was denounced as an affront to the honor and dignity of France. It was "unspeakable." Bristling with anger, Admiral de Bon declared that the French Admiralty was planning to build twelve capital ships and could not accept a holiday until 1931.

Hughes called in Jusserand the next day and told him, as ambassador, of Briand's friendly offer before he had left. "Although I dislike going over M. Sarraut's head," he said, "I feel that it is imperative to communicate with the Premier." Jusserand merely remarked that that would be quite within the Secretary's rights. The "personal message" which Hughes dictated was put into Briand's hands just as he was leaving Paris for London.

Success or failure of the conference hung on the word of France, Hughes told the Premier. If France were to make the same sacrifices that the other powers were making, her tonnage of battleships would be reduced to 102,000. "We do not ask this," Hughes hastened to add. His plan for France would allow her to keep all her 164,000 tons of dreadnoughts and even increase her quota to 175,000 tons. Likewise her pre-dreadnoughts could be saved, although all other countries were scrapping theirs.

"If it be said that France desires a greater relative strength," he argued, "the obvious answer is that this would be impossible of attainment."[17] The result would be no agreement; then the United States and Britain would shortly have navies, not of three to one in relation to France, but of six to one. "The proposed agreement," he drove home to Briand, "really doubles the relative strength of the French Navy." Should France insist on a quota of more than 300,000 tons, he concluded, she would wreck the conference and blight the hope of the world for relief from the burden of excessive armaments.

Unquestionably the French had padded their demand for capital ships in the hope of winning favorable concessions as to smaller craft and submarines.

[16] Author's interview with J. Reuben Clark, Jr., Dec. 12, 1948.

[17] *Foreign Relations, 1922,* I, 130ff.

When confronted with the risk of defeating all agreement, Briand cabled to Hughes: "With regard to the tonnage of capital ships—that is to say, ships of offense, which are the most costly—I have instructed our delegates in the sense you desire." [18] However, it would be impossible, he insisted, for France to accept corresponding reductions as to light cruisers, torpedo boats, and submarines.

Hughes thought this response ended the controversy so far as capital ships were concerned. But Sarraut, Jusserand, and Admiral de Bon insisted that Briand's acceptance of Hughes' proposal as to capital ships was conditional on the granting of France's desires as to light cruisers, flotilla leaders, destroyers, and submarines. Saying that he would resort to the language of the street, Sarraut ranted about France being "blotted out of the surface of the sea" and "cut into shreds and done away with piecemeal." [19] He read "confidential instructions" from his government to the effect that France must have an irreducible minimum of 330,000 tons of light cruisers, torpedo boats, and so forth, and 90,000 tons of submarines. Referring to Secretary Hughes' success in bringing the British and Japanese around to his point of view, Sarraut asked pointedly for a guarantee that, in return for France's acceptance of the capital-ship limit of 175,000 tons, France's other demands would be met.

Hughes rejected this fantastic high-pressure scheme, but the exorbitant French demand for auxiliary craft was untouchable. Once more he appealed to Briand for some indication, to be given in confidence, as to his minimum figures for the so-called "defensive" ships. The Premier promised to comply while he was still in London, but, back in Paris, where he was having trouble holding the confidence of Parliament, he dropped the idea. Eventually the French accepted the 175,000-ton limit on capital ships, but refused to go an inch beyond it.

This attitude spelled the doom of Hughes' hope for proportionate reductions in auxiliary craft. The United States had originally suggested a 90,000-ton limit on submarines for itself and Great Britain and a 54,000-ton limit for Japan. A later American plan called for 60,000 tons of submarines for the two largest naval powers, with Japan, France, and Italy keeping what they then had. Both France and Japan objected, and apparently nothing would induce the French to lower their demand for 90,000 tons, although their existing fleet of submarines was little more than one-third that size. The British had urged complete abolition of submarines, and in view of the fabulous French demand in this category Balfour was unwilling to accept any limit on destroyers or other small craft used to combat submarines. Both the British and Italians hinted at aggressive intentions behind the French demands, and this led to the bitterest row of the conference.[20] Since M. Briand had realistically

[18] *Ibid.*, p. 135. [19] *Ibid.*, p. 137ff. [20] *Conference*, pp. 574ff.

closed the door to any reduction of land armaments until the security of France could be guaranteed by other means, the French took the chief blame for limiting the achievements of the conference.

Feeling the necessity of getting some action as to submarines, the American delegation, with Root taking the lead, put through a treaty stating the rules of international law as to submarines and attempting to prohibit their use as commerce destroyers.[21] Any submarine commander violating the rules was declared to be subject to punishment, "as if for an act of piracy," by the military or civil authorities of any country. The same treaty undertook to prohibit the use of poisonous gases and chemicals in warfare. It was ratified by the United States, Great Britain, Italy, and Japan, but France held out until the treaty was superseded by a milder agreement at the London Naval Conference of 1930.

To prevent the building of larger cruisers to take the place of capital ships, the conference limited the individual size of auxiliary craft to 10,000 tons and the caliber of their guns to eight inches. Aircraft carriers were limited both as to the over-all tonnage each power might have and as to individual size. The American delegation at first proposed a limit of 27,000 tons displacement for aircraft carriers, but the Navy, fearing it would never get money out of Congress for carriers, conceived the idea of converting the battle cruisers *Lexington* and *Saratoga* into carriers. These vessels, designed to displace 43,500 tons, could not be stripped as carriers to less than 33,000 tons. So the treaty was written to retain the 27,000-ton limit, with an exception that any of the powers might convert into carriers two of their ships that would otherwise be scrapped, and these might be of a tonnage up to 33,000.

Taking advantage of this idea while the treaty was still in the drafting stage, the British inserted clauses permitting doomed ships to be converted to commercial or harbor use. Hughes raised a furor. "It is of vital importance," he said, "that nothing be done which would tend to impair the moral value of the *whole* treaty. No petty economies or fancied saving would compensate the destruction of the moral value. . . . Sincerity of purpose is the thing the treaty will be judged by." The world was looking for something comparable to the destruction of the German fleet at Scapa Flow and "would brook nothing which enabled these ships to be kept alive." Permit them to be converted to commercial and harbor use and they would all remain available in case of war. The average man would say "the treaty was a sham." [22]

Admitting the possibility of misunderstanding, Balfour asked if it was not difficult to defend conversion of the *Lexingtons* into aircraft carriers if the British were not allowed to economize by converting their old warships for

[21] *Report of the American Delegation*, pp. 36f.
[22] *Foreign Relations, 1922*, I, 189–192.

harbor service. Hughes could not see the comparison. A warm argument ensued. The American delegation was opposed, the chairman said, to having the treaty say one thing when meaning another. If necessary to avoid that blunder, he personally would eliminate the provision as to the two aircraft carriers. "I will not for the sake of ten or twenty millions of dollars," he declared, "spoil this treaty."

A strenuous discussion followed within the American delegation, with Hughes disposed to strike out the concession on aircraft carriers and Root and Underwood agreeing. Roosevelt saved the carriers by arguing that Congress might continue spending money on two ships under construction but probably would not appropriate for entirely new ships. Hughes went back to the committee of chief delegates and won his point without sacrificing the carriers. That was the logical outcome, for there was really no relation between converting battle cruisers into carriers, which the United States had a right to build in any event, and saving warships in excess of quotas by devoting them to civilian uses.

The American draft of the treaty was accepted largely because Hughes had had the foresight to put a group of experts to work on it shortly after the conference assembled. He personally scrutinized each new draft the experts produced, penciling in additions and corrections and clarifying the language. By January 4 the American draft had been approved by the committee of legal experts with only minor changes.

Fresh difficulties arose, however, as to the status quo agreement on fortifications and naval bases in the Pacific. The experts asked what should be the boundaries of the "Pacific region" in which no bulwarks should be built. The statement of December 15 said only that the region included Hong Kong and did not include the Hawaiian Islands, Australia, New Zealand, the islands composing Japan proper, and the coasts of the United States and Canada. That left many questions unanswered. What would be the status of the Aleutians? What of the British naval base at Singapore? What islands constitute "Japan proper"?

The British evolved a clever scheme based on a parallelogram bounded on the east by the International Date Line, on the north by the thirtieth degree of latitude, on the west by the 110th meridian and on the south by the Equator.[23] All the islands inside the parallelogram, including most of the American and Japanese islands, were not to be fortified. All the islands outside, including most of Great Britain's, would be unrestricted. Meanwhile the Japanese had put in a claim for exclusion of the Bonins and other islands several hundred miles distant from the Japanese coast.

[23] Harold and Margaret Sprout, *Toward a New Order of Sea Power*, pp. 244f.

Kato visited Hughes informally on January 16 and said that the nonfortifications agreement had been transformed into a political issue in Japan. Tokyo would not accept the British proposal. Apparently some of Kato's enemies at home were using the agreement to embarrass him. He asked the Secretary to give him a few days to see if he could work the problem out quietly without having to face the Naval Committee.

On January 22 Kato reported that acceptance of the British proposal would cause the Japanese Cabinet to fall and no treaty could then be ratified. Against the background of that ominous forecast, he offered a concrete proposal of his own. He would leave the United States free to fortify the Hawaiian Islands and islands adjacent to the mainland. Britain could fortify islands adjacent to Canada, Australia, and New Zealand; Japan could fortify any of her islands, except Amami-Oshima, the Bonin Islands, Formosa, and the Pescadores. Balfour immediately called for exemption of Singapore. After consultation with the Navy Department, Hughes wished to exempt, in addition to the Hawaiian Islands, the islands adjacent to "the coast of the United States, including Alaska and the Panama Canal Zone." He added to Kato's list of Japanese islands to remain unfortified Okinawa-Oshima and "any insular possessions in the Pacific Ocean which Japan may hereafter acquire."

Kato objected because this reference to Alaska would permit fortification of the Aleutian Islands, which extend in the direction of Japan. We cannot give up our right to fortify the Aleutians, Hughes replied, unless Japan, in return, will give up her right to fortify the Kurile Islands, which stretch out toward Alaska, and the Loochoo Islands, which point toward the Philippines. After cabling his government, Kato proposed that the Aleutians, the Kuriles, and the Loochoos be brought into the status-quo agreement and that Okinawa-Oshima be left out. This proposal was finally adopted.

The fortifications agreement, Colonel Roosevelt wrote in his diary, "leaves us, in my opinion, in a slightly better position than Japan. We trade certain fortifications which we would never have completed, for fortifications which they [the Japanese] would have unquestionably completed. We retain one outpost in the Pacific of great importance and they give up all but their mainland." [24]

Three days after Kato got his final instructions from Tokyo the naval treaty was completed. Secretary Hughes had compromised with the Japanese on fortifications and on the *Mutsu,* and the French had blocked agreement as to auxiliary craft. With these exceptions, he had won every major controversy with every delegation, and all the principles laid down in his initial speech were safely embedded in the text of the treaty. From beginning to end it had

[24] Jan. 29, 30, 1922. Quoted by Sprout, *op. cit.*, p. 251.

been Hughes' conference. "A powerful locomotive pulling a great express train gives a slight idea of the force and the speed of the Chairman of the conference," wrote one of the experts of the American delegation.[25]

Even in his hour of triumph, however, the Secretary was bedeviled by a minor irritation. Plans had been laid for printing the treaties with the equally authentic French and English texts in parallel columns. Hughes advanced the idea that, since the conference had been held in the United States, with English dominant in the discussions, the English text should have the more conspicuous place in the left-hand column. Jusserand was horrified. Sarraut is said to have threatened to withhold France's approval of the treaties unless the French text were given the "place d'honneur." [26] The vehemence of this demand, added to the arbitrary conduct of the French in the naval-treaty negotiations, aroused Hughes' Welsh-Irish ire.

After a spirited debate with Jusserand over the telephone, Hughes was discussing the controversy with Solicitor Fred K. Nielsen when Senator Lodge dropped in. "Mr. Secretary," the Senator remarked in his squeaky voice, "what's the difference?" [27] A smile of acquiescence crept over Hughes' face. While he had been human enough to haggle over a petty matter as the greatest drama in his career approached a finale, he was quick to recognize that his own precept of not letting insignificant details stand in the way of great achievements had been effectively turned against him.

The proud moment for presentation of the Naval Armaments Treaty to the conference came on February 1. Again Continental Hall was filled to capacity by a distinguished audience. But the tension of November 12 had given way to a quiet feeling of satisfaction and renewed faith in peace. With no manuscript before him, Secretary Hughes reported the details of the treaty, the ships to be scrapped and their tonnage, the deviations from the original American plan, the agreement as to fortifications, the miscellaneous provisions, and the processes of reasoning that led to agreement on each point. Nothing was missing. His associates shook their heads over this feat of memory as Hughes summed up:

> May I say that no more extraordinary or significant Treaty has ever been made. It is extraordinary because we no longer merely talk of the desirability of diminishing the burdens of naval armaments, but we actually limit them. (*Applause.*) . . .
>
> This Treaty ends, absolutely ends, the race in competition in naval armament. (*Applause.*) At the same time it leaves the relative security of the great naval Powers unimpaired.

[25] George H. Blakeslee, *The Recent Foreign Policy of the United States* (New York, Abingdon Press, 1925), pp. 236f. Copyright, 1925, by George H. Blakeslee.

[26] Chandler P. Anderson's diary, Feb. 6, 1922.

[27] Author's interview with Mr. Nielsen, July 21, 1949.

By Larry Keys in the *Columbus Citizen*, February 7, 1922.

PROOF OF THE PUDDING IS IN RATIFICATION

The significance of the Treaty is far more than that. In this Treaty we are talking of arms in the language of peace. The best thing about the engagement is the spirit which has been manifested throughout our negotiations and to which is due our ability to reach this fortunate conclusion. In other words, we are taking perhaps the greatest forward step in history to establish the reign of peace. (*Applause.*) [28]

[28] *Conference*, p. 248.

Chapter 47

THE FOUR-POWER PACT

THE destruction of weapons, standing by itself, is a negative achievement. It becomes positive in effect only when it is supplemented by better means of keeping the peace. The Washington Conference courageously attacked both problems. Much of its time was given to removing sources of friction, defining rights, and creating obligations that would eliminate any necessity for appeal to the arbitrament of arms.

Secretary Hughes concluded that four sources of unrest in the Pacific would have to be dealt with if the experiment in arms limitation were to have a fair chance of success: first, the Anglo-Japanese Alliance; second, Japanese imperialism on the continent of Asia; third, the Shantung controversy that was keeping Japan and China at daggers' points; fourth, the controversy over the mandated islands which had strained relations between the United States and Japan. If these sore spots could be healed and the naval race ended, the drift toward war could be arrested and future aggression would be made more difficult.

The exertion of pressure for modification of the Anglo-Japanese Alliance had started in the Wilson Administration. Secretary Hughes put increased vigor behind that policy. American public opinion was deeply hostile toward the alliance, for it legally bound Great Britain to go to war with the United States if Japan should do so. The British had attempted to strip the alliance of this obligation when it was renewed in 1911 by including a provision that it should not operate against a third power with which either ally might conclude a treaty of general arbitration. But the Senate had rejected the Anglo-American arbitration treaty. When the postwar tension between the United States and Japan reached its height in 1920 and 1921 and renewal of the Anglo-Japanese Alliance was under consideration, both Japanese and British spokesmen denied that it was a menace to the United States. Nevertheless, it was a fertile source of unrest in the United States, Britain, and Canada.

An inaccurate press report in June, 1921, gave Hughes the opportunity he had been seeking to voice his antagonism toward the alliance. "It is understood," said a dispatch dealing with the London Imperial Conference, "that the State Department has been kept fully informed of the plans of the British Government, and that it has been given assurances that in the renewal of the treaty every precaution will be taken to guard against the inclusion of anything inimical to American rights." [1] Hughes publicly denied that he was being kept informed and said that he had received no assurances; he did not wish the public to get "a false impression." The following day Ambassador Geddes hastened to the Secretary's office to ask if he wished to say anything in regard to the proposed renewal of the alliance.

Hughes replied that, since the defeat of Germany and the collapse of Russia had removed the original cause for entering into the alliance, the American people would regard its continuance as an alliance against them.[2] His chief emphasis, however, was upon the unfortunate encouragement the alliance gave to Japanese imperialism. There were no questions between the United States and Japan that could not be solved, he said. But the American Government had some very clear policies in the Far East, including the Open Door, the integrity of China, and now, in view of existing conditions, those policies embraced the integrity of Russia. If he could "speak freely in an informal and confidential way," the Secretary said, "he felt that if Great Britain and Japan had any arrangement by which Great Britain was to support the special interests of Japan, the latter might be likely, at the instance of the militaristic party . . . to take positions which would call forth protests from this Government . . . leading to a state of irritation among the people in both countries; that such a condition of affairs would be fraught with mischief; that if it were true that the policies of Great Britain in the Far East were like our own there should be cooperation between Great Britain and the United States, and it should be possible for the United States to find complete support on the part of Great Britain in their maintenance and execution. . . ." [3]

Geddes wondered whether it would not be possible "to have cooperation with Japan,—that is, on the part of the three nations." It was a bid for the United States to come into the alliance. Hughes made it plain that the United States would not accept such an arrangement. What he had in mind was pursuit of common policies. But he approved Geddes' suggestion for a common declaration of Far Eastern policies if it could be made to square with the principles he was trying to uphold.

Seizing every argument to impress upon the British the desirability of working closely with the United States, Hughes then told Geddes that a resolution for recognition of the Irish Republic would be introduced in Congress. In his opinion it would not pass, but in the debate the enemies of Great Britain would take full advantage of any relation between Great Britain and Japan indicating disregard for American interests. On the contrary, British action

[1] *Foreign Relations, 1921*, II, 313.
[2] Author's interview with CEH, Nov. 26, 1946.
[3] *Foreign Relations, 1921*, II, 314f.

indicating a desire to support the Far Eastern policies to which the United States was committed "would give great aid and comfort to those who were opposing such a resolution."

By this combination of persuasion and pressure Hughes sought to shift British influence from the Japanese side of the Far Eastern equation to the American side. The effect of the alliance had been to shield Japanese imperialism in China and Russia. Japan had interpreted it as a sort of hunting license on the continent of Asia, with her ally maintaining a benevolent hands-off attitude. The Japanese thus laid great store upon renewal of the alliance, and Hughes was equally determined, if at all possible, to bring the British into a tacit partnership for the purposes of holding the Japanese in check.

For a time the issue was clouded by another dispute about Ambassador Harvey's veracity. Geddes returned to the department on July 6 to confirm his understanding that the Secretary had informally said the United States would regret the renewal of the alliance. Hughes assured him that his understanding was correct. Sir Aukland then said that Harvey had given exactly the opposite impression in London.[4] In talking with Lord Curzon, Harvey had said that whether or not Great Britain renewed the alliance or made a special arrangement with Japan was of no concern to the United States. No such statement had been authorized, Hughes replied, and it did not represent the opinion of the Administration.

The Secretary cabled Harvey for an explanation, and pointedly reminded him that he was expected to "await instructions before expressing opinions as to policy." Harvey read part of the cablegram to Curzon and quoted the Foreign Minister as saying: "That is simply monstrous. Of course you never said anything of that kind and I never said you did." [5] According to Harvey, Curzon had asked him if he could give a hint as to his government's attitude toward renewal of the alliance, and he had replied that he could not but would be glad to submit any question Curzon might wish to ask. To another question he had replied that he personally thought the American people would look upon renewal of the alliance with disfavor and mistrust. Harvey had not bothered to pass along Curzon's query to the Secretary of State. Final responsibility for the conflicting assertions was never fixed.

By the time the Washington Conference assembled, the British appeared not only willing but also eager to modify their alliance with Japan. Curzon, Lloyd George, and even King George himself had confided to Harvey their desire to get rid of that bond.[6] Balfour came to Washington, therefore, with the problem of the Anglo-Japanese Alliance uppermost in his mind. Calling on Hughes the day before the conference opened, he spoke of the danger of

[4] CEH to Harvey, July 6, 1921. [5] Harvey to Hughes, July 8, 1921.
[6] Willis F. Johnson, *George Harvey: "A Passionate Patriot,"* pp. 322f.

wounding Japan's sensibilities, and of the need for control over Japanese action and for safeguarding the Dominions. The situation was very delicate. If the alliance were not to be continued, what could be substituted for it? Answering his own question, Balfour said he had sketched two memoranda of possible agreements.

Hughes assured Balfour that the United States was friendly to Japan and would not oppose natural and legitimate economic opportunities for the Japanese. Their need was not political expansion, he said, but economic opportunity. Balfour ultimately came back to his drafts. Hughes asked time to consider them, and reiterated that the United States would not enter an alliance. Remembering the Senate, he was even averse to the word "treaty" and preferred to talk of "a definitive statement of principles and policies" that would take the place not only of the Anglo-Japanese Alliance but also the Root-Takahira and the Lansing-Ishii notes. Especially the Root-Takahira agreement was "a coin to be reissued." Balfour then substituted "arrangement" for "treaty" and "alliance" wherever they appeared in his drafts and penciled a note to the effect that "arrangement" as used was "deliberatively vague." [7]

The Secretary scrutinized Balfour's proposed "arrangements" and decided that neither was acceptable. One contained the germ of what was later to become the Nine-Power Treaty, but only the germ. The other was little more than the old Anglo-Japanese Alliance rewritten to include the United States. Each of the trio would agree to respect the rights of the others in the islands of the Pacific and bordering territories and to consult together if any one of them thought its rights to be imperiled. If threatened, any two of the signatories would be at liberty "to protect themselves by entering into a military alliance provided (*a*) this alliance is purely defensive in character and (*b*) that it is communicated to the other High Contracting Party."

Hughes' high opinion of Balfour must have sagged as he analyzed this scheme. It offered the United States the shell of a tripartite agreement and allowed Great Britain and Japan to keep the nut of their military obligations in case of trouble. Any war threat in the Pacific could transform the "arrangement" overnight into the old alliance. Indeed, the alliance was not even specifically cancelled by the Balfour proposal.

Hughes concluded, moreover, that no three-party agreement would protect American interests. If we should join with two countries that had been allies for twenty years, he said, the American people would feel that their government had put its head into a noose. The only way to avoid the risks of a two-to-one combination, with the United States in the minority, he decided, was to bring in France. When Hughes broached this idea to Balfour in one of their

[7] Papers on the Four-Power Treaty, Hughes Papers.

early interviews, the latter not only welcomed it but also agreed to seek the consent of Japan.

"It was Hughes' idea to bring in the French," Balfour wrote to a friend, "in order to soothe their somewhat ruffled pride." [8] That motive undoubtedly entered into the decision, but it was incidental to his feeling that a four-power agreement was necessary to shake off the odium of the old alliance and remove the danger that "England and Japan might combine against us." If France were brought in and the old alliance were abandoned in favor of a mere consultation treaty, the Secretary thought he might be able to get it approved by the Senate.

On November 26 Shidehara brought in a tripartite proposal similar to Balfour's. The British and Japanese had frequently consulted together. Hughes thus found himself a minority of one, as he feared his country might if it entered the Anglo-Japanese scheme. Nevertheless, he clung doggedly to his own ideas, and a series of meetings won the British and Japanese delegations to his point of view.

There was much delay, however, in getting final instructions from Tokyo. Not a word had been said to the French delegation about the proposed quadruple agreement because of the delicate situation that would arise if Tokyo should object to the inclusion of France. Meanwhile the restive French delegates were a source of increasing apprehension. At the meeting of the Big Three on naval limitation on December 2 Hughes asked Kato if he could say anything as to Japan's attitude on the proposed four-power agreement. Kato replied that he had had no response to his cable. Foreseeing no objection, he thought it would be reasonably safe to approach the French, but Hughes was reluctant to take such a chance, and Kato promised to cable a request that his government expedite its reply.

Finally the word came that Tokyo would accept a quadruple agreement. Thinking he had to have something definite to show the French, Hughes went to work immediately to draft the treaty. A preliminary American draft prepared by Chandler P. Anderson, with an alternative preamble by James Brown Scott, both legal advisers to the American delegation, had been handed to Hughes a fortnight earlier. With all the previous drafts before him, Hughes wrote an entirely new document that was to become the Four-Power Treaty.[9]

The first article pledged each of the four powers to respect the rights of the others to their insular possessions and dominions in the Pacific, and in case of controversy between any two of the four powers "likely to affect the relations of harmonious accord now happily subsisting between them," they were to invite the other powers to a conference in which "the whole subject" could be

[8] A. Whitney Griswold, *The Far Eastern Policy of the United States* (New York, Harcourt, Brace, 1938), p. 310. Copyright, 1938, by Harcourt, Brace & Co.

[9] CEH to Underwood, March 11, 1922.

"considered and adjusted."[10] Article II was a pledge that, in case of an aggressive threat from the outside, the four powers would "communicate with one another fully and frankly in order to arrive at an understanding as to the most efficient measures to be taken, jointly or separately, to meet the exigencies of the particular situation." It was a reissuance of the Root-Takahira "coin." The agreement would remain in effect for ten years, and then might be terminated by any party on six months' notice. As soon as it was ratified, the Anglo-Japanese Alliance would be terminated.

Root and Lodge were the first to see the draft and they unhesitatingly approved it. After making a few verbal changes, Hughes showed it to Balfour and Shidehara and won their consent. Determined to put the French in a happier mood, he invited M. Viviani to his home on the evening of December 7. When he sprang his surprise offer to the French, giving them an advantage they had not even sought, Viviani rushed up to the Secretary and kissed him on both whiskered cheeks.

In a conference with Balfour, Viviani, Jusserand, Kato, and Shidehara, Hughes made skillful use of the Four-Power Pact as a prod to hasten settlement of the mandates controversy. Since the mandates treaty with Japan was not yet signed and negotiations with Great Britain as to islands south of the Equator had not even begun, he inserted a clause in the Four-Power Pact to the effect that it should "not be deemed as an assent" on the part of the United States to the mandates.

Shidehara, at this same session, handed around copies of a new draft of the proposed treaty. It provided that if a dispute arose in the Pacific, the two parties, "in mutual agreement with each other," should invite the other powers to a conference. That would give Japan a chance to prevent a conference from being called if her imperialistic policies should be challenged. Shidehara said, however, that the chief reason for his draft was to break up Hughes' first article into two parts since it contained two ideas. The group agreed to divide the article into two sentences, but rejected the Japanese joker.

Shidehara asked if the agreement extended only to insular possessions and dominions. Hughes replied with pointed candor that it was so limited, and the reason was "to avoid the difficulties connected with the mainland, especially as to China." There are matters, he said, which "still required adjustment."[11] Both the Balfour and Shidehara drafts had dealt with rights and interests in eastern Asia as well as the Pacific islands, but Hughes was not willing to give any suggestion of countenance to Japan's imperialism in Shantung or elsewhere in China. By the astute means of narrowing the geographical scope of the agreement, as Harold and Margaret Sprout point out, Hughes had transformed the project, in practical effect, "from an American recognition of

[10] *Foreign Relations, 1922*, I, 7, 8. [11] *Ibid.*, p. 14.

Japan's conquests in Asia, into a Japanese pledge to respect United States sovereignty over the Philippines." [12]

The most embarrassing mix-up of the conference came over the question of whether the Four-Power Pact included the main islands of Japan. Shidehara first raised the question at the December 8 meeting. Hughes said that, being both "islands" and "possessions," they would be included in the language of the treaty. Balfour agreed. Since the mainland of no other party to the agreement was included, Shidehara said he would like to have the main islands of Japan excluded. Balfour at once declared that he could not admit that Australia and New Zealand, which were definitely in the treaty, were less important than any other part of the British Empire. A spirited discussion ensued in which Hughes expressed his willingness to meet Japan's wishes in the matter, and Balfour remained skeptical. Shidehara then attempted to bring in all the regions bordering on the Pacific Ocean. Both Hughes and Balfour resisted this. Finally, the meeting broke up with the understanding that the Japanese delegates would further consider an exchange of notes stating that the agreement did not apply to domestic issues and did not cover the main islands of Japan.

When the same group met the next morning at Hughes' home, Shidehara completely retreated. Now he was satisfied to have the main islands of Japan covered by the agreement and no exchange of notes on that point would be necessary. But he wished to narrow the type of controversies falling within the agreement. Hughes, on the contrary, wished to make certain that questions affecting the security of island possessions could be brought into a conference under the treaty as well as questions directly arising out of the islands themselves. Balfour welcomed this attempt "to give the peace-making aspects of this instrument a wider scope." [13] Ultimately it was agreed to revamp the preamble. Article I was also somewhat altered to read as follows:

> The High Contracting Parties agree as between themselves to respect their rights in relation to their insular possessions and insular dominions in the region of the Pacific Ocean.
>
> If there should develop between any of the High Contracting Parties a controversy arising out of any Pacific question and involving their said rights which is not satisfactorily settled by diplomacy and is likely to affect the harmonious accord now happily subsisting between them, they shall invite the other High Contracting Parties to a joint conference to which the whole subject will be referred for consideration and adjustment.[14]

Eager to announce the treaty because of the prairie fire of rumor that was running through Washington, Hughes got permission to call a plenary session the next morning if Paris indicated its assent in time. Viviani called at the

[12] Harold and Margaret Sprout, *Toward a New Order of Sea Power* (Princeton, Princeton University Press, 1940), p. 174. Copyright, 1940, by the Princeton University Press.

[13] *Foreign Relations, 1922*, I, 23ff. [14] Report of American Delegation, p. 44.

Hughes home that evening with a favorable message from Briand. The fourth plenary session of the conference was thus held on December 10, with Hughes reporting for the Committee on Pacific and Far Eastern Questions and Senator Lodge presenting the Four-Power Pact in his best literary style. While Hughes himself had written the treaty and fought it through, he gave Lodge the honor of presenting it, with a shrewd eye upon its approval by the Senate. Root and Underwood were also to have their moments in the spotlight. The chairman's fair division of honors contributed much to the complete harmony and good will that prevailed in the American delegation.

The nature of the treaty was a surprise to the public. While it was generally hailed as a welcome substitute for the Anglo-Japanese Alliance, politicians and editors scrutinized it suspiciously. When members of the American delegation reported, in reply to questions from the press, that the terms of the agreement covered the main islands of Japan there was an outcry against the supposed "guarantee" to Japan without any reciprocal guarantee to the United States. But the furor subsided because no one who read the treaty carefully could find any guarantee to Japan.

Then a reporter asked the President, at his regular press conference on December 20, whether he understood the main islands of Japan to be included in the treaty. Hughes had explained the whole controversy to Harding, telling him precisely what Balfour and Kato had said and what the final outcome had been. But Harding had forgotten these details. "As I see it," he replied to the press, "the quadrilateral treaty does not apply to Japan proper. The mainland is no more included in the provisions of the treaty than is the mainland of the United States." [15]

News of the President's contradiction of his own delegation flashed and re-flashed around the world. Foes of the treaty shouted with delight. Even the Administration itself, they said sarcastically, was torn between conflicting interpretations of Hughes' "simple and direct" agreement. Suspicion as to the whole document deepened. Some jumped to the conclusion that Hughes had kept the President in the dark as to the meaning of the treaty. Others assumed there had been an open break between the President and the delegation. The conference was thrown into commotion.

Hughes and the other American delegates met immediately. Fearing that Hughes might wish to resign, Root expressed his indignation and offered to go to the White House as mediator.[16] But Hughes was neither excited nor in a mood to resign. Knowing Harding, he surmised what had happened. After reassuring his fellow delegates, he hastened to the White House to see what could be done about Pandora's box that had been opened.

[15] Text of statement in Hughes Papers.
[16] Author's interview with CEH, Nov. 26, 1946.

Harding was apologetic. "I shouldn't have said anything about it to the press," he confessed in a tone of self-accusation. "But, Hughes," he added honestly, "when they asked me about it, I didn't want to appear to be a dub." [17]

They both laughed and agreed that Hughes should dictate a corrective statement to be issued by the White House. Honest words in a case of this sort are a poor cushion; but Hughes softened as much as possible the bump that his chief was bound to take. "He [the President] has learned from the United States delegates to the conference," the statement read, "that they have agreed to the construction which includes the homeland of Japan in the term 'insular possessions and insular dominions,' and has no objection to that construction." [18] It was a complete retraction.

Meanwhile Shidehara, encouraged by senatorial criticism of the treaty, revived his request for exclusion of the main islands of Japan from its provisions. Hughes objected because such action would expose the conference to criticism on the ground that it had approved a treaty meaning one thing today and another tomorrow, but it was found that Australia and New Zealand did not object to exclusion of the Japanese home islands. Ultimately Hughes accepted Shidehara's proposed supplement, insisting only that it be recognized as a change in the treaty and not a mere afterthought.

Thoroughly fatigued as the conference adjourned, Hughes sailed to Bermuda for a brief rest. The Senate took up the Four-Power Treaty in his absence, and part of his time there was spent writing messages and letters in its defense. Opponents of the treaty assumed that it was an alliance imposing on each of the parties at least a moral obligation to aid the others by military or naval force in case of aggression from an outside power. Lodge had made it absolutely clear in his presentation of the treaty to the conference that it had no such implications. The delegates had merely "substituted a four-power agreement to talk for a two-power agreement to fight." But some Senators refused to believe that Great Britain and Japan had given up their alliance for such a flimsy pledge on our part. They formally requested the President to submit all records, minutes, arguments, debate, and conversations relating to its negotiation. Harding cabled to Hughes his proposed refusal to comply. Hughes corrected the President's assumption that all available records had been handed to the Senate and suggested that, while refusing to disclose memoranda of informal and confidential conversations, the President assure the Senate "that there were no secret understandings or exchanges of notes and no commitments whatever except as appeared in the Four-Power Treaty itself. . . ." [19] "President's attitude seems to me exactly right," he commented. "The freedom of the Executive in negotiating treaties should not be impaired by yielding to demands of this sort which can serve no useful purpose but would be re-

[17] *Id.* [18] Text in Hughes Papers. [19] CEH to State Department, Feb. 19, 1922.

sented by foreign powers and create distrust of our ability to respect reasonable amenities of negotiations."

For several weeks the debate continued. It was asserted that the Japanese or British had drafted the treaty, with implications that the American delegation had been taken into camp. Hughes responded with a letter to Underwood disclosing his own authorship of the draft that was finally accepted and sharply denying that there was any basis for suspicion concerning it. "Its failure," he wrote, "would be nothing short of a national calamity." [20] In a letter to Lodge he branded the continued rumors of a secret understanding as "absolutely false" and expressed an indignant hope "that the American Delegates will be saved further aspersions upon their veracity and honor." [21]

The Senate's performance was very depressing. Hughes wrote to his friend Judge Hiscock:

> I am at a loss to understand how those who have attained the high position of Senator can permit themselves to indulge in reckless characterization of other peoples and to manifest in a manner so injurious to the conduct of our foreign relations their opposition to the work of the conference. There is certainly cause for anxiety when the results of the most earnest endeavor under American auspices come so near to defeat at the hands of the Senate. . . . My solicitude in the matter transcends any personal feeling that I may have growing out of my relation to the matters under consideration, for we cannot protect our own interests and enjoy the prestige and influence which we should have in the world if we are thus betrayed in our own homes.[22]

The tirades of the Irreconcilables had the effect of rallying public support behind the treaty. One editor called Borah, Johnson, and their like "senatorial jackals" and accused them of introducing "the forensics of the gutter." Hughes was so angry that he thought this criticism was "entirely justified."

Eventually the Senate consented to ratification of the treaty, with a reservation asserting that it involved "no commitment to armed force, no alliance, no obligation to join in any defense"—all of which was obvious from the treaty itself. A majority came to realize that this Four-Power Pact was the cement of good faith that held together the settlements reached as to other issues. The consultation pledge afforded a means by which disputes in the Pacific could be settled if there was any will to settle them. But of much greater importance than the obligations it created were the obligations it removed. By destroying the Anglo-Japanese Alliance, Hughes detached the British from their tacit support of Japanese policy in the Far East and in effect aligned them with American policy. That is an achievement from which great historic consequences have flowed.

[20] CEH to Underwood, March 11, 1922. [21] CEH to Lodge, March 21, 1922.
[22] CEH to Frank H. Hiscock, March 24, 1922.

Chapter 48

STABILIZING THE FAR EAST

THE DISTRUST and turmoil that were festering in China could best be dealt with, Secretary Hughes concluded, by giving American policy in that area the sanction of international law. Ever since Secretary Hay had proclaimed the open door in 1899, the United States had consistently sought to prevent the powers from seizing Chinese territory and carving China into spheres of influence. In 1921 the need was not to devise a new policy but to make this old policy effective against the postwar imperialism of Japan. Hughes' first move in that direction was to reiterate, in notes to London, Tokyo, and Peking, the intention of the United States "neither to participate nor to acquiesce in" any schemes to create monopolies or spheres of influence in China.[1]

At the Washington Conference, Balfour initiated the discussion in this sphere on November 11 when he handed Hughes a proposed five-power "arrangement" on China. In the meetings of the Far Eastern Committee that followed, Root was given the responsibility of drawing up a joint statement of principles. Hughes seemed always to be present at these sessions, however, and on January 17 he offered a resolution on the open door that, with slight changes, was to become Article III of the Nine-Power Treaty. Under the influence of Hughes and Root, this instrument was shaped into "the most categorical and aggressive affirmation of the Far Eastern policy of the United States yet on record."[2]

The principles underlying the Nine-Power Treaty were agreed upon early in the conference. The Japanese balked only when the Americans insisted on translating those principles into specific pledges and obligations. All Hughes' powers of persuasion, Root's experience and moderation, and Balfour's shrewdness as a mediator were required to bring the Japanese into line. That is not strange, for the treaty erected the strongest barriers ever raised against Japanese imperialism in China. It was possible to wring such concessions from Japan only because a spirit of mutual trust prevailed. Hughes had lifted all suspicion that the United States had aggressive intentions. Expecting condemnation, Japan had been welcomed to friendly discussions; her prestige had been upheld by the Four-Power Pact; she could not afford to withdraw from the

[1] *Foreign Relations, 1921*, I, 439–446.
[2] A. Whitney Griswold, *The Far Eastern Policy of the United States*, p. 322.

world community. In these favorable circumstances the negotiators were able to compel Tokyo to forswear policies which it had been pursuing since the outbreak of the war.

The treaty was signed on February 6, 1922, by representatives of the United States, Great Britain, Japan, France, Belgium, China, Italy, the Netherlands, and Portugal. For the first time China became a party to the agreement of the powers about herself. The signatories pledged themselves (1) to respect the sovereignty, independence, and integrity of China; (2) to give China the "fullest and most unembarrassed opportunity" to maintain an effective and stable government; (3) to use their influence to establish and maintain equal opportunity for the commerce and industry of all nations in China; (4) to refrain from taking advantage of conditions in China in order to seek special rights or privileges that would abridge the rights of citizens of friendly states, and from countenancing action inimical to the security of such states.

By Article II the powers were bound not to make any agreements among themselves or with other nations that would infringe these principles. Article III was Hughes' open-door provision committing the powers not to support their nationals in seeking any superiority of commercial or economic rights in China or any monopoly or preference that would close the open door to any legitimate trade or industry sponsored by the nationals of other powers. Spheres of influence were specifically condemned. China agreed to prevent unfair discrimination as to railway traffic. Finally, the powers pledged themselves to "full and frank" discussion if any one of them should raise the issue of violation of the treaty.

The language could not have been more emphatic in avowing respect for the open door and the integrity of China. But it was a mutual promise of self-discipline, not a guarantee to use force. Hughes and Root had given new buttressing to the traditional American policy.

The Secretary also took advantage of this treaty to end what appears to have been the only secret protocol in American diplomatic history up to that time. Former Secretary Lansing had signed an agreement with Viscount Ishii of Japan in 1917 giving countenance to Japan's "special interests in China." [3] Apparently Lansing had no intention of recognizing any special Japanese *rights* in China. He attempted to offset his concession by obtaining from Ishii a memorandum which pledged Japan "to refrain from taking advantage of conditions in China in order to seek special rights or privileges which would abridge the rights of subjects or citizens of friendly states, and from countenancing action inimical to the security of such states." But he permitted the memorandum to remain secret. Openly stated, it would have been an effective moral weapon behind American policy in the Far East. Remaining under

[3] *Ibid.*, p. 216.

cover, it was useless. The world assumed that the open-door doctrine had been distorted in Japan's favor, and Tokyo acted as if the secret pledge were nonexistent.

Hating secrecy in public affairs and being loath to work under the handicap of this hidden protocol, Hughes laid a clever plot to bring it into the open. While Root was working out the principles to guide the Far Eastern Committee, the Secretary showed him the secret memorandum and asked him to embody it in the new treaty.[4] Root incorporated Ishii's secret pledge almost verbatim into the Nine-Power Treaty as Paragraph 4 of Article I. The Japanese could scarcely object, for after all they had agreed to it under cover. A much-criticized deviation from the open-door policy was thus eliminated, and the secret diplomacy into which Lansing had slipped was abandoned without revealing the existence of the suppressed document.

The public learned nothing about Hughes' shrewd coup in putting the secret protocol on record until 1938, when the State Department published the diplomatic correspondence related to the Washington Conference. But the impediment had been removed in 1922, and Japan had consented a year later to formal cancellation of the defunct Lansing-Ishii Agreement. The open-door policy had reached the zenith of its vigor.

To avoid any further resort to secrecy, Hughes induced the conference to provide for publicity concerning every treaty or agreement then in force or later entered into concerning China. Contracts giving concessions or franchises in China to the nationals of any of the powers were also to be brought into the light of day.

More delicate than any of the other Far Eastern issues that bedeviled the conference was the dispute between China and Japan over Shantung. At Versailles, Wilson had given way to the Island Empire's demands for control of Shantung, which it had wrested from Germany. China got only "the shell of the oyster." That settlement had aroused much bitterness in the United States and had been an important factor in the defeat of the Treaty of Versailles in the Senate. In the Far East it had kept hostility between China and Japan near the boiling point. Some readjustment was imperative if war clouds over the Pacific were to be dissipated.

China had refused to negotiate with Japan on the basis of the Versailles settlement or to take any step that would involve recognition of the wartime treaties Japan had wrung from her. Japan, being in the saddle, was eager for a settlement. Ambassador Shidehara approached Hughes on July 21, 1921, and said that if the Secretary could induce the Chinese to negotiate with Japan, his government would seek a settlement that would be satisfactory to China and all the other powers. Hughes asked what sort of terms Japan might be

[4] Author's interview with CEH, Nov. 26, 1946; *Foreign Relations, 1922*, I, 279n.

willing to make and was not satisfied with Shidehara's vague reply. A few weeks later he informed the ambassador that before approaching China he would have to know what the outcome was likely to be. If negotiations should be undertaken and fail, the outlook for the forthcoming conference would be worse and not better. Japan would have to have a satisfactory offer, therefore, if she expected him to have anything to do with it. But he would welcome a full statement by Japan, and if such a statement seemed to hold promise of a settlement he would suggest to China that negotiations be undertaken.

Shidehara came in with Japan's proposal on September 8. Hughes objected to various obscurities and said that he had reason to believe that China would not consent to the proposed joint ownership of the Shantung Railroad. He could not make a hopeful suggestion to China on this basis. Were the terms final? Shidehara said they were not. Hughes expressed his gratification and threw out the suggestion that it might be possible for Japan to offer a solution under which China could obtain complete ownership and control of the railroad by making compensation.[5]

While thus wangling the best possible terms out of Japan, Hughes also attempted to soften the Chinese. Peking was determined to inject the Shantung controversy into the conference itself. Hughes saw that a more practical approach would be necessary to achieve results. Japan was loath to permit reopening of the issue before any international body. And even if that hurdle could be cleared, China would be confronted by a group of powers—all of those present except the United States and the Netherlands—that had sanctioned the rape of Shantung at Versailles. Any attempt to force the issue into the conference in these circumstances might split it wide open and endanger everything it was attempting to do. Yet it was clear that the Sino-Japanese rupture would have to be healed if the conference were to achieve its aims. Hughes thought it doubtful that the Senate would approve a naval limitation treaty or any pact dealing with the Far East unless this threat to the peace could be removed. The best hope, he concluded, lay in direct negotiations between the Chinese and Japanese representatives to be carried on collaterally in Washington but not as part of the conference.

As the weeks passed, the Secretary increasingly turned his persuasive powers upon the Chinese in the hope of inducing them to negotiate. The Chinese resisted any compromise, insisting on full restoration of Shantung with no economic or political strings attached. When Balfour arrived in Washington, he and Hughes jointly offered their "good offices" to the disputants. Under heavy pressure in Peking as well as Washington, the Chinese finally caved in with the understanding that American and British observers would attend the direct

[5] *Foreign Relations, 1921,* I, 620.

negotiations. This idea of neutral observers sitting in to assure fair play between hostile negotiators is one of Hughes' significant contributions to diplomacy.

Hughes, Balfour, and the Japanese delegates met at the Pan American Building for the first of these sessions on December 1. They sat wondering what had happened to the Chinese delegates. Upon investigation, J. V. A. MacMurray, who was Hughes' right-hand man in all Far Eastern affairs, found the Chinese besieged in the bathroom of their Massachusetts Avenue Legation by an angry crowd of Chinese students who were opposed to direct negotiations with Japan. When Hughes heard of the siege, he telephoned the War Department and asked for a military escort to bring the Chinese delegates to the meeting if they wished to come. But MacMurray and a companion had no difficulty in bringing the beleaguered delegates out, and the conference went forward as scheduled.[6]

Thirty-six meetings were held before an agreement could be reached. After failure of the Japanese scheme for joint ownership of the Shantung Railroad, Shidehara got around to acceptance of Hughes' suggestion for restoration of the railroad to China in return for payments to be made over a series of years. But controversy continued over details of the arrangement. Several times an impasse was reached. On each occasion Hughes and MacMurray worked on the Chinese and Balfour on the Japanese until direct negotiations were resumed. The Chinese would not meet with the Japanese without American or British representatives present. At one point M. Viviani further bedeviled the negotiations by insisting that he or a French expert be admitted, although he had not been invited by either of the governments directly concerned.

When Hughes concluded that the Japanese had been pushed as far as they would go in making concessions, he turned all his persuasive powers upon the stubborn Chinese. The Secretary believed that if the conference should end without a settlement of the dispute, China would lose Shantung. She could not force the Japanese out. The idea of the United States going to war to put the Japanese out was unthinkable. Consequently, our own interests and those of China demanded support of the best compromise obtainable. After Shidehara had made numerous concessions, the question boiled down to this: Should China risk losing Shantung because the Japanese insisted on spreading China's payments for the railroad over at least five years and on employment of a Japanese traffic manager during that period?

Hughes invited the Chinese (along with Balfour) to his home on January 22 and talked to them with the utmost candor. The conference had produced a remarkable atmosphere of good will, he said. The Japanese had liberalized their original offer to an extent that had seemed beyond hope when the con-

[6] Author's interview with J. V. A. MacMurray, July 9, 1949.

ference opened. China's remaining objections were trivial beside the great advantage of regaining Shantung. It was "inconceivable," Hughes told them, that these objections should be allowed to stand in the way of a settlement. "Surely what China wants," he exclaimed, "is to see Japan out of Shantung." That fond hope of every Chinese could not possibly be attained by trying to "fire" the Japanese out. Only a conciliatory mood would bring the desired result. Continued standpattism might frustrate all that it was hoped to achieve in the conference for the good of China. Before making their decision, he declared, the Chinese should realize that if they chose to break off negotiations over trivialities and thus bring disaster upon themselves, they could not "count on any support either from public sentiment in the United States or from this Government." [7]

Balfour said afterward that he had never heard so "forceful an appeal." The Chinese must have been similarly impressed for they withdrew their last objections and signed the treaty with Japan in ample time to have it reported in a plenary session of the conference. Full sovereignty over Shantung was restored to China. Japanese troops were withdrawn. The railroad also went to China, with payments in Chinese treasury notes over a period from five to fifteen years. Japan retained a shadowy economic hold on the province, but the treaty was a substantial victory for China. It dried up the worst open sore in Far Eastern diplomatic relations and made it possible to consummate the other agreements that had been moving forward in the conference. In keeping with the prevailing spirit of accommodation, Balfour also announced that Great Britain would hand back to China the Weihaiwei leasehold on the Shantung coastline.

After the conference was over, Admiral Kato, back in Tokyo, candidly acknowledged that the Shantung settlement "was largely due to the good offices of Messrs. Hughes and Balfour" and paid a touching tribute to Hughes for "his unceasing care, intense earnestness and indefatigable industry as well as for the unalloyed sense of justice with which he discharged his duties." [8]

[7] Memorandum by Miles W. Lampson (later Lord Killearn) in the Hughes Papers.
[8] Philadelphia *Public Ledger*, May 12, 1922.

Chapter 49

IN RETROSPECT

AFTER GERMANY, Italy, and Japan had scourged the world with new wars in the thirties and forties, the whole idea of limiting armaments by mutual pledge seemed to fall into disrepute. Men desperate for an explanation of these calamities looked back to the Washington Conference and saw that it had wiped out a formidable fleet of battleships. With ships, tanks, and airplanes once more the main source of security, they impetuously denounced the conference of 1921–1922 for having intoxicated the world with a false idealism. It has not yet emerged from the cloud cast upon it by this superficial judgment.

There is a basic fallacy, however, in trying to judge any international conference by events two decades after the completion of its work. History moves in cycles, and what is wise or possible in one period may be utterly unwise or impossible in another. To appraise the Washington Conference fairly, it must be kept in its own setting of events and trends. Its sponsors had to deal with the problems before them and could not be expected to forsake the prospect for peace in the decade ahead in deference to uncertain objectives related to a more distant future.

The first important point about the conference, then, is that it admirably met the demands of its own time. Its achievements evoked almost universal applause. The Senate approved the Naval Limitations Treaty by a vote of seventy-four to one, and twenty of the twenty-one Senators who were absent took pains to have it announced that, if present, they would have voted for the treaty.[1] The explanation is clear. When the conference met, as Balfour said, a "spirit of deep anxiety" overshadowed the Pacific. Twelve weeks later the war clouds had vanished. Confidence took the place of distrust. "The conference produced a complete change in the attitude of mind of the nations there assembled," said Lord Lee of Fareham, "and, if I may so describe it, made them think in terms of peace rather than in terms of war." [2] Balfour said the conference gave "an expectant world all that anybody possibly could hope for, and far more than experienced statesmen ever dared to expect." Sarraut

[1] *Congressional Record,* Vol. 62, Pt. V., 67th Congress, 2nd session, March 29, 1922, pp. 4718f.

[2] Speech to Royal Colonial Institute, London, May 9, 1922; Hughes Papers.

called it "the loftiest precedent of mankind." Speaking for Portugal, Viscount d'Alte dramtically exclaimed, "America has justified her leadership of the world." [3]

It is true that there was much disappointment in France, for the conference had not been able to deal with that country's vital problem of security in Europe. In Japan the navy clique and part of the press were hostile to the treaties on the ground that Japan had been exposed to Anglo-American domination. "The most miserable is Japan," wailed the *Yomiuri*, ". . . the days of her unrestricted freedom of action are at an end." [4] But it was the common verdict among the Japanese delegates, according to K. K. Kawakami, the leading Japanese journalist at the conference, "that the happy conclusion of the naval negotiations, so skillfully and so patiently engineered by Mr. Hughes, is a master-stroke of American diplomacy even greater than the announcement of his naval retrenchment program at the very first sitting of the Conference." [5] The liberal government then in power in Tokyo courageously supported the treaties, and a large majority of the people were said to rejoice in the brightened prospect of peace. Prime Minister Takahashi called the treaties "a blessing to all mankind." [6]

In both Great Britain and the United States some protests were made by the big-Navy advocates, but they seemed scarcely audible. Prime Minister Lloyd George told Parliament that the conference was "one of the greatest achievements for peace that has ever been registered in the history of the world." The *Times* of London thought the day on which the Naval Treaty was presented would be "a great day for all time." The *Daily Chronicle* hailed the treaty as "a unique contribution to world peace," and the London *Outlook* said that it was "magnificent."

Enthusiasm in the United States bubbled up in the press, the pulpit, and street-corner talk. "Much the greatest [conference] . . . of all time," said the *New York Herald*. "A monumental contribution to international understanding and human progress," declared the New York *Tribune*. "The way to measure the importance of the naval treaty," reasoned the *World*, "is to remember what would have happened had there been no agitation for disarmament, no Washington Conference, no Hughes proposals, and no agreement." [7] A "stupendous success—the results epochal," concluded Walter McLean in the Baltimore *Sun*.[8]

Walter Lippmann accurately saw in the conference the beginning of a new policy of Anglo-American cooperation. "For the first time," he wrote, "the

[3] *Conference on the Limitation of Armament*, pp. 366ff. [4] Feb. 11, 1922.
[5] Kawakami, *Japan's Pacific Policy* (New York, Dutton, 1922), p. 28.
[6] *New York Times*, March 12, 1922.
[7] Quotations from Sprout, *Toward a New Order of Sea Power*, pp. 263–273.
[8] Feb. 20, 1922.

concert of powers in the East is not a concert of aggression, with America on the outside protesting, but a concert against aggression, with Japan on the outside resisting." It may well be, he added, that Hughes "has stopped the drift into a ruinous and indecisive war." [9]

Looking back to Hughes' opening speech, Senator Ransdell declared that "humanity breathed easier from that hour. I have never felt prouder of being an American citizen than on that occasion." [10] Indiana and New Jersey passed resolutions congratulating the Administration on the outcome of the conference. "If the world has hungered for a new assurance," said President Harding, "it may feast at the banquet which this Conference has spread." [11]

Nor was it a temporary intoxication. Three years after the conference the General Board of the Navy concluded that "the great accomplishment . . . was not in the fixing of a definite ratio of ships, with its attendant economies, but in effecting an agreement making aggressive warfare across the ocean more difficult." [12] The *New York Times* was still convinced that the conference was "a monument of peace-making, and no one who has the welfare of the human race at heart will attempt to undermine it." [13] Elihu Root's conclusion in 1925 was: "I think you will go far to find any public service to the world rendered with a higher order of ability or with more signal success than the service Mr. Hughes rendered in directing and controlling that Conference." [14]

Eight years after the event the New York *Herald Tribune* expressed a widely held view: "The Washington treaty stands as a monument to international accommodation and self-restraint, to cooperation in avoiding needless causes of national antagonism and in promoting peace." [15] The *World* then thought that the threat of conflict in the Pacific had vanished and that the conference still stood as "one of the great diplomatic achievements in modern times." [16] The least that can be said is that the conference put into effect a policy for which most of mankind was clamoring.

The second important point is that the conference did lay a proper groundwork for an indefinite period of peace in the Pacific. The Naval Treaty relegated rivalry among the powers to the economic sphere, and the Nine-Power Treaty provided a code of fair play to prevent commercial enterprises from evolving into political conquests. The Shantung settlement removed the poison from the well of Sino-Japanese relations. The Mandates Treaty settled the most irritating issue between Japan and the United States. The Four-Power Pact brought a sense of equality and, as Hughes said at the time, a "new state of mind" [17] in which friendly conferences were to take the place of naval competition. The limitation of navies fit into the picture as a sort of guarantee

[9] New York *World*, Jan. 29, 1922. [10] *Congressional Record*, March 15, 1922, p. 3906.
[11] *Conference*, p. 398. [12] New York *World*, Dec. 11, 1924. [13] April 8, 1924.
[14] Speech of Nov. 10, 1925. [15] Jan. 22, 1930. [16] Dec. 18, 1929.
[17] *Report* of the American Delegation, p. 88.

of good faith which made all the other agreements at once possible and meaningful.

Each country had to make substantial concessions to bring about these happy results. The United States' great concession was the scrapping of twenty-eight capital ships, thirteen of which were under construction. Great Britain's chief sacrifice lay in her abandonment of supremacy on the seas and in giving up her giant super-*Hoods*. Japan's concessions ran all the way across the board. In addition to her loss of battleships, she gave up her 10:10:7 demand, the Anglo-Japanese Alliance, her forged license for conquest in China, and her extreme claims in Shantung and the mandated islands. The treaties coming out of the conference unquestionably impinged more severely upon Japan's expansionist policy than upon the national policies of any other power.

It is sometimes said that the United States paid (in battleships) too high a price for the legal strait-jacket placed upon Japan. But this assumption, as we have already seen, rests on the false premise that the United States scrapped real ships while Great Britain and Japan merely burned their blueprints. Actually, Japan, with her smaller navy, scrapped sixteen ships, six of them under construction. The heart of the matter is that each of the three major navies was drastically reduced without disadvantage to any one of them. In this respect there were no victors and no vanquished at the conference.

Hughes had contributed only the principle of a proportionate reduction of naval strength and the idea of halting all building. It was the Navy that decided what ships each country would have to scrap to carry out this formula. If the American sacrifice could be shown to have been disproportionate, the blame would fall upon the admirals. But no such criticism is valid. The fact is that each country saved enormous sums of money without losing anything in terms of security. Completion of the 1916 program would have raised our Navy's annual operating costs alone by more than $200,000,000. Sixteen years after the conference a Congressman estimated that it had saved at least $4,000,000,000 for American taxpayers.[18]

Our relative naval strength could have been improved only by adding costly new shipbuilding ventures to the 1916 program, and Congress had emphatically rejected that policy before the conference was called. Eager as they were for relief from the burden of naval building, both Great Britain and Japan were determined to continue the competition in the absence of agreement. "Despite her financial burdens," wrote Hector C. Bywater, the distinguished British naval expert, "it is unthinkable that she [Great Britain] would have let the trident slip from her hands without making a strenuous effort to recover it." [19] Japan was still more energetic in pushing her ambitious pro-

[18] Congressman Robsion, *Congressional Record,* March 16, 1937, p. 2930.
[19] Baltimore *Sun,* Dec. 18, 1924.

gram of naval construction. Only our own Congress was hell-bent to disarm, unilaterally if necessary. What the conference did was to slow down the other powers to a pace that the United States could reasonably expect to maintain in the psychological climate of the twenties.

The absolute necessity of a naval limitation agreement from the American point of view is driven home with great force by subsequent events. The United States virtually abandoned naval building. All the other powers continued to add to their fleets vessels in the unrestricted categories. During the eight years from 1922 to 1930 Great Britain laid down or appropriated for 74 naval vessels; Japan, 125; France, 119; Italy, 82; and the United States, 11.[20]

Hughes had expected our Navy to be maintained at the 10:10:6 ratio. In October, 1922, he issued a direct warning against sacrificing by default the victory that had been won:

> This Government has taken the lead in securing the reduction of naval armament, but the Navy that we retain under the agreement should be maintained with sufficient personnel and pride in the service. It is essential that we should maintain the relative naval strength of the United States. That, in my judgment, is the way to peace and security. It will be upon that basis that we would enter in future conferences or make agreements for limitation, and it would be folly to undermine our position.[21]

His sound advice was not followed. Because of the United States' failure to maintain the 10:10:6 ratio, Japan made a powerful bid for a 10:7 ratio in heavy cruisers and other auxiliary craft when the London Naval Conference met in 1930. She succeeded in getting a ratio a little better than 10:6 in light cruisers and destroyers and equality in submarines. Premier Hamaguchi induced the Diet to ratify this compromise but at the cost of violent reactions on the part of the military and his own assassination.

When the powers again met in conference in 1935, Japan demanded a "common upper limit" for all navies and walked out when she failed to get it. Assuming that the United States would never build up to treaty strength anyway,[22] Tokyo had previously renounced the naval treaties of 1922 and 1930. All restrictions on naval building thus came to an end in 1936, not because any mistake had been made at the Washington Conference, but partly because the United States' failure to maintain the sensible balance of strength there established had convinced Japan that if the naval race were resumed she could win it. Her conclusion was not without foundation, for naval building in Japan was pressing against the treaty ceilings, while depression-ridden America

[20] Senate Document 202, 78th Cong., 2nd session.
[21] Quoted by Representative Vinson, *Congressional Record*, Jan. 30, 1934, p. 1607.
[22] Ambassador Grew in *Peace and War—U.S. Foreign Policy, 1931–1941*, pp. 20f.

needed 102 ships that would cost $380,000,000 to restore the expiring treaty ratios.[23]

In one other vital respect Congress undercut the policy of good will and cooperation that Hughes had inaugurated. Our relations with Japan had reached a high state of cordiality. The American people had generously aided Japan after her "bewildering devastation" by the earthquake of 1923. The gratitude of the Japanese strengthened the good relations that had taken firm root at the Washington Conference. Then suddenly this hopeful amity was poisoned by rancor because Congress intemperately wrote a Japanese exclusion clause into the Immigration Act of 1924.

Immigration from Japan to the United States had been controlled since 1907 by the so-called Gentlemen's Agreement between the two governments. The agreement was not wholly satisfactory because it allowed too many exceptions and did not permit effective control at the ports of entry. The State Department recognized a need for tightening the agreement or for giving Japan a quota under the Immigration Act. Instead, California legislators demanded absolute exclusion of aliens ineligible to citizenship—a sly way of striking at the Japanese without naming them.

Ambassador Hanihara called on Secretary Hughes and said that it would be quite impossible to make the Japanese people understand the general friendliness of the Americans toward Japan if an exclusion provision should be enacted. He wished to impress upon the American Government how seriously the issue would be regarded in Japan. The Japanese counselor of embassy also informed the State Department that the influence of the conciliatory party, meaning that group of public men who were disposed to work in conjunction with the United States, would be at an end if the exclusion policy should become law.[24] The militarists would insist that, with the closing of the American door upon the Japanese, the open door in the Orient could no longer remain open.

Hughes expressed his deep concern over the exclusion movement in a letter to Albert Johnson, chairman of the House Committee on Immigration and Naturalization, on February 8:

> The Japanese are a sensitive people and unquestionably would regard such a legislative enactment as fixing a stigma upon them. I regret to be compelled to say that I believe such legislative action would largely undo the work of the Washington Conference on Limitation of Armament, which so greatly improved our relations with Japan. The manifestation of American interest and generosity in providing relief to the sufferers from the recent earthquake disaster in Japan would not avail to diminish the resentment which would follow the enactment of such a measure, as this enactment would be regarded as an insult not to be palliated by

[23] Representative Vinson in *Congressional Record*, Jan. 30, 1934, p. 1607.
[24] Saburi to MacMurray, Jan. 9, 1923, memorandum in State Department.

any act of charity. It is useless to argue whether or not such a feeling would be justified; it is quite sufficient to say that it would exist. It has already been manifested in the discussions in Japan with respect to the pendency of this measure and no amount of argument can avail to remove it.

The question is thus presented whether it is worth while thus to affront a friendly nation with whom we have established most cordial relations and what gain there would be from such action.[25]

Hughes went on to show that if the exclusion section of the bill were eliminated, the effect would be to put immigration from Japan under quota. This would limit the number of Japanese immigrants to only 246 a year—fewer than were estimated to be coming under the Gentlemen's Agreement. "I am unable to perceive," he concluded, "that the exclusion provision is necessary and I must strongly urge upon you the advisability, in the interest of our international relations, of eliminating it."

The committee rejected the Secretary's plea and sent the bill to the House floor with the exclusion provision intact. One reason for this action, the committee report indicated, was the obscurity of the Gentlemen's Agreement, which consisted of diplomatic correspondence with Japan that had not been made public. Hughes felt this was a valid criticism. The meaning of the agreement had to be gleaned from a mass of diplomatic papers that he had not been able to submit to Congress without the consent of Japan.

When Hanihara called on March 27, the Secretary told him that he was troubled by two points in the committee report. The assertions that the Gentlemen's Agreement was secret and obscure and therefore ineffective, he said, ought to be met. Since the correspondence back of that agreement was long and detailed, there would be little point in merely producing it. Nor could the State Department properly undertake to outline Japan's activities under the agreement. Hughes cautiously suggested, therefore, without making a definite proposal, that the ambassador write him a letter setting forth the Japanese Government's understanding as to the intent and effect of the agreement and summarizing the agreement itself.[26]

Acting on Hughes' suggestion, Hanihara got the consent of his government and explored the problem with MacMurray. The State Department submitted a memorandum on the Gentlemen's Agreement to the Japanese Embassy. Hanihara finally completed his letter on April 10. It was an accurate résumé of the agreement, giving all the information of which the House had professed ignorance. In addition, Hanihara expressed his personal belief that Japan would willingly discuss proposed changes in the agreement. He recognized the right of the United States to control immigration into its own territories and denied any desire on the part of Japan to send her nationals where they were

[25] *Foreign Relations, 1924,* I, 217. [26] *Ibid.,* II, 337f.

not wanted. His plea was merely for "that proper consideration ordinarily given by one nation to the self-respect of another, which after all forms the basis of amicable international intercourse throughout the civilized world."

The temperate and persuasive qualities of the letter were lost to sight, however, because of two ill-chosen words in the following paragraph:

> Relying upon the confidence you have been good enough to show me at all times, I have stated or rather repeated all this to you very candidly and in a most friendly spirit, for I realize, as I believe you do, the grave consequences which the enactment of the measure retaining that particular provision would inevitably bring upon the otherwise happy and mutually advantageous relations between our two countries.[27]

Seeking the State Department's approval, Hanihara took the letter to MacMurray, who relayed it to Hughes. In reading it the Secretary's eye rested momentarily on the words "grave consequences." "That is a very unfortunate phrase," he said.[28] But he decided to ignore it. The words were couched in a friendly text. Obviously they meant only that the happy relations between the two countries would be impaired by an exclusion act, which was the simple truth. Any suggestion that the phrase be changed, moreover, would have put him in the position of approving the remainder of the letter, and Hughes was determined not to assume that responsibility. Finally, if this restatement of the Gentlemen's Agreement were to reach Congress before the exclusion amendment came to a vote, there was no time in any event to seek revision of it. Hughes wrote to Hanihara that the statement was in accord with his own understanding of the arrangement between the two governments and sent copies of both letters to the interested committees of the House and Senate.

Two days later the House passed the immigration bill, including an exclusion provision, by a vote of 323 to 71. Meanwhile a section of the press had given an inflammatory meaning to Hanihara's words, "grave consequences." On April 14 Lodge took up the cry in the Senate. Asserting that the letter was a "veiled threat" to the United States, he induced the Senate to reject the Hughes-endorsed amendment recognizing the Gentlemen's Agreement. Even the Senators who had supported the department's point of view bolted, and the amendment went down by a vote of 76 to 2. Passage of the Johnson bill then followed by a majority scarcely less stupendous.

Hughes had had no idea that Hanihara's indiscreet words would be so blatantly misinterpreted.[29] The hapless ambassador went to the department in sackcloth and ashes carrying a copy of the *Congressional Record* in which he had underlined the unbridled ranting of the Senators. The idea of a threat, he said, was the furthest thing from his mind. He had not "in any part of his

[27] *Ibid.*, p. 373. [28] Author's interview with J. V. A. MacMurray, July 9, 1949.
[29] Author's interview with CEH, Dec. 18, 1946.

body" the slightest feeling of unfriendliness or antagonism toward the United States. A few days later he wrote the Secretary a letter expressing his dismay over the hostile interpretation his words had been given.

Hughes accepted the explanation and expressed his deep regret over the incident and his feeling of complete assurance that no threat had been intended. It is unbelievable that any substantial number of Senators were really concerned about the alleged "threat." Rather, they were determined to adopt the exclusion policy in any event and seized upon the Hanihara letter to salve their consciences. A poll is said to have indicated a majority of fifty-four votes for exclusion in the Senate before the Hanihara letter was released.

President Coolidge attempted to avert the "grave consequences" of the incident by suggesting, while the immigration bill was in conference, that application of the exclusion clause be delayed for two years. In that period the State Department would negotiate with Japan a treaty so effectively restricting immigration that drastic legislation would not be necessary. Congress refused. Coolidge then bid for a one-year postponement, and was again rebuffed. Ultimately the President signed the exclusion measure because it was part of a comprehensive immigration bill and because a veto in the face of such overwhelming congressional support would have been a futile gesture. For the same reasons Hughes had not requested a veto.

Irreconcilable Senators whispered about the cloakrooms a tale that Hughes had written the Hanihara letter. His associates hotly denied it,[30] but the fact that he had suggested the letter in order to bring the agreement out into the open gave buoyancy to the rumor. Twenty years later Frederick Moore, who had been an adviser to the Foreign Office in Japan, asserted that the State Department had not only urged Hanihara to strengthen his "grave consequences" paragraph but had also approved the letter in its final form. "I have every reason to believe, and do believe," Hughes replied to an inquiry about this statement, "that the paragraph in question, and these words, were Hanihara's own and that their insertion was not advised, suggested, or approved, by any member of the State Department." [31] This was emphatically corroborated by MacMurray.[32]

Japan's reaction to the incident was prompt and violent. "No nation retaining the least trace of its self-respect," said the *Jiji*, "could tolerate the discrimination aimed at by the Johnson bill." As a people, the Japanese were deeply wounded in a way that is difficult for Americans to understand. Crowds picketed the American Embassy in Tokyo, some of them threatening to destroy American property and shoot Americans who would not leave Japan.[33] Suicides in protest against the Act were reported, and American goods were boy-

[30] William R. Castle's diary, 1924, pp. 178f.
[31] CEH to Miller Freeman, Aug. 31, 1944.
[32] MacMurray to Miller Freeman, Oct. 14, 1944.
[33] Castle's diary, 1924, pp. 203f.

cotted. The Japanese's sense of injustice brought gall and wormwood into relations that, since 1922, had been singularly happy.

The Secretary was badly jolted by the incident. Calling on President Coolidge while the latter was confined to his bed by illness, he declared that "it was enough to make a man resign." "Don't you ever think of leaving your position," Coolidge responded. "I agree with you in everything that you've done." [34]

In a letter to Judge Hiscock the Secretary got some of his disgust off his chest:

> It is a sorry business and I am greatly depressed. It has undone the work of the Washington Conference and implanted the seeds of an antagonism which are sure to bear fruit in the future. Of course there is no danger of war. Japan cannot threaten anybody. She is overwhelmed with her economic difficulties as a result of the earthquake. She had no idea of making threats. That makes the situation all the worse because she feels that we have chosen to affront her at such a time. The question is not one of war but of the substitution of antagonism for cooperation in the Far East, with all that that involves. Our friends in the Senate have in a few minutes spoiled the work of years and done a lasting injury to our common country.[35]

Calling in Hanihara, Hughes sought to minimize the damage that had been done by saying that the Act did not indicate a lack of friendship on the part of the American people for the Japanese. When Japan lodged her formal protest against the Act, the Secretary again attempted to soothe her wounded feelings while upholding the right of Congress to terminate the Gentlemen's Agreement by unilateral action.

Hanihara resigned in humiliation, and his successor, Ambassador Matsudaira, arrived in San Francisco amid a storm of recriminations across the Pacific. Hugh Wilson, chief of the Division of Current Information, suggested that the occasion be used to rekindle amiability. Dejected and pessimistic, Hughes nevertheless said he was willing to try. Wilson prepared a statement and summoned a group of correspondents to the Secretary's office. When he spoke to them, every trace of Hughes' discouragement had gone. "Like a prophet," he preached the gospel of good relations. So impressed were the newsmen that they spread his message through their stories and communicated its substance to their home offices. Editorials appeared all over the country. Matsudaira got a friendly reception, and the idea that "there was nothing between Japan and ourselves except a state of mind" was widely broadcast. "This episode," Wilson wrote many years later, "caused one of the most extraordinary reversals of public opinion that I have ever seen." [36]

[34] Beerits' Memorandum, XXVII, 10. [35] April 24, 1924.

[36] Hugh Wilson, *Diplomat Between Wars* (New York, Longmans, 1941), p. 188. Copyright, 1941, by Hugh R. Wilson.

In Japan, Shidehara, who had become Minister of Foreign Affairs, earnestly sought to calm the excitement of his countrymen, and some measure of cordiality was maintained. After Hughes left office, however, Secretary Kellogg let the United States drift into outright championship of China against Japan, even when China reneged on her treaty obligations. While Chiang Kai-shek was extending his conquests and consolidating his power by playing upon Chinese hatred of all foreigners and by inflicting violence and insults upon Americans and other Westerners, the United States and Great Britain seemed nevertheless to vie with each other for Chinese favor. Breaking away from the cooperative policy that had been established at Washington, the State Department suddenly negotiated a separate customs treaty with Chiang's Nationalists and began yielding to Chinese pressure for ending extraterritoriality. Alarmed by this division of the big powers in the face of China's repudiation of treaties, Japan sent Count Uchida to Washington in 1929 to find out whether the cooperative policy was dead. The only answer that he could get was that where concurrent action had not been agreed upon or had been tried and failed the United States considered itself free to act independently.

These deviations from the Hughesian policy of cooperation and even-handed justice necessarily weakened the liberal elements in Japan. In 1931 Shidehara's "friendship policy" was finally routed,[37] and the military launched its conquest in Manchuria. For a decade, however, the spirit generated at the Washington Conference had pervaded the Pacific, and it is clear that if the Hughes and Shidehara policies could have prevailed there would have been no attack on Pearl Harbor in 1941 and no war between the United States and Japan.[38] Incidentally, Shidehara returned to power in Japan after World War II and expressed the view that his country had been liberated—that the Japanese people were better off under American occupation than they would have been under a victorious Japanese military hierarchy.[39]

The invasion of Manchuria was the signal that a new policy in dealing with Japan was essential. Secretary of State Stimson saw that the gang then in control in Tokyo would respect only force and sought to find such force in collaboration with other governments and the League of Nations. Everywhere he was rebuffed. No nation was willing to use its economic or military strength to arrest aggression in the Far East. And the United States, racked by depression and weakened by neglect of the Navy, was neither inclined nor prepared to back its words with actions. The Nine-Power Treaty was at hand as an appropriate implement of pressure, but willingness to apply the pressure was lacking. Stimson could only fall back upon the lame device of refusing to recognize Japan's war spoils.

[37] Henry L. Stimson, *The Far Eastern Crisis*, p. 87.
[38] See *Documents on German Foreign Policy, 1918–1945*, Chap IV.
[39] Wayne Coy in *Washington Post*, March 9, 1947.

When the Franklin D. Roosevelt Administration took over the reins, the nonrecognition policy was reaffirmed. Secretary Hull, however, offered no leadership in collective resistance to Japan's imperialistic ventures.[40] Both Roosevelt and Hull clung to the twin policies of conciliation and arms reduction as tenaciously as Hughes had done under far more favorable circumstances. Three years after the conquest of Manchuria, the President instructed Norman H. Davis, chairman of the American delegation to the 1935 naval conference, to seek another 20 per cent reduction in navies in accord with the principles laid down in 1922. He wrote:

> The Washington Naval Conference of 1922 brought to the world the first important voluntary agreement for limitation and reduction of armament. It stands out as a milestone in civilization. . . . The important matter to keep constantly before your eyes is the principle of reduction—the maintenance of one of the greatest achievements of friendly relations between nations.[41]

A few months later, when Japan scuttled the Naval Limitation Treaties, Secretary Hull expressed his "genuine regret" because those treaties had "safeguarded the rights and promoted the collective interests of all of the signatories." [42] Even with the protective treaty structure a shambles, the Administration made no immediate move to strengthen the navy.[43] To be sure, the President had drawn upon "pump-priming" funds in 1933 to finance the construction of thirty-two naval vessels and the following year Congress had passed the Vinson-Trammell Act authorizing a navy of treaty strength. But appropriations continued to lag. The Washington and London naval treaties had been dead three and a half years and Hitler and Japan had gone on the warpath before any move was made toward building ships in excess of the old treaty levels.[44]

Japan's undeclared war on China in July, 1937, pointedly demonstrated the weakness of the American position under these changed conditions. For a time it appeared that the United States might take the lead in resisting this aggression. On October 5 the League's Far Eastern Advisory Committee declared Japan guilty of violating the Nine-Power Treaty and the Kellogg Pact and called the signatories of the former into conference. The same day President Roosevelt made a sensational speech in Chicago urging the "peace-loving nations" to quarantine war "like an epidemic disease." When the delegates of the nine powers (excepting Japan) met in Brussels, however, the Americans declared that the purpose of the gathering was not to coerce the belligerents

[40] A. Whitney Griswold, *The Far Eastern Policy of the United States*, pp. 440, 445.
[41] *Foreign Relations, Japan, 1931-1941*, I, 282.
[42] *Peace and War*, pp. 12, 244. [43] *Ibid.*, pp. 44, 316.
[44] Senator David I. Walsh, Senate Document 202, 78th Congress, 2nd session, p. 3.

but "to seek by agreement a solution of the present situation in China." [45] With Japan thumbing her nose at the conference, it was obvious that no conciliation was possible. After three futile weeks the conference adjourned with a mere reaffirmation of the principles of the Nine-Power Treaty. Here was final notice that only force could halt the Japanese militarists; yet it was not until 1941 and 1942 that large-scale naval building in the United States got under way.

Under the whip of war sentiment, the work of the Washington Conference was frequently derided, especially in the campaign of 1944. Speaking at the Democratic National Convention, Governor Kerr of Oklahoma accused the Harding Administration of having "scrapped and sunk more of our fleet than was destroyed by the Japanese at Pearl Harbor." [46] President Roosevelt, sick and weary, declared that "much of the strength of our Navy, and I ought to know it, was scuttled . . ." in the twenties.[47] Such distorted statements cut Hughes to the quick. Even before the campaign warmed up, he wrote to his son-in-law, Chauncey L. Waddell, from his winter retreat (he was then in retirement) in Tucson, Arizona:

> Your letter is a better tonic than the Arizona air. I have been greatly distressed by the unjustified criticism of the Washington Conference and your letter is balm to a wounded spirit. I have realized that it was wise for me to keep quiet as anything I might say would bring bitter and demagogical rejoinders, and I should only extend and magnify a controversy in which I couldn't hope to have the last word. I have no doubt that truth will prevail after the present emergency is over and there is a better chance for a correct historical perspective.[48]

The outstanding fact that the critics ignored is that the conference changed a prospective 100 to 87 naval ratio as between the United States and Japan into a 100 to 60 ratio. Whatever disadvantage the United States suffered in the final showdown with Japan was not a result of the Washington Conference but is solely attributable to the failure of subsequent administrations to maintain the fair naval ratio which the conference fixed and to the delay in recouping our strength after the treaties had been thrown overboard. Roosevelt shares the blame for our naval weakness when war came because of his adherence to the Hughes policy of 1922 long after the amicable relations that had blossomed in the twenties had been upset by Japanese fascism.

World War II also brought criticism of the agreement restricting fortifications. Deploring the cost in American lives of recapturing our insular possessions in the western Pacific, politicians and armchair strategists stressed the

[45] Griswold, *op. cit.*, p. 460; see also *Documents on German Foreign Policy, 1918–1945*, Chap. IV.

[46] *New York Times*, July 20, 1944.

[47] David Lawrence in New York *Sun*, Oct. 23, 1944.

[48] Feb. 21, 1944.

great advantage that bases at Guam and the Philippines would have given us. The trouble is that this view wholly ignores the impossibility of acquiring such bases under conditions that existed in the twenties and thirties. Had the United States insisted on the right to fortify the islands, there would have been no naval agreement. We should then have been more thoroughly outclassed in the ensuing competition than we were under the treaty.

Japan naturally feared the building of American bases in Guam and the Philippines, as we would fear potentially hostile bases in Bermuda or the Galapagos Islands. Hugh Wilson, who served in Tokyo while the Washington Conference was in session and who made a study of the problem of fortifying Guam, expressed fear that "those fortifications would never be completed, at least they would not be completed before battle had been engaged between the Japanese and American fleets, unless we have available in Pacific waters a fleet of much greater preponderance than the present one." [49] Even if a clash could have been avoided, the Japanese would have ringed our base at Guam with bases at Saipan, Palau, and Truk (as they did during the war), so that it would have been useless.

The historic fact is, moreover, that the Naval Limitation Treaty did not delay the fortification of Guam. After Japan threw off the restraints of the treaty, the Roosevelt Administration had five years in which to fortify the island—years in which events were moving inexorably toward the Pearl Harbor disaster. But the Hepburn Board had estimated the cost of such a project at $326,216,000, and the danger of precipitating war with Japan had increased. Chairman Walsh of the Senate Naval Affairs Committee stated flatly after the war had broken out: "No direct request for the fortification of Guam was ever put before the committees of the Senate or the House." [50] A small appropriation for dredging the harbor and building a breakwater was requested in 1939, but Secretary of the Navy Edison and Admiral William D. Leahy told congressional committees that there was no intention of fortifying Guam.[51]

Obviously, then, nothing was lost by Hughes' concession to Kato on fortifications. That agreement did make it impractical for the United States to use force in support of its Far Eastern policy. But the decision not to use force for this purpose had been made by Theodore Roosevelt and Secretary Hay at the turn of the century and was merely continued by Hughes. With the country in an isolationist mood, he could not have reversed that policy. He recognized also, as previous and subsequent administrations have done, that the Philippines could not be defended against an all-out attack from Japan. The Philippines were made a little more secure, however, by a direct pledge from the

[49] *Diplomat Between Wars*, p. 145.
[50] *Congressional Record*, Aug. 24, 1942, p. A3369.
[51] *Ibid.*, May 7, 1942, p. A1811; also Walsh report, pp. 4ff.

Japanese, in the Four-Power Pact, to respect their status and submit any unsettled dispute to a four-power conference.

Hughes rightly concluded that this was the best he could do. There was not a remote possibility that Congress would appropriate the enormous sums required for bases that would make our position in the Far East entirely secure. Equally important was the fact that the whole network of treaties coming out of the conference scrapped distrust as well as the sinews of war. The United States could not at once bid for a new order of live and let live in the Pacific and then insist on building bases that would menace another power. Finally, it is not to be forgotten that Hughes exacted a price for his concession on fortifications. By giving up the right to fortify the Kuriles, the Bonins, the Loochoos, and Pescadores, Japan sacrificed potential submarine bases from which American trans-Pacific shipping could have been menaced. When the war came it was the Japanese bases in the mandated islands that made the recapture of the Philippines and the defeat of Japan so difficult. The United States could have been fully informed about these bases if Secretary Hull had enforced the inspection rights that Hughes had forehandedly passed along to him. "It was not the Washington treaties," as Sumner Welles has pointed out, "but the subsequent shortsighted policies of the major powers, that enabled Japan to flout her treaty obligations with impunity." [52]

Nor should we forget that the Washington Conference laid the groundwork for the Anglo-American partnership that saved the world from fascist rule in the forties. When the Four-Power Pact was under debate in the Senate, Borah interpreted a speech by Paul D. Cravath, Hughes' former law partner, as indicating, on the authority of delegates to the conference, that a secret understanding had been established between Great Britain and the United States. Cravath vehemently denied it. He had not talked with any member of the conference.[53] While Hughes was irritated by Cravath's indiscretion and Borah's suspicion, and while he diplomatically refrained from making a point of his coup at the time, what he had openly done was to break the tie between Great Britain and Japan and give new emphasis to the common interests between Great Britain and the United States. "I doubt," said Root, "if any formal treaty ever accomplished so much by doing so little." [54]

"Had it not been for the Hughes policies," Sumner Welles commented nearly three decades later, "the British-Japanese alliance would have continued and Britain and the United States would have started a naval race. Anglo-American relations would have been poisoned with disastrous consequences for the democracies when the Axis rose to power." [55] Thanks to the

[52] *Washington Post*, Sept. 7, 1948. [53] Cravath to CEH, March 20, 1922.
[54] Address to American Society of International Law, April 27, 1922.
[55] *Washington Post*, Sept. 7, 1948.

Washington Conference, that potential misfortune was averted. When the great test came in 1941, Britain and the United States stood side by side in fighting Britain's former ally.

To summarize, the Washington Conference immediately dispelled the war clouds that had been rising in the Pacific by eliminating the worst sources of friction in that area; it "nailed open" the open door and gave the American policy of safeguarding the integrity of China the sanction of international law; it applied new pressure for Japanese evacuation of Siberia; it transferred the British from the Japanese side of the Pacific conference table to the American side; it held Japanese naval expansion in check for ten years; it saved billions of dollars for the taxpayers in each of the big naval powers; and, finally, it brought the United States back into world councils for the first time since the tragic debacle over the Treaty of Versailles. With all the Hughes treaties ratified by the Senate, America resumed a place of world leadership that had seemed impossible of attainment when the conference assembled.

By robbing these treaties of endurance, Japan minimized their impact on history. That was a tragedy for mankind. But it scarcely detracts from the stature of the man who planned this new order in the Pacific and brought it into being with such consummate skill. His performance proved to be the most effective blow that was struck for peace between the two great wars of this century. Since the conference effected the only general reduction of armaments in the history of the world, it will remain a challenge to statesmanship as long as massive armaments and national rivalries exist.

Chapter 50

PROTECTOR OF RUSSIA—FOE OF LENINISM

HUGHES' hatred of imperialism gave him a unique role—protector of Russia—that was almost forgotten in later years. Coming into office at a time when Russian industry and commerce were in a state of collapse and revolution was still rampant, Hughes feared that Russia was slipping into chaos of the sort that had made China easy prey for the imperialistic powers a few decades earlier. All the influence that he could muster was used to drive away the vultures while the Russian nation was going through its agony of rebirth.

The most dangerous threat came from Japan's continued occupation of large areas in Siberia and Sakhalin. The United States and Japan had jointly sent troops to Siberia in 1918—one of the strangest and least defensible missions ever assigned to American soldiers. The purpose loudly proclaimed at the time was to help a Czechoslovak force that had been isolated when Russia had dropped out of the war and was supposed to be fighting its way to Vladivostok. Actually, the Czechs had taken over the Trans-Siberian Railway, organized new governments in towns along the line, and did not intend to leave Siberia. Major General William S. Graves, who commanded the American expedition, later concluded that Washington officials knew this before he was given his orders and that the underlying purpose of sending troops to Siberia was to overthrow the Soviet régime,[1] although the War Department instructed him not to interfere in Russia's internal affairs. This cynical view of our Siberian adventure is consistent with President Wilson's flirtation with Admiral Kolchak, the counterrevolutionary who was trying to restore a monarchistic régime in Russia. On June 12, 1919, Wilson had agreed with the Allies, "To assist the government of Admiral Kolchak with munitions, supplies and food, to establish themselves as the government of all Russia." [2]

General Graves distributed American arms and supplies to Kolchak in accord with that agreement, but otherwise refrained from interfering with the course of the Russian Revolution. The expedition proved to be a "dismal tragi-comedy" which succeeded only in arousing the resentment of more than 90 per cent of the people of Siberia,[3] thus driving them into the arms of the

[1] Graves' *America's Siberian Adventure* (New York, Cape & Smith, 1931), pp. 346–355. Copyright, 1931, by William S. Graves.
[2] *Ibid.*, p. 355. [3] *Ibid.*, p. 347.

Communists. The American troops were ingloriously withdrawn early in 1920, but the Japanese remained and continued to run riot.

The understanding had been that the United States and Japan would each send about 10,000 troops; Japan had sent 72,000. These invaders broke up local efforts to restore order, smuggled in goods disguised as military supplies, and maltreated the population. Anti-Soviet soldiers, under the protection of Japanese troops, "were roaming the country like wild animals, killing and robbing the people." The invaders were in complete control, and there were many indications that they intended to stay. The Island Empire appeared to be bent on Japonizing the entire Russian Pacific littoral.

In a stiff note to Tokyo on May 31, 1921, Hughes told the Japanese that their continued hold upon strategic centers of Siberia "tends rather to increase than to allay the unrest and disorder in that region." The issue presented, he said, was that of scrupulous fulfillment of the assurances given to the Russian people by the United States and Japan that the expedition of 1918 would not be used as "an occasion to occupy territory, even temporarily, or to assume any military or administrative control over the people of Siberia." Hughes' pointed indictment continued:

> . . . in the present time of disorder in Russia, it is more than ever the duty of those who look forward to the tranquilization of the Russian people, and a restoration of normal conditions among them, to avoid all action which might keep alive their antagonism and distrust toward outside political agencies. Now, especially, it is incumbent upon the friends of Russia to hold aloof from the domestic contentions of the Russian people, to be scrupulous to avoid inflicting what might appear to them a vicarious penalty for sporadic acts of lawlessness, and, above all, to abstain from even the temporary and conditional impairment by any foreign Power of the territorial status which, for them as for other peoples, is a matter of deep and sensitive national feeling transcending perhaps even the issues at stake among themselves.[4]

Hughes frankly warned the Japanese that the United States would not recognize "any claim or title arising out of the present occupation." Nor would we acquiesce in any action which "might impair existing treaty rights or the political or territorial integrity of Russia." The Secretary went as far as any statesman could go (without making futile threats) in pressing the Japanese to pull in their horns.

When he called the Washington Conference, "the integrity of Russia" was given a prominent place on the agenda. The Soviet's Commissar for Foreign Affairs sent a slashing protest against Hughes' failure to invite Russia to the conference. Without acknowledging the note of the unrecognized Moscow régime, Hughes took upon himself the responsibility of protecting Russian interests.

[4] *Report of the American Delegation* (Arms Conference), p. 82.

"In the absence of a single, recognized Russian government," he announced, "the protection of legitimate Russian interests must devolve as a moral trusteeship upon the whole conference." [5] It was regrettable that the conference, "for reasons quite beyond the control of the participating powers," was not to have Russian cooperation. But Hughes could not conceive of the conference taking any action that would be prejudicial to legitimate Russian interests or would encroach upon Russian rights.

After the conference opened, the Secretary had his aides draw up a resolution reaffirming the idea of moral trusteeship and taking a firm position against any "further violation of the rights of Russia and her citizens." [6] Ambassador Shidehara probably anticipated what was coming. The moment Hughes mentioned the Siberian issue in the Far Eastern Committee on January 23, 1922, the ambassador was on his feet reiterating Japan's "good intentions" and announcing that Japanese troops were soon to be withdrawn.[7]

Hughes accepted these assurances, reasserted the American policy laid down in the note of May 31, 1921, and again drove home the point that good faith required the "complete withdrawal of Japanese troops from all Russian territory." Spreading both Japan's pledge and his own statement on the conference record, he placed Tokyo under the necessity of withdrawing its troops or acknowledging its words to be fraudulent.

When the United States was invited to participate in the Genoa Conference of 1922, Hughes took advantage of the occasion to reiterate that "this Government, anxious to do all in its power to promote the welfare of the Russian people, views with the most eager and friendly interest every step taken towards the restoration of economic conditions which will permit Russia to regain her productive power." [8] Even though the United States did not send delegates to this conference, the Secretary made it plain that any move on the part of the powers to take advantage of Russia's prostration would meet with sharp disapproval in America.

A few months later Japan evacuated Siberia; three years later her troops left northern Sakhalin. Historians point out that by this time she had gained valuable concessions, and occupation costs had become heavy. But Hughes' skillful mobilization of world opinion against the Japanese venture was one of the factors that made it too costly to pursue. Challenging the Japanese militarists without any European assistance, he earned the lion's share of the credit for saving Russia from continued exploitation and possible dismemberment.

This statesmanlike intercession in behalf of a prostrate power reflected not only Hughes' desire to curb Japanese expansion but also a genuine interest in the welfare of the Russian people. His friendliness toward the Russians was

[5] *Foreign Relations, 1921*, I, 70. [6] J. A. V. MacMurray to CEH, Jan. 12, 1922.
[7] *Conference on the Limitation of Armament*, pp. 139ff.
[8] *Foreign Relations, 1922*, I, 393.

further manifested by his aid to the movement which supplied $66,000,000 for the relief of suffering from the great Soviet famine of 1921–1922. But he could see nothing good for the Russians or for the world in Nicolai Lenin's Communist régime.

Wilson had not recognized the new Moscow government, and Hughes continued that policy in common with most of the foreign offices in Europe at that time. At St. Augustine in February, 1921, he was approached by Joseph Z. Dalinda, a Russian who was sponsoring a scheme to employ American engineers for the restoration of Russia's ruined industries. Hughes was cool and noncommittal. The following month the Soviet government suggested sending a special delegation to the United States to negotiate a trade agreement. The communication was crudely addressed to Congress as well as to the President and was released to the press before it was received.

"It is idle to expect a resumption of trade," Hughes replied, "until the economic bases of production are securely established. Production is conditioned upon the safety of life, the recognition of firm guarantees of private property, the sanctity of contract, and the rights of free labor." [9] Pointing to Russia's starvation and chaos, he insisted that her primary need was for relief and internal stability.

Through Secretary of Commerce Hoover, several American companies inquired of the State Department as to the possibilities of resuming business in Russia. "I do not think it advisable," Hughes replied, "to put any obstacle in the way of any American concern that desires to do business with Russia, or to endeavor to resume management of its property in Russia, always with the understanding that it is acting at its own risk. It is only through efforts of this sort that the difficulties in doing anything worth while under the present regime in Russia will be disclosed to the satisfaction of our business men." [10]

As to diplomatic relations, Hughes' stand was based on well defined principles and reflected no vindictiveness. He was not stiff-necked about recognizing a revolutionary government. "We are not concerned with the question of the legitimacy of a government as judged by former European standards," he wrote in reply to a letter from Samuel Gompers, president of the American Federation of Labor. "We recognize the right of revolution, and we do not attempt to determine the internal concerns of other States." [11] The Russians had a right to develop their own institutions. The Secretary also conceded that "long-continued acquiescence" on the part of the people in a régime actually functioning as a government should count heavily in its favor.

Beyond stability, however, was the all-important element of good faith. "Recognition," he said, "is invitation to intercourse. It is accompanied on the

[9] *New York Times*, March 26, 1921. [10] CEH to Hoover, March 22, 1922.
[11] CEH to Samuel Gompers, July 19, 1923; Hughes Papers.

part of the new government by the clearly implied or express promise to fulfill the obligations of intercourse." Soviet Russia made no pretense of accepting such obligations. Hughes knew, as Root said, "that the fundamental doctrine of the men who govern Russia now is that it is their mission in the world to overturn and destroy the government of the United States, of England, of France, of all the civilized nations of the western world." [12] Moscow had a new code of ethics which elevated bad faith to the status of a policy. Hughes refused to match it by making self-deception or hypocrisy a guide to action.

The Soviet officials had openly and unconditionally repudiated all foreign debts owed by Russia, including $187,000,000 the United States had lent to the Kerensky government. They had also ruthlessly confiscated property belonging to American citizens. Hughes had not the slightest idea of slipping into the role of the harsh creditor. "The United States," he said, "is not seeking to press debtors who cannot pay beyond their means. But indulgence and proper arrangements are one thing, repudiation is quite another." [13] How could there be any faith in a régime that adopted repudiation and confiscation as policies? The honest-minded apostle of justice who was Secretary of State simply could not bring himself to the point of rewarding the authors of those policies with diplomatic recognition.

The chief reason for turning a cold shoulder toward the Moscow régime, however, was its sponsorship of subversive activities in the United States. The State Department gathered an abundance of evidence as to what the world revolutionists in control of the Russian government were trying to do on this side of the Atlantic.[14] Hughes' attention rested especially on Trotsky's declaration to the young Communists that "revolution is coming in Europe as well as in America, systematically, step by step, stubbornly and with gnashing of teeth in both camps. It will be long protracted, cruel and sanguinary." [15] In his statement of July 1, 1924, the Secretary made his position clear:

> The essential fact is the existence of an organization in the United States created by, and completely subservient to, a foreign organization striving to overthrow the existing social and political order of this country. The subversive and pernicious activities of the American Communist Party and the Workers' Party and their subordinate or allied organs in the United States are activities resulting from and flowing out of the program elaborated for them by the Moscow group.[16]

To recognize Russia under these circumstances, Hughes concluded, would be to give the Communist régime an embassy in Washington as an official

[12] Root's Address of Nov. 10, 1925. [13] *The Pathway of Peace*, p. 63.

[14] *Hearings, "Recognition of Russia,"* before Senate Foreign Relations Subcommittee, 1924, 68th Congress, 1st session.

[15] *The Pathway of Peace*, p. 64.

[16] Charles Cheney Hyde, "Charles Evans Hughes," in *The American Secretaries of State and Their Diplomacy*, ed. S. F. Bemis (New York, Knopf, 1928), X, 287. Copyright, 1928, by Alfred A. Knopf, Inc.

headquarters for its subversive activities. That he steadfastly refused to do. To summarize, he denied the Soviet recognition for three reasons: (1) insufficient proof that it had been accepted by the people; (2) its unwillingness to meet the obligations of international intercourse; (3) its persistent efforts to destroy the governments whose recognition it sought.

Senator Borah, for reasons that have never been fully explained, became the spearhead of the movement for recognition of the Soviet. His demands for a conference to iron out differences between Washington and Moscow boomed through the Senate. Hughes felt that, without indications that the Soviet régime was ready to modify its conduct, a conference would be futile. Preparing a terse statement to this effect, he took it to President Coolidge for approval.

"Why shouldn't I say that?" was the President's response.

"Of course you could," Hughes replied. "But would it be wise to expose yourself to the criticism that will rain upon the head of the person who makes this statement public?" [17] He felt that it was part of his job to shield the President, whenever possible, from brickbats aimed at the foreign policy they were pursuing.

"I guess you are right," the calm little Yankee said.

Hughes then issued his statement:

> The American government . . . is not proposing to barter away its principles. If the Soviet authorities are ready to restore the confiscated property of American citizens or make effective compensation, they can do so. If the Soviet authorities are ready to repeal their decree repudiating Russia's obligations to this country and appropriately recognize them, they can do so. It requires no conference or negotiations to accomplish these results which can and should be achieved at Moscow as evidence of good faith.[18]

The Lion of Idaho roared his disapproval, and Soviet sympathizers protested so loudly that newsmen asked the Secretary if he would resign. Hughes snorted in the negative. His policy undoubtedly reflected the wishes of a majority in Congress and the country as well as those of the President. Secretaries Kellogg and Stimson later adhered to the same policy, and the latter reiterated Hughes' three chief reasons for withholding the hand of friendship. When recognition was finally accorded in 1933, it was upon the explicit pledge that the Soviet government would refrain from interfering in any manner in the internal affairs of the United States and would restrain all persons in its service and all organizations in receipt of any financial assistance from it from any act liable to injure the tranquility, prosperity, order, or security of the United States. Subsequent history heavily underscores Secretary Hughes' fears that, even if expressly given, such a pledge would rest upon bad faith.

[17] Author's interview with CEH, Dec. 10, 1946.

[18] Hyde, *op. cit.*, p. 286.

At no time, however, did his realistic understanding of the Communist dictatorship alter his interest in, or his friendship for, the Russian people. And he insisted on maintaining the amenities when dealing with Soviet representatives. When one of the latter came to the department seeking an interview in connection with a case before an American tribunal and the subordinate assigned to see him began letting off steam, Hughes cut him short. "Hold on," he said. "Mr. ——— has asked for an appointment with me. I cannot see him; but you must. He is entitled to a perfectly fair hearing and to be treated courteously." [19]

A decade later when the first Soviet ambassador, Alexander Troyanovsky, came to Washington, he called on Chief Justice Hughes in accord with time-honored custom. Their relations became "most agreeable," and on three separate occasions in the years that followed the Chief Justice and Mrs. Hughes were the guests of honor at large dinners at the Soviet Embassy. At the last of these fêtes in May, 1938, the two men sat together after dinner and surveyed at length the rising menace of Hitlerism in Europe, with the ambassador asserting rather emphatically that Hitler, as soon as he was ready, would attack France.[20]

To the end of his days Hughes remained alert to the menace of revolutionary and imperialistic Communism. He would neither countenance the despoilment of a prostrate nation nor compromise with bad faith. When the Russian people emerge from their era of terrorism, they may well count him one of their best friends during the dark days of Lenin.

[19] Hyde, *op. cit.*, p. 282. [20] CEH, Notes, p. 317.

Chapter 51

THE FRIENDLY NEIGHBOR

SECRETARY HUGHES picked up the reins of foreign policy in Latin America with vivid memories of his 1916 presidential campaign. Some of his severest criticism had been directed at Wilson's handling of the Mexican imbroglio. As Secretary of State, his central aim in regard to Latin America was to replace Theodore Roosevelt's big stick and Wilson's erratic interventions by the stabilizing hand of friendship.

The United States' meddling in Mexico and its general overlordship in the Caribbean area had provoked widespread resentment among the Latin American peoples. During World War I most of them had supported the United States; but, with the war over and with Europe notably weakened in relation to the Western Hemisphere, suspicion as to the motives of the "colossus of the North" had been reactivated. This suspicion was fed by the presence of United States troops in Santo Domingo, Haiti, and Nicaragua. The American flag was flying in more countries than ever before. Hughes' firm policy was to bring the flag and the troops home while helping our Latin neighbors to maintain their own freedom and national stability.

Ten days after he became Secretary of State, Hughes first enunciated his aim at a luncheon given by Dr. L. S. Rowe, director general of the Pan American Union.

> We have and will have no ulterior purposes with respect to the Republics of Latin America. We wish to help to a common prosperity, through the safeguarding of the opportunities of peace, the fostering of friendship and of mutually advantageous commercial intercourse. . . . We can have neither security nor peace, neither stability nor progress, unless reason rules and justice is assured. We are all collaborators in that greatest of endeavors and we are looking forward with the utmost confidence to an era of exceptional mutual benefits through our working together in a spirit of mutual trust.[1]

What had been done could not be undone overnight. No good would come from sudden withdrawal of our Marines, leaving to chaos the countries that had come to lean upon them for law enforcement. Lasting progress could be made only by eliminating the causes of unrest, preventing the growth of conditions prejudicial to the United States, and aiding our neighbors to settle their

[1] *New York Times,* March 15, 1921.

own disputes peacefully without imposing our will on them. Hughes summed it up by saying: "Our interest does not lie in controlling foreign peoples; that would be a policy of mischief and disaster. Our interest is in having prosperous, peaceful, and law-abiding neighbors with whom we can cooperate to mutual advantage." [2]

Two decades after this policy was put into effect, Professor Samuel Flagg Bemis of Yale University described it as the liquidation of imperialism. "Responding to the new situation," he wrote, "it was the policy of Secretary of State Charles E. Hughes . . . to liquidate the interventions of the United States in the Caribbean and Central America as promptly as political stability should seem to be established and the safety of foreign nationals reasonably assured." [3] Hughes heartily accepted this as an accurate statement of what he had tried to do. Others credited him with taking the first steps toward what became, under the second Roosevelt, the "good neighbor policy." [4] Certainly he emulated the good neighbor, though he had more difficult problems to meet in Latin America than Roosevelt and Hull encountered more than a decade later.

One reason for this similarity of the Hughes and Roosevelt policies in Latin America was Sumner Welles. As chief of the State Department's Latin American Division when Hughes took office, Welles immediately won his new chief's respect. His work proved him to be a diplomat of "exceptional ability, poise, and force of character." [5] Although Welles left the department early in 1922, he helped to shape Hughes' Latin American policy in its formative period. During a large part of the Roosevelt administration Welles was again in the department as Undersecretary of State.

Among the first fruits of the Hughes-Welles teamwork was the Central American Conference. The little countries south of Mexico were on the verge of war. Honduras and Nicaragua had accused each other of assisting revolutionists in the invasion of their respective countries. Salvador had also become involved, and Washington feared a general upheaval in the back yard of the Panama Canal. On a request from Nicaragua, Hughes first invited the Presidents of the three countries to a conference on the U.S.S. *Tacoma* in Fonseca Bay in August, 1922, in the presence of United States diplomats, and they succeeded in patching up a temporary agreement.

Seeking a more reliable means of settling such disputes, Hughes induced the President to call a conference of Central American countries. It met in Washington in December, 1922, with Hughes and Welles as the United States'

[2] *The Pathway of Peace*, p. 137.

[3] Bemis, *The Latin American Policy of the United States* (New York, Harcourt, Brace, 1943), p. 203. Copyright, 1943, by Samuel Flagg Bemis.

[4] James Grafton Rogers in *American Bar Association Journal*, July, 1941, p. 412.

[5] CEH. Notes, p. 327.

delegates exercising no right to vote. The Secretary was to make the opening address. When the day of the conference arrived, however, he had been so preoccupied with the reparations dilemma in Europe that he had nothing prepared. Calling in Welles, he hastily discussed the main points to be covered and dictated his speech—ten small pages—in precise, penetrating words comprehensively dealing with every essential point. While the speech was being typed he turned to other problems, but he was on time for the conference and delivered his address verbatim, with no manuscript before him, changing only about three words.[6]

"The Government of the United States has no ambition to gratify at your expense," he said, "no policy which runs counter to your national aspirations, and no purpose save to promote the interests of peace and to assist you, in such manner as you may welcome, to solve your problems to your own proper advantage. The interest of the United States is found in the peace of this Hemisphere and in the conservation of your interests." [7]

The conference produced a general treaty of peace and amity and eleven conventions dealing with the limitation of armament, extradition, agriculture, an exchange of students, and so forth. One convention set up a Central American Tribunal, the first court of arbitration in history. The United States became a party to the convention providing for international commissions of inquiry into a limited category of disputes not settled by diplomacy or arbitration. Another blow for stability was struck by reviving and tightening up the Tobar Doctrine of 1907. Each of the five republics pledged itself in specific detail not to aid or recognize any government coming into power in any of the other signatory countries by a *coup d'état*. They also agreed "not to intervene, under any circumstances, directly or indirectly, in the internal political affairs of any other Central American republic." Here was a model for the Treaty on the Rights and Duties of States that came into being at Montevideo in 1933.

The usefulness of the treaties was demonstrated when the failure of the presidential election in Honduras in October, 1923, threw that country into revolution. The Navy proposed that Marines be rushed in at once. Hughes would not tolerate it. Instead, he sent Welles to offer the good offices of the United States, and peace and order were restored. In the thirties the nonrecognition treaty broke down when a revolutionary government established itself in Salvador in spite of the disapproval of Washington and its neighbors. However, the Central American treaties kept the peace among these little nations "until they stepped into the larger Pan American peace structure set up at Montevideo and Buenos Aires in 1933 and 1936." [8]

Relations with Latin America were also much improved by the Senate's rati-

[6] Author's interview with Sumner Welles, Oct. 29, 1947.

[7] Address of Dec. 4, 1922; Hughes Papers.

[8] Bemis, *op. cit.*, pp. 208f.

fication of the treaty for payment of $25,000,000 to Colombia because of Roosevelt's seizure of the Panama Canal Zone. The treaty had been negotiated before Hughes took office, but he heartily approved it and sought to take full advantage of the clarified atmosphere on the Pan American horizon. The logical next step was the withdrawal of American troops from Latin American soil, and to this task the Secretary diligently applied himself.

Santo Domingo became the first test case. Wilson had sent naval forces to the Dominican Republic in 1916 to avert civil war. Hughes' study of the situation convinced him in 1921 that the time was opportune to seek withdrawal of these troops. His initial moves were to bring about the appointment of Rear Admiral Samuel S. Robison as military governor and direct the issuance of a proclamation to the Dominican people. The United States wished to withdraw its forces, the proclamation said, and turn over the administration of the republic's affairs to a responsible Dominican government established in accord with the Constitution of 1908. The plan was for the military governor to convene primary assemblies to prepare for an election and then to supervise the balloting to get a free expression of the popular will.

The Dominican people suspected a trick intended to prolong the occupation, and rejected Hughes' friendly gesture. He tried in vain to reassure them; then, instead of resenting their rebuff, he patiently sought a new approach. At the same time he curbed the rigors of the Navy's dictatorship. Six or seven young Dominicans had been imprisoned for publishing articles in the press attacking the application of the land law. Hughes denounced the sentences as "peculiarly unfortunate" and asked the Navy Department to suspend them at once and "to refrain, in the future, from taking official cognizance of purely political offenses of this character without the concurrence of the Department of State." [9]

In March, 1922, Francisco J. Peynado, former Dominican minister to the United States, came to Washington. He and the Secretary had no difficulty in modifying the evacuation plan so that it appeared acceptable in principle. Then Hughes sent word to the Dominican political leaders that they would be welcome in Washington if they wished to seek an agreement. When General Horacio Vásquez and Federico Velásquez arrived in Washington, they were in entire accord with the new evacuation plan. The President, at Hughes' request, appointed Welles commissioner to Santo Domingo for the purpose of ascertaining the wishes of the people and arranging for the final withdrawal. Welles had previously resigned as chief of the State Department's Latin American Division and had been succeeded by Francis White.

It was a proud moment for Hughes when President Vásquez was inaugurated on July 12, 1924, and a new era of independence began for the Dominican

[9] *Foreign Relations, 1922,* II, 37.

Republic. The American occupation forces were gradually withdrawn between June and September. Hughes had insisted that law, order, and constitutional government follow in the wake of the occupation; his liquidation of imperialism was not the abandonment of bankrupts to their fate but the rehabilitation of weak states so that they were capable of self-government.

The Secretary hoped to repeat this achievement in every country that was still occupied by American troops. In Haiti, however, the situation was less favorable. Frequent upheavals had left the people destitute and almost hopeless. In the last murderous orgy before American troops had restored order in 1915, former President Zamora and President Sam were both slaughtered, the latter being dragged from the French Legation, where he had taken refuge, and torn to pieces in the street. Reviewing this background of chaos and violence, Hughes sent John H. Russell, a civilian-minded brigadier-general, to Haiti early in 1922, with instructions to work in the closest cooperation with the local authorities. The new American High Commissioner was not satisfied merely to maintain peace and order. Agriculture and industry were revived; the currency was stabilized, the public debt reduced, and constructive public works undertaken. An American adviser attempted to establish a sound judicial system, and local government was strengthened. But, after a thorough investigation, Hughes was convinced that the withdrawal of American troops would plunge the country into bloodshed and revolution once more. He had to be content with a report of progress and a statement of his good intentions.

Nicaragua was a more hopeful case. American troops had been stationed in that country since 1912; order had been fully restored and a new electoral system set up by Harold W. Dodds, later president of Princeton University. Hughes told the Nicaraguans in November, 1923, that after the elections of the following year and the installation of the new President in January, 1925, the last of the Marine guard at the American Legation in Managua would be withdrawn. Meanwhile he offered to lend expert aid for the training of a Nicaraguan constabulary. A relatively fair and free election was held, and Carlos Solórzano was inaugurated president in February, 1925. Fearing an uprising from the defeated party, Solórzano asked that the withdrawal of the Marines be delayed, and the evacuation was not completed until a few months after Hughes had left office. A revolution followed, and President Coolidge sent the Marines back again.

In Cuba the Hughes policy took the form of forbearance. The significant thing about our relations with Cuba, he used to say, "was not that we went in but that we came out." [10] The Secretary was "vehemently implored" to rescue

[10] Charles Evans Hughes, *Our Relations to the Nations of the Western Hemisphere* (Princeton, Princeton University Press, 1928), p. 76.

Cuba from the corruption of the Zayas régime. While the reports he received from General E. H. Crowder, trusted American friend of Cuba, gave him many anxious hours and while intervention might have been justified under the Platt Amendment, Hughes preferred to use less drastic methods. By aiding the Cubans in straightening out their financial affairs and governmental machinery, he avoided any necessity for intervention.

Cuba was especially grateful to Hughes for his aid in getting the Isle of Pines Treaty ratified. Negotiated in 1904, the treaty had been pigeonholed by the Senate out of fear that the interests of American citizens in the island might be imperiled if our government definitely renounced all claim of title. The Secretary revived the treaty and interested a number of Senators in it over Borah's opposition. "The present undetermined status of the Isle of Pines," he wrote to Senator Robinson, "constitutes one of the few remaining questions capable of prejudicing the intimate relations between the United States and Cuba, and it is my earnest hope that the Senate in its present session will give its consent to the ratification of the Treaty." [11] The Senate responded in March, 1925, two months after this letter was written, with a vote of 63 to 14 for the treaty.

The Hughes policies in Latin America were given a secure philosophical base by his clear thinking about the Monroe Doctrine. Over the years people on both sides of the Rio Grande had made a practice of lumping together under the heading of the Monroe Doctrine all the ideas and practices by the United States that our neighbors found obnoxious. Secretary Olney's boast that "the United States is practically sovereign on this continent," Theodore Roosevelt's "Corollary" to the Monroe Doctrine, and Wilson's interventions were all linked in the public mind to President Monroe's famous declaration. Some went so far as to assume that a logical extension of the doctrine would sweep all the Caribbean area under the American flag. Such hateful connotations were a heavy liability for any national policy to carry.

Hughes took advantage of his address to the American Bar Association in Minneapolis on August 30, 1923, to strip our hemispheric policy of these excrescences. "The Monroe doctrine," he said, "is not a policy of aggression; it is a policy of self-defense. It was asserted at a time when the danger of foreign aggression in this hemisphere was very real, when the new American states had not yet established a firm basis of independent national life, and we were menaced by threats of Old World powers directed against republican institutions. But the achievements of the century have not altered the scope of the doctrine or changed its basis. It still remains an assertion of the principle of national security. As such, it is obviously not exclusive." [12]

He assumed that the United States would always reserve to itself the right

[11] *Foreign Relations, 1925*, II, 2. [12] *The Pathway of Peace*, p. 120.

of defining, interpreting, and applying the doctrine. He made no effort to share its enforcement with the other American states, as Secretary Stettinius succeeded in doing in the "one for all and all for one" arrangement worked out at Chapultepec in 1945. Hughes was well aware of Wilson's failure to interest Argentina, Brazil, and Chile in a Pan American treaty incorporating the Monroe Doctrine.[13] While persistently seeking hemispheric cooperation, he went no further in this matter than to encourage the other American states to maintain "Monroe Doctrines" of their own, which would have the effect of common resistance to any outside aggression. His chief contribution to the doctrine was his hard pounding on the point that it does not "infringe upon the independence and sovereignty of other American States." There was nothing in it contemplating a "protectorate" over any other country. It gave "no justification" for intervention in the affairs of our neighbors. "I utterly disclaim, as unwarranted," he said, "the observations which occasionally have been made implying a claim on our part to superintend the affairs of our sister republics, to assert an overlordship, to consider the spread of our authority beyond our own domain as the aim of our policy, and to make our power the test of right in this hemisphere."

In an address to the American Academy of Political and Social Science at Philadelphia on November 30, 1923, in celebration of the centenary of Monroe's declaration, Hughes further outlined the constructive aspects of his hemispheric policy. First, he recognized "the equality of the American republics, their equal rights under the law of nations." Second, he pledged respect for their territorial integrity. Third, he emphasized that each state has "duties as well as rights," including the duty of protecting the rights which citizens of other states have acquired under its laws. Fourth, he offered "friendly assistance" to promote the stability and strengthen the independence of those sister republics which were especially afflicted with disturbed conditions. Fifth, the United States would aid the peaceful settlement of disputes between the governments of the Western Hemisphere. Sixth, he urged limitation of armaments. Seventh, he promised "mutually helpful cooperation" through the Pan American conferences. Eighth, the United States would not seek preferential trade rights but unconditional most-favored-nation treatment. Ninth, it would rigorously protect its special interests such as the Panama Canal.[14] In Hughes' hands the Monroe Doctrine thus became the foundation for a positive policy of helpfulness.

He saw no inconsistency between the confraternity of the Western Hemisphere and the United States' position as a world power. American interest in the integrity of China and Russia and in world peace were sprouts from the same root that produced the Monroe Doctrine. In these broader fields, the Sec-

[13] Henry P. Fletcher to CEH, Jan. 10, 1923.

[14] *The Pathway of Peace*, pp. 155–163.

retary said, the United States was "pursuing under different conditions the same aims of independence, security, and peace which determined the declaration of Monroe." The Monroe Doctrine expressed our firm intention to retain security in the Western Hemisphere, but it also left the door open to action on the world stage in any degree that our future security might require.

Welles thought that Hughes' "painstaking and authoritative elucidation" of the Monroe Doctrine was one of his greatest services to the country. "Secretary Hughes brought it home to the American public in a manner more convincing than ever before," he said, "that the Monroe Doctrine was solely a policy of self-defense. . . ." [15] Hughes also gave greater endurance to his own concepts of international justice and fair dealing by weaving them into the fringe of the venerated doctrine.

[15] Welles' *Naboth's Vineyard* (London, Payson & Clarke, Ltd., 1928), II, 922f.

Chapter 52

REMOVING CAUSES OF FRICTION

SECRETARY HUGHES carried his message of friendship to the heart of South America when he attended the centennial of Brazilian independence at Rio de Janeiro in 1922. The Emperor Dom Pedro II had been a prominent figure at the United States centenary in 1876. To return the emperor's courtesy, Harding named Hughes head of a delegation that included also Representative Stephen G. Porter, Admiral Hilary P. Jones, Major General Robert L. Bullard, and Justice Edward R. Finch of the Supreme Court of New York.

The sailing of the official party from New York on August 24 aboard the S.S. *Pan America* was somewhat delayed by a striking incident that had no direct connection with the trip. As Hughes joined in the embarkation ceremonies, a New York lawyer determined to see him arrived hurriedly at the dock and followed the official party. It was Grenville Clark. Clark kept a watchful eye on the Secretary as the procession boarded the ship and went to the main saloon where the greetings and speechmaking took place. Then he followed the Secretary to his stateroom. The door was open. Hughes was unfastening his valise when Clark, standing in the doorway, made known his presence with a knock.

"Clark, what are you doing here?" the Secretary demanded sharply. "You are not going, are you? You will be left."

"I must speak to you," Clark replied, "about your having signed the document for the landing of the cable at Miami."

"How did you know about that?" Hughes asked.

"Stabler telephoned Root about it at Clinton and Root phoned me half an hour ago and was extremely disturbed," Clark said. "It was understood, as you know, that the cable would not be landed until the last South American country had consented, and, as you know, Argentina has not yet consented."

The controversy had arisen out of a prolonged fight between the American and British cable companies serving South America. All America Cables, Inc., maintained cable connections between the United States and Buenos Aires by way of the west coast of South America, where it held some monopoly rights. The Western Telegraph Company, Ltd., operated a monopolistic cable system on the east coast of South America. Through an alliance between this British company and the Western Union Telegraph Company, the east coast cable had been extended from Buenos Aires to within three miles of Miami—a formidable threat to the All America Company. Elihu Root, Jr., counsel for All America, had found a line of precedents under which the United States had forbidden foreign companies to land their cables on our shores if they held monopoly rights in other foreign lands with the effect of excluding the cables of American companies. Reasserting this policy, President Wilson had sent a government vessel to prevent the cable off Miami from being landed.

Suit had been brought, and Judge Augustus N. Hand had ruled that Wilson had exceeded his constitutional authority. While the case was pending before the Supreme Court, the All America Company had appealed to Congress to grant the President the needed authority, and an exciting race had ensued to get the measure enacted before the court could hand down its decision. Congress had won; the bill had become law; and the contending parties, after a number of conferences with Secretaries Hughes and Hoover, had entered into an agreement under which monopoly rights were to be abandoned on both South American coasts. It was understood that the cable at Miami was to be landed but only after all the South American countries had granted to the respective companies the landing licenses contemplated by the agreement.

To avoid further delay, Hughes had signed papers lifting the ban on the Miami cable before he left Washington, although there was still a question as to whether the reply of Argentina fully met the conditions on which the agreement between the cable companies was based. On learning this, Root (who was in Clinton, New York) had made every effort to telephone the Secretary, and, being unsuccessful, had asked his partner (Clark) to locate Hughes in New York and try to have the action revoked.

Hughes replied to Clark that the points he raised were technical and that he (Hughes) would see to it that Argentina's consent was forthcoming. "You young men have had a great success in holding off the landing of that cable all these years," he said, "and you ought to be satisfied. Now you must leave the ship at once."

"That is not quite the point, Mr. Secretary," Clark replied. "The point is that you have signed the document for the landing of the cable before Argentina's clear-cut consent has been received; and neither you nor anyone can absolutely guarantee what Argentina will do. If it goes wrong, the agreement is not fulfilled, and we are put in an impossible position."

"You have heard what I have said," Hughes retorted impatiently. "Now you must leave."

"I am sorry, then," Clark blurted out, "but I am obliged to charge a breach of faith by the Department of State."

"How dare you?" the Secretary exclaimed, his face flushed from indignation.

"I am indeed sorry to have to make that statement," Clark came back, "but I must repeat it; that is precisely what it is, a breach of faith." [1]

Hughes struggled for self-control. After a brief pause he rang for the steward and instructed him to go immediately to the captain and say that Secretary Hughes wished the ship to remain at the dock for an hour or until he sent word.

"Now, Clark," he said as soon as the steward had gone, "we have both raised our voices and become emotional. Let's take a fresh start. Sit down here quietly and we will cool off and talk it over, and I want you to take your time about it."

Hughes listened with only brief questions while Clark reviewed the main points of the whole controversy and, while holding to his position, again expressed regret that he had felt it necessary to use such harsh language. The Secretary then replied that Clark had done right to see him under the circumstances and that he had made a mistake in signing the cable-landing license before the question of Argentina's compliance had been fully cleared up. But he felt that the Argentine message constituted a substantial compliance, and that if Messrs. Root and Clark saw the entire dispatch they might change their minds. The upshot was an understanding that, if the license had not already been sent to the British-Western Union combine, Leland Harrison at the department could use his discretion as to holding it up until Root could examine the full Argentine dispatch. Hughes gave Clark a message to Harrison, repeating it several times so that Clark could learn it by heart and deliver it by telephone as soon as he got off the ship. Root saw Harrison the next morning. The net result was to delay delivery of the license by only a single day. The incident served, however, to reassure the American company, to alert the department, and to give Clark a "lasting admiration" for Hughes' sense of justice and self-control. At the same time, Clark's firm and persistent course evidently did not interfere with Hughes' esteem, as was shown by their confidential relations in later years.

Except for hot weather, the trip to Rio was a fascinating interval for the overburdened Secretary. He and Mrs. Hughes were lodged in the beautiful Guanabara Palace, home of Brazil's former emperors, and extensively entertained. On the centennial day, September 7, they were guests of President Pessôa of Brazil in reviewing 40,000 troops at Campo Sãochristovão, with American bluejackets and Marines leading the parade. At noon the whole city joined in a great noise-making demonstration, and in the evening more than 100,000 persons marched down the flag-draped Avenida Rio Branco.

In the following week Secretary Hughes delivered four addresses to Brazilian audiences. At the dedication of the site for the American centennial monu-

[1] Mr. Clark's memorandum for author, Nov. 21, 1949.

ment at Rio he made one of his most positive statements on Latin American policy:

> We shall also be glad to have this monument associated in the thought of our friends with a true appraisement of our North American ideals and aspirations. . . . We have our domestic problems incident to the expanding life of a free people, but there is no imperialistic sentiment among us to cast even a shadow across the pathway of our progress. We covet no territory; we seek no conquest; the liberty we cherish for ourselves we desire for others; and we assert no rights for ourselves that we do not accord to others. We sincerely desire to see throughout this hemisphere an abiding peace, the reign of justice and the diffusion of the blessings of a beneficent cooperation. It is this desire which forms the basis of the Pan American sentiment.
>
> . . . We have institutions dedicated to freedom, and we desire not simply the independence of might but the independence which rests secure in a prevailing sense of justice. We have different stocks and traditions but we cherish the same aspirations; the same longings for liberty under law. The differences are superficial, the resemblances fundamental.

On the return trip aboard the battleship *Maryland* a heavy storm arose. The Hugheses stood on the bridge for several hours watching a seventy-five-mile-an-hour hurricane curl foam-capped hillocks of water over the deck. When they went to their cabin, the lunging sea tore away the port and poured a series of fourteen-inch jets of water in upon them. Butler Wright found Hughes, wearing shorts and a quizzical smile, standing in the middle of the room, with several inches of water swishing back and forth and various articles of clothing floating about. Mrs. Hughes was sitting in a corner convulsed with laughter. Wright never ceased to regret that the scene was not recorded for the benefit of those who talked about Hughes' austerity.

The most troublesome chasm that Secretary Hughes had to bridge in Latin America was that between the United States and Mexico. A long period of turmoil in the land of Montezuma and Cortes had come to an end in September, 1920, with a constitutional election. The time seemed ripe for resumption of diplomatic relations and settlement of the voluminous claims of American citizens against Mexico. Tedious and complicated negotiations were necessary, however, to secure a meeting of minds between the two governments.

The unprincipled confiscation of American properties under Carranza, in the face of his explicit assurances to the Wilson Administration, had brought demands for armed intervention after the Armistice of 1918. But the Mexicans themselves had overthrown and assassinated Carranza. With General Obregón's claims to power confirmed by the election of 1920, Hughes felt that a steadying hand was the first essential in dealing with Mexico. He sought a treaty guaranteeing the protection of American interests [2]—a treaty of amity and commerce to be signed coincidental with the resumption of diplomatic relations. In expounding his Mexican policy on June 7, 1921, he said:

> The fundamental question which confronts the Government of the United States in considering its relations with Mexico is the safeguarding of property rights against confiscation. . . . Whenever Mexico is ready to give assurance that she will perform her fundamental obligation in the protection both of persons and of rights of property validly acquired, there will be no obstacles to the most advantageous relations between the two peoples.

But Obregón continued to angle for recognition with no strings attached. When he got around to making counterproposals on a wholly different basis, Hughes declined to consider them and asked for a statement of objections to his proposed treaty. The result was a complete impasse. Again the Secretary outlined his policy—a somewhat softened policy—in a speech before a mass meeting in Boston's Symphony Hall on October 30, 1922:

> Our feeling towards the Mexican people is one of entire friendliness and we deeply regret the necessity for the absence of diplomatic relations. We have no desire to interfere in the internal concerns of Mexico. We do, however, maintain one clear principle which lies at the foundation of international intercourse. When a nation has invited intercourse with other nations, has established laws under which investments have been lawfully made, contracts entered into and property rights acquired by citizens of other jurisdictions, it is an essential condition of international intercourse that international obligations shall be met and that there shall be no resort to confiscation and repudiation. We are not insistent on the form of any particular assurance to American citizens against confiscation, but we desire in the light of the experience of recent years the substance of such protection, and this is manifestly in the interest of permanent friendly relations. . . . The problem is a very simple one and its solution is wholly within Mexico's keeping.

Under the constitution of 1917, Mexico had broken up her large landed estates and permitted villages to regain or to acquire communal lands. She had also nationalized subsoil deposits, including petroleum, thus claiming valuable property which, under previous Mexican laws, the owners of the surface rights believed to be theirs. Many Americans, including the oil interests, had suffered severely under these expropriation and nationalization programs. In 1921 the Mexican Supreme Court handed down five decisions reassuring pre-1917 owners against any retroactive application of the nationalization laws,[3] but the government was extremely reluctant to make the amends that these judgments demanded.

[2] CEH, Notes, p. 322.
[3] S. F. Bemis, *The Latin American Policy of the United States*, p. 215.

Secretary Hughes was in sympathy with the fundamental policy of the Mexican law, which was to break up the big estates and to curb exploitation. What he objected to was the confiscation of property owned by Americans as a means of carrying out this policy. There was no suggestion in his attitude that Mexico should change her constitution to please the United States. All he asked was that she respect her own laws in dealing with United States citizens.

An intermediary finally suggested the appointment of commissioners to talk over the problems between the two governments. Hughes induced the President to name Charles Beecher Warren, former ambassador to Japan, and Judge John Barton Payne, former Secretary of the Interior, and they went to Mexico City in the spring of 1923 with instructions to seek (1) restoration or payment for lands taken from American owners prior to May 1, 1917; (2) assurances against confiscation of subsoil interests in lands owned by Americans prior to the same date; and (3) an appropriate claims convention. Ultimately Mexico agreed to respect the rights of American surface owners or lessees to subsoil privileges where some positive act had been performed prior to promulgation of the 1917 constitution and to grant certain preferential rights to landowners and lessees who had failed to perform such positive acts. It was a compromise that Hughes believed to be fair to both countries.

There was no difficulty in reaching an agreement that all the agrarian lands expropriated by Mexico should be paid for at their fair value. The claims of American citizens arising out of Mexico's ten years of revolutions were to be adjudicated before a commission under a Special Claims Convention, and a broader category of claims by the citizens of both countries was to be heard by a second commission. Both governments were to be represented on each commission, with a neutral presiding commissioner to be selected, if possible, by mutual agreement. Hughes had given way on many details, but underneath his policy of friendly conciliation the hard core of principle had been preserved intact. Mexico had acknowledged her international obligations. The Colossus of the North had demanded, not a pound of flesh or even a reservoir of oil, but only a common variety of justice that was everywhere recognized in international law.

Hughes derived great satisfaction out of this liquidation of the chronic feud across the Rio Grande. When General de la Huerta sought to fan the embers of revolution on the eve of the election that brought President Calles to power, Hughes responded to the plea of the Mexican authorities for arms and munitions to put down the rebellion. His object was to help a neighbor maintain its own constitutional processes. Huerta's movement was not instinct with the aspirations of an oppressed people, he said, but with personal politics.[4]

[4] *Our Relations to the Nations of the Western Hemisphere*, pp. 52f.

The work of the claims commissions was disappointing to the United States. The State Department magnanimously accepted a Panamanian umpire for the general commission and a Brazilian for the special commission. The United States finally accepted a lump sum amounting to only 2.64 per cent of its original claims before the special commission. In 1941 the claims before the general commission (other than petroleum expropriations) were similarly settled for a lump sum of $40,000,000. Mexico's big neighbor had tempered justice with extreme leniency. Faith and charity had triumphed over dictation and punitive expeditions. Losses were unquestionably suffered, but they ultimately became an investment in good feeling throughout the Western Hemisphere.

Being a realist, Secretary Hughes did not rely wholly upon peace machinery and expressions of good will. The best way of preventing war in the American family of nations was to heal the festering sores that spread the infection. Accordingly, he devoted himself to all manner of prophylaxis intended to promote a healthy international environment.

These activities extended to Canada as well as to Latin America. In 1923 he suggested the creation of an American-Canadian commission to be composed of an equal number of distinguished citizens from each country who would examine and report the facts underlying any question that might arise between them. His thought was that each country would be kept so well informed about the problems and sensibilities of the other that the infliction of unnecessary injuries or indignities could be avoided.

In Latin America he repeatedly minimized friction by thwarting the schemes of Americans who were trying to exploit or bully their less sophisticated neighbors. His influence was used, for example, to curb the Army's high-handed dealings with the natives of Panama. Thirty-six protests against the conduct of United States officials in the Canal Zone were sent to the State Department by the Panamanian Legation. Hughes asked Francis White, chief of the Latin American Division, to summarize these cases and suggest what should be done. White did so with fine regard for the department's policy of equal justice to all men and all countries. The Secretary allowed himself only fifteen minutes to read White's seventy-two page report before the Panamanian minister called. Yet he discussed each case with amazing familiarity with the details and agreed to satisfactory adjustments.[5]

Governor Jay J. Morrow of the Canal Zone, who seemed to be the antithesis of his brother Dwight, rushed to Washington to protest against the new policy of treating Panamanians as if they were human beings. The State Department, he told its chief, did not understand the Latin Americans. The only way to

[5] Author's interview with Francis White, April 22, 1949.

deal with them, he said, with the air of an old experienced hand, was to hit them between the eyes. Hughes froze the Governor with a glance, and told him flatly that hitting between the eyes was not the policy of the United States and was not going to be.

A well known Congressman came to the department with a financial scheme that he hoped to impose on Honduras. White threw cold water on it when he discovered that it would yield a million dollars in profits to its promoters. In a huff, the Congressman said he would go straight to the Secretary. Hughes gave the legislator a chance to present his plan a few days later and told him candidly, "I do not think it will bear examination." The Congressman sputtered that of course the details could be changed, but Hughes only repeated his firm conclusion.

The Secretary was eager to see American capital and American experts honestly at work developing the resources of neighboring countries. "This sort of 'economic penetration,'" he said, "may be regarded as the highest expression, from the material standpoint, of international confidence and good will." [6] Yet his awareness of dangers in the flood of Latin American bond issues that international bankers were unloosing upon investors in the United States led to the adoption of a precautionary policy. Hughes could not attempt, of course, to ascertain the economic soundness of these loans. All he could do was to prevent them from being used to thwart American foreign policy. Especially ominous was the prospect of bond issues being floated in the United States to finance revolutions or other militaristic ventures in Latin America. Called into conference at the White House, the investment bankers agreed not to sell foreign bonds to the American public without giving the State Department full information about each issue and an opportunity to raise objections.

When misunderstandings arose as to what this policy involved, the department issued a press release emphatically disavowing any attempt to pass on the soundness of any bond issue, directly or indirectly. Bankers were instructed that no prospectus or contract should in any way refer to the attitude of the Government toward any proposed issue. Salesmen nevertheless managed to convey, in some instances, an impression that the Government had endorsed the foreign issues they were peddling to gullible investors, and the department's policy was severely criticized, especially when the depression of the thirties left many of the bonds in hopeless default.

The outcome was certainly lamentable, but the department took the only course open to it at the time. It could not have permitted international bankers to thwart its policies in dealing with other countries for want of information as to what those policies were. Subsequent Administrations did not abandon but further tightened controls over foreign financing in the United States and set

[6] *Our Relations to the Nations of the Western Hemisphere*, p. 58.

up the Securities and Exchange Commission to compel the registration of all securities offered for sale to the public.

After Hughes settled the conflicting territorial claims of Panama and Costa Rica, many countries vexed by unsolved boundary disputes knocked at his door. According to Sumner Welles, the United States' efforts in this sphere were "singularly successful so long as Mr. Hughes was Secretary of State." [7]

In the case of the dispute between Colombia and Panama, the Secretary's contribution was merely a suggestion that the two countries undertake direct negotiations, which proved to be successful. At the request of Brazil, Colombia, and Peru he made a detailed study of their three-way boundary dispute and offered his final recommendations at five o'clock on his last day in office as Secretary of State. Brazil had brought the controversy to a head by protesting to Peru against the latter's ratification of the Colombia-Peru boundary treaty of 1922. Hughes suggested that the protest be withdrawn and that ratification of the treaty be completed. The third step he recommended was a convention between Brazil and Colombia accepting the Apaporis-Tabatinga line, with Brazil granting Colombia perpetual freedom of navigation on the Amazon and other rivers common to both countries. Within two hours an agreement on this basis was closed. According to Dr. Rowe, the settlement brought "universal joy" throughout Latin America.

Far more troublesome was the dispute between Chile and Peru over the desert provinces of Tacna and Arica. This feud had hung like a dark cloud over Latin America for forty years. However, both countries appeared to be in a mood of welcoming the good offices of the United States, and after sounding them out Hughes invited them to send representatives to confer in Washington in the spring of 1922. Secretary and Mrs. Hughes gave the delegates a brilliant reception on May 12 with more than a thousand guests present. A few days later the conference opened in the Hall of the Americas before a distinguished gathering of notables. Hughes was doing his utmost to provide a favorable atmosphere. "The only relief for a troubled world," he told the opening session, "is in resort to the processes of reason in lieu of those of force."

The idea behind bringing the Peruvian and Chilean delegates to Washington was that they might be able to agree upon certain points to be submitted to arbitration. At the close of the war between Chile and Peru in 1883, the disputed territory had been held by Chile. Their peace treaty, the Treaty of Ancón, had provided that after ten years there should be a plebiscite to decide whether these provinces should "remain definitely under the dominion and sovereignty of Chile," or should continue "to constitute a part of Peru." No such plebiscite had been held, and this fact had become the center of the acrimonious controversy. Asserting that 80 per cent of the population of the district was Peru-

[7] *Naboth's Vineyard* (London, Payson & Clarke, Ltd., 1928), p. 934.

vian in 1894 when the vote should have been taken, Peru charged that Chile had willfully obstructed the plebiscite until she could transplant enough Chileans to constitute a majority.[8]

Hughes worked indefatigably to narrow the area of disagreement. Patiently he argued the Chileans into acceptance of arbitration on the question of whether a plebiscite should be held. At the same time he persuaded Peru to give up her demand that the arbitrator proceed to decide the future status of Tacna and Arica if settlement by plebiscite should be discarded. At last both countries accepted the Hughes formula and, on July 20, 1922, signed a protocol of arbitration.

They had proceeded on the assumption that the President of the United States would be the arbitrator. Hughes had attempted to discourage this, suggesting instead an independent jurist, such as Elihu Root, or a board of jurists. Both sides refused to budge, however, because it was clear that if the President were named, the actual task of arbitration would fall on Hughes. The Secretary yielded because his refusal would have upset what seemed to be the only possible basis for agreement. In a showdown he always sacrificed his own personal wishes to pressing public duty.

Hughes named William C. Dennis to aid him, and they examined enormous volumes of historical data and arguments submitted by Chile and Peru. The first question that had to be decided was whether a plebiscite should be held. Hughes' answer was Yes. The Treaty of Ancón provided that the people of Tacna and Arica should decide their own destiny in a plebiscite to be held "*after* the expiration" of ten years. No time limit had been fixed. Failure of the parties to agree upon the terms of the plebiscite could not, therefore, be regarded as a breach of the treaty.

His second task was to prescribe conditions under which the plebiscite should be held. He laid down detailed rules as to who would be entitled to vote and called for supervision of the balloting by a Plebiscitary Commission consisting of one representative from Chile, one from Peru, and a chairman to be named by the President of the United States. Hughes had explored the idea of using American troops to supervise the balloting but dropped it because of his belief that Congress would not agree and because Chile had insisted, as a condition to her acceptance of the arbitral agreement, that she should retain administrative control over the territory until the dispute could be settled.[9]

As the Secretary's award was submitted on his last day in office, the Plebiscitary Commission, at first headed by General Pershing, functioned without his supervision. But in any case its task was hopeless. Peruvian sympathizers in Tacna and Arica were intimidated; some were forcibly deported as the date

[8] *Arbitration Between Peru and Chile,* "The Case of Peru," I, 206–251.
[9] CEH, Notes, p. 334.

for the voting approached. After postponing the plebiscite several times, the commission decided that no impartial expression of the will of the people in the disputed territory could be obtained, and the effort was abandoned. The effect of Hughes' arbitration was nevertheless to break the legal impasse that had prevented agreement. By establishing the fact that the plebiscite section of the Treaty of Ancón was still valid, he had proved to the parties that further direct negotiations would have to be undertaken to obtain a settlement. His formula, which Chile and Peru had accepted in 1922, foresightedly called for continued negotiations under the good offices of the United States if the other steps undertaken should fail, and such negotiations went forward in Washington. Although he was again practicing law in New York, Hughes kept closely in touch with these negotiations, and repeatedly advised with the department through correspondence and personal visits.

The settlement that was finally achieved in 1929 gave Peru the northern province of Tacna, where most of her lost citizens lived, and Chile retained Arica, the southern province to which many Chileans had migrated. Neither contender was reduced to bitterness or frustration. Of course, no such solution had been open to Hughes in his role as arbitrator. His duty lay in fair interpretation of a treaty rather than formulation of a new policy, but the background of good will he created and his later advice contributed enormously to the final elimination of the Tacna-Arica tinder box.

Still another boundary dispute was pressed upon Hughes after he had returned to the bench. Guatemala and Honduras had negotiated for six months without agreeing upon an arbitration formula, although both said that if such a formula could be found only one arbitrator—Hughes—would be acceptable. Francis White suggested that they leave to Hughes the points they could not agree upon, and both assented. Their century-old controversy was thus submitted in 1930 to a Special Boundary Tribunal consisting of the Chief Justice of the United States as president and two distinguished Latin American jurists—Dr. Luis Castro Ureña of Costa Rica and Dr. Emilio Bello Codesido of Chile. Burdened though he was by the work of the Supreme Court, Hughes decided that he should accept the appointment in the interests of eliminating another source of international friction.

The tribunal's first decision was that it should sit, not as the International Central American Tribunal, but as a special boundary tribunal. Since it was impossible to find the line specified in the treaty between Guatemala and Honduras in some parts of the area in dispute, Hughes and his colleagues fixed a new line following natural boundaries in so far as they were consistent with settlement of the territory, actual possession, and other equities. Aerial photographs were used for the first time in a case of this sort, and the new line was drawn on detailed maps so as to leave no question whatever as to its location.

It was a line of convenience and common sense which proved satisfactory to both countries and brought an exchange of friendly notes between them.

Hughes' great interest in the settlement of international disputes of a juridical character led him to work for a hemispheric arbitration system. At the Havana Conference in 1928 he helped to commit the American republics to a policy of obligatory arbitration. The next step toward transforming this pledge into international law was taken at the special Pan American Conference on Conciliation and Arbitration at Washington in the winter of 1928–1929. Secretary Kellogg was nominally head of the American delegation, but Hughes wielded the "laboring oar." His problem was complicated by the fact that the Senate, over a long period of years, had consistently rejected every arbitration treaty that did not make allowance for Senate approval of each separate case to be submitted to arbitration. Reviewing this disheartening history with Coolidge and Kellogg, Hughes said that he was not willing to go through the farce of drafting a convention that would merely pledge us to arbitrate when and if two-thirds of the Senate might feel so disposed after a dispute had arisen. If the Senate's attitude in the past had to be accepted as final, he hinted, he would not serve as a delegate.[10] The upshot was complete agreement on the part of the President, the Secretary of State, and Hughes to fight for arbitration without senatorial apron strings attached.

In the arbitration section of the conference the chief question was whether the general principle of arbitration, to which all were devoted, would be riddled by exceptions. The parties finally agreed to arbitrate all international differences of a justiciable nature that could not be settled by diplomacy. Specifically included were disputes over (*a*) the interpretation of a treaty; (*b*) any question of international law; (*c*) the nature and extent of the reparation to be made for any breach of an international obligation. Only two classes of controversies were excepted from the obligation to arbitrate: (*a*) those within the domestic jurisdiction of any of the parties and not controlled by international law; and (*b*) "those which affect the interest or refer to the action of a State not a Party to this treaty." [11] This latter exception was Hughes' language designed to protect the Monroe Doctrine.

In case the disputants could not agree on the tribunal to handle a specific dispute, the treaty provided that each should designate two judges and they should select a fifth presiding judge or leave the choice to two judges of the Permanent Court of Arbitration at The Hague. It was a long plunge toward acceptance of obligatory arbitration of all justiciable disputes. Especially notable was the absence of any provision for senatorial domination of the procedure, but this was also an Achilles' heel. The Senate let the treaty gather dust for six years and then riddled it by a reservation requiring senatorial approval

[10] Beerits' Memorandum, XVIII, 42.

[11] *Foreign Relations, 1929,* II, 659–663.

of each separate agreement. All but five of the Latin American countries put the treaty into effect, although with many reservations.

As to conciliation, the conference decided to build upon the Gondra Convention that had been worked out at Santiago in 1923. The Gondra commissions of inquiry set up in Washington and Montevideo were now authorized to act also in a conciliatory capacity. They were to take up any controversy between the parties that could not be settled through diplomatic channels, and to propose a basis of equitable settlement within six months if no prior settlement had been reached. This treaty was ratified by the Senate.

Except for his work on the Guatemala-Honduras boundary tribunal, this was Hughes' final contribution to the cause of a peaceful Western Hemisphere. For nearly a decade the business of living amicably with our neighbors had claimed a large share of his time and interest. No one can examine the soil in which the good-neighbor policy is rooted without being struck by the quality and extent of Hughes' contribution to it. His evacuation of troops from two of the occupied countries and his patience in restoring good relations with Mexico provided the essential ingredient of mutual trust. His settlement of boundary disputes removed sources of friction in several different areas. His clarification of the Monroe Doctrine afforded a philosophical climate in which the new Pan Americanism could flourish. And the specific improvements he made in the means of peacefully settling disputes nourished the belief that justice could be substituted for wars within the American continents.

Chapter 53

THE HAVANA CONFERENCE

SECRETARY HUGHES looked upon the quinquennial Pan American conferences chiefly as friendship festivals. They were more significant for the interchange of ideas, for the promotion of understanding, and for extension of cultural and commercial relations than for any formal treaties that might evolve out of them. Men had to learn to work together and to discuss their differences dispassionately before they could devise means of settling all the major disputes among themselves. The warp of confidence and the woof of law had not yet been woven into the fabric of hemispheric solidarity.

Originally Hughes intended to go to the Fifth International Conference of American states at Santiago in 1923 as chief of the American delegation. An avalanche of work and a stubborn case of grippe changed his mind. Henry P. Fletcher was brought back from his ambassadorial post in Belgium to head the delegation. The Secretary had to be content with sounding the keynote in a message read by Fletcher. Two facts about the conference stand out. First, it set up a commission of jurists to codify international law. Second, it adopted the Gondra Convention, a "cooling-off" arrangement designed to assure both ample time and expert assistance for the settlement of international disputes. Hughes praised the treaty as an "entirely practical" attempt to assure the maintenance of peace in this hemisphere, and the Senate gave its consent.

It was five years later that Hughes, then a private citizen, singlehandedly bent a Pan American Conference to his will. At the request of President Coolidge he headed the United States' delegation to the Sixth International Conference of American States at Havana. Among the actors in this hemispheric drama who disembarked from the U.S.S. *Texas* one brilliant Sunday morning in Cuba's springtime of 1928 were President Coolidge, Secretary of State Kellogg, Hughes, Ambassadors Fletcher and Morrow, former Senator Underwood, Ray Lyman Wilbur, James Brown Scott, former Justice Morgan Joseph O'Brien, and Leo S. Rowe, director general of the Pan American Union. At the dock the visitors were greeted by President Machado, and two hundred thousand spectators cheered them as they passed through beautiful Malecon Drive to the Presidential Palace.

On the morning of January 16 the delegates assembled in the National Theater to hear the opening speeches of Presidents Coolidge and Machado.

Two days later the first plenary session was held in the Magna Aula, or Great Hall, of the University of Havana—a chamber of awesome dimensions as well as rich decorations. This was the organization meeting. Hughes was assigned to the Committees on the Pan American Union and Public International Law.

In spite of the warm welcome, a good deal of tension hung over Havana. For the first time the Latin American republics were ready to challenge the "Colossus of the North" on real live issues, and the issue that arose most persistently was nothing less than the United States' interventions in the Caribbean area. Smarting under the restrictions the United States had imposed on the importation of Argentine beef in order to keep out the foot-and-mouth disease, the Buenos Aires government was especially eager to exploit the mounting resentment against "Yankee imperialism." Forebodings of a clash could be seen in every gesture of the Argentines.

The outlook for trouble was doubtless one strong reason for the appointment of Hughes, who had an enviable reputation for successful dealing with the Latin Americans. The State Department made no bones about handing him a hot potato. In a "Special Political Memorandum" the department directed attention to the "vigorous anti-American propaganda" that had swept through Latin America during the previous year and warned that "certain delegates" might attack the policies the United States had been following. The most prominent instruction to Hughes and his fellow delegates was to strive to keep off the agenda all controversial subjects not already there and to resist the doctrine of absolute nonintervention.

Fully aware of the explosive possibilities, Hughes had accepted the assignment with misgivings.[1] Some feared that, under his negative instructions, he could do little more than "sit on the lid." Mistrusting suppression, however, he himself brought the intervention issue out into the open and faced it squarely. His opportunity came at the dinner given in honor of the delegation by the American Chamber of Commerce of Cuba on January 21. His theme was the same as it had been at Rio six years before:

> It is the firm policy of the United States to respect the territorial integrity of the American Republics. We have no policy of aggression. . . . We do not wish their territory. . . . Nothing could be happier for the United States than that all the countries in the region of the Caribbean should be strong, self-sufficient, fulfilling their destiny, settling their problems, with peace at home and the fulfillment of their obligations abroad.

The delegates who had counted on pussyfooting from the United States were routed. A dispatch from Mexico City pronounced the speech the "finest expression of the American position that had been given in a quarter of a cen-

[1] CEH, Notes, p. 337.

tury," and the Nicaraguan delegate said that it "ought to convince our critics of the justice of the United States' efforts to establish peace in Nicaragua." [2] Argentina continued her baiting, but the Havana atmosphere had been cleared, and the conference went ahead with candid discussion of its numerous projects.

Social events lightened the delegates' labors. Will Rogers once told a New York theater audience how he and Mrs. Rogers, having invited Mr. and Mrs. Hughes and other guests to dinner in their Havana hotel suite, had debated whether "to serve or not to serve." Prohibition was still the law in the United States. Finally they put the cocktails off to one side where they would not be conspicuous. "When Mr. Hughes came in," Rogers said in his inimitable drawl, "he took one glance at the refreshments, parted his beard, drank a cocktail, and the party was a success."

Several radical reforms in the Pan American Union were urged as a means of goading the "Colossus of the North." Mexico contended that the chairmanship and the office of director general should be filled by rotation among the member countries in alphabetical order. And she wanted the governing board composed of special representatives who would not be subjected to the subtle influences that were supposed to sway Latin American ambassadors in Washington.

Instead of fighting these proposals, Hughes expressed entire sympathy with the idea of equalizing rights and privileges in the organization. The United States, he said, wished only to be a "co-worker and colleague, a true comrade." Without making any direct suggestions, he pointed out, however, the great advantage of leaving each country free to decide for itself how its representative in the union should be chosen. Either an ambassador or a special representative would act only under instructions from his government. Special agents would mean extra expense and the risk of divided counsel without in any way changing the nature of the Pan American Union. Responding to this logic, the delegates refused to rule ambassadors off the governing board, and the suggestion for rotation in the office of the director general was withdrawn.

The American delegation heartily supported the Mexicans' proposal that the Pan American Union should not "exercise functions of a political character." But Dr. Honorio Pueyrredón, head of the Argentine delegation, fought stubbornly to write into the preamble of the Pan American Union Convention a denunciation of international trade barriers. While Hughes sat silent, many Latin American delegates rose in committee to plead with Pueyrredón to abandon his intransigence. It was Argentina that was isolated. "The United States found itself in the Latin-American family," as William Hard wrote, "arguing against the stubbornness of what might be called the Colossus of the South." For Hughes did have his say before the controversy was over. "Let us

[2] *New York Times*, Jan. 23, 1928.

not destroy the Union," he declared, "by attempting to make it a tariff commission." [3] When the vote came, Dr. Pueyrredón stood utterly alone. The conference then went on to adopt, in the form of a convention, a sort of constitution for the Pan American Union. While the field in which it could operate was delimited in keeping with the nature of the organization, the union was placed on a firmer basis than ever before.

In spite of his reluctance to get out in front, Hughes emerged as the guiding spirit of the conference long before its dramatic close. Mark Sullivan's "confidential scout" at Havana wrote him:

> Hughes is walking away with the conference. In courtesy he out-Latins the Latins. There are only two or three first rate intellects among the delegates and Hughes looms head and shoulders above the best of them. In committee meetings the Latins tie themselves into knots from which escape seems impossible, and then Hughes gets up and in ten words unravels the tangle. He has the knack of remembering names and when he makes a flowery allusion to Senor So-and-So, he completely disarms hostility. From the tributes I have heard I am beginning to sympathize with Mr. Hilles' wish to "draft him" [for the presidential nomination in 1928].[4]

While he made use of Latin techniques, he was not swept away by them. In one of the sessions a speaker waxed eloquent in Spanish on the subject of Mr. Hughes himself. Sensing the trend of the remarks, Hughes said to his interpreter, "Don't bother to translate anything until he gets to *pero*"—meaning "but."

The standing of the American delegation was further strengthened by its vigorous support of a Mexican resolution denouncing aggression and pledging the American states to "employ all pacific means to settle conflicts which may arise between them." Hughes popped up with an endorsement so warm that he almost swept the semihostile Mexican delegates off their feet. "It is my happy privilege to say for the United States of America," he began, "that we would join most heartily in a declaration that there shall be no war of aggression in America." With visible emotion, Dr. Gonzales Roa, sponsor of the resolution, rose and bowed his acknowledgment while the audience thundered its approval.

The great event of the conference evolved out of a clash of national interests in the Committee on International Public Law. The committee had before it twelve projects for the codification of international law that had been submitted by the Commission of Jurists as a result of its meeting at Rio de Janeiro in 1927. Seven of these concerning the status of aliens, treaties, diplomatic agents, consuls, maritime neutrality, asylum, and the obligations of states in

[3] Proceedings of Committee No. 1, Feb. 13; Hughes Papers.
[4] Sullivan to CEH, Feb. 6, 1928.

the event of civil strife were adopted with little fuss and few modifications. Two others entitled "The Fundamental Bases of International Law" and "States—Existence, Equality, Recognition" threw the delegates into a fracas over the question of nonintervention.

On this subject the jurists at Rio had forsaken the prosaic task of codifying law already in existence in an effort to condemn the United States' action in Nicaragua. "No state," they had declared with misleading simplicity, "may intervene in the internal affairs of another." There had been no attempt to define "intervene" or "internal affairs," and both expressions were variously interpreted. It was a fragmentary and ambiguous pronouncement that satisfied some of the Latin American delegates but brought vigorous dissent from others.

Dr. Victor Maurtua of Peru, to whom this project had been referred as reporter for the Committee on International Public Law, discarded the oversimplified nonintervention gesture. Before attempting to codify the law, he said, the conference should define the fundamental principles on which the law was based. Dr. Maurtua offered in lieu of the Rio jurists' formula the Declaration of the Rights and Duties of States sponsored by the American Institute of International Law. It was the work of leading jurists of Latin America and the United States and had been endorsed by Hughes in 1923 when he was Secretary of State. It proclaimed the right of every nation to independence and freedom to develop itself "without interference or control from other states, provided that in so doing it does not interfere with or violate the rights of other states." [5] Recognized also was the right of every nation "to exercise exclusive jurisdiction over its territory, and all persons whether native or foreign found therein."

Hughes firmly supported Maurtua because he feared that "the balanced precepts of international law were . . . in danger of being forgotten in the zeal for a trumpet call in defense of the ideal of liberty to which we are all devoted." But they were in the minority. Gustavo Guerrero, chairman of the committee, insisted that the Rio jurists' nonintervention statement should be the basis of the committee's discussion. Delegates from thirteen states adhered to this view, with the notable exception of the Nicaraguans and the Cubans. To the latter "intervention" was a word of hope for oppressed peoples.

The sizzling controversy was referred to a subcommittee that met behind closed doors with Hughes in the chair. He labored mightily for agreement and at one point was said to have obtained unanimous approval of certain rights and duties of states, but when it came to phrasing the resolution Pueyrredón and Guerrero held out for complete nonintervention. Hughes told them he was there to codify international law, not to write up political theories and doc-

[5] American delegates' report, p. 14.

trines as law. While he was willing to condemn the domination of one country by another, he was not willing to cover up basic disagreements with loose phrases or to let Pueyrredón turn the conference into a propaganda siren.

When no agreement could be reached in the subcommittee, Pueyrredón finally shifted his position. At a banquet given in honor of Colonel Lindbergh, who had flown his *Spirit of St. Louis* to Havana in a gesture of good will, Pueyrredón told Maurtua that since there was no chance of reconciling the conflicting viewpoints, the issue should be postponed for another conference.[6] An informal discussion followed. Hughes and Raul Fernandes, of Brazil, also members of the subcommittee, were seated in the same group, but Hughes withheld his reply to Pueyrredón's proposal until he could consult with various other delegates. Having done so, he gave his consent the following morning on condition that Guerrero, chairman of the full committee, would agree. Pueyrredón talked with Guerrero, and as the committee assembled the latter came down to Hughes' chair and said he was willing to drop the jurists' proposal.[7] The committee then unanimously agreed that the whole subject of intervention should go over to the next Pan American Conference in 1933.

Frustrated by the failure of his general strategy and under pressure from his own government, Pueyrredón resigned both as delegate to the conference and as ambassador to the United States. At Montevideo, en route to Buenos Aires, he denied that he had fathered the move to postpone consideration of the intervention issue and said that the initiative had come exclusively from Hughes.[8] Later he contended that his suggestion had been to end discussion in the committee and carry the dispute to a plenary session of the conference then in being. This adroit misstatement enabled him to dodge criticism in Argentina, but there could have been no misunderstanding; his whole point in suggesting the postponement had been that the matter should not be further discussed because there was no prospect of unanimity. Hughes informed the State Department that "the action taken was precisely in accord with Pueyrredón's suggestion." Dr. Maurtua declared himself to be "absolutely in accord with Mr. Hughes' version,"[9] and their accounts were further sustained by Fernandes.[10]

The conference met for its last plenary session on February 18. The galleries of the Great Hall were packed with visitors and men of the press, although the conference seemed to have nothing more to offer than routine reports and addresses by dignitaries of the University of Havana. Late in the afternoon, however, the report of the Committee on Public International Law, with its

[6] Statement by Dr. Maurtua, June 19, 1928; Hughes Papers.
[7] Hughes to Francis White, May 14, 1928.
[8] Associated Press dispatch, April 12, 1928.
[9] Statement by Dr. Maurtua, June 19, 1928.
[10] Fernandes to Dr. Octavio Mangabeira, July 2, 1928.

proposal that the subject of nonintervention be left to the next Pan American Conference, brought the new chief delegate from Argentina, Dr. Laurentina Olascoaga, to his feet with an expression of regret that no agreement had been reached and a reaffirmation of his government's "irrevocable convictions" in this matter. The atmosphere of the Great Hall tensed as if a current of electricity had run through it. Delegates who had been drowsing sprang into action with the startled excitement of troops summoned from deep sleep to immediate battle.

The delegates from Haiti, Santo Domingo, Guatemala, and Colombia rose in rapid succession to record their hatred of intervention. Hughes and many others expressed regrets that a postponement had been necessary. A Guatemala delegate wanted to know why no agreement had been reached, which brought from Guerrero, the Foreign Minister of Salvador, the amazing reply that while the subcommittee had been divided apparently agreement now existed. If the conference were unanimous, as it appeared to be, he told the delegates, he could see no reason why the question of intervention should not be submitted to a vote. As a member both of the subcommittee and of the main committee that had explored the problem, he knew, of course, that no agreement could be attained. Apparently he was only airing his grievance; in any event, he offered no motion.

But Dr. Antonio Sanchez de Bustamente of Cuba, the chairman of the conference, apparently did not clearly understand the situation. To the surprise of the United States delegates, he asked Guerrero to draw up a formula of a general character. The Salvadorean then hastily jotted down a resolution ending with the previously discarded declaration: "No State has the right to intervene in the internal affairs of another." Its presentation to the conference brought thunderous applause from the galleries.

The debate was interrupted at this point by an invasion of the gorgeously gowned doctors of law, science, and philosophy from the University of Havana. While the professors spoke, however, the delegates whispered plans for renewal of the fight. Fernandes of Brazil and Olaya of Colombia came to Hughes and said that Guerrero was guilty of an intolerable breach of honor. Hughes replied that in spite of it he would not be placed in the position of trying to stop the discussion. He sent to Dr. Bustamente a request that he keep the conference in session under any and all circumstances "until this matter can be settled." [11]

When the debate broke out again, it raged more fiercely than before. Fernandes contended earnestly that there had been a misunderstanding—that while there was unanimous regret over the failure to reach an agreement there was no meeting of minds on the proposal now submitted for reconsideration. Spokesmen for Colombia, Costa Rica, Ecuador, and the Dominican Republic

[11] Author's interview with CEH, Dec. 3, 1946.

took the same view, but the effect was only to add fuel to the flames. Fiery speech followed fiery speech. One of the delegates, in denouncing the attackers, declared that they would take us back to life in the jungle—a red-flag phrase in Latin America. Hughes murmured, "Save us from our friends." Maurtua attacked Guerrero, and when Guerrero resorted to personal abuse in return an indignant Peruvian called him a "cheap watch salesman." Dr. Bustamente intervened to prevent the exchange from reaching a point where nothing but pistols for two would have been acceptable to wounded Latin American honor. For the galleries it was a Roman holiday. At last they seemed to have the Colossus of the North in a tight box where everyone could jab at him. Each hostile sally brought wild applause, while defenders of the United States were hissed. The anti-intervention faction appeared to be sweeping everything before it.

Hughes listened to the unrestrained abuse of his country in a state of rising agitation. He could see the achievements of the conference crumbling into rubble under the impact of this emotional temblor. The prestige of the United States appeared to be cracking dangerously. Could the impending disaster be averted? If the Guerrero faction had votes enough to pass the resolution, Hughes thought it would be better not to resist it. On the other hand, it would be a grave mistake to let this onslaught against the United States succeed if he had a fighting chance to prevent it. The strain on his discretion was terrific.

"I feel like Holmes when he was wounded at Antietam," Hughes whispered to Fletcher with a sigh that seemed to come from deep within him. "If I ever get out of this, I think I shall never love another country." [12]

Senator Underwood was pacing up and down the aisle saying, "Let me answer him." "No, Senator," Hughes replied; "I've got to deal with this myself." [13] As head of the delegation, he could not risk the appearance of having been put to rout.

At 8:00 P.M. the Great Hall was still ringing with the excited cries and applause of the noninterventionists. Every argument for the resolution had been made. Every epithet had been hurled. The Guerreristas were moving in for the kill. "The time has come," said the Costa Rican delegate to a companion, "for Mr. Hughes to speak." As a hush fell over the hall, he turned and saw that Hughes was already on his feet.

Over the years Hughes had learned patience and superb self-control. Now he demonstrated both. His rising was neither a moment too soon nor a moment tardy. Inside he was boiling with excitement and almost trembling with the awful realization of what hung upon his words. Never had he felt more keenly the responsibility of speaking for his country. Yet his appearance

[12] Author's interview with Henry P. Fletcher, Aug. 10, 1946.
[13] Author's interview with CEH, Dec. 3, 1946.

was that of easy self-command. It was the evening of a nerve-racking day, but he was as radiant as morning. "He was smiling. He glanced at the galleries with no anger, with no discontent, with no reproof. He stood erect, unembarrassed, wholly unapologetic, positively commanding, and yet utterly companionable. The effect was incredible. He dominated the hall by his mere rising." [14]

Necks were craned to see how the famous North American would react to the bludgeoning his country had taken. Ears were alerted to catch every word. Summoning the interpreter to his side, Hughes commanded, "Interpret sentence by sentence." It was too important to trust a translator's summary. Through all the resulting pauses he sustained the continuity and force of what he was saying. In the most direct and candid fashion he laid bare the details of the disagreement in the Committee on Public International Law and of the unanimous decision to postpone action until the next conference. Then he turned to an incisive analysis of United States policy:

> There is nothing to conceal. There are no hidden motives. . . . I merely recognized that this was a question which needed time and further study to resolve in principles which all could accept, and that was the view which I supposed that all my colleagues on the subcommittee, and on the full committee as well, entertained. I gladly acquiesced in their decision. Now what is the situation when we come to the actual facts of the case? There is no one here who does not have enjoyment in the free air of independence. My country was nurtured in the desire for independence. One hundred years ago we declared the policy that all the American republics should be recognized in their independence. We have given our arms and our blood for the independence of the American republics and are always ready to do so. We yield to none in the establishment of the ideal of sovereignty and independence for every one of the American republics from the greatest to the smallest.

Recalling his support of the Mexican antiaggression resolution, he hammered home the facts underlying the policy he had followed as Secretary of State:

> We do not wish the territory of any American republic. We do not wish to govern any American republic. We do not wish to intervene in the affairs of any American republic. We simply wish peace and order and stability and recognition of honest rights properly acquired so that this hemisphere may not only be the hemisphere of peace but the hemisphere of international justice.

After explaining the situation in Nicaragua, he continued:

> Now what is the real difficulty? Let us face the facts. The difficulty, if there is any, in any one of the American republics is not of any external aggression. It is an internal difficulty. . . .
>
> What are we to do when government breaks down and American citizens are in danger of their lives? Are we to stand by and see them butchered in the jungle [15]

[14] William Hard in New York *Herald Tribune*, Sept. 2, 1928.

[15] The phrase "butchered in the jungle" was modified in the official text, but Michael J. McDermott, who heard the speech, insists that this is the way Hughes spoke it.

because a government in circumstances which it cannot control and for which it may not be responsible can no longer afford reasonable protection? . . .

Now it is a principle of international law that in such a case a government is fully justified in taking action—I would call it interposition of a temporary character—for the purpose of protecting the lives and property of its nationals. I could say that that is not intervention. One can read in text books that that is not intervention. But if I should subscribe to a formula which others thought might prevent the action which a nation is entitled to take in these circumstances there might come later the charge of bad faith because of acceptance of a formula with one interpretation in my mind, while another interpretation of it is in the mind of those proposing the formula. So it was necessary to have a fair understanding.

Of course the United States cannot forgo its right to protect its citizens. . . . International law cannot be changed by the resolutions of this conference. The rights of nations remain, but nations have duties as well as rights . . . we cannot codify international law and ignore the duties of States by setting up the impossible reign of self-will without any recognition upon the part of a State of its obligations to its neighors. . . .

I have made this statement merely to avoid any possible misunderstanding. I am too proud of my country to stand before you as in any way suggesting a defense of aggression or of assault upon the sovereignty or independence of any State. I stand before you to tell you that we unite with you in the aspiration for complete sovereignty and the realization of complete independence. I stand here with you ready to cooperate in every way in establishing the ideals of justice by institutions in every land which will promote fairness of dealing between man and man and nation and nation.

I cannot sacrifice the rights of my country, but I will join with you in declaring the law. I will try to help you in coming to a just conclusion as to the law; but it must be the law of justice infused with the spirit which has given us from the days of Grotius this wonderful development of the law of nations by which we find ourselves bound.

As Hughes sat down, the galleries that had previously hissed the name of the United States gave way to a frenzy of admiration. Everyone seemed to realize that Guerrero's shoddy gesture had been beaten. A moment later Guerrero arose, and a hush once more fell over the Great Hall. In a voice that could scarcely be heard, he withdrew his resolution, saying that it was unnecessary to insist on a vote "since every resolution of the Conference to be valid must attain unanimity." [16] The reversal of his position, like the change in the temper of the audience, was complete. Hughes had routed an emotional tornado by the sheer force of his personality, the cutting edge of his logic, and the deep sincerity of his convictions.

It was ten-thirty o'clock that night when the delegates arrived at the dinner party given by the mayor of Havana. The Cubans had been leisurely waiting, and the festivities went forward with no apparent loss of the convivial spirit. Meanwhile the press and official circles in many lands fairly gurgled with

[16] Foreign Policy Association, Information Service, April 27, 1928, p. 72.

delight over Hughes' feat of snatching at least a show of harmony out of the very jaws of discord.

The *Springfield Republican* declared that the events at Havana "revealed once more to the American people in the person of Mr. Hughes their greatest living statesmen." "If Mr. Hughes' previous history had been by some black magic obliterated," commented the New York *Sun*, "the Havana speech alone would stamp him as one of the greatest Americans."[17] After the event had seasoned a few months, William Hard penned this panegyric: "If I live to be a hundred years old I shall never expect ever again to see anybody so great, so grand, so god-like, as was Mr. Hughes at Havana . . . an American statesman for the first time in our history had told to Latin America the truth and had received in return an ovation. Few equal triumphs of individual personality can be found written anywhere on the roll of recorded human time."[18]

In expressing his and the President's "deep sense of obligation," Secretary Kellogg wrote: "It is really an accomplishment of surpassing importance to the United States. . . . I have never seen the press so united and so enthusiastic." "I have heard you many times," observed the Costa Rican minister, "but never like this." A sheaf of letters from distinguished men was sprinkled with such glowing terms as "great accomplishment," "wonderful piece of work," "enthusiastic expressions," "wonderful impression," and "saved the conference from failure." President Coolidge wrote with typical conservatism:

> . . . you secured a decision on all questions on their merits, which left us nothing to fear. . . . It was a great service in creating understanding and friendly relations among the peoples of the western hemisphere.

Hughes himself went back to the practice of law with the feeling that he had never had a greater success in his life. As the years passed, he probably came to realize that his tour de force, much as it was admired, left a backwash of resentment among some Latin Americans. But he had saved the United States from humiliation and the conference from driving a wedge of ill will into the American community of nations. The conference at Montevideo in 1933 was to approve a Treaty on the Rights and Duties of States with a nonintervention provision, and at Buenos Aires three years later Secretary Hull would accept the doctrine of absolute nonintervention by any state acting alone. At that time, however, American troops were no longer in Haiti and Nicaragua and the Platt Amendment allowing intervention in Cuba had been abrogated. Hughes had prevented a premature plunge. His comments in his later years left no doubt, however, that he would have been happier about it if his Havana speech could have been devoted to hastening the end of interventions, as his persistent efforts as Secretary of State had been.

[17] April 11, 1928. [18] New York *Herald Tribune*, Sept. 2, 1928.

Chapter 54

THE HARDING TRAGEDY

REVERBERATIONS of scandal began to come out of the Harding Administration before it was two years old. Finding the President an amiable man and a lenient chief, the Ohio Gang established itself in the Little Green House on K Street and set up a lively traffic in everything from the protection of bootleggers to illegal concessions and appointments to office. Harry Daugherty, the crony who had wormed his way into the attorney generalship in order "to protect Harding from the crooks," was himself the center of an ugly tangle of rumors.

As Harding discovered one betrayal after another, he sought desperately to save his Administration from open scandal. Charles R. Forbes, the dashing playboy who had been a favorite at the White House while he mulcted the Veterans' Bureau, was sent to Europe with the understanding that he would resign. Twelve days after the Senate launched an investigation of the bureau, Forbes' closest assistant, Charles F. Cramer, the legal adviser, shot himself.[1] Less than three months later Jess Smith, simple, bumbling influence man, committed suicide in the apartment he shared with Daugherty. Harding was terribly shaken.

Between this aspect of the Harding régime and the State Department was a gulf that seemed as wide as the Atlantic. Secretary Hughes was not one of the President's cronies. He never attended the drinking parties on the second floor of the White House. Only once did he join Harding's poker circle—when cruising down the Potomac on the presidential yacht. Thoroughly preoccupied by his own bailiwick, he knew nothing of the corruption that was seeping into high places in the President's official family.

What did worry Hughes in the spring of 1923 was the President's failing health. Returning to his office after a few weeks of illness, Harding looked suddenly old and exhausted. His blood pressure, he confided to Hughes, was 175. "We have been worrying about Mrs. Harding," the Secretary commented to his wife that night, "but I think it is the President we should be more concerned about. No man can carry the burdens of the Presidency with a blood pressure of 175." [2]

[1] Mark Sullivan, *Our Times*, VI, 241.
[2] Author's interview with CEH, Dec. 10, 1946.

As friend after friend stooped to treachery, the President's appreciation of Hughes' steadfastness and complete loyalty seemed to be heightened. "If you find the associations incident to your official life agreeable and adding to your happiness," Harding wrote in one of his personal notes to the Secretary, "I shall never cease to rejoice that it was my fortune to call you to the high position which you are filling with such notable success."

In June, 1923, the President attempted to relieve his nervous exhaustion and deep brooding by going out to the country to "bloviate," as he expressed it. Weariness grew upon him as he stumped across the continent and then took a boat trip to Alaska. Returning to Seattle, he was seriously ill, and when he reached San Francisco the doctors put him to bed with pneumonia. A few days later, on the evening of August 2, apoplexy struck him down and plunged the whole nation into mourning.

Hughes' telephone tinkled ominously and persistently about midnight. A voice from the State Department informed him that the President was dead. Allen W. Dulles and a companion drove to the remote Macsfolly farm near Kensington, Maryland, where the Hughes family was spending the summer, and took the Secretary to the department. He talked unceasingly about Harding: the burden of the Presidency had killed him; Harding had been an admirable chief and had many fine qualities, but he could never deny a request from a friend. Hughes repeated the story that Harding himself had told in a flash of candor during an off-the-record talk to the National Press Club.

"Warren," his father had said to him, "it's a good thing you wasn't born a gal."

"Why?" Warren had asked.

"Because you'd be in the family way all the time. You can't say No."

News of Harding's death was carried to Calvin Coolidge, the new President, at his father's farm at Plymouth, Vermont. Awakened by a telegraph messenger from Bridgewater, eleven miles away, Colonel John Coolidge toddled up the narrow stairs and aroused his son in a voice trembling with excitement. Coolidge read the message under a kerosene lamp. At 2:30 A.M.—thanks to the quick work of telephone linemen in tapping the trunk line at Plymouth Union—he was talking with Secretary Hughes, the highest official in Washington.

Hughes advised the new President (he insisted that Coolidge had become President the moment Harding died) to take the oath of office and come to Washington at once. Coolidge recalled that it was a special oath he must take. Hughes already had the Constitution at hand and dictated the oath to Coolidge's secretary.

"It should be taken before a notary," he reminded the President.

"Father is a notary," Coolidge quickly responded.

"That's fine," Hughes replied.[3]

While farmer John Coolidge administered the presidential oath to his son before eight persons in the combination living room and office of his quaint old home, Hughes notified members of the Cabinet and all the American ambassadors and ministers abroad. To Mrs. Harding he wired: "There are no words that can express the depth of our sympathy and grief. May God sustain and comfort you. . . ." To the press he said: "A quiet, brave, strong leader has fallen over-borne by the burden he was carrying." Between tasks Hughes paced the floor of his office, moody and depressed, talking volubly about Harding and Coolidge to anyone who might be on hand to listen. He was glad to have had the privilege of sitting in Cabinet meetings with Mr. Coolidge, he said, for he now realized that there was something back of the New Englander's impassive face.[4]

Harding's funeral train, crossing the country to Washington, brought in an emotional deluge. A few sordid rumors about scandal in high places had been whispered during the President's trip, but these were silenced by the tragedy. The people knew only that a kindly President of good intentions had broken under the strain of his exalted office. Many thousands, including the new President and members of the Cabinet, packed Union Station when the body arrived. The whole city was in mourning on August 8 when the President, the Chief Justice, the Cabinet, and even former President Wilson followed Harding's flag-draped casket from the White House to the Capitol for a brief ceremony under the great dome.

Officials then boarded the funeral train for Marion, where the fallen son of Ohio was to be buried. Hughes lay awake in his berth most of the night watching the crowds that lined the tracks and jammed the station of every town through which they passed. Again and again the pall of silence was broken by the strains of "Nearer, My God, to Thee" and other hymns. The nation's heart had been deeply touched.

On the return trip to Washington there was an unseemly scramble to get the new President's ear—a scramble in which Hughes did not participate. Under questioning by Chief Justice Taft, however, he did drop a bit of information that was of much interest to Coolidge. Under no circumstances would he (Hughes) run for the Presidency in 1924. Taft, who loved a little friendly gossip, hastened to pass the word along to the calm little Yankee who had inherited the Republican landslide.

What Hughes had said to Taft was merely a repetition of what he had been telling friends ever since 1916. With his prestige greatly enhanced by his work as Secretary of State, many were loath to give up the idea of seeing him some

[3] Author's interview with Allen W. Dulles, July 6, 1949.
[4] William R. Castle's diary, 1923, p. 121.

day in the White House, but his own convictions remained firm, as indicated by a letter to his former secretary at Albany, Robert H. Fuller:

> . . . of course you understand that nothing in the world could induce me, even if the question should come up, and it is not likely to come up, to consider a candidacy. I have had enough of that sort of thing and under no circumstances would I be drawn into such a venture again. I greatly admire Mr. Coolidge and I believe that he will impress the country as a man of rare ability.

Coolidge was eager to give the appearance of carrying on the Harding policies, but he quickly turned his back upon the playboys, the hangers-on, the grafters, and the poker cronies. To those who had played upon Harding's inability to say No, Coolidge seemed almost incapable of saying Yes. Visitors found so little advantage in an interview with the President that they were often content to see his secretary instead. When Hughes went to the Executive Office in the afternoons with important State Department business, he would find the President alone, smoking a cigar and reading his papers.[5] Order, simplicity, and quiet dignity were to be the watchwords of the new régime.

Coolidge asked all members of the Cabinet to carry on. Shortly after his accession, he summoned Hughes to the White House and told him that he was the backbone of the Administration and "the greatest Secretary of State this country ever had." [6] During the next two years Hughes acted as a sort of premier, being consulted on all the important issues relating to the welfare of the country. The two men got along admirably together. While it was difficult to get a quick response from Coolidge, once his answer was given after careful deliberation he was not likely to change it, as Harding sometimes had done.

Several members of the Cabinet thought Coolidge should get rid of Attorney General Daugherty because of his failure to prosecute cases of suspected corruption. Coolidge resisted out of loyalty to Harding. "Mr. President," Hughes said to him one day at the conclusion of an interview, "if it would be of any help to you, I think I could arrange to have all members of the Cabinet place their resignations in your hands; you could then reappoint those you wish to retain."

"No, don't do that," Coolidge called across the room as he was making a hasty exit. "It might leave me alone with Daugherty!" [7]

The Senate's exposé of the oil scandals began in the autumn of 1923. At first Albert B. Fall's bold and aggressive defense of his oil leases seemed to undermine the extravagant charges that the newspapers were making. Fall had resigned as Secretary of the Interior some months before Harding's death. Many thought he was a victim of smearing. Both Coolidge and Taft suspected

[5] CEH, Notes, p. 253*b*. [6] Castle's diary, 1924, p. 54. [7] CEH, Notes, p. 253*e*.

a Democratic-Progressive plot to discredit the Administration. As for Hughes, he found it difficult to believe that Harding, lenient as he had been with his cronies, would have permitted them to sway his judgment in any matter affecting the nation's vital interests. His conviction on this point had been strengthened by the fact that the President had once stood by him (Hughes) in rebuking Fall for a false statement that had offended a foreign government.[8]

As the months passed, the Senate's relentless investigator, Thomas J. Walsh, wove a web of circumstantial evidence about the looters. Congress had set aside rich oil-bearing lands as reserves under control of the Navy. To prevent these natural reservoirs from being drained by adjacent private wells, Congress had given the Secretary of the Navy authority to make leases on the reserves when and if, in his judgment, the best interests of the nation required such action. The accommodating and gullible Secretary Denby had yielded that responsibility to the Interior Department under Fall's blandishments, and Harding had innocently signed the transfer order. Avoiding competitive bids, Fall had proceeded to lease to Harry F. Sinclair the Teapot Dome, from which the latter expected to garner a cool $100,000,000 in profits, and to Edward L. Doheny the fabulously rich Elk Hills reserve in California. Then he had obtained a $100,000 loan from Doheny.

As the magnitude of the scandal became unmistakably apparent, Harlan F. Stone, future Chief Justice of the United States, urged Coolidge to appoint a special prosecutor for the oil-scandal cases and suggested Owen J. Roberts of Philadelphia. When his advice was sought, Hughes heartily seconded this suggestion, although he then knew Roberts only by reputation. Coolidge responded by naming two special prosecutors, Roberts and Atlee Pomerene, an able lawyer and former Democratic Senator from Ohio.

With the smell of unprosecuted crime growing ever stronger, Hughes renewed his efforts to get Harry Daugherty out of the Cabinet. He and Hoover went to the White House together and tried to stiffen the President's backbone in this matter.[9] Similar pressure was coming from Senator Burton K. Wheeler and Senator Borah, who pressed his charges in a dramatic showdown with Daugherty at the White House. Coolidge was slow to act, but at last when Daugherty refused to give the Senate investigating committee certain papers in his office the President demanded his resignation. Stone then became Attorney General.

While these events were unfolding, Hughes was writing the Harding memorial address to be delivered before a distinguished audience in the House of Representatives on February 24, 1924. Timid friends suggested to him that stories about to break might make it advisable to tone down his estimate of his

[8] Author's interview with CEH, Dec. 10, 1946.
[9] *Id.;* Herbert Hoover to author, March 14, 1949.

dead chief. He refused to change a word,[10] for in writing the speech he had drawn only upon his personal knowledge of Harding. Recounting the achievements of the Harding Administration, he gave a warm personal appraisal of his subject: "President Harding had no ossification of the heart. He literally wore himself out in the endeavor to be friendly." At the same time Hughes was gently candid about Harding's shortcomings. A president, he said, "is under strong temptation to endeavor to be all things to all men. . . . The presidency is a super-office, but nature imposing her limitations upon the greatest has supplied no super-men to fill it." [11] Harding had given his life in the service of his country. No man could give more.

The speech was a masterpiece of careful statement. "There was not a sentence I would have wished to change in your wonderful eulogy," wrote the grateful Mrs. Harding. "I have heard all the memorial addresses in the House of Representatives for twenty years," Chief Justice Taft commented to a friend, "and I do not hesitate to say that none surpassed his." "It is a hard thing not to overpraise or undervalue," wrote George Wharton Pepper. "But even Pericles would admit that you did neither." [12]

In the years that followed the Teapot Dome exposé, some who did not question Hughes' personal integrity nevertheless accused him of having sat silent while rich oil lands were turned over to the robber barons. Could it be that he was negligent or a quiet accessory to the crime? The first pertinent fact is that the oil leases were never discussed or acted upon by the Cabinet. The charge occasionally heard that Hughes was in the Cabinet meeting when jurisdiction over the naval oil reserves was transferred to Fall is plain falsification. Coolidge was a faithful attendant at the meetings of the Harding Cabinet, and he heard nothing about oil leases.[13] Hughes issued a statement on January 31, 1924, when the issue was before Congress, to the effect that the oil leases had never been brought before the Cabinet for decision and that his opinion as to their propriety or legality had never been sought. Secretaries Hoover and Weeks made similar declarations. All these denials were reiterated when the New York *Evening World* raised the issue in the Hoover-Smith campaign in 1928, and Hughes added emphatically: "I had nothing whatever to do with any of them [the oil leases], directly or indirectly, and I knew nothing whatever about them." [14]

The only way in which Hughes could have discovered Fall's perfidy would have been to turn aside from his own pressing duties and attempt to investigate a fellow Cabinet member. Such an investigation in itself, not being requested by the President, would have been an act of disloyalty to him. Only an incorrigible busybody would have launched such a venture, and Hughes was

[10] Henry L. Stoddard, *It Costs to Be President*, p. 80.
[11] *The Pathway of Peace*, p. 303.
[12] Letters in Hughes Papers.
[13] White House statement, Jan. 26, 1924.
[14] Speech at Brooklyn, Nov. 1, 1928.

the antithesis of a busybody. When it became his specific duty to investigate corruption, he would strip to nakedness every wrongful act within the purview of the inquiry; but he was astonishingly tolerant of misconduct toward which he bore no responsibility. He had, as Everett Colby has pointed out, "none of the average reformer's passion for regulating the private life of the individual." [15]

This characteristic in Hughes has intrigued many of his closest associates. It was not indifference to how the world wags, for he lent a hand to innumerable reform movements. Nor was it any laxity in his moral code; no man in public life in our time has held himself more rigorously to a high standard of conduct. Rather, it was a deep reluctance to judge his fellow men unless it became his official duty to do so. In his old age he said frankly that if he had known what the Ohio Gang was up to he would not have joined the Harding Cabinet. But under no circumstance would he prejudge the men whom Harding had trusted or intrude into affairs that were not his business.

Now that passions have cooled, it is impossible to see that the oil scandal reflected upon Hughes in the slightest degree. He was an actor in that sordid drama only to the extent of urging clean-up operations. The Coolidge Administration as a whole was astonishingly successful in lifting its skirts above the scandal. At times there seemed to be more oil in the 1924 campaign than in the Teapot Dome and Elk Hills combined, and it was not the kind of oil one pours on troubled waters. But the men who would have been vulnerable to that sort of attack were no longer in office. Fall, Denby, and Daugherty were gone. Daugherty was later to be tried twice for misconduct of his office (both juries disagreed), and Fall, Forbes, and Alien Property Custodian Thomas W. Miller were on their way to prison. The Republicans were vigorously cleaning house.

Hughes met the oil-scandal issue as temporary chairman of the New York Republican State Convention on April 15, the first time he had ever participated in a political convention. His candor and sense of proportion had much to do with turning the public mind away from oil toward the rising tide of national prosperity:

> Let it be understood that we do not condone wrong; we extenuate no crime. . . . We would bring to the bar of justice every dishonest official and every perverter of administration in or out of office. . . .
>
> Neither political party has a monopoly of virtue or of rascality. There are crooks in every community and in every party. Now and then, one gets into office. Let wrongs be exposed and punished, but let not partisan Pecksniffs affect a "holier than thou" attitude. The corrupting currency may be found in Democratic satchels. One who is corrupt is as faithless to his party as to his government. Guilt is personal and corruption knows no party.
>
> Today, counsel of eminent ability and unimpeachable integrity, selected from

[15] *Scribner's,* May, 1928, p. 564.

both the great parties by a Republican President, are taking appropriate legal proceedings by which all the questions which have been raised as to the leasing of the public domain will be threshed out, every public interest will be safeguarded and every guilty person punished. These cases are in the courts where they belong, and the courts will decide. It would be foolish, false and unpatriotic to breed distrust either of the integrity of the Government or of the soundness of American life. That would be to assail the honor of the hosts of officials devoting their lives with unselfish fidelity to the country's interests.

Although Hughes forbade his associates at the State Department to engage in politics, he himself became the right bower of Coolidge's campaign. According to Chief Justice Taft, Hughes' effort at Cincinnati was "far and away the best speech of the campaign." It was "as exceptional as the one you delivered for me in 1908," Taft insisted, "and . . . I verily believe it will be equally effective." [16] Hughes bore down upon both of Coolidge's opponents, John W. Davis and "Fighting Bob" La Follette, with more skill than he had employed in his own behalf in 1916. It was an easy Republican victory; the G.O.P. was riding the wave of postwar prosperity. Nevertheless, the voters who swelled the Coolidge landslide must have concluded that the Administration had successfully purged itself of the corruption it had inherited. In this they were right.

[16] Taft to CEH, Oct. 5, 1924.

Chapter 55

ECONOMIC POLICIES

PROSPERITY, in Secretary Hughes' credo, was an intimate companion to peace. Settlement of international differences without bloodshed undoubtedly came first. But men do not live on peace, and their best plans and intentions are likely to go sour unless their economic endeavors are reasonably successful. The economic well-being of the war-sick world thus commanded an enormous amount of Hughes' energy during the four years of his Secretaryship.

On his first survey of the United States' commercial policy he concluded that it ought to be revamped. Our treaty of commerce and navigation with Great Britain was more than a century old, and various other treaties were equally obsolete. New products, new trade practices, and new nations had come into being without any recognition in our commercial agreements. In pursuit of a comprehensive new policy Hughes induced the President to set up a committee of advisers from the State, Treasury, and Commerce departments. The model draft treaty worked out by these experts was first accepted by Germany.

There were four principal sections to the treaty. It threw numerous safeguards around the rights of the nationals of each party living in the territory of the other. It spelled out the rights, immunities, and status of consuls. It set up a nondiscriminatory shipping policy and committed the contracting parties to unconditional most-favored-nation treatment for the exports and imports passing between them.

The latter policy was revolutionary in its effect upon American foreign trade. The most-favored-nation clause in our treaties had theretofore been interpreted as being conditional; that is to say, a most-favored-nation treaty between the United States and France would not give France the advantage of a concession we might make to Belgium unless France should give us in return a concession equivalent to Belgium's. This traditional policy of exchanging favor for favor had led to much bickering and uncertainty and had hampered international trade with a network of special conditions. Equality of treatment had been retarded instead of being advanced.

Before writing the unconditional most-favored-nation principle into his model treaty, Hughes had taken the precaution of securing the approval of the President and of Senator Lodge, chairman of the Senate Foreign Relations Committee. When the treaty with Germany reached Lodge's committee, however, he ignored it. Thinking it unwise to begin negotiations with other countries until the Senate had made its position known, Hughes undertook to answer every argument raised against the treaty in a series of letters to Senator Lodge. The practice of granting special concessions for special concessions, he wrote, had upset the equilibrium of international trade. It did not in fact produce equality of treatment but merely afforded opportunity to bargain for such treatment. In defense of its own interests, moreover, the United States had become the champion of the principle of the open door in international commercial relations. Consistency with this principle demanded that we interpret the most-favored-nation clause unconditionally.[1]

When Lodge died in November, 1924, Hughes discovered that none of his communications on the treaty had been submitted to the Foreign Relations Committee. He renewed his campaign and got an invitation from Senator Borah, the new chairman, to argue his case before the committee on February 2, 1925. He did so in masterful fashion, covering every point in controversy so thoroughly and so convincingly that opposition crumbled.

The most vehement protest against the treaty had been directed at its provision for reciprocal national treatment, rather than most-favored-nation treatment, as to cargo, tonnage, harbor, pilotage, and quarantine charges imposed on shipping. The United States would be untrue to its own interests, one coterie of Senators said, if it should bind itself in fresh treaties not to discriminate in favor of its own shipping. Our idle vessels could be employed only by giving them a privileged status. To this Hughes replied that discrimination would beget discrimination. "We are constantly insisting upon equality of opportunity," he said, "and we cannot expect to be successful in removing discriminations against us when we think them injurious and at the same time insist on discriminations in our favor whenever we see fit." And since the maritime powers imported more from the United States than the United States imported from them, our own shipping would suffer most from any policy leaving the door open to favoritism by each country of its own ships.

The Senate as well as the committee saw the logic of Hughes' argument and a week later consented to ratification of the treaty, with a minor reservation. The Hughes policies as to both shipping and trade were consistently written into other commercial treaties after his resignation, and they are still in effect more than a quarter of a century later. When the Reciprocal Trade Agreements Act was passed in 1934, it specifically retained the unconditional most-favored-nation principle.

Under the stimulus of Hughes' driving energy, the American policy of the open door also underwent a significant evolution. We have seen that he used

[1] CEH to Lodge, March 13, 1924.

the Nine-Power Treaty to prop open the open door in China, and that he forced Japan to recognize our commercial rights in the Pacific mandates. Possibly more important was the part he played in giving American oil companies a stake in the petroleum reserves of the Near East.

Oil had become the object of intense international intrigue in the years following World War I. It was apparent that the next war would be fought with gasoline-driven machines and that the lands seized from the crumbling Ottoman Empire were among the world's richest petroleum storehouses. With Germany prostrate, the British had turned over to France the former German interests in the Turkish Petroleum Company, which claimed exclusive rights to exploit the vast oil deposits of Iraq. In short, an Anglo-French-Dutch monopoly had been created in a mandated area in which the United States had equal rights. Hughes was determined to break this monopoly.

While the British denied any intention of discriminating against American companies in the mandates of the Near East, they claimed that the oil fields of Iraq had been leased to the Turkish Petroleum Company before the war and that the lease was still valid. Secretary Colby had resisted this claim, and Hughes exploded it by showing that no valid lease had been made by Turkey. In 1914 the Grand Vizier of Turkey had given a vague concession to British, Dutch, and German interests, but they had not obtained the required approval of the parliament, and no effort had been made to exploit the concession. Hughes argued that monopolistic arrangements of this sort should not be tolerated in the mandated territories unless such prior rights could be established by convincing proof.[2]

In March, 1925, the British caved in and relinquished half their shares in the Turkish Petroleum Company to seven American companies. The Iraq Government, under British mandate, granted a concession to this expanded international concern—a tacit admission of the dubious character of the 1914 lease. The final settlement, which gave the American companies a 25 per cent share in the concession, was negotiated by the companies themselves, but it was Hughes' intervention in behalf of fair play that made the victory possible.[3] The importance of this outcome was amply demonstrated by the part that Near Eastern oil played in World War II and is playing in the mechanized economy of the present day.

The Secretary's adherence to the policy of equal opportunity was consistent even when it worked to the disadvantage of American companies. On one occasion the Latin American Division sent to his office a scheme to grant a concession to an American national in one of the Caribbean countries under our control. Hughes smelled monopoly and asked A. C. Millspaugh, the depart-

[2] *Foreign Relations, 1921*, II, 82–110.
[3] Author's interview with Allen W. Dulles, July 6, 1949.

ment's economic adviser, to review the proposal. Millspaugh confirmed the Secretary's suspicions that the scheme would have sanctioned in the Caribbean precisely what the department had protested against in the Near East. The concession was denied.[4]

When the Sinclair Oil Company complained that the department was not supporting its efforts to obtain an oil concession in Persia, Hughes outlined his policy in a letter to President Coolidge on November 8, 1923:

> From time to time there has been some dissatisfaction expressed in business circles because this Department's attitude towards American business interests in the foreign field differs somewhat from the attitude in similar matters of the British, French and other European governments. The latter are not loath to interfere politically in support of the business interests of their nationals to a degree which is not followed by this Department. Our position is that we are always ready to give appropriate support to our nationals in seeking opportunities for business enterprise abroad, but we do not undertake to make the government a party to the business negotiations or use political pressure for the benefit of private interests in order to obtain particular concessions, or intervene in favor of one American interest as against another. We are persistent in our efforts to maintain the open door policy, or equality of commercial opportunity, but we do not attempt to assume obligations for the government, expressed or implied, which under our system we could not undertake to discharge.
>
> American companies which might prefer a policy of more direct interference on their behalf by the government are inclined, in my opinion, to overlook the fact that American prestige and reputation for fairness has [*sic*] been enhanced, and consequently business opportunities of our nationals have been increased, by the correct policy which this government has followed. I find that in many parts of the world American business is welcomed largely because foreign countries realize that they can deal with American interests on a business basis without fearing political complications.[5]

Entangled with the Near Eastern oil problem was the larger question of the United States' relations with the new Turkish republic. The Allies had attempted to impose on Turkey an unconscionable peace treaty, the Treaty of Sèvres, depriving her of vast territories and reestablishing all the pre-1914 encroachments upon Turkey's right to control her own fiscal, economic, educational, and judicial affairs and even adding new concessions. Rallying under Mustapha Kemal Pasha in a furious nationalistic movement, the Turks had rejected the treaty, driven the Greeks out of Anatolia and Constantinople, the French from Cilicia, and the Italians from Konya. The war-weary Allies had brought about an armistice between the Turks and Greeks in October, 1922. Then followed the Lausanne conferences in which the United States was ably represented by Joseph C. Grew, the minister to Switzerland.

[4] A. C. Millspaugh to author, May 17, 1949.
[5] *Foreign Relations, 1923*, II, 717f.

Just before the first conference met in November, 1922, the British ambassador told Hughes that the Turks were preparing to expel the entire Christian population of Constantinople and asked that the United States join in an ultimatum to the Turks. Hughes replied that he was using his utmost influence to curb atrocities growing out of the Turks' extreme nationalism, but he would not attempt to pledge the United States to go to war. Only Congress could do that. The ambassador said he had suggested only a threat of war, and Hughes retorted gingerly that his government did not indulge in idle gestures and could not associate itself with imperial ambitions in the Near East.[6]

When the conference opened, Hughes' inability to protect the rights of the persecuted and decimated Armenians in Turkey left him in an embarrassing position. Before his appointment as Secretary of State, he had been the "principal supporting pillar" of the American Committee for the Independence of Armenia. Early in 1919 he and Lodge and others had appealed to President Wilson for a positive American policy of protecting the Armenians. The country had been aroused by the Turks' atrocities against this Christian minority during the war, and Hughes felt that if we were going to intervene in their behalf the time to do it was when we had a large army abroad and were able to carry out any policy adopted. When the problem fell into his own lap a few years later, the possibility of American military intervention no longer existed. Most of our troops had been brought home; the Armenians in the region that had once been thought of as an Armenian state had been practically exterminated; and the victorious Turks were ready to resume fighting at the drop of the hat for what they regarded as their sovereign rights. They would give no guarantee whatever as to Armenian minorities. Secretary Hughes thus found it necessary to abandon a cause that Citizen Hughes had earnestly fought for, and the Armenians in this country probably never forgave him for it.

The first Lausanne conference was a flat failure. Due in no small measure to the moderating influence of Hughes and Grew, the second conference succeeded in hammering out a peace treaty. The United States did not sign that pact but negotiated a separate treaty with the Turks reestablishing diplomatic relations on much the same basis that the European powers had accepted. The capitulations through which Turkey had been held in a sort of vassalage were abandoned in favor of very limited immunities for foreigners. American religious, educational, and philanthropic institutions existing in Turkey before 1914 were recognized, and equality of commercial opportunity and freedom of the Straits were guaranteed. For the most part, however, the victorious Turks succeeded in imposing their own terms upon the Western powers.

[6] *Foreign Relations, 1922*, II, 952ff.

The Secretary was not pleased with the treaty, but he knew that it was impossible to secure any better terms than the Allies had obtained, and he believed that our interests in the Near East would best be protected by resuming diplomatic relations with Turkey as quickly as the other powers did. Unlike Russia, Turkey was ready to meet her obligations as a member of the family of nations. There was ample reason for recognizing the new republic and for approval of the treaty, but the Senate finally rejected it in January, 1927.

Hughes strongly resented the charges in some newspapers that the State Department had been influenced in negotiation of the treaty by the oil concessions Turkey had given to a group of Americans headed by Admiral Colby Chester, retired. The department had nothing to do with securing the concession. It had been granted before the treaty negotiations began. Britain and France had raised a furor because the Chester concession was in conflict with their claims in the Mosul oil fields, but Hughes had resisted requests that he intervene. The Turks insisted that the Chester concession was valid and that it had been granted because the Americans did business on business principles without resorting to governmental pressures.

The impact of prohibition in the United States upon our foreign relations gave Hughes an especially baffling problem. One horn of the dilemma was the section of the National Prohibition Act forbidding foreign as well as American ships to carry intoxicating liquors into our ports or through our territorial waters. The other horn was the hovering of foreign-flag smuggling vessels just outside the three-mile limit within which our domestic law could be enforced.

American-owned vessels shifted to British registry were transporting vast quantities of forbidden intoxicants from the Bahama Islands to Florida ports. They often carried two sets of clearance papers—one indicating they were bound with liquor cargoes to Halifax, Tampico, or St. Pierre and the other indicating that they were proceeding "in ballast" to an American port. If caught with the liquor, the former papers were used; if they succeeded in disposing of their liquor before being searched, the latter papers were used. Small, fast boats from these rumrunners delivered liquor direct to the American shore. To break up this traffic, Hughes asked Great Britain to agree that the authorities of each country might search the vessels of the other at any point within twelve miles of the shoreline.

Meanwhile the prohibition zealots were insisting that the Government reach beyond the three-mile limit for rumrunners without waiting for the consent of other countries, and the Department of Justice seized a number of such vessels on the high seas. In the Tariff Act of 1922 Congress specifically authorized enforcement agents to board, search, and seize vessels beyond the three-mile limit. Hughes insisted, however, that rights on the high seas are controlled by international law rather than by domestic law. The United States had always contended that the sovereignty of other nations ended at the three-mile limit and had once paid damages under international arbitration for the seizure of a British sealing vessel in disregard of that limit. In a Cabinet meeting Hughes secured an understanding that in the future no foreign-flag ship would be molested beyond the three-mile limit unless it was sending intoxicants to shore by small boats or otherwise violating the law within our territorial waters. Enforcement agents nevertheless detained seven vessels captured beyond the three-mile limit. Hughes sharply reminded Attorney General Daugherty of the understanding in the Cabinet and expressed hope that the seven ships would be released.[7] A month later five of them had been returned to their owners.

The British turned a cold shoulder upon Hughes' suggestion of a treaty to aid the capture of rumrunners. Nor would they concede any right on the part of the United States to seize liquor boats found to be communicating with the shore for illegal purposes from beyond the three-mile limit. When the United States persisted in capturing such boats, Lord Curzon, the British Foreign Secretary, warned that it would create "a very serious situation." [8] Hughes cited a British precedent for seizures under similar conditions and held steadfastly to the policy he had announced.

The two governments exchanged hot words over the seizure of the *Henry I. Marshall*, until the British Foreign Office acknowledged that it was an American vessel improperly using the British flag. An American note, which Hughes referred to as a "sockdolager," then pressed London not to espouse the cause of any British ship similarly engaged in this unlawful liquor traffic. The Foreign Office did not reply.

The United States Supreme Court added heat to the controversy in April, 1923, by holding that, under the Volstead Act, foreign ships could not enter American harbors carrying liquor cargoes or ships' stores of intoxicants even if they were under seal.[9] Protests from all parts of the globe rained upon the State Department. The United States, the complaints said, was egregiously departing from international comity.

Of course Hughes accepted the court's decision as the law of the land, but he had previously complained that the Supreme Court's view of the Eighteenth Amendment was "unnecessarily rigid" and that it would result in "great harm to the interests of our commerce." [10] There was no sense in trying to impose prohibition on foreign ships. Racking his brain for some practical means of relieving international commerce of this unreasonable restriction, he concluded that the Eighteenth Amendment itself did not forbid ships to bring intoxicants

[7] *Foreign Relations, 1922,* I, 576f. [8] *Foreign Relations, 1923,* I, 164.
[9] *Cunard Steamship Co.* v. *Mellon,* 262 U.S. 100.
[10] CEH to Harry M. Daugherty, Oct. 5, 1922.

within American waters if those liquors were sealed to prevent their consumption in the United States. Congress had gone further than it needed to go in providing for enforcement of the Amendment. It followed that Congress could remove the burden it had laid on foreign vessels. Indeed, Congress had already exempted from the penalties and forfeitures of the Volstead Act intoxicating liquors in transit through the Panama Canal, although the Amendment was applicable to the Canal Zone. The Supreme Court had noted this exercise of congressional discretion without objection. Hughes seized upon this fact to clinch his point. If determinations of this kind had not been removed beyond the legislative power, he reasoned, then they were still within the treaty-making power. In other words, he could straighten out the tangle over foreign ships bringing liquor into American ports by making treaties with the maritime powers.

Hughes also saw in this situation an opportunity to strike a blow at smuggling. The treaty that he offered to Great Britain and other powers in June, 1923, thus provided not only immunity for forbidden articles under seal on foreign ships in American waters; it also proposed to grant the authorities of each country permission to board and search vessels of the other suspected of importing forbidden articles, if such vessels should be caught within twelve miles of the shore. The Secretary was acting on the theory that one good turn deserves another.

But Curzon denounced the proposed liquor treaty in a House of Lords speech aimed directly at Hughes. Some American newspapers printed it in full. The Secretary took up the gage the next day at his press conference, speaking off the record to avoid clashing openly with Curzon over a supposedly domestic speech. "For three-quarters of an hour he shouted and pounded the table. . . ." [11] Then correspondents dashed to their typewriters, and wires to many parts of the world were soon sizzling with the Secretary's words. Through the press, he had replied to Curzon as effectively as if he had used Congress as a sounding board.

A change in the London atmosphere was immediately noticeable. In late summer Hughes discussed the treaty with Lord Birkenhead, former Lord Chancellor of England, at the American Bar Association's annual meeting in Minneapolis and later in Montreal. Returning to London, Birkenhead softened the attitude of his friend Curzon, and within a few months the Foreign Office submitted a counterproposal. It was so responsive to Hughes' original suggestion that a complete agreement was soon worked out. The Secretary did not like the British demand that search and seizures be permitted within one hour's run of the shore instead of a twelve-mile limit. That made the legality of each seizure depend upon the speed of the particular boat seized, but he agreed to

[11] Bertram D. Hulen, *Inside the Department of State*, p. 132.

it in deference to Britain's unwillingness to name any mileage figure that might conceivably compromise the three-mile limit. The treaty was signed on January 23, 1924, and the Senate consented to its ratification two months later. Before the close of the year six other countries had signed similar treaties.

Without any strain on our constitutional system, Hughes had eliminated an acute source of international friction and snatched from the smugglers the handiest device of their trade.

Chapter 56

THE STRUGGLE FOR POSTWAR RECOVERY

EUROPE'S ECONOMIC calamities resulting from World War I came to a head in 1922. Germany was prostrate under her burden of reparations. With her people in poverty and despair, production lagged, and the payments that the victorious Allies had anticipated to aid their own recovery were not forthcoming. "Look pretty much where you will today in Europe," Ambassador Houghton wrote to Secretary Hughes from Berlin, "you find men and women living under conditions of great hardship,—insufficiently nourished, insufficiently clothed, unprotected against the bitter cold of the approaching winter." [1] In a previous letter he had said, "It is a sort of quiet bleeding to death."

Across the Rhine from Germany, wounded France was sullen and defiant. Having been twice invaded in half a century, France's strongest determination was to make the Germans pay for the war to the last franc. Originally she had demanded 100 billion dollars, then 56 billion, then 33 billion—the figure fixed by the Reparation Commission. The fading hope of wringing any such sum out of Germany's inflation-ravaged economy made it increasingly evident that France would resort to coercive measures. All Europe seemed to teeter on the brink of ruin.

As early as April, 1921, Germany had appealed to the United States to mediate the reparations question and to fix the sum to be paid by Germany to the Allied powers. Then had come a plea for President Harding to nominate a commission of impartial experts to investigate Germany's capacity to pay. Hughes had declined to intervene, but he had informally acquainted the British and French ambassadors with Berlin's proposals. Neither London nor Paris was interested.

Hughes had been deeply worried about the outlook long before the crisis stage was reached. "The prosperity of the United States," he had said in one of his earliest speeches as Secretary of State, "largely depends upon the economic settlements which may be made in Europe, and the key to the future is with those who make those settlements." [2] A year later he told the United States Chamber of Commerce, "We have only begun to think internationally, and we find the attitude of the public mind to be still ill-adjusted to the magni-

[1] *Foreign Relations, 1922,* II, 172. [2] At Brown Commencement, June, 1921.

tude of our financial power and to the international interests which we have suddenly accumulated as the result of the World War." [3] After the arms conference was out of the way, the economic rehabilitation of Europe became his major interest.

In European capitals and among American economists there was a clamor for cancellation of all reparations and war debts. The $10,150,000,000 that twenty European countries owed the United States, largely for supplies obtained during and after the war, was a secondary millstone on the neck of Europe's economy. But Congress had set up the World War Foreign Debt Commission and instructed it that, in entering into debt-funding agreements, it should not cancel "any part" of the war debts and should not accept interest rates of less than 4½ per cent. With postwar disillusionment still running strong, there was no possibility of inducing Congress to wipe out these wartime obligations. Hughes insisted, with characteristic regard for political realities, that any gesture toward cancellation would destroy his only chance of being helpful.

In September, 1922, the Secretary reviewed the growing chaos in Europe with Myron T. Herrick, who was on leave from his ambassadorial post in Paris. Returning to France in October, Herrick took with him a definite suggestion from Secretary Hughes that the best way of dealing with the reparations dilemma was to let a group of eminent financiers determine what Germany could pay. The effect would be, Hughes thought, to break the deadlock among the politicians (all of whom were catering to sentiment in their own countries) and force the recognition of economic realities. But Premier Poincaré clung to the waning hope of obtaining fabulous reparations. At Hughes' request, Herrick again suggested an expert study, and on November 7 the Secretary took it up with Ambassador Jusserand in Washington.[4] The governments could not solve the reparations problem, he said, for they were committed; but they could ask a group of financial experts to work up a plan that would have a secure economic foundation. Governments could then accept the plan because of the favorable world opinion that would be marshaled behind it. Jusserand expressed himself as in agreement and said he would see if anything could be done along the line suggested.

Meanwhile conditions in Europe were going from bad to worse. Houghton reported from Berlin that the parliamentary system had broken down. Armed groups in Germany were "working toward dictatorship." The most active of these groups were headed by a young Austrian named Hitler, who was in control of 30,000 men. "By his vehemence and fanaticism," Houghton wrote, "he [Hitler] was rapidly becoming leader of a whole movement . . . following

[3] *The Pathway of Peace*, p. 252. [4] *Foreign Relations, 1922*, II, 178f.

the pattern of the Fascisti in Italy. These people," he concluded, "seem to me to be slowly going mad." [5]

France was still determined to make her enemies pay whether or not it was economically feasible. There were rumors that France would seize the state coal mines in the Ruhr. Hughes saw Jusserand again and talked earnestly about the interest of the entire world in the economic rehabilitation of Europe. He expressed doubt that the French really intended to occupy the Ruhr because that course would not give them the reparations they sought. There was no pot of gold in the Ruhr that the French could pick up.

French occupation of German territories, Hughes continued, would create a situation "which would seem to make war at some time inevitable if it were not otherwise redressed." No one wished to see Germany escape her just obligations. But a point had been reached, he said, "where it was necessary to put sentiment aside." In the interests of peace France could not afford to drive her former enemy to desperation. Force would accomplish nothing, he concluded, but France could win the favorable opinion of the world by offering to be guided by hard economic facts.

Poincaré remained cool to the idea, and there was an angry outburst in the Chamber of Deputies because of the impression that America was trying to tell France what she should do. Meanwhile a clamor arose in the United States against the drastic measures that seemed to be taking shape in Europe. The newspapers sensed the crisis, and, knowing nothing of what Hughes had been doing under cover to avert it, belabored him for following a do-nothing policy. Some of them assumed that the United States should step in and prevent occupation of the Ruhr. Senator Borah called for an international economic conference. Germany proposed an agreement with Great Britain, France, and Italy not to engage in war for thirty years unless war should be approved by a vote of the people. Fantastic proposals were legion; none of them offered any real hope of arresting the course of events in Europe.

Hughes' brooding over the dismal outlook was mingled with fitful sleep through the night of December 26, 1922. Suddenly he was awakened by what he later described to Castle as "the voice of God" [6] directing him to talk in New Haven about the European situation. He was to address the American Historical Association on the evening of December 29 on "Some Aspects of Our Foreign Policy." It would be a golden opportunity to get before the world the plan he had urged upon the French. Advance copies of the address had already been distributed to the press, but an annex could be added. Hughes was out of bed in a twinkling and worked through the small hours of the morning.

[5] Houghton to CEH, Nov. 21, 1922.
[6] Diary of William R. Castle, Jr., 1922, pp. 178–181.

Before breakfast he telephoned the White House for an appointment, and by 9:00 A.M. he was reading the annex of his speech to the President. Harding warmly approved. Two days later, when the Secretary delivered his address at New Haven, its historical aspects were completely overshadowed by his novel plan for dealing with the critical present.

"The economic conditions in Europe give us the greatest concern," he said. "We cannot dispose of these problems by calling them European, for they are world problems and we cannot escape the injurious consequences of a failure to settle them." Reparations were the crux of the difficulty. Germany should not be relieved of paying for the consequences of her aggression, but, on the other hand, economic recuperation in Europe would be impossible without German recuperation. "There will be no permanent peace unless economic satisfactions are enjoyed," Hughes declared. "We should view with disfavor measures which instead of producing reparations would threaten disaster."

The weak part of the speech was its lack of any promise of substantial aid from the United States. As this country had not asked for general reparations, Hughes was unwilling to relieve Germany of paying the costs of the American army of occupation. He would not permit German reparations to be linked with the war debts of the Allies to the United States, and he did not think the United States should assume the role of arbiter. But the United States would use its influence to obtain a settlement of the reparations issue on its merits. When that was done it would be easier to determine the capacity of the Allies to pay their debts to the United States.

The Secretary threw his challenge directly to the statesmen of Europe: "Why should they not invite men of the highest authority in finance in their respective countries—men of such prestige, experience and honor that their agreement upon the amount to be paid [by Germany], and upon a financial plan for working out the payments, would be accepted throughout the world as the most authoritative expression obtainable? . . . I have no doubt that distinguished Americans would be willing to serve in such a commission."

The speech caused a sensation in spite of the mildness of Hughes' proposal. It prompted the London *Morning Post* to comment that "only the truth can make statesmen free." The *Sunday Times* (London) thought Hughes' suggestion went "down to the heart of most of the difficulties retarding the world's recovery."[7] But Poincaré was moved only to anger. By inference Hughes had condemned the occupation of the Ruhr before it had begun and brought pressure upon France for a more reasonable settlement. Feeling the heat of world opinion, Poincaré denied that he had received any suggestion from the American Government along the lines of Hughes' New Haven speech.[8] It was a sheer falsehood. Herrick had twice presented the idea to Poincaré, and, at the latter's

[7] Quoted in *Literary Digest*, Jan. 13, 1923. [8] *Foreign Relations, 1923*, II, 46.

request, repeated it again in the form of a memorandum. Jusserand had likewise kept his government informed, and, through Jusserand, Poincaré had expressed to Hughes his "cordial appreciation" of the suggestion.[9] Jusserand was highly embarrassed by his chief's disingenuousness, and Hughes was especially irritated because he had kept his proposal secret for several months in the hope that the French would feel free to take advantage of it and claim the credit for initiating it themselves.

The French moved into the Ruhr early in January, 1923, and a new avalanche of "hectoring and abusive criticism" descended upon the Secretary of State. On one hand he was denounced for not pursuing a vigorous policy in Europe; on the other, for intermeddling in Europe's affairs. The Senate Foreign Relations Committee began to take a keen interest in the reparations issue. Hiram Johnson demanded the recall of the American "unofficial observer" with the Reparation Commission, and Lodge asked for and received full details on the activities of that official.

Lodge went to the department to discuss the repeated demands for an economic conference. Whatever we may think of the matter, Hughes told him, the Allied powers regard their war debts to the United States as part of the economic problem. "They do not want our advice," he added, "but merely relief from their debts. We of course could not arrange for a conference to discuss a subject and then decline to discuss what others considered relevant to that subject." [10] Since any mention of canceling the war debts chilled the marrow in congressional bones, the conference idea was dropped.

Under the lash of criticism, Harding asked Hughes to watch for a favorable opportunity to intervene in the European situation. Although the Secretary was hurt by the fury of many of his critics and although he longed to go back to the practice of law, he scrutinized each development with the faithfulness of a mother watching over a sick child. "Sometimes I wonder how the Secretary can stand the strain," Castle wrote into his diary, "as the Senate is behaving like the devil, trying to take on itself the conduct of foreign relations and attacking Mr. Hughes most unreasonably on all sorts of counts. He has been irritable lately, and had to be irritable unless he were Job himself.[11]

As the summer wore on, there was discussion in the department of the possibility of making the Rhineland a separate state in the Reich, of measures to end passive resistance in Germany, and of depressing the value of the franc to make France realize her failure. No one of the schemes held a glimmer of hope. Indeed, Hughes had previously concluded that any action suggestive of sympathy with Germany would enrage France and give her a chance to blame him for the failure of her venture. And to support France in any way might

[9] *Ibid.*, 1922, II, 182, 195.
[10] Memorandum of conversation, Feb. 1, 1923, in Hughes Papers.
[11] Jan. 22, 1923.

delay her withdrawal from an untenable position. He could only bide his time.

Meanwhile it was a comfort to know that some thoughtful observers understood and approved the policy he was following. George W. Ochs Oakes, editor of *Current History*, wrote to him:

> I think that your course has been prudent, statesmanlike, wise and eminently just. . . . I am writing this letter solely to let you know that amid the chorus of expletives and criticism hurled at you, there are some Americans, whose knowledge of foreign affairs qualifies them to speak, who unqualifiedly endorse your course.

Hughes replied on February 20, 1923:

> If I could talk to the country as one could in dealing with domestic affairs I should have little difficulty, for I feel so sure of the propriety of our course that I think I could carry the country if I could go into every detail and make "appeals to the people." But we cannot talk to our own people without enlisting the attention of the peoples abroad and then we create more troubles than we cure. In representing the country in its foreign relations, it is necessary to be *right*, not to be assured of approval of the Press of the moment in its hurried and often biased reviews, but of the calm verdict of the coming generation which will pass the final judgment upon our fidelity and intelligence at this critical time.

While the French tightened the thumbscrews on Germany, the British sent Stanley Baldwin, Chancellor of the Exchequer, to Washington at the head of a commission to settle their war debt. The conversations began on January 8, 1923, with Secretary Mellon as chairman of the American commission (of which Hughes and Hoover were also members) and with Ambassador Harvey as the chief intermeddler.

Harvey had been granted permission to return to Washington during the debt negotiations upon his own suggestion that his services might prove useful. The nature of the service Harvey would render came to light when Sir Auckland Geddes, the British ambassador, went to the Secretary's home and handed him a copy of a speech written by Harvey and sent to Baldwin for his use in addressing the two commissions the next morning. In a state of high indignation, Geddes averred that the Chancellor of the Exchequer was quite capable of making speeches without such assistance. Hughes read Harvey's suggested peroration, laughed at its audacity, and mollified Geddes by saying that it was solely a product of Harvey's overzealous interest in securing a debt agreement.

Baldwin delivered his own speech the next morning and made a very favorable impression on the American Commission. Britain planned to pay her entire debt, he said, and asked only a fair business settlement. The American Commission decided to go beyond the limits fixed by Congress and make the most liberal settlement that Congress might be expected to accept. The limit of what

Congress might be willing to do was left to the Senators and Representatives on the commission after sounding out the sentiment on Capitol Hill.

In spite of the conciliatory attitude on both sides, the negotiations reached an impasse on the question of interest rates. Prime Minister Bonar Law in London insisted that the American offer to reduce the interest rate from 4½ to 3 (later 3½) per cent did not go far enough. Baldwin sailed for home on January 20, and Hughes instructed Harvey to hasten back to London and explain to the Prime Minister that the United States had made its best offer.

Hughes then learned from Geddes that Harvey had told Bonar Law some months previously that Britain could expect settlement of her debt on the basis of 2 per cent interest.[12] That explained the Prime Minister's stand against the 3 per cent offer. In Washington, Harvey had also suggested to Sir Maurice Low that a great surprise was in store for Mr. Baldwin; namely, an interest rate of 1½ per cent on the debt. That tip had been passed along to the British negotiators, who began to think, along with Bonar Law, that the American Commission was merely fencing. The Secretary cabled to Harvey to see Bonar Law immediately and make him understand that no settlement could be reached unless the terms offered by the American Commission were accepted.

The impetuous Harvey threw into his interview with Bonar Law all his very considerable power of persuasion. But once more he slipped into reckless speculation. The American Government, he told the Prime Minister, intended to give Britain the right to raise a tax-free loan in the New York market. Geddes hastened to Hughes' home to learn the meaning of Harvey's latest brainstorm, and the Secretary could only lament once more that Harvey had spoken without authority. Together Hughes and Geddes went to Secretary Mellon's apartment to see if he could throw any light on the strange report from London. Mellon had never heard of such a proposal. With astonishing restraint, Hughes cabled Harvey that he should not discuss any departure from the terms offered by the American Commission.

Harvey was near the end of his rope. After his return to London, two hotels sent to the State Department substantial bills that he had incurred and left unpaid. Hughes sent them on to Harvey and later refused to visa vouchers covering "certain items"—meaning intoxicants—for which, under the law, the department could not pay. Harvey thought this was "very ungracious," considering his aid in the debt-funding negotiations, but in the end he apologized.

The Secretary was aware of Harvey's final influence in swinging Bonar Law and the British press behind the debt settlement. Yet it was a great relief when, six weeks after the death of President Harding, Harvey submitted his resignation without any suggestion from the State Department. Undoubtedly he knew that his maladroit ventures had been tolerated only because of the

[12] Memorandum of Interview, Jan. 21, 1923.

political debt that Harding owed him. Hughes accepted the resignation courteously, expressed appreciation for Harvey's services, and recommended former Senator Frank B. Kellogg as his successor.

The debt agreement with Britain was approved by Congress, but it had little effect upon the deepening chaos in Europe. By midsummer Hughes said that "between the Supreme Court liquor decision . . . the delay of the French to ratify the Naval Limitation Treaties, the pressure for action in the Ruhr situation, he really wished he was a woman and could cry." [13] A week later, however, the department celebrated France's ratification of the Naval Treaty and the Four-Power Pact, and other patches in the international sky began to clear. Lloyd George, the former British Prime Minister, started a fresh clamor for an expert inquiry into reparations. Speaking at Montreal, he noted that the ability of Germany to pay was still shrinking. "The greater the delay," Lloyd George said, "the closer the situation approaches chaos. I hope that serious consideration of Mr. Hughes' plan may be taken up even at this late date, and I repeat that it is the best hope of a successful settlement." [14]

The next day President Coolidge endorsed the Hughes plan. The effect was to give it new life. Lloyd George came to Washington, and at his own suggestion arrived an hour early at the dinner Hughes gave for him so as to get a firsthand explanation of the proposed inquiry. After their chat together he was so perturbed over Great Britain's neglect of the Hughes plan that, even though he was no longer in the government, he cabled London asking for immediate consideration of it. Britain then took the lead in urging its acceptance. Belgium and Italy expressed approval. France yielded an inch but still insisted that the amount of the German debt could not be changed and asked that the inquiry be limited to Germany's "present" capacity to pay. The French chargé went to the State Department to explain France's position and stayed to hear a powerful argument against the course his country was pursuing.

In defense of their position the French handed Hughes a technical memorandum on France's rights under the Treaty of Versailles. "But we have nothing to do with all this," he replied. "What we are interested in is whether M. Poincaré wants to get any reparations." [15] If so, the investigation would have to be broad enough to mean something. Finally, Poincaré said he would let the inquiry of the experts extend as far as 1930. Hughes replied that a study on that basis would be futile. Jusserand attempted to argue. "It is absurd," Hughes retorted, "for two old friends, as we are, to discuss this matter. You have reported what you were told to say and I know what I must do, so there is an end to it." [16] Once more the deadlock appeared to be unbreakable.

[13] Castle diary, 1923, July 5.
[14] *New York Times*, Oct. 9, 1923.
[15] Castle diary, 1923, p. 181.
[16] *Ibid*, p. 212.

At last the Reparation Commission itself backed into an inquiry of the type Hughes had suggested. Meeting on November 30, 1923, the commission unanimously voted to create a committee of experts to consider means of balancing the German budget and stabilizing the currency. A second committee of experts was instructed to estimate the amount of exported capital and suggest means of returning it to Germany. Louis Barthou, president of the Reparation Commission, earnestly requested the aid of American experts on these commissions of inquiry, and Hughes consented, with the understanding that the experts could investigate all the economic conditions in Germany essential to balancing the budget and stabilizing the currency. French opposition had been routed by giving a different name to the investigation of Germany's capacity to pay.

As the American experts to serve on the first committee, Hughes recommended General Charles G. Dawes and Owen D. Young. Both were appointed, along with Henry M. Robinson as an expert on the second committee. The Dawes Committee brought in its first report in April, 1924, recommending that French troops be withdrawn from the Ruhr; that a bank be set up as a depository and fiscal agent of the German Government; that Germany pay the Allies $250,000,000 from railroads, industry, and loans the first year and increasing sums thereafter; and that the Allies and the United States should lend Germany $200,000,000. The powers unanimously accepted the Dawes Plan and called a conference to meet in London in July to put it into effect. Dawes hastened to write to Hughes: "If our work contributes in a measurable way to peace and good will on earth to no one, more than yourself, is it due."

But the end of the controversy was not yet in sight. Ramsay MacDonald had come into power in Great Britain, and Édouard Herriot in France. They were soon at loggerheads over whether the Allies should approach Germany about the proposed new protocol before agreeing among themselves as to how the Dawes Plan should be put into operation.

While this wrangling continued, Secretary Hughes sailed for London, not as a delegate to the forthcoming conference, but as president of the American Bar Association leading two thousand American and Canadian lawyers and many of their families on an Old World pilgrimage. Chief Justice Taft had induced the lawyers to select Hughes as their leader because of the prestige he would give the expedition. The coincidence of the pilgrimage with the reparations meeting caused the New York *World* to jeer at Hughes as a "super-pussyfooter" and to assert that "America has sneaked into Europe by the back door." [17] European editors seemed to take special delight in ridiculing the idea that such a ceremonial visit by the Secretary could have any influence on the ravenous struggle for reparations. But, as formal American participation

[17] Aug. 1, 1924.

in the conference was out of the question, Hughes welcomed the opportunity the pilgrimage afforded for face-to-face discussion of the Dawes Plan on an unofficial basis.

The trip brought many memorable hours. Aboard the *Berengaria*, which had become a sort of lawyers' paradise, there was an outpouring of good fellowship and numerous gay parties. At one of these, a dinner of Harvard Law School graduates, Dean Roscoe Pound summoned the leader of the pilgrimage and conferred upon him a "degree" in these words:

> Charles E. Hughes—in diplomacy, like a planked shad, open and above board; in politics, like Caesar's wife, all things to all men; in international affairs, like the Venus de Milo, the greatest figure in disarmament; your spirit of aloofness we now know is as Mark Twain said about the rumor of his death—greatly exaggerated. In recognition of how we have come to regard you on this trip, we confer upon you the degree of Prince of Good Fellows, *ex Merito*.[18]

The extent of Hughes' unbending surprised even some of the lawyers who were closely associated with him. One afternoon as he was relaxing on the promenade deck a rather breezy young woman came up to him.

"Mr. Hughes," she said, "I don't know how we should address you. My father used to speak of you as 'Governor Hughes.' Afterwards I heard people saying 'Judge Hughes.' Now here on the boat I hear them say 'Mr. Secretary.' I don't know how you should be addressed."

A quizzical expression on Hughes' face gave way to a bland smile.

"Those who love me," he said, "call me Charlie!" [19]

Arriving in London, the Hugheses and many of their compatriots attended the Sunday services in Westminster Abbey while other visitors thronged Westminster Cathedral and old St. Paul's. Hughes lived over again the thrill of his first visit to the Abbey as a boy of eleven in 1873. How he had loved that trip! As his mind ranged back over half a century, he mused that few present that morning had visited this choice spot before he had.

The official program for the visitors opened Monday morning with a grand reception in Westminster Hall—the shrine of the common law. The visitors sat in semidarkness under the awesome spell of Westminster's high-timbered roof and the colorful glow of light from its great window. The very atmosphere seemed heavy with history. On one side stood members of England's junior bar in bob wigs and gowns. On the other side was a bank of county court judges wearing full curly wigs, violet stoles, and cuffs. Below were members of the English bar in full wigs, black silk robes, knee breeches, buckled shoes, and frilly cuffs; also the Canadian Privy Councilors in the gorgeous blue and gold of their rank. To the left were Secretary Hughes, Ambassador Kellogg,

[18] Hughes Papers. [19] Roscoe Pound to author, March 22, 1950.

Solicitor General James M. Beck, Justice Sutherland of the Supreme Court, and other distinguished Americans.

The hall was suddenly flooded with light upon the entrance of the Lord Chancellor's procession, giving added brilliance to the ceremony. The tipstaff led the march followed by bearers of the traditional mace and purse and by the Right Honorable Viscount Haldane, the Lord High Chancellor, stately in his black and gold robes. Next came the Lord President of the Council, a group of former Lord Chancellors, the Lord Chief Justice in scarlet and ermine, the Law Lords looking the part of knights about to take part in a splendid tournament, and the King's Bench judges garbed in scarlet. The trains of the great men of the bench were solemnly carried by bearers. The American visitors arose and stood in silence while the judges marched up the aisle and Lord Haldane took his place with the dignity of an old king.

The oratory began with brief addresses of welcome by Sir Patrick Hastings, the Attorney General, resplendent in his white frills; Sir Robert William Dibdin, president of the Law Society; and the Honorable Sir James Aikins, president of the Canadian Bar Association. Lord Haldane then delivered a major address, and Hughes and Sutherland responded in behalf of the American lawyers. Their plain morning dress was in sharp contrast to the elegant robes of the British judges. But Hughes stood on the raised platform with statuesque dignity, his eyes twinkling under heavy brow and his face an image of masculine strength and firmness. The words rolled from his lips with measured cadence. As was his custom, he spoke from memory, with every quotation exact and with a nice balance of tact, wit, and literary polish:

> Of all international contacts, none could be happier than this. We have no political ends to serve, no differences to compose, no policies to advance, except the highest good of all—the policy of understanding and good will. The fact that we are here is more eloquent than anything we can say here. We come rejoicing in an amity which has become, I am glad to say, a fixed habit of two peoples intent on cooperation in the interest of peace. We come to tighten the bonds of friendship. . . .
>
> We are not here to pay tribute to the corpus of the early law, still less to the formalism which has had so much to do with its development, but rather to the genius of the common law which brings us together with a definite realization of brotherhood. . . .
>
> The fundamental conception which we especially cherish as our heritage is the right to law itself, not as the edict of arbitrary power, but as the law of a free people, springing from custom, responsive to their sense of justice, modified and enlarged by their free will to meet conscious needs, and sustained by authority which is itself subject to the law—the law of the land. If, as Mr. Justice Holmes has said, "the life of the law is not logic but experience," the life of the common law has been the experience of free men. . . . There is still the need to recognize the ancient right—and it is the most precious right of democracy—the right to be gov-

erned by law and not by officials—the right to reasonable, definite and proclaimed standards which the citizens can invoke against both malevolence and caprice. We of the common law respect authority, but it is the authority of the legal order. We respect those who in station high or humble execute the law—because it is our law. We esteem them but only as they esteem and keep within the law. . . .

This meeting of those who enjoy a common tradition and cherish a common purpose cannot fail to heighten our sense of responsibility, as we find our strength renewed, our ardor quickened and our hearts deeply stirred as we sit together at the fireside in the old homestead.

Hughes' happy phrase about "the old homestead" resounded through the press and through many comments from the bar. On Monday night he was the guest of the Pilgrim Society of Great Britain at a dinner in the Hotel Victoria. Responding to toasts by the Duke of Connaught and his grandnephew, the Prince of Wales, Hughes delivered another memorable address, concluding:

I believe that Gladstone remarked in a time of great difficulty that public men ought not to suffer disenchantment. They ought to know that ideals in politics are never realized. Their progress in public life is a continual process of disillusionment, but the greatest of all illusions is that we can serve and achieve without faith. It was faith which made firm the Pilgrims' resolve. It is faith that brings us hither on this delightful journey, an unquestioning faith that some day humanity will enjoy an enduring peace and the reign of justice, and to that end we gladly pledge our lives.

Balfour said that it was "the most important speech ever delivered before a British audience by an American statesman."[20] Years later Hughes himself thought that in these London speeches he had reached his "top speed."

On Wednesday he took Mrs. Hughes to lunch with King George and Queen Mary at Buckingham Palace. It was a delightfully informal luncheon. The King talked freely and had a good deal to say about President Wilson, Colonel House, and Ambassador Harvey. He had been amazed, he said, by the fact that President Wilson was always shadowed by a number of secret service men while he was in Europe. "I never think of taking such precautions," the King said. "Often I go riding in Hyde Park in the mornings with a single companion." One morning as the King was riding along Rotten Row, he related, he was recognized by two Americans. "Hey, there's the King!" one of them cried. "Oh, hell," the other exclaimed, "where's his crown?" The idea that he should have a crown on his head while riding horseback was a source of much amusement to His Majesty.

The following day the King and Queen entertained the visiting Americans at a garden party at Buckingham Palace. By prearrangement Secretary and Mrs. Hughes met the royal couple near the palace. The King asked Hughes to

[20] London dispatch by J. D. Whelpley.

accompany him, and the Queen asked Mrs. Hughes to accompany her. Taking different routes, the two parties began making their way toward the royal marquee, the almost solidly packed crowd opening paths before them as they approached. During this walk, the King told Hughes that if he saw anyone whom he wished to introduce he should not hesitate to do so. The Secretary was very pleased and picked out of the crowd several prominent Americans for presentation to His Majesty, taking care, however, not to abuse the privilege.

Tea was served at the royal marquee to a group which included Secretary and Mrs. Hughes, Premier MacDonald, Premiers Herriot of France and Hymans of Belgium, Ambassador Kellogg, the Duke of Connaught, Prince and Princess Arthur of Connaught, and Princess Beatrice. Then the King and Queen moved to another marquee and received the officers and committee members of the American Bar Association. The crowd was standing obediently behind a line about 150 feet away, without any guards or police in evidence. Some Americans were shaking their heads in admiration of this discipline when a little Brooklyn girl broke away from the crowd and ran to the Prince of Wales for his autograph. The King laughed heartily and said, "I'm afraid she will capture my son"—not dreaming that that honor would go to a Baltimore girl and that it would cost the Prince his throne.

One other youthful effort to take advantage of royal graciousness was less successful. The seventeen-year-old daughter of a visiting lawyer attempted to go through the reception line a second time, assuming that, among the thousands present, she could not be recognized as a repeater. Instead of greeting her, however, Queen Mary said tartly, "I have already seen you."

Interspersed among the ceremonies were a series of informal discussions with the leading statesmen of Europe. Ambassador Kellogg invited Premier Herriot, M. Theunis, the French Minister of Finance, Baron Moucheur of Belgium, and the Italian ambassador to lunch at Crewe House, and Hughes spent two hours with them, pleading that the Dawes Plan be given a chance to operate. Herriot seemed sympathetic, but he feared that any concession he might make would be used against him at home by Poincaré. Pressed by Hughes' relentless logic, Herriot clapped his hands to his head and cried, "I'll fall! I'll fall!" Hughes' rejoinder was that the Premier would fall anyway if he did not carry out the plan.

When Herriot returned to the Inter-Allied Conference, a new spirit—the will to succeed—permeated the deliberations. Herriot began to make concessions that inspired counterconcessions. Meanwhile Hughes went to Paris, and in addition to being elaborately entertained by the French bar, had a heart-to-heart talk with Poincaré on the necessity of pulling together. "Here is the American policy," he said, referring to the Dawes Plan. "If you turn this down, America is through." Poincaré responded favorably. The clouds of pessimism began to lift. Even the French press began to reflect new confidence, with the result of strengthening the hands of Herriot in London.

In Brussels, Hughes' visit with the Belgians produced similar results. At a dinner at the American Embassy in Berlin he talked with equal candor to President Ebert, Chancellor Marx, and Foreign Minister Stresemann just before the German delegates went to the London Conference. If Germany did not accept the Dawes Plan, he said, she could look for no further aid or sympathy from the United States. The Germans pledged themselves to carry out the new reparations scheme to the letter.

The bankers came close to upsetting the apple cart by insisting that a representative of J. P. Morgan & Company be appointed as general agent to carry out the Dawes Plan. Hughes objected on the ground that the plan would have to have the full confidence of Germany for success. Then the bankers tried to swing the appointment to Norman Davis. The Administration's choice was Owen D. Young, but the bankers opposed him unless he would agree to hold the post for three years. Young was not willing to do this, but he was appointed with the understanding that he would get the machinery running smoothly before turning it over to S. Parker Gilbert.

As Secretary Hughes sailed for home, he was widely credited with having brought success to the London Conference without having attended it. "The solution of this reparations question, if it is solved," said a London dispatch "will date, I believe, from Herriot's luncheon with Secretary Hughes." [21] The London *Times* said of the conference:

> It has reestablished harmony among the Allies over the principal problem of Europe; it has taken France and Germany out of the cold atmosphere of frigid notes and curt conversations into that of amicable discussion; and it has sealed the participation, unofficial but extremely helpful, of the United States in the economic reconstruction of the Old World. The first tentative suggestion of Mr. Hughes in his famous speech at New Haven some 18 months ago . . . has now borne splendid fruit.[22]

The reparations adjustments thus effected saved Europe from economic collapse for six years. In the great depression of the thirties the whole flimsy structure of war debts and war penalties tottered and fell. Then it became evident that the Dawes Plan and the Young Plan had succeeded temporarily only because American and British investors had lent to Germany more money than she repaid in reparations. Actually it was these investors who paid the cost of rebuilding Europe. It would have been much better to have wiped out the war debts and to have confined reparations to such tangible German property as could have been removed without crippling the country. Vast sums

[21] New York *World*, Aug. 2, 1924. [22] Aug. 18, 1924.

simply cannot be transferred from one country to another year after year, except in the form of goods, and the United States and other countries had raised their tariff rates to prevent a larger flow of imports.

There is no evidence that Secretary Hughes foresaw the inevitable breakdown of the postwar settlements or that he fully appreciated the significance of the United States' shift from the position of a debtor to that of a creditor nation. He continued to support the Republican tariff policy, which made payment of the war debts economically infeasible. While he was clear-headed and insistent in warning the French that they could not get milk and beef from the same cow at the same time, he never undertook to warn the American people that they could not collect on the war debts unless they were willing to receive a much larger volume of European goods.

In appraising Hughes' efforts to cope with the economic dislocations resulting from World War I, however, we must avoid any easy comparison with the Marshall Plan which followed World War II. In the latter case the United States poured billions into the European recovery effort because the folly of expecting war and rehabilitation loans to be repaid had then been pointedly demonstrated and because the shift of military power in Europe to Soviet Russia made it imperative for the free nations to stand together. There were no such compulsions to unity of effort in the twenties. Nor was the dominant economic position of the United States so marked as it has since become. If, as Winston Churchill has pointed out, a man of great authority had had "the wit, ascendancy, or detachment from public folly" to declare the hopelessness of trying to make a defeated nation pay the cost of a modern war, no one would have believed him.[23]

A bolder attitude on Hughes' part might have enhanced his stature in history, but he was mindful of what had happened when Wilson overplayed his hand. It was prompt recovery in Europe and not a futile showdown that he sought. Root looked upon Hughes' course as the "only possible curative policy." It proved to be only a palliative, but the fact remains that it was the most constructive step taken to rescue Europe from its economic chaos in the postwar years when there was still hope that a second world war could be averted.

[23] *The Gathering Storm* (Boston, Houghton Mifflin, 1948), pp. 8–9. Copyright, 1948, by Houghton Mifflin Co.

Chapter 57

THE WORLD COURT

HUGHES' passion for justice and his deep interest in peace predestined him to become a strong supporter of the World Court. To his way of thinking the settlement of international disputes over legal issues in the cool detachment of the courtroom was the first logical step in the substitution of world law for force. "The desire for peace," he said, "must be supported by the institutions of peace." [1] Of course, no international court could become a cure-all. But an independent tribunal of able judges could settle numerous disputes on the basis of facts and law, and it could give peoples a new consciousness of justice operating on an international scale.

The creation of an international court had long been a cardinal feature of American policy. Secretary Hay had tried to interest the First Hague Conference of 1899 in such a tribunal, and the conference had set up the Permanent Court of Arbitration. As this body was only a panel of arbiters, Secretary Root had attempted at the Second Hague Conference to convert it into a real international court composed of full-time judges. The project had failed only because no satisfactory method of electing the judges could be found.

In his 1916 campaign Hughes had picked up the world-court idea from Hay, Root, and Theodore Roosevelt and given it warm support. After the United States had entered World War I and again in the 1920 campaign, he had voiced his devotion to the cause of an international court. With much interest, he had followed the work of the Commission of Jurists which had assembled at The Hague on invitation from the Council of the League of Nations. The jurists, including Hughes' highly esteemed friend, Elihu Root, had brought forth a carefully devised statute to set up the Permanent Court of International Justice, and the Assembly of the League had approved it on December 13, 1920—the very day that Hughes agreed to join the Harding Cabinet. His earliest acquaintance with the World Court plan had convinced him that one of his major tasks as Secretary of State would be to win adherence of the United States to it.

Despite Mrs. Harding's efforts to dissuade him, the President acquiesced in this conclusion. The revolt in the Senate against the League of Nations suggested caution, however, and Hughes' preoccupation with the Washington

[1] *The Pathway of Peace*, p. 67.

Conference through most of his first year in office compelled delay. Meanwhile a disturbing incident put him in the light of being hostile to the court.

Root had sponsored a provision in the World Court statute authorizing the nomination of judges for that tribunal by the members of the old Hague Court of Arbitration. By this means it was hoped to confine the nominations to eminent lawyers and judges in the various countries instead of having governments select nominees for political reasons. Judges to serve on the World Court were then to be elected from the list of nominees by separate votes of the League Council and Assembly. In June, 1921, Sir Eric Drummond, secretary general of the League, sent out requests that members of the old Hague Court panel nominate American jurists for the new court, but the letters went astray.

By Harry James Westerman in the *Ohio State Journal,* June 11, 1923.

CHARLES VS. SIMEON

Hughes told his press conference at the time that if the requests for nominations should come to the State Department they would be forwarded and that the Hague Court judges would act in accord with their own judgment. That was the last he heard of the matter until about August 14, when Root wrote him a letter and Oscar S. Straus called at the department to ask if the communications had been received. Hughes had seen nothing of them, but he launched an immediate search. Two days later he replied to Root:

> As soon as I received the latter [Root's letter of August 14] I had the files of the Department searched and found, to my great regret, that the communications from the Secretary General of the League of Nations, addressed to you, Judge Gray, Mr. Straus, and Mr. Moore had been received, placed on file, and not forwarded. How this happened I am unable to state. . . . Apparently the papers were received and filed without being referred to me and without appreciation of their significance.[2]

In belatedly sending out the League's invitations, Hughes also apologized to the other members of the panel. He was deeply chagrined. The primary fault lay, however, with the incompetent career service officer who had been letting all League communications pile up in a sort of dead-letter file.

As it was then apparent that the United States would not join the League, Root was uncertain whether the American group should attempt to nominate judges for the court the League had created. He cabled Drummond that he was trying to get his fellow panel members together "to determine whether under the circumstances we have authority to comply with your invitation." [3] When they met, Straus and Gray thought the nominations should be made in spite of the roadblocks the Senate had erected between Washington and Geneva. Root then went to Washington in September, 1921, and laid the panel's dilemma before Hughes.

The Secretary was then in the midst of his preparations for the Conference on the Limitation of Armaments. Realizing that treaties coming out of the conference would be worthless without the Senate's approval, he was wary of any step that might antagonize the Senate. The members of the Court of Arbitration, he reminded Root, had been appointed by the President, and any action by them would be regarded as in effect done by the United States Government. Consequently, he feared that compliance with the League's request "would involve serious risk of immediate controversy which might be very injurious to the success of the important policies the government is now pursuing. . . ." [4] At the same time, Hughes said, he had no request to make of the judges. He had spoken frankly because Root had raised the issue, but

[2] CEH to Root, Aug. 16, 1921.

[3] Reprinted by permission of Dodd, Mead & Company from *Elihu Root* by Philip C. Jessup. Copyright, 1938, by Dodd, Mead & Company, Inc.

[4] *Ibid.*, p. 426.

he felt that the judges should act on their own responsibility.[5] Root replied that he too was convinced that the nominations should not be made. With the consent of the other judges, he cabled to Drummond to convey the reluctant conclusion that the American arbitration judges were not entitled to suggest nominees for the new court.

Apparently Root's disclaimer of authority to make the nominations was his own idea. There would have been less embarrassment when nominations were later made by the same group, without waiting for the United States to ratify the World Court protocol, if Root had merely accepted Hughes' argument that it was inexpedient for the four Hague Court judges to act in the fall of 1921. Hughes never questioned their authority.

Unaware that Hughes was merely biding his time on the World Court issue, the pro-League forces unlimbered some of their heaviest artillery against him. Hamilton Holt directly accused the Secretary of preventing the American Hague judges from sending in their nominations. As the interests of the court were close to his heart, this sort of criticism was hard for Hughes to take. "What a wonderful thing it would be," he remarked, "to wear a mantle of complacency so thick and warm that you would never fear the cold comments of the world." But he was never to find such a mantle. In this instance, moreover, he could not divulge what his future strategy would be, and the disgruntled friends of the court had no means of reading his mind. His reply that Holt's statement was "in error" and that "the American Hague Judges acted in accordance with their own views of propriety" [6] was not enough to overcome an impression that Hughes and Root were out to scuttle the World Court.

While the critics were having their field day, Hughes worked quietly "through one of the most eminent and most influential friends of the League" to get a voice for the United States in the election of World Court judges.[7] His silence on the court issue was finally broken in a speech at Boston on October 30, 1922. By this time the Senate was less suspicious of his motives, and the Washington Conference treaties had successfully run the senatorial gantlet.

"We favor, and always have favored, an international court of justice for the determination according to judicial standards of justiciable international disputes," the Secretary said. "I believe that suitable arrangements can be made for the participation by this Government in the election of judges of the International Court which has been set up, so that this Government may give its formal support to that court as an independent tribunal of international justice."

A misinterpretation of this speech by Charles A. and Mary R. Beard demands correction because of the generally high standing of their historical

[5] CEH, Notes, p. 310. [6] CEH to Holt, July 13, 1922.
[7] CEH to Edwin Gay, Aug. 1, 1922.

work. "Secretary Hughes," they wrote, "made a declaration in favor of a world tribunal standing on an independent basis. That was a concession but as nearly all the nations of the earth were operating under the League court, there was a distinct air of hauteur in the American call for another institution of international justice. Perceiving this paradox, perhaps, Harding himself then indicated a desire to participate in the existing World Court if it could be so constituted 'as to appear to be . . . a world court and not a League court.' . . ." [8]

At no time did Hughes have any idea of proposing "another" court.[9] He spoke of arrangements for the United States to participate in the election of judges "of the *International Court which has been set up,* so that this Government may give its formal support to *that* court." (Italics supplied.) His reference to "an independent tribunal of international justice" was clearly a description of the court then in being. The suggestion that Harding stepped in to swing his Administration away from an impracticable State Department scheme to set up a new world court is especially ironical, for it was Hughes who was pushing Harding faster than he wished to move toward the existing World Court.

It was no accident that Hughes' first blow for the World Court was struck in Boston. That locale gave him a natural opportunity to sugar-coat his advocacy of the World Court with complimentary references to Senator Lodge, who was still chairman of the strategic Committee on Foreign Relations. As Lodge was confined to his home by illness, Hughes sent him a copy of the speech. The Senator replied that it was "a very great speech indeed." Back in Washington, Hughes found a favorable opportunity to see Lodge and elaborate the Administration's hopes and plans for ratification of the World Court protocol, with reservations. The wily New Englander refrained from expressing opposition in the face of Hughes' persuasive arguments, but his subsequent action was to prove that silence had not given consent.

Putting the most favorable interpretation on Lodge's passivity, Hughes again pressed for action at the White House. Harding once more indicated his approval, but he was eager to dispose of the merchant-marine bill and several other items on the legislative calendar before sending up a message on the World Court. Hughes agreed to wait a little longer.

February, 1923, rolled around, and Harding had made no move toward sending a World Court treaty into the senatorial lion's den. Confined to his home by an attack of grippe, with time to think about the court problem, Hughes decided to thrust the issue before the President in a form that would stimulate action. If Congress should adjourn before considering adherence to

[8] *The Rise of American Civilization* (New York, Macmillan, 1930), II, 691f. Copyright, 1930, by The Macmillan Company.

[9] CEH Notes, p. 311*b*.

the court, he thought, another year would be lost. Despite his illness, he dictated a long letter to the President outlining the steps he believed to be necessary to make adherence to the court feasible for the United States.

Ever mindful of the bitter-enders in the Senate, the Secretary took special pains to show that the Permanent Court of International Justice was not a mere tool of the League. The court statute had not become effective, he asserted, upon its adoption by the Assembly but only upon ratification of a special protocol by the participating powers. The court was open to nonmembers of the League. Its judges were jurists of the highest caliber from many nations, including a distinguished American—John Bassett Moore. To be sure, the judges were elected through the machinery of the League. It was this provision, giving the small nations a veto on judges through the Assembly and the large nations a veto through the Council, which had made the organization of the World Court feasible. Arrangements could now be made, he thought, for the United States to share in the election of judges on a basis of equality with the other states. "I am profoundly convinced," he concluded, "that this Government, under appropriate conditions, should become a party to the convention establishing the Court and should contribute its fair share of the expense of maintenance." [10]

Hughes offered four "conditions and understandings to be made a part of the instrument of adhesion": (1) our acceptance of the court statute should not be taken to involve us in any relation to the League; (2) the United States should be permitted to participate, on a footing of equality, in any and all proceedings of the Council and Assembly of the League for the election of judges; (3) our share of the expenses of the court should be determined and appropriated by Congress; (4) the court statute could not be amended without the consent of the United States.

Harding sent a copy of the Hughes letter to the Senate on February 24, along with a brief endorsement. Lodge came back with a tricky question. Did the President favor an agreement obligating all powers signing the protocol to submit to the court all disputes (of a specified character) which could not be settled by diplomatic efforts? A Yes answer would be fuel to the faggots the committee was piling up around the protocol. An answer of No would leave the court open to attack as a weak tribunal lacking compulsory jurisdiction.

The statute of the court gave it jurisdiction over only such cases as the powers might voluntarily submit to it, unless they had signed the optional compulsory clause, as only fifteen of the forty-six signatories had done. In his letter to the President, Hughes had carefully avoided asking for acceptance of the compulsory clause, knowing that it would be futile. Replying to Lodge, he found satirical amusement in pointing to the Chinese wall that the Senate

[10] *Foreign Relations, 1923*, I, 10–17.

had built against obligatory arbitration or adjudication of international differences. "In the light of this record," he wrote, "it would seem to be entirely clear that unless the Senate changes its attitude it would be a waste of effort for the President to attempt to negotiate treaties with the other Powers providing for an obligatory jurisdiction of the scope stated in the Committee's first inquiry. . . ." Lodge's boomerang thus smacked the Senate itself.

Hughes carried his case to the country in a speech before the American Society of International Law on April 27, 1923. We have a direct interest, he said, in seeing that "the best practicable method of judicial settlement" is applied to other nations' controversies as well as to our own. The faith of the American people in fact-finding and the application of law had been demonstrated by the participation of their government in more than seventy arbitrations. But it was unnecessarily expensive to create a separate tribunal for every case, and that practice resulted in a series of "sporadic utterances by temporary bodies" instead of the orderly development of international law that could be expected from a permanent bench of judges. An established court, moreover, would eliminate the increasing difficulty of finding impartial arbiters after a controversy had arisen.

The plan of the court, he declared, "gives every assurance against a successful attempt by any *bloc* to manipulate or control the elections." To the complaint that the court set up by the League was not a world court, he replied, "It is not too much to say that there will be no world court if this court cannot be made one, and whether or not it is to be in the fullest sense a world court depends upon our own action." As to the argument that joining the court would be an "entanglement," he asked, "In what do we become entangled?" Judicial settlement of international controversies had been a feature of American policy since the foundation of the government. "We have never considered this to be an entanglement," he asserted. "If you are to treat participation in a permanent court of international justice as an entanglement foreign to our institutions, you must rewrite American history."

Nor was it necessary to await the codification of international law. "We shall make no progress toward the prevention of war," he said, "if we adopt a perfectionist policy. Whatever else we should have, we need at once a permanent court of international justice. No plan to promote peace can dispense with it. . . . I hope that the United States, in deference to its own interests and in justice to its ideals, will do its part." [11]

This speech is one of the finest expositions of an intricate political problem in the English language. Hughes' persistent critic, Hamilton Holt, called it "by all means the most lucid, logical and irrefutable argument for the court that has appeared anywhere." [12] Rereading the speech a generation later,

[11] *The Pathway of Peace*, pp. 65–88. [12] Holt to CEH, April 28, 1923.

Judge Manley O. Hudson of the World Court was moved to write to Hughes, "It is a most accurate chart for us today, and I feel myself still inspired by your words of almost twenty years ago." [13]

The Secretary was constantly on guard against schemes to take the court out of its strictly judicial role. "The success of the Permanent Court of International Justice is too important," he wrote to Lewis Einstein, the American minister to Prague, "to permit it to be used for the purpose of dealing with questions which lie outside the appropriate determination of justiciable controversies. . . . We have steadily refused in this country to permit the Supreme Court to become a political agency and I feel that we must take a similar attitude with respect to the Permanent Court of International Justice." [14]

Hughes made another plea for the World Court in his address at the Kent Centennial Celebration at Columbia University on June 4, 1923. Two weeks later he told the alumni at Dartmouth College, "There is no path to the millennium other than the path of justice, and if we discard the best attainable instrumentalities of justice, to that extent we invite the decision of the sword."

When Coolidge succeeded to the Presidency, he too spoke out for the court, and both the political parties called for adherence to the protocol in their 1924 conventions. But the Senate committee continued to stall. Lodge had introduced a bill calling for a new world court in the image of the existing one, except that he omitted any mention of the League. "It does not change the character of the judges," Hughes commented, "to move them from one room to another." [15] On the day before Hughes left office, the House of Representatives expressed its confidence in the court by a vote of 301 to 28 without stirring the balky Senate to action.

Out of office, Hughes continued to pile up arguments for the World Court. He told the American Society of International Law, of which he had been elected president, that

> We have come to realize that war is not to be ended by war, that the seeds of another conflict have been plentifully sown, and that the spirit of man emerged from the fire of the struggle still unpurified, more restless if not more passionate, and less amenable to restraint. . . .
>
> It is precisely because we are dealing with civilization itself, which is nothing less than progressive self-restraint and an increasing capacity for cooperation to ensure the enrichment of the individual life, that we attach the greatest importance to the development of international law . . . the effort to promote the reign of law, as accepted, not imposed, may be after all the most important contribution to permanent peace.
>
> . . . it is not correct . . . to speak of peace, or the mere absence of war, as our ultimate goal. We wish to have the peace, not of the lowest forms of life, but

[13] Hudson to CEH, Dec. 12, 1942. [14] July 11, 1924.
[15] Castle diary, 1924, p. 151.

of the highest, with its inescapable longings and strivings. Peace is but an opportunity, and our chief concern is justice.

In Washington, however, timorous Senators had found a powerful ally in Judge Moore, who had returned from The Hague fearful that the court might abuse its power of giving advisory opinions. The court had set a sensible precedent when the League Council had requested an advisory opinion on the dispute between Finland and Russia over Karelia.[16] Because Russia, not a member of the League, withheld its consent, the court had ruled that it could

By Edwin Marcus in the *New York Times*, January 25, 1925.

ANOTHER ECLIPSE?

not give an advisory opinion in that case. It had concluded, moreover, that in any event advisory opinions could be given only in open court in conformity with the rules laid down for the handling of other cases. Not satisfied to have these sound rules established by a seven-to-four decision of the court itself, Moore sought to make them forever binding by writing them into an American reservation to the court protocol to which the previous signatories would be asked to assent.

Senator George Wharton Pepper sponsored a resolution embodying Moore's ideas. President Coolidge hastened to ask Hughes' advice. "I have never been able exactly to determine," the President wrote, "whether Judge Moore thinks we ought to go into the Court or stay out of it, though I suppose he is in favor of adherence." [17] The next day Coolidge wrote to Hughes again to ask

[16] Denna Frank Fleming, *The United States and the World Court*, pp. 61 f.
[17] Coolidge to CEH, Nov. 3, 1925.

"what possible authority there can be for the constant assertion that it [the court] has to declare the League law to be *the* law."

Hughes was cool to the Pepper-Moore draft. As to Judge Moore's elaborate reservation prescribing rules for the court in rendering advisory opinions, Hughes thought it was quite unnecessary, although he did not object to the principles laid down. "The United States," he wrote, with clear-headedness that seemed to be lacking in the Senate, "would not have responsibility for any opinion upon any question in the submission of which it did not take part." [18]

Nor did he see anything frightening in the "League law" bogey. There could be no "League law," he advised the President, except in the sense of agreements between members of the League or rules established by it, and in neither case could these deprive states outside the League of their just rights. The court was bound by its own statute to apply international conventions, international customs that had come to be accepted as law, and the principles of law recognized by civilized nations; it could also recognize judicial decisions and legal teachings as subsidiary means of determining the law. ". . . if we were to undertake to set up a Permanent Court of International Justice of our own making," he wrote, "we probably should not care to phrase its duty differently."

It was Judge Moore's voice, however, that prevailed with the Senate. After accepting Moore's ultracautious reservations, the Senate added one of its own. No American case should go to the World Court in any event without the consent of the Senate by a two-thirds vote. The Senate finally adopted its own emasculated version of the court protocol on January 26, 1926, nearly three years after Hughes' letter had gone to Capitol Hill.

Distasteful though the extreme reservations were, Hughes hoped that the other powers would accept the Senate's proposal. "The significant thing," he said, "is that the United States has reaffirmed its historic policy." [19] But the League powers countered with reservations of their own, and the United States remained outside the court. That is the price the country paid for rejecting Hughes' advice, for it is clear that his limited reservations would have been acceptable to the other powers.

In 1935 a modified proposal to take us into the court failed to get a two-thirds vote in the Senate. It was not until the United Nations came into being after World War II that the United States finally took its place in the International Court of Justice. Meanwhile Hughes had served as a judge on the international bench, and his unquenchable faith in the judicial settlement of disputes had given buoyancy to the continued struggle for a world amenable to law.

[18] CEH to Coolidge, Nov. 5, 1925.

[19] Speech of April 22, 1926.

Chapter 58

THE HUMAN ELEMENT

FROM the foregoing pages one might suppose that Secretary Hughes had little time to sleep and no time at all for the ordinary trivialities of living. Actually he crowded into his busy days a myriad of personal chores and pleasantries. He found time to "be with the boys" at college class reunions, to write old friends, to give advice to youths, to send greetings to dozens of gatherings, to speak for charitable causes, to have several portraits painted, and to joke about thousands of things that tickled his sensitive wit.

When Philip A. de László espied the Secretary in a white suit one summer day, he said that he would like to paint him in that attire and would make him a present of the canvas. Having sat for several portraits, Hughes at first replied that he could not spare the time that would be required, but later he consented on de László's assurance that it would not take more than two sittings. As he went to the Corcoran Art Gallery for the second sitting and discovered that the artist had obliterated almost everything he had previously done, Hughes was inclined to abandon the venture, feeling that the portrait could never be finished in the time allotted. At the end of the third sitting, however, de László handed over the finished canvas, and it is the best portrait of Hughes in existence.

The painting of the Hughes portrait that hangs in the Cornell Law School library gave its subject a different sort of experience. He and Simon Elwes, popular English artist, exchanged so many good stories and had such a good time together while Elwes was at work that the portrait acquired the air of a man about town. "All it needs is a boutonniere," Hughes remarked as he surveyed the finished painting, "to make me a boulevardier."

Old friends and new discovered that Hughes' office was a humming workshop but no ivory tower. When "Al" Smith called, the Secretary rushed out to the reception room to greet him and ushered the Governor into the inner office with a friendly arm around his shoulder. Such effusive greetings were rare, but several of Hughes' aides felt his arm on their shoulders as an expression of appreciation for some service superbly rendered.

The Secretary's prolific correspondence included numerous personal letters of advice, encouragement, and kind words to people in trouble. He found time to write thoughtful suggestions to mothers worried about their children, to advise veterans as to their careers, and to comfort friends who had suffered misfortunes. Something deep within his nature seemed to drive him to a full utilization of his powers, and the satisfaction that came from these casual acts of kindness was not very different from that derived from great achievements.

Blessed with an outgiving disposition, he naturally distributed most freely the intellectual coin that he possessed in greatest abundance. It would not be accurate to assume, however, that advice and cheer were his only gifts. His letters to relatives, friends, and organizations sometimes contained checks despite his limited means at this time. When the bread of kindness cast upon the waters returned in tangible form, he was cautious about receiving it. Such tokens of esteem as flowers, fruit, and incidental items of food he accepted, but he returned a package of cravats and many similar gifts. His invariable rule of not accepting compensation for his speeches caused him to return checks sent for that purpose in ignorance or disregard of his wishes.

Yet he continued to make an astonishing number of speeches that had little or no relation to his work as Secretary of State. On October 3, 1921, he presided over and addressed a gathering commemorating the six hundredth anniversary of the death of Dante. In memory of Helen, he spoke for the national and local tuberculosis associations. He laid the cornerstone of the National Baptist Memorial to Roger Williams and Religious Liberty, and spoke repeatedly on university campuses. The insistent demand for his speeches never turned his head or gave him any easy sense of mastery. A week before he was to deliver his scholarly address at the James Kent Centennial he wrote to his son, "I am terrified by the preparations to hear the address, which is still in the works."

The advent of radio induced him to change his speaking technique. As governor and as presidential candidate, he had been accustomed to enthusiastic audiences who would applaud the crescendoes of an extemporaneous speech. The radio audiences demanded more restraint and precision along with a conversational tone. This (plus the necessity of supplying copies to the press) meant that radio speeches had to be prepared in advance. At the same time Hughes was keenly aware of the dislike of American audiences for the reading of speeches. Finding himself frequently addressing an audience physically present as well as a larger radio audience, he took to memorizing what he wished to say. His Notes give the best account of his method:

> Fortunately I did not find it difficult to memorize a speech—even a long one. I have been blessed, to a fair degree, with visual or what is sometimes called a photographic memory. That is, having composed a speech, I find that reading it a few times—always from the same typewritten copy—fixes the type in my mind's eye so that in speaking I am almost reading the pages. When I wished to interpolate, introducing something that was suggested or required by the occasion, or paused

to answer a question, I put a mental finger at the place on the page, and after the interpolation or interruption I could easily resume where I had left off. Reporters sitting before me with copies of my speech have flattered me sometimes by saying that I had reproduced the written speech with verbal exactness. But that is an exaggeration. To follow the written speech so that the reporters were satisfied that I was not delivering a speech different from the one given out, answered the purpose.

His speeches were always prepared under pressure. "Aside from the Historical Address at Brown University (1914) and my lectures on the Supreme Court at Columbia (which because of so many references and details had to be worked over for some time)," he tells us, "I do not recall an instance in which I prepared an address with the pleasing consciousness that I could work at leisure and completely satisfy my ambition. Time was always of the essence, and one demand had to be got out of the way to make room for another on its heels." At no time in his life, however, did Hughes make use of a ghost writer. On one occasion he did incorporate a brief memorandum on the Near East in a speech covering a wide range of subjects, but when a book of his speeches was published in 1925 this part of the address was dropped out.

Because of their heavy social schedule, an evening at home or a quiet meal together was a luxury for the Hughes family in this period. Even an illness that would mean confinement at home had some aspects of a happy interlude. In February, 1923, the family was stricken by grippe, and Elizabeth, in spite of her fever, was charmed by the opportunity of monopolizing her mother for more than a week. A good deal of bantering passed between the sick rooms, and Elizabeth captured some of it in a parody of Longfellow:

> Loud from his darkened bed chamber, the deep-voiced
> neighboring Secretary
> Speaks, and in accents disconsolate answers the wail
> of the Madame.

Elizabeth was the only fledgling left in the nest. When the family had moved to Washington in March, 1921, Catherine had found an excuse to remain in New York as a guest in her brother's home, because she was in love. Within a month she was engaged to Chauncey Lockhart Waddell of New York, son of Mr. and Mrs. Edwin J. Waddell of Greenfield, Ohio, and notified her parents by letter. While Mrs. Hughes had liked Chauncey from the beginning, this unexpected news prompted her to call the car and go straight to the State Department with the letter in her hand. It was the only time she ever broke in upon the Secretary's work at the office to discuss a personal matter. "Catherine is engaged," she told him, "to a fellow she has seen only half a dozen times."

Hughes had met the fiancé only once and could not identify him among the several young men Catherine had introduced to him. But he seemed to have implicit faith in his daughter's judgment. He and Mrs. Hughes telephoned their congratulations and also sent a telegram. Then each wrote Catherine a letter, with Hughes looking back at his own romance as the source of his greatest satisfaction:

Dearest Catherine,

I long to see you and tell you how glad I am that the great decision has been made and that for you life's real happiness has now begun. I have no fatherly words of wisdom—only thoughts of love. I have had only a glimpse of Chauncey—but Mother has told me how much she had admired him, and I am sure that he not only has your love but also that sincere esteem—by reason of qualities of mind and character—which underlies the love and faith that endure no matter what experiences life may bring. You cannot realize all that this means to you both, but Mother and I do. We are thinking of you and Chauncey and sending our choicest blessing, realizing the fullness of the happiness of our thirty-two years together. The day we plighted our troth is as bright in the memory as ever and we have been reviewing those days of long ago with the tenderest thought of you.

Tell Chauncey that he will have the welcome of a son—and of the winner of a great prize.

Love and kisses from
Father

The marriage took place on June 10, 1922, in the Bethlehem Chapel of the National Cathedral in Washington and was the first Cabinet wedding of the Harding Administration. A distinguished gathering, including the President and Vice President, kept eyes fastened on the vivacious bride in her crepe-basque satin gown elaborately embroidered with pearls while the "I do's" were said. Then followed a reception at the Pan American Building at which the Secretary and Mrs. Hughes beamed almost as happily as the bride and groom. Hughes was already fond of his son-in-law—an affection that was to grow with the years.

More placid than her sister, Elizabeth nevertheless lived in a state of entrancement when men and women of famous names came to the Hughes household. In 1916 she had not realized her dream of bathing in the White House fountain, but that disappointment had long since been swallowed up by the fascination of being daughter to the Secretary of State. During the formal dinner parties given by her parents, she could not resist the temptation of peering at the guests over the banister from a secluded position on the second floor.

"Elizabeth," her mother used to say, "you'll come down with a crash some night."

But her curiosity was stronger than any fear of embarrassment. Hughes was well aware of the spell that famous people cast on her, and when Lloyd George came to visit him, he called Elizabeth in for a five-minute chat with the dynamic little Welshman. She walked out on air, as only a girl of sixteen can.

Sparks of humor and whimsy helped to dispel any clouds that gathered in either domestic or official skies. When Charles Junior wrote to acquaint his parents with some difficulty he had encountered, his father admonished him: "If you run into a course of bad luck, remember your grandfather's story of the man who bought a lot of pigs for one dollar apiece and drove them a long way to market, selling them for seventy-five cents apiece. When asked where the profit came in he said he had the company of the pigs on the journey. You are getting a most valuable experience."

Selected as one of the "burnt offerings" at the Gridiron Club's semiannual dinner, Hughes replied to the invitation: "I suppose the victims must at least utter a groan, if desired, and I shall endeavor to say a word . . . as requested." If a dinner put him in a jocund mood, he would sometimes dash off nonsensical rhymes, at least one of which has survived in the mind of a friend:

> Wives of great men all remind us
> We can make our wives sublime
> And departing leave behind us
> All the rest at dinner time.

Sitting with Balfour at a banquet during the Washington Conference, Hughes facetiously recalled a story about Balfour being questioned in the House of Commons on the arrest of a sixteen-year-old watchmaker's apprentice for yelling "Bloody Balfour" in the streets of Dublin. Suave Mr. Balfour had answered, Hughes recounted, that there were certain inaccuracies in the report: the person arrested was not a watchmaker's apprentice, but a shoemaker; he was not a lad of sixteen, but a man of forty-six; he was not arrested for shouting insults, but for being drunk; and while it was true that the prisoner had shouted "Bloody Balfour" en route to the jail, His Majesty's Government did not regard that as sufficient cause for the man's liberation. Balfour was much amused, but instead of verifying the story, he said simply, "I wish I could think I had said that."

Requests that flowed into the Secretary's office were sometimes a source of amusement. One woman solemnly asked Mrs. Hughes to secure the autographs of delegates to the Washington Conference on a tablecloth. A general, who was afflicted with what Hughes called a bit of the "divine inflatus," sent in a plan to settle all Europe's troubles and then publicly announced that he could not comment on the plan because it was under consideration by the State Department. Hughes telegraphed to the general a bit sharply that he was going to tell the people what his (the general's) suggestion was, "as we could not have it thought that the Department was preventing the world's salvation." [1]

There was good nature as well as humor in his day-to-day contacts. "This is Papapou speaking," the Secretary boomed into his telephone one busy day. He was exchanging a long-distance greeting with his little grandson in New York, who preferred his own contracted version of "Grandpapa Hughes."

"Bring me a bale of hay," Hughes invariably commanded his waiter when taking breakfast away from home. If the waiter were observant, he could detect the flicker of a smile playing around the corners of the Secretary's mouth. And if he hastened to bring a bowl of shredded wheat, amicable relations were at once established.

Fond memories were occasionally stirred by a note or a greeting from old friends on the Supreme Court. When Hughes received a book from Justice Holmes, he replied:

MY DEAR MR. JUSTICE:

I have always been glad to receive anything at your hand—except a dissenting opinion. . . .

I suppose that you are still plugging away at the Fourteenth Amendment.[2]

Yes, Joseph H. Choate was right. One has to have his pleasure from day to day if he is going to get it at all. Hughes had an enormous capacity for sandwiching the little amenities of life in between his herculean tasks. These lighter moments may have had little to do with the deeper satisfaction that he found in work well done, but they added savor to life; and they were as much a part of the complex character of Charles E. Hughes as were his moral qualities and his mental powers.

[1] Castle diary, 1923, p. 135. [2] CEH to Holmes, Nov. 24, 1924.

Chapter 59

RESIGNATION

The year 1925 made its debut upon the stage of time amid a normal American hubbub over Coolidge prosperity, prohibition, and flapper fashions. In Congress the most exciting issues were the McNary-Haugen bill and the soldiers' bonus. Except for the smoldering anger in Japan over the Exclusion Act, our foreign relations were placid. It was a favorable moment, Secretary Hughes concluded, to return to the practice of law.

The State Department as well as the policies it was following had become the lengthened shadow of Charles E. Hughes. In part that was because he kept his fingers on everything the department was doing and carried a very large share of the burden himself. But in part also it was due to the striking loyalty that he commanded. His example of diligence, his courtesy, and the little things he remembered about employees gave him a special hold on them. Michael J. McDermott, later press relations officer of the department for many years, was one of several hundred employees who had shaken the Secretary's hand on the day he took office.

"Mr. Secretary," McDermott had said, "I'm proud to serve in your administration."

Four years later, when the employees filed by to say farewell, McDermott was again in the line.

"Well, Mac," Hughes asked, "are you still proud?"

Such incidents were typical, and they became lasting bonds between Hughes and his aides.

"As long as I live," Castle wrote in his diary near the end of the Secretary's fourth year, "I shall consider association with Mr. Hughes one of the great privileges of life. It is inspiring to come into contact with his mind, the most perfect mental machine in the world; with his courage, which always dares to do the right thing. . . . If he was only mind he would be a leader, but not the great leader he is. I know no more splendidly human person, no one with a bigger heart or quicker sympathy."

Nor was Hughes' personal interest confined to the top-ranking employees in the department. A routine letter reporting to the Civil Service Commission that certain charwomen in the department were doing outside work in violation of the regulations brought an explosion when it reached his desk. Tossing the letter at the chief clerk with an angry gesture, Hughes said he would not tolerate such nonsense. If these women wished to work extra hours to earn additional money for their families, he would be the last person in the world, regulation or no regulation, to get them into trouble for it. Hughes had lifted morale in the department to a level that has seldom been equaled.

The relations between the State Department and Congress had also undergone something akin to a revolution. Hughes had in large measure subdued the unruly Senate by working with it instead of throwing treaties into its teeth. Never demanding the impossible, he made the treaties he did send up so reasonable that the Senate was virtually compelled to accept them. The result was to supplant hostility by trust and amicable discussion even though many differences remained unreconciled.

Out of Hughes' experience with Congress came a suggestion to bridge the gap between the Executive and the legislature. ". . . the separateness of the executive power under our system, while it has advantages which have been deemed to be of controlling importance," he said, "deprives the Executive of the opportunities, open to parliamentary leaders, of participation in parliamentary debates. . . . The Secretary of State, acting for the President, may negotiate an important treaty, but he has no opportunity to explain or defend it upon the floor of the Senate when its provisions are under debate."[1] To overcome this handicap, he suggested that Cabinet members be given the opportunity to speak personally in either house of Congress when important departmental measures and policies are under debate. The proposal was not original with him, nor did he succeed in getting it accepted. But it gave special point to his belief that our governmental system of divided powers can be made to operate more efficiently by the simple device of executive-legislative cooperation.

The fruitfulness of Hughes' cooperative attitude is a matter of record. During his four years as Secretary of State sixty-nine treaties were negotiated, not counting a few insignificant ones that were later withdrawn. Of these, sixty-three had been approved by the Senate when Hughes left office. Of the remaining six, four were later ratified. The only two that failed in the Senate were the general relations treaty with Turkey and the Geneva convention for suppression of obscene publications. In addition, the Senate turned a cold shoulder to two protocols—one providing adherence to the World Court and the other dealing with the relations of Costa Rica to the Panama Canal.

Hughes' only conspicuous failure in dealing with the Senate, therefore, was in respect of the World Court, and both the tests on this issue came long after his resignation. The Hughes record, said the *Christian Science Monitor,* "constitutes a chapter of cooperation between the Department of State and

[1] Address to University of Michigan, June 19, 1922.

the Senate without parallel in the relations between the executive and legislative branches . . . no administration ever had so great a proportion of its foreign treaties approved by the Senate." [2]

On the basis of his own experience, Hughes concluded that there was no need for changing the constitutional requirement of a two-thirds vote in the Senate for approval of a treaty. The rejection of the Treaty of Versailles had created a powerful argument for abolition of the two-thirds rule. While recognizing the disadvantages of an arrangement which sometimes results in minority decisions and which deprives the House of Representatives of a share in the treaty-making process, Hughes was more impressed by the vast scope of the treaty power. Whatever is pertinent to our international relations, he said, is within the sweep of the power to make treaties. If the President could ratify treaties with the advice and consent of only bare majorities in the House and Senate, he might unwisely commit the nation to policies that could not be changed, as domestic legislation may be. In Hughes' mind that danger outweighed the disadvantage of having a treaty occasionally rejected by the Senate.

Whether or not one agrees with this conclusion, the success of Hughes' way with the Senate is well established. He maintained congenial relations both with the Republican and with the Democratic members of the Committee on Foreign Relations. Individual Senators frequently called on him at the department, and he was always well informed as to what the committee was thinking and doing. Borah's accession to the chairmanship on Lodge's death was unquestionably disappointing to Hughes, and when the latter resigned shortly afterward it was widely suggested that Borah's enhanced power was the cause. Hughes steadfastly denied this, and there is no reason to doubt his candor; for he succeeded in establishing satisfactory working relations with Borah. It was a matter of principle with him not to let personal feelings disrupt the public business.

Hughes' decision to leave the Cabinet was taken shortly after the election of Coolidge to a new term in November, 1924. The relations between the two men were still close and cordial, although Coolidge showed no enthusiasm over the vigorous speechmaking campaign that Hughes had made in his behalf. When the Secretary reported on his journey, half expecting a warm expression of thanks, the taciturn Yankee, whose reputation for parsimony in all things was already well established, said with a slightly embarrassed smile, "Well, I hear you've been making some good speeches." That was all! Hughes knew that the President intended it as a genuine expression of gratitude, but was none the less amused by his restraint.

The Secretary's chief reason for resigning was that he had been working at

[2] March 9, 1925.

top speed with little relaxation and no extended vacation for eight years. Now he was worn out. As he approached the end of his fourth year in office, moreover, he had a strong yearning to earn some money. For twenty years he had been almost continuously in public service. His expenses as Secretary of State, as during his governorship, had greatly exceeded his $12,000 salary. With his sixty-third birthday approaching, he felt that his primary duty was to make a satisfactory financial provision for his family's future. Mrs. Hughes too was eager for relief from her heavy social burden. Having notified Coolidge of his intention in November, the Secretary formally tendered his resignation on January 5, 1925, to take effect on March 4.

When he told his family that he had handed his letter to the President, he was in high spirits. Nevertheless, he was a little surprised by Coolidge's ready acceptance of his resignation. Laughing a bit ruefully, he said, "I feel a little as if I had been fired." Then, in a serious voice, he added: "Much as I wish to return to private life, I have so enjoyed the wonderful cooperation of those fine men in the department that if he had said to me, 'Hughes, I earnestly ask you to stay,' I don't think anything could have driven me from the job!"

The President responded to Hughes' letter as follows:

> I can well appreciate that you are personally entitled, after twenty years of public service, to seek some of the satisfactions of private life. But I cannot refrain from expressing my feeling of personal loss at the prospect of your retirement, and also the loss that must inevitably ensue when one of your ability and experience goes out of an office which he is so well qualified to fill.
>
> I realize, however, that this is in the nature of things, and so wish to put my emphasis upon the appreciation that I feel for your loyalty at all times to me, your many expressions by word and deed of a friendship upon which I could not set too high a value, and the exalted character and disinterested nature of the important public service that has come so constantly under my observation. I trust that you may have a well-merited repose and that satisfaction which alone can come from a consciousness that the duties of this life have been well performed.

At Hughes' suggestion, Frank B. Kellogg was named to succeed him. Kellogg was a conscientious and hard-working lawyer with experience in the Senate and at the Court of St. James's, and Hughes thought he was the best man available. Whatever qualifications Kellogg may have had, they suffered by comparison with Hughes'. Amid the chorus of praise for the retiring Secretary were many minor notes of regret that Kellogg was not his equal.

"It is not too much to say," declared the New York *Sun*, "that in sheer weight of mental force, backed and buttressed by sound and rugged character, Mr. Hughes stands with the foremost figures of to-day, perhaps the greatest of all." [3] The *Evening World* said that Hughes had parroted the language of the

[3] Jan. 12, 1925.

Irreconcilables and that from this phase of his career even his well-wishers would prefer to "walk backward with averted gaze and hide the shame." [4] But the *World's* was a lonely voice. Sir Willmott Lewis, Washington correspondent of the *Times* of London, referred to Hughes as "the most compelling figure among the Foreign Ministers of the post-war period" [5] and said this fact was perhaps more clearly appreciated outside the United States. The London *Observer* concluded that "In the Conferences of Washington and London, American cooperation without the League did bigger things than the League without American cooperation." [6]

"Probably not since John Quincy Adams," asserted the *Forum*, "have we had a more capable director of our foreign affairs." [7] "It is something to be said on behalf of democracy, which often blunders," said the *Outlook*, "that during this most critical period after the war this self-governing people found a way of putting such a mind to work on the specially intricate problems of foreign affairs." [8] One of the most pertinent comments came from Arthur Brisbane of the *New York American*, which had fought Hughes so bitterly when he ran against Hearst for the New York governorship: "Mr. Hughes, working for the public for twenty years, has sacrificed not less than six million dollars, plus interest, by doing so." [9]

Eminent friends of the Secretary swamped him with congratulations. Chief Justice Taft declared: "He was a great Secretary, one of the ablest we have ever had, as he was a great Judge and a great Governor." [10] At a dinner on Lincoln's birthday Arthur Balfour scribbled a note on the back of an envelope and passed it over to Senator Fess: "Charles E. Hughes is the most dominating figure I have ever met in public life." [11]

Within the department and the Foreign Service the farewells were warm with sentiment. "I doubt if you can realize how deep and genuine is our feeling of regret at your going—how much loyal attachment will follow you into private life," wrote Hugh Gibson from Berne. "Since your resignation was announced I have heard nothing but regret such as I have never heard in regard to the going of any other public man." Hugh R. Wilson was so upset that he tried to persuade the Secretary to change his mind.[12] Still more touching was a letter in which "a humble, insignificant clerk" let herself go in a personal lament over the loss of her "beloved chief":

> I wanted you to know that not only I but every other woman in the Department appreciated more than I can tell you the unfailing generous courtesy with which you went out of your way to greet us when you saw us around the Depart-

[4] Jan. 12, 1925. [5] March 3, 1925. [6] Jan. 25, 1925.
[7] January, 1923. [8] Jan. 21, 1925. [9] Jan. 12, 1925.
[10] Claude M. Fuess, *Calvin Coolidge* (Boston, Little, Brown, 1940), p. 363, note 2. Copyright, 1940, by Claude M. Fuess.
[11] Original in Hughes Papers. [12] *Diplomat Between Wars*, p. 173.

By Carey Orr in the *Chicago Tribune*, January, 1925.

COMPLETED WITHOUT A BLOT

ment. It meant a great deal more to us than you have any idea of and it was quite understood that to meet you in the morning meant a happy day.[13]

The friendly sentiments that affected Hughes most deeply were expressed at a luncheon on March 3 at Rauscher's given by the staff of the State Department. Undersecretary Grew spoke for the group:

> We are at the parting of the ways with our chief, who, through four strenuous years, has held in unstinted measure our admiration and respect, our devoted loyalty, and, what is more, our deep personal affection. . . . If any greater monument to his work can be erected than the specific achievements of the last four years, it may be found in the inspiring and enduring influence he has exerted upon those around him. Because of it we shall always be better servants of the Government, better men.
>
> During the last four years the Department of State has attained a cohesion, an enthusiasm and an esprit de corps which has never before been equalled; a department where every man and woman works for the joy of working, and knows that his work is being directed into the right channels to constructive ends.[14]

When Mr. and Mrs. Hughes and their daughter Elizabeth left Washington on March 6, almost the entire Cabinet and diplomatic corps were at the station. Mounting the steps of a coach, Hughes held an informal farewell reception. After the last hand had been shaken and the train began to roll, he settled into a seat with the comfortable thought that his public career was over and he was now a free man for the remainder of his days.

The passing years have given Hughes additional stature as Secretary of State. He is repeatedly bracketed with the most eminent men who have held this office—Jefferson, Madison, John Quincy Adams, and Elihu Root. Sixteen years after Hughes' resignation James Grafton Rogers ranked him among "the little handful of major statesmen this country has produced." [15] The final conclusion of Charles Cheney Hyde is that "We have to go back for more than a century to find his equal in that office." [16] Sumner Welles' estimate likewise verges on the superlative:

> In his sheer intellectual supremacy, in his enlightened recognition of this country's permanent interests, and in his constructive patriotism, Charles Evans Hughes towers above all but a few of the truly great Americans of the past century.[17]

Greatness consists of many facets, but it is possible in Secretary Hughes' case to single out a few of special significance. First, there was seldom any doubt about where he stood. Muddling through was contrary to his nature. If Hughes did not know what our policy should be in any given instance, he

[13] Louise E. Lacey to CEH, March 4, 1925. [14] *New York Times*, March 4, 1925.
[15] *American Bar Association Journal*, July, 1941, p. 412.
[16] Prof. Hyde to author, July 15, 1947. [17] *Washington Post*, Sept. 7, 1948.

By "J. N. Ding" in the New York *Herald Tribune*, 1925.

NO WONDER HUGHES RESIGNED

probed into the facts until he had the answer. His subordinates were never left to flounder in confusion. Second, he thought in global terms. Before launching a policy in Latin America, the Near East, or Europe he sagely anticipated its repercussions in other parts of the world. Never did he play off the prejudices or hostilities of one area against those of another. His aim was nothing short of the welfare of the world, and all his major policies, from the limitation of arms to European economic recovery and the liquidation of imperialism in Latin America, point in that direction.

Third, he built no dream castles but worked with the men, the facts, and the ethos of his time, without losing sight of his long-range objectives. No one understood better than he that statesmanship is the art of the possible. Working against a tide of disillusionment and isolationism that he could not stem, he nevertheless reasserted world leadership in those areas of policy-making in which passion had not subverted reason. His stern refusal to abandon international cooperation because perfection could not be attained kept hope alight and eased the approach to collective security when a new opportunity arose out of World War II.

Fourth, his policies had a moral quality about them that overreached national interests in the narrow meaning of that term. Diplomacy with him was not a game or a matching of wits for the advancement of one country at the expense of others. Rather, it was the direction of international relations in accord with sound principles. "Our greatest interest," he once said, "is international friendship. National prestige may be associated with power, but it is never heightened by a brutal assertion of it. Indeed, our national prestige is inseparably connected with the demonstration of our sense of justice." [18]

Hughes' passion for justice was no less in evidence in his foreign policy than in his work on the supreme bench. He held steadily before him, as Sir Willmott Lewis pointed out, "the concept of the State as the embodiment of justice rather than force, with its corollary of the reliance on justice rather than force for the vindication of national policy." [19] There was no place for imperialism, "dollar diplomacy," or power politics in this concept. "The principle, each nation for itself to the full extent of its power," he once said, "is the principle of war, not of peace." [20] If a nation is truly devoted to peace, it must first substitute justice for force in its own dealings with its neighbors.

Here is the core of Hughes' policy. He had the courage to dethrone "My country right or wrong" and to deny sponsorship to every American cause that he believed to be unjust. That high moral attitude fused into working principles, without any taint of self-righteousness, lifts Hughes into the select company of our best and wisest molders of foreign policy.

[18] Speech of Nov. 10, 1925. [19] *Times* (London), March 3, 1925.
[20] *The Pathway of Peace*, p. 15.

Chapter 60

PRIVATE CITIZEN AGAIN

REST WAS the first item in Hughes' plan for his new era of freedom. With his wife and Elizabeth, he spent the spring of 1925 in Bermuda and then shifted to Lake George for the summer. Under this unusual pampering his reserve of strength was fully restored, and a thorough medical examination showed him to be in fine fettle.

The mood in which they returned to housekeeping in New York is suggested by a rhyme that he dashed off for Mrs. Hughes' birthday on September 14:

We're two old birds at best,
Building another nest,
It's up a tall tree
And between you and me
Our Avenue beats all the rest.

But why speak of age
When we're only more sage!
Is not wisdom the crown of life?
My darling in truth
Has perpetual youth,
Richest blessings upon my dear wife!

The years gliding by
Only strength the tie
That binds our hearts together.
Our love, strong and true,
Will pull us both through;
We're ready for any weather.

His first resumption of activity was not money-making but speechmaking. No longer bound by official restraints, he poured out a Niagara of ideas. His audiences were the American Society of International Law, many bar associations, chambers of commerce, patriotic, literary, scientific and political gatherings, and colleges. The public servant who had retired to a life of peace and freedom soon found himself getting up at 5:00 A.M. to write speeches for which he consistently refused compensation.

The public loved it. Frederic William Wile suggested that America ought to elect Hughes toastmaster for life. "In language, power of expression and that ebullition that must mark the ideal toastmaster," Wile declared, "Hughes is incomparable. He scintillates mainly because he likes to do that sort of thing. . . . It comes naturally. He can lapse from the sublime to the ridiculous without a strain. He can tell stories as well as Choate ever told them and in the next breath stir hearers to emotional enthusiasm with some appeal to their moral or spiritual sense." [1] Apparently these traits had something to do with the characterization of Hughes by a legal journal, *The Jealous Mistress*, as "a cross between Jehovah and Bernard Shaw . . . a cousin to Mark Twain and a brother of Santa Claus." [2]

It is in his speeches and civic activities that we find the best index to Hughes' thinking during this period. He was soon to be assailed as a tool of wealth blind to the interests of a democratic people. But the work he was doing outside of his profession reflects a keen interest in the free society of which he was a part and a sympathetic understanding of its problems. While he was representing many big corporations at the bar, those associations cast no shadow upon the strong current of liberalism that ran through the activities he pursued for the love of it.

Addressing the American Bar Association as its president at Detroit on September 2, he assailed the reactionary thinking that had caused Nebraska to forbid the teaching of the German language and Tennessee to suppress the doctrine of evolution:

> The most ominous sign of our time, as it seems to me, is the indication of the growth of an intolerant spirit. It is the more dangerous when armed, as it usually is, with sincere conviction. . . . We justly prize our safeguards against abuses but they will not last long if tolerance gets under way . . . the just demands of liberty are not to be satisfied even by a free and uncorrupted right of suffrage. Democracy has its own capacity for tyranny. Some of the most menacing encroachments upon liberty invoke the democratic principle and assert the right of the majority to rule . . . freedom is in danger of being slain at her own altars if the passion for uniformity and control of opinion gathers head. . . .
>
> I do not propose to discuss evolution, or a particular statute and litigation recently much advertised [the Scopes trial in Tennessee]. . . . I desire in a non-controversial spirit to emphasize the vast importance of the freedom of learning in the hope that our people instinct with the spirit of liberty will not lay hands on our public schools and state universities to set obstacles in the path of knowledge. . . . If we sum up the comforts, the conveniences, the privileges and the opportunities of our life in the twentieth century . . . we must realize that these benefits are due, not so much to governments, or politics, or the strivings and issues of campaigns, but to the ceaseless and unobtrusive endeavors, and the unquenchable zeal, of the pioneers and their devoted followers in the quest of knowledge, who in the study of the earth and the universe have enlarged the inheritance of the race and vindicated the capacity and worth of the human spirit . . . freedom of learning is the vital breath of democracy and progress.

[1] *Evening Star* (Washington), April 27, 1925. [2] October, 1925.

The speech as a whole was an inspiring appeal that the law be made "the servant of liberty wisely conceived" and "the expression of the righteousness which exalteth a nation." The assembled lawyers could scarcely contain their admiration. Columnist Walter Lippmann wrote: "It seems to me about the most useful speech that anybody has undertaken to make in America for a long time." [3]

Hughes' interest in education was closely related to his political philosophy. "The cure for the ills of democracy," he said, "is not more democracy, but more intelligence." [4] Nor were his efforts in behalf of freedom of learning confined to occasional exhortations. As a trustee of the University of Chicago, he joined with President Harry Pratt Judson and others in altering a provision in the charter requiring that two-thirds of the trustees and the president of the university be members of regular Baptist churches. During most of the thirty-eight years that he was a Fellow of Brown University he also worked for liberalization of its charter.

Hughes had been a member of the committee of nine selected in 1908 to reexamine Brown's charter of 1764 giving the Baptists substantial majorities among the trustees and fellows and requiring the president to be a Baptist. The committee had brought in powerful arguments for removal of all the denominational provisions from the charter. Conservative alumni had whipped up a storm of protest. One member of the board had argued with deep feeling that if Catholics were admitted to the councils of the university it would be a betrayal of the founders. Hughes had replied in friendly tone but with withering effect. One eyewitness reports that "his logic fell with the driving power of a sledge-hammer, relentless, crushing, pulverizing." [5]

So bitter was the opposition, however, that the committee had advised postponement of action. It was not until 1926 that the presidency of Brown was freed from the denominational requirement and broader representation was given to non-Baptists on the board of trustees. Hughes was a consultant to the committee which sponsored this compromise and helped to shape the bill which the General Assembly of Rhode Island finally passed. In 1940 President Henry M. Wriston of Brown revived the issue, and after a conference with Chief Justice Hughes, it was decided that the time had come for full achievement of the aims of the original committee. This time Brown's charter was completely stripped of all denominational requirements.

Hughes' hatred of bigotry led him to join with Newton D. Baker and S. Parkes Cadman in founding the National Conference of Christians and Jews. The conference was an outgrowth of a dinner sponsored by the Committee on Good Will between Jews and Christians on February 23, 1926. As

[3] Lippmann to CEH. Aug. 27, 1925, after examining advance copy.
[4] Speech in Faneuil Hall, Boston, June 17, 1925.
[5] Everett Colby in *Scribner's*, May, 1928, p. 560.

toastmaster and principal speaker, Hughes made a powerful plea for tolerance, freedom of learning, religious liberty, and interracial cooperation.[6]

The following year he sent out a letter which raised $25,000, and this served to launch the conference as a going concern. Adopting the broad aims that he had suggested—elimination of intergroup prejudices and promotion of justice, amity, understanding, and cooperation among Protestants, Catholics, and Jews—the conference soon became national in scope. In 1940 it presented a citation to Chief Justice Hughes for his work in bridging the gulfs between racial and religious groups. Responding, he pleaded for a "deep and abiding sense of human dignity and worth" and said that rancor and bigotry "are deadly enemies of true democracy, more dangerous than any external force because they undermine the very foundations of democratic effort."

In 1947 Hughes sponsored the application of the International Council of Christians and Jews for affiliation with the United Nations Educational, Scientific and Cultural Organization. Tolerance with him was not a policy but a deep-seated trait. His son's activity as chairman of the Mayor's Committee on Unity in New York from 1944 to 1948 and the extensive work of his daughter (Mrs. Waddell) in behalf of the United Negro College Fund enlisted his keenest interest and sympathy.

Meeting with other bar association presidents in New York, Hughes joined in urging the appointment of a joint committee to investigate ambulance chasing and other shady legal practices. When lawyers make the machinery of justice a device to snare the unfortunate, he declared, "the outraged sentiment of the entire Bar should find expression in investigation, condemnation and redress. It should clean house. . . . Our trouble is not simply in keeping the pestilence out of the temple, but in destroying it inside." [7] "We are ministers of justice," he said in another speech to the bar, "and no lawyer is worthy of any reputation in the profession, whatever his ability may be, if he does not regard himself first and last as a minister of justice in the community in which he practices." [8]

Several books by Charles E. Hughes came off the press in this period. *The Pathway of Peace* contains more than a score of his speeches while he was Secretary of State. In May, 1928, he delivered a series of lectures at Princeton University on "Our Relations to the Nations of the Western Hemisphere," and these were published in book form. His Sherrill Foundation lectures at Yale on "Pan American Peace Plans" in March, 1929, were also published.

The most important of these volumes is *The Supreme Court of the United States,* containing six lectures delivered at Columbia University in January and February, 1927. Hughes devoted many of his supposedly leisure hours to

[6] *New York Times,* Feb. 24, 1926. [7] To Bronx bar, Jan. 25, 1929.
[8] *American Bar Association Journal,* May, 1926, pp. 323–326.

gathering and arranging his data. Addressing laymen as well as lawyers, he produced one of the few first-class books that have been written about the Supreme Court. While it is in no sense an "inside story" and H. L. Mencken complained that it ignored some of the court's "most gorgeous feats of nonsense," the book is infused with a fine understanding of the court and its constitutional function. Professor Felix Frankfurter of the Harvard Law School, later to be Hughes' colleague on the bench, called it "the most compact story of the foundations of the Court and an excellent description of the Court at work." [9] The stipend for the lectures went back to Columbia, along with all the profits from the book, which was in its fourth printing in 1947. A similar course was followed in regard to the Princeton lectures.

"Success in the democratic experiment," Hughes said in one of his speeches, "lies in the extent to which the strong are harnessed, with bit and reins and blinders, and are induced to pull the democratic cart on a straight road without running away or upsetting it." Taking him at his word, numerous professional and civic groups "hitched" him to their causes as soon as he was out of official harness. In addition to being president of the American Bar Association, the Legal Aid Society, and the American Society of International Law, he was named vice president of the Pilgrims' Society, later president of the Association of the Bar of the City of New York, and president of the American Judicature Society. He became a member of a committee to finance a memorial to Woodrow Wilson, his political opponent of 1916, and chairman of a New York group seeking to raise a million-dollar endowment fund to promote the study of American history. He accepted the chairmanship of the American Committee of the World Conference on Faith and Order, the vice presidency of the National Municipal League, a place on the National Advisory Committee for the Institute of Law at Johns Hopkins University, and the chairmanship of the committee sponsoring the Byrd expedition to the Antarctic. He was elected vice president of the Brown chapter of Phi Beta Kappa and was awarded the Rosenberger medal at Brown. The Roosevelt Memorial Association medal was also added to his collection in 1928.

"Now, once more with us," said the New York *Sun*, "we have Hughes the great lawyer and Hughes the citizen, whose untiring hands go out to every public task."

Yielding to pressure from both political parties, Hughes accepted the chairmanship of a commission to effect a reorganization of the government of New York State. As we have seen, his first efforts to give New York a modern administrative system had been made while he was governor. His campaign had been carried on by others after he left Albany, and in 1925 they had secured the adoption of a constitutional amendment. The Republican leaders

[9] *American Bar Association Journal*, April, 1930, p. 251.

of the legislature then set up an unofficial commission to work out an organizational pattern in keeping with this mandate from the people.

Former Speaker H. Edmund Machold had been informally selected to head the commission, but the choice aroused fear that the Republicans might give the reorganization a political twist. John W. Davis, who had been the Democratic presidential candidate in 1924, suggested that Hughes be drafted for the chairmanship. Hughes reluctantly consented, and, being nominated by Machold himself, was unanimously elected. His first act as chairman was to assure the people that the reorganization plan would be shaped to their interest "with no partisan taint about it whatever." [10]

Hughes had an able commission, with John Lord O'Brian as vice chairman and men like Henry L. Stimson, John W. Davis, Henry W. Taft, James W. Wadsworth, Nicholas Murray Butler, and Robert F. Wagner among the members. Subcommittees were named to bring in detailed plans and suggestions in various different spheres of governmental activity. On the basis of reports from these groups the executive committee of which Hughes was chairman shaped its conclusions. Forgetting his initial reservations, Hughes almost wore out his committee with long intensive sessions. Once the members rebelled when he tried to keep them in continuous session without any lunch. His seeming insensibility to the pangs of hunger when there was serious work to be done was one failing that his associates never quite forgave.

Thanks largely to Hughes' driving energy, the report was completed in late February, 1926, and won a remarkably favorable response. Nearly 180 departments, commissions, and bureaus were consolidated into eighteen administrative departments under control of the governor. The Water Power Commission and various other floating ribs were marked for abolition with transfer of their powers to the regular departments. The reformers also recommended creation of a full-fledged executive budget, a four-year term and more extensive removal power for the governor, and better salaries for the governor and department heads. The central idea behind the plan was to increase the powers of the governor for efficient management of the state's affairs. In this respect the Hughes Commission did for New York State what the Hoover Commission was to do for the Federal Government more than two decades later.

Governor "Al" Smith thought the report was a "wonderful piece of work" [11] and gave it his enthusiastic support. Not a word reflecting a partisan motive had entered into the candid discussions. So great was the prestige of the commission that the legislature hastened to accept not only the organizational pattern but also the recommended changes in the law. Many contributed to this happy outcome, but it was the deft hand of former Governor Hughes that turned a hopeful experiment into a glowing success.

[10] *New York Times*, Nov. 20, 1925.

[11] Smith's address of Dec. 17, 1926.

Hughes also maintained a lively interest in national affairs. On his trips to Washington to argue before the Supreme Court, he was frequently invited to the White House, and Coolidge talked volubly and frankly about problems confronting his Administration. Sometimes the calm little Yankee would talk for an hour or more, almost without stopping, trying out on Hughes ideas and policies that were taking shape in his mind. Hughes replied with equal candor.

The President importuned Hughes to lead the American delegation to the Conference on Naval Limitation at Geneva in 1927. Hughes replied that his duties as special master in the Great Lakes case made acceptance of such an assignment impossible. Although he was still intensely interested in abolishing provocative armament, it is quite probable too that he foresaw the failure of this 1927 venture. He was never inclined to beat his head against a stone wall when the possibility of accomplishment was nil. However, he did accept appointment as an American member of the Hague Court of Arbitration to succeed Judge Gray—the only position he ever held involving so much dignity along with so little work. It was in this period also that he headed the American delegation to the Havana Conference and was a delegate to the Pan American Conference on Conciliation and Arbitration.

Hughes' boundless activity led many to suppose that he was out to capture the Presidency in 1928. When he was a guest at the Gridiron dinner in December, 1926, the funmakers of the press tried to tease him into an admission by singing a ditty with this refrain:

> You're as welcome as the flowers in May.
> Do you think you will come back to stay?
> For the White House has not moved away—
> Do you think that you'll come back some day?

"It is very pleasant to be sung to!" Hughes responded in the best of humor. "But the political flowers that bloom in the Spring and wither in the Fall have nothing any longer, thank heaven, to do with the case. I am glad to be here as an equal in the full enjoyment of my constitutional rights as a private citizen,—in this place dedicated to the freedom of the press. It was not ever thus! I have been here as a burnt offering, but now I am clad in the comfortable asbestos of private life. . . .

"Chief Justice Taft once said that a constitutional lawyer was one who had abandoned the practice of the law and had gone into politics. Well, for anyone who has left his profession to go into politics, the happiest road is the way back. I am with you no longer as a servant but as one of the millions of masters in this fortunate land where the Government is so organized that everyone has a chance to talk but can do as little harm as possible."

One group of Hughes enthusiasts suggested that he run for the Senate by unseating Senator James W. Wadsworth in the New York primaries. Instead, Hughes threw his support to Wadsworth. On May 21 the Republican State Committee talked of drafting Hughes to run against "Al" Smith for the governorship, but he issued a statement saying that even if nominated he would refuse to run. Plans were then laid to make him temporary chairman and keynote speaker at the state convention, but Hughes sailed for Europe on June 16, announcing that he would not be back for the convention.

At last Hughes was back to his exhilarating routine of earlier years—renewing his strength and recharging his batteries by European travel. Taking Mrs. Hughes, Elizabeth, and her friend Polly Hoopes, he toured Italy, Switzerland, France, England, and Scotland as if he were once more an adventurous youth discovering new lands. All worries were cast to the winds. They climbed Mount Vesuvius and looked down into the crater. Traveling by motor, they reveled in the Italian countryside and little villages and then sought variety in the art galleries and cathedrals of the cities.

In Rome the veteran tourist and his party spent two weeks seeing the sights. Vice Consul David Bruce hired the best known local guide to show the party around, but it was Hughes who read the Latin inscriptions and did most of the talking about the monuments and shrines and the history connected with them. Although it was his first visit to Rome, he displayed such an astonishing knowledge of Roman history that the guide refused to take any pay for his services, saying that he had profited from the tour more than Hughes could have done.[12] Hughes called on Mussolini and had an informal chat with Pope Pius XI. Everywhere he was recognized. Relaxed and in a holiday mood, he was an easy mark for autograph hunters. When a laughing group of girls cornered him and then filed by in a line to get his autograph, he probably enjoyed it as much as they did.

Leaving Mrs. Hughes at Ábano-Terme for some treatments at the springs, Hughes took Elizabeth and Miss Hoopes to Venice. The fairy city of canals and palaces, throned on her hundred isles, was one of his first loves, and now its beauty stirred fond memories as well as new emotions. Whether they were feeding the pigeons at St. Mark's or gliding through the moonlight in a gondola, as opera stars in adjacent boats filled the night air with music, every moment was a joy. Hughes' happiness bubbled out in the form of reminiscences, jokes, and fascinating talk about the people and their customs.

Switzerland was always heavenly—the food, the wine, and the quiet serenity of the mountains. Reinvigorated by a motor tour through the Alpine haunts they loved so well, the Hugheses turned to Paris and London. Another motor tour took them through the English lake country into Scotland and then

[12] David Bruce to author, Jan. 26, 1950.

down to the cathedral towns. They sailed for home on the *Leviathan* near the end of September more than ever delighted with the new-found freedom of private life.

On the return voyage Hughes blossomed out in an utterly new role so far as the public was concerned. He teamed up with Will Rogers, the Oklahoma cowboy-humorist, as an entertainer. In response to the President's appeal for funds to aid the victims of the Florida hurricane disaster, the captain of the *Leviathan* called a meeting of its distinguished passengers, and Hughes seconded Rogers' suggestion that the entertainers on board be organized into a troupe to raise money for the cause. Rogers was made chairman. Apparently the rope-twirling humorist was chary at first about adding Hughes to his troupe; the two had not previously met, and Rogers regarded Hughes as "a pretty cold blooded proposition" who might freeze a joke in its tracks. But, "calcalatin'" that somebody would be needed to make a serious appeal for funds, Rogers satirically billed Hughes for "Wisecracks" and himself for "Diplomatic Immunity."

"Well," Hughes responded, "I have been called everything else in my career but an entertainer, but I will do my best."

Rogers tells what happened:

> We gave the concert and he was supposed to be the serious end of our program and then I was supposed to come along and blackjack them out of what they had. Well he got out there and he was making such humorous remarks and such entertaining observations that he almost forgot to mention what the appeal was to be for, but then he switched on them and all I had to do when I went on was to have a bushel basket to put the checks in.[13]

Rogers began his performance with the air of one whose thunder had been stolen. "Say," he exclaimed, "we asked this old guy up here to be serious!"

The show was repeated on the two following nights for the second-class and third-class passengers, with Hughes racking his brain for new jokes and Rogers complaining that Hughes had outclassed him. All told, the troupers collected $42,000. "It broke all records for any collection at sea," Rogers recounted, "and it was mainly due to the hearty cooperation of Mr. Hughes. Say, if he had been running for President then he would have carried that boat, Democrats and all . . . if ever a man was misunderstood in regard to being a real genuine good fellow it's this Mr. Hughes." It was the beginning of a fast but never intimate friendship between the judge and the comedian.

Back in New York, Hughes campaigned unsuccessfully for Wadsworth and for Ogden L. Mills, who had been nominated as the Republican candidate for governor. Talk of Hughes as a presidential nominee persisted through the early

[13] Rogers' column in *Atlanta Journal*, Oct. 17, 1926.

months of 1927 as the popularity of Coolidge waned. On May 20, Hughes issued a statement designed to set all speculation at rest:

> There should be no doubt as to my own attitude. I am for President Coolidge, first, last, and all the time, and I believe that he will be renominated and reelected. I do not wish my name to be used in any contingency. I am too old to run for President and I would neither seek nor accept the nomination.

The speculation flared up again, however, as soon as Coolidge's cryptic "I do not choose to run for President in 1928" came sizzling over the wires from the Black Hills. Hughes was again spending the summer in Europe with his wife and Elizabeth, without a political thought in his head. After a restful trip through France, including the Pyrenees and the Riviera, he returned in September and found that Secretary Hoover was making an active bid for the nomination. Several Hoover supporters called on Hughes and let him know that if he intended to go out for the nomination he would have a fight on his hands. Hughes assured them that he was not in any sense a contender.

Charles D. Hilles, Republican National Committeeman for New York, sounded out the party leaders and announced on December 1, 1927, that the New York delegation would go to the convention prepared to back Hughes. A few days later that unwilling favorite son said once more that he would not accept the nomination. While he was strong and vigorous at sixty-five, he would be nearly seventy-one at the end of the term. That age would be a bar to renomination, he said, and a President needs more than four years to carry out his program.

"Besides," Hughes added, "I don't want the turmoil of being a presidential candidate. I had that turmoil once, and I don't want it again." [14]

Hughes declined, late in March, 1928, to make the keynote address at the Republican Convention. As in 1920, he refused to compromise his position by making a speech that might seem to encourage a nomination he did not want. When the delegates assembled at Kansas City, powerful elements in the party were still trying to stop Hoover. Mellon, Hilles, Senator Butler, and Chief Justice Taft had all gone to the White House hoping for some hint that the President was willing to be drafted.[15] Coolidge was willing, but he remained quiet because he knew that there was no popular demand for his renomination. In a last desperate effort to save the party from Hoover, Thomas W. Lamont of J. P. Morgan & Company went to Hughes' office. An important group at the convention was eager to see Hughes nominated and elected, he said. All that was necessary was for Hughes to give his consent, and this group would throw its full strength behind his candidacy.

[14] Richard V. Oulahan in *New York Times Magazine*, Sept. 9, 1928, p. 19.
[15] William Allen White, *A Puritan in Babylon*, p. 400.

"Do you think I could accept a nomination coming in that way?" Hughes asked, with resentment and courtesy vying for control of his voice. Before Lamont left, Hughes had squelched the last vestige of hope that he could be drafted by Wall Street.

After Hoover was nominated, Hughes gave him assurance of his support and then sailed, with his family and a companion for Elizabeth, for another summer of freedom in Europe. In Berlin he visited President von Hindenburg, took his family for an airplane ride over the city, and laughed at his daughter because she was frightened. Motoring to Dresden and Prague, they visited Tomáš G. Masaryk, the tall and courtly President of Czechoslovakia, in his old castle. After a conference with Chancellor Seipel in Vienna, they turned again to Switzerland. Always the Alps had to be included. At Saint-Moritz they celebrated Elizabeth's twenty-first birthday, and her father indulged his custom of writing a birthday rhyme, which reflects his gay mood:

Elizabeth—! 'tis of thee
Sweet age of liberty—
Of thee I sing—
Age of our daughter's pride
Parents at last subside
From each St. Moritz side
Let freedom ring!

Before Hughes returned about the middle of September, he had been made honorary chairman of a lawyers' committee to aid Hoover. Eager to get Hughes back to Washington, the Hoover forces made another vain effort to induce him to run for the Senate. However, his high esteem for Hoover and his lifelong habit of resting his confidence in the Republican Party did impel him into the thick of the campaign in spite of his affection for "Al" Smith, the Democratic nominee.

In his first speech at St. Joseph, Missouri, on October 23, he drew a balance sheet of the two candidates' qualifications and found Hoover to be best fitted for the Presidency. At Chicago he assailed Smith's criticism of Coolidge's economy record. At Buffalo he gave new emphasis to Hoover's charge of "state socialism" against some of the Democratic proposals. At Worcester he lauded Hoover's record. In Brooklyn he took up the tariff, water power, and prohibition. So impressed were Hoover and his managers with the power of Hughes' speeches that they induced him to close the campaign—a privilege usually reserved for the candidate himself—with a radio broadcast from his New York apartment at 11:30 P.M. the night before the election.

Before listening to this speech, Hoover wired: "The effect your speeches has been the most profound of any campaign in our history. I hear them from [e]very town and village across the continent." His sense of obligation to his former colleague was further enhanced by the Republican landslide on November 6.

The greatest honor that was paid Hughes in these busy years was the unremitting demand for his services on the stump, in governmental tasks, at the bar, in the civic forum, in the universities, and around the festive board. When the Bronx County Bar Association met to honor Hughes on January 25, 1929, because he was soon to enter upon a new phase of his career, William D. Guthrie compressed a popular appraisal of the man into three words: "the perfect citizen."

Chapter 61

LEADER OF THE BAR

WHEN HE was not traveling in Europe, making speeches, or slaving over some public-service assignment, Hughes intensively practiced law. Rejoining his old firm, Hughes, Rounds, Schurman & Dwight, he had everything to his own liking, including his complete independence at the bar. The Hughes name itself was sufficient guarantee that his practice would be large, varied, and lucrative. There was also, as he wrote in his Notes, "the privilege of once more enjoying an intimate professional relation with my son."

A thousand friends swarmed into the huge ballroom of the Hotel Astor on November 10, 1925, to welcome Hughes back to the bar and signalize his service to the cause of international good will. It was a gay dinner, with all the sparkle, wit, and good fellowship that the great men of the law could give it. Irving T. Bush, the toastmaster, read congratulatory messages from President Coolidge, Chief Justice Taft, and Secretary Hoover. The chief address by Root was one of the finest tributes that one eminent American has ever paid to another.

"I think we are not so much here to do honor to Mr. Hughes," Root said, "as to thank him for having done honor to us. (*Applause.*)

"Mr. Hughes is a lawyer. I claim him for the Bar. If there be unworthy lawyers—and there are some—range them all together upon one side of the account and I will put Mr. Hughes on the other side of the account and thank you to pay me the balance in my favor. (*Applause.*)

". . . it is not merely what Mr. Hughes has done that has shed honor upon all, upon all of his countrymen. It is what he has stood for. He never sought an office; he never administered an office with a view to keeping it longer, or with a view to getting another. (*Applause.*) He never attempted to build up a personal political machine for his own aggrandizement. He never abandoned or suppressed an opinion which he thought ought to be expressed, in order to please anybody. He never hated or abused or imputed sinister motives to an adversary who differed from him. . . . He always thought about his job and never about himself. He subdued his idealism to the uses of mankind. He never sought popularity by glittering generalities or noble sentiments, rhetorical or otherwise. He sought always the best possible means for weak and prejudiced and quarreling mankind, in order that a step might be taken towards the probability for betterment in the future. He never allowed the expediency of the moment to drive him off the bed-rock of sound principles of government and of international intercourse, in which he believed and which he openly and fearlessly and cogently declared and expounded."

"If this is the happiest moment of my life," Hughes responded, "it is also the most embarrassing. Words are useless . . . to requite such kindness and generosity, and what would be more becoming than 'a great, sweet silence'? But that is denied me. You have sent me forth to the doubtful combats of public life. Sometimes I have returned with my shield, and at least once I returned upon it (*Laughter*), but I have always come back. While it is a privilege to hold public office, it is the life beyond the political grave that is the best. In one respect the servant of the people is like the Apostle—he 'dies daily.' And his paradise of the blest, to which his hope fondly clings, is the old home with the kindred spirits who have not been estranged or deluded by the temporary official accouterment. It is their welcome and confidence that he prizes most."

The zest with which Hughes went back to the bar was thus matched by generous recognition on the part of his fellow practitioners. His first big case in this period was a suit involving about $18,000,000 brought in behalf of the receiver of the New York & Cuba Mail Steamship Company. A few weeks later the New York Attorney General retained him as a special deputy to protect the state's power rights in its boundary streams against encroachments by the Federal Government. In May he offered to help the United Mine Workers fight an injunction in West Virginia. Other big cases that were dropped into his lap involved land suits against New York City, alien property, railroad rates, taxes on "short sales" of stock, and the antitrust laws.

The comparative freedom of private practice was very satisfying after long years in public service. As Hughes sat in the Supreme Court waiting to argue his first case before that tribunal since his State Department days, John W. Davis asked if he was not a little envious of his former brethren on the bench.

"No," Hughes flashed back. "Can't you hear the clanking of their chains?" [1]

Taking only about half the cases that were brought to him, Hughes had an excellent opportunity of picking and choosing his clients. Any case that might involve a departure from his professional standards he rejected as a matter of course. "A capable lawyer," he once said, "has in his own office scales of truth which he uses before he resorts to the public weighing station." Furthermore, he declined to capitalize his special knowledge of American foreign affairs. While he was still in Bermuda in 1925, his son wrote to him that two oil magnates were eager to see him about proposals by the Russians to supply them with oil. "I think I should keep clear of matters . . . with which I dealt officially," Hughes replied. This became his invariable rule. Foreign interests

[1] Author's interview with Mr. Davis, Nov. 4, 1949.

THE DIFFERENCE BETWEEN WORKING FOR THE U.S.A. AT $12,000 A YEAR

AND BEING YOUR OWN BOSS WHERE SOUND LEGAL JUDGMENT IS APPRECIATED AND RESPECTED

By "J. N. Ding" in the New York *Herald Tribune*, 1925.

seeking his aid against the United States were turned down whether or not he had had anything to do with the matters in controversy as Secretary of State. His special knowledge of our foreign relations might unconsciously redound to the advantage of a foreign client in cases of this sort; such knowledge he would not sell for legal fees.

He was equally conscientious in not taking advantage of his former membership on the Supreme Court. Never would he permit lawyers to put his name on a brief (if he had no other connection with the case) on the assumption that it might carry weight with his former brethren on the bench. Nor would he pit Hughes the lawyer against Hughes the judge. If a case required arguments at variance with legal principles he had enunciated as Associate Justice, he declined to take it. This self-imposed rule did not, however, prevent him from arguing a case if he saw an honest distinction between the principle he had laid down for the court and the new point at issue.

The first question Hughes asked himself about a case submitted to his scrutiny was: Should it be argued? If he thought there was a valid argument to be made in behalf of a client, he never refused to take the case because that argument might be difficult or might arouse public criticism. It was evident that his assault upon the five-cent fare in New York on behalf of the Interborough Rapid Transit Company would bring the wrath of city officials and subway riders upon his head. But he was convinced that the company's demands for a seven-cent fare were just and reasonable and that the city's policy of pouring tax funds into the transit system was depriving the people of needed schools, hospitals, and other municipal improvements.

Arguing the case before the Supreme Court in Washington, in the presence of Mayor "Jimmy" Walker, political beneficiary of the nickel subway ride, Hughes contended that a more compensatory fare was required by the law and that it would benefit the city. "The policy which the city now asserts," he said, "will only impoverish its taxpayers, and yet the city and Transit Commission sit here opposing and blocking the company in its efforts to get fair compensation under a policy which would relieve the taxpayers of a burden." [2] Hughes lost the case on technicalities, and the city continued to pour vast subsidies into its subway systems to keep them operating on the five-cent fare, until Mayor O'Dwyer finally denounced that policy in 1948 as a means of "playing politics with the health of the people."

We can get some idea as to Hughes' fidelity to his clients and at the same time his high ethical standards by following him to Washington on one of his frequent trips to argue a case before the Supreme Court. In the "short-sales" tax case he was retained by William F. Unger, New York attorney, to make the argument. As they traveled to Washington together, Unger said, "I know

[2] *New York Times*, Jan. 16, 1929.

that you have many friends in Washington and I don't want you to feel obligated to take all your meals with me."

"I have only one purpose in making the trip," Hughes replied, "and that is to win this case. I do not intend to accept any social invitations but to spend my time discussing the case with you." [3]

During the next two days they took their meals together and walked together from the Mayflower Hotel to the Supreme Court, a distance of about three miles. For the greater part of this time Hughes insisted on talking about the case. He urged Unger to ask him questions in order to test his knowledge of the facts and the law. His former brethren on the bench would probably take great delight, he said, in trying to trip him up—a fear that proved to be unwarranted. Each morning he went early to the Supreme Court to read the authorities cited in Unger's brief. Hughes carried his absorption in the case so far that Unger was relieved when the ordeal was over.

The case was not reached for argument in the first session that Hughes and Unger attended. After the court adjourned they walked together down the corridor at the moment the Justices began to file across the hall from the old court chamber to the robing room. Chief Justice Taft, jolly and ponderous, espied Hughes, rushed over, and clapped him on the shoulder in his most jovial manner.

"Hughes, my boy, I am delighted to see you."

"Mr. Chief Justice," Hughes replied, politely but coolly extending his hand, "I am honored to see you."

Looking deflated, Taft proceeded with the other Justices to the robing room. Unger, unable to conceal his astonishment, asked Hughes why he had greeted the Chief Justice so coldly.

"I did it intentionally," Hughes replied, "as I intend to win my cases on their merits and not through friendship with the judges." [4]

On proper occasions Hughes could greet an old friend on the bench with both warmth and admiration, as indicated by the feeling that infused the notes passing between himself and Holmes. Taft too was an old and esteemed friend, but his effusiveness in greeting a lawyer about to argue before him embarrassed Hughes before other members of the court. Having been a judge himself, Hughes had only contempt for fawning, unctuous lawyers, and he would not permit even a suspicion to arise that he was practicing their art.

In the spring of 1927, owing to the pressure from his lectures on the Supreme Court, the hearings in the Great Lakes case, and his extensive practice, Hughes almost suffered a breakdown. "I argued my cases with difficulty," he later disclosed, "and one day, walking to my hotel from the Supreme Court I suddenly felt as though a curtain had fallen over my left eye. I went at once

[3] William F. Unger to author, May 20, 1949. [4] *Id.*

to an oculist and found that this was caused by the breaking of a small blood vessel. Fortunately no serious harm was done, but I was strongly advised to slow up my pace. I followed this advice so far as possible and soon regained my usual vigor." [5]

Big corporations and wealthy clients beat a trail to Hughes' door because he was the best known and certainly one of the ablest lawyers in the country. In behalf of the meat-packing industry, he challenged the validity of a consent decree of 1920, which had enjoined the "Big Five" interests from handling foodstuffs other than meat. In 1928 he argued the WYG case against the Federal Radio Commission before the United States Court of Appeals for the District of Columbia, contending that the General Electric Company had acquired a vested interest in the transmission channel it had been using. We shall hear more of this case later.

In the Duke-Haskell case Hughes' task was to save his client, the estate of the late tobacco manufacturer, James R. Duke, from the payment of damages amounting to $24,000,000. Haskell had sued under the antitrust laws, alleging that he had had a contract with Duke for the exploitation of bauxite deposits in Quebec and that he had been "frozen out" by a conspiracy between Duke and the Aluminum Company of America. A jury in the Federal district court had awarded Haskell $8,000,000, and his attorneys appealed the case in an effort to have the damages trebled under the punitive clause in the Sherman Act. Hughes also appealed and won a decision to the effect that Haskell had failed to establish a contract of agreement. The Circuit Court of Appeals said that the trial judge should have directed the jury to return a verdict in favor of the Duke estate.

Fat fees came rolling into Hughes' office in very satisfactory volume. As he was a lawyers' lawyer, most of his fees were fixed by other members of the bar. In his best year his straight legal fees amounted to $400,000. At last material fortune was smiling upon him in most generous fashion. Hughes could have doubled this income by giving all his time to his practice, but he was never thrown off balance by the idea of piling up wealth. Instead of money-grubbing, he sometimes argued against the fees other lawyers fixed for him. His old friend Meier Steinbrink came to him with an important tax case to get an independent check on the conclusions that he (Steinbrink) had already reached as counsel. Hughes hastily reviewed the facts and the proposed action, said that it was legally and morally sound, and made one minor suggestion. Steinbrink thanked him and asked what his fee would be.

"Don't you talk to me about a fee," Hughes replied. "A man who fought and bled with me in those dog days in Washington [during the aircraft investigation] is welcome to my advice any day for the mere asking."

[5] CEH, Notes, pp. 365f.

Steinbrink remonstrated that his client was able and willing to pay. "If you refuse to name your fee," he said, "I shall have to fix it myself." But Hughes good-naturedly insisted that his fee was nothing and he would not change it.

The next day Steinbrink sent a check for $500. Hughes called him on the telephone and said he would not accept it. "How ridiculous," he expostulated, "to send me $500 for fifteen minutes of work! Even if I were making a charge, it would not be more than $150. I shall return at least $350."

Once more Steinbrink insisted that the expert knowledge Hughes had brought to bear on the case was worth $500 and that his client did not think the fee excessive.

"I'll tell you what I'll do, Steinbrink," came the voice of sweet surrender over the telephone, "I'm going to retain you to capitalize my time for the rest of my life." [6]

Hughes was delightfully surprised in May, 1929, by the appointment of his son to be Solicitor General of the United States. Having no idea that his son's name was under consideration, he had recommended Randall J. Le Boeuf, a former student at Cornell, for the place. It was all the more gratifying that "Son's" nomination at the early age of forty stood entirely on its own merits—that it had come with no wire-pulling in his behalf. The younger Hughes had had the advantage of eight years of professional association with his father, but he had never coasted on his father's reputation. He was making an independent career.

In Europe at the time, the elder Hughes was impatient to have the nomination quickly confirmed. On May 12 he wrote to Mrs. Hughes:

DEAREST WIFIE,

I am a little anxious about Charlie's confirmation. I do hope that my business connections will not stand in his way, and that the Senate radicals will not make a disturbance. If there should be the slightest occasion, tell Charlie to cable me fully. I should give up every retainer if it would help him, in case there is criticism on account of his relation to me and my relation to "big business." It is hard for some persons to understand that when a lawyer of the right sort takes a public place, he brings to the public the same loyalty and singleness of purpose that he displayed in his relations to his private clients. . . .

Love to all my flock—now in the hands of the tender shepherdess. . . .

C.

The effect of the appointment was notably to diminish the elder Hughes' income, for a large percentage of his big cases had been against the Government and he no longer took cases of this sort. He could not imagine himself arguing one side of a case while his son argued the other. On November 11, 1929, he wrote to Attorney General Mitchell:

[6] Author's interview with Judge Steinbrink, July 24, 1947.

In order to avoid any possible misapprehension, and confirming what I believe is well understood by you, I think it proper that I should say that the sole reason for my withdrawal from further relation to the matter of the proposed merger of the Standard Oil Company of New York and the Vacuum Oil Company (which was the subject of an interview with you last spring) was that, in view of the appointment of my son as Solicitor General, I did not feel at liberty to continue to deal with any matters which might be the subject of consideration by the Department of Justice.

I may add that I have adopted the same policy with respect to all other cases in which the Government has any interest.

The Great Lakes water diversion case was the biggest legal problem that Hughes handled in the 1925–1930 period, and he took it not as counsel but as special master. As it was a dispute between states, the suit was filed directly in the Supreme Court. Being in no position itself to conduct a trial in such an intricate and far-reaching controversy, the court appointed Hughes special master to take the evidence and make findings of fact, conclusions of law, and recommendations for a decree. It was the most important case that had ever been entrusted to a special master.

During the next year and a half Hughes spent many weeks taking testimony and writing his report. ". . . although I am no longer even under the illusion of making history," he wrote to Jusserand, "I have been busier and more anxious in my smaller world than when the fate of 'American imperialism' was in my hands. . . . We have already taken over ten thousand pages of testimony and I am about to go to Washington for another session." [7]

At the conclusion of the hearings Hughes asked the lawyers if there was anything else that should go into the voluminous record. Newton D. Baker, chief counsel for the complaining states, replied that he was not certain whether or not his group had covered a certain point. "Yes, you did," Hughes shot back, citing the name of the witness and the day on which the testimony was given.[8]

The case had grown out of Chicago's use of Great Lakes water to flush her sewage into the Mississippi River. Having reversed the course of the Chicago River by means of a canal connecting it with the Mississippi, the Chicago Sanitary District was drawing 8,500 cubic feet of water per second from Lake Michigan. This diversion had lowered the level of the Great Lakes and caused heavy losses to citzens of the adjoining states.

Hughes found unmistakable evidence of damage suffered by navigation and commercial interests, summer resorts, parks, and riparian property generally in the Great Lakes states. Chicago was impairing the navigability of the Great Lakes to save itself the expense of building sewage-disposal plants. The special master concluded that Chicago had no authority to make or continue the

[7] CEH to Jusserand, March 11, 1927.

[8] Baker to J. Reuben Clark, Jr., to author.

diversion in question, although he concluded that a permit granted by the Secretary of War allowing Chicago to take 4,167 cubic feet of water was valid. He thought the court should uphold this permit and dismiss the bill of the complaining states without prejudice to their right to sue to restrain any attempted unlawful diversion in the future.[9]

Relying heavily on the master's report, the Supreme Court decided to enter a decree that would compel Chicago to end its illegal drainage. The opinion written by Chief Justice Taft expressed the court's "obligation to the master for his useful, fair and comprehensive report"[10] and referred the case back to him with instructions virtually to work out the details of a final decree. Further hearings were held and Hughes filed his second report in December, 1929. In an opinion by Justice Holmes, the court sustained all that Hughes had done. In effect, he had functioned as a special Supreme Court in disposing of an original jurisdiction case of enormous importance.

The question of Hughes' compensation for this work did not arise until after he had become Chief Justice. Then Holmes sought the advice of the counsel who had served in the case. A conference of the lawyers was held, and their recommendations ranged from $60,000 to $125,000. Newton D. Baker reported this fact to Holmes and added: "The work done by him was of the highest possible quality, and any compensation the Court awards him will have been richly earned."[11]

Holmes took the letter into the conference and laid the matter before his brethren. Hughes said immediately that he would not accept any such sum as Baker had suggested. So far as he personally was concerned, he said, he would be glad to take nothing. But that would set a bad precedent. As the court would occasionally need to call upon highly skilled lawyers to serve as masters, there should be no precedent that might make them feel they ought to serve without remuneration. With that, Hughes left the room so that his brethren could make their decision unembarrassed by his presence. They fixed his fee at $30,000, plus expenses, and this he "gladly accepted."

The most significant fact about Hughes in these last years of his practice is that he never lost his sense of being a "minister of justice." While most of his clients were wealthy corporations, they came to him because they needed a powerful advocate in a legitimate cause or an independent opinion on intricate legal issues. No one exercised a shadow of control over his thinking. He was the independent lawyer nonpareil, who also possessed a sensitive conscience that money could neither taint nor petrify.

[9] Master's report, House Doc. 178, 70th Congress, 1st session, p. 105.
[10] 278 U.S. 367. [11] Baker to Holmes, April 17, 1930.

Chapter 62

INTERNATIONAL JUDGE

WHEN JOHN BASSETT MOORE resigned as judge of the Permanent Court of International Justice in 1928, his mantle fell naturally upon Hughes. His proved capacity as a judge, his wide experience as Secretary of State, and his preeminence at the bar marked him immediately as the best choice. At The Hague he was also recognized as one of the warmest and oldest friends of the World Court. The two Americans who had done more than any others to take the United States into the court were Root and Hughes, and Root was now too old to be considered for a judgeship.

The real question was whether Hughes would accept such a nomination. Only three years had elapsed since he left public office to spend the rest of his days in "the comfortable asbestos of private life." There was no hankering on his part for new honors. Judge Moore suggested Edwin B. Parker as his successor, and Hughes (now one of the nominators by reason of his membership in the Hague Court of Arbitration) readily gave Parker his endorsement. It was Wickersham and Professor Manley O. Hudson of Harvard Law School who first urged Hughes to allow his name to be presented. Both argued that it was vital to have an American on the court, that Hughes' election would be assured, and that the election of any other American would be "very improbable." [1]

Hughes scouted these doubts and said that if there was fear that Parker might not be elected, his choice would be Wickersham. His own disinclination stemmed from the facts (1) that he was committed to act as delegate to the Pan American Arbitration Conference the following December; (2) that the election would be for only the unexpired two years of Judge Moore's term, and if it were known that he (Hughes) would not stand for reelection, as it should be known, the nations might prefer to choose a judge who would render longer service; and (3) that even two years abroad would give him a difficult personal problem because of Mrs. Hughes' desire to remain with her daughter until after her graduation from college.[2] The other nominators replied that service on the court would not prevent Hughes from taking part in the Arbitration Conference. Wickersham and Hudson also insisted that it would be all right to serve on the court for only two years, and as the annual session lasted

[1] Hudson to CEH, May 30, 1928.

[2] CEH to Taft, June 16, 1928.

only four months beginning in June, it would not seriously encroach upon his personal affairs.

The President added Newton D. Baker to the panel of the old Hague Court which was to make the nomination, and Baker immediately added his urgings to those of his colleagues. "I know nothing," he wrote Hughes, "that would do so much to make America's entry into the Court so likely as your presence on it as a judge." [3] Hughes replied on June 9:

> I deeply appreciate the generous way in which you support the suggestion made by Mr. Wickersham and Professor Hudson. . . . I have thought the matter over carefully, and I should be willing to accept the decision of yourself, Mr. Root and Judge Moore on the question whether my name should be presented. If you and they deem it advisable that I should serve, I am too deeply interested in our relation to the Court to decline.

Taft was "perfectly delighted" to hear that Hughes had been induced to accept the nomination. "It will be a great triumph for this country if you enter the court," he wrote. "And I doubt not you will greatly enjoy the work." [4]

Root, Moore, and Baker sent in the nomination while Hughes was in Europe, and twenty-six nations joined in presenting his candidacy. On September 8, just before he left Europe, he was elected a judge of the World Court by unanimous action of the League Council and an overwhelming vote in the Assembly. Four names were submitted to the delegates of the forty-eight nations that were voting. M. Walther Simons got five votes; Hughes, forty-one. He immediately cabled his acceptance and issued a statement expressing his deep interest in the court.

The event brought from the press of many lands generous praise of Hughes' work for an orderly world. Latin America was especially pleased. The *Jornal do Brasil* said that it was Hughes' "masterful diplomatic triumph" at the Havana Conference that had induced so many powers to sponsor his candidacy as a World Court judge, and the *Jornal do Comércio* hailed him as "the great advocate of . . . the reign of law in the relations between nations." The *Handelsblad* (Dutch) said that in Hughes "the American type is represented at its best." [5]

Telegraphing the "deep satisfaction" felt by all members of the court, H. E. Anzilotti, its president, expressed the belief that Hughes' election would be "of the greatest advantage to the Court in the fulfillment of its task of promoting the cause of international justice." [6] "No one could do so much as you," wrote Justice Harlan F. Stone, "to establish in that Court the traditions which have characterized the English and . . . American Courts. . . ." [7] Judge Moore

[3] Baker to CEH, June 6, 1928.
[4] Taft to CEH, June 22, 1928.
[5] Clippings in Hughes papers.
[6] Dec. 9, 1928.
[7] Sept. 11, 1928.

commented, ". . . you have shown again that you may be reckoned as somewhat of a specialist in subordinating your private interests to public service." [8] Taking advantage of the occasion to "rediscover" Hughes, William Hard described him as "our most extreme and exalted specimen of age veering toward youth." [9]

As a World Court judge, Hughes was doubtful whether he should go ahead with his plans to campaign for Hoover. While his high regard for his former associate in the Harding and Coolidge Cabinets swung him to an affirmative conclusion, he discussed only domestic issues. He also continued his practice of law until May 1, 1929, when he sailed for Europe to take up his new duties.

Hughes' departure brought forth another chorus of praise from Pound, Wickersham, Scott, John W. Davis, and others. Arriving in London, he was given a hearty welcome, and once more he was the guest of honor at a dinner given by the Pilgrims of Great Britain. The Lord Chief Justice of England, Lord Henry Hewart of Bury, toasted Hughes as "one of the few prophets who are not without honor even in their own country" and mistakenly assumed that "the spiteful voice of calumny" had never been raised against him. Quoting Burke's famous words—"calumny and abuse are essential parts of triumph"—Lord Hewart went on to ask: "Is there nobody waiting to seize an opportunity of pouring out upon him the accumulated venom of a defeated and mortified egotism? Apparently not; but you can never tell what the future may bring forth; nor from what unexpected quarter an omission of that kind may be supplied." [10]

His remarks were almost prophetic, for Hughes was only nine months away from the worst orgy of mud-slinging that he ever experienced.

"It is indeed an odd distinction," Hughes told the Pilgrims, "to come to Europe on the invitation of almost all governments except my own. But I am happy to think that . . . I may be taken as representing not only the detachment and impartiality which should characterize a judge of the World Court, but the earnest desire of the great majority of my fellow countrymen to promote the cause of international justice. . . .

"I come to you, and to my new duty, accredited by a force that is stronger than governments, the force of public opinion demanding the just settlements of peace."

The next day Hughes wrote to his wife, "I was overwhelmed by congratulations." The Hague welcomed him on May 13. Two days later he took the oath of office in the high paneled courtroom, looking very distinguished in his robe and lace "bib" hanging from his collar. It was a great day for the court. With Moore's resignation and the death of Lord Finlay of Great Britain, some

[8] Oct. 1, 1928. [9] New York *Herald Tribune*, Sept. 2, 1928.
[10] Copy of speech in Hughes Papers.

of the judges had previously been discouraged. Hughes brought in new buoyancy and confidence. Let Judge Max Huber, former president of the court, speak on this point:

> When you came in with your immense legal and judicial experience, your broad conceptions of a real statesman and your personality which inspires unlimited confidence, the conditions of work in the Court were entirely changed. The whole atmosphere was changed to such a degree that my decision, otherwise beyond discussion for me, to withdraw from the Court at the end of the period, was considerably shaken.[11]

Hughes entered into the work of the court with enthusiasm that was tempered only by his dislike for writing opinions and by the fact that he had temporarily left Mrs. Hughes in New York. Fond of Holland and its people, he also found delight in his meals, in the exhilarating walks that he took, and in the almost unbelievable freedom from pressure. For once a leisurely institution slowed him down to its own pace. At last he was on easy street. "I am about as happy here as I could be anywhere without you, my dearest," he wrote to his wife. "Life here is pretty close to the ideal." A week later he wrote again:

> How I dislike writing opinions! I prefer arguments—and let some one else have the responsibility of decision. But—once more—I must say how delightful I find the immunity of this life and these pleasant surroundings. . . . Certainly—for a "working man" I have found a good job and—knowing what other jobs are—I am content.

After Mrs. Hughes arrived, life at The Hague was still more stimulating. There was a good deal of entertaining, and the distinguished American judge and his wife were favorite guests as well as gracious hosts. The first reception given during the Economic Reparations Conference at The Hague that summer, with Briand and Snowden present, was an especially gala occasion. Before the summer was over, however, it was evident that Mrs. Hughes did not share her husband's enthusiasm for The Hague.

Some of the judges won Hughes' high esteem. B. C. J. Loder of The Netherlands, who had been the first president of the court, was a seasoned expert in international law. Huber of Switzerland was every inch a judge. Anzilotti, then president of the court, was an Italian jurist of wide experience in international law and an admirable presiding officer. But some of the others were men of little distinction and meager judicial attainments.

When the court was hearing a case to which states having no national on its bench were parties, it permitted the *ad hoc* selection of one additional judge to represent each such state. The practice was sometimes criticized as a means

[11] Huber to CEH, March 15, 1930.

of putting interested parties on the bench. But Hughes observed that it worked well and that some of the *ad hoc* judges were very able men. The important consideration, he thought, was to have every state taking a case before the court represented on the bench so that a judge from the losing state could assure his fellow countrymen that every point had been thoroughly weighed.

Hughes was favorably impressed by the court's thoroughness. It seldom took evidence aside from the documents submitted, but when the hearing began counsel could talk as long as they pleased without interruption. "How I envied them," Hughes said. It was the only court he had ever entered in which lawyers could ramble on without limit. He discovered that this was a great convenience for the judges; when the arguments were over, they knew all about the case. Every document had been read, all the evidence had been painstakingly reviewed, and weighty authority had been cited on every point.

With oral arguments closed, the court went into conference to dispose of preliminary questions, including that of jurisdiction. The day for submission of preliminary opinions was then fixed, and each judge proceeded to write his own conclusions without any consultation. This was "a rather thrilling experience," and Hughes reflected that it would be a fine thing for the judges of our domestic courts to write out opinions as the basis of their consultations. As a practical matter, however, he realized that such a judicial luxury could be enjoyed only by a court with plenty of time on its hands.

The tentative opinions were circulated among the judges; then came the consultation. Each question of fact and law was discussed without limit and voted on until the crucial point was decided. Two members were selected by secret ballot to join with the president of the court in drafting its judgment in accord with the majority vote. The judgment and award were circulated, and the full court met for further discussion until a majority could agree upon a judgment in final form. Any dissenting judges then had a chance to prepare opinions of their own before the judgment was finally reviewed, voted upon once more, and handed down. Hughes was a member of every drafting committee selected during his summer at The Hague.

A judicial atmosphere pervaded the court. "After sitting alone, with one's task, endeavoring to reach a conclusion as to the merits of a stubbornly contested dispute, wondering what one's colleagues think of the different points that have been laboriously argued," Hughes said, "one cannot but have a feeling of exaltation in reading the preliminary opinions as they come in, and in realizing to what extent the minds of men drawn from many countries move along the same lines of careful reasoning." [12] The court itself, he thought,

[12] Address to New York bar, Jan. 16, 1930.

was partly responsible for this. So thorough was its analysis of the facts and law that it was difficult for a judge not to deal with a case on its merits.

Returning to New York in September, 1929, Hughes felt that his work on the international bench had been "one of the most interesting experiences of my life." More than ever he was convinced that the United States ought to be a part of this agency that was making international justice a handmaiden of peace. To be sure, he saw two defects in the court. The election of its fifteen judges for nine-year terms, all expiring at the same time, opened the door to logrolling and made it possible to reconstitute the court with serious loss of prestige and continuity—a defect that was to be corrected in the new statute for the court adopted by the United Nations. The nominees for the court offered by the arbitration judges of some of the smaller countries were entirely unknown in international circles, thus exposing the Council and the Assembly of the League to the risk of choosing unfit judges. But these defects were minor compared to the high-grade judicial work the court was doing.

Having accepted the judgeship largely to bolster the confidence of the American people in the court, Hughes continued to urge his countrymen to ratify the protocol. "As a nation devoted to the interests of peace," he told the New York bar after a detailed analysis of the court's organization and procedure, "we have the utmost concern in this development. To hold aloof is to belie our aspirations and to fail to do our part in forming the habit of mind upon which all hopes of permanent peace depend." [13]

Hughes felt that there were two steps which could be taken to implement the pledge in the Briand-Kellogg Treaty for peaceful settlement or solution of all disputes that might arise among the signatories. The first, of course, was United States participation in the World Court; the second was consultation among the powers if any threat to the peace should arise. The latter suggestion was a direct outgrowth of the Four-Power Pact that he had negotiated in 1922. In that pact the Pacific powers had agreed to consult freely together on measures to be taken if the rights of any one of them should be threatened. What he now had in mind was a similar arrangement for the Atlantic powers. When he offered a general suggestion to this effect in a speech to the American Society of International Law on April 24, 1929, Secretary of State Stimson asked him to elaborate it. Stimson too felt strongly that the Briand-Kellogg Pact should be "supplemented by additional machinery to really make it effective." [14] But he feared that any conference of all the signatories would be unwieldy and the omission of some would be awkward.

Hughes did not think it would be necessary to invite all the signatories to such conferences. Most of the Latin American countries, for example, would

[13] *Id.* [14] Stimson to CEH, Nov. 18, 1929.

not care to enter a conference dealing with European or Far Eastern disputes. "My suggestion," Hughes replied, "is that the supplementary pact should be, like the Kellogg pact itself, very simple and should provide only for conference and not for any coercive process." The text he offered was:

> If there should develop between any of the High Contracting Parties any controversy which is not satisfactorily settled by diplomacy and there is a prospect of the disturbance of peaceful relations, the High Contracting Parties shall confer with one another fully and frankly in order to carry out the purposes of their said Treaty for the renunciation of war as an instrument of their national policy.
>
> To that end, any one or more of the High Contracting Parties may invite the Parties to such controversy to a joint conference for the purpose of consultation and conciliation. The Party or Parties issuing the invitation may include therein any others of the High Contracting Parties; and any one of the High Contracting Parties, who may not be so invited, shall nevertheless be entitled on its request to participate in such a conference.[15]

Hughes thought his plan would avoid interference with the League of Nations. At the same time it would enable conferences to move swiftly in any area of disturbance without assembling delegates from the whole world. It was, he thought, the most positive device for keeping the peace that stood any chance of approval by the United States Senate. Unfortunately, the plan was never followed up. Had it been adopted, the nations bordering the Atlantic would at least have had on hand a skeleton that could have been clothed with power (if there had been the will to so clothe it) when Hitler launched his aggressions.

Having thoroughly enjoyed life at The Hague, Hughes was looking forward to returning in the summer of 1930 and was even thinking seriously of accepting another nomination at the end of the two years for which he had been elected. As he refused to take cases involving the Government after his son became Solicitor General, his practice had sharply diminished. Everything seemed to favor his continuance on the international woolsack, except Mrs. Hughes' dislike for living abroad. The wife whom he adored, who had been sweetly deferring to his wishes for forty-one years, finally put her foot down and said that if he were elected to the court again he would have to go alone. Of course his utter devotion to her would have prevented him from going alone. A showdown was happily averted by his nomination on February 3, 1930, to be Chief Justice of the United States.

Hughes resigned from the World Court on February 15 amid a chorus of regret from The Hague. Judge Loder lamented that the resignation was "a blow we shall not easily overcome." Judge Huber was certain that nobody "equivalent" to Hughes would take his place, "because even a great country can have but one best man."[16] Anzilotti, the president, insisted that Hughes

[15] CEH to Stimson, Nov. 23, 1929. [16] Hughes Papers.

would remain a member of the World Court until the election of his successor in September and urged him to attend the summer session in spite of his new assignment. Concluding that the American people would not like their Chief Justice to sit in an international court to which this country had not yet given adherence, Hughes insisted that his resignation be effective at once. In spite of this, the Hague judges continued to claim him as a member and to pay his salary. He rejected it, and the sum was finally deposited to the credit of the court.

It was a matter of keen disappointment to Hughes that his service on the World Court was so brief. Until the end of his days he retained a lively interest in the court as an instrument of international justice. The spread of law-debasing fascism and communism and the kindling of passions that led to World War II were especially painful because they seemed to postpone the day when the World Court could operate in a hospitable climate. But Hughes took a long-range view of the court. It could render immeasurable service, he felt, if it did nothing more than apply the judicial process to disputes arising under the network of treaties governing international relations. What was needed basically was a willingness on the part of the peoples of the earth to accept justice rather than force in settling their disputes. Progress toward that end has been slow, but with the World Court retained by the United Nations as a going concern, and with American adherence to it, Hughes clung to the belief that a sound and promising start had been made.

Chapter 63

THE HIGHEST JUDICIAL OFFICE

Two decades had passed since the exalted office of Chief Justice of the United States had first been associated with the name of Charles E. Hughes. Five Presidents had weighed his singular qualifications to preside over the nation's highest court. Twice his simple adherence to what he believed to be his duty had stood between him and the office. When the call finally came in 1930, it was almost as if destiny had intervened, first to broaden his experience and temper his qualities and then to bring him to the Chief Justiceship fresh and vigorous in the hour of the court's greatest need for leadership.

Taft had noted, when he himself was elevated to the Chief Justiceship in 1921, the ironical circumstances that had kept Hughes out of the office. "I cannot but think," he had replied to Hughes' congratulations, "that I am to sit in a seat that would have been yours by right, had you not responded to what you deemed the highest call of duty, in two instances. I am conscious, too, how your preparation to fill the peculiar duties of the place would have been far better than mine. It is a source of great satisfaction to me, however, that you think I can fill the place acceptably." [1]

The first time that Hughes' response to "the highest call of duty" had denied him the Chief Justiceship was obviously in 1910. Taft's letter more than a decade later confirms the assumption that if Hughes had not accepted the Associate Justiceship in April, 1910, Taft would have named him Chief Justice after Fuller died in July of that year. Probably the second instance to which Taft refers was in 1916, when Hughes turned his back upon Chief Justice White's suggestion that Wilson would name him (Hughes) Chief Justice if he would remain on the bench and not run for the Presidency.

In 1921 Hughes had resented the speculation that he would head the Supreme Court, because he had put his hand to the plow as Secretary of State and did not intend to turn back.[2] In 1925, when Coolidge asked him if he wished to be Chief Justice as he was about to leave the State Department, he had tossed off a flat No because he did not take it seriously. At that time he was eager to get back into private life. In any event, Chief Justice Taft was then going strong. "I had no reason to doubt," Hughes commented later, "that he would outlive the time when by any chance I could be deemed available." [3]

[1] Taft to CEH, July 8, 1921. [2] CEH, Notes, 1930–1941, p. 1. [3] *Ibid.*

Taft was only five years his senior. The idea of ever being Chief Justice had thus been completely dismissed from Hughes' mind.

But when Hoover was elected in 1928, he seemed determined to bring Hughes back into public life. As President-elect, he asked Hughes to become Secretary of State. When Hughes declined, Hoover sent Henry M. Robinson, who had been one of the American representatives in formulation of the Dawes Plan, to urge reconsideration. Hughes agreed to think it over again for a few days, but his answer was the same. The President-elect was loath to accept a negative reply and telegraphed a further appeal saying, ". . . our Nation has no others who can give such competent guidance."

Hughes remained unmoved because he feared that if he resigned from the World Court, before he had even attended one of its sessions and following so closely upon Judge Moore's resignation, it might have unfortunate repercussions. "I do not feel that I could honorably resign to accept other appointment," he replied to Hoover. He was also reluctant to subject Mrs. Hughes once more to the heavy social demands that the Secretaryship entails, although this was a minor objection.

Some weeks before the inauguration Hughes visited the President-elect at the latter's home in Washington.

"I don't suppose you would care to go to England," Hoover said, obviously referring to the ambassadorship.

"No," Hughes replied. "There is certainly one man who does not wish any office, and that is myself." [4]

Hoover had other requests. Sending Hughes an advance copy of his inaugural address, the President-elect asked for criticism, especially of the section dealing with Latin America. Hughes strongly advised the deletion of two pages on the subject of intervention, which, he feared, "might largely destroy the good effects of your recent visit" to South America.[5] His counsel was followed.

Three weeks after his inauguration Hoover sought Hughes' help in organizing the new commission that was to delve into the appalling problem of enforcing the prohibition law. His suggestion was that Judge Moore be persuaded to return to the World Court long enough for the Law Enforcement Commission to be set up under Hughes' leadership. "I am led to write you in this vein," the President said, "because the opposition of Chief Justice Taft is such that it seems hopeless to secure Justice Stone, who would be willing to undertake the work if the Chief Justice approved—but at the moment this seems impossible. Outside of yourself and Justice Stone there is no man in the country who could adequately undertake this work. I have again canvassed the entire possible personnel and am most despondent about the whole enterprise,

[4] *Ibid.*, p. 2. [5] CEH to Hoover, Feb. 13, 1929.

although I am convinced that it is the outstanding necessity of the next four years." [6]

Hughes replied that Judge Moore could not resume his seat unless he (Hughes) should resign and Moore should be reelected. Even then the re-election could not take place before September, and the court was to meet in May. As there was no alternative to taking his seat at The Hague, Judge Hughes could only express his sorrow over the President's troubles. After Owen J. Roberts had also declined the thankless prohibition assignment, it went to Wickersham.

Chief Justice Taft failed rapidly in the last months of 1929. Visiting him on December 17 before filing a final report in the Great Lakes case, Hughes was shocked by the havoc that had befallen Taft's ponderous hulk. Shortly after they parted, Hughes went to Bermuda to spend the Christmas holidays, and Taft, desperately ill, sought rest in North Carolina. Near the end of January, Hughes learned that there was no hope for his old friend and that Taft was eager to see him (Hughes) in the seat under the eagle. "Hughes is young enough to wait," President Taft had said twenty years previously as he snatched away the prize that he had so recently held up before the young Governor of New York. Now at last he might redeem his implied promise by himself relinquishing the Chief Justiceship as death plucked him by the ear.

Taft had been fearful that, if he should die or resign, Hoover would advance Stone to the Chief Justiceship. That would be a great mistake, he wrote to his son, "for the reason that Stone is not a leader and would have a great deal of trouble *in massing the court*. . . ." [7] Late in January, however, Taft's powers were slipping away so rapidly that all hope for his recovery was abandoned, and it appeared that the best he could do was to resign while he was still capable of making a decision in the hope that his wishes would be respected. Robert A. Taft (later Senator) took word of his father's condition to the White House, and members of the Supreme Court informed Attorney General William D. Mitchell that Taft would resign as soon as the President indicated that he was ready to nominate a successor.

Mitchell reminded Hoover at their next meeting that he "would be confronted soon with the most important appointment that he would have to make as President, the appointment of a new Chief Justice." [8] From the first, Hughes was Mitchell's choice, but he did not wish to make a recommendation to the President without knowing that Hughes would accept the post. Having no authority from the President to make a direct inquiry, Mitchell sought the assistance of two members of the court. Justices Van Devanter and Butler dined with Hughes in his New York apartment on January 28 and subse-

[6] Hoover to CEH, March 25, 1929.
[7] Henry F. Pringle, *The Life and Times of William Howard Taft*, II, 1044.
[8] William D. Mitchell to author, Nov. 7, 1949.

quently held a long conference. Doubtless they conveyed to him Taft's wishes and urged him to accept the nomination if it should come. They came back to Washington convinced that he was willing and so informed the Attorney General.

Mitchell went to the White House and suggested Hughes for the place. Hoover asked him if he thought Hughes would acquiesce, and Mitchell said he felt sure of it.[9] The Attorney General concluded from what the President said at the time that he had independently decided that Hughes was the logical choice. Some years later Hoover confirmed this in a letter to Hughes:

> I at once discussed the question of his [Taft's] possible successor with the Attorney General. To my great satisfaction, Mr. Mitchell urged your appointment. The question required no consultation with others. It was the obvious appointment.[10]

Mitchell left the conference with the understanding that the President would inform Hughes that the mantle of Marshall, Taney, Chase, and Taft was to fall upon him. Meanwhile the Attorney General got word to the court that Hughes would be nominated as soon as Taft's resignation came in. Presumably this was relayed to Taft.

Hughes was summoned to the White House as he was glancing over an opinion that he had prepared for an oil company. "Hold up that opinion," he said as he put down the telephone receiver. "It may not go out."[11] Even though the opinion was finished, it was never released. A mere request to come to the White House while the Chief Justiceship was under discussion was enough to put his legal advice beyond the reach of private clients.

This time there was no cancellation of the White House call, as there had been in 1910. Hughes went to Washington on January 30 and ate breakfast with the President early the next morning. Taft's resignation had not yet come in, but the President said that it would undoubtedly be forthcoming and that he wished to be ready to announce the nomination of a successor instantly "and thus prevent all the political pulling and hauling that takes place over an open vacancy."[12] He offered the place to Hughes.

At no time since he left the bench in 1916 had Hughes yearned to return. Confinement to the bench, he once said, made him feel like a bird in a cage. His present judgeship in the World Court did not rob him of the freedom he loved so much; the Supreme Court would. Certainly he would not have accepted an Associate Justiceship.[13] Nor would he reach out for the highest judicial honor. "There are various reasons why you should not nominate me," he told Hoover, "one of them being that I'm too old." With his sixty-eighth birthday less than three months away, he felt that the responsibilities

[9] *Id.* [10] Hoover to CEH. Feb. 25, 1937.
[11] Author's interview with Ernest L. Wilkinson, February, 1949.
[12] Hoover to CEH, Feb. 25, 1937. [13] CEH, Notes, 1930–1941, p. 2.

of the Chief Justiceship were more than he should carry. A second reason was his reluctance to interfere with the career of his son, who would have to resign as Solicitor General after only eight months of service if his father should become Chief Justice. "Finally," Hughes said, "I think I've earned the right to finish life in peace." [14]

The discussion ran to great length, with Hoover advancing many reasons why Hughes should accept the post. The President was eager to keep Charles Junior in the government in some other equally important position. "It is your duty to take it," Hoover said flatly. "Your acceptance would bring confidence to the whole country and would meet great response on the part of the people." Finally he argued that Taft would more readily resign if he knew that Hughes would succeed him.

With Hughes' arguments against acceptance pretty well demolished, he laid down one final condition. "I don't want a fight over the nomination," he said. "I want you to ascertain whether my nomination will have support. I've been active in politics since 1916. As recently as 1928 I campaigned for you. I don't know whether this political activity has left sores. If you are convinced that the nomination will be confirmed by the Senate without a scrap, I will accept it. But I don't want any trouble about it." [15]

The President reassured him that there would be no difficulty about his confirmation. The two parted with the understanding that the matter was settled if no evidence of opposition were found.

Hoover had counted on Hughes' "sense of public service" to compel his acceptance. But the voice of conscience may have been less influential than that of his wife. Although she had opposed his continuance on the World Court, she strongly urged him to take the Chief Justiceship of the United States. To her, he was still "a man of destiny." To him, her wish, even when it took him by surprise, as in this case, was a powerful incentive to action.

Taft's resignation reached the White House on February 3, and Hoover announced it late that afternoon. Immediately the press began to speculate about Taft's successor. For some unknown reason George Akerson, presidential secretary, walked into the White House pressroom and whispered, "It's Stone." [16] That false report was flashed all over the country. Reporters were frantically writing stories about the promotion of Justice Stone when the President appeared and passed around slips of paper announcing the nomination of Hughes.

Akerson's blunder has never been fully explained, and it has given buoyancy to reports that the President originally wished to appoint Stone. Hoover and Stone were close personal friends. They went fishing and played medicine ball

[14] *Id.*, p. 3; also, Hoover letter of Feb. 25, 1937, and CEH to Hoover, Mar. 8, 1937.
[15] Author's interview with CEH, Nov. 12, 1947.
[16] J. Fred Essary in the Baltimore *Sun*, June 3, 1941.

together, and Hoover had previously offered the Justice several assignments. One version of the story is that Hoover confided to Undersecretary of State Joseph P. Cotton a desire to make Stone Chief Justice. Cotton is supposed to have said that it would be a good idea to offer the position to Hughes first but that Hughes would decline and then the President could name Stone.[17] Hughes' acceptance was thus supposed to have embarrassed the President. Another version of the story has Hoover, with tongue in cheek, offering the Chief Justiceship to Hughes over the telephone. It is known that Cotton was eager to see Stone promoted in the hope that his place as Associate Justice might be given to Judge Learned Hand, but beyond this the story is sharply contradicted by known facts.

When the rumor first appeared in print some years later, it "greatly disturbed" Hughes. Because of its inconsistency with what had passed between himself and the President, he assumed that the report was inaccurate but remained silent. In 1937 the story first came to Hoover's attention, and he voluntarily wrote to Hughes an indignant and emphatic denial of it.[18] Hughes then cited another version of the story, and Hoover, digging into his presidential files, wrote a longer letter declaring that he had not discussed the matter with Cotton and that "no telephone conversation as to your appointment as Chief Justice ever took place." Later he declared, "There was not a shred of truth in that Cotton story."

Buttressing Mr. Hoover's denial is the fact that he said nothing about Stone to the Attorney General. Mitchell had heard from other sources rumors that Stone was interested in the Chief Justiceship and made incidental reference to those rumors when he went to the White House to urge Hughes' nomination. "The President expressed surprise," Mitchell relates, "and I realized that he had not been considering Justice Stone or anyone else but Mr. Hughes." [19] Certainly the President could not have offered the place to Hughes expecting him to decline, for Mitchell had assured Hoover, on the strength of the report he got from Van Devanter and Butler, that Hughes could be persuaded to serve.

Through Justice Van Devanter, Hughes dispatched a warm note of regret to Taft:

> I cannot tell you how distressed I was at the news of your illness and that it seemed to be necessary for you to retire from the office that you have filled with such great distinction. . . .
>
> It is with deep emotion, with the keenest sense of opportunity and responsibility, that I shall endeavor, if the Senate confirms my appointment, to follow in your footsteps, inspired and heartened by your example.

[17] Henry F. Pringle in the *New Yorker*, July 13, 1935.
[18] Hoover to CEH, Feb. 19, and 25, 1937.
[19] William D. Mitchell to author, Nov. 7, 1949.

I trust that in these difficult days you may find rest and happiness, with no cause for regrets, conscious of noble aims nobly accomplished.

Believe me, my dear Chief Justice, as ever

Faithfully yours,

Acclaim of the Hughes appointment was almost unanimous. His daughter, Mrs. Waddell, asked, "What in the world did you want to do that for?" But the press and the hundreds of letters that streamed into his office were full of enthusiasm. "Never," said the *New York Times,* "was there a clearer case of the office seeking the fit man." The Democratic *World* said the appointment "has been received with universal approval." ". . . in the future that beckons so invitingly," concluded the *St. Louis Post-Dispatch,* "the political skids of 1916 may be accounted a beneficent intervention." From Maine to California the editorials were studded with such phrases as "a noble figure," "the greatest lawyer in the world," "the man to whom the people turn instinctively," "our most distinguished private citizen." [20]

Justice Brandeis said, "Confirmation ought to be made at once and ought to be unanimous." Judge Cardozo declared, "There has been a great choice of a great man for a great office." On Capitol Hill both the Democrats and Republicans appeared to be well satisfied. Senator Pat Harrison thought the nomination would be "universally endorsed." "There is no objection to the confirmation of Mr. Hughes," said Senator George W. Norris, Insurgent chairman of the committee to which the nomination was referred. "I think it will be unanimously voted by the Judiciary Committee." [21]

For a few happy days the designation of Hughes to be the eleventh Chief Justice of the United States seemed to be everywhere recognized as a fitting climax to his eminent career of public service. After the first wave of favorable comment subsided, however, an ominous stir was felt in the Senate—the sort of uneasy wind that rises before a storm. The Insurgent Republicans and a coterie of Democrats were trying to summon courage to defy the inevitable. At first their protests were a barely audible murmur. On February 8, for example, Senator Norris handed to the press, without explanation, a list of fifty-four cases in which Hughes had appeared as counsel before the Supreme Court since 1925. It emphasized what everyone knew—that Hughes had argued cases for many big corporations and wealthy clients. Still, Norris disavowed knowledge of any organized effort to withhold confirmation.

In the late afternoon of February 10, Norris took a favorable report from the Judiciary Committee to the Senate floor and said that he wished to be heard briefly. Majority Leader James E. Watson asked for unanimous consent

[20] Hughes Papers and family book of clippings.
[21] New York *Herald Tribune,* Feb. 4, 1930.

for immediate consideration of the nomination. For a moment it appeared that Hughes would be confirmed with nothing more than a token protest from the Insurgent committee chairman. But Coleman Blease, the hate-belching spellbinder from South Carolina, arose to object, and the nomination went to the calendar.

Norris then went ahead with his protest. For two "fundamental reasons" he thought the nomination was unwise. After Hughes had resigned from the Supreme Court to run for the Presidency and after he had amassed a fortune in practice that had come to him by reason of his former high position, Norris said, the President had returned him to the judicial tribunal which he voluntarily left to engage in politics and the amassing of a fortune. The Senator feared that such a precedent would encourage political activity on the part of Supreme Court judges. In the second place, he said Hughes had represented "untold wealth"; he had associated with Wall Street and lived in luxury. ". . . it is reasonable to expect," Norris concluded, in a sweeping generalization untainted by any relationship to fact, "that these influences have become a part of the man. His viewpoint is clouded. He looks through glasses contaminated by the influence of monopoly as it seeks to get favors by means which are denied to the common, ordinary citizen." [22]

Norris' attack was comparatively mild, but it drew blood that set the whole pack of Insurgents howling at Hughes' heels. The next day Borah took up the cry. Just as Norris had imputed to the nominee the opinions and failings of his clients, Borah linked him to the sins of the Supreme Court, of which he had not been a member for fourteen years. In striking down an order of the Maryland Public Service Commission, the court had said that the rate of return allowed a Baltimore transit company should have been 8 per cent instead of the 6.26 per cent allowed by the commission.[23] Borah pontifically warned the Senate that Hughes was "associated in his views with the contention which is sustained by the majority," which, if carried to its logical conclusion, "must result in great economic oppression to the people of the United States."

Actually, Hughes had had nothing whatever to do with this case. The conclusion reached by the court was in conflict with views he had expressed as Associate Justice, and he had no sympathy with it.[24] As a matter of policy, moreover, his antipathy toward excessive utility charges had been demonstrated in his fight for 75-cent gas in New York and in his successful campaign as governor for an effective public-service-commission law. But the Lion of Idaho, tossing his shaggy mane, roared that the Supreme Court had become

[22] *Congressional Record*, Feb. 10, 1930, pp. 3372f.
[23] *United Railways* v. *West*, 280 U.S. 234.
[24] Author's interview with CEH. Nov. 12. 1947.

an "economic dictator" on utility rates and that the Senate should not permit the President to add to the court a man holding extreme views "which exalt property rights above all other rights."

Abetted by Senator Wheeler, Borah then turned a barrage upon Hughes' arguments as counsel in the WYG case. Here perhaps a scintilla of justification for his fears may be found. Hughes had argued before the Court of Appeals in Washington that the General Electric Company, by reason of prior appropriation and long-continued use, had acquired a property right in the electrical impulses along a certain broadcasting channel. Senator Clarence Dill later took up this case in more detail, read extensively from the brief (which Hughes had not written, although his name was on it) and denounced the nominee for trying to set up "the doctrine of squatter sovereignty of the air."

This is one of many instances in which Hughes had been retained to lay before the court a case worked up by other lawyers. In doing so he made an extreme argument in favor of protecting the company's investment in Station WYG. It was clearly special pleading—the kind of plea to which Hughes had given short shrift on the bench. But under our system of jurisprudence, it is a lawyer's duty to his client to advance every legitimate argument to support his case. The judge will decide which arguments ought to prevail.

Three years after the confirmation fight Chief Justice Hughes was to hand down an opinion in another radio case running directly contrary to his own argument in behalf of Station WYG.[25] Under his leadership, the court would uphold a Radio Commission order transferring a frequency from two stations in Illinois to a station in Indiana as a means of equalizing public service. "Those who operated broadcasting stations," he would say, "had no right superior to the exercise of this power of regulation. They necessarily made their investments and their contracts in the light of, and subject to, this paramount authority." The views of the judge would push aside the advocate's arguments. Such is the common experience of active practicing lawyers called to the bench. The Insurgents failed to distinguish between the advocate and the judge—failed even to look impartially at the record Hughes had already made as Associate Justice.

The contribution of Senator Blease to the debate was a dark hint that "political intrigue" was at work, because of certain cases pending, "to get Mr. Taft off that bench for the purpose of putting on this man whose opinions have already been written in many of the cases in the form of arguments."[26] Demagoguery has seldom sunk so low.

The chief target of Senator Carter Glass' attack was Hughes' opinion as Associate Justice in the *Shreveport Case*. That decision, Glass inaccurately

[25] *Fed. Radio Comm.* v. *Nelson*, 289 U.S. 266.
[26] *Congressional Record*, Feb. 11, 1930, p. 3451.

The United States Supreme Court in 1930

Wide World Photo

Wide World Photo

The fiftieth year of marriage, Venice, 1938

declared, stripped from the states every right they possessed to control "interstate traffic." Here was a most ironical assault. Hughes was denounced because he had taken a broad view of the commerce clause—a view that had been twice sustained by the court after his resignation. In passing the Transportation Act of 1920, moreover, Congress itself had asserted precisely the same power that Hughes had upheld in the *Shreveport Case*. The excitement of the confirmation fight had led eminent Senators to grasp any stick to beat a judge. Connally, Borah, and several others took up the *Shreveport Case*. Senator Ransdell of Louisiana was the only one who undertook to analyze the court's opinion impartially.

While the debate waxed hotter with each passing hour in the Senate, Hughes was in New York in a state of mental agony. Always thin-skinned to criticism in spite of his extraordinary poise in public, he felt that his toil and faithfulness of a lifetime were being smeared over by a sickly smudge that might leave his name tarnished as long as it would be remembered. If he could have foreseen this tirade of abuse, which apparently no one foresaw, he never would have permitted his name to be submitted.[27] Now that the fight was on, however, he would not turn back. Nothing that was said in the Senate gave him the slightest twinge of conscience. His anguish was that of the builder who sees the temple he has erected defiled and hacked by wild, unthinking men in pursuit of what they suppose to be a noble cause. For a time it appeared that the almost universal acclaim which had greeted his nomination had been thrown into a chaotic reversal by some giant hand of fate. Nights were sleepless, and days were a continuation of chafing and waiting for a vote that did not come.

Senators Robert F. Wagner and Royal S. Copeland of New York gave Hughes their support, although both were Democrats. Senator Frederick H. Gillett pointed out that if the criticism leveled against Hughes for arguing cases in behalf of wealthy clients were to be taken seriously, no great lawyer could ever be confirmed as Chief Justice. The most effective defense speech was made by Senator Otis F. Glenn of Illinois, who contended that the arguments raised against Hughes would have been equally applicable to Lincoln; for Lincoln's best client was the Illinois Central Railroad. At the conclusion of his admirable rebuttal, however, Glenn took the wind out of his own sails by defending great mergers and combinations as being necessary in the public interest.

As the debate went on, venom increasingly took the place of argument. Intoxicated by his own slander, Senator John J. Blaine said that whenever the evil and blighting influences of monopoly had sought counsel their paths had "all converged in the office of Mr. Hughes." With complete emancipation from facts, Senator Dill ranted about Hughes having sat in the Harding Cabi-

[27] Author's interview with CEH, Nov. 12, 1947.

By "J. N. Ding" in the New York *Herald Tribune*, February, 1930.

CONCEDED TO BE ONE OF THE OUTSTANDING JURISTS
OF THE WORLD

net with Daugherty, Fall, and Denby without ever indicating that he "smelled anything." Senator George complained about Hughes' defense of Senator Newberry. Wheeler put in a derogatory plug about the Interborough fare case. Norris again raked over the Baltimore fare case in monotonous detail, assuming without a shred of justification that it reflected Hughes' reasoning. Then came Senator Thomas J. Walsh with a statement that he was switching his vote for Hughes in committee to a vote against him on the floor. To justify this change of front, he told a distorted story of the aircraft investigation of 1918, reviving the false claim that Hughes had suppressed a telegram that would have exonerated Colonel Deeds.[28] It was obvious that he had not read the testimony. Hughes' conscientious work in the aircraft inquiry brought one dividend, however. Senator Claude A. Swanson told his colleagues that Wilson had turned to Hughes to get "an honest and impartial investigation" and that "one to whom President Wilson gave that confidence we can afford to trust." Thanks largely to Secretary Stimson's influence on Minority Leader Robinson the Democrats did not make Hughes' confirmation a party issue.

In the late afternoon of February 13 Norris moved to thwart the nomination by sending it back to the Judiciary Committee. The motion went down by a vote of 31 to 49. The Senate then confirmed Hughes as Chief Justice of the United States by a vote of 52 to 26, with 15 Democrats and 11 Republicans taking the negative side.

Not since Jackson nominated Taney had the Senate raised such a furor over the confirmation of a Chief Justice. Never before had Hughes taken such a drubbing. In this one-sided contest he had suffered in silence while a tornado of accusation ripped through the Senate without warning. If calumny and abuse are essential parts of triumph, as Burke said, certainly the new Chief Justice had those particular qualifications for a place in history.

"My appreciation of the honor of the appointment is outweighed by a deep sense of responsibility," he calmly remarked when the ordeal was over. "The ideals and principles relating to public service with which I entered public life twenty-five years ago, and which I have tried to exemplify in public office, I hold unaltered. In facing this new and most important task, I am heartened by the generous expressions I have received from all parts of our land. I wish to express my most grateful acknowledgments." [29]

Probably the Senate's orgy on this occasion will never be fully explained, but certain aspects of it are understandable. America was in the first throes of the great depression of the thirties. The Insurgents were striking more at the Taft court and the Hoover Administration than at Hughes as an individual. For the moment Hughes was made an unwitting symbol of the philosophy which they believed to be responsible for the country's economic convulsions.

[28] See pages 379–382. [29] *New York Times*, Feb. 14, 1930.

The strange thing is that men who claimed to be "liberals" chose as their target one of the greatest champions of human rights in the current century.

Only the unprincipled demagogues cast any reflections upon Hughes' integrity. Most of his opponents paid respect to his impeccable character and his great achievements in the law. The fatal infirmity of their case was that they assumed Hughes was biased in favor of big corporations without making any effort to examine his record or his personal views. They ignored his work in the gas and insurance investigations, which at that time had given him the reputation of being such a dangerous radical that the leading trustees of his own university stayed away from the commencement that he was invited to address. They ignored his progressive record as governor, his devotion to human rights as a judge, his work in the Legal Aid Society, his magnificent defense of the five Socialists expelled from the New York Legislature, his great reputation for fairness and even-handed justice as Secretary of State, and even the spirit of liberty and equality that had infused his speeches. Closing their eyes to his life

By Clifford Berryman in the Washington *Evening Star,* February 24, 1930, when Hughes took his seat as Chief Justice.

of public service, they pretended to believe that he had sold his soul to the clients whom he had happened to represent momentarily at the bar.

No doubt many lawyers who are attached to great corporations most of their lives absorb the corporate point of view. But Hughes was never in that position. The very fact that he represented dozens of different clients in rapid succession—such varied clients as the State of New York, railway companies, and the United Mine Workers—makes it absurd to suppose that, chameleon-like, he acquired their intellectual predilections. "We liberals," Professor Chafee wrote, "cannot have it both ways. If we blame a prominent lawyer like Mr. Hughes for some of his clients, we are merely chiming in with those who constantly call the American Civil Liberties Union communistic because it has represented Communists along with the great many other defendants. . . . The doctrine of guilt by association is abhorrent enough in the criminal and deportation fields without being extended into the relation between lawyer and client." [30]

Beyond this is the fact that Hughes' convictions bearing upon the great constitutional issues of the day had not been acquired at the bar but in public service. And these convictions, which were amply spread on the record, showed him to be no mouthpiece of the moneybags but a seasoned champion of liberty and of a "marching Constitution." The favorite shibboleth of the old-school judges had been "freedom of contract." Hughes had demolished that bulwark of the propertied interests in the McGuire case. With Holmes, he had fought against the "yellow dog" contract in *Coppage* v. *Kansas* and pleaded for the right to a fair trial in *Frank* v. *Mangum*. Over Holmes' protest, he had written that grand declaration of freedom from peonage in *Bailey* v. *Alabama*. Any impartial investigator could have found overwhelming evidence that, on the bench (as he had indicated in the letter about his son's confirmation as Solicitor General), the people of the United States would be his only client.

The Insurgents got from the press a drubbing no less severe than that they had administered to Hughes. Under the heading, "The Senate at Its Worst," the New York *Herald Tribune* declared: "That 26 Senators should vote to reject so admirable a nomination as that of Mr. Hughes to be Chief Justice of the United States is a symptom of aggravated degeneracy in a body now habituated to disesteem and decadence." [31] As the years passed, several repentant Senators quietly expressed regrets for their conduct, and others sought to mitigate their error by commending Hughes' outstanding service on the bench.

"The decorations of our public servants," Hughes once said, "are mostly scars." [32] In the long run, however, he carried few if any scars from the

[30] Reprinted by permission of the publishers from *Free Speech in the United States* by Zechariah Chafee, Jr., pp. 358f., Harvard University Press, 1941.

[31] Feb. 14, 1930. [32] Speech of May 14, 1924.

bitter debate over his confirmation. The prevailing view seems to have been that not since the appointment of Marshall had any man taken to the Chief Justiceship qualifications equal to Hughes' experience, ability, and judicial temperament.

Chapter 64

INSIDE THE SUPREME COURT

"POPULAR interest naturally centers in the Chief Justice as the titular head of the Court. He is its executive officer; he presides at its sessions and at its conferences, and announces its orders. By virtue of the distinctive function of the Court he is the most important judicial officer in the world; he is the Chief Justice of the United States."

So wrote Charles Evans Hughes, attorney at law, in 1928.[1] Now he occupied the office. On February 24, 1930, he met with his brethren in the robing room at the Capitol (how familiar it was), and Holmes administered the oath of allegiance. Everyone had a cordial greeting for the new chief. At twelve o'clock the Justices crossed the corridor and took their places on the bench. Hughes, bringing up the rear, waited at the clerk's desk while the traditional "Oyez, Oyez, Oyez! God save the United States and this Honorable Court" resounded through the courtroom. With a quaver in his voice, Holmes then expressed regret over Taft's resignation. "We are happy to know," he said, "that in his place is to sit our old associate, Charles Evans Hughes." [2] Charles Elmore Cropley, clerk of the court, administered the judicial oath, and the marshal conducted the new Chief Justice to his seat at the center of the bench. Smiling happily, Hughes grasped the hand of Holmes on his right and of Van Devanter on his left and bowed to the other Justices and the audience. Then the business of the court went forward.

Hughes took over the reins with the easy grace of one long familiar with his task, although he had never presided over a court before. His piercing eyes and finely chiseled nose, his broad forehead, his white beard and bushy brows, standing out in contrast to his black robe, gave him the appearance of Mr. Justice himself. Never has a man been more appropriately cast for the highest judicial role.

The first lawyer recognized by the new Chief Justice was his son. Charles Junior had resigned as Solicitor General immediately upon his father's confirmation, but the resignation did not become effective until April 1. And since it was the Solicitor General's prerogative to lead off in presenting lawyers

[1] *The Supreme Court of the United States* (New York, Columbia University Press, 1928), p. 56. Copyright, 1928, by the Columbia University Press.

[2] *Washington Post*, Feb. 25, 1930.

for admittance to practice before the court, father and son briefly faced each other across the short distance from bench to bar.

That evening the new Chief Justice went to his son's home to dinner. Feeling chipper, he greeted both his son and his son's wife, Marjorie Stuart Hughes, with a kiss.

"Well," he said, his whiskers parting into a broad smile, "I suppose this is the first time the Chief Justice ever kissed the Solicitor General, and certainly it is the first time the Chief Justice ever kissed the Solicitor General's wife." [3]

The Chief Justice decided to give up his legal residence in New York and become for the rest of his days a voteless resident of the District of Columbia. Accordingly, he purchased the large commodious house at 2223 R Street, Northwest, and moved into it in September, 1930. Once more he completely severed his political connections; there would be no underground politicking on his part; nor would he serve as a backstage presidential adviser. Hughes promptly shut out every conceivable influence that might interfere with efficient and detached judicial service.

The heavy work of the Chief Justiceship compelled him to organize his time and utilize his energy with maximum efficiency. The innate sense of order that had characterized his life was thus crystallized into an almost invariable routine. He arose at the same time every morning, refreshed and full of ideas. Often he would jot down notes about a case before the court while he was dressing. Always his mind was keenest in the morning. At 7:30 A.M. he ate a light breakfast and then walked one mile. People living on Massachusetts Avenue could set their clocks by remembering the time at which he passed their door each morning. On his return he would be panting with eagerness to get his accumulated ideas on paper. At precisely 8:30 A.M. he was at his desk writing an opinion, making notes on cases to be presented to the conference, handling his correspondence, or holding interviews regarding the business of the court. On session or conference days he left home at 11:30 A.M., arriving at the court in time to give a few additional minutes to administrative details.

About five minutes before noon the Chief took his place in the anteroom where the judges assembled. As the other Justices arrived, there would be a general round of handshaking and affable chatting. At precisely the right moment Hughes would say, "Brethren, the time has come." Two pages would part the drapes, and the Justices would mount the bench together on the stroke of twelve with scarcely a second of variation. Not once in eleven years did the Chief permit the court to be one instant late.

From two o'clock to two-thirty the brethren lunched together. For Hughes it was a period of complete relaxation. On the bench, however, he would not permit a moment to be frittered away. Taking out the gold watch given him

[3] Author's interview with CEH, Jr., Aug. 13, 1948.

by his students at Columbia a half-century before, he held each speaker to exactly his allotted time. It is said, with some exaggeration, that once he called time on a leader of the New York bar in the middle of the word "if." When John W. Davis asked how much time remained and Hughes snapped, "Exactly one minute and a half," counsel suavely replied, "I present the court with one minute and a half." Hughes appreciated the humor, but he didn't alter his practice. He would call a new case for argument if only three or four minutes remained before adjournment. Sometimes when further argument seemed unnecessary, he would pass a slip of paper down the bench for the concurrence of his brethren and then say, "The court does not wish to hear any further argument in this case."

After court adjourned he disposed of administrative details with great dispatch and by five o'clock was on his way home. He and Mrs. Hughes would then go for a stroll and return for an early dinner. The evening was given to study, general reading, and family relationships. Promptly at 10:00 P.M. the Chief Justice went to bed feeling thankful for his sense of *bien-être,* which he attributed largely to his regular habits and his emancipation from smoking.

The fortune that Hughes had made at the bar brought his family all the comforts and some of the luxuries of life. Mrs. Hughes beautifully furnished the living quarters of their R Street home. The faithful services of Mary Dudley, the cook, and Lois Jones, the chambermaid, helped to keep the household running smoothly, and a chauffeur drove the family's shining limousine. Hughes would have none of the austerity that the wealthy Brandeises imposed upon themselves. Yet there was no splurging in his household—just comfortable living befitting the station of the Chief Justice.

By 1930 the Hughes family had shrunk to two members. On December 19 of that year, Miss Elizabeth, the youngest daughter, was married to Mr. William Thomas Gossett in a quiet ceremony at the Hughes home, with the Reverend Dr. Harry Emerson Fosdick and Dr. William S. Abernathy officiating and with only members of the family present. As a lawyer in Hughes' New York firm, Gossett had won a high standing with the father as well as the daughter. Later he was to be a partner in the law firm of his brother-in-law, Charles E. Hughes, Jr., until he left in 1947 to become vice president and general counsel of the Ford Motor Company.

Busy, happy, and self-sufficient, the Chief and Mrs. Hughes gave only one night a week—Saturday night—to entertainment, except when they were invited to the White House. This came to be generally understood in Washington's social circles, with the result that the Hugheses were booked up for every Saturday, sometimes nearly a year in advance, with only three Saturday evenings reserved for their own annual dinner parties.

These were occasions for complete relaxation, for indulgence in a glass of champagne, and full enjoyment of friendly relations. The majesty of the Chief Justiceship had not dulled Hughes' sense of humor. In conference, to be sure, his stories usually had a bearing upon the point at issue. But at a party humor for its own sake was always in order. He could even relish jokes on himself. When an unusual outburst of laughter went pealing through the Hughes home at one of their parties, it was safe to assume that he or Mrs. Hughes had brought out the "shirttail letter." Addressed to Hughes by May Markson, "auction editor" of the *Des Moines News,* the letter gave details of a scheme to raise money for the Red Cross "by selling at a big public auction here, kitchen aprons made from the shirttails of famous men, and others." It concluded:

> May we ask you to mail soon a shirt from your wardrobe to the Auction Editor, The Des Moines News, accompanying the same with an identification mark, and if possible, a short biography of the garment, as to what important events it has shared in your life?
>
> Whatever your decision, please do not make this letter public.

Hughes framed the letter, and it became a prized possession of the family. Incidentally, his fan mail while he was Chief Justice was said to be exceeded in volume only by the President's and Huey Long's—when the latter was in the Senate. One fan merely drew a picture of the famous whiskers on a card, and it was delivered without name or address.

People were insatiably curious about him. While the Hugheses were vacationing in the White Mountains one summer, the Chief took his grandson Dick Waddell to see the Old Man of the Mountain. Soon after they alighted from their car, they found themselves in a group of sightseers who had just arrived by bus. Some of the bus passengers whispered about that the bewhiskered gentleman was Chief Justice Hughes. But he and his young companion were laughing so gaily that others were skeptical. One woman who was sure that the illustrious Chief Justice would never indulge in such undignified mirth said to Hughes with a contemptuous smirk, "They think *you* are Chief Justice Hughes."

In Washington one day a young man passed Hughes on the sidewalk, staring hard, and then waited for the Chief to catch up with him.

"You know," the young man said, "you look like Chief Justice Hughes."

"Yes," was Hughes' only reply.

"Are you Chief Justice Hughes?"

"Yes," he again replied, much amused.

"Oh, no you ain't," the young man chortled and hastened away.

Even Mrs. John Lord O'Brian failed to identify the Chief Justice one Sunday morning—over the telephone. To Hughes' request to speak to Mr.

O'Brian, she replied that he was in the bathtub. "Please tell him," Hughes responded, "that the Chief Justice wishes to talk with him." Suspecting a joke on the part of her friend Charles P. Sisson, who had promised to call that morning, Mrs. O'Brian exclaimed, "Now look here, Charlie, you can't fool me." After a pause Hughes ventured, "But this really is the Chief Justice." Mrs. O'Brian apologized, and she and the Chief enjoyed a good laugh over the incident the next time they met.

During the weeks when the court was in recess for the preparation of opinions, Hughes worked all day in his chambers at home, taking time out only for a brief lunch with Mrs. Hughes. His chambers consisted of two rooms on the first floor, one of which was occupied by his secretary, Wendell W. Mischler, once described by the Chief as a man of "tact and discretion" who gave "meticulous attention to every detail . . . and never-failing devotion to duty." Hughes' office, a pleasant, squarish room with books covering two walls, was simply furnished with two overstuffed chairs and a davenport. He sat at a plain, flat-topped mahogany desk in the high-backed chair which he had used as governor and which had been given to him by the State of New York. Close at hand were his dictionary and a shelf of reference books. Looking down on him at his left above the clock was a picture of Chief Justice White, and nearby an engraving of "The Right Honourable Thomas Lord Denham, Chief Justice of the Queen's Bench." Behind the door, as if relegated to a secondary place, was a likeness of John Stuart Mill. Facing the Chief Justice from a high mantelpiece across the room was a bronze bust of Lincoln—the most conspicuous object in the room. From these modest quarters the Supreme Court was to be directed for eleven years.

Only three of Hughes' former associates on the bench were still there—the ineffable and seemingly ageless Holmes, the genial and versatile Van Devanter, and the narrow and tenacious McReynolds. Even in his felicitation of the new Chief Justice, McReynolds reflected the crabbed pessimism that had settled upon him. "As you well know," he wrote, "you are returning to slavery. But somehow it seems the common fate to end one's days in chains of some kind." [4]

"Yes; I know that," Hughes replied in blithe spirit. "I have experienced freedom but even freedom has its illusions." [5]

Van Devanter was delighted by the return of his good friend to the bench. Their mutual esteem ripened as they resumed their work together. Hughes noted that in conference Van Devanter was as lucid as ever, but his "pen paralysis" had become almost an affliction. When several months slipped by without opinions assigned to him being circulated in the court, he got no more cases from the new Chief Justice. Sometimes Hughes found it necessary, as the end of a term approached, to take back cases that he had assigned to Van

[4] McReynolds to CEH, Feb. 1930. [5] CEH's speech of May 8, 1930.

Devanter. But he did it with a flourish of good will that put no strain on their friendship. "You are overworked," he would say. "Let me relieve you of some of your burden."

Holmes was still a keen blade of the law. It was always a joy to work with him. Three days before Hughes' confirmation the Magnificent Yankee, who had been presiding over the court as senior Justice during Taft's illness, had written the new chief:

> This pressing affair that I expect to turn over to you very soon has delayed a little my telling you what I hope you know without my telling you, that I shall welcome you with a double delight—that I am to have my friend near me again and that we are to have such an able and competent head for our work. It is most satisfactory and once again I can sleep in peace at home or by your side. I hope that you are as happy as I am.

Hughes had replied on February 13:

> DEAR JUSTICE HOLMES,
>
> I am still somewhat dazed by the flash of the unexpected, but nothing could give me greater pleasure than your welcome. I can say with deep affection and esteem, and, I am sure—in your view—without irreverence—"Thou shalt guide me with thy counsel." I am indeed happy to return to our delightful association which I trust will long continue.
>
> Faithfully yours,
>
> CHARLES E. HUGHES

Holmes did continue to take his cat-naps on the bench, and this was a source of no little amusement among his brethren. One day an old colored man wandered into the court while arguments were being heard, settled into a front seat, and fell asleep. In the interest of maintaining the court's dignity, Hughes sent a page boy to wake the man up. Then he whispered to Holmes, with a twinkle in his eye, "We can't have that. Only Justices are allowed to sleep in this courtroom."

Nevertheless, Holmes was still full of zest and intense devotion to his task. Observing that the venerable philosopher and judge kept his notes of the arguments with the same care that he had demonstrated twenty years before, Hughes was amazed by his vigor. Nor was any abatement of his power evident in his opinions. Standing almost alone in his generation, he was ever of the present. "Within his breast," Hughes said, "he carries the secret of eternal youth, and he carries it with an incomparable grace." [6]

Holmes' ebullient personality continued to find expression in notes on the proof sheets of the brethren's opinions. On one of the Chief's first opinions

[6] Hughes' tribute to Holmes, *Harvard Law Review*, March, 1931.

he inscribed: "Wee-Mussoo OWH Ye crags & peaks, I'm with you once again." [7]

The new Chief Justice was on friendly terms with all the members of the court, having appeared before them frequently and having met them off the bench from time to time. Justice Stone, able, scholarly, and experienced, had been Attorney General in Coolidge's Cabinet during Hughes' last year as Secretary of State. Some of Stone's friends thought that he resented Hughes' accession to an honor that might otherwise have been his. But he offered his "heartiest congratulations" and worked along with the Chief without noticeable friction.

The friendship between Hughes and Justice Brandeis went back to the former's clerkship in the office of Walter Carter. Always eager to boost promising young lawyers, Mr. Carter had come to the door of the clerks' room one day with a keen-eyed, slender young man whom he introduced as "Louis Brandeis, the coming leader of the Boston bar." [8] Some years later the firm of Brandeis, Dunbar, and Nutter had been correspondent in Boston to Hughes' firms in New York. When the Boston crusader finally won his long fight for confirmation and took his seat on the supreme bench in June, 1916, Hughes had heartily welcomed him a few days before his own resignation.

Brandeis' poise and serenity in every discussion made him "a delightful companion." Nothing of importance escaped him because it might be minute; at the same time his mental vision ranged "far beyond the familiar worlds of conventional thinking." Basic differences between the two men not infrequently came to the surface, but these were always disposed of in a friendly fashion. More often they saw eye to eye. When Brandeis marshaled his legions of facts behind a thesis that Hughes had laid before the court in conference, the Chief would say to his intimates, "Brandeis weighs a ton." [9]

Another colleague who won Hughes' highest respect was Justice Owen J. Roberts of Philadelphia. Roberts succeeded Justice Sanford in May, 1930, after the rampaging Senate had rejected the nomination of another outstanding jurist, Judge John J. Parker of the United States Circuit Court of Appeals. A most engaging personality as well as a lawyer of ability, forcefulness, and forensic skill, Roberts had won national distinction in his prosecution of the oil-scandal cases. On the bench he was a strong judge, and Hughes found him a "most agreeable" companion throughout the eleven years they sat together. At no time was there any display of the Chief's affection for Roberts, but when the big Philadelphian broke his shoulder in a fall from a horse, the Chief visited him in the hospital every day, except Saturdays and Sundays, for three weeks.

Hughes had been well aware of the cleavage within the court. After he re-

[7] CEH, private papers. [8] CEH, Notes, 1930–1941, p. 10.
[9] Author's interview with William T. Gossett, June 14, 1949.

turned to the bench he agreed with Holmes: "We are very quiet there, but it is the quiet of a storm center." Pierce Butler, McReynolds, Van Devanter, and George Sutherland formed a tight little bloc of conservatism. All were men of character and conviction, but their common emphasis on property rights drove them into a sort of judicial phalanx against various types of welfare laws that Congress and the states were enacting with increasing frequency. Of course, they did not stand together on all issues. In his earlier days on the bench Van Devanter had written a number of liberal opinions, and Sutherland, a former senator from Utah, frequently took a broad view of civil rights and governmental powers. For example, Sutherland wrote the court's opinions sustaining the right of an accused Negro to counsel in a criminal case in a state court; [10] striking down a state license tax on newspapers; [11] and upholding the exercise of broad presidential powers in the sphere of foreign relations.[12] But the pattern of agreement among the "Four Horsemen," as the conservative Justices were flippantly called, was sufficiently consistent to make them a formidable power.

Butler was the most difficult man on the court. Tough-minded and unshakable in his convictions, he was always ready for intellectual battle. At the conference table he argued with typically Irish tenacity and force, sometimes with thrusts of wit and eloquence. Authoritarian by instinct, he brought all the power of an indefatigable and fearless personality to the support of his views. McReynolds shared Butler's inclination to make a fetish of the constitutional guarantee of property rights, and they (especially Butler) exerted a strong influence upon Van Devanter and Sutherland.

The four conservatives often conferred together as a little nucleus within the court. Their teamwork was stimulated by a common dislike for certain views held by Brandeis, and his elaborate and forceful exposition intensified opposition.[13] Butler was sometimes so ill-tempered in his outbursts aimed at Brandeis that the Chief would have to intervene to restore a judicial tone to the discussion. While Butler was the spearhead of the conservative bloc, McReynolds easily held first honors in acidity. The cantankerous bachelor from Tennessee felt in his bones that Brandeis was undermining the court. In addition he was bitterly anti-Semitic and declined many invitations to avoid meeting Brandeis socially. The Hugheses held two court dinners each year and carefully divided the Justices so as to avoid embarrassment and make it possible to invite other guests.

Other members of the court felt the sting of McReynolds' churlishness in a different manner. He liked to regard himself as a mentor of new Justices, and

[10] *Powell* v. *Alabama*, 287 U.S. 45.
[11] *Grosjean* v. *American Press Co.*, 297 U.S. 233.
[12] *U.S.* v. *Curtiss-Wright Corp.*, 299 U.S. 304.
[13] CEH, Notes, 1930–1941, p. 14.

if they did not care to be taken under his wing, they had to brace themselves for persistent ridicule of their opinions. "This statement makes me sick," McReynolds would say with reference to an opinion circulated in proof.[14] For Chief Justice Hughes, however, the splenetic Tennesseean had a good deal of deference.

At the opposite pole of judicial thinking stood Brandeis, Holmes, and Stone. Brandeis, at this period, was the most resourceful of the three. "As Justice Holmes became more and more conscious of the limitations of age he was inclined to depend upon the judgment of his close friend." [15] Taft had concluded that Holmes was "so completely under the control of Brother Brandeis that it gives Brandeis two votes instead of one." [16] While Stone often agreed with Brandeis, he was careful to maintain his independence, sometimes writing separate concurring opinions.

Left to themselves, these factions might have produced the worst judicial cacophony in our history. But the Chief Justice exerted a powerful moderating influence. In terms of judicial philosophy, as well as in the seating arrangement, he occupied the center of the bench. Roberts, too, charted an independent course somewhere near the middle of the stream. If Hughes and Roberts stood together on a controversial issue and could win the support of the four conservatives, the court would usually divide six to three. In other controversial cases, Hughes would win the support of the liberal wing, and the division would be five to four, with Roberts casting the deciding vote.

In voting on decisions and in writing opinions the Chief Justice has no more power than any other member of the Supreme Court. Because of his three special functions, however, he has a unique opportunity for leadership within the court: (1) he is the moderator of the conferences in which the judges make their decisions; (2) he presides over the open sessions of the court; (3) he assigns the cases to the judges for the writing of opinions. Through the exercise of these powers a strong Chief Justice may dominate the court. ". . . it is evident," as Hughes himself wrote when he had no idea of becoming Chief Justice, "that his actual influence will depend upon the strength of his character and the demonstration of his ability in the intimate relations of the judges." [17]

Hughes had thoroughly mastered the art of judicial administration. In his first period on the court he had learned from Chief Justice White what a presiding judge ought not to do. The unfortunate results of White's indecisive statements to the conference and the rambling debate that followed led Hughes to place great weight upon concise, forthright, and accurate statement of each

[14] Author's interview with Owen J. Roberts, May 21, 1946. [15] CEH, Notes, p. 14.

[16] Henry F. Pringle, *The Life and Times of William Howard Taft* (New York, Farrar & Rinehart, 1938), II, 969. Copyright, 1938, by Henry F. Pringle.

[17] *The Supreme Court of the United States*, p. 57.

case and confinement of debate to the points at issue. Through these administrative devices that White had neglected, Hughes was able to reduce controversy to a minimum (and to accelerate the work of the court) without sacrificing freedom or fullness of discussion.

Preparation for the Saturday conference began on Friday of the preceding week when each Justice received from the clerk of the court a copy of all the accumulated petitions for certiorari, jurisdictional statements, and motions, with accompanying records and briefs—often a stack of papers four feet high. Delving into them, the Chief's law clerk made extensive notes on every case. Hughes had the good fortune of being served in succession by four law clerks of exceptional capacity—Reynolds Robertson, Francis R. Kirkham, Richard W. Hogue, Jr., and Edwin McElwain. He relied upon these men for a comprehensive survey of the "certs." With the aid of his clerk's memoranda, he then focused his own photographic mind upon the records and briefs, inserting innumerable bookmarks and making occasional checks on the margins. Most of his attention was given to the records, as he preferred to go to the original source for his facts.[18]

The purpose of this first examination of the certiorari cases was to determine which the court would review in the interest of clarifying the law. Hughes could find no merit whatever in about 60 per cent of these petitions. Many of them were so obviously frivolous that he recommended denial without discussion in conference. His list of such cases (it was dubbed the "black list" by court personnel) was circulated among the Justices with the understanding that a simple request by any one of them would be sufficient to get discussion of a listed case in conference. In eleven years, however, the Chief's judgment as to these cases was not questioned more than half a dozen times.

The conference discussion was thus focused upon about 40 per cent of the applications for certiorari. In these cases Hughes made concise notes from his study of the record and his clerk's memoranda, usually confining himself to two five-by-eight-inch sheets for each case. Taking these notes, his clerk's memoranda, his marked copies of the records and briefs, and numerous lawbooks, Hughes would sit at the head of the conference table full of youthful exuberance and ready for any challenge. His thorough and obvious preparation was an effective warning to anyone who might disagree with him that he had "better know *all* the facts and know them well." [19]

With scarcely a glance at his penciled notes, Hughes would launch into case after case in rapid succession. Since a typical agenda for the Saturday conference would include twenty to thirty petitions for certiorari, half a dozen jurisdictional statements on appeal, a few miscellaneous motions, and ten to fifteen cases that had been argued during the week, only a few minutes could be given

[18] Edwin McElwain in the *Harvard Law Review*, Vol. 63, No. I, p. 13.
[19] *Ibid.*, p. 14.

to each "cert" if the conference were to reserve time for deliberation on the argued cases. The pressure for time put a special premium upon Hughes' knack for condensing facts. His brief analyses were nevertheless so complete, accurate, and objective that in many instances no other Justice felt any urge to supplement what he had said or to take exception to it. If a question were raised, Hughes would reach for one of his reference volumes full of white markers and either read or summarize the supporting data. "I do not remember an instance," Justice Roberts has reported, "when he was found to have erred in his original statement." [20]

The court always granted certiorari if four Justices so requested, and, not infrequently, if three, or even two, Justices strongly urged the grant. Nevertheless, about 80 per cent of these petitions were denied. The phrasing of the denials and all other *per curiam* decisions was left almost entirely to the Chief Justice. Hughes gave a good deal of attention to this phase of his work, believing that clear expression of the reasons for the court's summary decisions would discourage lawyers from bringing frivolous cases to the supreme bench.

Except at the beginning of a new term, when several conferences were necessary to dispose of the petitions for certiorari accumulated during the summer, Hughes always insisted on finishing all the business before the conference at a single session. This kept the court abreast of its work. Stone sometimes complained that the Chief was a taskmaster, and Brandeis left the conference if it ran beyond the scheduled closing hour of 4:30 P.M. On such occasions Brandeis would pick up the old-fashioned green bag in which he carried his papers and say to the Chief, "Your jurisdiction has expired and that of Mrs. Brandeis has begun. I am leaving my vote." [21] His vote would be cast as requested. Beneath these superficial protests against the intensity of Hughes' methods, however, there was deep appreciation of his adherence to system and his prodigious industry. Brandeis used to say that Hughes was the greatest executive genius he had ever encountered in law, in business, or in government.[22]

The cases which the court agreed to take soon came on for argument, with Hughes in the presiding chair. In this role he was nothing short of superb. His long experience at the bar, his close study of judicial conduct, and his native courtesy had given him an impeccable set of courtroom manners. With his urbanity, dignity, and resourcefulness in meeting every situation, he "radiated authority." [23] Apparently no one has mastered the art of presiding over the court to the extent that Hughes did.

To argue before the Hughes court was a trying experience for any attorney. The Chief always seemed to know as much about the case as counsel did, or

[20] Justice Roberts' memorial address before the New York bar, Dec. 12, 1948.
[21] Author's interview with CEH, April 30, 1946.
[22] Author's interview with Henry P. Chandler, Dec. 8, 1949.
[23] Justice Frankfurter in the *Harvard Law Review*, Vol. 63, No. 1, p. 4.

even more. That was not due solely to his unusual memory but also to his systematic use of his notes. If counsel moved expeditiously from one main point to another, with neither oratory nor evasiveness, Hughes was likely to sit and drink it in. But few lawyers made that kind of argument. Since there is no real Supreme Court bar, most of the lawyers who came before the court (except the Solicitor General and his staff and the senior partners of a few large firms) were relative strangers to it. Hughes had the faculty of sizing up these men "a split second after the first word was uttered," [24] and he saw to it that neither nervousness nor shallowness of thinking on their part should deprive the court of expert analysis of the crucial issues.

Breaking into a windy harangue by counsel, the Chief would concisely state the point the lawyer should have been making and ask if that was the gist of his argument. If the lawyer assented, Hughes would say, "Now the court would like to hear you on these other points." It irked him to have counsel evade a question by saying that it would be answered at the appropriate point in his argument. When such a reply was made to other members of the court, the Chief often rephrased the query and usually got a responsive answer. But he never harassed counsel. His questions were asked solely for the purpose of eliciting information and keeping peripatetic lawyers on the beam. "I know of no instance," said Justice Roberts, "where a lawyer had reason to feel rebuked or hurt by anything that the Chief Justice said or did." [25]

Sometimes the intensity of an argument before the court was too much for a lawyer to endure. Solicitor General Stanley Reed once fainted while arguing a case before his brethren-to-be. One day a private practitioner completely lost the thread of his argument and began to babble incoherently. Hughes tried to aid him by asking simple questions about the case. Seeing that this further bewildered the lawyer, Hughes took the brief and completed the argument that counsel was unable to make. "Isn't your argument so and so," he would ask in his most kindly manner as he went along. The baffled lawyer could only assent and express his unbounded appreciation.[26]

Not infrequently the tension in the courtroom was broken by flashes of humor. A utilities lawyer argued that a rate-making question had been left in "a state of confusion." Unable to suppress a pun, Hughes cut in with, "It was left in the State of California, wasn't it?"

When an attorney argued a tax case which turned on whether a jig-saw picture was a game or a puzzle, Hughes asked with a twinkle in his eye, "Would the court in that case be a game?"

"No, your honor," the attorney drawled. "The court is a puzzle."

There were other occasions when the utmost restraint was necessary to

[24] Edwin McElwain in the *Harvard Law Review*, Vol. 63, No. 1, p. 16.
[25] Justice Roberts' memorial address before the New York bar, Dec. 12, 1948.
[26] Author's interview with Randolph Paul, Feb. 9, 1950.

maintain the dignity of the court. One day a young man arguing before the nine patriarchs of the law got himself tangled in a complicated sentence and exclaimed, as if dictating to his secretary, "Strike that out!" A New York attorney argued so vehemently that his false teeth popped out of his mouth. With amazing dexterity he scooped up the errant dentures almost before they hit the counsel's table in front of him and flipped them back into his mouth, with scarcely a word interrupted. Not a smile ruffled the dignity of the bench, but the Justices' pent-up mirth broke into gales of laughter when they reached safe havens of privacy.

Cases on which arguments were completed were presented to the conference the following Saturday. In preparing for this task Hughes would extend, and, if necessary, revise, the notes he had previously made on each case. Former Justice Roberts gives us a vivid picture of how the Chief laid an argued case before the conference:

> His presentation of the facts of a case was full and impartial. His summary of the legal questions arising out of the facts was equally complete, dealing with the opposing contentions so as to make them stand out clearly. When this had been done, he would usually look up with a quizzical smile and say, "Now I will state where I come out," and would then outline what he thought the decision of the Court should be. Again in many cases his treatment was so complete that little, if anything, further could be added by any of the Justices. In close and difficult cases, where there were opposing views, the discussion would go round the table from the senior to the junior, each stating his views and the reasons for his concurrence or his difference with those outlined by the Chief. After the Chief Justice had finished his statement of the case and others took up the discussion, I have never known him to interrupt or to get into an argument with the Justice who was speaking. He would wait until the discussion had closed and then briefly and succinctly call attention to the matters developed in the discussion as to which he agreed or disagreed, giving his reasons. These conference sessions lasted from twelve o'clock sometimes until six, sometimes until six-thirty in the evening. . . . It is not hard to understand that, at the close of such a conference, most of the Justices were weary. The sustained intellectual effort demanded was great. The way the Chief Justice came through these difficult conferences was always a matter of wonder and admiration to me.[27]

It has sometimes been assumed that Hughes was domineering and even schoolmasterish in dealing with his brethren. The idea is absurd to anyone who knew the court from the inside. No man of any intelligence would have attempted to dominate Brandeis, Butler, or Roberts. Hughes recognized that the court was composed of judges of wide experience, deep learning, independent views, and profound convictions. Everyone's brains, as he used to say, were on the table. It was ridiculous to suppose that the brethren could be swayed

[27] Justice Roberts' memorial address before the New York bar, Dec. 12, 1948.

from any settled habits of thinking by high-powered arguments or emotional appeals. Consequently, Hughes made no such appeals. We have Stone's word that the Chief's influence upon "the efficiency and morale of the Court . . . cannot be exaggerated." But Stone attributes that influence solely to Hughes' "passion for the prompt and faithful performance of the work of the court" and to his "painstaking care and unflagging energy." [28]

Nor did the Chief Justice solicit support for his views outside the conference. He had only contempt for the kind of chief who would take a judge aside and say, "Can't you see the tight spot we're in; you've got to help us out." He knew, of course, that the four conservatives conferred together on specific cases. But he would neither join their circle nor sponsor a rival one. While his door was always open to any member of the court who wished to discuss any kind of problem, he reserved his views of cases before the court (with one or two exceptions) for expression at the conference where all the Justices would be present.

"What his conclusion was," Justice Roberts said, "none of us knew until he announced it at conference. He neither leaned on anyone else for advice nor did he proffer advice or assistance to any of us, but left us each to form his own conclusions to be laid on the table at conference in free and open discussion. A nice sense of propriety undoubtedly brought about this practice. . . . I am sure that this calculated course greatly strengthened his position and authority with his brethren." [29]

Hughes' mere presence tended to keep the discussions on a high-minded plane. "This high personal quality," says Roberts, "pervaded all the deliberations of the Court. Strong views were often expressed around the conference table, but never in eleven years did I see the Chief Justice lose his temper. Never did I hear him pass a personal remark. Never did I know him to raise his voice. Never did I witness his interrupting a Justice or getting into a controversy with him, and practically never did any one of his associates overstep the bounds of courtesy and propriety in opposing the views advanced by the Chief."

If discussion among other members of the court deteriorated into wrangling, Hughes would promptly cut it off. Every Justice had complete freedom to speak his mind, and rebuttals and general discussion were permissible. But as soon as heat began to supplant analysis and reason, the Chief would say, "Brethren, the only way to settle this is to vote." [30]

Regardless of how deep the controversy might run, Hughes closed the door upon it as soon as the conference was over. As Justice Frankfurter has pointed out, "he had no lingering afterthoughts born of a feeling of defeat, and thereby

[28] *American Bar Association Journal*, July, 1941, p. 407.
[29] Justice Roberts' memorial address before the New York bar, Dec. 12, 1948.
[30] Author's interview with CEH, Dec. 3, 1946.

avoided the fostering of cleavages." [31] One day the court rejected a decision proposed by Hughes just before the judges went to lunch. Without once alluding to the case, the Chief sat by the junior member who had taken the lead in opposing his view and chatted in his most fascinating manner throughout the lunch period. Grousing over a defeat was as foreign to his nature as gloating over a victory.

Aside from his genius for pulling the court together, the rules of the conference gave Hughes the dominant role. It is often erroneously assumed that in these conferences the Chief Justice gives his verbal opinion last. "On the contrary," the most eminent authority has written, "it is the tradition and regular practice for the Chief Justice to lead the discussion of each case by stating his opinion first and then to call for the views of the other Justices in the order of seniority. The mistaken notion is due to a confusion of the order of discussion with the order of voting. When the discussion has reached the point where the Justices are ready to vote, the Chief Justice calls the roll in the inverse order of seniority and thus casts the last vote." [32] The important point is that in each case the judges were faced with the question of agreeing or disagreeing with the Chief, and no one was inclined to disagree with him unless driven to it by some basic conviction.

Division in the court was also held in check by the ingenious reasoning that Hughes frequently advanced to give the contending factions common ground on which to stand. In some cases in which agreement had seemed impossible, dissents were thus avoided.[33] Hughes often modified his own opinions in order to win additional support for them if that could be done without compromising the integrity of the position the majority had taken. And when other Justices seemed fairly close together in the views they had expressed, he would suggest insertions or a little blue-penciling to avert a split decision. In these efforts he was highly successful because of the great respect within the court for his judgment.

While it is true, therefore, that Hughes was the dominant influence in the court, it was not because of any domineering attitude on his part. He "ran the court as it was never run before." [34] But he did it through the thoroughness of his work, the clarity of his statements, the power of his intellect, and the considerate treatment of his colleagues. It is his fellow workers who have most frequently described him as "the greatest of a great line of Chief Justices." [35]

In the assignment of opinions Hughes again followed principles that buttressed the court as an institution. This important function is left entirely to

[31] Justice Frankfurter in the *Harvard Law Review*, Vol. 63, No. 1, p. 3.
[32] CEH, Notes, 1930–1941, p. 15.
[33] Author's interview with former Justice Roberts, May 21, 1946.
[34] Edwin McElwain in the *Harvard Law Review*, Vol. 63, No. 1, p. 26.
[35] Justice Roberts' memorial address before the New York bar, Dec. 12, 1948.

the Chief Justice, except when he is in the minority, in which case the assignment is made by the senior Justice in the majority group. The Chief Justice may write all the major opinions himself or he may distribute them among the Justices whose views are closest to his. Hughes did neither. "My most delicate task," he wrote in his Notes, "was in the assignment of opinions. I endeavored to do this with due regard to the feelings of the senior Justices and to give to each Justice the same proportion of important cases while at the same time equalizing so far as possible the burden of work. Of course, in making assignments I often had in mind the special fitness of a Justice for writing in the particular case." [36]

Laying great store upon this "deployment of his army," Hughes would sit down at the end of each Saturday conference with his law clerk and a chart showing the position each judge had taken in each case. After pondering and trying various combinations, he would indicate his decisions by writing the number of each case opposite the name of the Justice who was to write the opinion. Most of the assignment slips were delivered that evening in deference to the eagerness of the brethren to know promptly what opinions they would write. But there were two exceptions. Justice Cardozo had suffered a heart attack before his appointment to the Supreme Court. Knowing that Cardozo went to work on his opinions immediately after getting his assignment on Saturday night, the Chief made a practice of withholding Cardozo's assignment slip until Sunday.[37] To keep Cardozo from suspecting that his health was being shielded, Hughes also held back the assignments of Justice Van Devanter, who was a neighbor of Cardozo in a Connecticut Avenue apartment house.

Hughes assigned to himself those cases which he believed to be of such importance that the country would expect the pronouncement of the court to come from the Chief Justice. But he also took a large number of run-of-the-mine cases. His constant practice was to write as many opinions as other members of the court in addition to his administrative load.

Sometimes he would assign a line of cases in a single field to one Justice, but he was careful not to carry specialization to extremes. To do their work properly, all members of the court had to be at home with tax law, admiralty, civil rights, and various other branches of the law. "Every judge," he said, "should have a chance to demonstrate through the writing of opinions the wide range of his reasoning powers and not be kept before the public as an extremist or specialist working in one particular groove." [38] If the court were sharply divided, he tried to avoid extremes by assigning the opinion to the Justice nearest the center, as when he gave Roberts the Agricultural Adjustment Administration case.

[36] Chapter XXIII, p. 16.
[37] Author's interview with CEH, April 30, 1946.
[38] *Id.*, Oct. 17, 1946.

When a Justice with a reputation as a liberal voted with the majority on the conservative side of a question, he usually got the opinion to write. The same was true in the case of a conservative voting on the liberal side. Hughes' constant effort was to enhance public confidence in the entire court as an independent and impartial tribunal.

In writing his own opinions the Chief set an example in both promptness and systematic workmanship. First, he reexamined his combined set of notes plus any memoranda he might have made on points emphasized in the conference. Then he outlined the points he would cover in his opinion and the order in which he would deal with them. His writing began only after this pattern had taken definite shape in his mind and he had thought out precisely what he wished to say.[39] A first draft was then scratched out in longhand with little regard for paragraphing or any refinements. As soon as one section was completed, he would call Mischler and dictate from this rough draft. While Mischler was typing the first section, the Chief would scribble out another segment, continuing that process until the opinion was completed. This first draft went to the printer with few changes. Corrections were made on the proof sheets, but Hughes never rewrote his opinions in proof.

The qualities that he sought to infuse into his opinions were accuracy, clarity, conciseness, and power. These were the four corners of good judicial craftsmanship. It was not the function of a judge to write literature. The struggle for catch phrases, rhetorical flourishes, and stylistic effects too often led to obscurities and equivocal statements. Hughes was fond of turning a subtle phrase in his speeches, but not in his opinions. The test of a good opinion was not whether it beguiled the public but whether it made the court's judgment unmistakably plain to the lower courts and the bar.

As he wrote, Hughes felt that he had a lawyer representing each party to the case looking over his shoulder and saying, "Now, you son of a gun, don't dodge this point." That is why he always made it evident in his opinions that every important point had been considered. The losing party should know precisely why he had lost. A Hughes opinion thus exudes an inexorable quality. Chief Justice Arthur T. Vanderbilt of the Supreme Court of New Jersey chose Hughes' opinions as a model of the argumentative style because of Hughes' "rare gift" for organization, rhythm, and power of expression.[40] His directness, simplicity, and vigor made each major opinion that he wrote an orderly march of facts to the music of reason.

The Chief followed a strict rule of not sitting in cases involving former clients or in cases in which a former partner was counsel. Under our system each judge decides for himself when he is disqualified, and the standards used to guide such decisions differ widely. Justice Brandeis, for example, did not

39 *Id.*, May 28, 1947. 40 *New York University Law Review*, October, 1950.

think it necessary to withdraw when former associates argued before the court, and sometimes he sat in cases involving corporations in which he had investments. He thought Hughes was too meticulous about disqualification. "Oh, Chief Justice," he would say, "there is no need to disqualify yourself because of some association in the remote past. No one will have the slightest question as to your impartiality." [41] But Hughes held to his rule.

Having argued the Duke-Haskell case, he stepped aside when another suit involving the Duke estate reached the high bench. For this he was severely abused by an ill-tempered Pennsylvania lawyer, who had the temerity to write the Chief Justice that he should either sit in the case or resign and make place for "a more courageous individual." Instead of ignoring the insult or "blowing his top," Hughes wrote to his impertinent critic a thoughtful letter on disqualification, in which Brandeis concurred. No matter who may be appointed to the bench, the Chief explained, he will be confronted by some cases in which he is not qualified to sit. If a judge should take part in a decision when he is disqualified, the letter continued, "he would, indeed, be subject to just criticism and might even in a grave case be subject to impeachment. If the judge is disqualified, the question is not one of courage but of propriety and honor." The fact that the withdrawal of one Justice may, in rare cases, leave the court evenly divided, he wrote, makes it the clearer that the deciding vote should not be cast by a disqualified judge.

In the second year of the Hughes period the spotlight seemed to focus on the court's most venerable member. Holmes celebrated his ninetieth birthday that year—March 8, 1931—and everywhere he was lionized. In the evening, as he sat in his library listening to tributes on the radio, he heard the Chief Justice say:

> He has abundantly the zest of life and his age crowns that eagerness and unflagging interest with the authority of experience and wisdom. . . . We place upon his brow the laurel crown of the highest distinction. But this will not suffice us or him. We honor him, but, what is more, we love him. We give him tonight the homage of our hearts.

Deeply moved, Holmes philosophized for a moment about the "little finishing canter" in the race of life and concluded with a priceless quotation from a Latin poet: "Death plucks my ears and says, Live—I am coming." [42]

When the court began its new term the following October, Holmes was slipping fast. "While he was still able to write clearly, it became evident in the conference of the Justices that he could no longer do his full share in the mastery of the work of the Court." [43] His drowsiness during arguments was so

[41] Author's interview with CEH, Nov. 26, 1946.
[42] Francis Biddle, *Mr. Justice Holmes* (New York, Scribner's, 1942), p. 193. Copyright, 1942, by Charles Scribner's Sons.
[43] CEH, Notes, 1930–1941, p. 11.

uncontrollable that his head would droop almost to the papers on his desk; then he would start up suddenly, writing with concentrated effort to keep awake. The Chief shielded him whenever possible, giving him only the easier cases. But Holmes' brethren began to fear that he would bring criticism upon the court. In January, 1932, a majority of them asked the Chief Justice to request Holmes' resignation.

Hughes was in a quandary. His brethren had asked him to perform the most distasteful duty he ever had to face—a task he would never have undertaken on his own initiative. Instinctively his mind played upon the numerous attempts of the court in the past to ease senile judges from its bench. After the first argument of the legal-tender case following the Civil War, the court had been afraid that Justice Grier would cast the deciding vote at a time when he was no longer able to address himself to the issues involved. A committee of judges, including Justice Field, had waited on Grier and urged his resignation. Years later Field himself had tarried on the bench after he was too old to meet the responsibilities of a judge, and his brethren had deputed Justice Harlan to remind the old man of what his committee had said to Grier. Harlan had aroused the venerable Justice as he was vegetating on a settee in the robing room. Did not Justice Field remember that he was one of the committee which had waited on Justice Grier? Did he not recall what the committee had said on that occasion? Suddenly alert, his eyes once more blazing with the fire of youth, the old man had retorted, "Yes! And a dirtier day's work I never did in my life." [44]

Harlan had related this experience to Hughes. Certainly it did not lighten the "highly unpleasant duty" now laid upon him. He consulted Justice Brandeis, Holmes' closest associate on the court, and Brandeis agreed that the time had come for the Magnificent Yankee to step down.[45] On Sunday, January 11, the Chief summoned all his tact and went to see the grand old man at his home. Gradually coming to the point of his visit, he told Holmes that he was under too heavy a burden; a man who had been forty-nine years on the benches of his state and nation should not strain himself by continuing to carry the load when his strength was no longer equal to it.[46]

Holmes was the soul of equanimity. Without the slightest indication of resentment, he requested Hughes to get out from the bookshelves the applicable statute and wrote his resignation with his usual felicity of expression. On Monday the aged jurist was full of sentiment as he sat with his brethren for the last time. Hughes wrote him a letter which all the Justices signed—a letter warm with affection and regret over the necessity of his leaving. "My Dear Brethren: You must let me call you so once more," Holmes replied. "Your more than

[44] *The Supreme Court of the United States*, p. 76.
[45] CEH, Notes, 1930–1941, p. 11. [46] Author's interview with CEH, Jan. 7, 1946.

kind, your generous, letter touches me to the bottom of my heart." Seldom have government circles witnessed a more tender parting.

To Hughes' great satisfaction, President Hoover named, as Holmes' successor, Chief Judge Cardozo of the New York Court of Appeals. "I am delighted," the Chief Justice wrote to his son, who had once been Cardozo's law clerk, "with the appointment of Cardozo. I had hoped that this would be possible." Ever since Hughes had met Cardozo as a lad in knickerbockers at Long Branch, they had been friends. Frequently they had met at the bar in New York, and when Cardozo went on the bench he followed a self-imposed rule of waiting twenty-four hours before making a decision in any case argued by this particular friend so as to avoid being overwhelmed by the power of Hughes' intellect and personality. In return, Hughes regarded him as "one of the outstanding jurists of his time, a rare spirit with whom it was a privilege and constant delight to be associated." [47]

With Cardozo's accession to the supreme bench early in 1932, there was to be no break in the membership of the court for more than five years.

[47] CEH, Notes, 1930–1941, p. 12.

Chapter 65

ORGANIZING THE COURTS FOR EFFICIENCY

HUGHES' passion for efficiency was felt throughout the federal judicial system. "We do not blink the fact," he said in one of his first speeches as Chief Justice, "that the greatest need in this country today is improvement in the administration of justice, especially of the criminal law." [1] Not content to re-energize the Supreme Court, he stimulated the lower courts to minimize delays, simplify procedure, and make "equal justice under law" a living reality.

Chief Justice Taft had inaugurated two great judicial reforms for the sake of efficiency. The Jurisdictional Act of 1925 had made it possible for the Supreme Court to concentrate its efforts upon cases involving questions of public importance and to keep its calendar up to date. To survey the work of the lower courts, Taft had also brought into being the Conference of Senior Circuit Judges, with the Chief Justice as its chairman. But the great tasks of devising a control mechanism for the judicial system and of improving procedure in the lower courts were still in their initial stages when Hughes took the helm.

One of the most pressing needs was the expediting of appeals in criminal cases. Congress passed two Acts giving the Supreme Court authority to prescribe rules for the federal courts with respect to proceedings in criminal cases after verdicts or pleas of guilty. A careful study of federal practice and procedure was laid before the Supreme Court, and Hughes took the matter up with the Senior Circuit Judges. The court promulgated its rules as to criminal appeals on May 7, 1934.

With the ice thus broken, there was a tremendous drive for procedural reforms in civil cases. For many years the American Bar Association had urged Congress to give the Supreme Court the same authority to provide for uniformity in federal procedure in actions at law as had been given with respect to equity practice. But a great deal of opposition had come from lawyers who wished to retain the practice with which they had become familiar in the state courts. Hughes threw his influence strongly on the side of modernization, and Attorney General Cummings brought the weight of the Roosevelt Administration behind the reform.

Congress responded in its Act of June 19, 1934, authorizing the Supreme

[1] Address to American Bar Association, Aug. 21, 1930.

Court to prescribe general rules to govern civil actions at law and, at its discretion, to set up a uniform system of procedure both for actions at law and suits in equity. Despite much opposition, the court decided that it would proceed at once to obtain a unified system, so far as that could be done without violation of any substantive right.

"It is manifest," the Chief Justice said, "that the goal we seek is a simplified practice which will strip procedure of unnecessary forms, technicalities and distinctions, and permit the advance of causes to the decision of their merits with a minimum of procedural encumbrances. It is also apparent that in seeking that end we should not be fettered by being compelled to maintain the historic separation of the procedural systems of law and equity." [2]

In devising the new rules the Supreme Court named an advisory committee of experienced practitioners and specialists from the law schools. The committee's preliminary draft of rules was widely distributed for the criticism of judges and lawyers before being adopted, with some changes, by the court. It became effective in 1938.[3]

The new Federal Rules of Civil Procedure have brought an enormous improvement in the administration of justice. The pretrial proceedings alone have helped to clear many federal court calendars by encouraging amicable settlements and stripping the cases that go to trial down to the real issues. The rule permitting examination of defendants as to their assets has eliminated a great deal of legal finagling. Not least in importance is the fact that these rules came from within the judicial system instead of being imposed upon it by legislative action. It was Hughes' hope that a tradition could be developed for leaving changes in procedural rules entirely to the courts.

Early in the Hughes period the Supreme Court also simplified various practices of its own. Hughes insisted that the court keep abreast of its work even though it had to dispose of about a thousand cases a year. To him, "justice delayed was justice denied." [4]

More important than rules was the human factor. "The spectacle of a weak and incompetent judge in action, or in inaction," Hughes said, "does more to undermine public confidence than abuse of the institution by hostile critics." [5] In cases where conscientious judges were swamped with work, he persistently sought additional judgeships through the Conference of Senior Circuit Judges. Under Hughes' stimulation, the conference also instructed the senior judge in each circuit to assign judges who had relatively little work to help out in other districts that were overburdened. The result was speedier trials in many jurisdictions.

Behind these improvements a larger idea was taking shape. It was the idea

[2] Address to American Law Institute, May 9, 1935. [3] 308 U.S. pp. 645–788.
[4] Justice Stone in *American Bar Association Journal*, July, 1941, p. 407.
[5] Asheville address, June 9, 1932.

of binding an array of separate courts, each operating independently with no effective check on its work, into a well managed judicial system. The people were complaining over the law's delays and occasional maladministration. If the courts could not put their own house in order, there was danger that Congress might sweep the judiciary under some sort of executive or legislative supervision, thus impairing judicial independence. Some judges were also complaining because they had to go hat in hand to the Attorney General for stationery, supplies, and office help. The Department of Justice itself was eager to be relieved of its duties of making budgets for the courts and buying their supplies. Under the impact of these pressures, Hughes began to vitalize the Conference of Senior Circuit Judges as "the nucleus of a supervisory organization" [6] and to project the conference idea into the circuits.

One of his first moves was to secure complete statistics on the work of the courts. The conference concluded that the gathering of statistics would have to be carefully supervised and suggested that a unit for tabulation of court statistics be set up in the Department of Justice. Meanwhile Hughes was advancing a proposal that a conference of federal judges be held in each circuit to deal with local problems of administration. Such voluntary conferences were already being held in some of the circuits. They afforded an admirable opportunity for bringing district and circuit court judges together, along with members of the bar, to consider their common problems.

At the invitation of Chief Judge John J. Parker, Hughes attended a conference of the judges of the Fourth Circuit at Asheville in June, 1932, which gave attention to various problems of efficiency in the judicial system. "I think that we should . . . put aside for a while the order of the day," he said, "in order to observe how the department to which we belong is working and what we can do to make it work to better advantage. We must do our duty as judges of particular cases, but we are more than that—we are guardians of an institution." [7] His plan was to have ideas of general interest that might be developed in the circuit conferences relayed to the annual gatherings of senior circuit judges in Washington. By this means national attention could be focused on the needs of the courts, while decentralized supervision would help to work out local problems and keep the judges on their toes.

While this evolution was going on, Attorney General Homer Cummings got out a bill to create an administrative office of the United States courts. Cummings' laudable object was to give the courts the management of their own housekeeping and better supervision of their work. His plan called for a director of the new agency with broad powers not only over administrative details but also to examine the dockets of the various courts and to recommend to the Chief Justice of the United States temporary assignments of

[6] CEH, Notes, 1930–1941, p. 38.
[7] *Asheville Times*, June 9, 1932.

judges to help clear up overloaded dockets outside their own districts or circuits. In this respect the bill was reminiscent of a provision in the court-packing bill of 1937 which called for a proctor to survey judicial calendars and authority for the Chief Justice to send judges wherever they might be needed most. Both measures would have made the Chief Justice a sort of czar over the federal judiciary.

Hughes laid the measure before his brethren of the Supreme Court without committing himself. It aroused general hostility. Brandeis was emphatically opposed to it. Apparently the chief objection of the brethren was that the measure would lay too heavy a burden on the Chief Justice, who was already overworked.[8] The Chief Justice would not have time to comb over the budget figures or to settle all the disputes that would arise over the temporary assignment of judges away from their home districts. Consequently, he might become an easy target for attacks that would reflect upon himself and upon the Supreme Court.

Hughes remained temporarily silent as this opposition to the bill developed; he did not wish to appear unwilling to assume the new burdens if Congress or others thought he should do so, and he was heartily in favor of pulling the federal courts administratively closer together by any appropriate means. In September, 1938, when Cummings came before the Judicial Conference with a plea for endorsement of his bill, Hughes was ready with a reply. He strongly approved the idea of freeing the courts from any reliance upon the Department of Justice for housekeeping services. Independent courts should not be beholden to the chief litigant before them for services essential to their operation. The opportunity of effecting this reform ought to be seized, he said, while an Attorney General willing to relinquish this power was in office.

There was definite need, moreover, for improvement in the work of federal judges. With district judges entirely free from supervision in 85 to 90 per cent of their work, their conduct sometimes became "czar-like and arbitrary." The bar was pressing for more supervision, and since the courts were peculiarly responsible for the maintenance of our form of government, it was of vital importance to keep their work in good standing before public opinion.

The trouble with the bill, as Hughes saw it, was not its aim but its method. He thought that better supervision of the courts could be achieved without the objectionable concentration of power in himself. "Instead of centering immediately and directly the whole responsibility for efficiency upon the Chief Justice and the Supreme Court," he said, "I think there ought to be a mechanism through which there would be a concentration of responsibility in the various circuits."[9] What he suggested was the creation of a judicial council in each circuit composed of judges who could supervise the making of budgets

[8] CEH, remarks to Conference of Senior Circuit Judges, Sept. 30, 1938. [9] *Id.*

and thresh out local problems without ever coming to Washington. As for the nation as a whole, the Conference of Senior Circuit Judges could act as a judicial council. It would need a permanent organization to do the administrative chores and keep statistics, but that agency would be a servant of the conference and the circuit councils instead of looming up as a potential master over district judges. The Supreme Court could be left entirely out of the picture.

With this magic touch of decentralization, Hughes eliminated most of the opposition to the Cummings proposal. But he did not wish the modified plan to go to Congress as "the Chief Justice's bill." To avoid that possibility, the conference agreed to the appointment of a committee to work out the problem and draft a bill in accord with Hughes' suggestions. Chief Justice D. Lawrence Groner of the United States Court of Appeals for the District of Columbia became chairman of the committee, with Senior Circuit Judges Parker, Stone, Evans, and Manton as members. Working with the Attorney General and the Judiciary Committees of the House and Senate, the committee drafted a bill that was enacted on August 7, 1939.

This Act brought into being the Administrative Office of the United States Courts, which has been a powerful agent in improving the quality of federal justice. It functions as a secretariat for the judicial system and is directly responsible to the Conference of Senior Circuit Judges (now the Judicial Conference of the United States), thus greatly expanding the influence and usefulness of that body. Hughes' idea of decentralized control was spelled out in the Act. A council of circuit judges was set up in each circuit and directed to meet at least twice a year. District judges were put under obligation "promptly to carry out the directions of the council as to the administration of the business of their respective courts." While there was no interference with the independence of judgment in the lower courts, the circuit judges were thus empowered to maintain a constant supervision over the work of the courts in their circuits.

Hughes became chairman of the committee named by the conference to supervise the Administrative Office. The plan he had outlined seemed to be coming to fruition without a hitch. When he suggested the name of an outstanding lawyer to head the Administrative Office, however, he ran into stout opposition. Justice Reed proposed as rival candidates several lawyers who were associated with the Executive branch, one of them sponsored by Thomas G. Corcoran, the ubiquitous fixer then in high favor at the White House. This maneuver won the support of the three other Roosevelt appointees to the court. With Justice Butler ill, the court was thus deadlocked, and for some weeks it was unable to make an appointment. At last the Chief, at the suggestion of Grenville Clark, brought Henry P. Chandler of Chicago to Washington to meet the members of the court, and he proved to be an acceptable compromise. Some of the judges were indignant over this little revolt against Hughes' leadership, but Chandler proved to be a happy choice; he set up the Administration Office with a combination of tact and skill that have made it a bulwark of the judicial system.

"This plan has rich promise," Hughes said. "The courts are now equipped to manage their own affairs and will have the correlative responsibility." [10]

Judges immediately felt the monitory hand of the conference. It instructed the Administrative Office to obtain reports from all district judges as to delayed cases and motions, also the titles of cases that had been at issue more than six months. Easy-going judges could no longer let procrastination drain the substance out of justice. Now they were answerable to a better informed public as well as to their fellow judges. Courts that were two or three years behind in their work began to hustle. Those that were actually overworked were given more judge power. Without any great expense or any loss of judicial independence, the courts were brought into a manageable system with remarkable improvement in the quality of their work.

Although many men share the credit for this achievement, it was Chief Justice Hughes who gave the new concept of judicial integration its distinctive touches and supervised the establishment of the essential machinery. This work gives him a high place among the architects of our judicial system.

While the Supreme Court was left untouched by this evolution in the judiciary system, it too experienced a momentous break with the past. After sitting for seventy-five years in the old Senate chamber in the Capitol—that "unique and hallowed spot"—the court moved in 1935 to its new marble temple across the plaza from the Capitol. For the first time the court had a home of its own—a magnificent structure symbolizing in stone and steel the idea of a permanent institution for the settlement of legal disputes in accord with constitutional principles.

The new building was a fulfillment of Taft's dream, but Taft did not live to see construction undertaken. Hughes succeeded him as chairman of the Supreme Court Building Commission and spoke for the court at the laying of the cornerstone in October, 1932. In spite of the depression that had paralyzed the nation, in spite of widespread misgivings and world unrest, he saw in the project an expression of confidence that "our people have political instincts and convictions which are not likely to be uprooted." We have pride and hope on this occasion, he said, "because we believe, without underestimating adverse influences, that the spiritual resources of the Nation, from which each generation draws anew its conceptions of fair dealing, are unwasted, and because we

[10] Address to American Law Institute, May 16, 1940.

Photo P. Stephens, Yonkers, N. Y.

The Hughes children and their families

This picture was taken in 1938 for the golden wedding anniversary
of the Chief Justice and Mrs. Hughes

Photo Apeda, N. Y.

In retirement at eighty

From a letter to his daughter: "You will receive a photograph, under separate cover, of the old man 'as is.' Mother is very desirous that you have it."

find in this building a testimonial to an imperishable ideal of liberty under law."[11]

One important decision concerning the building was literally handed down from the bench. A letter passed to the Chief Justice during an argument contained the architects' suggestion that the words "EQUAL JUSTICE UNDER LAW" be inscribed in the main frieze of the west portico and "EQUAL JUSTICE IS THE FOUNDATION OF LIBERTY" in the east portico. Hughes approved the first motto and passed the letter along the bench to Van Devanter with a note about the second: "I rather prefer 'JUSTICE THE GUARDIAN OF LIBERTY'." "Good," replied Van Devanter, and the east portico inscription was changed accordingly.

When "EQUAL JUSTICE UNDER LAW" began to gleam out from the white marble above the eight classical pillars at the front of the building, Herbert Bayard Swope accused the Chief Justice "of having permitted tautology, verbosity and redundancy, each of which is an abomination in good usage."[12] Hughes replied:

> Immediate judgment. Indictment quashed.
>
> The distress which led to your complaint may be somewhat alleviated if for a moment you will free yourself from the tyranny of the blue pencil and consider the history of the law. "Equal Justice" is a time-honored phrase placing a strong emphasis upon impartiality,—an emphasis which it is well to retain. [He quoted the phrase from two dictionaries, from Jefferson's first inaugural and from great opinions of the court.]
>
> There is a long history in that phrase. Try to bear with it.[13]

One day in 1934 the Chief learned to his astonishment that his own likeness had been chiseled into the stone of the pediment above the front entrance, without either the knowledge or consent of the building commission. Nine figures stand out from the pediment. In the center is Liberty Enthroned, holding the scales of justice, with Order and Authority on guard on either side. To the left of this symbolic trio is a likeness of Taft when he was a student, Elihu Root, and Cass Gilbert, architect of the building. Just to the right of Order is Chief Justice Hughes in a thoughtful mood; Robert Aitken, the sculptor of the pediment; and Chief Justice Marshall represented in his boyhood.

At first the court felt uncomfortable in its magnificent new chamber, with its walls of Ivory Vein marble from Spain, its rich red velour hangings, and its twenty-four columns of tinted Old Convent Siena marble from Italy. The elegance of its new home seemed strangely out of keeping with the compactness and simplicity traditionally associated with the court. Some of the Justices resented the change, and several declined to use the beautiful suites the

[11] *New York Times*, Oct. 14, 1932. [12] Swope to CEH, Jan. 25, 1935.
[13] CEH to Swope, Feb. 4, 1935.

new building provided for each. The Chief continued to write his opinions at home and used his new office only for appointments and administrative work.

Visitors who flocked to the Supreme Court in increasing numbers seemed to be more interested in its luxurious surroundings than in the work it was doing. But its distinctive new home gave emphasis to its status as a separate, coordinate branch of the government. Established in a sort of shrine to the majesty of the law, the court would be better fortified for the great struggle that was soon to ensue over its right to function as an independent agent of justice.

Chapter 66

MARCHING CONSTITUTION

ONE of the most striking characteristics of Hughes' work on the bench was his high degree of objectivity. He was neither a crusader, standpatter, nor reactionary; he was an open-minded judge. Butler and McReynolds held doggedly to a *laissez faire* conservatism. Brandeis, too, according to his biographer, "was inclined by the pressures and drives of his own nature to translate his own economic and social views into the Constitution itself." [1] In a large measure Hughes succeeded in freeing his judicial reasoning from any social or economic pattern.

A student asked the Chief Justice whether he regarded himself as a "liberal" or a "conservative." He replied: "These labels do not interest me. I know of no accepted criterion. Some think opinions are conservative which others would regard as essentially liberal, and some opinions classed as liberal might be regarded from another point of view as decidedly illiberal. Such characterizations are not infrequently used to foster prejudices and they serve as a very poor substitute for intelligent criticism. A judge who does his work in an objective spirit, as a judge should, will address himself conscientiously to each case, and will not trouble himself about labels." [2]

No man can attain complete objectivity. His judgments will necessarily be guided by his convictions and his concept of the society of which he is a part. Loyalties to groups, methods, and ideas are likely to color his conclusions. The human mind does not operate independently of its experience. But Hughes' basic loyalty was to the ideas of justice and constitutional government. No sympathy for any group, no interest in economic theory or social reform could stand against this powerful incentive. "His decisions," as Joseph M. Proskauer has said, "were legal decisions and not determinations of non-legal controversies. They reflected the ideals of the judge and not of the philosopher or economist." [3] Emotionally as well as intellectually Hughes was driven toward judicial conclusions. For him, justice was not the means to an end; it was the end.

Closely related to his passion for justice was his ingrained respect for facts. Holmes used to say that he hated facts, although he used them skillfully when

[1] Alpheus T. Mason, *Brandeis* (New York, Viking, 1946), p. 580. Copyright, 1946, by Alpheus T. Mason.
[2] Asheville speech, June 9, 1932.
[3] Address at Hughes Memorial Services in Supreme Court, Nov. 4, 1949.

occasion demanded. Brandeis liked facts and marshaled armies of them to support his theses. Hughes trusted facts and sought them out as a guide to the course he would take. In his early days at the bar it was said that he "believed in God but believed equally that God was on the side of the facts." His chief predilection was for exhaustive investigation before he would attempt to draw any conclusions. Yet Hughes never lost himself in any uncharted wilderness of facts. He knew how to balance the details of a case and "the felt necessities of the time" with the facts of history and constitutional law. His pursuit of facts was nothing less than a search for the bedrock of truth.

The Chief's judicial thinking was also influenced by an unshakable belief in the American constitutional system. That system made it possible for the people to use government as an agency for their own advancement. At the same time it was a bulwark against tyranny. Its basic guarantees were justice and freedom of the human spirit. Believing that the best hope of mankind lay in the protection of these principles and rights, the Chief Justice set his course by the star of constitutional democracy. The system underlying our way of life was infinitely more important than any conflicting expedient that might be advanced to cope with temporary problems.

Hughes felt a special responsibility upon the courts to safeguard this American heritage. The nature of this duty he outlined in his address to the conference of federal judges of the Fourth Circuit at Asheville on June 9, 1932, in words that should long be remembered:

> The supreme exercise of the judicial power of the United States is in maintaining the constitutional balance between State and Nation and in enforcing the principles of liberty which the Constitution safeguards against arbitrary power. This is an extraordinary demand upon judicial intelligence, but it is an integral part of our system, and the duty imposed upon our judges cannot be escaped. We cannot perform this duty in a narrow, technical spirit. Our dual system requires recognition of appropriate State power as well as Federal power. It demands freedom for state authority to meet local needs. It demands opportunities for experimentation and progress. We must ever keep before our minds the illuminating phrase of Marshall, "that it is a *constitution* we are expounding." That Constitution was made, as Justice Matthews observed, "for an undefined and expanding future, and for a people gathered and to be gathered from many nations and of many tongues." We should be faithless to our supreme obligation if we interpreted the great generalities of the Constitution so as to forbid flexibility in making adaptations to meet new conditions, and to prevent the correction of new abuses incident to the complexity of our life, or as crystallizing our own notions of policy, our personal views of economics and our theories of moral or social improvement. We should be equally faithless to our duty if we failed to remember that it is an *American* constitution we are expounding. It is permeated with American ideals, infused with an American conception of liberty.
>
> We cannot take the great phrases of the Constitution and disregard their his-

torical background and fundamental purposes. These purposes were so expressed as to permit a broad range for new methods and achievements, but they were expressed in limitations. These limitations were imposed so as to safeguard rights believed to be fundamental. As Madison said, the tribunals of justice would be "in a peculiar manner the guardians of those rights"; they were to be "an impenetrable bulwark" against encroachment upon them either by legislative or executive power. The extent of these fundamental rights is a subject of perennial debate. But that they exist is a postulate of our system that cannot be ignored. They are limitations, as I have said, in the interest of liberty, requiring a measure of freedom of opportunity which even legislatures must respect. We would be as faithless to our judicial obligation in failing to recognize these boundaries of power because of individual conceptions of the value of new social schemes resting upon coercion by a class, or upon unrestrained legislative will, as we would be in tightening conceptions to re-enforce particular economic views. . . . It is a highly difficult, but I think not an impossible task, to escape the errors of the extreme constructions which either would nullify, or would extend beyond their fundamental purpose, the great guarantees of individual liberty.

It is from this philosophical background that his work on the bench must be judged.

Tax laws ran afoul of Hughes' constitutional doctrines more frequently than any others; yet the period of his Chief Justiceship was marked by the tapping of many new sources of revenue and by the virtual abolition of intergovernmental tax immunities. His contributions to tax law are indicative of his belief in a marching Constitution.

Depression-emptied treasuries had given new popularity to sales taxes accompanied by "use taxes" on goods consumed within the state after being purchased outside—the purpose being to prevent evasion of the sales tax. To the surprise of many who knew how jealously it had guarded interstate commerce from all state-imposed burdens, the court upheld these levies. Hughes had previously written an opinion that sustained a Minnesota tax on cattle shipped from another state and held in stockyards for resale, on the ground that interstate commerce had come to rest.[4] When the use tax made its bow before the high bench, he reiterated that doctrine, got agreement, and assigned the opinion to Cardozo.[5]

But the Chief adhered literally to the doctrine that a state could not, in any form or under any guise, directly burden interstate business. When the court in 1940 appeared to relax this principle in *McGoldrick* v. *Berwind-White*,[6] he vigorously dissented with the concurrence of Roberts and McReynolds.

[4] *Minnesota* v. *Blasius*, 290 U.S. 1.
[5] *Henneford* v. *Silas Mason Co.*, 300 U.S. 577. [6] 309 U.S. 33.

For nearly a decade the Hughes court frowned upon double taxation. Its general thesis was that under the due-process clause of the Fourteenth Amendment a state could tax only property within its territorial jurisdiction or intangible property in the state where its owner was domiciled. To be sure, the court recognized some exceptions. Hughes wrote an opinion upholding a West Virginia tax on bank deposits and accounts receivable even though the steel company challenging the tax had plants, sales offices, and bank accounts in other states. The tax was saved by the fact that the company's business was completely directed from its Wheeling headquarters.[7] The Chief Justice also upheld New York in taxing the profits of a Massachusetts resident from the sale of a "right" appurtenant to his membership in the New York Stock Exchange, on the ground that the right by nature was localized in New York.[8] In 1939, however, when the court began to permit two states to tax the same intangible property and to let other states reach beyond their boundaries for revenue, Hughes consistently dissented.

It was an evolutionary process that swept away most of the labyrinth of intergovernmental tax immunities which had grown out of Marshall's thesis that the power to tax is the power to destroy. At first Hughes followed Holmes' reasoning in *Gillespie* v. *Oklahoma*,[9] giving the states and their agencies liberal immunity from federal taxation. He and Holmes led the majority in denying Congress the right to tax the sale of a motorcycle to a city,[10] with Brandeis and Stone dissenting. With a bare majority of the court, the Chief also clung to the precedents forbidding federal taxes on production of oil and gas from state school lands leased to a private company.[11] But a ferment was at work within the court, and Hughes himself became a part of it.

As early as 1931 Hughes spoke for the court in reversing a judgment that Congress could not tax profits from the sale of municipal bonds.[12] He accepted the doctrine that federal taxation of the interest from state and municipal bonds is forbidden, but that did not justify multiplication of immunities. "The power to tax should not be crippled," he said, ". . . by extending the constitutional exemption from taxation to those subjects which fall within the general application of non-discriminatory laws, and where . . . there is only remote, if any, influence upon the exercise of the functions of government." Three years later he again led the court in holding that railway trustees appointed by, and acting for, a state must pay the federal income tax.[13] Constitutional immunity from federal taxation, he said, was not a necessary result of being a state officer.

[7] *Wheeling Steel Corp.* v. *Fox*, 298 U.S. 193.
[8] *N.Y. ex rel. Whitney* v. *Graves*, 299 U.S. 366. [9] 257 U.S. 501.
[10] *Indian Motorcycle Co.* v. *U.S.*, 283 U.S. 570.
[11] *Burnet* v. *Coronado Oil and Gas*, 285 U.S. 393.
[12] *Willcuts* v. *Bunn*, 282 U.S. 216. [13] *Helvering* v. *Powers*, 293 U.S. 214.

In 1938 Stone spoke for the court in extending this principle so as to sweep away the entire maze of fine-spun immunities shielding government employees from taxation.[14] Millions of new taxpayers began to swell governmental revenues without the slightest loss of prestige or power to any federal or state agency.

Meanwhile Hughes and four of his brethren had upheld a nondiscriminatory West Virginia tax on a corporation doing work for the Federal Government.[15] Other Hughes opinions cleared the way for state taxation of contractors and their employees working on federal projects. After six years of such judicial erosion, Hughes also agreed to reexamine the precedents shielding private interests operating on public lands. In 1938 he wrote an opinion which upset both the Gillespie decision and *Burnet* v. *Coronado Oil and Gas* for which he had been in part responsible. "Mere theoretical conceptions of interference with the functions of government" could not give a cloak of immunity, he said. "Regard must be had to substance and direct effects." [16]

Finally, the court also swept away the immunity from income taxes that federal judges had long enjoyed. In the interval while Hughes was not a member of the court it had decided, in *Evans* v. *Gore*,[17] that judges' salaries could not be taxed because the Constitution forbids reduction of their compensation during their term of office. Holmes and Brandeis had vigorously dissented. In 1936 Congress had circumvented this decision by applying the income tax to the salaries of judges to be appointed after the law became effective. A test case came up to the supreme bench in 1939, and everyone except Butler agreed that the Act was constitutionally sound.[18] Hoping to avoid a direct repudiation of the court's previous judgment, Hughes assigned the opinion to Frankfurter, who skillfully laid *Evans* v. *Gore* on the judicial relic shelf instead of consigning it to a dishonorable grave.

When the opinion was circulated, the Chief suggested that *Evans* v. *Gore* be made to appear a "less casual" decision. "If I had been on the bench when *Evans* v. *Gore* was decided," he told Frankfurter, "I think I should have voted with Holmes and Brandeis. It means little to me to pay the tax. I am a rich man. But at least some of the brethren are poor men, and also I do not want to reflect on the prior views of members still on the court; if you can conscientiously indicate that there was ground for their decision, I hope it may commend itself to you to do so. But I want you to know that I am ready to sign the opinion as it now stands." Accordingly Justice Frankfurter inserted a few lines about Chief Justice Taney's letter to Secretary of the Treasury Chase

[14] *Graves* v. *O'Keefe*, 306 U.S. 466.
[15] *James* v. *Dravo Contracting Co.*, 302 U.S. 134.
[16] *Helvering* v. *Mountain Producers Corp.*, 303 U.S. 376.
[17] 253 U.S. 245. [18] *O'Malley* v. *Woodrough*, 307 U.S. 277.

saying that, while no federal judge would be qualified to sit in such a case, the application of the Civil War income taxes to judges' salaries was unconstitutional.

Out of approximately 350 opinions that Hughes wrote for the court as Chief Justice, thirty-nine are especially significant in their bearing upon the powers of the states. In thirty-two of these he sustained the state law or action that was challenged; in seven (including four tax cases) he administered a lethal dose of constitutionalism. Three times he dissented because a majority liquidated state laws he believed to be valid.

His self-restraint in passing upon state legislation was reflected in the first opinion he wrote after returning to the bench. The court held that Ohio was within its rights in denying its own supreme court the power to invalidate legislation if more than one judge dissented. ". . . it is not for this Court to intervene to protect the citizens of the State from the consequences of its policy," Hughes wrote in reply to a taxpayer's appeal, "if the State has not disregarded the requirements of the Federal Constitution." [19]

The cool logic of another Hughes opinion protected the powers of three governors against legislative irregularities. In defiance of gubernatorial vetoes, the lawmakers of New York, Minnesota, and Missouri had attempted to redistrict those states in accord with an Act of Congress reapportioning among the states the seats in the House of Representatives. The court ruled, in a test case from Minnesota, that the Constitution gives state legislatures no redistricting power outside the regular procedure of enacting a law, which the governor could veto. In case of a stalemate over redistricting, where the number of seats allotted to the state had been reduced, it would have to elect all its representatives at large.[20]

Hughes spoke for the court in upholding the New York workmen's compensation law,[21] a Louisiana Act for the purchase of books to be lent to children in private as well as in public schools,[22] an Oklahoma statute licensing cooperatives in competition with private business,[23] and a Nebraska law guaranteeing bank deposits.[24] Other Hughes opinions gave the green light to Texas in limiting the size and weight of trucks engaged in interstate traffic over its highways; [25] to Oregon in revoking the licenses of dentists for unprofessional conduct; [26] and to Minnesota in subjecting sexual perverts to examination akin to lunacy proceedings.[27]

His liberal view of the state police power is pointedly illustrated by his

[19] *Ohio ex rel. Wadsworth* v. *Zangerle*, 281 U.S. 74.
[20] *Smiley* v. *Holm*, 285 U.S. 355.
[21] *Staten Island Rapid Transit Co.* v. *Phoenix Indemnity Co.*, 281 U.S. 98.
[22] *Cochran* v. *Louisiana*, 281 U.S. 370.
[23] *Oklahoma* v. *Lowe*, 281 U.S. 431.
[24] *Abie State Bank* v. *Bryan*, 282 U.S. 765.
[25] *Sproles* v. *Binford*, 286 U.S. 374.
[26] *Semler* v. *Dental Examiners*, 294 U.S. 608.
[27] *Minnesota* v. *Probate Court*, 309 U.S. 270.

opinion sustaining Florida's regulation of sponge fishing by her citizens beyond the three-mile limit in the Gulf of Mexico. "If the United States may control the conduct of its citizens upon the high seas," he wrote, "we see no reason why the State of Florida may not likewise govern the conduct of its citizens upon the high seas with respect to matters in which the State has a legitimate interest and where there is no conflict with acts of Congress." [28] Even unseaworthy vessels could be brought under state regulation, the court held, so long as there was no collision with federal laws enacted under the commerce clause.[29] Hughes abhorred a vacuum of power.

Two interesting state cases give emphasis to the Chief's high standing with his brethren. Shortly after returning to the bench, he wrote a scholarly opinion holding that a Nebraska homestead law, as applied to a citizen of Norway, was not invalid because of conflict with an ancient treaty of amity and commerce between that country and the United States.[30] By way of expressing his approval, Holmes dipped into *Hamlet* and saluted the Chief with the admiring words of Ophelia about the Prince of Denmark:

> The courtier's, soldier's, scholar's
> eye, tongue, sword,
> The expectancy and rose of the
> fair state.
> Yes Sir,
> O. W. H.

Holmes had left the bench when the Chief wrote his learned opinion to the effect that the Principality of Monaco could not sue the State of Mississippi, without its consent, for the redemption of bonds that the state had repudiated.[31] But four of the other judges penciled generous comments on the proof sheets: "A skillfully drawn, masterly and judicious opinion. I agree." G. S. "Complete and convincing. I agree." W. V. "Yes. Handsomely done." L. D. B. "I agree. A notable opinion." B. N. C.

Only two state regulatory measures were wiped off the books by Hughes' opinions. Florida had passed a law subjecting private carriers engaged in contract hauling to a special tax and requiring them to obtain certificates of public convenience and necessity. Haulers of agricultural products and fish were exempted. The court concluded that "the constitutional guarantee of equal protection of the laws is interposed against discriminations that are entirely arbitrary." [32] The other case involved an Arkansas statute providing that no money paid or payable to any resident of the state as the beneficiary of a life-insurance policy could be seized through judicial process for the payment of

[28] *Skiriotes* v. *Florida*, 313 U.S. 69.
[29] *Kelly* v. *Washington*, 302 U.S. 1.
[30] *Todok* v. *Union State Bank*, 281 U.S. 449.
[31] *Monaco* v. *Mississippi*, 292 U.S. 313.
[32] *Smith* v. *Cahoon*, 283 U.S. 553.

any debt.[33] The profit of a business, Hughes pointed out, could thus be withdrawn from the pursuit of creditors by investing it in life insurance. The statute was condemned as an arbitrary interference with the "obligation of contracts." The right-wingers concurred separately and disagreed with Hughes' reasoning.

The Chief was also one of the majority which struck down the Oklahoma law regulating the ice business.[34] Declaring the manufacture and sale of ice to be a public concern, the legislature had forbidden anyone to engage in it without obtaining a license from a state commission. A licensed ice company sought an injunction for the purpose of driving an unlicensed dealer out of the business. Justice Sutherland's opinion for the majority recognized that "all businesses are subject to some measure of public regulation" but concluded that a statute denying to individuals the right to engage in "an ordinary business" of this kind offended against the due-process clause.

Brandeis, with the concurrence of Stone, strongly dissented on the ground that the decision as to when a private business should be converted into a public one ought to be left to the legislature. In the exercise of the court's power under due process to strike down measures that are "arbitrary, capricious or unreasonable," he said, "we must be ever on guard, lest we erect our prejudices into legal principles." This criticism has often been repeated, and subsequent judicial thinking leans strongly toward the broader rights of legislative experimentation for which the minority contended. Hughes himself thought the case was near the border line.[35]

The Chief's willingness to examine challenged statutes in a largeness of spirit was especially evident when the states' emergency measures enacted to mitigate the hardships of the depression were denounced before the high bench. The first major case of this kind involved the fate of the Minnesota Mortgage Moratorium Law of 1933. It was solely an emergency measure designed to postpone execution sales after mortgages had been foreclosed, thus extending the redemption period so that property owners would have a chance to save their homes. The law was attacked as an unconstitutional impairment of the "obligation of contracts."

"Emergency does not create power," the Chief Justice said in a sweeping opinion upholding the Act.[36] But "emergency may furnish the occasion for the exercise of power." A state could not adopt as its policy the repudiation of debts or the destruction of contracts or the denial of means to enforce them. "But it does not follow," he declared, "that conditions may not arise in which a temporary restraint of enforcement may be consistent with the spirit and purpose of the constitutional provision and thus be found to be within the

[33] *Worthen* v. *Thomas*, 292 U.S. 426.
[34] *New State Ice Co.* v. *Liebmann*, 285 U.S. 262.
[35] Author's interview with CEH, Jan. 2, 1947.
[36] *Home Building and Loan Association* v. *Blaisdell*, 290 U.S. 398.

range of the reserved power of the state to protect the vital interests of the community . . . if state power exists to give temporary relief from the enforcement of contracts in the presence of disasters due to physical causes such as fire, flood or earthquake, that power cannot be said to be non-existent when the urgent public need demanding such relief is produced by other and economic causes."

Reviewing all the cases directly bearing on his problem, the Chief Justice swept onward to his conclusion:

> It is manifest from this review of our decisions that there has been a growing appreciation of public needs and of the necessity of finding ground for a rational compromise between individual rights and public welfare. The settlement and consequent contraction of the public domain, the pressure of a constantly increasing density of population, the interrelation of the activities of our people and the complexity of our economic interests, have inevitably led to an increased use of the organization of society in order to protect the very bases of individual opportunity. Where, in earlier days, it was thought that only the concerns of individuals or of classes were involved, and that those of the state itself were touched only remotely, it has later been found that the fundamental interests of the state are directly affected; and that the question is no longer merely that of one party to a contract as against another, but of the use of reasonable means to safeguard the economic structure upon which the good of all depends.
>
> It is no answer to say that this public need was not apprehended a century ago, or to insist that what the provision of the Constitution meant to the vision of that day it must mean to the vision of our time. . . . the statement that . . . the great clauses of the Constitution must be confined to the interpretation which the framers, with the conditions and outlook of their time, would have placed upon them . . . carries its own refutation. It was to guard against such a narrow conception that Chief Justice Marshall uttered the memorable warning—"We must never forget that it is a *constitution* we are expounding" . . . "a constitution intended to endure for ages to come, and, consequently, to be adapted to the various *crises* of human affairs." . . .
>
> With a growing recognition of public needs and the relation of individual right to public security, the court has sought to prevent the perversion of the [contracts] clause through its use as an instrument to throttle the capacity of the states to protect their fundamental interests. This development is a growth from the seeds which the fathers planted. . . . The principle of this development is, as we have seen, that the reservation of the reasonable exercise of the protective power of the state is read into all contracts and there is no greater reason for refusing to apply this principle to Minnesota mortgages than to New York leases.

"Yes. Strongly put and interesting," Brandeis wrote on the proof sheets. "I approve of changes proposed. I gladly concur in this memorable opinion."

Sutherland wrote the dissenting opinion, with the concurrence of Van Devanter, McReynolds, and Butler, reading the Constitution "with exact literalness like a mathematical formula." It was a narrow victory for forward-marching constitutionalism. But there was wide rejoicing throughout the country over the broad scope and realistic tone of the Chief Justice's opinion. He spoke in deliberate, judicial terms the language that was on the lips of legislators, editors, and leaders of the Roosevelt Administration.

Hughes also took the lead in sustaining the law under which New York was fixing the price of milk in order to curb destructive price-cutting. Once more the court divided five to four. Justice Roberts is said to have paced the floor of his home until the early morning hours in the process of deciding which way he would turn. When he voted to sustain the act, Hughes promptly concluded that he (Roberts) was the best man to write the opinion. "It is clear," the court asserted, "that there is no closed class or category of businesses affected with a public interest. . . . The Constitution does not secure to anyone liberty to conduct his business in such fashion as to inflict injury upon the public at large, or upon any substantial group of people." [37] Due process was no absolute bar to price-fixing.

Nebbia v. *New York* is sometimes said to reflect a sharp breaking away from the doctrine of the Oklahoma ice case. Hughes did not so regard it. To be sure, the court abandoned Sutherland's obiter dicta about a business being "charged with a public use." But in the Oklahoma case Liebmann's right to sell ice had been upheld against what a majority of the court believed to be an arbitrary and capricious restriction. In the Nebbia case no one had been denied the right to sell milk. Perhaps the difference is only one of degree, as in most questions of due process, but a reasonable mind trying to strike a balance between individual liberty and governmental power to act in the public interest can support both decisions without inconsistency.

The great test of the court, so far as state police powers were concerned, came in *Morehead* v. *New York ex rel. Tipaldo* [38] in which the right to fix minimum wages for women was at stake. In 1923 the court had stricken down the District of Columbia minimum-wage law in *Adkins* v. *Children's Hospital* [39] by the slender margin of one vote. Its action had been widely criticized, and some states had enacted similar statutes in spite of the Supreme Court. Under the New York law, Morehead had been sent to jail to await trial for failing to pay the prescribed minimum wage and sought release on a writ of habeas corpus. New York resisted it on the ground that its law was distinguishable from the statute the court had invalidated. A majority of the court wished to deny certiorari, but Hughes, Brandeis, Stone, and Cardozo voted to take the case, and that was sufficient to put it on the docket.

From the beginning it was obvious that Roberts would cast the deciding vote. His opinion in the Nebbia case strongly suggested that he would not again impale a state police regulation upon due process unless the impairment of liberty

[37] *Nebbia* v. *New York*, 291 U.S. 502. [38] 298 U.S. 587. [39] 261 U.S. 525.

under it were beyond reason. The time was ripe for a bold assault upon *Adkins* v. *Children's Hospital,* but counsel for New York pursued a more cautious course. Meekly accepting the Adkins ruling, he asked the court only to differentiate the two statutes. Roberts thought that reasoning was disingenuous and voted with the conservatives.

Writing for the majority, Butler simply clung to the Adkins decision. This meant that the court benightedly looked upon minimum-wage laws as transgressing "the right to contract about one's affairs." The opinion provoked a powerful dissent from Hughes and another from Stone, Brandeis, and Cardozo. Butler then wrote additional arguments into his opinion. Its reactionary tone was very distasteful to Roberts, but he held to the position he had taken. The result was to subject the court to the severest drubbing it had experienced in many years. For in thus limiting the power of the states to cope with economic problems, while preventing congressional intervention in local affairs, it had created a dangerous power vacuum.

Hughes had not broken new ground when he urged his brethren to sustain the New York statute. As Associate Justice, he had riddled the freedom-of-contract doctrine, and in the case of the paper-box factory girl, he had thrown his support to the Oregon minimum-wage law.[40] *Adkins* v. *Children's Hospital* had been decided when he was not a member of the court, and Hughes looked upon it, as he did upon the Dred Scott decision, the income tax cases, and *Lochner* v. *New York,* as a self-inflicted wound for the court. Since four of the brethren were committed to the Adkins decision, however, he concluded that he would have a better chance of clearing the path for minimum-wage legislation if he made no direct assault upon that precedent.

There was a calculated difference between the District of Columbia and New York statutes. In the District, Congress had required a "living wage." Trying to avoid the shoals of due process, New York had added the idea of a "fair wage" corresponding to the reasonable value of the services performed. It was a slender distinction, but Hughes thought it was substantial enough to justify the court in taking a fresh look at the problem. The weakness of his case was that the New York Court of Appeals had found no material difference between the two statutes, and the Supreme Court usually considers itself bound to accept a state court's interpretation of a state law.

"The validity of the New York Act," he asserted, "must be considered in the light of the conditions to which the exercise of the protective power of the State was addressed." Women did not have equality in bargaining power. "Freedom of contract" as applied to them was illusory. Necessity forced them to accept whatever wages were offered. The legislature had found that harsh and overreaching employers had been cutting wages, reducing purchasing power, threat-

[40] CEH, Notes, 1930–1941, p. 32; also p. 313 this volume.

ening the stability of industry, and forcing women to go on relief at the expense of the taxpayer in order to live decently. "We are not at liberty," the Chief Justice continued, "to disregard these facts."

Citing numerous decisions upholding different regulations affecting employment, he drove home his point:

> While it is highly important to preserve that liberty [of contract] from arbitrary and capricious interference, it is also necessary to prevent its abuse, as otherwise it could be used to override all public interests and thus in the end destroy the very freedom of opportunity which it is designed to safeguard. . . . In the statute before us, no unreasonableness appears. The end is legitimate and the means appropriate. I think that the act should be upheld.

Brandeis, Stone, and Cardozo joined in the Hughes opinion, but in Stone's separate dissenting opinion they also hinted that the Adkins case should be overruled even though its reconsideration had not been asked.

The issue was finally settled in March, 1937, when the court reversed its previous decision and found the minimum-wage law of the State of Washington to be constitutional.[41] Roberts joined the four Justices who had dissented in the New York case to make a new majority of five. Since the highest court of Washington had sustained that state's minimum-wage law in spite of the Adkins decision, that precedent had been directly challenged. And the majority in the Tipaldo case had felt the lash of public opinion from the bar, the press, and indirectly from the electorate when it returned the Roosevelt Administration to power by a landslide vote in 1936. It is impossible to determine all the influences that weigh upon a judge, but in any event Roberts had in his Nebbia opinion a well-marked trail by which he could, and did, return to the Hughes camp.

In writing the majority opinion Hughes took note of the ironical fact that the Washington law had been in effect for twenty-three years. It was almost identical with the Oregon statute which he and Holmes had championed in 1915 and which had been sustained by an evenly divided court two years later.[42] Meanwhile the court had invalidated the District of Columbia, Arizona, Arkansas, and New York minimum-wage laws and probably discouraged the enactment of similar statutes in many other states. Certainly it was time to sweep away the inverted pyramid of confusion that the court had built up on the insecure basis of due process.

"In each case," the Chief Justice said, "the violation alleged by those attacking minimum wage regulation for women is deprivation of freedom of contract. What is this freedom? The Constitution does not speak of freedom of contract. It speaks of liberty and prohibits the deprivation of liberty without due process

[41] *West Coast Hotel* v. *Parrish,* 300 U.S. 379.

[42] *Stettler* v. *O'Hara,* 243 U.S. 629.

of law. In prohibiting that deprivation the Constitution does not recognize an absolute and uncontrollable liberty . . . the liberty safeguarded is liberty in a social organization which requires the protection of law against the evils which menace the health, safety, morals and welfare of the people."

The new majority concluded that *Adkins* v. *Children's Hospital* "was a departure from the true application of the principles governing the regulation by the State of the relation of employer and employed." The correct view was to be found in Holmes' dissent in that case. "What can be closer to the public interest," Hughes asked, "than the health of women and their protection from unscrupulous and overreaching employers? And if the protection of women is a legitimate end of the exercise of state power, how can it be said that the requirement of the payment of a minimum wage fairly fixed in order to meet the very necessities of existence is not an admissible means to that end?" The legislative response to the evils of the "sweating system" could not be regarded as arbitrary, he said, "and that is all we have to decide." The Adkins decision was flatly overruled.

Sutherland solemnly admonished his brethren that the judicial function "does not include the power of amendment under the guise of interpretation." But he spoke for only a minority.

The court's about-face on this vital issue is generally attributed to President Roosevelt's court-packing plan, which was announced in the interval between the two decisions. Actually that assault upon the court had no bearing whatever on the outcome, as will be shown in a later chapter. The West Coast Hotel case did, however, clinch the victory of the liberal-minded men within the court. With a few exceptions, state police powers have since been broadly interpreted.

The Hughes record as a whole shows a tolerant recognition of state powers. While holding fast to the basic freedoms, he used his influence to loosen the restraints upon social experimentation. In very large measure he succeeded in diverting the court from intermeddling in local economic and social policy-making to the role of guardian of an ordered liberty and the federal system.

Chapter 67

BALANCE WHEEL OF POWER

No MEMBER of the Supreme Court since the days of John Marshall has written as many opinions of far-reaching import as did Chief Justice Hughes in the fateful decade of the thirties. The nation was in a ferment. Economic dislocations, new social pressures, and changing political concepts sent a parade of constitutional issues into the highest court. As Marshall was called upon to give the Constitution the vitality of a workable organic law, Hughes was destined to adapt the great charter to the bewildering requirements of an economic and social transition.

One of the most delicate aspects of this task arose out of the repeated appeals to the courts to save public-service corporations from the consequences of rate regulation. On this subject the Hughes court had inherited from its predecessors mostly confusion and controversy. While there was general agreement that confiscatory rates could not stand under the due-process clause and the direct prohibition in the Fifth Amendment against taking private property for public use without just compensation, the Justices were far apart in their ideas as to what was confiscatory and what was not. Back in 1898, in *Smyth* v. *Ames*,[1] the court had laid down the rule that a utility is entitled to a fair return and that such a return should be calculated on the "fair value" of the property used for the convenience of the public. But the yardstick suggested by the court for measuring fair value was so all-inclusive that it multiplied confusion.

Conservative judges were inclined to interpret "fair value" as meaning the cost of reproducing a utility. After World War I greatly increased reproduction costs, this formula often led to exorbitant charges. Hughes had been the first judge to speak for the Supreme Court in rejecting the cost-of-reproduction formula when it gave utility property a speculative value. In working out the *Minnesota Rate Cases*[2] in 1913, he had pointedly exposed the injustice of valuing land in accord with the estimated cost of "reproducing" it.

When he returned to the court as Chief Justice, it was leaning toward general acceptance of the cost-of-reproduction formula. At every step it was being challenged, however, by Justice Brandeis, who had developed the "prudent investment" theory and was pressing for its acceptance by the court. Hughes threw his influence against commitment of the court to either theory. While he

[1] 169 U.S. 466. [2] 230 U.S. 352, 445, 450, 454.

agreed with Brandeis that the original cost of property devoted to public use was in most instances the best guide to its "fair value," it was not for the court to fix a rigid formula. Legislatures and rate-making bodies should be left free to adjust or change their formulas to meet changing conditions. Under some circumstances, moreover, a regulated utility might have real value that would not be reflected by the "prudent investment" formula. It was property of which a person could not be deprived without due process of law—not merely an original investment.

The Chief Justice tried to extricate the court from its tangle in two important cases. When a Los Angeles gas company attacked rates fixed by the Railroad Commission of California, the court refused to upset those rates because the company's value had been fixed on the basis of historical costs after examination of all the relevant data. "We do not sit as a board of revision," Hughes said, "but to enforce constitutional rights. . . . The legislative discretion implied in the rate making power necessarily extends to the entire legislative process, embracing the method used in reaching the legislative determination as well as the determination itself. . . . The Court may not interfere with the exercise of the State's authority unless confiscation is clearly established." [3]

Here was plain notice that the court would not thrust down the throats of rate-making bodies either the "prudent-investment" or the "cost-of-reproduction" yardstick. Brandeis put aside championship of his own particularistic formula and concurred. Butler dissented and gave vent to his fury both on and off the bench. Only Sutherland joined him.

The Chief realized that his course left a great responsibility upon rate-making bodies and that it might throw a heavy burden upon the courts. But he felt that the mistake of imposing a rigid formula from the bench must be avoided. And what labor was too great if it might "serve to buttress in any degree the institutions of an ordered liberty?" [4]

In a later opinion the court sustained the Chicago telephone rates fixed by the Illinois Commerce Commission. Trying to show that those rates were confiscatory, the company had swelled the record with expert testimony as to the cost of reproducing its system. Hughes swept it all aside. "Elaborate calculations which are at war with realities revealed by the financial history of the business," he said, "are of no avail in determining the adequacy of the rates prescribed for a public utility corporation." [5]

This time Sutherland agreed, and wrote on the proof sheets, "A hard job well done." Butler concurred in the result. Cardozo suggested that one paragraph be taken out; yet he concurred "in this extraordinarily fine opinion." Brandeis too was pleased and gave a copy of the opinion to Lord Keynes when

[3] *L.A. Gas & Electric Co.* v. *R.R. Comm. of California*, 289 U.S. 287.
[4] Address to American Law Institute, May 6, 1937.
[5] *Lindheimer* v. *Illinois Bell Telephone Co.*, 292 U.S. 151.

he came to Washington as an illustration of how the United States was meeting its economic problems.

To the embarrassment of his critics, who had assumed that he would favor exorbitant profits for utilities, Hughes consistently upheld rate-making bodies in allowing a 7 per cent return on the "fair value" of the property.[6] Since a unanimous court, with Cardozo as spokesman, invalidated gas rates yielding a return of only 4.53 per cent,[7] presumably the "line of confiscation" fluctuated, according to differing circumstances, between that figure and 7 per cent.

Another mounting problem for the court was the mushroom growth of administrative agencies that were impinging upon the rights and lives of the people. As one of the original fathers of this movement, Hughes was not hostile toward its progeny. He recognized

> that this development has been to a great extent a necessary one. Activities of vital importance to the public could not be left unregulated where legislatures were powerless to supply the details of regulation. Experience, expertness, and continuity of supervision, which could only be had by administrative agencies in a particular field, have come to be imperatively needed. But these new methods put us to new tests, and the serious question of the future is whether we have enough of the old spirit which gave us our institutions to save them from being overwhelmed.[8]

The controversy over the constitutionality of fact-finding by such bodies was settled by Hughes' opinion in *Crowell* v. *Benson*[9] handed down in 1932. An injured worker had been awarded benefits under the Longshoremen's and Harbor Workers Compensation Act of 1927. The claim that only the courts could make a final determination of the facts relating to the alleged injuries was rejected. If the deputy commissioner's findings were supported by evidence and within the scope of his authority, the Chief Justice said, without dissent, the courts should not interfere.

Harmony among the judges was shattered, however, when Hughes asserted that the courts had a right to determine the facts for themselves in deciding whether they had jurisdiction in the case. Brandeis made a vehement attack upon this view and was joined by Stone and Roberts. Sutherland, too, was at odds with the Chief in conference, but when he saw the finished opinion, he scribbled on the proof sheets: "I congratulate you upon a beautiful piece of work. You have effectively disposed of the proposed dissent. I fully concur."

The battle of wits between Hughes and Brandeis on this issue was renewed in the St. Joseph Stock Yards case.[10] The question before the court this time was whether the rates fixed for the company by the Secretary of Agriculture

[6] *Wabash Valley* v. *Young*, 287 U.S. 488; *Clark's Ferry* v. *P.S.C. of Penn.*, 291 U.S. 277.
[7] *West Ohio Gas Co.* v. *P.U.C. of Ohio*, 294 U.S. 63.
[8] Address to Federal Bar Association, Feb. 12, 1931.
[9] 285 U.S. 22; see also *Shields* v. *Utah Idaho Central R.R.*, 305 U.S. 177.
[10] 298 U.S. 38.

were confiscatory. The court had no difficulty in deciding that they were not. But the question of how far judicial review should go brought these two giants of the law into one of their sharpest controversies. The Chief Justice contended that the court could redetermine the facts when a constitutional right depended upon factual findings. Brandeis was willing to grant this as to personal liberty but not as to the protection of property rights.

If a legislature acts directly in fixing rates, Hughes declared, those rates are subject to scrutiny in the courts to make certain that the limits of legislative power have not been transgressed. The legislature could not preclude such scrutiny by making any finding of its own. Nor could Congress frustrate judicial review of the acts of its agents by authorizing those agents to find that they had kept within their powers. Some of these quasi-legislative agencies were expert and impartial; others were not. An unscrupulous administrator might be inclined to say, "Let me find the facts for the people of my country, and I care little who lays down the general principles." If the Constitution were to be maintained as the supreme law of the land, Hughes insisted, the court would have to intervene where the evidence clearly showed that the agency's findings were wrong and that constitutional rights had been infringed.

Brandeis agreed that, when constitutional rights were at stake, every question of law could be carried to the courts. Moreover, "a citizen who claims that his liberty is being infringed is entitled, upon habeas corpus, to the opportunity of a judicial determination of the facts." But in dealing with property, he declared, "a much more liberal rule applies." In these instances Congress was free to leave the final ascertainment of facts to an administrative tribunal.

To this Hughes replied: "You've no right to split the due process clause for the purpose of judicial convenience." [11]

Under the Fifth Amendment no distinction whatever is made between the human right to liberty and the human right to retain property. Hughes marshaled all his persuasive powers to prevent the court from writing such a distinction into its constitutional doctrines. In his opinion he declared:

> It is said that we can retain judicial authority to examine the weight of evidence when the question concerns the right of personal liberty. But if this be so, it is not because we are privileged to perform our judicial duty in that case and for reasons of convenience to disregard it in others. The principle applies when rights either of persons or of property are protected by constitutional restrictions. Under our system there is no warrant for the view that the judicial power of a competent court can be circumscribed by any legislative arrangement designed to give effect to administrative action going beyond the limits of constitutional authority.

Hughes emphasized that the court should give due weight to administrative findings. His only point was that the court must not wear any blindfold in-

[11] Author's interview with CEH, Nov. 12, 1947.

vented by Congress to prevent it from seeing an invasion of constitutional rights by way of clearly erroneous findings. While he carried a majority with him, Stone and Cardozo joined in Brandeis' concurring opinion.

The most spectacular fight over the conduct of administrative agents came in the Morgan cases.[12] Secretary of Agriculture Henry Wallace had found the rates of commission men for selling livestock on the Kansas City market to be exorbitant and had fixed maximum rates under the Packers and Stockyards Act. Morgan and others went to court with a complaint that they had not been accorded a fair hearing. The first time the case reached the supreme bench in 1936 it ordered the lower court to give the commission men an opportunity to show the nature of the hearing accorded them. ". . . there must be a hearing in a substantial sense," the Chief Justice said. "And to give the substance of a hearing, which is for the purpose of making determinations upon evidence, the officer who makes the determinations must consider and appraise the evidence which justifies them."

Secretary Wallace was then put on the stand in the lower court, and his testimony clearly showed that no fair hearing had been given. The evidence had been taken under his predecessor. "Sketchy and general" arguments had been heard by Assistant Secretary Tugwell. Wallace himself had then dipped into the bulky record, read the briefs and transcripts of the oral arguments, and conferred with the department's prosecutors in the case. Accepting the prosecutors' findings (save for the alteration of some rates), he had given the commission men no opportunity to be heard on those findings before issuing his order. Requests for a rehearing had been denied.

When this situation was laid before the Supreme Court, it held the Wallace order invalid and pointedly rebuked his department for laxity of procedure.[13] "The right to a hearing," Hughes said, "embraces not only the right to present evidence but also a reasonable opportunity to know the claims of the opposing party and to meet them. The right to submit argument implies that opportunity; otherwise the right may be but a barren one." The Chief Justice repeated what he had said in his previous opinion: that it was good practice to have an examiner receive the evidence and prepare a report as a basis for exceptions and argument, but this was not required procedure. The Secretary himself might conceivably hear evidence in some cases and make his own findings. But he could not accept as his own the findings "prepared by the active prosecutors for the Government" and impose those findings upon the commission men without giving them an opportunity to argue their objections. "That is more than irregularity in practice," the court said; "it is a vital defect." Only Justice Black dissented.

Wallace pretended that the court's criticism was aimed solely at the absence

[12] *Morgan* v. *U.S.*, 298 U.S. 468. [13] 304 U.S. 1.

of a trial examiner's report. He wrote a complaint to the Chief Justice and told the Senate that the error the court had criticized had been "committed not by this administration but by the preceding one." [14] In a public statement he accused the Chief Justice of indulging in "cloudy phraseology," [15] and the Solicitor General asked for a rehearing on the ground that the court had contradicted itself. Of course, the court had done nothing of the sort. Hughes might have written more clearly than he did in the second opinion, but a careful reading shows unmistakably that he was striking at the irresponsible practice of having one man hear the evidence, a bureau make the findings, an official hear the arguments, and another official make the decision. In a sharp *per curiam* opinion the court denied a rehearing, again spelled out the "vital defect" in Secretary Wallace's procedure, and declared that the Government's allegation of conflict between the two previous opinions was "wholly unfounded." [16]

It had been generally assumed that the $700,000 paid into the District Court by the commission men while awaiting the outcome of the case would go back to them under the Supreme Court's ruling. The lower court did so decide after the Supreme Court had tossed the case back to it a second time, but the Government again appealed. The Supreme Court said through Justice Stone that the fund should be held until the outcome of new rate-fixing proceedings could determine who was entitled to it.[17]

Not infrequently the court administered judicial correction to itself. These were always occasions for soul-searching on the part of the Chief Justice. Laying great store upon clarity and stability in the law, he was loath to see the court throw down a previous decision. The court, as Justice Frankfurter once said, "did not sit like a kadi under a tree dispensing justice according to considerations of individual expediency." General adherence to its own rules and precedents was indispensable to the idea of a government of law. Yet if experience and deliberation convinced Hughes that a previous decision was out of line with sound legal or constitutional doctrines, he would frankly face the necessity of correcting it.

Such a necessity arose in *Erie Railroad Company* v. *Tompkins*,[18] and the Supreme Court met it by discarding a doctrine to which it had given faithful adherence for nearly a century. The facts of the case were simple. Tompkins had been injured by a swinging freight car door on a passing train, and a federal court jury had awarded him damages of $30,000. The Court of Appeals had affirmed. Ordinarily that would have settled the issue. The Supreme Court granted certiorari only because the case came up to it after years of brooding

[14] Department of Agriculture release, May 12, 1938.
[15] *New York Times*, May 8, 1938.
[16] *Morgan* v. *U.S.*, May 31, 1938.
[17] *U.S.* v. *Morgan*, 307 U.S. 185.
[18] 304 U.S. 64.

by several of its members over the inconsistent practice of applying different versions of the common law in the federal and state courts.

Tompkins had got his case into a federal court because he was a citizen of Pennsylvania and the railroad that injured him happened to be incorporated in New York. The first Congress had provided in Section 34 of the Judiciary Act of 1789 that in such cases of diverse citizenship, where no question of federal statutory or constitutional law was involved, the federal courts should rest their decisions on "the laws of the several States." A question had arisen as to whether this meant only state statutes or included also the decisions of state courts, which some lawyers insisted were not laws. The Supreme Court had directed the lower federal courts to follow the decisions as well as the statutes of the state in which they sat. The result was that the federal courts applied different versions of the law in every state.

In 1842 the Supreme Court had decided in *Swift* v. *Tyson* [19] that the federal courts were bound to apply only the statutes of the state in which they sat and could interpret the common law in accord with their own judgment. This might create two different versions of the common law in each state, Justice Story acknowledged, but it would have the virtue of promoting uniformity of federal decision. The court hoped that the new "federal general common law" would gradually supersede state common law and thus evolve into an accepted unwritten law for the whole country. But in this it was disappointed. The only result was to build up conflicting versions of the unwritten law in each state. If two persons riding side by side were injured in the same accident, one claiming diversity of citizenship might go into the federal court and obtain damages while the other, confined to a state court, might be entitled to nothing. Equal protection of the laws became impossible.

Holmes and Brandeis had tried to overthrow *Swift* v. *Tyson* before Hughes returned to the bench.[20] Charles Warren, historian of the Supreme Court, had showed from examination of the original documents that Story had given an erroneous interpretation to Section 34 of the Judiciary Act in 1842.[21] As new cases arose, the conference of judges threshed out the advantages and disadvantages of reverting to the earlier rule. Each time the conviction that the 1842 precedent was wrong seemed to take firmer root. When *Erie* v. *Tompkins* brought the issue into sharp focus in 1938, Hughes laid the case before the conference with the comment, "If we wish to overrule *Swift* v. *Tyson*, here is our opportunity." [22] Every judge except Butler and McReynolds agreed that the time for a change had come.

The Chief Justice recognized Brandeis' leadership in bringing about the change by assigning the case to him. The dean of the court responded with a

[19] 16 Pet. 1. [20] *Southern Pacific Co.* v. *Jensen*, 244 U.S. 205, 222.
[21] *Harvard Law Review*, Vol. 37, pp. 49, 51–52, 81–88.
[22] Author's interview with CEH, June 4, 1947.

closely reasoned opinion showing that, "There is no federal general common law." To the surprise of his brethren, however, he did not stop with a reversal of the court's error in 1842. "If only a question of statutory construction were involved," he wrote, "we should not be prepared to abandon a doctrine so widely applied throughout nearly a century. But the unconstitutionality of the course pursued has now been made clear and compels us to do so."

Hughes was disturbed by this. He could see no point in dragging in a constitutional argument when the court was merely correcting its own misinterpretation of the Judiciary Act.[23] To be sure, *Swift* v. *Tyson* had departed from sound constitutional theory, but it had set up only a judge-made rule. The court was always free to rectify its mistakes whether or not a constitutional doctrine were involved. The Chief consulted Brandeis and learned that he had originally written his opinion without reference to any constitutional issue. Stone had induced him to change it by arguing that *Swift* v. *Tyson* had stood so long that Congress must be regarded as having accepted its doctrine. Consequently, it was necessary to invoke the Constitution to undo what the Supreme Court and Congress had jointly done. Hughes replied that there was no evidence that the issue had ever come squarely before Congress—that in fact only the court was at fault. For the sake of harmony in so important a decision, however, he and a majority of the brethren agreed to go along with the Brandeis opinion as circulated. Only Justice Reed insisted on writing a separate opinion, saying that the constitutional argument was surplusage, although the Chief Justice and apparently several other members of the court shared that view.

One writer has assumed that the judicial revolution effected by *Erie* v. *Tompkins* was a result of Justice Black's lone dissent in the Gamer case two months before.[24] But in this dissent [25] Black did not even mention *Swift* v. *Tyson*. More conclusive is the fact that he got no support from Brandeis, who voted with the majority. The court was brooding over a reversal of *Swift* v. *Tyson* long before Black came to the bench, and it is absurd to suppose that his lone dissent in the Gamer case had any influence on the momentous decision in *Erie* v. *Tompkins*. Most of the credit for this overturn goes to Justice Brandeis.

Hughes' disposition to keep the law attuned to the needs of the time may be seen in a notable opinion dealing with the Sherman Antitrust Act. To him, the virtue of the Sherman Act, like that of the Constitution, lay in its broad generalities. It was not to be interpreted in a spirit of narrow literalness but used with shrewd discrimination to protect the public interest against monopoly and the destruction of competition.

In the early thirties the coal-mining industry was in a state of acute de-

[23] *Id.* [24] Wesley McCune, *The Nine Young Men*, pp. 31–32.
[25] *N.Y. Life Insurance Co.* v. *Gamer*, 303 U.S. 161.

moralization. Several investigations had revealed a surplus capacity within the industry, cutthroat competition that was depressing both prices and wages, a breakdown in collective bargaining, heavy financial losses for the operators, and violence and disorder among the miners. A group of producers who controlled 73 per cent of the commercial production in their area formed a collective selling agency, with authority to set prices for coal from all the cooperating mines. The agency continued to meet sharp competition from mines in other areas and from other fuels, but it was prosecuted under the Sherman Act.

The Supreme Court refused to upset the venture, with Hughes writing in his most vigorous manner. A cooperative enterprise is not to be condemned as an undue restraint of trade, he asserted, because it may effect a change in market conditions, where the change would mitigate recognized evils and would not impair, but rather foster, fair competitive opportunities. The restrictions imposed by the Act were not mechanical or artificial. Its general phrases did not seek to establish a mere delusive liberty. "Reality must dominate the judgment," Hughes insisted. For "when industry is grievously hurt, when production concerns fail, when unemployment mounts, and communities dependent upon profitable production are prostrate, the wells of commerce go dry." [26] The Sherman Act did not require companies to merge in order to correct marketing abuses.

It was a statesmanlike application of the antitrust law in full accord with the needs of the times. "I agree entirely," Brandeis wrote on the proof sheets. "You have made our position clear and persuasive." Sutherland praised the opinion as "excellent, timely and helpful," and Cardozo as "a fine piece of work." Only McReynolds dissented.

A few months after Hughes had returned to the bench, with much opposition from the unions, he handed down a decision that made labor leaders sit up and rub their eyes. The court sustained an injunction under the Railway Labor Act of 1926 forcing the Texas and New Orleans Railroad Company to disestablish its company union and reinstate the Brotherhood of Railway and Steamship Clerks as collective bargaining agent.[27] Anyone familiar with Hughes' defense of the right of collective bargaining in *Coppage* v. *Kansas* back in 1915 would have expected this decision in 1930. Labor was taken by surprise because it had listened to the misleading tirades of the self-styled liberals in the debate over Hughes' confirmation.

"Freedom of choice in the selection of representatives on each side of the dispute is the essential foundation of the statutory scheme," the Chief Justice said. ". . . it is of the essence of a voluntary scheme, if it is to accomplish

[26] *Appalachian Coals* v. *U.S.*, 288 U.S. 344. [27] 281 U.S. 548.

its purpose, that this liberty should be safeguarded." Collective bargaining would be a mockery if the workers had to organize under employer coercion.

Nor was there any doubt as to the constitutional authority of Congress to prohibit such coercion. "The power to regulate commerce," Hughes asserted, "is the power to enact 'all appropriate legislation' for its 'protection and advancement.' . . . Exercising this authority, Congress may facilitate the amicable settlement of disputes which threaten the service of the necessary agencies of interstate transportation." Here is the precursor of Hughes' famous opinion in the Jones and Laughlin case, but that can be best discussed in a later chapter.

"You have made this matter entirely clear," Brandeis wrote on the Texas and New Orleans proof sheets. Van Devanter thought the opinion was "as near perfect as is humanly possible." Said John P. Frey of the American Federation of Labor: "It may well be that those who believe that the Chief Justice is over-conservative in his attitude toward human relations in industry are mistaken." [28] A news commentator said that Hughes had "shown himself to be just the sort of Chief Justice that his opponents insisted he never could be." [29]

The Texas and New Orleans opinion did not mean that the Chief Justice was pro-labor. Rather, it indicated a disposition on his part faithfully to enforce a policy laid down by Congress within its constitutional powers. His conclusions were no less forthright when he felt that the law compelled a decision against labor. Such a case reached the high bench in 1939 after the country had experienced an epidemic of sit-down strikes. Because the Fansteel Metallurgical Corporation had indulged in unfair labor practices and resisted organization of its employees, a group of them had seized its plants and fought furiously against dislodgment. After two pitched battles, many had been arrested and fined or sent to jail for violation of a court injunction. The strikers had been discharged for their misconduct, but the National Labor Relations Board had ordered them reinstated with back pay. Hughes wrote for the court an almost blistering denunciation of this attempt to condone the strikers' "highhanded proceeding without shadow of legal right." [30]

The employer's conduct was reprehensible, the opinion said, but it did not make him an outlaw or deprive him of the right to possession of his property. The remedy for the employees was a complaint to the NLRB. They also had the right to strike, "but they had no license to commit acts of violence or to seize their employer's plant." "To justify such conduct because of the existence of a labor dispute or of an unfair labor practice," Hughes declared, "would be to put a premium on resort to force instead of legal remedies and to subvert the principles of law and order which lie at the foundations of

[28] *International Labor News Service*, July 19, 1930.
[29] Oliver McKee, Jr., in *Outlook and Independent*, Oct. 7, 1931, p. 171.
[30] *NLRB* v. *Fansteel Metallurgical Corp.*, 306 U.S. 240.

society. . . . There is not a line in the statute to warrant the conclusion that it is any part of the policies of the Act to encourage employees to resort to force and violence in defiance of the law of the land."

Justices Reed and Black, dissenting, fell back upon the flimsy argument that both sides had erred grievously and that the courts should "not interfere with the normal action of administrative bodies."

The Fansteel decision was a powerful stroke for "ordered liberty" and helped to counteract the perilous doctrine that labor unions can do no wrong. It was followed by another notable decision to the effect that Illinois could restrain picketing conducted "in a context of violence." [31] In this instance Hughes assigned the opinion to Frankfurter. Black and Reed wrote separate dissents, with the support of Douglas, thus opening a breach between the Roosevelt appointees to the court that was to be greatly widened with the passing years.

In two labor cases involving the Sherman Act, Hughes found himself in the minority. The first of these, *Apex Hosiery Co.* v. *Leader*,[32] brought him into a memorable clash with Stone. The case arose out of a sit-down strike. Only eight of the company's 2,500 employees had been members of the union when the strike began, but union men from other factories descended upon the company's plants and held them for nearly two months, wrecking the machinery and completely stalling operations for a longer period. Stone condemned the strike as a "lawless invasion" resulting in "destruction of . . . property by force and violence of the most brutal and wanton character." Still he concluded that, in willfully preventing any movement of 134,000 dozen pairs of hosiery awaiting shipment, largely to other states, the strikers had not restrained commerce within the meaning of the Sherman Act.

To Hughes (who was joined by Roberts and McReynolds), this was an unwarranted contraction of the antitrust laws. In the Clayton Act Congress had given labor immunity to antitrust restraints in carrying out its "legitimate objects." The Chief Justice bore down on the fact that violence and willful obstruction of interstate shipments were not "legitimate objects." Where, then, could the immunity be found? Stone had taken refuge in the historic meaning of "restraint of trade," but Hughes pointed to the fact that the Sherman Act also condemns conspiracies in restraint of "commerce among the several States." "Commerce" had a definite meaning in American law. It embraced "commercial intercourse in all its branches, including transportation. . . ." Plainly there was a conspiracy here. Certainly there was restraint, and it was admitted that the restraint acted directly upon interstate commerce. Hughes unmercifully exposed the tangled logic on which the majority relied:

[31] *Milk Wagon Drivers Union* v. *Meadowmoor Dairies*, 312 U.S. 287.
[32] 310 U.S. 469.

> It would indeed be anomalous if, while employers are bound by the Labor Act because their unfair labor practices may lead to conduct which would prevent the shipment of their goods in interstate commerce, at the same time the direct and intentional obstruction or prevention of such shipments by the employees were not deemed to be a restraint of interstate commerce under the broad terms of the Sherman Act.
>
> This Court has never heretofore decided that a direct and intentional obstruction or prevention of the shipment of goods in interstate commerce was not a violation of the Sherman Act. In my opinion it should not so decide now. . . .
>
> Once it is decided, as this Court does decide, that the Sherman Act does not except labor unions from its purview,—once it is decided, as this Court does decide, that the conduct here shown is not within the immunity conferred by the Clayton Act,—the Court, as it seems to me, has no option but to apply the Sherman Act in accordance with its express provisions.

In the Hutcheson case [33] the court took another long leap toward freeing labor from the restraints of the Sherman Act. This was a secondary boycott case, the carpenters' union having launched a boycott against Anheuser-Busch beer because the company had given the machinists' union work the carpenters thought they should have. If the court followed its previous decision in *Duplex Co.* v. *Deering,*[34] it would have to rule that the Sherman Act prohibited such union conduct. Speaking for a majority, Justice Frankfurter avoided that result, without overruling the Duplex decision, by "reading the Sherman Law and Section 20 of the Clayton Act and the Norris-LaGuardia Act as a harmonizing text of outlawry of labor conduct."

This strained telescoping of different Acts passed at different times for somewhat different purposes shocked the legal profession.[35] The court had joined together what Congress had put apart. Many authorities believe that the old court, in its Duplex decision, had emasculated Section 20 of the Clayton Act, providing that none of the routine labor union activities specified should be held to violate any federal law. But if Congress had thought so, as Justice Frankfurter assumed, it could have reversed the Duplex decision. It could have written Section 20 of the Clayton Act into the Norris-LaGuardia Act. Instead, it deliberately restricted the latter Act to the control of injunctions in labor disputes. It said not a word about relieving unions from liability to prosecution under the Sherman Act for secondary boycotts.

Because of his "forked" opinion in the Apex Hosiery case, the Chief Justice refrained from writing a dissent in the Hutcheson case. But he conferred with Roberts and joined in his dissenting view, "that no court has ever undertaken so radically to legislate where Congress has refused to do so."

This clash high-lights two diverging concepts of the judicial function. In

[33] *U.S.* v. *Hutcheson,* 312 U.S. 219. [34] 254 U.S. 443.

[35] Charles O. Gregory, *Labor and the Law,* p. 273.

justification of the technique he had employed in the Hutcheson opinion, Justice Frankfurter cited Holmes' belief that if the legislature had "intimated its will, however indirectly, that will should be recognized and obeyed." ". . . the change of policy that enduces the enactment may not be set out in terms," Holmes had said, "but it is not an adequate discharge of duty for the courts to say: We see what you are driving at, but you have not said it, and therefore we shall go on as before."

Hughes was much less trustful of judicial acumen in reading the legislative mind. If the change of policy was not set forth in the law itself or indicated in its legislative history, how could judges be sure of what Congress was "driving at"? In a note to Frankfurter three weeks before the Hutcheson opinion came down, the Chief offered a substitute for Holmes' explanation to Congress:

DEAR JUSTICE FRANKFURTER:

Just a word "off the record"—prompted by your quotation from Justice Holmes but with humble deference to judicial technique:

"We have a notion that you may have had this in mind, but you stopped short of covering it, and we can't extend your statute so as to add what you left out. We await your pleasure." [36]

A strong bond of friendship had grown up between Hughes and Frankfurter, the chief legatee of the Holmes tradition. That friendship remained unruffled by any intellectual differences; still Frankfurter's acceptance of what he believed Congress was "driving at" and Hughes' more cautious policy of "awaiting the pleasure" of Congress suggests a wide difference in approach to the judicial task.

[36] CEH's private papers.

Chapter 68

GUARDIAN OF FREEDOM

A SINGULAR devotion to civil liberties had marked Hughes' advance to the headship of the judicial system. His soul-searching over the pardon cases at Albany, the tolerant spirit that infused *Bailey* v. *Alabama* and *Frank* v. *Mangum*, and his courageous defiance of popular prejudices to defend the five Socialists expelled from the New York Legislature had revealed the consistent liberality of his thinking in this sphere. The Chief Justiceship was to bring this dominant quality to full flower.

It was a crucial moment in the development of constitutional safeguards for civil liberty when Hughes returned to the bench. Even such basic rights as freedom of speech and freedom of the press seemed to hang by a slender thread when challenged by state governments. In 1920 the Supreme Court had sustained a wartime statute in Minnesota forbidding the advocacy of pacifism.[1] Holmes had acquiesced, and Brandeis, dissenting, had said he saw "no occasion to consider" whether this encroachment upon freedom of speech violated the Fourteenth Amendment. Two years later, in upholding the Missouri Service Letter Law, the court had said flatly: ". . . neither the Fourteenth Amendment nor any other provision of the Constitution of the United States imposes upon the States any restrictions about 'freedom of speech' or the 'liberty of silence' . . ."[2] Both Holmes and Brandeis had concurred.

Curiously, it was McReynolds who had been spokesman for the court when, in 1923, it had found enough freedom in the Fourteenth Amendment to knock out the Nebraska law forbidding the teaching of the German language.[3] Holmes and Sutherland had dissented. Then had come the Gitlow case in which the court assumed "for the present purposes" that "freedom of speech and of the press—which are protected by the First Amendment from abridgment by Congress—are among the fundamental personal rights and 'liberties' protected by the due process clause of the Fourteenth Amendment from impairment by the States."[4] It was the first time the court had transfused these basic guarantees from the First into the Fourteenth Amendment, and the transfusion seemed rather inconclusive, for the effect of the decision was to uphold the New York Criminal Anarchy Act and to suppress a Socialist pamphlet.

[1] *Gilbert* v. *Minnesota*, 254 U.S. 325. [2] *Prudential Insurance Co.* v. *Cheek*, 259 U.S. 530.
[3] *Meyer* v. *Nebraska*, 262 U.S. 390. [4] *Gitlow* v. *N.Y.*, 268 U.S. 652.

Holmes' dissent showed that by this time he and Brandeis had firmly embraced the Fourteenth Amendment as a shield to free speech, although he thought that principle might "be accepted with a somewhat larger latitude of interpretation than is allowed to Congress" under the First Amendment.

In 1927 the Criminal Syndicalism Act of California had been upheld,[5] but a little later the court had used the due-process clause to reverse a conviction under the Criminal Syndicalism Act of Kansas.[6] Such was the state of the law when Hughes came to the bench a second time. Under his powerful influence the pendulum might easily have swung backward or forward. His decision to push it vigorously forward is one of the most significant facts in our recent constitutional history.

On three successive Mondays in the late spring of 1931, Hughes spoke fluently and inspiringly for free speech, free thought, and freedom of the press. Twice he spoke for a majority of the court in overthrowing state policies of suppression. The man who had been denounced as "the greatest champion of property rights" was leading the way into a new era of civil liberties.

First came *Stromberg* v. *California*.[7] In a Communist camp a nineteen-year-old girl of Russian parentage, but American-born, had daily raised a red flag bearing the hammer and sickle and taught children to salute it as an emblem of opposition to organized government. California had convicted her under a vague "red-flag" law—a characteristic tool of suppression. Hughes insisted that she had a right to display a red flag so long as she did not "incite to violence and crime and threaten the overthrow of organized government by unlawful means." Stripping the case to the naked issue of freedom, he declared:

> The maintenance of the opportunity for free political discussion to the end that government may be responsive to the will of the people and that changes may be obtained by lawful means, an opportunity essential to the security of the Republic, is a fundamental principle of our constitutional system. A statute which, upon its face, and as authoritatively construed, is so vague and indefinite as to permit the punishment of the fair use of this opportunity is repugnant to the guarantee of liberty contained in the Fourteenth Amendment.

It was the sweep of the decision that gave the country a lift. Hughes made it clear that free speech was not to be cramped into any kind of narrow brackets. Instead of forcing citizens to curb their speech in accord with state rules, legislatures would have to accommodate their rules to a free market place of ideas. Only McReynolds and Butler failed to go along.

In the celebrated case of Douglas Clyde Macintosh four of the strongest men ever to sit on the supreme bench—Hughes, Holmes, Brandeis, and Stone

[5] *Whitney* v. *California*, 274 U.S. 357, 373.
[6] *Fiske* v. *Kansas*, 274 U.S. 380. [7] 283 U.S. 359.

—stood together and lost.[8] The majority, with Sutherland as mouth, denied citizenship to this Canadian-born professor of divinity at Yale University, because his pledge to fight in defense of the United States was qualified—he would fight only if he believed the war to be morally justified. To the majority, this meant that he was not attached to the principles of the Constitution.

Three years previously the court had denied citizenship to Rosika Schwimmer, and Holmes, dissenting, had made his classic plea for "freedom for the thought that we hate."[9] This time he joined Hughes in a quite different line of reasoning. The question was not, the Chief said, whether it was right to deny citizenship to applicants who refused to bear arms, but whether Congress had prescribed such a test. Where did the arms-bearing requirement originate? The statute itself provided only that applicants for citizenship should take an oath that they "will support and defend the Constitution and laws of the United States against all enemies, foreign and domestic, and bear true faith and allegiance to the same."

This naturalization oath, Hughes showed, is substantially the same as that required of civil officers. Certainly men with religious scruples against war could not be deemed disqualified for public office because they would have to take an oath to defend the Constitution. The bearing of arms was not the only important method of defense, even in time of war. "I think that the requirement of the oath of office should be read in the light of our regard from the beginning for freedom of conscience," the Chief Justice said. And since Congress had "reproduced the historic words of the oath of office in the naturalization oath," it should be read in the same way.

The practice of excusing conscientious objectors from military service further suggested that Congress had not expected every naturalized citizen to tote a gun. ". . . in the forum of conscience," Hughes pointed out, "duty to a moral power higher than the state has always been maintained. . . . The essence of religion is belief in a relation to God involving duties superior to those arising from any human relation. . . . There is abundant room for . . . maintaining the conception of the supremacy of law as essential to orderly government, without demanding that either citizens or applicants for citizenship shall assume by oath an obligation to regard allegiance to God as subordinate to allegiance to civil power. . . . The Congress has sought to avoid such conflicts in this country by respecting our happy tradition."

This powerful dissent won the support of the country and became the law of the land in 1946, when the Supreme Court overruled both the Schwimmer and Macintosh decisions.[10] Although Hughes was no longer on the bench, the court specifically went back to his dissent of 1931 and rested in his conclusion

[8] *U.S.* v. *Macintosh,* 283 U.S. 605.
[9] *U.S.* v. *Schwimmer,* 279 U.S. 644
[10] *Girouard* v. *U.S.*, 328 U.S. 61.

that Congress had not "set a stricter standard for aliens seeking admission to citizenship than it did for officials who make and enforce the laws of the nation."

On June 1, 1931, the Chief Justice completed his trilogy on freedom with an opinion which had the effect of wiping the Minnesota press-gag law off the books. It was the first time that the guarantee of liberty in the Fourteenth Amendment had been used completely to obliterate a state law. The Chief met with fierce opposition within the court, and Butler, Van Devanter, McReynolds, and Sutherland dissented. The decision stands out, however, as one of the great landmarks in the history of civil rights.[11]

The newspaper that Minnesota had suppressed was a vicious little scandal-sheet called *The Saturday Press*. Its vilification campaigns had been aimed chiefly at city officials of Jewish origin in Minneapolis. After much provocation, officials had moved against the publisher under a state law of 1925 providing that "malicious, scandalous and defamatory" newspapers and magazines could be enjoined as a "public nuisance." The Supreme Court of Minnesota had upheld the conviction, but from the center of the supreme bench in Washington, D.C., the state's action had the appearance of violating a great principle to punish a little scandalmonger.

Hughes found it "impossible to conclude" that freedom of the press "was left unprotected by the general guaranty of fundamental rights of persons and property." To be sure, it was not an "absolute right," and the state could punish its abuse. But this Minnesota statute condemned publications that officials might deem to be "malicious" without even requiring proof of malice. It permitted defense, not on grounds of truth alone, but only on the ground that the truth was published with good motives. Instead of prescribing punishment for libel, its aim was the suppression of newspapers that might be exposing political scandals. And after a newspaper had been suppressed, its publisher could be placed under court order for continued good conduct. "This is the essence of censorship," the Chief Justice exclaimed.

The government could forbid publication of the sailing dates of troop ships, he reasoned; it could protect community life against incitements to violence and uphold requirements of decency. But it could not suppress a publication to stop criticism of public officials. Laying great stress on the almost complete absence of "previous restraints upon publications" for a century and a half, he concluded:

> The importance of this immunity has not lessened, . . . the administration of government has become more complex, the opportunities for malfeasance and corruption have multiplied, crime has grown to most serious proportions, and the danger of its protection by unfaithful officials and of the impairment of the funda-

[11] *Near* v. *Minnesota,* 283 U.S. 697.

mental security of life and property by criminal alliances and official neglect, emphasizes the primary need of a vigilant and courageous press, especially in great cities. The fact that the liberty of the press may be abused by miscreant purveyors of scandal does not make any the less necessary the immunity of the press from previous restraint in dealing with official misconduct.

Stromberg v. *California* and *Near* v. *Minnesota* set the pattern for the Hughes court in shoring up civil liberties. In 1936 Sutherland wrote for the court in knocking out Huey Long's tax on the gross receipts of the larger Louisiana newspapers that were opposing him.[12] It was an obvious device for curbing freedom of the press. Two years later Hughes extended the doctrine of *Near* v. *Minnesota* to handbills, circulars, and tracts. Alma Lovell of the Jehovah's Witnesses had been sentenced to prison for fifty days for violating a city ordinance in Griffin, Georgia, forbidding the distribution of circulars or "literature of any kind" without permission of the city manager. The court was unanimous in recognizing this sweeping prohibition as an invasion of freedom of the press. The Chief Justice said:

We think the ordinance is invalid on its face. Whatever the motive which induced its adoption, its character is such that it strikes at the very foundation of the freedom of the press by subjecting it to license and censorship. The struggle for the freedom of the press was primarily directed against the power of the licensor. . . . Legislation of the type of the ordinance in question would restore the system of license and censorship in its baldest form.

The liberty of the press is not confined to newspapers and periodicals. It necessarily embraces pamphlets and leaflets. These indeed have been historic weapons in the defense of liberty, as the pamphlets of Thomas Paine and others in our own history abundantly attest. The press in its historic connotation comprehends every sort of publication which affords a vehicle of information and opinion.[13]

Freedom of assembly had a no less exalted standing in the court's scale of values. When Dirk De Jonge was sentenced to prison for seven years for helping to conduct a Communist Party meeting in Portland, Oregon, Hughes drew an unerring line between criminal conduct and peaceful assembly. The meeting had been an orderly protest against the shooting of strikers—until the police broke it up on the ground that it was sponsored by an organization advocating criminal syndicalism. Whatever the objectives of the Communist Party might be, the Chief Justice said, De Jonge still retained his right to make a speech and take part in a peaceful meeting:

The right of peaceful assembly is a right cognate to those of free speech and free press and is equally fundamental.

These rights may be abused by using speech or press or assembly in order to

[12] *Grosjean* v. *American Press Co.*, 297 U.S. 233.
[13] *Lovell* v. *City of Griffin*, 303 U.S. 444.

incite to violence and crime. The people through their legislatures may protect themselves against that abuse. But the legislative intervention can find constitutional justification only by dealing with the abuse. The rights themselves must not be curtailed.

. . . The holding of meetings for peaceful political action cannot be proscribed. Those who assist in the conduct of such meetings cannot be branded as criminals on that score.[14]

Sutherland made it clear in a proof-sheet note that he concurred because the opinion was carefully drawn "so as to safeguard the right of free speech & peaceful assembly without giving sanction to abuse of these rights." Brandeis wrote simply, "Yes Sir. This is grand."

The court again in 1939 went on record for freedom of assembly after Mayor Hague had attempted to prevent the Congress of Industrial Organizations from holding a public meeting in Jersey City.[15] An ordinance giving full discretion to the director of safety to grant or withhold permits for public meetings was held to be invalid on its face. There was no opinion of the court, but Roberts and Stone wrote separate opinions and Hughes partly concurred in both; McReynolds and Butler dissented. The following year the court overturned an Alabama statute forbidding "loitering and picketing," with Justice Murphy writing the opinion and only McReynolds dissenting.[16]

An opinion by Justice Roberts took the sting out of a Connecticut law requiring the approval of a welfare official for the solicitation of money for religious or charitable purposes.[17] No such strait-jacket could be placed on religious freedom, the court said. By this decision it completed the process of incorporating the entire First Amendment—freedom of religion, freedom of speech, freedom of the press, and the right of peaceful assembly—into the word "liberty" in the Fourteenth Amendment.

Attorneys for Tom Mooney dropped an enormous record, including twelve volumes of testimony, into the lap of the Supreme Court in 1934. Near the end of the summer Hughes called his secretary to New York and dictated an analysis of the celebrated case for presentation to the conference. The court concluded that Mooney should seek a writ of habeas corpus from California's highest court before sending his case to Washington.[18] The Chief laid a good deal of store upon the judicial proprieties. At the same time he jarred the California authorities by declaring that due process could not be satisfied "by mere notice and hearing" if in truth the court and jury had been deceived "by the presentation of testimony known to be perjured." His *per curiam* opinion was an invitation to Mooney to send his case back if he could not get justice from California.

[14] *De Jonge* v. *Oregon*, 299 U.S. 353.
[15] *Hague* v. *C.I.O.*, 307 U.S. 496.
[16] *Thornhill* v. *Alabama*, 310 U.S. 88.
[17] *Cantwell* v. *Connecticut*, 310 U.S. 296.
[18] *Mooney* v. *Holohan*, 294 U.S. 103.

Tyranny from any source found its nemesis in the Hughes court. The Chief was fond of quoting William Pitt's penetrating observation. "Where law ends, tyranny begins." Then he would assert, "And it is our business to see to it that when law begins, tyranny shall end." [19] In *Sterling* v. *Constantin* [20] he applied this rule to the Governor of Texas who was trying to enforce his edicts by martial law.

In the dark days of the depression Texas had sought to reduce the flow of oil from wells capable of producing five thousand barrels a day to a mere two hundred barrels. The legality of the order had been challenged, and a federal court had issued a temporary injunction against its enforcement. By way of retaliation Governor Sterling had shut down all the wells in several counties and tried to justify this resort to martial law by declaring that "insurrection and riot" in the oil counties were beyond civil control.

A three-judge federal court had found "no insurrection or riot in fact . . . no closure of the courts, no failure of the civil authorities," nor any condition resembling a state of war. In these circumstances, the Supreme Court concluded, the Governor could not interrupt the ordinary judicial procedure by military force. Hughes' opinion said:

> It does not follow from the fact that the Executive has this range of discretion, deemed to be a necessary incident of his power to suppress disorder, that every sort of action the Governor may take, no matter how unjustified by the exigency or subversive of private right and the jurisdiction of the courts, is conclusively supported by mere executive fiat. . . . What are the allowable limits of military discretion, and whether or not they have been overstepped in a particular case, are judicial questions.

The Governor's duty, Hughes concluded, was to aid the process of having rights determined, not to thwart it. The logic of this sound limitation on martial law—imposed upon governors for the first time in this Hughes opinion—would have saved the court from sanctioning the expulsion of the Nisei from the West Coast in World War II [21]—if the court had then been willing to apply it.

Hughes was always on guard against racial discrimination in the courts. The broad tolerance of his earlier opinions had ripened into unalterable convictions. After putting on the mantle of Chief Justice, he seized the first opportunity to speak his mind on this subject. A federal judge in the District of Columbia had refused to permit the questioning of jurors as to their racial prejudices, and the all-white jury thus selected had convicted a Negro of first-degree murder. Hughes reversed the judgment, with the comment that "no surer way could be devised to bring the processes of justice into disrepute" than to "permit it to

[19] Address to Federal Bar Association, Feb. 12, 1931.
[20] 287 U.S. 378. [21] *Korematsu* v. *U.S.*, 323 U.S 214.

be thought that persons entertaining a disqualifying prejudice were allowed to serve as jurors." [22]

The well-known Scottsboro case involving rape convictions against seven Negroes came twice to the supreme bench. The first time Hughes took the lead in reversing the convictions because the trial judge's appointment of counsel for the men had been a mere gesture.[23] Only Butler and McReynolds resisted this conclusion. In line with his policy of asking conservative judges to write liberal opinions, the Chief assigned the case to Sutherland.

Alabama tried the Scottsboro boys in another county, and they came back to the Supreme Court under death sentences with a plea that Negroes had been systematically excluded from jury duty. The statute itself did not discriminate against Negroes. But in Jackson County, where the indictment had been drawn, residents for more than half a century could not remember that any Negro had been called for jury service. In Morgan County, where the trial had been held, no Negro had ever been on a jury, although a large number were qualified to serve. This testimony in itself, Hughes said, "made out a *prima facie* case of the denial of the equal protection which the Constitution guarantees." [24]

The chief significance of this opinion lies in its realistic handling of the facts. The Supreme Court of Alabama had relied upon fiction—the fiction that if no Negroes were called it was because none was qualified. Hughes cut through that flimsy pretense by giving weight to facts that the state court had ignored. Nor did he require elaborate proof of intent on the part of the administrative officials to discriminate; that inference was drawn from the overshadowing fact that Negroes were never summoned as jurors.

Here is a striking illustration of the need for the Supreme Court to discard clearly prejudiced or incompetent fact-finding by lower courts or administrative agencies when necessary to protect a constitutional right. "That the question is one of fact," Hughes said, "does not relieve us of the duty to determine whether in truth a federal right has been denied. . . . If this requires an examination of evidence, that examination must be made. Otherwise, review by this court would fail of its purpose in safeguarding constitutional rights." All the brethren concurred, including Justice Brandeis, who a year later was vehemently to challenge this doctrine when the Chief Justice reiterated it in a case involving property rights.

The Chief's indignation boiled over when a shameful third-degree case came up to the high bench from Mississippi.[25] Three ignorant Negroes accused of murder had been tortured until they confessed and then convicted solely on the basis of the confession. One of the men had been hanged to a tree and then systematically beaten until he signed a statement dictated to him. The

[22] *Aldridge* v. *U.S.*, 283 U.S. 308.
[23] *Powell* v. *Alabama*, 287 U.S. 45.
[24] *Norris* v. *Alabama*, 294 U.S. 587.
[25] *Brown* v. *Mississippi*, 297 U.S. 278.

By Daniel R. Fitzpatrick in the *St. Louis Post-Dispatch*, February, 1937.

STILL A PLACE OF REFUGE

others had their backs cut to pieces with buckles on the ends of leather straps ". . . the transcript reads more like pages torn from some medieval account," Hughes wrote in his opinion, "than a record made within the confines of a modern civilization which aspires to an enlightened constitutional government."

Fairly scorching the authorities responsible for this outrage, he continued:

> The rack and torture chamber may not be substituted for the witness stand. The State may not permit an accused to be hurried to conviction under mob domination —where the whole proceeding is but a mask—without supplying corrective process. . . . It would be difficult to conceive of methods more revolting to the sense of justice than those taken to procure the confessions of these petitioners, and the use of the confessions thus obtained as the basis for conviction and sentence was a clear denial of due process.

Hughes, Brandeis, Stone, and Cardozo joined Roberts in an opinion freeing Angelo Herndon, who had been sent to prison for eighteen years after conviction under an ancient Georgia statute of attempting to incite an insurrection.[26] Herndon had been advocating "self-determination for the Black Belt," but there was no real evidence of insurrection.

In 1938 the Chief Justice wrote a strong opinion holding that a Negro student was entitled to admittance to the law school of the University of Missouri. The state admitted that the student, Lloyd Gaines, was scholastically qualified to take up the study of law. Missouri also acknowledged her obligation to provide Negro students with educational opportunities substantially equal to those provided for white students. But this obligation had been met, it was contended, by the declared intention of the state to set up a law school for Negroes "whenever necessary or practical" and meanwhile by paying the tuition of its colored law students at the universities of adjacent states to which they could be admitted. Hughes brushed aside this subterfuge. "Manifestly," he said, "the obligation of the State to give the protection of equal laws can be performed only where its laws operate, that is, within its own jurisdiction."[27] Nor could the discrimination be excused by its alleged temporary character. With only McReynolds and Butler dissenting, the court decreed that the University of Missouri law school should open its doors to Gaines.

Abuse of the "separate but equal" formula again brought a rebuke from the Chief Justice in *Mitchell* v. *United States*.[28] Congressman Arthur Mitchell had been compelled to give up his Pullman seat as the train on which he was traveling crossed the line into Arkansas. Confined to an "old combination" coach assigned to Negroes, he had been denied various accommodations available to white passengers. Hughes said the discrimination was unmistakable and

[26] *Herndon* v. *Lowry*, 301 U.S. 242.
[27] *Missouri ex rel. Gaines* v. *Canada*, 305 U.S. 337. [28] 313 U.S. 80.

repeated his conclusion in the McCabe case twenty-seven years before. If separate facilities were provided, they had to be substantially equal in spite of differences in demand on the part of white and colored passengers.

The Chief was also alert to racial discrimination and denial of civil rights in examining the *in forma pauperis* cases.[29] The law gives every citizen a right to proceed in any federal court without payment of fees, upon his execution of a pauper's oath. Consequently, murderers, madmen, bank robbers, and illiterates of all sorts who believe they are victims of injustice may address themselves directly to the Supreme Court. In Hughes' day all such unprinted documents addressed to the court, some of them scrawled illegibly in pencil, went to the Chief Justice and were reported upon by him at conference before any printing costs were incurred. Most of them were completely frivolous, but Hughes scanned them patiently because the smell of injustice could occasionally be detected despite the inadequacies of the petition.

Perhaps the most notable of these cases was *Bob White* v. *Texas*.[30] White, an illiterate Negro, filed a petition for certiorari *in forma pauperis* after his second conviction in Texas on a charge of raping a white woman. The meager papers he submitted gave the court no understanding of the underlying facts. Certiorari was denied. On a petition for a rehearing, however, the Chief somehow sensed that an injustice had been done and sent for the record.[31] It revealed that Texas Rangers had wrung a confession from Bob White by third-degree methods. A rehearing was granted; the court took the case and summarily set aside the conviction. Two irate Texans connected with the prosecution called on the Chief and accused the court of arbitrary conduct. He suggested that they file a petition for rehearing. Their petition failed to wash out the horror of the coerced confession; so the court reiterated its stand in an excoriating opinion by Justice Black. As a jury was being empaneled to try White a third time, he was shot by the husband of the complaining witness, and the killer was exonerated on the prosecutor's assertion that he had been forced to take the law into his own hands because the Supreme Court had thrown out the confession and the state did not have enough evidence to convict White without it. Such lawlessness in the name of law was sufficient to keep Hughes vigilant in examining the *in forma* cases.

As it became known that victims of injustice might win a case before the Supreme Court without a high-priced lawyer—sometimes by merely writing a letter to the court—crude petitions to the high bench were greatly multiplied. After the court ordered a new trial for an inmate of Alcatraz who had been denied the right of counsel,[32] a veritable bombardment of petitions came

[29] Edwin McElwain in *Harvard Law Review*, Vol. 63, No. I, p. 24.
[30] 309 U.S. 631; 310 U.S. 530.
[31] Edwin McElwain in *Harvard Law Review*, Vol. 63, No. I, p. 25.
[32] *Johnson* v. *Zerbst*, 304 U.S. 458.

out of that institution. Most of these went to the District Court at San Francisco and the Ninth Circuit Court of Appeals and got scant consideration because of their lack of merit. The Solicitor General did not bother to file opposing briefs in the "Alcatraz cases" that reached the Supreme Court. Disturbed by this casual attitude, Hughes induced his brethren to grant certiorari on a highly informal petition from two convicted bank robbers who had been given the brush-off in the District Court. Counsel was appointed, the cases were argued and sent back to the lower court with instructions to hold proper hearings in *all* cases,[33] including *in forma* pleas from Alcatraz. About the same time the Solicitor General made it a rule to file a brief in every case before the Supreme Court in which the United States was a party. The effect of the Supreme Court's vigilance seemed to permeate throughout the judicial system.

With all his zeal for the protection of civil rights, Hughes consistently resolemnized the marriage of liberty and order in his constitutional doctrines. When five Jehovah's Witnesses were convicted of parading on a public street in Manchester, New Hampshire, without a license, the court held that the state had a right to control the use of its highways for the public convenience and safety.[34] "Civil liberties, as guaranteed by the Constitution," Hughes said, "imply the existence of an organized society maintaining public order without which liberty itself would be lost in the excesses of unrestrained abuses."

In the flag-salute case of 1940 the court was compelled to choose between two important rights.[35] The children of Walter Gobitis, a Jehovah's Witness, had been expelled from the public schools at Minersville, Pennsylvania, because of their refusal, on religious grounds, to salute the flag. The question was whether the right of the state to use the flag-salute ceremony for training its youth in citizenship should supersede the right of the individual to follow the dictates of his conscience in such matters.

To most of the Justices, it was not a new issue. The underlying question had been settled when a unanimous court had concluded in 1934 that the University of California was within its rights in expelling conscientious objectors who refused to take a prescribed course in military training.[36] Cardozo had written a concurring opinion with the support of Stone and Brandeis. Four times the court had also unanimously found that it was not beyond the power of the states to make attendance in the public schools conditional upon saluting the flag.[37] Stone, Brandeis, Cardozo, Roberts, and the Chief Justice had all joined in these decisions.

When the Gobitis case arose, Hughes reiterated the established doctrine

[33] 312 U.S. 275, 342. [34] *Cox* v. *New Hampshire,* 312 U.S. 569.
[35] *Minersville School District* v. *Gobitis,* 310 U.S. 586.
[36] *Hamilton* v. *Regents,* 293 U.S. 245.
[37] See Justice Frankfurter's dissent in *West Virginia* v. *Barnette,* 319 U.S. 624.

that a state had a right to prescribe its own curriculum in its free public schools. If it wished to require a salute to the flag, as a symbol of liberty, that was its own affair. It was not an encroachment upon religious scruples. The liberty protected by the due-process clause did not extend so far as to require settlement of this question of educational policy in the courtroom.

Not a word of opposition to this view was uttered in the conference discussion. As several of the brethren left the room together, someone said that the Chief ought to write the opinion, presumably to clinch a settled issue. At Roberts' suggestion, Frankfurter turned back and repeated that idea to Hughes.

"No," the Chief replied emphatically, "I'm going to assign it to you."

Frankfurter wrote a persuasive opinion, and only when Stone failed to initial it did the brethren learn that he was writing a lone dissent on the ground that the required salute was an encroachment upon religious faith.[38] Within three years, however, this view became law. Justices Black, Douglas, and Murphy dramatically reversed their previous conclusion and joined a new majority in uprooting a West Virginia flag-salute requirement. Hughes, then in retirement, felt so strongly that the court had gone astray in this case that he broke his self-imposed rule not to discuss current decisions of the court in order to write his congratulations to Frankfurter on his powerful dissenting opinion.

While he thought Jackson had written a strong opinion for the majority, Hughes concluded that Frankfurter had "knocked out one of the main props of the decision in pointing out that the State, under the unanimous decision in *Pierce* v. *Society of Sisters* and other cases, could not constitutionally make attendance in its public schools compulsory." [39] The Chief was confident that Cardozo, Brandeis, and Holmes would have held to Frankfurter's position.

The Gobitis case is the only instance in which Hughes has been accused of voting against civil liberties. Actually his vote should not be so regarded here, for he upheld what he believed to be the prior right of the state to impose a condition upon the privilege of attending public schools. The decision gives emphasis to his restraint in not undercutting legislative policy with due process, unless basic rights were actually impaired.

Hughes' entire record in this field makes him one of the greatest modern exponents of civil liberties. Joseph Percival Pollard concluded as early as 1934 that Hughes had shown a "greater fondness for the Bill of Rights than any Chief Justice this country ever had." [40] While avoiding the distorted view that the entire Bill of Rights was absorbed into the Fourteenth Amendment, he made the fundamental freedoms living law in the states as well as the nation. The arch of due process had been chiefly used to shelter property rights. Hughes

[38] Author's interview with CEH. Nov. 12, 1947. [39] CEH to Frankfurter, June 17, 1943.
[40] *North American Review*, April, 1934, p. 357.

found under its protective expanse ample room for those human rights that are traditionally associated in the American mind with "liberty." Under his leadership, the court made freedom of the press and of religion, free speech, and free assembly so much a part of the law binding upon the states that they are never likely to be endangered so long as independent courts sit. To his everlasting credit also, he refused to eclipse the constitutional guarantee regarding property while he was amplifying the guarantees as to life and liberty.

Chapter 69

THE NEW DEAL IN COURT

THE MOST dramatic and far-reaching struggle involving the court came over the use of federal power to control the national economy. The depression of the thirties had thrust upon the government numerous obligations that it had never before assumed. Swept into office on a pledge of drastic action, President Franklin D. Roosevelt had launched a series of bold experiments with little regard for the limits of federal power. From the first days of the New Deal it was obvious that our constitutional system was undergoing a wrenching such as it had not experienced since the Civil War.

In the dark days of 1933, however, officials were thinking only of pulling the country out of the hole it was in. The banks had been closed to avert general panic. Industrial production was at a low ebb. Unemployment had reached an appalling total. Agriculture was being crushed by its own unmanageable surpluses. People were losing their homes, their savings, and their faith in the future. In the face of these conditions the country welcomed heroic measures.

The new Congress fell at once into the role of the little lamb to Roosevelt's Mary. Meeting in extraordinary sessions in March, 1933, it rushed through the President's emergency banking bill in a single day. In the turbulent weeks that followed the statute books burgeoned with legislation creating the Civilian Conservation Corps, the Tennessee Valley Authority, the Home Owners Loan Corporation, and the Agricultural Adjustment Administration for the control of farm production. To the AAA bill Congress also attached the slapdash Frazier-Lemke scheme to save farm mortgages from foreclosure and an amendment to inflate the currency and give the President broad powers to change the gold content of the dollar. Finally, came the National Recovery Act with its vast grant of power to the President and trade associations to harness business and industry under codes that could be enforced as law. In a little more than three months our sick and halting free economy had been brought under centralized national control.

Congress had not legislated in the ordinary meaning of the term. Rather, it had responded to the demands of the executive branch for power to meet an emergency. Most of the bills enacted had come straight from the White House. All of them had been drafted under great pressure—some by men with little experience in government. Veteran legislators had warned their colleagues that no such heedless unleashing of federal power could be sustained under the Constitution, but the prevalent feeling was that if constitutional obstacles were in the way, the reckoning would have to be left to less critical times.[1] Some of the young men who surrounded the President believed that the country was in a revolutionary era. In this expansive mood they felt no necessity for shaping their "new instruments of power" to the constitutional doctrines that had found acceptance on the bench. The Supreme Court was *passé*, and the idea that it might interfere with the forward march of the New Deal was heresy.

As between the principals in the approaching struggle, relations were cordial and friendly. Roosevelt had made his debut in public life as a member of the New York Senate the year that Hughes had left Albany to take his seat on the supreme bench. As a young anti-Tammany Democrat, F. D. R. had supported Hughes' reforms and had even crossed the party line to vote for the Republican Governor.[2] In later years Louis Howe had served as liaison between them. Howe had been an indefatigable Hughes supporter at Albany long before he became Roosevelt's closest political adviser. He appears to have kept Hughes' stock at a high figure in the presidential book in the early years of the New Deal.

On the eve of his inauguration in 1933 the President-elect had written to the Chief Justice:

> May I tell you how very happy I am at the thought that you will administer the oath to me. In addition to our long time friendship and to my admiration and respect for you, I think it is interesting that a Governor of New York is to administer the oath to another Governor of New York.
>
> I am looking forward with great satisfaction to our coming association and to seeing more of you than I have had the opportunity of seeing for many years.[3]

Hughes had replied:

> It gives me the greatest pleasure to receive your letter. It will be a high privilege to administer the oath of office and you will enter upon your great task with my heartiest felicitations and my earnest wish that you will have a most successful administration.
>
> I am glad to have the suggestion that you repeat the oath in full instead of saying simply "I do." . . .
>
> I cordially reciprocate the sentiments of friendship which you so kindly express, and I especially prize the opportunity of being associated with you in our great American enterprise.[4]

[1] Carl Brent Swisher, *American Constitutional Development*, p. 877.
[2] F. D. R. to CEH to author, interview of May 28, 1947.
[3] F. D. R. to CEH, Feb. 25, 1933. [4] CEH to F. D. R., Feb. 28, 1933.

Hughes did administer the oath with great dignity on that historic March 4; then the two men went their separate ways. Roosevelt sent Howe to consult the Chief Justice about a very important appointment in the State Department, and the executive and judicial heads occasionally chatted amiably at official receptions. That was the extent of their relationship. As constitutional issues began to loom large on the horizon, the President let it be known that he would welcome a chance to talk over these problems with members of the Supreme Court. One of his intimates gave that message to Justice Stone. Before his inauguration F. D. R. had written to Justice Cardozo: ". . . I hope that I can have at least in part the same type of delightful relations with the Supreme Court which I had with the Court of Appeals in Albany."[5] Intimations of the same desire reached the ears of the Chief Justice, although he was not directly approached.[6] Stone had been shocked by the suggestion, and any alert observer could determine that Hughes' concept of judicial duty would never sanction a back-stage discussion of issues or cases that were to come before the court for adjudication.

Through the newspapers Hughes was aware of the New Deal's unprecedented recovery program. The closer integration of society thus contemplated seemed to have his sympathy. On June 7, 1933, he told the graduating class at Deerfield Academy, including his grandsons, Charles E. Hughes, 3d, and Henry Stuart Hughes: "Now one increasingly finds himself controlled by a social urge. Economic independence is now difficult, if not impossible, to realize. We cannot save ourselves unless we save society. No one can go it alone." But the Chief was too much absorbed in his own task to give any detailed attention to the type of legislation Congress was passing, and another year was to elapse before any major New Deal law would come under his scrutiny.

A slight jar to the Administration's confidence was felt in February, 1934, when a unanimous court ruled that an economy measure was invalid in so far as it reduced the pay of retired judges of the lower federal courts.[7] Roberts' opinion pointed out that retired judges could be recalled to active duty; consequently, they still held the office, and, under the Constitution, their salaries could not be diminished. *Lynch* v. *United States*[8] was a further warning that the Supreme Court was not overawed by the so-called Roosevelt revolution. The court decided unanimously that Congress had overreached its power in taking away certain contractual rights under the War Risk Insurance Act, and Hughes diplomatically assigned the opinion to Brandeis.

When the "hot-oil" cases were argued in December, 1934, the court got

[5] *F. D. R.: His Personal Letters 1928–1945* (New York, 1950, Duell, Sloan & Pearce), III, 307. Copyright, 1950, by Elliott Roosevelt.

[6] Author's interview with CEH, May 28, 1947.

[7] *Booth* v. *U.S.*, 291 U.S. 339. [8] 292 U.S. 571.

an extremely unfavorable impression of New Deal methods. To his great credit, Assistant Attorney General Harold M. Stephens (later Chief Judge of the United States Court of Appeals for the District of Columbia) volunteered the information that the Petroleum Code had been enforced for about a year without a penal section. In a revision approved by the President, the section imposing penalties had been inadvertently left out, and the mistake had not been discovered until shortly before the "hot-oil" cases were argued. Men had been arrested, indicted, and held in jail for violating a law that did not exist.

The elusive character of the codes stimulated searching questions from the bench. Brandeis wanted to know who promulgated these codes that had the force of law. Stephens said it was the President.

"Is there any official or general publication of these executive orders?" Brandeis persisted.

"Not that I know of," Stephens replied.

"Well, is there any way by which one can find out what is in these executive orders when they are issued?"

"I think it would be rather difficult," the attorney candidly admitted, "but it is possible to get certified copies of the executive orders and codes from the NRA."[9]

In response to another question, Stephens estimated that several hundred codes and executive orders of this type had been issued. The judges were shocked by the extent and slipshod method of this executive lawmaking. Hughes decided to write the opinion himself. He found the root of the trouble in Section 9 (c) of the National Industrial Recovery Act. Congress had not laid down a policy to aid the states in controlling oil production or to regulate the flow of oil in interstate commerce. It had merely given the President "unlimited authority to determine the policy and to lay down the prohibition, or not to lay it down, as he may see fit." [10] And disobedience to his order had been made a crime punishable by fine and imprisonment.

From the beginning of the government, the Chief Justice said, Congress had conferred upon executive officers the power to make regulations to carry out the law. In every case the court had upheld such regulations, while recognizing that there were limits to the delegation of power that could not be transcended. "We think," he added, "that Section 9 (c) goes beyond those limits." It was no answer to insist that "deleterious consequences follow the transportation of 'hot oil.' " Even to meet recognized evils Congress could not "abdicate, or transfer to others, the essential legislative functions with which it is vested." To permit the delegation of such "unfettered discretion" to the President would be to invest him with "an uncontrolled legislative power."

[9] *Washington Post*, Dec. 11, 1934.
[10] *Panama Refining Co.* v. *Ryan*, 293 U.S. 388.

"Yes Sir," Brandeis wrote on the proof sheets when Hughes circulated the opinion. "Complete and even the layman can understand." Sutherland commented: "Clear, convincing and written with careful discrimination." Only Cardozo dissented, arguing that a sufficient standard to guide the President could be found in the Act.

The "hot-oil" decision was a severe jolt to the Administration. Now it was apparent that several New Deal statutes were in jeopardy. Tension gripped the country as hearings on the gold-clauses cases began the very next day after the "hot-oil" decision had come down. "The whole American economy was haled before the Supreme Court." [11] Under the Act of May 12, 1933, the President had reduced the gold value of the dollar by 40.94 per cent. The policy had been a failure so far as raising prices and stimulating business were concerned, but it had brought the dollar more nearly into line with devalued foreign currencies. The country had accepted the "59-cent dollar" and had been making contracts and settlements on that basis for about a year. Economists foresaw unimaginable chaos if the devaluation Act should be upset.

Two principal issues were argued before the court. The first was the validity of the gold clause in private contracts. For many years lawyers had been writing into bonds, mortgages, and contracts a standard clause to the effect that the principal and interest should be payable only in gold coin of the same weight and fineness as the dollar in circulation when the contract was entered into. Gold obligations of this sort outstanding in the United States probably amounted to a hundred billion dollars. Since Congress had forced the surrender of all gold to the Treasury, the holder of a railroad bond calling for an interest payment of $22.50 in gold dollars demanded $38.10 in the new devalued currency. To recognize such demands would vastly enrich the creditor class and plunge debtors into ruin.

The other issue involved the gold clause in the government's own obligations. John M. Perry contended that, in the absence of gold, the government should pay him $16,931.25 in devalued currency on a $10,000 Liberty Bond. The court seemed to have the alternative of increasing the public debt by about 60 per cent or of acknowledging congressional power to repudiate at any time the solemn bond of the United States. The Chief Justice bore down heavily on counsel in this case. "Here we have a bond issued by the United States Government . . . in time of war," he said, ". . . a bond which the Government promised to pay in a certain kind of money. Where do you find any power under the Constitution to alter that bond, or power of Congress to change that promise?" [12] The Assistant Solicitor General could only point lamely to the power of Congress to fix the value of money.

[11] Robert H. Jackson, *The Struggle for Judicial Supremacy* (New York, Knopf, 1941), p. 101. Copyright, 1941, by Robert H. Jackson.

[12] *New York Times*, Jan. 11, 1935.

While the Justices mulled over their momentous problem, tension became so acute that they ordered the clerk to announce at the end of each successive week that no decision in the gold-clause cases would be forthcoming the following Monday. President Roosevelt was so worried over the potential disaster of a decision holding the government to its promise to redeem its bonds in gold that he wrote a radio speech announcing his refusal to enforce such a ruling.[13] It was to be delivered, of course, only if the decision went against the government. The court knew nothing of it. On February 8, 1935, when the Justices dined at the White House "on the President's gold plates," the unmentionable gold cases and the secret repudiation speech must have haunted the table like Banquo's ghost.

The Chief worked the problem out in his own mind before he took the cases to conference. The gold clause in private contracts gave him no trouble. Back in 1911 his opinion in the McGuire case had made it clear that governmental powers could not be nullified by private contracts.[14] Now it was only a question of applying this principle to the gold-clause contracts. His conclusion was clear and forceful:

> Contracts, however express, cannot fetter the constitutional authority of the Congress. Contracts may create rights of property, but when contracts deal with a subject matter which lies within the control of the Congress, they have a congenital infirmity. Parties cannot remove their transactions from the reach of dominant constitutional power by making contracts about them.[15]

The Perry case was more difficult. Hughes was deeply perturbed by the spectacle of the great United States repudiating its word. The terms of the bond were explicit. While there was no question about the power of Congress to regulate the value of money, the promise to pay bonds in gold rather than currency was apparently intended to assure investors that they would not suffer loss through any depreciation of the currency. There was a clear distinction between asserting the dominance of this power over private contracts and using it to alter the government's own engagements. The Chief Justice feared that failure on the part of the Supreme Court to recognize the binding character of these promises might have a serious effect on the public attitude toward government bonds in the future.[16]

". . . The binding quality of the promise of the United States is of the essence of the credit which is so pledged," he said. "Having this power to authorize the issue of definite obligations for the payment of money borrowed,

[13] Arthur Krock in *New York Times*, Jan. 26, 1947.

[14] *Chicago B. & Q. Ry. Co.* v. *McGuire*, 219 U.S. 549; see also *Philadelphia B. & W. Ry. Co.* v. *Schubert*, 224 U.S. 603

[15] *Norman* v. *B. & O. R.R.*, 294 U.S. 240.

[16] Author's interview with CEH, April 30, 1946.

the Congress has not been vested with authority to alter or destroy those obligations."[17]

But Hughes' sense of responsibility would not let him stop there. To permit every owner of a $10,000 bond to collect $16,931.25 would constitute "unjustified enrichment" and place an appalling burden upon the government. The bondholder had not shown, or even attempted to show, that in relation to buying power he had sustained any loss whatever. Having suffered no loss because of the government's unconstitutional act, he could claim no damages.

It was an ingenious solution reminiscent of Marshall's *Marbury* v. *Madison*. While rebuking the political branches for their breach of faith, it gave them a victory that they would have to accept in order to save the government from financial catastrophe. In this respect it was a typically Hughesian performance. For while he was deeply concerned with the maintenance of integrity and constitutional principles, he also had a passion to make government succeed. This decision alone should be sufficient to dispose of any idea that he was actuated by hostility toward Roosevelt or the New Deal.

Seven members of the court agreed with the Chief that repudiation of the gold clause in government bonds was unconstitutional. Stone insisted that it was not necessary to pass upon the constitutional issue, but he concurred in the result. The four conservatives dissented from the result, contending that the bondholder should be allowed to take his pound of flesh. In the two other cases—those involving the gold clause in private contracts and the status of gold certificates[18]—Hughes won by a single vote. McReynolds blurted out one of the most acid dissents since Harlan's outburst in the Standard Oil case. The policy upheld meant "repudiations," he exclaimed, "spoliation of citizens . . . legal and moral chaos."

At first Hughes had contemplated assignment of the opinions to Stone. He changed his mind and wrote them himself when it became apparent that Stone would partly dissent in one case. It was obvious that all three opinions should be written by the same judge. Brandeis, Roberts, and Cardozo stood solidly with the Chief throughout. "The three opinions are clear and forceful," Brandeis wrote on the proof sheets. "You have said all that should be said in support of our view." Cardozo told the Chief that he was "100 per cent right" in saying that repudiation of the gold clause in government bonds was unconstitutional.[19]

The dominant feeling through the country was one of profound relief. "America thanks God for a man of independent opinion," one jubilant citizen telegraphed. "In history the name of Hughes will be greater than that of Marshall."[20] Although confused over the details of the decisions, the people

[17] *Perry* v. *U.S.*, 294 U.S. 330.
[18] *Nortz* v. *U.S.*, 294 U.S. 317.
[19] CEH's Notes, 1930–1941, p. 14.
[20] Hughes' papers, Supreme Court.

felt that sound judgment had prevailed on one of the most important issues ever to come before any court. "The Constitution has been stretched, perhaps," said the *San Francisco Chronicle,* "but not beyond its limit of elasticity." [21]

At the National Theater the night after the decision came down, the Chief Justice and Mrs. Hughes laughed heartily as Gilbert's and Sullivan's two Gondoliers decided that they should occupy the throne jointly so that "the validity of their acts" would not be questioned. Returning to the theater of reality, Hughes smiled whimsically as a newsboy shrieked at him, "All about the gold decision!"

During the next few months official Washington breathed easier. The Administration's margin of victory was narrow, but the court had demonstrated that a majority of its members were examining New Deal statutes with open minds. In several cases that could be decided on other grounds the court refused to pass on the constitutionality of congressional acts. May, 1935, however, brought an upset of the Act providing a compulsory retirement and pension system for railway employees. A majority of five, with Roberts as spokesman, concluded that the Act denied due process of law "by taking the property of one and bestowing it upon another." [22]

Hughes wrote a stiff dissent and was joined by Brandeis, Stone, and Cardozo. While admitting that there were defects in the Act, he struck powerfully at the majority argument that it was not a regulation of interstate transportation:

> What sound distinction, from a constitutional standpoint, is there between compelling reasonable compensation for those injured without fault of the employer and requiring a fair allowance for those who practically give their lives to the service and are incapacitated by the wear and tear of time, the attrition of the years? I perceive no constitutional ground upon which the one can be upheld and the other condemned. . . . The fundamental consideration which supports this type of legislation is that industry should take care of its human wastage, whether that is due to accident or age.
>
> The power committed to Congress to govern interstate commerce does not require that its government should be wise, much less that it should be perfect. The power implies a broad discretion and thus permits a wide range even of mistakes.

Meanwhile the Administration had been searching for a favorable case by which to test the validity of the NRA. By early 1935 the grandiose experiment was breaking down. Employers were rebelling, little business was complaining that the "Blue Eagle" meant monopoly, and consumers were disgruntled by higher prices. With suits multiplying, the NRA had to hasten a test in the Supreme Court or risk collapse of its enforcement program. A case involving

[21] Feb. 19, 1935. [22] *R.R. Retirement Board* v. *Alton R.R. Co.*, 295 U.S. 330.

the Lumber Code was chosen for the test,[23] but after it had advanced to the Supreme Court the more responsible lawyers in the Department of Justice discovered that some of the facile minds of the "brain trust" had tricked the lower court. To avoid resting a test on this slippery ground, the Solicitor General had the case dismissed.

About the same time a poultry dealer from Brooklyn asked the Supreme Court to review a Court of Appeals decision upholding the "Live Poultry Code," and the department found itself obliged to defend the NRA at one of its most vulnerable points. The arguments in the case high-lighted the petty local transactions that the NRA was attempting to control. The Schechter brothers had been convicted of selling an "unfit chicken" to a butcher, of permitting the "selection of individual chickens" from their coops, and of selling to unlicensed dealers. These trivial "offenses" had about as much effect on interstate commerce as a mosquito on a herd of elephants.

The Chief Justice presented the case to conference in his usual thorough and precise manner. Every judge agreed that the NRA was beyond the pale, and the importance of the case dictated that the Chief himself should write the opinion. He met the arguments of the government one by one. "Extraordinary conditions may call for extraordinary remedies," he conceded. "But . . . extraordinary conditions do not create or enlarge constitutional power." Officials exercising the limited powers of the national government "are not at liberty to transcend the imposed limits because they believe that more or different power is necessary." [24]

To the argument that the NRA was a cooperative effort among those engaged in trade and industry, he replied that it was also a coercive exercise of the lawmaking power. Violations of the codes were punishable as crimes. Obviously the NRA had to be treated as an exercise of governmental power. As such, it had two fatal weaknesses. It involved a surrender of lawmaking power to trade associations and the President, and it reached out to control local activities that had no real bearing upon interstate commerce.

As he had done in the "hot-oil" case, Hughes elaborated the difference between Congress laying down a policy, with provision for administrative details to be filled in, and turning over the lawmaking power to some other agency. "The Recovery Act," he said, "supplies no standards for any trade, industry or activity. . . . Instead of prescribing rules of conduct, it authorizes the making of codes to prescribe them." Of course, the codes had to have the approval of the President, and if he did not like a code drawn up by industry and labor he could discard it and substitute one of his own. But this only meant that the President had acquired the lion's share of the arbitrary lawmaking power that Congress had given away. "Such a delegation of legislative

[23] *U.S.* v. *Belcher,* 294 U.S. 736.

[24] *Schechter* v. *U.S.,* 295 U.S. 495.

power is unknown to our law," Hughes said, "and is utterly inconsistent with the constitutional prerogatives and duties of Congress."

Turning to the second fatal defect, he noted that the "Live Poultry Code" was not concerned with the transportation of poultry into New York or even with the sales of commission men to the Schechters. All the Schechters' business was wholly within the state. No "flow of commerce" into and out of the state was involved. The real question was whether the Schechters' local business "affected" interstate commerce so as to bring them within the scope of federal regulation.

It is often assumed that Hughes took a narrow view of the commerce clause in this case. The reverse is true. "The power of Congress," he said, "extends not only to the regulation of transactions which are part of interstate commerce, but to the protection of that commerce from injury. It matters not that the injury may be due to the conduct of those engaged in intrastate operations." It is the "effect upon interstate commerce," not "the source of the injury," he quoted from previous opinions, which is "the criterion of congressional power." To show the broad scope of this federal power, he went back to his own opinion in the *Shreveport Case,* in which the court had upheld federal control of local railroad rates when that was necessary to protect interstate commerce from unjust discrimination. Only a few months before the Schechter decision the court had also held that a conspiracy of market men, wholesalers, and a labor union to monopolize the poultry business in the New York metropolitan area was a violation of the Sherman Act because it obstructed interstate commerce.[25] Hughes strongly reiterated the doctrine behind these decisions in his NRA opinion. But in those cases the injury done to interstate commerce was direct and immediate. He searched in vain for any impact on interstate commerce from the Schechters' chicken coops. If the test case had involved a big interstate industry, NRA would still have gone down, but only on grounds of unconstitutional delegation of power.

The court did insist on maintaining a distinction between direct and indirect effects of local activities on interstate commerce. Hughes regarded the distinction as fundamental. Otherwise, he said, "there would be virtually no limit to the federal power and for all practical purposes we should have a completely centralized government." He also recognized the great difficulty of drawing the line between direct and indirect effects on interstate commerce and observed that the line may shift from decade to decade, but that did not obviate the necessity of drawing it from case to case for the sake of preserving our federal system.

Justice Cardozo wrote a concurring opinion to indicate why he was now

[25] *Local 167* v. *U.S.,* 291 U.S. 293.

going along with the court after dissenting in the "hot-oil" case. "This is delegation running riot," he declared. "No such plenitude of power is susceptible of transfer." Both Hughes and Cardozo emphasized the lack of federal power to regulate wages and hours in the Schechter establishment. But each confined his remarks strictly to wages and hours in a local business having no repercussions across state lines. There was no suggestion, as some critics have assumed, that Congress could not regulate wages, hours, and industrial relations in big enterprises operating across state lines. Nor were intrastate industries placed beyond the reach of Congress if their working conditions had a direct impact upon interstate commerce. In simple fairness to the court these opinions must be read in the light of the facts about the Schechter brothers' business.

Stone joined in the Cardozo opinion because he had disagreed with Cardozo in the "hot-oil" case and did not wish to give the impression of pulling away from his close friend. The unanimity of the court stands out starkly from the comments scribbled on Hughes' proof sheets. Brandeis' barb may be a little shocking to those who have thought of him primarily as a New Dealer. "Yes," he wrote. "This is clear and strong—and marches to the inevitable doom. It seems to me ready for delivery on Monday—and I hope that will be possible." Van Devanter commented, "Nothing essential is omitted and nothing said goes beyond what is appropriate." Sutherland responded with obvious delight: "You make the thing so clear that it is a marvel that anyone should think otherwise. I am glad to concur in so fine an opinion."

The knell for the NRA was accompanied by two other unanimous opinions—one striking down the Frazier-Lemke Act for relief of farm debtors and the other rebuking the President for his removal of William E. Humphrey from the Federal Trade Commission. Brandeis administered the *coup de grâce* to the recklessly drafted Frazier-Lemke Act.[26] All the brethren agreed that it authorized an unconstitutional taking of private property for a public purpose, without just compensation.

In the Humphrey case [27] the court said, through Justice Sutherland, that the Federal Trade Commission was an independent, nonpartisan body of experts charged with quasi-judicial duties. Unlike the postmaster whom the Taft court had held removable by the President, an FTC member could be ousted only for the causes specified by Congress, and F. D. R. had frankly admitted forcing the commissioner out because their minds ran in different channels. Humphrey was dead by the time the case was decided, but the decision came as a severe blow to the President's concept of his powers.

These three unanimous decisions made Monday, May 27, 1935, the black-

[26] *Louisville Joint Stock Land Bank* v. *Radford*, 295 U.S. 555.
[27] *Humphrey's Executor* v. *U.S.*, 295 U.S. 602.

est day in the history of the New Deal. The Chief Justice had raised a question as to whether three such jolts should be inflicted on the Administration in a single day.[28] Brandeis had replied that he could see no objection. Later he declared that the momentous session on May 27 was "the most important day in the history of the court and the most beneficent." [29]

When the news reached the White House, the first question the President asked was, "Where was Brandeis?"

"With the majority," replied one of his legal advisers.

"Where was Cardozo? Where was Stone?" he queried.

"They too were with the majority." [30]

For the moment the President seemed to find solace in the suggestion of his adviser that the court had relieved him of a political white elephant. He could not have been unaware of the fact that the NRA was breaking down of its own weight. But F. D. R. had invested much pride in this experiment. "History," he had grandiloquently predicted upon signing the bill, "probably will record the National Industrial Recovery Act as the most important and far-reaching legislation ever enacted by the American Congress." [31] His sense of personal injury quickened as the "palace guard" flocked in to bewail the audacity of the court. Four days later his anger boiled over in a press conference, and he accused the court of taking the country back to a "horse-and-buggy" definition of interstate commerce.

Speaking for an hour and a half, seriously, vigorously, and sometimes with biting satire, the President said that the destruction of the NRA was the most important Supreme Court ruling since the Dred Scott case precipitated the Civil War. The court had stripped the Federal Government of its power to deal with social and economic problems, he asserted, and the people would have to meet the issue thus raised. Ignoring the utterly local nature of the "sick-chicken" case, he assumed that the court would block any future federal control over the national economy.

Outside the Administration circle there were few mourners at the NRA funeral. Some experienced lawyers in the President's own following realized, moreover, that the court had merely done its judicial duty. General Hugh Johnson, former head of the NRA, later insisted that the Administration had brought defeat upon itself by "putting up to the Court the supernal absurdity that Kosher chicken killing of one gallinaceous bird in Brooklyn affected interstate commerce." [32] That feeling was sufficiently widespread at the time to bring an avalanche of criticism upon the President for his assault upon the

[28] Author's interview with CEH, April 30, 1947.
[29] Alpheus T. Mason, *Brandeis* (New York, Viking, 1946), p. 620.
[30] Confidential source No. 1.
[31] *The Public Papers and Addresses of Franklin D. Roosevelt*, II, 246.
[32] General Johnson's radio address, April 13, 1937.

court. If the President was then thinking of legislation to subdue the judges, he got a negative response from the country.

In the next two years the clash between the Administration and the Supreme Court moved toward a historic climax. Unshaken by the scolding from the White House, the court continued to wipe off the books acts for which it could find no constitutional footing. The next in line was a provision of the Home Owners Loan Act of 1933 authorizing the conversion of state savings and loan associations into federal ones in violation of state law. Justice Cardozo, speaking for the court, said it was an unconstitutional invasion of powers reserved to the states by the Tenth Amendment.[33]

Probably the most troublesome case the court had to deal with involved the validity of the Agricultural Adjustment Act. For the first time the government had undertaken to regulate farm production. Under this Act the Secretary of Agriculture estimated the amount of each basic crop that could be sold at specified prices and the number of acres required to grow the desired volume. Acreage allotments were then parceled out to each farmer, and if he reduced his planting accordingly he was entitled to benefit payments financed largely by taxes on the processing of the commodities. The case that reached the Supreme Court in 1936 was a suit by the government against Butler *et al.*, receivers for the Hoosac Mills Corporation, to compel payment of this tax.[34]

Hughes' analysis of the case led him back to an opinion on the general welfare clause that he had prepared for a private client in 1919. His research at that time had convinced him that Hamilton and Story had been right in contending that the Constitution gives Congress power to tax and spend for "the general welfare" beyond the scope of its enumerated powers. Madison had been wrong in trying to confine the taxing and spending power to the relatively narrow scope of the purposes mentioned in the Constitution. Hughes' notable achievement in the Butler case was in bringing the entire court to acceptance, for the first time, of the broad Hamiltonian thesis. He always felt that this was the most "significant and important ruling in the Butler case." [35]

For the majority, however, this liberal view of the spending power did not give the AAA a clean bill of health. It undoubtedly meant that Congress was free to make benefit payments to farmers. But the AAA was also controlling farm production. Was the government free to levy taxes for this purpose, without relating its action to any federal regulatory power?

Once more the court was confronted by an inept statute. Any alert constitutional lawyer should have known that the taxing power was not a secure foundation on which to rest a sweeping regulatory law. In 1922 the Taft

[33] *Hopkins F.S.L. Association* v. *Cleary*, 296 U.S. 315.
[34] *U.S.* v. *Butler*, 297 U.S. 1. [35] CEH, Notes, 1930–1941, p. 27.

court, with both Holmes and Brandeis concurring, and only Clarke dissenting, had ruled that Congress could not outlaw child labor by means of the taxing power.[36] On the same day the court had unanimously rejected an Act using the taxing power to control trading in grain futures on the Chicago Board of Trade.[37] Taft had taken pains to point out that the end sought could probably be accomplished under the commerce power, and a similar Act based on the commerce clause had then been passed and sustained. Yet Congress had set up the AAA under its taxing power in reckless defiance or ignorance of this pertinent history. It was blandly attempting to make a revenue power do the duty of a regulatory power, thus controlling local activities "irrespective of any relation to interstate commerce."

This experiment could be upheld under the Hamilton-Story-Hughes concept of the spending power only if the acreage controls were deemed to be voluntary. That is where the split came. A majority of six Justices concluded that the Act was coercive. Stone and Cardozo, believing that the purchase of compliance was not coercion, stood strongly for upholding the Act. Brandeis had not made up his mind when the vote was taken in conference and said that he would let the Chief Justice know later how his vote was to be recorded.[38] Ultimately he joined the dissenters.

Gossip has the Chief Justice denouncing his brethren for this decision and then changing his vote to avoid another five-to-four split. One story was to the effect that newspaper men standing in the corridor heard him shout above a tumult in the conference room, "Gentlemen! You are not only ruining this country, you are ruining this court." The Chief wrote his son that this gem of journalistic quackery was "manifestly absurd." [39] No newspaper men were in the corridor. If they had been, they could not have overheard the discussion in conference. At no time in his judicial career, moreover, did Hughes indulge in any such foolish emotional outburst. The rumor of Hughes changing his vote is equally void of substance. While he was zealous in safeguarding the prestige of the court, his profound sense of integrity never permitted him to alter his judgment in a case before the court for the sake of creating a better impression.

Roberts wrote the majority opinion, concluding that the processing tax was only a device for the unconstitutional regulation of farm production. While he stated the broad Hamiltonian doctrine as to the taxing and spending power, he limited its effectiveness in this case by saying the Tenth Amendment reserving the ungranted powers to the states was a bar to the type of taxing and spending that Congress had undertaken. This was because the majority regarded the benefit payments as coercive.

[36] 259 U.S. 20.
[37] 259 U.S. 44.
[38] Confidential source No. 2.
[39] CEH to his son, Feb. 22, 1937.

Stone's dissent was unusually bitter and this almost cost him the vote of Justice Brandeis. Accusing the majority of taking a stand "that must lead to absurd consequences," Stone declared: "Courts are not the only agency of government that must be assumed to have capacity to govern." His brethren of the majority felt that his words were unduly theatrical because of the narrowness of the difference between the two groups. Stone himself recognized that "the power to tax and spend" could "not be used to coerce action left to state control." [40] Likewise he acknowledged that the penalty taxes of the Bankhead Act of 1934 for the restriction of cotton acreage were "coercive," but drew a distinction between these and the AAA's benefit payment plan. The strong inference is that if the minority had thought the AAA controls to be coercive the court would have been unanimous. But Stone's view of the voluntary nature of the benefit payments has prevailed. Subsequent thinking has put the majority in the wrong on this point, and few commentators have taken the trouble to note how narrow the point really is.

While the casualties were heavy, the court also continued to sustain many Acts of Congress. It upheld the Trading With the Enemy Act,[41] the National Bankruptcy Act,[42] the Silver Purchase Act.[43] the Ashurst-Sumners Act prohibiting the shipment of prison-made goods in interstate commerce,[44] and the Chaco Arms Embargo Act. In the latter case Sutherland wrote a scholarly opinion confirming the broad sweep of the President's power in international affairs. In this field, "with its important, complicated, delicate and manifest problems," the court asserted, "the President alone has the power to speak or listen as the representative of the nation." [45]

Hughes wrote the opinion upholding the authority of Congress to build and operate the Wilson Dam in the Tennessee River.[46] The war and commerce powers gave ample authority for the project, he said, and the sale of power generated at the dam was an orderly disposition of government property under authorization from Congress. Since the broad-gauge program of the Tennessee Valley Authority was not involved in the case, the court expressed no opinion as to its validity.

Before taking its summer recess, however, the court struck down two more congressional Acts. A five-to-four decision, with McReynolds writing for the majority, sent the Municipal Bankruptcy Act of 1934 into the discard as an invasion of state sovereignty.[47] Hughes joined Cardozo, Brandeis, and Stone in a strong dissent, refusing to look upon voluntary petitions to which the state

[40] 297 U.S. 87. [41] 292 U.S. 449.
[42] *Kuehner* v. *Irving Trust Co.*, 299 U.S. 445.
[43] *U.S.* v. *Hudson*, 299 U.S. 498.
[44] *Kentucky Whip & Collar Co.* v. *Illinois Central R.R. Co.*, 299 U.S. 334.
[45] *U.S.* v. *Curtiss-Wright Export Co.*, 299 U.S. 304.
[46] *Ashwander* v. *TVA*, 297 U.S. 288.
[47] *Ashton* v. *Cameron Co. Water Dist.*, 298 U.S. 513.

itself gave assent as impairing any state's rights. More important was the three-way split within the court which left the Guffey Act a shambles.

The Guffey Act had been passed in 1935 to give the bituminous coal industry a new code after the invalidation of NRA and to sound out the Supreme Court once more as to how far federal regulation of distressed industry might go. The President had been advised that the bill was unconstitutional. But this had not cooled his sponsorship of it. He had sent a message to the hesitant subcommittee in charge of the bill saying: "An opportunity should be given to the industry to attempt to work out some of its major problems. I hope your committee will not permit doubts as to constitutionality, however reasonable, to block the suggested legislation."

When a test case reached the supreme bench, a majority of five rejected the Guffey Act with a flat declaration that the evils it was designed to correct "are all local evils over which the Federal Government has no legislative control."[48] Justice Sutherland's opinion spread on the record so narrow a view of the commerce clause that the President's "horse-and-buggy" tag seemed belatedly fitting. Not content to upset the controls over wages, hours, and working conditions, the court said that the price-fixing provisions would also have to go as part of the general scheme, although Congress had specifically made the two sections separable. Dissenting vigorously, Cardozo, Brandeis, and Stone defended the price-fixing provisions as applied to interstate sales and to local sales "where interstate prices are directly or intimately affected." They thought it was not necessary to consider the labor provisions.

Both wings of the court had broken away from the middle ground the Chief Justice had offered them. So he wrote a separate opinion speaking only for himself. He was in accord with the majority in saying that the heavy tax designed to force every coal producer to adhere to the code was not a real tax but a penalty; it could be imposed only so far as the commerce power extended. Mining is not itself commerce, he declared, but he again emphasized that Congress could protect interstate commerce from injury from any source and "provide for the peaceful settlement of disputes which threaten it." As Congress had ample authority to regulate the prices of coal sold in interstate commerce and to prohibit unfair methods of competition, he insisted that the inoffensive price-fixing section of the Act should be permitted to stand. The labor provisions he regarded as invalid chiefly because of the broad delegation of legislative power, without standards or limitations, and the arrangement under which one group of producers and employees could impose rules governing hours and wages on other groups not parties to the agreement.

A week later, as previously recounted, the court's revolt against innova-

[48] *Carter v. Carter Coal Co.*, 298 U.S. 238.

tion reached its climax in the Tipaldo case invalidating the New York minimum-wage law for women. Having blocked an orderly evolution of federal power in the name of states' rights, the majority suddenly turned and clamped the states themselves in the irons of standpattism. A rumble of discontent swept through the land. Many who had previously been reluctant to criticize the court now chorused angry protests. For the court had created a political vacuum into which no government was supposed to enter regardless of how serious economic and social conditions might become.

Hughes was deeply troubled. In three important cases within two weeks the court had repudiated his leadership. That in itself was a minor matter, but the Chief Justice was convinced, as his ringing dissent in the Tipaldo case showed, that the court was inflicting fresh wounds upon itself. Rumors of Administration plans to pack the court were beginning to circulate. An epidemic of proposals to curb the court's powers broke out on Capitol Hill. Everywhere the prestige of the judiciary was sinking.

The extremes to which the majority had gone in a few cases tended to cast a shadow over all the careful work the court had done to bring the New Deal into line with the Constitution. Most of its decisions overturning hastily drafted emergency laws were sound. No court could have accepted all the undigested and ill-founded legislation of that period without abdicating its constitutional function. We must remember also that, of the twelve decisions upsetting New Deal statutes, six were unanimous, and in two others the vote was eight to one.[49] When Hughes, Brandeis, Stone, Roberts, and Cardozo stood shoulder to shoulder and carried the more conservative Justices with them, it would be absurd to say that they were acting on caprice or illiberal bias. But in a few cases this liberal-moderate combination had broken up and left the court really vulnerable to criticism.

Its three errors that seemed to give some color of excuse for action against the court were the Tipaldo and Carter Coal decisions in both of which Hughes had dissented, and the AAA decision in which he had stood with the majority. In other words, the substantial counts against the court would have been reduced to one if the brethren had followed the Chief's leadership. And in those circumstances the court-packing venture might have been avoided.

In Hughes' mind there was no contest between the court and the New Deal. He had gone straight down the line of judicial duty, giving sanction to Acts that squared with the Constitution, as he understood it, and setting aside those that did not. Sometimes he was represented as shuttling erratically between liberal and conservative doctrines, but this was only because of the foolish notions that he was voting for or against the New Deal and that everything the Roosevelt Administration sponsored was liberal. The consistency of

[49] Senate Report 711, 75th Congress, 1st session, pp. 18, 45.

his struggle is inescapable if judged by his own objectives. Those objectives were to keep the law sensitive to the vibrant realities of his own day and at the same time preserve our constitutional system.

The tragedy of the situation, as this chapter in the court's history ends, is that Hughes seemed to be losing his fight in the squeeze between the judges who sought to petrify the law and the politicians who were determined to ride roughshod over the court if necessary to reach their goal.

Chapter 70

THE COURT-PACKING FIGHT

PRESIDENT ROOSEVELT watched the trend of the Supreme Court's decisions with mounting anger. He felt that the court was disregarding the national will and thwarting the national interest. As his recovery measures continued to go down, the President discussed with the Attorney General four possible remedies for "the court problem": a constitutional amendment enlarging federal powers, a statute limiting the court's jurisdiction, a law requiring more than a majority vote to nullify an Act of Congress, and enlargement of the court's membership. The President was not willing to wait for a constitutional amendment and did not think it was necessary. Although each of the other schemes had grave defects, "new blood" on the bench seemed to offer some hope of a solution. He ordered Attorney General Cummings to continue his research in this field.

Adding to the President's irritation was a feeling that the court had snubbed him. At the beginning of a new term it is customary for the Chief Justice to notify the White House that the court is in session and for the President to ask the Justices to call on him. In 1936 no such call was made. Two years later Roosevelt told Harry Hopkins that he had returned to Washington from a campaign tour to be present for the annual court visit and that no telephone call had come from the court. "After waiting three days," according to Hopkins' notes recorded by Robert E. Sherwood, "he had Marvin McIntyre get in touch with Justice Stone's secretary to find out what was going on. McIntyre was informed that 'There will be no visit to the White House this year.' "[1]

Obviously the President thought the court was nursing a grievance. But the ascertainable facts do not bear out his story. Actually the President was in Hyde Park on Monday, October 5, the day on which the court opened its new term.[2] He returned to Washington on Tuesday, but the court was then immersed in the work of disposing of its summertime accumulation of petitions for certiorari. Where McIntyre got his information is a mystery, for neither

[1] *Roosevelt and Hopkins* (New York, Harper, 1948), p. 94. Copyright, 1948, by Robert E. Sherwood.

[2] *Washington Post*, Oct. 6, 1936.

Justice Stone's secretary nor his clerk had any call from the White House in connection with the incident.[3] Nor could any one in the Chief's office or among the personnel of the court itself remember such a call. The known facts strongly suggest that, in the three days the President spent in Washington between campaign trips, there was no mutually convenient time for the court to make its call.

No one who knew Charles Evans Hughes would accuse him of indulging in a petty discourtesy. As Chief Justice no less than as Secretary of State, he gave meticulous attention to protocol. The fact that differences had arisen between the court and the President would have stiffened his insistence on observing the amenities. Justice Roberts and many others affiliated with the court are certain that "no snub was intended." [4] The President's resentment on this score appears to have been conjured out of thin air.

The decision to go ahead with a court bill was taken only after Roosevelt had won a whopping victory in the 1936 election. In his campaign speeches there had been no word about subduing the Supreme Court. On the contrary, his platform had pledged the Administration to meet the economic and social problems of the day "through legislation within the Constitution," or, if that should prove impracticable, to seek a "clarifying amendment." Some Republican orators had hinted that, if reelected, Roosevelt might pack the Supreme Court, but this line of campaigning had brought incensed denials from his supporters. "A more ridiculous, absurd, and unjust criticism of a President was never made," cried Senator Ashurst, the Democratic chairman of the Judiciary Committee.[5] Court-packing, he said, was a "prelude to tyranny."

But once the election was over, the President felt that he had a new mandate from the people—that if the court stood in his way the people would support him in brushing it aside. On his trip to South America in November, 1936, he took along two huge volumes of Department of Justice proposals to deal with the court, but found none of them satisfactory. Cummings then came up with the idea of naming new judges to supplant or replace the aged men on the bench. Recalling that Justice McReynolds, when he had been Attorney General in 1913, had recommended the appointment of substitutes for judges who failed to retire at the age authorized by law, Cummings felt sure that he had hit upon the right approach.[6] Even though McReynolds had exempted Supreme Court Justices from his proposal, the temptation to turn his own device against him seemed irresistible. The scheme got a warm reception at the White House, and the Attorney General, carrying his secret like a wise

[3] Gertrude Jenkins (the secretary) to author, March 25, 1950; Harold Leventhal (the clerk) in conversation with author, March 15, 1950.

[4] Justice Roberts to the author, March 21, 1950.

[5] Merlo J. Pusey, *The Supreme Court Crisis* (New York, Macmillan, 1937), p. 67.

[6] Alsop and Catledge, *The 168 Days* (New York, Doubleday, 1937), pp. 34–36. Copyright, 1937, by Joseph Alsop and Turner Catledge.

old owl, spent several tense weeks filling in details and giving the whole plan a veneer of judicial reform.

Meanwhile the President assured Congress in his annual message that the New Deal would go forward in spite of the court. On the evening of February 3, 1937, the President and Mrs. Roosevelt gave their dinner for the judiciary with eighty guests present, including all members of the court except Brandeis and Stone. Still treasuring his secret, the President was unusually gay; he was enjoying "one of those ironical little moments" [7] of which he was so fond. Two days later he sent his bombshell to Capitol Hill.

The bill was first disclosed to a small group of incredulous Cabinet members and congressional leaders on the morning of February 5. The President talked briefly without asking for advice, then hastened away to break the news in "the most jubilant press conference he ever had."

His drastic measure was represented as being a step to relieve the courts of congestion and avoid injustice. "Even at the present time," he said, "the Supreme Court is laboring under a heavy burden." Noting the large number of petitions for review denied in the previous year, he inferred that the court was keeping its calendar clear only by sloughing off its responsibilities. The general picture he drew was one of judges of "lowered mental and physical vigor" unable to meet the demands of a modern, progressive judicial system. This set the stage for his appeal for a "persistent infusion of new blood" into the judiciary. The only hint of his real purpose lay in his suggestion that if this bill were passed more fundamental changes in the powers of the courts or in the Constitution could be avoided.

The bill provided for a maximum of fifty additional judges. It called for a proctor to investigate the needs of the courts and aid the Chief Justice in dispatching what were later called "flying squadrons" of judges to district and circuit courts with congested calendars. But all this was sugar-coating. The central provision gave the President authority to appoint a sort of coadjutor for every federal judge who had been on the bench for ten years and who had not resigned within six months after reaching the age of seventy. In effect this meant that the President could enlarge the Supreme Court from nine to fifteen Justices.

Almost instantly the bill was stripped of the swaddling clothes of reform in which Roosevelt and Cummings had so diligently wrapped it. Congress was rent by the naked issue of packing the Supreme Court. Legislators who thought the end justified the means hailed the bill as a master stroke, and some of the Democratic wheelhorses hastened to endorse it to prove their party loyalty. But the constitutionalists of both parties acted as if the bottom were about to fall out of the American system. The first flush of anger and surprise gave

[7] *Ibid.*, p. 64.

By Eugene Elderman in the *Washington Post*, February 6, 1937.

TO FURNISH THE SUPREME COURT PRACTICAL ASSISTANCE

way to fear gnawing deep in the bowels of democracy, for it was generally assumed that the President's sweeping victory had given him the power to make his will effective. "Why," exclaimed Senator Glass in voicing his opposition, "if the President asked Congress to commit suicide tomorrow they'd do it."

Across the country came a rumble of protest. First it was the press. Then it was the press and radio echoing civic, patriotic, fraternal, religious, professional, and political organizations. The conscience of America had been deeply stirred. Indignation fed upon the deceptive nature of the President's message. The leaders of powerful groups in the President's following were also disgruntled because he had taken them for granted. Neither the Cabinet, nor congressional chieftains, nor party bigwigs, nor labor, nor farm leaders had been consulted.

As the conflict gained new intensity, the Supreme Court was the calmest spot in the Washington vortex. News of the bill reached Chief Justice Hughes while he was presiding in the courtroom. Always alert for information of interest to the court, the marshal, Thomas E. Waggaman, had secured copies of the President's message and bill and immediately distributed them to the Justices on the bench. Whatever inner excitement they may have felt, the judges maintained a stoic silence. Even in the seclusion of their offices and conference room, there was very little discussion of the bill.[8]

Without exception, however, the Justices were hostile to the scheme. Brandeis, the oldest member of the court and therefore presumably the chief target of the clamor for "new blood," was deeply wounded. Roberts, the youngest Justice who would not have been personally affected by the bill, nevertheless decided to resign if it were passed. Hughes, who was seventy-four, was determined to ride out the storm regardless of what might happen. "If they want me to preside over a convention," he said, "I can do it."[9] Under no circumstances would the court go down to humiliation and loss of confidence if he could prevent it.

President Roosevelt soothed the growing fears of his lieutenants by repeating a sort of standard refrain: "The people are with me, I know it." But in the office of the Chief Justice one got a very different impression. Thousands of letters and telegrams addressed to the court were almost unanimous in their opposition to the bill. Business men, professors, great lawyers, organizations of every description, and plain citizens of both parties gave vent to their wrath: "It makes my blood boil. . . . Every citizen resents this insult to the court. . . . Please do not allow the President to change this great court." Many letters "begged" the Chief Justice not to resign. "More power to you. . . . God bless you gentlemen and spare you to save our highest

[8] Author's interview with CEH, Nov. 19, 1945. [9] Confidential source No. 2.

court. . . ." [10] If there had been any doubt as to the standing of the court with the people, the flood of mail that went both to the court and to Congress quickly removed it.

After four weeks of mounting criticism the President recognized the necessity of making a gloves-off fight. In his address to the Democratic victory dinner on March 4, he openly accused the court of usurping power and of vetoing his program. Five days later he went to the people with a "fireside chat" full of appealing sentiment, plausible arguments, and deep indignation toward the court. He accused the Justices of acting as a "superlegislature" and took out of context, with torturing effect, Governor Hughes' impromptu remark: "We are under a Constitution, but the Constitution is what the judges say it is."

"We have, therefore," the President concluded, "reached the point as a Nation where we must take action to save the Constitution from the Court and the Court from itself." [11] The implication was unmistakable—the President, with the aid of his advisers, was a better judge of what the Constitution means than was the Supreme Court.

Meanwhile the opposition had been effectively organized. The first meeting of Democratic legislators hostile to the bill had been held at the home of Senator Millard E. Tydings. Among those present were Senators Wheeler, Byrd, Copeland, George, Burke, King, and Van Nuys. A few days later a group of Democratic and Republican Senators lunched together and selected Wheeler as their leader, the Republicans agreeing to remain discreetly in the background.

As hearings on the bill got under way on March 10 before the Senate Committee on the Judiciary, the opposition concluded that its first task was to dispel the myth of a senile court unable to keep abreast of its work. For this purpose an authoritative statement from the court itself was sought. The Chief Justice gives us the following account of his negotiations with members of the committee:

> As the opponents of the bill were about to present their case, Senators Wheeler, King and Austin called upon me—I think it was on Thursday, March 18th, 1937—and asked me to appear before the Committee. I was entirely willing to do this for the purpose of giving the facts as to the work of the Court. Even in appearing for such a purpose, however, I thought it inadvisable, in view of the delicacy of the situation, that I should appear alone. It seemed to me that at least one other member of the Court should accompany me,—preferably Justice Brandeis—because of his standing as a Democrat and his reputation as a liberal judge.
>
> I so informed the Committee. But when I consulted Justice Brandeis I found that he was strongly opposed to my appearing—or to any Justice appearing—before the

[10] Hughes papers, Supreme Court.
[11] Senate Report 711, 75th Congress, 1st session, p. 41.

Committee. I stated the desire of the Committee to have the facts as to the state of the work of the Court and suggested that I might, in response to a request, write a letter for that purpose. With that suggestion Justice Brandeis fully agreed. I found that Justice Van Devanter took the same view.

Accordingly, I telephoned to Senator King and to Senator Wheeler on the morning of Friday, March 19, 1937, that I had found that there was a very strong feeling that the Court should not come into the controversy in any way, and that it was better that I should not appear; but that if the Committee desired particular information on any matters relating to the actual work of the Court, I should be glad to answer in writing giving the facts.

Later—on Saturday, as I recall it—Senator Wheeler, who I understood had seen Justice Brandeis in the interval, called on me and asked me to write such a letter. He said that the Committee desired this letter so that it could be used on Monday morning at the opening of the hearing on behalf of the opponents of the bill. This gave me very limited time but I proceeded at once to assemble the necessary data, and on Sunday, March 21st, the letter was completed. I at once took it to Justice Brandeis and to Justice Van Devanter, and each went over it carefully and approved it.[12]

Wheeler called at the Hughes home for the letter late Sunday afternoon. "The baby is born," said the Chief Justice with a broad smile as he put the letter into Wheeler's hand. In the brief chat that followed Hughes said that he had had all the honor that he could expect from the American people and that he was not worried about the impact of the bill upon himself or upon his brethren. "But if this bill should pass," he declared, "it would destroy the court as an institution."[13]

There was a precedent for Hughes' proposal that he and Brandeis testify before the committee. In 1935 they and Justice Van Devanter had gone before the same committee to oppose Senator Black's bill providing for immediate appeals to the Supreme Court from lower court orders restraining compliance with federal laws. While he rigorously eschewed any discussion of politics or policy-making, the Chief Justice felt that, if requested, he should give Congress any information about the work of the court that might save it from legislating under a misapprehension. It was only Brandeis' vehement opposition that prevented the Chief from going personally before the committee.

The next time the judges met, Hughes told them he had hoped to consult with each of them about the letter but had found it impossible because of the short time allowed him for its preparation; he hoped they all approved his action.[14] Several said they did, and Hughes thought everyone acquiesced. Actually, however, Stone was merely concealing his irritation. While he never

[12] CEH, Notes, 1930–1941, pp. 20–21. A memorandum of the March 19 conversation with the senators is in Mr. Hughes' private papers.

[13] Author's interview with Burton K. Wheeler, April 4, 1950.

[14] CEH, Notes, 1930–1941, p. 21.

uttered a critical word about the letter in the presence of the Chief, he let other members of the court know that he resented Hughes' failure to consult the entire court. Considering the delicacy of the issue, Hughes' action with the approval of only two of his eight colleagues was certainly a tactical error.

Wheeler released the Chief's letter in dramatic fashion in his opening statement for the opposition. The letter itself was cool, judicial, and factual:

> The Supreme Court is fully abreast of its work. When we rose on March 15 (for the present recess) we had heard argument in cases in which certiorari had been granted only 4 weeks before—February 15. . . . There is no congestion of cases upon our calendar.
>
> This gratifying condition has obtained for several years. We have been able for several terms to adjourn after disposing of all cases which are ready to be heard.

Hughes then went into details as to how the court works, completely undermining Roosevelt's insinuations that full justice had not been done because so large a percentage of the petitions for certiorari had been denied. The ends of justice were met, he pointed out, when a litigant dissatisfied with the verdict of a district court had an opportunity to carry his case to the Court of Appeals. "If further review is to be had by the Supreme Court," he said, "it must be because of the public interest in the questions involved. . . . I think it is the view of the members of the Court that if any error is made in dealing with these applications it is on the side of liberality." His conclusion was:

> An increase in the number of Justices of the Supreme Court, apart from any question of policy, which I do not discuss, would not promote the efficiency of the Court. It is believed that it would impair that efficiency so long as the Court acts as a unit. There would be more judges to hear, more judges to confer, more judges to discuss, more judges to be convinced and to decide. The present number of Justices is thought to be large enough so far as the prompt, adequate, and efficient conduct of the work of the Court is concerned. As I have said, I do not speak of any other considerations in view of the appropriate attitude of the Court in relation to questions of policy.[15]

With equal ease, he disposed of the suggestion that an enlarged court might hear cases in divisions. "A large proportion of the cases we hear are important," he wrote, "and a decision by a part of the Court would be unsatisfactory." Besides, the Constitution authorized "one Supreme Court" not two or more Supreme Courts or two or more units functioning as separate courts.

In spite of its dispassionate tone, the letter blasted the court bill with bombshell effect. Its sincere recital of facts stood out in damning contrast to the transparent pretense of the President's message. Its restraint threw the

[15] Committee Report (see note 11), pp. 36–39.

dignity of the court into the balance against the bombastic charges in the President's recent speeches. "Others may speak for weeks or months," Henry L. Stoddard wired the Chief, "but you have closed the debate." [16]

One week later the judges seemed to give another disconcerting jerk to the rug on which the court-packers were standing. Shortly before Christmas, 1936, the court had voted four to four, in the West Coast Hotel case, to uphold the Washington minimum-wage law and overrule its six-month-old decision in the Tipaldo case. In this instance the Adkins decision had been directly challenged, and the question of overruling it had to be faced. Roberts had abandoned the standpatters and voted with Hughes, Brandeis, and Cardozo to sustain the Act. This meant that the Washington minimum-wage law would stand, for it had previously won the sanction of the highest court in that state. It meant also that Hughes would have a majority behind his broad interpretation of the state police powers as soon as Stone, who was ill, could return to the bench. To avoid a four-to-four decision on so important an issue, the case had been held temporarily. Stone had returned about February 1, 1937, and a majority of five overturned both the Tipaldo decision and *Adkins* v. *Children's Hospital*.[17] Before the opinions could be written and handed down, however, the court found itself under threat of being packed.

Hughes had been overjoyed by his success in swinging the court back into line with the Blaisdell and Nebbia cases. When Roberts, in a private chat, had divulged his intention of voting to sustain the Washington law, the Chief had almost hugged him. But now it was obvious that this triumph of liberal thinking *within* the court would be interpreted as a reversal under pressure. The court had no official spokesmen or ghost writers. Its conference proceedings were always kept secret. Hughes held back his opinion for a short time, to avoid the impression of an immediate response to the court-packing plan.[18] But that did not change the inevitable.

The story of how the court corrected itself in this case has never before been told. Hughes felt justified in disclosing the confidential details in his Biographical Notes "in defense of the Court's integrity." His most pointed comment was: "The President's proposal had not the slightest effect on our decision." [19]

On the same day that the Chief Justice dramatically reversed his court on the minimum-wage issue, three other favorable opinions came down. One of these upheld the National Firearms Act,[20] another the new Frazier-Lemke Act [21] recast to meet the court's objections, and a third the collective bargaining requirements of the Railway Labor Act as applied to shop employees.[22] The jubilant foes of the court bill dubbed the day (March 29, 1937) White

[16] Hughes papers, Supreme Court. [17] CEH, Notes, 1930–1941, p. 31. [18] Author's interview with CEH, May 7, 1947. [19] Chapter XXIII, p. 31. [20] *Sonzinsky* v. *U.S.*, 300 U.S. 506. [21] *Wright* v. *Vinton*, 300 U.S. 440. [22] *Virginian Ry.* v. *Federation*, 300 U.S. 515.

Monday in contrast to Black Monday when the NRA had been deflated. The court was said to be on the march. Some sponsors of the court bill regarded this performance as a Machiavellian plot to defeat the President's bill. Actually, however, a badly divided court had merely corrected one of its own mistakes and rendered independent judgment upon three acts involving no serious abuse of power.

Now foes of the court bill began to pray for a favorable decision on the National Labor Relations Act. Every day the fight to pack the court was losing momentum, although the President was still determined to force a showdown. The fate of the NLRB might be the decisive factor. Lawyers, legislators, and officials as well as curious spectators jammed the courtroom on April 12 expecting to see the court seal its doom or, possibly, rise to its salvation. They were not disappointed. After a few moments of preliminary business the Chief Justice began to deliver the court's judgment in *National Labor Relations Board* v. *Jones and Laughlin Steel Corporation.*[23] He read it magnificently, without a trace of histrionics or pomposity, yet with such a tone of authority that the law itself might have been speaking. Faces flushed and heartbeats quickened as his listeners realized that he was weaving a mantle of constitutionality around the NLRB.

The board had ordered Jones and Laughlin to reinstate ten employees dismissed for union activity, and the Circuit Court of Appeals had refused to enforce the order on the ground that it lay beyond the range of federal power. Hughes took note of the little empire that the company operated—its iron and steel plants in Pennsylvania, its mines in Michigan and Minnesota, its limestone properties in West Virginia, its steamships on the Great Lakes, its railroads, and its nineteen sprawling subsidiaries. Here was no Schechter chicken business but an interstate octopus. Congress had a right to protect interstate commerce from labor disturbances in such vast enterprises clearly beyond the reach of state power.

It was not necessary, he said, to relate the business of Jones and Laughlin to the "stream of commerce" cases.

> The congressional authority to protect interstate commerce from burdens and obstructions is not limited to transactions which can be deemed to be an essential part of a "flow" of interstate or foreign commerce. Burdens and obstructions may be due to injurious action springing from other sources. The fundamental principle is that the power to regulate commerce is the power to enact "all appropriate legislation" for "its protection and advancement." . . .
>
> It is thus apparent that the fact that the employees here concerned were engaged in production is not determinative. The question remains as to the effect upon interstate commerce of the labor practice involved.

[23] 301 U.S. 1.

In the Schechter case the court had found the effect to be so remote as to be beyond federal power. But repercussions from industrial strife in the Jones and Laughlin empire would be immediate and might be catastrophic. Hughes continued:

> We are asked to shut our eyes to the plainest facts of our national life and to deal with the question of direct and indirect effects in an intellectual vacuum. . . . When industries organize themselves on a national scale, making their relation to interstate commerce the dominant factor in their activities, how can it be maintained that their industrial labor relations constitute a forbidden field into which Congress may not enter when it is necessary to protect interstate commerce from the paralyzing consequences of industrial war? . . .
>
> Instead of being beyond the pale, we think that it presents in a most striking way the close and intimate relation which a manufacturing industry may have to interstate commerce and we have no doubt that Congress had constitutional authority to safeguard the right of respondent's employees to self-organization and freedom in the choice of representatives for collective bargaining.

Accompanying the Jones and Laughlin opinion were two other cases in which the Chief Justice found the Labor Relations Act applicable to a trailer company [24] and a men's clothing manufacturer [25] because of the interstate character of their businesses. With the basic principle of protecting commerce from labor disturbances established, it was evident that the court would apply it wherever the repercussions from labor strife upon interstate business might be substantial.

"Admirably done!" was Brandeis' comment. "Yes, sir," wrote Cardozo, "a magnificent opinion!" McReynolds, Van Devanter, Sutherland, and Butler dissented, writing a sort of "swan song of a dying philosophy." But even with a slender majority of one it was a momentous victory for liberal interpretation of the basic law. The legislators fighting to save the court from being packed were ecstatic, and lukewarm supporters of the bill fell away in droves.

"We did it," [26] chortled the President. At the same time he looked upon the decision as only a token victory that made it all the more necessary to press on with the fight for a court that would "cooperate." A five-to-four majority was not enough. With Tommy the Cork (Thomas G. Corcoran, counsel to the RFC) turning the heat on the opposition and with judicial appointments held up in states where the Senators were not "going along," [27] the President was still confident and refused to countenance talk of a compromise.

On May 18 the Judiciary Committee rejected the bill. A few days later the Supreme Court removed the last vestige of excuse for enlarging its membership by upholding the Social Security Acts. Both opinions, one giving

[24] *NLRB* v. *Fruehauf Trailer Co.*, 301 U.S. 49.
[25] *NLRB* v. *Friedman-Harry Marks Clothing Co.*, 301 U.S. 58.
[26] James A. Farley in *Collier's*, vol. 119, p. 11, June 21, 1947. [27] *Id.*

a clean bill of health to the tax supporting unemployment insurance [28] and the other to the old-age benefit plan,[29] were based squarely upon the broad concept of the spending power for which Hughes had won the court's approval in the AAA case. In writing the opinions Justice Cardozo specifically cited *United States* v. *Butler* as having settled the right of Congress to spend money in aid of the "general welfare." Since the federal unemployment compensation law did not operate directly upon the citizen but made it possible for each state to set up its own unemployment insurance system, the question of coercion, which had troubled the majority so much in the AAA case, was not present. The old-age benefit plan seemed to fall clearly into the pattern that the court had outlined in the AAA opinion. There were only two dissents in this case.

Only one other step was needed to complete the liquidation of the court-packing scheme. During his four years in office President Roosevelt had had no opportunity to name a Supreme Court Justice even though six of the men on the high bench were over seventy. From the White House it looked as if the old men were clinging to their posts in order to prevent Roosevelt from naming their successors. In an effort to refute this assumption and to enable the Administration to give up its court bill with a minimum loss of face, Justice Van Devanter notified the President on May 18 of his intention to retire in June.

The ironical fact is that both Van Devanter and Sutherland had wanted to retire before 1937.[30] Butler and McReynolds had tried to dissuade them, but Van Devanter at seventy-eight was eager to lay down his burden, and Sutherland, with his high blood pressure, could keep abreast of his work only by writing most of his opinions in bed. They had clung to their posts chiefly because of the unfairness of Congress to Justice Holmes.[31] After Holmes had resigned, relying on a congressional pledge to continue the salaries of judges over seventy stepping down after ten years of service, Congress had reduced his compensation. The Constitution afforded no protection, for it forbade diminution of judges' pay only "during their continuance in office." Supreme Court Justices did not then have the privilege of retirement (as distinguished from resignation) which was accorded to the judges of the lower courts. The result was that Justices who otherwise would have retired remained on the bench.

The Administration had gone ahead with the court-packing bill without offering the aged Justices an opportunity to retire with continuance of their salaries assured. It was only after the court fight had been launched that the

[28] *Steward Machine Co.* v. *Davis*, 301 U.S. 548.
[29] *Helvering* v. *Davis*, 301 U.S. 619.
[30] Author's interview with CEH, May 28, 1947.
[31] CEH, Notes, 1930–1941, p. 16.

opposition rushed through a retirement bill in the hope of thwarting the more drastic measure. Senator Borah then impressed upon his close friend Van Devanter the great service he could render the cause by stepping down at that time. The Chief Justice had nothing whatever to do with it.[32]

At the White House, however, this conciliatory gesture turned to gall and wormwood. Long before the court fight had begun the President had promised the first vacancy on the supreme bench to Senator Joseph T. Robinson, the majority leader who was now fighting to get the court bill through the Senate. The pledge was well known among Robinson's colleagues, and as soon as the Van Devanter resignation was announced they swarmed into the Senate to congratulate him.[33] But Robinson was a conservative Arkansas politician of sixty-five. To single him out for the first vacancy on the court while the President was clamoring for younger and more liberal judges, would turn the court fight into a roaring farce. To disregard the pledge would produce an explosion in the Senate. Now it seemed imperative to create places for several liberal Justices to balance the inescapable Robinson appointment.

While the President was wrestling with this dilemma, Senator King presented the Judiciary Committee's historic "Adverse Report." It was a devastating attack. The committee recommended that the bill be rejected "as a needless, futile, and utterly dangerous abandonment of constitutional principle." Its ultimate operation, said the report, "would be to make the Constitution what the executive or legislative branches of the Government choose to say it is—an interpretation to be changed with each change of administration."

"It is a measure which should be so emphatically rejected that its parallel will never again be presented to the free representatives of the free people of America." [34]

With the fight still going on, the court's summer recess became the signal for a new blast from the White House. The President said that the court had cleared its docket only by ordering reargued six cases that had already been argued. The judges were going off for a four-month vacation, he complained, leaving undetermined cases of vital concern to the PWA, the TVA, and the SEC.

Actually the court had disposed of every case that had been ready for hearing. Rearguments had been ordered in four cases partly because the government, although it had vital interests in the cases, had not been represented in the first argument. The court had also agreed to hear two cases involving the right of the government to finance municipal power plants; but these cases

[32] Author's interview with CEH, May 28, 1947.
[33] Alsop and Catledge, *op. cit.*, pp. 210ff.
[34] Senate Report 711, 75th Congress, 1st session, p. 23.

had not been ready for argument when the court adjourned, and the government had made no request for a summer hearing.[35] The President's criticism was significant only as a measure of his irritation with the court.

Throughout the fight the Chief Justice had maintained a complete silence, except for his letter to Senator Wheeler. In May he declined an invitation to speak on Constitution Day, feeling that he could not attempt "to deal adequately at this time with such an important subject." But when he visited Amherst College on June 19 to attend the graduation of his grandson, Henry Stuart Hughes, fighting blood was coursing through his veins.

Stuart was really the lion of the occasion, being president of his class, the class orator, and the recipient of the highest award for "excellence in culture and faithfulness as man and scholar." Grandfather Hughes beamed with pride. When it came his turn to speak, at the Amherst alumni luncheon, he was the antithesis of an old man doddering in conservatism. ". . . we know nothing of age," he declared exuberantly, "but what we have read in Cicero. We come to you with youthful hearts, with spiritual arteries not yet hardened. To have the zest of youth and the memories of years is one of the most precious of the blessings of life."

Without mentioning the court bill or its sponsors, he proceeded to drive home a lesson in public morals which could not have been more pointed if it had been part of the Senate debate:

> Nor is it fitting that I should discuss contemporary political questions. But there are fundamental needs which, I think, require emphasis at a time when the institutions of democracy are threatened by an authoritarian philosophy. . . .
>
> We shall always have crusaders. I should be swift to recognize our indebtedness to crusaders who have aroused a lethargic public in a war upon abuses. But crusaders may have more fervor than wisdom, and extreme demands may create an intolerable civil strife. Where shall we look for the balanced judgment, the sane appraisements and the reasonable methods by which civilized society may attain its purposes without surrendering the democratic principle to a regime of force? . . .
>
> I put first the passion for truth. Of course I do not refer to a mere philosophical aspiration. I mean the mental habit of thoroughness, the emotional drive of the will to know one's subject with precision, a mental habit which does not detract from but rather promotes alertness and vigor. I put that mental habit in contrast with a mere search for arguments to triumph in a controversy. I contrast it with the cultivation of facility, to quote Justice Holmes again, in "dodging difficulty and responsibility with a rhetorical phrase." I contrast it with contentment with showy superficialities, with the easy flippancy of cynical criticism, with the ambition to be plausible enough to "sell" something. . . .
>
> The tolerant spirit is as important as the crusading ardor. It is so easy to be unfair and vindictive. Ruthlessness in trampling upon the rights of individuals in the exercise of the brute strength of the majority, if unchecked, will inevitably lead to

[35] CEH to Prof. Douglas Johnson, June 10, 1937.

By S. J. Ray in the *Kansas City Star*.

REGARDLESS OF HOW THAT THIRD HORSE PULLS, HE'S CERTAINLY NIMBLE-FOOTED!

the entire overthrow of democratic processes and the substitution of the tyranny of force. Democratic society can never have the complete efficiency of a machine dominated by a single will. But it carries the banner of freedom and safeguards the priceless aspirations of the human spirit. Between liberty and progress there can be no lasting conflict,—for progress, if true, must be that of a community in which men enjoy the essentials of freedom in the exercise of their highest capacities and are not the mere puppets of the State.

Two days later Hughes addressed an alumni meeting at the Brown University commencement where Charles Evans Hughes 3d received his A.B. degree and gave one of the student orations and Charles Evans Hughes, Jr., received an honorary LL.D. Once more the Chief lashed out in general terms against the rise of totalitarianism in Europe and the attempt at judicial coercion in America:

We still proclaim the old ideals of liberty but we cannot voice them without anxiety in our hearts. The question is no longer one of establishing democratic institutions but of preserving them. . . . The question is not one of the adequate power of government, designed to keep clear the highways of honest endeavor, but how that power shall be used. . . .

The arch enemies of society are those who know better but by indirection, misstatement, understatement and slander, seek to accomplish their concealed purposes or to gain profit of some sort by misleading the public. The antidote for these poisons must be found in the sincere and courageous efforts of those who would preserve their cherished freedom by a wise and responsible use of it. Freedom of expression gives the essential democratic opportunity, but self-restraint is the essential civic discipline.

While the Chief Justice and Mrs. Hughes began a delightful summer at Jasper Park, Alberta, the Senate debated the court bill in Washington's July heat. By this time all prospect of enacting the original measure had disappeared. The debate was on a face-saving substitute, but, as the principle of court-packing was still at stake, the fight was waged with bitterness and tenacity. Eager to claim a place on the supreme bench as his reward, Senator Robinson was still trying to rally the Administration forces with an outward show of almost fierce determination. But his heart had never been in it. Secretly he had kept in touch with the opposition, sending word to Senator Wheeler whenever a supporter or an opponent of the court bill seemed to be wavering.[36] Sick and worried, Robinson succumbed to a heart attack alone in his room the night of July 13, and the fight was over. No one else had a chance of leading the shattered Administration ranks to victory.

After Robinson's funeral Vice President Garner, who had demonstrated his contempt for court-packing by going home to Texas in the midst of the struggle,

[36] Author's interview with Mr. Wheeler, April 14, 1950.

returned to the capital and negotiated the President's surrender to the jubilant Wheeler-Burke-King-O'Mahoney junta in the Senate. On July 22 the bill was finally recommitted to the Judiciary Committee, which is the Senate's way of administering euthanasia to its progeny that is unfit to live.

"Glory be to God!" exclaimed Hiram Johnson, and the country seemed to respond with a fervent, "Amen."

Chapter 71

TRIUMPH OF RESTRAINT

CONGRESS and the Supreme Court had won an incredible victory over President Roosevelt. The President's ablest lieutenant in the fight, Robert H. Jackson, has said that Hughes' letter to Senator Wheeler "did more than any one thing to turn the tide in the Court struggle." [1] Harold L. Ickes, Secretary of the Interior, put it this way: "The whole world knows that, while at first it appeared that the President would be strong enough to carry his reform through Congress, he was outmaneuvered in the end, largely by Chief Justice Charles Evans Hughes." [2] However one looks at it, Hughes' unwavering courage and cool restraint contributed powerfully to saving the Supreme Court from the most formidable attack ever launched against its independence.

The unsettled questions are how the Chief Justice achieved his victory and what price he paid. The prevalent belief seems to be that the court saved itself from being packed by reversing its opinions. "A switch in time saved nine," the flippant say. As the supposed planner and director of this supposed strategic retreat, Hughes is variously accused of resorting to Mephistophelean methods and praised for "judicial statesmanship"—sometimes with the insinuation that he trimmed his principles and browbeat his brethren to save the court as an institution.

In the introduction to his state papers published in 1941, Roosevelt took it for granted that the court had yielded to pressure. For two decades, he asserted, the Supreme Court "had been successfully thwarting the common will of the overwhelming majority of the American people." But after the "definite turning point" in 1937 the kind of government the people wanted was permitted to function. "For that reason," he boasted, "I regard the effort initiated by the message on the Federal Judiciary of February 5, 1937, and the immediate results of it, as among the most important domestic achievements of my first two terms in office." [3]

Certainly F. D. R. is right in saying that 1937 marks the beginning of a new era of harmony between Congress and the Supreme Court. The extreme conservatives on the court did not thereafter muster a majority on any vital issue involving the exercise of federal power. It is equally true, however, that the

[1] *New York Times*, June 24, 1943.
[2] *Saturday Evening Post*, July 3, 1948.
[3] *Collier's*, Sept. 13, 1941, p. 11.

extreme New Dealers did not thereafter regain control of the lawmaking branch. Was the court subdued by the White House, or was Congress subdued by the court?

The great about-face of the Chief Justice is supposed to have come in the Jones and Laughlin case. His opinion is superficially said to be a reversal of what he had written in the NRA and Carter Coal cases. Some shift in emphasis is undeniably apparent, but it may be traced entirely to the vast differences between the situations with which the court was dealing. In the NRA case the court found that the commerce power did not reach into the Schechters' chicken coop, and Hughes employed every legitimate argument to buttress that conclusion. In the NLRB case it was clear that the Jones and Laughlin empire could be reached through the commerce power, and he naturally emphasized that fact. This is the universal practice of judges. Once a decision has been made, they properly support it with the strongest arguments at their command.

The important point is that the same basic principle underlies all three of these opinions.[4] In each instance Hughes insisted that Congress may use the commerce power to regulate activities that are not in themselves interstate commerce if they directly affect that commerce. All three opinions drew the distinction between direct and indirect effects upon interstate commerce. Indeed, these principles had taken firm root in Hughes' mind during his first year on the bench, and he held fast to them before and after the court-packing venture.

This fact is widely recognized by judges and lawyers. Looking back at those early opinions, Attorney General (later Justice) Jackson said that "Hughes' vigorous championship of federal power under the commerce clause is reminiscent of Marshall." [5] Francis Biddle, soon to be Attorney General, also saw that Hughes was treading in his post-1937 opinions a new segment of the same path he had trod as Associate Justice. Chief Justice Stone spoke of Hughes upholding "the constitutional validity of the National Labor Relations Act, upon principles which twenty-four years before he had stated with clarity and precision in the *Minnesota Rate Cases*." [6] Speaking later of the vast reserve of federal power that Hughes had opened up in the *Minnesota Rate Cases* and the *Shreveport Case,* Stone said, "It is evident that when Congress, many years afterward, began to exercise that power on a large scale, in order to accomplish desired social and economic reforms within the states, *it was a legislative and not a judicial revolution which was being staged* . . ." [7] (italics supplied).

One must remember, too, that in the Texas and New Orleans case of 1930 Hughes had given strong underpinning to a congressional act protecting the right of railroad employees to bargain collectively. This opinion plus the

[4] F. D. G. Ribble in *Columbia Law Review*, November, 1941, p. 1199.
[5] *American Bar Association Journal*, July, 1941, p. 410. [6] *Id.*, p. 408.
[7] Address to Association of the Bar of the City of New York, March 16, 1946.

doctrine he had laid down in the *Minnesota Rate Cases* and the NRA case pointed unmistakably to *NLRB* v. *Jones and Laughlin.* The Chief Justice himself insisted that there was no change in his concept of governmental power in this sphere between the writing of these opinions,[8] and the record bears him out.

Nor did Hughes high-pressure his brethren. While he presented the NLRB case before the conference with vigor and thoroughness, this was his usual practice. Rumors that he assumed the role of schoolmaster and that he issued dire warnings to his fellow judges are pure fiction. Equally unfounded are the reports that he pleaded with Justice Roberts to save the NLRB,[9] although he was delighted to have Roberts' concurrence. Undue pressure on the part of the Chief Justice was scarcely less abhorrent to him than undue pressure from the President. Hughes gave reason its full sway, but threats and appeals to the emotions were as completely absent from the conferences during the period of the court fight as they had been before.

"Nor can it be supposed," Hughes wrote in his Notes, "that the President's proposal had any effect upon the views of Justices Brandeis, Stone and Cardozo in relation to the National Labor Relations Act. And as to Justice Roberts, I feel that I am able to say with definiteness that his view in favor of these decisions of the Court would have been the same if the President's bill had never been proposed. The Court acted with complete independence." [10]

Sweeping changes had indeed taken place, but they were largely in the character of legislation going up to the court. The New Deal laws of the early thirties had been drawn, as we have seen, with almost no regard for their constitutionality. In the National Industrial Recovery Act, Congress had attempted to sweep under control of the President *all* industry in virtually all phases of its activity, regardless of whether this activity had any substantial effect on interstate commerce. Likewise the Guffey Act had cut loose from any interstate-commerce yardstick of federal power, asserting control over "every" coal producer as if a sweeping new general welfare clause had been written into the Constitution. It was this loose assertion of unlimited federal power that caused most of the New Deal reverses in 1935 and 1936. After the NRA and the AAA went down, greater care was exercised in the drafting of bills. The young lawyers writing the Administration's proposed laws tardily discovered that the commerce clause was the proper measure of the Federal Government's regulatory power and that there were some limits to the reach of even the commerce clause. The Hughes court was not again asked to pass on a measure comparable to the NRA or even the AAA.

When the statutes invalidated by the court were reenacted with regard for

[8] Author's interviews with CEH, Nov. 19, 1945, and Dec. 3, 1946.
[9] *Id.* [10] Chapter XXIII, p. 33.

constitutional limitations, they were invariably sustained. In March, 1937, the court had given sanction to the revised Frazier-Lemke Act. In 1938 Hughes wrote the opinion upholding an amended version of the Municipal Bankruptcy Act.[11] Congress passed a new Bituminous Coal Act in 1937, correcting various provisions of the Guffey Act and leaving out the invalid labor provisions. and it was upheld in *Sunshine Coal Company* v. *Adkins*.[12] Pointing to these changes the court observed, through Justice Douglas: "There is nothing in the *Carter* case which stands in the way. The majority of the Court in that case did not pass on the price-fixing features of the earlier act. The Chief Justice and Mr. Justice Cardozo in separate minority opinions expressed the view that the price-fixing features of the earlier Act were constitutional. We rest on their conclusions for sustaining the present Act."

Taking the hint contained in the AAA decision, Congress based its new agricultural programs on the commerce clause, and they were sustained. In 1939 the Chief Justice spoke for the court in rejecting a challenge to the Tobacco Inspection Act.[13] Going back to the *Shreveport Case,* he said that the commingling of intrastate and interstate transactions in the tobacco markets did not restrict the overriding federal power. "It is the essence of the plenary power conferred," the Chief concluded, "that Congress may exercise its discretion in the use of that power. Congress may choose the commodities and places to which its regulation shall apply. . . ." A few months later the court gave an accolade to the new Agricultural Adjustment Act, which imposed its controls upon basic farm crops at the "throat" where the produce entered interstate commerce.[14] Justice Roberts wrote the opinion, as if to imply that the first AAA would have survived its test in 1936 if the commerce clause had been used as the measure of federal regulatory power.

Finally, in 1941, the court upheld the Fair Labor Standards Act[15] and overthrew *Hammer* v. *Dagenhart,*[16] in which the White court had upset the Federal Child Labor Act in 1918. Here again, however, a significant step toward that end had been taken before the court fight. On January 4, 1937, Hughes had delivered a unanimous opinion upholding the Ashurst-Sumners Act with the effect of forbidding the movement of convict-made goods across state lines in violation of state law.[17] Without overruling the 1918 decision, Hughes asserted that Congress was not estopped from exercising its power because convict-made horse collars were useful and harmless articles. He seemed to recognize also that Congress could prevent the interstate shipment of such goods irrespective of state consent. Only one more stroke was needed to cut off the limb on which *Hammer* v. *Dagenhart* rested. That strike came in

[11] *U.S.* v. *Bekins,* 304 U.S. 27.
[12] 310 U.S. 381, 396, 397.
[13] *Currin* v. *Wallace,* 306 U.S. 1.
[14] *Mulford* v. *Smith,* 307 U.S. 38.
[15] *U.S.* v. *Darby,* 312 U.S. 100.
[16] 247 U.S. 251.
[17] *Kentucky Whip & Collar Co.* v. *Illinois Central R.R. Co.,* 299 U.S. 334.

United States v. *Darby* with Stone writing for a unanimous court. The opinion was a sweeping recognition of congressional power to control the national market for the sake of protecting the public health, morals, or welfare.

The Hughes court did not, however, abandon the distinction between what is national and what is local. It merely recognized that the evolution of our economy had lengthened the reach of the commerce power. In a closely integrated economy interstate commerce was more sensitive to the impact of local interferences. Hughes again expounded his view in *Santa Cruz Fruit Packing Co.* v. *Labor Board,*[18] in which the court sustained the application of the National Labor Relations Act to a fruit canning and shipping company:

> . . . injurious action burdening and obstructing interstate trade in manufactured articles may spring from labor disputes irrespective of the origin of the materials used in the manufacturing process. . . . It is also clear that where federal control is sought to be exercised over activities which separately considered are intrastate, it must appear that there is a close and substantial relation to interstate commerce in order to justify the federal intervention for its protection. However difficult in application, this principle is essential to the maintenance of our constitutional system. The subject of federal power is still "commerce," and not all commerce but commerce with foreign nations and among the several States. The expansion of enterprise has vastly increased the interests of interstate commerce but the constitutional differentiation still obtains. . . .
>
> To express this essential distinction, "direct" has been contrasted with "indirect," and what is "remote" or "distant" with what is "close and substantial." Whatever terminology is used, the criterion is necessarily one of degree and must be so defined. This does not satisfy those who seek for mathematical or rigid formulas. But such formulas are not provided by the great concepts of the Constitution such as "interstate commerce," "due process," "equal protection." In maintaining the balance of the constitutional grants and limitations, it is inevitable that we should define their application in the gradual process of inclusion and exclusion.

What we have in the whole range of Hughes' opinions is a gradual unfolding of the vast scope of the commerce power. The fact that he used a checkrein when this great power was pushed beyond what seemed to him its constitutional limitations is an indication of commendable independence on the bench.

Along with his liberal concept of the commerce clause went a profound distrust of using the taxing power, or any other nonregulatory power, as a means of controlling local activities in the states. National controls resting on the commerce power were consistent with our federal system. National controls imposed through the taxing power knew no bounds. This vital distinction is often overlooked, as when Professor Swisher speaks of the Hughes court abandoning the Tenth Amendment as a check upon the expansion of federal power between the AAA decision in 1936 and the *United States* v. *Darby* in 1941.[19]

[18] 303 U.S. 453.

[19] Carl Brent Swisher, *The Growth of Constitutional Power in the United States*, pp. 34f.

In the AAA case the Tenth Amendment was invoked to arrest what the majority believed to be a misuse of the taxing and spending power to regulate local activities. The Fair Labor Standards Act upheld in the Darby case rested on the commerce power. Obviously the Tenth Amendment would not bar any legitimate use of the commerce power given to Congress specifically for regulatory purposes.

Both the written record and confidential testimony from the Justices who sat with Hughes through the conferences from 1937 to 1941 are utterly barren of evidence that he trimmed his principles, reversed his judgment, or high-pressured his brethren. It does appear that the travail through which the court passed in 1937 consolidated his leadership. During the next few years it was more distinctly a Hughes court than it had been before. But to assume, as some have done, that it became a "Roosevelt court" is grossly to distort the facts. F. D. R. had sought the delegation of power "running riot" as well as overriding federal controls that threatened to absorb the police powers of the states. What he got from the Hughes court was recognition of a broadened but still limited sweep of the commerce power, with delegation held in check and some semblance of balance retained in the federal system.

Undoubtedly several factors contributed to the temporary cut-off of decisions holding Acts of Congress to be unconstitutional. "New blood" on the bench soon minimized the influence of the old conservative wing. The changed temper of American democracy may have subconsciously influenced the thinking of some judges. But no other factor seems to be as important as the changes in the character of the legislation passed—the self-reversal on the part of Congress. Especially after it had saved the court from being packed, Congress was eager to avoid passing legislation that the court would have to invalidate.

What has been widely proclaimed as the self-reversal of the court narrows down, therefore, to the West Coast Hotel case, decided before the court-packing threat was made, and a few other cases in which it is assumed that, had they been decided before the court fight, Justice Roberts would have voted with the four ultraconservatives. Such speculation is futile. The one thing certain is that there was no sudden shift from conservative to liberal thinking on Roberts' part. Before 1937 he was on the liberal side of the court in the Blaisdell, Nebbia, West Coast Hotel, and gold-clause cases. Since there was no extreme stretching of federal power between 1937 and 1941, his acceptance of the federal legislation coming before the court in this period can be reconciled with his former record without reflecting upon his courage or his integrity.

Certainly there was no modification in the rock-ribbed conservatism of Butler and McReynolds. As for Hughes, Brandeis, Stone, and Cardozo, they had stood together in eight of the twelve New Deal cases and a majority of them were in full or partial accord in three others. To assume that all of them shuffled their principles in response to a threat against the court is an irresponsible surmise unrelated to any demonstrable facts. The constitutional doctrines on which these men agreed became the guiding principles both of Congress and of the Supreme Court in 1937 and the years immediately following.

What the record does show is a steadiness and moderation on Hughes' part both in passing judgment on New Deal legislation and in resisting the assault on the court. Under great stress he drove straight ahead without losing his nerve, his balance, or his high sense of integrity—without permitting himself to be drawn into a maelstrom of vindictiveness. His combination of restraint, courage, and tenacity to principle in piloting the court through its dark days is perhaps the best measure of the man in the high office of Chief Justice.

Chapter 72

CULMINATION

WHEN the Supreme Court assembled for its October term in 1937, it had a new member for the first time in five years. To succeed Justice Van Devanter the President had nominated Senator Hugo L. Black of Alabama, a fiery New Dealer and a stalwart fighter for the court-packing bill. It is said that Black was chosen primarily because he would be unacceptable to those who had beaten the court bill but would have to be confirmed nevertheless because he was a Senator.[1]

The Senate had voted confirmation amid muffled rumors that Black was or had been a member of the Ku Klux Klan. Later the press had dug up unmistakable evidence that Black had joined the Klan in 1926 when he ran for the Senate, and indignant protests against seating him in the court were heard through the rest of the summer. Returning from a tour of Europe, the new Justice admitted his former membership in the Klan while repudiating all that the Klan stood for. The episode thus ended on a note no less sardonic than the court fight itself.

When Black took his seat, however, Hughes greeted him with all the courtesy and cordiality that could have been bestowed upon the most distinguished jurist in the land.[2] Black was now a duly confirmed member of the court. That settled the matter so far as Hughes was concerned. In their subsequent relations there was not the slightest show of antagonism on the part of the Chief Justice because Black had voted against his confirmation in 1930 and worked to pack the court. Some of the Justices complained that the new member lacked judicial craftsmanship,[3] but not Hughes. While at first he assigned relatively minor cases to Black, that was the custom with all new members. In the conference Black had free rein to speak his mind. At no time did the Chief rebuff him or cut off expression of the views that went into his numerous lone dissents. Black thus came to have a high regard for Hughes' fairness, his intellect, and skill as a presiding officer, and a real affection for him as an individual.[4]

The Chief made a special point of giving Black opportunities to demonstrate

[1] Alsop and Catledge, *The 168 Days*, p. 299.
[2] Author's interview with Justice Black, Feb. 2, 1950.
[3] Marquis Childs in *Harper's*, May, 1938, pp. 587ff.
[4] Author's interview with Justice Black, Feb. 2, 1950.

that no taint of klanism influenced his thinking. When *Chambers* v. *Florida*[5] came up on petition for certiorari, Black voted against taking it.[6] There were plenty of other votes for hearing it because of the evidence that a group of Negroes had been forced to confess by third-degree methods. Hughes had almost scorched the earth of Mississippi a few years earlier for a similar third-degree conviction. After the Florida case had been heard on its merits and all the judges accepted the Chief's recommendation that the verdict be reversed, he assigned the opinion to Black. The latter wrote a strong denunciation of the third degree, and *Chambers* v. *Florida* has become one of his best known opinions.

Vacancies came fast after 1937. Justice Sutherland had decided to step down as soon as the Retirement Act was passed, but he waited until Van Devanter's seat had been filled to avoid creating two vacancies at the same time. He was succeeded by the able, steady, but unspectacular Solicitor General, Stanley F. Reed. The court was saddened in July, 1938, by the death of Justice Cardozo—the friend whom Hughes described as "a beautiful spirit, an extraordinary combination of grace and power." In his place President Roosevelt chose Professor Felix Frankfurter of Harvard Law School. During the years that remained to the Chief, the dynamic and scholarly jurist from Harvard was to become one of his most devoted friends. Indicative of their relationship is the following comment by Frankfurter after they had worked together about a year:

> No outside student of the work of the Court could be unaware of the intrinsic authority with which you have exercised your chief justiceship. But only one who has been privileged to sit under you as chief can possibly appreciate the sweep and impact of [the] resources and fruitful tradition and creative energy with which you lead the Court. Of your complete dedication to its functions in our national life it would be almost humorously impertinent to speak.[7]

Justice Brandeis was the fourth member of the "old court" to go. After suffering a heart attack at the age of eighty-three, "the master of both microscope and telescope" whose advice "weighed a ton," divested himself of his judicial burden in February, 1939, and was succeeded by William O. Douglas.

Up to 1939 Hughes' zest remained unabated. In nine years he had not missed a single session of the court or the conference, or indeed a single hour of the work of the court. His enjoyment of life was still keen, as indicated by the frequent trips he took with Mrs. Hughes to Europe and to various favorite spots in Canada and the United States. With astonishing ease, he could put

[5] 309 U.S. 227. [6] Confidential source No. 3.
[7] Frankfurter to CEH, Feb. 24, 1940.

aside the dignity of the Chief Justiceship for a pun, a joke, or a story. On one of their jaunts in New England he and Mrs. Hughes decided to drop in unannounced at Beverly Farms, the summer home of Justice Holmes, then in retirement. Earlier in the year Holmes had asked them to visit him, and Hughes had said it would be impossible. But their plans had changed, and Hughes seized the opportunity to surprise his old friend. Holmes himself came to the door wearing a quizzical smile.

"Well, Mr. Justice," Hughes began, with a grin playing around the ends of his mouth, "your invitation was so enticing that we just couldn't resist it. We changed our plans, and here we are."

Holmes put his thumb to his nose and waggled his fingers—his favorite gesture—then extended his usual salty welcome.

In the family circle Hughes continued to be an incorrigible tease. He seemed never to tire of bantering Mrs. Hughes on how young she looked. "Everyone says," he would tell her, " 'I didn't know the Chief Justice had married a second time.' "

In the presence of the family one day he said, "Your mother will live to be an old, old lady, and she'll be saying to you, 'Children, I can't quite remember what he looked like.' "

"Don't you dare say that!" Mrs. Hughes exclaimed, pulling his whiskers and laughing in spite of her exasperation. But the nature of her response assured repetition of his persiflage as soon as another favorable occasion arose.

The relationship between the Chief Justice and his bride of half a century was still that of a boy and girl in love. She was the object of his deep and unwavering adoration, and in return she almost worshiped her hero. Nothing was too good for him. Ever aware of his intellectual powers, she brought to him the serenity, the love, and understanding that alone made possible his sustained concentration upon public affairs.

On the Chief's seventieth birthday Mrs. Hughes had given him a memorable party attended by the Hughes children and grandchildren and a few other guests, including President and Mrs. Hoover, General Pershing, Justice Cardozo, former Undersecretary of State William Phillips, and Mrs. Hennen Jennings, a neighbor. The Hughesian custom of exchanging verses or notes of greeting on birthdays and other anniversaries persisted. Typical of the verses penned only for her eyes is the following:

Intent upon "opinions" terse,
I have no time or skill for verse.
How can I hope to meet your pleasure
In vain attempt to write in measure!
Enough—that hard judicial lives
Are made serene by charming wives.

April 11th. 1937.

2223 R STREET, N.W.
WASHINGTON, D.C.

My dearest and my gallant
"old Soldier" -

How can I be
grateful enough on this - your
75th birthday - that we are
to-gether, that we are well
and sound of mind and,
above all, that our love has
grown deeper and truer with
the years?

With these blessings we
can bear anything, even "the
slings and arrows" of an

outrageous Court plan; and let us face the future some-thing as follows.

"There, whatsoever wind doth blow.
My heart is glad to have it so,
And blow it East or blow it west,
The wind that blows, that wind is best."

Devotedly

Wifie

Here is the beginning of a little 'Poets Corner'"!

On one of their "days" Mrs. Hughes wrote a sentiment-laden rhyme beginning:

Darling, I am growing old!
More "silver threads" than can be told,
But dearer far you are today
Than any words of mine can say.

Hughes did not see it exactly that way. When they celebrated her seventy-second birthday that same year at the Plaza Hotel in New York, he attached to the present he gave her this warmhearted note:

How can it be true
That she's seventy-two!
So slim and so trim
With so graceful a carriage
I see her still as I saw her when
We clasped our hands in marriage.

From your old lover—May it be the happiest of birthdays.

Antoinette Carter Hughes returned the compliment when her husband reached the venerable age of seventy-five:

MY DEAREST AND MY GALLANT "OLD SOLDIER"—

How can I be grateful enough on this—your 75th birthday—that we are together, that we are well and sound of mind and, above all, that our love has grown deeper and truer with the years?

With these blessings we can bear anything, even "the slings and arrows" of an outrageous Court plan; and let us face the future something as follows:

"Then, whatsoever wind doth blow,
My heart is glad to have it so.
And blow it East or blow it West,
The wind that blows, that wind is best."

Devotedly,
WIFIE.

On their wedding anniversary in 1937—the year of the court-packing plan—the supposedly austere Chief Justice penned these sentimental lines:

To my Dearest—to whose care and love, unfailing watchfulness and encouragement, I owe everything—health, peace of mind, the most congenial companionship, and the unbroken happiness of forty-nine years. How could the evening of life be more glorious! How can I express the love that feeds upon the years!

The following year, on December 5, they celebrated their golden wedding anniversary. Their fifty years together had brought no disillusionment but only

Supreme Court of the United States
Washington, D.C.

Dec. 5 - 1937

To my Dearest — to whose care and love, unfailing watchfulness and encouragement, I owe everything — health, peace of mind, the most congenial companionship, and the unbroken happiness of forty-nine years — How could the evening of life be more glorious! How can I express the love that feeds upon the years!

Supreme Court of the United States
Washington, D.C.

December 5, 1938

Dearest,—

That was a stout young tree—the tree of our love, and each year—in storm and sunshine—it has grown in beauty and strength,—and under its spreading branches we have found rest and peace.—

It is a magic tree, which has never known blight and it has the perennial freshness of the evergreen with the sturdiness

of the oak.—Its roots have
run deep into the soil of our
Common interests and our
unity of spirit has been its
never failing vital force.—

Fifty years are all
too short for such happiness:-
All I have I owe to you.
If I could have my
dearest wish, it would be
that I should live with
you forever.—

C

deeper understanding and exaltation of marital love. It cannot be doubted that Hughes laid greater store upon his sustained romance than upon all the official honors that had come to him. The depth of his emotion and the ripening of his appreciation are beautifully caught up in the note that he wrote to his wife:

DEAREST,

That was a stout young tree—the tree of our love, and each year—in storm and sunshine—it has grown in beauty and strength, and under its spreading branches we have found rest and peace.

It is a magic tree, which has never known blight and it has the perennial freshness of the evergreen with the sturdiness of the oak. Its roots have run deep into the soil of our common interests and our unity of spirit has been its never failing vital force.

Fifty years are all too short for such happiness. All I have I owe to you. If I could have my dearest wish, it would be that I should live with you forever.

C.

In spite of his health, happiness, and success, Hughes was determined not to overstay his time on the bench. Within his family he had arranged for a secret ballot (the result of which would be communicated to him) if any one of his children felt that he was slipping into senility. No one had thought of raising such a question. In late February, 1939, however, his iron constitution began to waver, and it appeared that he might be the next to leave the court.

Hughes had agreed to address a joint session of the Senate and House of Representatives on March 4—the sesquicentennial of the meeting of the first Congress. About a week before the celebration, as he sat at the big table in the conference room after all the brethren had left, a gray-green pallor spread over his face. Wiping his hand across his brow, he acknowledged to Cropley, the court's faithful clerk, that he was ill. Cropley helped him to a couch. The Chief closed his eyes and looked as if he were about to expire.

"Cropley, where are you?" he called as the clerk moved toward the door with the intention of seeking a doctor.[8] He would not let Cropley leave the room. After a while he felt better, sat up, cautioned Cropley not to mention the incident, and then went home, refusing to let Cropley accompany him because some question might be raised as to the reason for it.

Feeling very weak, the Chief continued his work. On the day of the celebration the Justices and their wives gathered in the old Supreme Court chamber in the Capitol, Mrs. Hughes looking worried. Seeing Cropley's anxious expression, the Chief whispered, "I'm all right." They went on to the House chamber, which was crowded by members of Congress, ambassadors, chieftains of the Army and Navy, the Cabinet, and other dignitaries. Hughes took his seat with a feeling of terrible weakness pulling him down. The Speaker of the House and the president pro tempore of the Senate delivered their orations. At last

[8] Author's interview with Mr. Cropley, Jan. 18, 1950.

Senator Barkley, the majority leader, was introducing the Chief Justice of the United States. Hughes wondered if he could get to the rostrum.[9] Summoning all his reserve, he managed to walk the short distance without swaying and began to speak with something less than his usual gusto. Using no notes, he nevertheless spoke with precision and a Lincolnesque sense of dedication to his task:

The most significant fact in connection with this anniversary is that after 150 years, notwithstanding expansion of territory, enormous increase in population and profound economic changes, despite direct attack and subversive influences, there is every indication that the vastly preponderant sentiment of the American people is that our form of government shall be preserved.

We come from our distinct departments of governmental activity to testify to our unity of aim in maintaining that form of government in accordance with our common pledge. We are here not as masters, but as servants, not to glory in power, but to attest our loyalty to the commands and restrictions laid down by our sovereign, the people of the United States, in whose name and by whose will we exercise our brief authority. If as such representatives we have, as Benjamin Franklin said—"no more durable preeminence than the different grains in an hour glass"—we serve our hour by unremitting devotion to the principles which have given our Government both stability and capacity for orderly progress in a world of turmoil and revolutionary upheavals.

. . . If we owe to the wisdom and restraint of the fathers a system of government which has thus far stood the test, we all recognize that it is only by wisdom and restraint in our own day that we can make that system last. If today we find ground for confidence that our institutions which have made for liberty and strength will be maintained, it will not be due to abundance of physical resources or to productive capacity, but because these are at the command of a people who still cherish the principles which underlie our system and because of the general appreciation of what is essentially sound in our governmental structure.

Aside from intensity of his words, it was evident that the Chief was speaking under a great strain. His appraisal of our constitutional heritage was punctuated by several pauses. Once his voice faltered, and for a moment it appeared that he might not go on. Then came another wave of strength, and his voice built up to a dramatic conclusion:

I am happy to be here as the representative of the tribunal which is charged with the duty of maintaining, through the decision of controversies, these constitutional guarantees. We are a separate but not an independent arm of government. You, not we, have the purse and the sword. You, not we, determine the establishment and the jurisdiction of the lower Federal courts and the bounds of the appellate jurisdiction of the Supreme Court. . . .

But in the great enterprise of making democracy workable we are all partners. One member of our body politic cannot say to another—"I have no need of thee." We work in successful cooperation by being true, each department to its own

[9] CEH, Notes, 1930–1941, p. 46.

function, and all to the spirit which pervades our institutions—exalting the processes of reason, seeking through the very limitations of power the promotion of the wise use of power, and finding the ultimate security of life, liberty, and the pursuit of happiness, and the promise of continued stability and a rational progress, in the good sense of the American people.

Sick though he was, Hughes had compressed into a few ringing paragraphs his philosophy of the wise use of public power—a philosophy that is pregnant with meaning for the modern world. The concluding speaker was the President, but the occasion had already found its zenith in the words of the Chief Justice. He was overwhelmed with compliments both oral and written: ". . . your wonderful address . . . splendid . . . brilliant . . . gave me a thrill . . . a godsend . . . profoundest admiration . . . It was the most perfect piece of oratory I have ever had the pleasure to hear." [10] With the ceremony over, however, Hughes' chief interest was neither the glowing acclaim of his friends nor his own physical condition but the Saturday conference which the ceremony had disrupted.

"Well, come on, brethren," he said. "We have work to do."

"Oh, Chief Justice," Roberts remonstrated. "You have done enough today. Let the conference wait until next week." [11] Several other Justices joined in the protest, but Hughes was adamant. The conference had never been postponed since he had presided over it. It could not be postponed now. All afternoon until six o'clock he sat at the head of the table analyzing cases and directing the discussion. Then he made his assignments for the writing of opinions. That evening he and Mrs. Hughes gave one of their large dinners. When it was all over, the Chief went to bed feeling that the lifeblood had been drained out of him.

On Monday, Hughes called in his physician and learned that he had a bleeding duodenal ulcer and had sustained a serious loss of blood. For the next several weeks he was confined to his bed. Rest and diet soon cleared up the internal bleeding, and by April 11, his birthday, he was able to go for a walk again. Soon he was back on the bench. As the term closed about June 1, the Chief thought he detected a recurrence of internal bleeding symptoms, and his doctor put him to bed on a water diet for two days, but the subsequent exploration showed no serious trouble.

Justice Butler, looking the picture of health, dropped in at the Hughes home just before leaving on his vacation. "We'll never see the Chief again," was his gloomy prediction. He was right, but it was because of his own death in November of that year. After a summer of comparative rest the Chief Justice was in fine fettle once more. When he and Mrs. Hughes celebrated their wed-

[10] Hughes papers, Supreme Court.
[11] Author's interview with Justice Roberts, May 21, 1946.

ding anniversary on December 5, he was especially mindful of how she had nursed him back to health. His note to her said:

DEAREST—

The past year has had its difficulties—unusual because of physical troubles—but my dependence and your care have made my love more tender and more strong—if that be possible. Here's to the 52nd—my darling,—the best gift of life.

With the selection of Attorney General Frank Murphy to succeed Butler, the supreme bench had a majority of Roosevelt appointees. Hughes remained unquestionably the dominant figure in the court, but he found himself more frequently in the minority in controversial cases. Still there were numerous amenities. On February 1, 1940, the court celebrated its own sesquicentennial. The Chief would not agree to an elaborate ceremony, but he responded to commemorative remarks by Attorney General Jackson and Charles A. Beardsley, president of the American Bar Association. "Democracy is a most hopeful way of life," he said, "but its promise of liberty and of human betterment will be but idle words save as the ideals of justice, not only between man and man, but between government and citizen, are held supreme." Thanks in no small measure to his own efforts, he could proudly say that the court still stood, after 150 years, "as an embodiment of the ideal of the independence of the judicial function." [12]

"Not your greatest predecessor," commented Justice Frankfurter, "could have bettered what you said and how you said it." [13]

Later in the month all the brethren joined in saluting him and Mrs. Hughes on his tenth anniversary as Chief Justice. "We all look forward with joy," their message read, "to the continuance for years to come, of the association which means much to each of us." From his retirement Brandeis wrote, "You have, as Chief Justice, given to the Court ten great years." [14] Brandeis was telling his friends that in all his long experience Hughes was the best Chief Justice he had ever known.[15]

The war against Hitlerism in Europe had taken the spotlight off the Supreme Court and all other domestic concerns. As 1940 wore on, interest was divided between the clash of arms abroad and the clash of words at home, where another contest for the Presidency was in progress. Roosevelt was making his bid for a third term against a formidable challenge by Wendell Willkie. In spite of the President's assault upon the court, Hughes remained scrupulously aloof from the struggle. His attitude remained unchanged when, on October 17, he received a frantic appeal from Herbert Hoover. "I am about to make a suggestion that may impress you as fantastic," the former President wrote. "I would

[12] U.S. Reports, 309, pp. XIIff.
[13] Frankfurter to CEH, Feb. 1, 1940.
[14] CEH's private papers.
[15] Author's interviews with Justice Roberts and others.

not do it if I did not believe that the whole future of the American people hangs upon the decision of this election."[16] His "fantastic suggestion" was that Hughes resign the Chief Justiceship "with a declaration to the country of the complete necessity for a change in Administration."

Hughes did not reply in writing, but he told Lawrence Richey, who had delivered the letter, that such a gesture would be futile for the simple reason that there would promptly be another Chief Justice; the prestige of the office would not follow him in such a venture.[17] In any event, the Chief declined to think seriously of ending his career on the bench with a little partisan sputter.

Before and after the election he maintained pleasant relations with the President. When King George and Queen Elizabeth visited Washington in June, 1939, the Chief was undergoing his two-day physical exploration and could not attend the state dinner. Learning this, the President personally called Mrs. Hughes on the telephone, expressed his regrets, and said in his usual gay manner that he hoped she would come and that he was going to seat her next the King. And this he did.[18]

On January 20, 1941, Hughes administered the oath of office to Roosevelt for the third time. Some weeks later, as the two men sat on a sofa in the White House library after the judicial dinner, the inaugural ceremony came into the conversation, and Hughes confessed to the President, "I had an impish desire to break the solemnity of the occasion by remarking, 'Franklin, don't you think this is getting to be a trifle monotonous!' "[19]

Hughes' seventy-ninth birthday, April 11, 1941, was an occasion for almost a barrage of congratulations and good-will messages. One of them read:

DEAR CHIEF:

My affectionate regards & best wishes on your Birthday. You are not a day older—mentally or physically than I am—just 59!

As ever yours,

FRANKLIN D. ROOSEVELT

The Chief Justice replied the next day:

DEAR MR. PRESIDENT:

Your extraordinary appraisal of my youth has almost turned my head. While I am old enough to know better, I am young enough to like it.

It is most kind of you in the midst of your heavy responsibilities to send me such a generous and encouraging greeting. I heartily reciprocate your good wishes.

Very sincerely yours,

CHARLES E. HUGHES[20]

Several notes from the newer members of the court attest the cordial relations that prevailed. "It is comforting," wrote Justice Murphy, "to find you on

[16] Herbert Hoover to CEH, Oct. 17, 1940.
[17] Author's interview with CEH, June 4, 1946.
[18] CEH, Notes, 1930–1941, p. 33.
[19] *Id.*, p. 34.
[20] Mr. Hughes' private papers.

your birthday at the very zenith of your matchless intellectual and physical powers." Justice Reed commented: "You have come to be the symbol of the Court and one in which all of us take great pride. It is a great satisfaction to work in your team." Justice Frankfurter sounded a note that ran through many of the felicitations: "May you long be spared, in your superb vigor, for your country and your colleagues." [21]

Actually, of course, Hughes was far beyond the zenith of his powers, and he knew it. While he was still in good health and had not missed a day of work, except for the two occasions in the spring of 1939, he found the maintenance of sustained effort over long hours increasingly difficult. If he remained on the bench, he would have to slow down. As he had criticized judges for hanging on after they were unable to bring full vigor to their tasks,[22] he concluded early in 1941 that the time was approaching when he should follow his own advice. It is a mark of his greatness that he could apply an objective judgment to himself, even when it meant extinction of his power. No other Chief Justice has laid down the reins in good health since John Jay resigned in 1795 to become Governor of New York.

When he first decided to quit, Hughes was strongly inclined to resign outright and not claim the benefits of retirement. Having a fortune of about $1,200,000, he did not need the retirement allowance that Congress had made available. On full consideration, however, he concluded, as had Justice Brandeis, whose fortune was much larger, that a resignation would set an undesirable precedent—that in the interests of the court the policy of the Retirement Act should be maintained.[23] Accordingly, he wrote a brief note announcing his retirement, to take effect on July 1, 1941, and sent it to the White House just before he ascended the bench for the last time to preside over the final session of the term.

The message was telephoned to the President at Poughkeepsie, New York, and he wrote the following telegram in longhand:

> I am deeply distressed by your letter of June second telling me of your retirement on July first from active service as Chief Justice of the United States. This comes to me, as I know it will to the whole Nation, as a great shock for all of us had counted on your continuing your splendid service for many years to come. My every inclination is to beg you to remain; but my deep concern for your health and strength must be paramount. I shall hope to see you this coming week in Washington.[24]

Returning to the capital, F. D. R. invited the Chief to lunch at the Executive Offices to discuss the choice of his successor. Ever conscious of the value of experience on the bench, Hughes strongly recommended Stone,[25] who was then

[21] *Id.* [22] *The Supreme Court of the United States*, pp. 74–77.
[23] CEH, Notes, 1930–1941, p. 18. [24] Washington *Evening Star*, June 3, 1941.
[25] CEH, Notes, 1930–1941, p. 47.

senior Associate Justice. The President talked favorably of Stone and of Attorney General Jackson. Hughes thought well of Jackson, but he felt that Stone's record gave him first claim upon the honor. At Hughes' suggestion the President also consulted Justice Frankfurter, a close friend of Jackson, who urged the appointment of Stone, a Republican, in the interest of national unity in meeting the international crisis then gripping the country. Roosevelt responded in fine spirit, and Stone took the oath of office two days after Hughes' retirement became effective. The appointment is indicative of how far the President had retreated from his court-packing days in spite of his continued efforts to justify the course he had pursued in 1937. For Stone had voted to upset the NRA and five other New Deal Acts. He had stood with Hughes in the New Deal cases, excepting *United States* v. *Butler,* one point in the gold-clause decisions, and partial disagreement in the Carter Coal case.

One of Chief Justice Stone's first acts was to write his predecessor a humble note:

> When I reflect upon the fact that I have taken it [the oath of office] as your successor and upon the great service which you have rendered as Chief Justice, to the country and the Court, I bow my head in humility and pray that I may in some moderate degree prove worthy to be your successor.[26]

Hughes' retirement unloosed an avalanche of commendation. The formal letter from the court signed by all the brethren was heavy with conventional encomiums. Most of the Justices wrote warmer personal notes: Justice Black, "I would be untrue to my own impulses if I should fail at this time to tell you that as a result of our association I entertain for you a genuine personal affection." Justice Douglas, "Your generosity, kindliness and forbearance meant much to me. Your professional performance . . . was a real inspiration." Justice Frankfurter wrote to Mrs. Hughes, ". . . there can be no doubt that his name will be among the ultimate few who have served this country as the voice of law."

A host of distinguished friends seemed to vie for the honor of paying the most glowing compliment. Hoover wrote, "You have given the most distinguished service to America that she has had in your generation." William Allen White commented, "I wanted you to know how proud I am to have lived in the generation with you." From Henry L. Stimson came, ". . . you have stood as one of the great pillars of integrity and morality in public life"; from Secretary Ickes, "You have been a great Chief Justice and a great citizen and no man could ask more of life"; from William Hard, "You have surpassed them all [the public men he had reported] in the number and variety of your exploits"; from Senator Wagner, "Every phase of this great transitional era

[26] Stone to CEH, July 3, 1941.

By Leo Joseph Roche, *Buffalo Courier-Express*, June 7, 1941.

THAT'S THE QUESTION

By Harold Talburt, Scripps-Howard Newspapers, June, 1941.

"WE'VE COME A LONG WAY TOGETHER!"

bears the mark of your labors"; [27] from Attorney General Jackson, "The bar ranks Chief Justice Hughes in a class with John Marshall"; from Judge Learned Hand, "The Court will look back to him as one of its great figures"; from Chief Justice Lawrence Groner of the United States Court of Appeals, "When shall we look upon his like again? . . . I have heard from the lips of the judges who served with him that all regard him as the ablest Chief Justice in the history of the Court."

Some of the men who served under him were even less restrained in their praise. "God must have gotten his formulas mixed," said Thomas E. Waggaman, marshal of the court, "for he gave the Chief more intellect than any mortal was supposed to have." Cropley, the clerk, brought his veneration to a climax by saying that the Chief's "criticism left you richer than another man's praise." The press was equally laudatory. Hughes had made himself the "symbol of the integrity," "the very embodiment of justice," the exemplar of "equal justice under law," "the judge *par excellence* with no tag line to his integrity." The widespread similarity of the comment is indicative of the impact of his career upon the public mind.

Any appraisal of Hughes' eleven years as Chief Justice must recognize at least four outstanding facets of his work. His enhancement of efficiency within the courts would alone give distinction to a lesser figure. One eminent jurist regards the Act setting up the Administrative Office of the United States Courts —largely Hughes' handiwork—as "the most important legislation affecting the federal judiciary to be passed since the Judiciary Act of 1789." [28] This will be a lasting monument.

His mastery in presiding over the court and the conference of the Justices has probably never been equaled. An indefinable quality in his makeup kept the deliberations on a plane of high-mindedness and inspired those about him to put forth their best efforts. "Everyone who came into contact with him," as Justice Roberts has said, "was charmed by his personality," [29] and Hughes took full advantage of this fact to make his standards prevail.

Among his positive contributions to the law, the firm establishment of the four freedoms of the First Amendment as guarantees to the citizen against state action is an achievement of the first order. In the field of civil liberties his record is more consistent than that of Holmes; and Hughes, instead of becoming another great dissenter for freedom, succeeded in making most of his opinions the law of the land. In expounding the commerce clause his influence was perhaps even more profound. Chief Justice Marshall had given the commerce clause its initial standing as a great instrument of national power. Hughes adapted it to the necessities of our modern industrial economy.

[27] CEH's private papers. [28] Judge John J. Parker to CEH, June 5, 1941.
[29] Address to New York bar, Dec. 12, 1948.

Finally, of course, he was helmsman of the judiciary at a time when it had to be saved from executive domination as well as from ossified thinking. The nice balance that he maintained between sagacity and courage, determination and restraint, stands out in contrast to previous clashes between the President and the Chief Justice. When Jefferson attempted to remake the Supreme Court by impeaching Federalist judges, Chief Justice Marshall's courage sagged and he suggested that Congress reverse court opinions that it deemed unsound—an utter retreat from the great principle he had established in *Marbury* v. *Madison*.[30] In the Civil War period, following the tragic Dred Scott decision, Chief Justice Taney hurt the court by taking an openly hostile attitude toward the Lincoln Administration. Hughes judiciously avoided both precedents. As to the court's function and the constitutional doctrines he believed to be sound, he held steadfastly to his convictions. But he adroitly refused to get into a feud with the White House. His defense of the court without rancor and his treatment of the law as a progressive, living organism are among the finest fruits of our judicial tradition.

Here was the "meekness with power" that Hughes had once eulogized before a Baptist Sunday-school gathering. His leadership of the court through this troublesome period was essentially a triumph of character. It will occasion no surprise if, in the history of our constitutional system, Hughes' name is written beside Marshall's in the same relationship that Lincoln holds to Washington.

[30] Albert J. Beveridge, *The Life of John Marshall* (Boston, Houghton Mifflin, 1916), II, 177. Copyright, 1916, by Albert J. Beveridge.

Chapter 73

THE LITTLE FINISHING CANTER

RETIREMENT meant complete withdrawal from the life Hughes had known for nearly four decades. We get the key to his attitude from an incident that happened a year and a half before he left the bench. At Butler's funeral members of the court were seated as a body, with the two retired Justices at the end of the line. McReynolds thought it was improper to have the older retired members placed as if they were junior to the most junior active Justice. Roberts agreed and at a subsequent conference suggested to the Chief that on ceremonial occasions the retired brethren should have their old places in the line. Hughes sharply objected. "If I retire," he said, "there will not be two Chief Justices." [1]

It was not easy for Hughes to keep himself completely out of the limelight. At first he spent much of his time declining invitations. The American Bar Association asked him to be its guest of honor at Indianapolis in September, 1941, and President Roosevelt urged him to accept and discuss the Nazi peril in Europe. "As you know," he wrote, "it is a task of the utmost difficulty to make people realize what the effect of a German victory would be, and I know of nothing more effective than a speech broadcast by you." [2] Hughes had already declined the invitation. To the President he replied: "I feel that the time has come when I should be excused from preparing addresses and be spared the fatigue of public performance. I must leave to others the effort to inform, clarify and persuade." [3]

Three different bar associations in New York wished to give dinners in his honor. Then former Attorney General Mitchell came to Washington and urged him to consent to one dinner in which all the New York bar associations would join. Columbia University tried to induce him to deliver a series of lectures as the first Cardozo professor of jurisprudence. But in no instance would he budge from the quiet little world into which he had settled down with his family. The idea of going to a public function merely to hear himself lauded to the skies was repugnant. And he was so determined to do nothing that would in any way detract from the prestige of his successor that he even declined invitations to Sunday dinner from old friends on the court.

[1] Author's interview with Justice Roberts, May 21, 1946.
[2] F. D. R. to CEH, Aug. 25, 1941. [3] CEH to F. D. R., Aug. 30, 1941.

Those who tried to lure him into political activity found him even less receptive. Being still a member of the court, at least in theory, he felt that it was up to him to set a precedent for exemplary conduct in retirement. There was also the fact that he felt like an antediluvian. When he had been in harness, he had spoken with authority and conviction. Now he feared that whatever he might say would be mere words, and mere words to put in the newspapers were not worth his lifeblood.

Silent he might be, but he was not forgotten. His eightieth birthday, April 11, 1942, brought a fresh outpouring of good wishes from the press and many friends, including President Roosevelt. "Is there a more enviable American?" asked the *New York Times*. To one of his former colleagues Hughes replied:

> In my safe octogenarian harbor I welcome the friendly greetings from the staunch ships that are sailing the open sea. My pride is that I was once with them, and their messages to one who can no longer ride the waves outside are doubly precious. My best wishes for good voyages.[4]

As he took Mrs. Hughes for a walk in the sunshine, an old friend crossed the street to wish him many happy returns. Hughes replied, with a good-natured smile, that he had similarly greeted Root on his eightieth birthday, and Root had expressed precisely what he (Hughes) now felt: "I'm as good as I ever was—one hour a day."[5] Hughes himself gave a party at the Plaza Hotel in New York in celebration, as he put it, of "my 80th and Teddy's 14th"—referring to his grandson, Theodore Hughes Waddell. "Do not be disturbed," he wrote to his daughter, Mrs. Waddell. "I am giving this celebration (wifie and I are one)—a dinner to my children and such of my grandchildren as can come. No *presents* desired—just *presence*."

Hughes' role was now that of the proud father and grandfather. It was the second and third generations that were "sailing the open sea." His pride was magnified as three of his grandsons won distinction in the war. Lieutenant Charles Evans Hughes, 3d, fought through the battles of the Pacific on a destroyer in Admiral Halsey's fleet. Lieutenant Colonel Henry Stuart Hughes and Lieutenant Richard Hughes Waddell served in Europe, the former doing field research for the Office of Strategic Services.

There was one significant exception to Hughes' aloofness to public affairs. In April, 1944, Secretary of State Cordell Hull sought his advice, as a former Secretary of State, on the creation of an international organization to keep the peace. First, Myron C. Taylor called at Hughes' home, as a representative of Secretary Hull, asked his cooperation, and left him copies of a tentative draft of the United Nations Charter. The Chief said that, loath though he was to

[4] CEH to Justice Frankfurter, April 13, 1942.
[5] Author's interview with Sir Willmott Lewis, Oct. 24, 1949.

be drawn into any controversy, he would do his duty as a citizen. A few days later Secretary Hull spent an hour and a half at the Hughes home going over the problem in detail.

Hull stressed his desire to avoid Wilson's mistake in shaping the Covenant of the League of Nations. Accordingly, he had asked members of the Senate, including Republicans, to go over the project with him. It was to be kept on a strictly nonpartisan basis. Hull also said that he was trying to keep away from the idea of a world government. Hughes fully agreed, saying that Russia would not for a moment enter any superstate and certainly our Senate would not. In response to the Secretary's request, Hughes said that he would give his advice freely if he could be protected against being drawn into controversy over any of the questions presented.[6]

The Chief said there could be no effective international plan to keep the peace unless the United States, Great Britain, and Russia were prepared to work together. Hull, who had recently returned from Moscow, thought Russia would come along if the other powers were patient. While Hughes accepted the basic premise of the charter—that the Big Four, including China, would have to be in accord to apply force—he suggested a more liberal representation of the smaller powers on the Executive (Security) Council. The tentative plan called for four permanent members of the Council and four others elected annually. "As long as the great powers control the decision as to the use of force," Hughes urged, "there would not seem to be any harm in enlarging the number of smaller powers which would be in a position to be consulted and give their views." [7] Remembering the Washington Conference, he also put in a special word for France. The French were very sensitive, he said, and always wanted to be recognized in any international set-up. France was not at that time included as one of the permanent members of the Council.

Hughes objected to the sweeping nature of the provision then forbidding any member of the Council to vote in the decision of any dispute involving itself. If Russia should get into a squabble with Poland, he said, she would not be willing to stand aside and have it settled by the United States and Great Britain. As to the use of force, Hughes felt that it could be successfully employed against any new aggressions by Germany or Japan and to arrest any trouble among the smaller powers. But it would be futile, he agreed, to look to the use of force against Russia, Britain, or the United States, for that would mean another world war, which the organization was designed to prevent.

On May 5 the discussion was resumed in a conference attended by Taylor, John W. Davis, Nathan L. Miller (former Governor of New York), and Hughes at the latter's residence. The following day the Chief sent Taylor a memorandum suggesting seven specific changes in the proposed charter. The

[6] Memorandum of interview in Hughes Papers. [7] *Id.*

most important of these was his suggestion that the membership of the Council be increased from eight to eleven. If France insisted on becoming a permanent member, that would leave six members to be chosen by the Assembly. This suggestion became a part of the charter. Hughes thought the office of "President of the General organization" should be eliminated as being merely ornamental and a potential cause of strife. This too was accepted. He suggested that protective policies such as the Monroe Doctrine should be more specifically recognized; that justiciable disputes should go to the World Court rather than to the Council, unless the parties agreed to ask the Council for a "just and equitable settlement"; that in disputes growing out of internal issues, such as immigration, the Council be limited to inquiry, conciliation, and other means short of compulsion. He advised against a provision for withdrawal because it might weaken the organization, while recognizing that any great power wishing to leave would have its way in any case.

When Hull called on Hughes a second time, on May 7, he was troubled by the question of whether the President could order American military forces into action at the request of the Council, without the approval of Congress. Senator Vandenberg and others had raised that query. Hughes said that a strong President would not hesitate to use the force at his command, if he saw fit, without waiting for Congress to act; that he would be able to say that he was acting in accord with the treaty.

The next day Taylor asked the Chief to explore this problem further, and he replied that he "could not undertake to give any opinion on constitutional questions." Nevertheless, he offered his advice in discussing with Taylor the practical situations that would probably arise. "Our Presidents have used our armed forces repeatedly," Hughes pointed out, "without authorization by Congress, when they thought the interests of the country required it." [8] He assumed that the American representative on the Council would act under direction of the Secretary of State and the President. Any provision requiring the approval of Congress before these officials could back up the Council with armed force, he concluded, would be regarded as emasculating the treaty. He thought the plan might well go forward on the assumption that, with armed forces at his disposal, the President would use them at the request of the Council to carry out our international obligations.

Secretary Hull expressed his gratefulness for Hughes' "extremely helpful comments," [9] and the latter had the satisfaction of seeing a number of his suggestions come to fruition in the United Nations Charter adopted at San Francisco in 1945. He thought the charter "stood as a beacon in a darkened world." But he had no illusions about the efficacy of mere organization. "Structure of any sort, and any defined method," he wrote to the president of

[8] Memorandum of interview, May 11, 1944. [9] Hull to CEH, May 25, 1944.

the American Society of International Law, "will bring nothing but disillusion unless they are infused by good will and permeated by a spirit of reasonableness which alone makes possible the effective use of any form of organization that may be devised."[10]

His work on the United Nations organization was only an interlude. For the most part he and Mrs. Hughes lived for each other. Conscious of the fact that his long absorption in public affairs had deprived them of many happy hours together, he now lavished most of his attention upon her. When she was confined to Johns Hopkins Hospital for two operations in 1941, he motored to Baltimore every day to see her. His daughter, Mrs. Waddell, cautioned him not to wear himself out making so many trips.

"Don't you worry," he replied. "How *could* I get tired going to see my best girl!"

They spent happy days together in Jasper Park, in Arizona, at Skytop, and other favorite spots. In Washington they lived in delightful seclusion, with Hughes tending to his correspondence, working on his Biographical Notes, reading the newspapers, and dipping into history, philosophy, and biography. "If a person is philosophical or has intellectual interests," he said, "old age is a very agreeable time." [11]

Both were well and happy as they celebrated their fifty-fifth wedding anniversary on December 5, 1943, and Hughes penned his customary note with the ardor of a young lover:

> DEAREST—How precious are these years! Each one draws us closer together as in loving companionship we review the long past with its wonderful experiences and manifold blessings. *You are all in all to me.*

As she reached the venerable age of eighty on September 14, 1944, he was still courting her with devotion that knew no bounds, as indicated by this birthday note written at the Plaza Hotel:

> Happy Birthday to my best beloved!
> We "climbed the hill together"
> And, now that we are going down
> on the other side, we find the
> slope gentle and beautiful!
> And so we go hand in hand—
> in the eighties!
> Your "steady company"
> C

But these days were numbered. At Skytop in the summer of 1945 Mrs. Hughes had a fainting spell from vascular spasms, and Hughes learned from

[10] CEH to Frederic R. Coudert, read to ASIL, April 25, 1946.
[11] New York *Herald Tribune*, April 15, 1943.

her doctor that the end of their blissful union was not far off. She was looking frail and worn when they went to the Waddells' home in New York for dinner in honor of her eighty-first birthday. The next night she collapsed on the bathroom floor of their hotel and was taken to the hospital in an ambulance. When she seemed well enough a few weeks later, Hughes took her home to Washington and watched over her as her strength ebbed away. Every day he wrote the details of her condition to one of his children. At times she seemed to improve but would then suddenly collapse again. In late October she had difficulty in feeding herself and in speaking.

As her condition worsened, Hughes went by car to lonely Hains Point to take his walks so that he would not meet friends and have to talk about her illness. On November 26, 1945, he wrote to his daughter in New York:

> Do not worry about me. I am taking good care of myself and am as well as can be expected in these sad circumstances. I am sustained by the thought of the beautiful life I have had with Mother and by the constant manifestations of your devotion and that of Charlie and Elizabeth. Was ever a husband and father so blessed!

On the Hugheses' fifty-seventh wedding anniversary, December 5, Dr. B. W. Leonard, the family physician, noted a sharp deterioration in her condition and said the end was approaching. Still, Hughes was reluctant to have the children come. During the day he wrote to Mrs. Waddell:

> He [the doctor] knows our plans to have you come down and my reluctance to ask you to come before it is necessary. It would be a miserable business to have you just sitting around here waiting for Mother to pass. Dr. Leonard says that about the best estimate that can be made now is that it is a matter of four or five days and possibly less.
>
> Today is our 57th Wedding Anniversary! I am trying to fix my thought upon our long and beautiful companionship, a perfect union with a radiant spirit.
>
> So much love,
>
> FATHER

As he was eating breakfast alone the next morning, the nurse came in and said that Mrs. Hughes was dying. He rushed upstairs and saw that she was unconscious. A wave of hysteria swept over him. Almost running to the telephone, he called his daughter in New York. "Catherine! Catherine!" he shouted. His voice was broken—hysterical sounds akin to laughter alternating with sobs. "Mother is sinking rapidly," he managed to say. "Come as fast as you can." "Father!" she called to him, "Father! . . ." But he was too choked with emotion to reply.

When his storm had subsided, he calmly telephoned his daughter again and apologized for having lost control of himself. His son and both daughters hastened to his side, and Mrs. Hughes died peacefully at eight o'clock that night, December 6, 1945. The Chief was now in full control of his emotions and insisted on taking command of the arrangements. It was he who called the press and handed to reporters a brief biographical statement about her.

The body was taken to New York for a private funeral and interment in Woodlawn Cemetery. At the departure from Washington the funeral party found Union Station jammed with postwar travelers, but as the solemn procession made its way through the diplomatic entrance a hush fell upon the milling crowd. The people instinctively cleared a path; the men removed their hats; and everyone stood silent, many with bowed heads, while the casket was wheeled to the train and Hughes followed, haggard and completely oblivious to his surroundings. It was a touching tribute.

The Pennsylvania Railroad won the Chief's gratitude by providing a special funeral car and another special car for him and his children. As the casket was placed in this beautiful setting, he murmured, "Fit for a queen, and she was a queen!"

After the family was settled on the train, Hughes felt a temporary lifting of his grief and told the children the story of his courtship—a story never to go beyond the bosom of the family. At times he laughed and seemed almost gay. Then a deep gloom once more settled upon him. Not long after the funeral was over he was back in Washington. His son and daughters had tried to convince him on the night of Mrs. Hughes' death that he should give up his home and move to New York where he would be close to them—and away from the memories that would haunt him. While he had agreed at the time, the next morning he had changed his mind and said he would continue to live in the old home. It was too late to start a new life.

There was some comfort in the deluge of tributes to Mrs. Hughes. Everyone seemed to love her. William Phillips, who had been close to the Hugheses as Undersecretary of State, expressed what was in many hearts: "We can never think of you separately, for together you stand, and will always stand, for all that is finest and noblest in this world."

But the old home was a shell of loneliness. The servants were there to satisfy every whim. Mischler, his faithful secretary, was there. Old friends dropped in to cheer the Chief. His children became frequent visitors, and the author of these volumes claimed many hours of the great man's time. During intervals of this sort he was able, after a few months, to laugh, joke, and forget himself in reminiscences. But the gaping void of her absence always engulfed him again as soon as he was alone. Sometimes he grew impatient over his own longevity and wished that "the little finishing canter," as Holmes had called it, might end more abruptly. There was nothing left for him now. His chief dread was that he might become helpless, as Cardozo had.

There was no self-pity in his attitude, and he made a conscious effort to avoid being morbid. "You can always make yourself think of something else," he would say. In addition to this deliberate shifting of his thoughts to cheerful things, he kept reminding himself of how generously fortune had smiled upon him. "I have everything to be thankful for," he would say. But no philosophizing could overcome his loneliness or fill the void her absence left.

The living room of the R Street home became a shrine to Mrs. Hughes. Everything in the room was kept precisely as she had left it. The next night after her death he went to the dictionary to look up a word and almost sat in the chair that Mrs. Hughes had invariably occupied in the evening when she was reading or writing letters; but a sudden impulse checked his motion and he did not sit. "I can hardly bear to look at that chair," he said to the children. "But I know that the time will come when I'll get great comfort out of it."

Mrs. Waddell came to Washington to be with her father on the first anniversary of her mother's death. On December 5, the anniversary of his marriage, he was in a gay mood and talked all day about his courtship and his wedding trip, about the bright red bathrobe his bride had worn on that occasion and his own blue one, about their travels and happy times together. The next day he was immersed in gloom. "Do you know what day it is today?" he asked his daughter as evening approached. "Yes, Father," she answered, "I have been aware all day of what day it is."

After dinner he tried to read a newspaper, then impatiently turned on the radio. Nervous and agitated, he kept looking at the clock. He went to his room and a few minutes later was back again. It was not until eight o'clock, the hour of her passing, that his mood changed. Then quick as a flash he said, "Have you read Davenport's *East Side, West Side*? I think I should like to read some of it aloud and discuss it with you." At ten o'clock he was relaxed and ready for sleep.

For a change of scene after his wife's death Hughes spent his winters in Florida and his summers on Cape Cod. On the Cape he shared a cottage with his daughter, Mrs. Gossett, and her children. His chauffeur, Clarence Lucas, was always close by, and drives through the countryside were a favorite diversion. Being very fond of Lucas, the Chief made certain that pleasant accommodations could be provided for the chauffeur and his wife before deciding to spend his summer at the Cape. On some of his drives he insisted that Mrs. Lucas should accompany her husband in the front seat and took pleasure in showing her the sights.

At the Wianno Club cottage quiet hours of reading on a cool porch and a more intimate acquaintance with "Tibby" also lifted his spirits. Tibby was a lively, charming, and intelligent young lady of five—his granddaughter, whose real name is Elizabeth Evans Gossett. Finding that she had a way with her grandfather, she soon had him taking her for walks, playing games, and singing to her "The Golden Slippers," "In the North Sea Lived a Whale," and other favorites. Tibby claimed so much of his interest that he sometimes labeled his letters from the Cape as "reports from Tibbyland." On July 16, 1947, he wrote to Mrs. Waddell from this retreat:

> I am living in luxurious ease—never felt better. I never tire of sitting on our porch—with the view of the "neighboring ocean"—and the drives are charming.
>
> Tibby is a constant delight, with her never ending—"Tell me a story about the bears." And I put my old and weary brain to the test of imaginative feats. We are great pals!

One evening during the second summer at the Cape, Grandpa Hughes substituted for a baby-sitter, and Tibby saw no reason to respond to his efforts to get her to bed at the accustomed hour.

"I'm the Chief Justice now," she declared with feminine finality, "and I'm not going to bed."

"I'm sorry, young lady," her astonished grandfather retorted, "but I'm still the Chief Justice and you are going to bed."

She finally went.

On another occasion Mrs. Gossett returned to the cottage to find the retired Chief Justice draped in bath towels and Tibby kneeling reverentially by his side.

"Sh-h-h-h-h!" he whispered, raising his finger to his lips, "I'm a nun."

Before returning to Washington from Cape Cod, Hughes made a practice of stopping for a few weeks at the Plaza Hotel in New York. Here his children frequently dropped in to enjoy a quiet dinner with him in his room. He didn't care to go to the hotel dining room. "You know I am quite shy," he explained, "and don't like a lot of attention."

Florida claimed his interest from January to March each year. Members of his family visited him at Ormond Beach, and he spent pleasant hours reminiscing with Owen D. Young, whose Washington Oaks cottage was only twenty-five miles away. Hughes' moods were as variable as the winds. Returning from Florida by motor with Mrs. Waddell, he was exuberant the first day and (after a restless night) despondent the next. All day long he said little, and that evening in Wilmington, North Carolina, they subsisted on string beans and shredded wheat in a cafeteria because the hotel dining room had been taken over by service men. Mrs. Waddell was worried, tossed most of the night, and awoke with a cold the next morning. But her father was feeling gay. "I slept like a top," he said, slapping her on the knee. "I'm ashamed of feeling so young." He laughed heartily, sang off key, told stories, and recited Shakespeare, Goethe, and Schiller mile after mile.

His sense of humor was still keen. One day when he and Justice Frankfurter were talking about aged men not knowing when to quit, the Chief remarked that he had taken no chance of remaining too long on the bench.

"But you can't claim any credit for knowing when to quit," Frankfurter put in, "because God gave you a sense of humor."

"Sh-h-h-h-h!" Hughes replied, finger on lips. "I'm not supposed to have a sense of humor."

Sometimes he even reverted to bits of nonsense. When a crank wrote him a letter asking for a lock of his "silvery hair to put in a gold case," he sent it on to his daughter with this note:

> DEAR CATHERINE:
> Well, here is a true friend.
> He wants a lock of my hair.
> But I am sorry to say
> I have none I can spare.
> So much love,
> FATHER.

In Washington during both his spring and fall sojourns he gave an enormous amount of time, over a period of two and a half years, to answering the author's questions. He would sit in the governor's chair, with myself across the desk, and respond to any and every sort of query, talking so fast that he would need frequently to wipe his beard with his handkerchief. His mind was not only clear but amazingly sharp. His memory—stretching over fourscore years—was encyclopedic. At no point in his career was it possible to bring to light any hidden regrets, for he had never been consumed by ambition. Never had he sought an office, except to campaign after nominations without effort on his part. "It is better to take what comes," he would say. "Poor Harding would have been happier if ambition had not driven him beyond his depth." Hughes clung to his thesis that in order to be fit to wield power a man must be ready to relinquish it at any time. Even where failure had attended his efforts, he could truthfully say, "I did the best I could." His conscience was clear; his soul free.

One more brief moment in the limelight remained to him. In April, 1946, death suddenly beckoned to Chief Justice Stone, and after the funeral President Truman called Hughes on the telephone and asked if he might come to see him. Hughes replied that, if the President wished to see him, he would come to the White House. Within an hour he was there, and after greetings had been exchanged the President remarked that he wished Hughes himself were available for the Chief Justiceship. While the Chief interpreted this as only a friendly gesture, and while he said nothing at that time about the interview, except to his son, *Time* published his picture and said flatly that Truman had asked him to head the court once more.

Hughes went over the President's list of possible nominees and spoke highly of some of the judges on it. Then he volunteered an account of his conference with President Roosevelt when Stone had been named Chief Justice in 1941. F. D. R. had questioned him about both Stone and Robert H. Jackson. Hughes had spoken very well of both, preferring Stone because of his long experience. He had come away with the distinct impression that if Stone were not chosen the mantle would fall on Jackson. As Jackson had since proved his capacity and independence as an Associate Justice, Hughes recommended him to Truman as the best available choice.[12] The President, too, was reported to be favorable to Jackson at that time, but there were threats of resignations from the court if Jackson should be chosen, and the appointment went to Secretary of the Treasury Fred M. Vinson. When Jackson, who was in Nuremberg as United States prosecutor in the war crimes trials, learned of this knifing from two of his brethren, he issued a sizzling statement that made the feud within the court front-page news throughout the land. It was a pointed illustration of how morale on the high bench had sagged since Hughes' retirement. Some months before this Justice Roberts had resigned in a state of indignation and written to the Chief:

> To work under you was the greatest experience and the greatest satisfaction of my life. When you left the Court, the whole picture changed. For me it could never be the same.[13]

On April 11, 1947, Hughes attained the ripe age of eighty-five. "The only reason I have lived so long," he said, "is because I have never been absorbed in the past. Instead of brooding over disappointments, I have pushed what is done out of my mind and gone on to new activities."

As he sat in his room at the Plaza the telephone rang and a voice asked, "Is this Chief Justice Hughes?" Before he could answer there was a clatter on the wire and the connection was broken. A few minutes later the same voice asked the same question and was followed by the same sort of clatter. When the telephone rang a third time, he seized it irritably, prepared to cope with a practical joker taking advantage of the telephone strike. But this time a pleasant voice said, "This is Harry Truman," and there followed a warm birthday greeting from the President.

That evening Hughes was the guest at a family dinner given by his son.

[12] The details of Mr. Hughes' recommendation to the President were given to me in a confidential interview on May 29, 1947. Subsequently, Mr. Hughes looked over my notes of the interview and penciled in some corrections. He made no mention whatever of Secretary Vinson coming into his discussion with the President. When I took the matter up with the White House three years later, however, President Truman disputed my report that Mr. Hughes had recommended Justice Jackson and gave me a memorandum saying that Mr. Hughes had finally wound up his conversation by saying that, in his opinion, Secretary Vinson would be the best man for the Chief Justiceship.

[13] Roberts to CEH, July 16, 1945.

While he had "as wonderful a time as an old man can have," he could not help reflecting that he would never again see all his offspring together.

Early in January, 1948, he suffered a recurrence of his bleeding duodenal ulcer. Not until February 16 was he able to make his annual trip to Florida. In the interval he had lost twelve pounds and looked haggard and worn. In Florida he was very weak, and near the end of his stay he could scarcely walk to the dining room. Dr. Leonard had prescribed digitalis to stimulate the Chief's sluggish heart, but it nauseated him and left him only the choice between weakness from poor circulation and weakness from an upset digestive system. As soon as he arrived home in April he was put to bed with two nurses in attendance.

Most of his talk now was about his trips to Europe as a young man, his college days, and his grandfather's farm, although he continued to read the newspapers and magazines and the *Congressional Record*. His deepest thinking was of God and the hereafter. One night he told Mrs. Waddell that he felt he could demonstrate to his own satisfaction that there is a spiritual force operating in the world above the power and doings of men. She begged him to go on. He said he was too tired to make the explanation that night, but they would talk about it some other time. She never succeeded in getting him onto the subject again.

For every small favor his thanks were profuse. "So many people," he exclaimed one day, "to take care of an old relic. But the old relic," he added, "will not be bothersome much longer." Then, with an obvious effort at cheerfulness, he waved his hand to his daughter, wagging his fingers and smiling as he had done when she was a child. Soon he was singing. "How long since you last saw *The Pirates of Penzance*?" he asked. As if to make up for any neglect of Gilbert and Sullivan, he recited dialogue from their enchanting light operas until he was ready to sleep.

Hughes was well aware that the end was approaching. He talked frequently of death in a half-joking manner. It was always, "When I have turned up my toes . . ." By way of avoiding self-pity he would say, "I've been the luckiest man in the world. I've had everything. I've drunk the wine of life to the bottom of the glass. Now only the dregs are left."

But he would not sit around and wait for the Inevitable Intruder. Feeling weary and irritable in Washington, he decided to make the trip to Cape Cod in spite of his weakness. Dr. Leonard asked him if he really thought he was strong enough to go. "I have more reserve strength than you think," he replied. His nurse refused to accompany him alone, and Dr. Leonard took the same train without letting the Chief know about it. He was furious when he found out. There was no need for "babying" him in that fashion.

At the cottage near the Wianno Club, where he once more joined the Gossett family, Hughes seemed to experience a renewal of strength. But it was of short duration. When an attack of uremic poisoning and congestive heart failure struck him, he sank fast. The doctors put him in an oxygen tent, and Mrs. Gossett called her sister and brother. By the time they arrived he seemed a little better, and they were afraid that if they went in to see him he would know that the hour was at hand. Finally, Mrs. Gossett told him that she had called her sister and brother the day before when he had been so ill.

"They shouldn't have come," he said.

"Don't you want to see them?" she asked.

"You bet I do," he replied.

In his last hours, however, he said he would rather be alone. They waited on the porch outside his room. In the afternoon he lapsed into a coma; he did not suffer. His period of helplessness had been cut short. Fully prepared for the great adventure, he drew his last breath at 9:15 P.M. on August 27, 1948,

By Clifford Berryman in the *Washington Sunday Star*, August 29, 1948.

EPITAPH FOR A GREAT AMERICAN

as unpretentiously as he had drawn his first eighty-six years and four and a half months before. He had often remarked that it is almost impossible to come into or go out of this world gracefully, but such gracefulness as there can be in death he attained.

A wave of sadness went out over the nation. Pointing to Hughes' career as a "superb example of a life dedicated to reason and justice in human affairs," President Truman issued a proclamation ordering flags flown at half-mast until after the funeral service. Governor Dewey did the same in New York. Everywhere men realized that one of the great minds of the century had come to rest. To those who knew him best it was as if a towering peak had suddenly disappeared from the horizon.

The funeral was held in Riverside Church in New York. More than 1600 officials, judges, lawyers, former associates, and personal friends filled the church. The service was brief and simple but full of dignity and profound emotion. The Reverend Dr. Fosdick spoke feelingly of "strong nails that hold the world together" and of "forget-me-nots in the Alps"—the little human incidents among the towering peaks of achievement. As Hughes was laid to rest beside his wife in beautiful Woodlawn Cemetery, eulogies filled the press and dropped from many tongues. Great men searched for words to describe "so magnificent a mind, so elevated a character." But Hughes himself had penned the lines that seemed most appropriate:

> The most beautiful and the rarest thing in the world is a complete human life, unmarred, unified by intelligent purpose and uninterrupted accomplishment, blessed by great talent employed in the worthiest activities, with a deserved fame never dimmed and always growing.

His words had been spoken in tribute to Holmes, but they are a true reflection of his own career. On the strength of his own industry, character, and intellect he had touched the superlative. The sum of what he took from life is dwarfed only by the almost unfathomable total of what he gave in return.

Appendix I

DAVID CHARLES HUGHES

WE FIRST hear of Hugh Hughes, who hailed from Carnarvonshire, North Wales, when he joined the famous "farm and labour colony" at Trevecca, established prior to 1769 by Howell Harris, the fiery apostle of the Methodist Revival. When Harris' evangelical efforts were interrupted in 1751 by a breakdown in health, he decided "to sell all I have . . . and build an Alms House and School House and employ as many as I could of the followers." [1] Every member of the "Family" thus assembled at Trevecca was required to cast all personal possessions into the common purse and to submit to strict discipline, including three religious services a day, the first at five o'clock in the morning. Sixty trades were followed within the "Family," and so long as Howell Harris lived this "marvellous experiment, . . . a reformatory and monastery all in one," enjoyed "a strange success." [2]

In this stern spiritual environment Hugh Hughes courted and married Jane Owen in 1773. The eldest of their three children, Nathan Hughes, who was baptized February 9, 1780, was to become Charles Evans Hughes' grandfather. Nathan was apprenticed to the printing trade at Trevecca. Being "naturally gifted" and having "literary tastes," according to the records of the colony, he wrote and printed in Wales a short biography of Howell Harris. Sometime before 1828 he married Jane Evans from the Vale of Clivyd in North Wales, who contributed to her famous grandson his middle name. The couple moved to Tredegar in Monmouthshire, England, where he engaged in business and became a schoolmaster. It was at Tredegar that David Charles Hughes was born to them on June 24, 1832, the youngest of six children.[3]

Information as to the life of young David Charles before he migrated to the United States is meager. His father, Nathan Hughes, died at the age of about sixty-five when the lad was in his thirteenth year. His elder brother Samuel had not survived young manhood. The family consisted, then, of Jabez, John Richard, Jane, and Eliza Hughes in addition to their mother and young David Charles. The latter acquired a great respect for his brother Jabez, who was a man of wide reading, intellectual ability, independence of character, and kindly disposition. His brother John Richard was in the process of becoming an eminent preacher of the Calvinistic Methodist denomination. Having been brought up in a religious atmosphere and being fond of public speaking, young David Charles also had his eye on the ministry, but first he became a printer. He worked at his trade at Merthyr Tydvil and for a time was employed on the staff of the *Hereford Times*.[4] What schooling he had is not known, but "he was very studious and read widely, devoting himself

[1] Script, "The Hughes Family," sent to Charles E. Hughes by his cousin, Reverend Howell Harris Hughes.

[2] *Ibid.* [3] CEH, Notes, pp. 3–4.

[4] *South Wales News* (Cardiff), Nov. 7, 1916.

chiefly to history and biography." In speaking of his efforts at self-improvement, he often quoted from Bailey's *Festus:*

> I know what study is: it is to toil
> Hard, through the hours of the sad midnight watch,
>
> . . . . . .
>
> Wring a slight sleep out of the couch, and see
> The self-same moon which lit us to our rest,
> Her place scarce changed perceptibly in Heaven,
> Now light us to renewal of our toils.[5]

Apparently his first opportunity to preach came in 1854–1855 when he was licensed for that purpose and put on the Wesleyan Hereford Circuit. Then a new idea took firm root in his mind. He happened to read the story of another printer who had left his home and succeeded in making a name for himself in that new and thriving land called America. It was Benjamin Franklin's *Autobiography.* Young Hughes was deeply impressed. He had no friends in the United States, not even an acquaintance. Nor was there any opening or particular prospect that lured him. Yet he decided to leave his native land and become an American.

It may well be that the prospect of having to wait some time for a permanent assignment in England or Wales influenced his decision. One of the letters he carried with him to the New World said that he would have offered himself to the English Conference but was afraid that he would have to wait longer than was convenient in view of the number of applicants. Other reasons for his going, however, seem to predominate. Benjamin Roberts, superintendent of the Swansea Circuit, gave the young Welsh preacher a letter of recommendation which stated that "had this good brother offered himself to the full work of the Ministry in his native country, he would undoubtedly have been accepted and stationed on a circuit as soon as an opening should occur." But he thought it to be "his providential call to cross the Atlantic with a view to offer himself to the full work of the Ministry in the Methodist Episcopal Church of America." [6]

Underlying this desire to preach in America was a no less positive wish to be an American. David Charles Hughes was a republican by conviction; having gained an affection for the United States from the books he had read in the little print shops of England and Wales, he longed to identify himself with that challenging land across the sea. The fact that he intended to remain a preacher suggests that he sought neither fame nor fortune, but the idea of sharing the life and the experiences of a free people in a republic of their own making was alluring to him.

His family took a sharply differing view. Jane Hughes, his sister, who married Edward Jones, a colliery agent at Abertillery, Monmouthshire, a man of importance in that community, had only angry resentment for what she regarded as her brother's rash undertaking. With a woman of her dominating personality leading the family's opposition to his venture, David Charles must have spent some very uncomfortable days before his departure. But he held to his resolution and sailed for New York on the *Jacob A. Westervelt,* arriving on September 20, 1855, at the age of twenty-three.

[5] CEH, Notes, p. 7. [6] *Ibid.,* p. 8.

Appendix II

MARY CATHERINE CONNELLY

THE CONNELLYS are an old American family. Tradition handed down to successive generations says that they came from the province of Ulster (northern Ireland) to Ulster County, New York. "Michel Connolly" (the name is variously spelled) appears as one of the freeholders of Kingston who signed the "Agreement to Maintain Constitutional Rights," on July 1, 1775.[1] This same Michael Connelly, or a son by that name, was an officer in the Revolutionary War. He served with General Clinton, commander of the Revolutionary forces in New York [2] and later Governor of New York and Vice President of the United States. On July 11, 1777, General Clinton recommended his devoted follower to General Washington for a commission in the Continental Army. "The Bearer Mr. Connolly," he wrote, "is the Person I formerly mentioned to your Excellency as a supernumerary Officer, I having given a Warrant to him as a 1st Lieutenant after the 4 Companies officered by me were compleat." [3]

Among Michael Connelly's eight children was William Connelly, who was born in 1769 and lived until 1835. A printed obituary found in his Bible handed down through the Hughes family says that he was a physician of repute at Saugerties, about twelve miles from Kingston, and a Baptist minister. He married Lydia Merihew, who was of English descent. Their son, William Connelly, Jr., born in Shandaken, Ulster County, in 1807, became the grandfather of Charles E. Hughes. The younger William Connelly did not follow his father's profession, but made his start as a contractor and builder. Soon after his marriage to Margaret Ann Terpenning on July 11, 1829, he contracted to build some tanneries in the wilds of Delaware County. It was there among the beautiful hills near Margaretville—then still unspoiled--that Mary Catherine Connelly was born on November 22, 1830.

Her maternal ancestors were chiefly Dutch. The line has been traced back to Barent Burhans, a weaver, and his wife Elizabeth who had moved into Holland from Wesel, Germany, near the Dutch frontier, and were married at Deventer in 1593.[4] Apparently they were of "Holland extraction." Across the street from the Burhans home lived an ancestor of Justice Willis Van Devanter.[5] More than three hundred years later a descendant from each of those homes found time between the writing of opinions for the Supreme Court of the United States to speculate as to whether their ancestors hobnobbed together and chatted over their schnapps about the virtues of the remarkable new plant being imported from Virginia—"quite unable to imagine the part their remote descendants would be called upon to play in the marvelous new world." [6] One of Barent's and Elizabeth's three children was

[1] Schoonmaker, *History of Kingston*, 1888, pp. 517–518.

[2] *Public Papers of George Clinton as First Governor of New York* (published by the State, 1899), I, 566.

[3] *Id.*, II, 102, 103.

[4] Burhan's Genealogy, pp. 3, 4.

[5] Van Devanter to CEH, Nov. 2, 1935.

[6] CEH, Notes, p. 12*a*.

Jacob Burhans, who came to America as a soldier in the Netherlands service on the *Esopus* and settled at Wiltwyck (Kingston, New York) about 1660. The following year he was appointed "Collector" by the Honorable Lord Petrus Stuyvesant, and in 1666 he was elected and confirmed Schepen (justice-magistrate) of the court at Wiltwyck. Jacob's son, Jan Burhans, arrived in America in 1663 on the *Bonte Koe* (Spotted Cow). A decade later he was magistrate for the town of Swaenburgh and in 1693 he became magistrate of the Town Court at Kingston.

Mary Connelly was in the seventh generation from Jan Burhans. The line was Dutch, save for the infusion of German when Deborah Ostrander, great-granddaughter of Jan Burhans, married Leonard Krows. Leonard was born in Kingston, but his father, John Krows, was from Germany. Both fought in the Revolutionary War as soldiers in the First Regiment of Ulster County.[7] Leonard, who had enlisted when he was only sixteen, was wounded and received a pension.[8] His eldest daughter Mariah married Tjerck Vilie Terpenning (Tjerck's father, Henricus Terpenning, had also fought in the Revolution and received a commission from General Washington) and they were the parents of Margaret Ann Terpenning, who married William Connelly, Jr.

To William and Margaret Connelly their Old World connections seemed very remote. Yet they brought up their children in the traditions of thrift and self-reliance characteristic of Mrs. Connelly's Dutch ancestors. Mary Catherine, the eldest, became a little mother to her brothers and sister. Her brother, Henry Cantine Connelly, was her best loved companion. Later he became a successful man of business, first at New Salem and then at Kingston. Succeeding to his father's business at Eddyville, he greatly extended its operations and his firm (Connelly & Shaffer) at one time owned extensive slate quarries. His reputation for integrity and sound judgment took him to the State Senate in 1874–1875 and again in 1886–1887. The dignity of his manner and appearance in his full suit of black broadcloth made a lasting impression on his nephew, Charlie Hughes.[9] Mary Connelly's only sister, Cathalina, who was fourteen years younger than she, became Mrs. Alfred Van Nostrand of Kingston. Her younger brother, Carey Simpson Connelly, became active in Ulster County politics and for many years was employed in the Customs House in New York City.

[7] *New York in the Revolution* (published by the State, 1904), pp. 189, 206, 403.
[8] CEH, Notes, p. 12*b*. [9] *Ibid.*, p. 17.

INDEX

Volume One: pages 1–409
Volume Two: pages 411–810

Bei Fragen zur Produktsicherheit wenden Sie sich bitte an:
If you have any questions regarding product safety,
please contact:

Walter de Gruyter GmbH
Genthiner Straße 13
10785 Berlin
productsafety@degruyterbrill.com